CASEBOOK IN

AMERICAN BUSINESS HISTORY

SIR THOMAS SMYTHE, THE FIRST BUSINESS MAN TO HAVE A PROFOUND EFFECT UPON AMERICA

CASEBOOK IN AMERICAN BUSINESS HISTORY

N. S. B. GRAS
Straus Professor of Business History

and

HENRIETTA M. LARSON
Assistant Professor of Business History

Graduate School of Business Administration
Harvard University

APPLETON-CENTURY-CROFTS, INC.
NEW YORK

520

MANUFACTURED IN THE UNITED STATES OF AMERICA

PREFACE

The present volume of cases in business history, apparently the first to be published, is made up of forty-three cases or problems which have been taken chiefly from American experience. Of these, five cases from European business history have been selected for their unique contributions—Sir Thomas Smythe, Boulton and Watt, Josiah Wedgwood, John Law, and Hugo Stinnes.

The general emphasis in the cases is on business administration, that is, business policy, management, and control. The objective is the study of decisions made and actions taken under varying circumstances in the pursuit of private profit and social gain. Commonly, the individual case raises problems in production, distribution, finance, and industrial and public relations, to which no clear answer can be given. Some teachers and students may use this book in order to obtain factual information or neat pocket answers to problems, economic or social. Its purpose is to facilitate understanding of the various possible choices of action and the implications thereof. The training along this line lies in thinking of alternatives of action and in seeing the results of that action.

History is of value in the study of business because it presents a background for the present, provides a rich variation of settings for action, leads to the formation of a perspective, and often provides a more nearly complete and objective presentation than is possible in current cases. History is but the past on its way to the future via the present. The old problems arise again and again in business. We shall make little progress in profiting from past mistakes, either public or private, unless we develop a habit of learning from experience, which, in the busy-footed struggle of the present, is very difficult.

Actually, what an observer sees happening, as he watches the procession of business men pass by, is one group following another. In the early town (ancient, mediaeval, or modern) we see first the petty capitalist, then in the later towns the mercantile capitalist, followed by the industrial capitalist, the financial capitalist, and now the national capitalist. The great succession of men and efforts moves alternately to the encouraging music of prosperity and the dull rumble of depression.

The cases are of unequal value as bodies of historical information; they are of more nearly equal value as instruments of instruction. Some of them have been based on the accounts, minutes, and correspondence of firms, often checked by personal conversation with executives or workmen. Others are based on published sources which have to be used with great care because they are often prejudiced.

This casebook itself provides considerable aid for the use of the cases, not alone in the introduction but in the readings and questions appended to the individual cases. In addition, there is now available the outline entitled *Business and Capitalism: an Introduction to Business History,* written by N. S. B. Gras and published by F. S. Crofts & Co., 1939.

In a very real sense this casebook is the result of coöperation. Publication has been made possible by the generous assistance of a friend of business education. We owe a great deal to colleagues in the Harvard Graduate School of Business Administration, who have given advice and information whenever called upon. Our thanks are also due to colleagues in other institutions, particularly Professor Arthur M. Borak of the University of Minnesota and Professor Earl J. Hamilton of Duke University. Some of the original compilers of the cases here included are as follows: William T. Baxter, Philip Donham, Edward Edelman, Mildred L. Hartsough, Edward A. Horton, Jr., Merrit C. McElroy, Sterling Popple, Kenneth W. Porter, H. Maynard Rees, J. Owen Stalson, Mrs. C. P. Wright, and Philip Young. To them our best thanks for their coöperation and for the pleasant recollection of joint efforts made in common tasks. We feel sure that they will understand the rearrangement and abbreviation made necessary by the change from mimeographed to printed form. To Richmond Fletcher Bingham we are indebted for his aid in planning and for drawing the map facing page 29 and the chart illustrating the movement of wholesale prices. To the many authors and publishers who have so generously allowed us to quote from their works we are also very grateful.

We owe much to our closest colleague, Dr. Ralph M. Hower, assistant professor of Business History, who has compiled three of the cases (Josiah Wedgwood & Sons, Ltd., 1759–1920, New York Transatlantic Packet Services, 1817–1837, and N. W. Ayer & Son, Advertising Agency, 1869–1939) and aided in the revision of several others. We have had the benefit of his experience in teaching the cases and of his knowledge of the subject and its background.

The help of two members of our staff cannot be adequately acknowledged. Mrs. Elsie Hight Bishop has had the chief responsibility for the editorial preparation of the material and for the reading of the proof, work which, because of the nature of the material, has required both careful judgment and much patience. Miss Frances Carpenter has given constant assistance at all stages of the work and deserves special commendation for the final careful work of typing the cases for publication.

In a sense this *Casebook in American Business History* is just a segment of the continuous emphasis placed on the case method of research and instruction at the Harvard Graduate School of Business Administration. The method is very expensive in time and effort; but we have found abiding satisfaction in the experiment and are grateful to the School for the chance to participate in the working-out of both a new method and a new subject.

N. S. B. G.
H. M. L.

CONTENTS

INTRODUCTION

CASES IN BUSINESS HISTORY

LIST OF ILLUSTRATIONS

INTRODUCTION

GENERAL INTRODUCTION TO BUSINESS HISTORY

1. The Nature and Objectives of Business History

We may begin by saying that business history is primarily the study of the administration of business units of the past. This administration consists in policy-formulation and management. Policy includes organization, production, distribution, and finance. Management covers the same aspects of business but is concerned with the adaptation and execution of the policy. In practice, in actual business, all these are woven together into a living undivided stream of effort, partly conscious and partly unconscious.

Business arises only when business men come into being, that is, when men make a living chiefly out of providing goods and services for exchange with others. The Hottentot villager who makes an occasional sale of a few yams or the American subsistence farmer who parts with a few turkeys or fox skins obviously does not thereby become a business man.

Business arose in towns and spread to the rural parts. It is marked by the use of money as a means of exchange and a unit of credit. It creates, and flourishes, in a price economy. In the background everywhere are the elements of profit and service. As units of business become larger, the chance for profits increases. As units become larger, the towns grow until they reach the proportion of large commercial centers. We can trace the rise and shifts in business by studying the centers where business has flourished. The following is an approximate list of such centers that shows a rough sequence of development:

Ur, Babylon
Memphis, Thebes (Egypt)
Knossus (in Crete)
Tyre, Sidon, Rhodes
Ephesus, Smyrna, Babylon, Carthage
Athens, Corinth, Delos, Syracuse
Alexandria, Antioch, Rome
Antioch
Byzantium
Genoa, Venice, Florence; and Danzig, Bremen, and Lübeck
Bruges, Lisbon, Antwerp
Amsterdam, London
London, New York

We have simple business records on clay tablets from Babylonia earlier than 2000 B. C. We know a little about individual merchants of Asia Minor in the ancient period. Our first detailed information, however, comes from Greek and Roman cities.

Interesting as is the early history of business we shall find that we can discover the chief lessons of business history by studying the modern period, say, from about 1600. In the earliest part we would discover that significant facts are few and far between and that there was much repetition as one civilization followed another. Up to the eighteenth century A. D., it is probable that there were only two important types of private business men—first petty capitalists and then mercantile capitalists. If these two classes do summarize nearly five thousand years of private business history, then we may just as well study them in their later developments and thus learn the essentials about them.

But first let us raise the question why we want to study business history, that is, what we expect to get out of our efforts. First, we need a background and a perspective for our judgment as to the direction in which business has been going. Second, we need to appreciate the sense of eternal change in business. Third, we should learn to deal with situations and cases from any standpoint that may be uppermost at the time. History offers a wide variety of problems and puzzles to solve. Fourth, before attempting to solve its problems, we need to study the general circumstances in which any firm may find itself. History offers us a great array of problems in a wide variety of backgrounds. Fifth, we need to learn from history the part that business has played in civilization, and the extent to which it has grown to the stature of a profession along with teaching, preaching, medicine, and the law. There is little question that business has played a big part, but we have made only a beginning in understanding what it has actually done.

2. Petty Capitalism

We study this subject not because it is a major interest but because it is a necessary background for more important systems of business. Moreover, petty capitalists, although not now dominant, are everywhere in evidence, very important, and strongly championed by politicians.

Petty capitalism is the earliest form of business. It arises in towns, commonly develops gilds, and flourishes in small market areas (or groups of persons). It is at once petty and vulnerable but very persistent. It is the business system in which men learned the ways of exchanging goods and services. It is not big business but the cradle of big business in the ancient, mediaeval, and modern periods.

The chief examples of petty capitalists have been shopkeepers, storekeepers, and traveling merchants. The shopkeepers, rising in small towns everywhere and in every age, were small artisans who manufactured goods for sale to consumers who themselves ordered the wares or bought goods already made up. These shopkeeper artisans are exemplified by weavers, dyers, shoemakers, blacksmiths, joiners, and pewterers. They were fond of their work and proud of their skill. Their capital invested in tools and raw materials was for them considerable. They were spirited essential citizens in any town of importance. Of course, this group has persisted through the ages and is still very much with us, though lingering on with ever changing fortunes. Blacksmiths are disappearing but garage men have more than taken their places.

Storekeepers kept stores of goods on display and for sale to consumers. They manufactured nothing themselves, though they handled sundry goods made by artisans in the town or in the country. Probably the earliest examples were general storekeepers of whom all trace has apparently disappeared in ancient and mediaeval records. In American towns, however, they were very clearly the earliest storekeepers and long remained a vital nucleus in town life. In Europe the early storekeepers of whom there is record were bladers, vintners, drapers, mercers, ironmongers, salters, and spicers. These retailers bought their wares locally or from traveling merchants.

Traveling merchants are the key traders of the early towns. They brought in foreign wares and took out local products in return. Their main policy was to sell to storekeepers and shopkeepers by wholesale. Then they would like to be off to the next town. In the Middle Ages, however, the town magistrates commonly forced them to sell for a period to consumers before supplying storekeepers and shopkeepers. Thus, we must regard traveling merchants as both wholesalers and retailers in the mediaeval records which constitute our most voluminous source of information.

These traveling merchants were not merchant princes but men of little capital and great daring. They were periodically losing the profits hard earned on hazardous ventures. Robbed, shipwrecked, and trapped by changing market conditions, they frequently had to borrow money from the more successful traveling merchants who had retired or from urban landlords who added to their living by lending money. The form of the loans was often simple partnership ventures in which the lender (the stay-at-home partner) put up most or all of the capital and took a certain percentage of the profits if any profits were made.

The traveling merchant might own a small ship or a pack-horse. For the sake of safety against pirates at sea and robbers on the land, he preferred to travel with a group. In many cities and districts associations of such traveling merchants sprang up and attained considerable stability and power. Such associations or regulated companies are to be compared with the gilds of shopkeepers and storekeepers —the famous craft (one-craft or one-trade) gilds of history.

Petty capitalists held up the ideal of economic independence. They all united to buy freedom of action for their towns as against a feudal lord or any other power. They also clung to the ideal of no control by any other business man, no matter how rich or able that man might be. When forces turned against them, they had to bow their heads to richer men, but we may be sure it was with the sullen resolve ultimately to throw off any yoke imposed upon them. They wanted no control except that of the regulation of equals in associations—of merchants, storekeepers, or shopkeepers. We may sum up a good deal by labeling their public policy as democratic economic equality.

The rules of the associations or gilds of petty capitalists constitute our earliest important ethical codes. They aimed at fair dealing, high quality of work and goods, and equality for all masters. Each apprentice, it was assumed, would become a journeyman (day worker for wages), and each journeyman would become a master. For generations each master became a full-fledged member of his gild. The gilds became cultural associations as well as trade associations, for they provided a means of debate on public and private issues, a means of supporting Church and other worthy causes, and a means of providing public entertainment in the form of dramas and tableaux presented at the street corners and market places of the town. Occasionally, without plan, they provided general entertainment of an exciting kind when the members of one gild fought with those of another.

The traveling merchants, all unwittingly, developed a body of law and a set of procedures that have had considerable importance in legal development. We refer to the "law merchant" or mercantile law of the Middle Ages which in modern times in England was absorbed in the common law. In this mercantile law there were no lawyers. A court was improvised at a market place or at a fair—the so-called "dusty-footed court"—made up of the principal parties to the dispute and others near at hand who knew the facts or were familiar with the type of transaction at issue. In a short time, the parties standing, the trial might be decided and justice executed. This normally involved a payment in money or in goods. It resembles the procedure called "arbitration" which business men, notably since the eighteenth century, have intermittently sought to introduce.

3. Mercantile Capitalism

Petty capitalism gives way as a system to big business, and at this point the whole picture changes. This does not mean that petty capitalists disappeared but that the democratic economic equality of their system passed away. Henceforth there were bigger and richer men who tended to influence or control the petty capitalists' own business affairs and to dominate their gilds. The new power in the land was the sedentary merchant, the mercantile capitalist par excellence.

The sedentary merchants, of whom the most successful were called "merchant princes," came in as part of a new system. We may say that they *created* a new system. It is, of course, doubtful whether they were conscious of the full import of what they were doing.

The sedentary merchant arose because he had something to offer the world: that is why he won over the petty capitalists. He offered a type of business, which, using more capital and abler administration, would cater to a larger number of persons (extend the market, if you will), bring in goods from a wider area, and send out more wares. He became the protagonist in the large commercial city, ultimately in metropolitan economy.

The central part of the policy of the sedentary merchant was to remain at home. He had little of the spirit of personal adventure of the traveling merchant. He would send his ships out in charge of his supercargoes. He would remain at home—in his countinghouse, which was the throne room of the new class. Here in a single room were the accounts, letters, maps, money chest, money balance, and merchandise scales. Here was a chance to think, to plan, to work out policies, to arrange for others to do the detailed work. At this point big business was born. How often this class of merchants rose and fell in the ancient period we do not know. We do know, however, that the sedentary merchant began the era of big business in mediaeval Western Europe about the thirteenth century and that we have never lost the heritage of his efforts or the effect of his presence in history. Florence, Venice, Marseilles, Augsburg, Lübeck, Bremen, Bruges, Antwerp, Amsterdam, and London were centers in which the sedentary merchant rose to a position of dominance and power. In Florence one mercantile family, the Medici, became the ruling house in the government of the city and surrounding territory.

The rise of the sedentary merchant means the dominance of commercial capital, the supremacy of well-considered business policy, the victory of careful management, and the triumph of metropolitan economy. These cannot all be considered here. A partial summary of the whole would be that mercantile dominance pointed the way to bigger and better results. It is a curious fact that in a very general way the period of the rise and dominance of the mercantile capitalist, 1300–1800, was the very time when the dominating feudal-manorial lord lost his position to the small cultivator. Perhaps we may see in this a social compensation such as might have been arranged by a deity presiding over the affairs of men. The victories were in both cases incomplete, however, and the issues often confused.

There were certain functions performed by the sedentary merchant which we may call primary. He was first and foremost an importer, exporter, and wholesaler. He handled relatively large amounts of merchandise and preferred to deal only with "the trade." There were reasons, however, why the sedentary merchant was rarely, if ever, an out-and-out wholesaler. Town magistrates continued the policy they had developed to guide the traveling merchant, namely, that the merchant should sell to consumers for a period (about ten to forty days) before they sold to the trade. To be sure, it is uncertain how far such a rule was enforced. But far more important than town ordinances were the needs of the sedentary merchant himself. He probably always found it helpful, even necessary, to have a retail store at home, for instance, to dispose gradually of goods which he had not been able to sell in quantity to retailers.

In addition to the functions already mentioned, the sedentary merchant was active in other fields. A successful sedentary merchant bought ships or had them built for his use. These he found necessary to ensure transportation for his own goods. When his ships had vacant cargo space, he sought freight from other merchants, thereby becoming a common carrier. He also built or bought a warehouse in which, when not fully occupied, he would rent space to other traders, thereby becoming a common warehouseman. He would often insure the cargoes and ships of other merchants even more for the privilege of asking them to insure his own than for the premiums received. He would act as commission agent for other merchants, commonly receiving 5 per cent for his service. And he handled banking and exchange transactions for himself and others.

Often the sedentary merchant found it hard to get the supplies he needed for his business. These might be manufactured wares, minerals, fish, or lumber. Although he preferred to buy these and other goods from independent small masters, still he stood ready to help, influence, or even control these masters in order to get goods when he wanted them and of such a quality and quantity as his affairs required. Sometimes the small masters welcomed his participation in their affairs in so far as he provided capital and assisted in marketing, but frequently they resented the control that accompanied his help.

Often sedentary merchants got together to form incorporated joint-stock companies, particularly after 1400 in Italy and Southern Germany and later in England and Holland. These companies were promoted in order to engage effectively in commercial banking, mining operation, and distant foreign trade. The East India and West India companies of Holland, England, and France are illustrations. The trained abilities of sedentary merchants in the administration of their own affairs became indispensable to the management of the new corporations. Those countries, such as France, that allowed nonbusiness influence to creep in, suffered in rivalry with the nations, such as Holland and England, which gave the merchants a fairly free hand.

As the centuries went along and some sedentary mercantile families became rich and well established, there developed a tendency toward specialization in one function. Occasionally this occurred in ship operation, but more often it was found in banking, as in Italy and Southern Germany.

By the fifteenth century the merchant-banker had become an important factor in Genoa and Florence, and by the sixteenth century in Augsburg. He ordinarily combined trade in such commodities as cloth, copper, and spices with commercial banking. He might have offices in as many as a dozen or a score of cities from Naples to London and Portugal to Hungary. He developed the practice of selling drafts or bills of exchange on his branches for the convenience of both traders and travelers. Italy and Southern Germany were well on the way to something like financial capitalism when America was discovered and when, accordingly, economic power and commercial advantage shifted to the nations on the Atlantic. With this high promise in the field of finance went a culture that was without precedence except in the ancient period. It is of little advantage but some interest to speculate as to the glories that might have come to Italy and Southern Germany if the discovery of America had not spoiled their fair promise.

Europe (including England) experienced all the phases of development in mercantile capitalism. It took England till about 1650 to attain the stage reached by Florence in 1500. By 1750 England had surpassed all countries in the world in the development of mercantile capitalism and had begun to develop disintegrating specializations within the system. America lagged far behind. Hancock, Astor, and

Girard in the 1790's were more like Sir Thomas Smythe about 1600. It was the lot of America to skip from an *early form* of mercantile capitalism into the next stage —industrial capitalism.

4. Industrial Capitalism

This system followed mercantile capitalism. Under the new system there were a great many highly specialized business men or firms which took over the various functions of a sedentary merchant under mercantile capitalism; such functions as importing, exporting, wholesaling, retailing, warehousing, transportation, commission agency, insurance, banking, manufacturing, and so on, fell into the hands of specialists. Of course specialization had existed for centuries but it was largely confined to petty capitalists in small towns, such as shoemakers, bakers, grocers, and ironmongers.

There are two separate origins of specialization in big business. One lies in the disintegration of the sedentary merchant's functions, such as occurred when merchant-bankers (Medici and Fuggers) came into existence. The other, and more important, arose out of the Industrial Revolution in England in the eighteenth century.

The Industrial Revolution was a great movement in the direction of improved manufacture. Narrowly expressed, it called the factory system into being by introducing power machinery into the central workshop. This occurred first in textiles and then in the iron industry. Later, the power machinery was introduced into transportation in the form of locomotives and steamships. The framework of this story we are already familiar with, but we might all review it with profit by reading Mantoux's *Industrial Revolution*. This is a classic work that every serious student should own.

The implications of the Industrial Revolution for business history need special elucidation. We may note three points. First, the Industrial Revolution threw a bomb into the midst of business by introducing a challenging new technique of machine production. Second, it put a fresh strain on business to provide an unprecedented amount of capital for procuring the new equipment. And, third, it offered fresh hope to petty capitalists, so long submerged by mercantile capitalism, if only they could fit into the new picture, particularly through the adoption of machine production.

In the régime of mercantile capitalism the sedentary merchant had rarely stepped into the industrial arena except through a factor or agent who employed small masters to work for him or bought goods they had already manufactured. Now, however, the Industrial Revolution was producing power machinery too big and too expensive to be handled by small masters unless able and ambitious. Such equipment had to be put into large central workshops and had to be carefully managed for production on a large scale. This was a task not for small masters as such but for business men just as big as the sedentary merchants themselves. Accordingly, the only major alternatives were for a sedentary merchant to become a manufacturer or to specialize in some other function that he had performed in the past. If a sedentary merchant decided to enter the field of specialized manufacturing, he had to learn how to use machinery and develop mechanical power, and how to hitch the two together for effective production. To be sure, he might employ a mill agent to do this. This agent would commonly be a former small master—a wheelwright, carpenter, blacksmith, and so on. Then the new industrial capitalist himself would devote his attention to marketing the product, financing the enterprise, and general administration. Of course, he might find a sales agent to take over marketing, as was common in New England. This sales agent might be another sedentary merchant who was try-

ing to build up a new specialized commission business.

Mustering adequate capital was also a task. The most common device for the manufacturer was to take one or more partners and then if necessary to borrow on promissory notes. Earnings were plowed back into the business. In the case of the canals, highways, bridges, and railways, however, so much permanent invested capital was required that only the joint-stock company would meet the needs. Gradually joint-stock companies, generally incorporated, became the rule, and their securities became the common objects of buying and selling in brokers' offices or on public exchanges.

Petty capitalists got a new inning. They might become mill agents or mill superintendents. They might set up small factories of their own and watch them grow big. Many petty capitalists attained the proportions of successful industrial capitalists. Samuel Slater, Gordon McKay, Andrew Carnegie, Philip Armour, Harvey Firestone, and Henry Ford are examples in the field of manufacturing.

England *developed* the new fire that other nations *borrowed* to kindle themselves into the quicker life of industrial capitalism. Then ideas, machines, and men left England's shores in a way that could be compared only with the migrations from Phoenician and Greek cities of old. Slater came to America and Cockerill went to Belgium. The former developed the textile industry in his new home, and the latter the iron industry. The new technique was carried to the two continents with great rapidity. When the railway got under way in the 1830's, it spread as almost no other device ever known to man has spread, for all alike saw in it the emancipation of vast stretches of inland country hitherto backward and stunted unless located on a river. Soon Englishmen were in demand as engineers or superintendents in laying rails and building locomotives.

There is no reason to pity the old class of sedentary merchants as a group of business men who had outlived their usefulness. To be sure, some were too old or too inflexible to enter a new specialized business. But most of them entered manufacturing, transportation, commission agency, and so on. Some of them gave excellent management to their new enterprises because they could draw upon the severe training they had had as sedentary merchants. Above all, they could bring to their new business a power to coördinate production and distribution and to distinguish between the short-time and the long-time point of view.

At first, industrial capitalists had a rather easy time because their competitors were business men who used the old techniques. For instance, cotton spinners, woolen weavers, and iron manufacturers operating with power machinery competed with small masters using hand tools and machines; railroad operators competed with stage coaches; and steamship operators competed with sailing vessels.

As always, there came a time when trouble for the new system was at hand. The halcyon days of industrial capitalism were over in America by the time of the Civil War, except in the case of important new industries. Competition arose between rival firms having about the same technical knowledge and equipment. Generally speaking, industrial capitalists, certainly those who had come up from the ranks of petty capitalists, were stronger in production and distribution than they were in finance. When a depression came along, they were likely to be caught unprepared. And when the long downtrend which lasted from 1866 in America and 1873 in Europe to 1897 settled over business, industrial capitalists, especially in the old industries, were hard put to it to survive.

Severe and disastrous competition led to bankruptcy or near bankruptcy or it led to sharp practice to escape bankruptcy. In some firms, by great efforts the business was reorganized from within. In other cases there was no alternative to bankruptcy or to reorganization by someone on the outside. In other words, industrial capitalism had in a remarkably short time reached old age. Specialized industry was still promising but chiefly in new fields where there was a brisk market and not much competition. New processes in meat packing and flour milling were to produce such new industries, and automobiles performed the miracle of creating numerous new industries, large and small.

5. Financial Capitalism

The new system of financial capitalism arose to correct the weaknesses of industrial capitalism. Whilst the régime of industrial capitalism disappeared, many industrial capitalists remained. Indeed, it is a common feature of social evolution that the old system as a dominant system disappears while many of the old habits and units remain. And so under financial capitalism we find a new group of financial capitalists dominant but we also find industrial capitalists and, much more numerous, petty capitalists. To be sure, mercantile capitalists have almost wholly disappeared except in a few less developed parts of the world.

Financial capitalism arose (a) to promote the flow of capital into business through the efforts of money middlemen, (b) to follow up this promotion of investment by influence or control, and (c) in the case of the far-sighted to do this primarily in the interest of investors. The main emphasis is on successful investment as evinced by returns in the form of dividends and interest. As the investors received their reward, laborers earned their wages, landlords got their rent, and the government obtained its taxes. A dollar went to the investor and ten to other groups.

In France in the 1840's there began a movement in the direction of the promotion of industries and especially railroads through the help of banks formed for the purpose. The movement ended in 1871 with the fall of the Empire. Because of the lack of evidence of effective influence or control we may conclude that this was but an adumbration of the system and not full-fledged financial capitalism. The beginning made in France, however, at once flowered in Germany and during the period 1871–1914 was dominant—as financial capitalism. Germany developed the system because, poor in investment capital, it had to make what it had go a long way. Similarly the United States was to meet its needs for capital by adopting financial capitalism. England and France, however, having no such pressing need, have not developed financial capitalism, though they have not failed to adopt the system in many of their foreign economic undertakings.

It is the great historic rôle of J. P. Morgan & Co. to have been the first to develop in America the new system that was so strongly to influence American material progress. We might name the period 1879–1933 as the chief era of financial capitalistic experience in America up to date. In 1879 Morgan sold in London some of the holdings of W. K. Vanderbilt in the New York Central Railroad. The purpose was to help this road by getting rid of the dominance of the Vanderbilt family to which so much objection had developed in America. Henceforth Morgan & Co. played an important rôle in the affairs of the New York Central; whether it be described as "control" or more likely as just "influence" not always consciously exercised is of no great matter. At any rate the event proved to be important as Morgan's beginning in the active influence or control in American railroad affairs. The other date, 1933, is the beginning of the New Deal, or national capitalism. Of course, during the interim there had been a short period (1913–17) of the New Freedom of Woodrow Wilson which only threatened financial capitalism.

We do not need to analyze completely

the financial capitalistic group, but we may properly note some of the chief elements. At the head of the group are the investment bankers who had been gradually coming into existence after 1815 and who in the firm of Jay Cooke & Co. reached considerable heights. Until Morgan pointed the way, however, these bankers had been largely instruments for selling securities. Financial capitalism was born in America when the investment bankers became active in the affairs of the concerns the securities of which they handled. Commonly the activity came through the interlocking of directorates, which has been of great service to American business though it has also brought serious abuses.

Other members of the group of financial capitalists are certain commercial banks (notably those formerly possessing security affiliates), certain large insurance companies, certain investment trusts, and certain large private estates. It would be a proper subject of inquiry for the student to find examples within each category.

Thus, there has existed and does exist a group of large investors and money middlemen, financial capitalists, operating under the leadership of the chief investment bankers. Public opinion has been fanned to fury at times by what has happened. Journalists, who have written much that is false, have fed flames of misconception. Wall Street is a term of opprobrium, not very different from La Salle Street in Chicago, State Street in Boston, or the Board of Trade in Minneapolis. The Money Trust was a popular term around 1920. A better designation would be "a community of financial interest," for the financial capitalists have no constitution and no organization. The units that make it up are motivated primarily by the advantage of controlling production and distribution, in the interest of investors and of their own business and, lastly but surely, in the general interest.

A big and potent problem is the relation of financial capitalism to industrial capitalism. If industrial capitalists did certain things, they survived. If they did not, the financial capitalists would do those things for them. If this happened, then financial capitalism supplanted industrial capitalism. It is a major point that the weakness of industrial capitalists necessitated some such control, influence, or guidance as financial capitalists offered.

Industrial capitalists were commonly weak in failing to coördinate production and distribution, in sticking to specialization of functions, in holding to short-time points of view, and in failing to establish and maintain good credit ratings so as to get capital on favorable terms. There was a tendency for such capitalists to engage in cutthroat competition and to resort to acts of dishonesty. Bankruptcy was one outcome but bankruptcy was not in the public interest, for it meant sacrifice prices of goods, lower capitalization of reorganized firms, more severe competition, and so on.

Some industrial capitalists, such as Swift & Co., Henry Ford, and the Standard Oil group, corrected the above-mentioned tendencies toward weakness. They entered something like a financial phase of industrial capitalism. They continued to be free from banker influence. They needed no outsiders to put their houses in order. To be sure, many that have succeeded may some day need outside aid.

One of the reforms that an industrial capitalist had to make was to abandon specialization. If he did not do this, he would require aid from financial capitalists who would ordinarily insist on turning away from the specialization of the nineteenth century. This change involved (a) developing multiple economic functions on the part of the firm, (b) integrating these effectively, (c) combining units horizontally, and (d) diversifying products, services, and investments.

Thus, according to this view, financial capitalism introduces into business much-needed reforms and provides much-needed capital. The Marxian view is that it simply builds up big monopolistic units. A common American view is that it enables many middlemen to grow rich through the sale of securities. Choose which view you will accept, but no simple generalization is accurate.

Emphasis upon the reform and strengthening of business as the leading characteristic of financial capitalism does not preclude the secondary characteristics, which may or may not be permanent. The régime has been undemocratic, at times ruthless, tending to monopoly, and forgetful of public opinion. It has aroused the animosity of laborers, farmers, petty capitalists, industrial capitalists, and, of course, vote-getting politicians. It has been identified with internationalism and Jewish influence. It has been in an exposed position in a period of depression when it can be blamed for all that is unfavorable and be given credit for nothing.

6. National Capitalism

Just as financial capitalism first threatened and then overthrew industrial capitalism, so now national capitalism threatens financial capitalism and may in time supersede it. Although national capitalism is a new order of society, it is nevertheless keyed to operate within the circle of private business capitalism.

National capitalism is a régime of control of the flow and, to some extent, of the use of capital. It is set up in America specifically to counteract the influence of financial capitalists and to repair damage resulting from their mistakes. The latter will not be destroyed but their sway will be restricted and their predominance curbed. In other words, industrial capitalists and petty capitalists will have as their allies the national capitalists in their dealings with financial capitalists.

Beyond this control is a growing socialization of production and distribution. This has already begun in America in the provision of electricity from public water power. It threatens to extend to the railroads, munitions, life insurance, and so on. There is not a little to be said for socialization in the case of sick or dying industries and in the case of industries that have passed the pioneering stage and become purely routine. Private business capitalism is aided not injured by such developments, provided that the management of the transition is smooth and fair to all parties concerned.

It would be easy to find dangers and weaknesses in socialization, for they are inherent in the situation. The difficulties of effective operation through political groups are great, but the danger that the whole system will go over into communistic capitalism is the real source for worry on the part of those who believe in rewarding the fit and maintaining leadership. For the present, however, we should remember that national capitalism envisages only a limited amount of socialization.

Instead of control from New York and Wall Street we shall under national capitalism have to come under the economic dominance of Washington. The national capitalists are made up of politicians (policy formulators) and political executives (managers). The workers in the group will be the civil servants.

Workmen in private business should not be left out of the picture, especially the permanent worker and the less fit in the field of employables. Such are the ones who suffer first and longest in a depression and are discarded first because of age. They are not primary movers in the growth of national capitalism but they are the sick men in the party who cause those who adventure to slow down and stop for rest and relief. It is the unfortunate and the unfit who constitute a weak spot in the nation as in the ancient cities and mediaeval towns. Scheming politicians and irresponsible social reconstructionists can take advantage of their necessities and promise them much for their political support. This is embarrassing to accredited leaders of political and economic action. In periods of stress, such as a depression or the years following a war, the whole problem of employment, rate of wages, and relief of the unfit becomes acute.

Attention was given to the position of the workers on a large scale in Germany under Bismarck and in Britain under Lloyd George. In both cases there were two drives at work: one was to do justice to those who suffered—often through no fault of their own; and the other was to prevent the political and social dangers that arise from idleness and distress. By providing social insurance against old age and unemployment, Germany and Britain made a fine gesture and accomplished something solid. In making such reforms Germany did not seriously impair its financial capitalistic régime and Britain did not seriously impair its industrial capitalistic system.

The birthplace of national capitalism as a rounded system, however, is Italy. After the World War, Italy—always a land with limited natural resources—found itself financially weak, culturally stunted, socially disintegrating, and politically corrupt. Something had to be done to check the action of irresponsible trade union leaders and the disintegrating particularism of party political leaders. The leader who saw the dangers was Benito Mussolini, who had been an excessive social reconstructionist, indeed an international radical of extreme views. He turned to fight for nationalism, first, by extending Italy's borders, secondly, by strengthening Italy's government, and, thirdly, by creating an economic system that would support capitalism against the very forces that he himself had formerly led. The march on Rome (1922), the establishment of the corporate state, the war in Ethiopia, and the bold bid for world recognition, through the war in Spain (1936–39) and through support of an anti-comintern movement, are landmarks in the unfolding of national capitalism or fascism in Italy. The revolutionary labor leaders are in exile or otherwise taken care of, trade unions have been disbanded, investors are protected, and industrialists, large and small, are encouraged to produce. The aim of economic activity seems to be taxation, and the objective of all life in Italy seems to be preparation for a great war. Planes of living have lowered, and national financial impoverishment seems threatened. All men, however, are employed at a wage, and the rank and file seem enthusiastic.

After the World War Germany was distressed by defeat, reparations, inflation, and feeble government. By 1933 Adolf Hitler found a chance to seize power and to begin the unfolding of naziism. Trade unions were abolished as was the old political régime. Hitler's personal followers, largely young men to whom many promises and benefits were given, became dominant, and their opponents were sent to concentration camps. Unemployment ceased. No petty capitalists and no industrial capitalists, unless Jewish, needed to fear labor trouble or dispossession. Let every man produce and serve the state as a soldier, worker, or tax-payer. Socialization went on particularly in the building-up of roads and war equipment. Public capital was never so great and had, of course, to be taken from the citizens in one way or another. There have been no serious labor disputes, political dissensions, and no unemployment. On the other hand, there is no freedom for non-Nazis; there is a lowering plane of living; and there is an increasing weight of taxes. Whether the end is anything but war remains to be seen.

Richer in resources than Italy or Germany, America got into difficulty in its economic system at a later date (1929), but still national capitalism was introduced with startling rapidity by Franklin D. Roosevelt in 1933. He had promised economy in the election campaign of 1932 but he reversed himself, threw over the Democratic Party platform, and almost took as his own the socialist platform of Norman Thomas. The *reforms* that he introduced were not national capitalistic, except in so far as they were aimed at financial capitalists. The New Deal was aimed at preventing the full fruition of some of the unfortunate situations of 1932–33 of which the following is a partial list: factories closed; unemployed camped near Washington; farmers stopping products going to market and preventing foreclosure sales of goods, stock, and land; citizens losing their mortgaged homes; youth tramping the country begging and stealing as they went; banks and insurance companies dangerously weakened.

Various groups needed assistance: the workers needed work, the petty capitalists needed credit, the farmers needed higher prices for their products, the industrialists needed credit and business, and the investors needed assurance that their interests would be considered. The weak had to be assisted either by taxing the rich or by drawing upon the credit of the government.

We all remember something of what was done in the hectic period 1933–36 to help the forgotten man, to restore business, and to enable the average citizen to regain his confidence. Roosevelt gained great credit for his innovations in 1933–35, but many of those innovations were unsound as permanent policies or institutions. The Supreme Court killed the N R A and part of the A A A. Then Roosevelt attacked the Supreme Court and thereby roused the country to a fear of where he was tending to go. In 1938 his party was again victorious but on a reduced scale, and his personal candidates were commonly defeated. The domestic situation has since been complicated by the threatening conditions of foreign affairs. Roosevelt's strong policy of preparedness is suspected by many as looking toward war as a way out in case the policies of the New Deal fail.

Certainly in America, as in Italy and Germany, accomplishment has been at the expense of a heavy mortgage on the future. Public debt comes to be a burden on business and a damper on enterprise. Heavy taxes create tax dodgers and lead men to invest in safe rather than forward-looking ventures. Who will run the risk of loss when most of the gain goes to the government? The very system that was founded to protect private capitalism by creating benefits for workers comes to a place where it threatens the existence of private capitalism and therefore also of workers. The issue seems to become one of going back to financial capitalism or on to communistic capitalism. It is still conceivable, however, that by careful administration national capitalism can keep an even keel and avoid retrogression.

Already in the depression that began in 1937 men have called out for the leadership of financial capitalists who during the period of their chief power, 1893–1929, kept the wheels of business turning. They say, "Let us have a few mistakes so that we may have a lot of prosperity." It is good for society, we may decide, to have two systems—financial and national capitalism—competing with one another.

National capitalism was born in the trough of despair in the downward secular trend that began in the country in 1920 and extended to the town in 1929. We recall that industrial capitalism saw its start in the downtrend of 1815–43 and financial capitalism in the downtrend of 1866–97. Each of these movements—industrial and financial capitalism—reached its height in the following uptrend. By analogy we might expect (if we wished to prophesy) that national capitalism would reach its height in the period from the 1950's to the 1980's, that is, during the next secular trend upward. On the other hand, we may argue that national capitalism will destroy itself by excessive taxes and bloody war.

In judging national capitalism the humanist will think of liberty and welfare, the politician of national power, and the economist of business. In the field of business the important considerations are whether there will be planning for new enterprises, such as involve new plants and new factories, and whether there will be a continuous flow of wealth into the coffers of the nation—most of which may go for consumptive uses and some for aid in production. It is a matter of doubt whether men will indefinitely save and turn over their savings to the government for uses which they often have no understanding of or no sympathy with and which may even compete with their own private activities. The working-out of any new system is difficult, and national capitalism is no exception to the rule.

Not only is the position of capital uncertain—over the long run—but the position of labor is clouded. Some persons think that labor is given a privileged position under national capitalism. This may be true in the early stages, as under Roosevelt in America and Blum in France. But, as time goes on, it may be expected that labor will be subordinated and disciplined as democratic forms of government give way to autocratic. When national capitalism is introduced by a revolution, as in Italy and Germany, then labor quickly goes to a position of honorable subordination. Men get work at low rates—such conditions are mingled with parades and low-priced railroad transportation. Perhaps this is the most that can be expected under such general conditions of economic and political distress as we are now experiencing.

For business as for the whole of society the future is problematical. The great need of today is to regulate the economic system in the interests of the whole, while at the same time leaving room for that initiative which is the leading instrument of efficient production. One of the significant lessons of business history is the importance of planning and execution of policy and management. Another lesson is that no form of organization is permanent. For the business man and for the individual, who through the vote or through public opinion helps set up instruments of regulation, the question is not one of abstract ideologies or systems but of what works best. An outstanding need for business history at this time comes from the necessity of understanding how our economic life actually operates.

SUGGESTIONS ON THE USE OF THE CASEBOOK

The first objective of this book is to provide material for use in training for better business administration and for a clearer understanding of business as it is today. A further objective is to enrich the field of historical study by presenting material on a significant aspect of social effort which has touched closely all phases of life—economic, religious, intellectual, and social. This book has been designed principally with a view to the first, and the suggestions that follow herewith have to do with its use in the study of American business history.

One general idea is basic to this casebook: that the heart of business is administration, and that administration can best be studied through the individual business man or enterprise. Business history according to this view should begin with the individual concern and should aim as far as possible to present business as it has operated in a dynamic setting.

While emphasizing the individual unit, the book recognizes that business men must operate within the conditions in which they live. Systems of thought, forms and policies of government, and general business conditions are among the more important larger influences which bear upon the work of the individual business man. The cases on economic thought and systems, the American government, internal markets, and business trends are concerned with those larger influences and factors. That they are in a measure the results of business does not minimize their significance as conditioning factors which bear upon the work of the individual in business.

There are forty-three cases in this book. These are by no means designed as a rounded or finished whole. Business history is young as a special field of historical study, and the subject has therefore been only partly worked. Expediency and design have both entered into the selection of subjects. There are necessarily important omissions. For instance, petty capitalism has hardly been touched upon; the South and the Far West are conspicuous in their absence; marketing organizations have been inadequately dealt with, and public utilities not at all. The book does, however, include cases on all periods in American business history and on many aspects of the work of business in the different periods.

The lack of cases on certain subjects can in part be overcome by those who use the book. It would be a very stimulating exercise for the classroom student himself to write new cases. As monographs are published in business history, the reader may find valuable data for cases. New cases could also be written from the records of local enterprises which would not be available in other districts. Indeed, really effective business history must inevitably be the coöperative work of many students.

In the use of the cases it should be remembered that they are first and foremost exercises in experience and in judgment and not things to be memorized for their own sake. The facts presented are tools to be used in making observations, analyses, and judgments or conclusions. In any given situation should be seen, on the one hand, the forces at work and the problems that have presented themselves and, on the other, how business men have met those problems—what policies they have followed and what managerial methods and techniques—and with what results.

The structure and quality of the cases vary greatly. Many have been written after exhaustive research in primary material, usually in the records of the enterprise or individual concerned. Some have been written from material easily available—often biased and superficial. Four skeleton cases—on Lloyd's, the American system of government, the American merchant marine, and flour milling—give merely suggestions of studies which the student may carry further.

The cases contain special aids for the reader. The list of dates is designed, not to stress the importance of the dates themselves, but to give a quick view of the subject of the case: some readers might find the list most useful for review after the case has been read. The readings are not a complete bibliography of materials used in the case; they indicate sources of more detailed information for those who would like to carry further the study of the case. The questions at the end of each case are designed to point to significant problems in the case; readers might well supply other questions which would be as pertinent and as useful. The map of the United States facing page 29 gives important transportation lines and cities that appear in the cases.

First and last, it should be kept in mind that the *Casebook* must be supplemented with material from other sources. No case can possibly give all that is necessary for its understanding. No field of history makes a stronger demand on the student than does business history. He must learn that the larger forces at work are vital to business at all times, and, while in those forces the economic is of prime importance, the political, social, and psychological factors are also of great significance. In business it is the individual who perceives, analyzes, and translates the various elements in a situation into policy and action, and in that process the individual becomes important. In essentially similar exterior circumstances why does one business man fail and another succeed? The question can never be completely answered, for all factors cannot be reconstructed and placed in their exact and real relationship. It is clear, however, that no approximate answer can be found without considering both the individual and the conditions under which he has worked.

The *Casebook* assumes a general knowledge of history, such as is obtained from college courses in American history. For additional general works on an important adjoining field, that of economic history, the following list of books is suggested:

N. S. B. Gras, *An Introduction to Economic History* (New York, 1922).

Herbert Heaton, *Economic History of Europe* (New York, 1936).

George M. Calhoun, *The Business Life of Ancient Athens* (Chicago, 1926).

Tenney Frank, *An Economic History of Rome* (Baltimore, 1927).

M. Rostovtzeff, *The Social and Economic History of the Roman Empire* (Oxford, 1926).

James W. Thompson, *An Economic and Social History of the Middle Ages, 300–1300* (New York, 1928), and *Economic and Social History of Europe in the Later Middle Ages, 1300–1530* (New York, 1931).

E. Lipson, *The Economic History of England,* 3 vols. (London, 1915, 1923, 1931).

W. J. Ashley, *An Introduction to English Economic History and Theory,* vol. i, parts i and ii (London, 1888, 1893).

P. J. Mantoux, *The Industrial Revolution in the Eighteenth Century: an Outline of the Beginning of the Modern Factory System in England* (Marjorie Vernon, translator, New York, 1927).

Arthur Redford, *The Economic History of England, 1760–1860* (London, 1931).
Clive Day, *Economic Development in Modern Europe* (New York, 1933).
Davis R. Dewey, *Financial History of the United States* (New York, 1934).
I. Lippincott, *Economic Development of the United States* (New York, 1927).
Edward C. Kirkland, *A History of American Economic Life* (New York, 1939).
Harold U. Faulkner, *An American Economic History* (New York, 1938).

To have meaning, the cases must be placed in their proper setting in the history of business. This the *Casebook* obviously cannot do. The book, *Business and Capitalism,*[1] has been written as a companion volume to the *Casebook,* and, since it is the only volume available for that purpose, its reading should be the first approach to the subject.

For a course of study of business history the following outline is proposed. It has been made with a view to use in a two-semester course given three hours a week. It is impossible to give full bibliographies on the various topics. On some topics little if any material exists outside the contemporary sources. There is a wealth of material on the periphery of many subjects which does not reach into the central interest of business history, that is, policy and management, but by careful selection the student can cull even from such material much that is useful and even valuable.

OUTLINE OF A COURSE IN BUSINESS HISTORY

(Arranged for three hours a week throughout the year) [2]

First Semester

1. Topic: The Origin of Private Business.
   Readings: N. S. B. Gras, *Business and Capitalism* (New York, 1939), chaps. i and ii; see readings for chap. ii.
2. Topic: The Rise and Development of the Sedentary Merchant.
   Readings: Gras, *Business and Capitalism,* pp. 67–119; W. A. S. Hewins, *English Trade and Finance Chiefly in the Seventeenth Century* (London, 1892); H. R. Fox Bourne, *English Merchants,* vol. i (London, 1866).
3. Topic: The European Merchant in the Planting of Early Colonies.
   Readings: W. F. Craven, *Dissolution of the Virginia Company* (New York, 1932); Frances Rose-Troup, *The Massachusetts-Bay Company and Its Predecessors* (New York, 1930), and *John White* (New York, 1931); C. M. Andrews, *The Colonial Period of American History,* vol. i. (New Haven, 1934); J. Franklin Jameson, *Willem Usselinx, Founder of the Dutch and Swedish West India Companies* (Papers of American Historical Association, vol. ii, no. 3, 1887); William T. Davis, editor, *Bradford's History of Plymouth Plantation* (New York, 1908); *Records of the Governor and Company of Massachusetts Bay in New England,* 5 vols. (Boston, 1853–54).
4. Case: Sir Thomas Smythe and the Virginia Company, 1558(?)–1625.
5. Topic: The Economic Revolution in the Colonies: the Development of Colonial Business and Management.
   Readings: *Bradford's History of Plymouth Plantation; Records of the Governor and Company of Massachusetts Bay in New England;* Curtis P. Nettels, *The Money Supply of the American Colonies before 1720* (Madison, 1934), and *The Roots of American Civilization* (New York, 1938); A. M. Davis, *Currency and Banking in the Province of Massachusetts Bay,* 2 vols. (New York, 1901); C. M. Andrews, *The Colonial Period of American History,* vols. i–iii (New Haven, 1934–37); W. B. Weeden, *Economic and Social History of New England,* 2 vols. (Boston and New York, 1890).
6. Case: William Fitzhugh's Proposals for a

[1] By N. S. B. Gras, published by F. S. Crofts & Co. in 1939.

[2] The numerals in this outline refer to class hours, estimated as ninety for the year.

Constant Factorage in Virginia, 1683–1687.

7. Topic: The Framework of Business History.
Readings: Pages 4–15, above; Gras, *Business and Capitalism, passim.*
8. Case: Robert Keayne, Boston Merchant, 1596–1656.
9. Topic: Religion and Business.
Readings: Gras, *Business and Capitalism,* pp. 151–157; E. A. J. Johnson, *American Economic Thought in the Seventeenth Century* (Cambridge, 1932); Samuel E. Morison, *Builders of the Bay Colony* (Boston, 1930); Albert Hyma, *Christianity, Capitalism, and Communism: a Historical Analysis* (Ann Arbor, 1937); Werner Sombart, *The Jews and Modern Capitalism* (London, 1913), and *The Quintessence of Capitalism* (London, 1915); Herbert I. Bloom, *The Economic Activities of the Jews of Amsterdam in the Seventeenth and Eighteenth Centuries* (Williamsport, Pa., 1937); Max Weber, *General Economic History* (F. H. Knight, translator, New York, 1927); H. M. Robertson, *Aspects of the Rise of Economic Individualism* (Cambridge, England, 1933).
10. Case: John Hancock, 1737–1793.
11. Topic: Colonial Business Men of the Eighteenth Century.
Readings: W. T. Baxter, "Daniel Henchman, a Colonial Bookseller," *Essex Institute Historical Collections,* vol. lxx (1934), pp. 1–30; Edward Edelman, "Thomas Hancock, Colonial Merchant," *Journal of Economic and Business History,* vol. i (1928–29), pp. 77–104; Paul H. Giddens, "Trade and Industry in Colonial Maryland, 1753–1769," *ibid.,* vol. iv (1931–32), pp. 512–538; Elizabeth Donnan, "Eighteenth-Century English Merchants: Micajah Perry," *ibid.,* vol. iv (1931–32), pp. 70–98; Susie M. Ames, "A Typical Virginia Business Man of the Revolutionary Era," *ibid.,* vol. iii (1930–31), pp. 407–423; David D. Wallace, *The Life of Henry Laurens* (New York, 1915); Elizabeth Donnan, editor, *Documents Illustrative of the History of the Slave Trade to America,* vols. iii and iv (Washington, 1932 and 1935); Leila Sellers, *Charleston Business on the Eve of the Revolution* (Chapel Hill, 1934); Virginia D. Harrington, *The New York Merchant on the Eve of the Revolution* (New York, 1935); Nettels, *The Roots of American Civilization.*
12. Case: John Jacob Astor, 1763–1848.
13. Topic: Late Sedentary Merchants in America.
Readings: Gras, *Business and Capitalism,* pp. 165–169; E. P. Oberholtzer, *Robert Morris, Patriot and Financier of the American Revolution* (New York, 1903); K. W. Porter, *John Jacob Astor, Business Man,* 2 vols. (Cambridge, 1931); John B. McMaster, *The Life and Times of Stephen Girard,* 2 vols. (Philadelphia, 1918); John C. Brown, *A Hundred Years of Merchant Banking* (New York, 1909).
14. Case: Early Economic Systems, Especially Mercantilism.
15. Topic: Merchants' Policies and Mercantilism.
Readings: Suggested readings, pp. 115–116, below; and Gras, *Business and Capitalism,* pp. 120–129.
16. Case: An American System of Government and Business.
17. Topic: Foundation Stones of American Business.
Suggestions: This large topic, on which there is much scattered but no concentrated material, may be handled in a number of ways. Foundation stones other than the system of government could be considered, such as the population (including social, political, religious, intellectual, and economic background), the resources of the country, and the institutions of importance to business. The reception and adaptation of the common law is one of the institutional foundations which had great significance. The following have been selected from a large mass of material which touches the subject but does not deal with it fully: Simeon E. Baldwin, "History of the Law of Private Corporations in the Colonies and the States," *Select Essays in Anglo-American Legal History,* vol. iii (Boston, 1909), pp. 236–255; George Cairnes, *Enquiry into the Law Merchant of the United States* (New York, 1802); R. C.

Dale, "Adoption of the Common Law by the American Colonies," *American Law Register,* vol. xxi (1882), pp. 553–574; F. A. Henry, "English Common Law in the United States," *The Western Reserve Law Journal,* vol. viii (1910); O. W. Holmes, *The Common Law* (Boston, 1881); James Kent, *Commentaries on American Law,* 4 vols. (Boston, 1896); Nathan Isaacs, "The Merchant and his Law," *Journal of Political Economy,* vol. xxiii (1915), pp. 529–567; H. Pope, "The English Common Law in the United States," *Harvard Law Review,* vol. xxiv (1910–11), pp. 6–30; Roscoe Pound, *Outline of a Course on the History and System of the Common Law* (Cambridge, 1919), and "The Place of Judge Story in the Making of American Law," *United States Law Review,* vol. xlviii (1914), pp. 676–697; P. S. Reinsch, *The English Common Law in the Early American Colonies,* Bulletin of the University of Wisconsin (1898); H. T. Terry, *Some Leading Principles of Anglo-American Law* (Philadelphia, 1884); *Two Centuries' Growth of American Law, 1701–1901* (New York, 1901); Charles Warren, *A History of the American Bar* (Boston, 1911); Samuel Williston, "History of the Law of Business Corporations before 1800," *Harvard Law Review,* vol. ii (1888), pp. 105–124, 149–166.

18. Topic: Weaknesses of Mercantile Capitalism and the Rise of Industrial Capitalism.
    Readings: Gras, *Business and Capitalism,* pp. 160–165, 169–195.
19. Case: John P. Cushing as an Investor, 1828–1862.
20. Topic: Forces Driving Business toward Change, 1815–43.
    Suggestion: For this topic may be substituted Business Difficulties and the Emergence of Specialization in a Period of Declining Prices, 1815–43, pp. 664–682, below.
21. Case: The Rise and Decline of the American Merchant Marine.
22. Topic: Risk and Early Methods of Meeting Risk.
    Comment: There is no history of risk in business ("uncertainty in regard to cost, loss, or damage") nor is there any comprehensive general historical work on ways of meeting risk. On the problem of risk the broadest treatment in English is Charles O. Hardy, *Risk and Risk-Bearing* (Chicago, 1923). Many institutions have been important in spreading the effect of losses, such as the family, the community, the partnership, and the corporation. Risk-bearing emerged early as a separate function in business, and the only general work on its early history is C. F. Trenerry, *The Origin and Early History of Insurance, including the Contract of Bottomry* (London, 1926).
23. Case: History of Lloyd's, an Association of Underwriters.
24. Case: Thomas Willing & Company, a Study of Early Marine Underwriters in Philadelphia.
25. Case: The Philadelphia Contributionship for the Insurance of Houses from Loss by Fire, 1752–1938.
26. Topic: The Early History of Life Insurance.
    Readings: Trenerry, *The Origin and Early History of Insurance;* A. F. Jack, *An Introduction to the History of Life Assurance* (London, 1912); J. A. Fowler, *History of Insurance in Philadelphia for Two Centuries, 1683–1882* (Philadelphia, 1888); C. K. Knight, *The History of Life Insurance in the United States to 1870* (Philadelphia, 1920); James M. Hudnut, *Semi-Centennial History of the New-York Life Insurance Company, 1845–1895* (New York, 1895); [Henry Tyrrell], *Semi-Centennial History of the Northwestern Mutual Life Insurance Company of Milwaukee, Wisconsin, 1858–1908* (Milwaukee, 1908).
27. Topic: The History of Early Banking in Europe.
    Readings: Gras, *Business and Capitalism,* pp. 148–151; C. A. Conant, *History of Modern Banks of Issue* (New York, 1927); Heinrich Sieveking, *Genueser Finanzwesen mit besonderer Berücksichtigung der Casa di S. Giorgio,* 2 vols. (Freiburg, 1898–99); A. P. Usher, "Deposit Banking in Barcelona, 1300–1700," *Journal of Economic and Business History,* vol. iv (1931–32), pp. 121–155; J. J. van Dillen, "La Banque d' Amsterdam,"

Revue d'Histoire Moderne, May-June, 1928, pp. 161–187; Eli F. Heckscher, *Sveriges Ekonomiska Historia,* part i, vol. ii (Stockholm, 1936), pp. 623–633; Richard D. Richards, *The Early History of Banking in England* (London, 1929); J. E. T. Rogers, *The First Nine Years of the Bank of England* (Oxford, 1887).

28. Case: The Massachusetts Bank, 1784–1903.
29. Topic: Early American Banking.
Readings: Gras, *Business and Capitalism,* pp. 186–189; A. M. Davis, *Currency and Banking in the Province of Massachusetts-Bay;* Nettels, *The Money Supply of the American Colonies before 1720;* H. E. Miller, *Banking Theories in the United States before 1860* (Cambridge, 1927); N. S. B. Gras, *The Massachusetts-First National Bank of Boston, 1784–1934* (Cambridge, 1937); Allan Nevins, *History of the Bank of New York and Trust Company, 1784 to 1934* (New York, 1934); John H. Michener, *The Bank of North America* (New York, 1906); James O. Wettereau, "New Light on the First Bank of the United States," *Pennsylvania Magazine of History and Biography,* July, 1937.
30. Case: Second Bank of the United States, an Experiment with Branches.
31. Topic: The Early Industrial Revolution.
Readings: Gras, *Business and Capitalism,* pp. 92–103, 175–181; P. J. Mantoux, *The Industrial Revolution in the Eighteenth Century: an Outline of the Beginnings of the Modern Factory System in England* (New York, 1927); George Unwin, *Industrial Organization in the Sixteenth and Seventeenth Centuries* (Oxford, 1904), and *Samuel Oldknow and the Arkwrights* (Manchester, 1924); T. S. Ashton, *Iron and Steel in the Industrial Revolution* (London, 1924); Herbert Heaton, *The Yorkshire Woollen and Worsted Industries* (Oxford, 1920).
32. Case: Boulton & Watt, 1775–1800.
33. Topic: Industrial Stages.
Readings: Gras, *Business and Capitalism,* p. 93, and *Industrial Evolution* (New York, 1930).
34. Case: Samuel Slater and the American Textile Industry, 1789–1835.
35. Topic: Spread of the Industrial Revolution in America.
Readings: (1) General: V. S. Clark, *History of Manufactures in the United States, 1607–1860,* vol. i (New York, 1929). (2) On the Boston Manufacturing Co. and the textile industry on the Merrimac: Nathan Appleton, *Introduction of the Power Loom, and Origin of Lowell* (Lowell, Mass., 1858); Caroline Ware, *The Early New England Cotton Manufacture* (Boston, 1931). (3) On the reaper: W. T. Hutchinson, *Cyrus Hall McCormick: Seed-Time, 1809–1856* (New York, 1930). (4) On precision instruments and standard parts: J. W. Roe, *English and American Tool Builders* (New Haven, 1916); Denison Olmsted, *Memoir of Eli Whitney* (New Haven, 1846); W. P. Blake, "Sketch of the Life of Eli Whitney," *Papers of the New Haven Historical Society,* vol. v (1894), pp. 109–131.
36. Case: Josiah Wedgwood & Sons, Ltd., 1759–1920.
37. Topic: The History of Crises and Fluctuations in Business.
Readings: Gras, *Business and Capitalism, passim;* "Crises," *Encyclopaedia of the Social Sciences;* H. Hauser, "The European Finançial Crisis of 1559," *Journal of Economic and Business History,* vol. ii (1929–30), pp. 241–255; R. Ehrenberg, *Capital and Finance in the Age of the Renaissance* (H. M. Lucas, translator, New York, undated). N. W. Posthumus, "The Tulip Mania in Holland in the Years 1636 and 1637," *Journal of Economic and Business History,* vol. i (1928–29), pp. 434–466; W. R. Scott, *Constitution and Finance of the English, Scottish, and Irish Joint-Stock Companies to 1720,* vol. i (London, 1912); Willard L. Thorp, *Business Annals* (New York, 1926).
38. Topic: The General Situation in Western Europe in the Early Eighteenth Century.
Readings: Herbert Heaton, *Economic History of Europe* (New York, 1936), chaps. xiii–xiv; Witt Bowden, Michael Korpovich, and Abbot Payson Usher, *An Economic History of Europe since 1750*

(New York, 1937), chaps. i and ii; W. F. Reddaway, *A History of Europe from 1715 to 1814* (London, 1936); W. C. Abbott, *The Expansion of Europe* (New York, 1938), chap. xxix.

39. Case: John Law, Financier and Speculator.

40. Topic: Business Promotion and the Corporation in America in the Late Eighteenth Century.
Readings: Robert A. East, *Business Enterprise in the American Revolutionary Era* (New York, 1938); J. S. Davis, *Essays in the Earlier History of American Corporations,* 2 vols. (Cambridge, 1917); E. M. Dodd, *The First Half Century of Statutory Regulation of Business Corporations in Massachusetts* (Cambridge, 1934); Shaw Livermore, *Early American Land Companies; Their Influence on Corporate Development* (New York, 1939).

41. Case: William Duer, Contractor and Speculator, 1747–1799.

42. Topic: The Flow of Investment Capital under Early Industrial Capitalism.
Readings: Gras, *Business and Capitalism,* pp. 218–223; John P. Cushing as an Investor, pp. 119–130, below; L. H. Jenks, *The Migration of British Capital to 1875* (New York, 1927); Henrietta M. Larson, "S. & M. Allen—Lottery, Exchange, and Stock Brokerage," *Journal of Economic and Business History,* vol. iii (1930–31), pp. 424–445, and "E. W. Clark & Co., 1837–1857," *ibid.*, vol. iv (1931–32), pp. 429–460, and *Jay Cooke, Private Banker* (Cambridge, 1936); G. H. Evans, "Early History of Preferred Stock in the United States," *American Economic Review,* vol. xix (1929).

43. Case: Jay Cooke & Co., 1861–1873.

44. Case: The Development of the New York Stock Exchange.

45. Topic: The Rise and Development of Commodity and Stock Exchanges.
Readings: "Fairs," *Encyclopaedia of the Social Sciences;* N. S. B. Gras, *The Evolution of the English Corn Market from the Twelfth to the Eighteenth Century* (Cambridge, 1926); Abbot Payson Usher, *The History of the Grain Trade in France, 1400–1710* (Cambridge, 1913); E. Vidal, *The History and Methods of the Paris Bourse* (National Monetary Commission, Washington, 1910); William Parker, *The Paris Bourse and French Finance* (New York, 1920); A. P. Poley, *The History, Law, and Practice of the Stock Exchange* (London, 1907); James E. Boyle, *Speculation and the Chicago Board of Trade* (New York, 1921), and *Cotton and the New Orleans Cotton Exchange: a Century of Commercial Evolution* (New York, 1934).

46. Case: Business Prosperity and the Victory of Specialized Business in a Period of Rising Prices, 1843–1866.
Suggestion: This case may be omitted here and considered at the end of the course with the other cases on secular trends.

47. Topic: Summary of Chief Developments in Business History so far Considered.

Second Semester

48. Topic: Review of Petty Capitalism, Mercantile Capitalism, and the Beginnings of Industrial Capitalism.
Readings: Gras, *Business and Capitalism,* pp. 27–237.

49. Case: New York Transatlantic Packet Services, 1817–1837.

50. Case: Cornelius Vanderbilt, 1794–1877.

51. Topic: Early Railroad Promotion and Management.
Comment: Since American railroad history has not been written with a view to administration and management, material on this subject must be sought chiefly in original sources. Something can be gleaned from *Hunt's Merchants' Magazine,* annual reports of railroads, and the *American Railroad Journal,* but the richest sources are the private papers of the men concerned.
Readings: George P. Baker, *The Formation of the New England Railroad Systems; a Study of Railroad Combination in the Nineteenth Century* (Cambridge, 1937); Caroline F. MacGill, *History of Transportation in the United States before 1860* (Washington, 1917); J. L. Ringwalt, *Development of Transportation Systems in the United States* (Philadelphia, 1888).

52. Topic: Stages in the Development of the Market, with Special Reference to the Metropolitan Market.
Readings: Gras, *Business and Capitalism*, pp. 127–132, and *An Introduction to Economic History*, pp. 181–340.
53. Case: Cincinnati Southern Railway: Struggle between Two Rival Cities for Metropolitan Dominance, 1860–1929.
54. Case: The Development of Internal Markets: Metropolitan Economy.
55. Topic: Changes in Market Organization, 1815–1890.
Readings: Gras, *Business and Capitalism*, pp. 195–207; Ray B. Westerfield, *Middlemen in English Business, Particularly between 1660 and 1760* (New Haven, 1915), and "Early History of American Auctions—a Chapter in Commercial History," *Transactions of the Connecticut Academy of Arts and Sciences*, vol. xxiii (1920); Richardson L. Wright, *Hawkers and Walkers in Early America* (Philadelphia, 1927); Lewis E. Atherton, *The Pioneer Merchant in Mid-America* (Columbia, Mo., 1939); F. M. Jones, *Middlemen in the Domestic Trade of the United States, 1800–1860* (Urbana, Ill., 1937); John B. Jones (pseudonym for Luke Shortfield), *The Western Merchant, A Narrative, Containing Useful Instruction for the Western Man of Business Who Makes His Purchases in the East; also, Information for the Eastern Man whose Customers are in the West; Likewise, Hints for those who design emigrating to the West. Deduced from actual Experience by Luke Shortfield* (Philadelphia, 1849), and also by the same writer, *Life and Adventures of a Country Merchant* (Philadelphia, 1854); N. S. Buck, *The Development of the Organisation of Anglo-American Trade, 1800–1850* (New Haven, 1925); Hermann Hagedorn, *Brookings: A Biography* (New York, 1936); H. J. Thornton, *The History of the Quaker Oats Company* (Chicago, 1933).
56. Case: James J. Hill and the Great Northern Railway, 1876–1916.
57. Topic: Railroad Management.
Readings: Gras, *Business and Capitalism*, pp. 181–186; C. F. and Henry Adams, *Chapters of Erie, and Other Essays* (Boston, 1871); F. C. Hicks, *High Finance in the Sixties* (New Haven, 1929); *A Century of Progress, History of the Delaware and Hudson Company, 1823–1923* (Albany, 1925); Edward Hungerford, *The Story of the Baltimore & Ohio Railroad, 1827–1927*, 2 vols. (New York, 1928); James B. Hedges, *Henry Villard and the Railways of the Northwest* (New Haven, 1930); J. G. Pyle, *The Life of James J. Hill*, 2 vols. (Garden City, 1917); George Kennan, *E. H. Harriman*, 2 vols. (Boston, 1922); E. G. Campbell, *The Reorganization of the American Railroad System, 1893–1900* (New York, 1938), pp. 9–144; John Moody, *The Railroad Builders* (New Haven, 1919).
58. Case: Chicago, Milwaukee, St. Paul & Pacific Railroad, 1852–1938.
59. Topic: Industrial Capitalism and Social Engineering in the Manufacturing Field.
Readings: Gras, *Business and Capitalism*, pp. 227–234; W. M. Leiserson, "Contributions of Personnel Management to Improved Labor Relations," *Wertheim Lectures on Industrial Relations* (Cambridge, 1929), pp. 125–164; J. D. Hackett, *Labor Management* (New York, 1929); G. D. H. Cole, *Robert Owen* (Boston, 1925); W. H. L. Leverhulme, *Viscount Leverhulme, by his Son* (Boston, 1927); J. A. Williams, *The Firm of Cadbury, 1831–1931* (New York, 1931).
60. Case: Dennison Manufacturing Company, 1844–1938.
61. Topic: Andrew Carnegie as an Industrial Capitalist.
Readings: Gras, *Business and Capitalism*, pp. 192–193; Burton J. Hendrick, *The Life of Andrew Carnegie* (New York, 1932).
62. Case: N. W. Ayer & Son, Advertising Agency, 1869–1939.
63. Topic: The Business Auxiliary.
Readings: Gras, *Business and Capitalism*, pp. 49–51, 207–214, 293–297.
64. Case: John Wanamaker, 1838–1922.
65. Topic: History of the Department Store.
Comment and Suggestions: There is no satisfactory work on this subject. Books on individual stores are either useless as business history or are written from too

narrow a point of view to be entirely satisfactory. In G. d'Avenel's *Le Mécanisme de la vie moderne* (Paris, 1902), the chapter on "Les Magasins de Nouveautés" is suggestive; and R. M. Hower's brief article in the *Bulletin of the Business Historical Society,* vol. xii (1938), pp. 91–101, points to a promising study of the department store in America.

66. Topic: The Weaknesses of Industrial Capitalism and the Beginning of Specialization.
Readings: Gras, *Business and Capitalism,* pp. 234–246. The case, Business Difficulties, with a Tendency to Combine and Integrate, in a Period of Declining Prices, 1866–1897 (pp. 706–725, below) may be read in connection with this topic or may be considered at the end of the course with the other cases on secular trends.
67. Case: Two Metropolitan Banks: First National Bank of Boston and First National Bank of New York.
68. Topic: Early Financial Capitalists.
Readings: Gras, *Business and Capitalism,* pp. 246–259; Ehrenberg, *Capital and Finance in the Age of the Renaissance;* article and bibliography on Saint-Simon in *Encyclopaedia of the Social Sciences* or in *Britannica;* André Liesse, *Evolution of Credit and Banks in France* (National Monetary Commission, Washington, 1909); Jacob Riesser, *The German Great Banks and their Concentration in Connection with the Economic Development of Germany* (National Monetary Commission, Washington, 1911); Count Egon Caesar Corti, *The Reign of the House of Rothschild, 1830–1871* (New York, 1928); G. W. Edwards, *The Evolution of Finance Capitalism* (London, 1938).
69. Case: Two Life Insurance Companies: the Mutual and the Equitable, of New York, 1842–1938.
70. Topic: Two Investigations of Financial Concentration.
Readings: The report of the Armstrong Investigation (*Report of the Joint Committee of the Senate and Assembly of the State of New York Appointed to Investigate the Affairs of Life Insurance Companies,* 7 vols., Albany, 1905–06), and the report of the Pujo Investigation (*Money Trust Investigation: Investigation of Financial and Monetary Conditions in the United States,* 62nd Congress, 3rd Sess., 1912–13), are invaluable sources on the subject of financial capitalism in the United States. The latter must be used critically, but for both investigations the hearings give much information on the interrelation of financial institutions.
71. Case: J. Pierpont Morgan, 1837–1913.
72. Case: International Mercantile Marine Company, 1901–1937.
73. Case: Elbert H. Gary and the United States Steel Corporation.
74. Topic: Financial Capitalism and Capitalists in America, 1901–1938.
Readings: Gras, *Business and Capitalism,* pp. 251–293; Kennan, *E. H. Harriman, A Biography;* Cyrus Adler, *Jacob H. Schiff, His Life and Letters,* 2 vols. (Garden City, New York, 1929); Anna Robeson Burr, *The Portrait of a Banker: James Stillman, 1850–1918* (New York, 1927); "William Rockefeller," *Dictionary of American Biography* and *Who's Who in America,* 1922–23; T. W. Lawson, *Frenzied Finance* (New York, 1905).
75. Topic: Strength and Weakness of Financial Capitalism in America.
Readings: Gras, *Business and Capitalism,* pp. 305–322.
76. Case: Armour & Company, 1867–1938.
77. Topic: Swift & Company.
Readings: L. F. Swift, *The Yankee of the Yards* (Chicago, 1927); T. W. Goodspeed, *Gustavus Franklin Swift, 1839–1903* (Chicago, 1921); R. A. Clemen, *The American Livestock and Meat Industry* (New York, 1923); U. S. Federal Trade Commission, *Report on the Meat Packing Industry,* parts i–vi (1919).
78. Case: The Flour-Milling Industry in the United States.
79. Topic: Phases of Industrial Capitalism.
Readings: Gras, *Business and Capitalism,* pp. 189–195.
80. Hugo Stinnes, German Industrialist.
81. Topic: Associations and Combinations.
Readings: Gras, *Business and Capitalism,* pp. 266–292; L. H. Haney, *Business Organization and Combination* (New York,

1934); Eliot Jones, *The Trust Problem in the United States* (New York, 1921); *The International Cartel Movement* by L. Domeratzky, U. S. Dept. of Commerce, Trade Information Bulletin, no. 556, 1928; H. Levy, *Monopolies, Cartels and Trusts in British Industry* (London, 1927), and *Industrial Germany* (Cambridge, 1935); D. Warriner, *Combines and Rationalisation in Germany, 1924–1928* (London, 1931); Thornton, *The History of the Quaker Oats Company.*

82. Topic: Secular Trends in Business.
Readings: Pages 000–000, below; Gras, *Business and Capitalism,* pp. 215–218, 297–304; W. C. Mitchell, *Business Cycles* (New York, 1927).
83. Case: Business Difficulties and the Emergence of Specialization in a Period of Declining Prices, 1815–1843.
Suggestions: If any of these cases have been used earlier, they should be reviewed here, but it would not be necessary to discuss them fully again unless they were handled from another point of view.
84. Case: Business Prosperity and the Victory of Specialized Business in a Period of Rising Prices, 1843–1866.
85. Case: Business Difficulties, with a Tendency to Combine and Integrate, in a Period of Declining Prices, 1866–1897.
86. Case: Business Prosperity and the Recombination of Business Functions, in a Period of Rising Prices, 1897–1920.
87. Topic: Recent Trends, 1920 to the Present.
Readings: F. C. Mills, *Economic Tendencies in the United States* (New York, 1932), and *Prices in Recession and Recovery* (New York, 1936); J. M. Clark, *Strategic Factors in Business Cycles* (New York, 1934); Conference on Unemployment (1921), Committee on Recent Economic Changes, *Recent Economic Changes* (New York, 1929); H. V. Hodson, *Slump and Recovery, 1929–1937* (London, 1938).
88. Case: Recent Economic Systems.
89. Topic: National Capitalism.
Readings: Gras, *Business and Capitalism,* pp. 323–372; L. E. Hubbard, *Soviet Trade and Distribution* (London, 1938); Adolf Hitler, *Mein Kampf* (New York, 1939); F. L. Schuman, *The Nazi Dictatorship: A Study in Social Pathology and the Politics of Fascism* (New York, 1936); W. G. Welk, *Fascist Economic Policy* (Cambridge, 1938); Frieda Wunderlich, "Germany's Defense Economy and the Decay of Capitalism," *Quarterly Journal of Economics,* vol. lii (May, 1938), pp. 401–430.
90. Topic: Summary of Chief Developments in American Business History.

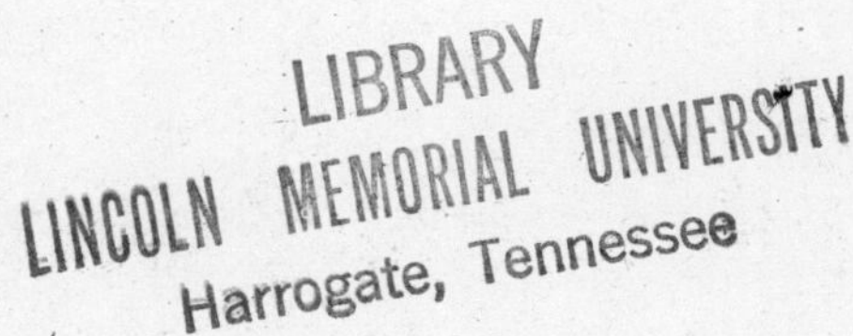

CASES IN BUSINESS HISTORY

MERCANTILE CAPITALISM

I. SIR THOMAS SMYTHE AND THE VIRGINIA COMPANY 1558(?)–1625

1. General Statement

Sir Thomas Smythe, one of the greatest merchants of his day, was closely associated with the most important English trading companies of the late sixteenth and early seventeenth centuries. Born in that decade which saw the beginning of a new capitalistic system of enterprise in English foreign trade, Sir Thomas Smythe lived long enough to help finance or to manage most of the great English joint-stock companies of his day. A shrewd, self-confident, businesslike make-up won him the admiration of King James's court and the London exchange. An ability to manage corporations, first shown in the Levant Co., led to his selection as governor of the Russia and Virginia companies and gave him the opportunity to reorganize and strengthen them. A clear-headed financier, he recognized the advantages of combinations of "moneyed capital" and of agreements and common understandings among the outstanding London companies. Always in the foreground helping to project new plans and adventures, he was one of those who sent Hudson to Hudson Bay, Thomas Button to discover the Northwest Passage, and William Baffin to the Arctic.

Despite the fact that British seamen gave his name to headlands, bays, islands, and capes scattered throughout the world, Smythe was hated by hundreds of powerful English gentlemen and Virginia colonists. Plutocratic, a believer in autocratic government and the monopolistic control of trade, a protector of corporation interests during his brief term in Parliament, a bit lax in his attention to the details of managing the Virginia Co., the bold leader of a feud with Sandys (one of the heads of the English Liberal movement), he could hardly be expected to pass through life unscathed by the tumultuous attacks of his enemies.

The real issue from which arose the opposition of Sandys to Smythe was the failure of the Virginia Co. to make profits. Accused of mismanagement and even dishonesty in his administration of the affairs of the Company, Smythe was forced to resign. His crime actually was that he had not produced dividends. But even the Liberal Sandys, his successor, similarly failed to produce profits. The result was that the Company, virtually bankrupt, in 1624 lost its charter. Thus the two opposing factions, one led by a prominent London business man and the other by an outstanding English Liberal, failed in the New World.

2. Important Dates in the Career of Sir Thomas Smythe

1558(?)	Birth. His grandfather had been a yeoman haberdasher and clothier, and his father was a haberdasher in London.
1580	Admitted to the Haberdashers' Co. and the Skinners'. Within a short time was a rich man.
1599	Governor of the Levant Co. and one of the sheriffs of London.
1600	First governor of the East India Co., serving only four months.
1601	Falsely charged with aiding the rebellion planned by the Earl

1601	of Essex. Imprisoned in the Tower.
1603	Knighted.
1603–21	Governor of the East India Co., except in 1606–07.
1604	Special ambassador to the czar of Russia. Seems to have been concerned with the Russia trade and the Russia Co.
1606	Helped organize the Virginia Co. of London.
1607–20	Governor of the Russia Co.
1609–19	Treasurer of the Virginia Co. Obtained a new charter for the Company in 1609.
1619	Forced to resign, giving way to Edwin Sandys.
1624	Sandys lost control of the Company which was bankrupt.
1625	The Virginia Co. dissolved. Smythe died.

3. Early English Joint-Stock Companies

To understand the operations of the Virginia Co. of London it is necessary to keep in mind that this enterprise was but a part of the far-flung efforts of England to develop foreign trade which had been active from about the middle of the sixteenth century. Thus London merchants had half a century of experience in corporation management of trade when the Virginia Co. was established. Though operations were carried on under difficulties and severe reverses were suffered, the profits had generally been astonishingly high. The East India Co. was very profitable even during many years when the American enterprise was languishing. The following summary of the experience of three companies is meant to illustrate the activities of London merchants in general and Sir Thomas Smythe in particular.

A. The Russia, or Muscovy, Co. was probably the first joint-stock company to be organized in England. Before its time regulated companies had been formed for important trading operations. The regulated company was an association of single merchants or partnership groups which provided protection and facilities for trade that a single unit could not alone provide but left the actual trading to the individual.

Hakluyt gives some information about the formation of the Russia Co.[1] Its object was to open up new trade for England, "seeing that the wealth of the Spaniards and Portuguese, by the discovery and search of new trades and countries was marvelously increased." The promoters moved cautiously, choosing "certain grave and wise persons in manner of a senate or company, which should lay their heads together, and give their judgments and provide things requisite and profitable for all occasions." These wise men proposed that every man willing to join the "society" contribute £25, through which course £6,000 was gathered and three ships were purchased.

A significant fact about the Russia Co. is that it was at the beginning a joint-stock enterprise. Sebastian Cabot, governor of the Company, made it clear in his "Ordinances" of May 9, 1553, that the Company was not to be run on the regulated plan. He specifically forbade individuals from doing any selling or buying, implying that such trade would "hinder or prejudicate the common stock of the company." [2] The original joint stock was kept intact until 1586, when the interests of the Company were sold to a second Russia Co.

The Russia Co., the "Mysterie of the Companie of Marchants Adventurers for the discoverie of regions, dominions, islands and places unknowen," had a varied career. It sent out strongly armed vessels —in the absence of any protection from

[1] Richard Hakluyt, *The Principal Navigations, Voyages, Traffiques, and Discoveries of the English Nation,* vol. ii (Glasgow and New York, 1903), pp. 239–240. Spelling has been modernized throughout this and all long quotations printed in the case. No changes in grammatical structure or punctuation have been made.

[2] *Ibid.,* p. 201.

the government—to explore and trade. Almost at once it secured from Ivan the privilege of trading freely in Russia, and from England a monopoly of that trade. It also, in 1566, secured a route through Persia for trade with the Orient. The Company met many problems, such as dangers from attack, freezing in the Arctic, competition which disregarded its monopoly, and the tying-up of capital in long-time credits to the queen for naval stores imported. During its first ten years, it had to make assessments on its shareholders; but from 1566, when a route to the Orient was secured, until 1581, when the oriental trade ended, the Company flourished. As the outcome of one of its so-called "unsuccessful voyages," 106 per cent was paid on each share. But in 1581 the Persia trade ceased. Owing to its dependence thereafter on the unprofitable Russia trade—unprofitable in part, some think, because of the corruption of its agents, the original Company took a downward course until it was reorganized in 1586.

This second company likewise failed, and in 1593–94 a third was formed. It united with the East India Co. in an expedition to discover a northwest passage to India. Its problems also were many. It was attacked in the House of Commons for exacting high prices for cordage and, because the directors "had made one purse and stock of all," for existing as a monopoly. Meanwhile its governor was suspected of having manipulated its accounts.

In 1607 Sir Thomas Smythe entered into the administration of the Russia Co. The third company at that time made a bargain with the earlier adventurers and a fourth joint-stock company was formed with Smythe—who had held stock in the concern inherited from his grandfather, one of the founders of the Russia Company—as governor. Under his administration the Company went into the whaling trade, having secured a monopoly of that industry from Parliament. This venture was very successful; it made a total profit of 339 per cent, an average of about 42 per cent per annum, during its first eight years. But it, also, ran into trouble; in 1618 it was forced to borrow money from different sources, including the East India Co., and at that time its monopoly was threatened by James I, who wanted to grant the trade to another enterprise. Smythe's company was finally forced to sell out to a newly formed Russia Co. which lasted until 1669.[3]

B. A second company with which Smythe was associated was the Levant Co. This concern had been established in 1581—the year the Russia Co. began to be unprofitable—to trade with Turkey. Smythe was one of its twenty founders. The Levant Co. was given a monopoly of the English trade with Turkey and received from Queen Elizabeth £40,000, as a loan or an investment, from the prize money resulting from Drake's privateering voyages. This Company seems for many years to have traded as a joint stock. Agents were kept in Turkey and a considerable trade was carried on. The profits of the enterprise were large, but success aroused the animosity of the Venetians and the Spaniards. The latter were defeated in 1588, and the former were struck at through the grant to the Levant Co. in 1592 of a monopoly of English trade with the Venetians. The Company had high profits, while it held its monopoly, particularly from the current trade; but the loss of the monopoly brought disorganization in the trade, and in 1599–1600 the joint-stock concern

[3] The principal sources used for this summary: W. R. Scott, *The Constitution and Finance of English, Scottish, and Irish Joint-Stock Companies to 1720,* vols. i, ii (Cambridge, England, 1912, 1910); Richard Hakluyt, *op. cit.*, vol. ii; Edward A. Band, editor, *Russia at the Close of the Sixteenth Century* (pub. by Hakluyt Society, 1856); C. D. Morgan and C. H. Coote, editors, *Early Voyages and Travels to Russia and Persia* (pub. by Hakluyt Society, 1886).

was changed into a regulated company.[4]

C. The most important of England's early joint-stock trading companies and the one in which Smythe was most active —serving as its governor from 1603 to 1621—was the East India Co. Merchants who had been in the Russia and Levant companies were among the founders of this new undertaking. Various circumstances led to its formation, notably the profitableness of the East India trade to the Portuguese and the Dutch and the (by then) almost complete exclusion of the English from the Mediterranean. Members of the Levant Co. led a movement for a company which might send ships to the Indies by way of the Cape of Good Hope,[5] and in 1599 London merchants subscribed £30,133 for the formation of the East India Co.

A group of 218 persons was in 1600 granted a charter to trade "in a joint and united stock" for fifteen years, with the privilege of renewal, "from the East Indies into the countries, and parts of Asia and Africa, and into and from all the places . . . of Asia, Africa, and America, or any of them beyond the Cape of Bona Sperancia [Good Hope], to the Straits of Magellan."[6]

While the East India Co. traded as a single joint-stock concern until 1613, a separate joint stock was organized for each voyage. The business of the Company was to plan individual voyages and obtain royal sanction for each voyage, receive subscriptions to its fund, buy the necessary ships and goods, conduct the venture, and finally divide the profits.[7] The temporary character of the stock came from the conditions existing at the time and the personal characteristics of some of the adventurers.[8] A group's liability was limited to the separate voyage to which it subscribed; but, if fresh capital could not be raised from a new group of subscribers, those concerned might be forced to subscribe to a further venture. Participation in a group for a voyage was not always actually limited to the Company's own members. Control was in the general court or meetings of the Company, and the complicated business of management was carried on mainly by the governor and committee men, a body similar to the board of directors of today.[9]

The earliest voyages of the Company were of varying degrees of success.[10] The joint voyage with the Russia Co. in 1602 to discover a northwest passage failed, and the subscribers lost their money. In the India trade the losses from shipwrecks, pepper crop failures, and conflicts with traders of other countries were more than offset by the profits from trade and plunder. From 1609 to 1612—when large fleets were sent, possibly for strength against the Dutch and the Portuguese—the profits were unusually high. The Company was the talk of the times—James I honored Governor Smythe by placing a great chain with a medal around his neck.[11] Table 1 summarizes the financial history of the Company during the period of separate

[4] On the Levant Co. see the following: Scott, *op. cit., passim; Calendar of State Papers, Domestic, Elizabeth,* 1591–1594 (London, 1867), pp. 58, 88–89, 169–170; M. Epstein, *The Early History of the Levant Company* (New York, 1908); A. C. Wood, *History of the Levant Company* (Oxford, 1935).

[5] According to Scott, *op. cit.*, vol. ii, p. 91, at least 23 out of the 101 organizers of the East India Co. can be identified as members of the Levant Co.

[6] Henry Stevens, editor, *Court Minutes of the East India Company,* 1599–1603 (London, 1886), Sept. 25, 1599, p. 8; "East India Company's Patent," in Samuel Purchas, *Purchas His Pilgrimes,* vol. ii (Glasgow, 1905), pp. 366–391.

[7] W. W. Hunter, *A History of British India,* vol. i (London, 1899), pp. 261–262.

[8] Scott, *op. cit.*, vol. ii, pp. 96–97.

[9] Hunter, *op. cit.*, p. 263; Stevens, *op. cit.*, Jan. 11, 1602, pp. 200–201.

[10] The principal sources used: Scott, *op. cit.*, vols. i and ii, *passim;* Hunter, *op. cit.*, vol. i, especially pp. 275-293; Stevens, *op. cit., passim; First Letter Book of the East India Company,* 1600–1619 (London, 1893).

[11] Hunter, *op. cit.*, vol. i, p. 288.

TABLE 1. FIRST NINE VOYAGES OF THE EAST INDIA CO., 1601–12

As shown in the India Office folio of "Marine Records," with the profits added from Bruce's "Annals"

	Date of voyage	Capital	Exported in money	Exported in goods	Cost of ships & victuals	Ships sent out	Profits on the venture
First	1601	£68,373	£21,742	£6,860	£39,771	4	95 p.c.
Second	1604	60,450	11,160	1,142	48,150	4	95 p.c.
Third	1607	53,500	17,600	7,280	28,620	3	234 p.c.
Fourth	1608	33,000	15,000	3,400	14,600	2	Both ships wrecked
Fifth	1609	13,700	6,000	1,700	6,000	1	234 p.c.
Sixth	1610	82,000	28,500	21,300	32,200	3	121⅔ p.c.
Seventh	1611	71,581	19,200	10,081	42,500	4	218 p.c.
Eighth	1612	76,375	17,675	10,000	48,700	4	211 p.c.
Ninth	1612	7,200	1,250	650	5,300	1	160 p.c.
		£466,179	£138,127	£62,413	£265,841	26	

voyages.[12] It should be remembered that these profits represent income on both English imports and exports, on the coastwise trade, on port-to-port barter, as well as on prize goods taken from rival traders in India. Moreover, the capital for a voyage was at times tied up for six or eight years, and the division of the returns to the subscribers was sometimes in the form of spices.

In 1612 came two important changes in the Company's affairs. The Englishmen won several naval battles with the Portuguese in the East, which enabled them to obtain trading concessions on the India mainland and thus to begin British penetration of India. And in that year the Company decided to abandon its plan of separate voyages and to organize expeditions for several years under one stock. Apparently a factor in bringing about this change was the bickering between the agencies of the different voyages in the East and dissension at home,[13] but no doubt the London company saw the advantage in the strong centralized organization of its chief competitor, the Dutch East India Co. The Dutch company, further, was not paying out all its profits in dividends, but was using some of its profits to construct forts and otherwise to strengthen its position in the East.

The East India Co. prospered under the first permanent joint stock. It got control of more and more of the eastern trade as it won supremacy over the Portuguese on the coast of India and finally in 1622, with the aid of Persian land forces, drove the Portuguese from the Persian Gulf. Four voyages including 29 ships were sent out, 1613–16, under the so-called First Joint Stock of 1613. Though the voyages of the First Joint Stock ended in 1617 and the accounts could not be wound up for several years, its shares in 1617 sold at 207 per cent.[14] Such was the success of the Company that an observer wrote in 1617: [15]

[12] *Ibid.*, p. 291 (with the permission of Longmans, Green & Co., Ltd.). For comparison, Scott, *op. cit.*, vol. ii, pp. 23–125, may be consulted. Scott does not altogether agree with Hunter's figures on number of voyages and capital employed or profits for each voyage. The former's enumeration of twelve voyages comes from the fact that he considered as separate voyages three which the latter counted as parts of voyages. The profits gained are figured on different capital bases per voyage.

[13] S. A. Kahn, *East India Trade* (London, 1923), p. 4; Earl of Northampton to Sir Thomas Lake, *Calendar of State Papers, Colonial*, 1513–1616, vol. ii (London, 1862), p. 261.

[14] For statistics on these voyages see Hunter, *op. cit.*, vol. i, p. 307.

[15] *Calendar of State Papers, Colonial, East Indies*, 1617–1621, p. 15.

"Our East India Company are in great bravery, having closed their books for underwriters the last of January and find adventurers for 1,400,000 £ for the four following years, which in truth is a very large sum and a great deal more than was expected, but divers have underwritten for 10, 12, and 14,000 £ a piece."

But the optimism of 1617 was to see reverses. The Second Joint Stock, which operated from 1617 to 1630, suffered severely from the Dutch. The "Hollanders" were willing to sacrifice profits in order to drive out the English,[16] and the result was bloody war between the two in the East. For six years the English East India Co. fought to hold its ground in the Spice Islands, but the destruction of the English agents and factories at Amboyna finally gave the Dutch a complete victory. From 1618 to 1630 the stockholders of the English company received an average of only 3 per cent on their investment.[17]

4. The Virginia Company

The Americas provided new opportunities for profits through group action. One kind of opportunity prevailed in Central and South America; and of that the Spanish took advantage through conquest which brought rich returns in precious metals. In North America the English used other means. The first enduring effort, the settlement of Virginia, was an attempt to make profits through production and trade.

The Virginia Co. is a case in company promotion and administration in a new field. Administration had to keep in mind profits as its aim. Its policy and management are very significant from the point of view of both the old individual system of organization and the new corporate form. We see the mistakes made. Did Smythe and Sandys and their mercantile contemporaries of London also see them? If so, how can one explain the errors of so seasoned a merchant as Sir Thomas Smythe?

A. Organization and the beginning of colonization and trade.

Encouraged by the success of the early trading voyages to the Virginia coast in the opening years of the seventeenth century, a group of adventurers applied to the government for a patent allowing them to found a settlement in Virginia. There were three elements among those early promoters of Virginia: (1) prominent London merchants, foremost among whom was Thomas Smythe; (2) an influential and powerful group led by Lord Robert Rich and his son, the second Earl of Warwick, who were best known for their participation in Elizabethan piracy; and (3) a miscellany of small merchants of a speculative turn, adventurous country gentry, and great lords who looked upon the venture as a means of employing their wealth and leisure for profit and, especially, for honor.[18]

A charter was granted by the king on April 10, 1606. The settlers were expected to furnish their own means of transportation and were not to be governed by a joint-stock company but by the King's Council of Virginia. The Virginia Company itself was to profit by the permission granted it to control the settlement's trade, inward and outward, for five years, in from one to three joint stocks, and to supply all commodities purchased by the settlers.[19]

In 1607 a settlement was made in Virginia at Jamestown. Houses were raised, wheat planted, and some timber and sassafras immediately sent to England from the colony. Trade in Virginia was in the hands of the Company, and cargoes were stored in the "magazines" under the charge of a "cape-merchant," who sold to the set-

16 Hunter, *op. cit.*, vol. i, pp. 364–382.

17 Scott, *op. cit.*, vol. i, p. 196.

18 W. F. Craven, *Dissolution of the Virginia Company* (New York, 1932), pp. 25–27.

19 Charter printed in Alexander Brown, *Genesis of the United States* (Boston, 1890), vol. i, pp. 52–64; Scott, *op. cit.*, vol. ii, p. 248.

tlers and remitted the proceeds to the Company in London.

W. R. Scott says of this venture: [20]

> "It was not long before there were signs that those, who had provided the capital to fit out the first expeditions, expected an immediate, or at least an early return. . . . It was expected that, if possible each voyage should pay its expenses, and if it made a serious loss, it was unlikely that capital would be readily forthcoming for a further expedition. . . . The local council was warned that hitherto it had fed the adventurers, 'but with ifs and ands, hopes and some few proofes' while the settlers were warned that if they could not make some return for the supplies sent them, which had cost between £2000 and £3000 'they were like to remain as banished men.' "

It soon became clear that without effective coördination of colonization and commerce the enterprise would fail. The necessary changes were effected by the charter of 1609, which incorporated a joint-stock company under the title "The Treasurer and Company of Adventurers and Planters of the City of London for the First Colony in Virginia." In this company each stockholder was to have a vote, regardless of the size of his holdings. It was to be governed by a council and treasurer and to be represented by a governor in Virginia. The produce of the colony was to be collected by the cape-merchant and sent to England for the account of the joint stock.[21] Thus the colonizing and commercial activities were joined, and the Company had the authority for raising capital, transporting planters, and surveying and dividing lands as well as for trading.[22] This change virtually made the whole project a business enterprise and placed upon the Company greater freedom but also great problems in its administration of the colony and its activities.

While the charter was under consideration, the problem of financing the enterprise was taken in hand. A letter sent by the Company to the "Lord Mayor, Alderman, and Companies [gilds]" of London, concerning a contribution for transporting London paupers to the New World, is significant. It stated that a "bill of adventure" would be furnished for £12 10s., and that those going to the colony should "have meat, drink and clothing, with a house, orchard and garden, for the meanest family, and a possession of lands to them and their posterity, one hundred acres for every man's person that hath a trade or a body able to endure day labor, as much for his wife, as much for his child." His "Lordship and your Brethren" were at the same time offered participation as subscribers under very liberal conditions, the cause being commended to them for the advancement of religion and the honor, safety, and trade of England, "and many secret blessings not yet discovered." [23]

B. The administration of the Virginia Co. under Smythe.

In 1609 Thomas Smythe became treasurer of the Virginia Co. He had been active in its formation and he had supported it in its early stages. His task was a heavy one. The Company had wide powers and some capital, but it had much work to do. The first essential was settlers. Next came the problem of government of the colonies and management of the economic life so as to sustain the colonists and to produce a surplus. And, lastly, there was the trade between the colony and England and Europe. Throughout all his work for the colony Smythe had to keep in mind that the object of the enterprise was profits for eager shareholders.

The first task confronting the new administration was to provide the colony with

[20] *Ibid.*, pp. 248–249. (This and other quotations from this author are used with permission of Cambridge University Press.)

[21] *Ibid.*, p. 250.

[22] *Ibid.*, p. 249.

[23] Brown, *Genesis*, pp. 252–253.

people. Several expeditions were sent out while Smythe was treasurer. The total number sent from 1609 to 1619 was about fifteen hundred.[24]

The next task was to organize production. Smythe's first plan for the management of the work of the colony has been described as follows: [25]

"[to establish] a plantation system . . . the colonists working in gangs under officials as overseers, eating at common tables, and living in common barracks. . . . The governor at Jamestown, as well as each outlying plantation, was to perform the double duty of military commander and overseer. The same was true of all the officers under him, and they all bore military titles. . . . The day was so divided that the hours of labor in the morning continued from six to ten o'clock, and in the afternoon from two until four. These periods began and closed with the beat of drum, and at their close all the settlers were marched to the church to hear prayers. Under the supervision of officers all tools were taken day by day for use from the storehouse and returned thither again."

But this system was not productive, according to one of the men of the colony.[26]

"When our people were fed out of the common store, and laboured jointly together, glad was he [who] could slip from his labour, or slumber over his task he cared not how, nay, the most honest among them would hardly take so much true pains in a week, as now for themselves they will do in a day: neither cared they for the increase, presuming that howsoever the harvest prospered, the general store must maintain them, so that we reaped not so much corn from the labors of thirty, as now three or four do provide for themselves."

Smythe at first worked for diversification of production, ordering the colonists to attempt to make pitch, tar, soap ashes, steel, iron, hemp, flax, silk, and other things. Rolfe's experiments in growing tobacco in 1612 were so successful that the colony would have gone very soon to the exclusive cultivation of tobacco if Governor Dale had not forced them to plant other crops. Until 1616, eleven commodities were shipped annually to the mother country, "in the hope that the Colony would soon be able to compete successfully with foreign merchants in supplying the English people with the articles which they were now compelled to purchase abroad." [27] The production of tobacco was in 1616 encouraged, however, by the discovery of a method of curing which made Virginia tobacco rate higher than it had done in the English market.

The colony, in the meantime, had not had the financial success for which the shareholders of 1609 had hoped. Even the first expedition sent out under the new charter proved a great disappointment. "When the adventurers saw the expectance of such a preparation come to nothing, how great a dampe of coldness it wrought in the hearts of all may easile be deemed." This situation brought a serious financial problem, for many shareholders had counted on the profits of the first installment on their shares to meet the second. A number refused to pay the second installment, and even more, the third.[28]

The situation brought a serious financial problem to the administration. In the absence of working capital Smythe had to borrow, largely on the security of unpaid calls, to finance further expeditions. One who was close to the Company wrote thus to the Lord Chancellor of England: [29]

"The said Treasurer and Company were forced to engage themselves and their credit for very great sums of money which they

[24] Alexander Brown, *The First Republic in America* (Boston, 1898), pp. 71, 97.

[25] H. L. Osgood, *The American Colonies in the Seventeenth Century,* vol. i (New York, 1904), pp. 63–64, 71–72.

[26] Edward Arber, editor, *Travels and Works of Captain John Smith,* pt. ii (Edinburgh, 1910), "Out of Master Hamor's Books," p. 516.

[27] P. A. Bruce, *Economic History of Virginia in the Seventeenth Century,* vol. i (New York, 1896), pp. 218–219.

[28] Scott, *op. cit.,* vol. ii, p. 251.

[29] Brown, *Genesis,* vol. ii, pp. 627–628.

the more readily and willingly did adventure to do for the general cause in hope to be freed and saved harmless by the money to be received from the said adventurers, which they assured themselves every one as he was bound in honesty and conscience, would pay in his due time according to that which he had underwritten."

It is possible that means would not have been secured had it not been for Smythe's personal influence. Enough was secured, however, to send out Lord de la Warr's expedition in 1610. By 1612 the situation had become so bad that suits were instituted against a number of shareholders who had refused to pay their installments.[30]

The Company succeeded in securing two new sources of funds in 1612. It obtained the sum of £2,000 by selling to the Somers Island Co. its rights (actually nonexistent) to Bermuda; and through its third charter of 1612 the Company received the privilege of conducting lotteries for securing working capital.[31] The lottery yielded large profits. It was the mainstay of the Company for seven years—without it the Virginia settlers could hardly have been kept alive during those years. One of the peculiar provisions of the "Great Standing Lottery" held in 1614 and 1615 was that any person who ventured £12 10s. in the lottery, and then renounced his prizes before the drawing took place, was awarded one share of the Company's stock.[32]

These sources of support proved insufficient, however, and Smythe, aided by a few other adventurers, carried much of the burden of supplying necessary funds. His attitude, when most of the stockholders abandoned the Virginia enterprise between 1613 and 1616, is expressed in a statement of the Council for Virginia:[33]

"Which when those gentlemen the adventurers here saw, and that the expectation of so great a preparation brought nothing home but adverse success and bad reports, they for the most part withdrew themselves, in despair of the enterprise, and so gave it over, not enduring to repair the ruins. . . .

"By whose inconstancy and irresolution the hope of that plantation, together with the lives of our people there, had then utterly perished, had not . . . a very small remnant of constant adventurers, that with Sir Thomas Smythe (their Treasurer and Governor from the beginning) in all that time of three years disaster, were never discouraged, nor withdrew themselves from weekly courts and meetings, yielding their purses, credit, and counsel, from time to time, to make new supplies, even beyond their proportion, to uphold the plantation."

Some important changes in the management of the colony came in the years 1614 and 1616. In keeping with the provision in the charter that land would be distributed in seven years, at the end of the period of apprenticeship, a distribution was made to 81 persons in 1614.[34] Since more became entitled to land in 1616, and, it is said, because Smythe and the directors believed the colony to be in a "prosperous condition,"[35] a land division was again made. Every shareholder who paid the Company £12 10s. for another share, thus furnishing money for the expense of survey and allocation, received 100 acres of land. "Adventurers of their persons" received a like share. When the adventurer had settled the land he had obtained, he received another 100 acres together with 50 acres for each person transported to his estate.[36] A further step was taken in that members of the Company organized subordinate joint-stock ventures for settling their land dividends.

The land division put trade on another basis. While the individuals became responsible for the outlay on their lands,

[30] S. A. Kingsbury, *Records of the Virginia Company,* vol. iii (Washington, 1933), pp. 34–39.

[31] Scott, *op. cit.,* vol. ii, pp. 252–253.

[32] Brown, *Genesis,* vol. ii, p. 763; for further particulars on the lottery, see pp. 537 ff.

[33] *Ibid.,* p. 776.

[34] Craven, *op. cit.,* p. 35.

[35] Scott, *op. cit.,* vol. ii, p. 255.

[36] *Loc. cit.*

which took some of the burden off the Company, they also became the owners of what the land produced. This meant that the Company had to buy the goods, and, since it did not have sufficient working capital, it formed a subsidiary joint-stock company to carry on the trade. "The Society of Particular Adventure for Traffique with them of Virginia in a joint-stock," known as the "Magazine," was to exchange commodities from England for tobacco and to market the tobacco in England. It was closely attached to the original company and was directed by Alderman Johnson, Smythe's son-in-law. The total capital subscribed and paid up by the adventurers in this enterprise was £7,000.[37]

A second subsidiary joint stock was organized during Smythe's régime, the "Joint-Stock, for Transporting Men and Divers Goods on a Fishing Voyage." It is likely that the purpose of this enterprise was not only to fish but also to bring out colonists to Virginia at the start of the fishing voyage.

Since the efforts of the Company itself brought little in the way of results, and no profits, much dissatisfaction was expressed and the Virginia Company came to experience "a state of faction and strife not uncommon to a failing business."[38] There was much criticism of conditions in the colony. There was too much dependence on one commodity, tobacco. The Magazine was said to charge too high prices for English goods—it raised its prices because the colonists demanded a high price for their poor tobacco. The cry of oppression arose against Governor Argall of the colony.[39]

Out of discontent in Virginia and faction in London arose an opposition to Smythe within the Company which was led by Sir Edwin Sandys. This movement was strengthened by the feeling of many that Virginia had great promise if properly administered; indeed, a number of influential and important adventurers were planning by 1618 to send colonists to settle individual plantations.[40]

The movement led to radical changes in the administration and management of the enterprise. While this occurred under Smythe's treasurership and was planned and put into effect under his leadership, it was clearly influenced by the Sandys opposition. The nature of the changes is indicated by the instructions given to the new governor by "the Treasurer and the Companie."[41] With respect to the economic life of the colony the plan was to encourage diversified production so as to make Virginia more nearly self-sufficient, to encourage private enterprise by further division of lands and restrictions on the Magazine, to reëstablish the public lands in the hope of financial benefit to the Company, and in general to build a stronger colony as a base for the operations of the Company. Recognition of law and order as basic to the successful working of the colony brought other changes. "The reform of greatest immediate importance," says a recent study of the Company, "was the abolition of martial law and the substitution of the English common law."[42] Best known, however, is the institution of the assembly in Virginia as an instrument for the improvement of the administration of the colony, which might be looked upon not so much as a liberal reform as an extension of the older council to tie together scattered settlements in the colony.[43]

Smythe was not to lead the Company under the new rules. At the meeting of the Company of April 28, 1619, he declined to stand for election—evidence reveals that

[37] Craven, *op. cit.*, pp. 33–34; Scott, *op. cit.*, pp. 255–256; Kingsbury, *op. cit.*, vol. i, pp. 74–75; N. W. Stephenson, "Some Inner History of the Virginia Company," *William and Mary Quarterly*, vol. xxii (1913–14), pp. 92–93.

[38] Craven, *op. cit.*, p. 34.

[39] *Ibid.*, pp. 34–40, 44.

[40] *Ibid.*, pp. 45–46.

[41] Kingsbury, *op. cit.*, vol. iii, pp. 98–109, gives instructions of Nov. 18, 1618.

[42] Craven, *op. cit.*, p. 70.

[43] *Ibid.*, pp. 77–78.

he would not have been elected had he been a candidate.[44] A coalition of the two groups of Smythe's enemies—the forces of the pirateering Warwick, who had broken with Smythe over the management of the affairs of the Somers Island Co. in Bermuda,[45] and the Sandys faction, composed largely of the minor adventurers—brought about his overthrow. The patronage which the treasurer of the Virginia Co. could bestow and his power and influence, in general, were important factors in the situation. The astute politician, Sandys, had coveted the office, and nothing was more natural than that he should make a bargain with the Earl of Warwick to secure the prize.

C. The administration of the Company under Sandys.

Sandys was primarily known as a leader in a movement for political and religious reform. He had earlier brought forward a radical measure favoring the reform of law so that persons accused of crime could employ counsel in their own defense, and he had asked for free trade and the overthrow of monopolies and for the control of the Crown by the electorate. A founder of the Virginia Co. and an influential member of the East India Co. at an early date, he had turned his entire attention to trading companies after 1614. He had acted as Smythe's assistant from 1617 to 1619.

Sandys held the position of treasurer of the Virginia Co. for a year. Though he was not reëlected in 1620, the Earl of Southampton, who became the treasurer at that time, was in fact his lieutenant, and through him Sandys was virtual treasurer until shortly before the dissolution of the Company. As leader of the Company "Sandys presents an interesting study in that combination of public and personal interests which moved men of Stuart England to support colonization." [46]

The election of Sandys brought no real change in policy. It was his job to erect upon the basis of the reform instituted in 1618 a healthy economic structure in Virginia. "The chief importance and interest in his administration is to be found in an heroic attempt to work out the economic salvation of the company by building a few enfeebled and scattered settlements into a prosperous colony serving the ends of mercantilism and fulfilling the adventurer's hope of profit." [47] This meant the encouragement of private plantations, immigration, the establishment of free trade, and the setting-up of the new form of government for which provision had been made before Sandys' election.

Two lines of effort are especially significant. Sandys aggressively promoted emigration to the colony and he attempted to encourage a more diversified production.

It was essential to promote migration to Virginia so that the public lands, from which much of the income of the Company was expected, might be occupied and new commodities be produced. Various means for securing settlers were used with considerable success. Tracts were distributed to advertise the rich promise of Virginia. For seven years' service on the Company's lands one such appeal promised each colonist full provisions for a year, complete equipment of weapons, tools and implements ("both of house and labour"), and a share in the profits. Skilled workers were sought—brewers, iron-workers, shipwrights, weavers, and many others.

Sandys tried to turn Virginia away from too heavy a reliance on tobacco. He wanted the colony to provide the forest products, iron, wines, fruits, salt, silks, drugs, gums, sugar, and other products which England had to buy from abroad. The iron industry, which could draw on the forests

[44] Kingsbury, *op. cit.*, vol. i, p. 212. There is an excellent summary of the opposition to Smythe in Craven, *op. cit.*, pp. 81–87.

[45] The feud between Warwick and Smythe had been intensified when Warwick's sister eloped with Smythe's 18-year-old son.

[46] Craven, *op. cit.*, p. 93. (Reprinted with the permission of the Oxford University Press.)

[47] *Ibid.*, p. 88.

for charcoal, was pushed with vigor. Skilled iron-workers were brought to the colony and some £5,000 was spent on developing the new industry. Wine production was likewise promoted, with the import of vignerons and vines from France and the Rhineland. Skilled workers were brought from Hamburg to develop shipbuilding. And "silkworm seed" was sent to the New World to start a new industry. At the same time Virginia was encouraged to produce to supply her own needs.[48]

Sandys' great plans for peopling Virginia ended in dismal failure. Of the 5,000 in the colony at some time during his period of control—about 1,000 when he became treasurer and 4,000 new settlers—only 1,275 were in the colony in February, 1624.[49]

Two particular reasons can be given for the tremendous loss of life. One reason was bad management. Many colonists were sent who were poorly suited for the hard life they had to live. Shiploads of colonists were sent without adequate provisions for the trip and were unloaded on a colony which had insufficient to meet its own needs until the harvest of the next year. The responsibility for the situation falls first on the deputy-treasurers (the Ferrars) and the committee in charge of the shipment of colonists and supplies, but there was obviously weakness at the top. Sandys himself was busy with a multitude of other affairs within and without the Company, and his work was made more difficult because of the long illness of his wife which kept him for some time in Kent. The unfortunate situation continued, even though Governor Yeardley repeatedly urged the sending of more provisions and equipment. When the colonists were ready to mutiny in 1620, Yeardley wrote to Sandys "to advise you that you do not run into so great matters in speedy and hasty sending so many people over hither and undertaking so great works before you have acquainted me and have been truly informed by me of the state of the Plantation and what may be done here." If this was not done, warned the governor, Sandys would fail in the execution of his projects.[50] The other main reason for the loss of life, that is, the Indian massacre of 1622, was also in a sense a failure of management. The colony was composed of groups which were scattered and very poorly armed. Apparently friendly, the Indians fell upon them without warning; killed between 300 and 400 men, women, and children; and left many more destitute. Some of the settlements were abandoned and the unfortunate people were crowded into other settlements.[51]

The promotion of production in Virginia was likewise unsuccessful. Iron production, which had been entered upon with so much expense and enthusiasm, failed, apparently from the lack of ore and the death of the workers. The silk project died with the perishing of the cocoons on the way to America. The wine experiment proved unproductive. The same was true even of other industries for which Virginia was better fitted.

The only profitable product was tobacco. Though Sandys had tried to discourage the dependence on tobacco production, 20,000 pounds were exported in 1619, 40,000 in 1620, and 60,000 in 1622.[52]

Several things, however, worked against the adventurers in the tobacco trade. The old agreement with the Virginia producers kept the price up in the colony even at a time when increased production in the West Indies was driving down the price in London, thus narrowing the margin between the buying and selling prices. The competition of Spanish tobacco, which was superior, endangered Virginia tobacco in England. Moreover, a duty was set on tobacco imports in England, contrary to the charter of the Virginia Co., a cost which

[48] *Ibid.*, pp. 99–103.
[49] Scott, *op. cit.*, vol. ii, p. 286.
[50] Craven, *op. cit.*, pp. 157–158.
[51] *Ibid.*, pp. 195–197.
[52] Bruce, *op. cit.*, vol. i, pp. 262–263.

the Company could not shift to either producers or consumers. In 1620 a group of men was granted a monopoly of the tobacco trade in England, while the Virginia and Somers Island companies were permitted to bring in annually an amount much smaller than they had recently been importing. The Virginia Co. turned to the Dutch market, but the product had to pass through England and pay a duty.[53]

"A little consideration will show," says Scott in his *Joint-Stock Companies,* "that the whole financial superstructure rested on the receipts from lotteries, since, the colony not being able to exist without further capital expenditure, this was the sole source of funds for that expenditure." [54] Smythe had secured much help from the lotteries, but Sandys plied them even more diligently. Indeed, in the first two years of his control of the Company the lotteries had provided the greater portion of its revenue.

In March, 1621, however, the Company's license to conduct lotteries was withdrawn. England was getting tired of the lotteries and there was complaint of irregularities. There seems to be no question but that it was the "royal pleasure" to discontinue the lotteries. The king's antagonism to Sandys—whom James I disliked as a Liberal, aside from other considerations—was apparently fanned by the Smythe faction. When James' order against the reëlection of Sandys was obeyed by the election of the Earl of Southampton, one of Sandys' men,[55] Sandys could no longer expect anything from the king.

By the summer of 1621 the Company was practically bankrupt. To carry on, it was necessary to get new sources of capital. This was sought through subsidiary companies. Several were floated in 1621, among them a "Joint-Stock for providing Apparel and other Necessaries," the "Joint-Stock for Transporting 100 Maids to be Made Wives," a joint stock for a glassworks, one for a trade in furs, and probably at the same time an iron bloomery venture. The only one of these ventures that was at all successful was the one for transporting maids.

While these ventures were being put into operation, a new effort was made to save the tobacco trade. In 1622 Sandys proposed that the Virginia and Somers Island companies be granted the monopoly of tobacco import in England. The management of the scheme was discussed in the Court of the Virginia Co. Sandys expected to become the director "upon whom the whole success of the business almost depended." The Court was amazed at the proposal that the director be paid £500, the treasurer £400, and the eight assistant directors £50 each. When it was said that "divers gentlemen and other sufficient men" would do the business for less, a Sandys supporter, apparently referring to Smythe, answered that he had "found by experience that some that had for conscience sake served this Companie had for conscience sake undone it." [56] The quarrel over salaries took such form that, though the proposal was ratified, bitter strife ensued which even spread to the Somers Island Court and split the companies into open factions. The Warwick group fought the contract, even opposing it before the king, and the result was that the lord treasurer refused to grant the contract to the companies. They had to continue importing tobacco under unprofitable conditions.[57] Failure in this effort was a severe blow to Sandys and his Company.

The quarrel over the tobacco contract was only one of many sources of serious friction within the Company. The instance illustrates strikingly that economic man is not wholly rational and that business is

[53] Craven, *op. cit.,* pp. 181–183; Scott, *op. cit.,* vol. ii, pp. 272–275.

[54] *Ibid.,* p. 272.

[55] *Loc. cit.;* Craven, *op. cit.,* pp. 183–184.

[56] Kingsbury, *op. cit.,* vol. ii, p. 152.

[57] *Ibid.,* pp. 147–152; Scott, *op. cit.,* vol. ii, pp. 282–283; Craven, *op. cit.,* pp. 233–248.

not only a matter of the working-out of impersonal forces or even of wise policy. In Sandys' administration, as in Smythe's, there were personal dislikes, grudges, injured feelings, and rivalries of individuals and groups which kept the Company as a whole in a constant state of friction.

One of the earliest sources of friction under Sandys' leadership was Smythe's accounts. It was agreed in 1620 to have the accounts audited, but unfortunately the three men who were to head the auditing had been active in bringing charges against Smythe's accounts. The investigation of the accounts was long drawn-out. Fearing that his old accounts—which had been accepted earlier by the regular auditors—would not be given a fair examination, Smythe objected at almost every point.

He offered, however, to make up out of his own purse any apparent discrepancy, but Sandys was unable to decide what Smythe's indebtedness was. Though Smythe's books were undoubtedly unsatisfactory, his greatest fault was probably carelessness and too great a dependence on his subordinates. Sandys himself denied that he intended to cast any reflections on Smythe "further then [sic] of neglect and that through multitude of business." [58] It would have been far better if Sandys had compromised by agreeing with Sir Thomas on an estimated sum. As the matter dragged on, it came to be said around London that Smythe refused to pay his debts. After four years of bitter feeling over the matter, Sandys finally decided in 1624 that Smythe owed the Company £800.[59]

The attempt to audit the accounts of the Magazine also led to trouble. Sandys, needing capital for the Virginia Co., believed that some of the Company's funds had been illegally used by the Magazine. There is no evidence on which to base any conclusions about these accounts, but it was unfortunate that what was at best a difficult job should have been approached in such a way as to reflect in advance on the honesty of Johnson, the leading officer of the Magazine and Smythe's son-in-law. The effect was to antagonize both Sir Thomas and Johnson.

One dispute led to the loss of Warwick's support for Sandys. The two men had been united by a common dislike of Smythe. Sandys was not the man to make concessions to keep Warwick's goodwill—"His was a straightforward course designed for a definite purpose to which he was passionately attached, and whatever act the interests of Virginia seemed to demand he executed regardless of the cost." [60] Sandys' effort to bring former Governor Argall, an associate of Warwick, to trial for his misgovernment of Virginia aroused Warwick's wrath. This matter was before the council of the Company for a long time. About the only thing accomplished was to drive the Warwick faction into friendly relations with the Smythes.

The final blow came in the spring of 1623, when Captain Butler, the governor of Bermuda who had visited Virginia, made known the real condition of the colony. He prepared a document which made sensational disclosures: [61]

"I found the plantations generally seated upon mere salt marshes full of infectious bogs and muddy creeks and lakes, and thereby subjected to all those inconveniences and diseases which are so commonly found in the most unsound and unhealthy parts of England. . . . The colony was this winter in much distress of victuals so that English meal was sold at the rate of thirty shillings a bushel. . . .

"Their houses are generally the worst that ever I saw, the meanest cottages in England being every way equal (if not superior) with the most of the best. . . .

"I found not the least piece of fortification: three pieces of ordnance only mounted at

[58] *Ibid.*, pp. 106–111.

[59] *Ibid.*, pp. 111–112.

[60] *Ibid.*, p. 120.

[61] Kingsbury, *op. cit.*, vol. ii, pp. 374–376. The spelling in this quotation has been modernized.

James City and one at Flowerdue Hundred but never a one of them serviceable; so that it is most certain that a small bark of 100 tunns may take its time to pass up the River in spite of them. . . .

"Expecting according to their printed books a great forwardness [in the production] of divers and sundry commodities, at my arrival I found . . . the iron-works were utterly wasted and the men dead and the furnaces for glass and pottery at a stay and in small hope. . . . Tobacco was the only business and, for aught that I could hear, every man . . . little thought or looked for anything else.

"I found the old plantations of Henrico and Charles City wholly abandoned and left to the spoliation of the Indians who not only burned the houses . . . but fell upon the poultry, hogs, cows, goats, and horses. . . .

"There having been, as it is thought, not fewer than ten thousand souls transported thither there are not, through the aforementioned abuses and neglects, above two thousand of them at present to be found alive, many of them also in sickly and desperate state. So that it may undoubtedly be expected that, unless the confusions and private ends of some of the company here, and the bad execution . . . by their agents there, be redressed with speed by some divine and supreme hand, instead of a plantation it will shortly get the name of a slaughter house and so justly become both odious to ourselves and contemptible to all the world."

This revelation led to much investigation. "Sandys and the Ferrars were charged," says Scott, "with suppressing information as to the true state of the plantation and of causing misleading reports to be sent from it, which were written with the intention of making it appear that the colony was in a satisfactory condition." There was, according to Scott, a considerable basis for these accusations.[62] The result was that faction reigned.

The commission of inquiry found the Company bankrupt. Sandys lost control of the Company in 1624, but the Sandys faction refused to recognize a new government under Smythe. Finally in May, 1625, an act of James I dissolved the corporation. Though the colony continued to exist, the business corporation which had been responsible for its establishment thus disappeared.

D. Statistics of the two administrations.

(1) Smythe's administration.

The population of Virginia, 1609–19

Colonists surviving in 1609	less than	109[63]
" sent out by Smythe		1,500
" surviving when Smythe resigned		1,000[64]

Survey of finances, 1609–19

The Virginia Co.

Receipts to April, 1619[65]

Total capital (subscribed £52,624) paid in	£36,624
Profits of lotteries	20,000
Borrowings and debts due (partly estimated)	5,000
Miscellaneous receipts " "	5,500
	£67,124

No monetary gain was received by the holders of the "General Stock." Their only dividends were in land.

Subsidiary stocks.

"The Society of a Particular Adventure for Traffique with them of Virginia in a Joint-Stock," commonly called the "Magazine," established in 1616 had a sub-

[62] Scott, *op. cit.*, vol. ii, p. 281.

[63] Brown, *First Republic,* pp. 71, 97.

[64] Scott, *op. cit.*, vol. ii, p. 286. Perhaps the figure 1,000 is excessive.

[65] *Ibid.*, pp. 258, 288.

scribed and paid-in capital of £7,000. The stockholders probably never secured any dividends, but after the Magazine had been suspended there was a division of £4,000.[66] The "Joint Stock, for Transporting Men and Divers Goods on a Fishing Voyage," established in 1618, had capital subscribed to the amount of £1,800.[67] Nothing is known about dividends on this stock.

(2) Sandys' administration.

The population of Virginia, 1619–24 [68]

Colonists surviving when Sandys took charge	1,000
Persons transported	4,000
Total population of Virginia in 1624	1,275

Survey of finances, 1619–23 [69]

The Virginia Co.

Total capital subscribed (nothing paid in)	£ 237
Profits of lotteries, 1619–1620	9,000
No dividends were paid on the general stock	

Subsidiaries

Joint-Stock Capital Subscribed for:

A Fishing Voyage (1620)	£1,000
A Magazine (1620)	1,000
Providing Apparel and other Necessaries (1621)	1,800
A Glass Furnace in Virginia for Making Glass and Beads (1621)	"nearly" 1000
Transporting 100 Maids to Virginia to be made Wives (1621)	800
A Trade in Furs (1621)	900
Transporting Shipwrights to Virginia (1621)	1,000

It is estimated that the receipts of capital from all sources which were expended upon the plantation between 1619 and 1623 under Sandys were £80,000 to £90,-000. This includes the estimated expenditures of private adventurers.

What returns these investments brought it is impossible to say. The only joint stock which was profitable was that for "Transporting 100 Maids to Virginia," which is said to have brought its subscribers "great contentment."

5. Suggested Readings

For background:

Clive Day, *A History of Commerce* (New York, 1922): "Development of the Economic Organization," pp. 139–148; and "England: Survey of Commercial Development," pp. 198–206.

Edward P. Cheyney, *European Background of American History* (New York, 1904): "Commercial Companies," pp. 123–146.

Edward P. Cheyney, *A History of England from the Defeat of the Armada to the Death of Elizabeth* (New York, 1926), pp. 309–518.

On enterprises and individuals considered in the case:

A biography of Sir Thomas Smythe is found in Alexander Brown, *Genesis of the United States* (Boston, 1890), vol. ii, pp. 1012–1018.

For a full discussion of individual companies, see W. R. Scott, *Joint Stock Companies,* vol. ii (Cambridge, 1910).

A very readable and scholarly one-volume work on the Virginia Co. is W. F. Craven, *Dissolution of the Virginia Company* (New York, 1932).

[66] *Ibid.,* pp. 273–288.

[67] *Ibid.,* p. 288.

[68] *Ibid.,* p. 286.

[69] Most of the figures for this section come from Scott, *op. cit.,* vol. ii, pp. 273, 276–277, 288–289. Scott does not separate the figures for the Smythe and Sandys administrations. N. W. Stephenson, *op. cit.,* pp. 89–98, 160–168, also contains many figures on the finances of the Virginia Co.

On the economic experience of the Virginia colony, see P. A. Bruce, *Economic History of Virginia in the Seventeenth Century,* vol. i (New York, 1896), pp. 189–275.

A judicious recent consideration of the Virginia Co., particularly as to politics and personality, is C. M. Andrews, *The Colonial Period of American History,* vol. i (New Haven, 1934), pp. 98–178.

6. Suggested Questions

1. Explain the use of subsidiary companies by the permanent company. Are there any analogies today?
2. What were the weaknesses in organization and administration of the Virginia Co., especially in 1609–19?
3. If you had been a stockholder of the Virginia Co., living in London in 1625, would you have voted for Sandys' administration or favored the return of Smythe? Explain at length. Are there any more recent analogies?
4. What evidence is there for the view that capitalism was making progress in London about 1600?
5. Could a regulated company have colonized Virginia?
6. Could the English government have colonized and opened up overseas trade in the early seventeenth century?

II. WILLIAM FITZHUGH'S PROPOSALS FOR A CONSTANT FACTORAGE IN VIRGINIA, 1683–1687

1. General Statement

William Fitzhugh arrived in Virginia about 1670. He was a lawyer, planter, merchant, a representative in the House of Burgesses, and a local military leader. He was a typical early planter—restless, active in work and play, socially ambitious, and eager for literary and historical knowledge. He compiled for publication the early laws of Virginia. He was a voluminous letter-writer, a fact to which we owe our knowledge of his career. Indeed he has left behind him 213 letters covering the period 1679–99. At his death in 1701 he possessed a large estate—lands, slaves, indentured servants, stock, furniture, and money. His wealth came to him through practising law, buying and selling real estate, growing tobacco, buying tobacco for sale, selling imports to his neighbors, and probably handling bills of exchange for his district.

He was ambitious to establish a constant factorage or mercantile business and made proposals therefor: first, to two persons apparently in New England; secondly, to his commercial agent, John Cooper, in London; and thirdly, to a Liverpool merchant. So far as we know, none of the proposals was accepted. If such an arrangement had been made, towns might have developed in the South and the course of American history might have been somewhat changed.

2. Letter of Fitzhugh to Mrs. Eleanor Cutt and George Jeffries (of New England?), February 5, 1683 [1]

"At the instance of Mr. Jackson, though unacquainted, this comes to acquaint you that I apprehend you are mistaken in carrying on any trade in our parts by your sending your goods to purchase her [the ship's] own loadings. This puts a necessity upon your dealer to sell for the speed of his market [a] great deal cheaper than you need. If you could afford a stock beforehand to lie in some factor's hands in this country and who would then take the opportunity of his market and could reduce the whole loading to lie in some certain places to be immediately taken in upon the arrival of your vessel—which those that come to purchase their loading are forced to go from place to place for, so that the profit of

[1] "Letters of William Fitzhugh," *The Virginia Magazine of History and Biography,* vol. i (1893–94), pp. 108–109. For the sake of readability and clarity, the spelling and capitalization of these letters have been modernized.

the voyage, if you purchase very cheap (which is uncertain), is eaten up by the length of stay necessarily occasioned by going from place to place to fetch the several parcels of wheat, besides the uncertainty of the market—those things would be taken away by settling a constant factorage here, and whatever commodity you had a mind to, or gave advice of, might be reasonably and certainly every year purchased and the vessel that comes for it quickly dispatched. Thus, the first stock of money being dead about five or six months gives these advantages a certain and sure market, an easy change, and a quick dispatch, which is the life and profit of every trade. What I have said is not to court your employ but to satisfy Mr. Jackson."

3. Letter of Fitzhugh to His London Agent, John Cooper, March 10, 1683 [2]

"This comes by Capt. Smith where you'll find 19 hhds. of tobacco consigned to yourself as per bills of loading will appear. I can assure you it is as good a parcel of tobacco as ever I saw of the sort, most of it of my own crop, which I myself took care to see well handled and sorted; the remainder, which is 7 hhds., I saw well packed and therefore am sure it is good; if this does not suit the market and get a price, it's in vain for me to think of shipping any more tobacco. Just as I am writing I have news of Capt. Norrington's arrival, by whom I expect to hear farther from you; all that I have yet this year received was one letter per Capt. Harris. Business and the small encouragement tobacco gave was the occasion I wrote no oftener and larger to you last year, but this year, being sure the first is something abated and in hopes the latter is amended, I shall be more ample and frequent in my letters and advices. The first thing that I have of necessity to advise you is that I have charged bills upon you payable to Mr. Jno. Bowden for the use of Capt. Elisha Mellowes of Barbadoes for £35 2s 10d at eighty days sight, which I hope you have effects of mine to comply with before the time of payment. I took so large a time that I might have a full opportunity of advising you thereof and of remitting the effects.

"Sir, I have a proposal of trade if you or any of your friends approve of it, the manner this: To send a small vessel of about 200 or 250 hhds. burden at most, which I will undertake to give her notes for loading, within a month at farthest after her arrival and that within twenty miles compass, which is but a small distance here, upon this condition: to have well-bought goods and bought with ready money delivered at my landing at 10 shillings per hundred pounds without any advance or, if you think that not convenient because of the uncertainty of the market, then give me an allowance of 21 lb. of tobacco in the hundredweight of tobacco more than the general market goes at in our parts, upon the arrival of the said vessel, for my commission, expedition, storage and insurance of the whole and all other incident charges that traders here necessarily lie at, provided the ship comes not before some time in Dec. and I have notice thereof by the forward ships in Sept., Oct., or Nov., though I desire none of the goods till her arrival. By this trade here [there] will be a great charge saved in the long stay ships generally make here, being oftentimes forced to run from one end of the country to the other almost, which eats out the profit of a good market, besides sloop hire, the allowance to your factor, and merchants, the uncertainty of purchasing tobacco and if purchased many times lying out and behind [outstanding and overdue] and some bad debts never to be recovered. On the other side, as soon as your ship arrives, she may be taking in tobacco, her whole loading certain, the distance the tobacco lies at small, so that two or three flats will presently load her and by that means save sloop hire. About one-third or nearly one-half of the loading will be in one place together, which she may well take in four days. As soon as I see Capt. Norrington (which I now every day expect) I shall discourse [with] him further thereon; and, if he thinks the proposal will be approved, I shall then be more large by the next conveniency and withal manifest to him something of my method to proceed therein and shall desire him to give you an account whether I am fully fitted and capable for such an undertaking."

[2] *Ibid.*, pp. 116–118.

4. Extract from a Letter of Fitzhugh to John Cooper, May 18, 1685 [3]

"Our river this year produces little consignments of tobacco, and I suppose no great quantity will be carried from us to you thither, for other parts have found an advantageous trade to themselves here and profitable to us per the good prices they give for our tobacco, in which you might have been a considerable sharer if you had thought convenient to have accepted my offers I made you about three years since."

5. Letter of Fitzhugh to Thomas Clayton, of the Firm of Clayton and Richmond, Merchants in Liverpool, April 26, 1686 [4]

"The trade and dealing that I have had with Mr. Greenhahgh this year, and by that means the converse, society and acquaintance with Mr. Jno. Marshal [who] is fully able and I suppose will readily inform you, and whose persuasions and advice give me the opportunity and you the trouble of this present overture for a quick, constant and certain and I believe advantageous trade, which in my apprehension you have not hitherto hit on. The offers I have to make are but of two sorts. The first for a quick and speedy Dutch trade. The second for a quick and sudden trade and dispatch here, and a ready and full compliance to your whole ship and cargo and so on. As to the first, which is the Dutch trade, to have a ship of 200 hhds. burden here the beginning of October, and to have her whole loading ready by the 15th and on board by the 25th of the same month, that she might be dispatched out hence by the 27th at farthest, and by that means have first choice of the crops here, and the first and best of the Dutch market there. In which design I myself would go a quarter, or, rather than fail, a third part, and engage to have my whole loading ready by the 10th of October at farthest. But [I] doubt [fear] your own remoteness and the indexterity of most of your factors in the course of trading you are now in, will not admit so ready a compliance [on your part as] that concern requires [in order] to be profitably carried on. [I] shall be no more particular therein, but refer you to Mr. Marshal for a more ample account thereof.

"As to the second, for a quick and sudden dispatch, and so on, I have this to offer: at 16s 8d per hundred pounds I will engage to load a ship of 200 hhds. after this manner, that is, let her arrive any time by the 10th November; immediately upon her arrival after the 10th November aforesaid, I will give her notes for one-third of her loading; as soon as ever she has dispatched those notes and got the tobacco on board, I will then give her notes for one-third more of her loading, and, when she has dispatched them, I will then give her notes for the remaining part of her full loading, which, beginning the 10th Nov. may be easily perfected and performed by the 28th of the same month, and she ready to sail by the last of the same month or beginning of December at farthest—provided the master be a diligent, industrious man, such a one as I can assure you Mr. Marshal is. And whatever stay she makes for want of my notes aforesaid, I will be bound to pay damage money per day to the full of the ship's charge. The convenience of tobacco and readiness of getting it on board, Mr. Marshal can pretty well inform you [on], and I must also tell you that nearly one-half thereof must come off my own plantation, nearly a third more at one particular rowling house or landing, and the whole remainder not above twenty miles distance, which in this country is a very inconsiderable matter. The 200 hhds. at 460 [pounds] per hhd., which will certainly be the smallest weights of forward tobacco, will amount to 92,000 lb. of tobacco, which at 16s 8d per hundredweight comes to £766 13s 4d; half of this money I would [have] deposited in such hands as I shall appoint and the other half in goods salable for [in] this country. The money there deposited, I covet not the disposal of, nor the goods hither sent the possession of, till I have first answered my contract per the delivery of notes for good tobacco. Thus I have shortly touched at the trade proposed, and, if you doubt in anything, I refer you to Mr. Marshal, with whom I have more amply discoursed thereof and who is fully able to inform you of my capacity and ability for

[3] *Ibid.*, p. 273.

[4] *Ibid.*, pp. 399–403.

performance, and the convenience that will be in it. By this way of trade your ship has no stay, your men a full employment, your goods a certain sale, your ship a certain loading, yourselves but one-half of the risk by reason one-half the money is left in England, no fear of bad or slow debts, no doubtful, careless or giddy factors to overthrow the voyage. And reckoning the charge of the ship's stay upon [under] the course [method] of trade you are now in [using] and the bad debts left [resulting] the same quantity of tobacco must needs stand you in a great deal more money, with all the hazards and disadvantages aforesaid.

"What is before said for the forward ship's arrival and dispatch in November, I have the same to propose in the same circumstances, and under the same conditions for the said ships or some other of the same burden arriving here, by the 10th of February, which may likewise be as suddenly dispatched; but the weights of the hhds. round cannot be expected so great as the first ship's, yet may, and I believe will hold out 420 [pounds] per hhd., which will amount to 84,000 lb. tobacco at 16s 8d per hundred lb., [which] is 700£, which money I would have likewise ordered as the former, half there deposited and half in sortable goods as before. This latter ship will be dispatched before most if not all your ships that come hither under the course of trade you are now in. By this means one ship will readily and easily perform two voyages in one year, the seamen kept in full employment and consequently deserve their wages, the master busily and constantly employed, and the ship according to the intent of her building in a continual run; and since, above all, things [will be] in certainty and what loitering time is made (provided the master be diligent and dextrous) [will be] at my charge, which I believe well weighed and considered, [the ship] will deliver tobacco in England at cheaper rates than it is now purchased [at] by those that make the cheapest purchases.

"If this method and proposal be acceptable, then care must be taken to give me for the first year timely and speedy notice, either per the last Sept. or beginning of October at farthest, of the acceptance and continuance for at least three years, provided we live so long, but mortality must separate, because the contract is personal. Now the directions that I have to propose for your methods to take therein [are] to give Mr. Nicholas Hayward, notary public, near the Exchange, London, notice thereof, who will give me a speedy and sudden account of it; also to pay the money for the first and second ships into his hands, or else to take such care as shall be to his satisfaction for the payment thereof, together with such caution for the same as he shall approve. After notice of the same from him, I shall be ready then to make my full compliance in tobacco as aforesaid. And for the goods, sort them, as if you were to send a cargo to purchase your loading here (with this caution that it [be] well bought and with ready money) which is this way advantageous that, in case of my mortality, it may suitably fit you towards your loading, according to your present course of trading and will most properly suit me for my second ship's loading; and such suitable goods in your second ship will suitably prepare me for my summer's market, and your next forward ship's punctual and ready compliance. To Mr. Nicholas Hayward, I refer the security and receiving [of] the money payable in England as aforesaid, and therefore expect the application and compliance first to be made to him, who will by the first opportunity and timely enough give me notice thereof to make preparation accordingly. For that reason do expect to receive my first letters from you subcover of his, and upon reception of them shall take care to be provided pursuant thereunto. And whereas I have set the sum of money according to the weights of tobacco I guess at, if the weights of the hhds. fall short, bulking [not packed in hogsheads] may make up the complement; or, if it overdoes your matters, orders must be large enough to make an allowance. Also as to the set times of 10th November and 10th February for the giving [of] the first notes, I have set them down because of certainty and as boundaries to the proceedings; but, if the ship arrives before either of the times, immediately upon her arrival she may keep doing [start loading] and if I have sufficient tobacco ready by me, she may get her dispatch; but, if for want of seasons or receipts, I should [at a later time] not have tobacco to make compliance, I may then have as much time given me afterwards, before I pay damage money, as

I gave them employment by my notes before the prefixed time aforesaid. Also if the ship, by contrary winds or bad weather stays longer before her arrival than the times prefixed, I do not expect that exactness, of three times for the delivery of notes, but they may have notes for the whole or the half according to the time of their stay immediately upon her arrival. Now, my intentions being to make a full compliance of 400 hhds. at the time and under the penalties in the manner and method beforementioned for the money and goods there expressed, if I have been defective in anything that may relate to your interest, provided the main intention be kept good upon notice thereof, I shall be ready to supply that defect. Or, if I have been deficient in any particular relating to my own interest, the main being kept whole, I expect the same measure, for every particular perhaps may not occur to my memory, in a bargain of this weight and nature, but in general if you approve I will make a full and sure compliance which is the needful at present from

"Worthy Gent. Your Wff. [W. Fitzbugh]"

6. Extract from a Letter of Fitzhugh to Nicholas Hayward, Notary Public in London, January 30, 1687 [5]

"My proposals of trade I have heard nothing of, neither from Liverpool nor elsewhere. I suppose the lowness of tobacco gives a stop to those proceedings, for as yet I neither hear nor know of any Liverpool man in the country and very few other ships are yet arrived. Those that are here say the lowness of the commodity occasions so few ships and no more are to be expected, but we are apt to believe that bad weather and contrary winds keep many out."

7. Extract from a Letter of Fitzhugh to Nicholas Hayward, April 18, 1687 [6]

"Since the waiting [writing] of the former I have received a letter from Mr. Clayton of Liverpool, who writes me that the lowness of tobacco will not answer to give my settled price therein mentioned of 16s 8d, but yet is mighty willing and desirous to be concerned in a trade with me and highly approves of the dispatch, desiring me to propose a lower price or other methods which I have now done, as per the enclosed copy of the letters sent him you'll perceive. And the reason I send the copy to you is because I continued my designs (if he approves of any of the propositions therein mentioned) in lodging what money I can conveniently spare in your hands, and have ordered Dr. Ralph Smith, my brother-in-law by the marriage of my sister, as I informed you in my last, to direct in the sorting of the goods and ordering some of the money there to be deposited in your hands."

8. Letter of Fitzhugh to Thomas Clayton, of Liverpool, April 8, 1687 [7]

"Sr. Yours by Mr. Marshal I received, though have not seen nor certainly heard where he is, so consequently [have] not [had] the opportunity of consulting him, nor indeed thoroughly to understand your meaning, for I find you are willing to be concerned in a trade and approve of the dispatch, but withal give me a particular account of the lowness of tobacco and the several great and incident charges thereunto. From whence you conclude that, unless tobacco [can] be purchased very low here in the method of trade you are now in, you cannot possibly advantageously continue the same, in all which I fully agree with you and must now plainly say, as in my last was intimated, that your purchase had need be very low here to make a profitable return to you there, when I consider the length of your stay here, the charge your ships lie at, the charges of storage and drinkage, the commissions you give to your factors or agents, the uncertainty of a market when you arrive here, the many debts necessarily contracted, the difficulty afterwards of getting those debts when they are due from responsible persons (and many of them never to be got nor any possibility of getting), the hazard of sending in a careless or negligent factor of your own or of employing one here, as great a hazard of meeting

[5] *Ibid.*, vol. ii (1894–95), p. 25.
[6] *Ibid.*, p. 134.

[7] *Ibid.*, pp. 136–139.

with an honest or substantial person, or, if your Master has the management of the merchandising affairs as well as the ship's, he must necessarily neglect the one or the other, for each of them requires a whole man, so that, if he be industrious on the cargo's account, either the idleness or carelessness of his own crew will give at least a month's stay in the ship's concerns or, if he neglect that, then want of employment will hinder as much.

"All which considered makes me concur with you in [your] opinion. But the method in my last proposed took off all those inconveniencies, and all things considered, I believe comes as near of [to] purchasing tobacco almost as cheaply, if not altogether, as the other way, especially most years, though I must confess [that] this year the scarcity of ships and plenty of tobacco cause an alteration. But I will, according to your desire, [make] this further offer, that, upon the same terms and under the same circumstances, I will let you have the quantity of tobacco at the times therein limited and mentioned at 12s 6d per hundredweight, which, considering the dispatch of the ship and indeed the ship's cargo in her stay, I estimate goes a great many [ways] in your purchase. And by this means she may as easily make two voyages as one in the year and at both times after arrival may be in continual and full employment, no arrears left behind nor hazard of negligence, insufficiency, or falsehood, being [provided that] you part with neither money nor goods, till you have a full satisfaction for the same.

"But if you are unwilling to give that settled certain rate, then I will make another offer: that is, I will make the dispatch as I before mentioned for your forward and latter ships' loading, allowing 2 shillings per hundred lb. more than the current market price at the time of the ship's arrival and 15 per cent commission, bearing all charges myself and running the hazard of all debts, every year sending you the full produce of your whole cargo. If yet you think that may be uncertain because of the rising and falling of the market, I will agree the market price to be 8s 6d per hundred lb. and accordingly will make you your return yearly; this way your dispatch may be in a month or five weeks time at farthest, and [I] should be willing that each ship or the ship at each time could carry 300 hhds. and could as easily dispatch her as the ship of 200 or 250 hhds. mentioned in my letter last year. If this method still likes you not, I will once again propose that I will fill you two ships, a forward and a latter one, with the same celerity and dispatch as I mentioned in my former at 25 per cent commission and £30 sterling extraordinary for each 300 hhds., and make you full return according to the market price or settled price before proposed of 8s 6d per hundred lb. But you can expect no further account of sales from me than the market price or settled price mentioned because your first ship's loading must be put on board out of my own tobacco, for before I have sold a pennyworth of your goods or indeed before I desire a pennyworth of them in my custody, according to my method in my last year's letter, I must have given notes for all, [or] if not, the greatest part of your first ship's whole loading so that the goods may be properly, after their arrival, accounted my purchase according to the market rate, or the prices there mentioned, and not sold to procure the tobacco. Upon this last proposal I'll make remark to you [that] 10 per cent is the ordinary and agreed allowance for receiving tobacco, 5 per cent the same for sales of goods, 3 per cent it comes to for storage, and, I am sure, in dealing with our country planters, less than 2 per cent will not afford drinkage insurance of the whole, [which] cannot reasonably be accounted for less than 3 per cent. And I believe I should make no extravagant computation if I should reckon the dispatch as I propose—with the leaving [of] not one pound of tobacco behind, [even] though in good, sure hands—to be worth at least 7 per cent all [of] which reckoned together comes to more than I ask by 3 per cent and better, reckoning the £30 extraordinary also.

"In my opinion, if you accept of this last proposal, the better way would be to let your forward ships be of about 200 or 300 hhds. and the latter ship a good flyboat of about 600 hhds. for these reasons:

"*First*. Such a flight [voyage] is sailed almost with the same charge as one of your country ships, in the method you are now in, are [is] because such ships are built rather for the profit of merchants than the accommodations of masters, being of a large hold and little cabin, and the only ships indeed for this country trade.

"*Secondly*. I had as lief fill such a ship for a latter ship than one of less burden, provided I had timely notice and assurance of the same; and she might also be filled with the same speed and ease too, provided sloops and flats were provided beforehand against her arrival, by which easy charge and great quantity of tobacco carried your freight would be mighty low.

"But I must thus caution you that I expect the goods bought well and with ready money, and the custom and other incident charges particularly mentioned and not an advancement of the goods to make up those charges, as is in frequent use and practice. Sir, according to your desire I have once again made you other overtures. If you like any or either of them, give but timely and speedy notice to Dr. Ralph Smith of Bristol, by whom this is conveyed to your hand, and he will take effectual care to give me timely account thereof. Or, if you doubt in anything or every particular is not so full and plain as you desire, I have given him full orders and instructions to make everything plain and conclude the same with you as well as if I were there myself. But [I] must desire you to write to him, and subcover of him to me, timely to come with the first ships, though you like not to accept of any of these proposals. If you accept of any of these proposals and acquaint Dr. Smith therewith, he will, in my behalf and according to my instructions given to him, direct in the suiting [selection] of your cargoes and what quantity of money is to be ordered for my use to Mr. Nicholas Hayward."

9. The London Agent

The London agent was expected to do his best in the sale of colonial produce, though the market might be glutted. He was asked to buy for the planter a great array of commodities but without being given explicit instructions. On one occasion Fitzhugh asked to have sent to him "Kerseys, Cotton, blue linen, nails and shoes for the product [tobacco]."

The planter would ask the agent to supply bricklayers, carpenters, blacksmiths, and housekeepers. At times it was some literary work or household plate. Once the agent, John Cooper, failed to buy the plate called for, because it seemed extravagant. Fitzhugh was furious and wrote to his notary in London for the same. The plate came just in time to be displayed before the governor of Virginia. Needless to say the notary was henceforth a favored person. The agent was expected also to receive, at times even to board, the sons of planters sent abroad for an education.

The agent was often rich, but there is little evidence of great wealth from the Virginia trade alone. The planter tended to overdraw his account—that is, he rarely sent wares of the value of the goods he sought. We cannot charge Fitzhugh with this carelessness, however, for he was a good manager. In case the agent did allow the planter to overdraw, the tendency was for the agent to take advantage of the planter in future dealings, believing that he had the upper hand. Fitzhugh, however, was too shrewd a business man to get himself into this position. He sought agents in places other than London but seemed to have little luck.

When the London agent was flooded with colonial products, he did not send a ship to the colonies; this meant loss and despair for the planter. In 1692 ships were plentiful, but in 1693 not a London ship entered the Potomac. To be neglected was intolerable. The tobacco would rot, and needed supplies were absent. There seemed no remedy for this, except for the planters to provide ships for themselves. We may well speculate as to why they did but little in this direction. The London middleman was alternately praised and blamed for his deeds; his was a difficult position.

10. General Conditions of the Time

In making up our minds as to why the English merchants declined to accede to

Fitzhugh's plan, we should not fail to take into consideration the general condition of affairs on land and at sea. Although England was not at war during the years in question, 1683–87, nevertheless there was international uncertainty on the Continent of Europe. Within England itself there was a pretty stew. Catholics were plotting a return to full power within the State. The Crown had attacked the validity of the charter that gave to the City of London its autonomy. Whigs and Tories were in a ferment. Actually civil war occurred in Monmouth's Rebellion. And then, along the coast of Virginia, as on the high seas generally, pirates plied their daring game of plunder. English merchants might naturally hesitate to lay plans for the future under such circumstances.

11. Readings

General background:

For economic life in Virginia at the time, see P. A. Bruce, *Economic History of Virginia in the Seventeenth Century,* 2 vols. (New York, 1907), especially vol. i, pp. 424–459, on the cultivation of tobacco; and vol. ii, pp. 331–391, on the sale of imported goods in Virginia.

On the early development of British colonial policy, consult G. L. Beer, *The Old Colonial System, 1660–1754,* part i, "The Establishment of the System, 1660–1688," vol. ii (New York, 1912), chap. viii, especially pp. 105–167, and C. M. Andrews, *The Colonial Period of American History,* vol. iv (New Haven, 1938).

An excellent description of the commercial mechanism in Virginia is given in L. C. Gray, *History of Agriculture in the Southern United States to 1860,* vol. i (Washington, 1933), pp. 419–428.

A description of the work of a London merchant in the Virginia-Maryland trade is found in *Journal of Economic and Business History,* vol. iv (1931–32), pp. 70–98, "Eighteenth-Century English Merchants: Micajah Perry," by Elizabeth Donnan.

On Fitzhugh:

Fitzhugh and the handling of trade in Virginia—the man and his setting—are both considered in J. S. Bassett, "The Relation between the Virginia Planter and the London Merchant," *American Historical Association Report for the Year 1901,* vol. i, pp. 551–575.

12. Suggested Questions

1. What business policies did Fitzhugh recommend?
2. Why did Fitzhugh want to establish a constant factorage in Virginia?
3. Why did the English merchants hesitate to accept Fitzhugh's plan?
4. What important changes occurred in the maturing of Fitzhugh's plans?
5. Do you accept Fitzhugh's statement of economies to be expected?
6. How do you explain the fact that the London merchant and agent seldom gained great wealth?
7. What bearing has the situation in this case upon (1) the general economic development of the South and (2) the American Revolution?

III. ROBERT KEAYNE, BOSTON MERCHANT, 1596–1656

1. General Statement

Robert Keayne (or Cain), a shopkeeper and member of the Merchant Tailors' Co., of London, came to Boston in 1635 with considerable capital accumulated in the course of his business. In Boston he imported goods, such as bridles, nails, and buttons, from London. He kept a retail store and came to own several shops and houses in Boston. In London, and probably also in Boston, he had taken the money of others in charge, paying no interest, so far as we know. By 1653 his chief property was in his farm near Boston (at Chelsea), his cattle, houses, and household goods. Our principal interest in Keayne, however, lies not in his wealth but in his business methods and management. In the struggle between the two ideals of market price and just price in America, he occupied a place somewhat similar to that of Jacob Fugger in Europe.

Keayne's difficulties over price marked the culmination of an old issue in Boston. The regulation of prices and wages was almost as old as the Massachusetts Bay Colony itself, but the early attempts to set maximum limits were not successful. In 1634 the court introduced another method when it limited the rate of profits on most imports to 4 pence on the shilling of the cash cost in England. Though this law was repealed the following year, the "wrongs" were left generally indictable, and the records show that fines were actually imposed for charging a price which was above 4 pence on the shilling.

Under the leadership of the Reverend John Cotton, the question of price became an important moral issue in Boston. Having been educated at Cambridge and having won a dangerous reputation as a liberal clergyman in England, Cotton sought refuge in the Massachusetts Bay Colony in 1633. A man of great learning and sincerity, he was soon given a high position in the church in Boston. What he preached often became either the law of the colony or the practice of its church. In his work Cotton diligently sought to make the rule of the Church effective over things both spiritual and material, to establish a theocracy in Massachusetts.

Many conditions seem to have played on the work and influence of Cotton and Keayne and helped to determine the outcome of the controversy over price. There were the rich and the poor; there was country against town; there were also those who stood for discipline and regulation as against those who wanted freedom. But most important, perhaps, were the changing economic conditions of the colony. In the year 1637 expired the monopoly of the importation of goods held by the associates who had established the colony, which event opened that trade to all. In 1638 three thousand new settlers came in three months; these new arrivals brought a heavy demand for imported goods in both town and country. Trade, accordingly, developed rapidly in 1638 and 1639, and prices rose. In 1640, however, conditions changed: with the Puritan Revolution in England, immigration almost ceased; sellers were many and buyers were few; money was scarce; and prices fell even as low as one-fourth of what they had been in the preceding boom. Several laws to help debtors were passed. In 1641 the tide of depression appears to have been at its lowest ebb, and not until 1648 did commodity prices again reach a level that might be considered normal.[1]

2. Important Dates in the Career of Keayne

1596	Born about this year, son of a butcher, Windsor, England.
1606	Apprenticed to John Heyfield (merchant?), London.
1615	Admitted to Merchant Tailors' Co., London.
1626	One of 42 English stockholders agreeing to sell their equity in Plymouth Co. to planters in Plymouth.
1635	Migrated to Boston.
1636	Received into Boston church and made freeman of colony.
	Supposed to have seized unlawfully poor woman's sow, which increased hard feelings between rich and poor. Keayne acquitted, 1642.
1638	High wages and prices complained of in New England.

[1] Marion H. Gottfried, "The First Depression in Massachusetts," *New England Quarterly*, vol. ix (1936), p. 656.

1639	Received 400 acres of land from colony. On November 5 fined £200 for charging excessive prices.
1640	Accused about this year of not returning money entrusted to him. £120 of the fine of £200 remitted.
1646	Speaker of General Court of Massachusetts for one day.
1649	His first will and testament.
1653	His final will and testament.
1656	Death in Boston.

3. Last Will and Testament of Keayne, 1653

This will, occupying 36 pages, was written by Keayne in his own hand and at different times between June 1 and November 15, with an addition dated December 15. It is difficult to exaggerate the importance of this document for the early history of American business. The will is really the autobiography of one of Boston's first merchants. It lists the various bequests, public and private, describes the estate, sets forth the business records, and justifies certain commercial transactions.

To his widow Keayne gave one-third of his wealth, and the same proportion to his son. The rest was divided among other kinsmen, friends, servants, and public institutions. He desired especially to establish a market, a conduit, and a library for divines and scholars. His gift, which was more than doubled by popular subscription, made possible the first State House of Massachusetts (1667–1711), also used as an exchange. He bequeathed part of his wealth to assist in the support of a granary, the poor of his church, a free school, and Harvard College.

Charity to the poor was a personal obligation, in the view of Robert Keayne. Even before leaving England, he had set aside one penny out of twelve (not ten as the Bible prescribes) as a fund to be used either to help others or himself when in need. This poor man's "stock" was also invested in sea voyages. Just how much of it the poor people actually saw is quite uncertain, for Keayne himself tapped it frequently. But the poor box was found—not empty—after his death.

The records used in business are listed and briefly described. There was a daybook containing items of sales and purchases. There were various debt books not fully analyzed. It is his ledger which he calls his "book of creditor and debtor in which is the sum of most of my accounts contracted, wherein there is accounts between myself and others, with the accounts balanced on either side, as also an account of what debts I owe and how far they are discharged." In his inventory book he casts up his whole estate —generally every year. In his records he distinguishes debts by book and by bill; those that were "desperate and doubtful" he kept apart from the others. He had a receipt book of money that he had already paid, thus saving himself from the danger of paying twice. In a pocketbook he accounted for daily or weekly expenses for diet, clothes, and housekeeping.

He balanced his books with man and with God. He read and synopsized religious books. He always knew just where he stood in relation to others. It was with some satisfaction that he recorded the following: "whether I have justly deserved what here I have undergone, either by words or actions, the whole passages of my life in all my dealings since I was an apprentice, being to be found in one book or another, written by my own hand."

For forty or fifty years he had been in trade, on the average earning less than £100 a year net. "I did ever drive a great trade not only since I came hither but especially in England." Bringing £2,000 or £3,000 to this country in 1635, he had only about £4,000 in 1653; but he noted that he had lived well in Boston. He thought of his business as twofold: turning and managing his own stock and receiving goods from England sent by other men. These activities seem to have been what we should call retailing and importing.

His attitude of defending himself continues throughout the will. Although his fortune was about £4,000, he had put it down for tax purposes at £1,000, his excuse being that undervaluation was the practice everywhere.

From sources other than his will we learn that he was one of the founders of the Artillery Co. of Boston. We should remember that he was "Captain" Keayne and very active in the militia of Boston. His son, Major Keayne, apparently saw military service abroad (perhaps in Cromwell's armies), though his chief interest may have been to get away from an unfortunate marriage in Boston. In the make-up of our hero we see a common trinity of business, war, and religion.

4. Inventory

When an inventory was made of Keayne's property, after his death, the total value of houses, land, and movables was found to be £2,426 2s. 1d. Among the items listed are the following:

	£	s.	d.
Cash	14	0	6
Two negroes and a child negro	130	0	0
A negro maid and a suit	20	0	0
The great house with garden and orchard	570	0	0
The new house and yard	300	0	0
The house and farm at Romney Marsh (Chelsea)	750	0	0
Land near by	80	0	0
Cattle	201	18	0
Horses	70	0	0

In addition there are debts listed to the amount of £446 7s. 2d., among which are the loans made to Major Keayne, his son, amounting to £239 9s. 2d.[2]

5. Excerpts from the Will of Keayne, 1653 [3]

"But the truth is that [I have received] unkindness and ill requital of my former love, cost, and pains, both in Old England and here, which I have taken to promote the good of the place, being answered by divers [persons] here with unchristian, uncharitable, and unjust reproaches and slanders since I came hither (as if men had the liberty of their tongues to reproach any that were not beneficial to them), together with that deep and sharp censure that was laid upon me in the country and carried on with so much bitterness and indignation of some (contrary both to law or any foregoing precedent, if I mistake not, and I am sure contrary or beyond the quality and desert of the complaints that came against me, which indeed were rather shadows of offenses) [more] out of a desire of revenge made great by the aggravations of some to make them heinous and odious than that they were so indeed (and this not in my own judgment only, which may be looked at as partial, but in the judgments of hundreds that have expressed themselves, both then and especially since). And yet by some it was carried on with such violence and pretended zeal as if they had had some of the greatest sins in the world to censure, [and] that had it been in their power or could they have carried it, they would not have corrected or reformed but utterly have ruined myself and all that I had (as if no punishment had been sufficient to expiate my offense) for selling a good bridle for 2s. that [than which] now worse are sold without offense for 3s., and [for selling] 6-penny nails for 7d., and 8-penny nails for 10d. per hundredweight, which since and to this day are frequently sold by

[2] See the inventory of Apr. 23, 1656, in the Suffolk County Court, Supreme Court records.

[3] The will is printed in *A Report of the Record Commissioners of the City of Boston* (1886), document 150–1886. The excerpts are from pp. 27, 30–32, 35. The form has been modernized.

many for a great deal more, and so in all other things proportionably, as selling gold buttons for 2s. 9d. a dozen that cost above 2 in London and yet were never paid for by them that complained.

"These were the great matters in which I had offended, when myself have often seen and heard offenses, complaints, and crimes of a high nature, against God and men, such as filthy uncleanness, fornications, drunkenness, fearful oaths, quarreling, mutinies, sabbath breakings, thefts, forgeries, and such like, which have passed with fines or censures so small or easy as have not been worth the naming or regarding, which I cannot think upon but with sad thoughts of [the] inequality of such proceedings, which have been the very cause of tying up my heart and hands from doing such general and public good acts as in my heart I both desired and intended.

. . . .

"I did not then, nor dare not now, go about to justify all my actions. I know God is righteous and does all upon just grounds, though men may mistake in their grounds and proceedings. Councils have erred and courts may err, and a faction may be too hard and outvote the better or more discerning part. I know the errors of my life; the failings in my trade and otherwise have been many. Therefore, from God it was most just; though it had been much more severe I dare not so open my mouth against it, nor never did, as I remember, but justify him. Yet I dare not say, nor did I ever think (so far as I can call to mind), that the censure was just and righteous from men. Was the price of a bridle, not for taking but only asking 2s. for it which cost here 20d., such a heinous sin, [such bridles] which have since been commonly sold and are still for 2s. 6d. and 3s. or more, though worse in kind?

"Was the selling of 2 or 3 dozen of great gold buttons for 2s. 10d. per dozen, that cost 2s. 2d. ready money in London and bought at the best hand, such a heinous sin (as I showed to many by my invoice, though I could not at that instant find it when the court desired to see it, and since was confirmed by special testimony from London, and yet the buttons not paid for when the complaint was made, nor, I think, not yet)? Neither did the complaint come from him that bought and owed [for] them, nor with his knowledge or consent, as he has since affirmed, but merely from the spleen and envy of another, whom it did nothing concern. Was this so great an offense? Indeed, that it might be made so, some out of their ignorance would needs say that they were copper and not worth 9d. per dozen; but these were weak grounds to pass heavy censure upon.

"Was the selling of 6-penny nails for 8d. per pound and 8-penny nails for 10d. per pound such a crying and oppressive sin? Though as I remember it was above two years before he that bought them paid me for them; and [they were] not paid for, if I forget not, when he made that quarreling exception and unrighteous complaint in the court against me (he then being of the court himself), as if I had altered and corrupted my book in adding more to the price than I had set down for them at first delivery. Which if I had set down 8d. for that after 2 years forbearance, which I would have sold for 7d. if he had paid me presently, I think it had been a more honest act in me than it was in him that promised, or at least pretended, to pay me presently, that he might get them at a lower price than a man could well live upon, and when he had got my goods into his hands to keep me 2 or 3 years without my money, and though all that while there was no fault found at the prices but when he could for shame keep the money no longer, yet he will requite it with a censure in the court.

"For my own part, as I did ever think it an ungodly act in him, so I do think in my conscience that it had been more just in the court to have censured him than me for this thing though this was the chief crime alleged and most powerfully carried against me and, [though] other things [were] drawn in to make this the more probable and to help to make up a censure, [such] as some farthing skeins of thread, etc.

"But the truth of the thing was this: This man sent unto me for 2 or 3 thousand of 6-

penny nails. I sent to him a bag full of that sort just as they came to me from Mr. Ffoot's of London, never opened nor altered by me. These I entered into my book at 8d. per pound, thinking he would have paid me in a very short time. It fell out that these nails proved somewhat too little for his work. He sent them again and desired me to let him have bigger [nails] for them. I took them and sent him a bag of 8-penny nails of the same quantity at 10d. a pound. Now, because I was loath to alter my book and to make a new charge, I only altered the figures in my book and made the figure of 6 a figure of 8 for 8-penny nails, and the figure of 8 that before stood for 8d. a pound, I made 10d. Now, though he knew of the change of these 6-penny nails for 8d., which I had quite forgot through my many other occasions and the length of time that they had stood in the book unpaid, yet this he concealed from me and from the court also. But to make the matter more odious, he challenged me and my book of falsehood, supposing that because he had kept me so long from my money, therefore I had made the price higher by altering the figures than at first I had charged them down and that I required 10d. per pound for 6-penny nails. And so [he] carried it in the court, who was the more easily believed because he was a magistrate and of esteem therein (though it was a most unjust and untrue charge, and only from his own imagination) till I cleared it by good testimony from an honest man in his own town.

". . . [This was the man] whom he sent for the first nails and did so bring them back and received the bigger nails for them, who came to me of his own accord and told me he heard there was a difference between such a man and I which he said he could clear. And [he] related the matter fully to me, which I was very glad to hear, which brought all things to my mind and what was the ground of altering the figures in the book, which before I had forgot, though I saw it was done with my own hand. And this was the very truth of the thing.

"I presently acquainted our honored governor, Mr. John Winthrop, and some others, who were very glad that the truth of that reproach was so unexpectedly discovered and cleared. And many, if not most of the court, was satisfied with it and saw the thing to be very plain in my debt book. But the party, himself, would not be satisfied but [that] they were 6-penny nails set down at 10d. per pound, though [he], himself, saw the figure of 8 as plain as the figure of 10.

"Now I leave it to the world to judge, or any impartial man or any that has understanding in trade, whether this was a just offense, or so crying a sin that I had such cause to be so penitent for (this being the chief [charge] and pressed on with so great aggravation by my opposers), except it should be that my actions innocent in themselves were so misconstrued and I knew not how to help myself. Especially considering it was no oppressive price, but usual with others at that time to sell the like so, and since, for almost half as much more frequently (as I think all know), and yet both given and taken without exception, or at least without public complaint.

"Yes, and the same gentleman, himself, since he has turned merchant and trader seems to have lost his former tenderness of conscience that he had when he was a buyer and [seems] not to be so scrupulous in his own gainstaking. For (if I be not misinformed and I think I had it from very good information, of some of his neighbors yet living, that knew well what they said), he agreed with some of the neighbors in his own town that he would send for or bring with him £1,000 worth of English goods for the good of the country, which they should have at easy rates and he would take wheat, peas, or any sort of corn and cattle for the pay. They provided their pay according to agreement.

"But he failed them in their first expectation, having no goods come at all. Yet another year he had a less quantity come, and amongst them nails, and I believe taken up upon credit and not paid for before they came. Yet, when they were come, corn nor cattle would not serve for pay, nor trust he would not, but his demands are ready money. And for the gains he will have 6d. in the shilling profit (which was oppression and exaction in the highest degree when he was a buyer).

"But that was not all either, for, if they paid in Spanish money, they must pay him there dollars at 4s. 6d. a piece, which here went currently at 5s. And for his nails, they being scarce at that time, his neighbors being in want would have given him any price or pay for them, but he would part with none of them. No necessity would prevail except they would buy all his other goods with them (which no doubt came at prices high enough, which made his parcel lie somewhat long upon his hands and possibly was fain to fall both in his price and pay after so many had refused them) and to retail some of them, for I was shown myself some cloth bought of him at 18 or 20s. per yard that, if some others had sold the like at 15s. per yard, it would have been thought worthy [of] complaint.

. . . .

"It is true that in anything wherein I might justly take shame or sorrow to myself God inclined my heart not to withstand it. For he that hides his sins shall not prosper, but he that confesses and forsakes them shall find mercy. In many this [things?] we sin all, and who can say his heart is clean. Yet, for the chief of the things that was most urged against me in court and for which the sentence [was] passed against me (as the gold buttons, the bridle, the nails, the falsifying of my books), I did justify and stand to maintain that they were evident mistakes and that I was wronged about th** [them?] (as that they were 8-penny nails at 10d. per pound and not 6-penny, that the buttons were gold and not copper and that they cost 2s. 2d. per dozen in London [and] sold here at 2s. 10d. per dozen and that there was no oppression in that price, that though the figures in my book were altered, yet it was not for any such end as was pretended and urged against me but upon that very cause that before I have related here). I had no cause of penitence or confession of guilt except it was for that I had been so used and reproached about them against all equity. But, if they should have cast me out of the church 20 times for this, I should have chosen it rather than to have confessed myself guilty, for the satisfaction of any, wherein I knew myself (better than anyone else did) to be innocent. . . ."

6. Commentary of John Winthrop,[4] Governor of Massachusetts, 1629–34, 1637–40, and 1646–49

"Mo. 9.) At a general court holden at Boston [1639], great complaint was made of the oppression used in the country in sale of foreign commodities; and Mr. Robert Keaine, who kept a shop in Boston, was notoriously above others observed and complained of; and, being convented, he was charged with many particulars; in some, for taking above six-pence in the shilling profit; in some above eight-pence; and, in some small things, above two for one; and being hereof convict, (as appears by the records,) he was fined £200, which came thus to pass: The deputies considered, apart, of his fine, and set it at £200; the magistrates agreed but to £100. So, the court being divided, at length it was agreed, that his fine should be £200, but he should pay but £100, and the other should be respited to the further consideration of the next general court. By this means the magistrates and deputies were brought to an accord, which otherwise had not been likely, and so much trouble might have grown, and the offender escaped censure. For the cry of the country was so great against oppression, and some of the elders and magistrates had declared such detestation of the corrupt practice of this man (which was the more observable, because he was wealthy and sold dearer than most other tradesmen, and for that he was of ill report for the like covetous practice in England, that incensed the deputies very much against him.) And sure [since] the course was very evil, especial circumstances considered: 1. He being an ancient professor of the gospel: 2. A man of eminent parts: 3. Wealthy, and having but one child: 4. Having come over for conscience sake, and for the advancement of the gospel here: 5. Having been formerly dealt with and admonished, both by private friends and also by some of the magistrates and elders, and having promised reformation; being a member of a church and commonwealth now in their infancy, and under the

[4] Winthrop's *History of New England from 1630 to 1849*, vol. i (Boston, 1825), pp. 313–317. Some of the notes to the *History*, added by the editor of the edition of 1825, have been omitted. Slight changes have been made in the text.

curious observation of all churches and civil states in the world. These added much aggravation to his sin in the judgment of all men of understanding. Yet most of the magistrates (though they discerned of the offense clothed with all these circumstances) would have been more moderate in their censure: 1. Because there was no law in force to limit or direct men in point of profit in their trade. 2. Because it is the common practice, in all countries, for men to make use of advantages for raising the prices of their commodities. 3. Because (though he were chiefly aimed at, yet) he was not alone in this fault. 4. Because all men through the country, in sale of cattle, corn, labour, &c. were guilty of the like excess in prices. 5. Because a certain rule could not be found out for an equal rate between buyer and seller, though much labour had been bestowed in it, and divers laws had been made, which, upon experience, were repealed, as being neither safe nor equal. Lastly, and especially, because the law of God appoints no other punishment but double restitution; and, in some cases, as where the offender freely confesseth, and brings his offering, only half added to the principal. After the court had censured him, the church of Boston called him also in question, where (as before he had done in the court) he did, with tears, acknowledge and bewail his covetous and corrupt heart, yet making some excuse for many of the particulars, which were charged upon him, as partly by pretence of ignorance of the true price of some wares, and chiefly by being misled by some false principles, as, 1. That, if a man lost in one commodity, he might help himself in the price of another. 2. That if, through want of skill or other occasion, his commodity cost him more than the price of the market in England, he might then sell it for more than the price of the market in New England, &c. These things gave occasion to Mr. Cotton, in his publick exercise the next lecture day, to lay open the errour of such false principles, and to give some rules of direction in the case.

"Some false principles were these:—

"1. That a man might sell as dear as he can, and buy as cheap as he can.

"2. If a man lose by casualty of sea, &c. in some of his commodities, he may raise the price of the rest.

"3. That he may sell as he bought, though he paid too dear, &c. and though the commodity be fallen, &c.

"4. That, as a man may take the advantage of his own skill or ability, so he may of another's ignorance or necessity.

"5. Where one gives time for payment, he is to take like recompense of one as of another.

"The rules for trading were these:—

"1. A man may not sell above the current price, i. e. such a price as is usual in the time and place, and as another (who knows the worth of the commodity) would give for it, if he had occasion to use it; as that is called current money, which every man will take, &c.

"2. When a man loseth in his commodity for want of skill, &c. he must look at it as his own fault or cross, and therefore must not lay it upon another.

"3. Where a man loseth by casualty of sea, or, &c. it is a loss cast upon himself by providence, and he may not ease himself of it by casting it upon another; for so a man should seem to provide against all providences, &c. that he should never lose; but where there is a scarcity of the commodity, there men may raise their price; for now it is a hand of God upon the commodity, and not the person.

"4. A man may not ask any more for his commodity than his selling price, as Ephron to Abraham, the land is worth thus much.

"The cause being debated by the church, some were earnest to have him excommunicated; but the most thought an admonition would be sufficient. Mr. Cotton opened the causes, which required excommunication, out of that in 1 Cor. 5. 11. The point now in question was, whether these actions did declare him to be such a covetous person, &c. Upon which he showed, that it is neither the habit of covetousness, (which is in every man in some degree,) nor simply the act, that declares a man to be such, but when it appears, that a man sins against his conscience, or the very light of nature, and when it appears in a man's whole conversation. But Mr. Keaine did not appear to be such, but rather upon an errour in his judgment, being led by false principles; and, beside, he is otherwise liberal, as in his hospitality, and in church communion, &c. So, in the end, the church consented to an admonition." [5]

7. Commercial Laws Drawn Up by the Reverend John Cotton as Part of a Code for Massachusetts, 1636 [6]

These proposals were not actually adopted, but they illustrate the survival of the mediaeval attitude to price and interest. The author had in mind the attitudes found in the Old Testament to which he frequently refers. The proposal concerning wages reflects contemporary practice in England.

"1. First it shall be lawfull for the Governour with one or more of the Counsell, to appoint a reasonable rate of prizes upon all such commodities as are out of the Ships, to be bought and sould in the Countrey [Province].

. . . .

"3. To the intent that all oppression in buying and selling may be avoyded, it shall be lawfull for the Judges in every Towne with the consent of the free Burgesses to appoint certaine select men, to set reasonable rates upon all commodities, and proportionably to limmit the wages of workemen and labourers, and the rates agreed upon by them, and ratified by the Judges, to bind all the Inhabitants of the Towne. The like course to be taken by the Governour, and Assistants, for the rating of prizes throughout the Countrey, and all to be confirmed if need be by the generall Court.

. . . .

"6. No increase [interest?] to be taken of a poore brother or neighbour, for any thing lent unto him."

It is notable that the genuine legal code of Massachusetts, adopted in 1641, simply fixed the maximum rate of interest—at 8 per cent. Apparently nothing was said about prices or wages. This code was drawn up by another clergyman, the Reverend Nathaniel Ward, who had studied and practised law in England.

8. Readings

On just price in mediaeval times:

For the position of leaders in the mediaeval Church see W. J. Ashley, *An Introduction to English Economic History and Theory,* pt. i (London, 1888), chap. iii, sec. 16, on Aquinas and just price, and pt. ii (London, 1893), chap. vi, sec. 63, on canonist economics.

The rise and nature of the spirit of business enterprise is considered by W. Sombart in *Quintessence of Capitalism* (New York, 1915), pp. 125–129, which deal with the art of calculation, and pp. 251–262, which consider Protestantism in relation to free enterprise.

Economic thought and enterprise in and around Boston:

The price controversy in which Cotton and Keayne were the leaders is summarized in E. A. J. Johnson, *American Economic Thought in the Seventeenth Century* (London, 1932), pp. 123–130.

[5] For this unusual instance of moderation in the church, whose corrective hand in such an offense had been more appropriately exercised than that of the magistrate, we may find two reasons: 1. Keayne's principal accuser belonged to the country; the sympathies of Boston people, of whom many (being traders) must have felt the futility of several of the allegations against their craft, were therefore less strongly excited; 2. Wilson, the pastor of the church, was his brother-in-law. Keayne, in his will, says Winthrop was prejudiced against him, but changed his opinion on the matter shortly before his death and designed to have moved the court for restitution of the fine.

[6] [John Cotton], *An Abstract of the Lawes of New England as they are now established* (London, 1641). Reprinted in Peter Force, *Tracts,* vol. iii (Washington, 1844), chap. ix, pp. 10–11.

For a discussion of economic conditions in the colony, see W. B. Weeden, *Economic and Social History of New England* (Boston, 1890), vol. i, pp. 47–87 and 117–148.

9. Suggested Questions

1. Compare the personality and policy of Robert Keayne and John Cotton.
2. What general forces at work in 1639 were inimical to Keayne?
3. What were the charges against Keayne?
4. Of what did Keayne complain in return?
5. What was Keayne's defense?
6. What difficulties did the court have in convicting Keayne?
7. Has the concept of just price any validity today?
8. Which leader of thought should we emphasize in our day—Thomas Aquinas or Conrad Peutinger? Study these two persons independently.

IV. JOHN HANCOCK, 1737–1793

1. General Statement

John Hancock was a general merchant in Boston. He became a prominent figure in politics, but for present purposes he is more interesting in his business relations. He belonged to the old category of nonspecialized merchants, active and outstanding for centuries.

In business Hancock was bold and self-confident, proud of his general position as a merchant, yet often ignorant of his real financial situation. He was habitually tardy in meeting his obligations. Many other practices of his have also been called into serious question. Keep in mind, however, that during the years with which this case is chiefly concerned business was suffering from the deflation following the Seven Years' War, and the relations between the American colonies and the mother country were strained.

Hancock was a tall man, dignified, and fond of brilliant costume. He was liberal, suave, and anxious to attain popularity. It is doubtful whether he was by disposition a man of business. Politics suited him well.

2. Outline of John Hancock's Life

1754	Graduated from Harvard.
1754–60	Apprenticed in uncle's business.
1760–61	In London, learning other side of foreign trade.
1763	Partner in Thomas Hancock & Co.
1764	Succeeded his uncle as head of the firm.
1765	Hard pressed for money from about May.
1768	His sloop *Liberty* seized for smuggling. Troops brought to Boston. Definite opposition to British government.
1770	Boston Massacre. Led committee to request removal of troops.
1771–73	Broke with revolutionary party of Adams.
1773–74	Business dull. Hancock's Boston Massacre oration. Turned against England.
1774–83	Deserted business for national affairs.
1783–93	Returned to business, but devoted practically all his time to politics.

3. Hancock's Trade with London

A. He said in part in a letter to his London agents, Barnards & Harrison, on February 7, 1765: [1]

". . . Times are very precarious here you must make the most of your remittances as Money is Extremely Scarce, & trade very dull. If we are not reliev'd at home we must live

[1] Substantially all the letters and accounts in this case have been taken from the Hancock manuscripts in the Baker Library and the New England Historic Genealogical Society of Boston.

upon our own produce & manufactures—we are terribly burthen'd our Trade will decay we are really worth a saving. . . ."

B. It seems that business was very poor and John Hancock was almost continually short of funds from the time of his uncle's death on August 1, 1764. This is an example of his foreign correspondence during the early Stamp Act days. He hinted that credit was being given to others and not to him.

"My demands latterly of goods from you I confess have been very small, owing partly to the little Demand here, & in a great measure owing to the great Number of Importers many of whom are oblig'd to Sell their goods at all Events, & of Course must go very low, that Really I had better lay by than Carry on Business to a Loss; it has been no Difficult thing for anyone to obtain Credit on your side, which has hurt us much, & I believe you not a little, but I think things must Take a Different Turn, & the Man of Capital will Carry on Business to some advantage.—By next oppor'y I shall Remitt you my whole Ballance."

C. Hancock seemed not to know how much he owed to his English agents. From the time of his uncle's death he continually wrote to London complaining because his bills were not honored, and stating that he wished a detailed statement of account so that he might know how he stood. In almost every letter to his London agents he confessed that he did not know how much he owed them, yet when he finally got a bill of his account with a large interest charge he was overwhelmed. The following is a typical example. It is part of a letter to Harrison & Barnard on October 31, 1766.[2]

". . . cannot omit taking Notice of the Charge made of £216..3..1 for Interest, it may be right in the most strict punctuality for what I can say at present as to the contrary not having Examind the account & which I will show no objection or aversion against paying, but must beg leave to say that it is a Circumstance I never Expected would have taken place, Considering the Extent of my Business & the various profitable Branches of it, & stricter or nicer Calculations could not have been render'd to the most indifferent Correspondent you have; it is needless to mention the amount of my Concerns with you for Two years past as you have the Books before you but upon the whole I cant but think it a little too severe upon me, but will pay you if you Desire it.

"This has brought me to a Resolution of closing all my account & then I can exactly determine my remittances so as to avoid the Censure of not making timely remittances, & the Charge of Interest which is a Destructive thing, and I now earnestly desire that you will please as soon as possible to convert all my Consignments of oyl Potashes etc. into cash & credit my account for their produce, & Compleat my account Current & send it to me, that I may have a Rect. in full— The Goods I have wrote [for] I pray may not come in the Spring unless this matter can be Effected first, or at least I would have them carried to an Entire new account for I am invariably determind ever in future to have the State of my account before me, at least as perfect as I can, & will never again subject myself to the demand of interest when I may avoid it. . . . I have not the least Disposition to evade the payment of this Charge of Interest, but will rather Chuse to pay it, but seriously say, it shall be the last farthing of that sort."

D. He said in his letter to Harrison & Barnard, dated December 17, 1766:

". . . . With Respect to the Charge you make to me for my order (as you Term it) to Arthur Savage of £300 Sterlg. in the first place I utterly deny any such order. It is very true I wrote you (Copy of which letter I now inclose you) that for goods you might Supply him to the Amount of £300 I would See you were no losers, but for no further Sum, in Consequence of that letter it seems you gave him a Large Supply of Goods & debit me for the £300 in part pay for those Goods. Now Gentlemen how could you with any propriety

[2] This house changed its name from Barnards & Harrison to Harrison & Barnard in 1766.

charge me that Sum, when Mr. Savage himself told me that he had remitted you very near the Sum my Letter mentioned, & I Expect that the first monies he remits you to the amount of £300, entirely cancells my Letter & to be open & Honest, I now tell you I will never cede to it otherways, really Gentlemen it is making a meer Fool of Me, I am not so void of Common Sense as to give way in this contrary to my own Judgment but I wave expressing fully My Sentiments as to your Transaction in this matter but will only say, that I expect you will Credit my account for the £300 & Interest charg'd upon it, which if I have not an account from you of it being done in the first Letter I receive from after this reaches you, I will upon my Honour & Reputation, send a Single writ down to Casco Bay & take Savage & secure myself for the £300 with Interest. I will Strictly abide by all my letters, but this Treatment really Vexes me, & I see so much of the World that I am almost Tempted to say I will not Concern myself in Trade any longer. —I Beg your attention to these matters & that I may hear from you by the Very first opportunity for I will not loose the £300. I will as things are Circumstanc'd obtain it if to be had above ground. I cant but think myself very severely dealt with, better Treatment Gentlemen I think without Vanity I merit, tho' I must say I see no difference between me & the most insignificant Correspondent you have. In Short Gentlemen you seem of late to try to put me out of Temper & express very little Satisfaction in my Conduct, that I am almost tired. No man can have a higher opinion of you than myself, nor has anyone strove more to promote your interest here than myself. I cannot live in constant Disputes I will live as agreeable & Easy as I can & unless I can carry on Business without being Involved in so many perplexities as of late, I will either leave it off, or carry it on in another Manner. But I hope you will redress me. . . ."

Since Hancock did not keep his word with regard to remittances, frequent appeals of this kind to his English agents received scant attention.

E. One letter reveals a final break with his London agents:

"Boston October 16th 1767

"Gentlemen:

". . . . Capt. Davis arriv'd here last Night but not a Letter from you No News of Scott, Marshall or Watt. Capt. Daverson senior arriv'd here yesterday by whom I receiv'd your Letters of 15th July which I heartily wish had got here in a tolerable passage as if it had Gentlemen suffer me to tell you, it would from the Contents have much alter'd my plan of Business this Fall; such a Letter I despise, It is what no man who had any knowledge of me would have dared to address to me for God's sake Gentlemen what can be your intentions. If your aim is to injure my reputation you will fail in your attempt, neither is it in your or any man's power to hurt my Credit in this part of the World, but it appears to me you are injuring yourselves. I mean as to connections in Business. & tho' by experience I find I have no influence with you, let me tell you I am one of no small influence here. & am greatly offended at the Liberties you take with me in your Letter. & is what I should have disdain'd to have wrote a Man of much less consequence than myself. You can be at no loss to determine what particular passages in your Letter I refer to, but will in the first place mention your Letter to Mr. Palfrey upon the same Subject with the Paragraph in yours respecting that Gentleman. You say you receiv'd his letter & pay a proper Respect to him & my recommendation, but as you are determin'd to retrench your trade, you must beg to be excus'd sending his Goods. In your letter to me you say. 'We have wrote Mr. Palfrey by this opportunity acquainting him that we must decline his order, we have the highest opinion of your good intentions toward us. & you will we doubt not excuse us.' How Repugnant is your Conduct to your expressions in your Letter, to say you have the highest opinion of my good intentions; & to act so contrary, nay openly & in Effect to say that I am not of Reputation & Credit enough to answer for the Goods; you say you want to retrench your trade, why Gentlemen am I the first object of your Trial. I should not have expected this from those with whom the whole extent of my Business centers; that I should be one of the first to be Refus'd Goods is truly very astonishing to me, that an Invoice sent home to you for a few goods to stock my own Shop under the direction of W. Palfrey should be refus'd is as high an Affront as I could receive and what I shall not very readily put up with. I look'd upon my recommendation & Credit to be of some weight with you, but I find it otherways. if 500 shopkeepers were recommended by some they would be instantly supplied, & if I can't be on at least the same footing with them, it is time to withdraw my Connections in Business & retire I could have wish'd you had not shipd my Goods you might with equal propriety have refus'd me, in this instance as well as the other; & Your Conduct towards me Gentlemen is unaccountable. I am really much troubled & look upon myself extremely ill us'd. I cannot see how you can reconcile it. Another instance of your Extraordinary Conduct is in the Refusal of the Goods to Mess. Cazneaus who I so strongly recommended to you with this additional agravation that they sent you my Bill of £200 in part pay for the Goods is not this Conduct a very great Slight upon me & paying very little Credit to my recommendation or my Bill it is in effect protesting my Bill. I am amaz'd & it wholly divests me of all manner of patience.

"Sometime ago you sent me a General power of Attorney, as also one to Mess. Amorys, desiring me to be assiduous in any Matters that should occur which might affect your Interest. I should have strictly adher'd to your desire in all Respects, but now find out that without even waiting for my Reply, you have from the Recommendation of Mess. —— appointed Mr. Price your attorney which with respect to me is not altogether so genteel, but I must learn to bear all things; I have no objection to Mr. Price but think you need not have been so sudden in the matter; in short Gentlemen I find others have so much more influence over you than myself, & I am of little consequence & repute with you, that I am at a loss how to account for it; but upon the whole Gentlemen I have to say that from what I have mentioned, from the Circumstances of Delano being preferred to Scott & Lyde for freight, I cant but think it most advisable for all our Navigation to be sold as it is not worthwhile to keep Vessells upon Expence without any prospect of Freight.—

"I am now to Desire you will please to order my whole account to be Got out & Sent me & if after Examination they appear to be Right I will instantly order you the full Ballance with many Thanks for your many Services hitherto, but I must add, Gentlemen, from the Treatment I have had, that unless matters can be better Reconcil'd I must wave any Connections. I Stand Ready at an hour's warning to pay every Debt I owe in the World, but as I can't be thought by you to be Responsible for £500, I must apply to those who have a better opinion of me than you have.

"I always Chuse Gentlemen to be open & explicit. I have wrote Mr. Hayley by this opportunity on the Subject of connection in & Business & propos'd opening a Correspondence with him, at least till I can have an explanation from you. I look on myself a Man of Capital, & am not to be put on a footing with every twopenny Shopkeeper that addresses you. I am greatly amaz'd at Your Conduct I think I am very freely treated, & I suppose the only instance in Town. I doubt not when Scott arrives he will bring Goods for every Shopkeeper that deals with you. & to refuse me Goods Gentlemen is what I can't bear I am ready to pay you every farthing I owe you, & it shall be done before I deal another Shilling with you. You have affected me in the tenderest point; I have determind to send my Invoice to Mr. Hayley for a Spring Supply, & let me tell you, you are obligd to me for some of your best Correspondents who would naturally be induc'd to deal with the man I engage with, & will follow me, & although my Business is not worth your attention, yet it may be an object of acceptance of many a Man in England, with thanks besides & I believe Mr. Hayley will think so.

"Many other Paragraphs of your Letter require a particular reply but I must wave that until Mr. Jackson's Brig goes, which will be in a few days, when I shall write you more particularly. Mr. Cazneau whom you dissapointed in his Goods is going to England, to whom I shall give a more extensive Credit than I did before, & dare say Mr. Hayley will readily accept his Commission. As to Mr. Palfreys goods I shall write for them myself to Mr. Hayley, & am in no doubt he will readily oblige me in sending them.

"I have many more things to say but time

fails me as I keep this Vessell wholly for my Letters. All my Friends & Connections are amaz'd at your Conduct, but I suspend adding till next oppy. till when I am

"Gentlemen Your humble Servant."

From this time on, John Hancock used Hayley as his agent in England. This letter, obviously to Harrison, Barnard & Spragg,[3] was unaddressed in the copy found in the letterbook.

F. Gleanings from other letters of John Hancock to his London agents:

Hancock often purchased oil, whalebone, or potash, for other merchants either in America or in England at a regular commission of 5 per cent. (November 26, 1764)

Hancock continued to demand credit and to refuse money until urged to send it. (May 21, 1765)

Hancock was hard pressed for payment but, since bills owing to him were unpaid, he could not meet his obligations. The Stamp Act was doubtless a factor in the local curtailment of trade. (Letters of July–December, 1765)

Shared ownership of a cargo with London agents:

"I Note what you say in Regard to the Cargo of the Liberty. I very freely made you an offer of a part of her Cargo; in consequence of which you were earnest to hold ¼ part which I consented to; but now find you decline that concern from which [I] conclude that money will be lost on that Cargo. I have only to say, Gentlemen, that I am quite content to take the loss on myself, but must beg leave to say that in future I must decline leaving my concerns at such an uncertainty, & take profits & loss to myself as it may happen. I mean exclusive of our connections in Vessell. I imagine if money had been made by that Cargo you would not have Declin'd the Concern. . . ." (April 17, 1766)

Hancock's bill on another house had been declined by Harrison & Barnard, the chief London agents, to whom he wrote:

"... . I rec'd a letter from those Gentlemen of 10th August acquainting me that they had Drawn on you at 60 days for the amount of my provisions but that it was not convenient for you to pay the Bill on those Terms, & that they had chang'd it to six months adding £8..13..6 for the Interest. This I know not how to account for, & shall only [say] that the Consequences will clearly show my opinion of it, & is what I should not have done to any of my Connections. In short I cannot have the face to send to those Gentlemen for any future Supplies, without sending Bills with my orders, & how to apologize to them I know not. I do not think I am well us'd but I must learn to Bear all things." (October 7, 1766)

Hancock's agents, thinking that Hancock did not know enough about whale oil and bone to purchase it wisely, offered to send him a man to help him purchase and inspect the oil. Such an act would, of course, have made him an object of ridicule in the eyes of his fellow merchants. (September 18, 1767)

Hancock turned from his old agents to a new one, Hayley. Still he continued correspondence with the old agents, Harrison, Barnard & Spragg, for about a year longer, indeed until they had a misunderstanding over finances. (October 16, 1767)

The London agents threatened to send a representative to collect from Hancock. Such a threat made Hancock "uneasy," as he mildly put it. (April 13, 1768)

In 1770 a credit of £11,597 was given by his London agents, Hayley and Hopkins, chiefly for goods sent them by Hancock, while £10,553 was charged against him for bills and merchandise. (Account of 1770)

Hancock shipped to his London agents, Hayley and Hopkins, four tons of pig iron for Nicholas Brown & Co. (November 19, 1770)

In 1772 Hancock's chief agents credited his account with £10,299 for cargoes and remittances, while they paid bills and charged to his account £13,354. Next year

[3] Harrison & Barnard became Harrison, Barnard & Spragg in 1767.

he sent several shiploads of goods which reduced his indebtedness. (Account of 1772)

Business, 1764–74: purchases of Hancock greatest in 1765; business of 1773 fairly good; decline in 1774 as Hancock turned to politics. (Receipt Book, 1764–84)

In 1783 Hancock learned that he had a balance of £500, left over from before the war. (Letter of November 14, 1783)

4. Hancock in the Whale-Oil Trade [4]

Thomas Hancock had long dealt in whale oil,[5] and it was only natural that John Hancock should carry on this type of business. It was partly because of special circumstances, however, that John became more heavily interested in oil cargoes than his uncle had ever been. One of these circumstances was the new supply situation in the whale-oil market in 1763 and 1764. The French and Indian War in America had come to a close in 1763, and in that year the whale fisheries began to get back to normal. The "catch" had been negligible during the war years, because the French had destroyed the fisheries. The price of oil still held high after the war: the oil was selling at £27 and £28 per ton in London in 1763 and 1764, whereas it normally sold at about £20 per ton. These top prices prevailed even after Thomas' death, in August, 1764, and helped to draw John into the market.

A second important consideration was the rivalry that had existed between Thomas Hancock and Rotch, of Nantucket, during Hancock's last years. The nephew was forced to manage the whole concern during the several months in which his uncle was an invalid; being young and incautious he was gradually aroused to the spirit of battle—ready to buy more and more oil to gain a possible competitive advantage over his rival, even outbidding his competitor, who had a very strong position in the trade.[6]

At this point it is well to keep in mind the organization of the whale-oil trade of the time. The leading American primary market for whale oil was New Bedford, Massachusetts; the leading secondary market was Boston, where the American price was determined; and the world center of the trade was London. Boston merchants bought outright or took oil on consignment from the factors in the primary markets—New Bedford, New York, Nantucket—and sold to the merchants in London. Boston was, however, only one of the possible outlets for whale oil, so that in dealing with the factors Boston merchants had to meet those other demands. In 1763–64 one of the strongest demands must have come from the association of manufacturers of spermaceti candles, called the United Company of Spermaceti Candlers. These manufacturers attempted to establish a monopoly in their line by taking all the oil of the kind they used that was brought into American ports.[7]

One of the leading factors in the primary market was Rotch. His strength is indicated by the fact that he was one of a small group of factors specifically chosen to purchase whale oil for the powerful association mentioned above for a year beginning April 13, 1763.[8] The friendship or enmity of Rotch meant much to Hancock, for Rotch knew the whale-oil business near the source of the product, and he was a strong factor in the trade.

A. A letter recorded shortly after the death of Thomas shows the growing per-

[4] Whale oil was used as an illuminant at that time and occupied the place now held by our modern oils as a lubricant.

[5] See Edward Edelman, "Thomas Hancock, Colonial Merchant," *Journal of Economic and Business History,* vol. i (1928–29), pp. 77–104.

[6] Letter of Hancock to Harrison & Barnard, July, 1764.

[7] *Commerce of Rhode Island,* vol. i (Massachusetts Historical Society Collections, seventh series, vol. ix), pp. 87–92, 97–100.

[8] *Ibid.,* p. 98.

sonal rivalry between Rotch and John Hancock. From this letter of August 17, 1764, to Messrs. Barnards & Harrison it appears that Hancock is ready to compete openly with Rotch:

". . . I am determin'd to increase rather than lessen my concerns in it [oil]. My visit to Nantucket was very agreeable. I found such connections as to prevent any dissapointment, I can have what oyl I please of the best men there which of course takes from the other Channell and is very Chagrining to Mr. R—h [Rotch] but he knows my mind. . . ."

On the same date Hancock wrote Barnards & Harrison further about his plans:

"We shall be glad you will be Explicit in Your opinion respecting oyl & whether You would chuse a Concern in more than what will load the Ship and Brig. The whole of the oyl will center with you, Champion & Haley, and Buxton & Symmes. You will have a large quantity in the Fall, for we are determined the plan they have laid shall not take effect, and should they have any Conversation with You on the subject, pray be cautious how You open Yourself to them and keep them ignorant of our Concerns, for J. H. is determined to pursue this business, which takes from the Channel of R—h and Centers it with you. Pray, in all Your Letters inform us what you can of oyl etc. & be frequent in your advices, this may be of use to us."

B. According to a letter to Barnards & Harrison, April 5, 1765, Hancock was then evidently bidding for the coöperation of Rotch:

". . . You do not consider the number of oyl Buyers here, who, not considering the consequence give any price for oyl for the sake of getting their ships away tho I am full in the belief that the number of ships in the London trade must soon be Lessen'd. . . . I shall however be better able to write you by next opportunity as I can know more of Mr. Rotch's plans and designs and whether he is inclinable to be on amicable terms tho he this day call'd upon me, and mention'd what his friends wrote and that he was disposed to Effect their plan, and desir'd we might conferr together on the Subject, and I appointed a day for him to dine with me and no one else when we shall talk matters over after which I will acquaint you with the Result. . . ."

C. After the conference referred to above, Hancock wrote again to Barnards & Harrison (April 18, 1765):

". . . I have had a long conference with Mr. Rotch agreeable to your desire Respecting the oyl trade. He appears dispos'd to be upon amicable terms and to be aiding & tells me he will strictly abide by the instructions he has received from Buxton Symmes & Enderby, how farr, Time can only discover. You are not so well acquainted with that Gentleman as I am but I will for once try him, which but for your desire, I should never have even had a thought doing. . . ."

D. Hancock wrote to the same London agents on July 6, 1765:

". . . the price of oyl [has] not yet broke, tho I have heard notwithstanding the positive agreement made with Mr. Rotch, that, his son has offerd £15 Stg. for oyl, I am fearfull it will not break under that. I am now come to a Resolution never again to be under any Limitations but to be at Liberty to act as I shall judge best."

E. The same to the same, February 25, 1766:

". . . I have now severall Whaling Vessells of my own, & in about three Weeks shall fit them out, that with Common Success I shall have a large Quantity of oyl & Bone, with my own Vessells . . . I propose being pretty largely concern'd the coming year in purchasing oyl; beg your opinion as early as possible as to oyl & Bone."

F. The same to the same, April 17, 1766:

". . . As to my coming into any kind of conversation, connection or concern with Mr. R—h I must beg leave utterly [to] decline even the thought of such a thing, but with respect to Folger Barker & Garn [?] ready to Consult for the good of the whole tho' I generally Chuse to Carry on my own Business in my own way, but on this Occasion I will Talk with these Gentlemen with whom I am connected & do all I can to forward what you Recommend."

G. The same to the same, November 8, 1766:

". . . I have now so well Establish'd myself with those concern'd in the Whale Fishery, that I can have the refusal of almost all their oyl, & I think Mr. R—h has had small success in purchasing, & by far the greatest quantity of oyl will be in your hands which is my aim."

H. Though oil had been almost steadily dropping in price since 1764, Hancock plunged into the market with greater determination than ever in 1766, and in the fall of that year he sent a considerable number of ships loaded with his oil to London. Suddenly, in the winter and spring of 1767, just as his vessels reached England, oil dropped between 15 and 20 per cent.

I. Analysis of the purchase and sale of a cargo sent to London in November, 1766.

Hancock wrote to his agents, Harrison & Barnard, November 10, 1766: [9]

"I have already wrote you by this oppory to wch refer, since which I have rec'd a letter from our Freinds Josiah Barker & Co. of Nantucket who write me the Brige. Whale Bone is almost Loaded, & will soon sail to you with a Load of oyl & desire me to write for Insurance on her & am now to desire on Rect. of this you will please to make Insurance. . . . The Vessell & Cargo is at present ownd, one third by me, & two thirds by Barker & Burnell . . .

"I shall soon write you by Bass with oyl & shall forward you all my oyl as fast as possible"

The cargo referred to in the above letter was shipped late in November, 1766: [10]

"Nantucket, November 20, 1766

"Account of Oil Shipt on Board Brigt Whale Bone Benjamin Jenkins Comndr for London on acct and risque as pr Invoice

"Gallon		Ton		£ [s][d]	£ [s] [d]
24495 White Sperms oil		97–1–20	at	24	–2332–18– 1
1769 Brown " "		7–0– 5	"	22	– 154– 8– 8½
2710 Whale " "		10–6–1½	"	18–13–4–	200–15– 6
2069 Whale " "		8–1–22	"	21– 6–8–	176– 1– 8
1008 White " "		4– –	"	25– 6–8–	101– 7– 8
11 thousand Staves	at			2– 3 –	23–13– 0
Binding and gagueing 127 ton	"			–8– 8 –	55– 5– 0
Wharfage of do	"			–0– 8 –	4– 5– 0
Storeing and trucking of 645 bbls				–4–	10–15– 0
310 gallon whale oil at 21–6–8					26–03–10
Binding and gagueing at 8–8					10–10
Wharfage of 10 bbl at 1					–10
Commission att 5 pr Ct					154– 6– 3
Primage Paid Capt Jenkins					4– 4
				"Lawful Money	3244–15– 4
				"John Hancock 1/3	1081–11– 9

"Errors Excepted—Josiah Barker & Company
"Examined, J. H.—small errors only"

[9] John Hancock's Letterbook, New Eng. Hist. Gen. Soc., on deposit in Baker Library, Harvard University.

[10] Hancock Mss., Baker Library. £100 "lawful money" of the province was equal to only £75 sterling.

The oil was sold by Hancock's London agents and partners in the spring and summer of 1767. The following shows the returns from the venture.[11]

"Sales of 789 Casks oil Received by the Whalebone Capt Jenkins at New England by consignment of Messrs Josiah Barker & Co on accot in thirds between John Hancock Esqr. Josiah Barker & Co & our Selves.

"Jan. 26, 1767	*£ Sterling*	
To Cash paid Duty, Entry fees, Oath & Sufferance	73.. 6..	
Lighterage, Wharfage, Landing, Houseing, Laying Down, etc.	34..15..4	
Warehouse Rent	16..18..	
Landwaiters, Surveyors, Weighers' fees and expenses	7..17..	
Cooperage & Gauger	31..12..6	
Lighterage, Wharfage, Landing & Staves	2.. 2..6	
Brokerage at 1/2 p. Ct.	12..10	
Freight & Pierage	326 – 4	
		505.. 1..8
To our Commission on £2500 — 9 at 2 1/2 p. Ct		62..10..
To John Hancock Esqr. accot. Current for 1/3 Net Proceeds	644.. 3..½	
To Messrs Josiah Barker & Co. ditto for 1/3 ditto	644.. 3..½	
To H B & S for 1/3 ditto	644.. 3..	
		1932.. 9..1
		2500.. –..9"

"(Sales of the Oil)

"1767	
"April 20	
By Moore & Smith . . . 17 3/4 Tons 46 gallons Whale Oil at £18 5s	327.. 5..5
"May 14	
By Moore & Smith . . . 66 Tons 20 Gallons White Oil £21 10s	1420..14..1
"Jany. 31	
By Cash received for 8200 Barrel Staves	20..10..
"May 14	
By Moore & Smith . . . 36 Tons 42 Gallons brown oil at £19 10s	705.. 5..
"July 16	
By John Reynolds for 9 Casks Oil Sold him . . . 1 1/4 Ton 34 Gallons at £19	26.. 6..3
	2500.. –..9"

"Errors Excepted London 20th August 1767
"Harrison Barnard & Spragg"

5. Retail Business of John Hancock

A. Hancock had a retail store of his own in which he sold many articles which he had himself imported, according to an advertisement of December 25, 1764:[12]

"Store No. 4, at the east end of Faneuil Hall Market, a general assortment of English and India Goods, also choice Newcastle Coals, and Irish Butter, cheap for Cash. . . ."

B. The following goods were sold at wholesale but some also at retail: account books, *Aesop's Fables,* blankets, buckram, butter, buttons, canvas, cartridge paper, cloves, combs, fans, felt hats, handkerchiefs, hatbands, hosiery, indigo, leaf twist, mackerel lines, mitts, molasses, nails, paper, pepper, pigeon shot, pork, ribbons, rigging, salt, sea coal, tea, trunks, window glass, and wines. (Waste Book, 1764–67)

C. Hancock wrote to Harrison & Bar-

[11] Hancock Mss., Baker Library. Forms modernized.

[12] A. E. Brown, *John Hancock, His Book* (Boston, 1898), p. 60.

nard, his agents in London, January 18, 1766, as follows:

"... Inclos'd you have an invoice of Goods to be put up & Sent me in the Spring as early as you can if the Stamp Act be Repeal'd, other ways not. These goods I beg may be well Chosen & Pack'd, & Charg'd at the lowest Rates. My design being to put them in a Shop for Retail, in which I shall place a young Man who has been with me since my late Uncle's Death, as my Brothers Leaveing the Store occasion'd my wanting more help just at that Juncture as I had a multiplycity of affairs to attend to; of whose abilities I have a high opinion, & shall now make Tryall as well for his advantage as my own, & if it answers I shall order the Goods after these to be charg'd to his account. The Goods wrote for in the Inclos'd Invoice you will please to mark ..., Consign them to me in a separate Invoice & Bill Lading, & let them be all of the Best. ..."

D. Retail partnerships: Hancock wrote to his London agents, Hayley and Hopkins, as follows:

"... You have also Inclos'd an Invoice of Goods which I Beg the Favour of you to give orders to be particularly attended to in the Choice of the Articles. Let them be Charg'd at the lowest Rates, Consign'd to me & Charg'd to my account. Mark them H B T. These goods are for a most commodious well Scituated Shop of mine to be kept by Mr. William Bant who is an excellent Shopkeeper, & in which we are Jointly Concern'd; this is the Gentleman to whom you Shipt Goods by Scott; & as he will in a few days remove into my Shop with his goods. ..." (Letter of April 29, 1771)

6. Banking Transactions of John Hancock

A. Concerning money left in the care of Thomas Hancock.

Hancock wrote to Captain David Allen in London:

"Boston, July 6, 1765

"Sir

"A Multiplicity of Affairs having devol[v]ed upon me since the Event of the death of my late uncle which has Engaged my whole attention & prevented my writing you till now—

"I am now to acknowledge the receipt of yours of 14 Nov. & 12 Jany. and agreeable to your desire now inclose you the State of the Treasurers Notes you left in the care of my late uncle. I also inclose your account as it stands on his Books, by which you will see you have Credit for the Cash received of Mr. Wallace, and as my late uncle wrote you he could not get it into the Treasury, it has lain ever since for your order, you will observe that the whole of the notes become due next June, after which time I dont think it can be Continued, as the Province is in no want of Cash, and they have offers of the Loan of any sum at 5 per cent. I should think it would be most for your Interest to order it home, as I could not advise you to put it into the hands of people here I should judge it too precarious this I submit to you and whatever Resolutions you may take respecting it you may depend on a punctual & cheerful compliance from me, the Prizes in the New London Lottery I fear will never be recover'd—

"You will please to let me know your determination about your monies & your orders shall be Executed—

"My best wishes attend you, & I am with Tenders of my best Services

"Sir

"Your most obedient & humble Servant

"Treasurers Notes belonging to Capt. David Allen left by him in the care of the late Thomas Hancock Esq. which are now in the hands of John Hancock & lay on account & risq of said Capt. Allen—Viz

"One note	dated	16th Feby. 1763	payable	20 June 1766	£445
One do	–	2d June 1764	– –	20 June 1766–	140
One do	–	30 Mar. 1763	– –	20 June 1766–	123
One do	–	6 July 1763	– –	20 June 1766–	134
					£842"

"Int. on above Notes due from the Dates"

Allen later wrote to Hancock:

"Haverford West, South Wales,
"1st April 1767.

"Sir

"In Consequence of the first & only Letter I have received from you, acquainting me that the Treasury would not long [sic] & advising me to draw my money home as more to my advantage. I have wrote to you, I believe, ten Different Times, requesting that you would as soon as possible remit me the Interest Due upon the Capital as also the Money paid into your Uncles Hands by Mr. Hugh Wallace, which has been laying dead for so long a Time.

"I must now once more make the same Request that you will remit me the Interest of the aforesaid Capital, likewise the money paid by Mr. Wallace, viz 526½ Spanish Dollars and if the Capital should no longer be invested in the Treasurey, you will please to remit that at the same Time, but should it still be invested you will notwithstanding remit it if it can be drawn & negotiated without Loss.

"I did mention in all my former Letters for the money remitted to Childs's, but that is a matter of Indifference; you may send me Bills for the Amount if more agreeable to you, of 30 days for which you can never be at Loss at Boston, but the former would be rather more agreea. . to me, as it is a Chance if I shale have any Business to call me to Town, but which ever you should fix on, yo. . will please to advise me of it by the earliest opportunity.

"My best Respects wait upon Mrs. Hancock

"I am
Sir
Your most Obedient
Humble Servant
David Allen"

B. Concerning another sum left with Thomas Hancock:

"Boston November 16, 1768

"Sir

"Having been much hurried & Engag'd prevents my writing you so fully by this oppory as I intended. I must therefore Defer it to the next Ship which will be in about a Week, when I shall write you further & Inclose you your whole account. I have now only Time to inclose you my Bill on George Hayley Esq. Merchant in London of this Date No. 90 for Three Thousand pounds Sterling in part of the Monies left by you in the hands of my late Uncle for which I am accountable to you, & when paid you will please to Credit my Account therefor By Captain Daverson who will Sail in a Week. I shall Transmitt you your whole Account & Send you an order for the full Ballance of that account when you will please to give up the Receipts my late Uncle gave you for the Monies left in his hands—

"My Aunt Joins me in best Compliments to you & I am with much Esteem Sir

"Your most Obedient humble Servant

"His Excellency Thomas Pownall Esq.–"

C. Brief notices:

"Messrs. Burnall & Barker Dr. to cash for my Bill on Barnard & Harrison No. 9 of this date for £200 Stg" (October 3, 1764). This was Hancock's entry of a bill given apparently to a Boston firm desirous of transferring cash to London, and doing so through Hancock and his London agent (the latter usually charging ½ of 1 per cent for the service).

"Messrs. Barnard & Harrison of London Dr to cash paid their bill to Samuel Griffith. Sterling 10.–" (November 26, 1764). Here we find Hancock's record of payment of a bill drawn upon him by his London agents in favor of a client of theirs, presumably someone traveling to America.

"Jonathon White Dr to merchandise for his order paid David White 14 . 1 . " (February 6, 1767). This entry in Hancock's books indicates that he was paying out goods or money to people at the order of his customers.

"Benjamin Gerrish Esq. Dr to cash paid Maurice Cavenaugh by his order for the use of their Nova Scotia Packett £8 Halifax Currency & His Receipt in Full 9 . . 12 . . 0" (April 10, 1767).

7. Hancock and the Customs

A. As early as November of 1764 Hancock was having difficulties with the customhouse. In a letter written on November 17, 1764, to Barnards & Harrison he says:

". . . You have Inclosed a Certificate of Landing the Tea by Marshall, also a Naval Store Bill. I must beg at all Events you return me a Certificate of Landing the Staves & whalebone at London, as I am under Bonds here, & things at present under such circumstances with the Custom House that it is very difficult to carry on business & unless redress Trade must dwindle that without you return a Certificate my Bonds will be put in Suit."

B. Special instructions to the London agents:

". . . You will please to observe by the Invoice there is a quantity of Head Matter I have Shipt by Scott which I beg your care to get pass'd unotic'd, & I have no Doubt but you will Effect it as heretofore. . . ." (Letter of January 18, 1766, to his agents Barnard & Harrison)

". . . You will please to observe that I have Shipt by the Boston Packett 137 Cask Head Matter Mark'd per Invoice H N 1 to 137. This I must Beg your care to get pass'd without Notice. I have heretofore frequently ship'd parcells to Harrison & Co. & they have met with no trouble. I pray your care of this. . . ." (Letter of December 15, 1767, to his new agent, George Hayley)

C. Letter of Hancock to Hill, Lamar & Bissett, January 20, 1767.

"Gentlemen:

"I wrote you by way of London that I should send a Vessell to you for some Wines which Letter hope you have Receiv'd. This goes by the Sloop Liberty Nath Barnard Master to your address. & Inclos'd you have Invoice and Bill Lading of a few Articles ship'd by him for my Account which on its arrival with you I pray you will dispose of to the best advantage & Credit my Account with the Neat proceeds and am to desire you will please to ship me by my Sloop Liberty the following Wines vizt Four pipes of the very best sterling Madeira Wine that you can possibly procure for my own Table. I do not stand for price I like a Rich Wine, & if in addition to the four pipes you can Ship me a pipe of Right Sterling Old Madeira pale and good you will send it me cost what it may. I need say no more than that they are for my own use and I pray they may be the very best mark . . . & pray distinguish them from any others on board. You will please also to ship me four pipes and four Quarter Cask of good Saleable Madeira Wines for our Markett I would have them good & such as would suit our publick Houses where the best Company Resorts mark them H K & do let them be of good Quality.

"You will please also to ship by my Sloop two pipes of the best Madeira Wine consign'd to me in Separate Invoice and Bill Lading specifying the freight mark them H G T they are for the Treasurer of our Province [Harrison Gray] & you will please to let them be good.

"The Neat Proceeds of the Articles ship'd by Capt. Barnard you will invest in those Wines & for the Ballance you will please to draw Bills on my Friend George Hayley Esq. Merchant in London to whom I have wrote to honour your Bill. I beg that the Wines for my own use may be of the very best kind. And if Bills will purchase Better Wines than can be procur'd with the Articles shipd by Barnard, I should chuse you should invest the Neat proceeds of them in Saleable Wines & draw for the Amount of my wines tho' I should wish it was as agreeable to you to draw for the Ballance. I leave it to you only let my Wines be good.

"Messrs. Jonathan and John Amory write you for two pipes of Wine to be sent in my Sloop and they desire you to draw on their Friends Messrs. Harrison, Barnard & Spragg for their Cost in Compliance with their Request to me as they are Strangers to you, I am to acquaint you that you may Rely their Bills will meet with due honour and they are Gentlemen of Character and Reputation here.

"I shall be much obliged if you or any of your Friends should have any freight to ship this way that you would give my Sloop the preference she is a good Vessell and well found. I shall also be obliged to you to give Capt Barnard any advice or assistance he may need.

"I shall be glad you will send me two

bushells Madeira Nutts and 2 Boxes Citron charging them to my Account.

"You will please to send me by the Return of my Sloop my Account ballanced & shall be obliged to you to give the greatest dispatch to the Sloop as I shall not only want the Wines but the Sloop & I hope she may be here in March.

"I am with much Respect Gentlemen Your Most obedient Servant. . . ."

D. *The Advocate General* v. *Hancock*, 1768.[13]

"Before the Honorable Robert Auchmuty Esq.

"Province, etc.

"Be it remembered, that on the 29th day of October in the ninth year of the reign of his Majesty, George the Third (1768), Jonathan Sewall Esq., Advocate General for the said Lord the King, in his proper person comes and as well on behalf of the said Lord the King, as of the governor of this province, gives the said court to understand and be informed, that on the ninth day of May last, a certain sloop called the Liberty, arrived at the Port of Boston in said province, from the islands of Madeira, having on board one hundred and twenty-seven pipes of wine of the growth of the Madeira's; of which said sloop, one Nathaniel Barnard was then master; and that in the night time of the same day the said Nathaniel Barnard with intent to defraud the said Lord the King of his lawful customs, did unlawfully and clandestinely unship and land on shore in Boston, aforesaid, one hundred of the aforesaid pipes of wine of the value of thirty pounds sterling money of Great Britain, each pipe, the duties thereon not having been first paid, or secured to be paid, agreeable to law. And that John Hancock of Boston, aforesaid Esquire, was then and there willfully and unlawfully aiding and assisting in unshipping & landing the same one hundred pipes of wine, he, the said John Hancock, at the same time well knowing that the duties thereon were not paid or secured and that the unshipping and landing the same, as aforesaid, was with intent to defraud the said Lord the King as aforesaid, and contrary to law. Against the peace of the said Lord the King and the form of the statute in such case made and provided, whereby, and by force of the same statute, the said John has forfeited treble the value of the said goods, so unshipped and landed as aforesaid, amounting in the whole to the sum of nine thousand pounds sterling money of Great Britain, to be divided, paid and applied in manner following: that is to say, after deducting the charges of prosecution, one third part thereof to be paid into the hands of the collector of his Majesty's customs for the said port of Boston, for the use of his Majesty, his heirs and successors, one third part to the governor of said province, and the other third part to him that informs for the same.

"Whereupon as this is a matter properly within the jurisdiction of this honorable court, the said Advocate General prays the advisement of the said court in the premises, and that the said John Hancock may be attached and held to answer to this information, and may by a decree of this honourable court be adjudged to pay the aforesaid sum of nine thousand pounds to be applied to the uses aforesaid.

"Jonathan Sewall, Advocate for the King."

Hancock was actually arrested on the night of November, 1768. He gave bail, and finally came to trial on January 2, 1769. After a long trial the case was dropped on March 26, 1769.

E. William DeGrey made a legal analysis of the smuggling case for the benefit, as it seems, of the English government. He told at length how the wine was illegally landed and how one officer reported the matter to the customs officer at Boston. His comments on the situation in Boston are especially pertinent in this relation: [14]

". . . It will be necessary to observe here, that the Populace at Boston, had long before this shewn a great Disaffection to the Revenue Laws, and seemed to want nothing but a pretext for their proceeding to open Violences, wherefore the Officers of the Customs thought

[13] The case of *Jonathan Sewall* v. *John Hancock* as given in Quincey's *Massachusetts Reports*, pp. 457–458.

[14] William DeGrey, Case of the "Liberty," in *M. H. S. Proceedings*, vol. lv (1921–22), pp. 273–276.

it prudent that the Vessell, when seized, should be delivered with the Charge of the *Romney* Man of War, then lying at Boston for Security.

"On the same 10th of June Mr. Harrison Collector and Mr. Hallowell Comptroller of the Customs went on board the Liberty and made a Seizure of her, but while they were delivering her over to the care of the *Romney,* a great Number of People had collected themselves together, some of whom swore that the Vessell should not be taken into Custody, that they would throw the *Romney's* people Overboard, and used other Menaces to interrupt the Officers in the Execution of their Duty. From Menaces they proceeded to Violence, laying hold of the Ropes of the Vessell as she was towing towards the *Romney,* and pelting the Officers, 'till the Vessell was at last got from them by Force; and on the Return home of the Collector and Comptroller, they were surrounded by the Mob, which at that Time consisted of about 4 or 500 Persons, and were so much beat and wounded by them, that it was with the greatest Difficulty they Escaped with their Lives, nor did the Fury of the Mob stop here, Every Officer of the Customs they could meet with felt their Resentment, and narrowly escaped being murthered; the Windows of the Houses of the Collector, Comptroller and Inspector General were intirely demolished, and in short their Threats were so violent against all the Officers of the Customs, that the Commissioners, in order to save themselves, sheltered themselves in the Houses of their Friends for that Night, and afterwards took Refuge on Board the Romney, and have since been conveyed to Castle William for greater safety.

"On Saturday the 11th of June a Proposal was verbally made to Mr. Harrison, the Collector, on behalf of Mr. Hancock, that upon the Vessell being returned to him, he would give his own Bond as a Security for her forthcoming, and for redelivering her in case upon the Matter being heard in the Admiralty Court, a Decree should be obtained in favour of the Revenue Officers.

"At the Time this Proposal was made, the Populace still continued in a great Ferment, and seemed ready to proceed to every Outrage unless their Humour was complied with, and it was intimated to the Officers of the Customs, that the Cessation of Violence was only to continue 'till the Monday following, and that if the Proposal was not accepted by that Time, very terrible Consequences would ensue, wherefore the Collector and Comptroller acquiesced in the Proposal; and the Collector, seeing the Danger to which himself and the whole Town of Boston were exposed, went further, for by a Letter to Mr. Hancock he agreed to take his Word only as a Security for the Ship, and the Officers understood that everything was settled, and that the Vessell was to be restored to Hancock on the Monday, but on Sunday Evening a Message was brought them, that Hancock had advised with his Council and Friends and would settle nothing with them, but would let the Business take its Course.

"Things being in this Situation, the Commissioners, not knowing what Steps to take in so critical a Dilemma, have represented the above Facts to the Lords Commissioners of his Majesty's Treasury, and transmitted to them several Depositions and Letters relating thereto (Copies of which are herewith left) and their Lordships have been pleased to direct that a Case be laid before Mr. Attorney General for his immediate Opinion. . . .

"July 25, 1768 Mr. DeGrey"

8. Estate of John Hancock at His Death, 1793

A. Inventory of assets.

"Cash, U. S. Bonds, State Notes, and Bank Stock		£ 6500
Balance due on Notes of Hand and Account		10367
House Furnishings, Books, etc.		1935
Real Estate in Boston:		
Mansion House	£5000	
Hancock's Wharf and Buildings	7500	
Miscellaneous	5850	18350

Real Estate outside of Boston:		
Suffolk County	£ 1072	
York "	1142	
Lincoln "	13090	
Cumberland "	502	
Hampshire "	578	
Worcester "	1672	
Lancaster "	180	
Fairfield "	90	
Strattford "	404	
Hillsborough & Cheshire Counties (N. H.)	2743	
Grafton County (N. H.)	150	
Hampshire " " "	1203	22826
Total		£59978"[15]

B. Debts.

"Paid by October 22, 1799	$19,475	
Unpaid " " "	20,495	
Total debts and Claims		$39,970"[16]

In 1902 and 1903, the Probate Records show that claims were filed against the estate on several different occasions but no further action was taken.

C. Total Assets of John Hancock Estate.

Assets	£59,978
Liabilities	8,224
Value of Estate	£51,754

Since £41,176 of his assets were real estate, which was probably considerably overvalued, this sum should be discounted considerably. Most of this was wild, unused land which had been given to him for his services during the Revolution, at one time a gift of 40,000 acres being recorded.

By report Hancock had received from his uncle in 1764 about £70,000. By 1793 this had apparently shrunk to only £51,486 or perhaps much less.

[15] Probate Records of Suffolk County, vol. xciii, pp. 11–25, 781–794; vol. xcv, pp. 653–661; vol. cxiii, pp. 90–91.

[13] *Ibid.*, vol. xcvii, pp. 504–508; vol. cxiii, p. 73.

The estate was not finally divided, it seems, until 1815, because of numerous claims outstanding against it. His wife Mary and his brother Ebenezer inherited the proceeds.

9. Suggested Readings

Background:

For a brief general exposition of the development of American colonial commerce and British regulation, see H. U. Faulkner, *American Economic History* (New York, 1935), chaps. v and vii.

A more detailed treatment of regulation of colonial trade is given in E. Channing, *History of the United States*, vol. iii (New York, 1924), and C. M. Andrews, *Colonial Period of American History*, vol. iv (New Haven, 1938).

The reaction of the colonial merchants to British regulation is considered in A. M. Schlesinger, *The Colonial Merchants and the American Revolution* (New York, 1918), chaps. iii and (especially) vii.

On Hancock:

A. E. Brown's *John Hancock, His Book* (Boston, 1898) is recommended as the best, though not a satisfactory, study of Hancock's life. It quotes generously from his business correspondence.

Edward Edelman's "Thomas Hancock, Colonial Merchant," *Journal of Economic and Business History,* vol. i (1928–29), pp. 77–104, is recommended for the earlier story of the firm.

10. Suggested Questions

1. What profit (if any) did Hancock receive on the cargo of oil shipped to London late in 1766 and sold in 1767? Answer in pounds sterling.
2. Describe the different kinds of trade that Hancock was carrying on. What was the bearing of the general situation on management?
3. What was Hancock's policy with regard to partnership?
4. Whence came Hancock's business policy? Was it as successful as his management?
5. Do you regard Hancock as a typical example of a sedentary merchant in America?
6. Should Hancock have entered the whale-oil trade?

V. JOHN JACOB ASTOR, 1763–1848

1. General Statement

John Jacob Astor was one of the last of the great sedentary merchants and one of the first of the great specialists. Beginning in a small way as a retailer of musical instruments he soon became one of America's greatest merchants, combining foreign trade, both European and oriental, and the fur trade. His business reached from the leading markets of the Old World and the Orient to the Indian villages and the camps of the lone trappers of the great American wilderness. A typical sedentary merchant, Astor at first combined many functions but he later felt strongly the impact of the revolution that came in business about 1825. From the earliest part of his career he had been investing in real estate in a small way, particularly in New York City. With the great internal development in the United States, growing out of the building of canals and railroads, Astor was one of the many who deserted the merchant's countinghouse for other business. Just as Patrick Tracy Jackson, a Boston merchant, had seen the possibilities of the new power-driven textile factory, Astor foresaw the effect of the great development of New York's hinterland upon real-estate values on Manhattan Island. The man who had been known as one of America's outstanding foreign merchants was, at the time of his death, the greatest landlord of New York.[1]

2. Chronological Summary of Astor's Life

1763	Born in Waldorf in the German Rhine country.
1777	Confirmed in Lutheran church; left school to help father.
1779–83	Worked in London.
1784	In April came to New York. Returned to London to sell furs he had bought.
1785	Married Sarah Todd in New York.
1786	Set up small shop for sale of musical instruments and carried on fur business.
1788	Fur trade became Astor's leading business interest. Bought furs in Montreal to ship to London and Rotterdam.
1789	Made his first two purchases of New York real estate.
1794	Bought land in New York's back country.
1795	Jay's Treaty opened direct trade with Canada and required the British to give up frontier posts on United States territory.

[1] The materials for this case, and often even the exact wording, have been taken almost entirely from Kenneth Wiggins Porter, *John Jacob Astor, Business Man* (Cambridge, 1931). Other sources used will be indicated.

1797	Astor's importing business included dry goods, cutlery, powder, and shot.
1799	Began to advertise sale of oriental goods.
1800	Said to be worth $250,000. Owned share in vessel sent to China. Began to invest in New York City real estate.
1807–08	Foreign trade checked by international difficulties and Embargo.
1808	American Fur Co. organized by Astor with capital of $1,000,000.
1808–09	Astor's *Beaver* sent to China despite Embargo, returning with cargo of teas, silks, and nankeens.
1810	Pacific Fur Co., with capital of $400,000, organized to establish Astoria on the Northwest Coast.
1811	Post established at Astoria. The South West Co. organized by Astor.
1812–14	Astor's business badly deranged by the war.
1813	Bought $2,000,000 of a United States loan.
1813	Astoria and Pacific Fur Co. gave way to British.
1816	Act passed giving Americans monopoly of fur trade in United States. Astor gained foothold in St. Louis and extended his interests in the Pacific.
1819–48	Astor left work of management chiefly to son, who had become his partner in 1815.
1822	United States factories for trade with the Indians closed. Establishment of Western and Northern departments of American Fur Co.
1825	Astor discontinued using his own ships in the China trade, except for a brief period in 1827.
1828	Astor's Pacific trade brought to a close. Had monopoly of fur trade in United States.
1834	Withdrew from American Fur Co.
1834–48	Interested exclusively in investments and in lending money on real-estate security.
1848	Died, leaving a fortune of about $20,000,000.

3. Notes on John Jacob Astor, the Man

From a portrait of John Jacob Astor painted in his fifties Dr. Kenneth W. Porter has drawn the following impressions of the man. Astor was of medium height and somewhat heavy and unwieldy of body. He had a high and broad forehead, a prominent and strongly arched nose, a straight and thin-lipped mouth, and a jaw of iron. His eyes, deeply set, had a characteristically shrewd and keen expression. His countenance reveals a nature that was good-humored but at the same time aggressive and inflexible. The portrait gives the general impression that Astor was a man of intense mental activity and strong self-confidence.

In his relations with those who were close to him, Astor showed both kindness and indulgence—there was much of the patriarch in him. With his family he was affectionate and generous; and he was comparatively liberal with those of his agents with whom he had close personal contact—some of his men stayed with him for twenty or more years. But Astor's imagination was too narrowly limited by the practices of his own class and generation, and by the lack of contact with the distant parts of his empire, to feel the same responsibility for the hundreds and thousands of men who worked for him, or to have any feeling for the Indians or *engagés* in the fur country or the commoners cutting the Hawaiian sandalwood. Indeed, his attitude toward the men with whom he did not come in personal contact was inevitably similar to that which he had toward bales of fur.

Astor's life was business, and he had a passion for profits and an abhorrence of waste or loss. Vincent Nolte tells of an incident which occurred when Astor was under the observation of a Parisian doctor. One day, when Astor and the doctor were out for a ride, Astor acted as if he were "suffering from some secret pain or trouble." When the doctor urged him to tell what was wrong, Astor replied: "Look ye! Baron! How frightful this is! I have here in the hands of my banker, at Paris, about 2,000,000 francs, and cannot manage, without great effort, to get more than 2½ per cent. per annum on it. Now, this very day I have received a letter from my son in New York, informing me that there the best acceptances are at from 1½ to 2 per cent. per month. Is it not enough to enrage a man?" As in the case of so many men who have devoted their lives to the accumulation of vast wealth, apparently merely for the sake of amassing it, neither Astor nor society derived the benefits which could so easily have been secured.

It is significant that, while Astor wanted to make good profits, he did not speculate. A contemporary says that "he had a strong aversion to illegitimate speculation, and particularly to gambling in stocks. . . . It was his pride and boast that he gained his own fortune by legitimate commerce, and by the legitimate investment of his profits."

Many contemporary stories point to Astor's seeming niggardliness. It was characteristic of him to pretend that times were hard and profits low. On one occasion he subscribed to Audubon's *Birds of America,* the price of which was $1,000. But—so the story runs—when Audubon asked him to pay, he would not because "money is very scarce; I have nothing in bank; I have invested all my funds." On the author's sixth visit to Astor, he found the father and son together. Again pleading the scarcity of funds, Astor turned to his son, who had not followed the conversation, and asked him if they had any money in the bank. On the son's enumeration of $220,000 in one bank, $120,000 in another, and so on, Astor interrupted him with orders to write a check for $1,000.

Astor was a man of regularity and decision and one who kept his contracts. It is said that, in spite of the multiplicity of his interests and the personal attention he gave to details, he "did not bestow at his countinghouse more than half the time most merchants feel compelled to give their concerns." He went to his office early in the morning, transacted the necessary business, and left at two in the afternoon. A contemporary's characterization is significant in this connection: "He possessed marked executive ability. He was quick in his perceptions. He came rapidly to his conclusions. He made a trade or rejected it at once. . . . He made distinct contracts. These he adhered to with inflexible purpose." "In trade," it was said, he was "an autocrat in bearing," yet withal "he was represented as being a pleasant man to do business with, seldom being ruffled in temper or intemperate in speech."

Astor's efficiency in conducting business gave him time for other interests. After business was over in the early afternoon he had dinner. This, it is said, was followed by exactly three games of checkers and a glass of beer. Then came a ride around Manhattan on his horse, Astor keeping a lookout for promising pieces of land for sale. In the evening he frequently went to the theater or had musicales at home.

This solid man of business had many cultural interests. Astor could not write the English language without marvelous errors in grammar and spelling, but he enjoyed reading literature and history, and he gave aid to several men following a literary career and became a close friend of a few. Fitz-Greene Halleck, the poet, was Astor's confidential secretary from 1832 until Astor's death, and Washington

Irving, who wrote *Astoria* about Astor's western enterprise, became a close friend of the merchant. It was no doubt Astor's interest in literature and history and his friendship with writers which led him to endow the Astor Library in New York City.

Astor also had many friends among important public men. He seems always to have been on good terms with the dominant party. Those of his associates who were active in political life were predominantly Federalists before 1800, Jeffersonian Republicans until about 1824, and Jacksonian Democrats until about the time of his retirement. "He aroused no enmity among any group by conspicuous advocacy of the claims of some other, and so had little difficulty in securing favorable consideration from whatever party was in power."

No definite connection can be traced between Astor's religion and his business life. "In most respects he seemed, and doubtless was," says Dr. Porter, "a perfectly orthodox if somewhat inactive churchman." His philosophy was definitely secular—"Make the best of things" was his motto in adversity. Astor supported the church and assisted missionaries where he traded. This was good business, but he was no hypocrite and made no claims of Christianizing the savage. In his later years he took a considerable interest in the question of immortality, which he discussed at length with one of his secretaries. "Cogswell did not seem altogether sure of Astor's final decision upon the principal subject of their nocturnal discussions, but we can be confident that if he ever formed an opinion it was upon arguments tested and found valid by his own reason."

The great business man becomes in a real sense a public figure, and his work is subjected to the test of public judgment. Obituary comments on John Jacob Astor varied; no one doubted his greatness as a business man, but much doubt was expressed about the methods by which he had acquired his wealth.

4. Some Explanations of Astor's Success

Though widely accepted, the myths about the origin of Astor's fortune do not bear careful examination. The story about his finding Captain Kidd's treasure is an obvious fabrication; the author, himself, stated that he wove the yarn for the entertainment of some vacationists in Maine. Another tale, that of Astor's securing from the governor of the East India Co. a permit to trade in its monopoly ports, which enabled the merchant to send a ship to Canton at a huge profit, is also without foundation. The fact that Astor is said to have told it himself does not prove the truth of the tale but perhaps merely bears witness to his ingenuity in attempting to satisfy curiosity.

More challenging are the numberless statements which point out directly, or at least imply, that Astor's wealth was built through questionable business methods. A few of these are herewith given by way of illustration.

Gustavus Myers in his *History of the Great American Fortunes* attacks both the methods of Astor and the system under which he was working: [2]

"It is of the greatest importance to ascertain Astor's methods in his fur trade, for it was fundamentally from this trade that he reaped the enormous sums that enabled him to become a large landowner.

. . . .

"By means of Government favoritism and the unconcealed exercise of both fraud and force, he obtained a complete monopoly [of the fur trade in the region east of the Rocky Mountains and south of the Great Lakes], as complete and arbitrary as ever feudal baron held over seignorial estates. Nominally, the

[2] Gustavus Myers, *History of the Great American Fortunes* (Chicago, 1907), vol. i, pp. 111, 113–114, 115, 182. (This material is also found in the 1936 edition.)

United States Government ruled this great sweep of territory and made the laws and professed to execute them. In reality, Astor's company was a law unto itself. That it employed both force and fraud and entirely ignored all laws enacted by Congress, is as clear as daylight from the Government reports of that period.

. . . .

"If there was any one serious crime at that time it was the supplying of the Indians with whisky. The Government fully recognized the baneful effects of debauching the Indians, and enacted strict laws with harsh penalties. Astor's company brazenly violated this law, as well as all other laws conflicting with its profit interests. It smuggled in prodigious quantities of rum. The trader's ancient trick of getting the Indians drunk and then swindling them of their furs and land was carried on by Astor on an unprecedented scale. To say that Astor knew nothing of what his agents were doing is a palliation not worthy of consideration; he was a man who knew and attended to even the pettiest details of his varied business. Moreover, the liquor was despatched by his orders direct by ship to New Orleans and from thence up the Mississippi to St. Louis and to other frontier points. The horrible effects of this traffic and the consequent spoliation were set forth by a number of Government officers.

. . . .

"It was at this identical time, in the panic of 1837, that Astor was phenominally active in profiting from despair. 'He added immensely to his riches,' wrote a contemporaneous narrator, 'by purchases of State stocks, bonds and mortgages in the financial crisis of 1836–37. He was a willing purchaser of mortgages from needy holders at less than their face; and when they became due, he foreclosed on them, and purchased the mortgaged property at the ruinous prices which ranged at that time.' "

On the death of Astor, James Gordon Bennett, the Hearst of his time, expressed himself thus in the issue of his *New York Herald* of April 5, 1848:

"We give in our columns, an authentic copy of one of the greatest curiosities of the age —the will of John Jacob Astor, disposing of property amounting to about twenty million dollars, among his various descendants of the first, second, third and fourth degrees. . . . If we had been an associate of John Jacob Astor . . . the first idea we should have put into his head, would have been that *one-half of his immense property—ten millions, at least—belonged to the people of the city of New York*. During the last fifty years of the life of John Jacob Astor, his property has been augmented and increased in value by the aggregate intelligence, industry, enterprise and commerce of New York, fully to the amount of one-half of its value. The farms and lots of ground which he bought forty, twenty, ten and five years ago, have all increased in value entirely by the industry of the citizens of New York. Of course, it is as plain as that two and two make four, that the half of his immense estate, in its actual value, has accrued to him by the industry of the community."

Sundry other charges have been made against Astor's business character and methods. He is said to have been mean in his dealings with ship captains and stingy in paying for furs. He is said to have corrupted State and territorial governments to further his trade interests. His land policies have been attacked severely; he is alleged to have tried to rob Putnam County farmers by purchasing the claims to their lands, to have encouraged dissolute heirs to borrow on their estates only to be foreclosed in due time, to have bought land to hold for unearned increment without improving, and to have introduced the European practice of leases in place of sale, thereby running counter to the land policy of the patriots of the American Revolution.

Fortunately for our understanding of John Jacob Astor's business career, the myths, legends, and accusations which have grown up around him have been tested. The biography of Astor by K. W. Porter is the result of a careful study of the sources dealing with the merchant and landlord, and it lays bare, in great detail and with honesty and detachment, his business life.

5. The Business Career of John Jacob Astor

A. Gaining a foothold in American business.

In 1784 John Jacob Astor, aged 20, landed in Baltimore with seven flutes and about five guineas in his possession. Born in the German Rhine country, the youngest son of a none-too-prosperous butcher, John Jacob, after attending school until 14 and then helping his father for a time, had at the age of 16 set out for London, where an older brother was a maker of musical instruments. Young Astor had remained in London four years, during which time he had probably worked for his brother and a musical instrument firm, had learned English, and had saved money. On the long passage across the ocean—so it is told—he had learned much about the American fur trade from some passengers who were in that business.

Young Astor arrived in New York in April, 1784. He had another brother there, in the horse-and-cart stage of the butcher's business. Putting his flutes out to be sold on commission, the young immigrant worked at a number of occupations. He began by peddling bakery products for a baker. But it was not long before he found employment with a furrier. While thus employed he also traded for himself. Before the year was over he was back in London with furs which he had bought in New York. He sold the furs, invested the proceeds in merchandise, and returned to New York.

Shortly after his return occurred an event which was of great significance to Astor's business career. In 1785 he married Sarah Todd, the daughter of a sea captain. She had excellent connections in New York, a dowry of $300, and a great talent for business.

In 1786 Astor opened a shop of his own in a room in his mother-in-law's house. Tradition says he first sold German toys, but newspaper advertisements reveal that he had for sale different musical instruments and other articles in the music line. It is probable that Sarah Astor tended the shop while John Jacob attended to his fur business, but the wife also helped with the furs. One contemporary, Scoville, remarks that Mrs. Astor knew more about the value of furs than her husband, and that, "when they became very affluent, she used to make him pay her $500 an hour for using her judgment and knowledge of furs to promote his commercial plans."

By 1788 the fur business had attained primacy over the trade in musical instruments. Astor was then making regular fur-buying excursions into the back country of New York. Going out with Indian goods, at first with a pack on his back and later on a horse, he returned with furs. Through forest and swamp he sought out the Indians and the white trappers.

Early in the 1790's he seems to have ceased his personal purchase of furs in the backwoods. By then he had agents and correspondents, such as Peter Smith of Utica, who collected peltries for him on commission. A few years later he was sending young men out to represent him. A letter to Peter Smith, introducing a young Frenchman whom Astor was sending upstate to buy furs, shows something of how he tried out a young agent:

"Acting Causiously I Gave him but 500$ & a Cridet of 500 or 1000 more an Albany now it apears he is gone your way & without making use of the Cridet at Albany So that he has but abaut 500$ with him with which you know he Can not purshas much furr. I would there for be glad if in Case he shauld Lay aut his Little money if you would eighter pay him for my account from five to ten hundred Dollars—or pass his Bill on me for that amount this hawever youil observe is to be done only in Case that you have no reason to belive that he maks any bade use of the money."

By 1788 Astor had begun his annual fur-buying trips to Montreal, the capital of the American fur trade, and he had established connections with a Montreal merchant who was to ship $3,000 worth of furs for him to London, to be reshipped to Rotterdam and New York (direct shipment was not then allowed from Montreal to New York). It is significant that only four years after his arrival in America, Astor had sufficient funds or credit to purchase furs in Montreal for $3,000. In 1789, "describing himself for the first time under the resounding title of 'John Jacob Astor of New York . . . Merchant,'" Astor was again in Montreal. This time he reached further westward by an agreement with a Detroit merchant to furnish him 15,000 "Good and Merchantable Musquash Skins." Astor continued his trips to Montreal, leaving New York in the summer, staying in the fur city about two months buying and shipping furs, and returning to New York City in October or November.

The center of Astor's operations was New York. There he prepared the furs for shipping and managed their sale. He also had a considerable importing business. To his import of pianos and music supplies were soon added Indian goods to be used in the purchase of furs; this was followed by goods for supplying Astor's merchant-correspondents in the backwoods. By 1800, however, his chief European imports came to be arms, ammunition, and wool, purchased principally through London merchants.

In those early years Astor was already investing in real estate. In 1789 he purchased from his brother two lots and four half-lots on the Bowery Road on Manhattan Island. The next year he bought two more lots. In 1790 he bought a store at 40 Little Dock Street which became the headquarters of his business. The purchase of two more lots rounded out his early purchases in New York.

John Jacob Astor fell a victim to the common ailment of the time, the frontier real-estate fever. He tried to buy a large tract of land in Canada but failed; he succeeded, however, in upstate New York. There he, another New York merchant, and Peter Smith, of Utica, bought 37,200 acres on joint account in 1794.. This proved not to be a very profitable venture. For several years there were disputes over the title to the lands, and not till the late 1820's did Astor dispose of his share.

The management of these lands remained in the hands of Peter Smith for about 30 years. For his work Smith received no remuneration from his partners in the venture. On one occasion Astor collected Smith's share of a small attorney's fee of 20 years' standing with compound interest; but, when the latter asked for some compensation for his years of work, Astor wrote in reply, "I believe the agreement was that you ware not to Charge any."

Occasional glimpses are seen of Astor's finances in those early years. Though his business was steadily growing, he was not without his difficulties. In 1792, commenting on the number of bankruptcies, he wrote that they had caused him great loss and had "affaceted my property but not So as to affacet my business." Probably referring to the Duer Panic of 1792, Scoville remarks that "those who suppose Mr. Astor had an easy time in money matters, are greatly mistaken. He has often paid old Prime, in Wall Street, very large interest and a large commission to get long paper discounted."

In the fall of 1795, on returning from Europe, Astor found his "business here very mush Derangd So that I Shall am afraid fall short of Cash Even to Comply with my Engagements." Early in September he was still in the same condition, according to a letter to Peter Smith: "I

Can not Describe to you on Black & white how much I am in want of Cash theare for If you Can Sent me any it will oblige me mush be the Sum ever So Smale."

Though Astor was at times hard pressed, he was making a success of his business. By 1800 he is said to have been worth "something like $250,000." In that year he established a residence apart from his business, and there is evidence to suggest that he was not without some standing socially.

B. Expansion of Astor's business, 1800–15.

John Jacob Astor's entrance into the China trade followed almost inevitably from his progress as a fur trader and general merchant. No stock-in-trade of a general merchant was then complete without a line of oriental goods. In 1799 and 1800, Astor began to advertise such eastern goods as India silks, "very excellent Hyson and Souchong Tea," nankeens, and black India lute-strings. It was logical to add Canton to London and Continental ports as fur markets and sources of goods to be brought home and to send vessels to carry them.

In 1800 Astor became the principal owner of one vessel, and by 1805 he began to have ships built especially for the China trade. This trade was checked in 1807 and 1808 by the American Embargo on foreign trade, but in 1809 Astor had five ships engaged in the trade with the Orient.

During his first decade of participation in the China trade, Astor's commercial policy was simple, straightforward, and unoriginal. His ships would, if possible, leave for Canton in May and return in a year. "The China goods would be advertised in the New York press, some sold over the counter of his store, a part disposed of by some well-known auction firm, another part, perhaps, shipped to some other eastern city for sale, to Canada, or even to Europe."

The following is an interesting account of the cargo of the *Severn,* which left New York for Canton in May, 1804:

". . . First, there were 51 'Keges' of 'Specia,' valued at $140,000; next in value were 7 casks of furs, containing 2,570 rabbit skins, 1,322 otter skins, 166 beaver skins, and some seal and fox skins, invoiced at $8,000; 53 casks of ginseng containing 117½ piculs were valued at $6,000, but of these only 38 bore Astor's unmistakable mark (HA). Eighteen bales of cotton, estimated at $1,000, formed another feature of the cargo. To the above must be added some additional kegs and boxes of specie to the value of $11,000, none of which, however, bore Astor's personal mark. The entire value of the outward cargo, then, was $166,100, of which something over $153,000 is known to have been on Astor's account.

"We have a pretty good idea, also, of the source of these goods. The furs were doubtless the choicest of those purchased by Astor at Montreal the previous autumn or secured by his agents in the backcountry of New York. The ginseng, too, probably came from New York State, collected by the same agents who were there engaged in purchasing peltries. In July, 1799, Astor had informed Peter Smith that 'Gensang will Sell 3/6 to 4/ prlb if not too large aquantey is Caured.' The cotton, of course, had come up from Charleston, Baltimore, or other southern ports on some of the coasting vessels which occasionally brought goods consigned to Astor. It was not always easy to acquire enough specie for a China voyage. Astor seems to have had an arrangement with Gerrit W. Van Schaick, cashier of the Bank of Albany, by which Astor took up the notes of that bank which appeared in New York City and transmitted them to Albany, receiving payment in dollars. . . ."

The Embargo on American trade of 1807–08, which was intended to protect American interests from becoming involved in the Napoleonic struggles in Europe, led to an incident which has meaning with respect to Astor's business career. Instead of dismissing his captains, laying up his ships with tar barrels over the mastheads, and philosophically settling down to wait for the inevitable repeal of the repressive acts, or at the most besieging Congress and the President with threats, pleas, and petitions directed against the Embargo and its authors and supporters, Astor, by a stroke of ingenious and not too admirable trickery, actually caused the president to suspend the Embargo in his favor. The thing seemed perfectly innocent to President Jefferson. A Chinese mandarin, who had been to America on business and had suddenly been called home, "where the affairs of his family and particularly the funeral obsequies of his grandfather, require his solemn attention," applied to President Jefferson for permission to "depart for his own country with his property in a vessel to be engaged by himself." The President granted the mandarin's request both as an act of courtesy and a "means of making our nation known advantageously at the source of power in China." Not so did certain merchants of Philadelphia regard the matter, but their warning to the government officials was disregarded. John Jacob Astor's *Beaver* was the ship that undertook the mission, and there can be no doubt that the mandarin was a fabrication to override the Embargo.

The *Beaver's* outbound cargo consisted of only 3,000 otter skins and 5 piculs of cochineal. But, though she had been granted permission to bring back merely the proceeds of goods shipped by citizens of the United States before the Embargo went into effect, the *Beaver* returned, it was alleged, with "two hundred thousand dollars more than she left with," a cargo which was unusually large and was made up of a variety of China goods. Whether the stipulation about the return cargo was adhered to is not known, but the result was that Astor was able to import China goods when other merchants could not do so.

Astor's China trade continued to grow but eventually ran into a serious snag, the War of 1812. While before the war he had sent at least one ship a year to the Orient, during the years 1812–14 not a single voyage was both commenced and completed. During the first year of the war he had the good fortune to receive two cargoes of tea from China despite the British cruisers. His principal connection with the China trade during the war was the sale of the goods brought by those ships.

While he was pushing the China trade, Astor also was forming great plans for the fur trade and was making progress toward realizing his plans. We shall first consider the situation as it was from 1808 to 1815.

At the beginning of the period, two Canadian fur companies—the North West and the Michilimackinac—practically monopolized the fur trade. They secured most of their fur from the territory of the United States, by agreement limiting their operations to certain portions of the country. As a consequence of their strength Astor and other American fur traders were practically forced to buy their peltries in Montreal, often at a higher price than the furs would bring in London.

In view of the strength of the Canadians, nothing but a strong move on the part of other traders would succeed. Astor first organized the American Fur Co., a corporation with a capital of $1,000,000 chartered by New York State. The preamble to the charter was as follows: [3]

"Whereas John Jacob Astor has presented his petition to the legislature, representing, among other things, that he is desirous of forming a trading company, for the purpose of carrying on an extensive trade with the native Indian inhabitants of America; but that an undertaking of such magnitude would require a greater capital than any individual or unincorporated association could well furnish, and who would be less able to support a fair competition with foreigners who are at

[3] *Private Laws of the State of New York, passed at the Thirty-First Session of the Legislature* (Albany, 1808), pp. 160–161, as quoted in Porter, *op. cit.*

present almost in the exclusive possession of the fur trade; and has prayed that he and such other persons as may be associated with him, may be incorporated, the better to enable them to carry into effect this design: *And whereas,* such an establishment may be of great public utility, by serving to conciliate and secure the good will and affections of the Indian tribes toward the government and people of the United States, and may conduce to the peace and safety of our citizens inhabiting the territories bordering on the native Indian tribes."

This preamble notwithstanding, the American Fur Co. was in reality John Jacob Astor. Having secured for the project the blessings of President Jefferson, to whom he had explained the beneficial effects which it would have for the United States, Astor was ready to go ahead.

The great period of the American Fur Co. came after the War of 1812. Before that time Astor had made two important moves through what might be considered subsidiaries of the American Fur Co. In his campaign for securing a monopoly of the American fur trade, Astor struck his first blow on the Northwest Coast. To begin with, he formed an alliance with the Russian American Co. on the upper Pacific Coast, promising to supply them with goods. The ship *Enterprise,* Captain Ebbets master, was sent with a cargo for the Russians. A letter of instructions to the captain shows something of Astor's attention to detail:

"New york 13 Nav^{r}. 1809.

"Dear Sir

"I give you note of furrs as I am in hopes you will find Some Land furrs which will be worth brining here at all events beso good & bring with you from every port you Stop at Some few Skins of easch kind & keep a memrandum of where thy cam from also particular account of where easch kind are the most plenty Henry Merschel Whom you have on Board has Some knowlage of the quality as also how to preserve tham all kind of Skins Should be put in Cask Say rum punchions to be [s]crewd[?] but not to hard except Deer & Muss Skins which are to Large for Casks & Should beput in Bales—at foot you have price &c all Skins are the better for being keept from the air in a cole place & where it is not Damp as other wise thy grow Mauldey Do not omit to writ to me as often as you can if you find many Land furrs of good quality it may well be worth while to trade for tham & bring tham here Say Minck & Martin Skins as also fisher & Silver fox and Musrat Skins if any all these take Little Room and will Sell here Say Martin Skins from 4 to 8/—Minck from 2/ to 4/ Fischer from 4 to 8/—Mush Depends on the coller of the Martin and Mink the Darker the better & providd thy are taking in Season wild Catts are worth from 4 to 8/—gray fox 2 to 4/—wolf from 4 to 8/—Beare Skins black are worth from 8 to 40/—thy aught to be thick and Long fine haire—Deer Skins in red haire of the wight of 2 lb to 2 1/2 lbs are worth 6 to 7/ pr Skin those in gray Blue haire wighing 3 lbs are worth 6/—those of long gray haire & thin Lether are not worth anything Deer Skins Should have thick Lether & thin haire—furrs the Skins Should be thin & the furr thick—Racown Skins if well furrd & Large are worth 4/—Muss Skins if thick 16/—Musrat Skins 3/ if very good you may find Still Same ather Skins & if So bring Some

"and ob[li]ge Dear Sir your Hbl Svt

"J. J. Astor"

After he had completed his trading with the Russians and the purchase of furs on the Coast, Ebbets, as instructed, headed for Canton. There he sold his cargo of furs to Kingqua at a very good price (one batch which cost $27,000 was sold at $47,000). He purchased China goods for $40,000, which he shipped to New York via the *Beaver*. Ebbets loaded his own boat with goods, including beads, for the Indian trade and the Russian settlement. Again loading with furs on the Coast, Ebbets returned to Canton. From there the *Enterprise* returned to New York. In her absence of two and one-half years, she had laid the foundations of Astor's Pacific Coast trade.

In the meantime Astor's Pacific Fur

Co. had come into being. For his associates in the undertaking Astor had sought out experienced western fur men. There were Wilson Price Hunt, of St. Louis, and Ramsay Crooks, Robert McClelan, and Joseph Miller, who had all been engaged in the fur trade on the Missouri; the first-named had also been connected with one of the Canadian companies. From Canada came David and Robert Stuart, and the veteran North Westers, Alexander McKay, Donald McKenzie, and Duncan McDougall.

An agreement was made between these associates for the establishment of the Pacific Fur Co., a partnership having as its object the establishment of a trading post on the Columbia River. Astor was to manage the business and furnish the necessary funds, not in excess of $400,000; and he was to bear all the loss for 5 years, though any profit should be apportioned according to the shares. Astor took 50 of the 100 shares. Hunt was to reside on the Coast as agent.

Astoria proved an unfortunate undertaking. The *Tonquin,* sent out to establish the post, was badly captained and, after unloading some of the partners and goods at the Columbia, was destroyed by the Indians. The War of 1812 interfered greatly with the operations of the post. But it was the opposition of the Canadian North West Co. which finally broke the enterprise. In 1814 the partners of the Pacific Fur Co. who were on the Coast finally sold out the property of the company to the North West Co. Thus, for all practical purposes, closed the career of both the Pacific Fur Co. and Astoria, as well as Astor's hopes of founding a great fur empire and possibly a new nation on the Pacific Coast.

Astor's second move in strengthening himself in the American fur trade looked toward the extension of his activities in the interior. He had offered to buy out the Michilimackinac Co., and in 1810 representatives of the company offered him shares in it. This offer Astor would not then accept, and as a result the two Montreal firms organized a new company to carry on trade for a year. This made Astor all the more aggressive, and the result was that the Montrealers joined Astor in 1811 in forming the South West Fur Co.

This company was to last for five years, unless earlier dissolved by mutual consent. The trade was to be conducted for the joint account of Astor and the Montreal firms, each bearing half the expense and sharing the profit and loss equally. It was also agreed with the North West Co. that after 1811 it should give up every separate interest in the Indian trade in the United States east of the Missouri and the Rockies. The South West Co. agreed, at the same time, to stay out of Canada except in a certain area in the region of Lake Huron.

Astor took advantage of the War of 1812 to establish closer connections with the Missouri region. Not a great deal was accomplished in St. Louis, however, probably because the merchants in that city were strong enough to keep out the intruders.

All Astor's fur interests were vitally struck by the War of 1812. During the war his activities in the border region were concerned with the salvaging of his property, particularly in saving the furs at Mackinac from seizure by the British. His actual fur trading was confined principally to the regions within the limits of the United States in which he had for some time been established. Even there he met many difficulties, "including lack of transportation facilities, great scarcity of some kinds of furs, an oversupply of others, and a general lack of funds for purchasing those which were available."

Astor's fur trade suffered in two other respects during the war. His importation of goods from Europe to be used in the Indian trade and the shipment of furs to European markets were almost stopped by the war. The result was scarcity on the one hand and a glutted fur market on the other. Between March, 1813, and late 1814 no ships arrived at New York with goods for Astor. To relieve this condition, Astor tried every device for getting his vessels to Europe. His ingenuity may be illustrated by one case. On the pretext that the *Hannibal* was to carry back to France the anti-Napoleonic general, Moreau, permission was gained from the British for the ship to pass unmolested. A cargo was carried for Astor worth $60,000 and goods for others which brought more than $27,000 in freight. Astor's object in dispatching the vessel was probably that it would be advantageous to have a ship in Europe in the event of peace. That Astor was not always so fortunate as in the case of the *Hannibal* is proved by the capture and condemnation of another of his ships, the *Caroline*.

Any intention Astor might have had of sending additional ships would probably have been dissolved by the very effective British blockade of 1813 and 1814 and the Embargo laid by Congress from December, 1813, to April, 1814. It was not surprising, then, that Astor should write Peter Smith in February, 1814, that he was to "withdraw from almost every kind of business & I mean to remain so."

While the war brought difficulties to Astor, it also opened up new business. With idle funds on hand he was in a position to take advantage of other opportunities. He bought sterling bills on London and Amsterdam guilders to hold for a rise, but his biggest operations were in government loans.

When the government loan of 1813 failed to sell through popular subscription, Astor, Girard, of Philadelphia, and Parish, of Hamburg, took the remainder, of which Astor subscribed for $2,056,000 at 88 with a commission of one-quarter of one per cent. Since the expected peace and rise in price of the bonds failed to come soon, Astor began to dispose of his portion through his own countinghouse and agents in Boston, Philadelphia, and Baltimore. The bonds held up well for several months but then fell, reaching 75 during the year. Astor, therefore, ceased selling and began buying government bonds of both 1813 and 1814. When the bonds were low, he ordered a Boston broker to borrow funds at 2 per cent a month to invest in governments. That Astor profited by this operation is seen from the fact that, as he wrote, "My losses by Sea are made up in the peace by the rise on my Stocks of which I have something more than 800m$."

Astor came out of the war in a very good condition, comparatively speaking. His losses had been large, but gains from his government securities were to be considerable. Dr. Porter comments thus on his war-time policy: "He had avoided greater loss by keeping himself 'practically withdrawn from business,' 'doing nothing . . . ever since the unhappy war,' avoiding commercial ventures involving any considerable element of risk, and abstaining from speculation as much as was possible under the abnormal conditions then prevalent. In May, 1814, he wrote, 'it will be well for men who wish to live in comfort to be out of debt, I am more so than I have been for many years, of notes I have scarse any out, I owe some on acc[t]. of Stock [United States bonds] & to the custom-house.' " Astor welcomed peace. He was not one to choose the speculative risks of war times—he preferred peace as it "puts every thing on safe ground & I can always make money if I will be prudent."

C. The height of Astor's China and fur trade, 1815–34.

At the end of the war Astor, with his capital practically unimpaired and his vigor at its height, was ready for his last and crowning score of years in business. With a large capital, a fleet of nine vessels mostly purchased at the low prices prevailing during the war, a firm position in the American fur trade and in the New York–

Europe and New York–Canton trade, and with a beginning in the Pacific trade, Astor was in a position to do a large business when peace and order were again established.

The prospects of a great business made Astor look about for a partner. He chose Albert Gallatin, a Swiss-American distinguished for his political service to his adopted country. On offering Gallatin a partnership Astor explained that he had a capital of about $800,000 engaged in trade from which he expected net profits of from $50,000 to $100,000 a year. Gallatin refused the offer. His 18-year-old son could not visualize his father as a partner of Astor, who "ate his ice-cream and peas with a knife!" Perhaps Gallatin was too much aware of Astor's commercial tricks—he had been secretary of the Treasury at the time of the *Beaver* affair. Probably Gallatin was not interested in entering business. At any rate, the fact that he was offered the position of minister to France gave him an excellent pretext for refusing Astor's offer.

Astor thereupon decided to make his son, William B., his assistant and partner. Young Astor was then still in Europe as a student, having as a tutor the famous Baron von Bunsen and as a friend, Schopenhauer. He was in Paris studying French literature when he received a peremptory order from his father to return home. A few days later he was at Liverpool ready to sail. The scholar soon became the business man.

Two general policies dominated Astor's business in the decade after the war: the building-up of a very complicated foreign trade and a drive toward dominance in the fur trade.

Astor greatly extended his foreign trade after the war. Canton and New York were no longer the only ports concerned, for various European ports as well as the Pacific Coast of America came to be closely associated with the Orient. Sometimes three fleets of vessels belonging to Astor would be operating simultaneously, one between New York and Europe, another between New York and China, and a third in the Pacific Ocean.

In this complicated trade, in which a ship might be gone several years on a trading voyage, it was necessary to have efficient, resourceful ship captains. "It was Astor's policy to take into consideration every situation which might conceivably arise and give minute instructions as to his captains' conduct in each contingency, but he also strove to secure shipmasters who would not only follow his instructions to the letter in all cases for which he had made provision, but could also, when need arose, take measures on their own initiative and carry these to a successful conclusion."

A significant product added to Astor's trade in the Pacific at this time was the sandalwood of the Hawaiian Islands, which was much in demand for incense-burning in Chinese joss houses. Sandalwood was a royal monopoly and was cut on shares for the king by the chiefs, the work being done by the commoners for little or no compensation. An ingenious captain and an unscrupulous chief could even get together on the trade to their mutual profit—indeed, Astor recommended this as more expeditious, though "clandestine." In exchange for the wood, the king and the chiefs bought large quantities of goods. Astor's large capital enabled him to sell superior goods at a low price, so that his captains had a distinct advantage over their rivals. Those low prices were conditioned on receiving payment in wood at once, and thus a minimum of time was expended by Astor's ships at the Islands. The result was that the ships would arrive in Canton early in the season, secure the best prices in the market, and get back to New York before the market was flooded.

The complicated nature of the foreign trade of Astor, and the place of the Pacific in that trade, can best be indicated by an excerpt from Dr. Porter's study:

"Let us imagine, then, that in some particular year after the end of the War of 1812 Astor finds himself in possession of a considerable quantity of assorted furs. Some of these are sold in the fur market of New York; a few are shipped to other ports in the United States. Those in which we are particularly interested are, however, sent as freight to various ports in England and on the Continent, of which London, Hamburg, and Le Havre are typical examples.

"In return for these furs, from London come drygoods and hardware, such as blankets, cutlery, and muskets. From Hamburg, perhaps, are received iron, lead, and gin. Le Havre gives drygoods of a somewhat finer quality than those furnished by London. At New York some of these goods are, perhaps, offered in the open market. Some of the blankets, cutlery, muskets, lead, iron, gin, and other suitable articles are sent into the interior to be sold to the Indians for furs. But those which we are especially concerned in following are loaded on a vessel, intended for the Pacific Ocean. This vessel, perhaps, touches first at one of the Hawaiian Islands, where a miscellaneous assortment of goods from her cargo is sold on short credit because of the low prices made possible by Astor's large capital. Rum is popular, as are the fine textiles from Le Havre. Leaving the natives to collect the sandalwood for which the goods are exchanged, the vessel sails next for Norfolk Sound to trade with the Russians for seal skins and the fur of the sea otter. At Norfolk Sound, also, rum is popular, but there is a demand for general merchandise of all kinds. Perhaps some muskets and ammunition will be sold to the natives, if this can be done without arousing the suspicions of the Russians. Then the vessel may drop down to the vicinity of the Columbia River and sell guns, powder, shot, knives, rum, and all sorts of metalwork to the natives. On the coast of California general merchandise again meets a ready market among the inhabitants, though before 1818 one must be on the lookout for the Spanish authorities. Having pretty well disposed of the cargo they took on board at New York, the captain and supercargo decide to return to the Islands. Here they take on the sandalwood which has been cut for them in their absence on the Coast, and with this and the furs from Norfolk Sound, Columbia River, and California—perhaps some silver and pearl-shell from the last-named place—they sail to Canton.

"Here sandalwood and furs are bartered for teas, silks, nankeens, chinaware, sugar, spices, etc.—a cargo sure to meet with a ready sale at New York. But there are markets nearer to Canton than any city of the United States. Back to the Hawaiian Islands they head. The wives of the chiefs are impressed by the beautiful Chinese silks. What matter that their storehouses are already piled with goods sufficient to last a generation? There is plenty of sandalwood on the mountains, plenty of commoners to cut and carry it to the seashore free of charge. Soon a part of the Canton cargo has been sold and the ship's sails are again set for the coast of the Americas. This time the cargo is not so suitable for the Indian trade, but the Russians at New Archangel and the Spaniards of California are ready to purchase teas, silks, and nankeens in exchange for seal skins, sea-otter furs, silver, and pearl-shell. Moreover, farther to the south are Ecuador, Peru, and Chile, which have recently cast off the Spanish yoke and thrown open their ports to the trade of the whole world. So ho for Guayaquil, for Callao, for Coquimbo, where the rest of the cargo taken on board at Canton may be sold for red copper and white specie! Then back to the Islands to stow away odorous sandalwood beside the bales of glossy skins of the seal and the otter, the copper ingots, and the kegs of specie.

"Once again at Canton, a China cargo is taken on board, but this time the vessel at last clears for her home port from which she sailed three or four years ago. At New York the China cargo is unloaded. Some of the goods are sold at auction, some over the counter of Astor's own shop, some are shipped as freight to other ports in the United States and to the West Indies. Some, perhaps in company with furs from the Great Lakes and the Missouri, are shipped to Hamburg and Le Havre. We, however, shall devote our attention to those which are loaded on brigs and schooners, sometimes belonging to John Jacob Astor or to the Astor firm. The vessels clear for the Mediterranean, and sail away through the Straits of Gibraltar and on to the eastern end of the great inland sea. Here at Smyrna part of the China cargo is exchanged for Turkey opium. The brig then turns back on her course to Gibraltar, where the remainder of her China cargo is exchanged for quicksilver, specie, and lead, and the vessel clears once more for her home port.

"At New York the vessels are unloaded. Some of the opium and quicksilver may be advertised for sale in the New York newspapers, but a large proportion of the products of this Mediterranean cruise—opium, quicksilver, lead, and specie—is loaded on board an Astor vessel. Beneath the hatches are also stowed away bales of the choicest furs from the interior of North America, red-fox skins, beaver, and land-otter furs, much inferior in value to the sea otters and seals of the North West Coast, but still of a type to meet with a ready sale in the Canton fur market. There are also a number of kegs of ginseng and perhaps a little cotton and cochineal. This time the vessel proceeds directly to Canton, sells her cargo for the usual teas, nankeens, silks, chinaware, and cassia, and returns at once to New York, having been gone for less than a year. There her cargo is dispensed in much the same way as the cargo of the ship which we followed on her return from the Pacific.

". . . Is it surprising, in view of the number of times that goods were turned over between the departure and the return to New York, and the unsophisticated character of at least two of the races from whom Astor obtained the most important types of the commodities utilized in this commerce—from the Indians furs and from the Hawaiians sandalwood—that Astor became a multimillionaire of commerce at a time when simple millionaires were a rarity? Of course we must not forget that all this process was not as simple as it may sound. This program itself required careful planning based on long and hazardous experience, wise selection of subordinates, and a large capital which had been amassed from literally nothing by means of hard labor and the same foresight and willingness to venture on a small scale which he was now exhibiting in a large field. Otherwise Astor would not have emerged from the ruck of China merchants."

After the war Astor's fur trade grew along the lines which he had planned at the time of the organization of the American Fur Co. in 1808. Though the Astoria enterprise had proved a failure at the hands of the Canadians, the Treaty of Ghent and an act of 1816 requiring the licensing of alien traders on the soil of the United States checked some of Astor's strongest rivals. The one dominating policy of the Company came to be to drive toward a monopoly position in the fur trade.

Astor had two policies with respect to his rivals in the fur trade. Individual traders and small, weak companies would be speedily and ruthlessly crushed by means of the force of his financial and political power. The more efficient of the vanquished might be employed by Astor or allowed to trade on shares. But if a company put up a stubborn fight, rather than waste time and money Astor usually bought out or admitted the concern to the American Fur Co. on fairly generous terms.

Political power was used in the many ways which the situation made possible. It was always the object of Astor and the American Fur Co. to stand well with the government. Astor's friendship with President Monroe was close, and Governor Cass of Michigan Territory did much to help keep out alien competition and otherwise to assist in the Northern Department. Significant is the fact that Senator Benton of Missouri was at one and the same time attorney for the American Fur Co. and leader of the opposition which destroyed the government factory system, a system of government houses carrying on trade with the Indians which stood in Astor's way. The agents of the Company reached down to the humblest officer of the government —any officer, said one notoriously lawless agent, could be bought for a quarter-keg of wine.

Astor has especially been accused of flaunting the law in debauching the Indians with whiskey. As a matter of fact, however, he did not at first follow the practice of many traders in this matter. Indeed, because of the favorable position which his financial power gave him the exclusion of liquor from the Indian country would have been to his advantage. But that very financial power made other traders depend on liquor as a competitive tool in the trade. Astor at first urged the strict enforcement of that law but, when that appeared impossible, he set out to beat his rivals at rum-selling.

It was Astor's policy to secure the most efficient men for his organization. His strongest assistants were Ramsay Crooks and Robert Stuart, both veterans in the fur country, who were given positions of great responsibility. Crooks was a general assistant to Astor with particular responsibilities in the Western Department, while Stuart headed the Northern Department. Both worked for a salary and a small percentage of profits as partners in the American Fur Co. For the subordinate positions the most successful traders were chosen, men who knew the business, who had influence with the Indians, and who were unscrupulous as traders. Some of the agents of the Company were notorious for their lawlessness and their ruthless methods. It must be remembered that such methods were then the rule in the fur trade.

Astor's strongest competitive tool was his financial strength. With his immense credit and capital and his standing in the large markets he could use all the possible means for underbidding his competitors. In the price war he had the greatest endurance.

By the force of its strength the American Fur Co. drove toward monopoly. Its first victory was in the region of the Great Lakes, which in 1822 became the Northern Department with Stuart as its head. In the same year the Western Department was organized with headquarters at St. Louis. In 1827 the last serious rival at St. Louis, Bernard Pratte & Co., became a partner in the Western Department, sharing equally with the American Fur Co. in the profits or losses on the Mississippi below Prairie du Chien (Wisconsin) and on the Missouri and its tributaries. Also in that same year the Columbia Fur Co., veteran and ruthless traders operating in both the Northern and Western departments, joined the American Fur Co. in establishing the Upper Missouri Outfit (to be managed by the leading partner in the Columbia Fur Co.) and abandoned the trade elsewhere.

When opposition to the American Fur Co. had been driven off in a given area, the territory was organized as a part of a department and responsibility was definitely allocated. As heads of departments, Stuart, Crooks, and to some extent the St. Louis partners were responsible to Astor. The head of each outfit, or subdivision, was responsible to those in charge of the department; the clerks at trading posts were under the trader who managed the outfit, and the *engagés,* who went out for furs, were the humble servitors of the trading-post clerk.

Astor profited from the fur trade in several ways. As a partner in the American Fur Co. he participated in its profits. As a partner in John Jacob Astor & Son he purchased goods to be used in the fur trade and sold furs for the American Fur Co. in the large markets, for which he received a commission and expenses. As an individual he furnished capital to the fur company, on which he received interest.

The returns to Astor were respectable. From 1817 to 1823, when the competitive war was on, his profits from the American Fur Co. were not great. But for over a decade beginning in 1823 the Company made good profits. It is estimated that from the operations of the fur company in the years 1817–34 Astor "cleared in dividends, interest, commissions, etc., not less than a million dollars, and probably nearer two million."

These profits were apparently made mostly in the Indian country. As the Astor concern acquired strength it virtually subjected the traders and made them purchase goods at whatever prices the former thought proper; credit terms were dictated and furs purchased on the same principle. The result of this policy was that the small independent traders, as well as the *engagés* and *voyageurs* hired by the Company, were a poverty-stricken lot. The traders tried to protect themselves by using "fraud and deceit towards the men they have in their employ."

It must not be gathered that Astor's success came only from bludgeoning his competitors. "It had been," says Porter, "through sheer perseverance, foresight, and a process of profiting by the mistakes of himself and of others that Astor had become the wielder of this tremendous capital which now made him king of the fur trade." Those very qualities served him well in that trade. No one excelled him as a buyer of goods or as a seller of furs. He dominated the fur market in New York and Canton; and even in London, where he met the competition of the powerful Hudson's Bay Co., his position was a commanding one.

One of the significant things about Astor's career is the fact that on several occasions, when a certain business seemed still to be profitable, he withdrew from it. In 1823 he began to withdraw from the China trade conducted in his own vessels, and by 1825 his withdrawal was practically complete. In the very next year there was a heavy fall in the tea market. Had he foreseen the results of overexpansion in the China trade? His withdrawal from the Pacific trade came only a short time later; in fact, the Pacific trade could hardly exist alone. The exhaustion of sandalwood, following a period of reckless cutting of the wood to meet the king's heavy debts, caused a collapse of that trade in Hawaii and struck a mortal blow to the business.

In 1834 Astor withdrew from the American Fur Co. He had for some time talked of retiring. Though he complained of the state of the fur business, the fact that he had passed threescore and ten and was in ill health probably accounts sufficiently for his retirement. His interest in the Western Department was sold to Pratte, Chouteau & Co., of St. Louis, and the Northern Department was taken over by a group headed by Ramsay Crooks. After a short period of liquidation of his interest, in 1835 ended his connection with the fur trade and with commerce, the business in which he had been engaged for fifty years.

D. Astor's investments, principally real estate.

In his fur trade and foreign trade Astor was a business man of the old order. In his interest in railroads, banks, insurance companies, hotels, theaters, and real estate in general he was making a transition to the new order, that of specialization. Those newer interests indicate the many-sided character of Astor's mind and of his business activities.

Astor seems to have followed closely the rise of new investment opportunities. From his purchase of a share in the Tontine Coffee House in 1792 in New York until late in his life he is known to have invested in a number of insurance companies. From 1816 to 1838 he was sufficiently interested in insurance at various times to hold directorships in one or more of four companies, but he was never heavily interested in this field as compared with some of his other types of investments.

Like most moneyed men of his time Astor was interested in banking. As early as 1791 he held shares in New York's first bank. He took an active part in the organization of the second Bank of the United States—"I wish to God we might get a national Bank & that quickly," he wrote in 1815. Astor subscribed heavily to the stock of the bank and became one of its directors representing the government as well as president of the New York branch. From 1819 to 1826 he took little part in American banking since he spent most of his time in Europe. At some time or other after 1829 he purchased stock of more than a dozen banking institutions. Usually he bought to hold for investment, though in the case of the Louisiana Bank he purchased on speculation. In 1832 he wrote, "I will have to receive in the course of this month from 20 to 30m dollars, which I would like to invest as a permanent investment in some safe stock—no objections to large dividends, but whether that be a little more or less is not so much a matter, as to have it perfectly safe." A large part of his investments were in banks in Albany, Utica, Oswego, and Rochester, but he also invested heavily in the banks of New York City. In his will were mentioned from 500 up to 1,604 shares in such corporations as the Bank of North America, the Manhattan Co., the Merchants Bank, and the Mechanics Bank, the first-named a Philadelphia bank and the other three of New York.

About the time that Astor retired from shipping he became interested in advancing inland transportation, at first canals but principally railroads. He participated in 1826 in the organization of the Mohawk & Hudson Railroad—the first railroad out of New York City; he took 500 out of 3,000 shares of this road and served as director. In the next 20 years his investments in transportation were few but not small—for instance, 70 shares of the Camden & Amboy, which paid at one time a dividend of 12 per cent and sold at a good premium; investment in the Philadelphia & Trenton, which for the years 1837 to 1848 brought semiannual dividends of about $250; and a loan to the Delaware-Raritan Canal of $150,000. For some time after the panic of 1837 he was not particularly interested in railroads, but by 1847 he was convinced that they had good promise and he started to invest heavily in them shortly before his death.

Another form of investment in which Astor became interested was the bonds of municipalities, States, and the federal government. His first investment of this kind was the purchase in 1792 of United States six per cents to the amount of $2,500. In 1813 he bought United States securities for $2,000,000. In the 'thirties he purchased United States securities in Europe below par to hold till they were to be redeemed shortly thereafter. The retirement of the United States debt during Jackson's administration ended Astor's investment in the early federal loans. The Mexican War loans again placed federal securities on the market, and Astor bought heavily, probably for trust funds for his heirs.

Astor similarly invested in State "stocks." His half-million dollars' worth of New York bonds received in payment of the Morris claims was the largest single acquisition. Some of these he soon sold at home and in London but a large portion he retained. Ohio was another State the investments of which he purchased heavily. In 1826 and 1828 he bought $1,100,000 of Ohio 6 per cent bonds. These rose considerably after he had acquired them. He also invested heavily in Pennsylvania loans and took smaller amounts of the loans of Louisiana, Massachusetts, Indiana, and other States.

The outstanding investment interest of Astor was real estate. In this he was following the general practice of the sedentary merchant, who, since there were few (if any) bonds available for investment, had characteristically turned to land for the investing of his surplus capital. During his whole business career Astor invested in lands. At first this was merely a side interest; he purchased land when he thought an especially good opportunity presented itself or he acquired it on mortgage. In the last years of his life, real estate came to be Astor's dominating interest, partly because his son and business heir, William B. Astor, was very successful in real estate.

Two interests closely related to Astor's activities in lands need be noted. In 1806, in company with another New Yorker, he bought the Park Street Theatre for

$50,000. Astor's long-standing interest in the theater from a cultural and recreational standpoint may have influenced him to purchase the "Old Park." The theater was rented, however, for $8,400 a year. It was rebuilt, after a fire, in 1822. In 1828 the theater rented for $16,000 while its estimated value was $150,000.

Hotels were Astor's other interest of this kind. In 1828 he bought the City Hotel, the largest in New York. This hotel was run part of the time by a manager and at other times on lease. More important was the erection in 1834 of the Astor Hotel (at first the Park). The hotel, containing 300 rooms, and the shops were not managed by Astor but were leased. The hotel, itself, which Astor valued at $750,000, was leased unfurnished for seven years at a rental beginning with $16,000 the first year and increasing to $20,500 by the fourth year. The shops were leased for 5 years at about twelve hundred dollars yearly. When the first lease expired, the hotel was again leased for an annual rental of $30,000.

Astor's real-estate interest was, however, chiefly in lands and not in improvements on them. Indeed, it is notable that he rarely improved the lands which he owned and was sometimes accused of holding lots that were an eye-sore to their neighbors.

The most notorious real-estate transaction of Astor was that in Putnam County, New York. Though relatively insignificant in size it is important as revealing something of his business methods.

In 1809 Astor purchased for about $100,000 the claim of certain Morris heirs to 50,000 acres of land confiscated by New York State from Revolutionary loyalists. This land had been sold to various individuals, who considered it theirs. The heirs seem to have given up all hope of recovering the land when Astor learned—someone has hazarded the guess that Aaron Burr made the discovery—that Roger and Mary Morris, from whom it had been taken, had had only a life interest in the estate. In that case their children would be legally entitled to the land on the death of their parents; it was any claim they might have which Astor purchased.

There was no certainty as to the validity of the claim purchased by Astor, and in any event it could not be tested until Mary Morris had died. Unfortunately for Astor she lived on until 1825. In the meantime, however, Astor had sold shares in the claim. For instance, one undivided fourth of the claim had been sold for $50,000 (half of what Astor had paid for the whole). Though Astor sold shares to several men, it is probable that the shares reverted to him, since he held 90 per cent when the claim came to trial. Long before Mrs. Morris died, Astor offered to settle with the State of New York for $300,000, the State having sold the land to individuals. Six years later he offered to settle for $415,000.

After the death of Mary Morris in 1825, Astor offered again to settle with the State. The legislature offered to pay him $450,000 in State bonds bearing 5 per cent on certain conditions, one being that the United States Supreme Court decide in his favor and that, before the matter could be brought to the Supreme Court, Astor should win in three out of five ejectment suits. While he was dickering with the State, Astor started ejectment suits. The first went to trial late in 1827, and Astor's claim was represented by noted lawyers. The State maintained that there had been no marriage settlement, and, if there had been, the remainder had been destroyed by the act of attainder. Astor's counsel produced witnesses to the marriage settlement and declared that an act of attainder would not operate against a right belonging to another. The State might base its case on the ethics of the situation, but legality won for Astor. Since this case made it clear to the legislature that Astor's claim was strong, an act was passed in 1828 completely extinguishing any claim remaining to the Morris heirs. By 1832 Astor had won the required number of ejectment suits, and he received in satisfaction of his claim over $550,000 in New York State bonds. It was characteristic of him that he protested over the fact that the bonds stated that quarterly interest was payable on the first Monday of the month when it was due instead of the first day of the month as Astor maintained. It is estimated that this affair brought Astor over a period of 25 years a return after expenses of 350 per cent.

Not all Astor's many real-estate transactions were profitable. In the Mississippi and Great Lakes country he acquired land in connection with trading posts or on mortgages given in return for loans to luckless traders. An example of such a transaction is one which took place at Green Bay, Wisconsin. In 1834 Astor, Crooks, and Stuart took 2,790 acres of land in satisfaction of a balance owed the American Fur Co. by the old Green Bay Co.

The three owners made an agreement with James Doty, who was soon to become governor of Wisconsin Territory, whereby he purchased a quarter interest at $2,500 and agreed to serve as local agent of the partnership (which reminds us of Peter Smith's position in Astor's venture in New York State). The plan was to lay out the town of Astor at Green Bay and sell lots to capitalists or to individuals who expected to locate there. Doty followed the tactics of the typical town promoter. The sum of $40,000 is said to have been offered for the project, which Doty considered a fair valuation, but Astor held out for $100,000. In 1836 the project boomed, and the associates disposed of seven-sixteenths of their interests for $126,455, receiving total down payments of only about $21,376. Early in 1836 Astor began to fear that land speculation was overdone, and in 1837 sales and collections came to a standstill. Something might have been accomplished if steamboat service had been secured for Green Bay. As it was, the project languished and in the end proved unprofitable.

Several reasons may be seen for the failure of this enterprise. It was severely injured by the panic of 1837; the lots were sold to absentees who did not develop them; the management was divided between individuals long distances apart; and Astor, who by this time lacked energy and also intimate knowledge of the situation, did not allow the agent to follow his own judgment.

The real-estate ventures which made Astor a rich and famous landlord were those which took place on Manhattan Island. Tables 1 and 2, on page 96, show the nature of Astor's Manhattan transactions.

Dr. Porter holds that up to 1820 the bulk of Astor's real estate was purchased with profits from his commercial business, the China and fur trade. There is a close correlation between the rise and fall in land investments and changes in income from the China and fur trades. From 1820, however, another source of funds for land investments became of much greater importance than commercial profits, that is, the income from real estate. From August 1, 1826, to May 1, 1831, for instance, Astor collected rents to the amount of $190,000. From 1820 to 1834 he disposed of lands in fee simple or on long lease for over $386,000. During the whole period (1820–34) his land investments amounted to only $445,000. In other words, his lands yielded enough to account for his land investments in those years. For the period 1835–48 Astor's income from rents, alone, was much more than the amount invested in land.

We have next to consider from what sources Astor acquired his real estate. He has been accused of securing his lands at unreasonably low cost through foreclosures, purchases from indigent heirs, favorable long-term leases, and the purchase of water-lots from New York City at a small remuneration.

During the period 1800–19 Astor acquired most of his land through outright purchase, but an important proportion of his investments was in long-term leases. During the years 1820–48 leases were less important.

Two types of leases are especially significant. The more important was the purchase in 1803–05 of the Trinity Church leases from Aaron Burr, who was forced to sell because of debts. This parcel of somewhat over 241 lots was purchased at approximately $120,000, the lease to expire in 1866. The other was the lease of water-lots from the city; that is, Astor was given the right to reclaim land under water, below the high-water mark, which bordered on land owned by him. In 1806–29 he received 12 or 15 such grants, for which he usually agreed to pay at the rate of $32.50 annually—in many cases he secured a reduction of the rent on its remission for 30 years. The understanding was that Astor should fill up the lots granted to him and otherwise improve them, but he did not do as agreed and sometimes his lots became public nuisances.

During the years 1800–19 Astor acquired a few pieces of land through foreclosures. Of about 100 conveyances, only 8 were made by a master-in-chancery and one by a United States marshal; in 5 of these Astor was the complainant, and the other 3 he bought at auction. Of the 152 conveyances to Astor from 1823 to 1848 there were 58 by the master-in-chancery or the sheriff; all occurred after 1832 and 53 in the years after 1837.

From 1835 onward Astor was concerned as grantee in mortgage sales of mortgaged property of over $448,000, about $100,000 of which arose from conveyances he, himself, had made, taking as security mortgages the conditions of which were not fulfilled. During his entire career he was mortgagee in 500 separate transactions and became owner of 70 pieces of property by foreclosure. Frequently he carried mortgages beyond the time agreed upon if the mortgagor paid the interest; otherwise, he promptly foreclosed.

Most of Astor's real estate on Manhattan was acquired by purchase in fee simple. His largest purchases were made in 1800–09, 1826–34, and 1835–37. Astor knew when to buy. He has been much criticized

Table 1. CONVEYANCES OF MANHATTAN REAL ESTATE TO ASTOR

In fee simple		On long-term lease	
1789–91	$ 6,898.75	1789–91	...
1800–09	425,784.19	1803–05	$119,628.83
1810–19	152,447.00	1810	18,000.00
1822	10.00	1824	751.52
1826–34	438,650.80	1827, '30–'32	6,876.00
1835–47	764,551.70	1835, '38, '40, '42–'48	68,127.98
	$1,788,342.44		$213,384.33

Table 2. CONVEYANCES OF MANHATTAN REAL ESTATE BY ASTOR[a]

In fee simple		On long-term lease	
1803–04, '06–'09	$ 75,313.66	1806, '09	$ 1,025.00
1811–12, '18–'19	106,899.18	1812, '14–'15, '18–'19	8,745.34
1820, '22–'23, '26–'34	271,985.24	1824–34	114,682.39
1835–39, '41, '44, '46	531,931.28	1835–36, '40–'41, '47	76,200.00
	$986,129.36		$200,652.73

[a] This table leaves short-term leases by Astor, for an annual rental, out of account.

for buying the farm of Medcef Eden, which had been lost on a mortgage. He has also been criticized for buying well over $100,000 in land from George Clinton of New York, who had spent too much in politics, and from his more or less distressed heirs. That Astor profited from the low prices following the panic in 1837 is seen from the fact that in the three years 1837–39 he invested in Manhattan real estate an annual average of $160,000.

In acquiring Manhattan real estate Astor had a definite policy as to the location of his lands. He did not generally buy the highest-priced lands in the heart of the city, but he chose rather to buy far enough out so that prices were still low and yet in a location close enough to the center so that the land would soon be in greater demand.

Let us now examine Astor's methods of managing his real estate. Before 1820 his object was to dispose of his lands outright, at a good profit and as quickly as possible. Leases, either long-term or short-term, were a side issue and were apparently used largely in the management of the Trinity lots which could not be handled in any other way. After 1820 long-term leases sank to a subordinate position and the great bulk of the sales was in fee simple, for which Astor frequently took mortgages, say for 5 years at 7 per cent.

Since leases played such an important though subordinate part in Astor's real-estate transactions, it is well to see how they were handled. The lessee agreed to pay all taxes, duties, and assessments upon the lots, except for the trifling ground rent to Trinity. The lessee had the nominal right to remove any buildings erected on the lots within 10 days after the expiration of the lease. Otherwise, Astor should buy the improvements at a fair valuation or renew the lease. The length of time for which leases were granted fell in 1820–40 from about 42 years to 25 years, and after that only yearly or relatively short-term leases were granted.

A typical example of Astor's handling of long-term leases is found in his dealings with Daniel H. Turner. In 1832–35 and 1840–41 Astor sold Turner several leases to May 1, 1866, for about $56,000. The prices of these leases ranged from $900 in 1832 to above $4,000 in 1841. Most of the leases were then mortgaged to Astor for more than their original prices, above $94,000 in all. These mortgages were to cover the value of the lots and money advanced by Astor for improvements.

In the later years of Astor's life the short-time lease came to occupy a leading position, surpassing both outright sale and long-term leasing. The main reason was that, because of the growth of New York, rental values were rising rapidly. There was the added reason that Astor's Trinity leases expired in 1866. Most important for the land held in fee simple was the fact that the Astors preferred to hold land when values were increasing so rapidly.

When Astor died in 1848, his property was conservatively estimated to be worth from $20,000,000 to $30,000,000. "All agreed," says Dr. Porter, "that the greatest source of his wealth was to be found in the increase in value of his lands on Manhattan Island." It was through his almost unique vision of the future of New York City that he was able to invest his profits from trade so that with little personal exertion he became the richest man in America. Just before he died Astor is said to have made the statement, "Could I begin life again, knowing what I now know, and had money to invest, I would buy every foot of land on the Island of Manhattan."

6. Readings

K. W. Porter, *John Jacob Astor: Business Man* (Cambridge, 1931). Chapters xiii, xvi, and xx especially recommended.

Arthur D. Howden Smith, *John Jacob Astor* (Philadelphia, 1929). A light, popular account and a good character sketch of Astor, the best that could be done with outside material.

Fortune, vol. viii (Oct., 1933), "The Astors," pp. 71 ff. This is a popular account carrying the Astor real-estate interests down to the present time.

7. Suggested Questions

1. Characterize Astor's early general business policy, with criticisms.
2. What were the major shifts in Astor's business activities? Are such changes socially desirable?
3. Do you think Astor would have had so successful a business career if he had settled in Baltimore or in Montreal, or if he had come to New York a hundred years later? Discuss.
4. What was Astor's policy in the acquisition and the management of real estate?
5. Was Astor conscious of the dawn of an era of specialization?
6. What was the core of Astor's business ability?
7. Did Astor shift from mercantile capitalism to industrial capitalism?

VI. EARLY ECONOMIC SYSTEMS, ESPECIALLY MERCANTILISM

1. General Statement

Mercantilism has various shades of meaning but it has a central theme. It is a mercantile, commercial, or trading policy. It is favorable to the market place, the shop, the store, and the bank. In this respect it reversed one thousand years of Church policy which emphasized brotherly love and just dealings. For social justice it emphasized market facts. For the needs of men it substituted the advantageous and disadvantageous positions in which men found themselves. It recognized ability in trade and agreed to the reward of that ability.

Within this general policy are various types of policy, two of which are outstanding. One holds that the nation should build up most or all aspects of its economic life, particularly manufacturing; the other, that a nation should emphasize its foreign trade and make sure that it exports more than it imports, so as to have a "favorable" balance of trade. Thus, it would have gold and silver flow into its midst for use as money and for the building-up of a full national treasury; in this way the nation prepares for war, something the youthful state of the early modern period had always to keep in mind. On the other hand, to have the desired "favorable" balance it was necessary to export valuable commodities; these would ordinarily be manufactured wares. Accordingly, whichever avenue the mercantilist took he arrived at an emphasis upon manufacturing.

Observe whence mercantilism came and whither it went. It was nurtured by sedentary merchants and tradesmen in mediaeval towns but got no place until the power of the Church was broken by the modern state. Then, as the national state became an empire it was extended to colonies and other possessions. Mercantilism has cut a wide swath across human history. Displaced for a period by laissez faire, it has come back to us as neomercantilism.

Keep in mind the various economic systems, but emphasize mercantilism. Study all shades of this policy but do not forget the actual background of sedentary merchants, petty artisans, small retailers, private bankers, and a horde of others, such as stockbrokers, promoters, and insurance underwriters.

2. List of Significant Events in the History of Mercantilism

1558	Burghley, the mercantilist, gained power in England.
1651	First English Navigation Act.
1661	Colbert, French mercantilist, in office.
1664	Publication of Mun's *England's Treasure by Forraign Trade* helped put mercantilism upon a theoretical basis.
1678	England prohibited importation of chief French products.

ECONOMIC SYSTEMS

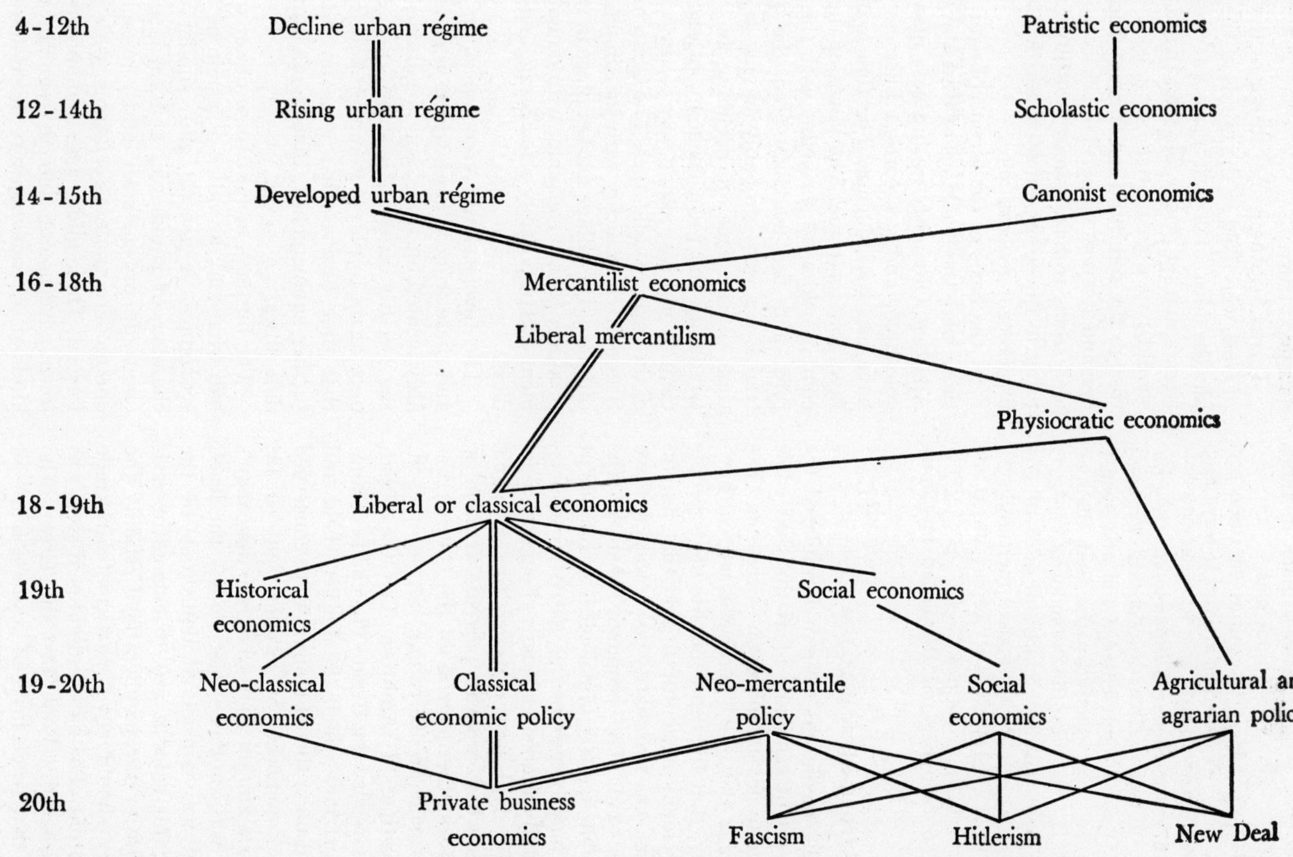

NOTE: Double lines indicate business interest and policy. Not all lines of influence and connection have been drawn.

1700	England prohibited use of silks and calicoes made in India, Persia, or China.
1719	Heavy penalties on those persuading artisans to leave England.
1767	Steuart's *Inquiry into the Principles of Political Economy* presented a full and sympathetic treatise from the mercantilist standpoint.
1776	Adam Smith's *Wealth of Nations* exposed mercantilism.
1791	Hamilton's "Report on Manufactures."
1786–1860	England abandoned mercantilism.

3. Before Mercantilism

The mediaeval Church formulated the first set of economic ideas that has come down to us in unbroken succession. Remember that the Church was a great hierarchy, that the economic life of its people was chiefly agricultural, and that its emphasis was on charity as a way to save one's soul. The economic ideas of the Church had a chronological development and may be grouped as patristic, scholastic, and canonist economic thought.

We shall first consider the economic ideas which we call patristic economics. This was the doctrine of the Church Fathers, such as Tertullian, St. Jerome, St. Augustine, St. Ambrose, Leo the Great, and Gregory the Great. The chief economic doctrines which the Fathers held and urged upon their followers were concerned with commerce. St. Jerome went so far as to maintain that what was one man's gain was another's loss. To say the least, trade was considered dangerous to the soul; far safer it was to engage in agriculture or the handicrafts. Certainly the clergy should never participate in trade for profit. The most enlightened view was expressed by Pope Leo the Great, who said that trade in itself was not bad—all depended upon the way in which it was carried on. This reminds us of the recent concession that there can be such a thing as a good trust.

It was St. Augustine, author of the *City of God,* who fixed in the minds of the people the idea of a just price (as distinct from a market price). He said that a man should pay a just price for a book even though the seller did not himself know or demand its real value. The basis for the idea seems to have been the utility of the thing in question—an idea not developed until recent generations.

At the basis of these concepts and attitudes were the teachings of Christ and the Apostles. Obviously no business man was consulted, and yet current business may have had its influence. The time was unfavorable for trade. The towns of the Ancient World were shriveling with the Empire, and the merchant and the petty tradesman were probably having a hard time in the face of declining business. Gradually the town economy of the Ancient World was giving way to the village of the early Middle Ages. The Church's attitude fitted in nicely with the simple conditions of the village market place in which producer sold to consumer with no middlemen, except possibly a few straggling peddlers.

The towns slowly grew up again here and there from villages which were favorably located for trade, and, beginning with the twelfth century, business men came once again to play a dominant rôle. Since that time business has gone on without further submergence, though not without difficulties.

The business men of these newer towns had what may be called a system of town economics. A general gild, similar to a chamber of commerce, and then special one-trade or one-craft gilds, resembling our modern trade associations, were soon formed. These gilds came to dominate the town government and to regulate most kinds of economic activity, including such handicrafts as weaving, shoemaking, and baking. The provisions trades, however, were commonly reserved for municipal regulation. The business men of the time quite clearly had a policy, which was regulation of the town's trade largely on behalf of the townsmen, and, in all but the provisions trades, on behalf of the producer. They believed in allowing all persons in trade and industry to pass up from apprenticeship to journeymanship and thence to mastership.

The formulation of economic thought in this early period of town economics in the twelfth and thirteenth centuries was also the work of the clergy. The result is known as scholastic economics. Learned teachers in Italy, France, England, and other countries examined the problems of belief and conduct which the Fathers had already dealt with and other problems which the Fathers had overlooked or had failed to consider seriously. Their two chief concerns were the old just price and the almost new doctrine of no "interest."

One of the most learned of the Scholastics was the southern Italian, Thomas Aquinas. In his *Theological Summary* he deals briefly with the two doctrines just mentioned. He asks a number of questions which indicate that the business men of the newly developing towns were taking their problems to the Church. Is it lawful to sell a commodity for more than it is worth? Is sale unlawful because of a fault in the thing sold? Is the seller bound to divulge a fault in the thing he is selling? Is it lawful to sell an article for more than was paid for it? Generally speaking, Aquinas made exceptions to the old doctrines of just price, which while quite casuistic at times nevertheless lent themselves to the needs of the period.

Aquinas was much concerned with interest, or usury as it was then called. He considered whether it was a sin to take usury for money lent. He was willing to allow the taking of interest in case the creditor had incurred a loss through the loan. Of all the many curiosities of reasoning the most interesting is that a good Christian might borrow money at "interest" but he might not lend it. In effect this meant salvation for the Christian borrower and damnation for the Jewish lender. Was it the influence of the new secular learning, particularly of Aristotle's *Politics* and *Ethics,* which was turning the later Scholastics from the ethical code of their own school, or was it the demands of business and business men that forced Aquinas at least to make exceptions in favor of a freer market?

One of the puzzles of the Middle Ages is how business men carried on their business and yet remained adherents of the Church. There are plenty of legal documents which point to subterfuge as a chief means of escape from the bonds of the Church. Instead of paying usury for a loan a business man borrowed free for a period and then paid an indemnity for not returning the money, though he had of course not intended to return it then. This indemnity was called interest. A second means of evading Church prohibitions was as follows. Instead of making a loan to a traveling merchant, a stay-at-home capitalist entered into a temporary partnership, sharing the profit or loss when the ship or packhorse returned. The older word, usury, a payment for the use of money, came to mean in the early modern period just an excessive rate of interest.

Though the business man played no direct part in formulating theory in the Middle Ages, he was creating a situation which someday would demand attention. Successful men were creating a capitalistic industry and commerce on a small scale. They were making over gilds into livery companies of large masters. They were reducing some of the small masters to practically the position of their workmen. In the fifteenth century they were creating a spirit of commercialism which was in anticipation of the nineteenth and twentieth centuries.

Again the Church responded to the facts. Scholastic economics gave way to the canonist system. This was a body of law which was growing up slowly and which concerned both laymen and clerics. The Church courts and the canon lawyers were becoming powerful as their jurisdiction was being extended. Into the Church courts went cases of marriage, legitimacy, heresy, intestacy, and usury. Through such cases grew up an elaborate code of canon law. This was more liberal than the earlier patristic and scholastic ideas. Interest was permitted as before. Sea-partnership, bottomry, and respondentia loans were allowed. It was permissible to buy rent charges, if one wanted to provide for one's old age or to serve the state or Church. Simple usury was permitted in the case of loans to the poor by pawnbrokers in order to cover expenses, but the rates must not be high.

The dominance of the economic thought of the Church ended about the fifteenth century. As the Western Church was split and as local sects shared its position, the old ethical codes were thrown over rather quickly, particularly in Switzerland, parts of Germany, England, and Scotland. Even the Church itself changed its policies. Such a faithful adherent as Jacob Fugger stood out for market price against any ecclesiastical notions of a just price. Within the Church, notably in Fugger's own town of Augsburg, there was a movement in favor of changing the doctrines of the Church.

4. Mercantilism

On the ruins of the canonist economics there was erected a secular system of mercantile economics. It is essential to observe that it had its beginnings in the towns, in the efforts of gilds and municipalities to give advantage to their own business men at home and to further their trade with other towns. Thus the Italian cities, the North German, the French, the Dutch, and the English had become urban mercantilist communities which furthered business at home and presented the strength of a unified policy in their exterior commercial relations. Urban mercantilism sometimes expanded into a larger regional or territorial system, of which the Hanseatic League is a most striking example. But eventually both the urban and the regional unity gave way to the larger national state. The mercantilist system reached its highest development under the state, which instead of hampering business accepted trade as the means to accomplish what was desired, namely national strength and self-sufficiency. Though the new mercantilist state policy was frankly political in its aim, the means used were to encourage business men in every way possible. This meant working toward free trade within the national state, encouragement of agriculture, mining, fishing, and industrial enterprise, and the regulation of foreign trade to secure a favorable balance.

A. Early mercantilist thought and policy.

One of the early expressions of mercantilist thought in England appeared in *Discourse of the Common Weal of this Realm of England* published in 1549. The analysis of business classes which is found there is of particular interest at this point: [1]

"And now that we are talking about business men, I will classify them as follows: (1) those who send money out of the country, (2) those who spend within the country what they get, and (3) those who bring treasure into the country.

"Among the first I would place all mercers, grocers, vintners, haberdashers, milliners, and

[1] This is a modernization of pp. 91–92 and 63–65 of *Discourse of the Common Weal of this Realm of England,* Elizabeth Lamond, editor (Cambridge, 1893). The author of this volume is uncertain. So recent a work as E. A. J. Johnson's *Predecessors of Adam Smith, the Growth of British Economic Thought* (New York, 1937), ascribes it to John Hales. Jean Yves le Banchu, however, in his *Ecrits Notables sur la Monnaie* (Paris, 1934, p. lxxx), concludes that the author of the work, as published in 1549, was Sir Thomas Smythe, statesman, scholar, and author, and that it was modified either by him or by his nephew, William Smith, and published by the latter in 1581 under the pseudonym, W. S.

such as sell wares produced beyond the seas and, thereby, export our treasure [gold and silver]. I consider these tolerable, but they could be spared more easily than any others. If we did not have those who brought treasure into the realm, these would cause us great loss. In the second group I would place shoemakers, tailors, carpenters, masons, tilemakers, butchers, brewers, bakers, victuallers of all kinds; they spend what they make in this country but they import no treasure. We must, therefore, encourage the third group. They are the clothmakers, tanners, capmakers, and makers of worsteds, who are the only ones I know who bring in any treasure.

"As for our wool, hides, tin, lead, butter and cheese, these commodities come from the soil and require the work of few people. If we should depend on them, alone, and carry on no other lines of work, a few persons would supply us such commodities. Then the realm would be better supplied with animals than men and would be subject to despoiling by other nations. This is the more to be feared and avoided because, as said above, such a country is more likely to produce such things as are needed for cattle than goods for the nourishment of men. . . .

"We must take heed that we buy no more from foreigners than we sell to them, for by so doing we would impoverish ourselves and enrich them. He is not a good manager who, having no other yearly income to live off but that of his business, buys more in the market than he sells. Keeping that in mind, we might save much of our treasure in this realm if we would.

"I marvel that no man takes heed of what an amount of trifles comes hither from beyond the seas, for which we pay inestimable treasure every year. These we might get along without altogether or produce in our own realm, or we might exchange substantial wares or necessities for them for which we might receive great treasure. Among those commodities I have in mind are looking and drinking glasses, glass windows, dials, tables, cards, balls, puppets, penhorns, inkhorns, toothpicks, gloves, knives, daggers, pouches, brooches, aglets, buttons of silk and silver, earthen pots, pins, points, hawks' bells, paper both white and brown, and a thousand similar goods that we might either get along without altogether or else make in sufficient amounts for ourselves within the realm.

"Some things, which we purchase from abroad, are made out of our own products and returned to us, which gives work to foreigners and exhausts the treasure of our realm. For instance, of our wool foreigners make cloth, caps, and carsies; of our hides they make spanish skins, gloves, girdles; of our tin they make salt holders, spoons, and dishes; of our broken linen, cloth, and rags, they make paper, both white and brown. What amount of treasure do you think goes out of our realm for each of those things? The treasure exported for all of them exceeds my imagination.

"No man is contented with gloves not made in Spain or France; or carse but of flemish dye; or cloth except it be of french dye, or fresadow [a cloth made with a high nap, like frieze]; or brooch or aglet not from Venice or Milan; or dagger, sword, gridle, or knife but of Spanish make; no, not so much as a spur but it must be fetched from the milliner [one who deals in wares of Milan manufacture]. I have known a time in these twenty years when there were not in all London a dozen of those haberdashers who sell French or Milanese caps, glasses, daggers, swords, gridles, and such things. And now, from the Tower to near Westminster, every street is full of them. Their shops glisten and shine with looking as well as drinking glasses; yes, with all manner of vessels of the same stuff; there are painted cruses, gay daggers, knives, swords, and gridles that would tempt any man, who looked at them, to buy though he did not need them.

"Why should anyone go beyond the sea to Peru or such far countries, or search the sands of the Tagus River in Spain, Pactolus in Asia, or the Genges in India, to get small grains of gold; or dig in the bowels of the earth for gold or silver mines, when they can make more good gold, than many gold mines would yield, out of unclean clay, not far to seek, or pebble stones and fern roots? I think that of our treasure more than a hundred thousand pounds a year is paid for things of no value in themselves except for the labor of those who worked them at our cost. What kind of people are we that we see and allow a despoiling of our goods and treasure by such means? Particularly, that we allow our own produce to go to foreigners to be worked up and returned to us? They bring them hither to be sold again. And note, I pray you, how much they make us pay again, at the end, for our stuff, that is, for the custom charge of the foreigners, for workmanship, color, and, lastly, for the tariff on returning the wares again to our realm. If the same were worked up within our realm, our own men would be working at the cost of foreigners. Tariffs should be borne by foreigners and be clear gains to the realm."

The first national mercantilists were apparently administrators such as Lord Burghley in England. Burghley was a civil servant who came to be the lord treasurer of England under Queen Elizabeth. He was the cool, calculating, worldly ambitious statesman who saw clearly that a state to be strong and independent had to be rich and economically prosperous. Burghley, as well as his successors, thought that trade and industry could best be encouraged by means of monopoly. To those merchants who joined the regulated companies or who formed joint-stock companies was given the sole right, so far as Englishmen were concerned, to trade with the Baltic peoples, Russia, the Levant, the East Indies, and so on. Their chartered corporations were their guarantee both of monopoly and of the support of the home government. To prospective manufacturers and inventors were given patents of monopoly which would guarantee them a high price for the goods they manufactured. This system was not so bad, in itself, but it easily developed abuses such as we nowadays identify with trusts.

Fortunately the long period of Burghley's power (1558–98) witnessed the careful husbanding of almost all of England's productive capacities. In France, however, the corresponding mercantilist, Colbert, was less balanced in his policy, and his period of office (1661–83) was much shorter. It is true that Colbert sought to remove barriers to the internal trade of France, but at the same time he tried to impose upon France many of the restrictive regulations formulated and elaborated by mediaeval town merchants. He would have cloth made so wide and with such and such a weight per yard. That prospective customers in distant lands did not require such cloth was of little concern to Colbert. Of course, at a time when France was competing with Holland and England for overseas trade such a policy was most unfortunate. In agricultural matters the French superintendent of finance, for that was Colbert's title, was far from judicious. Anxious to prevent the recurrence of periodic famines, he restricted or prohibited the export of grain. Accordingly, the French cultivators tended to grow less and less grain, thereby aggravating the danger of dearths and famines.

On the whole France probably gained much from Colbert's policy. Certainly French business men had favored the new policy before Colbert had come into power, as they continued to do after he had left his office. It was Montchrétien, a French iron-master, who wrote the first treatise which used the term "political economy." This mercantilist pamphlet was published in 1615.

B. Some merchants' thoughts on national wealth and policy.

There early developed in mercantilism an emphasis which, though unevenly spread, came to be regarded by some mercantilists as the distinguishing mark of the whole system. This emphasis was the insistence of each nation upon a favorable balance of trade. Each trade or industry was judged according to its capacity to create a favorable balance. The idea was to export more goods than were imported so as to bring into the country a large supply of gold and silver. Whether this notion came originally from the administrator's emphasis upon a plentiful supply of the precious metals for use in time of war or arose out of the business man's tendency to apply to the public situation what he found desirable in his private affairs, namely a monetary balance, is not clear. At any rate, the mercantilist came to regard gold and silver as superior to general merchandise.

Certainly the doctrine of the favorable balance of trade was actually carried to extremes, not only when it led to a total prohibition of trade with a single country (as in the case of England dealing with France) but also when it caused antagonism to certain kinds of trade, such as England's trade with the East Indies, which so many merchants regarded as the most profitable commerce of the day. Many of the early fleets of the East India Co. took out a greater value of silver than of wares. This seemed to threaten the supply of precious metals in the state. It was, indeed, the old story of the drainage of silver to India, drawing off the precious metal into a bottomless pit.

But here arises a situation of greatest importance: certain merchants came to perceive the error in the theory of a favorable balance when they saw their own interests threatened by its application. They checked the theories of statesmen from their own experience. Outstanding among the merchants who wrote on this great problem of national policy were Mun, Child, and North.

Thomas Mun, a London merchant active in the Mediterranean trade, as early as 1621 pointed to the fallacy in the current reasoning on the India trade.[2] He defended that trade on various grounds: it brought to England necessary drugs, spices, raw silk, indigo, and calico, which would cost more if purchased through other channels; it also gave employment to English ships and men; further, it could furnish England with naval stores and it brought income to the state in customs and imposts. But, above all else, Mun defended the East India Co. against the charge of diminishing England's treasure by exporting its specie. About a quarter of the wares from the East Indies could rightly be said to be consumed in England, while the remaining three-quarters entered into production for foreign trade or were resold abroad, thus bringing treasure back to England. Mun even went beyond his defense of the East India trade to a defense of trade in general, insisting that through trade England could dispose of her "superfluities" and receive in exchange necessary wares and treasure.

This broader defense of trade was later much more effectively developed by Mun in his *England's Treasure by Forraign Trade,* which was published in 1664. This book presented systematically and with insight an analysis of the basis of national wealth. Foreign trade, held Mun, was the "rule of our treasure," for the reason that, since England had no mines, she had no other means to increase her wealth but by foreign trade. The way in which England's wealth could be increased was "to sell more to strangers yearly than wee consume of theirs in value." The object of Mun's treatise was to set forth the particular means of doing this.

In this matter Mun spoke not as a theorist but as a merchant, frequently giving illustrations from his own experience.[3] First, he mentioned such obvious means of increasing England's balance as to refrain from the consumption of foreign wares in diet and dress and to be frugal in the use even of their own products, always avoiding the waste of rapid change of fashions; if they would be prodigal, however, it should be with their own materials and manufactures. Further, he urged the full utilization of England's labor in the production of goods and in giving services. Encourage fishing: "The Fishing in his Majesties seas . . . is our natural wealth, and would cost nothing but labour, which the *Dutch* bestow willingly, and thereby draw yearly a very great profit to them-

[2] *A Discourse of Trade* (London, 1621).

[3] The following discussion on Mun is based on *England's Treasure by Forraign Trade* (New York, 1910), pp. 7–30.

selves by serving many places of Christendom with our Fish, for which they return and supply their wants both of forraign Wares and Mony, besides the multitudes of Mariners and Shipping, which hereby are maintain'd. . . ." Trade in English ships, "for then we get not only the price of our wares as they are worth here, but also the Merchants gains, the charges of ensurance, and fraight to carry them beyond the seas;" these "are exceeding great" in long voyages, for which reason voyages to distant countries are especially profitable for the Kingdom.

Mun placed great emphasis on the development of manufactures in England. Use taxation for this purpose, he urged:

"It were policie and profit for the State to suffer manufactures made of forraign Materials to be exposed [sold] custome-free, as Velvets and all other wrought Silks, Fustians, thrown Silks and the like, it would employ very many poor people, and much encrease the value of our stock yearly issued into other Countreys. . . . And it is certain, that if the said forraign Commodities might be exported from hence, free of custome, this manufacture would yet encrease very much, and decrease as fast in *Italy* and the *Netherlands*. . . . It is needful also not to charge the native commodities with too great customes, lest by indearing them to the strangers use [raise the price too high], it hinder their vent [sale]. And especially forraign wares brought in to be transported again should be favoured, for otherwise that manner of trading . . . cannot prosper nor subsist. . . ."

As to domestic production:

"In all things we must endeavour to make the most we can of our own, whether it be *Natural or Artificial;* And forasmuch as the people which live by the Arts are far more in number than they who are masters of the fruits, we ought the more carefully to maintain those endeavours of the multitude, in whom doth consist the greatest strength and riches both of King and Kingdom: for where the people are many, and the arts good, there the traffique must be great, and the Countrey rich."

Two points which he emphasized went far beyond these more or less obvious considerations. One clearly reveals the merchant's concern over proper pricing:

"In our exportations we must not only regard our own superfluities, but also we must consider our neighbours necessities, that so upon the wares which they cannot want, nor yet be furnished thereof elsewhere, we may (besides the vent of the Materials) gain so much of manifacture as we can, and also endeavour to sell them dear, so far forth as the high price cause not a less vent in the quantity. But the superfluity of our commodities which strangers use, and may also have the same from other Nations, or may abate their vent by the use of some such like wares from other places, and with little inconvenience; we must in this case strive to sell as cheap as possible we can, rather than to lose the utterance of such wares. For we have found of late years by good experience, that being able to sell our Cloth cheap in Turkey, we have greatly encreased the vent thereof, and the *Venetians* have lost as much in the utterance of theirs in those Countreys, because it is dearer. And on the other side a few years past, when by the excessive price of Wools our Cloth was exceeding dear, we lost at the least half our clothing for forraign parts, which since is no otherwise (well neer) recovered again than by the great fall of price for Wools and Cloth. We find that twenty five in the Hundred less in the price of these and some other Wares, to the loss of private mens revenues, may raise above fifty upon the hundred in the quantity vented to the benefit of the publique. For when Cloth is dear, other Nations doe presently practise clothing, and we know they want neither art nor materials to this performance. But when by cheapness we drive them from this employment, and so in time obtain our dear price again, then do they also use their former remedy. So that by these alterations we learn, that it is in vain to expect a greater revenue of our wares than their condition will afford, but rather it concerns us to apply our endeavours to the times with care and diligence to help our selves the best we may, by making our cloth and other manufactures without deceit, which will encrease their estimation and use."

Mun also tried to refute the common opinion that the export of money in trade decreased England's treasure:

"First, I will take that for granted . . . that we have no other means to get Treasure but by forraign trade, for Mines wee have none which do afford it. . . . For it is in the stock of the Kingdom as in the estates of private men, who having store of wares, doe not therefore say that they will not venture out or trade with their mony (for this were ridiculous) but do also turn that into wares, whereby they multiply their Mony, and so by a continual and orderly change of one into the other grow rich, and when they please turn all their estates into Treasure; for they that have Wares cannot want mony. . . . It is not therefore the keeping of our mony in the Kingdom, but the necessity and use of our wares in forraign Countries, and our want of their commodities that causeth the vent and consumption on all sides, which makes a quick and ample Trade. If wee were once poor, and now having gained some store of mony by trade with resolution to keep it still in the Realm; shall this cause other Nations to spend more of our commodities than formerly they have done, whereby we might say that our trade is Quickned and Enlarged? no verily it will produce no such good effect: but rather according to the alteration of times by their true causes wee may expect the contrary; for all men do consent that plenty of mony in a Kingdom doth make the native commodities dearer, which as it is to the profit of some private men in their revenues, so is it directly against the benefit of the Publique in the quantity of the trade; for as plenty of mony makes wares dearer, so dear wares decline their use and consumption. . . ."

Trade, he said in conclusion, should be considered as to its end; looking only at beginnings would be like observing the sower like a madman casting away seed, without considering that the harvest would bring the increase.

In 1675 another merchant, who was primarily a banker, Sir Josiah Child, governor of the East India Co., published *A New Discourse of Trade* which dealt with the same problem of national wealth. Child was much concerned over the fact that Holland, particularly, was so much more successful in trade than was England. He enumerated the reasons for the success of Holland, such as: membership of experienced merchants in the councils of state; the standardization and careful packing of products; encouragement of invention and discovery; the efficiency of their ships, and sailing in fleets with convoy; their thrifty living; education of both their sons and their daughters, so that they wrote good hands and knew arithmetic and merchants' accounts, infusing in both sexes a love of and aptitude for commerce; low customs and high excise tax; careful provision for and employment of the poor; the use of banks; toleration, which attracted industrious people to the country; quick and cheap justice through the "law merchant;" rapid settlement of debts through transfer of bills; public registry of sale and mortgage of lands and houses; and low interest.

To increase the balance of trade Child made specific recommendations:

(1) "Increase hands in trade" by the following means: a liberal act of naturalization; liberalizing the regulations as to societies of merchants; an easier, freer admission of merchants and artificers to become burghers of cities and boroughs; not limiting the servants or tools a man could employ; lowering the interest on money; relaxing ecclesiastical laws which excluded or drove people from England; employing, educating, and relieving the poor; and giving honor and preferment to merchants in the affairs of the nation, which "will doubtless increase their number."

(2) Increase England's trading capital through the following means: lowering the rate of interest by a law for transference of bills of debt, which by making for speed in transfers would bring more rapid turnover; limiting the trade with England's colonies to England; having his Majesty's subjects provide timber, masts, boards,

and pipe-staves, now imported; preventing export of wool, thereby encouraging woolen manufactures; encouraging fishing trades; encouraging linen manufacture in Ireland by privileges to first undertakers; encouraging especially those trades that sold most of their manufactures, imported materials for manufacture, or furnished commodities for carrying on other trades; punctual payment of the king's obligations; lessening the number of holidays; increasing trade by paying back customs on imported wares exported.

(3) Make trade easy and necessary and make it to England's interest to trade by: "a law for transference of bills of debt;" a court-merchant; cheapening and speeding up service at the customs; reducing the rate of interest to 4 per cent; supplying regular convoys for ships so that goods need not lie long in ships; and reducing the impressment of seamen, which discouraged merchants by unmanning their crews.

(4) Make it to the interest of other nations to trade with England by: "being in a good condition of strength at home, in reference to the navy, and all other kind of military preparations . . . will render us wise and honourable in the esteem of other nations, and consequently oblige them not only to admit us the freedom of trade with them, but the better terms for, and countenance in, the course of our trade;" furnishing "them at as cheap or cheaper rates [prices] than any other nation can or doth;" "the well contrivement and management of foreign treaties;" "public justice and honesty" in making a public seal represent exactness "in length, breadth, and nature, according to what they ought to be by their seals;" receiving from other nations "the fruits and commodities of their countries, as well as send them our's," but preventing "as much as may be, the importation of foreign manufactures;" and discouraging "Venetian manufactures where we can now make them as well ourselves in England."

In 1691 Sir Dudley North, a London merchant who had gained wealth in trade with the eastern Mediterranean, published his *Discourses upon Trade,* which carried the argument on trade still further than had Child. North was especially concerned with refuting the currently expressed belief "that were there more Specifick Money, Trade would increase, and we should have better Markets for every thing." He attacked the arguments for lower interest, debasement of coinage, coining of much money, retaining gold and silver in England, and so on, with the object of increasing the quantity of money. North's position may be seen from certain "paradoxes" which, he says, are "no less strange to most men, than true in themselves:" [4]

"*That* The whole World as to Trade, is but as one Nation or People, and therein Nations are as Persons.

. . . .

"*That* There can be no Trade unprofitable to the Publick; for if any prove so, Men leave it off; and wherever the Traders thrive, the Publick, of which they are a part, thrives also.

"*That* To force Men to deal in any prescrib'd manner, may profit such as happen to serve them; but the Publick gains not, because it is taking from one Subject, to give to another.

"*That* No Laws can set Prizes [prices] in Trade, the Rates of which, must and will make themselves: But when such Laws do happen to lay any hold, it is so much Impediment to Trade, and therefore prejudicial.

"*That* Money is a Merchandize, whereof there may be a glut, as well as a scarcity, and that even to an Inconvenience.

"*That* A People cannot want [lack] Money to serve the ordinary dealing, and more than enough they will not have.

"*That* No Man shall be the richer for the making much Money, nor have any part of it, but as he buys it for an equivalent part. [It must represent value.]

. . . .

"*That* The sinking [debasing] Money by Allay [alloy] or weight is all one.

[4] Excerpt from an edition published in Edinburgh, 1846.

"*That* Exchange and ready Money [payment by clearing bills and by cash], are the same, nothing but Carriage and re-carriage being saved.

"*That* Money exported in Trade is an increase in the Wealth of the Nation; but spent in War, and Payments abroad, is so much Impoverishment.

"*In short, That* All favour to one Trade or Interest against another, is an abuse, and Cuts so much of Profit from the Publick."

North summed up all his argument in the brief statement that "It is Peace, Industry, and Freedom that brings Trade and Wealth, and nothing else." Indeed, his *Discourses* contains statements which seem like the morning light before the dawn of David Hume and Adam Smith.

Thus the merchants, of whom Mun, Child, and North are but outstanding examples, helped to formulate a broader and a more realistic basis of thought for mercantilist policy. They uncovered some of the fallacies involved in the policy of severe regulation with the favorable balance of trade as the immediate goal. Out of the movement which they started came a more liberal mercantilism, the so-called Tory free-trade policy. This was still mercantilism—it was still a theory of a favorable balance of trade, but it was a balance liberally and not narrowly interpreted. And it was a system that recognized the business man and trade as the chief builders of England's wealth.

C. Adam Smith's conception of mercantilism, 1776.

About a hundred years after Mun, Child, and North, Adam Smith examined mercantilism as a system of thought and policy. The following quotations from his *Wealth of Nations* give his idea of mercantilism as it was popularly understood: [5]

"I thought it necessary, though at the hazard of being tedious, to examine at full length this popular notion that wealth consists in money, or in gold and silver. Money in common language, as I have already observed, frequently signifies wealth; and this ambiguity of expression has rendered this popular notion so familiar to us, that even they, who are convinced of its absurdity, are very apt to forget their own principles, and in the course of their reasonings, to take it for granted as a certain and undeniable truth. Some of the best English writers upon commerce set out with observing, that the wealth of a country consists, not in its gold and silver only, but in its lands, houses, and consumable goods of all different kinds. In the course of their reasonings, however, the lands, houses, and consumable goods, seem to slip out of their memory, and the strain of their argument frequently supposes that all wealth consists in gold and silver, and that to multiply those metals is the great object of national industry and commerce.

"The two principles being established, however, that wealth consisted in gold and silver, and that those metals could be brought into a country which had no mines only by the balance of trade, or by exporting to a greater value than it imported; it necessarily became the great object of political economy to diminish as much as possible the importation of foreign goods for home consumption, and to increase as much as possible the exportation of the produce of domestic industry. Its two great engines for enriching the country, therefore, were restraints upon importation, and encouragement to exportation.

"The restraints upon importation were of two kinds.

"First, Restraints upon the importation of such foreign goods for home consumption as could be produced at home, from whatever country they were imported.

"Secondly, Restraints upon the importation of goods of almost all kinds from those particular countries with which the balance of trade was supposed to be disadvantageous.

"Those different restraints consisted sometimes in high duties, and sometimes in absolute prohibitions.

"Exportation was encouraged sometimes by drawbacks, sometimes by bounties, sometimes by advantageous treaties of commerce with foreign states, and sometimes by the establishment of colonies in distant countries.

[5] *An Inquiry into the Nature and Causes of the Wealth of Nations* (London, 1904), vols. i and ii.

"Drawbacks were given upon two different occasions. When the home-manufactures were subject to any duty or excise, either the whole or a part of it was frequently drawn back upon their exportation; and when foreign goods liable to a duty were imported in order to be exported again, either the whole or a part of this duty was sometimes given back upon such exportation.

"Bounties were given for the encouragement either of some beginning manufactures, or of such sorts of industry of other kinds as were supposed to deserve particular favour.

"By advantageous treaties of commerce, particular privileges were procured in some foreign state for the goods and merchants of the country, beyond what were granted to those of other countries.

"By the establishment of colonies in distant countries, not only particular privileges, but a monopoly was frequently procured for the goods and merchants of the country which established them.

"The sorts of restraints upon importation above-mentioned, together with these four encouragements to exportation, constitute the six principal means by which the commercial system proposes to increase the quantity of gold and silver in any country, by turning the balance of trade in its favour. [vol. i, pp. 415–417]

. . . .

"Though the encouragement of exportation, and the discouragement of importation, are the two great engines by which the mercantile system proposes to enrich every country, yet with regard to some particular commodities, it seems to follow an opposite plan: to discourage exportation and to encourage importation. Its ultimate object, however it pretends, is always the same, to enrich the country by an advantageous balance of trade. It discourages the exportation of the materials of manufacture, and of the instruments of trade, in order to give our own workmen an advantage, and to enable them to undersell those of other nations in all foreign markets; and by restraining, in this manner, the exportation of a few commodities, of no great price, it proposes to occasion a much greater and more valuable exportation of others. It encourages the importation of the materials of manufacture, in order that our own people may be enabled to work them up more cheaply, and thereby prevent a greater and more valuable importation of the manufactured commodities. [vol. ii, p. 141]

. . . .

"The encouragement given to the importation of the materials of manufacture by bounties, has been principally confined to such as were imported from our American plantations. [p. 143]

. . . .

"The exportation of the materials of manufacture is sometimes discouraged by absolute prohibitions, and sometimes by high duties.

"Our woollen manufacturers have been more successful than any other class of workmen, in persuading the legislature that the prosperity of the nation depended upon the success and extension of their particular business. They have not only obtained a monopoly against the consumers by an absolute prohibition of importing woollen cloths from any foreign country; but they have likewise obtained another monopoly against the sheep farmers and growers of wool, by a similar prohibition of the exportation of live sheep and wool. The severity of many of the laws which have been enacted for the security of the revenue is very justly complained of, as imposing heavy penalties upon actions which, antecedent to the statutes that declared them to be crimes, had always been understood to be innocent. But the cruellest of our revenue laws, I will venture to affirm, are mild and gentle, in comparison of some of those which the clamour of our merchants and manufacturers has extorted from the legislature, for the support of their own absurd and oppressive monopolies. Like the laws of Draco, these laws may be said to be all written in blood. [p. 146]

. . . .

"The laudable motive of all these regulations, is to extend our own manufacturers, not by their own improvement, but by the depression of those of all our neighbours, and by putting an end, as much as possible, to the troublesome competition of such odious and disagreeable rivals. [p. 159]

. . . .

"It cannot be very difficult to determine who have been the contrivers of this whole mercantile system; not the consumers, we may believe, whose interest has been entirely neglected; but the producers, whose interest has been so carefully attended to; and among this latter class our merchants and manufacturers have been by far the principal architects. In the mercantile regulations, which have been taken notice of in this chapter, the interest of our manufacturers has been most peculiarly attended to; and the interest, not so much of the consumers, as that of some other sets of producers, has been sacrificed to it." [p. 160]

D. Alexander Hamilton on America's industrial policy, 1791.[6]

The policy which had dominated England in her drive for economic supremacy was followed by the new United States. The mercantilist leader in America was Alexander Hamilton, British in origin and a friend and associate, as a lawyer, of many prominent business men of New York. The following quotations are from his writings:

"It is now proper to proceed a step further, and to enumerate the principal circumstances from which it may be inferred that manufacturing establishments not only occasion a positive augmentation of the produce and revenue of the society, but that they contribute essentially to rendering them greater than they could possibly be, without such establishments. These circumstances are:

"1. The division of labor.

2. An extension of the use of machinery.

3. Additional employment to classes of the community not ordinarily engaged in the business.

4. The promoting of emigration from foreign countries.

5. The furnishing greater scope for the diversity of talents and dispositions, which discriminate men from each other.

6. The affording a more ample and various field for enterprise.

7. The creating, in some instances, a new, and securing, in all, a more certain and steady demand for the surplus produce of the soil.

"Each of these circumstances has a considerable influence upon the total mass of industrious effort in a community; together, they add to it a degree of energy and effect, which are not easily conceived. Some comments upon each of them, in the order in which they have been stated, may serve to explain their importance.

. . . .

"Experience teaches, that men are often so much governed by what they are accustomed to see and practise, that the simplest and most obvious improvements, in the most ordinary occupations, are adopted with hesitation, reluctance, and by slow gradations. The spontaneous transition to new pursuits, in a community long habituated to different ones, may be expected to be attended with proportionately greater difficulty. When former occupations ceased to yield a profit adequate to the subsistence of their followers; or when there was an absolute deficiency of employment in them, owing to the superabundance of hands, changes would ensue; but these changes would be likely to be more tardy than might consist with the interest either of individuals or of the society. In many cases they would not happen, while a bare support could be ensured by an adherence to ancient courses, though a resort to a more profitable employment might be practicable. To produce the desirable changes as early as may be expedient, may therefore require the incitement and patronage of government.

"The apprehension of failing in new attempts, is, perhaps, a more serious impediment. There are dispositions apt to be attracted by the mere novelty of an undertaking; but these are not always those best calculated to give it success. To this, it is of importance that the confidence of cautious, sagacious capitalists, both citizens and foreigners, should be excited. And to inspire this description of persons with confidence, it is essential that they should be made to see in any project which is new—and for that reason alone, if for no other—precarious, the prospect of such a degree of countenance and support from government, as may be capable of overcoming the obstacles inseparable from first experiments.

"The superiority antecedently enjoyed by nations who have preoccupied and perfected a branch of industry, constitutes a more for-

[6] Arthur H. Cole, editor, *Industrial and Commercial Correspondence of Alexander Hamilton* (Chicago, 1928), pp. 256–257, 266–267.

midable obstacle than either of those which have been mentioned, to the introduction of the same branch into a country in which it did not before exist. To maintain, between the recent establishments of one country, and the long matured establishments of another country, a competition upon equal terms, both as to quality and price, is, in most cases, impracticable. The disparity, in the one, or in the other, or in both, must necessarily be so considerable, as to forbid a successful rivalship, without the extraordinary aid and protection of government.

"But the greatest obstacle of all to the successful prosecution of a new branch of industry in a country in which it was before unknown, consists, as far as the instances apply, in the bounties, premiums, and other aids, which are granted in a variety of cases, by the nations in which the establishments to be imitated are previously introduced. It is well known (and particular examples, in the course of this report, will be cited) that certain nations grant bounties on the exportation of particular commodities, to enable their own workmen to undersell and supplant all competitors, in the countries to which those commodities are sent. Hence the undertakers of a new manufacture have to contend, not only with the natural disadvantages of a new undertaking, but with the gratuities and remunerations which other governments bestow. To be enabled to contend with success, it is evident that the interference and aid of their own governments are indispensable."

E. Schmoller's historical view of mercantilism.

Gustav Schmoller's historical consideration of national mercantilism as a politico-economic system, in his *The Mercantile System and Its Historical Significance,*[7] has become a classic. Below are reproduced a few paragraphs:

"The whole internal history of the seventeenth and eighteenth centuries, not only in Germany but everywhere else, is summed up in the opposition of the economic policy of the state to that of the town, the district, and the several Estates; the whole foreign history is summed up in the opposition to one another of the separate interests of the newly rising states, each of which sought to obtain and retain its place in the circle of European nations, and in that foreign trade which now included America and India. Questions of political power were at issue, which were, at the same time, questions of economic organisation. What was at stake was the creation of real *political* economies as unified organisms, the centre of which should be, not merely a state policy reaching out in all directions, but rather the living heart-beat of a united sentiment.

"Only he who thus conceives of mercantilism will understand it; in its innermost kernel it is nothing but state making—not state making in a narrow sense, but state making and national-economy making at the same time; state making in the modern sense, which creates out of the political community an economic community, and so gives it a heightened meaning. The essence of the system lies not in some doctrine of money, or of the balance of trade; not in tariff barriers, protective duties, or navigation laws; but in something far greater:—namely, in the total transformation of society and its organisation, as well as of the state and its institutions, in the replacing of a local and territorial economic policy by that of the national state. With this accords the fact recently pointed out with regard to the literary history of the movement, that what is peculiar to all the mercantilist writers is not so much the regulations of trade which they propose for the increase of the precious metals as the stress they lay on the active circulation of money, especially within the state itself.

"The struggle against the great nobility, the towns, the corporations, and provinces, the economic as well as political blending of these isolated groups into a larger whole, the struggle for uniform measures and coinage, for a well-ordered system of currency and credit, for uniform laws and uniform administration, for freer and more active traffic within the land,—this it was which created a new division of labour, a new prosperity, and which liberated a thousand forces towards progress. As the territorial policy had rested on the

[7] Edited by W. J. Ashley and published in Gustav Schmoller, *The Mercantile System and Its Historical Significance,* in 1895. The excerpts are from pp. 50–78; footnotes in the material quoted have been omitted.

overthrow of independent local and town policies, on the limitation and modification of local institutions, upon the increasing strength of the general interests of the whole territory, so now there followed, for centuries, a struggle between state and district, between principality and province,—a task which was doubly difficult in those cases where the state did not yet include the whole nation. This struggle was primarily an economic one; it had to do with the removal of all the old economic and financial institutions, and with the creation of new joint interests and of united institutions. It was a process which in Italy and Germany reached its full conclusion only in our own day; which in France was not quite finished in 1789; which even in Great Britain was not completed till late; and in the Republic of the United Netherlands halted midway in its course.

. . . .

"It is a consideration of the economic history of France that most clearly brings out the fact that the mercantilism that was everywhere making its way was at least as much a matter of transformation and union at home as of barriers against the world outside. Louis XI. (1461–1483) cast down the great houses of Burgundy and Anjou, of Orleans and Bourbon, resisted the narrow selfishness of the corporations, sought to bring about uniform weights and measures in France, and forbade the importation of foreign manufactures. The edict of 1539, which introduced freedom of trade in corn in the interior of France, particularly between the several provinces, sets out with the assertion that in a united political body the several districts should, at all times, help and support one another. The declaration in 1577 that trade, and in 1581 that industry, belonged to the *droit domanial* had not so much a fiscal as a centralising significance; as was the case generally with the ordinances dating from the time of the great de l'Hôpital (Chancellor 1560–1568). Richelieu's razing of the fortresses of the nobility has often been extolled as one of the most important steps towards internal freedom of intercourse within France; his active measures for the creation of a French marine were among the most important contributions towards the development of an independent commercial policy in relation to other countries. Colbert's administration (1662–1683) was, primarily, a struggle against the municipal and provincial authorities; of whom Chéruel says that it was they really who hindered economic progress and the improvement of trade and manufactures. The submission of the towns to a uniform ordinance, the partial abolition of the provincial Estates, the diminution of the power of the provincial governor, and his replacement by the intendent; these were measures which, like his great road and canal works, his interest in posts and insurance, in technical and artistic education, in exhibitions and model buildings created by the state, in private and public model industrial establishments, his reform of river tolls, his union of the inner provinces in a uniform customs system,—all aimed at the one thing, to make of the French people under its brilliant monarchy a noble and united body, united in civilisation as well as in government, and worthy of the name of nation. The great laws of Colbert, the *ordonnance civile* of 1667, the *édit général sur les eaux et les forêts* of 1669, the *ordonnance criminelle* of 1670, the *ordonnance de commerce* of 1673, founded the legal as well as the economic unity of France; even economically they are more important than the tariffs of 1664 and 1667, for these did not succeed even in removing the differences between the *pays d'états* and *pays d'élection*.

. . . .

"If we pause for a while to consider this foreign and external economic policy of the European states of the seventeenth and eighteenth centuries,—which it has hitherto been the custom to regard as the essential feature of the mercantile system,—it is not, of course, our purpose to describe the details of its several forms. The general features of its regulations are well enough known. Difficulties were put in the way of the importation of manufactured goods; and their production and exportation were favoured by the prohibition of the export of raw materials, by bounties on export, and by commercial treaties. Encouragement was given to domestic shipping, to the fisheries, and to the coasting trade by restricting or forbidding foreign competition. Commerce with the colonies, and the supplying of them with European wares, was reserved for the mother country. The importation of colonial produce had to take place directly from the colony itself, and not by way of other European ports; and everywhere an attempt was made to establish *direct* trading relations by great privileged trading companies, and by state aid in manifold ways. England promoted the export of corn and the prosperity of agriculture at the same time by the payment of bounties; France hindered the export of corn for the benefit of industry; Holland, in its later days, sought to create very large stores of corn and a very free trade in corn, so as both to ensure a due domestic supply and to encourage trade. But, as we have already said, an account of these several measures would go beyond the purpose of this essay. The general features are known; the details have even yet not been subjected to due scientific investigation. Our only purpose here is to grasp the fundamental ideas of the system; which, naturally, found varying expression, here in high duties, there in low, here in the prevention, there in the encouragement of the corn trade. The thought pursued everywhere was this: as competition with other countries fluctuated up and down, to cast the weight of the power of the state into the scales of the balance in the way demanded in each case by national interests.

"In proportion as the economic interests of whole states, after much agitation of public opinion, found a rallying-point in certain generally accepted postulates, there could not fail to arise the thought of a national policy, of protection by the state against the outside world, and of the support by the state of great national interests in their struggle with foreign countries. The conception of a national agriculture, of a national industry, of national shipping and fisheries, of national currency and banking systems, of a national division of labour, and of a national trade must have arisen before the need was felt of transforming old municipal and territorial institutions into national and state ones. But, as soon as that had taken place, it must have seemed a matter of course that the whole power of the state, in relation to other countries as well as at home, should be placed at the service of these collective interests; just as the political power of the towns and territories had served their municipal and district interests."

5. Liberalism

Mercantilism marked a victory for the sedentary merchant and for business in that it recognized as never before the importance of business as a producer of wealth. But the form which mercantilist regulation took was not always to the merchant's liking. We have already seen how merchants of England's great mercantilist era worked for a more liberal mercantilism. Later, movements arose which challenged the very idea of regulation and helped to establish laissez faire as the leading principle ruling the relations of government and business.

In France economic thinking took a special turn in the doctrines of the physiocrats. Indeed, theirs was almost an anti-business system of thought. The merchant and manufacturer were regarded as useful but unproductive. In short, productivity was limited to the soil. That system would work best which left each person to follow his own interests, which meant that there should be complete freedom of trade, no monopolies, and no privileges. It is not easy to explain the incoming of this one-sided economics, but it must be remembered that France had earlier gone through a period of intensive but not too successful regulation under Colbert, that she had suffered severely from the commercial and financial panic attendant upon the failure of the system of John Law in 1720, that she was predominantly agricultural, and that her influential court was closely allied with landed interests.

Physiocratic economics made its contributions even though it did not help business directly. Its leader, Quesnay, was a physician who worked out the distribution of income, possibly on the analogy of the circulation of blood in the human body. Henceforth distribution was to be a problem for thinkers on a par with production. It is in itself of little moment that the term "economist" was first used and popularized by the physiocrats. The term reflected a situation: there was a large body of persons thinking about production and distribution who were not business men and not even administrators. Here we have at least an adumbration of the subsequent professionalization of economics and its divorce from business.

The opposition to mercantilist regulation reached its highest point in nineteenth-century England, when it developed into the system of thought best known to business men and students as classical economics. This was the joint product of Adam Smith, a Scottish professor of moral philosophy, and of David Ricardo, a Jewish stockbroker and private banker. Economics became a logical and intricate study, and it was the stockbroker even more than the professor who made it such. Although there are many shades of variation in doctrine held by these two and other leaders, there is a substratum of thought and attitude which underlies the whole system. The emphasis is upon the profits of the business man not only as an object of private business but as a means to public gain. In order to facilitate business there should be the maximum of freedom. Here was the economic man and here the new economic order.

Under the banner of the classical school business men could enroll. Such business leaders as Sir Robert Peel and later Richard Cobden, the former the son of a manufacturer and the latter an industrialist, found themselves at home in the new system. The Manchester Chamber of Commerce could assume an effective leadership in the movement for free trade in England and ultimately in the whole world. The navigation laws, apprenticeship rules, and tariffs were made to drop from the body politic as chains from a liberated slave. England first convinced herself and then other peoples that a new order of emancipated business was at hand. Practically all the countries of Europe were converted to the new system, and many Americans were convinced that the future belonged to free trade and unrestricted profit-taking.

Business men could then feel that they had realized their highest destiny. Their work was recognized as the most vital in the state. Their insistence upon more liberalism than had been found in the old mercantilistic doctrines had been accepted. In short, the victory of the business man's point of view, knocking at the door of patristic, scholastic, canonist, and mercantilist economics, was now established.

6. Suggested Readings

For a general survey of the history of economic thought as it relates to the business man and his work (from which survey a large portion of this case has been taken), the following article is recommended: N. S. B. Gras, "The Business Man and Economic Systems," *Journal of Economic and Business History,* vol. iii (1931–32), pp. 165–184.

On mercantilism:

Gustav Schmoller, *The Mercantile System and Its Historical Significance* (New York, 1895). This work is strongly recommended to anyone interested in the political and Continental aspects of mercantilism.

E. Lipson, *The Economic History of England* (London, 1931), vol. iii, chap. iv, "The Mercantile System." This selection is recommended as an excellent detailed treatment of the nature and operation of the mercantilist system in England. For a brief survey see Professor Lipson's "England in the Age of Mercantilism," in the *Journal of Economic and Business History,* vol. iv (1931–32), pp. 691–707.

A. J. Sargent, *The Economic Policy of Colbert* (London, 1899). A short description and evaluation of Colbert's theories and their application in France.

E. A. J. Johnson, *Predecessors of Adam Smith* (New York, 1937). Recommended for its discussion of the thought of outstanding writers on economic questions in England in the mercantilist period, especially chapters on Hales, Malynes, Misselden, Mun, and King.

J. W. Horrocks, *A Short History of Mercantilism* (London, 1925). This is a useful but not very scholarly summary of the subject.

Eli F. Heckscher, *Mercantilism*, 2 vols. (New York, 1935). This is by far the most comprehensive study of mercantilism as state policy.

7. Suggested Questions

1. What is the meaning of economic systems? Illustrate.
2. Has the analysis of business men, made in 1549, any value?
3. What was mercantilism?
4. Why was mercantilism brought into being? What was its relation to the sedentary merchant and to mercantile capitalism?
5. Who began the practice of appealing to the nation for favors?
6. What changes have occurred in mercantilism?
7. Wherein is mercantilism weak on the side of administration?
8. What was the emphasis of Hamilton?
9. Why did mercantilism lose favor? Has it done any harm?
10. Compare mercantilism with the New Deal and with fascism.

VII. AN AMERICAN SYSTEM OF GOVERNMENT AND BUSINESS (AN OUTLINE)

1. General Statement

This case is here presented in outline rather than in full, not because the subject is unimportant but because the background and content, being more familiar than most topics in this *Casebook,* can be supplied by users of the book. The construction of a case is in itself good training. It should be an especially helpful exercise where the materials used are somewhat familiar but where the problems involved require a new approach or a fresh point of view.

The reaction in the American colonies to the "tyranny" of England brought an emphasis on local freedom and individual liberty, in the late years of the Revolution and the early years of independence, which worked toward the establishment of what was virtually a town and provincial system of economy. Yet the business life of the new States had been geared to an entirely different setup. Before the Revolution colonial business had been part of the metropolitan mercantilist system centered in London; during the Revolution the basis of a metropolitan organization of business, growing out of war needs and a considerable foreign trade, had been laid in America. The question was whether the town or the metropolitan system should prevail. The issue came to be drawn between business and nonbusiness interests and between creditor and debtor.

Out of the conflict came the Constitution, which devised the framework of our government and made possible the adoption of certain governmental policies which were of fundamental importance to business. Those policies were later upheld and even strengthened by the Supreme Court. The position of the judiciary and, indeed, of the legislative and administrative branches of the government has varied from time to time, as different interests—of which the terms Hamiltonian and Jeffersonian have become symbolic—have held a dominating influence; but in the ebb and flow of policy certain constants have given assurance to business. Our strong government has not only preserved peace and order and established free trade at home and respect for the United States abroad, but it has also maintained the inviolability of contracts, the protection of private property under the law, and freedom of private enterprise. In recent years American business has been puzzled to know whether we are now experiencing a revolution which may change these fundamentals or whether the New Deal is only a phase of that cyclical movement which has been characteristic of American politics. There are those who believe that it would be helpful to study the making of the Constitution and the policies established in the early years of the federal government.

2. Important Dates

1781 Weak union of States established.
1783 Emigration of Loyalists. Short postwar boom.
1783–88 Depression, varying in degree from time to time and between industries.
1784 Establishment of the Bank of New York and the Massachusetts Bank.
1785 *Empress of China* returned from Canton.
1786 Shays' Rebellion.
1786–87 Business men fearful of debtor movements.
1786–90 Recovery and prosperity.
1787 Constitutional Convention met in Philadelphia.
1789 New government established under the Constitution.
1789–91 "Hamiltonian system" established.
1790 Slater's first spinning mill established.
1790–95 Prosperity with short breaks.
1791 Active speculation, particularly in bank stocks. Organization of the Society for Establishing Useful Manufactures. First Bank of the United States established.
1792 Short financial panic, especially in New York.
1794 Whiskey rebellion put down, proving federal strength.
1795 Treaties with Spain and England improved conditions of trade.
1796–98 Depression, particularly in the North.
1798 Difficulties with France. War scare.
1799–1801 Revival and prosperity.
1801 Jeffersonian Democracy threatened Hamiltonian system.
1802–03 Recession and depression.
1803 *Marbury* v. *Madison* marked beginning of Marshall's work in strengthening federal government.

3. American Business, 1783–90

A. Legacy of the Revolution: a new group of entrepreneurs with considerable capital and experience in large-scale enterprise; postwar deflation; loss by independent States of rights and privileges enjoyed as British colonies; spirit of localism, which threatened to oppose metropolitan system of business as well as strong central government.

B. Business conditions and developments, 1783–89: the price trend and the business cycle; the experience of different industries and interests; the growing strength of the new entrepreneurs.

4. The Movement for a New Government

Leading business men and large property owners and other prominent men urge the need of a stronger government; The Constitutional Convention—members, plans for strengthening government, and significant political ideas.

5. Provisions in the Constitution of Direct Importance to Business

Powers of Congress and limitations on its powers; limitations on the States; other provisions important to business; the first ten amendments.

6. The New Government in Operation

Early acts of the new Congress which establish confidence in the security of property and in the administration of business; growing strength of the government at home and abroad; the Supreme Court on the powers of the federal government.

7. Selected Bibliography

On business, 1783–90, the following works are suggested: R. A. East, *Business Enterprise in the American Revolutionary Era* (New York, 1938); A. H. Cole, *Wholesale Commodity Prices in the United States, 1700–1861* (Cambridge, 1938); S. E. Morison, *The Maritime History of Massachusetts, 1783–1860* (Boston, 1921); J. B. McMaster, *A History of the People of the United States from the Revolution to the Civil War*, vol. i (New York, 1890); Edward Channing, *A History of the United States*, vol. iv (New York, 1927); E. W. Spaulding, *New York in the Critical Period, 1783–1789* (New York, 1932); *The American Museum*, vols. i, ii, iv.

On the movement for a new government: A. C. McLaughlin, *The Confederation and the Constitution, 1783–1789* (New York, 1905); Allan Nevins, *The American States during and after the Revolution, 1775–1789* (New York, 1924); C. A. Beard, *An Economic Interpretation of the Constitution of the United States* (New York, 1935); Max Farrand, editor, *The Records of the Federal Convention of 1787*, vols. i–iii (New Haven, 1911); *The Federalist* (New York, 1863), especially essays number i and x; and the correspondence of prominent leaders.

On the new government in operation: the Constitution of the United States; Hamilton's reports on the public credit and the bank; the acts of the first Congress on the tariff, the bank, and the public debt; Jay's and Pinckney's treaties; and early decisions of the Supreme Court which strengthened the federal government; *Magazine of American History*, vol. **xxix** (1893), pp. 324–330; petitions in *American State Papers, Finance*, vol. i, pp. 5–10; J. S. Bassett, *The Federalist System, 1789–1801* (New York, 1906); E. S. Corwin, *John Marshall and the Constitution* (New Haven, 1919); C. A. Beard, *Economic Origins of Jeffersonian Democracy* (New York, 1915).

8. Suggested Questions

1. The following have been put into lists of foundation stones of American business by a group of students. Do you agree?

Protestantism	American Revolution
Market price	Laissez-faire policy
Slave trade	Loose business morals
Labor shortage	Smuggling
The corporation	

2. Comment: Englishmen ascribe part of their success to the absence of a constitution and Americans ascribe part of theirs to a constitution.
3. Comment: With our federal Constitution came prosperity, and without it prosperity would fade.
4. Why have socialists been particularly unfriendly to the Supreme Court?
5. Does the alleged conflict of human rights and property rights enter into the question of the foundation stones of American business?
6. Our banking system is perhaps the most distinctively American part of our business. Has it been a foundation stone of business?
7. Consider the question whether the long upward secular trend of business (lasting to 1815) began in 1787, 1788, or 1789.

INDUSTRIAL CAPITALISM

VIII. JOHN P. CUSHING AS AN INVESTOR, 1828–1862 [1]

1. General Statement

John Perkins Cushing played a part in both the mercantile and industrial systems of capitalism. He started on an office stool and rapidly became a merchant prince of the old order; then, wearying of wharf and market place, he washed his hands of business, bought an estate, and settled down to comfortable inactivity. But first he entrusted his wealth to William Sturgis, who invested it judiciously in securities of the companies that were just then being formed to run the banks, canals, railroads, and factories of the new era. And as a rentier Cushing was as fortunate as he had been when a sedentary merchant.

Cushing's career illustrates several important changes in American business in his time. His life neatly epitomizes the rise and decay of America's great commerce in the Far East and the transfer of capital from foreign trade to internal development. His career, moreover, illuminates the process of building that composite which we call American culture. For the later period it illustrates the separation of ownership and management, with the concomitant rise of an investor class, and is closely bound up with the early development of American investment management and investment banking.

[1] Except where specific references are given, the facts on Cushing's life have been taken from the T. H. Perkins Papers in the Massachusetts Historical Society, Cushing's Diary in the Boston Athenaeum, and the Cushing Papers and the Bryant & Sturgis Papers in Baker Library, Harvard University.

2. Important Dates in Cushing's Career

1787	Born near Boston.
1803	Went to Canton, China, as clerk.
1805	In charge of the Perkins business at Canton.
1806	Partner in Perkins & Co., Canton.
1807	Visited the United States.
1828	Perkins & Co. dissolved. Cushing returned to Boston.
1828–59	William Sturgis managed Cushing's investments.
1829	Cushing's property valued at $637,908.
1829–30	In Europe, buying goods for the China trade.
1830–31	Returned to Canton to close his business.
1831	Returned to Boston, married, and retired from business.
1859–62	Investments managed by J. M. Forbes.
1862	Died, leaving an estate worth $2,435,941.

3. Business Career of Cushing

Cushing entered business as a clerk in the countinghouse of his uncles, James and Thomas Handasyd Perkins. The Perkins firm, which had been engaged in trade between America and Europe and had entered the Northwest Coast and China trade almost at its beginning, in 1803 sent a resident agent to Canton. John Cushing, then 16 years old, accompanied this agent as clerk. The agent was forced to leave Canton because of illness in the fall of 1805, and young Cushing was left in charge of the business. His work proved so very satisfactory that in 1806 he was made resident manager and partner in Perkins & Co., a commission house established by the Perkinses to handle their rapidly growing Canton trade. Cushing headed Perkins & Co. in Canton for over twenty years; he is said to have become the most wealthy and the most highly respected foreign merchant in Canton,[2] and for a time he served as American consul there.[3] His success was in large measure the result of his infinite care in handling the details of the business. He seems to have stood well with the native merchants, notably with Houqua, a man remarkable for his wealth, culture, and high business ethics.

Except for a brief visit home in 1807, Cushing remained in China until 1828. We do not know exactly why he then left Canton, but a reasonable explanation would be that he had had enough of living in the foreign quarter. The Chinese officials forbade foreigners to bring their families to Canton and imposed other restrictions which made it impossible to establish homes there.[4] A reflection of Cushing's attitude toward life in the factories may be seen in his advice to young Thomas Forbes to remain in China no longer than was necessary for financial reasons. The immediate cause of Cushing's return to America was apparently the unsatisfactory state of his health, which made him seek a better climate.

Perkins & Co. was dissolved before Cushing left Canton, and young Thomas T. Forbes, a nephew of T. H. Perkins and a cousin of Cushing, was left to close the firm's affairs. After returning to Boston, Cushing arranged to withdraw $180,000 from Canton.[5] He instructed Forbes to invest $80,000 of this in such goods as the latter thought would pay, suggesting $12,600 in teas and the rest in silks and nankeens (cottons), to be consigned to Bryant, Sturgis & Co., of Boston, on Cushing's account; $100,000 was to be lent to Russell & Co., of Canton and Manila, from whom 8 per cent might be obtained, or to the merchant Houqua, if a good risk. The money left in the East should, however, be placed so that it could be withdrawn on three months' notice.

When Cushing returned to Boston he was 41 years old. Shortly after his return he estimated that his wealth totaled $637,908. What should he do with his time and capital? He might have continued in the China trade. This he considered. A reorganization was about to take place in the Perkins firm of Boston, and T. H. Perkins and his son-in-law, Samuel Cabot, asked Cushing to join them in forming a new partnership. Cushing was at first willing on condition that he was left free of all work, that the capital was strictly limited to $1,000,000 contributed equally by the three partners, and that the activities of the firm were confined to the China trade. He proposed that the Canton end of the business should be in the hands of a new house, with a working capital of $200,000 furnished by himself at 5 per cent a year; Forbes would manage this branch in return for a quarter share of its profits. The longer Cushing stayed in Boston, however, the less was he inclined to join the Perkins firm. He discovered that his views about business differed from those of Perkins and Cabot. Since Cushing felt that the latter was unpopular and the former too old to take his full share of responsibility, he believed that much of the responsibility would rest on himself. But he was tired of work and wanted to be free to go where

[2] Samuel Eliot Morison, *Maritime History of Massachusetts* (Boston, 1921), p. 66.

[3] H. B. Morse, *The Chronicles of the East India Company Trading to China, 1635–1834* (Oxford, 1926), vol. iii, p. 191.

[4] On this see *ibid.*, vol. iv, chap. lxxxviii; and K. S. Latourette, *The History of Early Relations between the United States and China, 1784–1844* (New Haven, 1917), pp. 24–26.

[5] The firm was a heavy creditor of the Cantonese merchant, Manhop, who had gone bankrupt, owing $1,900,000 (Morse, *op. cit.*, vol. iv, p. 173).

the climate best suited him. Moreover, he found that he had the strongest dislike of business as it was done in Boston, which he characterized as "totally different from what I have been accustomed to." He would not "for all the money in the universe" carry on business in Boston's way —he said that it would kill him in a month. In fact, he felt disgusted with everything pertaining to business. He, therefore, finally decided not to enter into any partnership.

Cushing planned, however, to continue in the China trade to a certain extent by taking occasional ventures with Perkins & Co. and his old friends, Bryant, Sturgis & Co. During 1829 he joined the two firms in sending to China three ships in which he took a quarter share. To Forbes, who was in charge of his interests in Canton, he wrote voluminous letters with instructions as to purchases.

4. Liquidating His Mercantile Interests

Shortly after his return to Boston, Cushing began the transfer of his capital from foreign trade to investments at home. He turned a considerable amount over to his friend, William Sturgis, of Bryant, Sturgis & Co., who had agreed to pay his bills and make investments for him. By January 9, 1829, Sturgis held $50,000 on Cushing's account; about a year later he held $150,000, which Cushing characterized as a "'nest egg' and apart from my business concerns."

In the summer of 1829 Cushing crossed to England with the immediate object of making purchases for the *Margaret Forbes* and the *Bashaw,* which were being sent to the East by himself, Perkins & Co., and Bryant, Sturgis & Co. These boats were loaded in England with iron, English cloths, and opium. While in England, Cushing made some interesting observations on the China trade. It would not do, he said, to ship silks or nankeens to the United States or Europe, since these could be "made cheaper in this country & France than in China to say nothing about the difference in duty." In the future teas would have to be looked to as a return cargo; when tea exports were not excessive and Canton prices moderate, there was a chance of profit.

In the autumn he sought a better climate on the Continent. It is unlikely that he would have stayed there long—he did not care a "pin" for Europe—but his stay was interrupted by the news of young Forbes' death at Macao near Canton. Cushing promptly boarded the *Bashaw* for China, giving various reasons for going. One was to manage the sale of the Canton-bound cargoes and look after his own and the Perkins firm's interests; moreover, he saw the possibility of making a "cool" $100,000 by an expedition to France and Holland, arranging with the Barings and the Hopes to send out two ships to carry back tea cargoes. To his friend Sturgis he confided his homesickness for Canton and the fact that he did not care much for "being amongst the good people of this hemisphere," among whom "I feel as much a stranger now as I did when I first reached home."

Before leaving London, Cushing made some disposition of his affairs. He asked Sturgis not only to look after the $150,000 already invested but in addition to manage all remittances on account of completed ventures and the liquidated Perkins firm. By this time he had $200,000 in the hands of Sturgis; he planned that the latter should receive $180,000 more from Canton in the ensuing six months and eventually handle the profits of the season's ventures and the remainder of Cushing's interest in the Perkins firm.

Cushing landed in Canton in August, 1830, and remained there until March, 1831. During his few months in Canton he succeeded in selling a portion of the European goods, though for much less than he had expected. He bought a considerable quantity of Chinese goods to be shipped to the United States on his own account. In addition he made arrangements for the purchase of tea cargoes to be sent to Europe and for the settling of other matters connected with his interests in the East.

Cushing found the Canton market unsatisfactory in 1830–31. There was too much competition in the trade, and too many ships were bringing British goods and opium. He believed that the export of British goods to Canton should be discontinued except for small amounts of certain things; he recommended that shipments be suspended altogether during the following year. A serious problem was the growing scarcity of specie, which the opium trade was draining out of China. In his letters he emphasized that the only goods worth taking from China to the West were teas—if they could be purchased at low prices. Nankeens superior to the Chinese product were made, he said, in Germany and France to sell at little more than half the price. No doubt, also, he foresaw that the certain discontinuance of the monopoly of the East India Co. in 1833 would flood the Canton market with other British traders. The cargoes he ordered for the *Bashaw* and the *Margaret Forbes,* costing $397,930, consisted almost exclusively of tea.

After Cushing's return to Boston in 1831 he was determined to retire from business. As has already been seen, he at first planned to employ a part of his capital in trade by engaging in ventures with Perkins and Cabot, Bryant & Sturgis, and with Houqua, the Hong merchant. He continued to do this, largely under his own direction, for a few years. Finding excellent opportunities for investing at home, however, he soon decided to withdraw his capital altogether and rid himself of all the risk and bother of trade. This took several years, for goods moved slowly in the oriental trade. The rate of liquidation of Cushing's mercantile capital is shown in Table 1.

Table 1. CUSHING'S CAPITAL, 1832–42

Year	Invested in foreign trade	Invested at home
1832	$454,500	$ 356,149
1833	266,210	670,658
1834	432,380	502,841
1835	267,501	682,828
1836	195,127	822,991
1837	124,283	946,452
1838	21,586	1,008,510
1839	6,800	1,067,429
1840	6,800	1,090,533
1841	6,800	1,113,960
1842	...	1,117,692

5. A Country Gentleman

In the summer of 1831 Cushing returned to Boston. Not long after his return he married "the very pretty and amiable Louisa Gardiner,"[6] a daughter of the rector of Trinity Church in Boston, and settled down to lead the life of a country gentleman. He quit "fagging," he said, to live.

His first step was to acquire a very beautiful estate, called Belmont, in Watertown. He had Chinese servants and filled his home with delicate eastern furnishings, until its atmosphere became one of oriental beauty and luxury. His wine cellar must have been superb, judging from the inventories of the wines which he carefully set down in a Miscellaneous Account Book. He collected a considerable library and had a standing order with London bookdealers for the latest books and the best periodical publications. A French manufacturer of rolls for a "self-performing organ" (music box) supplied him regularly with classical music and "popular works" like Mozart's. He imported a piano from Europe.

Following but improving upon the example of T. H. Perkins, Cushing made much of his gardens, which became known

[6] L. Vernon Briggs, *History and Genealogy of the Cabot Family, 1475–1927* (Boston, 1927), vol. i, p. 384.

far and wide.[7] He spent a fortune in importing flowers, shrubs, and fruit trees from China and Europe.[8] He also imported Chinese hogs, cattle—which gave little milk but were "beautiful animals," goats, fowl, geese, peacocks, and the best milk cows obtainable in England. He wrote to a friend, "I have become quite a farmer & find it affords me both occupation & amusement." As a matter of fact, he had become somewhat of a recluse, finding in his books and his estate satisfaction for the cultural interests and tastes which he had acquired in China.

6. The Management of Cushing's Investments

Through the thirty years following his retirement from active participation in business Cushing spent an average of almost $50,000 a year. Yet his fortune, which had been about $800,000 at the beginning of those years, had tripled by the end of his life.

Cushing himself actually did very little in the way of managing his capital. In 1832 he commissioned J. M. Forbes, of Canton, to send him from $50,000 to $100,000 of tea each season when prices were low, Forbes to charge commission or receive a fourth interest in profits without any charge for capital. At the same time Cushing suggested to Houqua that they take some joint ventures in tea. His letterbook, however, reveals few transactions with those Canton friends, and in 1840 he wrote to Canton that he was so nearly out of business that he did not know much about trade.

He might have managed his capital if he had continued to employ it in trade, but he knew nothing of investment opportunities at home. The situation was complicated by the mercurial state of American business, which was then rapidly undergoing fundamental changes, and by the fact that there were no specialized investment agencies to which Cushing could turn.

In this dilemma Cushing turned to his friend, William Sturgis.[9] Like Cushing, Sturgis was a foreign merchant. He had started in a Boston countinghouse at the age of 16 and had gone to sea at 18; by the time he was 30 he had been sea captain, Indian diplomat, and trader in the Northwest Coast-China trade. In 1810 he had settled in Boston as an importing and wholesaling merchant, soon joining in the partnership of Bryant & Sturgis, which became one of America's outstanding mercantile firms. For about a decade this firm had put most of its profits into the expansion of its trade; like Perkins & Co., however, it was in the 1820's investing at home, a very considerable portion of its profits going into banks, insurance companies, and manufacturing concerns.

Bryant & Sturgis continued in the China trade till the late 'thirties, confining their imports mainly to teas. The Opium War between England and China, 1840–42, put a stop to this activity, and in 1841 Bryant, Sturgis & Co. was dissolved. Bryant and Sturgis withdrew altogether from trade but formed a new partnership principally for the investment of their own capital.[10]

William Sturgis had come to be looked upon as one of Boston's soundest capi-

[7] A. J. Downing, *A Treatise on the Theory and Practice of Landscape Gardening Adapted to North America* (New York, 1857), pp. 55–56; Justin Winsor, editor, *Memorial History of Boston* (Boston, 1881), vol. iv, p. 633.

[8] Careful record was kept of these in his Diary, where they were listed by name and number when acquired.

[9] The source of the information about Sturgis and Bryant & Sturgis is the Bryant & Sturgis Papers, consisting of letterbooks and account books, in Baker Library, Harvard University.

[10] No definite statement to this effect has been found, but they did business as Bryant & Sturgis, and after the death of William Sturgis in 1863 the holdings of Bryant & Sturgis were equally divided between John Bryant and the estate of William Sturgis (Bryant & Sturgis Account Book, 1857–66).

talists. He was a man of considerable wealth, wide acquaintance with domestic investments, and conservative business principles. From his early years as a Boston merchant we find such statements as this in his letters: "We do not hold goods on speculation for a rise, but believe in a quick turnover with low profits; we do not trade in the East on credit." He gave advice to railroads in the 1840's: "You ask our opinion as to the expediency of reducing dividends, to conform to diminished receipts. Upon this subject *we have not the shadow of a doubt*. Our rule of action for ourselves, & our advice to others, always is, to *earn* money before dividing it, & to let corporations *get out of debt, & keep out of debt,* so far as the nature of their business will permit." Another bit of advice to a railroad is interesting: "It is often said (and sometimes truly) that the increase of business upon Rail Roads is sufficient to justify an increase of capital to absorb these additional earnings, but it is much better policy to invest the surplus earnings in improvements on the road without resorting to increase of capital for this purpose, and when the increase becomes too great (an event not likely to happen very often) let the rates of transportation be reduced, and thus most effectually stave off competition."[11]

Bryant & Sturgis now became in a very real sense a private investment house, and as such they illustrate one of the main sources of our modern investment business, a very large proportion of which had its origin in mercantile business. Except for the partnership, however, the only persons for whom they acted were Cushing and a few relatives. They invested in loans to railroads and individuals (many in the West), in stocks and to a smaller extent bonds, in insurance companies, in banks of New York and Boston, in eastern railroads, and in New England manufacturing concerns. It is well to note that until the Civil War there were only small amounts of United States securities on the market. The purchases of Bryant & Sturgis were made directly or through brokers, in New York mainly through the private banking firm of Prime, Ward & King.

By far the largest outside account handled by Sturgis was that of Cushing, whose investments he managed until in 1859, charging a commission of 2.5 per cent on annual income. Cushing, indeed, seems to have avoided money like the plague; Bryant & Sturgis paid his private debts, sent off his subscriptions to charities, managed his investments, and reinvested income as it accumulated. From the records of these transactions it is possible for us to watch the workings of what was practically an early investment trust, and also to see how Cushing's financial stature was greatly increased despite his lavish spending.

Unfortunately the records of Cushing's fortune are complete only for the period 1836–51, although certain figures are available for the other years. Most of the information given below is therefore concerned with the shorter period.

Some of the accounting procedure in the Cushing ledgers is not in accordance with modern methods; for instance, canal shares were treated as manufacturing securities instead of being classed with railroads. Accordingly it was thought advisable to make a number of minor adjustments and to prepare a new set of accounts. An attempt has been made to exclude all property from which no revenue was derived, such as Cushing's private residence at Watertown, and to show only those types of assets which a modern investment business would own. Similarly, personal outlays have been separated from the investment expenses and charged to a private drawing account. Owing to the lack of information, it was inevitable that there should be a certain amount of guesswork in this division.

Table 2 gives the amounts placed in

[11] Quotations are from the Bryant & Sturgis Letterbook, Dec. 28, 1842, and Feb. 10, 1849.

Table 2. CUSHING'S INVESTMENTS IN THE UNITED STATES, 1835–51 [a]

Year	Cash balances	Notes and personal loans	Bonds		Stocks				Real estate	Total
			Govern-ment	Rail-road	Insur-ance	Bank	Manufac-turing	Railroad & canal		
1835	$318,876	$167,636	...	...	$36,990	$ 41,003	$149,204	$ 33,712	$ 37,734	$ 785,158
1836	182,125	193,636	...	...	65,202	115,452	181,654	47,309	90,913	876,295
1837	181,139	251,636	...	...	79,744	139,152	216,404	50,309	90,913	1,009,299
1838	192,515	256,431	...	...	89,958	139,152	233,417	54,854	90,913	1,053,243
1839	169,298	268,217	...	...	85,958	81,979	242,467	127,866	90,913	1,066,702
1840	167,909	209,283	...	...	89,558	139,711	244,467	152,184	90,913	1,094,030
1841	76,298	303,353	...	...	77,284	139,711	266,467	193,941	90,913	1,147,970
1842	96,149	303,353	$ 4,720	...	69,034	139,711	271,467	205,254	90,913	1,180,604
1843	9,258	284,377	24,953	...	51,034	143,751	280,267	232,897	91,638	1,118,180
1844	13,243	342,902	24,953	...	39,116	138,701	284,567	238,638	82,647	1,164,771
1845	6,538	341,220	44,953	...	36,616	149,701	340,970	239,435	82,647	1,242,084
1846	9,876	335,273	44,953	...	35,146	149,701	367,470	278,107	82,647	1,303,177
1847	5,738	301,500	44,953	...	46,905	149,701	397,720	321,593	82,647	1,350,760
1848	4,691	319,500	23,240	...	49,009	149,701	417,720	350,339	82,647	1,396,850
1849	10,094	320,000	24,920	$42,450	49,009	149,701	443,544	324,789	82,647	1,456,157
1850	3,778	390,750	24,920	25,000	58,608	149,701	443,544	363,074	82,647	1,542,025
1851	8,372	306,550	44,920	30,684	58,608	149,701	427,169	392,023	156,899	1,574,930

[a] The figures are taken from annual balances for Dec. 31 compiled under the direction of Mr. William Baxter from the original Cushing account ledger of Bryant & Sturgis. The stock and real-estate values are given at cost.

various types of investments throughout the period studied.

From the same accounts have also been drawn the following statements which show the condition of Cushing's investments and the income from them in 1844 and in 1851, that is, at the middle and at the end of the period studied.

BALANCE SHEET, December 31, 1844

Assets

	Fixed interest investments	Fluctuating income investments	Total
Notes and Personal Loans			
Amounts Due by Bryant, Sturgis & Co.	$ 13,243.72		
Notes	342,902.26		
	$356,145.98		$ 356,145.98
Securities			
Bank		$138,701.86	
Manufacturing		284,567.79	
Railroad and Canal		238,638.05	
Insurance		39,116.68	
Government	$ 24,953.71		
	$ 24,953.71	$701,024.38	725,978.09
Real Estate		$ 82,647.50	82,647.50
	$381,099.69	$783,671.88	$1,164,771.57

Liabilities

Capital			
Balance as in 1835			$ 938,654.58
Profits			
Net Gains and Losses from Assets Sold:			
As of Dec. 31, 1843		$-11,163.23	
Gains, 1844		3,417.66	
		$ -7,745.57	
Net Gains from Shipping and Trade, as of Dec. 31, 1837 [a]		65,680.38	
Interest and Dividends, as of Dec. 31, 1843	$546,521.22		
Additions during Year 1844	91,885.49	638,406.71	
		$696,341.52	
Less Private Drawings, as of Dec. 31, 1843	$421,512.66		
Additions during Year	48,711.87	470,224.53	226,116.99
			$1,164,771.57

[a] Certain shipping ventures were still being wound up in 1836 and 1837, and this figure represents the profits on these transactions. Since the information is incomplete, too great a reliance cannot be placed on this result.

PROFIT AND LOSS STATEMENT, 1844

	Fixed interest investments	Fluctuating income investments	Total
Income			
Notes	$14,325.66		$14,325.66
Securities			
Bank		$ 8,140.50	
Manufacturing		43,085.59	
Railroad and Canal		17,707.50	
Insurance		5,980.00	
Government	$ 1,440.00		
	$ 1,440.00	$74,913.59	76,353.59
Real Estate		$ 3,665.16	3,665.16
Total Income	$15,765.66	$78,578.75	$94,344.41
Expenses: Commissions and Miscellaneous			2,458.92
Net Income			$91,885.49

BALANCE SHEET, December 31, 1851

ASSETS

	Fixed interest investments	Fluctuating income investments	Total
Notes and Personal Loans			
Amounts Due by Bryant, Sturgis & Co.	$ 8,372.81		
Notes	326,550.00		
	$ 334,922.81		$ 334,922.81
Securities			
Bank		$ 149,701.86	
Manufacturing		427,169.63	
Railroad and Canal	$ 30,684.92	392,023.17	
Insurance		58,608.42	
Government	24,920.00		
	$ 55,604.92	$1,027,503.08	1,083,108.00
Real Estate		$ 156,899.53	156,899.53
	$ 390,527.73	$1,184,402.61	$1,574,930.34

LIABILITIES

Capital			
Balance as in 1835			$ 938,654.58
Profits			
Net Gains and Losses from Assets Sold:			
As of Dec. 31, 1850		$ – 6,003.68	
Gains, 1851		–24,375.00 [a]	
		$ –30,378.68	
Net Gains from Shipping as of Dec. 31, 1837		65,680.38	
Interest and Dividends as of Dec. 31, 1850	$1,263,241.80		
Additions during Year 1851	97,515.80	1,360,757.60	
		$1,396,059.30	
Less Private Drawings, as of Dec. 31, 1850	$ 719,547.78		
Additions during Year	40,235.76	759,783.54	636,275.76
			$1,574,930.34

[a] This includes depreciation written off:

150 shares of Eastern Exchange Hotel Co.	$10,000
12 shares of Chickopee Mfg. Co.	2,875
38 shares of Lowell Mfg. Co.	11,500

PROFIT AND LOSS STATEMENT, 1851

	Fixed interest investments	Fluctuating income investments	Total
Income			
Notes	$21,454.25		$ 21,454.25
Securities			
Bank		$11,847.00	
Manufacturing		15,336.75	
Railroad and Canal	$ 1,820.00	32,364.08	
Insurance		8,020.00	
Government	[a]		
	$ 1,820.00	$67,567.83	69,387.83
Real Estate		$ 9,210.80	9,210.80
Total Income	$23,274.25	$76,778.63	$100,052.88
Expenses: Commissions and Miscellaneous			2,537.08
Net Income			$ 97,515.80

[a] Arrears paid in 1852.

The figure for the value of the investments in the foregoing statements shows their book value, that is, cost less a certain amount of depreciation written off and noted in the 1851 balance sheet. A more nearly correct view is obtained when current market values, so far as they are ascertainable, are substituted. Table 3 shows the figures for 1851 and for 1858 (for the latter year Bryant & Sturgis' own figures are quoted). In considering the depreciation in 1858, it should be remembered that there was a severe panic in 1857, which reduced the value of all the investments.

Table 3. BOOK AND MARKET VALUES[a] OF CUSHING'S INVESTMENTS

	1851			1858		
	Book value	Market value[b]	Depreciation[c]	Book value	Market value[d] (Oct. '58)	Depreciation[c]
Fixed interest investments						
Notes	$ 326,550.00	$ 326,550.00	...	$ 526,000.00	$ 526,000.00	...
Bonds						
Railroad	30,684.92	30,684.92	...	237,597.93	219,935.00	$ 17,662.93
Government	24,920.00	24,920.00	...	28,378.00	21,000.00	7,378.00
Total fixed interest	$ 382,154.92	$ 382,154.92	...	$ 791,975.93	$ 766,935.00	$ 25,040.93
Fluctuating income securities						
Bank	$ 149,701.86	$ 156,344.00	$-6,642.14	$ 210,751.62	$ 215,694.00	$ -4,942.38
Manufacturing	427,169.63	349,820.17	77,349.46	389,835.63	260,230.00	129,605.63
Railroad	392,023.17	389,608.43[e]	2,414.74	559,205.45	446,954.00	112,251.45
Insurance	58,608.42	62,262.92	-3,654.50	58,608.42	64,200.00	-5,591.58
Total fluctuating	$1,027,503.08	$ 958,035.52	$69,467.56	$1,218,401.12	$ 987,078.00	$231,323.12
Grand total	$1,409,658.00	$1,340,190.44	$69,467.56	$2,010,377.05	$1,754,013.00	$256,364.05

[a] Where the latter is not ascertainable, the book value has been substituted.

[b] These are the averages between the high and low quotations for the year, as shown in Martin's *History of the Boston Stock and Money Markets* (Boston, 1898).

[c] Minus sign indicates appreciation.

[d] Bryant & Sturgis' own estimates.

[e] Very few quotations available.

Cushing's investments seem to have been distributed in line with certain general principles: (1) investment in concerns with which Sturgis was personally acquainted; (2) investment with a view to getting earnings rather than speculative profits; and (3) wide diversification.

One striking characteristic of the investments was that they were largely limited to Boston and its immediate hinterland. Loans on notes to individuals or companies were almost exclusively local. A few loans were made to individuals out West, but those borrowers were apparently natives of Boston. Real-estate investments were also local. Securities were, however, slightly more scattered. The first investment made outside New England was the purchase of 200 shares of the Atlantic Insurance Co. of New York in 1832. These and shares of another New York insurance company were sold before the middle 'forties. From time to time a total of 700 shares of the second Bank of the United States was purchased, but these were sold in 1839. In that year were bought 700 shares in the Bank of Commerce, of New York, an institution of more than local importance. The year 1839 also saw the first purchase of railroad stock outside New England. Shortly thereafter an interest was acquired in several short roads in the Mohawk Valley; in 1845, shares in one New Jersey and two Ohio railroads; in 1846, in several Pennsylvania coal roads; in 1851, in the Philadelphia, Wilmington & Baltimore; in 1853, the Michigan Central; and late in the 1850's, in the Chicago, Burlington & Quincy. The only non-New England government bonds purchased were New Orleans city bonds acquired in 1845 and federal loans of the Civil War.

The investments outside New England constituted a very small proportion of the total. Emphasis on New England came in some measure from the fact that the investment market in the United States was, certainly until the 'fifties, largely local. Sturgis could and did purchase securities through New York brokers, but he apparently chose to deal principally with individuals or firms personally known to him or in whose development he had taken a part. Also, since New England was then one of the chief investment fields in the United States, it was hardly necessary to go outside that section of the country.

The second striking characteristic of Cushing's investments is the almost complete indifference they show to speculation. The three outstanding fields of speculation in the United States in those decades are noticeable because of their absence: canals, western State and municipal bonds, and western lands.[12] Indeed, investments in the West were avoided almost entirely. There is, moreover, no evidence of buying and selling securities for the purpose of taking speculative profits. Cushing's investments at his death were, with few exceptions, the sum total of purchases made from year to year. The exceptions, on some of which considerable losses were taken, were apparently sold because they were not worth holding. The most striking illustration is the stock of the second Bank of the United States, which was acquired between 1833 and 1837. This was purchased presumably on Nicholas Biddle's successful record as a commercial banker and before he had come to stand as a sponsor of questionable internal improvements and as a manipulator of the English cotton market. It is to the credit of Sturgis that he sold these shares at $71,435, which meant a loss of but $11,607, only a short time before their market value collapsed.

Cushing's investments were, therefore, apparently made with a view to securing income from earnings. Stocks and bonds were purchased in concerns which were meeting a developed need—railroads in unquestioned paths of commerce, industrials of good promise, and banks and in-

[12] Two local canal projects and the New Orleans bonds were the only exceptions, and they stand on their merits.

surance companies on a sound earnings basis. In connection with the securities held by Cushing at the time of his death it is interesting to note that 4 of the 6 banks are still existing, as are also about 20 of the 26 New England manufacturing concerns, and almost all the railroads.

The third characteristic of these investments was extensive diversification. This is indicated by Table 2, p. 125.

Real estate was relatively unimportant in Cushing's investments; it consisted principally of his home estate. A large part of the capital was always in cash balances and loans to individuals and companies on notes. These loans were generally made to run for several years, not infrequently as many as seven. Judging by the names of the borrowers, these funds may have gone extensively into mercantile enterprises. A considerable amount also went to manufacturing concerns, particularly in the later years. The relatively small amount of bonds simply reflects the fact that such borrowing by corporations was not at the time well developed. Federal loans were available only in small amounts when available at all except during the Civil War.

Within each group there was also considerable distribution. In 1835, the loans to 9 individuals averaged $22,905; shares in 3 banks, $13,668; in 6 insurance companies, $5,248; and in 10 manufacturing concerns, $10,636. In 1859, the last year entered in Cushing's summary account books, loans to 33 individuals and companies averaged $16,242; bonds of 11 concerns, mostly railroads, averaged $24,179; shares of 6 banks, $35,125; of 8 insurance companies, $7,326; of 16 manufacturing concerns, $24,364; and 16 railroads, $34,950.

The final test of an investment lies in the income which it brings and in its long-run value. Among the Cushing Papers is

Table 4. PERCENTAGE YIELDS FROM THE VARIOUS CLASSES OF CUSHING'S INVESTMENTS

	Fixed interest investments				Fluctuating income investments						
	Notes and personal loans	Bonds			Stocks						
Year		Government	Railroad	Total	Bank	Mfg.	Rail and canal	Insurance	Real estate	Total	Grand total
1836	5.5	...	...	5.5	4.1	10.9	15.1	15.2	3.0	9.3	7.3
1837	5.3	...	...	5.3	6.3	4.4	1.3	9.8	5.1	5.6	5.4
1838	4.8	...	...	4.8	6.5	9.2	4.5	8.5	6.3	7.6	6.4
1839	5.3	...	...	5.3	8.4	10.9	4.5	7.1	5.5	8.2	7.0
1840	6.3	...	...	6.3	5.1	4.6	6.9	9.4	7.1	6.1	6.2
1841	7.0	...	...	7.0	6.7	8.7	8.3	14.2	5.2	8.4	8.0
1842	4.7	...	...	4.7	6.2	3.0	8.7	19.5	5.9	7.0	6.2
1843	5.2	9.7	...	5.4	5.9	6.9	7.7	16.5	6.5	7.6	6.9
1844	4.4	5.8	...	4.5	5.7	15.2	7.5	13.3	4.2	9.9	8.3
1845	6.4	5.4	5.1	6.3	6.0	16.2	10.2	14.5	6.6	11.6	9.8
1846	5.3	6.8	6.1	5.5	6.5	11.9	10.8	6.1	6.7	9.9	8.4
1847	5.8	3.2	5.2	5.4	6.8	7.5	8.9	9.5	6.6	7.8	7.1
1848	5.7	14.8	5.5	6.4	7.4	4.7	10.4	9.6	6.4	7.2	7.0
1849	5.9	7.8	6.8	6.0	7.9	6.3	8.2	9.1	6.3	7.2	6.9
1850	5.6	3.5	6.9	5.5	7.8	5.8	15.0	17.6	6.0	9.7	8.5
1851	6.0	0.0[a]	6.5	5.6	7.9	3.5	8.6	13.6	7.7	6.7	6.4
Average	5.6	6.3	6.0	5.6	6.6	8.1	8.5	12.1	5.9	8.1	7.2

[a] Since the arrears for 1851 were repaid in 1852, the average should be higher.

an account book in Cushing's own hand which contains what is apparently a copy of Bryant & Sturgis' annual statement of his investments and income, together with calculations made therefrom. These record the average income from the property for the years 1833–58 as 7.282 per cent. This was, of course, in addition to the estate and personal property, which brought no money returns. A more realistic picture is gained from a statement of the annual yield of the different types of assets as given in Table 4 on the preceding page.

It may be of interest to show also the percentage yields of the different classes of securities. The figures in Table 4 were obtained by finding the relation of income to capital for each class of investment. Owing to the fact that during many of the years the holdings were increased, an artificial figure (the average of the book values at the beginning and end of the year) has been used as the cost of the capital invested. The results cannot, therefore, be regarded as absolutely accurate, but they will serve to show the general trends.

The inventory of Cushing's estate (Table 5) filed with his will shows that, as stated above, his wealth had tripled during the period of his retirement.

7. Readings

For general background read Clive Day, *A History of Commerce* (New York, 1922), pp. 498–527.

K. W. Porter, *John Jacob Astor: Business Man* (Cambridge, 1931), especially pp. 589–685 and 852–1024, is recommended for comparison with Cushing's experience. Further information on the China trade may be found in K. S. Latourette, *The History of Early Relations between the United States and China* (New Haven, 1917), and in Samuel Eliot Morison, *Maritime History of Massachusetts* (Boston, 1921).

8. Suggested Questions

1. Explain the transition in business (mercantile to industrial capitalism) exemplified in this case.
2. What were the various possibilities which Cushing might have followed in investing his capital after returning from China?

Table 5. INVENTORY OF CUSHING'S ESTATE AS OF JULY 26, 1862

	Fixed interest investments	Fluctuating income investments	Total
Notes and Personal Loans	$ 669,213.32		$ 669,213.32
Securities			
Bank		$ 204,260.00	
Manufacturing		305,210.00	
Railroad and Canal	$ 343,785.00	423,831.00	
Insurance		67,520.00	
Government	109,522.00		
	$ 453,307.00	$1,000,821.00	$1,454,128.00
Real Estate		176,600.00	176,600.00
	$1,122,520.32	$1,177,421.00	$2,299,941.32
Private Estates, etc., valued at		$109,000.00	
Furniture, etc.		27,000.00	136,000.00
Grand Total			$2,435,941.32

3. Can you justify his withdrawal from foreign trade?
4. What was the relation between Cushing's investment policy on the one hand and the federal Constitution and the Hamiltonian program on the other?
5. Criticize the investment policy followed as to rate of gain, turnover, spread of investments, and so on.
6. What changes do you see in Cushing's investment policy? How do you explain the change in the fixed interest investments?
7. In what ways would a modern investment policy differ from that followed in investing for Cushing?
8. Were Bryant and Sturgis investment bankers?

IX. RISE AND DECLINE OF THE AMERICAN MERCHANT MARINE (AN OUTLINE)

1. Introduction

From the very first, shipbuilding and shipping were two of the chief occupations of the British colonies in North America. Both were established in New England by 1640, and during the next two centuries they throve all along the Atlantic shore from Maine to the Carolinas.

Although the Dutch held most of the carrying trade of the world during the first half of the seventeenth century, the British thereafter succeeded in capturing supremacy at sea. The British regulations restricted American shipping in certain directions, but the net effect was undoubtedly to promote shipping and shipbuilding by Americans.

Favored by natural resources and the native genius of their shipwrights, colonial New England and New York built large numbers of ships for sale abroad as well as for the use of American owners. The possession of cheap and efficient ships, together with the development here of foreign trade, privateering, and the fishing and whaling industries, enabled colonial shipping to advance rapidly during the pre-Revolutionary period. On the eve of the Revolution more people in Maine and New Hampshire were engaged in shipping and shipbuilding than in agriculture, and Massachusetts is said to have had one seagoing vessel for every 100 inhabitants.[1]

Since the ratification of the Constitution of the United States, this nation has played an increasingly important part in the commerce of the world. From the beginning the federal Congress attempted to foster commerce and encourage shipping in American vessels. About 1790 began a phenomenal growth in American shipping which continued to the Civil War with only minor setbacks.

At the end of the Civil War the tonnage engaged in foreign trade was little over half of the previous peak. From this level it did not recover until the World War, although the foreign trade of the United States grew almost constantly year by year. It is well to seek the causes which contributed to this decline and inquire whether any concerted effort was made to prevent it. Further, it may be asked whether the decline was inevitable or whether something could have been done to counteract it.

2. Important Dates

1789	Navigation Acts passed to protect American shipping.
1793–1815	Wars in Europe.
1807	Jefferson secured an embargo on American shipping which lasted two years. The *Clermont,* the first successful American steamboat, appeared on the Hudson.
1812–14	War between England and the United States.
1815	First American legislation urging reciprocity of trade on all nations.

[1] Hans Keiler, *American Shipping, Its History and Economic Conditions* (Jena, Germany, 1913), pp. 1–25.

1818 First line of sailing packets (American) began operating between New York and Liverpool.

1819 First Atlantic crossing in a vessel using steam for part of the voyage.

1821 First iron steamship built in England.

1828 Last of the Reciprocity Acts passed by Congress.

1833 First Atlantic crossing in a vessel using steam for the entire voyage.

1838 First line of steam packets (British) began operating on the Atlantic.

1839 A mail subsidy granted to Cunard for an Atlantic steam-packet service.

1843 First iron-screw steamer appeared in the Atlantic service.

1845 First clipper ship, the *Rainbow,* launched at New York.

1846 England took the first step towards the repeal of her Corn Laws.

1847 Congress granted the first American subsidy for a service from New York to Bremen via England and from New York to Havre. Collins was granted a subsidy for a service between New York and Liverpool.

1849 The California gold rush began. The British Navigation Acts repealed.

1851 France began to grant mail subsidies.

1852 The Australian gold rush began.

1858 Congress allowed all subsidy contracts to lapse.

1861–65 The Civil War and the dissipation of our merchant marine.

1864 Subsidies revived in America.

1872 A drawback of duties allowed on certain goods imported for building wooden sailing ships.

1875–77 Subsidies again became unpopular and were allowed to lapse.

1881 France instituted general bounties on shipbuilding and shipping.

1885 Italy adopted general bounties on shipbuilding and shipping.

1886 Germany began to grant mail subsidies.

1890 Japan began to grant mail subsidies. United States freed all shipbuilding materials from import duties.

1891 Mail subsidies resumed by the United States. Loans to shipowners at low rates first instituted by Austria.

1912 Seaworthy foreign-built ships not more than five years old and owned by citizens of the United States admitted to American registry for foreign trade.

1914 The age limitation of 1912 and other restrictions on the admission of foreign-built ships to American registry removed.

1936 United States abandoned mail subsidies in favor of direct subsidies for the construction and operation of ships.

3. The Development of American Shipping, 1789–1840

The effect of the Revolution; the policy of the new federal government; effect of the Napoleonic Wars; American success in the intense competition of 1815–40.[2]

4. British Shipping, 1789–1840

British law favors British ships; the rise of rival shipping in 1793–1815; difficulties of British shipping, 1815–40.

5. Strong Competition with Great Britain, 1840–58

Iron and steam begin to change shipping; mail subsidies help develop steamship lines; Britain's liberal commercial policy and the Crimean War aid Ameri-

[2] See case XXII, pp. 348–359, below.

can shipping; the clipper ship brings brilliant success to America.

6. The Decline of the American Merchant Marine after 1858

Dissipation of merchant marine during Civil War; sectional division brings weak subsidy policy and adverse taxation in the United States while aid to shipping spreads in Europe; America lags in improving shipbuilding; high cost of building and operating ships hampers American shipping; comparative advantage in other fields works against American shipping; the World War furthers American shipping; retrogression after the War.

7. Bibliography

There is no single book that gives a satisfactory history of American shipping. Most of the published material is concerned with technical aspects of ship construction and subsidy policies. Almost nothing is available on costs of building and operation. The following list is representative of books on the subject: Robert Greenhalgh Albion, *Square-Riggers on Schedule* (Princeton, 1938); Arthur H. Clark, *The Clipper Ship Era* (New York, 1910); John Codman, *A Letter . . . on the Navigation Interest* (Boston, 1869); John Codman, *Review of the Report of the Special Committee on the Navigation Interest* (Washington, 1870); Henry Hall, *American Navigation* (New York, 1880); E. R. Johnson, G. B. Huebner, and A. K. Henry, *Transportation by Water* (New York, 1935); Hans Keiler, *American Shipping, Its History and Economic Conditions* (Jena, Germany, 1913); J. D. J. Kelley, *The Question of Ships* (New York, 1884); A. W. Kirkaldy, *British Shipping, Its History, Organisation, and Importance* (London, 1914); S. E. Morison, *The Maritime History of Massachusetts, 1783–1860* (Boston, 1921); John R. Spears, *The Story of the American Merchant Marine* (New York, 1910); David A. Wells, *Our Merchant Marine* (New York, 1882).

A great deal of material on American shipping can be found in various government reports and investigations. The reports of the Commissioner of Navigation and of the Bureau of Navigation in the Department of Commerce give much important material—for a continuous series of shipping statistics see *Merchant Marine Statistics,* 1935, published by the Department of Commerce. Another useful work published by the Department of Commerce in 1916, and in a revised edition in 1925, is G. M. Jones, *Government Aid to Merchant Shipping.* Government investigations and hearings, mostly concerned with the question of subsidy, are invaluable, though their controversial nature must be kept in mind. Most valuable is the *Lynch Report,* that is, the report of a select committee of the House, 41st Congress, 2d Sess., 1869–70, on the "Causes of the Reduction of American Tonnage and the Decline of Navigation Interests."

8. Suggested Questions

1. What were the principal factors in the prosperity of the American merchant marine before 1856?
2. Discuss in detail the bearing of British experience on the history of the American merchant marine during the period from about 1820 to about 1890.
3. What has been the policy of the federal government with regard to American shipping since 1789? Has it helped or hindered the development of a strong merchant marine?
4. What are the chief elements which account for the changed position of American shipping after 1856? In the light of your own analysis criticize the conclusions of the Congressional investigations.
5. What has been the effect of specialization on the fortunes of the American merchant marine?
6. What emphasis do you put on the downward secular trend of business, 1866–97, as a factor in the history of the merchant marine?
7. Does the experience of the American merchant marine contain any special lessons for business today?

BUSINESS MEN AND THEIR ASSOCIATIONS AND COMBINATIONS

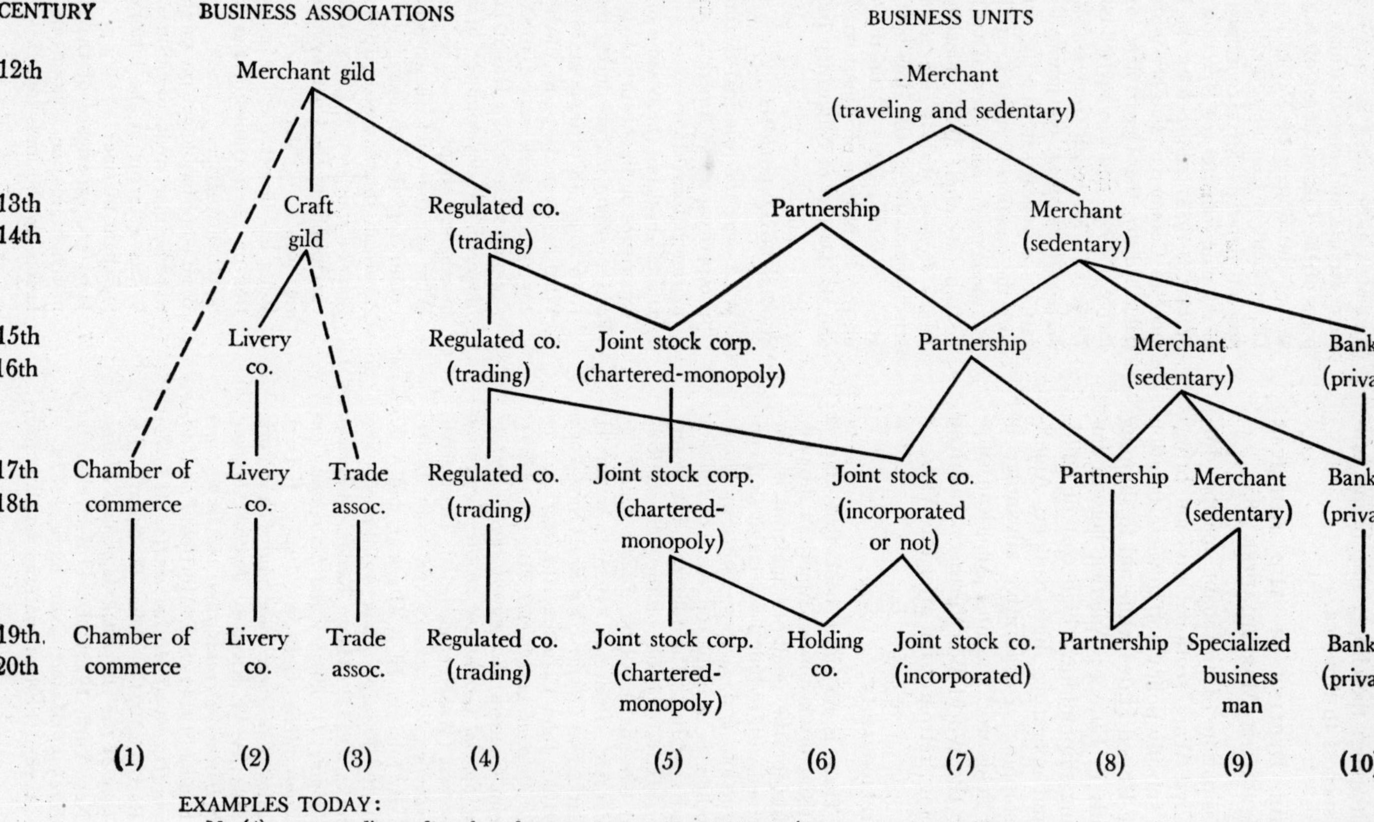

EXAMPLES TODAY:

No. (4) – commodity and stock exchanges, Corporation of Lloyd's (insurance underwriters).
No. (5) – Hudson's Bay Co., public utilities.

X. HISTORY OF LLOYD'S, AN ASSOCIATION OF UNDERWRITERS (AN OUTLINE)

1. General Statement

Probably no other commercial organization of today reveals within itself such sharp contrasts of mediaeval and modern business methods and ideals as are exhibited in the history of Lloyd's. Lloyd's is sixteenth-century England in basic concept, but it is also as new as tomorrow in adjustment to current requirements. Here is individualism enthroned—but regulated. The development of this institution parallels the rise of England in world trade; it is a development peculiarly and inevitably British in character and is deep-rooted in English customs, commerce, and politics.

It is no great exaggeration to say that the history of Lloyd's is the history of modern marine insurance in England. Through about 250 years it records the slow, uncertain awakening of the underwriters to group consciousness and the transition of underwriting from an activity intermittently attended to by early merchants and others to the highly specialized, full-time employment of experts which it is today. Other insurance enterprises have risen, and most of them have fallen; but Lloyd's has continued to grow.

2. Important Dates

1397 The modern form of a marine policy already fixed in Italian commerce.

1547 English underwriting marine risks.

1574 Office of Assurances established in London.

1601 Court of Assurances set up in London, by Act of Parliament. Of little effect, and abolished in 1688.

1689 Edward Lloyd conducting a coffee house in London which was a popular meeting place for those interested in shipping.

1695 Lloyd began publication of his *News,* containing shipping information. Later issued in penned form.

1700 Marine risks underwritten by various business men but a tendency toward specialization was evident.

1720 Monopoly of underwriting of marine risks granted to the Royal Exchange Assurance Corporation, the London Assurance Corporation, and to the private underwriters. The last-named tended more and more to congregate at Lloyd's.

1734 *Lloyd's List* supplanted the *News;* it also carried financial information.

1760 First group action of underwriters at Lloyd's in the formation of the Society to publish a *Register of Shipping.*

1769 The exodus of a group of (79) underwriters from "old Lloyd's to the new Lloyd's" gave further evidence of group consciousness among Lloyd's underwriters.

1774 Move into Royal Exchange marked the beginning of present-day Lloyd's. This, the third positive group action, led to the adoption of the first regulations.

1779 Joint action of private underwriters at Lloyd's to formulate a standard policy form, thereafter to be printed.

1810 Attempt to break the monopoly led to insurance investigation. Lloyd's had 1,400 members.

1824 Monopoly ended; many new corporations underwrote marine risks. Lloyd's did not admit partnerships or corporations.

1856	Specialized salvaging association formed.
1858	Beginning of guarantee fund through deposits by members.
1866	New member posted securities as protection for his insureds; this action became the basis for a policy of vast significance to Lloyd's.
1870	Lloyd's incorporated. The underwriting element was dominant.
1900	Lloyd's underwriters had begun to accept other than marine risks.
1918	Signing Bureau set up.
1927	A magnificent new building completed for Lloyd's.
1935	All normal insurance risks, excepting only life, underwritten at Lloyd's.

3. Marine Insurance in Early England

Italian origin of English marine insurance; the Office of Assurances; London business turned to the coffee houses in the seventeenth century; Edward Lloyd's Coffee House.

4. Growth of Marine Insurance at Lloyd's, 1700–69

Insurance monopoly in 1720 aided Lloyd's underwriters; *Lloyd's List; the Register of Shipping.*

5. Steps which Led to Formal Association of Underwriters, 1769–79

The exodus, 1769, and the establishment of a definite group; the printed policy, 1779.

6. Development under the Pressure of Wars, 1779–1811

Membership at Lloyd's and insurance practices, 1779–93; war problems, specialization, and the development of a group spirit, 1793–1811.

7. Creating the Modern Lloyd's, 1811–70

Instituting the system of Lloyd's agents; termination of the coffee house as a private enterprise, 1823; further challenging of the supremacy of Lloyd's; changes in the information services at Lloyd's; further changes in membership at Lloyd's; the Salvage Association; deposits and guarantees; Lloyd's incorporates.

8. Present-day Lloyd's

Character of the membership at Lloyd's; the Signing Bureau; Lloyd's as the universal insurer; the strength of Lloyd's; estimate and conclusion.

9. Bibliography

Charles Wright and C. Ernest Fayle, *A History of Lloyd's* (London, 1928). This book is the work of authors who had available all the records and documents possessed by Lloyd's. One of the authors is a member of Lloyd's. Examination of other sources has made abundantly clear that this history has gathered and fairly interpreted the major facts relating to Lloyd's. Much of the material dealing with the last century is nowhere else available to the general reader. The book is profusely illustrated, well documented, and well indexed.

Henry M. Grey, *Lloyd's: Yesterday and Today* (London, 1926). This is a shorter history of Lloyd's. It is more journalistic in treatment and approach.

Lucy Stuart Sutherland, *A London Merchant, 1695–1774* (London, 1933). This book is valuable in connection with this case chiefly because it has a chapter on a merchant's experience with marine underwriting at Lloyd's during the period of the monopoly. The merchant is shown to have shifted gradually in his business activities from foreign trade to pure risk-bearing.

Violet Barbour, "Marine Risks and Insurance in the Seventeenth Century," *Journal of Economic and Business History,* vol. i (1928–29).

Solomon S. Huebner, *Marine Insurance*

(New York, 1920). For those interested in the principles of marine insurance as practised in America today.

William D. Winter, *Marine Insurance, Its Principles and Practice* (New York, 1929). Another modern text. This is the work of a practising insurance executive. It contains the fullest description of policy terms and their legal significance.

Parliamentary Papers, 1810. *Reports from Committees of Commons,* vol. ii. This contains the evidence taken by the Select Committee and its report, which is a mine of information anent Lloyd's and marine insurance practices of the day.

10. SUGGESTED QUESTIONS

1. Account for the fact that Lloyd's was able to maintain more or less of a monopoly in marine insurance in the eighteenth but not in the nineteenth century.
2. Why was there no collective effort toward building up guarantee funds until the 1850's?
3. Why have we not had in the United States the development of a marine insurance association similar to Lloyd's?
4. Examine the organization and policies of some of the various so-called American Lloyds (see *Best's Insurance Reports,* 1938, pp. 729–737).
5. Comment: The experience of Lloyd's may offer some valuable lessons to commercial groups now suffering from slackness both in ideals and in competitive conditions.
6. What business organizations in America resemble Lloyd's in structure and service?

XI. THOMAS WILLING & COMPANY: A STUDY OF EARLY MARINE UNDERWRITERS IN PHILADELPHIA

1. GENERAL STATEMENT

In the seventeenth century merchants were constantly menaced by the risks incidental to the shipping of goods by sea. Ships were not seaworthy, and a large percentage of them vanished as victims of the elements; nations were frequently at war with one another; and privateers, sailing with letters of marque or reprisal, harried commerce. The percentage of loss was large, and many a man faced insolvency owing to unavoidable losses at sea.

In Europe, and especially in London, marine insurance was so highly developed by the latter part of the seventeenth century that insurance on most voyages could be obtained at a price. In London a definite insurance exchange had been established where brokers and underwriters met daily to write insurance on maritime ventures. In the Americas it was somewhat different: the risks to the merchant existed to an even greater degree, but the local facilities for insurance were undeveloped. Merchants wrote to their correspondents in London to obtain coverage on various voyages but had to write in advance, and by the time the ship sailed conditions might have changed so materially that the insurance was invalidated. Thus, a colonial merchant never knew positively that his ventures actually were insured. A variety of such factors caused local marine insurance to spring up in the ports along the Atlantic seaboard, especially in Philadelphia.

2. IMPORTANT DATES IN THE DEVELOPMENT OF UNDERWRITING

1682	Marine underwriting was highly developed in London.
1702–13	Colonial merchants experienced difficulty in obtaining insurance.
1721	John Copson established insurance office in Philadelphia.
1725	Francis Rawle, of Philadelphia, suggested establishing local insurance company.
1749	Joseph Saunders established insurance office.
1757	Thomas Willing & Co. began business.

1762	Protective association of underwriters established. Kidd and Bradford began to underwrite.
1776	Insurance upset by war.
1781	Insurance returned to normal.
1783	The *Philadelphia Prices Current,* an underwriters' magazine, established.
1784	A group of professional underwriters, with a permanent capital, were operating in America.

3. The Background of Colonial Insurance

A writer on insurance in 1682 said concerning insurance in London: [1]

"The *Policies* now-a-days are so large that almost all these curious Questions that former Ages, and the Civilians according to the Law Marine, nay and the Common Lawyers too, have controverted are now out of debate; scarce any misfortune that can happen, or provision to be made, but the same is taken care for in the Policies that are now used; for they ensure against Heaven and Earth, stress of Weather, Storms, Enemies, Pirates, Rovers, &c.; or whatsoever detriment shall happen or come to the thing ensured &c. is provided for."

The following advice concerning insurance was published in London in 1693: [2]

"So soon as you hear of a certain that a Loss is happened, you must inquire at the Office for the Insurers (if you know them not) and acquaint them of the Loss, and how you come to know it, and desire them to inform themselves of the Truth of it if they please, and are not satisfied with your report. When they are satisfied there is a real Loss, there is generally an abatement of 10 *per Cent.* for prompt payment; for if they are punctual Men, and value their Reputations, they will presently pay you; if not they will shuffle you off, and endeavor to find out flaws, and raise Scruples for a larger abatement than ordinary; and sometimes will keep you a Year or two out of your Mony, and many times never pay; but generally get, in case of Loss 15 or 20 *per Cent.* abated, I have known 40 *per Cent.* abated, upon very small Pretensions; which makes a common Proverb about such Insurers, *What is it worth to Insure the Assurers?* Be careful therefore to deal with Honest Men; that value their Reputation when you have any thing to be Insured."

The quotations above give some insight into the stage of development of insurance in London toward the end of the seventeenth century. The problems of the colonies in availing themselves of London's insurance facilities are suggested in the quotations which follow.

From Philadelphia in May, 1704, James Logan wrote in a letter to William Penn in London: [3]

"I have lately wrote four several ways [four copies by as many ships] to John Askew to insure £300 on thy account on John Guy from Carolina, some of which must needs come to hand. Isaac Norris has done the same, as William Trent also to his correspondent T. Coutts. I know not what to say of that vessel: when that voyage was projected, nothing could promise better, there being a great probability of making our money sterling, but instead of that nothing could have happened worse . . . there is not any probability of any convoy again from these parts this year, and it was upon this we wrote for insurance, as before; but now we much fear whether it will be possible to persuade the master to sail, or to get men to go home, and that, instead of sailing directly from Virginia, according to our orders, which there wait him, he will come in hither."

The following was written to Logan by Penn, from London under date of "16*th* 11*th-mo.*, 1704–5": [4]

[1] Quoted from *De Jure Maritimo et Navali* (London, 1688), bk. 2, chap. vii, sec. vii, by J. A. Fowler, *History of Insurance in Philadelphia for Two Centuries, 1683–1882* (Philadelphia, 1888), p. 3.

[2] Quotation by Fowler, *op. cit.*, p. 7, from W. Leybourn's *Panarithmologia* (London, 1693), appendix xxxviii.

[3] Quotation from *Correspondence between William Penn and James Logan,* printed for the Historical Society of Pennsylvania, 1870, vol. i, p. 301.

[4] *Ibid.*, pp. 352–353.

"The Barbadoes fleet, coming home so late, met both with storms of wind and guns, the French falling in among them; so that of 120 sail, not above 80 and odd got in, where out of 40 odd hogsheads of sugar, I have lost 30, and Edward Singleton carried into France. They freighted upon five vessels, one burnt, which Edward came out in, had 10 hogsheads, and two were taken that had 10 hogsheads each . . . as for Guy, no news yet. . . . J. Askew ensured £100 upon thy letter, but the ensurer broke, and the 20 guineas [war premium upon risk of £100] lost. This done upon the former intimations. Ensurers fail much."

On January 3, 1706, Logan wrote to Penn, in the postscript to a letter written the preceding day: [5]

"I wrote thee in my former letter to get insured upon the ship *Diligence,* Barth Penrose, master, burthen about 150 tons, the value of £500 or £600 sterling. She is to be sent from hence to Virginia, there to load, and thence to England, with convoy directly for London, if any offers; if not, then north about Scotland, and accordingly she ought to be insured from hence to Virginia and thence as aforesaid. But money comes in so very slow that I shall be hard put to it to make good my intentions. However, I shall strain to my utmost. I beseech thee not to be scrupulous in insuring, for if I have any right notion of the matter, 'tis as just and lawful as any other part of trade."

The difficulty of obtaining London insurance on colonial ventures caused a constant desire on the part of colonial merchants to develop local marine underwriting.

4. The Early Underwriters and Brokers in America

Francis Rawle—writing on the subject, *Ways and Means for the Inhabitants of Delaware to Become Rich*—in 1725 made the following remarks on insurance, which show that insurance in America was relatively unknown but not altogether untried at the time.[6]

"Having this far discours'd of most of the Branches of Trade we are capable of, there is yet one great Encouragement . . . namely an *Insurance-Office* in one or more of these Colonies; which is the interesting of divers in the Loss or Profit of a Voyage, and is now become so much the Practice of England, that Insurance may be had in divers Cases as well against the Hazards at Land, as Casualties at Sea, which must be acknowledged not only to be safe, but a great Encouragement to Adventure; for it may so happen that a Person may sometimes adventure his ALL, and then in case of a Loss he may be rendered uncapable of a future Trade, to the Disadvantage of the Publick, and (it may be) to the Ruin of himself; whereas could he get a part of his Interest either of Ship or Cargo insured, (tho' in Case of safe Arrival he parts with a part of his Profit, yet) in Case of Loss, he is secur'd of such part as he insureth, which may be a sufficient Bottom to begin a new Adventure: How far this may conduce to the Trade of this River is obvious to any Man of Thought. Now whereas there has been some Attempts made at *Philadelphia,* which dropt and prov'd abortive, (for what Reasons we never could learn) we humbly propose to the Legislature that an Office be erected and supported by a Fund arising out of the Interest of the Loan-Office. This will be a good and safe Bottom, and cannot be easily overset by a few losses; and we conceive will contribute to keep up the Value of our Paper-Credit by promoting of Trade, Navigation and Building of Ships, and in Consequence, of great Advantage to this River: which we refer to the Consideration of the Merchant."

In the *American Weekly Mercury,* printed and sold by Andrew Bradford, there appeared, as of May 25, 1721, the following notice: [7]

"Assurances from Losses happening at Sea, &c., being found to be very much for the Ease and Benefit of the Merchants and Traders in general; and whereas the Merchants of this

[5] *Ibid.,* vol. ii, p. 197.

[6] Francis Rawle, *Ways and Means for the Inhabitants of Delaware to Become Rich* (Philadelphia, 1725), pp. 62–63.

[7] Fowler, *op. cit.,* p. 11.

City of Philadelphia and other Parts have been obliged to send to London for such Assurance, which has not only been tedious and troublesome, but even very precarious. For remedying of which, An Office of Publick Insurance on Vessels, Goods and Merchandizes, will, on Monday next, be Opened, and Books kept by John Copson, of this city, at his House in the High Street, where all Persons willing to be Insured may apply: And Care shall be taken by the said J. Copson That the Assurers or Under Writers be Persons of Undoubted Worth and Reputation, and of considerable Interest in this City and Province."

This was evidently the first attempt to open an insurance brokerage office in Philadelphia. The exact arrangement between the merchants, broker, and underwriters at that time has never been known.

There is some reason to believe that before this time shippers had banded together and mutually agreed to share losses on certain voyages, but no definite records of this type of transaction are extant. However that may be, by 1721 there was a definite attempt to form an insurance brokerage office in Philadelphia. Just how successful this attempt was we have no method of knowing.

By 1749 Joseph Saunders, a general merchant dealing in all types of commodities on Reese Meredith's wharf, was operating a brokerage office for marine insurance. It was in this office that John Smith, who later was concerned with the founding of the Philadelphia Contributionship, had his ships insured and where he was actively engaged as an underwriter by 1750. The method of arranging for insurance was simple. The shipper having a venture to be insured went to the broker, where a policy was made out and the rate of premium determined. The policy was left with the broker, and various capitalists came in and signed the policy, each noting after his name the percentage of the full amount for which he would be responsible. When the full amount had been subscribed, one copy of the policy was given to the insured and one copy was kept by the broker. In case of the safe arrival of the ship the premium money was divided among the underwriters. In case of loss the broker was forced to collect the various amounts from the underwriters and turn them over to the shipper. By 1752 we find the following notice concerning Joseph Saunders appearing in the *Pennsylvania Journal:* [8]

"Notice is hereby given, That the INSURANCE OFFICE for Shipping and Houses is kept by Joseph Saunders at his House, where Israel Pemberton, sen., lately lived, near the Queen's Head in Water-street."

This is a combination advertisement for the Philadelphia Contributionship which had just been organized and for the marine insurance brokerage business of Joseph Saunders. It is to be noted that the early members of the Contributionship were mainly underwriters from the office of Joseph Saunders. Saunders advertised again on October 23, 1760: [9]

"JOSEPH SAUNDERS is removed from his late Dwelling, near Chestnut-street Wharff, higher up Chestnut-street, between Front and Second-streets, and next Door, but one, to John Reily's, where he continues to sell sundry Sort of Goods, and Keeps an Insurance office for Shipping, as usual, and hopes his Friends who have been pleased to employ him in that Way will still continue their Favours."

Other brokers were also appearing. In 1752 Thomas Wharton opened an insurance office in Philadelphia, but evidently little came of it. In 1756 Walter Shee published the following: [10]

"NOTICE is hereby given, that Walter Shee, in Front Street, at the corner of Chestnut-street, in Philadelphia, hath opened an office for the insurance of ships and merchandize. All persons who want to have insurance made, may apply at said office, where all risks will be underwrote."

[8] *Pennsylvania Journal,* June 25, 1752.
[9] *Pennsylvania Gazette,* Oct. 23, 1760.
[10] *Ibid.,* Sept. 23, 1756.

These cases point out the loosely organized character of early colonial underwriting. It is pertinent to remember that for every broker there had to be a large number of underwriters.

By 1759 out-of-town competition was being felt in Philadelphia. On September 13, the following notice was published: [11]

"The New York *Insurance Office* is opened at the House of the Widow Smith, adjoining the Merchant's Coffee House; where all Risks are underwrote at moderate Premiums. Constant attendance will be given from the Hours of Eleven to One in the Forenoon, and from Six to Eight in the Evening, by Anthony Van Dam, Clerk of the Office."

It must not be thought that early developments in marine underwriting were confined to Philadelphia. Boston and New York were prominent cities at the same period. All shipping which connected these ports with Europe, especially England, made shippers acquainted with the marine insurance practice of the old country.

The following policy, dated Boston, 1746, is without doubt typical of policies written in the colonial cities, policies apparently being taken over, at first unchanged, from foreign insurers.[12]

"676 5063

"In the Name of God, Amen, *Thos. Fayerweather* as well in his own Name, as for and in the Name and Names of all and every other Person or Persons to whom the same doth, may or shall appertain, in part or in all doth make Assurance, and causeth himself and them, and every of them, to be insured, lost or not lost, 300/100 the Sum of Three hundred / One hundred more Pounds old Tenor *from Maryland to Surranam upon any kind of goods, also upon the Body, Tackle, Apparell &c of and in the good Sloop called the Ranger* whereof is Master under God, for this present voyage, *James Tucker* or whosoever else shall go for Master in the said Vessel, or by whatsoever other Name or Names the same Vessel, or the Master thereof is or shall be named or called; beginning the Adventure upon *the said Vessel & Goods from this Vessel sailing from Maryland & so shall continue & endure during the voyage afores & until said Sloop be arrived as afores and there moored at anchor Twenty four hours in good Safety.*

"And it shall be lawful for the Vessel, &c. in this Voyage, in Cases of Extremity and Distress, to proceed and sail to, and touch and stay at any Ports or Places whatsoever without Prejudice to this Insurance: Touching the Adventures and Perils which we the Assurers are contented to bear, and do take upon us in the Voyage; they are of the Seas, Men of War, Fire, Enemies, Pirates, Rovers, Thieves, Jettizons, Letters of Mark and Counter-Mark, Suprizals, Takings at Sea, Arrests, Restraints and Detainments of all Kings, Princes and People, of what Nation, Condition or Quality soever; Barratry of the Master and Mariners, and of all other Perils, Losses and Misfortunes that have, or shall come to the Hurt, Detriment, or Damage of the said *Vessel & Goods* or any Part thereof. And in Case of any Loss or Misfortune, it shall be lawful to the Assureds, their Factors, Servants, and Assigns, to sue, labour, and travel for, in and about the Defence, Safeguard, and Recovery of said *Vessel & Goods* or any Part thereof, without Prejudice to this Insurance; to the Charges whereof we the Assurers will contribute each one according to the Rate and Quantity of his Sum herein assured. And that in Case of an Average-Loss not exceeding five pounds per Cent. the Assurers by Agreement with the Assured are not to pay or allow any Thing towards such Loss. And in Case of any Loss the Money to be paid in thirty Days after Proof of the same. And it is agreed by us the Insurers, that this Writing or Policy of Assurance shall be of as much Force and Effect as the surest Writing or Policy of Assurance heretofore made in Lombard-Street, or in the Royal Exchange, or elsewhere in London. And so we the Assurers are contented and do hereby promise and bind ourselves, each one for his own Part, our Heirs, Executors, and Goods, to the Assureds, their Executors, Administrators, and Assigns, for the true Performance of the Premises, confessing ourselves paid the Consideration due unto us for this Assurance by the Assureds at

[11] *Ibid.*, Sept. 13, 1759.

[12] Ms. in the keeping of the Insurance Library Association of Boston.

and after the Rate of *Seventeen* Pounds per Cent. And in Case any Dispute arising hereupon, the Matter in Controversy shall be submitted to and decided by Referrees chosen by each party.

"In Witness whereof, We the Assurers have subscribed our Names and Sums Assured in Boston in New England.

Ye 13 Day of March, 1746.

£ 100 *I Joshua Cheever am Content for One hundred Pound.*

100 *Joseph Dowse in behalf of John Gooch One hundred Pound.*

£ 100 *J. J. A. Boutmeau for One hundred Pound.*

£ 100 *Joseph Dowse for One hundred Pound.*

Insurance Office kept in King Street
Near the Long Wharffe by
Joseph Dowse."

Thus this early period was marked by the development of underwriting and of independent underwriters and insurance brokers. The brokers were general merchants, commission agents, or tavern-keepers. At first the underwriters shifted from one broker to another and underwrote any risk that suited their fancy. Usually the premiums received were not distributed immediately but were held until the ship had made the voyage in safety. The brokers adjusted the losses between the underwriters and the insured. Thus when an underwriter had several policies with one broker he soon had an open account. When a number of policies were underwritten, premiums tended to offset losses. Underwriters followed the practice of building up a reserve of cash with the broker, which was usually accomplished by allowing the premiums to accumulate. The cash reserve bound the underwriter more or less firmly to the broker and was a step toward the accumulation of capital permanently engaged in the insurance business. The formation of small groups of underwriters who consistently worked together through a broker paved the way toward the next development.

5. The First Temporary Insurance Association

After a group of underwriters had done business together for some time and had developed a more or less permanent capital for use in the insurance business, it was but a logical step for them to form temporary associations to underwrite as a unit. The first of these was Thomas Willing & Co. Thomas Willing, the promoter of this organization, came from a family which had for some time been prominent in the commercial life of Philadelphia. In 1726 Charles and Thomas Willing, two wealthy Englishmen, had established a mercantile house in the city. They engaged in shipping, in merchandising, and to some extent in private banking. Thomas, the son of Charles Willing, and Robert Morris entered business life as clerks in the organization. In 1754 they organized the firm of Willing, Morris & Co., which successively became Willing, Morris & Inglis and Willing, Morris & Swanwick. The articles of partnership of Thomas Willing & Co. follow: [13]

"Articles of Agreement indented made and concluded the eighth Day of October in the Year of our Lord one thousand seven hundred and fifty seven Between Thomas Willing, Attwood Shute, Charles Stedman Alexander Stedman, John Kidd and William Coxe all of the City of Philadelphia Merchants.

"Whereas the Insurance of Vessels and Merchandize has proved a great Encouragement to Trade, and that by Companies is most secure to the Insured Therefore to establish a Company for insuring Ships Vessels Goods and Merchandize on reasonable Terms We the above named Thomas Willing Attwood Shute Charles Stedman Alexander Stedman John Kidd and William Coxe have and each of us hath mutually and reciprocally for himself his Heirs Executors and Administrators covenanted and agreed and by these presents do and each of us doth covenant and agree to and with the other and with the Executors

[13] William Bradford Papers, Historical Society of Pennsylvania, Philadelphia, vol. ii, pp. 101 ff.

and Administrators of the other in the following Manner that is to say.

"First That we and each and every of us our and each and every of our Heirs Executors and Administrators Shall and will punctually and bone fide pay one full equal sixth part of all Losses Total and Partial which may happen or arise to or upon all such Vessels and Merchandize as shall be underwrote or insured by us or any of us in the Name and Stile of Thomas Willing and Company according to the Terms true Intent and Meaning of every Pollicy underwrote by us or any of us under that Name and Stile.

"2 That we the said Thomas Willing and Company shall not nor will for any Premium whatsoever underwrite more than six hundred pounds lawful Money of Pennsylvania nor less than fifty pounds of like Money upon any one Bottom or Risque whatsoever

"3 That we nor any one or more of this Company shall not nor will underwrite any policy of policy of [sic] Insurance whatsoever in his or their own Name or Names respectively but that the Name and Stile of Thomas Willing and Company shall be solely made use of in all policies underwrote by us or any of us for the Account Risque Benefit and Behoof of all the said parties to these presents equally.

"4 That there shall be a Sett of Books provided by and at the Expense of us the said Thomas Willing and Company parties hereto wherein all and every of the premiums or other Consideration received or to be received for underwriting policies of assurance conformable to these present Articles shall be fairly and regularly entered and kept and Accounts thereof as well as of all payments made for Total or Average Losses and all other Charges and Expenses attending the effectual prosecution of these presents.

"5 That the said Thomas Willing shall be Cashier of the said Company and shall have the Care and Custody of the Books and Effects belonging to the said Company which Books shall be kept in the Counting House of the said Thomas Willing in Front Street.

"6 That in the Books of the said Company a regular and just entry shall be made of the Names of each Vessel insured and of every Thing material in the respective policies likewise of the Vessel and Vessels Names on board of which the Merchandize insured or to be insured by this Company shall be.

"7 That each and every of us the said parties to these presents shall and may at all Times have free access and Inspection of all or any of the Books in which the Accounts and other Entries relating to this Company shall be kept as aforesaid.

"8 That the Accounts of the said Thomas Willing and Company relating to or consequent of these presents and of all Gain and Loss issuing thereupon shall be regularly fairly and punctually settled and adjusted the Stock divided and Ballance paid at the expiration of every three Months the first Settlement to be made the Seventh Day of January next and so on from quarter to quarter during the Continuance of the present Agreement.

"9 That these Articles shall continue in Force for and during the Space of one Year next ensuing the Date thereof.

"10 Provided nevertheless that in case of the Decease of any of us the said parties these Articles shall cease and be of no effect immediately on such Decease respecting any further Insurance to be made.

"11 That the Executors or Administrators of any of us the said parties to these presents who may first happen to dye shall be entitled to a full and equal sixth Part and Share of the neat Gain and Profit that may have accrued to the said Company by underwriting.

"12 And therefore such Executors or Administrators shall be lyable to pay sustain and make good a full and equal sixth part of all Losses sustained by the said Company by underwriting and shall remain subject to a like sixth Part or Proportion of all Risques which shall be out and underwrote by the said Company before the Decease of the said party.

"13 Lastly for the true performance of all and singular the Covenants Articles and Agreements aforesaid each and every of the said Parties to these presents doth hereby bind and oblige himself his Heirs Executors and Administrators unto the other five of the same parties and to their Executors and Administrators in the penal Sum of two thousand pounds lawful money of Pennsylvania to be forfeited and paid by the party failing in the Observance hereof to the party or parties performing the same. In witness whereof we the said Thomas Willing, Attwood Shute,

Charles Stedman, Alexander Stedman, John Kidd and William Coxe have hereunto sett our Hands and Seals the aforesaid eighth Day of October 1757.

"Thomas Willing L. S.
Attwood Shute L. S.
Charles Stedman " "
Alex. Stedman " "
John Kidd " "
Will. Coxe " "

"Sealed and delivered in the presence of
Wm. Bradford
D. Conduit"

This first temporary insurance association was composed of a number of underwriters who were accustomed to underwrite as a group through the insurance broker, William Bradford, at his tavern, the London Coffee House for Merchants and Traders. Bradford by this time was becoming very influential in the affairs of Philadelphia. He engaged in a lengthy dispute with the Society of Friends over the question of the morality of armed protection of their homes and ships. He believed that men had a right to defend their property from aggression. In this belief he was upheld by John Smith. In 1754 he established his Coffee House, which at once became the center of a group of merchants and underwriters. Subsequently Bradford became an insurance broker and an underwriter in his own right.

It is to be noted that when the year (in which Thomas Willing & Co. had been organized) expired, there was an immediate reorganization with but one change: Attwood Shute withdrew and Robert Morris took his place.[14] Thus Morris advanced from ownership of a fractional part of a share to a full partnership.

6. Protective Associations of Underwriters

By 1762 a variety of disagreements had arisen between the brokers and underwriters. The latter then organized a protective association to draw up a body of rules by which all were to abide. We reproduce them here: [15]

"At a Meeting of the underwriters on the 12th of February 1762 whose names are below the following Rules were agreed to. That the Several Brokers in whose Offices they shall hereafter Subscribe Policies shall be Accountable for all the premiums arising from such Subscriptions being allowed thereon by us the underwriters a commission of one & a quarter pc. for standing the Risques of such Premiums, collecting & paying the Same in the following manner.

"That such Brokers shall settle each underwriters Account every three months & pay the Ballance due thereon exclusive of all Premiums arising from Policys which have not been Subscribed above one Month, & in the Intermediate time between such settlements shall pay all losses due from us out of the Premiums on Policys which have been underwrote more than one month, or so far as such Subscriptions extend.

"That the three following Clauses shall be inserted in each Policy they may Subscribe after the first day of March next.

"That the Broker shall be allowed half p cent. by the assured on all Losses that shall happen on Policies underwrote after that date.

"That the underwriters shall pay but 98 p Cent. for any losses that may happen on such Subscriptions.

"On all Salt, Wheat, Indian Corn, Malt, Peas, & dried Fish stowd in Bulk & Tobacco in Casks, no loss shall be paid on Policys Subscribed after the said first day of March covering an Interest on those Articles so stowd unless it be a general Average or the Vessel stranded in either of which Cases they will pay as on other goods.

"Henry Harrison	Child & Stiles
Peter Reeve	Thos. & Wm. Lightfoot
Amos Strettle	
Conyngham & Nesbitt	Abram Judah
Scott & McMichael	James & Drinker
Samuel Purviance	Samuel Oldman
John Wilcocks	John Mifflin
Willing Morris & Co.	Reed & Pettit
Samuel Mifflin	Acquila Jones"

According to this agreement we may infer that it was customary to pay the

[14] *Ibid.*, p. 101.

[15] *Ibid.*, p. 104.

broker only 1.25 per cent of all premiums collected plus .5 per cent of all claims paid. This is in striking contrast to the remuneration exacted by the English brokers, who took 5 per cent of all premiums collected and abated 10 per cent to 16 per cent of all claims paid. Another plan of payment of the English broker was 5 per cent of all premiums collected plus 10 per cent of all underwriting balances in his hands after a certain period of operating. Whether this substituted for the above plan or was an additional exaction is not clear from the sources examined. But it is not unlikely that the English broker got 5 per cent of all premiums plus 10 per cent to 16 per cent of all claims paid plus 10 per cent of balances as indicated (that is 10 per cent of profits). Perhaps this greater income of the English broker may be ascribed to the greater dominance of his position in the business compared to that of the American broker. He was a man who secured risks for the underwriters to insure, collected premiums and held them in his own name, subsequently offering the risks for underwriting to private underwriters and companies. But in the colonies, as we have seen before, the broker was mainly merchant, agent, or tavern-keeper (stage leading to specialized brokerage) at this time and did little more than provide a table and books for recording. He held funds, if at all, more as a trustee, so to speak, for the underwriters than as a possession which involved him in any obligations to individuals. Finally we may believe that, at about the time that the broker in this country was to emerge as a significant party in the marine insurance business, he was robbed of any further development by the sudden emergence of partnership and later by corporate organizations among the underwriters. That he probably joined, or even took the lead, in this practice we have already suggested. But it may easily be inferred that this group possession of the "Fund" had the effect of pushing the broker back into a position of subservience. He remains there today in this country, however much he may be an expert adviser of insureds and business-getter for underwriting firms.

The disagreements between underwriting elements were not solved by the agreement quoted above. By 1766 unrestricted competition among insurance underwriters had driven insurance premiums down so low in a period of peace that the underwriters attempted to reach an agreement concerning the rates to be charged. The agreement follows: [16]

"Phila May 6, 1766

"The Subscribers hereunto being convinced by sad experience that the premiums of ensurance have of late been Inadequate to the Risques underwrote in this City and fearing that the Consequence of there continuing so will be an entire loss of so necessary & useful a branch of Business as most of the present underwriters are determined to decline the pursuit of it, unless some regulation of the premiums are made and generally agreed to. Wherefore We do each of us promise to and agree with each other.

"That we will not subscribe our names to any Policy or Policies of Assurance at any less premium or rate than are Specified in the list annexed hereunto signed by the Brokers–

"Secondly That we will not Cover or Assure any Vessel, Freight, Goods, Wares or Merchandize in any other Manner than by subscribing Policies of Assurance–

"Thirdly That we will not employ or cause any Person to be employed to Subscribe Policies for our account and risque at any premiums less than mentioned in the annexed List.

"Fourthly That If any Policies of Assurance are offered us on such Voyages as are not specified in this List every Person shall be at Liberty to use his own Judgment in fixing the Premium on such Risques.

"Fifthly That If any Persons now in the Practice of underwriting in this City, do refuse to sign and agree to these articles we will not subscribe any Policy of Assurance to cover any Ship, Freight, or Goods the Property of such refusing Underwriters other Pol-

[16] *Ibid.*, pp. 105 ff.

icy, which the Refusing Underwriter may have signed.

"Sixthly If any Person or Persons becoming Underwriters while this agreement is in Force and refuse to sign the same the foregoing Article shall be binding on us with respect to such Person or Persons.

"Seventhly The Premiums now fixed to stand without Alteration until the last day of June next and on the first day of July a meeting of the Subscribers to be Called to make such alterations therein as the Season will then Require.

"Eighthly The Premiums fixed the first of July to stand until the last day of October and on the first day of November a new list of premiums from that time until this Contract expires to be fixed at a meeting of the Subscribers then to be called and a Majority of those who do meet on the day appointed to determine in case of dispute.

"Ninthly That we will Subscribe no Policies but what comes from an Office Keeper–

"Lastly We do unanimously agree that the Several foregoing Articles shall be binding on us for one year from the date hereof when we hope it will be found that the Trading Interest and our own have been mutually benefited by this contract."

This attempt to regulate prices and competition evidently did not succeed; while most of the underwriters of Philadelphia signed the agreement, they scratched out their signatures and withdrew from the association.

Again comparison with English experience of the same period is of interest, for English underwriters and brokers were becoming class conscious and were about to take formal steps toward self-regulation. This, even then, was but tardy recognition of the already powerful influence of group sentiment in the matter of underwriting practices as exercised over recalcitrant fellow-frequenters of the Coffee House on Lombard Street.

7. War Upsets Insurance

During the Revolution the insurance business was thoroughly upset. Some underwriters, such as William Bradford, entered the army, but a greater number became privateersmen. The control of the port of Philadelphia by the enemy drove ships away, and with them went the business of underwriting.

With the return of peace Philadelphia developed a constantly growing ocean commerce, and insurance increased in proportion. The older generation of brokers and underwriters returned and with them came many newcomers. By 1783 brokers and underwriters had become so numerous and so important that Captain John Macpherson, a former privateersman, commenced publishing a semimonthly paper known as the *Philadelphia Prices Current*, which devoted itself mainly to insurance news. The publication of this periodical acted as a stabilizing influence on insurance rates in Philadelphia. Insurance practice, modeled after that of Lloyd's in London but somewhat changed by precedent and experience, had become fixed. Insurance underwriters, while numerous, were becoming closely banded together under different brokers through the custom of doing business together and the use of open accounts. A more or less permanent capital had been accumulated by the brokers through the policy of not allowing the underwriters to withdraw premiums until all the voyages should have been successfully terminated and all accounts paid. Everything was now prepared for the next development, the coming of the permanent joint-stock insurance companies as previously indicated.

8. Suggested Readings

John A. Fowler, *History of Insurance in Philadelphia for Two Centuries, 1683–1882* (Philadelphia, 1888). Rich in specific contracts, names of insurance people, quotations from sales booklets, and rates—in other words, a source book.

T. H. Montgomery, *A History of the Insurance Company of North America of Philadelphia* (Philadelphia, 1885). A statement about an American company, and one of the good company histories.

Charles Wright and Charles Ernest Fayle,

A History of Lloyd's (London, 1928). An excellent and interesting account of the founding and growth of the Lloyd's underwriters. It is at the same time our best history of marine insurance.

Lester W. Zartman and William H. Price, *Yale Readings in Insurance: Property Insurance* (New Haven, 1914).

S. S. Huebner, *Marine Insurance* (New York, 1920).

William D. Winter, *Marine Insurance: Its Principles and Practice* (New York, 1929). An outstanding text on marine insurance: comprehensive in plan, detailed in execution, and effective in presentation.

9. Suggested Questions

1. What part did the desire for profits play in the minds of early insurance underwriters?
2. What factors tended to force underwriters to form temporary associations?
3. Why did the attempt to organize the Philadelphia underwriters fail?
4. Is any type of business still conducted on the same plan as early insurance?
5. Compare the Lloyd's associations and the reciprocal insurance associations in America today with Thomas Willing & Co.

XII. THE PHILADELPHIA CONTRIBUTIONSHIP FOR THE INSURANCE OF HOUSES FROM LOSS BY FIRE, 1752–1938 [1]

1. History of Fire Insurance

Fire has undoubtedly been recognized from earliest times as a great destroyer as well as a great benefactor. Community life, we may believe, has generally compelled the formulation of plans of action for fire prevention, fire fighting, and even for replacement of losses caused by fire. History provides us, however, with no record of fire insurance, as practised today, antedating 1667. The reasons which underlie this postponement disclose something of the nature of fire insurance as well as something of its history.

When the communes of Assyria, 2,500 years ago, followed a plan for replacing losses of the individual resulting from accidental fires by assessing all members of the commune, they employed a method which is not unlike state insurance. If under such a plan each individual could claim protection as a right, enforceable in the courts, we should have present most of the elements of compulsory assessment fire insurance, administered by the State. But if the State should make replacements or not to suit itself, then the guarantee to the individual—the very core of insurance—would be lacking.

One very sufficient reason that there has been no insurance to protect the individual from losses caused by fire, even in comparatively recent times, may be that few persons have had much to lose. Houses, except those of the very rich, have been insubstantial and for the most part readily replaced. Personal property of a movable character has been scant in quantity, insignificant in value, or, as in the case of herds, little subject to fire risk. Another reason may well have been the sense of group solidarity which, in variously modified forms, has prevailed until comparatively recent times. Possibly property, whether consisting of buildings or movable goods, has been viewed more or less as communal possessions; it would be but natural that its loss should be accepted as a group, and not as an individual, loss. Insurance replaces loss to the individual. When he has no sense of individual loss he requires no such aid as insurance. Marine insurance of a kind had taken root a thousand years before Christ. One would expect that business men must have discov-

[1] Mr. J. Somers Smith, treasurer of the Philadelphia Contributionship, has given generous assistance in the preparation of this case. The material has been secured largely from the original records in the offices of the Contributionship.

ered fire insurance by simple analogy. Whether they did or not we are unable to say. Even if they saw the parallel, they may well have rejected the device for other reasons. Marine risks were of short duration; they began at a sailing date and ended with the return or loss of the ship. Customarily these risks did not extend over periods of more than a year or two. But a building might not burn down during the lifetime of the owner or of the insurer. This long-term uncertainty of loss was too great a responsibility to assume. That the risk might have been broken up into time units does not seem to have occurred to these business men. To be sure, prospective or potential insurers might have felt baffled in trying to fix a rate. This hypothesis does not carry much conviction, however; although rates may affect the volume of business transacted, they do not usually determine the existence of such a service. We must, therefore, assume that fire insurance did not enter the minds of business men as a reasonable possibility until the late Middle Ages.

Perhaps we should say that the conditions which were eventually to lead to the institution of fire insurance had their origin, as have so many modern devices, in the commercial life of northern Italy in the twelfth and thirteenth centuries, for out of that bright outburst of enterprise and achievement came capitalistic method and individualism. At any rate, with the subsequent increase in the quantity and value of personal property, with the wider distribution of its ownership, with the awakening of merchants to the hazard of business losses through fire, with the waning support of the individual by the community, with the rise of marine risk-bearing under policies of insurance, came the demand for individual security against fire losses. Information concerning definite early developments is very scant. Certainly a plan was suggested to Count von Oldenberg in 1609 by which he should undertake to recompense fire losses of his subjects in return for a payment from each of them equal to 1 per cent of the value of the properties to be insured. The rate suggested is interesting because it is one which makes the modern reader believe that earlier generations knew something of the risk involved. Other plans were formulated and advanced from time to time during the seventeenth century, but nothing seems to have come of them.

In 1666 occurred that major calamity, the London Fire. This conflagration lasted for four days and nights, spread over hundreds of acres of land, destroyed more than 85 per cent of the buildings of the city, and resulted in property losses which have been put at $300,000,000 in terms of modern values. Such an event could hardly pass lightly out of mind. Nor did it. One of the fruits of its contemplation was a quickened interest in security against fire. This expressed itself in many ways: building restrictions, fire-fighting plans, and a plan for fire insurance.

In the year after the fire Nicholas Barbon, of London, opened an office in which he underwrote risks of fire loss on buildings. He was a private underwriter. His plan must have met with success, for in 1680 we find him continuing his "Fire Office" as a partnership. His contract of insurance guaranteed to indemnify in case of complete loss or to repair in case of damage. The insured had no liability beyond his premium.

The City of London made an abortive effort to go into the fire insurance business at about the same time but abandoned the plan of 1683. In that year, also, there was formed a sort of mutual fire company which went under the name of the "Friendly Society." This enterprise did business for a hundred years. Its plan of operation was to charge a yearly premium, collect with the first premium a sum equal to five additional annual premiums, and secure simultaneously a signed agreement from the insured to share losses of the society up to a certain percentage of the face of his policy. The deposit was a guarantee of payment of premiums or assessments; at the termination of the insurance, or at intervals, reckonings of experience were computed and settlements made with each assured. This is not unlike the Philadelphia Contributionship. The Philadelphia company was apparently, however, more directly influenced by the Amicable Contributionship, which was founded in London in 1696.

Charles Povey in 1706 inaugurated, as a private underwriter, a London business by which he insured personal (i. e., movable) property. A little later he formed a similar firm to underwrite fire risks not only in London but throughout the nation as well. In 1710 the firms were combined into one enterprise known first as the "London Insurers" and later as the "Sun Fire Office." It was then and is today a partnership.

During the next 15 years many partnerships were formed to underwrite fire insurance. Two companies, more prominent in marine insurance than in fire, received charters of incorporation in 1720; they appealed to those who wished to insure fire risks on the alleged merits of possessing large funds, of making no assessments, and accepting large risks. There was a great interest in fire prevention during the whole of the eighteenth century; the fire companies organized fire-fighting units. By 1803 there were in London alone some 50 units; for economy's sake some of them were consolidated in 1825, and all of them by 1833. But not until 1866 did the city itself take over the job.

France had fire insurance companies before 1791, but the Revolution wiped them out. Modern stock companies in France date from about 1818, from 1827 in Russia, and from 1828 in Austria.[2]

[2] Chaps. iii and iv of Lester W. Zartman and William H. Price, *Yale Readings in Insurance: Property Insurance* (New Haven, 1914), give a more detailed narrative of early fire insurance history.

2. The Beginnings of American Fire Insurance

There is no reason to doubt that the colonists knew about the home country's development of fire insurance. On the other hand there is no reason to believe that any colonial goods or buildings were insured against fire by English firms during this early period. With marine insurance it was different; in that case the risks involved might well concern English business men.

As might have been expected, the fire-prevention and fire-fighting activities took root first. Philadelphia authorized an increase in civic fire-fighting equipment in 1730. In the colonial towns strict rules were laid down, and scrupulously adhered to, in an effort to reduce fire losses. Volunteer fire companies were organized and equipped. Despite precautions, however, fires were numerous, and often enough the more fortunately circumstanced residents were called upon to make contributions toward the support of those whose buildings had been destroyed and whose resources were inadequate.

But this early period had its share of insurance plans too. At least two unsuccessful attempts, one in 1728 and another in 1748, were made to start fire offices in Boston. In Charleston, South Carolina, a mutual society existed from 1735 to 1740.[3] The really continuous growth began in 1752, however, with the organization of the Philadelphia Contributionship.

3. Founding of the Contributionship, 1752

The Contributionship was probably the result of a movement for the establishment of a fire insurance company which had its beginning in the Union Fire (Fighting) Co. in 1750.[4] The "Minutes" of the Union

[3] *South Carolina Historical and Genealogical Magazine,* Jan., 1907, pp. 46 ff.

[4] See Harrold E. Gillingham, "Philadelphia's First Fire Defences," *The Pennsylvania Magazine of History and Biography,* Oct., 1932, pp. 368–370.

show that the Union had a fund which, it was proposed, should be used to insure its own members and that in August, 1751, Benjamin Franklin, who had been an active member of the Union since he helped found it in 1736 and who had firsthand knowledge of fire insurance in London, proposed a meeting of representatives from various fire-fighting companies to consider a scheme for the insurance of houses. Franklin and Philip Syng were appointed to attend such a meeting. What happened at the proposed meeting is not known. On February 18, 1752, however, the *Pennsylvania Gazette* carried the following announcement of a subscription to a new company:

"All persons inclined to subscribe to the articles of insurance of houses from fire, in or near this city, are desired to appear at the Court-House, where attendance will be given, to take in their subscriptions, every seventh day of the week, in the afternoon, until the 13th of April next, being the day appointed by the said Articles for electing 12 Directors and a Treasurer."

The articles of insurance herein mentioned evidently became the "Deed of Settlement" of the Contributionship, which was organized on April 13, 1752. The organization for which the articles made provision was a kind of partnership consisting of the subscribers or contributors. The articles had the following provisions: [5]

Company name	Philadelphia Contributionship for the Insurance of Houses from Loss by Fire.
Membership	All who contributed to (that is, were insured in) the company.
Management	In the hands of 12 directors, elected by contributors.
Risks	Houses in Philadelphia, or within 10 miles of city limits.
Term of coverage	Seven years.
Premium	A single deposit of money equal to a fixed percentage of the face of the policy.
Plan of business	The deposits were to be invested; the income was to be employed to meet expenses and pay losses. In case this income was insufficient to meet these drains, then the principal could be drawn upon. An account was kept for each contributor; it was credited with excess earnings, debited for excess costs of business. Such accounting took notice of the ratio of each contributor's deposit to total deposits. Surplus *earnings* were to be credited to contributors.
Rates	There were only two classifications: Brick houses (four kinds) and timber houses. The charge was from 15 shillings per £100 (of the amount insured) to 40 shillings on the timber houses (that is, from 0.75 to 2 per cent).
Assessments	Fifty per cent of each contributor's deposit.
Restrictions	Damage caused by stored gunpowder voided the contract.
Fire fighting	The directors were instructed to reward those active in extinguishing fires.

The first private citizen to sign the Deed of Settlement was Benjamin Franklin (the lieutenant governor of the Province of Pennsylvania having signed it), and among the early signers were Samuel Morris, John Mifflin, and Israel Pemberton, Jr. Frank-

[5] The original deed of settlement is in the offices of the Philadelphia Contributionship, 212 South Fourth Street, Philadelphia, Pennsylvania. It is on a roll of parchment 44 feet long, which also contains the signatures of about eighteen hundred early members.

lin was also one of the original directors. John Smith was chosen treasurer, an office which he held from 1752 to 1756 when James Pemberton succeeded him. The first clerk was Joseph Saunders, an insurance broker, who served for two years. According to an announcement in the *Pennsylvania Gazette* of June 11, 1752, Saunders carried on the business of the Contributionship in his own insurance office.

John Smith, as the first treasurer of the Contributionship, was its first administrative head. His background is significant. He had, no doubt, made the usual entry into commerce as a clerk. As his diary records, he went to sea as supercargo on one of his father's ships. Later he became a partner of Abel James in the shipping and selling of general merchandise. Smith and James availed themselves of whatever insurance facilities the city offered in protecting themselves against marine perils to their ships and goods. Through the office of Joseph Saunders they joined with others in similar underwriting for the security of other merchants. Here they associated with experienced underwriters: Abram Judah, John M. Nesbitt, Pemberton & Edwards, Kidd & Bradford, John Shee, Amos Strettell, and Willing, Morris & Co.

Just what stimulated Smith's interest in fire insurance is not clear. The theory has been advanced that he visited England and while there became acquainted with either the Amicable Contributionship or the Friendly Society. He was a member of the Hand-in-Hand Fire (Fighting) Co. and often mentions it in his diary. Unfortunately, the diary stops just before 1752, but it contained the following entry, according to Fowler,[6] as of August 26, 1748: "In the evening rode to Stenton; took with me a plan of the damage done by the fire in London, and gave it to the old gentleman [James Logan, Smith's father-in-law]."

[6] J. A. Fowler, *History of Insurance in Philadelphia for Two Centuries, 1683–1882* (Philadelphia, 1888), p. 297.

The earliest policy in the possession of the company is policy number 40, made out to Susannah Dilwyn and dated July 15, 1752. It is reproduced in full below: [7]

"No. 40.

"THIS INSTRUMENT OR POLICY WITNESSETH, That *Susannah Dilwyn of the City of Philadelphia*—

having become, and by these Presents becoming a Member of the PHILADELPHIA CONTRIBUTIONSHIP, for insuring Houses, Etc. from Loss by Fire within the City of PHILADELPHIA, and ten Miles round the same, in PENNSYLVANIA, pursuant to a Deed of Settlement, bearing Date the *25th* Day of *March*, 1752. And for and in Consideration of the Sum of *Three pounds fifteen shillings* .... in Hand paid by the said *Susannah Dilwyn* .... to the Treasurer of the said Contributionship, being the Consideration for insuring the Sum of *Three hundred* .... Pounds unto the said *Susannah Dilwyn her* Executors, Administrators and Assigns, upon *her House & Kitchen, situate the North west Corner of Second & Sassafras Street where Dr. Peter Nigh Dwells, the house being 18 foot front & 39 foot back, Piazza & Kitchen 12 by 24 foot, & the Wash house 16 by 18 foot valuing the house at £225, the Piazza & kitchen at £50—Wash house at £25* .... during the Term of Seven Years from the Date hereof: Which said Sum of *Three pounds fifteen shillings* .... is hereby declared to be deposited by the said *Susannah Dilwyn* .... as a Pledge or Caution for the Performance of the Agreements comprised in the said Deed of Settlement on *her* Part from henceforth to be performed. Now we the Directors of the said Contributionship, for and in Consideration thereof, do hereby order, direct and appoint the Treasurer for the Time being of the said Contributionship, according to the said Deed of Settlement, to pay and satisfy unto the said *Susannah Dilwyn her* .... Executors, Administrators, or Assigns, the Sum of *Three Hundred* .... Pounds, at the End of three Months next after the said *House, Kitchen etc.*—shall be burnt down or

[7] This policy has the same form as policies 19 and 20 previously issued to Benjamin Franklin.

demolished by or by Reason or Means of Fire; and in like Manner shall pay the Sum of *Three Hundred* Pounds so often as any *House, kitchen etc.* of the same Value and Goodness, built in the Room thereof, shall be burnt down or demolished by Reason or Means of Fire, during the Time this Policy remains in Force, and thereupon to endorse each and every such Payment on this present Policy. AND ALSO, That We the Directors aforesaid, do hereby further order, direct and appoint, that when and so often as the said *House Kitchen etc.* or any *House, Kit'n, etc.* built in the Room thereof, shall happen to be damnified or injured by or by Means of Fire; such Damages shall be made good, according to the Estimate thereof, or repaired and put into as good Condition as the same was or were before such Fire or Fires happening. And We likewise order and direct the said Treasurer for the Time being of the said Contributionship, at the End of the said Term of Seven Years, to repay unto the said *Susannah Dilwyn* .... his Executors, Administrators or Assigns, the said Money so deposited as aforesaid, or so much thereof as shall not in the mean Time be apply'd towards Losses, and the unavoidable Expence of the said Insurance Office, pursuant to the said Deed of Settlement [of March 25, 1752].

"PROVIDED, and it is hereby declared and agreed, That if the said Deposite Money shall not be demanded at this Insurance Office within the Space of One Year next after the Expiration of the said Term of Seven Years, then the Payment thereof shall cease, and the same shall be sunk and remain to the Benefit of the said Contributionship.

"PROVIDED ALSO, That if it should so happen, that the whole Stock of the said Contributionship should ever be insufficient fully to pay and discharge all the Losses sustain'd by the Members of this Contributionship, in such Case a just Average shall be made, and the Payment to be demanded in Virtue of this Policy shall be a Dividend of the said Stock in Proportion to the Sum insured, agreeable to the Tenor and true Intent of the said Deed of Settlement.

"IN WITNESS whereof, We have hereunto set our Hands and Seals this *Fifteenth* Day of *July* .... in the *Twenty sixth* .... Year of the Reign of King GEORGE the Second, Annoq; Dom. 1752—

"SEALED AND DELIVERED IN THE PRESENCE OF US

Samuel Rhoads [seal]

Sam. Pemberton
Jos. Saunders

Jos. Morris [seal]
William Griffitts" [seal]

4. Pertinent Recent Insurance Conditions

It may be of some value now to step forward almost two hundred years and look back at the beginning of fire insurance in America in the light of intervening experience.

First, let us consider organization. The Contributionship was a type of mutual. Today we think of mutuals in the fire field as generally pertaining to one or another of the following types: *Locals*—These are limited by law to small areas where the membership is such that a mutual responsibility will be felt; this results in the selection of good risks only; the members do the work of administration free or at nominal fees; members of such a group seldom attempt fraud; few, if any, taxes are paid; locals insure mainly farm property (for which reason they are often referred to as Farm Mutuals); obvious disadvantages inherent in these locals are little knowledge of business, small capital, and the fact that a bad year or two bears down heavily on them. *State Mutuals*—They are much the same as locals but have permission to do business over a wider area; customarily a local may begin with $50,000 in risks, whereas a State mutual must have $750,000 in risks. State mutuals' merits lie just between the advantages of a local and those of a national company; they miss the economy and good selection of their smaller brothers as well as the efficiency of their larger brothers; failures have been numerous in this class. *Factory Mutuals*—These are by far the most interesting. They got under way in the period from 1835 to 1870; they are exactly what their name implies; they have a fine record of service to the whole industry, for they initiated the policy of charging rates to suit the hazard involved. Mainly their work was to study causes of fires, means of preventing fires, plant construction, and manufacturing process adjustment in the plant, with the aim of reducing fire hazard; their action revolutionized the fire insurance business. Fundamentally the Contributionship is a local, according to the classifications just described, but now it has a State-wide business.

But present-day fire insurance is, for the most part, in the hands of stock fire insurance companies; they do more than 90 per cent of the business. Typically, they do a national business. Each company divides the country into five or six sales districts, each district being in charge of a general agent; the latter sells through some two or three thousand local agents located throughout his district. The local agent is furnished with company forms and blank policies which he is authorized to sign, his signature being binding upon the company. In large cities the local agents tend to be supplanted by brokers. The company employs special agents to travel to supervise the local agents; these "specials" discover new local agents, inspect risks, gather information, report on fires, and settle claims. The home office receives daily reports of new business written and employs expert examiners to check these new policies for character and moral hazard. If they do not approve of a policy, they return it to the local agent for his immediate cancellation.

The Contributionship has never needed an elaborate organization. During the very early years it accepted only residence risks. (In fire insurance terminology "risk" designates the property insured, "hazard" the danger insured against.) But the large modern company today insures properties of widely different degrees of hazard. For their aid and guidance in fixing a rate that shall represent fairly the hazard involved in each case the companies have classified risks much more elaborately than the founders of the Contributionship would ever have dreamed necessary. Ordinarily this classification begins by dividing the country into areas; then it grades cities into five or six classes, having in mind the fire-fighting facilities, attitude of the community to property, and so on; next, a base rate is set for a typical one-story brick building in a given area, and another base rate is set for a typical one-story frame building in a given area; finally, the rate fixed by the above classification is modified by plus or minus charges to take account of innumerable other details, such as construction, type of work going on in building, private fire protection provided, and exposure to hazard from neighboring buildings.

We have mentioned only the physical aspects of the hazard; a most important item in fire insurance is really the moral hazard. Companies want to know whether the owner is under financial pressure, whether his property is objectionable to his neighbors, whether his property is more valuable to him burned (if insured) than standing. Moral or personal hazards are hidden and presumed rather than known; they are hard to measure or to subject to classification.

Contributionship risks were close at hand; they could be seen by company managers; their owners were known to contributors. Probably two classifications were adequate for them at the beginning, but their modest approach stands in sharp contrast to the infinite division and subdivision of today's classifications.[8]

Setting fire rates has been compared to setting taxes. They are, in the end, arbitrary. Measuring hazards accurately, and to the satisfaction of all concerned, is a difficult task; information is hard to get

[8] For a good statement of rating and ruling schedules read chapters x–xiii, of *Insurance and Real Estate* (New York, 1911), part i, "Fire Insurance," by Edward R. Hardy.

and costly; conditions within an industry or within a plant are constantly changing. The Contributionship management resorted to what is known as the judgment plan of rate-making; that is, they inspected a risk and pronounced a rate for it. The trend since then has been to continue that plan with gradual accumulation of bases for finer and finer distinctions in classifying risks. In contrast to the judgment plan we have today what are ambitiously called "Scientific Rating Systems." The most famous of these are Moore's "Universal Mercantile Schedule" and Dean's "Mercantile Tariff and Exposure Formula for the Measurement of Fire Hazards." All such tariffs leave much to be desired; they are administered in such a way as to leave still more to be desired; but they look in the right direction.

Zartman, in one of his Yale lectures on fire insurance, stated that these ratings resulted (in themselves or in their administration) in discrimination between insureds. Too high a rate is charged on private houses because the companies can actually collect an excessive charge on them; too low a rate is charged on factories because the owners thereof are so vocal and insistent on better classification, resorting to legislative pressures on obstinate companies to force their wishes; finally, they discriminate between specific risks which should be identically classified. The latter discrimination is the result of pressure upon the companies by their agents and brokers who offer a company blocks of risks, the good mixed with the bad, "take all or none." Some of this discrimination could be eliminated if the companies were allowed to coöperate with one another in controlling classifications, regulating rates, and fixing commissions. The public will not tolerate "compacts," however, between the companies. This is but another evidence of the great American phobia against monopoly.

5. Early Growth and Early Problems of the Contributionship

The exact amount of insurance in force during the early years is not definitely known. At least the original policies remained in force, but otherwise the business lagged. The early losses are given in Table 1.[9]

Table 1. LOSSES BORNE BY THE CONTRIBUTIONSHIP, 1754–92

Year	Loss	Year	Loss
1754	$388.26	1770	$ 209.71
1755	32.40	1779	1,012.52
1761	160.00	1780	436.12
1767	8.01	1790	139.14
1769	191.18	1791	1,016.14
		1792	619.00

By 1763 it had become well known that the Contributionship was not growing. People had come to believe that the company was fundamentally unsound so long as it continued to pay out its earnings in the form of dividends. This belief became so common that in April, 1763, the board voted that the interest money arising from the stock should be carried to one common account to be applied as directed by Article 21 of the Deed of Settlement in discharging the expenses of the office. They voted that the surplus should be applied toward satisfying any loss by fire and that no part of the deposit money should be expended until the balance of the interest money was paid.[10]

Following this action the company developed the policy of accumulating as large a reserve as possible against the contingency of a disastrous fire. This provision seems to have engendered confidence in the Contributionship, whose growth was henceforth rapid.

On February 20, 1768, the lieutenant-governor and the proprietaries of the Prov-

[9] The tabulations in this case are compiled from original sources in the offices of the Philadelphia Contributionship.

[10] Minutes of the Board of Directors, April, 1763.

ince of Pennsylvania passed an act for incorporating the Philadelphia Contributionship, confirming the Deed of Settlement of 1752 under which the Contributionship had until then operated. This act was ratified by the King-in-Council on March 6, 1769. The Contributionship was probably the first American fire insurance company, therefore, to receive a royal charter. (The semi-charitable Presbyterian ministers' fund had been incorporated in Pennsylvania in 1759 to insure the lives of ministers of that denomination.)

By 1769 the company discovered that its insurance in force covering wooden buildings was not profitable. It had two alternatives: to increase the deposit necessary for the insurance of wooden buildings or to refuse to insure them. It chose the latter. On April 10, 1769, it was voted: "That no Insurance be hereafter made on any Wooden Buildings." This reduced the losses considerably.

Next it was discovered that the greatest losses came from houses which were surrounded by green trees. Therefore, on April 9, 1781, it was voted that (1) no house should be insured that had a tree or trees planted in the street in front of it; (2) if a tree or trees stood in the street in front of an insured house, the policyholder should not be allowed to renew; and (3) if any policyholder planted a tree or trees in front of his house, his insurance should be forfeited unless he removed the tree or trees within three months.[11]

This act created a storm of objections, since many of the contributors valued their shade trees highly. The result was that a minority of the contributors, having shade trees, seceded and formed an insurance company of their own, known as the Mutual Assurance Co. for Insuring Houses from Loss by Fire. This company was established on October 12, 1784, and became well known by the name of the "Green Tree." This company made an additional charge to compensate for the increased risk. Both companies subsequently rescinded their action in regard to trees.

Upon its establishment the Contributionship followed the practice of the English companies of placing its firemark, cast of lead, on the front of each building insured. The Contributionship chose a mark of four hands clasped. The idea was that in case of fire the volunteer fire companies, being composed to a large extent of fellow-contributors, would see the mark, know the building was insured by their company, and increase their efforts to prevent loss. These early firemarks, being made of soft lead, could easily be melted and rumor has it that most of them were used in making musket balls during the Revolution, but a few may still be seen in the older parts of Philadelphia.

Fire fighting was in a very undeveloped state during the early years. Public fire departments were inadequate. There were, however, many private associations composed of the householders of various localities. In order to stimulate these fire fighters the Contributionship offered rewards to the organizations which put out the fires on property that it had insured and indicated with its firemarks. Competition became very keen among the companies and at several points in the papers of the Contributionship we find notices to the effect that, unless the companies cease fighting with each other and pay more attention to the fire, they will not be given any more gratuities. Then the situation took another curious turn. With the growth of the city there seems to have developed a feeling on the part of many people that, if a building had a firemark on it and was adequately insured, there was no need to attempt to save it from destruction. Possibly that is part of the reason for the eventual unpopularity of the firemark.

From 1763 to 1792 the company experienced a very remarkable growth. The volume of insurance increased steadily. The losses were considerably less than the income from the investments of the com-

[11] *Ibid.*, April 9, 1781.

pany. It is to be noticed that during this period insurance was officially for a period of seven years but actually it was perpetual. After a householder had made his deposit, he did not have to make further payments; and at the end of seven years he simply signed another contract.

6. The Period of Growth, 1792–1852

During this period the Contributionship experienced a slow but steady growth in volume of insurance. By 1810 there was general recognition that most of its policies of insurance were in fact perpetual, and in that year the Deed of Settlement was amended so as to make all policies officially perpetual.[12] By 1852 the amount at risk was $7,944,707.35, and the book value of the assets was $694,545.27. Losses for the period are given in Table 2.[13]

In most years losses were small, but in 1851 a fire swept through the oldest section of Philadelphia. It was there that both the Contributionship and the Green Tree had the bulk of their perpetual policies. The result was that both had heavy losses while the other companies escaped. The company that year had a decrease in assets of $35,735.34. Despite this fact the income of the Contributionship in the following years was greater than its expenses and losses, and its assets continued to increase steadily.

We see here that the Contributionship was able to survive what is known as a conflagration. This calls attention to the nature of that problem in the fire business. It is the view of authorities that fire losses should be viewed as the result of two types of hazards—the ordinary hazards and the conflagration. Unfortunately this view is not widely held. Conflagration hazards, of course, occur mainly in cities; farms, except for forest fires, are conceived as beyond this hazard. And, peculiarly, it is on those city risks that the lowest rates are granted, partly owing to competition and the effectiveness of brokers in pitting one company against another in trying to

[12] *Ibid.*, April 9, 1810.

[13] Compiled from the company's records.

Table 2. FIRE LOSSES OF THE PHILADELPHIA CONTRIBUTIONSHIP, 1793–1852

Year	Loss	Year	Loss	Year	Loss
1793	$ 17.06	1813	$1,403.86	1833	$ 1,922.24
1794	no losses	1814	286.78	1834	1,730.97
1795	3,733.33	1815	58.40	1835	6,226.68
1796	2,864.18	1816	5.25	1836	3,501.34
1797	4,261.60	1817	8.69	1837	1,313.71
1798	11.70	1818	314.17	1838	1,719.66
1799	1,430.54	1819	924.25	1839	13,930.53
1800	1,933.83	1820	778.35	1840	35,829.07
1801	no losses	1821	2,224.00	1841	1,077.98
1802	926.79	1822	225.88	1842	10,310.98
1803	1,905.40	1823	3,639.49	1843	1,541.62
1804	650.00	1824	4,394.00	1844	1,351.67
1805	112.00	1825	173.33	1845	7,914.12
1806	113.50	1826	353.28	1846	5,890.34
1807	4,390.24	1827	4,909.95	1847	2,023.55
1808	6.56	1828	2,054.76	1848	2,529.91
1809	7.74	1829	1,538.07	1849	1,028.58
1810	645.15	1830	3,549.58	1850	1,569.50
1811	40.21	1831	640.34	1851	85,953.82
1812	1,418.82	1832	874.66	1852	8,932.23

secure for their clients the best possible rates. But the really great issue is how to plan for conflagration losses. They are rare in occurrence; they are hard to average; they do not lend themselves to statistical treatment (the only proper basis for rate structures). This latter criticism is of course properly made against even the ordinary classifications, since American companies do not pool their experience for the better guidance of the whole industry as is done in England. The result is that, although reserves are on the whole properly made for ordinary hazards, no separate reserve is set up for conflagration losses, which are really additional losses and not the increase of ordinary losses. It is customary now for many companies to reinsure part of their largest individual lines and also to provide against conflagration losses by taking excessive reinsurance.

7. The Struggle for Control, 1852–94

James S. Smith had been treasurer from 1842 to 1859. His son, James Somers Smith, succeeded him, holding office from 1859 to 1894. It was expected that his grandson, J. Somers Smith, Jr., who had been employed in the office for seven years, would be the next treasurer, but at the meeting in 1894 several unforeseen events occurred.

A group of policyholders, headed by Richard M. Elliott, Thomas D. Hunter, and Clifford Pemberton, Jr., led the opposition to the election of J. Somers Smith, Jr., to succeed his father. The reform group also nominated a new board of directors and named as treasurer Clifford Pemberton, a great-grandson of Israel Pemberton. This action was unexpected, and the group formerly in control took advantage of the fact that they could have the election cover more than one day. This gave them time to see to it that the great body of the contributors voted. The fight was bitter.

One form which the fight took was a small pamphlet war. A pamphlet distributed by the opposition contained the following statements: [14]

"The Philadelphia Contributionship was incorporated February 26, 1768, for the purpose of affording its contributors indemnity against loss or damage by fire, upon payment of the smallest possible premium consistent with safety and prudence. Today the corporation, in spite of its age and wealth, is a failure, inasmuch as it does not approximate its objective points as closely as its competitors. The average fire insurance company pays 30% of its premium receipts in expenses, leaving the balance (70%) for losses and profit. The Philadelphia Contributionship pays 113% to 120% of its premium receipts in expenses alone, to which, of course, must be added whatever losses have to be borne, and, which in the past 10 years have been 80%; or, in other words, it costs the Philadelphia Contributionship $200 every year to get $100, and when it is further considered that the corporation issues only perpetual policies, and that the deposit money can be withdrawn by the insurer upon demand, and that the company gets the interest alone upon the sum deposited, the result is even more lamentable.

"The average increase added to the premium account annually during the past 20 years has been but $162, and to attain this, the corporation has expended annually $24,847 or it has cost them $153 to get $1. Today, while other companies are actively striving for profitable business, the Philadelphia Contributionship appears to be entirely indifferent to securing insurance; its office hours are from 10 A. M. to 2 P. M. and it declines to write any policy under $3,000, and insists that in all cases the premium shall be paid before the policy is written, and frequently requires a month to write the policy. It also in every case requires a survey to be made of the property insured.

"The Philadelphia Contributionship should assume among insurance corporations the position to which it is entitled by its age, its wealth, and its objects, and it is our purpose to place in nomination for the ensuing year for your board of directors a more progressive management, men who are intimately

[14] From a clipping, apparently from the *Philadelphia Press* sometime in 1894, in a scrapbook in the office of the Contributionship.

connected with the interests of the building of dwellings, and men who are so situated as to bring to the company's office a large share of the business to which it is entitled, and to so conduct the company as to render insurance to the individual contributors at the least possible cost consistent with safety."

The opposition took court action, with the result that a master was appointed to conduct the election. Although the election was contested hotly, it was soon apparent that the old board possessed a decided majority. When the votes were finally counted, it was determined that the old board had won by a seven to one majority and that J. Somers Smith, Jr., had been elected treasurer.

8. The Recent Period, 1894–present

One of the first things the reëlected directors proposed to do was to make conditions such that a repetition of the raid of 1894 would be an impossibility. In order to accomplish this they called a special meeting of the members, who amended the articles to provide that the directors should hold office for four years and that only one-fourth of them should be elected each year. Nevertheless, there was still considerable dissatisfaction on the part of many of the contributors with the fact that the company should go on accumulating assets far beyond the needs of safety and that no one should benefit therefrom. In response to this feeling the directors in 1895 declared a 10 per cent dividend on the deposit money on all policies in force. Moreover, they resolved that all new deposits received after that date would have to remain with the company ten years before they would be entitled to dividends. Ten per cent dividends have been paid annually ever since, totaling to April 30, 1939, over $2,300,000.

The growth of the insurance in force and the assets of the Contributionship are indicated by Table 3.

Table 3. ASSETS AND AMOUNTS AT RISK, 1895–1938

Year	Assets at par value	Amount at risk
1895	$ 3,789,359.82	$14,738,948.69
1900	4,253,641.83	14,654,111.69
1905	4,744,851.96	15,229,924.66
1910	5,586,909.77	18,793,340.66
1915	6,745,823.44	23,719,440.66
1920	7,933,779.05	33,546,556.33
1925	9,402,174.78	44,292,481.00
1930	10,941,494.67	54,686,626.01
1935	12,030,185.25	61,352,651.01
1938	12,534,442.25	67,338,172.01

The growth of the surplus resulted from the fact that losses were consistently smaller than income.

Table 4. FIRE LOSSES OF THE CONTRIBUTIONSHIP 1895–1938

Year	Loss	Year	Loss
1895	$11,348.40	1917	$ 4,775.15
1896	6,735.07	1918	9,953.88
1897	16,055.79	1919	11,040.67
1898	11,582.77	1920	24,604.58
1899	33,462.78	1921	8,834.24
1900	49,231.34	1922	13,153.39
1901	10,404.01	1923	26,589.55
1902	28,568.55	1924	14,617.16
1903	14,468.61	1925	11,889.59
1904	15,178.40	1926	16,705.53
1905	20,055.31	1927	14,631.30
1906	7,790.61	1928	17,561.27
1907	19,539.90	1929	14,837.70
1908	4,401.91	1930	23,733.62
1909	7,253.93	1931	14,176.43
1910	8,872.82	1932	8,999.72
1911	13,156.49	1933	4,247.15
1912	8,479.03	1934	8,883.70
1913	14,863.33	1935	10,121.45
1914	11,838.98	1936	12,236.89
1915	11,377.70	1937	19,603.98
1916	6,547.85	1938	14,748.93

The company is now doing business throughout Pennsylvania, 25 per cent of its risks coming from outside Philadelphia. There are no restrictions as to the kind of risks they accept, but the practice is to underwrite only those which would ordinarily be classified as "preferred." In or near Philadelphia risks are inspected by the company's own staff engineer; he is also sent to more distant places, where there is sufficient business, but otherwise distant points are taken care of by the inspection organization which serves the mutuals. Of the total amount of business offered the company at least half of the face amount is rejected, either because of certain defects discovered upon inspection (if the owner declined to remedy) or because the company was unwilling to write as large a line as desired, or because the risk was not considered "preferred" (being at least 40 per cent frame or in a hazardous neighborhood). About 90 per cent of new business comes through properly licensed Pennsylvania brokers, who collect the deposit premiums (which are roughly twelve to fifteen times the usual annual premium, with a minimum rate of 2 per cent) and are given a commission of 10 per cent.

9. Suggested Readings

John A. Fowler, *History of Insurance in Philadelphia for Two Centuries, 1683–1882* (Philadelphia, 1888). The history of the Contributionship is considered in the broader history of fire insurance in Philadelphia in part ii.

Lester W. Zartman and William H. Price, *Yale Readings in Insurance: Property Insurance* (New Haven, 1914). Excellent selection of readings on fire insurance and guide to literature in the field. Two chapters on the history of fire insurance in Europe and the United States.

Centennial Meeting of the Philadelphia Contributionship for the Insurance of Houses from Loss by Fire, Second Monday of April, 1852 (Philadelphia, 1852). A short history of the company.

Charles W. Burpee, *One Hundred Years of Service: Being the History of the Hartford Fire Insurance Company* (Hartford, 1910). Full of details about the work but especially valuable because it contains the main currents in fire insurance history.

H. R. Gall and W. G. Jordan, *One Hundred Years of Fire Insurance; Being a History of the Aetna Insurance Company, Hartford, Connecticut, 1819–1919* (Hartford, 1919). A company history of the better type.

William F. Gephart, *Principles of Insurance*, vol. ii, *Fire* (New York, 1922). A good text on fire insurance.

10. Suggested Questions

1. Why did fire insurance develop later than marine insurance?
2. What do you think of a company that does not try to expand?
3. What is the significance of the struggle for control in 1894?

XIII. THE MASSACHUSETTS BANK, 1784–1903

1. General Statement

Established in 1784, the Massachusetts Bank was the first commercial bank in Boston and indeed the first in New England. The Bank of North America in Philadelphia had been founded in 1781, however, and the Bank of New York a little earlier in 1784.

The Bank had to learn banking as it went along. It had no real bankers for many years after its foundation. It saw many changes and weathered many storms. It had periods of prosperity and periods of difficulty, but it still lives on—in the form of the First National Bank of Boston, with which it was merged in 1903.

The Bank is older than the American Constitution and the American dollar. It came with the first flowering of our national history and lived through the War of 1812 and the Civil War without harm to itself and also without making any special effort to aid so distant an organization as the American government. It saw the first Bank of the United States (1791–1811) and the second Bank of the United States (1816–36) come and go. It opened its doors before there was any bank legislation in the State and it survived the various laws designed to help or hinder it. Although it had no relish for the national banking system of 1863, it joined that system in 1865. We can study the history of this bank from its own records—minutes and accounts.

2. Chronology

1782	Massachusetts incorporated the Bank of North America of Philadelphia.
1783	Boston merchants and capitalists wrote to the president of the Bank of North America about the problems involved in the founding of a bank.
1784	Massachusetts Bank received a State charter on February 7. Opened for business, July 5.
1785	Nonspecie basis for circulation, June 21, 1785–January 2, 1786.
1785	Reduction in the Bank's capital, October 14.
1786	Charge made for keeping deposits, January 4. Discontinued 1791.
1790	No discount for less than $100 and none for over $3,000 unless secured.
1791	Bank's capital doubled. Deposits kept without charge.
1791–92	Bank's loans considerable and specie reserve low. Prosperity in the East.
1792	Massachusetts law limited loans and circulation to twice capital. Bank's capital doubled. Accounts began to be kept in dollars and cents, July 4. Two rival banks in Boston.
1803	A third rival in Boston.
1807	Bank to loan no money on a note with one person as promisor and endorser for over $70,000.
1808	Bank's capital doubled.
1810	Capital again doubled.
1811	Fourth rival in Boston.
1821	Capital reduced by half.
1837	Bank's first suspension of specie payment of its circulating notes.
1857	Second suspension.
1859	Aggregate loans to directors limited to $350,000.
1860	Aggregate loans to directors limited to $450,000.
1861	Bank's third suspension.
1865	Bank joined the national banking system.
1873	Bank suspended currency payment.
1884	Panic, after which the Bank showed little recuperative power.
1897	Dividends passed for whole year.
1899	Bank examiner ready to close the Bank. Weeks group gained control.
1900	Wing became vice-president.
1903	Massachusetts Bank and First National Bank merged.

3. The Founders of the Bank and Their Aims

There were six men in Boston who wanted to establish a bank and who saw no reason why they should not do so, since the charter of the Bank of North America had ceased to be in effect in Massachusetts in 1783. Though the Bank of North America had never actually opened a branch in Massachusetts, the threat had been made. A bank was needed in Boston, but local pride indicated that it should be locally owned and managed.

The six Bostonians who were willing to sponsor a bank were one active merchant, three merchants well on toward retirement, one retired merchant, and one judge. The retired merchant, William Phillips, was really an investing capitalist and as such took naturally to a bank. He was to become the brains, the motive power, and the brakes of the new institution. His son and grandson were to play their parts. For over a generation the new institution might well have been called Phillips' Bank. This is the family that founded the two academies—at Andover and Exeter.

Four aims were set forth: (1) The new institution was to provide loans at reasonable rates, which meant in Massachusetts at the time not over 6 per cent. (2) Punctuality in the paying of bills was to be inculcated. Here was one of the greatest problems which confronted business of the time. The aristocrats of Europe and the farmers of America, knowing their credit to be good, had long cheated their creditors by delaying the payment of bills and the meeting of other obligations. The two ingredients of bad habits and dishonesty constituted a sore trial to honest and prompt merchants. (3) A place for the safe deposit of money was to be provided without cost. (4) A circulating medium was to be supplied for Boston's use. Such were the motives as put forth in the preamble of the Act of 1784 which chartered the Bank. How far the motives were followed out in practice is a very different matter.

Perhaps, if we cast aside the points that were openly made, we may discern others more general and possibly more motivating. First, merchants had been accustomed to get together to serve one another by mutual aid. They had long insured their marine ventures this way. The new Bank would appeal to many of the stockholders on this ground—granting aid in financing their business. Second, there was the more driving and dynamic purpose of profits which investing capitalists or retired merchants might seek. Third, there was the feeling, perhaps not very conscious, that a bank would complete the freedom declared in 1776 and won politically in 1783. When the Revolutionary War was over, dependence upon the rich merchants of London and through them on the merchant bankers and Bank of England was very real. In the long run this would be expensive for Boston because of the tendency that indebtedness to London merchants had to tie American merchants to one single trading house in the great metropolis. When tied to one foreign firm the American merchant would be given no bargains. If local loans and discounts could be secured, then Boston merchants would be in a better bargaining position in London—and, we may add, elsewhere.

4. The Bank Is Organized

The stockholders of the Bank selected the president and directors and passed the laws which were to govern the Bank. These laws were taken over almost completely from the code used by the Bank of North America.

There can be little doubt that William Phillips was the moving force. He was probably influential in having James Bowdoin made president. Thereupon Phillips became the real power behind the throne occupied by a popular leader who was soon to be elected governor of the State. Probably much of the actual organizing of the new bank was the work of Edward Payne, the broker of the insurance office in which William Phillips and other supporters of the Bank underwrote marine insurance. Indeed, it seems that the substantial and enduring supporters of the Bank were patrons of Payne's office. Thus, the financial group that had come into existence to carry on the business of private marine insurance underwriting grew into a larger financial institution.

The executive officers of the Bank were the president and directors. The directors were meant to direct, not just to formulate policies at occasional meetings but to function in management. To relieve the president of onerous day-to-day duties the office of sitting director was provided for, as a kind of chief executive for the time being. The sitting director, one following another in rotation, was to be on hand to make decisions and to perform certain duties too important to entrust to a member of the staff. The directors chose the staff, designed to be made up of six persons but soon to be reduced to about three or four. The directors saw to it that the staff accountant went to Philadelphia to learn the method of keeping bank accounts followed by the Bank of North America. This calls to our attention the fact that no one in the Boston group knew a bank at first hand. The advice that came from Philadelphia was to follow the ordinary procedure of mercantile bookkeeping, adding a few extra books such as specie book and discount book. Further, the directors adopted the laws and ordinances of the Bank of North America almost verbatim. They decided that the monetary unit should be the Mexican milled dollar, which was to be divided not into 100 cents but into 72 local pence.

The early accounts of the Bank are in Mexican dollars and 72nds thereof. In Philadelphia the same dollars were divided into 90ths. These divisions were grounded in the practices of the States in valuing the Mexican coins. In Massachusetts, the value of a Mexican dollar was 6 shillings or (6 × 12 =) 72 pence. Let us recall that the American dollar, made up of 100 cents, came into being only in 1792 and was adopted by the Bank in that year. How clumsy the 72nds were can easily be imagined.

Finally, the Bank opened on July 5, 1784. The staff was nervous and the directors were present to help in an emergency. Deposits were made and discounts granted. M. M. Hays, a Jewish insurance broker, was the first customer. He deposited $10,000 and bought a draft for $600. Perhaps we may say that New England's political independence began on July 4, 1776, and its financial independence on July 5, 1784.

5. The Bank's Capital and Its Reduction

The stockholders were to pay for their stock in full in bills of exchange on London or in gold or silver coins. Each share was worth $500 par.[1]

[1] In 1821 the par value was reduced to $250, and in 1890 to $100.

Table 1. NUMBER OF SHARES OF THE MASSACHUSETTS BANK

1784	511	1808	1,600
1785	200	1810	3,200
1791	400	1821–65	3,200 (par reduced to $250)
1792	800		

The increases in capital, the result of profitable business prospects, may be dismissed without further consideration. The reduction in capital, both in 1785 and in 1821, merits attention.

As seen in Table 1, the 511 shares subscribed in 1784 were reduced to a round 200 in 1785. The 311 were called the "withdrawn shares." The directors invited such stockholders as wished to withdraw to do so and promised that they would be paid 50 per cent of their stock (basis not stated) at once, the rest as soon as possible. Note that this was not a reduction by a diminution of the par value, but an actual withdrawal of more than half the shares.

Here is a puzzle. Just what happened? We have the account of the withdrawn shares but no statement of the reasons for the withdrawal. We may observe that the number of shares left was exactly 200. This looks like engineering or planning, but let us see.

First, was the Bank overcapitalized? It had paid 4 per cent dividend for the second half of 1784 and for the first half of 1785 only 2½ per cent. Dividends in those days reflected earnings very closely. Although the Bank was later to earn more money, still the first year was a success from the standpoint of profits. Secondly, we remember the ideal that the founders had in mind—punctuality in payment of loans. The directors' records show that notes had to be renewed and renewed. It seemed impossible to force some to pay up, notably those who had put up the best of security—the Bank's own stock. Moreover, if the Bank did not force stockholders to pay up in full on time, how could it effectively force the others to pay? And so it seemed that the Bank was about to fail in one of its important ideals. How else meet the situation except by asking these stockholders, some of them politicians, to withdraw?

There is a third possibility of great interest, namely keeping the Bank a creditors' bank. Old-time banks in Massachusetts had been planned along lines of banking on credit (with nominal collateral of land, produce, and personal promise). This Massachusetts Bank, founded by the conservatives of Boston, seemed about to go down the primitive path of its predecessors which in colonial days had been mercilessly slaughtered by British authorities. The old banks had had no capital and this new bank seemed about to lose much of its capital. Probably the directors believed that there was a major policy at issue. A creditors' bank might succeed; a debtors' bank could not, at any rate under the circumstances prevailing.

Coupled with this point is a fourth, namely that Phillips was coming to see that he was the Bank's chief stockholder and the only one who had its future on his conscience. If he could squeeze the others out, he could have a good conservative institution. He could force punctuality and could keep the capital at all times unimpaired. In this way something like a revolution in the interest of good banking was brought about. A battle was fought and won.

6. Development of a Discount Policy

Loans were made by the Bank at not more than 6 per cent (slightly more on a discount basis) and in the form of discounts—on bills of exchange and on promissory notes. The promissory notes had one or two names as surety or had goods or government bonds as collateral. The main point, however, is that at last there was a market for commercial paper in Boston. This was a great day for business and a landmark in the business history of New England. For centuries European banks had received deposits and transferred credit and loaned money to princes on security of jewels and revenues, and loaned to merchants through the discounting of bills of exchange, and ventured into commercial speculation. But now, in Boston, the sober business of loaning on paper which represented actual commercial transactions had begun in New England—more than a century later than in Old England. A measure of financial independence lay in the new procedure, for the paper need not henceforth center in London. Boston was taking on financial functions in its progress toward full metropolitan autonomy.

The merchants and investing capitalists who were responsible for the inception of the Bank were fully aware of the responsibilities involved in the function of discounting commercial paper. They expected that they themselves and their friends and foes would apply for discounts. The decisions should be wholly impartial. Accordingly a mechanism of free secret voting was set up. Each director should walk to the corner of the room and there put a white or a black ball into the box in balloting on each discount. One black ball would preclude a discount. Thus the central job of the Bank—making discounts—was not left to members of the staff, to the president, or to the sitting director. In passing we may note that capitalists were using the secret ballot long before democracies ostentatiously adopted it.

The discounters belonged to various classes. First and foremost were the sedentary merchants. Then came the financial group of capitalists concerned with making private loans, underwriting insurance, and acting as brokers in the insurance, foreign trade, and real-estate businesses. Next were the many retailers of Boston. Finally there was a group of gentlemen, politicians, lawyers, and doctors. Farmers as such were excluded in practice: few outside Boston entered the picture. New England as a whole was not considered for several generations and then only to be rejected. The

State of Massachusetts, however, right from the first was a favored customer, rather dramatically in 1787–88 when the agrarian disturbances (Shays' Rebellion) threatened State and Bank alike. The average amount of income derived from discounts per week in the year 1791 was over $955, though the average for 1785–91 was only $340.

As we might expect, the directors of the Bank had few ideas concerning discount policy when the Bank was in the process of formation and when it was taking the first steps. It seemed wise to profit by the experience of the Bank of North America by taking over its policies at many points including discounting. For instance the period of discount should be 30 days and the rate 6 per cent. The usual three days of grace were allowed for repayment. Most of the rules for discounting had to be developed. In 1790 no discount was to be made for less than $300 or more than $3,000 on an unsecured note. In 1792 the State limited the total amount of loans to be made. In 1807 the Bank decided to loan not over $70,000 to one person as promisor and endorser. Later the aggregate amount to be loaned to directors was limited. No loans could be made to members of the staff. Discount loans were to be promptly paid back but in practice often had to be renewed, frequently on a scaling-down of the amount. Rates had to be lowered and the length of the period increased as competition with other banks had to be met.

7. Policy of Issue and Specie Reserve

From the earliest times American banks have been institutions for issuing circulating notes, and many of the early banks had virtually no other function. How far did the Massachusetts Bank follow this precedent?

Certainly our Bank began its career by issuing notes of $1.00 to $100, including denominations of $1.50, $2.50, $3.50, and $4.50. These latter unusual amounts were designed to help alleviate the shortage of small change experienced in 1784 and subsequent years till well into the nineteenth century. Opposition soon arose to any denominations under $5.00; legislation was enacted accordingly in 1792.

At first the Bank was cautious as to the amount of notes it put out, as is indicated by Table 2.

Table 2. PERCENTAGE OF SPECIE RESERVE TO CIRCULATION AND DEPOSITS

(Weekly average)

1785	144.9	1789	55.2
1786	97.0	1790	57.4
1787	64.5	1791	20.1
1788	60.2		

The year 1791 was inflationary, as is shown by these figures. The climax of the boom was reached when a panic broke out in New York the following year. A Massachusetts law of 1792 stipulated that the loans and circulation of the Bank should not exceed double its capital. In the years to follow, for instance up to 1811, for which we have figures the circulation fell far below the maximum. This is indeed the situation for the rest of the Bank's career. For whatever reason, the Massachusetts Bank was conservative in its issuance of circulating notes. In the years 1876–77, and again in 1884–99, the Bank's notes outstanding were surprisingly small—about $45,000.

There was one experience away back in 1785 which is significant. The Bank undertook to put out a new issue of notes, this time not demand notes but notes carrying a promise of only deferred specie payment. Specie payment was to be made only when the Bank was dissolved. This was a dangerous practice probably induced by the bad business conditions of the year of the withdrawn shares. Certainly the practice was soon corrected by the Bank and stood out as a wart on a record which, at least for the period subsequent to 1791, was high indeed. Those interested should study the situation in 1785—bad business, demand-note policy, and discount policy.

We cannot fail to be impressed with the undeveloped character of banking in America at the time of the foundation of our banks, first in the eastern cities in 1781–91 and later inland as settlement gradually moved westward from 1792 onwards. In the big cities, conservative merchants had a feeling for strong banks created to handle commercial paper and to issue notes primarily in answer to the needs of local business. Banks in smaller communities, particularly near the fringes of settlement, commonly had a very different attitude toward circulating notes. The notes were put out in the form of long-term loans on produce and real estate, essentially to provide a permanent fund for all kinds of ventures including real-estate speculation. The notes were not thought of as going out and coming in, according to fluctuating grade, but as going out and staying out.

The Massachusetts Bank, correcting its policy of 1791, soon came to be known as a safe institution. Its specie reserve was kept high in relation to its circulation and deposits. In 1815 the Bank was a tower of strength. In 1837 and 1857, years of severe panic, it suspended specie payment only at the request of the other banks and with a realization that an isolated course would in the long run be disastrous. In 1861, when the Civil War was threatening to disturb business and finance, it suspended specie payment somewhat more readily, though its own liquidity was clear enough.

There stands the Bank, then, since 1792 priding itself on remaining strong and liquid, and so far away from the danger line that conservative persons would turn to it with the confident feeling of safety.

8. Policy of Deposits and Interest

Originally the Massachusetts Bank was thought of as an institution that would accept deposits but would not emphasize them very much. Indeed this attitude is very much like that of the old-time private bankers, the merchant bankers, of Europe: they would accept deposits but would not emphasize them, except in years of great prosperity when they might go so far as to pay interest on them.

The founders of the Bank stated that one of the Bank's contributions to Boston's business would be to keep deposits safely and without charge. Nevertheless a charge for keeping deposits was actually made in 1784–91 and the income therefrom was an appreciable, though small, sum. From 1791 to the end of the Bank's experience deposits were accepted without charge. In the boom year of 1791 the Bank must have observed that deposits loaned out on commercial paper might become a considerable source of profit.

The average deposits on hand at the end of the week in a seven-year and a three-year period, respectively, were: 1785–91—$40,099, and 1809–11—$587,424. Statistics for the period 1865–1900 show much less increase than we might expect. Table 3 is instructive.

Table 3. CONDITION OF THE MASSACHUSETTS NATIONAL BANK
1865–1900

(Average of annual statements reported to the Comptroller of the Currency)

Loans and discounts	$1,577,370
Individual deposits	1,000,883
Surplus and undivided profits	156,244
Circulation	212,649

The Massachusetts Bank was no more eager to hold balances of other banks than it was to obtain deposits from individuals. Beginning in 1818, however, it did accept deposits from savings banks which developed into something like time deposits. The years of the war of 1812–14 showed a surprisingly large array of deposits from banks located in neighboring towns. The practice did not become fixed, however, nor did it grow. Indeed, peace brought decline.

Here is an amazing situation. Our Bank

allowed New England to develop without discovering any great opportunity for service in the region. It had begun as a bank for the sedentary merchants and retailers of Boston. It might look abroad, along the coast to New York and Philadelphia and beyond, but it hardly turned its vision inland. Once when it did make a loan apparently secured by Iowa lands after the Civil War, it lost. But just here we are interested primarily in the fact that "the Old Massachusetts" never became a bankers' bank. Its slowness to join the national banking system established in 1863 is an indication, in part, of its lack of interest in becoming a reserve bank.

As to the payment of interest on deposits we find but little evidence of the existence of the practice in Massachusetts Bank records. During the period 1825–44, while other banks in and outside Boston increased their practice of paying interest, the Massachusetts Bank deferred action. Just as Boston lagged behind New York in paying interest on deposits (for instance on bank balances after 1863), so did the Massachusetts Bank lag behind other Boston banks.

9. Redemption and Coöperation with Other Banks

The Massachusetts Bank, the pioneer of modern banks in Boston, felt its unique position. When new banks arose in the period 1792–96, the old Bank resented the intrusion. Later it just ignored the increase which was notable between the War of 1812 and the Civil War. Preferring to play a lone hand, the Bank was forced by circumstances to suspend specie payment when the other banks did. It gladly united with the other banks in forming two associations (1832 and 1847) to discover and punish counterfeiters. And it joined in forming a Clearing House Association in 1856. There is doubt, however, whether the Massachusetts Bank ever actually took the lead in any coöperative movement of banks.

The great opportunity for coöperation among banks arose when the redemption of bank notes became a problem. Boston bank notes offered no special problem, for they could be presented for redemption every day. Country bank notes, however, were different. As early as 1796 they were envisaged as a potential difficulty. It was only in 1824, however, that an efficient system arose for meeting the situation. Leadership was supplied by the Suffolk Bank (established in 1818), though there had been temporary arrangements before that time.

This is no place to describe in detail the Suffolk system of redemption which has become a notable landmark in our banking development. In brief, it was an association of Boston banks created for the purpose of maintaining a healthy condition of circulating notes in New England at a time when no governmental organization or law provided for the same. The various banks agreed to deposit a large sum, free, in the Suffolk Bank, and that bank undertook to be the clearing house for country bank notes and to send them back to the issuing banks for redemption in specie. Imagine the distress of the country banks!

Note that the Massachusetts Bank was not the central institution in the association. Note also that it soon withdrew from the association. It felt that, on the whole, it did not have enough country bank notes to justify the maintenance of such a large free deposit as was required. It would have been willing to coöperate on a pro rata basis for service rendered. What a clear confirmation of the unimportance of New England to the Massachusetts Bank!

10. Operating Results

Over a long period dividends indicate profits, especially in an institution in which surplus and reserves were unimportant. Table 4 is revealing.

Table 4. DIVIDENDS, 1784–1903

Paid (Average per cent per annum)		Passed	
1784–1792	12.4	1892	—2nd half
1784–1865	7.3	1894	—1st half
1865–1903	4.8	1897–1900	—3½ years

During the last years of the old Bank (1900–03), however, dividends of 4 per cent were paid. Since this restoration of earning power belonged to the future and to another story, we may pass it at this point.

In banks, as in other business firms, there was for a long time no thought of reserves or surpluses except to meet some obvious obligation. Until 1837 our Bank had slight reserves. From 1844 to 1865 they were sizable. Then, in the period 1865–73, they were increasing but during the period 1873–96 decreasing. On the whole we may almost disregard the subject of reserves and surpluses.

The reasons for the diminution of earnings of the oldest bank in Boston are naturally of interest. We do not get far in our search for the causes of the Bank's difficulties without coming upon trust company competition in Boston. In 1871 the New England Trust Co. was formed, and in 1873 the Massachusetts Loan and Trust Co. By 1890 there were 10 such companies in Boston and by 1900 there were 15, all chartered by the State. If these new institutions had confined their activities to trust and safe-deposit business, the old commercial banks (national) would have been very little concerned. Actually, however, they were aggressive and successful in commercial banking. They paid interest on deposits, whilst the Massachusetts National did little or nothing along that line. They were not required to keep so high a reserve as the national banks. They could make larger loans to individuals. And, finally, they were freer in making loans on real estate. Add to these advantages the virility of young institutions and you have before you a potent rival for the Massachusetts Bank and the other Boston banks struggling for business in a metropolis which since about 1857 had seen more and more of its big accounts go off to New York as the sales agencies of New England's industries came to be located in the larger and more vigorous center.

In addition we should note that two of the periods of low earnings and heavy losses were 1812–44, when the average annual dividend was 5.1 per cent, and 1877–97, when it was 3.9 per cent. During both these periods prices were going down and business success becoming more difficult. Moreover, during the first period the ownership of the Bank's stock was falling into the hands of executors, administrators, and trustees. This stock had stood as a gilt-edge investment which business men left to their heirs or bequeathed to institutions. During the second period too many of the directors were older men whose chief distinction was long and honorable service. Perhaps these factors are enough to explain why undue losses occurred and how the capital became impaired.

It is instructive to glance at the presidents of the Bank. The first, James Bowdoin, was a figurehead. All the others who held office up to 1874 (for more than a few months) were sedentary merchants or their immediate descendants. Indeed the last, John J. Dixwell, had personally been a partner in the oriental business of a Boston firm and had been resident abroad. From 1874 to 1900 there were three presidents, all of whom were chiefly identified with the smaller affairs of Boston business.

From 1863 to 1900 there were only two cashiers. Promotion, seniority, long service, and loyalty were the supreme qualities found in the Bank. We are reminded of management conditions that prevail in some older insurance companies.

Perhaps it may be said that the directors used a telescope when concerned with the Bank and the cashiers a microscope. When we try to discover dynamic leadership, such as would have given to the Bank hegemony in New England and such as would have reached out to share in the new industrial and transportation developments in a vigorous way, we find only a disappointing lack of such leadership.

11. The Rescue, 1899–1903

The savings banks of Boston had come to own a considerable amount of the stock of commercial banks located in Boston. The savings banks were not active in the matter until dividends began to drop seriously or to disappear. Then they began to make known their needs and to call for a solution. At this point two investment companies entered the scene. The first was Kidder, Peabody & Co. and the second Hornblower & Weeks. The former consolidated a group of banks to form the National Shawmut Bank in 1898, while the latter turned to the Massachusetts Bank and ultimately built up a similar aggregation.

Two men played a dominant part in putting the Massachusetts Bank on its feet again during the years 1900–03. The first was John W. Weeks, one of the founders of Hornblower & Weeks, brokers and bankers of Boston. Weeks was a man of many friends and great influence among the people of money in Boston. He was not so much a day-to-day manager as a planner and supporter of projects. Much of his work was done through his own firm.

The refinancing consisted chiefly of securing a loan of a million dollars for use during the reorganization and then raising more capital by a levy of $50 on each share of stock. Only such procedures, carried through rather quickly toward the end of 1899 and early 1900, saved the Bank. Two other national banks failed in Boston and the money stringency in America and England threatened further trouble. One of the national bank examiners, Daniel G. Wing, stood ready to close the Bank, but the unfolding of Weeks' plans saved the institution.

When the reorganization was accomplished, Weeks became president and Wing vice-president. Wing was the second figure of vital importance in the reorganization. Weeks planned success for the Bank; Wing attained it. For 35 years he was successively vice-president, president, and chairman of the board. His accomplishments belong chiefly to the period since 1903 when the Massachusetts Bank bought the First National with Wing in command.

The new success, following 1900, came through three circumstances. The first was an upward swing in prices and an improved condition of business, 1897–1920–1929. The second was new management, in which Wing figured prominently. The third was a policy that fitted the times—mergers to create greater lending power, integration of banking functions, hustling for business, the payment of interest on virtually all deposits, and so on.

12. Readings

The sole printed source is *The Massachusetts-First National Bank of Boston, 1784–1934* (Cambridge, 1937), by N. S. B. Gras.

13. Suggested Questions

1. What was the nature of the change in capital structure in 1785?
2. Was there any connection between the withdrawing of shares in 1785 and the issuance of notes carrying the deferred specie payment clause?
3. Was there any contradiction in the Bank's two policies—refusing to let stockholders borrow on the Bank's stock and willingness to have directors borrow large sums?
4. Was there any justification for not paying interest on deposits?
5. What were the chief errors in Bank policy?

6. What contributions did the Bank make to the solution of banking problems in Boston, 1784–1903?
7. If you had been called in for advice in 1811–12, 1820–21, 1865–66, and 1884–85, what would you have recommended?
8. Can you see any alternative to merger after 1884 or after 1896?

XIV. THE SECOND BANK OF THE UNITED STATES: AN EXPERIMENT WITH BRANCHES

1. General Statement

The second Bank of the United States, established in 1816, was a striking experiment with a central bank having a dual ownership and control and a dual objective. Although it was chartered and in part owned and controlled by the national government, it was mostly private in ownership and management. The Bank was expected to supply the leadership which would bring about greater uniformity in American currency and banking, while as a business enterprise it was supposed to earn profits.

It was difficult enough to start a new bank in the period of postwar deflation, but, when to the business of banking was added the task of bringing order out of the chaos which had grown up in American finance, the task assumed tremendous proportions. This condition in banking and currency had developed out of a number of circumstances, particularly from the failure to recharter the first Bank of the United States in 1811 and the War of 1812, which together had brought a mushroom growth of State-chartered banks of issue lacking in uniformity and reliability. Such was the situation that led to the suspension of specie payments in all regions except New England. So bad had been the effect on private business and government finance that the very men who had killed the first Bank of the United States had forgotten their earlier constitutional scruples and sponsored the establishment of the new national bank.[1]

The administrators of the Bank faced nice problems in policy and management. First, to be effective the institution had to serve different and conflicting regional and local interests. How could the Bank at one and the same time meet the needs of Boston's State Street financiers, who served highly developed commercial and manufacturing interests, and the needs of the Mississippi Valley and its land speculators and new farmers, whose incomes were in the distant future and uncertain at best? Secondly, the proper function of a bank of this nature, in a rapidly expanding economy such as the United States, was at the time not clear. Should the Bank do a conservative commercial business, supplying short-time credit for financing trade, earning moderate profits, and becoming at the most an outstanding but not a dominating bank, or should it serve the longer-time needs of American business, dealing in securities and long-time loans, at a greater risk but also with a greater chance of earning profits and assuming leadership in American finance? In the third place, the executives of the Bank had, moreover, to square the Bank's business with its responsibility toward the government as a depository and a collecting and disbursing agent and as an instrument for bringing about the resumption of specie payments and restoring uniformity of value to American currency. Finally, there was the problem of politics. How could the opposition, arising from inevitable conflicts with local interests or with other banks or business

[1] The material for this case up to 1836 is taken from R. C. H. Catterall, *The Second Bank of the United States* (Chicago, 1903). Catterall has used the printed sources with great care and judgment and has in addition had access to valuable manuscript material in private hands. Exact references will be given only where material is quoted verbatim from Catterall or where other sources have been used.

enterprises which profited from individualism in banking, be kept from uniting politically with the traditional American fear of monopoly to prevent the renewal of the Bank's charter?

2. Important Dates in the History of the Bank

1816	National charter obtained.
1817	Central office opened at Philadelphia; 17 branches put into operation; specie payments resumed by other banks in February as result of Bank's action.
1817–19	Rapid expansion in Bank's business; fraud in management.
1819–23	Rescue by Cheves from impending failure.
1823	Nicholas Biddle became president in January.
1829	Bank considered very successful. President Jackson attacked Bank.
1832	Jackson vetoed bill for recharter.
1832–33	Trouble from overexpansion in Southwest and West.
1833	Bank began to contract in August. Removal of government deposits started in October.
1834	Panic, January–July, owing to severe contraction.
1834–35	Bank prepared to close.
1836	Pennsylvania charter obtained on March 3.
1837	Bank severely weakened by panic. Helped peg United States credit abroad.
1839	Biddle resigned as president in March. Biddle's pegging scheme failed in September.
1841	Bank closed.
1856	Final distribution to Bank's creditors.

3. Structure and Administration

The form of the organization of the Bank was specified in the Act of Incorporation, which gave to the institution a federal charter to run 20 years from March 3, 1816. One-fifth of the capital of $35,000,000 was to be subscribed by the United States government, and the government was to select 5 of the 25 directors, who were to constitute the central management. Rules covering the election of directors were designed to keep the administration in the hands of American citizens and to make it reasonably democratic. The Board was to choose annually one of its members as president and to appoint such officers and clerks as were necessary. This central board was instructed to establish branches in accordance with definite regulations and to draw up rules for their management and to elect directors for each branch from among the citizens of the United States living in the State, Territory, or District (D. C.) in which that branch was located.

The Act of Incorporation set specific limitations to the activities of the Bank. The institution was forbidden to own real estate beyond what was needed for housing the offices or was in good faith acquired on a mortgage or in satisfaction of a debt. The debts of the corporation at any one time, "whether by bond, bill, note, or other contract, over and above the debt or debts due for money deposited in the bank," should not exceed $35,000,000, unless authorized by a law of the United States. The Bank was forbidden to "trade in anything except bills of exchange, gold or silver bullion, or in the sale of goods really or truly pledged for money lent and not redeemed in due time, or goods which shall be the proceeds of its land." It was, further, forbidden to "purchase any public debt [State and municipal] whatsoever," or charge more than 6 per cent interest.

Certain safeguards were also specified. Bills or notes issued by the Bank should be signed by the central president and cashier. All bills or notes should be payable on demand (except those for sums not less than $100, payable to the order of a specified person or persons, which might run not over 60 days) and were receivable for all payments to the United States. The Bank was forbidden at any time to suspend or refuse specie payment on "its notes, bills, or obligations" or on its deposits. Moreover, the head of the Treasury Department should on request be furnished a statement of the Bank and allowed to inspect its general accounts, and a committee of either house of Congress, appointed for that purpose, might examine the books and proceedings of the Bank. The Bank had to serve the government without compensation; it was to transfer funds for the government within the United States and pay public creditors. In return public funds should be deposited with the Bank and its branches. For its privileges the Bank was to pay $1,500,000 to the United States.

4. Organization and Trouble, 1816–19

The establishment of the Bank followed immediately upon the completion of the subscription to its stock in August, 1816. William Jones, the secretary of the Treasury who had been appointed director by the government, was elected president. In January, 1817, the central bank at Philadelphia was opened for business. By March, sixteen cities had been selected as sites for branch offices: Boston, New York, Baltimore, Charleston, New Orleans, Washington, Richmond, Savannah, Norfolk, Lexington (Kentucky), Cincinnati, Portsmouth (New Hampshire), Providence, Middletown (Connecticut), Chillicothe (Ohio), and Pittsburgh.[2]

The first task of the Bank was to bring about the resumption of specie payments and the transfer of public deposits from other banks to itself. By making promises to the associated banks of New York, Philadelphia, Baltimore, and Richmond which were disadvantageous to itself, the Bank secured in February, 1817, the promise that those banks would resume specie payments and use their influence to get other banks to do likewise.

[2] J. J. Knox, *A History of Banking in the United States* (New York, 1900), p. 57; Catterall, *op. cit.*, p. 23.

Specie payment was thus nominally though not actually attained. Specie not only continued very widely to command a premium over bank currency, but the premium even increased. In 1820 the secretary of the Treasury said that throughout the greater portion of the time since specie resumption, "the convertibility of bank notes into specie has been rather nominal than real in the largest portion of the Union."[3]

The transfer of government funds from the State banks to the national bank was similarly difficult. According to the agreement of the banks, transfer should be made on July 1 with interest, though the Bank assumed in February the burden of paying government drawings up to $8,800,000. The Bank extended further concessions to banks in the interior, but even so some banks in western Pennsylvania and in Virginia and eastern Ohio did not perceive that any advantages could result to them from the arrangement.

Immediately after opening, the Bank started on a career of rapid expansion. It was "urged thereto," says Catterall, "by the government, and by the briskness of trade and the opportunities for favorable investment."[4] In July, 1817, a dividend of 2.6 per cent was declared. The statement of the Bank for July, 1818, showed the following results: discounts, $41,457,000; funded debt of the United States, $9,430,000; adverse balances with European bankers, $572,000; balances with State banks, $2,463,000; circulation, $9,045,000; public deposits, $7,967,000; other deposits, $4,786,000; and specie, $2,357,000. In 1818 a total dividend of 7½ per cent was declared.

The Bank early ran into difficulty with its branches. By July, 1818, there were 19 active branches. Communication with some of them was a matter of weeks. Each branch looked to its local needs, loaning on mortgages, renewing notes, using race-

[3] *Ibid.*, p. 38.

[4] *Ibid.*, p. 28.

horse bills (payment of one bill of exchange by the purchase of another), and issuing bills and drafts without furnishing means of payment at the branch drawn on. The branches issued notes almost without limit, which found their way for redemption to eastern offices of the Bank. The disequilibrium between the various offices of the Bank, the Southwest and West drawing more than they were drawn on, resulted in the transfer of the capital of the Bank to those debtor sections.

The Bank could have done something toward restoring regional equilibrium by forcing State banks to pay their debts and adverse balances to the Bank and its branches in specie. Local influences exerted through local stockholders paralyzed the Bank, however, with the result that the State banks were in reality able to expand their discounts and issues. Local feeling was, moreover, so strongly against the Bank that every effort was made to profit by presenting its notes for redemption in order to secure specie. The result was that the Bank had to import specie, which it did at a loss.

Another difficulty of the Bank came from speculation and fraud, especially in the Baltimore office. Catterall says that "a clique of Philadelphia and Baltimore stock-jobbers controlled the bank as soon as it was organized." [5] The Bank's business was managed in such a way as to raise the stock in the open market. The Bank discounted on stock security for the payment of the second installment on its shares, disregarding the regulation about the payment of a portion in specie. With the excuse of extending the Bank's discounts in order to make profits, stockholders were granted discounts on stock as collateral at 25 per cent above par. An office was established in London to pay dividends to foreign stockholders "at the par of exchange, at the risk and expense of the bank." As a result of these machinations the stock rose to a premium of from 50 to 56 per cent.

As has been noted, the branch at Baltimore was the worst offender. The local controllers of the branch made up a company to speculate in the Bank's stock. In the first two years Baltimore discounts were from five to twelve and one-half millions; those large discounts were in great measure deliberately made for the purpose of raising the value of the stock. For purchasing stocks the manipulators borrowed $1,957,000 at the Philadelphia Bank and $1,629,000 at Baltimore on stock security; the loans were renewed even after the borrowers were known to be insolvent. The conspirators actually loaned themselves over a million on no security whatsoever and overdrew their accounts heavily.

It is pertinent to contrast the loose management of branches by the second Bank of the United States with the definite and orderly management of the same type of organization by the first Bank of the United States. Though our knowledge of the operation of the earlier institution does not go very far, it appears that the administrators of the newer system might have profited from the example of those of the earlier bank, who fixed the capital available for the use of the individual branches and maintained close supervision over their operations.[6]

The panic which came in the fall of 1818 made the central Bank check up on the branches. The Baltimore branch manipulated its report so as to cover up the enormous stock loans to individuals. When President Jones resigned early in 1819, retribution fell on the Baltimore speculators. However, by that time the Bank had lost $1,401,000 through their machinations.

Several months earlier the Philadelphia directors had tried to save the Bank when

[5] *Ibid.*, p. 40.

[6] James O. Wettereau, "New Light on the First Bank of the United States," *Pennsylvania Magazine of History and Biography*, July, 1937, pp. 277–279.

its immediate demand liabilities were $22,-372,000 and its specie fund was $2,357,-000. The Bank ordered certain branches to curtail discounts and others to call in balances due from banks. It sent out orders for restricting the purchase of bills of exchange and for selling drafts at par. The Bank ordered branches to cease drawing on each other; it called on the southern and western branches for $700,000 in specie; it forbade the acceptance of notes of banks not redeeming on demand in specie; and it refused Cincinnati, a bad offender, credit till its balances overdue were discharged. Thus the Bank tried to control the branches in the interests of the whole institution.

Had these measures been effective, says Catterall, they would have spelled ruin for thousands. But the Bank, though it helped to precipitate the panic, was not strong enough to make the measures effective. The East curtailed; the West and South to a considerable measure either directly disobeyed or circumvented the orders—indeed, the West could not contract. In attempting to curtail in the West and South the Bank won the bitter enmity of the States, banks, and people.

5. Saving the Bank, 1819–22

When Langdon Cheves of South Carolina took over the presidency of the Bank, the financial condition of the institution was as follows: it had specie totaling $2,-666,000; a balance with State banks of $2,624,000; $7,391,000 in funded debt; $35,785,000 in discounts (a large portion suspended debt); a circulation of $6,563,-000; public deposits of $2,856,000; other deposits of $2,936,000; and an unfavorable balance with European banks of $812,-000. The secretary of the Treasury believed that suspension was inevitable.

Cheves immediately took strong emergency measures. Southern and western banks were directed not to issue notes, while the Bank itself ceased to purchase and collect on exchange on those regions. The curtailment of discounts was continued, orders were issued to collect balances due from State banks; the government was asked to give the Bank time to make transfers of funds from the place of collection to the place of disbursement; and $2,000,000 was borrowed for three years from European banks. In this way the storm was weathered.

The first task thereafter was to improve the capital of the institution. It was decided not to declare any dividends until after the restoration of the original capital. The active funds were reduced by retaining the $3,795,400 in shares surrendered by the Baltimore debtors, by investing as far as possible in the funded debt of and loans to the United States government, and by writing off the suspended debt of $10,000,000. This left an active capital of about $8,000,000. The capital of the Bank had been restored by January 1, 1821, and a dividend of 1.5 per cent was declared.

Cheves tried to get a better distribution of the capital of the Bank. When possible the funds of the Bank were transferred from western and southern to northern offices by means of remittances in specie or in bills of exchange on Europe or the North; there still remained, however, vast sums locked up in Baltimore, the South, and the West. Specific portions of the capital were assigned to the different offices to be used as their working capital. By January, 1823, permanent capitals had been fixed in the northern and southern offices, ranging from $200,000 at Portsmouth, New Hampshire, to $1,000,000 at New Orleans, $1,500,000 at Charleston, $2,500,-000 at New York, and $24,000,000 at Philadelphia. Capital had not been assigned to the western offices—indeed, their business had almost disappeared.

The next problem was to keep the amount of capital stationary in the places to which it had been assigned. One difficulty was to stop the movement of the note issues of offices in the South and West to the North for the payment of government dues. Cheves finally ordered that no notes should be issued by those branches which had unfavorable exchanges. To help make the capital stationary it was ordered that any office could draw bills on other offices only to the extent to which it had funds in those particular offices, and such bills were limited to 60 days and sale at par. The offices should, furthermore, furnish each other monthly reports, and the central board should make detailed weekly reports about the exchange business.

Another serious problem was to control relations with State banks. These banks, as we have noted, had drawn heavily on the Bank and its branches. Cheves held them to strict accountability. He required the reduction of the State-bank debts to the Bank and branches, the settlement of balances at specified intervals, and the presentation by the Bank and branches of the notes of the State banks for specie. Some of the debts to the Bank and its branches were settled by accepting real estate.

Other changes looked toward improvement in management. Incompetent directors and officers were weeded out and criminals prosecuted. Cheves tried to reduce the number of branches but succeeded only in closing the office at Cincinnati. Expenses were cut to the lowest possible figure.

Cheves's reforms are reflected in the Bank's statement for January 1, 1823. Discounts, balances with State banks, and circulation had decreased during his administration, while the funded debt held, specie, and public and other deposits had increased.

Though he put the Bank in a more secure position, Cheves by no means succeeded in solving the Bank's problems. His own policies were not without flaw; he allowed discounts on long dates and on the Bank's stock as security, and he was satisfied to have the issues of the branches circulate only locally. However, he ran into many difficulties not of his own making: he was unable to restrict overdrawing at Philadelphia or at the branches and he did not get sufficient control of the branch officers.

The State banks continued, moreover, to make trouble for the Bank. Their issues were in a bad condition, even in New England. In 1819–20 failures were common in the North, while throughout Cheves's administration conditions were depressed in the South and West, where few banks redeemed their notes in specie. The adoption of relief measures in the West prevented creditors from collecting. The Bank accordingly curtailed its dealings, with the result that the South and West were without means of securing loans and a sound currency. "Convinced that the bank was to blame for all their woes," says Catterall, "the entire population of the South and West spent their nights and days in reviling it as a rapacious, greedy, oppressive, and destructive monopoly." [7] Some did more than that, for in both the West and the South banks openly rebelled against the Bank, the Georgia banks, for instance, carrying on open warfare with Cheves. The Planters' Bank and the Bank of the State of Georgia, both of Savannah, had escaped paying their debts under Jones. Cheves asked them to redeem their notes in specie and to reduce to $100,000 their balances with the Savannah branch. "The Georgia banks considered the propositions monstrous, refused to pay the excess, and declined haughtily to suffer the indignity of daily settlements for their notes." [8] They delivered their ultimatum, and the Bank had to make concessions. "No concessions could satisfy the Georgia banks, for they were resolved to do business far in excess of what was commercially justifiable." [9] They represented the Bank as the monster that was devouring all their wealth. The struggle was nominally won by the Bank in the Supreme Court of the

[7] Catterall, *op. cit.*, p. 84.
[8] *Ibid.*, p. 85.
[9] *Ibid.*, pp. 86–87.

United States,[10] but the verdict of public opinion was to all appearances different.

6. An Effective Central Bank, 1823–31

In January, 1823, Nicholas Biddle was elected president of the Bank of the United States. He was then 37 years old. He was of a distinguished Philadelphia family, a graduate of Princeton, and had lived in Paris and London. By profession he was a lawyer, and he had served in the senate of his State. His avocation was literature; he wrote poetry and prose and he had edited Lewis and Clarke's *Journal* on the exploration of the Northwest. In 1819 Biddle had been appointed director of the Bank of the United States. Versatile as he was, he had dug deeply into economic theory in general—Adam Smith, Ricardo, and the French economists—and banking and monetary questions in particular. He had become one of the most prominent among the directors of the Bank.

Catterall gives an excellent summary of Biddle's character and personality: [11]

"He was a man of eminent tact, conciliatory in temper, versatile, untiringly industrious, quick of apprehension and quick to act, strong-willed and tenacious of his own opinions. His prominent fault was the possession of an over-sanguine temper. On the whole, it would have been difficult to secure a more capable man for the position."

Jones had built up a tremendous business but had almost ruined the Bank. Cheves saved the Bank but almost destroyed its business. Biddle aimed to maintain the Bank's stability, while making it an effective national banking institution. He had definite ideas on how to accomplish this end though his ideas were neither consistently adhered to nor completely enforced.

In his early years as the head of the Bank, Biddle favored a policy of conservative commercial banking: [12]

"We have had enough and more than enough of banking in the interior. We have been crippled and almost destroyed by it. It is time to concentrate our business—to bank where there is some use and some profit in it, . . . to make at present the large commercial cities the principal scene of our operations."

Biddle believed that the Bank could dominate the State banks so as to raise the standard of the country's bank currency. He maintained that the Bank should use its own notes, instead of reissuing the notes of State banks as done under Cheves, and return the notes of other banks to be exchanged for specie. This the Bank could do by keeping itself a creditor to the others.

The policy of collecting specie would shift some of the pressure for specie from the Bank of the United States and would make possible an expansion of the Bank's currency without endangering its convertibility. This would, as a result, allow wider circulation of the branch notes, which should circulate as widely as the notes of the mother bank. This was a departure from Cheves's policy of limiting the area of circulation of branch issues. In keeping with his general aim to increase the Bank's usefulness and power Biddle favored a considerable expansion of discounts. He opposed loans on real estate and stock as security, however, and he wanted loans to run only 60 to 90 days, or in exceptional cases 120. Even when demand was slack, he thought a conservative policy should be followed. To escape the dangers in discounting on personal security he emphasized the safety in buying bills of exchange—"Our great object is business men and business paper," he said.[13] He thought that a surplus and the holding of a considerable amount of government securities were further safeguards.

[10] *Bank of the United States* v. *The Planters Bank of Georgia.*

[11] Catterall, *op. cit.*, p. 93.

[12] *Ibid.*, p. 95, quoting a letter of Biddle to R. Lenox, Feb. 3, 1823.

[13] *Ibid.*, p. 100.

Biddle's ideas on branch management differed considerably from Cheves's. He believed in giving branches more latitude, in removing Cheves's allocation of specific amounts of capital, and in setting aside restrictions on the circulation of notes. He believed that the first essential was to have strong men as cashiers of the branches.

The first consideration to note for the period 1823–31 is how Biddle organized the institution. As noted above, he wanted strong cashiers. McIlvaine, a man admirably suited for the place, was made cashier of the head office at Philadelphia. The new branch cashiers were generally chosen from among the trusted men in the Philadelphia bank, who were familiar with its policy and were freer from local influences than if chosen from a branch's own community. Biddle was unable to place cashiers of his own choosing in all the branches. At Nashville, for instance, a local man, appointed on the recommendation of President Andrew Jackson, carried on such reckless and reprehensible banking that he became a source of great trouble to the Bank.

Biddle devised other means for centralizing control in the mother bank. Holding that local cashiers should be subject to orders from Philadelphia, even though these orders might be contrary to the action of the local board, he required regular reports from them. The branch boards and presidents continued, of course, to be local. Several devices were adopted for checking the officers of the branches: unofficial observers reported to Biddle on their condition, and any member of the central board residing at the location of a branch was expected to act on the local board, with power to advise and discuss. To further centralize control, two assistant cashiers in the Philadelphia office were created in 1826, one to supervise the work of the branches, especially the accounts between the branches and their exchange business, and the other to take charge of the real estate and the suspended debt of the Bank and branches.

Biddle inherited from his predecessors the task of making the banks of the country resume specie payments. In his skillful handling of that problem he showed his own and the Bank's capacity for leadership. By increasing circulating notes of the Bank, so as to free it from the necessity of using State-bank notes, and by regulating its business so as to put it in a creditor position toward the State banks, Biddle was able to compel the State banks regularly to redeem their notes in specie. The Bank was aided by the government's refusal to take non-redeemed notes. So strong did his institution become that Biddle could say that there were "very few banks which might not have been destroyed by an exertion of the power of the bank." [14]

By 1830 it had become possible to force the banks everywhere to pay the Bank and its branches in specie. In accomplishing this, however, the Bank had won much criticism, for it was the accepted practice among banks not to demand specie from one another. Moreover, the Bank took nothing below $5 notes, and its influence, therefore, did not extend to the smaller currency—it was hardly strong enough with the public to follow its specie policy to the limit.

We find in this period of the Bank's history the emergence of the idea that such an institution should be somewhat of a reserve bank and should be able to cushion the shock in case of sudden and extreme changes in business. In the panic of 1825 the Bank's reserve helped tide over the period of stringency. Unfortunately, in 1828 when times again were hard the Bank was not in a condition to give that service.

The Bank's circulation was greatly expanded in those years. The amount issued was increased from $4,361,000 in January, 1823, to $21,355,000 in January, 1832.

[14] *Ibid.*, p. 438.

Actually, however, the circulation was somewhat larger. In the rapid expansion of business in the earlier years of Biddle's term, when the issues were kept down by the requirement that the president and the cashier of the mother bank sign the notes, Biddle adopted the branch draft as a substitute for notes. Legally they were different but they served the same practical purpose, being used especially in the newer sections.

The Bank currency was highly satisfactory. It circulated freely. Both branch issues and the issues of the main office had a high degree of convertibility. The issues were fairly flexible, but elasticity was hampered by the heavy deposits and drawings of the government, which brought expansion and contraction with little relation to business needs. The slowness of the presentation of notes for redemption, moreover, sometimes delayed contraction. Though there was neither true convertibility nor perfect elasticity, says Catterall, slight changes in the laws regulating the currency "would undoubtedly have given the country an excellent paper currency, completely convertible and sufficiently elastic." [15]

[15] *Ibid.*, p. 429.

Table 1. SELECTED ITEMS FROM THE GENERAL STATEMENTS OF THE BANK OF THE UNITED STATES, January, 1823–32
(000 Omitted)

Date	Discounts on Personal security	Discounts on Bank [a] stock	Discounts on Other securities	Domestic exchange	Real estate	Funded debt	Balances [b] with European bankers
1823	$22,597	$6,149	$ 50	$ 1,940	$ 626	$11,018	$-1,268
1824	24,324	6,708	75	2,323	1,302	10,874	414
1825	23,170	5,655	258	2,727	1,495	18,422	-2,383
1826	27,104	3,131	69	3,118	1,848	18,303	170
1827	24,330	2,933	326	3,347	2,039	17,764	180
1828	26,452	1,928	280	5,022	2,295	17,624	-1,111
1829	29,854	1,375	298	7,689	2,345	16,099	482
1830	30,654	1,002	315	8,691	2,886	11,610	1,530
1831	32,827	665	83	10,456	2,629	8,674	2,383
1832	48,852	731	18	16,691	2,136	2	-1,356

Date	Balances [b] with State banks	Specie	Circulation	Public deposits [c]	Other deposits	Profits On discounts	Profits On exchange
1823	$ 1,407	$ 4,424	$ 4,361	$ 4,275	$3,347	$ 573	$ 49
1824	1,287	5,813	4,647	10,181	3,520	678	67
1825	2,130	6,746	6,068	6,702	5,330	558	78
1826	747	3,960	9,474	5,769	5,444	711	107
1827	1,683	6,457	8,549	8,982	5,337	721	101
1828	-1,697	6,170	9,855	8,354	6,142	697	190
1829	1,723	6,098	11,901	10,697	6,364	823	274
1830	1,199	7,608	12,924	9,654	6,391	876	372
1831	- 734	10,808	16,251	9,131	8,165	889	401
1832	1,993	7,038	21,355	12,589	8,107	1,254	584

[a] Of the second Bank of the United States.
[b] Minus sign indicates balances against the Bank.
[c] Deposits by United States Treasurer and other public officers.

A most striking development is the rise of the Bank to dominance in the field of exchange. Under Biddle the Bank entered heavily into foreign exchange, which had been largely in the hands of merchants. Its dealing in foreign exchange began to be of some consequence in 1826. This business was based on the sale of the products of the South, chiefly cotton, the Bank buying foreign bills in the South and selling them in the North. It also dealt in China bills, being effective in stopping specie exports to China and the East Indies. From 1827 the Bank practically controlled foreign exchange.

The same was done in domestic exchange. Since the State banks had not had a proper organization for handling the business, particularly in the West and Southwest, inland exchange had been largely in the hands of private bankers and brokers. Catterall has estimated that the inland bills purchased by the Bank totaled $8,980,000 in 1823 and $46,532,500 in 1831. Throughout those years there was a gradual increase in the proportion of exchange transactions of the Bank in the West and Southwest so that by 1831 over half of the total was made in that region. The Bank had decided advantages over its competitors, and it is not strange that, because of its low rates and the regularity of its business, it practically dominated the whole domestic exchange market by 1832.

Other aspects of the business of the Bank are seen from Table 1, which sets forth the business of the Bank as reported in January of each year.[16]

Up to 1831 Biddle's administration appears to have been strikingly successful. The Bank had furnished a sound currency and low rates of exchange. It was doing a large business and maintaining its strength. In 1825 it had helped tide over the panic. It was at the same time doing well by its stockholders, its dividends rising from 4.25 per cent in 1822 to 7 per cent in 1829, the latter rate being maintained through 1836.[17] The suspended debt had been reduced from $10,426,000 in 1822 to $3,633,000 in 1831; the emergency loan of 1821 had been paid; and a surplus of $1,698,102 had been built up.

7. Overexpansion in the Southwest and West, 1831–32

We need only to examine its business to see that, although the Bank was apparently in a strong position in 1831, it was headed for trouble. It had extended its business heavily in the Southwest and West, and 1831 saw further expansion of its activities in those regions. By the Southwest and West is meant the Ohio and Mississippi valleys, which had 9 of the 26 offices of the Bank, all depending largely on recent agricultural development, much of it speculative. Biddle saw the dangers in the interior business, but he may have felt that the management had been sufficiently improved and the Bank sufficiently strengthened to take risks in the interior. Table 2 shows concretely what was happening.[18]

Table 2. BUSINESS OF BRANCHES IN SOUTHWEST AND WEST COMPARED WITH REST OF SYSTEM
1828–32
(000 Omitted)

	Discounts	Bills of exchange	Totals
May 1, 1828			
Southwest and West	$10,701	$ 2,996	$13,697
All other offices	21,959	3,696	25,655
May 1, 1829			
Southwest and West	12,001	4,757	16,758
All other offices	21,623	4,509	26,132

16 23d Cong., 2d Sess., *Sen. Doc.*, no. 17, pp. 194, 210–222; 25th Cong., 2d Sess., *Sen. Doc.*, no. 128, pp. 208–211.

17 23d Cong., 2d Sess., *Sen. Doc.*, no. 17, p. 194; 24th Cong., 2d Sess., *Ex. Doc.*, no. 118, pp. 136–137.

18 Catterall, *op. cit.*, p. 137.

May 1, 1830 [a]			
Southwest and West	$14,164	$ 6,577	$20,741
All other offices	19,640	4,237	23,877
May,[b] 1831			
Southwest and West	15,872	9,144	25,016
All other offices	20,061	5,822	25,883
May,[b] 1832			
Southwest and West	22,467	13,952	36,419
All other offices	24,905	9,100	34,005

[a] As of April 30.
[b] Date not given in source.

Certain circumstances of the time suggest why the Bank's business was thus shifted. One was the payment of the government debt, which forced Biddle to invest elsewhere the seven millions which the Bank had kept in the United States funded debt. He tried to put them into State loans of Pennsylvania, Louisiana, and Mississippi, but he failed to get the loans. Catterall maintains that Biddle also tried to invest in the East and South but did not succeed. There was a plethora of capital in eastern markets. Safe loans could be made there but at low rates. At the same time a strong expansion movement, offering lucrative investments, was developing in the West. The Erie Canal, the increasing use of steam on western rivers, and the beginning of railroad building were important in giving this movement the momentum which it had attained by 1832.

Presumably Biddle expected to conduct the inland business on safe principles. There is no denying, however, that that business was based on crops, which meant longer-time loans at best with inability to pay and renewals of loan if the crops failed. Biddle's plan to deal heavily in exchange was sound if properly carried out and based on legitimate commercial transactions. This he tried to bring about by requiring that the inland branches deal only with New Orleans in their exchange transactions and not with other branches, New Orleans conducting the branches' business with the South and East. The business was thus to be centralized in a strong office whose cashier was a trusted and competent graduate of the head office. In other words, responsibility for the region was to be centered in one office. This reminds one not a little of regional leadership in the Federal Reserve System.

As a matter of fact the rule that western exchange should be centered in New Orleans was widely disregarded. Much of the traffic in bills of exchange was illegitimate. It was more profitable to sell a bill than to discount a loan; the interest rate on discounts was limited by the Bank's charter to 6 per cent, while bills with the premium on exchange brought 12 per cent, which was the market rate. Disregarding Biddle's earlier order that the transactions should be limited to 60, 90, or at the most 120 days, bills were sold for six months. Worst of all, when the six months were over, the bill was frequently paid by the drawing of another bill on another branch. Although Biddle was informed of many irregularities, he did not take sufficient action to curb them.

This bad business was flagrantly carried on in Louisville, Nashville, and even in responsible New Orleans; these branches, together with Lexington, in 1829 to 1832 did four-fifths of all the exchange business of the West and Southwest. New Orleans' participation suggests that there must have been a dearth of legitimate business. In that case, should the Bank and branches have contracted their activities accordingly?

Such banking business could not stand a severe shock. The shock came in 1831 and 1832 when the cotton crop was short. The liquidation of loans was dependent on the sale of crops, and the imports of foreign goods for the whole country were largely dependent on bills drawn on the cotton crop. In the absence of such bills, specie went abroad. At the same time the United States Treasury demanded $6,000,000 of its deposits.

Biddle saved the situation, temporarily,

by borrowing $1,000,000 beyond his usual credit with Barings in London and securing a longer time in which to meet the government's demand for its $6,000,000.

He tried to improve the Bank's condition by ordering a contraction of its loans beginning in October, 1831. But contraction was not easy. Boston, New York, Philadelphia, and Baltimore succeeded in contracting, but the expansion inland had gained such momentum that instead of contraction, or even just renewal of loans, there was actually expansion until sometime in May, 1832. Eastern contraction during that time did not equal western expansion. It is significant that, though the Bank did not actually curtail in the West and Southwest, the slowing-up of expansion caused very much distress and increased the feeling that the Bank was an enemy of the interests of that region.

8. The Political War on the Bank, 1832–34

Biddle had learned his lesson and he might have profited by the experience, but the Bank of the United States was not free to work out its own salvation. The length of life of a private business institution is determined largely by its profits. The existence of the Bank was determined by its enemies. These were many: those whose constitutional scruples made them oppose the Bank; the States or cities which objected to the encroachment of the Bank of the United States on their own business; that legion of State banks, private bankers, and brokers who objected to the way the Bank ruled them and took away their business; Jackson and his kind, in command of the Democratic Party; and the debtor elements in general. Against its enemies the Bank could array solid and substantial friends, but they were not many in number.

Biddle early became aware of President Jackson's hostility and tried to defend his institution. Thinking the time favorable, he brought up the question of recharter in 1832, drawing the bill so as to satisfy the States and the State banks. In spite of determined opposition from the South, Southwest, and West, the bill passed both Houses, but it was vetoed by Jackson. The charges on which the Bank was convicted are disproved by the facts of the case, says Catterall. Although the President considered his reëlection in 1832 as approval of his attitude toward the Bank, the Bank still showed signs of strength in Congress.

In 1833 the war was carried to another front when Jackson began the removal of government deposits from the Bank. Heavy drafts were given to State banks and drawn without any notice to the Bank of the United States. In the first half of 1833, $6,000,000 was withdrawn, but of this action the Bank had ample warning. From July, 1833, to July, 1834, the government deposits were further reduced $3,837,000. In July, 1834, government deposits remained in the Bank to the amount of $2,675,000.

Before the government actually began to remove the deposits, Biddle started to prepare for such a contingency. He gave instructions that discounts should not be increased and bills should be drawn only on short time and on eastern offices. These early measures were not unduly severe and were calculated to transfer the Bank's capital eastward in order to make it more easily available in case of call.

At this point Biddle failed to reckon with public psychology. Moved in a measure by the necessity of meeting withdrawals, but also angered by the President's action and hoping to force the recharter of the Bank by showing how business would suffer without it, Biddle continued to order contraction. Discounts were decreased, stringent rules were enforced for contracting the exchange business, thereby mobilizing the Bank's capital ultimately in the East, and debts due from State banks were collected in specie or drafts on eastern cities.

The result was a tremendous contraction. From August 1, 1833, to September 1, 1834, there was a decrease of $17,200,000, or 27 per cent, about equally divided between discounts and bills. State-bank balances were reduced from $2,200,000 in October, 1833, to $500,000 in the following April. From the first of August, 1833, to October 1, 1834, the circulation was reduced $3,200,000, and the specie in the Bank was increased over $5,000,000. Altogether there was a reduction of $25,000,000 in one year.

The effect on the country was severe. Money became very tight, discount rates rose, wages and prices fell, unemployment increased, and bankruptcies were numerous. By January business houses and banks were failing in large eastern cities and a real panic was on. Times remained very hard until the Bank relaxed its contraction policy in July.

By this severe contraction the Bank had put itself into a strong financial position. But the suffering it had caused and the exhibition it had made of its strength increased its enemies. The people had seen what havoc the monster could bring. The election of 1834 sealed the Bank's doom.

9. Preparing to Close the Bank, 1834–36

The conduct of the Bank in the last year and a half under its national charter undid some of the evil of the years immediately preceding. Contrary to expectations the business was expanded but in

Table 3. SELECTED ITEMS FROM SEMIANNUAL STATEMENTS OF THE BANK OF THE UNITED STATES
1833–36
(000 Omitted)

Date		Discounts on: Personal security	Bank[a] stock	Other securities	Domestic exchange	Real estate
1833	January	$40,085	$ 687	$ 2,854	$18,069	$1,855
	July	37,032	827	3,833	21,676	1,809
1834	January	33,703	912	3,993	16,302	1,741
	July	29,932	1,031	3,459	16,601	1,741
1835	January	29,933	1,006	3,686	17,183	1,760
	July	32,132	1,860	6,228	24,976	1,758
1836	January	31,356	3,043	5,961	19,824	1,486
	March 3[b]	20,148	3,060	17,385	17,750	2,570

Date		Balances with European bankers	Balances[c] with State banks	Specie	Circulation	Public deposits	Other deposits
1833	January	$3,106	$1,596	$ 8,951	$17,518	$12,752	$7,518
	July	1,911	485	10,098	19,366	6,512	9,868
1834	January	1,801	1,536	10,031	19,208	4,230	6,734
	July	3,827	408	12,823	16,641	2,675	6,735
1835	January	1,922	1,490	15,708	17,339	2,621	7,844
	July	2,378	−2,065	13,429	25,332	1,686	9,558
1836	January	73	1,427	8,417	23,075	627	4,369
	March 3[b]	1	2,653	5,595	21,109	324	3,390

[a] Of the second Bank of the United States.
[b] Date of expiration of charter.
[c] Minus sign indicates balances against the Bank.

such a way as to prepare for the final liquidation early in 1836.

Table 3 reflects the changes in the Bank's policies and condition from 1834 through 1836.[19] (See preceding page.)

The central policy underlying the Bank's activities was so to conduct the business as to get control of the capital without exerting pressure on business. The object was to move the capital eastward and to get it into such shape that the affairs of the Bank could easily be liquidated.

In carrying out this policy exchange transactions were for some time large. Bills on the smaller branches in the West and Southwest were diminished while those on New Orleans and the eastern cities were increased. Discounts on personal security were contracted and converted into longer-time discounts on stocks and bonds as security. The real estate of several branches and the debts due to branches were sold largely in return for long-time loans also based on stocks and bonds, a reversal of Biddle's earlier policy. It was thus hoped to transfer the Bank's assets to Boston, New York, and Philadelphia and to get them into such shape that they could be liquidated without unnecessary loss and disturbance of business. It should be noted that some of these new loans ran as long as 20 years and that a large proportion were on stock security. In the Bank's efforts to secure control of its capital, the plentifulness of money, the good condition of business, and the rapid expansion in the security business were of great assistance.

The preparation for the winding-up of the Bank's affairs was proceeding satisfactorily when, in the fall of 1835, it was decided to continue the Bank under a State charter. The liquidation was then stopped. In February, 1836, the Bank was rechartered by Pennsylvania. It was arranged that the new institution should pay the United States government for its shares at the rate of $115.58 a share in four installments from 1837 to 1840.[20] When its national charter expired on March 3, the assets and liabilities of the Bank were as follows: [21]

STATEMENT OF THE SECOND BANK OF THE UNITED STATES

March 3, 1836

Assets	
Bills and Notes, including those protested	$57,368,018.62
Real Estate	1,483,219.21
Banking-houses	729,170.58
Mortgages and Navy Agent	96,181.84
State Banks, Balances and Notes	4,933,178.02
Specie	5,595,077.25
Deficiencies	149,796.94
Expenses	166,803.16
United States (disallowed)	5,267.32
	$70,526,712.94

Liabilities	
Capital	$35,000,000.00
Circulation	21,109,352.23
Dividends Unclaimed	253,937.43
Due to Baring Brothers	371,777.40
Contingent Interest	502,933.98
Due to Bank and Offices	1,548,869.31
Public Debt	120,621.87
Due to Depositors	3,594,048.25
Discount, Exchange, and Interest	602,713.39
Profit and Loss	3,765,031.55
Foreign Exchange Account	925,019.60
Fund for Banking-houses	1,104,223.09
Contingent Fund, less losses chargeable	1,628,184.84
	$70,526,712.94

10. Leadership in Panic, Boom, and Depression, 1837–41

The Bank continued from March 3, 1836, under the Pennsylvania charter as

[19] 23d Cong., 2d Sess., *Sen. Doc.*, no. 17, pp. 94, 124; 25th Cong., 2d Sess., *Sen. Doc.*, no. 128, pp. 2, 38, 61, 208–211.

[20] According to Treasury Records quoted by Knox, *op. cit.*, p. 79, the United States made a profit of $6,093,167.07 on its investment.

[21] 24th Cong., 2d Sess., *Ex. Doc.*, no. 118, p. 100.

it was under the old charter.[22] The new Bank took over the business of the old Bank, but it did not have the backing of the government and the prestige and business which that gave. Biddle, however, hoped even under a State charter to make the Bank a leader among the banks in the United States.

Circumstances very unfavorable to the Bank made its later career difficult: (1) the Bank was required to give a heavy bonus to the State for its charter; (2) it inherited from the old Bank a vast quantity of long-time loans based on stocks and bonds as security; (3) the panic of 1837 (May) all but annihilated the securities on which those loans were based, and upset business seriously throughout the country; and (4) European capital sought American investment and helped foster a boom which flourished until 1839.

Table 4 (p. 186) indicates the nature of the Bank's business and its condition through its first year and a half under its Pennsylvania charter.[23]

When the panic came and suspension spread the country over, the Bank was forced to suspend. Thereby it lost any power over the currency of the country that it had retained after losing its national charter.

The Bank was caught with fixed obligations, while the securities and goods with which to meet the obligations greatly decreased in value. The same was true of the whole country. Should business be liquidated at once, or should attempts be made to forestall liquidation? Biddle chose the latter. The first problem was to stop the export of specie and satisfy foreign creditors before things had gone so far as to force liquidation. Biddle hoped to assume leadership in American finance and to rescue American credit.[24]

The first step was to liquidate the immediate obligations of the United States to Europe. Biddle, therefore, called a conference of New York and Philadelphia bankers and proposed a plan. The result was the issue of a large amount of "post-notes" (short-term, interest-bearing notes) by the Bank of the United States, followed by smaller issues by four other banks. These notes immediately commanded a premium in New York and were received so favorably in London that they were taken by the Bank of England at the very time that it was trying to reverse the flow of gold to the United States.

This step led to the bold effort to peg the price of cotton. In exchange for post-notes the American banks received cotton bills. These had to be protected from a fall in the cotton price. Indeed, American credit, generally, leaned heavily on the price of cotton abroad, for cotton was the principal commodity used in settling American foreign mercantile balances in the 'thirties. Biddle accordingly devised a scheme for pegging cotton prices. Through Bevan & Humphries, Philadelphia merchants, cotton was bought in the South by means of notes on the Bank of the United States and consigned, at first to Baring Brothers and shortly to a new firm, Humphries & Biddle, of Liverpool. In the meantime, Baring Brothers having withdrawn their open credit granted to the Bank of the United States, Biddle had established Samuel Jaudon as the financial agent of the Bank in London. When the cotton bills on Humphries & Biddle became due, that house drew on Jaudon instead of selling at low prices. To cover payments Jaudon issued post-notes of the Bank of the United States, which were redeemed when due by the proceeds from the sale of secu-

[22] R. C. McGrane, *The Correspondence of Nicholas Biddle* (Boston, 1919), p. 307, letter of Biddle to John Forsyth.

[23] 25th Cong., 2d Sess., *Ex. Doc.*, no. 79, pp. 362–391. Table 4 is a contraction and rearrangement of the table from which it was taken.

[24] L. H. Jenks, *The Migration of British Capital to 1875* (New York, 1927), p. 89; R. C. McGrane, *Foreign Bondholders and American State Debts* (New York, 1935), pp. 15–16.

Table 4. STATEMENT OF THE PENNSYLVANIA BANK OF THE UNITED STATES

1836–37

(000 Omitted)

RESOURCES

	Bills and notes discounted	Loans [a] on stock	Bonds, judgments, and mortgages	Bills of exchange	Real estate and other property	Expense account	Due by other banks	Notes and checks of other banks	Credits not included under preceding heads	Specie	Total [b] resources of the Bank
August, 1836	$42,814	$2,880	$132	$11,867	$1,501	$ 85	$ 1,285	$1,604	$53,074	$4,696	$119,859
January, 1837	43,965	...	...	13,246	1,287	124	38,707	1,206	2,677	2,638	119,322
June, 1837	43,140	...	...	17,805	1,225	138	36,484	1,212	6,342	1,468	128,908
November, 1837	33,617	...	...	8,643	1,561	137	38,497	997	21,378	3,349	128,004

LIABILITIES

	Notes in circulation	Due to other banks	Due depositors	Discount, exchange, and interest	Profit and loss	Contingent fund	Debits not included under preceding heads	Capital stock	Total [b] liabilities of the Bank
August, 1836	$11,805	$ 1,655	$1,944	$1,913	$4,291	$5,943	$57,171	$35,000	$119,859
January, 1837	11,447	33,282	2,259	1,164	4,291	1,276	9,819	35,000	119,322
June, 1837	8,602	30,640	2,520	1,566	4,755	1,145	15,601	35,000	128,908
November, 1837	6,748	29,082	2,817	987	5,191	1,202	20,394	35,000	128,004

[a] Apparently stock of the Bank of the United States.
[b] Totals include some minor items omitted from table.

rities for the Bank of the United States, of Pennsylvania.

The scheme worked. At the end of eighteen months the cotton pool had made $800,000 for its operators, chiefly officials of the Bank of the United States, while the rise in cotton brought the desired improvement in the cotton industry and in American credit abroad.[25]

The very success of the Bank in pegging American credit abroad led to further complications. That success enabled the Bank to weather the panic and the subsequent recession, but kept it from making use of a possible chance to strengthen its own position by the liquidation of its assets and the contraction of its business. Instead the Bank continued to involve itself more deeply in long-time investments. Some of this was inevitable. But into some of it Biddle was led by his success and his enthusiasm for internal improvements, particularly for projects which gave promise of strengthening Philadelphia against its rivals. In the late 'thirties he became one of the country's greatest supporters of canal and railroad building. By such a policy the Bank which might have checked inflation only served to increase it.[26]

For internal improvements extensive credit was needed. American securities, issued in vast amounts, supplemented the post-notes in securing credit abroad. This was obtained through the London agency of Biddle's institution and through other channels in Europe. Biddle's reputation and the fact that the shares of his Bank were held abroad in large proportions enabled the Bank of the United States to market considerable amounts of stocks in England.[27] In doing this the Bank practically became the guarantor of vast sums loaned to American corporations, especially in the West and Southwest. In addition the Bank itself loaned heavily to various American enterprises, notably to those in Pennsylvania.

The vast credit structure thus built up was to be the ruin of the Bank. Unfortunately a very complicated set of adverse circumstances broke cotton prices in England in 1839. The credit of the Bank of the United States no longer sufficed to hold up the price. A second cotton pool failed in September to the amount of $900,000, much of the loss falling on the Bank of the United States,[28] and the credit of the Bank practically collapsed. European shareholders came to the aid of the Bank temporarily. This assistance was later covered by loans from the Paris Rothschilds and the Amsterdam Hopes on bonds of Mississippi, Illinois, Indiana, and Pennsylvania as security.

The Bank of the United States never recovered, and American credit did not for two decades regain the prestige it had lost. Biddle had resigned from the presidency of the Bank in March, 1839, and the Bank was closed in 1841.[29]

The following balance sheet, compiled from the report of the Bank of December 21, 1840, shows the condition of the institution just before it expired.[30]

STATEMENT OF THE BANK OF THE UNITED STATES, OF PENNSYLVANIA
December 21, 1840

ASSETS

Discounts	
Active	
on personal security	$ 8,023,967.63
on other security	2,552,553.17

[25] Jenks, *op. cit.*, pp. 90–91.

[26] See *Hunt's Merchants' Magazine*, vol. i (1839), pp. 508–509.

[27] Jenks, *op. cit.*, pp. 93–95.

[28] *Ibid.*, pp. 97–98.

[29] The following statement of a Philadelphia banker in the 1850's indicates what happened to the Bank: "All the circulating notes of the Bank of the United States together with the deposits, were paid in full, principal and interest, and the accounts of the assignees were finally settled in 1856. There were no funds, and no dividend was paid to the stockholders of the bank; the whole twenty-eight millions of dollars were a total loss to them" (Knox, *op. cit.*, p. 79).

[30] 26th Cong., 2d Sess., *Ex. Doc.*, no. 4, pp. 154, 157.

Suspended	
on personal security	$ 7,101,887.57
on other security	961,468.43
Domestic Bills of Exchange	
Active	1,610,590.30
Suspended	1,736,444.58
Stocks	31,665,553.66
Real Estate, &c.	3,662,673.53
Bonds and Mortgages	819,906.31
Balances with Foreign Agents	578,195.41
Foreign Bills of Exchange	557,847.75
Bonus for Charter	2,600,000.00
Due by State Banks	8,714,800.23
Notes of State Banks	1,148,101.93
Specie	2,171,722.97
Resulting Balances	697,428.99
Total	$74,603,142.46

LIABILITIES

Total Circulation	$11,223,658.99
Unclaimed Dividends	$ 31,386.80
Loans in Europe (due 1841–47)	12,575,301.97
Bonds in Europe	502,222.22
Bond to United States	633,643.83
Guarantee of Planters' Bank	550,000.00
Guarantee to State of Michigan	1,944,750.00
Due to State Banks	6,334,221.32
Due Depositors	3,164,354.50
	$36,959,539.63
Capital Stock	35,000,000.00
Surplus	2,643,602.83
Total	$74,603,142.46

The nature of the assets of the Bank of the United States may be seen from Table 5, which gives the individual items for two classes of the assets listed above.[31]

[31] *Ibid.*, pp. 155–156.

Table 5. SELECTED ITEMS FROM A STATEMENT OF ASSETS, December 21, 1840

(1) Stocks and bonds	Amount	Total
On hand at Bank of United States		
State loans		$ 380,988
City loans		172,625
Bank stock:		
Morris Canal and Banking Co.	$ 961,380	
Banks in Natchez, Mississippi	465,700	
Grand Gulf "	205,300	
Vicksburg "	120,855	
Other places "	48,800	
New Orleans	333,800	
Louisiana	99,200	
Tennessee	228,100	
Other States	169,865	
		2,633,000
Texas bonds and Treasury notes		137,015
Incorporated companies:		
Located in Pennsylvania:		
Loan to Cumberland Valley Railroad	$441,000	
Danville & Pottsville Railroad	647,011	
Sandy & Beaver Canal	647,011	
Philadelphia, Wilmington & Baltimore Railroad	152,500	
Williamsport & Elmira Railroad	350,000	
Union Canal	247,300	
Stock of Reading Railroad	208,800	
Stock and loan to Little Schuylkill Navigation, Railroad and Coal Co.	960,792	
Other companies	871,346	
		3,995,834

Located in other States:		
Loan to New York, Boston, & Providence Railroad	$501,592	
Delaware & Chesapeake Canal	375,893	
Other companies	370,350	
		$ 1,247,836
Bank of United States stock—Balance unsold, 24,714 shares		2,471,400
On hand at agency, New Orleans		56,774
On hand at agency in London:		
Indiana 5 per cents	$162,000	
Maryland 5 " "	179,000	
Illinois 6 " "	33,000	
Michigan 6 " "	272,000	
Other State bonds	4,000	
Ohio Life and Trust Co. bonds	1,000,000	
Farmers' Loan and Trust	234,000	
American Life and Trust	627,555	
Reading Railroad	411,111	
Texas bonds	184,204	
		3,106,871
Deposited as security for loans in Europe:		
Pennsylvania 5 per cents	$5,117,906.16	
Mississippi 5 " "	3,086,000.00	
Maryland 5 " "	400,000.00	
Indiana 5 " "	596,000.00	
Michigan 6 " "	3,583,000.00	
Illinois 6 " "	1,368,000.00	
Farmers Loan and Trust bonds	300,000.00	
		14,450,906.16
On hand with R. Alsop and J. A. Brown, special agents:		
Pennsylvania 5 per cents	$1,160,000.00	
Camden & Amboy Railroad bonds	522,222.22	
Hazleton Coal Company bonds	231,481.48	
Philadelphia, Wilmington & Baltimore Railroad bonds	811,111.11	
		2,724,814.81
Pennsylvania 5 per cents		16,487.21
Special loan to Commonwealth		271,000.00
Total		$31,665,553.66

(2) Due by State Banks[a]

To Bank of the United States:	
North American Trust and Banking Co.	$ 357,000.00
Banks in Natchez, Mississippi	2,683,982.32
Banks in Vicksburg, "	1,429,166.74
Gas Light and Banking Co.	2,151,799.44
Banks in Florida	436,298.86
Other banks	395,425.89
Bonds of Planters' Bank	550,000.00
To offices and agencies	711,126.98
	$8,714,800.23

[a] Most of these banks were weak.

11. Readings

For fuller information on the Bank of the United States until 1836 see R. C. H. Catterall, *The Second Bank of the United States* (Chicago, 1903).

A good brief account of the history of the Bank is given in Davis R. Dewey, "The Second United States Bank," in *Banking in the United States before the Civil War* (Washington, 1911).

As background for the history of the Bank in 1837–41 read Reginald C. McGrane, *Foreign Bondholders and American State Debts* (New York, 1935), chap. i; and L. H. Jenks, *The Migration of British Capital to 1875* (New York, 1927), chap. iii on Anglo-American finance.

For comparison with the first Bank of the United States, see James O. Wettereau, "New Light on the First Bank of the United States," *Pennsylvania Magazine of History and Biography,* July, 1937, pp. 270–285.

12. Suggested Questions

1. Could the movement of the capital of the Bank to the less developed sections of the country have been prevented?
2. What improvements could have been made in Biddle's management of the branches?
3. Is there any similarity in the basis of the opposition to branch banking in Biddle's time and today?
4. Was the Bank denied a charter for economic or for political reasons?
5. Is it correct to say that Biddle forgot that he was a banker and became a speculator?

XV. BOULTON & WATT, 1775–1800

1. General Statement

In the partnership of Matthew Boulton and James Watt we have the union of an inventor and a capitalist. Watt's contribution to the enterprise was inventive genius, training in a craft which especially required skill and accuracy, namely the mathematical instrument-maker's, and acquaintance with scientific theory and its application through his association with the brilliant group of scientists at Glasgow University. Boulton, in addition to finding the capital to finance experiments and to keep the concern going during its first decade, brought to the partnership an up-to-date factory at Soho (near Birmingham), practical experience in the metal industries, a wide acquaintance with men and affairs, and a breadth of vision and an energy of mind that enabled him to give constructive attention to many undertakings. Without Boulton, Watt undoubtedly would have accomplished great improvements in the steam engine; but, by Watt's own testimony, his lack of resources, his inexperience and timidity in money matters, and his difficult temperament must have delayed for many years the practical fruition of his ideas and experiments and would probably have prevented his reaping any material rewards.

In the affairs of Boulton & Watt may be seen not only the development of the steam power so necessary to large-scale industry but also the gradual building-up of an industrial unit, the evolution of an efficient organization, and the slow mastery of technique by the workers. Further, Boulton & Watt helped to lay the foundations of the engineering industry, and the growth of their firm was contemporary with the emergence of the engineering profession in England.

2. Important Dates in the History of Boulton & Watt

1728	Birth of Matthew Boulton.
1736	Birth of James Watt.
1764	Soho Manufactory built by Boulton and Fothergill.
1765	Watt invented the separate condenser for the steam engine.

1775	Boulton & Watt partnership formed and a new patent obtained.
1776	First Boulton & Watt engine installed.
1782	Manufacture of rotary steam engines begun.
1794	The sons of Boulton and Watt admitted to partnership.
1795	Soho Foundry built.
1800	Expiration of Watt's patent, withdrawal of James Watt, Sr., and formation of Boulton, Watt & Co.
1809	Death of Matthew Boulton.
1819	Death of James Watt, Sr.
1842	Death of Matthew Robinson Boulton.
1848	Death of James Watt, Jr.

3. Matthew Boulton's Enterprises

On leaving school, Matthew Boulton entered the business of his father, a silver stamper and piercer in Birmingham. He soon introduced new articles and improvements in the manufacturing processes. In 1759 he inherited a large fortune from his father, and his marriage in the following year to an heiress made Boulton a wealthy man. After taking into partnership John Fothergill, who was able, active, and familiar with foreign markets, Boulton moved (in 1762) to a new establishment at Soho, two miles north of Birmingham. Two years later, at a cost of £9,000, he completely rebuilt the factory which became the home of the Engine Manufactory until 1795.[1] Between 1770 and 1780 the hardware business lost £11,000 out of a capital of £20,000, partly because of the adverse business conditions of the time, but mainly because of the firm's overexpanded productive capacity. In 1782, upon Fothergill's death, the partnership came to an end just as financial recovery was setting in.

The extent of Boulton's interests and productive facilities at this time is manifest in a partial list of Soho products: metal filigree and inlay work, steel buttons and buckles, watch chains, trinkets, plated and solid silverware, candlesticks, ornaments in bronze and ormolu, gold plate, and—of greater significance for engineering and factory methods—clocks.[2]

Die-sinking, the striking of medals, and the making of coins or tokens were among the activities at Soho before Watt's entrance into the firm. For a number of years (about 1768 to 1775) Boulton purchased from Wedgwood[3] earthenware vases, which he decorated with metal bases and fittings and resold. Previously Boulton and Fothergill had bought Wedgwood's wares on their own account and distributed them on the Continent, especially to Spain and ports on the Baltic.[4]

Some of the numerous operations carried on at Soho required power which was furnished by a water wheel or, in times of drought, by horses. The insufficiency of the water power and the expense of the horses caused Boulton to turn his attention to other sources of power. His own experiments with "fire engines" were unsuccessful, as were those of his friends, and he heard with interest of Watt's experiments. There was evidence of similar demands for power in other quarters. Thus in 1771 a Birmingham friend wrote to Watt:[5]

"A friend of Boulton and me in Cornwall sent us word four days ago that four or five copper-mines are just going to be abandoned because of the high price of coals, and begs me to apply to them instantly. The York Buildings Company delay rebuilding their engine . . . waiting for yours. Yesterday ap-

[1] Erich Roll, *An Early Experiment in Industrial Organisation* (London, 1930), pp. 7–8.

[2] *Ibid.*, pp. 10–11; Samuel Smiles, *Lives of the Engineers: The Steam-Engine. Boulton and Watt* (London, 1874), pp. 119–124.

[3] Josiah Wedgwood, who greatly advanced the Staffordshire pottery industry, was one of Boulton's most intimate friends.

[4] Eliza Meteyard, *Life of Josiah Wedgwood*, vol. ii (London, 1866), pp. 27 f., 55 f., 76, 96 f., 479 ff.

[5] Quoted in H. W. Dickinson and Rhys Jenkins, *James Watt and the Steam Engine* (Oxford, 1927), p. 35. (By permission of The Clarendon Press, Oxford.)

plication was made to me, by a mining company in Derbyshire, to know when you will be in England about fire-engines, because they must quit their mine if you cannot relieve them."

An excerpt from one of Boulton's letters to Watt throws further light on Boulton's motives: [6]

"I was excited by two motives to offer you my assistance which were love of you and love of a money-getting ingenious project. I presumed that your engine would require money, very accurate workmanship and extensive correspondence to make it turn out to the best advantage, and that the best means . . . would be to keep the executive part out of the hands of the multitude of empirical engineers, who from ignorance, want of experience and want of necessary convenience, would be very liable to produce bad and inaccurate workmanship. . . . My idea was to settle a manufactory near to my own . . . where I would erect all the conveniences necessary . . . and from which manufactory we would serve all the world with engines of all sizes. By these means and your assistance we could engage and instruct some excellent workmen (with more excellent tools that would be worth any man's while to procure for one single engine). . . . It would not be worth my while to make for three counties only [as Dr. Roebuck [7] had suggested], but I find it very well worth my while to make for all the world."

Watt was dissatisfied with the workmanship in Glasgow. Deeply impressed with the unique organization and excellent workmanship which he found at Soho, he favored Boulton's entrance into the business; but Roebuck's financial difficulties prevented the conclusion of any agreement for several years. Roebuck owed over £630 to Boulton and Fothergill and about the same amount to Boulton personally. When Roebuck's affairs were finally settled, in 1773, his two-thirds share in Watt's engine was made over to Boulton in discharge of the indebtedness. Watt was unable to go to Birmingham until 1774, by which time the patent had run for six years and Boulton refused to invest further capital until the monopoly was renewed or extended for another term of years. By May, 1775, an Act of Parliament was obtained, granting Watt a monopoly in the manufacture of his steam engine for 25 years.[8] The partnership therefore ran from June 1, 1775, and the principal details were set forth in a letter from Watt to Boulton, dated July 5, 1775, part of which follows: [9]

"1. I to assign to you two-thirds of the property of the invention on following conditions:

"2. You to pay all expenses of Act or others incurred before June, 1775, and also the expense of future experiments, which money to be sunk without interest by you being the consideration you pay for your part, but the experimental machines to be your property.

"3. You to advance stock-in-trade bearing interest, but having no claim upon me for any part of that further than my Intromissions, but the stock itself to be your property and security.

"4. I to draw one-third of the profits so soon as any arise from the business, after paying the workmen's wages and goods furnished, but abstract from the stock-in-trade excepting the interest thereof, which is to be deducted before a balance is struck.

"5. I to make drawings, give directions and make surveys, the company paying travelling expenses to either of us when upon engine business.

"6. You to keep the books and balance them once a year.

"7. A book to be kept, wherein to be marked such transactions as are worthy of record, which, when signed by both, to have the force of the contract.

"8. Neither of us to alienate our share without consent of the other, and if either of us

[6] *Ibid.*, pp. 30–31.

[7] John Roebuck, a Birmingham doctor, had been attracted to Glasgow by his interest in chemistry. In the 1750's he formed a company for the manufacture of iron at Carron. In 1768 he obtained a two-thirds share in Watt's invention in exchange for substantial financial assistance in the project. Roll, *op. cit.*, pp. 12–17.

[8] *Ibid.*, pp. 13–18.

[9] *Ibid.*, pp. 19–20.

by death or otherwise shall be incapacitated from acting for ourselves, the other of us to be sole manager without contradiction or interference of heirs, executors, assignees or others, but the books to be subject to their inspection and the acting partner of us to be allowed a reasonable commission for extra trouble.

"9. The contract to continue for twenty-five years from the First of June, 1775, when the partnership commenced, notwithstanding the contract being of a later date."

A new partnership was formed in October, 1794, to permit the entrance of the sons, Matthew Robinson Boulton, James Watt, Jr., and Gregory Watt. Shares in the new partnership were held in the proportion originally laid down. The old firm was to continue, but future business was to be handed over to the new one. When the original partnership was dissolved in 1800, shares were equally divided between the Boultons and the Watts, and at the same time James Watt definitely retired from the business.[10]

The financing of the engine business proved more difficult than Boulton had probably anticipated. "He mortgaged his lands to the last farthing; borrowed from his personal friends; raised money by annuities; obtained advances from bankers; and had invested upwards of £40,000 in the enterprise before it began to pay." Watt would have gone on experimenting indefinitely, but Boulton pushed for the erection of the first engines,[11] a necessity from the marketing standpoint. Marketing, however, seems to have been less of a problem than financing. In 1776 a deputation from the copper mines in Cornwall came up to examine the engine at Soho and another which had been erected at a nearby colliery, and orders from Cornwall followed soon. Owing to stagnation in the copper trade, it became difficult to get cash payments from Cornwall; accordingly, in 1780, Boulton & Watt began to accept shares in some of the mines in lieu of the premiums due. At the same time many of Boulton & Watt's friends were induced to take an interest, and both John Wilkinson and Josiah Wedgwood purchased shares in Cornish mines as a result.[12]

"Boulton now made it his business to attend the meetings of the adventurers. . . . He found their proceedings conducted without regard to order. The principal attention was paid to the dining, and after dinner and drink little real business could be done. No minutes were made of the proceedings; half the company were talking at the same time on different subjects; no one took the lead in conducting the discussions, which were disorderly and anarchical in the extreme.

"Boulton immediately addressed himself to the work of introducing order and despatch. He called upon his brother adventurers to do their business first, and talk and drink afterwards. He advised them to procure a minute-book in which to enter the resolutions and proceedings. His clear-headed suggestions were at once agreed to; and the next meeting, for which he prepared the agenda, was so entirely different from all that had preceded it, in respect of order, regularity, and the business transacted, that his influence with the adventurers was at once established." [13]

Meanwhile, since it was becoming apparent that few more orders could be obtained from Cornwall for pumping engines for mines, Boulton was considering new markets. In June, 1781, he wrote to Watt: [14]

"The people in London, Manchester and Birmingham are *steam mill mad.* I don't mean to hurry you, but I think that in the course of a month or two we should determine to take out a patent for certain methods of producing rotative motion from . . . the fire engine."

[10] *Ibid.*, pp. 163–164.

[11] Dickinson and Jenkins, *op. cit.*, p. 115.

[12] Roll, *op. cit.*, pp. 88 f. For a more extended discussion of the firm's finances, see John Lord, *Capital and Steam Power, 1750–1800* (P. S. King & Son, Ltd., London, 1923), chap. vi.

[13] Smiles, *Lives of Engineers*, pp. 214–215.

[14] Dickinson and Jenkins, *op. cit.*, p. 55.

By the next year patents had been obtained, a rotative engine erected at Soho, and a cornmill put up for the purpose of gaining experience in driving it by steam power. In spite of an order in 1783, Watt seemed to have little faith in the commercial possibilities of the rotative engine and welcomed an inquiry from the Fen district for a pumping engine. Boulton, however, wrote: [15]

> "For my part, I think that mills, though trifles in comparison with Cornish engines, present a field that is boundless and that will be more permanent than these transient mines, and more satisfactory than these inveterate, ungenerous and envious miners and mine lords."

To hasten the demand for steam engines for grinding corn Boulton interested himself in a project for erecting the Albion Flour Mill at Southwark, London. The mill, which started working in 1786 after many delays, was successful technically, but had not proved a paying proposition up to 1791 when it unfortunately burned down. Boulton lost about £6,000 and Watt £3,000.[16]

In spite of such untoward events the affairs of Boulton & Watt had meantime improved, and by 1784 the payments on engines erected had become sufficient to enable Boulton to begin paying off his indebtedness. The multiplicity of his undertakings, however, seems to have prevented him from freeing himself for some time.[17]

Another business in which both Boulton and Watt were concerned arose out of Watt's invention of a method of copying letters. A patent was taken out in 1780, and James Watt & Co. started to exploit it. Watt had a half-share and Boulton and a friend had one-quarter each in this company until 1794; at that time the patent expired, and the company was reorganized.[18] In this, as in the other concerns, Boulton was the driving spirit without which success would have been unlikely.

While Boulton was in Cornwall in 1780 on the steam-engine business, the Birmingham manufacturers had agreed to form a company to make brass, which was the raw material for their manufactures. They wrote to Boulton asking him to take a lead in the business. He drew up a scheme for a company with a capital of £20,000, to be divided into 200 shares, of which no person was to hold more than four, and every holder was to covenant to purchase from the company one ton of brass per annum for every share that he held. The company was formed on the plan suggested by Boulton, who, disapproving of Birmingham as a site for the works, resigned from the committee after he had taken great trouble in experimenting with brass.[19]

Boulton's reforms of the administration of the Cornwall mining companies were not sufficient to solve the chief problem confronting the Cornish miners. Forced because of inadequate capital to realize promptly on their output of ore, they were at the mercy of a combination of smelters. They were also facing severe competition from recently opened mines in Anglesey; these were under the control of Thomas Williams, a customer for Boulton & Watt's engines and an able and enterprising business man who was pushing sales. Finally, in 1785, the Cornish Metal Co. was formed, largely through Boulton's initiative, to buy up the ore from the various mining companies at agreed standards, to have this ore smelted at fixed prices, and then to sell the copper. Boulton took a considerable proportion of shares to sell among his friends and thus obtained control of the company. Under this scheme the mines flourished for a time, but the company accumulated large stocks of unsalable cop-

[15] *Ibid.*, p. 57.

[16] *Ibid.*, pp. 64–65.

[17] *Ibid.*, p. 63; Smiles, *Lives of Engineers*, pp. 288–291.

[18] Roll, *op. cit.*, pp. 129 ff.

[19] Henry Hamilton, *The English Brass & Copper Industries to 1800* (London, 1926), pp. 217–224.

per. They were eventually forced to sell out to the Anglesey company and were so fortunate as to escape with practically no loss.[20]

Possibly to create a market for the stocks of copper on hand, Boulton in 1786 revived a project which he had formerly discussed with Watt, that of applying the steam engine to the coining of money. In that year he coined over one hundred tons of copper for the East India Co.; later he executed contracts for Russia, Denmark, Spain, Mexico, Calcutta, and Bombay; in 1797, after much propaganda against the disgraceful state of the coinage had appeared, he inaugurated an improved coinage based on the specimens submitted ten years before. His improvements in coining machinery were considered so valuable that he was employed to arrange the new mint in London and to direct the manufacture of the machinery and steam engines for it. He also supplied mints for the Russian, Spanish, Mexican, and Danish governments.[21]

In his coinage business Boulton demonstrated again a remarkable ability for visualizing new methods and processes which Watt and others could translate into practical machines, while he showed a genius for industrial management which no contemporary could approach and few successors could match for the next century. Coinage operations were arranged to facilitate the flow of materials through successive processes. Hot ingots were rolled into sheets; the sheets were fine-rolled cold in polished steel rollers; blanks were then cut and shaken in bags for cleaning, after which they were moved rapidly down an inclined plane to the coining machines, some of which could turn out 200 pieces a minute. Steam provided all the power, and the machines were so nearly automatic in operation that mere boys and girls could tend them with ease.

[20] *Ibid.*, pp. 168–213.

[21] Smiles, *Lives of Engineers,* pp. 310–322; Roll, *op. cit.*, pp. 132–135.

Various other projects connected with the copper industry engaged Boulton's attention after 1785, and he became a shareholder in the Rose Copper Co., formed about 1793 to produce copper for the shareholders and for the market.[22] Meanwhile he had taken, with Wedgwood, the leading part in forming and running the General Chamber of Manufacturers, formed to represent manufacturing interests before the government.[23]

Boulton's son, Matthew Robinson Boulton, began to take an active part in the steam-engine business, particularly, in the 'nineties, but Boulton still devoted much time to coinage and to his other affairs. The following list shows the number of manufactures in which Boulton was directly interested in 1800: [24]

"*Buttons in general,* gilt, plated, silvered, semilor, pinchbeck, platina, inlaid with steel, hard white metal, fancy compositions, mother-of-pearl, polished steel and jettina and steel tags, polished steel watch chains, patent cork screws, &c. Boulton & Scale.

"*Patent latchets and buckles:* silver, strong-plated, pinchbeck and steel. Boulton & Smith.

"*Plated and silver wares:* in general for the dining table, tea table, sideboard vessels of various kinds, candlesticks, branches, &c. Matthew Boulton & Plate Co.

"*Medals* in general and of various metals. By Matthew Boulton.

"*Rolled Metals* of all kinds and mixtures. By Matthew Boulton.

"*Iron Foundery:* Patent steam engines with rotative motions for mills of every kind or with reciprocating motions for pumps or mines, or for any other mechanical purposes, requiring different powers from 1–200 horses acting together. Pneumatical apparatus, large or portable for preparing medicinal airs. By Boulton & Watt & Sons.

"*Copying machines*—large for counting houses and portable for travellers. By the sons

[22] Hamilton, *op. cit.*, pp. 227–236.

[23] Roll, *op. cit.*, pp. 135–139.

[24] *Ibid.*, p. 128. (Reprinted with permission of the author and Longmans, Green & Co., Limited.)

of Messrs. Boulton & Watt under the firm of J. Watt & Co.

"Mercantile trade carried on in Birmingham to Europe and America. Matthew Boulton."

Within a few months of his death at the age of eighty-one, in August, 1809, Boulton was still going daily to the works. As a master and as a friend he seems to have been kindly and generous. He was patient with Watt's many attacks of despondency and considerate of his partner's frailties. He was held in high esteem by commercial and industrial leaders of the time, and on more than one occasion he was influential in shaping national policy.

4. The Manufacture and Erection of Engines, 1775–95 [25]

In 1775, when Boulton and Watt began their partnership, there were no engine-building works in existence, and engine-fitting as a separate craft had not yet arisen. Newcomen [26] engines were put together at the mine and, in case they were to be employed for pumping water for the supply of water wheels, at the mill. The erection was supervised by an engineer—who in some instances entered into a contract to supply an engine but usually seems to have worked for a wage—and the engine parts and materials were purchased directly by the owner of the mine or mill, who also paid the workmen employed on the job. The principal parts bought in a condition ready for use were the cylinder, cylinder bottom, and the working barrels of the pumps. The bored cast-iron work (cylinders and pump barrels) all came from one of the four iron works, Coalbrookdale, New Willey, Bersham, or Carron.[27] The smaller castings were sometimes obtained from the same place as the cylinders, at other times locally. The boiler, the wrought-iron work, and the wooden beams were made on the spot. Accordingly the engineer had under him a staff of smiths, carpenters, plumbers, and masons for building the engine-house.

Although in the petition to Parliament for the extension of the period of Watt's patent it had been urged that great sums of money would have to be expended in the erection of a manufactory for the production of the new engines, as a matter of fact Boulton & Watt did not embark on any considerable engine-making venture until a number of years later. They acted chiefly as consulting engineers and whenever possible left the construction to local engineers. The main reason for this arrangement was the lack of sufficient capital to build an extensive foundry works, but other factors entered in: Boulton's time and attention were taken up with the established hardware business; John Wilkinson had a monopoly on the improved method of boring cylinders; and the use of local engineers removed one source of opposition to the entrance of Boulton & Watt into certain areas.[28]

In the 'eighties the valves and nozzles were the only parts of the engine made regularly at Soho. The cylinder, its cover and bottom, the piston, the air pump, and the condenser were made at Bersham, then in the hands of John Wilkinson, who made nearly every one of Boulton & Watt's cylinders up to the year 1795. Pistons, piston rods, castings, and other parts were obtained from various ironmasters.

[25] Except where otherwise noted, this section consists of summaries and extracts from Dickinson and Jenkins, *op. cit.*

[26] Thomas Newcomen (1663–1729), a blacksmith and ironmonger of Dartmouth, evolved the first practicable steam engine. A full account may be found in *Transactions of the Newcomen Society*, vol. iv (1923–24).

[27] At Coalbrookdale, Shropshire, smelting by coal instead of charcoal had been established on a commercial scale by Abraham Darby as early as 1709. New Willey and Bersham belonged to the Wilkinsons; Carron, Scotland, was started by Dr. John Roebuck and others in 1760. See T. S. Ashton, *Iron and Steel in the Industrial Revolution* (London, 1924), for accounts of these iron works.

[28] Roll, *op. cit.*, pp. 24 ff.

Engine parts were ordered from the various makers by the customer, or by Boulton & Watt on his account. Payment was sometimes made through Boulton & Watt, however, and occasionally the firm even advanced the money for the parts.[29] Boulton & Watt sent the necessary drawings and instructions and kept a staff of men to supervise erection if the local engineer could not undertake it successfully. These men were paid by the person for whom the engine was being erected. It was one of the great difficulties to get together and to retain a suitable staff of erectors. The work required skill, accuracy, and ingenuity. The men were in danger of being seized on the way by press-gangs for the navy. At a later period they were subject to bribery by competitors or to seduction by foreign manufacturers anxious to start engine-works abroad. The best of their erectors was William Murdock.[30]

A good deal of planning and organization was necessary in order that the different parts from these widely separated localities might be brought together at about the same time, for example, for the erection of an engine in Cornwall. Since there was a frequent and direct service of ships between the Thames and one or other of the Cornish ports, the transport of goods made in London was the simplest problem of all. The goods from Soho and Birmingham were carted to the canal, along which they were taken to Stourport on the Severn. They were transshipped into a coasting vessel which completed the transit. The goods sent directly from Bradley could be loaded into the canal barge at the works. The Bersham goods were sent by road to Chester and there shipped to a Cornish port.

It was difficult to get ships with hatchways big enough to pass the cylinders. At ports where there was no crane, the cylinders had to be lifted from the ship's hold by such expedients as presented themselves and rolled ashore. The handling of the cylinders was generally an awkward affair. "There is no danger in throwing a cylin-

[29] *Ibid.*, pp. 55, 150.

[30] William Murdock (1754–1839), like Watt of Scottish birth, had been brought up to his father's trade of millwright and miller. He was engaged as a common mechanic at Soho in 1777 and soon earned promotion from his first employment of pattern-making to the erection of engines. In 1779 he was sent down to Cornwall where his sobriety, his dexterity, and his resourcefulness in erecting new engines and repairing old ones made him invaluable. Boulton reported of him in 1782 (Dickinson and Jenkins, *op. cit.*, p. 291):

"Murdock hath been indefatigable, ever since they began he has scarcely been in bed or taken necessary food, for everyone seems helpless in comparison of him. . . Friday last, he recd. a letter from Wl. Virgin in the West insisting upon his coming over directly as they could not set their engine to work, & if he did not come instantly they would let out ye fire. He accordingly went on Saturday morng., set ye engine to work, wch. went on very well dureing 5 or 6 hours, & then left it & returned back to ye Consd. Mines about 11 at night and was employed about the engines till 4 this morng. & then went to bed. I found him this morning in Poldice cistern, searching for pins & cotters that had jumped out, and I insisted upon his going home to bed for he had a bad cold."

When Murdock started in Cornwall in 1779 he received £2 a week. Twelve months later he wanted an increase to two guineas. Boulton sympathized, but Watt objected and thought it would be wrong to give this sum; "an example of that kind would ruin us by stimulating every other man we had to similar demands." Boulton managed to stave off the difficulty by persuading one of the mine companies to make Murdock a present of 10 guineas, to which he added another 10 on behalf of Boulton & Watt. Murdock remained loyal to Boulton & Watt in spite of tempting offers from Cornish engineers and miners. He invented a steam carriage, made many improvements on the engines, and experimented with gas lighting. In 1795 he was sent for to assist with the plans for the new foundry, and four years later he left Cornwall and became the right-hand man of the younger Boulton & Watt. He was offered a partnership in Soho Foundry in 1810 but preferred to take a salary of £1,000 a year. A picturesque account of him is given in Samuel Smiles, *Men of Invention and Industry* (New York, 1885), and a more accurate one in Dickinson and Jenkins, *op. cit.*, pp. 290–297.

der from a waggon on soft earth, . . . I would sooner trust to throwing it off the waggon there *than to their cranes*."

Delay frequently resulted because Boulton & Watt were dependent upon the enterprise and efficiency of many suppliers, some of whom were slack—Wilkinson was sometimes a bad offender in making tardy deliveries. Further difficulty sometimes arose through the lack of suitable agents to receive and forward goods in transit. The most serious cause of delays in the erection of the first engines, however, was the lack of skilled labor and exact machinery. Boulton & Watt were pioneers in the engineering industry and had not only to build a factory but also to train and organize their laborers.[31]

The engineering establishment at Soho was opened about 1775 in a blacksmith shop furnished with two hearths. It could not have been a very large building, although Boulton referred to it at this date as "formidable" and later called it "our great smith's shop." It served also as the fitting shop and probably boasted at least one lathe. Whether the patterns were made in the same building is not clear, but the firm seems to have made its own patterns from the beginning. At an early date Watt complained of the pattern-maker's drunkenness and dishonesty and proposed to replace him or get the work done outside. A few weeks later, however, there was reform; the pattern-maker, Watt reported, had been working very diligently and was well on with the nozzle patterns. Toward the end of April, 1777, an additional lathe for turning piston rods was set up, but the first piston rod met with several accidents. First it was reported: "Dickson has forged a very good piston-rod;" next, "Dickson's piston-rod was badly welded & we have had to take it asunder and re-do it;" then, "Cleobury-iron has turned out damned bad, the piston-rod for Huel Bussy was very well forged by Dixon and upon heating it to float it fell in two at the shooting —Dixon is now faggotting one out of Swedish small bars." [32]

One of the first engines to be erected by Boulton & Watt was put up for Wilkinson, in 1776, for blowing an iron furnace, and by the middle of the next year a total of four engines had been erected for him. During the early years most of the engines erected were pumping units for mines or waterworks, but forge and ironworks account for 17 engines during the period 1778–85,[33] and others were already being used in the textile, pottery, and flour-milling industries.[34]

In 1777, when Watt went to Cornwall to superintend the erection of his first engine in that county, he found that Soho prices for engine work were considered too high, and he wrote to Boulton: "Our prices so much exceed what they are done for here that we shall never get our bills pleasantly paid, and to be paid with a grudge, and to lose the business at the same time will never suit . . . we must give up the manufacturing of any parts of the large engines excepting the nozzles." This was the policy of the firm for many years, although in 1778 Boulton wrote: [35]

> "We are systematizing the business of engine making, as we have done before in the button manufactory; we are training up workmen and making tools and machines to form the different parts of Mr. Watt's engines, with more accuracy, and at a cheaper rate than can possibly be done by the ordinary methods of working. Our workshop and apparatus will

[31] Roll, *op. cit.*, pp. 57–60.

[32] Cleobury was an iron forge in Worcestershire which supplied iron for piston rods.

[33] Roll, *op. cit.*, pp. 29 and 47.

[34] For analysis of the engines by industry and geographical location, see Lord, *op. cit.*, chap. viii.

[35] To John Smeaton, who introduced the term "civil engineer" and who is best known for his Eddystone Lighthouse. He had made some improvements on the Newcomen engine. See Smiles, *Lives of Engineers*, vol. iv (London, 1874).

be of sufficient extent to execute all the engines which are likely to be soon wanted in this country, and it will not be worth the expense for any other engineer to erect similar works for that would be like building a mill to grind a bushel of corn."

In 1781 Boulton was occupied with plans for a new engine-shop, a two-story building that was completed by the end of the year at a cost of about £110. The firm also considered the erection of a foundry in Cornwall but speedily relinquished the idea, although later on Boulton made the suggestion of setting up a workshop there.

For some time both Boulton and Watt had been trying to devise machinery for the purpose of obtaining rotary motion from the steam engine, in order to increase its value for purposes other than pumping. Watt had completed and patented such a mechanism, the "Sun and Planet gear," early in 1782; and before the end of the year it was applied to an engine at Soho to work a forge hammer. The first engine embodying the new rotative principle to be supplied to a customer was for a forge hammer in Wilkinson's works at Bradley. With the introduction of the rotative engine more and more of the engine work was done at Soho. At the mines there were to be found the necessary tools and workmen capable of making and putting together the parts, and the mine owners were accustomed to buying the various parts and materials themselves and paying the cost of erection; but when it came to putting up engines in breweries, mills, and other factories, the conditions were altogether different. The proprietors wanted an engine, and they rarely had the workmen or equipment that would permit them to undertake their own construction. They preferred to give an order and to have no further trouble or responsibility. The tendency was, of course, to throw more work upon Soho (see Table 1).[36]

Between 1790 and 1795 the works went through a period of transition: of some engines only the nozzle and the working gear were made at the works; in other cases the entire engine was put together there.

[36] Roll, *op. cit.*, appendix ii. The figures under "Gross" refer only to the manufacturing side of the business.

Table 1. ENGINE PRODUCTION AT SOHO, 1787–1801

Year ending	New engines made	Men employed		Gross					
				Profit			Loss		
		In the yard	Erectors	£	s.	d.	£	s.	d.
1787	16	15–22	9				588	0	4¼
1788	10	21–22	14				576	17	9½
1789	12	19–22	9				707	14	1¼
1790	14	18–24	9				762	17	1¼
1791	15	25–38	12				1884	1	0¼
1792	26	35–42	12				299	9	9½
1793	23	40–50—later reduced to 32	18	104	19	10½			
1794	17	32–26	11				1499	3	7
1795	9	26–45	11				880	16	10½
1796	30	50–55	..	1585	19	0			
1797	30	...	..				123	2	7½
1798	25	...	..	611	17	0			
1799	34	...	..	2345	12	8½			
1800	41	...	..	1929	14	11½			
1801	52	...	..	4030	2	0			

Table 2 shows the volume of goods sent from Soho, together with the proportion of work performed outside.[37]

Watt did not take any active part in directing the engine-works or in improving the methods of production. He had an office in his house at Harper's Hill, and there he carried on his work, calculations, drawings, and correspondence. The mere bulk of the product forms abundant evidence that he worked very hard. Frequently many days elapsed between his visits to Soho to inspect the progress of any new schemes on hand and to discuss business matters with Boulton. With increasing business Watt's work became very heavy, and Boulton was constantly urging him to get an assistant. In 1781 Boulton suggested a number of young men, among them John Southern. "He is now with his brother as surgeon, . . . yet he had rather have been employed under you as a draughtsman and assistant, and if you wish to have him I know he will gladly come. He draws tolerably neat." After a second urging, Watt replied: "If you have a notion that young Southern would be sufficiently sedate, would come to us for a reasonable sum annually, I should be very glad to engage him for a drawer, provided he gives bond to give up music, otherwise I am sure he will do no good, it being the source of idleness." In June, 1782, Southern, then at the age of 24, started with Boulton & Watt on a three years' agreement and soon proved a valuable assistant. In 1790 the drawing office was moved to the Soho Manufactory. In October, 1794, a new partnership, Boulton, Watt & Sons, was formed to take over the old firm. The new partnership included both Matthew Boulton and James Watt, but it is clear from the extant correspondence that the old partners had already begun to retire from the business, leaving the sons in active control.[38]

It was Boulton who managed the works, kept an eye on costs, and sought to improve both the methods of production and the parts used. For instance, he wrote from Cornwall that cast iron was not a suitable material for the racks and sectors for op-

[37] *Ibid.*, appendix ix.

[38] *Ibid.*, pp. 163–165.

Table 2. GOODS SENT FROM SOHO, 1791–94, WITH PROPORTION OF WORK DONE BY FOUNDERS EMPLOYED BY BOULTON & WATT

		£	s.	d.
1791	Goods sent from Soho	11,895	6	9
	Deduct founders' account	7,300	17	3
		4,594	9	6
1792	Goods sent from Soho	10,552	11	11
	Deduct founders' account	6,155	4	5
		4,397	7	6
1793	Goods sent from Soho	10,819	15	9
	Deduct founders' account	4,007	6	1
		6,812	9	8
1794	Goods sent from Soho	6,329	13	2
	Deduct founders' account	3,104	7	3
		3,225	5	11

NOTE: The figures of founders' accounts include, in addition to cast-iron work, brass and wrought-iron work and fitting.

erating the valves, and suggested that "it would be safer to forge them of steel & cut them down with a cutter in the mill." Again he suggested that to have the collars made of brass instead of steel would save time and expense in nozzle-fitting. The need for improvements may be seen from the difficulties he reported from the Albion Mills, where he was working from ten in the morning till ten at night. "The gudgeons of the sun wheel are loose in the iron shafts from bad fitting. . . . the iron segments of circles which separate ye 2 rows of teeth in the sun wheels were badly made of bad iron & are obliged to be remade as they are broke to pieces." The working gear also was defective, that of the steam valves "doth not open them quick & even requires ye hand to assist sometimes or a weight." The upper nozzle too was cracked and other defects apparently manifested themselves every few days.

Bad workmanship and bad materials continued for years to be causes of complaint. In 1793 the owners of a cotton mill in Nottingham reported the following difficulties with an engine that had been started twelve months before: the wheels of the sun-and-planet motion were so bad that it had been necessary to replace them with new ones; the connecting-rod top had broken; the badly forged coupling-link had broken in three places; the brasses of the coupling-link and the connecting-rod gudgeons had broken and had had to be replaced; the fastenings for the gland of the piston-rod stuffing box and the gland of the air-pump stuffing box had broken; the top and bottom exhaust spindles were made of bad iron, and they had broken; the racks and sectors for the valves were badly fitted and very much out of order; the spring box at the top of the exhaust rod was in a very bad condition; "and many other matters."

One of the most important innovations made by Boulton was the manufacture of certain spare parts for stock in order to reduce the delay which the replacement of broken parts usually involved.[39] This practice implied a certain amount of standardization, and in 1782 Boulton suggested to Watt that some of the difficulty of making engines could be overcome by the use of pattern cards. In the same letter Boulton wrote that they should confine themselves to standard types and sizes of engines, a proposal which was gradually put into practice as the demand for engines increased.[40]

At the very outset the partners guaranteed free repair of their engines during the first year of operation, provided that the damage was not the result of carélessness on the part of the buyer's workmen.[41] Both Boulton and Watt, anxious to establish a good reputation for their firm, insisted on having the highest quality of workmanship available at the time.

This concern for their reputation is seen particularly in the many cases in which they were asked to adapt existing "common" engines to the new design. Only where this could be done profitably from the point of view of the buyer did they agree. Another proposal that was frequently made to them, namely to attach their condenser to the "common" engine, did not receive their approval. The reasons, set out in a letter to Smeaton, throw an interesting light on their business policy: [42]

"Though it might have enabled them [the miners] to have gone deeper with their engines, yet the savings of fuel would not have been great in comparison to the complete machine. . . . By tacking the condenser to engines that were not in good order, it would have ushered our engine into that country [Cornwall] in an unfavourable point of view and without such profits as would have been satisfactory either to us or the adventurers . . . and thereby curtailed our profits and perhaps our reputation. Besides, where a new machine is to be erected and equally well executed in point of workmanship and mate-

[39] *Ibid.*, pp. 85–86.
[40] *Ibid.*, p. 267.
[41] *Ibid.*, p. 28.
[42] *Ibid.*, p. 36.

rials I cannot find by my estimates the old kind of engine of the same power can be erected materially cheaper than ours, our boiler and cylinder being so much smaller."

Another reason advanced later against the suggestion of granting licenses to Cornish engineers for adapting the condenser to the "common" engine was that there were very few engines in Cornwall, and that they could, consequently, convert them all into Soho engines in one year.[43]

The insistence on high quality of materials and workmanship made for a rather rigid system of supply, high prices, and delays in execution, but the firm thereby gained a reputation which stood them in good stead after the expiration of their monopoly.

The work suffered many interruptions through such labor difficulties as drunkenness, carelessness, and inefficiency of the workers. Also, in 1790 a dispute over work rates almost caused a strike. Although the laborers claimed that the new engine-works clerk had instigated the enlistment in the army of one of the apprentices, their real grievances undoubtedly were connected with the lowering of wages, the elimination of evasion of payments to the Sick Fund, and the necessity of contributing to the payment of the extra watchmen engaged because of the riots in Birmingham.

5. Payments

Had Boulton & Watt been able to manufacture the engines or at least to assemble them at Soho, the question of payments would have been relatively simple, but neither Soho nor any other manufactory could in 1775 have undertaken such a task. Hence the system of payments, like that of manufacture, was complicated and changed from time to time.

In April, 1775, Boulton informed Watt that he had stated to a Cornish visitor to Soho: [44]

"That we will undertake and contract to make an engine or engines capable of doing any quantity of work that shall be requested and described, for as little money as comn [common] engines will cost that are capable of doing as much work, & we will guarantee them to do the work with half the expense of fuel that common ones will require; provided we are allowed a sum that shall be equal to its further savings over and above the said half."

This letter led to a discussion of the subject by the partners, and within two months the plan of taking one-third of the savings had been decided upon. In 1776 Watt wrote to one of the engineers in Cornwall: [45]

"Our profits arise not from making the engine, but from a certain proportion of the savings in fuel which we make over any common engine that raises the same quantity of water to the same height. The proportion of the savings we ask is one-third part to be paid to us annually for twenty-five years, or if our employers choose it they may purchase up our part at ten years price in ready money."

To calculate the savings it was necessary to compare the coal consumption of the Boulton & Watt engine with that of a Newcomen engine capable of doing the same work. The coal consumption of the Newcomen engines was ascertained from sworn statements by the engine men.[46] The work done was calculated from the diameter of the pumps, the height to which the water was raised, and the number of strokes made by the engine. This last factor was determined by a counter fixed to the engine beam. In view of the relation between the price of coal and the annual premium, the partners decided that where coal was unusually cheap some adjustment should be made. Finally, however, they

[43] *Ibid.*, pp. 36–37.

[44] Dickinson and Jenkins, *op. cit.*, p. 345.

[45] *Ibid.*, p. 344.

[46] These sworn statements were required in order to obtain a drawback of the customs duty on sea-borne coal. This drawback was allowed on the coal consumed by pumping engines in the tin and copper mines of Cornwall.

adopted a standard minimum price of 5 shillings per ton as a basis for their calculations.[47] Although fair, the arrangement had its drawbacks; one was that those months in which there was the most pumping to be done, and consequently the highest premiums to be paid, were also those in which the mines were least productive; another was that it was difficult for the adventurers to know what the premiums would be until the end of each month, so that they could not budget their expenditures. Moreover, the procedure used in calculating was extremely complicated and gave rise to disputes. Finally, there were suspicions as to the reliability of the counters, for in several instances their records were plainly wrong.

As a result, opposition arose to this method of assessing the premiums, and certain of the mine operators requested that it be replaced with a fixed rate for each engine according to its size. For small engines the idea of compounding the premium into a lump sum appeared to Boulton & Watt to be convenient, and the arrangement was made once in 1775 and several times thereafter. For large engines of the original type the partners proposed to adhere to their original arrangement. However, Boulton soon recognized the advisability of meeting some of the objections raised, and in 1780 a policy was adopted of fixing annual or monthly premiums, according to the size of the engine.[48]

The use of these methods of payment accounted for the importance which Cornwall assumed in the eyes of the partners. The price of coal was high there, and the engines required by the copper mines were large. The premiums, if all paid, would have amounted to a very large sum, but the depressed state of the copper trade and the struggle against Watt's patent seriously reduced payments.

With the rotative engine, the system of payment by savings was not applicable, and the other plan of a fixed rate was adopted. Very soon, however, a rate per horsepower was fixed upon, that is, five pounds per horsepower per annum for engines. All the premiums, it will be understood, were payable until 1800, when Watt's patent would expire unless it should before then be annulled by the courts.

The development of the market for rotative engines gradually forced Boulton & Watt to undertake an increasing amount of manufacturing and assembling of parts. As a result the plant had to be expanded, and the firm began to require large amounts of capital for this purpose. Partly for this reason and partly because their monopoly was soon to expire, the partners decided to sell engines for a single lump sum. Accordingly, after 1795 the price of an engine to the customer was calculated to cover (1) the cost of materials, (2) a flat percentage of the material cost to compensate the firm for undertaking the risk and work of construction, and (3) the compounded premiums. In 1798, as the end of the patent approached, the following prices were established:

1. Engines for abroad: "Metal Materials" plus 50 per cent
2. Engines for London: "Metal Materials" plus 45 per cent
3. Engines for country: "Metal Materials" plus 33 per cent

During the following year the last two figures fell to 33 and 25 per cent, respectively. In 1801 competition forced the firm to reduce its prices somewhat, and for the next twenty years engines were sold at cost of materials plus about 25 per cent, without any local discrimination. It is important to note that the firm kept careful and elaborate records of all costs, and that the item "Metal Materials" covered the calculated cost of all engine parts, including material, direct and indirect labor, and general overhead or burden charges. In computing overhead expenses they allowed

[47] Roll, *op. cit.*, pp. 30–31.
[48] *Ibid.*, pp. 77 ff.

5 per cent for depreciation and charged interest on capital invested in the business.[49]

At the outset, and for many years thereafter, only a small part of the engine was made at Soho and supplied by Boulton & Watt. As time went on the practice grew—particularly in connection with rotative engines—for the customers to order all the engine materials through Boulton & Watt. Then, in 1795, as the period of the patent was drawing to a close, the firm decided not to make the premium a separate charge but to price the engine so as to cover the premiums for the remaining years of the patent.

6. Rivals and Litigation

In 1775, at the beginning of the Boulton & Watt partnership, a number of engineers were occupied in building the Newcomen engine for public water supply and for pumping in mines. In Cornwall the Newcomen engine soon disappeared entirely, but elsewhere these men and their successors continued the work. In fact, at least as many atmospheric engines were installed in the last quarter of the eighteenth century apparently as in the preceding quarter.[50] The reason for this survival lies in the fact that the chief advantage of Watt's engine over Newcomen's—economy of fuel—was of little consequence to colliery owners who could use unsalable coal for the purpose.

As the Boulton & Watt engine gained ground and reports spread of the royalties which the firm was receiving, still more inventors entered the race. Boulton and Watt considered it wrong for anyone else to try to improve the steam engine; and, although they had a very poor opinion of the value of the rival projects, they were considerably annoyed. Urged on by his competitors' activities, Watt started upon expansive working and upon the rotative engine before he had planned to do so. In the 'nineties this rivalry became a serious matter. Most of the Cornish mine owners had almost from the beginning been very dissatisfied with the heavy payments to Boulton & Watt, in spite of the savings in fuel.[51] Watt said: [52]

> "The truth is that had the savings made by their invention been only ¼ of the fuel formerly used, instead of ¾, and B. & W. had taken only ⅓ of the savings, there would have been no complaint, although the mines would have saved a comparatively small sum. It is the magnitude of the sums which were justly due to B. & W. which have excited all this envy and malevolence. If they had gained little or been loosers by their services, they would have been more highly praised, though they would have merited it less."

The rapid development of factories, iron manufacture, and coal mining, and the resulting demand for power, caused a very considerable call for steam engines from Boulton & Watt. In some cases they were not able to fill orders with reasonable promptness, and in others the power users were opposed to paying the premiums asked; but there were always engineers who would undertake to erect the engines without, as they thought or stated, infringement of Watt's patent; it was, nevertheless, practically impossible for them to make any substantial improvement without infringing in one way or another. Watt claimed that the patent covered every one of his "principles," whether used together or separately. The patent, indeed, practically checked any advance by other engineers. Possibly doubting sincerely the validity of Watt's patent, some of them boldly embodied a number of his devices in their engines.[53]

Finally it became impossible to overlook the infringements. Customers began to ask why they should keep on paying premiums to Boulton & Watt for inventions of which their competitors made free use, and the partners were forced to take

[49] *Ibid.*, pp. 123, 237–249, 254.

[50] Dickinson and Jenkins, *op. cit.*, p. 298.

[51] *Ibid.*, pp. 298–299.

[52] *Ibid.*, pp. 334–335.

[53] *Ibid.*, p. 299.

action. A suit, brought in 1793, resulted two years later in an indecisive judgment. The result made it clear that there was reasonable doubt about the validity of Watt's patent, and it probably accounted for the greater number of infringements about this time. Boulton & Watt obtained injunctions against the infringers, and by June, 1796, all had submitted except two Cornish engine-makers who sought better terms than the other infringers had accepted. The suit which followed resulted in another verdict for Boulton & Watt. The defendants appealed on a writ of error and the case was retried before the King's Bench. In 1799 the judges decided unanimously in favor of Boulton & Watt. Thus, in the year before its expiration, the validity of Watt's patent was established. A number of actions were still pending, but the infringers all finally submitted and paid the premiums which Boulton & Watt demanded.[54]

John Farey, the patent expert of the early part of the nineteenth century, says of the matter: [55]

"According to the ordinary practice of the courts of law in other cases, Mr. Watt's patent ought to have been annulled, for the insufficiency of specification. . . . If this specification had not been supported by the testimony of many scientific artists, who stated that it was sufficient in their opinion, and if the merit of Mr. Watt's engine had not been so universally allowed at the time of those trials, as to have obtained a leaning in his favour, his right could not have been established."

7. Statistics of Output

See Table 3 (p. 206) for the industrial distribution of engines erected by Boulton & Watt in England from 1775 to 1800.[56]

The Soho works from 1775 to 1866 produced [57] 1,878 steam engines, (nominal h.p. 70,958, actual h.p. 250,000), consisting of 319 pumping engines, 1,090 rotative engines for manufacturing purposes, and 469 marine engines.

8. Changes after 1795

It was obvious from the increasing number of patent infringements after 1790 that fierce competition would set in as soon as the Boulton & Watt monopoly had expired. Unless, therefore, the partners altered the character of their business, the expiration of the monopoly would probably mean the extinction of the firm. This factor undoubtedly played an important part in Boulton & Watt's decision to build their own foundry in 1795. They had originally set out to be consulting engineers, but they had already been forced to manufacture some engine parts, and their customers were demanding completed engines. Matters were simplified because the partners now had at their disposal adequate capital, an established position as engineers, and a body of skilled workmen, trained and organized for the assembling and fitting of steam engines. The entrance of their sons into the firm in 1794 had infused new life into the business.[58] At the same time a

[54] *Ibid.*, pp. 325–326.

[55] John Farey, *A Treatise on the Steam Engine, Historical, Practical, Descriptive* (London, 1827), pp. 649–650.

[56] This table is taken from Lord, *op. cit.*, p. 175 (reprinted with permission of the publisher). Dickinson and Jenkins, who have given more careful study to the records, mention 44 engines as the number erected in Cornwall up to 1796, of which 33 were in existence and 29 working (p. 335). Lord's figure of 22 for copper mines must, therefore, be wrong. Note that there is an error in two totals (1,296 for 1,292 and 4,543 for 4,539).

[57] Samuel Timmins, editor, *Birmingham and the Midland Hardware District* (London, 1866), p. 64.

[58] The Soho Foundry partners were Boulton and his son and James Watt, Jr., and his brother, Gregory, who died in 1804. Shortly before the death of James Watt, Jr., in 1848, Gilbert Hamilton, Jr. (a cousin), and Henry Wollaston Blake became partners. Blake carried on the Soho Foundry until 1895 when the machinery and buildings were sold. Thus, James Watt held no share in the Soho Foundry which was operated as a concern separate from the Soho Engine Manufactory. Dickinson and Jenkins, *op. cit.*, pp. 278–279.

quarrel between the Wilkinson brothers, resulting in the closing-down of their Bersham works in 1795, was endangering the supply of engine cylinders upon which Soho had depended. The partners decided, therefore, to enlarge the whole engine manufactory, and, after careful consideration of the matter, they chose a new site (about a mile distant from the old works) with frontage on the Birmingham Canal in order to obtain easy transportation by water. Building operations began in the summer of 1795, and the foundry was opened early in the following year.[59]

It took time to get the place into working order, and there was difficulty in securing men. One of Wilkinson's men from Bersham had been engaged as foreman or manager of the foundry, and the firm advertised in the newspapers for moulders and furnace men. Apparently other workmen from Bersham were taken on, because Watt wrote from Bath on July 19, 1796, to Matthew Robinson Boulton: [60] "In respect of J. Wilkinson's men, I think you ought by no means to take any more of them, your doing so would be cruel and blameable, the men should therefore be positively refused unequivocally." Southern went up to Leeds to try for men, but he found that moulders and founders were in great demand everywhere because of the rapid increase in iron-founding.

Since the smith's work and the greensand castings were not satisfactory, Murdock and Abraham Storey, the foundry manager, were sent up to Yorkshire in 1799 to investigate the methods used there, by

[59] Roll, *op. cit.*, pp. 149–165.

[60] Dickinson and Jenkins, *op. cit.*, p. 271. The younger men had no love for the crafty old ironmaster who had been cheating the firm for years.

Table 3. INDUSTRIAL DISTRIBUTION OF ENGINES ERECTED BY BOULTON & WATT IN ENGLAND, 1775–1800

Industries	1775–1785		1785–1795		1795–1800		Total	
	E.	H.P.	E.	H.P.	E.	H.P.	E.	H.P.
Cotton Mills	2	9	47	736	35	637	84	1,382
Wool and Worsted Mills	..	...	2	60	7	120	9	180
Rope and Flax Mills	..	...	3	64	1	8	4	72
Bleachery	..	...	1	12	2	34	3	46
Calico Printing	..	...	1	4	..	...	1	4
Dyehouses	..	...	2	32	..	...	2	32
Calenderers and Glaziers	..	...	..	...	1	12	1	12
Canals	3	71	11	152	4	38	18	261
Collieries	5	100	22	220	3	60	30	380
Water Works	7	93	3	91	3	57	13	241
Corn Mills	2	34	6	68	1	16	9	118
Copper Mines	22	440	..	...	..	...	22	440
Foundry and Forge	17	428	9	150	2	40	28	618
Breweries	1	4	11	91	5	52	17	147
Potteries and Glassworks	2	16	2	22	2	46	6	84
Rolling Mill	2	17	..	...	..	...	2	17
Paper Mill	..	...	1	10	..	...	1	10
Salt and Lead Mines & Works	..	...	3	28	3	52	6	80
Distilleries	..	...	5	114	1	20	6	134
Tannery	..	...	1	6	..	...	1	6
Shot Mill	..	...	..	...	1	...	1	...
Other	3	26	14	149	8	100	25	275
Totals	66	1,238	144	2,009	79	1,296	289	4,543

Murray particularly. M. R. Boulton reported that they: [61]

> "returned from their excursion highly delighted and full of panegyricks upon Murray's excellent work. Abraham is now entirely convinced of his inferiority, &, what is more, of the possibility of amendment, & he is now *actually* making trials of different substances to mix with the sand with the view of getting a better skin to the castings. . . . They were admitted into every part of Murray's manufactory, & spent two evengs. with him. & by virtue of a plentiful doze of ale succeeded in extracting from him the arcana & mysteries of his superior performances."

Matthew Robinson Boulton and James Watt, Jr., deserve credit for the careful attention which they gave to the scientific organization and management of the new works. From 1795 to 1800 progress was slow, but the years from 1801 to 1803 mark a period of great extension and systematic planning and organization at Soho. Careful analyses of production methods were made, and processes were broken up in order to increase the division of labor. The existing speeds of machine operation were studied and new standard speeds established; power requirements were calculated and planned for; machinery and shops were arranged to facilitate the movement of material in proper sequence through the various stages of production. From the casting of the metal to the assembling and fitting of the finished parts, production was planned and coördinated and routing schedules were established. For the purpose of setting standard piece and wage rates and controlling costs of production, the partners had averages prepared of the time and expense involved in making various parts. All this involved the standardization of parts and processes to an extent which was unusual if not unique at the time. The principle of payment by results was applied as far as possible in every branch of production; and, where piece rates could not be set satisfactorily, the firm introduced the granting of "gratuities" or bonus additions to the daily wage, based on the amount of work finished.[62]

The following titles of papers in the Boulton & Watt Collection of the Birmingham Public Reference Library show the nature of some of the studies undertaken: [63]

> "Estimates of the different proposed methods of communicating motion to the machinery of Soho Engine Manufactory, Dec. 15, 1800."
>
> "Average cost of centring & turning Rot. shafts, main end gudgeons, pistons & covers, cylinder lids, air pump buckets & lids, rotative wheels & crank pins, July 1801, at Soho."
>
> "Memorandum of sundry articles wanted for the completion of the new & alteration of the old machinery at Soho, 1801."
>
> "Arrangement of Soho Engine Manufactory, December, 1801."
>
> "Arrangement of Workmen and Distribution of work at Soho Foundry, September 14th, 1801."
>
> "Specification of the fitting of Engine Materials and the Shops where it is to be done, December 3rd, 1801."
>
> "Account of the work done by the day and by the piece in the Engine Yard, Soho, June, 1800."
>
> "Particulars of the work done by piece at Soho Foundry, 1800."
>
> "Calculations for ascertaining piece-rates for the fitting of steam cases."
>
> "Proposed piece-prices for the fitting of different sizes of steam cases."
>
> "Table and calculations for proportioning premiums to ye borers. Table for the cylinders."
>
> "List of premiums upon various sizes of air pumps and cylinders, proposed to be paid to the borers."

The wisdom of the decision to manufacture complete engines was made manifest by the constant stream of orders and by

[61] *Ibid.*, p. 273.

[62] Roll, *op. cit.*, pp. 166–188, 208 ff.

[63] Dickinson and Jenkins, *op. cit.*, pp. 275–276; Roll, *op. cit.*, appendices xxii and x–xviii.

the financial success of the new undertaking (see above, p. 199). To some extent, at least, the results of more scientific management are reflected in the manufacturing figures for 1800 and 1801, as shown in Tables 4 and 5.[64]

In spite of many competitors and the high range of Soho prices, Boulton & Watt engines were much sought after for many years. Fulton's first successful steamboat engine was made by Boulton & Watt.[65] Marine engines became an important factor in the output. For a time gas-making apparatus was manufactured. With the exception of the manufacture of apparatus for pneumatic railways the Soho firm had little part in the railway era, but in addition to engines and boilers it contributed mill gearings, sugar mills, coining machinery, and similar equipment to Britain's export trade.[66]

Soho Manufactory was carried on as a separate establishment, but along with Soho Foundry until 1848, after the death of M. R. Boulton and of James Watt, Jr., when it was dismantled. A like fate befell Soho Foundry in 1895. James Watt, Jr., died unmarried. On M. R. Boulton's death, at the request of his executors, the name of Boulton was withdrawn from the firm, and it became James Watt & Co.[67]

[64] *Ibid.*, pp. 256–257.

[65] H. W. Dickinson, *Robert Fulton, Engineer and Artist, His Life and Works* (London, 1918), pp. 167–181.

[66] Timmins, *op. cit.*, pp. 340, 644–645; Smiles, *Lives of Engineers*, vol. iv, pp. 346–350.

[67] Timmins, *op. cit.*, p. 558.

Table 4. STATEMENT OF PROFIT AND LOSS, YEAR ENDING 1800

Loss	£	s.	d.	Profit	£	s.	d.
Brass Foundry	130	6	11½	Pattern Manufactory	451	4	1
Wrought Iron, Raw	2	6	4	Smithy	112	7	8½
Copper, Brass, etc.	0	0	4	Boilers	300	7	9½
Pneumatic Apparatus	64	10	0	Fitting Department	983	19	7½
				Engine Erectors	69	19	5½
				Commission on Foundry Engines	208	18	9
	£197	3	7½		£2,126	17	5
					197	3	7½
				Balance in favour of profit	£1,929	13	9½

Table 5. PROFITS FROM MANUFACTURING OPERATIONS, 1801

	£	s.	d.
Pattern Manufactory	294	19	3½
Smithy	289	14	10½
Brass Foundry	476	15	2½
Boiler Account	504	6	0
Pneumatic	38	14	9
Fitting Department	2,005	1	0
Engine Erectors	127	5	2
Commission on Foundry Engines	293	5	8½
	£4,030	2	0

9. Readings

General:

John Lord, *Capital and Steam-Power, 1750–1800* (London, 1923), pp. 75–88. An analysis of the effect of steam power, especially upon the capital requirements and organization of industry.

Paul Mantoux, *The Industrial Revolution in the Eighteenth Century* (New York, 1927), pp. 318–346. An excellent general study.

On Boulton and Watt:

H. W. Dickinson and Rhys Jenkins, *James Watt and the Steam Engine* (Oxford, 1927), a memorial volume, especially rich in illustrations and technical data.

H. W. Dickinson, *Matthew Boulton* (Cambridge, 1937). Though this work emphasizes the technical, it contains much that is of great value on the business; it is the only critical life of Boulton that exists.

Erich Roll, *An Early Experiment in Industrial Organisation* (London, 1930). A study of the firm of Boulton & Watt, based largely on its own records and stressing its business activities and management.

10. Suggested Questions

1. Explain the various difficulties which this partnership had to face.
2. What were the chief elements of the firm's business policy?
3. Why did the firm decide to manufacture engines complete?
4. What was the importance of the firm for the Industrial Revolution?
5. Is it strictly true to say that James Watt was the inventor of the steam engine?

XVI. SAMUEL SLATER AND THE AMERICAN TEXTILE INDUSTRY, 1789–1835

1. General Statement

The transition from mercantile to industrial capitalism is in no case better illustrated than in the work of Samuel Slater in the American textile industry. With the knowledge of the new machine processes which he had gained in England, Slater came to America in 1789, and almost at once he began to build spinning machinery in Pawtucket, Rhode Island, for the important mercantile firm of Almy & Brown.

Very soon Slater rose from the position of mechanic to a partnership in the firm. Next he branched out independently of the merchants, and before long he became a successful and a strong industrial entrepreneur concentrating on the manufacture of textiles.

We are fortunate to have voluminous records of the business of Samuel Slater. In the Rhode Island Historical Society are the papers of Almy & Brown, and Baker Library at Harvard University has a very large collection of the records of Slater's mills and also some of Slater's personal papers.

2. Important Dates in the Career of Samuel Slater

1768	Born in Derbyshire, England, son of yeoman farmer and timber merchant.
1783–89	Apprenticed to Jedediah Strutt in cotton spinning, acting as general overseer in the later years.
1789	Left secretly for America. In touch with Moses Brown, of Providence.
1790	Began building new spinning machinery in Pawtucket mill. Entered partnership with Almy & Brown.
1800	With partners built the "White Mill" at Rehoboth.
1803	John Slater arrived from England.
1806	William Almy, Obadiah Brown, and the Slaters built a mill at Slatersville.
1808–09	Difficult times for textile industry.
1812	Erected "Green Mill" at Oxford (Webster) with Bela Tiffany as partner.

1812–15	Great prosperity in textile industry.
1815	Started a woolen mill at Oxford with Edward Howard, an Englishman.
1816–19	Depression in textile industry. Slater missed opportunity of installing power looms.
1818	Tiffany retired from the "Green Mill."
1819	Sold out interest in "White Mill" to partners.
1823	Purchased cotton mills at what is now North Village, Webster, and at Jewett City, Connecticut. First power-loom weaving.
1826	In May became owner of one-half the mills at Amoskeag Village in New Hampshire. In December conveyed all but one-fifth to others.
1827	The first steam mill erected at Providence by Slater and associates.
1829	Financial difficulties brought a great change in Slater's holdings.
1830	Became proprietor of Providence Steam Cotton Mill and of mills in Wilkinsonville, Massachusetts.
1831	The two mills at Amoskeag incorporated. Interest in Jewett City Manufacturing Co. conveyed to his brother John.
1832	Repurchased with John the mills at Slatersville, running them under name of S. & J. Slater.
1835	Died at East Webster.

3. Introduction: Slater and the Browns

Slater came to America at the age of 21. He was a skilled mechanic, having served since the age of 14 as a clerk and overseer in the cotton mill of Jedediah Strutt, the former partner of Sir Richard Arkwright. He was a steady, persevering, self-contained, blunt young man, capable of new enterprise, and with infinite concern for detail. He did not believe that the cotton industry in England would always maintain its high prosperity, and he inferred from advertisements in American papers that any man experienced in the manufacture and use of the new textile machinery would be welcomed in the United States. The British government, anxious to maintain its industrial supremacy and following a policy already a century old, had forbidden the exportation of textile machinery and of models and diagrams relating thereto, as well as the emigration of mechanics skilled in the use of the new machines. It was for this reason that Slater, in the guise of a farmer boy, quietly slipped away to London and embarked for New York. It was his intention to secure the advantages, financial and otherwise, of being the first to introduce the improved English textile machinery into the United States.

Though most people in the United States were uninterested in if not actually adverse to the establishment of manufactures, a few individuals inspired both by motives of financial self-interest and by the desire to make the new country independent of Great Britain, industrially as well as politically, worked hard toward that end. A number of experiments had been made in the commercial manufacture of textiles, but none had been actually successful and most had failed, owing to ignorance of the technology of the manufacture and of the use of the necessary machinery.

Among those who were most interested in textile manufacture and who had enjoyed the greatest measure of success, entirely inadequate though it was, was the firm of William Almy and Smith Brown, of Providence. Almy and Brown were sedentary merchants of great promise, with considerable mercantile attainments. On capital furnished by the wealthy Moses Brown, father-in-law of one and kinsman of the other, they had made some progress toward the commercial manufacture of textiles.[1] Almy & Brown's mechanical equipment and methods in spinning are described in a letter written by Moses Brown to Samuel Slater in December, 1789:[2]

"We have two machines of this kind, one of thirty-two spindles, the other of twenty-four. They have been worked, and spun about one hundred and fifty skeins of cotton yarn, from five to eight skeins of fifteen lays round a reel of two yards to the pound; but the person whom we let the mill to, being unacquainted with the business, and the mills probably not perfected, he could not make wages in attending them, and therefore they are at present still. We then wrought hand roping and the carding machine was not in order. We have since got a jenny, and are putting on fine cards to the machines: these with an eighty-four and a sixty spinning jenny, and a doubling and twisting jenny, compose the principal machinery about our manufactory. We have from Ireland a man and his wife, who are spinners on the jennies, but we are destitute of a person acquainted with the frames. We shall be glad to be informed what quantity of yarn your mills spin in a day on one spindle. What number of spindles a lad can, or does attend, and at what age? How your roping is made, what fineness, whether twisting harder or softer than for jennies? Whether the cotton is soaped before carding, as that for the jenny, or not at all? What the wooden rollers in the mills are covered with? Ours have been done with calf-skin. How the taking up is regulated. Ours is by leather strings? On what the spools play and run, on irons?"

Since the cloth was woven from their own yarn, the following account of cotton goods produced by Almy & Brown from about June 11, 1789, to the end of the following year indicates that the firm must have been doing considerable spinning by this time:[3]

Corduroy	45 pieces,	1090 yds.	sold from	3s. 6d.	to 4s. per yd.
Royal Ribs, Denims, &c.	25 "	558 "	" "	3s.	" 4s. " "
Cottonets	13 "	324 "	" "	2s. 6d.	" 3s. " "
Jeans	79 "	1897 "	" "	2s.	" 2s. 6d. "
Fustians	26 "	687 "	" "	1s. 8d.	" 2s. " "
Total	188 pieces	4556 yds.			

4. The Mechanic Joins the Merchant in Machine Spinning, 1790–1800

A. Formation of the partnership and establishment of the Pawtucket mill.

It was natural that Samuel Slater upon his arrival in America should hear of Almy & Brown and should make an application to them. Slater joined the Providence firm to build and operate a mill for them, and he shortly entered into a partnership including Almy, Brown, and Slater. The conditions of this partnership are stated in their agreement of April 5, 1790:[4]

"The following agreement, made between William Almy and Smith Brown of the one part, and Samuel Slater of the other part, —Witnesseth that the said parties have mutually agreed to be concerned together in, and carry on, the spinning of cotton by water, (of which the said Samuel professes himself a workman, well skilled in all its branches;) upon the following terms, viz:—that the said Almy and Brown, on their part, are to turn in the machinery, which they have already purchased, at the price they cost them, and to furnish materials for the building of two carding machines, viz:—a breaker and a finisher; a drawing and roving frame; and to extend the spinning mills, or frames, to one hundred spindles. And the said Samuel, on his part, cove-

[1] Caroline F. Ware, The Industrial Revolution in the New England Cotton Industry (Ms. thesis, Radcliffe), p. 46, based on Almy & Brown Papers, Ledger, 1789–93. Also the same author's book, *The Early New England Cotton Manufacture* (Boston, 1931), pp. 19–20.

[2] George S. White, *Memoir of Samuel Slater* (Philadelphia, 1836), pp. 64–65.

[3] *Ibid.*, p. 65.

[4] *Ibid.*, pp. 74–75.

nants and engages, to devote his whole time and service, and to exert his skill according to the best of his abilities, and have the same effected in a workmanlike manner, similar to those used in England, for the like purposes. And it is mutually agreed between the said parties, that the said Samuel shall be considered an owner and proprietor in one-half of the machinery aforesaid, and accountable for one half of the expense that hath arisen, or shall arise, from the building, purchasing, or repairing, of the same, but not to sell, or in any manner dispose of any part, or parcel thereof, to any other person or persons, excepting the said Almy and Brown; neither shall any others be entitled to hold any right, interest, or claim, in any part of the said machinery, by virtue of any right which the said Slater shall or may derive from these presents, unless by an agreement, expressed in writing from the said Almy and Brown, first had and obtained—unless the said Slater has punctually paid one half of the cost of the said machinery with interest thereon; nor then, until he has offered the same to the said Almy and Brown in writing upon the lowest terms; that he will sell or dispose of his part of the said machinery to any other person, and instructed the said Almy and Brown, or some others by them appointed, in the full and perfect knowledge of the use of the machinery, and the art of water spinning. And it is further agreed, that the said Samuel, as a full and adequate compensation for his whole time and services, both whilst in constructing and making the machinery, and in conducting and executing the spinning, and preparing to spin upon the same, after every expense arising from the business is defrayed, including the usual commissions of two and one-half per cent. for purchasing of the stock, and four per cent. for disposing of the yarn, shall receive one half of the profits, which shall be ascertained by settlement from time to time, as occasion may require; and the said Almy and Brown the other half—the said Almy and Brown to be employed in the purchasing of stock, and disposing of the yarn. And it is further covenanted, that this indenture shall make void and supersede the former articles of agreement, made between the said Almy and Brown and the said Slater, and that it shall be considered to commence, and the conditions mentioned in it be binding upon the parties, from the beginning of the business; the said Samuel to be at the expense of his own time and board from thence forward. And it is also agreed that if the said Almy and Brown choose to put in apprentices to the business, that they have liberty so to do. The expense arising from the maintenance of whom, and the advantages derived from their services during the time the said Almy and Brown may think proper to continue them in the business, shall be equally borne and received as is above provided for in the expenses and profits of the business. It is also to be understood, that, whatever is advanced by the said Almy and Brown, either for the said Slater, or to carry on his part of the business, is to be repaid them with interest thereon, for which purpose they are to receive all the yarn that may be made, the one half of which on their own account, and the other half they are to receive and dispose of, on account of the said Slater, the net proceeds of which they are to credit him, towards their advance, and stocking his part of the works, so that the business may go forward.

"In witness whereof the parties to these presents have interchangeably set their hands, this fifth day of the fourth month, seventeen hundred and ninety.

"Wm. Almy
Smith Brown
Samuel Slater

"Witnesses—
Oziel Wilkinson, Abraham Wilkinson."

Slater found that the old machines at Pawtucket were not worth improving[5]—the spinning frame made very poor yarn. He, therefore, set about building new machines with capital furnished by Almy & Brown. He would not, however, begin building the Arkwright machine until he had been promised a man to work on wood who should be under bond not to steal the patterns nor disclose the nature of the work.[6] When he had been satisfied on this

[5] *Ibid.,* p. 84.

[6] This precaution was of little avail. Despite Slater's attempts to prevent diffusion of technical knowledge relating to textile manufacturing, there is evidence that Slater's mills, through employees and in other ways, inspired others to set up similar factories.

point, he at once set to work behind closed shutters and drawn blinds in Ezekiel Carpenter's fulling mill to build water frames, carding machines, and the necessary roping and drawing frames. The wooden parts of the spinning machines were cut out by Sylvanus Brown after Slater had chalked their outlines on the wood. Oziel Wilkinson, the blacksmith of Pawtucket—Slater's future father-in-law and like his partners a Friend—with whom Slater boarded, made the ironwork of the machines with the assistance of his sons and under Slater's directions. Pliny Earl of Leicester, Massachusetts, another Friend, made the cards.

The power was at first supplied by a wheel propelled by an old Negro, Samuel Brunius Jenks, but later water power was installed. At the start the water wheel was so exposed that it froze every night; in the morning it could not be started without first breaking the ice. Since no one could be found to do this, Slater, it is said, had to spend two or three hours before breakfast every morning in this occupation.[7] The effects of this exposure stayed with him the rest of his life.

Slater apparently did not begin spinning until December 20, 1790. There is no definite information available as to the amount of yarn produced in this establishment. Some idea of the success of the undertaking is given by two items from the records of Almy & Brown: [8]

1. Credit to Samuel Slater:

"Nov. 25th, 1792. By the one half of the proceeds from the sales of yarn spun at the mills, and of credit taken to our account, and accounted for by us as sold—£882 4s. 11½d."

2. Charged to Samuel Slater:

"To the one half of our account against spinning mills for machinery, &c. up to Feb. 11, 1792, £252 1 6
"To one half of do. for stock up to same date, 210 19 1¾"

The account book containing Almy & Brown's accounts with Slater for the Pawtucket mill from 1793 through 1804 gives information concerning the extent of the business and the source of its capital. It is the account of stock furnished to the spinning mill by Almy & Brown, for which they advanced the necessary capital to be repaid out of the profits. This account contains records of expenditures for building materials for the "Old Mill," for labor, cotton, and a miscellaneous lot of things used in maintaining the business.

Some excerpts from the mill account with Almy & Brown follow.[9]

"Spinning Mills for Stock to Almy & Brown—Dr.

[1795]						
8 Mo.	5.	To 2 lb Cotton wg. 486 @ 2/6	60..15			
		" 1 do. 120 lb @ 2/	12			
		" 1 do. 178 " 2/	17..16			
		" 1 do. Georgia wg. 53 lb @ 1/8	4.. 8..8	94	19	8
	15.	" Cash pd. for Truckg			1	10½
9 Mo.	4	" Cash pd. for Sea Coals			2	8
10 Mo.	26	To 249 lb Cotton @	28.. 0..3			
		" pd. for Cartg. do	.. 1..2½			
		. . . .		28	1	5½

[7] Perry Walton, *The Story of Textiles* (Boston, 1925), pp. 172–173.

[8] White, *op. cit.*, p. 76.

[9] Almy & Brown's Account with Spinning Mills, 1793–1833, Slater Papers, Baker Library, Harvard University.

Spinning Mills to Almy & Brown		Dr.	
1793			
1 Mo. 31.	To 4 lb of Candles @ 9 d	3	
	" Cash pd. for flat file	2..4	.. 5 4
2 Mo. 6.	" Cash paid for listing		.. 6 6
14	" 1 Gross Wood Screws carried forwd to p 8		
15	" paid Cash for a Bill		 6
23	To pd. for Carting to Pawtucket) 1918 feet white pine Boards) 1987 ft. yellow Pine do. 105 ft.) 6 Maple do. & 6 Barrs Iron)		..16 –
	To 1918 ft. White pine Boards for mill		5 15

. . . .

1794			
12 Mo. 3	To Cash pd. fr 2 Gross, 1 in. Screws	7.4	
	" do for 1 do. 1¼ inch	5	..12 4
9	" Cash pd. for wire		..13 4

. . . .

[1795]			
[3 Mo]			
7	To Masoning done by Elisha) Brown as Pr his Bill)	2.. 9..6	
	" Cash pd. Jacob Balcom p. Slats. drd.	3 —	5.. 9.. 6
12	" Cash pd. Israel Wilkenson) for Cartg. Iron pr Slaters Ords.)		.. 3 –"

[The following is a statement of the account with Almy & Brown, to the end of 1803: [10]]

"Dr.	Spinning Mills in Acct Current with Almy & Brown				Cr.
1803			1803		
12 Mo 31	To our Acct to date as rendered on the other side	149,061.61	12 Mo 31	By Spinning Mills a/c to date	$163,100.41
	To [be] accounted for with Saml Slater the other Owner of the Mill for the ballance in our settlement with him, say —.	18,031.77		By the Interest on $20,903.94 the differrence between our Debit and the Mills Debit 12 Mo. 31. 1801.—	3,992.97
		$167,093.38			$167,093.38

North Providence
9 mo 27. 1804

Errors Excepted per
Almy & Brown"

[10] *Ibid.*

B. Labor.

The first record of employees begins with Monday, December 20, 1790, though some say that the new machinery began producing yarn as early as October. During the first week four boys, Turpin and Charles Arnold, Smith Wilkinson and Jabez Jenks were employed for the full time. On the next Monday (December 27) Eunice Arnold, on Wednesday of the same week Otis Borrows, and on Thursday John and Sylvanus (Varnus) Jenks commenced work. On the following Monday (January 3) Ann Arnold was added to the list and during that week all the nine operatives, seven boys and two girls, worked the full time of six days. The same operatives also continued in the fourth week, though either "Varnus" Jenks or Smith Wilkinson (there is an error in the record which makes this point uncertain) worked only five days, while Turpin Arnold was absent two half-days. All these workers were children of from seven to twelve, according to Smith Wilkinson, Slater's brother-in-law, who began work for Almy, Brown & Slater at the age of ten "by tending the breaker." [11] The family basis of this employment is shown by the fact that among these nine early workers only four family names were represented, there being four Arnolds, three Jenkses, a Wilkinson, and a Borrows.

Since Pawtucket at that time contained only about a dozen houses, at first it was difficult to secure operatives for the mills. On this account Slater was obliged to persuade families to emigrate to Pawtucket. His son, H. N. Slater, tells of a family named Arnold, with 10 or 11 children, living in a lean-to cabin of slabs with a stone chimney. The wife and mother, on being consulted about moving to Pawtucket, stipulated that they should be provided with as good a house as the one they would be leaving.[12] It may be that this family contributed the Arnolds mentioned in the first time list.

We have some information about working and living conditions among Slater's workers. Wages ranged from 80 cents to $1.30 and $1.40 per week.[13] The daily hours of labor 30 or 40 years later ordinarily averaged 12, so they were probably not any less during the 1790's.[14] The indoor work was too confining to be attractive, and, there being neither school nor church,[15] nothing in Pawtucket compensated for this disadvantage. Slater tried to remedy some of these conditions by establishing in 1793 a Sunday school in his own house for the children working in the mills and those of the adult employees who had not received an elementary education. At first he taught them himself, but he later hired students from Rhode Island College, now Brown University. Later, day schools were established.[16]

Slater's strict paternal discipline was not always well received. He attempted to introduce the English apprenticeship system, but it did not suit the American temperament and had to be abandoned. One boy, who found the work too hard and discipline too strict, complained to an older companion who replied sagaciously, "Very well, act like the devil and Slater will let you off." [17]

The cotton, spun into yarn in the mills constructed by him and his associates, was put out to poor families to be cleansed and whipped at from 4 to 6 cents per pound, the rate depending on the cleanliness of the cotton. This was delivered in bags of about 100 pounds each and carried sometimes for many miles, usually on horse-

[11] William R. Bagnall, *Samuel Slater* (Middletown, Connecticut, 1890), pp. 44–45; White, *op. cit.*, p. 99. According to Moses Brown the work was done by children of from eight to fourteen, not a material discrepancy.

[12] *Slater Mills at Webster, 1812–1912* (Worcester, Massachusetts, 1912), p. 18.

[13] *Ibid.;* Walton, *op. cit.*, p. 174.

[14] White, *op. cit.*, pp. 128–129.

[15] *Slater Mills at Webster, 1812–1912,* p. 18.

[16] Bagnall, *op. cit.*, p. 49; Walton, *op. cit.*, p. 174; White, *op. cit.*, p. 107.

[17] *Slater Mills,* p. 18; Walton, *op. cit.*, p. 174.

back, and gave employment to many women and children at their homes.[18]

C. Marketing.

The marketing of the goods produced in the mill of Almy, Brown & Slater was handled by the mercantile firm of Almy & Brown. Samuel Slater had nothing to do with the sale of these goods, except to see that they should be of such a quality as to be easily salable. Even before joining with Samuel Slater, Almy & Brown must have made some advances toward the establishment of a market for the products of their mills.[19] Their Ledger A, 1789–93, shows that they sold cotton, woolen cloth, and stockings at retail in their Providence store. They may have disposed of yarn in the same way.

The first machine-spun yarn went to market in June, 1791, about six months after the spinning had started. The first lot of 116 pounds brought £35 3s. 4d. It was sold principally near Providence but in some instances as far away as Norwich, Connecticut. During this year and the next most of the sales were to people in either Providence or that neighborhood, for instance, Pawtucket and Warwick, though some were to customers in Norwich, Hartford, and Charlestown. The records for about the next eight years are lost, but later records show that the situation changed considerably in that time.[20]

By 1798, as we see in a letter of January 9 to Hussey, Faber & Co.,[21] a Boston firm with a branch in Lynn, the market must have been extended at least to Boston, since Almy & Brown promised to send this firm an invoice of yarn in care of Joseph Hussey, Boston, to be forwarded to them. This letter acknowledged the receipt of a payment and granted the firm the privilege of selling yarn on credit, accounting with Almy & Brown semiannually and assuming the risk. Hussey, Faber & Co. received the yarn at the wholesale price and they were to sell it at the retail price. Almy & Brown promised to keep the firm well supplied with yarn and urged that its sale be vigorously promoted.

A letter of January 22 to John B. Dockray (address not given in copy) indicates the sending of a consignment of yarn on six months' settlement, but the seller "being Desireous to spread the use of the yarn We matter not so much as to the punctual payment of the same, unless sold, provided it be in safe Hands."

On March 19, 1798, Almy & Brown wrote to "Oziell Wilkenson" mentioning that they had sent him something over $400 worth of cotton goods and cotton yarn, which they wished him to sell for money or barter for grain, or, failing to do so, leave in the hands of Harris and Peter Colt, Hartford, or some other responsible person who would handle their sale. The yarn was invoiced at the wholesale price so that Wilkinson would receive the ordinary retail profit. He was authorized to sell on a credit of ninety days, "with good security, such as on enquiry thou would be willing to take was the Property thy Own." The goods were not to be sold for grain unless the price was such that the grain could be freighted to Providence without loss to Almy & Brown. He was also asked to hunt up some suitable person in Hartford to sell yarn for knitting.

A letter of March 26, 1798, to a William Brown (no address) gives some insight into their marketing methods. Brown was informed that "We are free to furnish You with any quantity of yarn you can dispose of either by the Bundle or Pound. Neither do we intend So long as you give us satisfaction to supply any others on your Island with the same to sell on Commissions. But should there be application to Purchase the

[18] White, *op. cit.*, p. 106; *The Two Samuels, Slater and Batchelder,* Scrapbook (Boston, 1791), p. 5.

[19] White, *op. cit.*, pp. 64–65.

[20] Ware, *New England Cotton Manufacture,* p. 32.

[21] The Almy & Brown letters, quoted in this section, are from their papers in the Rhode Island Historical Society, Providence.

Yarn of us We expect to sell the same as heretofore."

On May 1, some cotton yarn "Spun by Water," as they were careful to explain, was sent by Almy & Brown to one Jacob Merritt, who with his brothers Daniel and Isaac had been recommended by a certain John Barker as "suitable persons to sell the same." It seems likely that Merritt was in New York State, as his brothers were, since Almy & Brown stated that since "this was sent only on Tryal it would be most agreeable to you to sell it on Commissions as several others do in Hutson Albaney & elsewhare." The yarn was charged at the "Retale Price," and Merritt was expected "to sell it at that Price & for us (Almy and Brown) to allow thee a Commission of 5 p. cent for doing the Business for us (after paying) & (for us) to pay all expenses attending the Transportation (&c)." The words in parentheses are crossed out in the original copy. It is evident that Almy & Brown felt that this yarn was a commodity not very familiar to the section of the country in which Merritt lived. Consequently they carefully explained the different grades and how they were sold. "The yarn," they wrote, "is sold Without any Trouble of Weighing, every skain of which haveing been Weighed to ascertain the (Price) No. the skain answering thereto, viz. No. 7½ is 7½ skains to the Pound, in order to make that easy, the Purchaser has his choice either to take 7 or 8 skain, paying for the ½ skain or having it deducted either as is most agreable." Although the Merritt brothers were strangers to Almy & Brown, still "from the recommendation given We hereby entrust you with the yarn," requesting a notification upon its arrival and on the "Prospect of selling the same."

In May, 1798, another letter contained a refusal to send further yarn to a client until a settlement of accounts had been made. This letter stated that, in view of the fact that Almy & Brown had to pay for their material and labor regularly, they had to place their yarn where they would be sure of payments at stated times.

A letter of July 26 to Benjamin Chamberlain, Philadelphia, regretted that no whitened yarn was on hand and instructed him to pay Elijah Waring, their agent at Philadelphia, for the yarn already sold. Another letter of October 7, evidently in reply to a letter of inquiry from Stephen Hoyt (Poughkeepsie), gave the terms under which, in this case, they would allow him to sell their yarn, namely at 5 per cent commission, Almy & Brown to pay all expenses of transportation, advertising, postage, and so on. Another, December 15, to their Philadelphia agent, Elijah Waring, instructed him to settle with Benjamin Chamberlain, receive the yarn left on his hands, return the yarn not likely to be sold, and put the rest in the hands of Letchwork or some other person "either to sell on our acct. [or?] their own." A letter directing Chamberlain to settle with Waring followed. The impression given is that it had been thought best to sever the connection and that the reason was Almy & Brown's dissatisfaction with the way in which Chamberlain was handling the business.

Apparently by this time their yarn was disposed of easily, as is seen in a letter of December 21 to Hussey, Faber & Co. This letter acknowledged the receipt of a sum of money and an order for yarn but stated that in the future the commission would be smaller since we "think that 5 per cent on yarn Sold at whole Saile now a considerable quantity is and probably more will be vended, is rather too high a Comishons when the Sales of it was only getting introduced we thought we might give that premium, but now we apprehend that two & half per C[t] would be as much as is usually given . . . if that would be agreeable to you to receive the yarn at in future, we shall be glad to furnish you with as good an assortment as we can from time to time." Whether or not Almy & Brown made this reduction effective, it is evident that they felt that their yarn had been firmly established.

There is here a gap in the correspondence. The next letter of interest appears March 10, 1801. Stephen Hoyt, of Poughkeepsie, complained that during the last year he had not been furnished yarn of satisfactory numbers and quantity. He had been applied to by a factory in Connecticut to take a supply from them but preferred the Pawtucket yarn if he could get it. He promised to pay the balance of his account as soon as he could sell some farm produce for cash. It was evident that the difficulty of Almy, Brown & Slater was now in supplying the yarn rather than in securing a market.

By 1801 Almy & Brown were selling to storekeepers in Portland, Newburyport, Marblehead, Salem, Boston, New Bedford, Nantucket, and in the Rhode Island and Connecticut ports; were shipping a large proportion of their product to New York City, Albany, Hudson, Philadelphia, and Baltimore; and were finding it hard to fill the orders.[22] Although the quantities sent to each place were small—only Portland, Boston, and Philadelphia took $1,000 worth, yet the market widened. A little was bought, not by storekeepers or merchants, but by manufacturers who put it out to be woven or knitted. Prices had been raised in 1801; finer numbers were being spun; there was still a sellers' market, though competition was beginning. This was 10 years after the formation of the Almy, Brown and Slater partnership.

5. Increased Production and Competition, 1800–12

A. New mills.

The Pawtucket mill had proved to be a success. This earliest pioneering work preceded a period of expansion in the textile interests of Almy, Brown & Slater as well as in the industry as a whole. It is significant that this later growth of Slater's interests was not wholly along the lines of the early partnership with Almy & Brown.

Slater, who for a decade had been engaged in only one enterprise, the partnership with Almy & Brown in the Pawtucket mill, in 1800 joined his father-in-law, Oziel Wilkinson, and his brothers-in-law, Timothy Greene and William Wilkinson, in the "White Mill." Slater's interest was one-half, Oziel's one-fourth, and that of the other two one-eighth each.[23] It is very likely that Slater's capital for this venture came from his years in the "Old Mill," though he may have received some help from his father's estate.

Slater was superintendent of both mills, receiving $1.50 per day from each. Oziel Wilkinson, who had made the ironwork of the spinning frames used in the "Old Mill," doubtless constructed the machines for the "White Mill." It is not known who handled the commercial side of the business. Slater, with his superintendence of both mills, could hardly in addition have done the buying and selling, even though he had formed the habit of working sixteen hours a day. Oziel was busy with his machine shop. The two junior partners probably handled the business.

That Almy and Brown objected to the building of the mill is seen from the fact that they had refused Slater permission to build on a site which they owned jointly. Slater finally secured a jury decision bringing a partition of the land and mill privileges. The letter below suggests that there may at other times have been differences between Slater and his first partners:

"Providence 8th *mo* 21 1798

"Respected Friend
"Saml Slater

. . . .

"In reply to thy suggestions, that we do not pay attention to the settlement of our accts with thee, that a long period of time has elapsed since their commencement,—that they lies in a precarious situation—and that

[22] Ware, *New England Cotton Manufacture*, pp. 32–33.

[23] Bagnall, *op. cit.*, p. 53.

thou thinks it high time that they were settled, We say that we have always been ready to make a settlement with thee, at any given time since our accts were opened,—that we have repeatedly manifested that readiness—and that we are now also ready to close them whenever thou will attend to it. Whence, therefore, this very extraordinary Paragraph in thy Letter, that on 'Monday next, being the 27th Inst. I *will* stop making rovings, so that all the rovings there are on hand may be spun in the course of a few days, in order to weigh off all the yarn, and stock on hand, so that we may complete our settlement.' If indeed, thou means that after that period thou shalt decline having concern in the mill and withdraw thy personal attention from the business it would be a subject of consideration & discussion how far that would comfort with thy engagements,—but if thou means a total stopping and derangement of the business, we now inform thee that we can by no means consent to such a measure.—We have not indeed invested in that business our Propperty and exerted our Credit as Extensively to effect the establishment, and continuance of it, to have it put a period to and made a sacrifice of, whenever it may suit the supposed Interest or *Will* of any Individual.—there are a variety of ways and means that that may be devised to ascertain the yarn & stock on hand unattended with such unnecessary derangement & loss.

"Upon the whole, notwithstanding the terms in which thine is couched, we must suppose, thou meant it as a proposition merely, which having so fully expressed our disapprobation of, we rest, depending that thou will not fulfill so infamous a measure, as it must eventually prove to thyself as well as to us.

"We are respectfully fds
"Almy & Brown"

The building of the new mill did not, however, occasion a break with Almy and Brown. On the contrary, in 1806 Slater with his brother John as an added partner entered into another project with them. It was probably the pressure of work as well as the desire for knowledge of the most recent technical advances that had caused Slater to send for his brother in 1803, instructing him to visit Oldham and Manchester before leaving England.[24] As an expert mechanic John could take much of the burden from Samuel's shoulders. The brother's coming encouraged the erection of the Slatersville (R. I.) mill, the site of which was selected by John Slater. Each of the four partners apparently held one-fourth share in this partnership. John may have brought money from England, from his father's estate or his own earnings, or Samuel may have advanced him money toward his share. A recent investigation calls attention to the fact that "it was very easy to start a mill with only a few thousand dollars. . . . Machinery was commonly made on the premises, not purchased. . . ."[25] John Slater was superintendent of this mill.

No new mills were added to the Slater interests from 1806 to 1812. While labor conditions and available capital were undoubtedly in some respects favorable to industrial development in New England during the Embargo years, that very situation encouraged a competition which became serious, especially in the New England market.

B. Marketing problems.

Marketing was a serious problem for Almy, Brown & Slater in those years. The pioneering work which they had done had made their yarn favorably known over a considerable area. This accomplished, they hoped to improve their marketing system. The Almy & Brown correspondence with agents, 1803–04, shows that they were trying to build up a superior demand and to extend their market farther south into the newer West. They were attempting to hold their old customers but also to add new ones, and particularly to increase direct sales at a discount for cash. In 1803 Obadiah Brown, who had become a partner in Almy, Brown & Slater, made a trip through Maryland, Delaware, Pennsylvania, New

[24] Walton, *op. cit.*, pp. 182–183; Bagnall, *op. cit.*, p. 64; White, *op. cit.*, p. 109 n.

[25] Ware thesis, cited above, p. 53.

Jersey, and New York, securing new customers and pushing sales. In a letter of April 8 from New York City he mentioned that he had been in Newport, Troy, and Eastown, taking orders for cotton yarn, stocking yarn, and sewing cotton. In a letter of May 20 from Carlisle, Pennsylvania, he wrote that he had been traveling about through that State with Elijah Waring, visiting possible or former customers in Philadelphia, Lancaster, Carlisle, and Yorktown, and taking orders for cotton yarn, bedticking, and stocking yarn, some to sell on trial and some for cash. At this time Almy & Brown also began to encourage hand weaving, extending credit to master weavers.

These efforts brought several problems. Credit in the country trade was one; Almy favored selling on commission only to city merchants or merchants with city backing. The firm found also that its agents, instead of accepting lower commissions, demanded higher rates and even favored lowering of prices. Further, some city agents were annoyed by Almy & Brown's attempts to widen their market.

Conditions became especially hard in the years from 1806 to 1810. Even before the Embargo, Almy & Brown had complained of the competition of the new mills in their old market. The increase in the New England mills, on the one hand, and the Embargo and the parallel contraction in the New England markets, on the other, made conditions worse. To one agent they wrote in March, 1807: [26] "If thou can dispose of yarn when your river is open we will send thee an assortment as we are extending our business in that line, and as others are also getting into the same business, in consequence of which we shall probably have to extend our sales, we therefore wish to keep all our old correspondents supplied."

The Embargo hit the commercial towns, which were their chief market. In 1808 new devices were used for strengthening the market. Almy & Brown ordered their agents to advertise and print handbills announcing the superiority of their yarn. They aggressively sought new customers. They offered extensive credit. They agreed to accept produce of various sorts and tried to exchange their goods for other goods to be sold in their store. They tried to get wholesale agents to sell in small lots. They even considered sending out peddlers, but feared the difficulty of securing good men. They tried to maintain a *price monopoly* among manufacturers. At the same time the agents were writing them of generous offers made to them by other mills.

A word might be said on price maintenance. Almy & Brown, who had originally set the price, had made it their policy to maintain price. "As we were the first that undertook the business of spinning cotton yarn in this country," they wrote in 1808, "consequently we were the first that made a price for the article, which price has, as far as we have any knowledge, been adhered to by those who are concerned in the business. Should any vary the price, we should be very much obliged by being informed of it, and the quality of their yarn, conceiving a mutual understanding among the makers and venders of the article would be mutually beneficial." [27]

One way of increasing the demand for their yarn was to encourage hand-loom weavers. At this early period we have no information whatsoever concerning Slater's relations, if any, with the problem of weaving, but the practices of his partners are indicated in their correspondence. In June, 1808, they wrote to John Wintringham, a master weaver of Poughkeepsie:

"We are glad to hear that thou art extending thy business by setting more looms up, as we

[26] Almy & Brown to J. Rogers, Mar. 10, 1807, Almy & Brown Papers, Rhode Island Historical Society.

[27] Ware, *New England Cotton Manufacture*, p. 44, quoting Almy & Brown to Phillips, Oct. 24, 1808, Almy & Brown Papers.

are desirous to encourage the manufacture of the yarn into cloth, by others rather than by ourselves, wishing to promote the industrious mechanic and manufacturer of cloth. We wish thee to increase thy sales to the full extent of the sales of cloth in the part of the country where thou lives, having ourselves been obliged to get our yarn wove into blue stripes etc. in order to sell the same, but if we can sell the yarn to the weaver and be certain of our pay, we shall prefer doing that to manufacturing it ourselves."

A letter of December 9, 1808, to N. Rice, a merchant weaver near Boston, on arranging with him to have cloth woven for them gives some light on their "putting-out:"

"We are to allow 5¢ per yard for ⅞ sheeting, 5½¢ per yard wide, and 9¢ for 9⁄8 sheeting for weaving the same. The cloth to be made for our satisfaction and delivered in Boston, thou to charge us back the yarn as per invoice and commission of 5% and to settle with or remit us the amount of account sale once in six months. Please to be particular and charge thy weavers to make good cloth. . . . If the cloth suits us and we do not get a sufficiency made at our factories we shall want as much as thou can get made, but as soon as thou can, send us a specimen of the cloth before thou puts out much of the yarn."

The above is the only case that has been discovered in which Almy & Brown placed or tried to place the management of "putting-out" into the hands of others. For the most part they put out webs directly to weavers in the vicinity of the spinning mills—paying them in due bills on their store—or, in the case of the Warwick mills (in which Slater was not concerned), had them woven in shops connected with their own factories. The rest of their yarn they sold directly to master weavers and shopkeepers and through selling agents. They disliked the irregularity in quantity and quality of output inherent in the domestic putting-out system and preferred to have their cloth woven in supervised shops, wherever possible. In a letter to John Wintringham, January 17, 1809, they wrote: "We have several hundred pieces now out weaving, but a hundred looms in families will not weave so much cloth as ten at least constantly employed under the immediate supervision of a workman." Through 1808, indeed, they preferred selling yarn rather than having it made up into cloth, because of the difficulty of getting satisfactory work done. A letter of December 22, 1808, to this same master weaver, Wintringham, mentions this problem.

Even with their strong efforts to extend the demand for their yarn, in the spring of 1809 Almy & Brown had piled up in their factories or in the hands of agents 100,000 pounds of yarn, including a three years' supply of one kind. They recommended that agents try to sell bedticking at auction.[28] They secured agents at Richmond and Norfolk. After the removal of the Embargo, Almy & Brown tried to maintain the demand for their goods, in the face of English competition, by insisting on the superiority of their own product. By 1810, however, partly because of the rapid expansion of the western market, the conditions were becoming more favorable to the American manufacturer.[29]

6. The Industrialist Becomes Independent of the Merchant

A. Acquisition of additional mills.

The comparative quiet of the years 1806 to 1812 was followed by a time of marked expansion in Slater's cotton interests, as in the textile industry in general. Not only did the war years bring inflated prices and demand, but they brought also an extension of the western market. A Buffalo merchant advertised in 1812 that he was regularly supplied with

[28] Letters to Waring, June 6 to 21, 1809, Almy & Brown Papers, Rhode Island Historical Society.

[29] Much of the above information on marketing was secured from chap. iii of Ware's *New England Cotton Manufacture.*

goods from the mills of Brown and Slater.

Slater's first new venture was partly the result of the need for more hand-loom weavers to weave yarn spun in his mills, for the increased supply could not all be woven in the vicinity of Providence. Labor and water power for spinning were also of importance in determining the location of new mills. Lyman and Bela Tiffany, employees of Slater, suggested Oxford (Webster) in southern Worcester County, Massachusetts, as a good location. At Slater's request Bela Tiffany made a careful survey, and upon his favorable report the "Green Mill" was erected in 1812, with Bela a member of the firm. How much capital the new member had is not known. It is probable that he was taken into the company for his personal ability rather than for any capital he may have furnished. The Ledger for 1812–13 shows the firm indebted largely to Slater and hardly at all to Tiffany.

Slater's next venture, inspired by the War of 1812, was the establishment in 1815 of a woolen mill at East Village, Oxford, in partnership with Edward Howard, an Englishman. Let it be noted that this was an entirely new departure in Slater's interests. Slater probably furnished most of the capital, while Howard superintended the mill. The Slater-Howard Ledger, 1823–26, shows the firm indebted to Slater for thousands of dollars and to Howard for hardly a hundred.

Slater was now concerned one-third in the "Old Mill" at Pawtucket,[30] one-half in the "White Mill" at Rehoboth, and one-fourth in the mill at Smithfield (Slatersville), Rhode Island. All these mills were either in Rhode Island or in Massachusetts close to Providence, and the first two were under Slater's own supervision. He also possessed a share, the size of which is not clear but which was probably large in proportion to the other partners' shares, in the "Green Mill" and the woolen mill at Oxford (Webster). In 1818 Tiffany retired from the "Green Mill" after only six years of the partnership, and Slater became sole owner. There seems a logical connection between this event and Slater's selling out his half-interest in the "White Mill" to his partners in 1819. He seems to have divided his time at this period between Oxford and Providence and doubtless, no matter from whom came the initiative in the matter of the sale of his interest in the Rehoboth mill, he found it necessary to pay more attention to the Worcester mills than could be given consistently with his duty to his earlier partners and engagements. The death in 1818 of his son, and namesake, who had begun some years earlier to take a part of the burden from his father's shoulders, was even in a purely material sense a grievous blow to him.

In 1820 the woolen mill burned, but Slater, still in connection with Howard, built a new mill at South Village (Oxford, or Webster as it was later called). The year 1823 saw the beginning of his purchase of mills in the establishment of which he had had no part. One of these was the Braman, Benedict & Waters cotton mill located in the same vicinity as the "Green Mill" and the woolen mill. It marked a further step toward increased attention to the Worcester County mills. The same year, with John Slater he bought the cotton mills at Jewett City, Connecticut, from the Jewett City Cotton Manufacturing Co., these mills being in London County, southeastern Connecticut, near the Rhode Island State line and closer to the Providence mills than to those in Worcester County, Massachusetts.

In 1826, with Larned Pitcher and Ira Gay, he bought the mills at Amoskeag Village in New Hampshire, Slater taking one-half, thus extending his holdings into a fourth State. Before the year was over,

[30] From the agreement of 1819 it is evident that he no longer held the half-interest with which he had started.

however, Oliver Dean, Willard Sayles, and Lyman Tiffany were taken into the firm, the last-named being an ex-employee of Slater and a brother of his ex-partner, Bela Tiffany. By this realignment Slater was left with only a one-fifth interest. In 1827 the first steam mill was erected at Providence by Slater and his associates, chiefly with capital furnished by the former. This mill was said to spin the finest yarn in the country. By 1827 Slater had been concerned in eight partnerships involving at least seventeen persons besides himself. Only two of these had been dissolved, one by the sale of Slater's interest and one by his purchase of his partner's interest.[31]

B. Slater's marketing methods.

We have already examined the system of marketing used to dispose of the goods produced in the mills superintended by Samuel Slater when this side of the business was handled by Almy & Brown according to the terms of the agreement of 1790. It might be asked whether Slater's method of doing business differed from that of the firm of Almy & Brown and, if so, how? Unfortunately there are very few Slater letters which throw light on his marketing methods. Some letters, written between 1814 and 1818 and reproduced in White's *Memoir of Samuel Slater*, may now be mentioned.

A few of these letters are enlightening. One is addressed to Elijah Waring, of Philadelphia, Almy & Brown's first agent. In view of the excellency of Slater's yarn, one of the factors which enabled Almy & Brown successfully to meet competition, it is probable that when Slater set up for himself he inherited some of the trade which had formerly gone to the mills in which Almy & Brown were interested. A letter to Waring, of February 23, 1814, is interesting in this relation. It concerns Slater's securing "a permanent agent" for the Philadelphia market—apparently Waring had been acting for him previously. The letter also reveals something of the production in the factories and of the market for the goods produced. Slater expected annually to produce $100,000 worth in the Oxford factory, "more than half of which I should wish to send to Philadelphia." Evidently, too, there was some talk of eliminating that portion of the 1790 agreement whereby Almy & Brown were to market all the goods produced in the factories in which they were concerned and of having, instead, each partner market his own share. Only two years previously Slater had erected a factory in Worcester County, Massachusetts, and it is probable that Almy & Brown felt that his work of superintendence over the mills in which they were concerned had suffered thereby. Other business letters, which present miscellaneous facts concerning the conditions and methods of business at various times, do not give so much information as the Waring letter on the methods of marketing, though one letter deals with such questions as interest and bad debts.

The acquisition by Slater in October, 1827, of an interest in the store of George S. Wardwell & Co. at Providence undoubtedly had some relation to his marketing system.[32] Wardwell's seems to have been a mercantile firm dealing chiefly in provisions, such as flour, coffee, sugar, and the like. After Slater became interested in the concern, it purchased wool and cotton and also acted as agents for disposing of starch, glue, syrup, and other produce received from correspondents, as well as for shipping thread, yarn, and other products to Baltimore, Philadelphia, and elsewhere.

On the whole it seems probable that Slater followed the example of Almy &

[31] Information on Slater's mills was secured from the following sources: White, *op. cit.;* Bagnall, *op. cit.;* Walton, *op. cit.;* and *The Slater Mills at Webster, 1812–1912.*

[32] Letters of Oct. 23 and 27, 1827, Slater, Wardwell & Co. Letterbook, 1821–36, Slater Papers, Baker Library.

Brown in his marketing and that his methods were similar to those which appear in the Almy & Brown correspondence. Such letters as do appear certainly show no difference worthy of mention.

C. Labor in Slater's mills.

As an aid to the study of working conditions in Slater's mills up to 1827, we have one time book, beginning in 1813 and continuing into 1836, and a book of accounts between Slater and his employees for 1817–19.[33]

Scant though it is, the information contained in the earliest time book, beginning February, 1813, does tell us a few things. From the names of the workers, it is seen that they were what would be called today "old Americans," "Nordics," or "Anglo-Saxons." The names recorded for the first month were such as Tiffany, Hitchcock, Green, Phettiplace, Holmes, Fuller, Simmons, Munyan, Howland, Johnson, Hill, Cady, Chase, Worsely, Benson, Learned, Reynolds, Stone, Weaver, Wilmoth, and Sheldon. The Christian names showed that the Puritan leaven was still at work.

By 1831 a change was coming in the nationality of Slater's workers.[34] Contracts were made with at least five men whose names were typically Irish: Coyle, Ryan, Corcoran, Burns, and Callaghan, the last two signing their names with a cross, though Ryan was the high-salaried ($500 per annum) dyer. In 1833 more Celts—Mooney, Dentt, Callahan—joined the force. In 1834 came Moore and Davit, both literate. But in 1836, the year after Samuel Slater's death, we find contracts with O'reille, Burk, Davitt, Doyle, and Kelly, each signed with "his X mark." Not until 1837 came the pioneers in the French or French Canadian invasion, Peter and Oliver Bargue, both "X" men.

Out of the 36 workers on the roll for February, 1813, according to the names, 10 were girls or women, 26 men or boys. The women put in 111½ days, or an average of a little over 11 each; the men 393½ days, or an average of a little over 15. Evidently the work was rather irregular this first month, since only 3, all men, put in the full working time of 24 days, and only 5, all men, worked more than 20 days; 22 men and 7 girls worked over 10 days; 4 men and 3 girls under 10 days. For one man whose name was on the list no work was recorded.

There is no definite record of the age situation in 1813, but it was probably not much different from the situation in 1790 when the work was done by boys and girls of from 10 to 15 years. We have a hint of this in the surname groupings of the listed workers. Out of the 36 names listed in February, 1813, there were only 21 different family names. Five of these family names covered 20 of the workers. Evidently the workers were made up chiefly of family groups, which probably consisted largely of minor children. It is difficult to ascertain the extent to which parents worked with the children. There were two Willard Howlands in the February list, possibly father and son.

Nearly a year later the workers had increased to 40 males and 17 females. The average number of days put in during the month had risen from 14¼ to nearly 18½. As usual the men worked longer on the average than did the women. Nine men worked the full time of 24 days, 27 men and 7 women more than 20 days, 33 men and 12 women over 10 days, 7 men and 5 women under 10 days. Three men who were listed did not work. The men worked on an average a little more than 19 days, the women nearly 17. By this time the mill was evidently operating more steadily. By this time, too, the family groups had become even more prom-

[33] Time Book, 1813–36, and Accounts Settled, 1817–19, Slater & Tiffany, Slater Papers, Baker Library.

[34] Time Book, 1831–37, Dudley Manufacturing Co., Slater Papers, Baker Library.

inent. Out of 57 workers there were only 23 family names. Twelve family names were shared by 46 workers, or about 80 per cent of the total. One family name included six workers; three, five; three, four; three, three; two, two. This indicates an increase also in child labor. Names show that at least two fathers were working with their sons and daughters.

Fourteen years later the number of laborers had grown to 144. Of these, 79 were males and 65 females. Family groups were still as conspicuous as they had been in 1813. The 114 workers had only 62 family names, and a little over half of the family names (33) included more than 80 per cent (116) of the laborers. Evidently minors still made up the bulk of the laborers. There were eight pairs of males possessing the same name, with the addition of "Jr." or "Sr." Evidently there were at least eight fathers working with their children. This may be compared to the situation in 1814 when there was a minimum of 2 fathers, out of a total of 23 families represented, who were working with their children.

The next question concerns the condition under which these people worked and lived. The normal working day was 12 hours, as may be seen from the time book for 1813–36. Wages varied widely, as is natural from the great variation in age. There are no pay rolls available for the years before 1827, and information concerning wages must be gleaned from the books recording the somewhat irregular settlement of accounts between Slater and his employees, sometimes at intervals of as much as half a year. The earliest of these books is the "Accounts Settled, 1817–1819," which tells us a good deal about wages and other conditions of employment. The heads of families signed this book in acknowledgment of the receipt of the wages of the members of their families and of their own. The wages of men in 1817 seemed to vary around a normal standard of 6s. per day. The shilling then being worth about 17 cents, $1.00 a day seems to have been the most common wage. Some men got as low as 4s. 6d. a day, or about 75 cents. Many of the women worked at piecework—doffing, reeling, mule-spinning—but there is no record as to how much they could do in a day. Where the daily wage is given it seems to have overlapped with that of the more lowly male laborers. It was the wages of children which hit bottom. Children were apparently always paid by the day, while men, in this period, were paid by the week. Children received sometimes as little as 3s. a week. Reduced to cents this would be about 50 cents per week or 6d. (8⅓ cents) for a day of 12 hours. Wages increased steadily with an increase in age, until the highest-paid minor found in this period received 25s. 6d. per week or 4s. 3d. a day (70 cents), only a little less than the lower-paid adults.

At this time workers in the mill who had no homes in the villages were "boarded-out" to various local families whose members worked in the mill. Apparently Samuel Slater paid for the board of such workers to the heads of the families with whom they boarded at the same time that he paid the family wages to the family heads, subtracting these payments from the wages of the boarders when settlement was made with them. The charge for women's board per week in 1817 was 7s. or 8s., about $1.20 to $1.35. Men, on the other hand, were uniformly charged $2.00 per week.

D. Delay in the adoption of the power loom.

The work performed by power at the Slater mills, as at all other New England mills until 1814, was limited to making yarns which were sold or given out to be woven on the account of the owners of the mills at so much per yard or cut. Though Almy & Brown put out yarn as early as 1800 to be made into coarse cloth, such as bedticking, Slater apparently did not become connected with handloom weavers until the inauguration of his factory at Oxford in 1812.[35]

Slater's weave book for 1812–13 records the amount and quality of yarn taken out and the date; then the amount and kind of cloth returned, the date, and the price due for the weaving, which was paid in due bills on the store. The cloth woven was sheetings, stripes, ginghams, and plaids at from 6 cents to 11 cents a yard, the last two being the most expensive. Slater had various devices for keeping track of his webs. He had adopted the English system of accompanying each web with a ticket containing a description of the yarn sent out and the kind of cloth into which it was to be woven. This ticket had to be returned with the cloth and unused yarn. Some of these tickets can be found between the pages of the Slater weaving books.

Until about 1818, as seen from the Hand-loom Weavers' Book for 1818–22, practically all Slater's webs were put out to be worked up in private homes; and as a consequence, owing to the conditions mentioned by Almy & Brown, a great many weavers had to be employed. From 1816 to 1820 there were 566 weavers on his books. None of these was making his or her sole living by weaving, as appears from the fact that webs were taken and cloth returned very irregularly. Some of the more industrious took only three weeks or a month between webs, but some took three or even six months. Three months seems to have been the limit of a reasonable delay, since there was a note on the margin of the account of Isaac Munyan, 1818–19, who had taken out a web on November 2, stating "Wrote February 18." Even with this reminder the cloth, according to the account, was not brought in until March 26.

As a result of this irregularity in the time taken Slater began, between 1818 and 1820, to put out webs to subcontractors who could give personal supervision to the weavers and attend to the tedious details of accounting, which must otherwise have eaten up the commissions saved to Slater by doing "the putting-out" himself.[36] Moreover, by the use of subcontractors the work could be done farther away.

There is a rather close family connection between the spinning-mill workers and the hand-loom weavers, as ascertained by a study of the family names included in both groups in the year between early 1813 and early 1814. During this period 62 family names are found among the spinning-mill workers and, as is natural in view of their greater irregularity of work and consequent increase in numbers, 139 family names are among the hand-loom weavers, while 29 family names are common to both groups. In other words, nearly half the families working in the spinning mills had members who at least occasionally did hand-loom weaving. In some cases children worked in the mill, and the father and mother—in their spare time or during slack seasons in their ordinary occupations—did hand-loom weaving, assisted perhaps by other children who were not employed in the mill. Not only the family names but the Christian names of those included in both groups are identical. Probably certain adults, during slack seasons in their usual occupations, entered the mills and worked till they could profitably return to their ordinary vocations supplemented by spare-time weaving. In hand-loom weaving usually the name of only the family head would appear on the weavers' book, since with him the contract was made, to him the money was paid, and on him lay the responsibility. He might, however, actu-

[35] Accounts with Hand Loom Weavers and Pickers, Slater & Tiffany, 1812–13, Slater Papers, Baker Library.

[36] Ware thesis, p. 97. Much of the material, in this section on weaving, was obtained from the same study.

ally do little or none of the work, that being left to his wife and children.

Hand-loom weaving seems to have reached its height between 1820 and 1825. During that period 600 weavers were individually receiving yarn from the mills, to say nothing of a large number whose names do not appear on the list; the latter were receiving webs through the medium of subcontractors to whom "the great bulk" of the webs went.[37] The irregularity of the individual weavers was still conspicuous. Of all the weavers during these 5 years only 65 returned as many as 25 webs, or an average of 5 per year. This irregularity extended also to the cloth. On the flyleaf of a weave book is a list of 33 names with comments: on 23 "good," 1 "middling," 9 "poor," and on individual accounts such notes as "it is desirable that he should weave no more."

Just as Slater had been driven to Worcester County because the vicinity of Pawtucket and Providence had become "saturated" with yarn, so did the expansion of spinning in Oxford force an extension of the territory occupied by hand-loom weavers serving his mills. Some of his webs went 20 miles and one of his subcontractors actually lived at that distance, a fact which must have extended the territory. This most distant subcontractor received, in addition to the commission, 50 cents per cut payable in yarn for transporting the yarn and cloth both ways.

Slater's mills adopted the power loom much later than did some other New England mills. When in 1815 a Scotch mechanic, familiar with the construction of power looms, visited the mill at Smithfield, John Slater favored the installation of the power loom; but he was overruled by Samuel, who preferred to adhere closely to spinning.[38] According to the Slater Consignment Books, Slater continued to have ginghams made by hand loom for the Philadelphia market. He paid higher rates for hand-loom weaving than did other mills.[39] The volume of his sales increased from $22,612 in 1815 to $92,763 in 1821.[40] In 1823 he began, however, to do power-loom weaving.[41] In 1824 a sharp decline occurred in Slater's weaving rates. In 1825 and 1826 speculation in England affected the American market. Slater shipped his last ginghams in 1828.[42] By 1829 he had ceased using the hand loom, having adopted the power loom [43] many years after its use had been found definitely advantageous in other mills in New England.

Account books of Slater & Tiffany in Oxford show that the cloth was also dyed outside the mill. One account book with the Oxford Dye House covers the years 1816–29. It contains a statement of type and amount of cloth, color, and charge for dyeing. The Slater Papers fail to show when the dyeing and finishing processes were actually brought into the Slater mills.

7. Concentration of Slater's Interests

Slater, who had successfully weathered earlier periods of business depression, was severely tried by the panic of 1829. He is said to have owed, at the time, not over $1,000 personally and to have held $50,000 in mortgages on real estate, but he was responsible for his partners' debts and for the debts of two neighbors whose paper he had endorsed.

[37] *Ibid.*, p. 100.

[38] Bagnall, *op. cit.*, pp. 61–62; White, *op. cit.*, p. 339; Walton, *op. cit.*, p. 184.

[39] Ware, *New England Cotton Manufacture*, p. 74, comparing the weave books of the Slater and Troy companies.

[40] Consignment Books, 1815–22, Slater & Tiffany, Slater Papers, Baker Library.

[41] Ware, *New England Cotton Manufacture*, p. 74.

[42] *Ibid.*, p. 76.

[43] Hand-loom Weavers' Book, Slater & Tiffany, 1825–29, and Weaving Book, 1827-30, Slater & Tiffany, Slater Papers, Baker Library.

Slater's financial situation can best be seen from his letter below: [44]

"N. Providence, Jan. 7th, 1829.

"Gentlemen,—In my last, under date of the 31st ult., I wrote you that I had drawn on you, for ten thousand dollars, on four months, in favour of the Steam Cotton Manufacturing Company, in order to meet a demand nearly due in Philadelphia, since which, have altered a five thousand draft into three, two of $1500 each, and one of $2000, all payable at the same time.

"It is rather a pinching time here for money; though many of the money borrowers say times are becoming more easy. Since the failure of Mr. Hurd, money-jobbers and anti-tariff folks have propounded almost every one, who has seen, or at least touched of late a cotton or woollen factory, that he must go down stream, and amongst them, some whose chins are barely above water, are (friendly) afraid that I have a very heavy load on my back, &c. It is true, I am on two neighbours' paper, but am partially secure, and hope in a day or two, to be fully secured against an eventual loss, providing Mount Etna should not extend its lava much beyond the usual limits. Last week, my sons George, John, and Nelson, bought out my old friend Edward Howard, in the woollen business, which relieves my mind considerably. The business in future will be transacted by myself and sons; and as it respects the Amoskeage and Steam Cotton Manufacturing Company, including the woollen factory and all my private concerns, (which I consider very trivial,) I think I can boldly say, after the whole company debts are paid, (all of which I have to meet,) there will be left from 800,000 to 1,000,000 of dollars to all concerned. I barely mention these circumstances to in some measure rebut any flying reports that may reach your city, and of course will not retard your acceptance of my paper so long as you have my funds in your hands to make you perfectly secure: I shall probably spend (at least) several weeks here, therefore, if you have not already forwarded your last quarter's sale and account current to Oxford, you will send it to Pawtucket. In great haste, your obedient servant,

"Samuel Slater."

Later he wrote a letter to the same firm, in which he shows evidence of increasing financial trouble.[45]

"North Providence, June 15th, 1829.

"Gentlemen,—Since I wrote you under date of 12th inst., there has been a dreadful storm in and about Pawtucket. I believe on Friday last, Samuel B. Harris made an assignment of his property without even consulting his endorsers, A. I. & W. On Saturday A. & I. W. made an assignment of their property, and as a great amount of paper was lying over, both of their own, and that which they had endorsed for W. Harris & S. B. Harris, as soon as the alarm was given in Providence, the Providence people, with their lawyers and sheriffs, were busy enough here until midnight on Saturday night, but the conjecture is, they were too late. It will not be necessary for you to make known the name of your informant of the above. Yours, &c.

"S. Slater."

In July, 1829, a letter told of further troubles: [46]

"Gentlemen,—

". . . Since I wrote you last, D. W. has gone down the falls. His failure is a serious one, and it affects my mind and body seriously, and purse too for the present, but hope eventually to meet with but little loss.

"Nelson started the Kennedy factory on my account last Monday, I hope shortly to have some goods for you. Today Jonathan Congdon & Sons, Charles Hadwin, and others, made assignments; so we slide along. I should write you oftener would my health and spirits permit.

"Yours, &c.
"Samuel Slater."

[44] Letter from White, *op. cit.*, p. 246. The Edward Howard mentioned had become Slater's partner in the woolen business in 1815.

[45] *Ibid.*, pp. 246–247. Refers to Abraham and Isaac Wilkinson, Slater's brothers-in-law.

[46] *Ibid.*, p. 247. This D. W. was David Wilkinson, one of Slater's brothers-in-law (*ibid.*, pp. 93, 127, 187).

And finally in a letter of the next month to the same firm: [47]

"N. Providence, August 3, 1829

"Gentlemen,—Your two letters under dates of the 27th and 28th ult. are at hand. In regard to my indorsements for D. Wilkinson, they are heavy without doubt, but I am secured for the whole eventually. The steam mill is in debt to a large amount, but as $70,000 have been paid in, and as the *whole* establishment is holden for her debts, I conceive, taking all things into view, that the depreciation will not exceed the amount paid in. As I have to look up entire new friends to aid me in my unexpected liabilities, makes my task more arduous.

"There is coming due at different periods, at the Merchant's Bank, Providence, on D. W. and J. K.'s account, about $62,000, which some of the directors say I can have my own time to pay.

"Respectfully your obedient servant,
"Samuel Slater."

From these letters it appears that Slater's obligations at the time of the crisis were very serious. He was unable to take up all his endorsed paper without great sacrifice. Yet he knew that with some accommodation he could meet all demands. He applied to his partner, William Almy, for aid, only to be disappointed. Slater thereupon was forced to announce that, without some accommodation, he would have to close his mills. "This circumstance," says Slater's contemporary biographer, "increased the alarm and shook credit, in Rhode Island, to its centre." [48] Slater finally sold his third in the "Old Mill" in Pawtucket, and his fourth of the Smithfield property. William Almy became the purchaser of these places. The biographer does not mention any ulterior motive in Almy's refusal to aid Slater, though he thinks it "passing strange." The opportunity Almy saw for obtaining possession of two of Slater's large holdings, at a price undoubtedly modified by the latter's need, is probably a sufficient motive.

Though Slater was forced to give up two of his mill properties, he also gained some new ones. In 1829 he and his three sons, as noted in a letter above, became associated in the woolen business by buying out Howard—a letter of Slater's, written at this time, implies that the business methods of Howard were not satisfactory to his partners.[49] Slater also became the proprietor of the mills in Wilkinsonville owned by David Wilkinson, whose debts Slater paid in 1829. In 1830 he found it necessary to take over the whole of the steam mill at Providence. All these changes may be traced to the panic of 1829.[50]

Soon thereafter Slater made several other changes in his business. He conveyed his interest in the Jewett City Manufacturing Co. to his brother, John. The following year he and John bought the whole of the Smithfield establishment, in which both had been interested, Samuel having been forced to sell his share to Almy in 1829. Another interesting event occurred in 1831. The two mills at Amoskeag, in which Slater was a partner, were incorporated. The partners received shares according to their respective interest in the partnership.[51]

At the time of his death in 1835 Slater owned the cotton mills at Webster, the woolen mills at the same place with his sons as partners, the mills at Smithfield in partnership with his brother John, the Providence Steam Cotton Mill, the mills at Wilkinsonville, and one-fifth of the shares in the Amoskeag mills. Geographically his interests had come to be quite definitely centered in southern Massachusetts, and his partnership policy had

[47] *Ibid.*, p. 248. J. K. was evidently the Kennedy mentioned in the preceding letter. His debts amounted to $115,000 (*ibid.*, p. 247).

[48] *Ibid.*, pp. 244–245.

[49] *Ibid.*, p. 245.

[50] *Ibid.*, pp. 245–246.

[51] Bagnall, *op. cit.*, pp. 65–67.

changed from a number of partners and partnerships to that of sole ownership and family partnerships and, in one instance, of a corporation.

8. Suggested Readings

For a brief summary of early manufacturing in America see Edward C. Kirkland, *A History of American Economic Life* (New York, 1939), pp. 293–331.

A more detailed description of the early American textile industry is found in Caroline F. Ware, *The Early New England Cotton Manufacture* (Cambridge, 1931), pp. 1–78.

George S. White's *Memoir of Samuel Slater* (Philadelphia, 1836), while not a satisfactory biography, contains much source material.

9. Suggested Questions

1. Why was weaving not brought into factory production at the same time that spinning was introduced?
2. What tendency or tendencies do you observe in the organization of Slater's various industrial enterprises? To what do you ascribe this trend (or trends)?
3. To what extent must Slater accept the responsibility for the introduction of child labor into American industry? What do you consider the reasons for the use of child laborers in Slater's mills?
4. Estimate Samuel Slater as a man, as a mechanic, as a production manager, as a business man. In which, if any, of these aspects does he appear the greatest, and why?
5. Does this case throw any light upon the social significance of the profit motive?

XVII. JOSIAH WEDGWOOD & SONS, LTD., 1759–1920

1. General Statement

The history of the pottery industry in England illustrates much of the general evolution of industry and commerce and reflects many of the changes caused by the Industrial Revolution. Until the seventeenth century pottery manufacture in England was not localized, and, since it usually shared with other occupations the attention of the potter, it was little more than a household industry. In the course of the seventeenth century, owing to the growing scarcity of firewood, the manufacture of pottery became localized in North Staffordshire where both clay and coal were available in large quantities. Localization and improved transportation facilities naturally led to specialization, which in turn resulted in many technical developments, particularly after 1690.

During the eighteenth and nineteenth centuries important changes occurred, not only in the technical processes of English pottery manufacture, but also in artistic decoration, transportation of materials and ware, distribution of the finished goods and in the size and nature of the units which were producing the pottery.[1]

2. Important Dates

1730	Birth of Josiah Wedgwood.
1759	Started in business for himself at Burslem, Staffordshire—foundation of present firm.
1765	Opened retail store and showrooms in London.
1768	Arranged with Matthew Boulton to sell ware in Continental Europe.
1769	Wedgwood took Thomas Bentley as partner.
1771	Adopted satisfaction-or-money-back policy.
1777	Regular sales promotion started among provincial dealers in England.
1782	Boulton & Watt steam engine installed. Wedgwood organized Cornish Clay Co. to supply raw materials.

[1] Except where otherwise indicated this account of the Wedgwood firm is adapted from Ralph M. Hower, "The Wedgwoods, Ten Generations of Potters," *Journal of Economic and Business History,* vol. iv (1931–32), pp. 281–313, 665–690.

1795	Death of Josiah Wedgwood. Business carried on by Josiah Wedgwood II and Thomas Byerley.
1829	Closing of London showrooms and abandonment of the practice of making sales directly to public.
1839	Ownership in clay mines sold.
1875	Showrooms reopened in London for display of wares and sales to dealers.
1899	Experiment with retail-store ownership begun.
1906	Company sales branch established in New York.
1911–13	Electrical power introduced in factory; plant considerably expanded.
1914–18	War period—growth of foreign business. Production difficulties.
1919	Program of further plant expansion adopted.
1935	Decision made to move to new site and construct model factory and village.

3. Origin and History of the Firm to 1795

Members of the Wedgwood family were engaged in potting from about 1612, and several of them made important contributions to the development of ceramic technique, especially in the period from 1690 to 1750. As a result of the technical changes which were taking place the economic organization of the pottery industry was changing. Earthenware had previously been shaped by hand on the potter's wheel, but the use of molds was developed at this time for many kinds of vessels, calling forth specialized block-cutters, flatware and hollow-ware pressers, and casters. Until about 1740 the same clay body had served for both lead and salt glazes, but potters began to specialize in one or the other and to use different bodies and mixtures in the process. In consequence it was necessary to import clays from other parts of England and to find a wider market for the finished wares.

Josiah Wedgwood was able to build upon the foundations which four generations of his ancestors had helped to lay. After the death of his father in 1739 Josiah went to work at the age of nine for his brother, Thomas, to whom he was formally apprenticed in 1744 for a period of five years. Josiah's right knee became permanently affected as a result of smallpox, and ultimately his leg had to be amputated. The injury prevented him from working steadily at the "Art of Throwing and Handleing" to which he had been apprenticed, with the result that he began to practise other branches of his craft, to exercise his natural tendency to experiment, and to supplement his three years of schooling by reading and study. At the end of his apprenticeship Thomas refused Josiah's proposal to join him in a partnership with the object of pushing trade and improving the manufacture of pottery by means of further experiments.

Since he lacked money to start out for himself, Josiah worked as journeyman for his brother until 1752, when he entered into a partnership with John Harrison of Newcastle-under-Lyme, a tradesman who had invested money in a potworks near Stoke. According to tradition Wedgwood improved the business appreciably and, receiving no increase in his share of the profits, brought about the dissolution of the partnership. In 1754 Wedgwood formed a new partnership, this time with Thomas Whieldon, a progressive and successful potter whose wares had become famous. The details of the agreement are lost, but it is clear that Wedgwood was to carry on experimental research for the benefit of the partnership without any obligation to reveal his discoveries to anyone. Most of the pottery made was of the useful or table variety, but such articles as snuffboxes were produced and sold to Birmingham and Sheffield hardware men who, after mounting them with metal, disposed of the finished product to retailers.

In 1759, the agreement with Whieldon

having expired, Wedgwood established himself in Burslem. His business expanded rapidly from the start; after the first year he rented additional quarters and hired more workmen; and shortly afterwards he moved into a still larger potworks. In the winter of 1765–66 he opened showrooms in London for the purpose of selling his wares to the public, and in 1766 he took into partnership his cousin, Thomas Wedgwood, who had previously worked for him as journeyman. Thomas acquired a one-eighth share in the production of useful, as distinct from ornamental, earthenware; Josiah held the remaining seven-eighths interest in the useful ware branch and owned all the ornamental ware branch.

Josiah purchased land near Hanley in 1766 as a site for an entirely new pottery. About the same time he invited Thomas Bentley to join him in the business. Bentley was a close friend and for several years had been Wedgwood's Liverpool agent for the forwarding of clay to Burslem and the exporting of finished ware, especially to America. In reply to Wedgwood's proposal of a partnership Bentley protested his ignorance of potting, but Wedgwood argued "you have taste, the best foundation for our intended concern . . . and for the rest it will be soon learn'd by so apt a scholar." Bentley agreed to the plan in May, 1767, but the formal agreement was not sealed until August 10, 1769.

Wedgwood and Bentley agreed "to be . . . copartners . . . in the Art . . . of making and vending Ornamental Earthen Ware . . . the said parties have in equal Shares and proportions made up . . . a Capital Stock . . . of 1441 Pounds." They were to share profits equally, but Wedgwood was to receive 7.5 per cent interest out of the partnership for sums advanced in building the new potworks, and 5 per cent for money advanced to Bentley. Bentley did not, however, relinquish the partnership which he had formed some years before in Liverpool with James Boardman; and the warehouse of Bentley & Boardman served for many years as an outlet for Wedgwood ware.

Work on the new factory (henceforth called Etruria) proceeded slowly. The formal opening took place in June, 1769, but the final removal from Burslem was not made until 1772, and the entire factory was not completed until 1774. There were two separate units—one for "useful" ware, the other for "ornamental," each with its own ovens, yards, and workshops. Wedgwood & Bentley were concerned only with ornamental ware, and useful ware was produced by Josiah and Thomas Wedgwood; both types were handled in the London showrooms. As soon as ordinary tableware began to bear decoration, a difficulty arose over the distinction between useful and ornamental. Wedgwood pacified his partners by getting Boardman to agree that useful ware should include "such vessels as are *made use of at meals,*" and persuading Thomas Wedgwood to consent to the making of ornamental teapots by Wedgwood & Bentley.

Death removed the two partners—Bentley in 1780 and Thomas Wedgwood in 1788. Meanwhile, the founder had begun to train his nephew, Thomas Byerley, and his three sons, Josiah, John, and Thomas, in the business. All four were made partners in 1790, but John and Thomas withdrew in 1793, and when the first Josiah died (January 3, 1795) he left the works to Josiah II, with Byerley owning a one-fourth interest.

The first Josiah was also interested in other partnerships. Between 1782 and 1794 he held a three-fourths interest in the Cornish Clay Co., while its production manager owned only a one-fourth interest in the concern. In 1775, when there seemed to be an opportunity of combining pottery and metal for ornamental purposes, Wedgwood & Bentley agreed to a partnership with William Storer, of Norwich, who had patented a kind of metal ornament. Wedgwood & Bentley were to supply £1,000 each and lend Storer the difference between the value of his equipment and £1,000, in order that he should have a one-third interest in the project. Storer got into financial difficulties and the agreement was canceled, but the incident throws light on Wedgwood's business policy. In 1791 Wedgwood joined with thirteen other potters of the district to form the Potters Clay Co. in order to get control of adequate supplies of good clay, and he agreed to supply half the capital required.

In this connection it is worth noting that in 1784 Thomas Byerley was a member of the firm of Haywood, Griffin & Byerley, flint-grinders, while he was employed by Josiah Wedgwood.[2] Since Byerley had no capital of his own, it is almost certain that his uncle was responsible for his share in the company.

4. Production, 1759–95

"Preface to Wedgwood's 'Experiment Book' [3]—

"This suite of Experiments was begun at Fenton Hall, in the parish of Stoke-on-Trent, about the beginning of the year 1759, in my partnership with Mr. Whieldon, for the improvement of our manufacture of earthenware, which at that time stood in great need of it, the demand for our goods decreasing daily, and the trade universally complained of as being bad and in a declining condition.

"White Stone Ware was the principal article of our manufacture. But this had been made a long time, and the prices were now reduced so low, that the potters could not afford to bestow much expense upon it or to make it so good in any respect as the ware would otherwise admit of. And with regard to Elegance of form, that was an object very little attended to.

"The next article in consequence to Stone Ware was an imitation of Tortoiseshell. But as no improvement had been made in this branch for several years, the country was grown weary of it; and though the price had been lowered from time to time, in order to increase the sale, the expedient did not answer, and something new was wanted, to give a little spirit to the business.

"I had already made an imitation of Agate, which was esteemed beautiful and a considerable improvement, but people were surfeited with wares of these variegated colours.

"These considerations induced me to try for some more solid improvement, as well in the Body, as the Glazes, the Colours, and the Forms, of the articles of our manufacture.

"I saw the field was spacious, and the soil so good, as to promise an ample recompense to any one who should labour diligently in its cultivation."

Lack of capital compelled Wedgwood to start in a small way. He made most of his own models and mixtures, superintended the firing, and was even his own clerk and warehouseman. He aimed at producing a cream-colored earthenware for table use. This involved repeated and expensive trials. Wedgwood had even to invent or improve tools, punches, molds, lathe apparatus, and other equipment. Disregarding his health, he worked in the evenings and even for whole nights, designing patterns and instruments and preparing for the next day's work. By 1761 he had made considerable progress with cream-colored ware, but his success was not complete until after 1768, when the Staffordshire potters learned that true China clay (kaolin) and felspathic stone were to be found in Cornwall. Wedgwood finally produced a tea set for Queen Charlotte, which so pleased her that she allowed him (1768) to call his product "Queen's Ware." Naturally, Wedgwood's business profited greatly from news of the royal patronage.

Meanwhile, Wedgwood was seeking to develop his ornamental ware along classical lines in accordance with the taste of the time. For years the potters of the dis-

[2] Ground flint is an important ingredient of earthenware.

[3] Reprinted in Josiah Wedgwood & Sons, Ltd., *The Story of Wedgwood, 1730–1930* (Wisbech, 1930), pp. 11–13.

trict had been making a black basalt or "Egyptian black" body by the use of an iron oxide and manganese. Wedgwood saw in this an opportunity to reproduce antique vases; by 1769 he had improved the body to give it a fine grain, a smooth surface, and a richer color, and he had decorated it with red encaustic painting, unglazed in the ancient Etruscan manner.

Between 1773 and 1776 Wedgwood perfected the body which came to be known as jasper.[4] This is the most beautiful and original of all the ceramic materials with which he worked and is the product which the public usually associates with the name of Wedgwood. Wedgwood saw an opportunity to meet the demand for classical reproductions by placing white relief figures in jasper against colored backgrounds of the same material. A serious problem in modeling at once confronted him. William Hackwood did much of the work, but so urgent was the need that although six modelers were employed in 1775, Wedgwood wrote, "we want half a dozen Hackwoods."

The chief object in obtaining a satisfactory body and glaze was to obtain a suitable background for decoration by printing, painting, or design in relief. The printing was done by Sadler & Green, of Liverpool, who in about 1755 had invented the process. As early as 1761 Wedgwood was sending them ware to be printed. The printers supplied the designs at first; but, as cream-colored ware reached perfection, Wedgwood became more particular and began to supply his own designs and subjects. This involved considerable expense, but the imitation of his patterns by competitors forced Wedgwood to produce new designs constantly. As the printing process was improved, patterns for enameled ware were frequently printed in outline to be filled in instead of having the decoration done entirely by enamelers. Wedgwood apparently promoted the use of this process to save time and skill. It is said that in 1763 he bought the right to do his own printing. At any rate printing was being done in the Chelsea workrooms in 1770, and Wedgwood had his own engravers in the 1780's. However, ware continued to be sent to Liverpool for the printing of certain patterns until after Wedgwood's death.

The painting of ware was at first done at or near Burslem, but in 1768 Wedgwood employed an artist in the London warehouse "to do Crests, or any other pattns by ordr, to take sketches, &c," and he proposed having a modeler, too, "to send to any Lady's favourite Antique for a coppy." In 1769 it was decided to have all decoration done on the firm's premises in London, in order that "the same Press, Printer, Clerk, & Master" might serve for all the decorators. A further motive was to enable the artists to attend the various art exhibitions in London.

Wedgwood searched everywhere to find materials for designs. He copied natural objects like fruit, flowers, and shells; he adapted ideas used in Birmingham metal work; he took hints about color and decoration from Chelsea, Dresden, and other china products. He bought or borrowed books, prints, and modern and antique porcelain; armed with introductions from patrons like Lord Gower and Sir William Meredith, he visited the houses of many of the nobility in order to inspect collections, make sketches, or receive orders for ware. He gave Bentley the task of searching treatises on Greek, Etruscan, and Roman art; and, when he began to produce medallions, intaglios, and bas-relief decoration, he was no longer content to rely on pictures and sketches but ordered casts of antique gems from Rome.

Wedgwood was tireless in his search for competent artists. The following excerpt shows both the type of artist he

[4] Jasper is a semi-vitreous body with a fine, smooth, but not glossy surface, although it will take a high polish. It can be produced in pure white and in various colors.

hired and the source of some of his designs:

"I have hired a Modeler for three years, the best I am told in London, he serv'd his time with a silversmith, has work'd several years at a China work, has been two or three years carving in Wood & Marble for Mr. Adams the famous Architect, is a perfect Master of the Antique stile in ornaments, Vases &c, & works with equal facility in Clay, Wax, Wood, Metal, or Stone."

When Bentley complained of the scarcity of painters, Wedgwood replied, *"we must make* them. There is no other way . . . & you must be content to train up such Painters as offer to you, & not turn them adrift because they cannot immediately form their hands to our new style."

In 1787 Wedgwood sent John Flaxman and Henry Webber to Rome. The precise arrangement with Flaxman is not known, but Webber was to tour Italy "for the purpose of making Models, Drawings & other Improvements in the Arts of Modelling and Designing for the Benefit and Advantage of the said Josiah Wedgwood in his Manufactory." Wedgwood was to pay all expenses and Webber's usual salary of £250 a year; in return, Webber was to submit all drawings to Josiah Wedgwood and remain in his service for nine years.

Wedgwood restricted the production of fine pieces of ornamental ware in order to avoid spoiling the market. With useful ware, however, he saw the advantage of producing standard designs and tried to avoid special orders. Referring to one such order he wrote: "I could sooner make £100 worth of any ware in the common course that is going, than this one sett, It is this sort of *time loseing* with *Uniques* which keep ingenious Artists who are connected with Great Men of taste, poor & wod make us so too if we did too much in that way." The following excerpts throw further light on Wedgwood's policy:

"I have more expectations from showy cheapish flowerpots in the country shops than in our warehouse in Greek Street [London], & if the present do not hit their fancy we must try again."

"Some of the Ladys say the same thing that occur'd to you & me abot the Sugr dish Vases, that they are like the things on the tops of Clock cases, or Beds heads— They are certainly not Antique, & that is fault enough to D—m them for with most of our customers."

Wedgwood was troubled from the outset because some of his rivals were pirating his ideas and designs. In 1769 he tried to meet the problem by taking out a patent, but the difficulties which arose in enforcing it soon led him to abandon the idea of obtaining legal protection from piracy, and no further patents were sought. Indeed, before the patent was granted Wedgwood and Bentley had decided to disregard the possibility of imitation and to be "released from these degrading slavish chains, these mean selfish fears of other people copying my works." The decision was adhered to, for five years later Wedgwood wrote: "We must not forget a good resolution we have long since made of not permitting any apprehension of being robbed of our inventions, prevent our putting them into execution, when we think it proper in other respects."

Wedgwood had to wield a large body of skilled and unskilled workmen into an efficient organization. He appears to have carried labor specialization to a greater extent than it had previously been applied in the industry. He often complained about the inefficient methods used by his workmen and worked constantly at training them. In 1769 he wrote:

"I am giving my people lessons upon the loss of clay, and with it the loss of credit [reputation] in making heavy ware, but all will not do. I have bot them half a doz. pair of scales, but there seems one thing wantg still, which I propose to have soon, a *Clerk of Weights and Measures,* whose constant business it shall be to weigh the goods as they are got up—he will save me three times his wages in *Clay,* & ten times as much in *Credit.*"

In the following year he wrote:

"In my first essays upon Vases I had many things to learn myself, & everything to teach the workmen, who had not the least idea of beauty, or proportion in what they did, few, or none of our productions were what we should now deem tolerable, & the prices were fixed accordingly, but after so long practice from the best models, & drawings, such a long series of instruction, as our workmen have gone through, & so very expensive an apparatus, or rather collection of apparatus's as we are now masters of, & all to enable us to get up *good things,* I think we ought not . . . return back again to make such things as we first started with. . . . The same hands who at first finish'd the serpent & other Vases with white bodys at about 3/6 or 4/6 each were content with earning 7 or 8/ per week, but they now are improv'd in their *wages,* as well as in their *workmanship,* to double that sum."

It is not definitely known how many workmen Wedgwood employed in all, but he had 120 workmen in November, 1769, and 150 in 1770 at Etruria alone; in addition a large number were employed in the production of useful ware at Burslem and in decorating at Chelsea. Early in 1769 the demand for his products was so pressing that in order to meet it Wedgwood had to resort to repairing and "doctoring" faulty ware, and by 1770 production at Etruria was increased to over £100 of ware a week. The total output of ornamental ware at Etruria from August, 1770, to August, 1771, was £5,756. This amount should be compared with the annual production of £100 to £200 which was typical of most potters in the district about 1715. In addition, of course, Wedgwood was producing useful ware; he estimated the total production of useful ware for 1769 to be £12,000. By 1772 the situation had changed. Business was slack and there was not enough work to keep the men busy: "I am sadly puzzled to know what to do with our hands. 'Tis a pity to part with those which have been so many years in making if one thought they would be wanted again in any reasonable time." Wedgwood attempted to meet the situation by cutting the piece rates; when this aroused opposition, he allowed the men to turn out larger quantities, in an effort to pacify them. In January, 1773, Wedgwood wrote: "We begin, after 3 weeks rest, to work again on Monday. If you can make us any orders pray send them for I really do not know what to set them to work upon, however they must begin for they attacked me all in a body yesterday morng & insisted on being either *employ'd* or *discharg'd.*" In the early 1780's, however, the supply of ware constantly lagged behind demand, and on one occasion it was even necessary to close the London showrooms. About 1785, production began to be more than adequate for the existing demand.

Wedgwood's factory was one of the first, not only in the pottery industry but also in other fields, to use steam power. Water power had been employed from the seventeenth century onwards for grinding flint and mixing materials, and at least one pottery firm had installed a Newcomen engine prior to 1782 to pump water for a water-mill; but the further application of steam had to wait for the development of Watt's engine. Wedgwood was a personal friend of both Watt and Boulton, and he had long been interested in the various attempts to construct a practical "fire-engine." It is therefore not surprising that he was among the first to order a Boulton & Watt engine (1782). Indeed, he had installed two at Etruria before even one was put to work (1787) in the Lancashire textile industry, which is usually credited with taking the lead in applying steam to factory production. Wedgwood's first two engines were probably used to pump water, but another was ordered in 1793 with the specific intention of using it directly to grind and mix materials.[5]

5. Marketing, 1759–95

Until the eighteenth century the task of distributing pottery was accomplished almost exclusively by hawkers and cratemen, who bought the goods at the potteries and peddled them about the country either on their own backs or by means of pack-horses. As the Staffordshire ware was improved and the market extended, the more enterprising merchants opened business communications with London and other large towns, either taking their ware in person or consigning it directly to general dealers who acted as middlemen. This was the situation when Josiah Wedgwood began to market his product. Bentley handled goods at Liverpool, most of which were for export; and crates of ware were sent off daily by wagon to London after 1765, when Wedgwood established a warehouse there with his brother John in charge. Retail shops, even in the north of England, were supplied from this center; if the orders exceeded Wedgwood's output, he sometimes filled them with ware bought from other manufacturers.

Shortly afterward Wedgwood hired rooms in Grosvenor Square, where patterns were shown and orders were taken. These quarters soon proved to be too small; Wedgwood wanted a larger place,

> "not to show or have a large stock of Ware in Town, but to enable me to shew various table and dessert services completely set out. . . . The same, or indeed a much greater variety of setts of Vases shod decorate the Walls, and both these articles may every few days, be so alter'd . . . as to render the whole a new scene. . . . Every new show, Exhibition, or rarity soon grows stale in London, & is no longer regarded, after the first sight, unless utility, or some such variety as I have hinted at above continue to recommend it to their notice. . . . I have done something of the sort since I came to Town. . . . The two first days after the alteration we sold three complete setts of Vases at 2 & 3 Guineas a sett, besides many pairs of them, which Vases had been in my Rooms 6–8 and some of them 12 Months, & wanted nothing but arrangement to sell them.—& besides room for *my Ware,* I must have more room for *my Ladys* for they sometimes come in very large shoals together."

The showrooms were accordingly moved to a larger house (August, 1768), and in 1774 the firm opened still larger quarters in Soho.

A large stock of goods was maintained with Bentley & Boardman in Liverpool, and in 1772 showrooms were opened in Bath, a watering place much frequented by society at the period. The sales in Liverpool were apparently on a commission basis, but the Bath branch, like the London rooms, was the property of Wedgwood & Bentley, who paid all the expenses and received all the profits. After the discovery of dishonesty among the London employees, Wedgwood suggested that the sales should be by commission, with the seller bearing all expenses "to interest sellers in care of Stock, reduce expense, stimulate attention & by holding comn till cash pd would improve collection." Later documents indicate that this proposal was not adopted in London, and in 1779 Wedgwood was trying to induce the manager at Bath to take over the shop on his own account.

All goods which were sold in London were originally charged with the expense of transporting them to London. Complaints were made, but Wedgwood felt that he could not raise the prices sufficiently to cover the extra expense, and he estimated that if he paid the carriage it would make a difference of £500 a year in his

[5] John Thomas, "The Pottery Industry and the Industrial Revolution," *Economic History,* Feb., 1937, pp. 399–414. Thomas states that Wedgwood's was "the *first* factory to have a Watt steam-engine installed" (p. 406), but present evidence does not support his implied assumption that it was used to drive machinery rather than to pump water.

profits. The following excerpt from a letter to Wedgwood's wife (1769) reveals his final decision and throws light on other selling policies:

"I had quite forgot to send you a copy of the Advertisemt I intend for next week. let me have yr Criticisms by Saterdays post & it may save me some shame perhaps.

"Queens Ware & Ornamental Vases

"Manufacture of Josiah Wedgwood, Potter to &c—are sold at his Warehouse . . . & at no other place in Town. Orders are executed on the shortest notice as above, or at his Manufactury in Burslem in Staffordshire. He does not now charge carr[iag]e to London, sells for ready money only, & the lowest price is mark'd on each Article."

In 1771 Wedgwood drafted an advertisement for Bentley's approval, part of which follows:

"The Goods are deliver'd safe & carre free to London, for ready money only, as usual: or if order'd from the works to any other part, the Carre is paid so far as the first carrier takes them. . . . Mr. W. engages that every piece shall be deliver'd whole at their houses in any part of England, provided that they are not order'd to go upon any River Navigation, or if any of the goods are broke the deficiency shall be made up either in goods, or by deducting so much from the bill, at the option of the purchacer, whŏ shall likewise be at liberty to return the whole, or any part of the goods they ordr (paying the carre back) if they do not find them agreeable to their wishes."

The following is a part of the note which accompanied the proposed advertisement:

"I am aware that insureg the goods to their own houses & giveing them the liberty of returng them will be an addition to our trouble & expence: but I think the disadvantage will not be equal to a £5000 stock: nor indeed, so great as one might at first imagine: for at present my Customers do return their goods if they do not like them, & they are out of humour if the breakages are not made up to them in some way or other; but this advertisemt will acquaint thousands who at present know nothing of it, that they run no risque at all (except paying a little carre of the goods back) by ordering goods from me, & I make no doubt will induce numbers to order services who, without such intelligence wod not think of doing so."

Additional information about Wedgwood's advertising policy is contained in the following excerpt:

"I have a letter from Mr. Ward [manager of the Bath showrooms] wherein he tells me he has advertised in the papers, & is now going to deliver *hand bills* at the Pump Room every morning, as the China-men &c do, which I am very sorry to hear.—We have hitherto appeared in a very different light to common Shopkeepers, but this step (in my opinion) will sink us exceedingly. . . . have wrote to Mr. Ward to desire he would not deliver any more hand bills as coming from us, it being a mode of advertiseing I never approved of."

In 1777 the partners decided that their ware should be made known through the country by personal agency. Wedgwood's nephew, Thomas Byerley, assumed the task of traveling over England and selling ornamental ware. The plan was to find wholesale dealers who, if they sold a sufficient quantity, would be given exclusive selling rights in their respective districts; but the traveler was to call on retailers also and was not to refuse orders from private individuals when offered.

Pricing always gave difficulty. Accurate cost accounting in the pottery trade is impossible even today, and with the simple bookkeeping of the eighteenth century Wedgwood could do little more than guess at costs. Prices, therefore, were fixed arbitrarily and represented Wedgwood's judgment as to what the market would bear or what competitors were charging. Wedgwood even instructed Bentley "in the future when any new articles come to you be so good to proportion the price yourself to the other things in the Warehouse." In 1771–72 competition and bad times compelled the partners to adjust their prices downward; the reductions, however, had little effect, and Wedgwood decided that "Great Folks do not regard a *little difference* in price, & that *little difference* may not reduce them low enough for *middleing People*."

In 1773, when some of the potters made an agreement to lower prices, Wedgwood wrote to his partner: "Do you think we can stand our ground in London @ 5/P [dozen] for plates, when every body round us will be selling @ 2/6 & 3/ — We must endeavour to make our goods better if possible—other people will be going worse, & thereby our distinction will be more evident."

Wedgwood insisted that his finest pieces "should not have a fixed & invariable price like a quart mug," but should be priced "according to their comparative merit." Much of the ware then as today was classified as "seconds" or "thirds" and sold, usually in large lots, at very low prices. The "firsts" were absorbed mainly by the London market, while the faulty ware was disposed of in the country or abroad.

Because he was selling to the public as well as to retailers and wholesalers, Wedgwood was obliged to work out a system of trade discounts. In 1766 he proposed to allow Bentley 10 per cent discount on goods for export, with 5 per cent for "ready money." In 1771 he advised his partner: "I shall write to Mr. Farrier . . . that we shall allow him 10 P Ct—Pay the Carre & breakage. That he must not . . . sell Ornaments from or for any other Person, that he must send us an acct of sales monthly, & a reme every 6 Mos." In this case as in many others Wedgwood & Bentley sent the dealer an assortment of goods, and allowed the 10 per cent discount on those sold, so that they, rather than the merchant, assumed the risk involved. For export trade at this time the discount was only 5 per cent. By 1773 the partners had evidently adopted a settled policy of allowing six months' credit or an extra 5 per cent discount.

In the same year Wedgwood wrote to Bentley as follows:

> "We wish to sell these things abroad in quantitys, but it wod be in vain to expect it at the prices we sell them *Retail* in our Rooms in London.
>
> "Many reasons concur to induce us to sell them lower to the Merchts.—They take quantitys— Are not so nice, so that a kind of 2nds will generally do.—There is no Carre to London— No expence of Sale upon them. These are Capital considerations, & all together including their taking such things as will not sell in our Rooms, may amot to near 30 P Ct.
>
> "We shod then have two prices if we mean to *make any point* of the Wholesale business. But how much shall we lower the Articles, besides the 10 P Ct the Merchts expect."

Before the end of the century the trade discount was fixed at 20 per cent on useful and 40 per cent on ornamental ware.

With regard to foreign trade the prevailing practice until about 1770 was not to sell directly to foreign middlemen but to dispose of the goods to general exporting merchants in Liverpool, Bristol, Hull, or London, who made up assorted shipments which they exported. Wedgwood's export trade, consequently, was opened chiefly by sales to English and foreign merchants in London and Liverpool. As early as 1768 Matthew Boulton helped to develop Wedgwood's trade on the Continent by buying ware at Etruria and exporting it on his own account to consignees in Cadiz and various ports on the Baltic. Before long, however, direct contacts with overseas markets began to be established. In 1768 Wedgwood visited Boulton at Soho, "where we settled many important matters, & laid the foundation for improving our manufactures, and extending the sale of it to every corner of Europe." By 1769 Wedgwood had a direct trade with New York of considerable importance, and in the same year he opened his trade with Amsterdam and St. Petersburg. In 1770 an agent undertook to introduce goods from Wedgwood & Bentley and Boulton into Italy on a commission basis, with the understanding that goods which remained unsold could be returned within a limited time. Before the end of the century Wedgwood ware was being sent directly by the firm to North America, the West Indies, and all parts of Europe, and, indirectly through agents, to South America, India, and other parts of the world.

In 1772 it was decided to open a warehouse in Amsterdam with a Netherlander in charge. Apparently the goods were sold on a commission basis. Wedgwood opposed this arrangement because "if the stock be ours, I am afraid we shall not meet with any Agents who *watch over its increase*." Wedgwood's judgment proved to be correct. By August, 1775, the stock of useful ware at Amsterdam had grown to £2,583 and the ornamental ware to £849. The partners had to sell the stock off as best they could during 1776 and early in 1777. The agency was then given to a man named Veldhuysen. "And in the future our connection is to be the same as I have with any other Mercht abroad. That is a credit fix'd in England, & supposing the house in England & Mr. V. should both fail between the time of the acceptance of my draft & its becoming due, it would only be the loss of one parcel of goods." The new arrangement was evidently satisfactory; in 1778 Wedgwood wrote: "Mr. Velthuson pays very well & bids fair to be a first rate customer to us both. Should not we make him some little complimt for his translating & dispensing our catalogue gratis?"

Trade with France at this time was severely restricted, but Wedgwood took a prominent part in the negotiations leading to the treaty of 1786 which enabled English manufacturers to trade with France on favorable terms. The outbreak of the French Revolution, however, prevented the development of a great market for Wedgwood ware in France.

In the autumn of 1771 a showroom was opened in Dublin. The entire risk of the venture was assumed by Wedgwood & Bentley, their agent selling on a commission. In 1773 they urged the agent to take over the stock and assume all expenses and risks. He, however, could not raise the necessary money, and in the following year Wedgwood, after noting that the Dublin sales for the year would again be about £1,200 with a sales expense of only 14 per cent ("1 Per Ct less than Bath or London") suggested that "we may give it a little farther tryal without any great risque." This branch was finally sold in 1777.

In 1773 an order was received from Catherine the Great of Russia for a service of 952 pieces, decorated with English scenes, no two of which were to be alike. Bentley estimated that the set cost £2,410 10s. 5d., but Wedgwood is supposed to have received only £3,000 for making it. A tremendous amount of work and expense was involved in obtaining the designs, and the undertaking attracted much attention throughout England. The service was exhibited in London before being sent to Russia.

In 1786 Wedgwood started to make a reproduction of the famous Barberini or Portland Vase. Three years of hard work and experimentation were necessary before a satisfactory copy was made, probably Wedgwood's greatest technical achievement. Josiah II and Thomas Byerley took one of the finest copies, after it had been shown in London, on a Continental tour, exhibiting it with a collection of ornamental ware in The Hague, Amsterdam, Hanover, Berlin, and Frankfort.

6. Related Activities of Josiah Wedgwood I

Wedgwood saw that progress in pottery manufacture would depend in a large measure upon improved means of transportation, and in 1760–61 he joined other potters of Burslem in their efforts to obtain good roads in place of the ill-kept lanes which served the district. By 1763 the bill for a road from Burslem to Liverpool was passed, and pack-horses for the first time in the history of the potteries gave way to carts and wagons. Transportation by land, however, remained nearly twice as expensive as by water, and goods which were sent by river were subject to so much delay, breakage, and pilfering that it was a highly unsatisfactory means of transport. Consequently Wedgwood, although still active in the movement to obtain turnpikes, in 1765 began to urge the construction of a canal to connect the Trent and the Mersey. He was made treasurer of the company, and it was largely owing to him that the Grand Trunk Canal was completed in 1777.

In 1783 Wedgwood was made a fellow of the Royal Society in recognition of his work in developing instruments for measuring high temperatures. Five of his papers were published by the Society, three on his pyrometer and two on chemistry and the composition of clays.

Wedgwood's activities and talents made him the acknowledged leader of the master potters, and in 1784, when the Association of the Manufacturers of Earthenware was formed, he was made chairman and delegated to represent the organization before Parliament. When the leading English industrialists organized the General Chamber of Manufacturers, Wedgwood was the first chairman.

7. Ownership of the Firm from 1795 to 1895

Between 1795 and 1810 the ownership of the business was vested in Josiah Wedgwood II and Thomas Byerley, who held a one-fourth interest. In 1800 the partners estimated the assets to be worth £35,600. In 1823 Josiah Wedgwood II took his eldest son, Josiah III, into the firm; and in 1827, when another son, Francis, entered the business, the firm adopted its present name, Josiah Wedgwood & Sons. Josiah Wedgwood II withdrew from the firm in 1841, agreeing at the same time to rent the factory, fixtures, and premises to his sons for an annual rent of £1,285. Josiah III withdrew the next year, leaving his brother Francis in sole charge. Francis then formed a partnership in 1843 with John Boyle, each partner owning a half interest. Boyle's death ended this partnership in 1845, and in 1846 Francis took Robert Brown into the firm. Brown agreed to pay Francis two-fifths of the value of the business and for the first four years of the partnership was to receive two-fifths of the profits, after which he was to be considered half-owner and entitled to half the profits. At the same time, part of the land occupied having been given up to Josiah II, the annual rent for the premises was reduced to £950. Brown died in 1859, and, in the settlement which followed, the business (including £11,360 due from customers) was valued at £37,064.

Immediately on Brown's death Francis took his son Godfrey into the business, giving him a one-fifth share which was later increased to a fourth. The other sons were admitted shortly afterward—Clement Francis in 1863 and Lawrence in 1868; and in 1870 Francis retired, leaving his three sons equal partners in the firm. Three years later they purchased for £17,000 the land, buildings, and fixtures which they previously had rented from the estate of Josiah Wedgwood II. At the same time they drew up an agreement whereby each partner was to be allowed to introduce "as a clerk and pupil" one son who might succeed his father as partner only after he was 21 years of age and had been a pupil for three years. As a result a new agreement was drawn up in 1891 with Cecil (Godfrey's son), Francis Hamilton (Clement Francis' son), and Lawrence Wedgwood as partners. This agreement lasted until 1895 when the business was incorporated.

8. Production, 1795–1895

Until 1806 the younger Josiah contented himself with visiting the works at Etruria only two or three times a year.

Consequently Thomas Byerley was left with the responsibility of managing the business and had to divide his time between the works at Etruria and the showrooms in London.

In spite of the uncertainties of the times, the partners made substantial improvements at the Etruria works. In 1799 Byerley urged the advantage of a steam engine for grinding materials and driving throwers' wheels, and in 1802 Boulton & Watt installed one of their engines. About the same time the partners decided to enlarge the works. By 1807 Wedgwood was complaining that too much money had been put into improvements, and Byerley proposed that they should "put a check to the extension of the works at the Mill and get rid of the gang of Millwrights."

No information is available about further mechanical changes in the Wedgwood plant during this period. For the industry as a whole there was a decided growth in the use of steam power and mechanical devices for preparing materials and shaping wares, especially between 1840 and 1880; and specialization of labor and standardization of product increased in extent. Prices lowered as the producers drew abreast technically, and serviceability of the ware (if anything) improved, but there was some loss in craftsmanship and artistic merit. Much handwork continued to be essential, however, and skilled labor remained of paramount importance in every stage of manufacture.[6]

Byerley apparently lacked the technical knowledge required for the proper supervision of production. Costs were high (see Table 1, p. 244 f.),[7] the ornamental ware department was losing heavily, and complaints had been made about the quality of the ware sent out. One cause of the difficulty was the shortage of skilled labor caused by enlistments and the consequent necessity of hiring very young and inexperienced workmen.

As far as possible the firm continued to employ the artists who had helped to establish its reputation; and some of the designs, for printed ware at least, were even superior to those produced before 1795. All the molds which had been made by Flaxman, Webber, and other artists were kept and used. Competitors, however, were producing good imitations of Wedgwood ware, and the company was losing the advantages which it had formerly enjoyed.

In 1801 Byerley wrote to the clerk in charge of the London showrooms, "You will oblige me infinitely by a frequency . . . of suggestions, whether practicable or not. . . . These things must be perpetually occurring to you in your daily business, and arise from the observations of your customers. . . . I want to urge you to a full and constant practice of picking up and furnishing me suggestions."

Later he stressed the advisability of producing china "something like the old French Fayance," because earthenware was "becoming so common that it will very soon grow out of fashion with persons of fortune." This suggestion was later adopted, probably in 1812. Early in 1815 Wedgwood wrote, however, "I have been a very short time a China maker & the Continental trade for Earthenware being now flourishing, I am discontinuing to make China."

In criticizing a border design which had been submitted to him Byerley wrote to Wedgwood: "It is only a repetition of what one sees in every glass and earthenware shop window in town. . . . It will add but little to the fame of your establishment, always characterized by originality. To maintain that character requires depth of research." In spite of keen competition from Spode, Adams, and other potters, Byerley's partners evidently did

[6] Thomas, *op. cit.*, pp. 408–410; J. H. Clapham, *An Economic History of Modern Britain* (Cambridge, 1938), vol. iii, pp. 187–189.

[7] Wedgwood Manuscripts, E–12643 (Sept. 2, 1798). This collection of manuscripts is in the Etruria Museum, Etruria, Staffordshire. This material is an exact copy of the original except that the figures have been adjusted to the nearest pound.

not respond with enthusiasm; on learning that Davenport, probably the largest English pottery manufacturer at that time, had obtained exhibition rooms in London, Byerley wrote, "I am not at all frightened at this if I could once see a little fondness in you and your brother for our own ornamental branch."

In 1841, when the Wedgwoods apparently employed about 500 workers, William Davenport & Co., of Longport, employed from 1,200 to 1,400; Copeland & Garraths, of Stoke, 780; Adams & Sons, of Stoke, in three of their four plants employed 648; and there were at least four other companies which were quite as large as the Wedgwood works. The Mintons in 1846 employed from 800 to 900 people, about the number employed at the Wedgwood works in 1930.

During the period 1810–60 Wedgwood ware was apparently excelled by the productions of the Minton factory, but the Wedgwoods continued to make improvements in body, glaze, and design. Josiah III made substantial improvements in transfer printing, and in 1860 the firm brought out a majolica ware which surpassed that made by the Mintons. In the same year the Wedgwoods obtained the services of Emile Lessore, a French artist who left the Sèvres works because his style was in advance of the times and caused dissension among the other designers there. Coming to England in 1858, Lessore spent two years with the Mintons and then went to the Wedgwoods, for whom he designed until his death in 1876. In 1878 the Wedgwoods resumed the manufacture of china (porcelain), and in 1880 they began the manufacture of decorative tiles.

9. Marketing, 1795–1895

The London showrooms were closed in 1829, and the other retail outlets apparently had been abandoned long before. Later the firm adopted the policy of stimulating public interest by displaying Wedgwood ware at international exhibitions: for example, London in 1851, 1862, 1871; Paris in 1855, 1867, 1878; Vienna in 1873; and Sydney in 1879. In 1875 the firm again opened showrooms in London, but on this occasion the object was to display samples and facilitate sales to retailers; no attempt was made to sell ware to the public. At least one traveling salesman was used during this period to sell "to the trade." No sales figures have survived.

10. Profits, 1795–1895

A statement, compiled in 1799, calculated the profits for the years 1795, 1796, and 1797 to be £24,288, or a yearly average of £8,096. For 1800 the profits were £8,000, and it was estimated that those for 1801 would be about the same. The net worth of the company in 1810 was estimated to be £35,383. Between 1847 and 1888 the net annual results ranged from a loss of £211 in 1870 to a profit of £13,614 in 1882, with an average annual profit of £6,830 for the period. The net value of the assets for the period averaged between £40,000 and £50,000. The calculation of profits was, however, exceedingly rough, and standards varied widely from year to year, so that the figures for any one period mean little.

11. History of the Company since 1895

Early in 1895 the Wedgwood company was incorporated under the "Limited Liability" Act of 1862. Out of an authorized capitalization of £100,000 the company at once issued £33,000 in preference shares and £33,000 in ordinary shares, all of which were taken by members of the family. Dividends on the preference shares were originally cumulative, but in 1912 the holders surrendered this right. The company also created £20,000 worth of 4 per cent first-mortgage debentures of which £10,000 were issued immediately.

A heavy loss was incurred in the first year after incorporation (1895), and the

Table 1. OPERATING ACCOUNTS FOR THE FIRST HALF OF 1798

[To the nearest pound sterling]

Useful Ware

		Disct.		
Sales at Etruria	6,347	612		
Sent to London	4,254	851 (20%)		
" " Liverpool	121	12 (10%)		
" " Enameling Works	642	128 (20%)		
	11,364	1,603		
Net Produce			9,761	
Charges:				
Wages	3,067			
Coals	997			
Clay	315			
Flint	455			
Lead	380			
Packages	376			
Carriage	432			
Incidents	145			
Goods bought	120			
Rent	201			
General Charges	244			
5% on net produce for probable charges not yet brought in	488			
5% for subsequent loss	488			
			7,707	
Profit				2,054

Ornamental Ware

		Disct.		
Sales at Etruria	622	115		
Sent to London	1,808	723 (40% for if they sell there to merchants they allow 20%)		
	2,430	838		
Net Produce			1,592	
Charges:				
Wages	1,010			
Coals	126			
Incidents	109			
Rent	69			
General Charges	43			
5% for charges not come in	80			
5% for subsequent loss	80		1,517	
				75
Profit				

The U and O works reciprocally do business for each other not taken into this account.– Balance probably against O, because many materials are drawn from U for the use of O —This branch of our business then appears to be carried on without profit.

Enameling Works

			Disct.		
Sales at Etruria		1,426	130		
Sent to London		1,837	735 (40%)		
		3,263	865		
Net Produce				2,398	
Charges:					
Wages		632			
Incidents		90			
Rent		30			
General Charges		57			
E'ware Stock	641				
Disct.	128	513			
2½% for charges not come in		60			
5% for subsequent losses		120		1,502	
Profit					896

London Warehouse

Sold Useful and Enameled	7,286		
Ornamental	1,257		
	8,543		
Income of London Warehouse, to go against its charges			
20% Disct from Manufactury U	851 (This is perhaps to[o] little by 10%)		
40% Disct from Manufactury O	723		
40% Disct from Enameling Works	734	2,308	
Charges:			
Wages & Incidents	348		
Salaries of Clerks	258		
Taxes	83		
Insurance whole year	82		
Enam. works, wages &c	456		
Rent	250		
5% for charges not come in & losses by bad debts	427	1,904	
			404
Increase of stock, London, deducting 9% expense of sales			863 *
Total profits			4,292
*too large—allow Disct	272		
Breakage	100		
	372 = 490 increase		
the profits are therefore			£3,921
Allow reserves Useful	976		
Ornamental	159		
Enameling Works	180		
London	427		1,742
			£2,179

total net profits for 1896 and 1897 together were only £1,268. The outbreak of the Spanish American War brought cancellations of valuable American orders, and the Boer War not only injured the home trade but also took the two most active directors to South Africa for two and a half years. In their absence the business was evidently not well managed and losses were incurred. In 1901 the net loss was over £6,000, and it was decided to close the decorative tile department which had been losing money for several years with no prospect of improvement. In 1902 the firm suffered an operating loss of over £10,000, part of which was caused by the closing of the tile department, part by a large inventory loss resulting from a drop in the prices of china ware, and nearly £1,500 by extra expense incurred in complying with the demands of the British Home Office that fritted lead be used in glazes to reduce lead poisoning among the workmen. The three directors, who had formerly received £500 each per year, agreed to serve without compensation until the company was put on a more profitable basis.

Meanwhile efforts were made to increase sales and reduce expenses. In 1895 a traveling agent, who had been sent to India and Australia, was dismissed because his volume of sales was low in comparison with the expense involved. In the same year one of the designers was released, "the Company being unable to afford the expense of two designers because of the lack of rich sales and low selling prices." Efforts were made to obtain aggressive agents in France and Germany, and the Continental traveler was sent to develop a market in Norway, Sweden, and Denmark. These measures having brought little improvement, the company reduced selling expenses by arranging to have its travelers represent the Belleek Pottery Co., an Irish firm of long standing, in all markets except Ireland where the Belleek Co. was to sell Wedgwood ware. It also sent ornamental ware "on sale or return to certain shops in London and elsewhere," with considerable success. In 1896 expenses were further reduced by having one traveler cover both the home and American markets, thus eliminating one salesman, and by replacing the Continental traveler with another man at a lower salary. Another saving was effected by letting the ground floor of the London showrooms and confining the Wedgwood quarters to the upper rooms. To increase the sales of tiles the company took part in several tile exhibitions and tried to stimulate sales in America; but the results were not satisfactory, and as said above the department had to be closed.

With a view to reducing the expense of sales promotion in America, the Wedgwoods joined with the Worcester Royal Porcelain Co. and T. Webb & Sons, Ltd. (a firm of crystal glass manufacturers in which the Wedgwood company held an interest from 1885 to 1920) in appointing an agent to handle their goods in the United States, Canada, Mexico, South America, and the West Indies. The company also joined other pottery manufacturers in a movement to raise prices to a remunerative basis, and an increase of 8⅓ per cent was actually applied on all earthenware; but this, coming at the opening of the Boer War, only depressed sales further.

In 1899 the Wedgwoods, to safeguard themselves against a bad debt, combined with the Worcester Royal Porcelain Co. and T. Webb & Sons, Ltd., to finance Messrs. Phillips, Ltd., a retail shop in London, taking debentures on all assets as security and receiving preferential trading agreements. In the same year the Wedgwoods opened a retail shop at Douglas, Isle of Man, under the name of Messrs. Gibson & Son and purchased another business at Harrogate, Yorkshire. In reporting these ventures the directors stated "that these steps had been forced upon them by the fact that the trade with retail houses was becoming annually more and more unremunerative and insecure, owing to the concentration of the retail trade in large departmental stores and the consequent beating down of prices to their lowest level."

Owing to bad management the Douglas shop proved a failure and was sold in 1902. The Harrogate shop, also unprofitable, was retained for some years until a satisfactory purchaser could be found. Matters fared little better with the Phillips Co. Its purchases from the Wedgwood company increased steadily, but after disastrous trading losses in 1902 the business had to be taken over by the debenture holders and reorganized. Fortunately it subsequently became a successful concern, and the Wedgwoods were later able to dispose of their interest in it without loss.

As soon as Cecil and Francis Wedgwood returned from South Africa, a determined effort was made to improve the position of the company. In order to obtain closer control the directors (now four in number) divided the task of supervising the business so that each became responsible for the operation of specified departments. The tile department having been closed, they seriously considered the advisability of selling or renting the china works which sometimes had shown a loss. However, since the difficulty of assigning overhead costs to the three departments with any accuracy made an intelligent decision impossible at the time, the production of china was continued. The directors decided to divide the home market into two territories and engage a second traveler.

Although the total volume of sales declined in 1904, the business showed a net profit for the first time in four years. The following year produced even better results and the directors felt justified in drawing £200 each for their services. In 1906, as the result of a gift from a member of the family, the Etruria Museum was opened for the preservation of historical pieces and documents relating to the Wedgwood company and family. Later in the same year the company opened its own branch office in New York with Kennard L. Wedgwood in charge. To improve working and living conditions among its employees, the company in 1908 appointed a welfare worker, apparently the first in the pottery industry.

American trade dropped sharply in 1908, as the result of which the Wedgwood branch office lost over £1,000 and caused a small net loss for the company. It was then decided to reduce expenses by adding to the New York office the agency of T. Webb & Sons, Ltd.

Public interest in Wedgwood ware was stimulated in 1909 through an exhibition in London of representative pieces lent by the Tsar from the famous service made by Josiah Wedgwood for Empress Catherine II. About this time the company added "powder blue" decoration and china lustre ware to its line of products, and started a women's school of free-hand painting at Etruria in order to guard against too severe standardization of design.

In 1910 the directors started in a small way a system of bonus payments to staff members, which they have extended and made a permanent part of the company's policy. The practice of taking part in international exhibitions was continued; the firm displayed at Brussels in 1910, and Turin in 1911, and won the *grand prix* on each occasion. In 1911 the New York office for the first time showed a profit, and the company's net profits increased accordingly, notwithstanding extra expenditures involved in applying electric power to outlying machinery in the works and in opening new showrooms in London.

In 1912 profits decreased partly because a coal strike closed the works for five weeks and partly because (as a result of social legislation in 1911) the company thenceforward had to contribute over £2,500 annually for health and unemployment insurance, amounting in 1912 to over 4 per cent of sales. In spite of this, with sales steadily improving and the American office at last on a paying basis, it was clear that the Wedgwood company had successfully passed its critical period, largely through the efforts of Cecil and Francis Wedgwood in England and Kennard Wedgwood in America.

In 1913, to provide for the expanding volume of business, new potters' shops were built and electrified, and the old Boulton & Watt steam engine was replaced with one of modern construction. At the same time the company joined others in sending an agent to develop trade in South America and coöperated with the Marshall Field Co. in a special exhibition of Wedgwood ware in Chicago. Directors' meetings, which had often been from four to six months apart, were now held once a month, records and accounts were kept in greater detail, more searching analyses were made of costs and sales, and sixty of the largest accounts were changed from a half-yearly to a monthly basis of settlement. Total sales for 1913 rose to £66,932, the largest in the company's history up to that time. Prices in the industry had displayed a rising tendency since about 1900.

The outbreak of the World War closed Continental markets and brought cancellations from other customers. With nearly £2,000 tied up in Germany and Austria and other credits probably frozen, the financial position of the firm was threatened. Directors' fees were stopped, salaries were reduced, the works were closed two days a week, and all single men under thirty were urged to enlist to help the country and leave more work for the married men remaining. By November, 1914, orders were improving and full-time production (allowing for the absence of 52 enlisted workers) was resumed. Good orders were reported from Spain, Italy, and America, but as other markets were injured and more workmen enlisted the company faced a decreased turnover. Economies were made wherever possible, and the works closed down on Saturdays after March 1, 1915. At this time increases in wages and the cost of coal and materials forced the first of the many price advances which were to come with war-time inflation. Moreover, circumstances made it extremely difficult to keep up the quality of ware produced.

Despite these difficulties the firm not only took part in the British Industries Fair but also sent exhibitions to Australia and New Zealand. Orders began to increase rapidly, particularly from America, and by September, 1915, practically all departments were working overtime, some even on Sundays. Ninety men (over 10 per cent of the total working force) were in the service, and the probability of further enlistments made imminent a serious labor shortage. By July, 1916, as many as 102 of the 185 eligible men employed in 1914 had enlisted, and production was falling far behind orders. Nevertheless the directors reported, "In view of the after war legislation and intense German competition which must affect the U. S. A. market, a special effort is about to be made to establish ourselves unassailably in the Canadian market."

Late in 1917 production was so hopelessly behind orders that, when the company was left without a traveler for the northern home market, no attempt was made to cover the territory, because, although the market had to be "kept alive," fresh orders were undesirable. The situation had not improved in March, 1918, and steps were taken to close smaller accounts and concentrate on supplying the larger customers. After the United States had declared war, American sales slackened until in June, 1918, an actual decline began which continued throughout most of 1919. Much of the later decline, however, came from the fact that during the War American customers were given preference, whereas after the Armistice, when orders still amounted to double the output, all customers were dealt with on an equal basis. By November, 1919, American sales experienced the recovery which had been evident for months in other markets. Total sales for 1919 reached £120,000 and in 1920 they leaped to £170,000, in spite of a slackening at the end of the year. When due allowance is made for price increases, the sales volume for 1920 was not much above that of 1913, but it must be remembered in this connection that the volume of sales would have been doubled if production facilities had permitted. For the first half of 1920, for example, sales totaled £84,000 while orders amounted to £169,000.

To provide for this increased demand the directors agreed late in 1919 upon a program of expansion which included new potting shops, additional kilns, a new printing shop, further electrification, and a dining-room for the workers. Some of the improvements were undertaken at once, but additions were made only as rapidly as the required craftsmen could be obtained and the necessary readjustments in plant and personnel organization made. In October, 1920, the directors voted, "That in view of (1) the present high cost of building which must sooner or later come down, (2) the uncertain trade outlook, (3) the financial stringency, high rates of interest and possible financial panic, all outlay should be cut down to absolute essentials, and only such expenditures should be incurred as can be met by (a) present finances, (b) current profits and (c) the reissue or deposit with the bankers of the debentures which the company now holds." [8] A modified program of plant expansion and improvement was adopted which was to cost £52,350, of which £35,900 was to be spent in 1921 and 1922. None of the technical improvements has displaced much skilled labor in the Wedgwood plant. The actual shaping and decorating of the ware requires much hand labor even today, and the craftsman still dominates the machine in this and other concerns which produce high-grade china and earthenware.

Between 1891 and 1920 the home trade, allowing for war inflation, maintained a fairly constant volume of sales, amounting to about £35,000; both the American and other foreign markets showed an upward trend. The changing proportions in the three markets are shown in Table 2.

Table 2. WEDGWOOD SALES IN VARIOUS MARKETS, 1891–1920

(Percentage of total)

Year	Home	American	Other foreign	Total foreign
1891	82.3	...	...	17.7
1892	80.2	...	...	19.8
1893	80.3	...	...	19.7
1894	76.8	...	...	23.2
1895	66.3	...	...	33.7
1896	65.8	...	...	34.2
1897	71.3	...	...	28.7
1898	67.0	...	...	33.0
1899	71.6	15.6	12.8	28.4
1900	70.5	18.3	11.2	29.5
1901	70.6	18.8	10.6	29.4
1902	69.5	19.2	11.4	30.5
1903	64.8	22.6	12.6	35.2
1904	64.9	18.3	16.8	35.1
1905	63.2	17.8	19.0	36.8
1906	60.3	19.0	20.7	39.7
1907	59.5	19.5	21.0	40.5
1908	65.8	13.2	21.0	34.2
1909	61.8	19.2	19.0	38.2
1910	59.6	19.1	21.3	40.4
1911	56.4	20.3	23.3	43.6
1912	56.1	19.4	24.5	43.9
1913	54.2	22.9	22.9	45.8
1914	51.8	23.2	25.0	48.2
1915	50.0	34.8	15.2	50.0
1916	46.1	37.4	16.5	53.9
1917	49.4	38.2	12.4	50.6
1918	56.2	31.1	12.7	43.8
1919	59.1	21.3	19.6	40.9
1920	55.3	23.8	20.9	44.7

The company in 1917 began to set aside a substantial reserve for postwar advertising and made new arrangements for agents in South America, India, and Australasia; and in 1920 it sent out an overseas travel-

[8] Directors' Minutes, Oct. 22, 1920.

ing exhibition which was to visit each of the British colonies during the next two years, "rather from an advertising point of view for future trade than for immediate orders." In view of the increased volume of American sales, the directors decided late in 1919 to create a subsidiary corporation—Josiah Wedgwood & Sons, Inc., of New York—as the sole agent for sales in the United States, Canada, and Central America. The capital ($74,000) was supplied entirely by the Etruria company, which also holds the voting control. The great majority of accounts in the United States are dealt with on what is called the "laid down" basis; i. e., goods for these accounts are invoiced to the American company which reprices and reinvoices to the dealers. All accounts in Canada and several of the larger ones in the United States are invoiced in sterling direct from Etruria. The New York office receives a commission for handling both types of business.

Two regular travelers handle the home market and another is assigned to Continental Europe. All three are controlled directly from Etruria. The Australian and New Zealand markets are supplied through an agent, resident in Sydney, who handles the products of other firms and receives a commission plus an expense allowance. The South American, South African, and other markets are dealt with almost exclusively through shippers or through London houses with branches abroad.

In the three principal markets the usual practice is to reserve a number of patterns to be handled exclusively by certain customers in given areas, but the company does not have a general policy of exclusive agencies. Since 1920 the company has begun to advertise regularly in the English and American markets, but no other important change in marketing policy has taken place.

In 1936 the Wedgwood management reached a decision which will undoubtedly loom large in the future development of the company. A part of the newspaper account of the announcement follows: [9]

"The historic Wedgwood works at Etruria are to be moved to a country site. . . . Wedgwood wares will be manufactured in a works which will be the last word in lay-out, equipment and firing technique—totally without smoke—and the factory will be the centre of a garden village, having eventually 500 workpeople's houses, playing fields, and truly rural amenities."

A total of 380 acres of land was purchased on the edge of Barlaston, about five miles from the present works. One-third of this area is to be kept as open space. The management expects the new factory to be ready for operation before the end of 1939.[10]

The ownership and management of the Wedgwood company today (1939) is still in the hands of members of the Wedgwood family, which has been actively connected with the pottery industry for ten successive generations.

12. Readings

Eliza Meteyard, *The Life of Josiah Wedgwood* (London, 1864–65), 2 vols. A detailed biography emphasizing the personal and artistic sides of the subject but containing also a wealth of information about Wedgwood's business activities. Many illustrations.

Josiah C. Wedgwood, *Staffordshire Pottery and Its History* (London, 1913). A good general history of the potteries, with information on nineteenth-century developments not to be found elsewhere.

Ralph M. Hower, "The Wedgwoods, Ten Generations of Potters," *Journal of Economic and Business History,* vol. iv (1931–32), pp. 281–313, 665–690. A brief account of the Wedgwood firm's history devoted chiefly to business aspects.

13. Suggested Questions

1. What factors in the contemporary eco-

[9] *Staffordshire Evening Sentinel,* May 14, 1936, p. 1.

[10] *The Times* (London), Dec. 24, 1937, p. 15.

nomic situation favored the business success of the first Josiah Wedgwood? Have they continued to favor his descendants in the business?

2. Criticize the steps taken before 1800 to build up a retail trade.
3. If you had been in charge of the Wedgwood company from 1895 to 1905, wherein would your policies have differed from those actually followed?
4. If you were in charge of the Wedgwood company's sales promotion, would you recommend that the company produce only eighteenth-century designs?
5. What should be the Wedgwood company's marketing policy with regard to the selection of retail dealers?
6. What was the general economic and social situation that lay behind the marketing problems of the period 1790–1890?

XVIII. JOHN LAW, FINANCIER AND SPECULATOR

1. Introduction

John Law lived in a time of innovation and experimentation in banking. The needs of ambitious national states and of an aggressive and expanding business had led men to think of money and credit and to devise institutions for supplying them. The Bank of St. George of Genoa, the Bank of Sweden, the Bank of Amsterdam, and the young Bank of England were examples of what banks could do. These institutions represented various objectives and various methods, but on the whole they were cautiously managed, serving business passively. As time passed, however, greater emphasis came to be placed on the need for more currency and credit, and new methods were proposed for meeting the need. The wide interest in land banks in England—banks issuing notes on land as security—illustrates the tendency to push the furnishing of credit beyond the limits of the earlier institutions.

Basic to the development of banking were two questions, much considered at the time: What is money, and what are the functions of money? The discussion on the nature of money was chiefly concerned with paper money. Bank notes had for some time been issued by a few institutions. But what gave paper money its value? And what was the advantage of bank issues over state issues and coins? As to the function of money, was it a servant of commerce to meet existing needs? Or was it a master, a leader in expansion and in correcting bad economic situations? This was an old issue. Again and again since ancient times, rulers and statesmen had regarded money as something to be manipulated toward certain ends.

John Law's emphasis was on credit. In the history of economic thought he is significant because of his contributions to the theory of credit and its uses. In the history of business his importance lies in his attempt to put his theories into practice. The "System" which he worked out in France was a significant attempt at economic control through monetary means and credit.[1]

2. John Law and His Early Experience and Ideas

John Law was handsome, clever, and brilliant. He had a strong imagination, no

[1] The whole story of Law's experiment is not known. Though there is a wealth of literature on the subject, relatively little has been found on the actual operation of Law's Bank and almost nothing on the management of the Company of the West or the Company of the Indies. Sometime scholars may discover the actual business records of the Bank and of the companies. Professor Earl J. Hamilton is at present doing significant work along a new line, which will no doubt add richly to our knowledge of Law's operations. For the present, though the information available is incomplete and far from satisfactory, consideration of the subject in the light of what is known can be justified. This case can ask questions though it cannot satisfactorily answer them.

end of daring, and little if any power of self-criticism. While he had a gambler's sense of honor, he seems not to have been strong in what is commonly known as character. He was the promoter par excellence though with more than the usual mental capacity of the promoter.

Law's early life prepared him for his later career. He was born in Scotland in 1671, the son of a goldsmith and banker. He studied at the University of Edinburgh, where he distinguished himself in mathematical subjects. After completing his education he went to London. There his fast life led to a duel in which he killed his opponent. Law was twice sentenced to be hanged; the first time he was freed and the second, he escaped. He was then 24 years of age. He fled to Amsterdam, at that time the commercial metropolis of Europe, where he studied the work of its sturdy bank. Thence he wandered from city to city, winning a reputation as a brilliant gambler.

In his wanderings Law observed business keenly. He thought much about money and credit and he discussed them with prominent men. He approached several governments with suggestions for improving their finances. His first serious move to establish a bank came in 1705, when he submitted to the Scottish parliament a plan for a land bank. Law believed that Scotland was languishing from an insufficiency of capital and proposed a banking system designed to provide an abundance of currency, in his mind the key to prosperity. The following excerpt from his *Money and Trade Considered,* containing his proposal for a land bank in Scotland, gives his early ideas on the relationship between the quantity of money and national wealth and power.[2]

"Domestick Trade depends on the Money. A Greater Quantity employes more People than a lesser Quantity. A limited Sum can only set a number of People to Work proportion'd to it, and 'tis with little success Laws are made, for Employing the Poor or Idle in Countries where Money is scarce; Good Laws may bring the Money to the full Circulation 'tis capable of, and force it to those Employments that are most profitable to the Country: But no Laws can make it go furder, nor can more People be set to Work, without more Money to circulate so, as to pay the Wages of a greater number. They may be brought to Work on Credit, and that is not practicable, unless the Credit have a Circulation, so as to supply the Workmen with necessaries; If that's suppos'd, then that Credit is Money, and will have the same effects, on Home, and Forreign Trade.

. . . .

"The use of *Banks* has been the best Method yet practis'd for the increase of Money. . . .

. . . .

"Last War, *England* set up a Bank to have the Conveniencies of that at *Amsterdam,* and by their Constitution to encrease Money. This Bank was made up of Subscribers, who lent the King 1200000 *lib.* at 8 and a Third *per Cent,* for 11 years, on a Parliamentary Fund; And were privileg'd Bankers for that time. The Sum due by the Government was a Security to the People, to make good any Losses the Bank might suffer.

"This Bank was safer than the Goldsmiths Notes in use before. It made a great Addition to the Money, having a much greater Sum of Notes out, than Money in Bank. And the Sum lent the King . . . had the same Effect in Trade as Money.

. . . .

"From what has been said about the nature of Money, *Chap.* I. it is evident, that any other Goods [than silver] which have the Qualities necessary in Money, may be made Money equal to their Value, with Safety and Convenience. There was nothing of Humour or Fancy in making Silver to be Money; it was made Money because it was thought best Qualified for that use.

[2] John Law, *Money and Trade Considered* (Edinburgh, 1705), pp. 13, 36, 38, 60–61, 89–91.

"I shall endeavour to prove, that another Money may be Establish't, with all the Qualities necessary in Money in a greater degree than Silver; with other Qualities that Silver has not: And preferable for that Use, tho silver were the Product of *Scotland*. And that by this Money, the People may be Employ'd, the Country Improv'd, Manufacture advanc'd, Trade Domestick and Forreign be carried on, and Wealth and Power attain'd.

. . . .

"The Paper-money propos'd will be equal in value to Silver, for it will have a value of Land pledg'd, equal to the same Sum of Silver-money, that it is given out for. If any Losses should happen, one 4th of the Revenue of the [governing] Commission will, in all appearance be more than sufficient to make them good.

"This Paper-money will not fall in value as Silver-money has fallen, or may fall; Goods or Money fall in value, if they increase in Quantity, or if the Demand lessens. But the Commission giving out what Sums are demanded, and taking back what Sums are offer'd to be return'd; This Paper-money will keep its value, and there will always be as much Money as there is occasion, or imployment for, and no more. . . .

"After the Method propos'd, the Quantity being always equal to the Demand for it, it will keep its Value, and buy the same Quantity of Goods 50 years hence, as now: unless the Goods alter in their Value, from any Change in their Quantity, or in the Demand for them.

. . . .

"Land has a more certain Value than other Goods, for it does not encrease in Quantity, as all other goods may. . . ."

3. Conditions in France Favor Law

Some ten years after he had proposed a bank for Scotland, Law took definite steps toward establishing a bank in France. There conditions were ripe for experimentation, and Law found a hearing.

France was almost bankrupt financially, and its economic life was in a bad way. A series of wars, the latest that of the Spanish Succession (1701–13), and the extravagance of Louis XIV had left the state's credit low, its treasury empty, its public debt tremendous, and its revenues pledged years in advance. Postwar readjustment and monetary deflation had brought a severe crisis. Bankruptcy, unemployment, idle workshops, agriculture in distress, and an almost stagnant commerce were then the rule in France. This primary postwar depression apparently began in 1715 and lasted until sometime in 1718.

France had no adequate leadership to cope with her financial problems. Her nobility, both lay and clerical, to which she might have looked for guidance, was degenerate. Having lost their function of leadership under the rising power of the kings and having been encouraged, especially by Louis XIV, to leave their estates for the life of the court, the members of the nobility had become a part of a social order which was unfit to deal with the crisis that France was facing.

Political leadership centered in the Duke of Orleans, Regent for the five-year-old Louis XV. Orleans was urged by the courtiers to declare France bankrupt, but he refused to consider that way of freeing his country from its burden of public debt and chose instead to experiment with devices for meeting immediate needs. Some of his measures might be considered forms of repudiation, though by certain modern economists they are looked upon as attempts at reflation following and remedying the deflation of 1713–15. The worst in its effect was probably the augmentation of the nominal value of coins, that is, depreciation of their real value. Some of the Regent's measures were wise but worked too slowly to meet the crisis then upon France. Fraudulent paper currency and dishonesty in the government aggravated the difficulties. Unfortunate France in 1715 seemed on the brink of even a greater period of stress than that which had just ended.

Such was the situation that gave Law an opportunity. On the one hand was the corrupt court, a gambling, fast-living crowd, open to the advances of a man with the personality, reputation, and boldness of a Law. On the other hand was the Regent, a daring individual with considerable imagination, driven by the necessity of doing something. Law had for some time been laying the basis for his appeal to French leadership. He had established relations with several members of the court, including Orleans, at the time of the War of the Spanish Succession. There is even some evidence which suggests that the ministers of Louis XIV had been interested in his scheme.

4. Dates in the History of Law's System

1715–18 Primary postwar depression in France.

1716 Law's General Bank established.

1717 Company of the West organized.

1718 Company obtained tobacco tax contract. Attack on Bank by the Parlement of Paris. "Anti-System" established. General Bank made Royal Bank with branches. Bank notes made redeemable in coin subject to change in tariff.

1719 Law appointed director of Royal Bank. Company of the West merged with two others to form Company of the Indies. Much new stock issued. Great increase in bank notes in summer. Company granted farming of the mints. New shares issued. Law promised dividends of 12 per cent. Livre content of gold louis reduced. Company granted farming of taxes in exchange for assumption of state debts. New shares issued. Beginning (in September) of great inflation in note issues, prices, and business. Company absorbed functions of receivers general of taxes. Law started tax reform. Disposition, in November, to realize on shares checked by decrees strengthening bank notes. Speculation in shares reached mania in December. Dividends on shares of Company fixed at 40 per cent of par.

1720 Law made Controller General of Finances of France. Ordered forced redemption of government *rentes,* apparently to stimulate demand for shares. Decrees strengthened bank notes relatively to coin and bullion. Royal Bank absorbed by Company in February. In March shares pegged at 9,000 livres; shares and bank notes made mutually exchangeable; value of coins in terms of livres reduced. Beginning of great bank-note inflation. Decree of May 21 ordered gradual reduction in price of India stock to 5,000 livres and 50 per cent reduction in denominational value of bank notes. Law removed from office of Controller General. Decree of May 21 withdrawn without restoring support of Company shares. Throughout summer Law and Regent tried to save System by contraction of bank-note circulation. Conversion of bank notes ceased in November. Rapid price decline and depression began in December. France returned to specie basis. Law fled to Belgium.

1721 Liquidation of Law's System began in January. Company of the Indies lost all privileges except commercial monopoly.

5. The Establishment of Law's Bank in France [3]

Law diagnosed the trouble in France as follows. He saw that France was rich in natural resources and people but poor in credit and badly deranged in her economic life. Confidence and sound credit would, he believed, bring recovery. That is, he believed that France was in a condition of economic disequilibrium, with idle factors of production, and that the backward elements could be raised and economic life brought into balance by the use of the twin levers, currency and credit. By these means, thought Law, France could be made to prosper.

The following excerpts from Law's writings in the summer of 1715 show the direction that his thinking was taking:

(1) From Law's "Memoir on the Bank." [4]

"It is evident that the richest states do not have sufficient specie to employ their people and to increase trade to the point to which it might be brought. The specie of England has been computed to be at the most between 14 and 16 millions sterling, about 200 millions in the silver of France. This sum would not be sufficient for that state, on the present scale of its manufactures and commerce, without the help of credit, as has been noted; and it may be assumed that if England lost this aid and were reduced to getting along with specie only, her manufactures and commerce would be cut in half. Credit, therefore, is necessary and useful for the good of the state and of commerce, in times of peace as in times of war, and the prince who does not establish it in his state is like him who has mines which he does not allow to be worked. [p. 555]

"Credit well established and regulated brings great benefits, but where there are faults in its organization, or where it is badly managed, it may cause a great deal of damage. [p. 556]

"The bank is a general credit which produces commodities and advantages for all parts of the state, principally for trade. [p. 578]

"The Bank of England . . . does not keep on hand all the sums for which it gives notes; it puts a large part of those sums to good use. . . . There are, ordinarily, about the same sums of money brought to the bank for notes as of notes to be converted into money. Hence it is not necessary to keep in the cash department the value of all the notes; but since it frequently occurs that the demand for one exceeds the demand for the other by 2 or 3 millions, it is necessary for the bank to keep cash for sustaining its credit. With 50 millions it has more specie than is needed to sustain the credit of 100 millions of notes. It thereby brings about a real increase of 50 millions and a profit to the company. [p. 581]

"Thus, the 50 millions, say, in the cash department support the credit of 100 millions of notes, and those 100 millions have the same effect that 300 million in specie might have; the bank by its credit and the greater circulation which it procures produces the same benefit to the state as if the quantity of money were increased by 250 millions. [p. 581]

"A bank which is well established need never lose its credit, assuming that the prince does not wish to destroy it, because it is very easy to foresee the events which might harm it. Supposing, however, that through lack of foresight the cash department of the bank were not strong enough to pay the notes which might be presented, then the bank would fail to pay, but it would not lose its credit, having in good investments funds exceeding the value of its notes. [p. 595]

[3] The statements of fact relating to the history of Law's system in France, as given in pages 254–273 of this case, have been drawn chiefly from the following sources: Marmont du Hautchamp, *Histoire du système des finances sous la minorité de Louis XV* (Paris, 1739), vols. v–vi; Paul Harsin, editor, *John Law, œuvres complètes* (Paris, 1934), vols. i–iii; A. M. Davis, "An Historical Study of Law's System," *Quarterly Journal of Economics,* vol. i (1887), pp. 289–318, 420–452; Earl J. Hamilton, "Prices and Wages in Southern France under John Law's System," *Economic History,* vol. iii (1937), pp. 441–461, and "Prices and Wages at Paris under John Law's System," *Quarterly Journal of Economics,* vol. l (1936), pp. 42–70; and E. Levasseur, *Recherches historiques sur le système de Law* (Paris, 1854).

[4] Translation of selections from Law's "Memoir on the Bank" in Eugène Daire's *Economistes —financiers du XVIIIe siècle* (Paris, 1843).

"By means of these establishments traders make their payments by settlements of accounts without cashiers; they avoid this expense and risk, the cost of sacks, of carriers of silver, of counterfeit or light money. [p. 557]

"The credit which Law proposes to establish will be different, in its organization and its conduct, from those which are in use. Suited to this monarchy and its present state of affairs, instead of following other projects, his will serve as the model which will be followed in the future. [p. 561]

". . . It is thought that in the beginning of this credit system those who receive notes from the royal officers will take them to the bank, as soon as they have received them, to buy their value in silver, not having confidence as yet in the system. However, as soon as merchants and other individuals have seen that notes are paid promptly, they will be induced to accept notes because of their convenience." [p. 569]

(2) The effect of the Bank on the interest rate.[5]

"Because, as I have already remarked, the price of all things is regulated according to quantity and demand; the quantity of money being considerably increased, and the demand not having been increased in the same proportion, its price, or interest, has greatly diminished, and it is logical to hope by means of the bank to reduce natural interest to 3 per cent or lower. The laws will not produce these results, but the abundance of money, which that establishment will produce, ought to do it; likewise, the indebtedness of the state will be noticeably decreased, and the subjects better able to meet the taxes which the king will need to levy."

Law conceived of a bank in France which would combine the main features of the Bank of Amsterdam and the Bank of England. The former was a bank of deposit, the merchant depositing a sum of money to establish credit, in terms of a fixed standard, on which he drew by order on the bank. The capital of the Bank of England was a loan to the government, that is, its capital was government credit. Like the Bank of Amsterdam the Bank of England was also a bank of deposit, but unlike the other bank it early began to issue bank notes and thus became a bank of issue.

Law's first proposal for a bank in France was submitted to an extraordinary meeting of the Council in October, 1715. The proposed bank would be founded on royal funds and administered under the authority of the King. It was described to the Council as follows: [6]

"The idea of this bank is to cause all the revenues of the King to be brought to the bank; to give to the receivers general and the tax farmers notes of 10 crowns, 100 crowns, and 1,000 crowns, weight and standard of that day, which will be called bank notes; these notes will thereupon be brought by the said receivers and farmers to the royal treasury, which will furnish them valid receipts. All those to whom payments are due from the King will receive at the royal treasury only bank notes, which they can redeem at the bank without delay, no person being obliged to keep them or to receive them in trade. But Law claims that their utility will be such that everybody will be glad to have bank notes in preference to specie, on account of the ease with which payments in paper can be made, and on account of the certainty of receiving payment for them whenever it is desired."

The project was opposed by a number of merchants and bankers who appeared before the Council. It was rejected under the strong leadership of the Duke of Noailles, then head of the finances of the government of France.

Law soon submitted a second proposal for a bank, a privately owned but chartered bank subject to inspection by the government. With the strong support of the Regent he obtained letters patent for such a bank in May, 1716. The following

[5] Excerpt from letter of Law to Desmaretz, July 26, 1715, Harsin, *op. cit.*, vol. ii, p. 52.

[6] Translation of selection from original record of the meeting as given in Levasseur, *op. cit.*, pp. 39–40.

selections indicate the nature of the new institution.

(1) From the decree of May 2, 1716, establishing the Bank.[7]

"I. That the said Law and his company alone have the right and privilege to establish on their own account a general bank in our realm, and to keep and maintain it for 20 years, counting from the day of the registration of these presents. We allow them to make contracts, to keep their books, and to issue notes, payable in crowns of specie, under the name of bank crowns, by which will be understood crowns of the weight and standard of that date. . . .

"II It is our will that the said bank be free from and relieved of all taxes and impositions, and that the shares of the bank and the sums in the treasury belonging to foreigners shall not be subject to the right of aubaine [right of king to property of deceased aliens], of confiscation, or letters of reprisal, even in case of war between us and the princes and states of which the said foreigners are subjects, which rights we expressly renounce by these presents.

. . . .

"VII. All persons will be free to take their money to the bank, for the amount of which they will be given bank notes, payable on sight.

. . . .

"IX. Our very dear and much loved uncle, the Duke of Orléans, shall be the protector of the bank, on which he shall report, to himself or to those who shall be appointed by him, whenever it seems desirable to him; and he shall appoint the inspector, whom he shall replace or change as he thinks proper; and the rules and plans for the management and operation of the said bank shall be presented to him for approval and shall, whenever necessary, be confirmed by us."

(2) Selections from the letters patent on the Bank.[8]

"I. The funds of the bank shall consist of 1,200 shares of 1,000 crowns each. Hence the capital will be 1,200,000 bank crowns [a bank *ecu* was worth about five livres, a livre being an old French money of account about the equivalent in value of one franc before the World War], that is six million in silver of current value.

. . . .

"V. The bank shall begin to do business as soon as subscriptions are made amounting to 1,200 shares and the stockholders have met at the office of the bank to elect the officers necessary for the administration and operation of the said bank and for regulating and arranging for the payment of shares.

"VI. In this meeting and in other general meetings of the stockholders of the company, everything shall be decided by the plurality of votes, which shall be counted in the following manner: those who have five shares and less than ten, shall have but one vote; those who have ten shares and less than fifteen, shall have two votes, and so on by fives; and those who have less than five shares shall have no vote.

. . . .

"IX. The bank's treasure shall be divided into the general cash department and the ordinary cash department; the general cash department shall be closed by three different locks and keys, one of which shall be kept by the director, another by the inspector, and a third by the treasurer, the office not being opened except in the presence of these three persons.

"X. The ordinary cash department shall be entrusted to the treasurer and shall not hold more than 20,000 bank crowns; each of the cashiers shall have not over 20,000 crowns, and they shall give sufficient surety for the sums entrusted to them.

"XI. The bank notes shall be signed by the director and by one of the associates, who shall be chosen by a plurality of votes in the first assembly [of the stockholders], and approved by the inspector. And at the same time the quantity required will be determined, the notes to be registered by number, date, and amount in a book kept for this purpose.

. . . .

"XIII. When the cashiers need coined money, the treasurer shall furnish it, at the

[7] Translated from du Hautchamp, *op. cit.*, vol. v, pp. 77–79.

[8] *Ibid.*, pp. 82–86.

same time retiring its value in notes; he shall likewise furnish notes and retire their value in coin. The same operations shall be made between the office of the treasurer and the general cash department.

. . . .

"XVI. To facilitate trade the bank shall take charge of the cash of individuals, both for receipts and for payments, and shall, according to their preference, make payments by cash or by transfers on accounts, charging at the rate of five bank sous for 1,000 bank crowns. The company shall appoint two agents to have charge of the ledgers for recording accounts and for the receipts and payments for individuals.

"XVII. It shall discount bills or letters of exchange in the manner to be prescribed by the company.

"XVIII. In order that this establishment shall not bring injury to individuals, merchants, bankers, or business men, the bank shall not carry on any trade in goods on land or sea, nor handle marine insurance; and it shall not handle the business of merchants on commission, either within or without the realm.

"XIX. The bank shall not issue notes payable at a stated future time, but they shall all be payable on sight. . . ."

It is impossible with the evidence at hand to trace the details of the development of the Bank or to give any definite statement as to the degree of its success. Judging from the evidence available, however, the Bank was apparently successful from the beginning of its business in June, 1716. It is said to have had an immediate and beneficial effect on trade and manufactures.[9] The Bank's note issue was reasonably conservative in its first two years of existence; a decree of April, 1717, states that the notes had already established their credit at home and abroad. At that very time the government gave open support to the Bank in requiring tax receivers to accept and redeem its notes and to make remittances in that paper. This act had been urged by Law as a means of giving the Bank the support of an absolute monarch, which he considered the strongest possible support for a bank.

6. The Development of Law's "System:" Union with a Commercial Company

In a letter to the Regent, Law had written: [10] "The bank is not the only nor the grandest of my ideas. I will produce a work which will surprise Europe by the changes which it will effect in favor of France,—changes more powerful than were produced by the discovery of the Indies or by the introduction of credit." Was this an allusion to a policy which brought the union of the Bank and a great trading company?

In August, 1717, letters patent were granted to the Company of the West, which was headed by Law. The Company was given the monopoly, relinquished by Crozat, of the colonial affairs, including mining and trade, of the great territory of Louisiana, and of the beaver trade of Canada. Two hundred shares of stock were issued, the stock being exchanged at par (500 livres) for depreciated *billets d'état;* these were converted into 4 per cent *rentes* (annuities or bonds), thus relieving the market of nearly one-half of the floating debt of the state.

The failure of a large proportion of the subscribers to pay for their stock brought action in support of the Company of the West. In June, 1718, it was announced that subscribers might pay one-fifth in *billets d'état* at that time and have an extension till November 1 for the payment of the rest; the time was later extended to January 1, 1719. In August, 1718, the Company obtained a contract for collecting tobacco taxes at a compensation of 4,020,000 livres. In November the Company of the West bought the Company of Senegal, which meant entry into the trade with

[9] Davis, *op. cit.*, p. 302.

[10] *Ibid.*, p. 305.

Africa and which gave to Law's company a considerable store of merchandise and eleven vessels. For the Company of Senegal with its privileges 1,600,000 livres was paid.

In the meantime strong opposition to Law's System had developed on two fronts. The Parlement of Paris, a body which had some power to check the King, on August 12, 1718, attacked the Bank by orders which, if enforced, would have seriously limited if not destroyed that institution. The Regent answered the attack by a coup d'état which practically destroyed the power of Parlement. More serious was the organization of the "Anti-System"—a company formed by Paris Brothers, strong bankers and enemies of Law—which was granted the monopoly of the collection of taxes known as the general farms.

The next significant step in the development of Law's system was the conversion of the General Bank into the Royal Bank in December, 1718. The King became its sole proprietor by reimbursing shareholders in coin for the *billets d'état* with which they had purchased their bank stock; since those *billets* had been converted into shares in the Company of the West, the Company was to that extent the property of the Bank and of the King. The notes of the Bank were henceforth to be under the sanction of the Council. Branches of the Bank were established in Rochelle, Tours, Amiens, Orléans, and, after delay owing to strong opposition, at Lyons. In January, 1719, Law was made director of the Bank.

The System was then launched. The conversion of the General Bank into the Royal Bank would seem to have been a realization of Law's original plan. Controlling the Bank on the one hand and the Company of the West on the other, Law was at last in a position to test his principles. "In addition to the ordinary channels of business," says Davis, "he had at his command the development of Louisiana, from which to gain that activity of circulation which was his measure of prosperity."

There was a portentous provision in the decree of December, 1718, concerning the Bank. It was ordered that the bank notes should be payable not only in bank crowns, as before, but also in *livres tournois,* which were subject to change in denominational value. Thus was reversed the previous conservative policy of having notes of fixed value.

Soon after the Bank had become royal a number of decrees were issued which had to do with the Bank's notes. One ordered that in cities which had offices of the Royal Bank payments exceeding 600 livres should be made in notes and not in silver. In January notes were issued in *livres tournois*. In February it was ordered that notes could be redeemed in gold as well as in silver, redemptions and payments to be at current rates, that is, at the market value of the metals. A decree of April, on the contrary, ordered that bank notes should not share in the decreases in actual value to which silver was subject. Authorities differ in their interpretation of Law's responsibility for this decree, but in view of his power at the time those scholars may be right who hold him responsible for strengthening the notes even though that was contrary to the decree of February.

The Company of the West, which had languished in 1717 and 1718, in 1719 came to life. By May it had 3,577,000 livres in its treasury, merchandise in its warehouses in France, and ships in port and on sea. But shares in the Company were still at a discount in current money. Law, it is said, therefore, began to stimulate the market for its shares; he is said to have paid 40,000 livres for the privilege of calling for 200 shares at par in 6 months, and before the contract matured the stock had risen to a price 10 times par.

Before the six months had passed, however, a great change had come in the affairs of the Company. In May it merged with the French China and East India companies to form the Company of the Indies. The addition in June of the rights of trade with the Barbary States virtually gave to Law control of French maritime commerce with the four quarters of the globe.

The formation of the Company of the Indies brought extensive operations in stock. Fifty thousand shares, at a par of 500 livres, were issued to pay off creditors of the old companies and to supply working capital. Shares were sold at a premium of 10 per cent, the premium being paid on subscription and the rest in 20 monthly installments. This issue brought the total capital up to 250,000 shares.

Various things served to encourage the demand for the shares. Certificates for partial payments could be traded in the market. The requirement, apparently to put a limit to subscriptions, that every subscriber should own four old shares (*mères*), in order to be eligible to subscribe for one new share (*fille*), may in truth have been designed to encourage speculation. Law is also said to have employed matched sales to hold up the securities. And loans on stock made by the Bank at low interest increased in size per share with the rise in the price of India shares. The result was rising prices and increasing speculation in India shares.

The new Company had a strong effect on the Bank. The increased trading in shares and contracts for futures helped give bank notes a preference over coin. As a result the coin in France was brought to the Bank, and Law even provided for bringing in the *piastres* of the Colony of Louisiana. The increased demand necessitated an increased issue of notes, notwithstanding the fact that it had been stated in April that the 110,000,000 livres which had been issued during that year made enough notes for trade. In June, 50,000,000 livres were issued and in July, 240,000,000. Shortly thereafter came what has been said to have been an attempt to cripple the System by an unexpected demand for the redemption in coin of several millions of livres. On July 25 a decree reduced the value of the gold louis in terms of livres, with the result that the conspirators, to escape loss, converted into bank notes the coin which they had withdrawn. It is a question whether this decree was an attempt to defeat an attack on the System or merely a part of the policy to keep the coin of France in the Bank.

In the summer of 1719 various moves were made further to strengthen the Company of the Indies. In July the Company was given the farming of the mints, which made all the mints of France branches of the Bank. Fifty million livres, to be paid in 15 months, was the cost of this new privilege. Fifty thousand additional shares (par 500) were issued and sold at 1,000 livres a share to pay for the mint privilege. To attract people of small means it was provided that shares could be paid in 20 monthly installments and that certificates for partial payments could be sold on the market, certificates being issued for as little as one share. This latest issue of shares was called *petites filles*.

It was announced about this time that dividends of 12 per cent per annum would be paid on the stock. Law's opponents contended that it would be impossible to pay such a dividend. One might well question the financial practice of declaring dividends that one merely hoped to earn. On this question Davis has the following to say: [11]

"The 4,000,000 livres per annum from the *rentes* [French debt owned by the Company] was a fixed income; but the estimated profits from the tobacco farm, from the coinage, and especially from the commercial companies, made up a set of doubtful items. . . . Levasseur figures the probable income of the company at the time at 16,500,000 livres, putting the commercial profits at 3,500,000 livres; but Dutot puts this item in 1720 at 10,000,000 livres, so that here we have a difference

[11] *Ibid.*, pp. 425–426.

which shows how Law might have justified his faith in twelve per cent earnings."

In August came the greatest stroke in the advancement of the activities of the Company. It was granted the farming of the taxes in France, for which Paris Brothers (Law's enemies) held a contract for 5 more years, and the privileges of the Company were extended for 50 years. The Company promised to lend the King 1,200,000,000 (later raised to 1,500,000,000) livres at 3 per cent a year, to be used for redeeming the *rentes, billet d'états,* or other government obligations. Thus the Company was on the way to becoming the sole creditor of the government.

To raise money to meet this new obligation the Company was authorized to sell either *actions rentières au porteur* (unregistered debenture bonds) or *rentes* bearing 3 per cent. But, since those securities apparently did not sell well, it later became necessary to sell more stock. Three hundred thousand shares were, therefore, issued at 5,000 livres (par 500), to be paid in 10 equal installments, hence known as *cinq-cents*. Certificates were issued for as little as one share.

Those shares found a ready market. Decrees of August 31 and September 5 had provided for the redemption of the government obligations (in notes or in coin, as the bearer chose). Thus, at a time when the decline in interest and the rise in real and personal property seemed to cut off the ordinary avenues of investment, the creditors of the government were forced to dispose of their notes or securities. This virtually drove them to investing in Law's securities. Moreover, the Bank was loaning at 2 per cent on stock valued at 2,500 a share. Further aid to speculation was the postponement of payments on the *cinq-cents* to help those operating for a rise. The Company, which two years earlier had found it difficult to dispose of 100,000,000 livres of capital, at this time was besieged with applicants for the issue of shares amounting to 1,500,000,000 livres. So great was the eagerness of the public to secure the *cinq-cents* that the street on which the Company's offices were located was thronged with carriages and crowds. On the payment of 500 livres a certificate was received for one installment on a share; when fully paid that share shortly rose to 8,000 livres. The old shares were consequently offered for sale, and early in October, when the market price of new shares stood at 8,000, the price of the old, which represented the same proportion of profits of the Company, was only 4,000 livres.

By the middle of October the amount which the Company of the Indies had received, assuming all subscriptions paid, was as follows:

Stock	Livres
Original stock or *mères* (invested in *rentes*)	100,000,000
Filles (premiums and 5 monthly installments)	8,750,000
Petites filles (4 monthly installments)	10,000,000
Cinq-cents (1 monthly installment)	150,000,000
	268,750,000

In the autumn of 1719 Law's activities were extended far beyond the immediate administration of the Bank and the Company. On October 12 the power of the Company was widened to include the rights and duties of the receivers general of taxes, including making direct advances to the Crown. This gave Law the opportunity to institute reforms which he had been advocating. He abolished many annoying taxes in Paris and elsewhere; he did away with taxes on the grain trade between provinces; and he consolidated the several tobacco taxes into one. In general he worked to remove restrictions from trade, both domestic and foreign. He also undertook a number of public works, including several projects for improving water transportation within France, and offered to develop the fisheries.

Some of Law's efforts for the general improvement of France at this time may seem not to have been consistent with his attempts to get monopoly rights for his Company. Levasseur explains that he was not seeking monopoly control for a group but a uniform administration for the good of the whole of France. In other words, it might be said that Law was working not for an economy of privilege for the few but for an economy administered and controlled for the advantage of the many.

France was at this time experiencing a general inflation in business which had the character of a boom. There was a great rise in prices, especially toward the end of the year. Old industries were revived and new ones arose; so great was the increased purchasing power that the factories and the markets could scarcely supply the demands of purchasers. The opera had never seen such prosperous days, and imports of luxuries rose. Governments, central and local, carried on a number of useful building projects, including, as noted above, the improvement of waterways, thus making markets more accessible. Agriculture and commerce, alike, profited from the benefits given.

The rise of prices and increased business activity brought the need for more bank notes. From September, 1719, to February, 1720, there was a very great increase in note issue. Notes for 120,000,000 livres were issued in September and also in October, and in December came the greatest of all issues, 360,000,000 livres, making the total note issue for the year 1,000,000,000 livres.

Speculation in stocks of the Company of the Indies reached a mania in the autumn of 1719. Guards had to be placed in the Rue Quincampois, the center of the speculative activities. "The attention of all Europe," says Davis, "was concentrated upon this narrow street, the dwellings in which, from basement to attic, were converted into offices." Provincials and foreigners flocked to Paris to take part in the speculation. In November shares sold for 10,000 livres in spite of the fact that in one week the Company put 30,000,000 livres of shares on the market.

Late in November a disposition to realize in coin appeared. This was checked by several decrees: for instance, the monopoly of refining and separating the precious metals was given to the Company; bank notes were placed 5 per cent above current coin in value; the use of silver was limited to payments under 10 livres, and gold under 300 livres, while the payment of foreign letters of exchange was to be in notes only. At the end of the year the stockholders' meeting of the Company fixed dividends for 1720, in anticipation of income, at 40 per cent. This would have been only 2 per cent on current market price of shares, while the *rentes,* which had been converted, had paid 4 per cent. The estimates of the Company show, however, that 40 per cent could not have been paid on capital from current earnings.

In January, 1720, Law was made Controller General of the Finances, virtually prime minister of France. Thus he came to be in a stronger position than ever to carry out his theories on economic control through credit. It is significant that at this time Law acquired, in addition to his many town houses, a number of places in the country, including four beautiful seignorial estates.

Among Law's first acts as controller were several decrees to force the redemption of government *rentes,* clearly with the object of stimulating the market for shares in the Company of the Indies. Many *rentiers* had not turned in their *rentes,* the redemption of which had been ordered in the preceding autumn. For those far from Paris the time had been too short; for all there was the problem of getting satisfactory investments in exchange—about the only investments available were the securities of the Company of the Indies, which were very high in price in proportion to their possible income. By February 6 four decrees had been issued which practically provided for forced redemption of the old *rentes* into a 2 per cent *rente* if not converted before the first of the next July. Criticized for his attack on the *rentes,* Law answered in the *Mercure* that the annuitants would not amount to a hundredth part of France, "and of them there's not a Hundred who are reduced to live on Annuities only, and who do not gain more by all the other Funds than they lose by this." [12]

It is not positively clear what Law's motive was in forcing the redemption of the *rentes*. Apparently the object was to foster speculation by increasing the demand for shares, though Law asserted that it was to discourage dealing in futures and thus to check an unwarranted rise in the stock. One decree offered shares at 11,000 livres, 1,000 in cash for which the subscriber would secure a *prime* (these were later known as the old *primes*). Thus for 1,000 livres one could secure a certificate with which to speculate. But this opportunity was not received so enthusiastically as had been anticipated, because, it is said, of the fact that there had already been much dealing in contracts for future delivery. This fact apparently accounts for a subsequent decree which forbade individuals to deal in contracts for futures.

Affairs at this time were not too encouraging for Law. It is true that shares of the Company actually sold for a hundred times the original real cost of shares held 28 months, but that very situation encouraged realizing. To stop realizing, Law resorted to control of coin. A decree of January 20 authorized search of all houses for coin—even the houses of secular and religious communities. A few days later the Company was authorized to visit all houses and palaces and confiscate specie, above 500 livres, the confiscated coin to go to the informer. Shortly, goldsmiths were forbidden to manufacture or offer for sale any but a few specified articles of silver or gold. Even the wearing of diamonds, pearls, or other precious stones was forbidden. On January 28 it was decreed that bank notes should have currency throughout the kingdom. The denominational value of coin was also changed. This was not a new thing—there had been several reductions in the preceding year, but the changes came more frequently at this time. On January 1 the value of the gold louis, one of the coins reduced, was changed from 32 to 31 livres; apparently to restore confidence and prevent flight abroad, its value was augmented to 36 livres on January 22; scarcely had a measure of confidence been restored when on January 28 there was a reduction to 34 livres. In addition, the Bank was authorized to issue 200,000,000 livres in notes (although it had been promised in December that no more would be issued), under the nominal pretense of replacing endorsed notes.

These measures brought much trouble, especially the confiscation of coin. The rewarding of the informer led to the setting-up of an effective system of espionage. Refuge in religious communities gave no protection. Seven million livres sent by Paris Brothers to Lorraine were seized on the way. "One heard no conversation," says Levasseur, "except about seizures: one day it was 26,000 marks seized at the home of a stockjobber; another day, 50,000 marks at a merchant's; an old servant of Louis XIV, Chancellor Pontchartrain, was forced to carry to the mint 50,000 louis which he had carefully saved." [13]

Criticism of Law was widespread at this time. The French clergy had taken a stand against speculation. The English were critical. To this was added the opposition of those—particularly the *rentiers*—who had suffered loss from Law's System. Law found it necessary to make a statement. In a letter which appeared February 21,

[12] *The Present State of the French Revenues and Trade* (London, 1720), p. 41.

[13] Levasseur, *op. cit.*, p. 208.

1720, in the *Mercure,* he made the following defense of his system: [14]

"And indeed what Rank of People, and what Profession, has not shared in the Riches that have arisen from the New System. Lands and Houses are at double, nay, treble the Value to the Seller, and will increase considerably in Revenue to the Purchaser. The Military and Civil Officers receive their Pensions or Salaries, which they had lost all Hopes of. The Merchants and Workmen have not enough to answer the Demand of the Buyers. The common People, and even those who by the meanness of their Fortune, can scarcely be ranked in any Class, all of them, in short, find a way to Live, to Thrive, and Inrich themselves; and even among the distrustful and blind, or ill-affected Declaimers, how many Debtors have delivered themselves from the Oppression of their Creditors? And how many Creditors have got in their desperate Debts?"

On February 23 came the final move in the completion of Law's System. By the union of the Bank and the Company, Law reached the height of his power. The Company now controlled the Bank and all its privileges; it held the royal funds; it collected the taxes; and it had almost complete control of the monopolies of France. Law, the head of the Company, was also at the head of the finances of the government of France.

The following translation of the decree of February 23 gives the rights and responsibilities of the Company under the new arrangement: [15]

"I. His Majesty has entrusted the Company of the Indies with the administration and management of the Bank for all the time remaining until the expiration of the charter of said Company. He wishes that the said Company enjoy the profits and benefits of the Bank, even those subsequent to the declaration of December 4, 1718, which converted it into a royal bank; he allows the appointment of such persons in such numbers and places as the Company may deem desirable for the operations of the bank.

"II. Inasmuch as the Bank is royal, the King guarantees to the public the value of the notes of the Bank; the Company of the Indies will be responsible to His Majesty for the administration and management of the bank, for which purpose the 1,600,000 loaned to His Majesty by said Company and the capital derived from the sale of shares shall be especially assigned; further, His Majesty forbids the directors to issue new bank notes, except in pursuance of decrees of the Council, following the decisions of the stockholders' meeting of the Company of the Indies.

"III. His Majesty directs that the Company of the Indies shall be held responsible for the receipts and expenditures, by true statement to the Council as well as in the court of the exchequer, in the form and manner prescribed by articles XIII, XIV, and XV of the deliberations of December 4, 1718. . . .

"IV. And in view of the granting to the Company of the Indies of the profits and benefits of the Bank, His Majesty orders that the said Company shall not exact the five per cent on specie which shall be brought to the offices of the Bank, nor receive or pay out coin except according to the current price. His Majesty also wishes that the payments below 100 livres shall be made in coin, and that in the future nothing shall be paid out but notes of 10,000 livres, 1,000 livres, and 100 livres. As for 10-livre notes, for two months they may be either taken to His Majesty's bureaus of payment in payment of taxes, with the exemption of four sous a livre according to the decree of January 29 last, or exchanged for specie either there or at the office of the bank at the option of the borrower.

"V. His Majesty gives and has given to the Company of the Indies 50,000,000 of his own shares in the Company, of the fifth issue; the said shares shall be sent to the treasury of said Company by the treasurer of the Bank.

"VI. For the price and value of said 50,000,000 shares, the Company of the Indies shall pay to His Majesty the sum of 900,000,000 livres—that is, 300,000,000 in the course of the present year, 1720, and the 600,000,000 remaining in 10 years, month by month, from January 1, 1721, at the rate of

[14] *The Present State of the French Revenues and Trade,* pp. 41–42.

[15] Du Hautchamp, *op. cit.,* vol. vi, pp. 32–37.

5 million a month—no deduction being made from the 900,000,000 for the amount which His Majesty owes to the Company, inasmuch as His Majesty is bound by Article XII of the decree of August 31 last, and by that of October 12 following, not to redeem for 25 years the *rentes* he established for the profit of said Company, which His Majesty shall continue to pay at the rate of 3 per cent.

. . . .

"VIII. His Majesty declares that at no time and for no reason whatever shall the Company of the Indies be required to make advances for his use, and that the Bank shall make payments for His Majesty only after the funds have been deposited in the Bank. Consequently he forbids the keepers of the royal treasury to draw on the Company or on the Bank for more than the sums which His Majesty shall have on deposit and forbids the cashiers and treasurers of the Company and of the Bank to pay beyond said sums, on pain of becoming answerable and responsible for them in their own and private name.

. . . .

"X. And since it is the intention of His Majesty to redeem completely the perpetual *rentes* against the *Hôtel de Ville,* even those which are not free from seizure and other limitations appertaining to bondholders, and since he wishes to secure for his subjects the means of assuring them of a fixed income and to employ profitably the sums which they cannot use, he has allowed and does allow the Company of the Indies to create preferred stock bearing fixed income for 10,000,000 at the rate of 2 per cent a year, making 500,000,000 of capital; these shares shall be deposited at the will of the bearer and listed in the book of free shares or in that of shares used as collateral, in such form as His Majesty shall designate in the future.

"XI. And, lastly, His Majesty has appointed the Controller General of Finances [Law] inspector general of the Company of the Indies and of the Bank, and commands Sr. le Pelletier de la Houssaye (ordinary councilor of state), the mayor of Paris, assisted by two of the oldest sheriffs in service, together with the judge and the first consul of the consular jurisdiction, to inspect the cash departments and books of the Bank four times a year and more often if they deem it advisable, without being required to give any notice; and all necessary letters patent for carrying out this present decree shall be served."

7. The Downfall of Law's System

Though Law had said that "if all the French and foreign traders should distrust of his project, it would not prevent him from succeeding," one thing, especially, made him immediately dependent on the confidence of the public. That was the Company's indebtedness to the King incurred in the absorption of the Bank, the sum of 300,000,000 livres having to be paid in the year 1720, which sum the Company was authorized to raise through the sale of *actions rentières* bearing 2 per cent. How could a 2 per cent security be sold when it had been impossible to sell 3 per cent shares in exchange for the suppressed *rentes?* It must be remembered that Law had taken on another large obligation when he had promised to pay a dividend of 200 livres a share on 524,000 shares.

The first effect on the market of the union of the Company and the Bank had been to raise the shares, but, says Levasseur, "when it was realized that the guaranties were illusory, that nothing supported the paper but the chimerical protection of another paper, and that private fortunes had no more security than before, the fall began." This brought a renewal of Law's efforts to sustain the notes by getting control of coin and bullion.[16]

On March 5, 1720, came a very important decree. It converted all the obligations of the Company into one kind of share, pegged shares at a high price, made shares and bank notes mutually exchangeable, and increased by one-third the value of coins. Selections from the decree follow: [17]

[16] Levasseur, *op. cit.,* p. 213.

[17] Du Hautchamp, *op. cit.,* vol. vi, pp. 49–53.

"The King . . . deeming it necessary to reduce to one kind of shares the old shares, the subscriptions, and the premiums [*primes,* or agreements for furnishing shares] delivered by the said Company, and at the same time to establish a fixed ratio between the shares of the Company of the Indies and the bank notes; wishing also to increase the circulation of money . . . has ordained and does ordain:

. . . .

"II. His Majesty has fixed and does set the shares of the Company of the Indies at 9,000 livres per share.

"III. His Majesty ordains that the subscriptions and premiums which the Company of the Indies has delivered, shall be brought in the course of the present month to be converted into shares.

"IV. His Majesty orders the cashier of said Company to receive them; that is, the subscriptions of which four payments totaling 2,000 livres, while 3,000 remain to be paid, have been made, at the rate of 6,000 livres each subscription; the old premiums [of January 10, 1720] at the rate of 1,050 livres; and the new [of February 29, 1720] at the rate of 5,000 livres each; and in exchange the said cashier shall deliver to the bearers of such securities, shares on the basis of 9,000 livres a share.

"V. His Majesty wishes that beginning on the 20th of the present month, a bureau shall be opened at the Bank to convert, in accordance with the wish of the bearer, the shares of the Company of the Indies into bank notes and the bank notes into shares of the said Company, which shall be both received and delivered on the basis of 9,000 livres for each share, the cashier having no power over said conversions.

. . . .

"VII. His Majesty orders that, beginning on the day of the publication of the present decree, and until otherwise ordered, money shall circulate and shall be received by the Bank and at the mint: the louis coined according to the decree of May, 1718, for 48 livres, the halves in the same proportion; those of the coinage ordered by the decree of November, 1716, for 60 livres, the halves and quarters in proportion [and so on, augmenting the value in livres of the different kinds of specie].

. . . .

"IX. Observe that the bank note is a form of money that is not subject to any variation . . . that the bank notes will be received at the rate of 110 for 100 by all the bureaus and receivers of the land tax, the poll tax, and other taxes which are not subject to the said four sous per livre. . . ."

Opinion differs as to the source and import of this decree. Levasseur thinks Law designed it to support the shares. Daire considers it the keystone of Law's System, since through the convertibility of shares and notes Law could control the circulating medium. Louis Blanc says the decree saved several great lords. Dutot, a cashier of the Company at the time, says it was a mortal blow to the System because Law could not support both; he holds the Regent responsible and the enemies of Law in that they made the move necessary through their attacks on the System. Professor Hamilton holds that the object was to check a decline in the price of shares from January quotations.

The decree of March 5 was soon followed by another, that of March 11:[18]

"Louis, by the grace of God, King of France and of Navarre: To all those to whom this present letter may come, greetings. To procure for our subjects the diminution of the price of goods, to sustain public credit, to facilitate circulation, to increase commerce, and to aid manufactures, we have judged it expedient to diminish the price of specie, abolish the use of gold coin, and to convert the crowns into money more convenient for trade. . . .

"I. That gold coin may continue to have currency in commerce and to be received in the offices of the Bank at the rate given in Article VII of the decree of our Council of the 5th of the present month until the 20th of the said month in Paris and next April 1 in the provinces; and that it may be received

[18] *Ibid.,* pp. 55–56.

for the *marc* during the same time at our mints, also gold bullion, at the rate fixed by Article VIII of said decree. . . .

"II. We forbid for all time our subjects and strangers in our kingdom, of whatever quality or condition, to have, in whatever place it may be, after the first of next May, any gold coin of France or foreign countries, or even gold bullion, except according to the following article, on pain of confiscation to the profit of the Company of the Indies of all the movable property of individuals and communities found to have in their possession said coin or gold.

"III. We give permission to goldsmiths and other workers whose work requires the use of gold to have it as apportioned to them according to their work, provided always, and not otherwise, that those workers prove that they have obtained said gold from the offices of the Company of the Indies. . . .

"IV. Similarly we forbid, for all time and under the penalties stated in Article II of our present declaration, all our subjects or foreigners to have, after the last day of next December, any silver bullion or any silver specie of France or foreign countries other than the sixths and twelfths of crowns, made in consequence of the declaration of December 19, 1718, and also with the exception of those silver livres the manufacture of which was ordered by the decree of the month of December, 1719.

. . . .

"XII. We order that beginning with the said 20th day of the present month, the price of all gold coin be diminished by an eighth at Paris alone, so that it shall not circulate except at this rate: namely, the *louis* at the rate of 25 to the *marc,* made in consequence of a decree of May, 1718, for 42 livres, the halves in the same proportion; those of the coinage ordered by the edict of November, 1716, at the rate of 20 to the *marc* for 52 livres 10 sous, the halves and quarters proportionately [and so on for the various kinds of coin].

"XIII. We wish, similarly, that beginning with the first day of next April, current silver coin, other than the sixths and twelfths of crowns or the silver livres, shall be diminished in all our kingdom and shall not be received except at the following rate: the crowns of the last coinage, or 10 to the *marc,* for 7 livres, the halves, quarters, and tenths in the same proportion [and so on, changing the livre content of a long list of coins]."

At the time of the issue of this decree Law made an appeal for support. In this new System, he said, "the whole Nation becomes a Body of Traders, who have for their Cash the Royal Bank, in which by Consequence all the Advantages of Commerce, Money and Merchandize, reunite." [19] Law tried to justify the efforts to bring coin into the Bank's vaults, and he tried to quiet people's fears that the coin might not be safe in the hands of the Bank. They need not fear, said Law, that there was not so much cash in France as the value of the shares in the Company—the houses in Paris likewise represented more than all the coin in the kingdom. Neither should the people fear despotic power; disquiet and agitation and the public which held the System back were the real dangers.

An immediate consequence of the decree of March 5 was the need for more bank notes. To purchase the shares offered, the issue of more notes became necessary. From March 26 to May 1 the circulation was increased 125 per cent. By May the quantity of money in circulation in France was actually about twice the estimated quantity when the Bank was chartered. Inflation was accompanied by a rise in prices. Hamilton says of the price increase: [20]

"The heavy note issue, the disparity between the market rate and the natural rate of interest, the spread of speculation from securities to goods, and the loss of confidence in the System were chiefly responsible for the rise in prices. A similar revolution of commodity prices did not occur at London, Paris, Madrid, or Philadelphia."

19 *The Present State of the French Revenues and Trade,* p. 44.

20 "Prices and Wages at Paris under John Law's System," pp. 69–70.

It is obvious that the whole matter depended to a great extent on the success of the Company in its own operations. Concerning that, however, little is known. In the absence of specific records of the operations of the Company we shall turn to Law for his statement of the affairs of the Company of the Indies in April, 1720: [21]

". . . we must inquire, Whether those who have bought, and are Members of the Company of Commerce, can hope from the fix'd Revenues of the Company, and the Produce of the Trade they undertake for the Revenue of the Six Milliards in Specie, plac'd upon the best Funds, for to that Sum amounts the Value of all the Shares at the Rate of Two Thousand a-piece.

"If we compare the Shares with what we call real Estates, such as Lands and Houses, 'tis certain that they are not yet arriv'd at their just Value, since as real Estates are now purchas'd, the fix'd and determinate Revenues of the Company alone will produce almost as much as the Six Milliards laid out in Land and Houses.

"By fix'd Revenues I understand the Rents assign'd to the Company on the King's Farms [fermes], which they receive with their own Hands, those on the Clergy, the different Cities, Provinces of the Kingdom, and the Countries that have a right to Tax themselves, &c. These Revenues alone will give near one pr *Cent.* of the Six Milliards, at which I reckon the Funds of the Sharers. We now buy Houses and Lands almost at this Rate; but if we consider that the Company will always have part of their Shares in Cash, and that the Rents of this will increase to others, their fix'd Rents will at least yield 1½ pr *Cent.* If besides we observe that the Diminution of Species will diminish the Incomes of Lands and Houses, and that Money lay'd out that way is an alienated Fund, with which one can't so easily assist themselves as with Shares. It will be agreed, that considering only the fix'd Rents of the Company, Shares are better worth the Price, than Lands and Houses at the Rate we now buy them.

"But the Rents are not a quarter of the Profit which the Company may reasonably expect from their Undertakings, they take in the Commerce of the Bank, of the whole inhabited World, and of all the Finances of the Kingdom.

"The Particulars of their Undertakings would require more Room than I can spare here; a very small Observation is enough to give one a View of the immense Profits which the Company may make annually.

"We have still a fresh Idea of the vast Fortunes which have been made in *France* by the *West India* Trade. The Company will renew them to the Profit of the Partners, and restore a Trade which the separate Interests of private Persons have ruin'd. Their Exports will be proportion'd to the Demand, and they will not debase themselves by exporting exorbitant Quantities. The Price of Goods, when not lessen'd by Rivals, will keep up. *French* Men will no more ruin one another, but keep the Advantage they have of their own Clothes, Silk, Gold, and Silver Stuffs, and the other Merchandise of their own Product.

"The Trade of the *East Indies,* and *China,* will likewise be another Source of Wealth to the Company, both sure and extensive. We must not compare its Commerce with those of the weak *French* Companies that formerly carry'd it on; they had neither the like Wealth, Understanding, nor Authority. The private Views of those who govern'd it clash'd with their common Interest. The Expiration of their Bonds forc'd 'em to buy and sell at a loss. They paid exorbitant Interest. Time alone ruin'd them, and the Nature of their Obligations was such as they could not fulfill. This Trade has made a certain Nation to flourish, whose Country is almost depriv'd of the Gifts of Nature.

"Our Alliance with them will be no less useful to us both in *Asia,* than 'tis in *Europe.* Commerce is never ruin'd, but rather augmented by the Number of Traders, and 'tis profitable and flourishing in no Places more than where they have the greatest Number of Traders, and those too of different Nations. When they are united among themselves, Navigation is more sure and commodious; their joint Strength guards them against the Insults to which Strangers are too

[21] *The Present State of the French Revenues and Trade,* pp. 58–65. According to Harsin, *op. cit.,* vol. iii, p. 112, this letter appeared in *Mercure de France* in April, 1720.

much expos'd in remote Countries; the Discoveries of the one serve the other, and the mutual Credit they give multiplies their Stock. Thus we shall join to the Commerce of *Asia* that of *Europe* in *Asia* it self, and carry the Fruits of the Peace to the uttermost Parts of the World.

" 'Twould be too long to run through all the other maritime Trade which the Company carries on, such as those of *Senegal* and *Louisiana,* so necessary for one another. The Plantation of *Louisiana* will be an immense Object. I know there must be Time to form a Colony, and to reap all the Advantage we expect from it; but if we consider the first Fruits we have had from thence in Tobacco, Silk, Indigo, and Silver, the Happiness of the Climate, the Goodness of the Soil, the Choice we may make in its vast Extent, the mild Temper of the Natives, the many Settlements that rich private Men and Companies make there from Day to Day, we are to hope in a little while to see more prosperous Times, than either our Neighbours or our Selves, who have not had those Helps, have seen for many Years.

"But we have in *France* more speedy and plentiful Objects.

"By how many different Canals is Gold and Silver convey'd with Profit into the Treasures of the Company.

"The Trade in Goods which is allow'd to them only, brings into their Hands what comes from all Parts into the Kingdom. The Bank brings them successively all the trading Money. The Finances convey immense Treasures into their Cash which lay useless in the King's Coffers; all the Specie returns also to them by the Coinage; besides that, this prodigious Quantity of Silver makes them Masters of all the Trade they have a mind to undertake. The Fountains which convey the Money to them, and have hitherto rais'd the greatest Fortunes, yield considerable Profit every Day.

"People were uneasy at the sudden Fortunes which in all Times a great Number of Persons rais'd by the Bankers Trade, and the negotiating of Effects, because they thought it was at the Expence of the Publick. But here the Advantage of the Company will be the Benefit of the Publick, because they are the greatest part of it, and that contenting themselves with a moderate Profit, it will diminish the Loss which others have by Trade.

"I know that in the handling the Finances, they wont make the same Profit as the Receivers did in the last Reign, upon Contracts more burdensome to the People than advantagious to themselves.

"But this Diminution which makes a difference in behalf of the People, of above One Hundred and Forty Millions levy'd upon them every Year in extraordinary Affairs, will turn to the Advantage of its Commerce, facilitate the same, and augment the ordinary Revenues of the Finances; for if this Maxim of the Finance be true, *That Imposts destroy Property,* the contrary must also be true, and the Imposts being taken off must add to what remains, and the Company will always have lawful Profits, which a good Administration, the Multiplication of Specie, a greater Consumption, and the publick Wealth, will render more and more plentiful.

"Even the Recoining of the Money after the Diminutions directed, will yield them 10 pr *Cent.* upon all the Money of the Kingdom, and the Profit will be renewed during nine Years, as often as the Interest of Trade join'd with the Interest of the Company, don't prevent it.

"To ask then from whence the Company will reap their Profit, is to ask, what has been the Spring of all the Fortunes that have hitherto been rais'd in *France* of what Nature soever? But their Opportunity is still greater, for all those Advantages which lay dispers'd, how ever great they might be, are not comparable to the whole reunited in one Company; which by their Re-union is in no danger of those Inconveniencies occasion'd by Opposition of Interests, that are so apt to diminish, and ev'n to destroy the best Businesses. Besides which, they find in one Branch of their Affairs and Trade what will support the other.

"The Commerce of the *West* favours that of the *East*. The Privilege of having Materials facilitates the Purchase of foreign Merchandize. The Manufactures which they support furnishes 'em with Means to have the Materials. The Trade in Blacks advances the Establishment of the Colonies. The negotiating their Actions keeps them up to their just Value. The Finances, the Bank, and Merchandize, mutually assist and increase one another. The Concurrence of all those Things carries the Power of the Company to such a height as no other ever arriv'd to. But that is not all, the State of the Company is fix'd for Time to come, for what becomes a general Thing in a State, must last as long as it does.

"We have often seen one Sort of Estates attack'd, and one part of a State suffer some Change in a Government, but no Body ever saw, or will see, such a Change as attacks all Estates together, and makes every one suffer at one and the same Time, because in those Changes, 'tis usually one part of a State that, abusing its Authority, sacrifices another to its own particular Advantage, either Real or Imaginary. Besides, a general Mischief can't be hid under any Disguise. This would be so plain, that the Prince must needs perceive it to be an Attack upon his own Power. The Concurrence of so many Advantages, ascertains the Continuation of the Company, and that being ascertain'd, turns that to be a settled Fund for the Company, which hitherto has only been a casual Profit. This Article deserves a particular Attention.

"Traders, Bankers, and Financiers, never look'd upon their Business, and the Profits of it, as a settled Fund, or a fix'd Revenue, because Death, Sickness, Revocation, Rivals and Misfortunes, might deprive them of it, and did indeed often deprive them of the Means by which they got those Profits. In a Word, Their Trade and Imploys were no constant Fund. But in the Hands of a Company which has perpetual Succession, and never dies, which by its immense Riches, and different Fountains of Profit, is in a Condition to bear up against any Loss or Misfortune, which being the Glory, the Riches, and the Power of the State and the King, has nothing to fear, but every Thing to expect from the Sovereign Authority. This Company, I say, is to look upon its Profits as a fix'd Revenue, a settled and immense Fund, whose Value is as much above the real Estates of *France,* as the Profits of Industry are above a real Estate, so that 'tis a constant and assur'd Fund, since being a Continuation to the same Company of the Privileges granted it, to take away the Fund from them, is not to acquire them for one or another, but to destroy them. A superior Authority might indeed so ruin *France,* but would inrich no Body, and, on the contrary, destroy the whole People. I think this a sufficient Security from that despotical Authority which is continually opposed to the New System."

In April and May a number of efforts were made to protect Law's System. As noted above, between March 26 and May 1 there was a staggering inflation of bank notes. On April 6, moreover, all stipulations for payment in coin were declared null and void. And on May 16 the Company was authorized to issue 4 per cent *rentes!*

Five days later came the most drastic effort to save the System. This was the decree of May 21 providing for the gradual deflation of the denominational value of the bank circulation and the value of shares in the Company: [22]

"The King, having had examined in his Council the state to which the realm was reduced before the establishment of the Bank, in order to compare it with the present condition, saw that the high price of money brought more injury to the realm than all the expenses to which the late King had been driven by the different wars, the avarice of money lenders having risen to the point of exacting higher interest per month than the law had established for the whole year. This usury had so weakened the kingdom that the revenues of His Majesty were paid only when compulsion against the tax payer was increased; the price of provisions scarcely sufficing to pay the cost of tillage and taxes, the landlords received nothing. This general distress had forced a part of the nobility to sell their land at a low price in order to support themselves in the service of His Majesty; and the other part of this nobility had its property seized. The indulgence of the King was their only recourse, and His Majesty was without the means to help or even to pay the salaries of the officers and the pensions which had been granted as recompense for services. Industry, commerce, and navigation had almost ceased. The business man was reduced to bankruptcy, and the laborer was

[22] Du Hautchamp, *op. cit.,* vol. vi, pp. 95–101.

forced to leave his native land to seek work with foreigners. Such was the condition to which the King, the nobility, the business men, and the people were reduced, while the money lenders alone lived in luxury; and the realm might have fallen into general disorder had not the King found a prompt remedy for this evil. By the establishment of the Bank and the Company of the Indies, the King has restored order into its affairs; the nobility have found in the increase in the price of their land a means of clearing themselves; industry, commerce, and navigation are restored; the lands are cultivated, and the artisan is working. But in spite of the obvious advantages which these institutions have brought, there are persons sufficiently evil-intentioned to plan to destroy them. Such persons forced His Majesty to give the decree in Council of March 5 last, to sustain by the augmentations of the money the credit of those useful and necessary establishments. By this decree His Majesty reduced the different kinds of securities of the Company of the Indies to one kind and ordered that the shares be converted into bank notes, and these notes into shares, following the ratio which was then the most fair in accordance with the value of specie. This depreciation of the money and the great popularity of the shares have given debtors the means of freeing themselves. It remained for His Majesty to give attention to the employment of the sums which should be refunded to minors, hospitals, religious communities, and others of the more privileged creditors; and at the same time to reestablish the value of money at a point favorable for foreign commerce and for the sale of produce. His Majesty has made provisions for these various objects by decrees, and particularly by the declaration of March 11 last, which ordered the reduction of the price [livre content] of specie. But since these reductions would necessarily produce a decrease, not only in the price of provisions and of chattels but even in the price of land and other fixed goods, His Majesty has decided that the general interest of his subjects demands that the price or money value of shares of the Company of the Indies and of bank notes be diminished in order to maintain those things in a just ratio with specie and other property in the realm; to prevent the high value of specie from lowering public credit; to give at the same time to privileged creditors the means of employing more favorably the reimbursements which would be made to them; and finally to prevent the losses sustained by his subjects in foreign trade. And His Majesty has decided upon this reduction the more readily because it will likewise be useful to owners of shares of the Company of the Indies and of bank notes, inasmuch as the distributions or dividends of these will be made more advantageously and because they will be convertible into hard money, which will produce at least 50 per cent more in specie or silver bullion after the reduction than at present. Upon which, having heard the report of Law, councilor of the King in all his Councils, Controller General of the Finances, His Majesty in his Council, with the advice of the Regent, the Duke of Orleans, has ordained and does ordain:

"I. That the shares in the Company of the Indies be reduced; that is, beginning on the day of the publication of the present decree, to 8,000 livres; on the first of July to 7,500 livres; on the first of August to 7,000 livres; on the first of September to 6,500 livres; on the first of October to 6,000 livres; on the first of November to 5,500 livres; and on the first of December to 5,000 livres.

"II. That the bank notes be likewise reduced, after which they will not be received in payments; that is, on the day of the publication of the present decree, those of 10,000 livres to 8,000 livres; those of 1,000 livres to 800 livres; those of 100 livres to 80 livres; and those of 10 livres to 8 livres. [Followed by monthly reductions until] December first of the present year, the said notes shall remain reduced and fixed; that is, those of 10,000 livres at 5,000 livres, those of 1,000 livres at 500 livres, those of 100 livres at 50 livres, and those of 10 livres at 5 livres.

"III. His Majesty, foreseeing that those of his subjects who find themselves holders of considerable sums in bank notes may convert them with advantage into shares in the Company of the Indies, and wishing to protect those who have not sufficient wealth to use in this way, orders that in the course of the present year, and until January 1, 1721, the bank notes shall be received in the payment of the land and other taxes in the generalities of the *Pays d'Election* as well as in those of the *Pays d'Estats*, in His Majesty's Bureau of Farms and likewise in the salt warehouses, according to the full value which the notes had before the reductions ordered by the present decree, without, however, the refunding of four sous a livre or of the 10 per cent allowed by the decrees of January 29, March 5, and April 28 last. And the said bank notes will likewise be received at their full value at the office designated for the distribution of *Contracts des Rentes Viagères* [life annuities] ordered by the decree of the Council of the sixteenth of the present month. . . ."

Let us see what Law had to say of this effort to save the System. The following selection is from a letter of May 22, 1720: [23]

"This arret does wrong to no Body.

"It does none to the Actionier [shareholder], who preserves the same Revenue. The Company has the same Funds to divide. The Dividend will be the same. The Action gave Two Hundred Livres Revenue, it will give the same still, and has the same prospect of Increasing.

"At the Years end, when all Reductions shall be made, the Actionier will be as rich with his Action reduc'd to Five Thousand Livres, as he was before the Arret with Nine Thousand Livres.

"The Arret does no wrong to the Bearer of the Bank Bill, all that he could desire was to have the same quantity of Bullion as he carried to the Bank or the Mint. He will have just the same. He carried in his Silver at the rate of Sixty, Seventy, and Eighty Livres a Mark, which Silver is to be reduced to Thirty Livres. The Bank Bill is reduc'd only in the same Proportion.

. . . .

"The real worth of an Employment is deriv'd from its Revenue. The Revenue of an Action is not diminish'd, by consequence the real Value of the Action is not diminish'd."

Law wrote in support of this decree, and there is some evidence that he was responsible for its appearance at that time.

[23] *The Present State of the French Revenues and Trade*, pp. 106–107.

He may again have forgotten reality; his plan may have been proposed earlier when times were more favorable; there are those who hold that the decree may have been the work of Law's enemies. We do not know positively. Davis notes that "his responsibility for doctrines whose enforcement would legitimately lead to such arbitrary methods as those contained in the decrees of March 5, 11, and May 22, cannot be denied."

The decree of May 21 brought the end of the System. Steuart says that "the *arret* was no sooner published than the whole paper fabric fell to nothing. The day following, the 22d of May, a man might have starved with a hundred millions in his pocket." [24] This is a glaring overstatement, though there was a considerable fall in the price of shares. With the fall in confidence, which immediately followed, went Law's position as controller —he was removed by the Regent and his enemies came into power. One thing remained, the royal guarantee of the bank notes. According to Hamilton, that guarantee saved France from a complete financial debacle.

8. Liquidation

Seeing its dire results, the Regent revoked the deflationary decree on May 27. He also made Law privy councilor, general intendant of commerce, and manager of the Bank. But the System was dead, and the revocation of the decree and the bringing back of Law brought no restoration of lost confidence.

The Regent and Law tried to save something. They could not, of course, restore specie payments, but they attacked the problem in various ways. With a view to decreasing the circulation, they offered in exchange bonds based on the revenues of Paris and the provinces and stocks and bonds of the Company of the Indies, and

[24] James Steuart, *An Inquiry into the Principles of Political Economy* (London, 1767), vol. ii, p. 268.

they destroyed 1,000 and 10,000 livre notes in the possession of the Bank. They withdrew 700,000,000 livres, for which they gave deposit credit on the books of the Bank which was transferable but not withdrawable. The failure of these efforts led to the announcement in October that on November 1 acceptance of bank notes in exchange for certain securities would cease.

December brought serious developments. The efforts to save the situation had by then definitely failed. Law fled, and France went back to a specie basis. About this time began the great drop in prices which marked the beginning of a severe depression which lasted until July, 1721, when the price level stood at about 38.7 per cent below its apex under Law.

In January the Council took steps toward the final liquidation of Law's System. A decree of January 26 called for an examination of claims against the System. Settlement was, ironically, placed in the hands of former enemies of Law, notably Paris and Crozat. The result of their work is summed up briefly by Hamilton thus: [25]

"The holders of bank notes and India stock apparently received on the average about two-thirds of the nominal value of their claims, but the fortunes acquired through speculation were amerced by as much as 95 per cent."

The Company of the Indies was reorganized with a smaller capital, losing all privileges except its commercial monopoly.

9. Statements on Law and His System Made after the Failure

A. By Law himself, (1) on the revenues of the Company: [26]

"The Company had promised a dividend of 200 livres per share, which was 40 per cent on the original capital [at 100 livres per share], or 4 per cent on the basis of 1,000 livres per share, the price at which the Company had sold stock when it redeemed the King's debt. It based this dividend partly on the circulation of bank notes. Since it had on hand 200,000 shares set aside for the amount of notes in circulation, there were in the hands of the public only 300,000 shares which drew a dividend; and, supposing that the circulation of the bank notes had been cut in half, then there would have been in the hands of the public 400,000 shares, the dividends on which would have amounted to 80,000,000.

"The resources of the Company for paying it were:

Rentes on the tax farms	48 millions
Profits from the tax farms	12
Tobacco	6
Receipts general	1
Commerce of the Indies, etc.	12
Profits on the mints	12
Total	91 millions

"Since 80,000,000 would suffice to pay the dividend, there remained according to this statement 11,000,000 to take care of the shortage which might occur in some parts."

(2) On the deflationary decree: [27]

"All the financial operations spoken of were successful; they produced an abundance and caused alarm abroad, but, since the disease was acute, extreme measures had to be taken; all this placed the System in danger of having an end less happy than its beginning. In spite of the great amount of and the increase in the number of bank notes and the high price of shares, the resources of the kingdom were more than sufficient to pay their total value, particularly after the discharge of the larger part of the debts. But public opinion had waned, and it is its caprices which settle everything. The credit of the Bank reached the point where it was based only on necessity and authority. For several months Law had foreseen that it would be impossible to sustain it. For that reason he decided to increase the notes by the purchase of shares, with the idea of forcing all debtors to pay their debts, and it was, so to speak, the last service that he expected from those notes. He was prepared to perform an operation to moderate

[25] Hamilton, "Prices and Wages at Paris under John Law's System," p. 61.

[26] Harsin, *op. cit.*, vol. iii, pp. 212–213.

[27] *Ibid.*, pp. 375–376.

the excess of those which he had already performed and to enable himself to introduce order and confidence into business, as well as to establish eventually another credit fitted to the needs of commerce, which would be solid because the causes of waste had ceased. The kingdom being relieved and wholly renewed, it remained only to conserve its forces and keep it in a healthy condition. That situation made him conceive the celebrated decree of May 21, 1720, which he had communicated to Orléans, who was satisfied with it. He considered it the solution of the difficulty brought about by the vast quantity of paper money of different kinds. The Keeper of the Seals was the only one to whom it was communicated and he saw to it that no one shared the secret. He approved heartily because he inwardly regarded it as a favorable occasion for ruining Law, and from that moment he started to make plans which would mature on the publication of the decree. The moment was favorable for his schemes, for that decree would not fail to alarm and antagonize the public. By successive diminutions from month to month, the bank notes and shares would be reduced by December 1, 1720, to half their numerical value, so that everyone could count on having lost half of his property and would have little faith in what remained. . . .

"There were, however, some clear-seeing persons who thought that that decree represented the only means of straightening out matters in general and putting business on a firm foundation; they believed that it was based on sound principles of credit and of trade."

B. By Steuart, an eighteenth-century English economist: [28]

". . . Had, indeed, the French nation perceived upon what bottom the security for the paper stood, during the year 1719, perhaps the credit of the bank might have been rendred precarious; but they neither saw it or sought after it: and the men of speculation were all of opinion, that as long as there was no more paper issued by the bank *than there was coin in the kingdom,* there could be no harm done. . . . I desire no farther proof of the total ignorance of the French in matters of this kind, than to find them agreeing, that bank paper is always good, providing there be coin in the nation to realize it, although that coin be not the property of the bank.

. . . .

"Law saw also, that credit supported itself on those occasions, where it stood on the most ticklish bottom: he saw bank notes to the amount of more than two thousand millions, issued in payment of the King's debts, without occasioning any run upon the bank, or without suggesting an idea to the public that the bank should naturally have some fund, to make them good: he saw people, who were in possession of a value in paper exceeding 6000 millions of livres, 60 to the marc, . . . look calm and unconcerned, when in one day, the coin was raised in its denomination to 80 livres in the marc; by which operation, the 6000 millions of the day before lost 25 *per cent.* of their real value. He saw that this operation did not in the least affect the credit of the bank paper; because people minded nothing but denominations.

"He saw further, that by the operation proposed, the whole debt of the King would be transferred upon the company. He saw that these debts, being turned into bank notes, would not be sufficient to buy above 200,000 actions, at the value they then sold for. He knew that the Regent, who had bought 400,000 of these actions at 5000 livres apiece, that is, at half price, would remain in possession of 200,000 actions, after selling enough to draw back the whole of the bank notes issued for the payment of the debts; and he saw that the company of the Indies had a yearly income of above 80 millions to enable them to make good their engagements: besides, he saw a power in the King to raise the denominations of the coin at will, without shocking the ideas of the people.

. . . .

"Until the bubble burst, no body *could* know where it was to end: every thing appeared very extraordinary indeed; and the fatal catastrophe might have been expected from the greatness of the undertaking, merely. But if there had been any roguery in the plan itself, it must have appeared palpable long be-

[28] Steuart, *op. cit.,* pp. 244–246, 262–264.

fore; because the whole of the operations in which only *it could* consult, were public.

. . . .

"My intention is . . . to prove, that an ill concerted system of credit may bring ruin upon a nation. . . ."

C. By the economist Levasseur: [29]

"In the midst of these vicissitudes, Law always remained the same in good as in bad fortune; inflexible theorist, he pursued with unshakable self-confidence the accomplishment of the work which he had envisaged: the creation of wealth by the abundance of cash and the transformation of the state into an immense society of credit and commerce. Up to the last moment, even in the decree of May 21 which marked the downfall of the System, he sought to regulate credit in the name of the state and to regulate, as he had always advised, the 'quantity of money in accordance with demand.'

"He acted with the precipitation and the violence of a man who, impregnated with his own ideas, walks straight to his goal, without being disturbed as to whether or not the crowd understands and follows, and who is irritated with the obstacles which nature imposes upon him and which he has not foreseen. He himself confessed his error: 'I do not pretend,' he says, 'that I have not made mistakes; I admit that I have made some, and that, if I had to begin all over again, I should act otherwise. I should proceed more slowly, but more surely, and I should not expose the state and my person to the dangers which must accompany the upset of a general system.' But, if he recognized his failure in the choice of methods, he persisted in believing that he had found the true secret of the wealth of nations, and he did not cease even to the end of his life to proclaim the power of credit. After the downfall of his System, he still could write these words from the depths of his exile: 'Do not forget that the introduction of credit has led to more changes among the powers of Europe than the discovery of the Indies, and that it is the part of the sovereign to give it and not to receive it, and that the people have such a great need for it that they come back to it in spite of themselves and in spite of their distrust of it.'

"We must do justice then to this man, such justice as he deserves. He was not, as is sometimes said, an adventurer come to France to profit from the weakness of the Regent. He was the first financier to give serious study to the phenomena and the causes of the production of wealth. If that political prudence which guides peoples was foreign to him, and if he deceived himself in his theories, at least he had clearly formulated principles, and he devoted his life not to the making of his fortune but to the assurance of the glory of his ideas. 'When I engaged in the service of the King,' he wrote to the Duke of Orléans, 'I had as much property as I desired; I owed nothing and I had credit; I leave the service of the King without property. Those who have had confidence in me have been forced to go into bankruptcy, and I have nothing to pay them.' He was right: France let him die poor; and, moreover, if the misfortunes caused by the ruin of his System had not been too recent to be seen in their true perspective, France would have been grateful for the generous ideas which he had given forth; he labored to extend trade, to reëstablish shipping, to found colonies; he suppressed burdensome taxes; he wished to abolish the venal magistracies, to create an administration of imposts less tyrannical and more simple; finally he set up a bank which, if it had outlived him, would have powerfully served trade and increased in a very real way the wealth of the country.

"If Law had understood that we exchange in trade only value for value and that gold itself is used as money only because it is merchandise, he would not have attempted to substitute for the metals paper which had no intrinsic value; if he had absorbed this truth, that credit has as its function simply to represent values which the debtor undertakes to pay, that in consequence it has natural limits and should be in proportion to the means of the borrower, he would not have abused with fatal imprudence the resources of this credit, and he would have founded a more lasting establishment.

"Still, he would have failed to gain the confidence of the public. Now, this confidence does not yield to chance. It is independent

[29] Levasseur, *op. cit.*, pp. 323–327.

and suspicious; when we do violence to it, it disappears at once; when we conceal from it the secret of our operations, it fears deception and it retires: in a credit institution, transactions should be independent and accounts publicly discussed. Law thought, on the contrary, that property could be prescribed and that an absolute government was more capable than any other of bringing it about because it was more powerful. Results have proved the reverse to be true. The excesses of the Regent, who according to Law, had the greatest interest in directing the Bank well, partly wrecked it; the debauchery of notes could not be stopped because there was no other body that could moderate the impulses of absolute power, and Parliament, which tried it, had neither the rights nor the power necessary for success; finally, as soon as the discredit had begun, the fears of the crowd, which did not know the true situation of affairs, exaggerated the evil. If Law had been less certain of the infallibility of his system, he would have sought to prevent those abuses which some of his contemporaries predicted. 'However good this establishment may be in itself,' said Saint-Simon, 'it could be good only in a republic, or in a monarchy such as England, the finances of which are governed absolutely only by those who provide them and provide them at their pleasure; but in a state, fickle, changing, more than despotic, such as France, solidity, and consequently confidence, was necessarily lacking.' "

10. Readings

The best account of John Law in English is A. M. Davis, "An Historical Study of Law's System," *Quarterly Journal of Economics,* vol. i (1887), pp. 289–318, 420–452.

Two recent articles by Earl J. Hamilton give significant new information on prices and business conditions in Paris and other leading French cities during the operation of Law's System and for some time after its fall: "Prices and Wages in Southern France under John Law's System," *Economic History,* vol. iii (1937), pp. 441–461; and "Prices and Wages at Paris under John Law's System," *Quarterly Journal of Economics,* vol. li (1936), pp. 42–70.

The most comprehensive collection of Law's works is Paul Harsin, *John Law, œuvres complètes* (Paris, 1934), vols. i–iii.

11. Suggested Questions

1. State briefly your understanding of Law's system or systems.
2. If there was a livre in coin for every livre in note issue, how do you explain the depreciation of the notes?
3. Compare events in France 1713–20 with those in America 1929–33. Consider particularly the decrees of March 5 and May 21, 1720.
4. What were Law's chief mistakes?
5. If you had been put into Law's place about May 1, 1720, and if you had been given full power, what measures would you have taken?
6. Compare the factors at work in the crisis of 1720 in Paris with those operating in 1929 in New York.
7. What lasting effect did Law's failure have upon France?
8. Did Law introduce financial capitalism, national capitalism, or something else?

XIX. WILLIAM DUER, CONTRACTOR AND SPECULATOR 1747–1799

1. General Statement

Born in England, educated at Eton, Duer first entered the army, then business. Apparently he turned some of his family's capital into the lumber business in New York State, to which he had migrated on receiving a contract to supply the British navy with spars. Then he took army contracts in the struggle against Britain, speculated in land after the Revolution, and finally pledged his career and fortune to speculation in securities.

Belonging to a family of social standing,

and being himself amiable, persuasive, ambitious, self-confident, and energetic, he became a great success in New York—until the moment of his undoing.

2. Outline of Duer's Life

1747	Born in England.
1764–68	Went to India as aide-de-camp to Governor-General Clive, but soon returned home because of fever. Inherited a moderate estate from his father and entered business. Went to New York with contracts to furnish lumber to British navy.
1768–75	In the lumber business up the Hudson, participating in local political affairs.
1775–83	On the Revolutionary side in the War, holding important offices. Contracted to furnish supplies to Colonial army and carried on other business. Apparently wealthy at end of War.
1782	Wife inherited considerable estate.
1784–92	Engaged heavily in speculation in United States securities.
1786–89	Secretary to the federal Board of Treasury.
1787–90	Interested in Scioto Land Scheme.
1788–90	Concerned in international banking schemes.
1789	Became assistant secretary of the Treasury, serving seven months.
1791–92	Organized and headed S. U. M. corporation.
1792	Failed in March during panic.
1792–99	In debtors' prison most of time till his death.

3. Duer, as Described by a Modern Investigator [1]

". . . Duer was a cautious man, whose right hand often was not suffered to know what his left hand did; he was careless of correspondence and memoranda, preferring face to face dealings and trusting much to his memory; and he saw to it that, so far as possible, papers containing 'incriminating' information regarding his connections and operations were destroyed.

. . . .

". . . His genial personality, his opulence and hospitality, his business aptitude, all won him friends. He was made a justice in the county courts (Charlotte County) and a colonel in the local militia.

. . . .

" 'In this august assembly [Continental Congress, 1777] he soon became distinguished for the ardor of his patriotism, and, although one of the youngest of its members, for the wisdom of his counsels. In eloquence he was unsurpassed.'

"Certainly he immediately made a large place for himself by his untiring energy and affability. Within two weeks he was appointed on no less than seven different committees, two of which were of importance.

. . . .

" 'Colonel Duer . . . lives in the style of a nobleman. I presume he had not less than fifteen different sorts of wine at dinner, and after the cloth was removed, besides most excellent bottled cider, porter, and several other kinds of strong beer.'

"He was also fond of quiet, friendly little parties at which business and pleasure could be smoothly combined. 'The most intimate friends of the family were Alexander Hamilton and Robert Troup,' but there was a large circle of others.

. . . .

" 'He is a gentleman of the most sprightly abilities, and has a soul filled with the warmest benevolence and generosity. He is made both for business and the enjoyment of life, his attachments strong and sincere, and diffuses happiness among his friends, while he enjoys a full share of it himself.'

. . . .

" 'I cannot finish this letter without speaking of another American, whose talents in fi-

[1] J. S. Davis, *Essays in the Earlier History of American Corporations* (Harvard University Press, Cambridge, 1917), vol. i, pp. 112, 114, 117, 126, 136, 158, 251, 262, 282, 334–338.

nance are well known here; it is Colonel Duer, secretary of the board of treasury. It is difficult to unite to a great facility in calculation, more extensive views and a quicker penetration into the most complicated projects. To these qualities he joins goodness of heart; and it is to his obliging character, and his zeal, that I owe much valuable information on the finances of this country, which I shall communicate hereafter.'

. . . .

"Especially considering Barlow's inexperience, Duer's neglect of him while abroad was inexcusable. This is traceable partly to Duer's native tendency to procrastinate, especially in letter writing; partly to the multitude of his interests; partly, perhaps, to a lack of sympathy between them which was suffered to grow. It bears testimony, however, to a fundamental weakness in Duer's make-up as a business man.

. . . .

"Many causes contributed to the failure of St. Clair's campaign [1792]. The troops were a heterogeneous and ill-disciplined lot; the officers were unacquainted with Indian warfare; the season was poorly chosen; the quartermaster-general was incompetent. But a heavy share of the responsibility belongs to Duer as contractor. Inept at long-range dealings in any case, it was impossible for him to devote due attention to this enterprise and at the same time to promote and float a large manufacturing company and to engage vigorously in stock speculations—to mention only his principal interests; and the army suffered.

. . . .

"The indications are that in the main the associates were bullish. Duer and Macomb were both of a sanguine temperament; Duer was a born bull leader. Moreover, he had successfully speculated on that side before. Stocks had risen so much, why should they not rise more?

. . . .

"Like other men of large calibre, however, Duer had both large talents and large deficiencies. He was first and foremost an initiator. He possessed in marked degree three essential talents of a promoter—ability to draft large and plausible schemes, ability to secure the adhesion of capitalists to these schemes, and ability to push and guide them through the troublous early stages. Witness the Scioto enterprise, the Brissot-Clavière association, the S. U. M., to mention only the clearest instances. Furthermore, he had a keen eye for a whole situation: he could always see the forest as well as the trees. At the same time he had a grasp of details, of distances and costs, of men, high and low, their strength and their weaknesses. He had a long-range vision. What is more, he had a dynamic conception of life, never assuming the *status quo* as normal, always counting upon change and development. Perhaps his dominant characteristic was a sanguine temperament. He might well have uttered the maxim attributed to the late J. Pierpont Morgan: 'Never be a bear on your country.' He had boundless energy. He had a fund of wholesome good nature and good fellowship, and he cultivated to a high degree the fine art of hospitality. Men liked him warmly, till they lost by him, and even then not all deserted him. In face to face intercourse he revealed a remarkable persuasive power. Men were carried away by his talk and would yield to him or give him support even if they did not altogether understand him. Doubtless his intimate knowledge of men enabled him to bring pressure to bear in appropriate fashion, but familiarity with the details of his career convinces one that his edifice was built up on voluntary and not on involuntary support. Moreover, he could and did invest heavily of his own funds in enterprises which he promoted, and he was not backward about making advances in their behalf. He knew how to keep matters to himself; even his intimates were not apprised of his ideas and interests and activities unless communication clearly suited his purpose.

"But while an effective promoter, Duer lacked essential characteristics of a successful entrepreneur. Good at planning, he was quite inferior in execution. He could start things, but he could not carry them through, especially if their accomplishment extended over large distances and a considerable period of time. In a significant sense one might say he had 'dash,' but not endurance. Excellent in close-range dealing, he was execrable in negotiations at long range. Perhaps in the twentieth century he might have fared better with the telephone, extra-fare express trains, and a corps of stenographers. As it was, correspondence annoyed him. His disinclination to commit too much to paper and his physical laziness about letter writing resulted in leaving his correspondents perplexed, uneasy, or exasperated, if not entirely in the dark; whereas his interviews usually left people clearheaded and enthusiastic, or at the worst vaguely satisfied. Furthermore, Duer had a most unfortunate tendency to undertake too many jobs at once. In view of the part which he proposed to play in his different enterprises, this may seem excusable, for none demanded more than a portion of his time. But when, as it often happened, the different enterprises required serious attention all at once, Duer was utterly unable to give the attention which they required. This was his principal difficulty in 1790–92. The successful man *par excellence* is he who recognizes not merely his powers and his opportunities, but as well the precise limitations of both. Duer did not know when to stop expanding.

. . . .

". . . Few speculators have had, in proportion to the materials available, a better command of information regarding the object of their speculation or the prospects of success. Moreover, he was never charged, as far as I can ascertain, with circulating false rumors. It is by no means clear that he directed fictitious sales of stocks, though it is not certain that this was contrary to his principles. It does appear probable that he attempted a corner in stocks. In the main, however, he was a typical bull operator in a boom period.

. . . .

". . . Certainly he was criminally careless about settling up his accounts with the government, and had it not been for his good fortune to be on excellent terms with such men as Hamilton, Wolcott, and Knox, his reputation might be still worse.

"In his business dealings with subordinates and other business men Duer was culpably lax and unduly disregarded their interests. He failed to write letters when the lack seriously hampered his agents not only in their relationship to him, but in their private capacities. . . .

". . . Taken as a whole, his course deserved neither success nor imitation. He was too much of a 'bull in a china shop' to be safely at large in the business community. Yet one cannot but regret that his unusual abilities were not linked with slightly more of caution and considerateness and infused with a keener moral sense, for all his abilities were greatly needed in the critical, dynamic period in which he lived."

4. Land Speculation

A. Explanation.

The Seven Years' War had ended in 1763. Britain had come out of it the possessor of both India and Canada. Now that the dangers of French aggression had been removed from the frontier, speculation in land became very common all along the western reaches of the American colonies. After Independence this greatly increased. The speculation which is of moment here had to do with a tract of over six million acres in and around Marietta and Cincinnati in Ohio.

In 1786 a group of New Englanders, of whom the Rev. Manasseh Cutler, General Putnam, General Parsons, and Major Sargent were the most prominent, organized the Ohio Company of Associates to purchase land. Many New Englanders, who expected to become colonists, actually subscribed. There were two difficulties, however, one to get an adequate grant from Congress, the other to raise the large sum necessary to pay for the lands.

In order to raise the necessary funds a second group, William Duer and associates of New York, was brought in, or was allowed to come in. A second company, the Scioto Co., was formed to provide about one-third of the money needed for the first payment. The 30 shares of this company were divided as follows: 13 went to William Duer, 13 to Cutler and Sargent, and 4 were for sale abroad. Both Duer, on the one hand, and Cutler and Sargent, on the other, proceeded to bring in others to whom were allocated parts of their shares. This group was almost wholly speculative. It cared little about actual settlement. Indeed it did not propose to go far in the direction of raising funds, though Duer himself made considerable contributions in order to get the enterprise started.

The Scioto Co. sent Joel Barlow to France and Holland to secure a loan on the Scioto option, or to dispose of it. The group at home did not care to develop the land and were interested in it only for purely speculative purposes. Feeling that he could dispose of the option or pay for the land in no other way, Barlow planned to sell to settlers. Encouraged by an Englishman named Playfair, and in league with a French lawyer called Soissons, he formed a third company, the Compagnie du Scioto, in July, 1789, into which were brought six Frenchmen, like the others rank speculators. Barlow contracted to hand over to this French company 3,000,000 acres of land at 6 livres per acre. Because of the fact that Congress had not actually given the title to the land companies, Barlow and associates were selling something they did not own. The French purchasers of shares thought they were buying a title, while in fact it was only an option. Nevertheless, the sale was made and settlers actually went out to the Ohio territory, with unfortunate results.

B. Duer's plan for obtaining the Scioto lands from Congress, 1787, as revealed in Manasseh Cutler's diary.[2]

"Friday, July 20. This morning the Secretary of Congress furnished me with the Ordinance of yesterday, which states the conditions of a contract, but on terms to which I shall by no means accede. Informed the Committee of Congress that I could not contract on the terms proposed; should prefer purchasing lands of some of the States, who would give incomparably better terms, and therefore proposed to leave the City immediately. They appeared to be very sorry no better terms were offered, and insisted on my not thinking of leaving Congress until another attempt was made. I told them I saw no prospect of a contract, and wished to spend no more time and money on a business so unpromising. They assured me I had many friends in Congress who would make every exertion in my favor; that it was an object of great magnitude, and (I) must not expect to accomplish it in less than two or three months. If I desired it, they would take the matter up that day on different ground, and did not doubt they should still obtain terms agreeably to my wishes. Colonel Duer came to me with proposals from a number of the principal characters in the city, to extend our contract, and take in another Company, but that it should be kept a profound secret. He explained the plan they had concerted, and offered me generous conditions, if I would accomplish the business for them. The plan struck me agreeably. Sargent insisted on my undertaking, and both urged me not to think of giving the matter up so soon. I was convinced it was best for me to hold up the idea of giving up a contract with Congress, and making a contract with some of the States, which I did in the strongest terms, and represented to the Committee, and to Duer and Sargent, the difficulties I saw in the way, and the improbability of closing a bargain when we were so far apart; and told them I conceived it not worth while to say anything further to Congress on the subject. This appeared to have the effect I wished. The Committee were mortified, and did not seem to know what to say, but still urged another attempt. I left them in this state, but afterward explained my views to Duer and Sargent, who fully approved my plan. Promised Duer to consider his proposals.

"We had agreed last evening to make a party to Brookline, on Long Island. . . . Duer, Webb, Hammond, Sargent, and others were of the party. . . . I spent the evening (closeted) with Colonel Duer, and agreed to purchase more land, if terms can be obtained, for another Company, which will probably forward the negotiations. Bill 4s. 6d.

"Saturday, July 21. Several members of

[2] W. P. and J. P. Cutler, *Life, Journals and Correspondence of Rev. Manasseh Cutler, LL.D.*, vol. i (Cincinnati, 1888), pp. 294–297.

Congress called on me early this morning. They discovered much anxiety about a contract, and assured me that Congress, on finding I was determined not to accept their terms, and had proposed leaving the City, had discovered a much more favorable disposition, and believed if I renewed my request I might obtain conditions as reasonable as I desired. I was very indifferent, and talked much of the advantages of a contract with some of the States. This I found had the desired effect. At length told them if Congress would accede to the terms I had proposed, I would extend the purchase to the tenth township from the Ohio and to the Scioto inclusively, by which Congress would pay near four millions of the national debt; that our intention was an actual, a large, and immediate settlement of the most robust and industrious people in America; and it would be made systematically, which must instantly enhance the value of federal lands, and prove an important acquisition to Congress. On those terms I would renew the negotiations, if Congress was disposed to take the matter up again.

. . . .

"Monday, July 23. My friends had made every exertion in private conversation to bring over my opposers in Congress. In order to get at some of them, so as to work powerfully on their minds, were obliged to engage three or four persons before we could get at them. In some instances we engaged one person, who engaged a second, and he a third, and so on to a fourth, before we could effect our purpose. In these maneuvers I am much beholden to the assistance of Colonel Duer and Major Sargent.

"The matter was taken up this morning in Congress, and warmly debated until 3 o'clock, when another ordinance was obtained." [3]

C. Ordinance for the sale of the Ohio and Scioto lands.[4] In Congress, July 23, 1787.

"That the Board of Treasury be authorized and empowered to contract with any person or persons for a grant of a tract of land. . . . The price to be not less than one dollar per acre for the contents of the said tract, excepting the reservations and gifts aforesaid, payable, in specie, loan-office certificates reduced to specie value, or certificates of liquidated debts of the United States, liable to a reduction by an allowance for bad land, and all incidental charges and circumstances whatever: *Provided,* That such allowance shall not exceed, in the whole, one-third of a dollar per acre. And in making payment the principal only of said certificates shall be admitted, and the Board of Treasury, for such interest as may be due on the certificates rendered in payment as aforesaid, prior to January 1, 1786, shall issue indents for interest to the possessors, which shall be receivable in payment as other indents for interest of the existing requisitions of Congress; and for such interest as may be due on the said certificates between that period and the period of payment, the said board shall issue indents, the payment of which to be provided for in future requisitions, or otherwise. Such of the purchasers as may possess rights for bounties of land to the late army, to be permitted to render the same in discharge of the contract, acre for acre: *Provided,* That the aggregate of such rights shall not exceed one-seventh part of the land to be paid for: *And provided also,* That there shall be no future claim against the United States on account of the said rights. Not less than 500,000 dollars of the purchase-money to be paid down upon closing of the contract, and the remainder upon the completion of the work to be performed by the geographer or other officer on the part of the United States. Good and sufficient security to be given by the purchaser or purchasers for the completion of the contract on his or their part. The grant to be made upon the full payment of the consideration money, and a right of entry and occupancy to be acquired immediately for so much of the tract as shall be agreed upon between the Board of Treasury and the purchasers.

"Ordered, That the above be referred to the Board of Treasury to take order."

[3] This ordinance was rejected but a more favorable one, passed on July 27th, was accepted by the Scioto Associates.

[4] *The Life and Public Services of Arthur St. Clair arranged and annotated by William Henry Smith* (Cincinnati, 1852), vol. ii, pp. 618–620.

D. Letter of Cutler and Sargent to the Board of Treasury, dated July 26, 1787.[5]

"We observe by the act of the 23d instant, that your honorable board is authorized to enter into a contract for the sale of a tract of land therein described, on certain conditions expressed in the act. As we suppose this measure has been adopted in consequence of proposals made by us in behalf of ourselves and associates, to a committee of Congress, we beg leave to inform you that we are ready to enter into a contract for the purchase of the lands described in the act, provided you can conceive yourselves authorized to admit of the following conditions, which, in some degree, vary from the report of the committee, viz:

"The subordinate surveys shall be completed as mentioned in the act, unless the frequency of Indian irruptions may render the same impracticable without a heavy expense to the company.

"The mode of payment we propose is, half a million of dollars when the contract is executed; another half a million, when the tract, as described, is surveyed by the proper officer of the United States; and the remainder in six equal payments computed from the date of the second payment.

"The lands assigned for the establishment of a university, to be as nearly as possible in the center of the first million and a half of acres we shall pay for; for to fix it in the center of the proposed purchase, might too long defer the establishment.

"When the second payment is made, the purchasers will receive a deed for as great a quantity of land as a million of dollars shall pay for, at the price agreed on; after which we will agree not to receive any further deeds for any of the lands purchased, only at such periods, and on such conditions, as may be agreed on betwixt the board and the purchasers.

"As to the security, which the act says shall be good and sufficient, we are unable to determine what those terms may mean, in the contemplation of Congress, or of your honorable board; we shall, therefore, only observe, that our private fortunes, and that of most of our associates, being embarked in the support of the purchase, it is not possible for us to offer any adequate security, but that of the land itself, as is usual in great land purchases.

"We will agree so to regulate the contract that we shall never be entitled to a right of entry or occupancy but on lands actually paid for, nor receive any deeds till our payments amount to a million of dollars, and then only in proportion to such payment. . . .

"If these terms are admitted, we shall be ready to conclude the contract."

E. Cutler to the agents of the Ohio Co., 1787.[6]

In this letter Cutler answers attacks made upon him by stockholders of the Ohio Co., who protested against his action in letting Duer and the rest of the Scioto group into their deal with Congress.

"Gentlemen:

. . . .

"After I had had many conferences with ye committee of Congress on terms of purchase to ye amount of 1,000,000 Dolrs (for I had, at that time, no tho't of contracting for more) they seemed to insist on 5. per Acre, tho' ye price was not so decidedly fixed as ye terms of payment—the terms which they positively fixed were, one half down, ye other as soon as the exterior line was run. So fixed were ye terms of payment that I was certain they would not receed [sic] from them. To raise 500,000 dollrs. instantly, circumstanced as our company then was, appeared to me absolutely impracticable. . . . I therefore proposed to give up ye idea of a purchase and to return home. This determination I mentioned to ye Comm & particularly to Judge Holton & Mr. Dane— Thus far I acted alone in the business.

"At this juncture, proposals were made to Majr. Sargent & myself for purchasing another tract of land, adjoining ye boundaries we proposed for ye Ohio Company, and an

[5] *Ibid.*, pp. 620–621. The contracts with the government were based upon this letter and the Congressional Ordinance of July 23, 1787. The Ohio Co., according to the survey, was to get 1,781,760 acres of land, and the Scioto Associates were to get 4,901,480 acres.

[6] A copy of this letter is in the Treasure Room of the Harvard College Library.

offer was made of 100,000 dolrs. to ye Ohio Company, if wanted, to complete their first payment, which sum was afterwards to be refunded. It appeared to us, likewise, probable that by connecting ye two purchases we might extend ye second payment until a line was run around ye whole, which would not only give us longer time to dispose of shares & collect ye money, but we would gain a large sum of indents of interest to ye funds of ye Ohio Company, on ye 2nd payment. These appeared to me important advantages to ye Company—neither could I suppose it would make any difference in ye view of Congress, whether one, two or three Companies were concerned in ye purchase yet it might make an essential difference to ye Ohio Company, in particular, if we, at that time, kept ye separate purchases out of sight; which we did until we went to N. York, to complete ye contract—then we informed the Board of Treasury that ye purchase was made for two Companies, and desired two distinct contracts—to which they consented without making ye least objection.

. . . .

"Accordingly, application was again made to ye Commtt.—they consented to reduce ye price to 4 pr acre—that 500,000 dolrs. should be paid down upon closing ye contract—& ye remainder on the survey of ye exterior line of ye whole tract being completed. These were ye best terms they would admit—& tho' we did not acceed to them, they tho't proper to report them to Congress, & an ordinance passed ye 23rd of July, authorizing ye Board of Treasury to contract with any *person or persons* on those terms. This Resolve was sent to us, enclosed in a letter from ye Board of Treasury, requesting us to inform them whether we were disposed to contract on those terms, or not. After consulting ye agent for ye other Company, we stated to ye Board . . . . in answer to their letter, the terms, on which we were willing to contract. Our letter was sent by ye Board to Congress, who approved the terms, excepting that interest should be paid on the installments, in which the other lands were to be paid for . . . . the Ohio Company's lands are perfectly designated, & unconnected with ye other tract—for we are to receive a deed for ye whole of those lands as soon as the second payment is made.

"We then entered into a formal contract with William Duer and his associates for ye lands we had agreed for, over & above ye Ohio Company's purchase, with this reservation that those persons who had at that time, taken an active part in forming, & carrying into execution ye designs of ye Ohio Company, should have ye liberty, if they pleased, to be concerned with ye said William Duer & his associates, in a part of those lands, on their giving bonds to pay such proportion of expenses & losses as might arise in ye prosecution of their plan. And in ye same contract, ye said William Duer obligated himself to pay to the Ohio Company one hundred thousand dollars in the following words—'And whereas ye purchase of ye above described lands, depends on ye punctual payment, on ye part of ye Ohio Company, of ye one moiety of ye purchase money of the part contracted for in their behalf, it is hereby agreed that ye said William Duer shall (if it be found necessary) advance on account of their said contract, 100,000 dolrs. provided that whatsoever sum, so paid, be reimbursed to ye said Wm. Duer out of ye monies, which ye said Sargent & Cutler may afterwards receive for subscriptions.' "[7]

F. Letter of Joel Barlow to Colonel William Duer.[8]

"Paris, November 29, 1789.

"My Dear Sir:—

"I have now the pleasure to inform you that the contract was completed on the 3d of this month. It is for the sale of three millions of acres—the price six livres the acre, to be paid either in cash or in American funds at ninety per cent., at the choice of the purchasers. It is probable that the greater part will be paid in the American French debt . . . some, however, will be paid in our domestic debt, and some in money. . . . The object of the company . . . is an immediate settlement, by the sale of portions to individuals and by sending cultivators in the service of the com-

[7] Actually $143,278.43 was supplied by Duer and his associates.

[8] This letter, as given here, was printed in Theodore Thomas Belote, *The Scioto Speculation and the French Settlement at Gallipolis* (Cincinnati, 1907), pp. 75–76.

pany. This they expect will raise the reputation of the lands to such a degree that they will sell them all off in the course of one year at a great profit. . . . The present circumstances of the kingdom are favorable, the object is popular, many portions are already sold, and the people preparing to embark in January. As I mentioned to you before, Major General Duportaile and Major Rochefontaine give me reason to hope they will go at the head of the establishment. Now, although my contract, in the letter of it, does not depend on the success of this or any other enterprise, yet in such great affairs no remedy can be had for any breach that a company may make either from choice or necessity. The only assurance against a violation of their engagements is never to suffer them to conceive it for their interest to violate them. For this purpose the utmost prudence and energy are necessary on both sides of the water; the manager here and the agents going with the people, will be perfectly in our interest. I have written to the gentlemen at Muskingum pointing out their duty in the strongest terms possible, which I wish you would enforce by your authority without delay, by writing them your reflections on the subject. I have advised them without delay, 1st, to ascertain the boundary between the 17th and 18th ranges of townships, at least the southern part of it—as these people will be there by the last of February—to begin their operations opposite the Great Kanawha on the 18th range—2d, to built them there a few huts and ovens, at least for the accommodation of one hundred persons,—3d, to send a person of activity from their settlement to Alexandria to make all the preparations on the route and at the fort for their reception and journey to the Scioto, and to wait at Alexandria to conduct them. For it can not be too much insisted on that the success of their sale of acres here, consequently their payment to us, will depend almost entirely on the accounts written back by the first people that arrive. It is an immense undertaking to the poor creatures who adventure in it . . . they . . . trust their lives and fortunes to the representations that I make to them. The confidence is slight; it will be strengthened or destroyed in the minds of those who are still to be engaged, by testimony of those who first arrive. If the first one hundred persons find things easy and agreeable as it is within our power to make them with a little attention, the stream of emigration will be irresistible. Twenty thousand people will be on those lands in eighteen months and our payments will be made in twelve. Do, my friend, exercise your rapid imagination for a moment in writing to those gentlemen—the subject lies with weight on my mind; it is, though small, one of the most essential services that now remain to be done. Whenever you shall know the complication of difficulties I have struggled with in bringing this unwieldy business thus far, you will excuse the warmth of my entreaties and believe that they are founded on the maturest reflection, as well as on the most ardent desire to serve the interests of the concern.

"The object which I recommended to you in my last is likewise in my opinion indispensable. I enclose here a duplicate of that part of my letter, lest you may not have received it. It is the only possible means of bringing a mere pre-emption into that shape in which it could be fairly offered for certain sale. It is absolutely necessary to us, it is the only reliance that the first purchasers of portions can have for their titles. The Secretary of Finance will certainly see the interests of the United States in making that arrangement, as it is their object to sink their debt by the sale of lands, as they are perfectly secure in this case as in the other, as it gives us the means of succeeding in the whole operation, and as the success of this will be followed by other sales to the extinguishment of a great part of the debt. I must add, as a further reason why you should not fail of making arrangements as recommended, that I have proceeded, as tho it were already done, by giving the company here power to resell portions before they make first payment on the contract, requiring as my security the deposits of the payments for those portions. This they have already acted on to a considerable amount. It is further to be considered that it is possible that their first payment will not be made to us in season for us to make ours to Congress before the people will arrive; should the people not be put in possession of their small purchases on their arrival, we are ruined. It will be but a few acres, I imagine not above five thousand, that those who shall arrive by the first ship shall have purchased. The secretary can run no risk by allowing them to take possession of so small a portion before it is paid for, as he can not suppose we would sacrifice the advantage of all our contract for the sake of cheating Congress out of so small a sum. But if no other means will do, you must make a deposit of five or ten thousand dollars to get possession of such a number of acres opposite the mouth of the Great Kanawha to be afterwards recovered towards our contract. Dispatch such leave of entry to your friends in the West, but do not let the European settlers know the manner of this proceeding . . . but that the lands were all our own before. I hope you will be of my opinion on these subjects, and that nothing will prevent the people being put perfectly at ease on their arrival. . . . I can think of no argument in addition to those I have formerly used to induce you to write to me; my reflections on that subject are painful beyond description. . . . I am, dear sir, with sincere regards,

"Your obedient servant,

"J. Barlow."

G. Letter of Joel Barlow to Colonel William Duer.[9]

"Paris, 25th Jan'y, 1790.

"My Dear Sir,

"Enclosed is a duplicate of my last, in addition to which, order the Treasurer to draw on me for one hundred thousand livres—the affair goes extremely well; it is true the payments are not made, but they certainly will be. The sales increase rapidly.

"Don't for God's sake fail to raise money enough to put the people in possession—make any sacrifice rather than fail in this essential object. If it fails we are ruined. All our fortunes and my character will be buried in the ruins. I know I have run a risk in suffering the people to go till I could get possession, especially as I could get no information from you, but the risk was absolutely necessary, and the proposition to the Secretary of Finance which I have often mentioned is so reasonable that it can not be rejected. Tell him that twenty millions of acres may be sold here in two years after it is known that these people are quietly in possession of their lands. You can certainly among all your Connexions raise one or two hundred thousand dollars for a few months. I pledge the faith of an honest Man for the payment. If necessary draw on me at Ninety days for a second hundred thousand livres—advise me of it at the earliest possible. I shall be more particular in a few days."

H. Petition of French emigrants to the agents of the Ohio Co., December, 1795.[10]

"The French inhabitants of Gallipolis by their Agents Matthew Berthelot, Peter Bureau, and R. J. Meigs, take liberty to lay before them the following Memorial:

"In the Year 1789 appeared at Paris Joel Barlow Esq., agent of a Company by the name of the Scioto Company, & by his Sub-agents Messrs. Playfair & De Soisson, offered for Sale large quantities of Land, lying in the Western Territories, a plan of which Lands were exhibited for the Information of those who wish to become purchasers, which included the Lands, opposite & below the Great Kanawha (in the Ohio Company's Purchase) in which general Plan was included that of a City to be situated opposite the Mouth of the Great Kanawha, a considerable quantity of those Lands were purchased by us—also a number of City Lots, to be chosen by us, out of the City Lots so designated by the said Plan. Possession of all of which were to be delivered immediate upon our Arrival.

"Upon our arrival from France to Alexandria, we finding no agent, or arrangements made by Mr. Duer, the Superintendent of the Scioto Company (as had been promised) for transporting across the Mountains, we sent to Col. Duer, who sent Col. Franks as his agent to negotiate with us, relative to the expenses of our delay at Alexandria & other matters incident to our Situation.

"Colonel Franks, & other agents of Mr. Duer then engaged, as a Compensation for our expenses incurred at Alexandria, that the Scioto Comp'y should grant to each of the

[9] *Ibid.*, p. 78.

[10] *Ibid.*, pp. 70–73.

purchasers among us one City Lot and one four-acre Lot adjacent to the said City.

"In the meantime the Scioto Comp'y finding the Lands they had sold us in France belonged to the Ohio Company, negotiated a Contract with the Ohio Company by Messrs. Duer, Flint & Craigie of the part & Messrs. Putnam & Cutler Directors of the Ohio Company on the other four parts of those Lands they had sold in France, in order to fulfill their Engagements with the purchasers, & a right of Entry was given by Messrs. Putnam and Cutler. In Consequence of the said Contract, & such right of Entry, the Scioto Co. proceeded to lay out the Town of Gallipolis for the fulfillment of their Contracts with us, who after long & expensive journeys, arrived at Gallipolis.

"Major Guion, Agent for the Scioto Company at Gallipolis, proceeded to designate by the Choice of the Purchasers to them the Lots sold in France, next by the drought the City Lots & four acre Lots engaged at Alexandria, as aforesaid, & lastly to sell in behalf of the Scioto Company other City & four-acre Lots for which he received in many Instances immediate payment.

"In this situation, under these Circumstances & Assurances, we have proceeded to clear, occupy & build, indiscriminately upon the City and four-acre Lots, not in the least doubting but that we should receive from the Scioto Company Sufficient Titles to the Lots so assigned. But our Expectations are disappointed by the failure of Mr. Duer, & the Lands we are upon belonging to the Ohio Comp'y.

. . . .

"(Confiding in the Scioto Comp'y we have paid for the Lands we occupy, our resources have been exhausted by long Voyages and Journeys & by Improvements upon those Lands which we now find not our own, & being satisfied the Ohio Comp'y would not wish to reap from us the fruits of our labours, & gain an acquisition by our Loss, we request the Ohio Comp'y to grant to us so much of the Land relinquished to the Ohio Comp'y by Mr. Craigie, as shall include the Town of Gallipolis & the four-acre Lots adjacent thereto, if the residue of the Lands relinquished by Mr. Craigie will defray the expenses which the Ohio Comp'y incurred relative to that Negotiation between the Ohio Comp'y and the Scioto Comp'y.)

"(These Circumstances we wish the agents of the Ohio [11] Comp'y to take into consideration & grant our request.)

"P. Bureau,

"R. J. Meigs, Jun.

"Marietta, Decr. 17, 1795."

5. Purchase of the American Debt to France, 1788–90

A. When America gained independence the government was heavily in debt to its own citizens, to the French government, and to Dutch bankers. When in 1788 and 1789 it seemed that this debt would be paid with interest, speculators both in America and in Europe began to consider the possibility of gain through the purchase of government securities. One of the most promising plans was the formation of a group of American and French speculators for the purchase of American securities, especially the debt of Congress to the French government.

B. A contract was entered into in October, 1788, between J. Peter Brissot de Warville for himself and Stephen Clavière of the Kingdom of France and William Duer and Andrew Craigie of the State of New York.[12] It was agreed to use whatever influence was necessary on the Court of France and the Congress of America in regard to the United States debt, to carry on trade in America and especially in government securities, and to perform whatever domestic or international banking operations that would involve.

C. King's memorandum on an international banking organization.[13]

[11] The paragraphs in parentheses were erased in the original document by the mutual consent of both parties, and the French instead requested that they be allowed to buy the land in question.

[12] Complete text will be found in Davis, *op. cit.*, pp. 159–161.

[13] These statements were taken from Charles R. King, editor, *Rufus King's Life and Correspondence*, vol. i (New York, 1894), pp. 623–624.

"New York, 21 December, 1788.

"Some days since Col. Duer mentioned to me that his situation required that he shd. pay some attention to his pecuniary Concerns, and to the establishment of some permanent provision for the Decline of Life and the support of his Family. He remarked that M. de Warville, who lately returned to France, came to this country with a view of looking into its Debt & Resources, to be able to give good information to such European capitalists as may be disposed to speculate in the American funds. That M. de Warville, who was a Geneva Banker, had devised a plan of purchasing the Debt due from the U. S. to France; that Capitalists of France would embark in the Purchase; that they proposed the association of Americans to the amount of a moiety of the purchase; that he had been consulted on the Subject and the plan had been submitted to him, and (he) proposed to me a concern in the project—my answer was ambiguous and indefinite.

"Yesterday Col. Duer renewed the conversation and told me that he had conferred with Wadsworth, Genel. Knox & Mr. Osgood on the Subject—and that he had informed them that Rob. & Gov. Morris had in view something of the same nature with Clavière's plan; that they had proposed to unite with him (Duer), and that Gov. Morris was going to Europe, with this among other views. That he had in some sort assented to the Morris proposals, and given letters to Govr. to the associates of Clavière, having previously shewn them to Warville. That the design of Govr. was that Duer, R. Mor. & Govr. Morris shd. be the principal Americans, that Constable & Duer's friend (Osgood) shd. be admitted and such other shares as shd. become absolutely indispensable shd. be taken into the Association; and that beyond these shares or *Portions* (which Govr. seems to have in view to limit) the surplus gains shall be equally divided between Duer, R. M. & Gouvr. Morris.—That the operation or effect of the letters given to Govr Morris wd go no farther than to admit him & R M as individual associates, on a common footing.—That the intention of Clavière & Warville was to make a conditional convention for the Transfer of the Debt due to France, the convention to become valid when ratified by Congress. But shd. this fail, the Idea of the Morrises and of Clavière and others is that the measure might be accomplished by the Influence of an American Minister in Holland.—R. Morris & the few friends of Govr. Morris would push his appointment.—Duer conceived that Mrs. Knox had been assailed on the subject, that Knox might be influenced in its favor, &c., said that he had therefore in company with Wadsworth freely conversed with Genl. Knox concerning the whole project—and that Knox & Wadsworth had requested him to apply to me and to know whether I would accept a public appointment to Holland;—that he had fully conversed with Osgood on the subject, and that Knox, W. & Osgood concurred in the entire propriety of my appointment. I told Col. Duer that I was not indisposed to a foreign appointment—and that the honor & Duties of such an office wd. be my Sovereign rule of Cond., & that, if in perfect consistence with the Duties & Dignity of the Office I cd. promote the interest of my Friends, it would be a great satisfaction to me. But that I desired not to be considered as giving an answer any way at present, that although Knox might prefer me to Govr. Morris, yet the opinions of Mr. Jay & Col. Hamilton were of consequence in my mind; that previous to any Decision on my part I must be ascertained of their opinions.

"Duer observed that there were some reasons why I should make an early Determination, such as the undecided state of Genl. Knox's mind and the probability of a direct application for his Influence from Robert Morris."

D. Final failure.[14]

"The Duer-Craigie-Parker-Brissot-Clavière undertaking is probably best interpreted as an effort to establish an international banking house, modelled upon those of the great Amsterdam firms, which should supplant them in the negotiation of American loans and rival them in commercial negotiations and in speculations in lands and securities. With their larger capital, their established prestige, their well-knit organization, the Dutch proved more than a match for the newcomers—scattered in distance, busy with various other

[14] Davis, *op. cit.*, p. 173.

interests, loosely organized, distrusting one another—and the new enterprise 'died aborning.' "

6. The First New Jersey Business Corporation, 1791

A. The idea of a Society for Establishing Useful Manufactures was developed in the Treasury Department by Hamilton and Coxe, but Duer was the principal organizer of the Society. He not only secured subscribers for much of its stock, but lobbied to obtain its incorporation by the New Jersey legislature. He was the first governor of the company and continued in office until his failure in 1792.

Because the manufactures of the company were to compete with those of European countries, and because the capital stock was so great, the scheme was felt to be a particularly new and venturesome one. A cotton mill and a canal which were eventually built by the company proved very unsuccessful. The company gave up its manufacturing operations, but its water-power rights and real-estate holdings brought the stockholders a very profitable return after about 1825, when the town of Paterson had developed. The corporation apparently still gets a return from various water rights which have been leased to other companies.

B. Selections from an act to incorporate the contributors to the Society for Establishing Useful Manufactures, and for the further encouragement of the said society, 1791.[15]

"Sect. 1. Be it Enacted by the Council and General Assembly of this State, and it is hereby Enacted by the Authority of the same, That all those Persons who have already subscribed, and who, according to the Terms hereafter mentioned, shall subscribe for the purpose of establishing a Company for carrying on the Business of Manufactures in this State, their Successors and Assigns, shall be and they are hereby incorporated by the Name of the 'The Society for establishing useful Manufactures,' and by the same Name, they and their Successors and Assigns are hereby constituted a Body Politic and Corporate in Law, and shall be able and capable to acquire, purchase, receive, have, hold and enjoy any Lands, Tenements, Hereditaments, Goods and Chattels, of what Kind or Quality soever, to an Amount in Value not exceeding Four Millions of Dollars. . . .

"Sect. 2. And be it Enacted by the Authority aforesaid, That the original or capital Stock of the Said Society or Company, shall not exceed the Sum of One Million of Dollars, to be employed in manufacturing or making all such Commodities or Articles as shall not be prohibited by Law, and to that End purchasing such Lands, Tenements, and Hereditaments, and erecting thereupon the Buildings, and digging and establishing such Canals, and doing such other Matters and Things as shall be needful for carrying on a Manufactory or Manufactories of the said Commodities or Articles.

"Sect. 3. And be it further Enacted by the Authority aforesaid, That the said Corporation shall not deal, nor trade, except in such Articles as itself shall manufacture, and the Materials thereof, and in such Articles as may be really and truly received in Payment or Exchange therefor.

"Sect. 4. And, the more effectually to encourage so useful and beneficial an Establishment; Be it further Enacted by the Authority aforesaid, That all the Lands, Tenements, Hereditaments, Goods and Chattels to the said Society, belonging, shall be and they are hereby declared to be free and exempt from all Taxes . . . . for the Term of ten years only, after which Term it shall be lawful to lay such Taxes for the Use of the State. . . .

. . . .

"Sect. 6. And be it further Enacted by the Authority aforesaid, That the Original or Capital Stock aforesaid, shall consist of One Hundred Thousand Shares, each Share being One Hundred Dollars; and that any Person, Copartnership or Body Politic, may subscribe for such Number of Shares in the Stock of the said Company which yet remain to be subscribed, as he, the [she] or

[15] *Acts of the General Assembly of the State of New Jersey,* 16th Assembly, 1st Sitting (1791), pp. 730–746.

they, shall think fit, until the whole Number of Shares subscribed shall amount to Five Hundred Thousand Dollars, after which it shall be in the Discretion of the Directors to permit or not, further Subscriptions from Time to Time, and in such proportions as shall seem to them expedient, not exceeding on the Whole the said Sum of One Million Dollars . . . all which Subscriptions, made prior to the said first Election of Directors, shall be payable, One Half in the funded Six per Cent. Stock of the United States, or in Three per Cent. Stock at the Rate of Two Dollars of such Stock for one, and the other Half in what is commonly called Deferred Stock, or, at the Option of the Party subscribing, such Subscriptions may be paid for in Specie, Computing the said Six per Cent. Stock at Par, and the said Deferred Stock according to the present value thereof at the Time of Payment, which Value shall be determined by a Calculation founded upon a Rate of Interest of Six per Centum per Annum, during the Period for which the Interest of the said Deferred Stock is suspended; and the Payments for such Subscriptions as shall be made prior to the first Election of Directors shall be made in four equal Parts, that is to say, the first within Forty-five Days after the Period of such first Election, the second within Six Calendar Months after the Time of the first, the third within Six Calendar Months after the Time of the second, and the fourth within Six Calendar Months after the Time of the third Payments. . . .

"Sect. 7. And be it further Enacted by the Authority aforesaid, That so much of the Capital Stock of the said Company as may consist of Public Debt, shall be placed on the Books of the Treasury of the United States in the Name of the said Corporation, except so much thereof as may be converted into Stock of the Bank of the United States; and that it shall be lawful for the Directors thereof to invest any Monies which may be received on Account of the said Capital Stock in the Purchase of such Debt, and likewise to invest both the said Debt and Monies, in Stock of the Bank of the United States in the Name of the said Corporation; and that in either Case the said Directors, on the Request of any Stockholders, shall grant to him a License to inspect and examine the Amount of Stock which may at any Time stand in the Name of the said Corporation, either on the Books of the Treasury of the United States, or on the Books of the Bank of the United States. . . .

. . . .

"Sect. 11. And be it further Enacted by the Authority aforesaid, That at every such Election Thirteen Directors shall be chosen by Ballot, and the Directors so chosen shall at the first meeting after their Election, not less than a Majority of the whole Number being present, elect from among themselves one Person to be Governor, and another to be Deputy Governor. . . .

[Selections on organization and powers of directors follow.]

. . . .

"Sect. 17. And WHEREAS it may be necessary, for the beneficial Extension of the aforesaid Plan, to cut Canals, and clear and improve the Channels of Rivers. . . . Be it Enacted, That . . . it shall be lawful for them, their Engineers, Artists and Labourers, to enter upon all such Land, and Land covered with Water, as shall be necessary for effecting such navigable Canal or Canals or for opening or clearing such River or Rivers, and to contract and agree with the owners of any Lands and Tenements for the Purchase of so much thereof as shall be necessary for the purpose of making, digging, and perfecting such Canal or Canals, or opening and clearing such River or Rivers. . . .

. . . .

"Sect. 20. And it be further Enacted by the Authority aforesaid, That it shall and may be lawful to . . . demand and receive of or from the Persons having the Charge of all Boats and Vessels, and Rafts of Timber, Boards, Plank or Scantling, passing through such Canal and the part of such River rendered navigable, and the Locks thereto belonging, such Tolls and Rates as . . . shall not exceed Fifteen per Centum on the Sums expended in making and establishing such Canal, or in opening and clearing such River, over and above the Expenses of maintaining and repairing the same, together with the necessary Works, and of collecting the said Tolls and Rates. . . .

. . . .

"Sect. 25. And Whereas the first Attempts towards the Establishment of Manufactories by the said Society may be attended with Loss, so as to impair and diminish the Capital thereof. . . . Be it Enacted by the Authority aforesaid, That the Society be, and are hereby authorized and empowered by one or more Lotteries, to be drawn within this State, according to such Scheme or Schemes, and upon such Terms, as the Directors of the said Society shall Institute, Publish, and Declare, and under the Management of such Persons as the said Directors shall for that purpose appoint, to raise, for the Benefit of the said Society, a Sum or Sums not exceeding in the Whole, One Hundred Thousand Dollars over and above such Charges and Expenses as shall have been incurred in and about the Management and Drawing of the said Lottery or Lotteries.

. . . .

"Sect. 37. And be it further Enacted by the Authority aforesaid, That this Act shall in all Things be construed in the most favorable Manner for the said Respective Corporations; nor shall any Nonuser of the Privileges hereby to the said Corporations respectively granted, create any Forfeiture of the same, and notwithstanding the Members of the said respective Corporations should fail to meet, and hold their Elections as is hereby specified, the said Elections may be afterwards holden, and made in such Manner as shall have been prescribed by the Laws and Ordinances of the said respective Corporations, and the Officers for the Time being shall continue to hold and exercise their office until others shall be duly elected to Succeed them at some subsequent Meeting."

C. An advertisement of the Society for Useful Manufactures.[16]

"The Legislature of the State of New-Jersey, having by their act of the 22d of November last, incorporated with the consent of its inhabitants, a district, not exceeding in contents, the number of acres contained in six miles square, for the purpose of establishing within the same, the principle seat of the Society for useful Manufactures; and the said Society being desirous to afford to every part of the State, which may possess the most important requisites, an opportunity of supporting their pretensions; GIVE NOTICE, that they will receive proposals, in writing, from any bodies corporate, township or individuals, in the State of New-Jersey, who may be desirous of securing the emoluments, which will result from this establishment. In these proposals, the applicants must specify particularly, the following points, viz:

"The advantage of water, for the purpose of erecting mills and other hydraulic machines, necessary for the establishment of a cotton manufactory on an extensive scale. The statement ought to be accompanied, if possible, with an actual survey, shewing the course of the waters, the different levels, and the nature and position of the adjoining lands:—the advantages of fuel, not only for *present* but for *future* use; in this statement it may be proper to detail, as accurately as possible, the quantity and price of wood, coal or turf, within the proposed district, and the resources which may be calculated on for the continuance of a very extensive supply for a series of years—the advantages of subsistance. This statement ought to shew the average price of wheat, corn, rye, beef, mutton, pork and other principal articles of provisions, and the means to be relied on in future, for a constant supply on reasonable terms to a populous town.

"The advantages of population; this statement ought to detail with accuracy, not only the number of inhabitants within the proposed district but of the country surrounding for the space at least of thirty miles.

"The advantages of building materials, detailing the present price of Oak and Pine timber, boards, plank, shingles, brick, stone, lime &c. and the resources which may be relied on for a series of years, for a plentiful supply of those articles, at reasonable rates.

"The advantages of intercourse with the principle commercial towns. In this statement must be shewn, the distance of the

[16] Davis, *op. cit.*, pp. 403–404, quoted from a New Jersey gazette.

proposed district, to the following places; the city of New-York—the city of Philadelphia—the city of New-Brunswick—the city of Amboy—the city of Burlington—Trenton—Elizabeth-Town—Newark—together with the price of transportation, by land and by water, to the respective places above mentioned.

"The advantages to be held up to the Society for employing within the proposed district, an active capital of ONE MILLION OF DOLLARS. In this statement the applicants must specify in particular, what quantity of land, or, land covered with water, they will be willing to give or sell to the company and on what conditions as to price and time of payment; with such other circumstances as may induce a preference to their respective proposals.

"The Society having fixed on the 17th of January next, to meet at the city of New-Brunswick, in order to determine finally on the principle seat of their Manufactories; all proposals must either be delivered to the board of Directors on that day, or previous thereto, be forwarded under an address to the subscriber in the city of Philadelphia, or to Archibald Mercer, Esq. Deputy Governor of the Society, at Millstone, in the State of New-Jersey. In case of conveyance by post, the postage must be paid. *By order of the Society for establishing useful Manufactories,*

"WILLIAM DUER, Governor.
"New-Brunswick, December 12, 1791."

7. Speculation in Securities and Panic of 1792

A. Speculation in government securities had begun to take place during the Revolutionary War, when certain moneyed men gathered up a large amount of State and Continental interest-bearing certificates of indebtedness, which were then worth very little. The prices of these securities went up quite rapidly between 1789 and 1791, as the Constitution was accepted, as the new government became stabilized, and as Hamilton's refunding plans progressed. Bank funds also rose rapidly in the general speculative movement, as did also the stock of the S. U. M. Corporation after it had been put on the market. At this time the New York Stock Exchange had its beginnings, and stockbrokers flourished. Newspaper quotations of stock began to appear, and stock gambling was rampant. In August, 1791, prices took a sudden drop, but by December they were higher than ever. In January and February speculation reached its peak, and during the middle of March the first panic in the United States was precipitated.

B. Duer and Macomb.

Duer formed a partnership with Alexander Macomb for speculation during the year 1792 in the debt of the United States and the stock of the Bank of New York. Macomb had accumulated considerable capital in the fur trade and the mercantile business, but he was less experienced than Duer in security dealings. Others of Duer's coterie also joined the speculation. Rumor had it that Duer sought to corner at least the United States six per cents.

Concerning the financing of the Duer-Macomb speculation, Davis has the following to say: [17]

"In this speculative firm Duer was the advising partner, and the principal financial member as well. He turned in not only his own available wealth, including what he had left of the sums received from the Treasury on account of his recent army contracts, but all that he could lay his hands on besides. The New Jersey country seat of the late 'Earl of Stirling,' his father-in-law, was sold at auction at the Coffee House February 7. Despite his later protestations, there is little doubt that he loaned from his right hand to his left the bulk of the $10,000 entrusted to him by the manufacturing society for procuring print cloths and workmen from abroad. Some $50,000, practically the entire cash surplus of the society, with the investment of which Macomb was charged, was borrowed at seven per cent, on deferred stock as collateral. Through Walter Livingston, a wealthy up-state member of the well-known Livingston clan and formerly a member of

[17] Davis, *op. cit.*, pp. 284–286; footnotes are omitted.

the Board of Treasury, the partners sought to obtain the surplus funds of the state of New York on much the same terms. Probably in the same way they 'borrowed the Funds of a Lottery to build a bridge over the Raritan in New Jersey and seventy or eighty pounds of money raised by a charity sermon.' Funds were doubtless secured also from the bank on collateral. Duer further borrowed heavily without collateral, either by giving his own notes supported by endorsements from friends like Macomb, Walter Livingston, Richard Platt, John Pintard, George Knox, Isaac Whippo, and one Bush, or by endorsing notes which he got such men to sign. The support of Macomb and Livingston in particular was of the greatest value, for both were reputed wealthy. After exhausting his credit with business associates and friends, Duer went farther afield. His personal notes, bearing very high rates of interest, were offered to the smallest savers. 'Allurements were held out to lenders of too tempting a nature for most persons to withstand,' wrote Watson to Wadsworth March 14. 'Usurious interest became frequent & almost fashionable—Multitudes came to Pintard's office where any sums not less than five hundred dollars were taken at all times from two to four P Cent pr Month.' 'Persons of all descriptions,' 'merchants, tradesmen, draymen, widows, orphans, oystermen, market-women, churches, etc.,' 'Besides a host of Usurers never before discovered,' were interested. It was stated in April that 'Duer's Notes for Certificates amounted to Thirty millions of dollars,' and while this was certainly an exaggeration, even his friends admitted that they were 'a surprising amount.'

"Macomb coöperated in this financing, especially as it concerned the manufacturing society, and he seems to have staked his own wealth completely in the speculation. He loaned his credit to Duer, as well as used it directly by giving his own notes in payment for securities. In spite of this their relationship was kept, with remarkable effectiveness, a profound secret. Macomb, while doing rather less of the financing, was the figure chiefly in the limelight in making sales and purchases, for cash or more often for future delivery, using notes whose maturity by no means invariably coincided with the execution of the contract to deliver. Yet it is highly probable that on occasions other men were used to make purchases for the firm when that policy promised better. Duer kept himself, as usual, very much out of sight, of necessity seeing excitable Frenchmen or his agents on Scioto or army business, but preferring his own choices for conferences and quiet consultations with those whom he called. Both men, it seems clear, devoted themselves very largely during these two or three months to their common object, though in January and February they were occupied during several different days with directors' meetings or committee meetings on behalf of the manufacturing society."

C. Letter from New York describing the panic.[18]

"March 29, 1792

"We have the devil to pay! Col. Duer has failed for they say three millions of dollars, and has taken in almost every person in the city, from the richest merchants to even the poorest women, and the little shopkeepers, women and butchers. He is now in the new jail and they even talk of breaking it open to take him out and tear him piecemeal, and to hang every indorser of his notes if everything is not shortly settled. How it will end God only knows; it has put a stop to general business and money is so exceedingly scarce that his runners go about with his printed notes indorsed and signed, but no sum inserted, and if they could find a lender they would pay four per cent. a month, and put it in the note. Walter Livingston and Company have stopped payment, and many more must, as nobody will lend a shilling."

D. Extracts from *Dr. Rush's Commonplace Book*, 1792.[19]

"March 30, 1792

"The conversation during the month turned very much on the fall of the Funds from

[18] In Thomas Jones, *History of New York*, vol. ii (New York, 1879), p. 589.

[19] L. A. Biddle, editor, *A Memorial containing Travels through Life or Sundry Incidents in the Life of Dr. Benjamin Rush* (Philadelphia, 1905), pp. 134–136. Some of the statements in the selection are not true, but the complete picture of the panic gives a good contemporary view of the situation.

25% to 20% occasioned by the failure of William Duer of New York. This man, it was said, aimed at monopolizing all the 6% (amounting to $17,000,000) of the United States and selling them afterwards to foreigners for 27s. or 30s. in the pound. In this attempt he contracted immense debts to merchants, tradesmen, draymen, widows, orphans, oystermen, market-women, churches, etc. He failed, it was said for two millions and a half of dollars, and so angry were his creditors that he was obliged to shelter himself from them by flying to a gaol. He ruined several brokers and injured many trading people by his failure. His failure was ascribed to all the banks ceasing to discount and calling in their credits. By these events a great and universal demand was created for money and many persons in New York and Philadelphia gave from 2% to 8% for temporary loans of money, and some 1% per day to make good their engagements to the different banks. The spirit of speculation ran high during the whole of last winter, so as to destroy patriotism and friendship in many people. 'Is it true,' said a spectator to me, 'that the President of the United States intends to resign?' 'I do not know,' said I, 'but what makes you ask that question?' 'A true answer,' said he, 'would determine me to buy in or sell out of the Funds.' Two or three Expresses generally passed between New York and Philadelphia every twenty-four hours to convey the prices current of stock.

. . . .

"April 14

"Failures numerous in New York and Philadelphia. Mr. McComb a wreck in New York; once worth £100,000 sterling, failed this week. . . . Walt Livingston and many others followed him as bankrupts. Several happened this week in Philadelphia, as J. M. Taylor, Summers, etc. Duer's Notes for Certificates amounted to Thirty millions of dollars. It appears that he borrowed the Funds of a Lottery to build a bridge over the Raritan in New Jersey and seventy or eighty pounds of money raised by a charity sermon, both of which he had wasted. Thousands, it is said, will be injured and hundreds ruined by him. . . .

. . . .

"April 18

"Bankruptcies continue to increase in New York and Philadelphia. A gentleman just arrived from New York says that he scarcely entered a house in which he did not find the woman in tears and the husband wringing his hands. . . . The Bank of New York observed that few of their old notes came in to them, owing, it was thought, to their being secreted by the bankrupts. Many of the brokers who have failed had bespoke carriages and some of them four horses. As yet I have heard of not one instance of insanity and only one of suicide, and he was a Frenchman who had lost by Duer's failure. Real property, which had risen 300% in some parts of our City, especially Market and Chestnut Streets, into the last of which the brokers crowded, suddenly fell to its former value. Two houses above Third Street in Chestnut Street belonging to Sam Pleasants were sold for $10,000 to two brokers. It was currently said that $2000 had been offered to Mr. Pleasants to take them back again. Chestnut Street was now called 'Lame Duck Alley.'"

E. Causes of the panic of 1792. Hamilton to Short.[20]

"Treasury Department, April 16th, 1792
"Sir:

"The fluctuation of the price of the stocks in the United States, is a circumstance that cannot have failed to attract your attention, nor to excite a temporary feeling in the minds of foreigners. Though I doubt not it will be well explained by the agents of those citizens of other countries who have vested their moneys in our funds, I think it necessary that some ideas should be communicated to you, on which you can found a true opinion, either for your own satisfaction or that of persons interested in our national welfare, with whom you may have occasion to confer.

"The moderate size of the domestic debt of the United States appears to have created the most intemperate ideas of speculation in the minds of a very few persons, whose natural ardor has been increased by

[20] John C. Hamilton, editor, *The Works of Alexander Hamilton,* vol. iv (New York, 1851), pp. 217–219. Short was Minister to Holland at this time.

great success in some of the early stages of the melioration of the market value of the stock. To combinations of private capitals thus acquired or increased, sums of specie, obtained as well at the most extravagant rates of premium as at common interest, were added, and to these were joined purchases of stock on credits, for various terms, so as to create a delusive confidence that the concentration of so much stock in a few hands would create a very high market rate. This expectation was increased by comparing the market values of the several species of our funds with those of the same species of stock in Great Britain, the United Netherlands, and other parts of Europe, without due allowance for the deductions which should have been made on account of the great difference in the value of money, and the objections arising from our distance from those European money-holders whose capitals they expected to attract, and other relative circumstances. At the time when many heavy engagements thus formed were becoming due, some contentions among the dealers in, and proprietors of, the debt, took place, and counter-combinations were formed to render the crisis of payment and speculation as inconvenient and disadvantageous as possible. By these means those eventual contracts, it was probably hoped, could be more cheaply complied with; and, moreover, that a reduced market would afford further opportunities of beneficial speculation. The extreme indiscretion of the first mentioned speculations, and the distress which, it was manifest, they must produce, excited perhaps and animated the movements of the other party, and brought on a scene of private distress for money, both artificial and real, which probably has not been equalled in this country. It happened in the winter season, when the influx of cash articles of trade, as returns from abroad, is nearly suspended, and when quantities of specie were sent from the sea-ports to the interior country, for the purchase of produce to supply the demand for the spring exportation.

"The banks, who can always perceive the approach of these things, were influenced to limit their operations, and particularly the Bank of the United States, which was then preparing for the opening of its branches, or offices of discount and deposit, in Boston, New-York, Baltimore, and Charleston.

"The United States, you would presume, could not be insensible of so fit a moment to make purchases of the public stock, and the Treasurer was accordingly authorized to buy; but, though the appearances of private distress for money were so great, he could not obtain for several days the sum of fifty thousand dollars, at the highest rates at which the public purchases had before been made. The holders who were free from engagements were averse to selling; the principal persons who were under engagements they could not comply with, were obliged or disposed to place their effects in the hands of their creditors, who did not choose to add to their own disappointments of great profits actual losses by unseasonable sales of the bankrupts' property. The stock in the market, therefore, was really made scarce. A quarter's interest has just been paid. Some of the cautious moneyed people have begun to purchase. The specie is returning from the country, and the heaviest private engagements having now fallen due, the declension of stock may be considered as arrested. There is little doubt that the difficulty for money among the dealers in the debt will be at no time so great as it has been, after the present week, and that changes of a favorable complexion are to be confidently expected; at first moderate, perhaps, afterwards such as will carry the funds up to their due value." [21]

8. After the Panic

A. Duer's New York property was probably secured by his creditors after his failure, but he had much outlying property including a share in an option for 2,000,000 acres of Maine land at ten cents per acre and some land in Vermont. Duer was trying to keep this land from his creditors, and he finally did succeed in selling his rights to the Maine option for $50,000.

Duer never made a proportional assignment of his property to his creditors after

[21] The day this was written Hamilton's agent wrote that stocks had become plentiful, and hundreds of persons were offering their stocks to the government's agent at New York.

his bankruptcy. With the proceeds from the Maine lands he invested in a cotton mill in the Bronx and he also seems to have been interested in a Virginia land deal. Later he lost the capital which he had held together. He died a pauper.

B. Duer proposes sale of rights to Maine lands.[22]

"My dear Friend:

"Governor Jackson has informed me of the Circumstances which prevent at present your Paying a Visit to this City. I regret it Extremely, but as no person but you and myself can arrange together what I wish relative to the First Two Million Purchase. I must still hope to see you on that Business in the Course of a month. My Interest, my dear Friend, in that Business is my Sheet Anchor, and there are only two principles on which I can make it the basis of a system for extricating myself from my present Embarrassments. The 1st—To purchase of you, on Principles to be agreed on, the whole of the Right you have in the Two Million Purchase.—the 2d—To define and divide the interest I hold in it. It is not possible to treat on this Subject, at least to Come to a Conclusion, by Correspondence.

"With Respect to the last Purchase, though my Embarrassments have compelled me to relinquish to others who have made the advance (of) my money in the Pre-emption—Yours remains perfect. It is so understood by Flint, and myself. But then my Friend you must of course continue to make the Proportion of advances.

"You may rest assured that Every Insinuation which may be made of my Intentions to Reserve Property to myself, at the Expense of those who have Claims on me, is false. You know me too well to suppose me capable of such a line of Conduct, or to imagine that I consider Poverty in that horrid Point of View as to sacrifice Character, rather than submit to it.

"The State of my Affairs, owing to an Indiscreet Confidence in others, and a too great Vanity of Object, compels me to take time to point out the source of my Losses, and to collect the Scattering Fragments of my Resources. When this is done, and I have secured some Claims of a Nature not to be dispensed with, I will manifest to the World. Then I will not reserve more than the Clothing of myself and Family. You shall have no Occasion to blush for your Friend.

"Ogden has got the Title for the Land. I consider our Contract on this Subject Valid,—but I must desire you in Confidence not to give the title to Walker 'till we meet when I will Explain the Reason. If he writes further tell him that you and myself have depending Accounts to Settle before that can be. You must guard in the Strictest Confidence what I say on this Subject. God help you, my Friend, and preserve you from the malice of your Enemies, and the Reverses of Fortune. As for myself,—severe affliction was in fact Necessary to Cure me of that Over Confidence in Men and Things, which has proved the Source of all the Calamities I have Ever Experienced. I still, however, maintain Firmness, and look forward with Confidence to better days.

"Yours affectionately,
"Wm. Duer

"New York, May 5th, 1792."

[22] Letter from Duer to Knox in *Knox Papers,* vol. xxxi, p. 74 (Knox Papers are in the Mass. Hist. Soc. Collection).

9. Readings

J. S. Davis, *Essays in the Earlier History of American Corporations* (Cambridge, 1917), vol. i, pp. 174–212. This essay is recommended as the best biography of Duer and as an excellent short discussion of the various undertakings in which he was concerned.

10. Suggested Questions

1. Do you consider that Duer was responsible for the panic of 1792? What men have occupied similar positions in other panics?
2. What were the probable intentions of (a) Hamilton and (b) Duer in the formation of the S. U. M.?
3. Why did Duer, and the Scioto group generally, join with the Ohio Co. in making contracts with Congress, in-

stead of securing a separate grant of land directly and openly from the federal government?

4. What were Duer's chief mistakes in business policy? Explain.

5. Would Duer have succeeded better in the years 1921–29 than in the late eighteenth century?

6. Does the Duer case throw any light on the service of a promoter?

XX. JAY COOKE & COMPANY, 1861–1873

1. General Statement

The history of banking in America may be divided into three general periods. In the first period, banking services were provided by the merchants, who transferred funds and dealt in credit as a part of their varied mercantile business. In the second, banking became a specialized business, often with its base in mercantile capital and experience and also often growing out of handling currency and specie. While the investment banker and the commercial bank of this period thus acquired independence, they long occupied a passive position. They served the merchant, the industrialist, and the carrier, but they did not dictate to them or dominate them; nor did they provide much active leadership in American business. The third period, that of the banker who became the leader and the coördinator of business, marked the full development of banking power as represented by J. Pierpont Morgan and others of his time.

Jay Cooke & Co. belongs chiefly in the second of these periods. The firm's particular significance lies not in the fact that it represents the banking of that period, however, but in the fact that it reveals the weaknesses of the specialized banker in a highly dynamic business situation. Jay Cooke & Co. failed. Did this company fail because it tried to do too much? Or, because it did not go far enough? [1]

2. Important Dates in Jay Cooke's Career

1821	Born at Sandusky, Ohio.
1835–36	Worked in store in Sandusky.
1836–37	Clerk in store in St. Louis.
1838	In office of Washington Packet & Transportation Co., Philadelphia.
1839	Entered office of E. W. Clark & Co. as clerk.
1843	Partner in E. W. Clark & Co.
1847	E. W. Clark & Co. sold Mexican War bonds.
1854	Began to buy western lands on joint account with other Pennsylvanians.
1857	Retired from E. W. Clark & Co.
1858–60	Interested in Pennsylvania canals, Franklin Railroad, Vermont Central, and western land.
1861	Jay Cooke & Co. established at Philadelphia.
1861–65	Jay Cooke served United States Treasury during Civil War, selling its loans totaling over a billion dollars.
1862	Washington house of Jay Cooke & Co. established.
1866	New York house established.
1866–69	Jay Cooke & Co. specialized in government securities.
1869–73	Jay Cooke & Co. served as financial agent for Northern Pacific.
1871	Jay Cooke, McCulloch & Co. established in London. Jay Cooke's American firms consolidated. The Cooke firm organized and managed syndicating of government loan.
1873	Failure of Jay Cooke & Co. Jay Cooke retired from banking.
1878–79	Jay Cooke regained fortune through silver mine.
1905	Jay Cooke died.

[1] Since this case is based on one volume, which contains references to sources (Henrietta M. Larson, *Jay Cooke, Private Banker,* Cambridge, 1936), further references will be omitted herein.

3. Business Career of Jay Cooke before 1861

Jay Cooke & Co. was established in Philadelphia in 1861 by two partners, Jay Cooke and his brother-in-law, William G. Moorhead. The latter was a man of considerable experience and prestige in Pennsylvania transportation; at the time of the formation of the partnership he was president of the Philadelphia & Erie Railroad. Moorhead never took an active part, however, in the affairs of the bank. Jay Cooke was the active partner from the beginning, and he, more than any other person, determined the policies and directed the work of the firm until its failure in 1873.

Jay Cooke's earlier life had given him excellent preparation for establishing his own bank. He was born in 1821 in Sandusky, Ohio, of New England and Revolutionary stock; his father was a lawyer. Jay attended school until he was fourteen years old, when he went to work in a general store in Sandusky. In 1836 he went to St. Louis to work for some merchants from New York, a position he held until the panic of 1837 broke his employers. The spring of 1838 found him in Philadelphia writing advertisements, soliciting passengers, and keeping books for the Washington Packet Co. His brother-in-law and later partner was president of this company, which owed its charter as well as most of its capital to political influence. Jay at this time earned his board and room by serving evenings as bookkeeper and clerk at the Congress Hall Hotel. The packet company failed, and in the spring of 1839 Jay accepted an offer of a clerkship with E. W. Clark & Co., a domestic exchange house of Philadelphia.

The Clark firm was a part of a development which was coming to hold an important place in American business, that of private banking. There were in America, as in Europe from mediaeval times, two distinct streams of private banking effort and development. One was that which grew out of the capital and experience of the foreign merchants, such as Stephen Girard's Bank (started in 1812 and incorporated in 1832) and Brown Brothers & Co. The mercantile banks had their roots in foreign trade and followed essentially the methods of their older contemporaries in London. More nearly indigenous in that it rose directly out of domestic needs and opportunities was the other stream of private banking development, the domestic exchange house. While the mercantile bankers looked abroad, the domestic exchange brokers looked inland. Since their work was at first principally that of dealing in money (at a time when bank notes could not generally be taken at their face value and the specie current came from the far corners of the Americas if not of the world) and of transferring funds, they did not need a large capital. To supplement their work, they took to dealing on commission in lotteries or stocks. As the exchange houses which survived gradually built up their own capital or credit and received deposits and secured loans, they began to discount and to invest for themselves in securities. Thus they became full-fledged commercial bankers and to some extent investment bankers. On the whole, however, their position was largely passive. They aggressively sought business, it is true, but they did not take a strong hand in the direction or management of the activities or enterprises which they served.

E. W. Clark & Co. was an exchange and stock brokerage concern when Jay Cooke joined it as clerk in 1839. It had been established in 1837 by Enoch W. Clark and Edward Dodge with a capital of $15,000, mostly borrowed. Its chief assets were the character, ability, and experience of Enoch W. Clark. Clark had received his training with S. & M. Allen & Co., which had had its beginning in a printer's dealing in lottery tickets in Albany around 1810 and which had moved to New York in 1815.

The Allen firm had a network of offices in important centers east of the Appalachians, in New England, the Middle States, and the South. Each office had a resident partner. Domestic exchange was the heart of the Allens' business, while lottery tickets and, later, stocks were important side lines. Indeed, the investment business proved the undoing of the Allens in the crisis of 1837. Having changed from brokers to investors or wholesalers, they were caught with inadequate funds to meet their obligations and were forced to suspend. Such a background of experience was invaluable to Enoch W. Clark. Like the Allens, he aggressively sought new business; unlike them, he believed in keeping "snug," that is, in such condition as to be able to meet his liabilities.

The history of the Clark firm from 1839 to 1857 reveals rapid growth in organization and function. From 1839 to 1842 the firm did principally an exchange business on commission—about the only business that was safe for a firm with little capital in a period of deflation. In 1842 they established a branch in St. Louis, in 1844 in New Orleans, in 1845 in New York City, and later in Burlington, Iowa, and in Springfield, Illinois (a chartered bank formed to issue notes when private bank notes were outlawed). By the middle 'forties they were doing a deposit and discount business. The war with Mexico brought them into government finance and gave them their first big business in securities and added considerably to their capital. By the 'fifties Clark's was one of the largest domestic exchange houses in the United States, and it was also doing a large business as security brokers and jobbers.

Jay Cooke became a partner in the firm in 1843, without supplying any capital; in 1854, on the retirement of the founder of the firm, he became the leading partner. In the speculative years of the middle 'fifties he—as Enoch Clark would have done—tried to keep his houses from expanding too far. But in such a speculative time it was impossible to hold oversanguine partners, on whom there was no effective check, to a conservative position. The result was trouble in 1854 and disaster in 1857.

On the reorganization of the Clark houses after the panic of 1857 Jay Cooke retired, apparently because he wanted to set up his own business. In the years 1858, 1859, and 1860 he was, as he said, on "free foot." But he was not idle. He participated in the organization of companies to buy Pennsylvania's State canals, managing the organization of a company which purchased one of the larger canals. He also managed the reorganizing and rebuilding of a small railroad, the Franklin. At the same time he led a fight on the part of a group of mortgage bondholders against the notorious management of the Vermont Central Railroad.

In the meantime the affairs of the old Clark firm had been settled, business conditions had improved, and Jay Cooke had increased his capital. Late in 1860 he was ready to join Moorhead in establishing a bank in Philadelphia. He was warned to watch the threatening clouds of southern opposition to the federal government, but that did not deter him. At the beginning of 1861 Jay Cooke & Co. opened its doors on South Third Street in Philadelphia.

4. Jay Cooke & Co. in Government Finance, 1861–65

Jay Cooke & Co. was a private bank. It had no specific capital, but the assets of the partners were to be at the bank's disposal when needed. Moorhead estimated that at the time of the organization of the bank he was worth half a million, the greater part in first-class transportation securities. Cooke valued his holdings at \$150,000, distributed as follows: a mortgage, \$15,000; real estate in Baltimore, \$35,000; Philadelphia residence, \$12,000; western land, \$25,000; Vermont Central stocks and bonds, \$40,000; other stocks and bonds, interest in E. W. Clark & Co., and miscellaneous assets, $23,000.

The keystone of the firm was Jay Cooke himself. He had a splendid physique, unusually good health, and tremendous vitality. Mentally he was quick and imaginative rather than critical. Emotionally he was a person of strong feeling, of deep sensitiveness to other people, and apparently remarkably free from conflicts within himself. Jay Cooke had a deep religious faith which gave him a sense of responsibility and a feeling of security and self-confidence, and he was a man of high integrity and of strong principle according to conventional standards. Altogether he was a typical extrovert. One of the sources of Jay Cooke's power was his ability to win and hold friends and supporters—his radiant health and spirits, his positive optimism, his kind and sympathetic nature, and his integrity were attractive qualities.

From the very first Jay Cooke seems to have been interested in government business growing out of Civil War needs. His experience in selling the Mexican War bonds in the Clark firm and the influential position in Ohio politics of his father and his brother, H. D. Cooke, who was editor of the *Ohio State Journal* at Columbus, certainly in part explain this interest. A letter written to Jay by his father, March 25, 1861, shows that the possibilities of the situation were already then recognized: "By the way, I took up my pen principally to say that H. D.'s plan in getting Chase into the Cabinet & Sherman into the Senate is accomplished, and that now is the time for making money, by honest contracts out of the govt. In perfecting loans —& various other agencies." On May 23, 1861, H. D. wrote to Jay: "We are just beginning to get 'inside the ring,' and there are several 'good things' in prospect, which a little management and patience will bring out all right." On June 1 another brother expressed the thought that the mantle of Morris, of Philadelphia, who had financed the Revolution, would fall on Cooke, of Philadelphia. Shortly thereafter Jay Cooke won much favorable attention for his successful sale, in coöperation with Drexel & Co., of a three-million-dollar Pennsylvania loan in spite of the fact that Pennsylvania's credit was low. Cooke sent information of the success of the loan to the president of the Confederacy, the secretary of the United States Treasury, and *The Times* (London), as well as to newspapers in the United States.

While Cooke and Drexel were selling the State loan, the national government was with difficulty securing money for its growing expenses by selling notes and bonds through the assistant treasurer in New York or receiving bids directly from banks. The unstable political situation, which made business men cautious, and the chaotic condition in banking and currency made the results of these early efforts very discouraging to Chase, the secretary of the Treasury.

In the fall of 1861 Cooke was appointed agent of the government in the Philadelphia territory for the sale of a fifty-million-dollar loan. Following the methods used in selling the Pennsylvania loan, he employed traveling agents and advertised widely. He succeeded in selling about one-fourth of the whole loan. By this time Chase was convinced of the value of Cooke's methods, which were for the time unique, and from then on the relations of the two men became closer and closer.

Encouraged by his success in selling government loans, his growing influence with Chase, and the prospects of a long and costly war, Jay Cooke took steps to prepare for more extensive participation in the sale of government loans. He proposed to establish a Washington bank in company with Anthony J. Drexel. On the latter's refusal to take this step without a guarantee of government business, Jay Cooke & Co. established its own house there in the summer of 1862.

The Washington house was a separate

partnership made up of the two Philadelphia partners and H. D. Cooke and Harris C. Fahnestock. Fahnestock was a young man, of the Bank of Harrisburg, who had impressed Cooke strongly when the two worked together on the Franklin Railroad and the Pennsylvania loan. He proved to be a banker of unusual ability. In directness, as well as in his ability to get at the heart of a problem and to make a decision, he was like Jay Cooke. He was unlike Cooke, however, in that he was influenced less by sentiment and more by cool calculation. H. D. Cooke was a lawyer by training and a newspaper editor by profession. He had a great deal of self-confidence. As a banker he was no good; as a manipulator of politicians he was a man of the first rank. H. D. Cooke and Fahnestock were the resident partners in Washington. Since young Fahnestock owned little property and Cooke was heavily in debt, the Washington house had scant capital beyond what the Philadelphia house could furnish.

After the passage of the National Banking Act, the influence of Jay Cooke & Co. was further broadened by the organization of the Philadelphia and Washington First National banks. The Philadelphia bank was practically controlled by the Cookes and the Clarks; that of the capital city was almost wholly owned by the Cooke partners.

Twice, on the failure of attempts to use a large number of banks as agents for the sale of government loans, Jay Cooke was given the agency for selling the loans. He received the agency for the sale of the "five-twenties" (redeemable in from 5 to 20 years) in November, 1862, and for the "seven-thirties" (notes bearing 7.3 per cent interest) in February, 1865. As sole agent he was to use his best efforts to sell the bonds at par, but he made no guarantee as to the amount to be sold. He was to have complete charge of the advertising and sale of the bonds and of their distribution after proper certification by the Treasury. Jay Cooke was to receive a commission which ranged from 3/8 to 3/4 of 1 per cent for different loans or portions of loans. Out of his commission he was to pay agents, salaries and commissions, and all other costs, the proportion to be paid to agents and for advertising being stipulated. The principal and the accrued interest on the bonds were to be paid in legal tender to the Treasury on delivery of the bonds.

Two great problems faced Jay Cooke in selling these loans: (1) how could enough buyers be found, and (2) how could the loan be managed without causing stringency in the money market? Cooke's plan was to draw in the money gradually from small as well as large investors, the country over. To accomplish this he created such an organization as had never before been used in America. He organized a system of agencies and subagencies which included not only bankers but, in some cases, insurance companies and even leading "capitalists" in small towns where there were no banks. In the New England and New York areas he delegated the management of sales to prominent bankers, like Spencer, Vilas & Co., of Boston, and Fisk & Hatch, Vermilye & Co., and Clark, Dodge & Co., of New York. In the rest of the country he won the close coöperation of larger bankers, for example, Preston, Willard & Kean, of Chicago, and also used a comprehensive system of traveling agents. These agents appointed local agents, established national banks (after the passing of the Banking Act), distributed advertising material, kept in touch with editors, and reported voluminously to Jay Cooke on the public opinion, resources, and so on, of the places visited. Agents were sent to California and to areas where northern troops were successful in the South. Night agencies were established in the cities. Thus the sale of the loans reached all classes of people far and wide.

Jay Cooke was a superb manager of sales. He sent circulars to agents, called them together in groups, or talked with them personally to build and maintain their enthusiasm. In advertising and publicizing the loans he was notably resourceful. Appeals were made to the public through posters, handbills, and pamphlets distributed by agents and through extensive advertising in newspapers. Never before had so comprehensive a system of advertising been used in the United States. Samuel Wilkeson, a New York journalist, was employed as a writer of editorials and advertisements. Through Peaslee's and Pettingill's advertising agencies and through agents the country over, arrangements were made with newspapers and periodicals to help popularize the loan, and material was distributed to the newspapers—even French, German, and Italian—and to the religious press. The papers received payment for advertisements but carried editorial articles gratis. So comprehensive was the advertising that there were few, if any, papers within territory under federal control that did not carry Jay Cooke's advertisements when his selling campaigns were at their height. One characteristic of Cooke's advertising was the fact that it gave full information about the loans in simple terms—no one who could read could fail to understand his famous "Questions and Answers" and "Facts and Figures."

Appeals were made to both patriotism and the purse. The people were urged to place their money as well as their sons on their country's altar. The security of property was said to depend on the success of the North. The bonds were said to be a first mortgage on the private and public wealth of the country. The richness of the resources of the United States was emphasized by elaborate statistics. A public debt was even pictured as a blessing, if properly managed, for it would give a basis for credit to be used in the development of the country. Since the selling of the loans obviously depended on the success of the North, Cooke tried to strengthen its cause by playing up the wisdom of its leaders and the success of its armies.

He went far beyond publicity, however, to strengthen federal loans in the market. He advised Lincoln to remove General McClellan because of the effect of the failure of his campaigns on the loans. When northern losses depressed bonds and greenbacks, advances were obtained from the Treasury with which to manipulate the bond market to the advantage of government credit. And when gold speculation threatened to drive currency downward and weaken faith in the government, Jay Cooke entered the gold market to break the mounting gold price. The gold panic of 1864 was brought on by such an effort.

Cooke's bond campaigns were in every instance successful. He sold considerably above one billion of five-twenties and seven-thirties. Thus he accomplished—by means of a powerful organization, strong publicity, and some effort to control the market—what the Treasury had earlier in the war despaired of doing through the banks of the country.

Jay Cooke's gains from the sale of government bonds were varied. His actual profits cannot be determined. He received from the Treasury a total of $7,167,717 for selling the loans, but nine-tenths of this amount was paid to subagents. In fact, at one time Cooke offered to work without any commission if the government would pay expenses.

Indirectly, however, Jay Cooke profited greatly from the war loans. Though he paid interest to the government on balances from sales, those balances gave him a working capital for his firms' own dealings. The government agency, furthermore, gave Jay Cooke & Co. an advantage in the market in governments—since Jay Cooke & Co. was concentrating on selling new issues rather than on trading or speculating, this advantage was more apparent than real. Something was unquestionably done, however, in the way of trading. On a day in January, 1863, a clerk in the Philadelphia house reported for that day a profit of $500 on the sale of government certificates, treasury notes, and gold. Some idea of the success of the Cooke houses is gained from the fact that their dividends to partners from 1861 to 1865, inclusive, totaled $2,057,303.

An unmeasurable gain from the work of selling government loans was increased prestige. The extensive advertising of Jay Cooke for several years, at a time when such advertising was not common, made Jay Cooke and Jay Cooke & Co. household words. "Allow me to say," wrote a man from California, "that the name of *Jay Cooke* is as familiar and as well known almost, as that of *Abraham Lincoln* our lamentable President. It is a passport to favor." Even more important was the fact that the Cookes had established good relations with a large number of the banks of the country.

Of notable significance to the Cooke houses was the great change which Civil War finance brought in American banking. The national banking system simplified domestic exchange and destroyed the work of the exchange house, which had grown out of a chaotic currency and the lack of uniform banking standards. Very significant is the fact that under the leadership of Jay Cooke security distribution was revolutionized. The old system of selling small issues through bankers who reached relatively few investors gave way to large-scale, high-pressure selling through an aggressive sales force which reached into the savings of the small man and was supported by a measure of control of the market.

5. Adjustment to a Peace Basis, 1866–69

At the end of the war the Cookes occupied a commanding position in American banking. Their prestige, their extensive experience in war finance, and their many contacts with bankers and other business men seemed to be a strong foundation on which to build in the years ahead. The refunding of the United States loans, private dealings in governments, and the expected economic growth of the country promised to provide adequate work. There were, however, certain elements of weakness in their position. Jay Cooke & Co. did not have a strong capital. In view of the disruption in the government and the inflation in business brought by the war, moreover, it was questionable what business the future would hold. The situation was not altogether unlike that which confronted J. P. Morgan & Co. at the end of the World War.

Jay Cooke and his partners were confident, however, that they would have good business in the future. The basis of Jay Cooke's business creed was his faith in the rich resources of the United States. Endless primeval forests and prairies and rich mines, the productive powers of which were beyond calculation, waited only for capital and credit to turn them into profits. Regardless of what the immediate future held, Jay Cooke was a bull on the long-run prospects of American business.

So strong was the confidence of Jay Cooke and his partners that they set to work at once, the better to fit themselves to fill the position in which their great success had placed them. They spent large sums of money on real-estate improvements. As soon as the war ended, Jay Cooke started to build a mansion on an estate north of Philadelphia. This mansion (at Ogontz) was spacious and was furnished almost without regard to cost—the new home was estimated to have cost over a million dollars. At the same time the Philadelphia office of Jay Cooke & Co. was rebuilt and refurnished at a cost of $60,000. The result, said the *Philadelphia Inquirer* of January 9, 1866, was "undoubtedly the most magnificent and most costly establishment of its kind in the United States." These expenditures, though unusual in amount, point to the fact that the Cookes were heavy spenders and believed in good living. Although Jay Cooke apparently would not have justified the spending of such large sums in 1865–66 on personal grounds, he considered it a fitting expression of the prestige of his banking houses.

Of great promise in the advancement of Jay Cooke & Co. was the addition of a New York house. It is clear that the Cooke organization built up during the war was not suited to the needs of postwar business. With the end of the war, the focal point of the business in governments shifted to New York, the central securities market. Also, New York had become the unquestioned leader in commercial finance and the greatest reservoir of capital in the country. A New York firm would give the Cookes a base in the center of America's private financial operations, just as the Washington house had given them one in public finance.

The new firm began to do business in March, 1866. The partners were Jay Cooke, William G. Moorhead, H. D. Cooke, Harris C. Fahnestock, and two new men, Pitt Cooke and Edward Dodge. Pitt Cooke, the oldest of the three Cooke brothers, had been in the real-estate and commission business in Ohio and the West. He was honest, conscientious, loyal to Jay, and unaggressive. The younger men of the firm affectionately called him "Uncle Pitt." He was worth about $150,000, largely in real estate. Edward Dodge, because of his knowledge of the New York stock and bond business, was brought into the firm from Clark, Dodge & Co. Dodge probably added a fair amount to the wealth of the group, but he never won the complete confidence of his partners. They mistrusted his business judgment and thought he did not give enough attention to his work. As in the other houses, no contribution of capital was required, but the partners were at liberty to keep money on deposit and were expected to help out with money and collateral when needed. The resident partners were Fahnestock, who was brought from Washington, Pitt Cooke, and Dodge.

The opening of a London house was also considered at this time. Jay Cooke saw in Europe a potential market for government refunding loans. But how could bonds be sold in countries which had during the war become so cool on the question of American investments? "The only successful plan," held Cooke, "will be a popularization there after the American plan & in this American agencies of foreign houses are of no account whatever." He concluded that, in case they should get refunding to do, they would have to go to work in London. The Cookes looked around for a partner for a London house, but the actual realization of their plans depended on the government's decision as to refunding.

The three Jay Cooke & Co. houses were separate partnerships. Jay Cooke, head of the Philadelphia house, was considered the head of the whole group. This was in recognition of his prestige and his ownership of about a one-third share in each house. He did not follow the details of the business in each place, but he received weekly reports from the New York and Washington houses and visited them frequently. All important business and all matters of policy were referred to him. In fact, it appears that the partners never as a group acted on matters of policy or program but conferred individually with Jay Cooke and practically always accepted his decisions. H. D. Cooke was the resident head in Washington and Fahnestock in New York.

Each of the firms maintained its business as an independent unit; that is, except where dealings were arranged on joint account, their operations were entirely separate. They were liberal in making advances to each other, but payment of interest was required and generally the deposit of collateral. Each house adjusted its affairs to meet local conditions: the Washington house did general banking; the New York house received deposits from inland banks, made payments for them, and dealt heavily in securities; the Philadelphia house did a large amount of general banking and managed joint-account bond deals. Both New York and Philadelphia dealt heavily in bonds for themselves and on commission. With all this independence there was much specialization. Government lobbying for the whole group was the *raison d'être* of the Washington house. The Philadelphia and Washington First National banks, so closely related to Jay Cooke & Co., served as government depositories and made advances to the Cooke banks. New York's special contribution was its closeness to the stock and bond market. Philadelphia served as headquarters and general clearing house for all the firms. The New York house soon became the leader in the group.

All the houses did a general deposit and discount business. None of their account books has been saved, but an idea of the nature of their deposits and discounts may be gathered from the correspondence of the partners. The Washington house, and probably the Washington First National, had only a local discount and deposit business. There was always much trouble with loans in both Washington banks. Their customers were of the type that required long-time loans and could give little security, or at best only real estate. Politicians, since they were in a position where it was difficult to deny them favors, were a special problem in this respect. Fahnestock and Jay Cooke were continually urging the Washington banks to cut down their loans on poor securities and to keep their assets liquid. "Can't some of that be called in without damage," wrote Fahnestock to Jay Cooke, March 25, 1867, referring to accommodation loans. "You must watch that very carefully, or the whole capital of the Bank will be loaned out irreclaimably to parties who cannot respond when called on."

The Philadelphia and New York houses had large deposits. Many accounts were for local individuals or business firms. After the war it became popular for bankers, especially westerners, to have deposits with Jay Cooke & Co., chiefly in New York. The proportion of deposits by banks and business men, other than local, came to be much larger in New York than in Philadelphia. Interest was paid on demand deposits, at one time as high as 5 per cent.

The discount policies of the Philadelphia and New York houses were about the same, the New York house probably being the more concerned about keeping its assets liquid. The conditions on which they loaned out money varied, of course, from time to time according to the bond and money market. "We are not primarily lenders of money," said Jay Cooke. Generally speaking, they let money out on loans with reference to the needs of their investment business. When they could not profitably employ the money otherwise, they lent it, principally to banks and other business men, on call. The New York house, especially, worked on the theory that "there are no 'friends' here in a tight money market" and that they could not afford to lend money at 6 per cent when they could make more in investments. "Every deviation, every departure from Cash assets," wrote Pitt Cooke, "weakens the power of a Banker to make money with his tools." As collateral, governments were preferred and very often required, at least until 1869. Dodge of the New York house worried his partners a great deal by accepting stock as security for loans, though he generally took it on a low valuation.

When they could profitably use more funds than they themselves had, the Cooke houses borrowed from each other or from other banks. In making advances to each other they were liberal, though the New York house complained of the heavy demands of the Washington house as well as of the First National Bank and even the Philadelphia house. All the Cooke banks borrowed from other banks: from the First National in Washington and in Philadelphia, and in New York from Clark, Dodge

& Co. or other bankers or banks. They gave their own securities as collateral and are known to have used securities left with them by their customers. Jay Cooke & Co. established the National Insurance Company of the United States of America for the purpose of securing its financial aid.

Jay Cooke & Co. seems not to have been interested in commercial paper. Before the establishment of the bank in 1861 Jay Cooke had bought notes to hold till maturity (he called it his "patent banking scheme"), but his banks followed the policy of keeping out of that business. A suggestion that they establish a note-broker department in 1868 was apparently unheeded by the Philadelphia and New York houses.

The biggest interest of Jay Cooke & Co. in the late 'sixties was government securities. This took two forms: (1) aiding the Treasury directly in the purchase of the short-term obligations or their conversion into long-time securities; and (2) carrying on an extensive trade in governments by mail and over the counter.

Their work for the Treasury did not develop so far as the Cookes had hoped. Jay Cooke had expected to play a strong hand in refunding operations after the war. He worked hard to bring about the passing of a general refunding act to lower interest on the long-term bonds, but such an act was not passed until 1870. The Treasury did, however, take up the short-time obligations, either by direct purchase or by conversion into long-term loans. In the years 1865–69, the United States Treasury purchased its loans to the amount of $2,312,444,656 and sold new loans amounting to $2,217,067,978. The Cookes took a considerable part in these transactions, some on commission and some by outright purchase and sale. They also from time to time did other work for the government, such as protecting its loans on the market or aiding in holding the money market steady. The fact that these operations for the Treasury were generally secret aroused very much opposition to Jay Cooke & Co.

There were two sources of opposition to the Cookes' relations with the Treasury. One grew out of a widespread feeling that Jay Cooke & Co. had made enormous profits in selling the war loans. The other had its source principally in growing competition in the investment business.

To understand the work of Jay Cooke and his firms in the late 'sixties and early 'seventies it is necessary to keep in mind that investment banking had developed greatly during the war. It had emerged from the conflict a more or less specialized institution with a technique of its own. Moreover, under the stimulus of an increasing trade and particularly of war finance, many new banking houses had been established which were largely interested in the investment business. Most of the leading private banking firms—such as J. P. Morgan & Co., J. & W. Seligman & Co., L. P. Morton & Co., and, of course, the houses which had grown directly out of war finance, that is, Fisk & Hatch, Henry Clews & Co., and Vermilye & Co.—had grown up during the war. The only important houses of earlier origin were Jay Cooke & Co., which was established at the beginning of the war, Brown Brothers & Co., and Drexel & Co.

The position of the Cookes with the Treasury weakened after the war was over. So strong did the opposition to the Treasury's employment of Jay Cooke and his houses become that they were given only minor jobs to do when they were employed at all. Criticism forced Secretary McCulloch to be very cautious, and the inauguration of Grant in 1869 and the appointment of a new secretary brought into strategic places men who had no particular friendship with the Cookes and who knew it was politically dangerous to maintain too friendly relations with them.

The Cookes' business in governments in 1865–69 was primarily not commission work for the government in great refunding operations, as they had hoped it would be, but trading in securities on their own account. Indeed, their most important work in the early postwar years was of that type. The two Washington firms—Jay Cooke & Co. and the First National Bank—did not carry on much local trade, but the Philadelphia and New York houses dealt with the Treasury, with brokers and bankers, and with individuals. They were in the nature of wholesalers or jobbers rather than commission dealers or retailers.

The center of their trade in governments was in their New York house, chiefly because New York was the national market for securities and money and had the advantage over other cities in following the market in those pre-ticker days. Moreover, Jay Cooke was a broker not a trader, while Fahnestock in the New York firm was a masterly trader.

The correspondence of the partners gives insight into the trading of the New York house in government securities. Until about the end of 1866 the New Yorkers carried on a large and lucrative trade in bonds. Much of their buying in 1866 and 1867 was in anticipation of Treasury needs, but they also sold a great deal to bankers who disposed of American securities abroad. They were usually "long" in the market; their correspondence does not reveal a single instance of their selling "short" in 1866, though their supply of bonds was often low. A letter of Fahnestock's illustrates their position in those years:

> "As nearly as I can carry in memory (Statement not made up yet this Evg) we have [the following government securities on hand:]
>
> | | |
> |---|---|
> | 62^s –450 to 500th
64 –150th
65 –200
10 40–
81
7–30–2300
——
3150–" | to which add 2¼ Millions Compounds bot up for a big trade with Treasy which we had first put in working shape and had been turning nicely the past four days |

The extent of their trading is suggested by the following random selections from letters: turned $800,000 government today, bought $600,000 and sold $500,000 at advance of ¼ to ¾; bought $350,000 and sold $700,000 at advances of ⅛ to ¼; business today of $2,000,000; hold $2,500,000 seven-thirties; $2,000,000 to $3,000,000 trade today.

The year 1867 began with falling prices and general uneasiness. Throughout the year the market was more uncertain than in 1866. At times the New Yorkers were short on some bonds and long on others; their daily turnover was sometimes large, but frequently there was little trading. Their biggest business in this year was probably meeting the demands of the Treasury.

The year 1868 was unsatisfactory. Both in the spring and in the fall there were long periods when the Cookes' trading was at a minimum. The Treasury was buying less. Political conditions and a tight money market made Fahnestock curtail buying. Unfortunately he was in Europe during the difficult times in October and November. At the end of the year the New Yorkers were in a pinch and were appealing to the Philadelphia and Washington houses for aid.

The situation became even worse in 1869. It was made all the more difficult by a growing difference between Jay Cooke and Fahnestock over the New Yorker's trading. Strange as it may well seem, in view of his later venture with the Northern Pacific, Jay Cooke was not a speculator. His Philadelphia house loaned more money and borrowed less and depended more largely on the commission business than did Jay Cooke & Co., of New York. There were two good reasons for this. Besides being more of a broker and banker than a trader in investments, Jay Cooke had a bearish attitude toward business in the period from 1867 to 1869 and thought security prices were headed downward. He, therefore, believed in keeping the firms' resources liquid and safe. Much of the time he favored a quick turnover of their government securities, and he almost always urged that only a small stock of bonds be held. Fahnestock, on the other hand, was fundamentally a trader, though he recognized the dangers in trading. Moreover, he had a more optimistic view of the current market than did Jay Cooke, and he sometimes chafed at Cooke's bearish recommendations and did not always heed them.

Owing to the uncertainty of the market throughout much of 1869, the differences between the two leading partners reached a climax in that year. Jay Cooke had been a bear on governments almost ever since the war, and in 1869 he became more strongly convinced than ever that those securities were heading for a drop and he urged Fahnestock to go short or curtail buying. On his urging, Fahnestock went short a million in certain governments in January at a loss of $10,000, a loss which was more than covered by going long on other bonds. February told the same story, and also March. Fahnestock at this point protested against Jay Cooke's policy:

"Since the high pressure war times (our first season in N. Y.) I have not taken large risks, and in our present movement I have kept our stock [of governments] within 3 mil.—but of course only for a short turn. As I remarked, there are times when I go short because it pays, but at this time the state of the market is such that precisely the reverse is the case, and bonds will all *certainly* be *higher*. Please remember that my government dept has made nearly all the money that has been made in N. Y. and the bulk of it by *having stock* [bonds] *on* a rising market. . . . And do you know that you have *never once* advised me to buy governments since I have been there, always contending that they were too high and must tumble and therefore recommending me to sell out."

Yet the New York partner recognized that the business in governments was "simply speculative" and that the Cookes might, "like any of the gold room people, be right or wrong."

Against Jay Cooke's wishes the New York house carried from one to two and one-half million dollars of governments in April at a gross profit of $64,000. In May they carried $3,000,000 at a paper profit of $75,000; in June they carried bonds at an apparent loss of $37,000; July brought a paper profit of $131,000. From that time on there was a steady shrinkage in values, but Fahnestock believed that influences at home and abroad would "overrule the possible vagaries of politicians which may after a while cause temporary trouble *but cannot prevail.*"

Though Cooke protested strongly, Fahnestock persisted in going long on bonds for some time. They were, he said in the summer of 1869, the heaviest government dealers in New York. He wrote Jay Cooke: "You are pleased when we control the market and are the leading house in all the government purchases, . . . and yet you want us to take no risks —that is to keep our bonds down to a sum which, while it would be ample in Phila or Boston, would oblige us to *relinquish* our leading position, take rank with the *smallest* dealers and would absolutely render it IMPOSSIBLE to make any considerable amt of money. . . . We cant sell the Government millions *unless we have them. . . . We cant make money* unless we are willing to run risks. The brokerage part of the business is a bagatelle—any thirty second man can do it." According to Fahnestock, even expenses could not have been made out of the commission business during the year just past.

The autumn found Fahnestock less sure of his position. He recognized at the end of the summer that the days of rapid trading in bonds were gone; he believed that the trade thereafter would be close and at a comparatively small profit on each transaction. It was the gold panic of Black Friday, September 24, that finally broke his courage. The panic left the Cooke partners a chastened lot, none more than Fahnestock. The gold mess had taught him a lesson; he wrote to Jay Cooke: "We have got to find a different way to make money from the way in which *all our New York* money has been made."

Unfortunately there are no records from which to get conclusive information about the relative income of the three houses from the various lines of business in those years. In the three and a half years of the New York house, said Fahnestock, $1,638,000 had been made in government securities (both from commissions and from their own trading), while the other business totaled $493,000. Almost one-half of the last figure resulted from Treasury gold commissions; the stock profits were $240,000, against which $52,500 in losses had already been charged off, while $290,000 was tied up in two bad stocks, Mariposa and Atlantic Mail. Only $71,390 had been made until November in 1869. It was clear that, at least for the time being, the business of trading in governments was almost dead.

6. Readjustment in 1869

The condition of the Cooke firms in 1869 is suggested by Table 1, which gives the annual dividends of the three houses for several years.

Table 1. DIVIDENDS OF COOKE BANKING HOUSES, 1866–69

	New York	Philadelphia	Washington	Combined
1866	$500,000	$100,000	$100,000	$700,000
1867	415,000	150,000	100,000	665,000
1868	200,000	100,000	none	300,000
1869	none	150,000	none	150,000

These figures furnish the basis for Fahnestock's statement in a letter to Jay Cooke of December 27, 1869, that "if the business were always to be as now we had better quit." Fahnestock's position reflects the despair that ran through the whole Cooke organization after Black Friday of September, 1869.

What was the trouble with the Cooke houses, and how could their difficulties best have been met? There may have been weaknesses in organization and personnel. If so, were these fundamental? Did Fahnestock's emphasis on the speculative side of the business, as contrasted with Jay Cooke's emphasis on commission trading, reflect a keener grasp of the possibilities of the investments market at the time? If so, what were the reasons for this? Did it indicate stronger competition among investment bankers or a condition arising from a change on the buying side of the market? Unquestionably the business in governments was decreasing. But was not this loss more than balanced by the expansion of business and the appearance of new investment opportunities in the United States at the time? The West was developing rapidly, and with this came extensive railroad building. Industrials may have offered some opportunity, for the textile, leather, and iron and steel industries were rapidly expanding at the time. Mining had increased greatly during the war; like most interests, however, it had experienced a depression soon afterward. Even if such opportunities existed, did Jay Cooke & Co., which had specialized in governments, know how to handle those types of investments?

Some effort was made to put the concern in a stronger position. Jay Cooke firmly advised his partners to get into cash assets as far as possible. Some attention was given to expenses. Fahnestock urged discontinuing the Washington house, which had apparently become both useless and dangerous. With the shrinkage of the government business the reason for its existence practically disappeared; and H. D. Cooke, its resident head, was dangerously impairing the assets of the whole Cooke organization by extravagances which made him indebted to his firm for nearly half a million, by liberal loans to indigent politicians, and by investments in and commitments to questionable enterprises. But the house was retained—H. D. Cooke promised to reform and turned his residence over to the firm as security for his debts.

The leading partners were expansionists by nature: Fahnestock wanted to do a big business or none at all, and Jay Cooke had been so successful and had so much faith in the United States, based fundamentally on the country's rich resources, that to speak of retrenchment was to him heresy. There was another element, however, to be considered. The Cookes were weak in capital but strong in prestige. Would curtailment mean a weakening of their strongest asset? Here was a first-class question of policy.

Fahnestock urged the extension of their commercial banking, especially in the foreign field. Foreign commercial banking was then developing rapidly, and such houses as the Morgans, Mortons, Drexels, and Seligmans were profiting thereby. Fahnestock urged the establishment of a London house to compete in the foreign business—without a London office, he said, they could only sit by and watch the others reap the harvest.

A fundamental difference in the interests of the two leading partners is revealed at this time. While Fahnestock thought that Jay Cooke & Co. should build up foreign commercial banking through a connection in London, Jay Cooke held that they should concentrate on the issue of bonds on commission. This was a reflection of the partners' opinions as to the importance of Europe to American business. The Philadelphian was interested in the development of the West, and he did not forget that one of the biggest financial enterprises of the time, the Civil War, had been financed by American money. Fahnestock, on the other hand, had gained, through his work in New York and a business trip to Europe, a feeling for the financial power of England and the Continent and for the opportunities offered by the commercial business between Europe and America.

For the time being, however, the interest of the Cooke organization continued to be focused on the investment business. What were the possibilities there?

Jay Cooke had consistently refused to enter projects which were new to him or which had not yet become recognized as profitable. Silver mining, in particular, was to him anathema. The oil boom of the early 'sixties had not interested him. Indeed, he was afraid of anything that seemed highly speculative.

In some other fields he had tried and failed. In 1868 he had entered the life insurance business in the organizing of the National Life Insurance Company of the United States of America, the only insurance corporation ever chartered by the federal government. His object had ostensibly been to give his banking house financial support. A comprehensive organization had been established, and the concern had been widely publicized. The venture did not, however, bring the immediate results for which Jay Cooke had hoped, probably because it was established at a time when life insurance was overexpanded.

Coal and iron had likewise proved unprofitable for Jay Cooke and his partners. In war times they had entered into several mining ventures in Pennsylvania, all of which had proved very troublesome. The postwar years were difficult ones in the iron and coal fields. Andrew Carnegie succeeded even then, but he knew the iron business and could concentrate on management. The Cookes were bankers and not industrial managers, and they were unable to secure good managers. The burden of Jay Cooke's advice to his partners was to get their money out of coal and iron.

The investment field which then bore the greatest promise for bankers was railroad finance. There Jay Cooke was at home. To understand the possibilities of his house in railroads it is necessary to know something of the general development in railroad finance and of Jay Cooke's position in it.

Railroad building did not reach its greatest postwar importance in investment finance until about 1869. In the earlier years, government securities had dominated the investment market, and in concentrating on governments the Cookes and other bankers had been doing the most profitable and the safest thing. "We cannot afford to build R R's & neglect our manipulations of Govt Securities," a Cooke partner had maintained in 1866, voicing the opinion of the group. Jay Cooke had had the further objection that identifying themselves with railroads might draw them into dangerous entanglements.

Yet the Cookes had not entirely neglected railroad finance. They had done very little in eastern roads, presumably because while they were engaged in government finance other bankers had preëmpted that field. The western roads had only then been getting under way, however, and there the field was open to anyone. In 1866–67, the Cookes, Clarks, and Drexels had with only moderate success sold the bonds of a Missouri road. This experience no doubt in part explains Jay Cooke's refusal to go into the Union Pacific. At the same time various influences, such as extensive land purchases and a visit to Duluth, had been encouraging Jay Cooke's interest in the upper Mississippi country. When the road projected to connect Lake Superior at Duluth with the Mississippi at St. Paul had appealed to the Cookes in 1868, Jay Cooke had been ready to participate. The Cookes and the Clarks purchased on joint account a small part of the road's bond issue and later agreed to sell more on commission. Though Europe proved uninterested, so well did the bonds sell in New York and elsewhere in the East that the financing venture was a great success. The loan, which in 1869 was spoken of as the most successful negotiation on Wall Street, left the Cookes enthusiastic about both the Northwest and railroad finance.

By that time railroad finance had grown to boom proportions. Old roadbeds and equipment were being replaced; smaller roads were being reorganized into larger systems; and new roads were being built at a staggering rate—4,999 miles of new road in 1869 as compared with the increase of 1,742 miles in 1866. Speculators, promoters, and politicians were again seeing in western railroad extension great opportunity, and the high interest rates offered by railroad bonds proved too much for the sales resistance of the owners of government bonds, for which Europe was offering a ready market.

By this time, however, the older roads had established relations with bankers, and such bankers as Jay Cooke & Co., who had long been busy with the affairs of the Treasury, had to look to new roads. Henry Clews had joined the Rock Island. Fisk & Hatch had made a magnificent job of financing the Central Pacific, and in the summer of 1869 they undertook to sell the bonds of the Chesapeake & Ohio, which work Jay Cooke had refused. And the Ciscos—a new house—had succeeded in selling the bonds of the Union Pacific, which Jay Cooke also had refused to undertake when he was occupied with governments.

Certain dramatic events transpired in American transportation in 1869. In that year the Pennsylvania system gained control of a continuous line to Chicago. The consolidation of three railroads—the New York Central, the Hudson River, and the Lake Shore & Michigan—gave Vanderbilt a practically continuous control to the same western terminal. But, most important, in May, 1869, the meeting of the Union Pacific and Central Pacific in Utah completed the first transcontinental.

The day after the last spike had been driven in the first transcontinental, the Northern Pacific again knocked at the door of Jay Cooke & Co. When that road had in 1865, 1866, and 1867 approached

Jay Cooke, he had not been interested. But this time it was different; the promoters were not only heard but even welcomed. It was not that in the meantime there had been any fundamental change in the project. The company was in 1869 still a promotion organization only, the result of a generation of discussions, surveys, and proposals for a railway from the Great Lakes to the Pacific. Having failed as a New England concern, the Northern Pacific Co. under the leadership of J. Gregory Smith of the Vermont Central Railroad had attached to itself a number of the leading railroad men of the country. With an imposing array of names, an immense land grant, and the right to mortgage the projected road and its telegraph line, the company again turned to Jay Cooke for aid.

After some investigation Jay Cooke drew up the terms on which he would consider financing the construction of the road. In a week he signed a preliminary agreement to attempt to sell $100,000,000 of the road's 7.3 per cent bonds and serve as its banker, provided that after preliminary surveys and investigations he considered the project a feasible one.

In the summer and fall four preliminary steps were taken. Extensive surveys of the Northern Pacific route convinced Jay Cooke that the country traversed bore great promise and that the estimated $100,000,000 would be sufficient to build the northern road and support it for a time. A very extensive publicity campaign attempted to build up favorable opinion concerning the Northwest and its projected road. Congressional leaders were consulted in the matter of federal aid, with no encouragement. And, lastly, the aid of the Rothschilds—which the Cookes thought would make success easy—was sought, but without success.

Moorhead, who had gone to Europe to secure the Rothschilds' aid, sent back very gloomy reports of his progress. His conclusions are illustrated by the following extract from a letter of October, 1869, about his conversation with the head of the house of Rothschild in London:

> "The old gentleman said they never engaged in anything that required risk, or trouble, in the management. This he regarded involved both. The amt too he said was very large. And there was no road built—no considerable amt of cash capital paid in—he said it would be impossible to sell the bonds. They could not offer them. He discussed evry point. I argued the value of the lands—refered to the Ill Central bonds—which were based on land &c &c, but without the least avail. He is determined and no power in America, or England, can change his mind. . . . The English and Germans, require finished roads with cash capital to induce them to purchase, or agree to sell large amounts of bonds. There may be individual speculators on this side who would go into an enterprise of this kind—but they are not to be found among the successful bankers—nor among those possessing large capitals. . . . Any house who undertakes to furnish the money for the rapid building of the N. Pacific RR. will (in my opinion) swamp—it can't be done unless the parties undertaking it have a capital of 20, or $30,000,000 to invest & thus give character to it, before they rely upon the sale of bonds abroad. . . . If you could secure Com. Vanderbilt and a few other RailRoad Capitalists—who would put in a few millions of dollars, & who would give some attention to the management—you would make a strong point—but to get the money from outside persons, who have no R. R. connections & place it in the hands of the Co. to be expended as they may think best, I fear would not accomplish your object. . . ."

There was from the first a strong division of opinion among the Cooke partners regarding the Northern Pacific. Moorhead was against it without qualification; Fahnestock and Pitt Cooke were skeptical and, at times, also strongly against the proposition.

Black Friday and the consequent depression in the fall of 1869 impressed on the Cookes that the Northern Pacific might be the way out for them—to sell bonds on commission at least did not carry too great a risk. Even so, with no prospect of securing government aid or European support, Jay Cooke as well as his partners shrank from undertaking the enterprise. Jay Cooke, therefore, proposed a modification of the original plan, that is, that the road for the present be built only to the Red River and that a request for government aid be deferred until that section had been completed. Encouraged by President Smith's assurance that they had no disposition to build more rapidly than they could prudently and economically do and that they would curtail or stop work at any time when conditions made it advisable, Jay Cooke finally decided in favor of the Northern Pacific.

On January 1, 1870, Jay Cooke & Co. agreed to the tentative contract of the previous May, with some qualifications. The conditions of the final agreement were briefly as follows. At a nominal cost Jay Cooke & Co. was to get 12 of 24 shares representing about 80 per cent of the $100,000,000 capital stock of the road; the firm was to receive the remainder as a bonus at the rate of $200 for every $1,000 in bonds sold. Jay Cooke & Co. was to select 2 of the 13 directors of the road and 2 members of the executive committee. Thirty-year bonds, bearing interest in gold at the rate of 7.3 per cent and payable in gold, were to be issued to the extent of $100,000,000, to be secured by a first mortgage on the railroad and all its lands and property; these bonds could be used in payment for the lands of the road at 110. Jay Cooke & Co. was to be the sole fiscal agent of the road and to have exclusive control of the sale of its bonds. The Cookes guaranteed to sell $5,000,000 of bonds in 30 days, but beyond that they made no guarantee as to the amount of bonds to be sold; they were to credit the railroad with $88 in currency for every $100 sold. Balances with the Cookes above $50,000 should draw 5 per cent interest. Jay Cooke & Co. should advance the road a maximum of half a million at one-half of 1 per cent a month on bonds as security. Further, they should purchase iron, rolling stock, and other material needed by the road. A land company was to be organized in connection with the road to own and improve town sites, Jay Cooke & Co. receiving 12 of its 24 shares.

7. Introducing the Northern Pacific, 1870–71

Jay Cooke's strategy in Northern Pacific financing was as follows. The first move was to secure the means with which to finance the building of the road from Lake Superior to the Red River, that is, to the western boundary of Minnesota. On the strength of the success of this first effort would be based two other moves: a campaign would be launched for selling bonds abroad and at home, and an appeal would be made for government aid. The stimulation of immigration was expected to settle the lands eventually, providing funds from land sales with which to repurchase bonds and in time furnishing traffic for the road.

The foundation of Jay Cooke's hopes for the Northern Pacific was its land grant. Bond sales would have to bear the immediate burden of construction, and it was hoped that the government would guarantee interest or give other tangible aid. But the fundamentals were land sales and traffic. An understanding of the whole negotiation hinges upon an awareness of the significance of the lands in Jay Cooke's plans for the Northern Pacific.

It was the Illinois Central, with its long and successful experience in selling its lands, which encouraged Jay Cooke to have faith in lands as a support for railroads. A circular issued by Jay Cooke & Co. on April 24, 1871, illustrates the banker's position:

"If the land grant of the Illinois Central has enabled the road to pay a large dividend annually, and to maintain its stock upon the market at $140 per share, what will a land grant of much better quality and six times as great per mile, enable the Northern Pacific Railroad to pay to its stockholders? . . . It is calculated that the sale of 287,000 acres of land annually, at only $4 per acre, and the investment of the proceeds in Northern Pacific bonds, as a Sinking Fund, compounded semiannually, will pay off the whole debt of the Northern Pacific Railroad Company before maturity."

It is important to note that under the land grant the Northern Pacific was to acquire title only as construction proceeded. Moreover, Jay Cooke could act only in an advisory capacity in the setting-up or directing of the organization which was to sell and colonize the lands. It was characteristic of him that he did not protect his plans by assuming a considerable measure of control of the project concerned.

Jay Cooke proceeded at once to organize a pool to furnish means for building to the Red River. The terms of the agreement were very attractive. For $5,600,000, to be paid over 15 months, the subscribers were to receive $5,000,000 of Northern Pacific bonds; also 12 shares out of the 24, that is, the half allotted to Jay Cooke & Co., representing $41,000,500 of stock; and half interest in the land affiliate of the Northern Pacific, which also owned a part of the land affiliate of the Lake Superior & Mississippi. Jay Cooke looked upon the land company as the best feature of the whole scheme. Proxies for the stock in the Northern Pacific were to be left with Jay Cooke & Co.

The pool campaign was a great disappointment. The Cookes failed to get prominent railroad men or capitalists to subscribe. But Jay Cooke's energy and drive brought success of a kind. The whole $5,600,000 was sold, the Cookes making heavy advances to carry subscriptions. Fahnestock warned Jay Cooke that to sell bonds on the strength of his recommendation and by personal influence might be extremely dangerous.

The next step was to secure from Congress the right to mortgage the land grant as security for the bonds. A resolution to this effect in Congress instigated a bitter fight which lasted for four months. The Cookes used all their influence with the press and their skill at lobbying and gave favors to politicians with the ostensible purpose of winning their support. The proposal was opposed especially by the middle tier of States across the continent and by rival interests. The Philadelphia *Public Ledger & Transcript,* which was owned by the Drexels, attacked the project bitterly. It is significant to observe, however, that the opposition was not chiefly against the mortgaging of the land grant. The resolution asked for a change of route which meant a considerable addition to the original land grant. On the grounds that the Northern Pacific's grant was already twice as large per mile as that of any other road, the pretext for the attack was principally this extension. It is plain that other factors, such as a growing antagonism toward railroad corporations and the feeling that Jay Cooke had already profited too much at the public expense, were behind the attack.

Though the Cookes and their road won (except that an amendment limited the iron used by the Northern Pacific to the American product), this episode is mentioned for two reasons. The debates in Congress and the publicity in the press advertised the weaknesses of the Northern Pacific; and the hard fight to pass the measure revealed clearly how little hope there was for either Jay Cooke & Co. or the Northern Pacific to get further help from the government.

In the meantime Jay Cooke & Co. made another invasion of Europe. An agreement was made with the young and weak firm of Jacob H. Schiff and Henry Budge of New York, formerly of Frankfort, whereby they should organize a group on the Continent to sell a large portion of the bonds. George B. Sargent, of Duluth, a typical western real-estate promoter, was engaged to accompany and aid the bankers as the representative of Jay Cooke & Co.

The results were unfortunate. A group of German bankers was organized to sell $50,000,000 of bonds. The German press was subsidized, and the Northern Pacific was represented conspicuously by Sargent. But a strong counter-publicity arose, apparently inspired by the Philadelphia *Ledger* of the Drexels, and the German market did not respond well. The project was therefore carried to England, which was already flooded with American railway securities and not favorably disposed toward them. It was soon clear that the Northern Pacific could hope for nothing substantial there. Then the Franco-Prussian War broke out. The first effect was panic and paralysis; and, when it became evident that the conflict would be a long one, the market settled down into inactivity and a strike of capital followed. Sargent still hoped for success with one firm, but at the end of the year he cabled, "Bischoffsheim delayed go ahead with loan America."

The beginning of the year 1871 found Jay Cooke planning to begin the public sale of the Northern Pacific loan in America. Why did he not wait until conditions were better? The answer probably lies in the Cookes' entanglements in the Northwest. The subscribers to the five-million pool who had bought the bonds on Jay Cooke's personal recommendation bound him to support the Northern Pacific, the construction of which had been started in Minnesota. His firm's heavy investments in the Lake Superior & Mississippi Railroad were threatened by the fact that the alliance of Chicago-Milwaukee transportation interests was strangling the Duluth road, and Jay Cooke was drawn into a heavy net of alliance and political intrigue to save his road. Moreover, Jay Cooke was pledged to further the well-being of Duluth and the land affiliates along the two roads for which it was a terminal. Lastly, the threat of competition on the part of the St. Paul & Pacific in northwestern Minnesota made the Northern Pacific purchase that road. Altogether, this meant great obligations for others and heavy investments on the part of Jay Cooke & Co. Since the whole structure was largely dependent on the Northern Pacific, it is clear that it would not have been a simple matter for Jay Cooke to lessen his support of the Northern Pacific in 1871.

Accordingly, the bond campaign was opened. The bankers of the country were organized for selling on commission; the press was again called upon to carry on a vigorous campaign; and Jay Cooke used all his personal influence to gain support for the project. But the bonds and the lands of the Northern Pacific sold slowly. This was the result not only of the weaknesses of the Northern Pacific but also of the apathy of a market which was becoming satiated at a time when it was flooded with investments, some much stronger than the Northern Pacific bonds.

In the spring of 1871 Jay Cooke was encouraged, by peace in Europe and the agreement of the United States and Great Britain, to submit to arbitration the controversy over the claims arising from the destruction of the *Alabama,* again to undertake negotiations abroad for the Northern Pacific. Both in England and in Germany capital came out of hiding and interest in railroad bonds increased. The New Germany, especially, was ready to put its young strength and its French indemnity into whatever promised good returns.

The European loan campaign of 1871 was carried on principally in Germany. The first move was to approach the rich Oppenheims of Cologne, one of the strongest banking houses in Germany. There Fahnestock, who headed the negotiation, ran into serious difficulties. Though the Budge associates were doing nothing to promote sales, their contract to sell Northern Pacific bonds was still in force and stood in the way of negotiations. Jay Cooke

& Co. finally disposed of them by repurchasing their $600,000 in bonds and releasing them from their contract. The aggressive house of Bischoffsheim & Goldschmidt—clever and unscrupulous bankers experienced in the railroad business, who had agreed to help negotiate the loan in England—also stood in the way of the Cookes. (Since those London bankers made no effort to sell Northern Pacifics, one is inclined to believe their only object was to maintain a connection with Jay Cooke & Co. in case refunding should again come its way.) Finally, however, a satisfactory agreement was made with the Bischoffsheims. But by that time the Oppenheims had learned that the loan had long been hawked about Europe.

Fahnestock had in the meantime established contact with the Union Bank in Vienna. This bank and a number of associates organized a group to sell the loan on condition that commissioners sent to inspect the Northern Pacific and its route reported favorably. But nothing resulted from this effort. It was a matter of months for the commissioners to inspect the route, and neither Jay Cooke and his firm nor the Northern Pacific spared any efforts in impressing the Germans. The report which they finally made was in many respects favorable, but it suggested the establishment of a reserve fund to carry interest until traffic had developed sufficiently, a condition which the road could not meet.

In 1871 a serious situation arose for Jay Cooke & Co. in its relations with the Northern Pacific. Though the bonds sold slowly, the road drew rapidly on the bankers. As early as January, Jay Cooke was disturbed by overdrafts on his houses; by autumn he was almost in a panic. He urged the executives of the road to slow down on construction, to stave off payments, and to seek more economical use of the means available. By December Jay Cooke had warned the executives of the danger of dishonoring their road's credit. But the correspondence of the president and the treasurer of the railway shows that the banker got neither the sympathy nor the coöperation of the executives of the road.

Jay Cooke threatened at the end of the year to resign from the agency if matters were not improved. At that time he made a statement to President Smith of the Northern Pacific which is very significant:

> "You must remember that my responsibility is greater than that of all the rest put together, as the money thus to be expended comes in 90 cases out of a hundred from those who purchase simply on my word. . . . If failure should occur, scarcely a word would be said or an imputation cast upon anybody but myself."

8. Reorganization and Expansion of Jay Cooke & Co.

The year 1870, which had brought profits to the Philadelphia house only and those merely paper profits, forced the Cookes again to take stock of their affairs. Though sound banking pointed toward the discontinuance of the Washington house, it was feared that such a move would weaken the Cookes' standing with the government. This might be serious at a time when they hoped to get federal aid for the Northern Pacific and some work in refunding the government debt. Certain salutary though not important changes were made in the membership of the Cooke houses. More promising was the consolidation of the three houses into one partnership and the adoption of new rules. Most significant was the effort to build up a stronger capital by placing a check on the disbursement of profits and on the freedom of the partners to make individual commitments.

At the time of the formation of the new Jay Cooke & Co., it was later estimated, the firm could command assets as given in Table 2 on the next page.

It is important to note that most of the property held by the individual partners and also a large portion of the firm's holdings could not have been made available for the firm's use on short notice. Some of the items included in the estimates below, such as real estate and stocks and bonds, were considerably overvalued.

In 1871 Fahnestock succeeded in turning his house to the development of foreign banking. For some time his firm had been doing a considerable business in importing railroad iron on commission, making foreign payments through the Browns and the Morgans. His first move was to try to establish an account with the Rothschilds or the Barings. It was probably the failure of this move, coupled with the fact that several American houses were at the time establishing branches in London, which induced the Cookes to establish a London house. Jay Cooke, McCulloch & Co. was opened in London early in 1871 with Hugh McCulloch, American banker and former secretary of the Treasury, as resident head.

The London house was expected to conduct an exchange business, loan money on government and other bonds, cash coupons, purchase railroad iron, and negotiate the sale of railroad and other securities. In other words, it was to do "everything in the way of business transactions between the two countries."

The first move was to secure the London account of the United States Navy, with the obvious purpose of getting a strong working capital in the form of government deposits. The account was not easy to secure. Both the Navy Department and the State Department accounts were then in the hands of the Barings. Any banker who took the account from them would probably lose their friendship if not also that of other bankers. And if the change should be made, there were other bankers as hungry for the business as the Cookes. Their strongest rival was Morton, Rose & Co., and the Cookes planned that, if the Mortons were given the State Department account, the Cookes would get the Navy. Jay Cooke & Co. got the Navy account, but the State went to Clews, Habicht & Co., the Mortons refusing it from fear of offending the Barings.

Fahnestock looked toward making foreign exchange, including the extension of commercial credits, the most important feature of his house. A man of excellent experience with Dennistouns in London was hired to assist French, a leading clerk in the New York house, in managing the business. Jay Cooke took little active part in this work; recognizing his partner's knowledge of that line of business, he left its management completely to him. On the strength of the foreign business, Fahnestock expected not only to make the New York house self-sustaining but also to sup-

Table 2. ESTIMATED ASSETS OF JAY COOKE & CO., AS OF JANUARY 1, 1871

Undivided profits			$737,773.34
On deposit with the firm by	Jay Cooke	$210,000.00	
	Moorhead	140,804.02	
	Fahnestock	66,727.74	417,531.76
			$1,155,305.10
Estimated value of property of	Jay Cooke	$2,697,786.69	
	Moorhead	1,691,517.74	
	Fahnestock	526,152.18	
	Pitt Cooke	250,000.00	
	Jay Cooke, Jr.	35,000.00	
	Thomas	67,364.13	
	Garland	......	
	H. D. Cooke	349,658.95	5,617,479.69
			$6,772,784.79

port the London house and carry a part of the weight of the Washington house.

While working toward a better organization and reaching out for new work, Jay Cooke and his partners tried to discontinue some of their more risky business and develop safer methods. After 1869 they did not speculate in gold. In 1871 the New York house disposed of "that heavy load *The Stock Desk*." Most significant was the adoption of the underwriting syndicate in the floating of new security issues. Some elements of the underwriting syndicate had no doubt been employed earlier in the United States—Jay Cooke used a full-fledged, modern underwriting group for the first time in connection with a small bond issue of the Pennsylvania Railroad in 1870; but the first dramatic use of such a group for a large loan was in the sale of the government loan of 1871.

Jay Cooke and his partners continued to hope for work for the government, but after the passing of the hard-fought refunding act in 1870 there was a mad scramble among bankers to get a hand in refunding. The Cooke partners, who had proved their ability to sell government loans, found that especially the Mortons, Drexels, and Seligmans stood in their way. Influenced by the clamor of the press and the urgings of rival banking houses, Secretary Boutwell entrusted the sale of $200,000,000 of the loan to national banks and a large number of bankers. Since the commission was low, the price of the bonds was not especially attractive, and there was no centralization of selling effort or manipulation of the market, the result was what Jay Cooke had foreseen.

Facing the failure of the loan, Boutwell finally turned to Jay Cooke, who undertook to organize a European and an American syndicate to underwrite $25,000,000 with an option on the remaining $105,000,000. In organizing the syndicate, however, Jay Cooke ran into much skepticism and some rivalry. The Drexels, Mortons, Barings, and Rothschilds refused to subscribe. Jay Cooke was, therefore, forced to rely on his old friends in America and, principally, on German-Jewish bankers in London.

After the two syndicates had taken $25,000,000, the rest of the loan was subscribed at once. Then came the task of helping the subscribing bankers to sell the bonds without disturbing the market. With the reluctant aid of the Treasury, Jay Cooke & Co. manipulated the money and bond market at strategic times in favor of the loan. The operation was carried out successfully and smoothly.

The sale of this loan strengthened Jay Cooke & Co. The direct profits were estimated at a quarter of a million, and the indirect profits—from trading on the market—were apparently large. The operation also greatly raised the prestige of Jay Cooke's firms. Even Morton said that it was a wonderful negotiation and that it would put Jay Cooke & Co. head and shoulders above any European banking house doing American business and make them the peers of the proudest European banking houses. Again Jay Cooke looked toward the Rothschilds, as is indicated by a reference to them in a letter to Fahnestock: "Could you not make an alliance with them which would be permanent & give us vastly additional power?"

In spite of the difficulties met, 1871 was the most profitable year that Jay Cooke's firms had ever experienced. The new London house earned the handsome sum of £100,000. The New York house divided $650,000 among its partners and its charity account, the first dividend since 1868. The Philadelphia house divided $500,000. The Washington house, alone, had nothing to divide.

9. The Fall of the Banking House of Jay Cooke, 1872–73

In spite of the Cookes' strenuous efforts, sales of Northern Pacifics were very low throughout most of 1872. There were good reasons for this: a resolution in Congress proposing an investigation of the affairs of the Northern Pacific; the statement of a senator from New England (whose campaign was aided strongly by Jay Cooke & Co.) that the lands of the road were not worth 5 cents an acre; circulars ridiculing Jay Cooke's "Banana Belt" and denouncing Jay Cooke & Co. as swindlers; but, most serious of all, the growing heaviness of the bond market, resulting from stringency in the money market and satiation of the securities market with railroad bonds.

Had the original understanding with the Northern Pacific—that the road should be built only as the sale of bonds provided the means and that it should never require an advance from the bankers of over $500,000—been adhered to, the slow sale of bonds would have made no material difference to Jay Cooke & Co. except for commissions. But this stipulation was disregarded. The officers of the road made their plans and entered into contracts for construction far ahead of the sale of bonds and expected the bankers to meet payments as they came due.

By March, 1872, the situation had become serious. Jay Cooke urged that big sums should not be disbursed without consultation with him. He especially protested against the purchase of iron for the West Coast for $800,000—paid in cash—a year before it was to be used and against the purchase of a steamboat on the Missouri long before the road reached that river. By August overdrafts totaled $1,500,000. The banker asked the directors to cover the overdrafts with their notes, but the notes were discounted by Jay Cooke & Co. At the end of the month overdrafts stood at $2,000,000, while bond sales were hardly sufficient to pay for advertising. Jay Cooke held that payments to contractors should be staved off, though he conceded that pay rolls should be cared for. The answer of the treasurer of the road was that Jay Cooke would have to bear the responsibility for the consequences of such action, if taken.

It is obvious that Jay Cooke had neither the coöperation nor the sympathy of the road's executives. They disregarded some of his rights under the contract, such as to consult him in advance about expenditures, and nonchalantly refused to take responsibility. President Smith was too busy with the Vermont Central to give much attention to the Northern Pacific, and even the directors—mostly prominent railroad men—were too occupied with their own work to follow the affairs of the Northern Pacific adequately.

By March, 1872, it was clear that Jay Cooke & Co. would suffer if matters did not improve. Fahnestock urged an appraisal of the whole business of the Cooke firms. He especially pleaded for consideration for the London house—"in a year our bills shall be unequivocally prime & shall rate always with the four bills in this city classed as such." He urged that the Philadelphia house be run on a self-sustaining basis. Instead of taking a firm stand with the railway, Jay Cooke characteristically attempted to patch up the situation. He warned the treasurer of the road to be careful about payments; he requested the president to sell the iron purchased for use in Washington Territory; he appealed to Fahnestock to secure another government deposit for the Navy account in London; he wrote with aggressive enthusiasm to McCulloch concerning the progress of the Northern Pacific, urging the London house to sell $10,000,000 in bonds; and he appealed to Puleston of Jay Cooke, McCulloch & Co. again to seek the coöperation of the Rothschilds.

The New York partners became fearful during the near-panic in the money market in April and May, 1872. The country was then financially in an unhealthy state. The great indebtedness to Europe for government and railroad bonds and the rapid tying-up of capital in fixed and unproductive investments were regarded as sources of danger. The failure of funds to return to New York from the inland as rapidly as usual in the spring served to aggravate their fears. Indeed, so bad was the situation early in May that a repetition of Black Friday of 1869 was feared.

By June Fahnestock was pleading for decisive action. He made a scorching indictment of the relations of Jay Cooke & Co. with the project. He said, "The present actual condition of the N. P. if it were understood by the public would be fatal to the negotiation of its securities." The most serious aspect of the matter to Jay Cooke & Co. was the fact that, through his strong recommendation of the bonds, Jay Cooke had become morally responsible for the honesty, good management, and success of the enterprise. Fahnestock recommended that Jay Cooke & Co. so divorce itself from the affairs of the Northern Pacific as to stand in relation to it merely as a broker and that a capable management be secured for the railroad.

In the summer of 1872 Jay Cooke could have reversed his policy on advances, which was well within his rights under the contract—he would no doubt have been severely criticized by holders of some $15,000,000 of Northern Pacifics for thus endangering the road, and Jay Cooke & Co. would have had to carry the burden of advances already made. But to Jay Cooke such action would have involved sacrifices, not of profits, for there was no longer any question of profits, but of prestige and pride. Moreover, he felt a genuine responsibility for the bondholders who had purchased on his recommendation, and as a trustee of the bondholders he had a moral and even a legal responsibility. It may be asked why he did not feel a similar responsibility for the depositors of his banking houses. Had the issue been clearly that of saving one or the other, Cooke's earlier career leads to the conclusion that he would probably have chosen the depositors. In his opinion, however, there was still a chance of saving both. If the management of the Northern Pacific could be improved and Jay Cooke & Co. given the work of refunding the government loan, or if settlement and traffic or government aid should strengthen the road, the threatened failure might turn to success. Even if everything else failed, improvement in general business conditions would help to save both the road and the banking house.

The minor panic in the money market in September, 1872, caught the New York house in a fearful condition. It held no balances for the Philadelphia house; Washington was overdrawn; and its own advances to railroads stood at about $2,600,000. It tried to borrow, but in vain—"money can hardly be raised on Govts—let alone paper of a R.R. Co. in these times." The Treasury, on Jay Cooke's urging, purchased government bonds for $3,000,000 in time to relieve the money market. On October 4 the New York house stood $3,000,000 in advance to railroads; on October 3 and 4 its deposits had been drawn down through the clearinghouse to the extent of $900,000; on October 4 the Northern Pacific had drawn $100,000 for the St. Paul & Pacific. George F. Baker then proved the friend in need: "Garland managed to have H. D. stir up Comptroller Knox to date the Banks Statement as of Yesterday Thursday 3 Oct. & that let Baker of 1st [National] loose & we took *500,000* of him at ¼ to 3 [fourths] which just let us squeak through."

Jay Cooke was caught in a trap, and he knew it. When his New York and London partners turned on him, blaming the Northern Pacific for their plight, he accused them of lukewarmness and urged them to have faith and to get to work. The protests of the partners were fully justified; as conditions were then, however, little could be done to improve matters. In the existing money market the least effort to rid Jay Cooke & Co. of the Northern Pacific would have invited disaster. Jay Cooke thought the only thing was to keep going without letting the firm's weakness be known. When the road reached the Missouri, when existing contracts for construction had been fulfilled and there would be some chance of traffic, he would throw the responsibility on the railroad.

In the meantime strenuous efforts were made to improve matters. Jay Cooke tried to keep a strong hand on the United States Treasury—he always maintained that it should stabilize the money market. He secured a salutary change in the administration of the Northern Pacific, which adopted policies more in keeping with the means available. Jay Cooke & Co. supported Grant and the Republicans in the election of 1872, hoping for favors and better business conditions under their administration.

Yet December proved to be the most difficult month Jay Cooke & Co. had ever known. The New York house, in which all the business of the firm centered, was in a position where the least run on its deposits would be fatal. It was paying 5 per cent, compounded monthly, on demand deposits, while, according to Fahnestock, no other respectable private bank (and only the Importers and Traders Bank among the chartered institutions) was paying over 4 per cent. On the evening of December 9 the New Yorkers were overdrawn $140,000 on the Bank of Commerce, with no balance to meet next morning's clearings and absolutely no collateral in the house —"without any exaggeration we are in a perfectly helpless position." The London house was at the same time in desperate need of funds—"They do not at all exaggerate the miserable poverty of the concern," said Fahnestock—and McCulloch was constantly worrying the New Yorkers with letters and cables pleading for help. During the last week of December the deposits of the New York house fell off heavily.

At this time we observe something that is both strange and significant. Though 1872 had been a difficult year, Jay Cooke & Co. had made excellent profits. The Washington house as usual had nothing to show for the year, but Philadelphia divided $500,000, London had earned a profit of £100,000, and New York reported net earnings of $505,529.

It is important to note the kinds of business which had produced such profits. The Philadelphia house apparently made most of its gains from commissions on the sale of Northern Pacifics; because of advances to the road these profits cannot be said actually to have been realized. The earnings of Jay Cooke, McCulloch & Co. speak eloquently of the success of the London house in banking growing out of foreign trade. The figures for the New York house, as shown in Table 3, are most interesting of all.

Table 3. EARNINGS OF NEW YORK HOUSE, 1872

Type of business	Amount of profit
Governments	$216,965.19
Northern Pacifics	39,721.09
Interest	89,302.95
Commissions	12,817.05
Gold Department	80,516.42
Iron Business (estimated)	100,000.00
Foreign Exchange	88,900.00
	$628,222.70

These figures need some explanation. The substantial profits in governments point to a considerable revival in the trading in government securities on the part of the New York house. It would be extremely interesting to know the source of the profits on the interest account, particularly since the house was paying 5 per cent on demand deposits; some of it came, of course, from advances to the Northern Pacific. The iron business consisted of the importing of English iron on commission, which the head of the New York house had built up. Fahnestock reports a significant fact with respect to the foreign-exchange account. The work of his house in foreign exchange during 1872 had brought earnings of $215,278 shared equally on joint account with the London house. But in the period of stringency in October, 1872, the London house had been caught so short of funds that the New Yorkers had to remit in a very difficult exchange market at a loss of $37,472. This loss, wrote Fahnestock to Jay Cooke, "resulted only from the condition in which we were obliged to keep the account because of the other enforcements of which you know (that in N. P.)."

The winter of 1873 brought no relief. The Cookes played their last trump in joining their enemies (the Mortons, Drexels, Morgans, Rothschilds, and others) and deserting their associates of 1871 in an effort to syndicate a refunding loan. The loan fell flat, which meant loss of prestige and profits for the Cookes. Congress, chilled by the revelations of corruption in the building of the Union Pacific, turned a cold shoulder to the Northern Pacific's request for aid. Worst of all, the stringency which had appeared in the money market in September, 1872, continued with only a slight interruption in the winter—"the most protracted monetary pinch which has been known for a quarter of a century," according to the *Commercial & Financial Chronicle*. Money rates rose to unusual heights; New York bank reserves fell; both Europe and America refused the plethora of railroad bonds offered; inflation was urged; and fear settled upon business.

At the same time the Northern Pacific was making remarkable progress. In June the Missouri was reached from the east and the Columbia River–Puget Sound Division was almost completed in Washington Territory. (For railroads see map facing p. 29.) In both regions there was considerable promise of traffic, and settlement was pressing into the Red River country. The Northern Pacific had also acquired some 10,000,000 acres of rich forest and agricultural land. Freight and passenger receipts were beginning to come in.

Yet necessary expenses, together with the payment due on the Oregon Steam Navigation Co. and interest payments, far outstripped all receipts. Only the boldest strategy might save Jay Cooke & Co. and the Northern Pacific. Jay Cooke accordingly tried to organize a syndicate to take the $9,000,000 in bonds remaining of $30,000,000, with the inducement that for the remainder of the bonds the interest would be lowered to 6 per cent! The effort failed in spite of Jay Cooke's aggressive salesmanship, and his promises later to take back bonds unsold. By this time many bonds had been thrown on the market—Jay Cooke regretted he did not have the means with which to bring the market price up to 95.

The improvement in business for which the Cookes had hoped did not materialize. Instead, conditions became worse. In August bonds hardly moved, interest rates rose, gold exports increased, New York bank reserves fell, and fear broke confidence.

Jay Cooke & Co. was in a hopeless condition. Table 4, drawn from the accounts of Jay Cooke & Co., shows that it was carrying a heavy load of advances to the Lake Superior & Mississippi and the Northern Pacific. (See p. 322.)

In the second week of September, 1873, the storm broke. First went the New York Warehouse & Security Co., which had been financing the Missouri, Kansas & Texas; next, Kenyon, Cox & Co., which had endorsed paper of the Canada Southern to the extent of $1,500,000.

The first break in Jay Cooke & Co. came in New York. Owing to the seasonal westward movement of money and particularly to the prevailing uneasiness over railroad securities, for several weeks there had been a steady diminution of deposits in the New York house. At the same time the Philadelphia house had continued to draw on New York. The New Yorkers, having used everything that looked like cash and converted everything possible into cash, had nothing to fall back upon when trouble came. The First National Bank of Washington had been drawn upon for some weeks; its advances to Jay Cooke & Co. from August 18 to September 18 totaled over half a million. By the morning of September 18 things had come to such a pass in the New York house of Jay Cooke & Co. that Fahnestock called in the heads of several of the leading banks in New York to advise him. The result was that just before eleven o'clock of the same morning Jay Cooke & Co., of New York, was closed.

Jay Cooke first knew of the closing of the bank after it was an accomplished fact. The result, however, could hardly have been different had he been informed of the state of affairs. There was no chance of getting advances on the paper of Jay Cooke & Co. in such a money market as then existed. The Clarks, who might have aided them, also suspended the same day. Indeed, all the friends of Jay Cooke & Co. were heavily involved in railroads. The Philadelphia house of Jay Cooke & Co. was closed at eleven, and a little later the Washington house and the First National Bank, of Washington, D. C.

The failure of Jay Cooke & Co. came at the beginning of a severe panic in New York. It was difficult to convince the "Street" that the "foremost American banking-house" was unable to meet its obligations, and, when it was realized, "dread seemed to take possession of the multitude." On the announcement that Jay Cooke's Philadelphia house and the First National Bank of Washington had suspended, the scene on Wall Street became indescribable. The stock market broke, and securities were sacrificed in the most ruthless manner. Depositors drew their money. Loans were called. Business became paralyzed. On September 21, for the first time in its existence, the New York Stock Exchange was closed.

A summary of the assets and liabilities of Jay Cooke & Co. made about a year after closing is significant, not as to the value of assets since they had shrunk

Table 4. ADVANCES OF JAY COOKE & CO. TO TWO RAILROADS AS OF AUGUST 15, 1873

(1) Lake Superior & Mississippi Railroad Co.

	Dr.	Cr.
Advanced on first mortgage bonds	$ 296,873.73	
" " second " "	1,139,350.07	
" " third " "	106,434.70	
Balance on book account, Philadelphia	56,875.43	
" " " " New York	1,347.50	
Stumpage account	264,565.38	
Total	$1,865,446.81	

(2) Northern Pacific Railroad Co.

	Dr.	Cr.
Balance on book account, Philadelphia	$1,910,359.79	
" " " " New York		$116,454.17
Notes, New York	1,898,240.00	
" Philadelphia	1,400,000.00	
Total	$5,208,599.79	
	116,454.17	
	$5,092,145.62	

greatly but as to their character. The combined liabilities of the houses and partners were $11,134,879, and of this $8,481,646 was unsecured. Assets definitely appraised, consisting of $130,333 in cash, bills receivable, and well over a million due on book accounts and bank shares, pig iron, and various bonds and stocks, amounted to $3,310,010. The homes of the partners, miscellaneous real estate in Ohio and the East, almost ninety thousand acres of land in the Middle West, various railroad securities, particularly bonds of the Sterling Iron & Railway Co. and the Northern Pacific Railroad, and a miscellany of other things were given an uncertain appraisement of $3,930,018. There remained, unappraised, thousands of shares of stock in various concerns, railroad bonds, town lots, and sundry other things.

The bankruptcy records, unsatisfactory though they are, show that Jay Cooke & Co. was very heavily invested in railroads. The roads were almost exclusively northwestern lines, the Northern Pacific or related roads. Jay Cooke & Co.'s relations with these enterprises are indicated by Table 5, which shows their interests in the various roads.

Within fifteen years after the failure of Jay Cooke & Co. the Northern Pacific was completed. Reorganization did away with heavy fixed interest charges. Efficient management cut costs. In the year 1876 receipts exceeded expenditures. In the late 1870's projected connections and branches in Minnesota and the Red River were completed about as planned by Jay Cooke, and settlement advanced in the Red River Valley, providing a market for the pine which the Northern Pacific carried westward from the forests. By 1880 the road was in a condition to attract capital, and an agreement was made with Winslow, Lanier & Co., A. Belmont & Co., and the Drexel-Morgan houses to furnish funds for construction to the Coast. Henry Villard succeeded in purchasing control of the road, and J. P. Morgan and August Belmont became

Table 5. SUMMARY OF JAY COOKE & CO.'S INTERESTS IN WESTERN RAILROADS

Bonds held:		
Value at par		
Northern Pacific Railroad Co.[a]	$5,600,000	
Lake Superior & Mississippi Railroad Co., first mortgage	437,000	
Lake Superior & Mississippi Railroad Co., income bonds	1,946,000	
Minneapolis & St. Louis Railroad Co.	226,000	
Minneapolis & Duluth Railroad Co.	55,000	
Stillwater & St. Paul Railroad Co.	116,500	
Iowa Central Railroad Co.	263,000	
Indiana & Illinois Central Railroad Co.	62,000	
	$8,705,500	
Value at cost to Jay Cooke & Co. at average of 80		$6,964,400
Cash advanced:		
Northern Pacific Railroad Co., on Oregon Steam Navigation stock	$1,500,000	
Lake Superior & Mississippi Railroad Co., on stumpage	268,822	
Lake Superior & Mississippi Railroad Co., on scrip	252,439	
Iowa Central Railroad Co., on scrip	21,942	2,043,203
Total		$9,007,603

[a] Includes those held as collateral for insolvent debtors, valued at cost.

directors. In 1883 the Northern Pacific reached Puget Sound via the railway of the Oregon Steam Navigation Co. along the Columbia River; in 1888 its own line was completed to Tacoma.

Though the Northern Pacific survived, Jay Cooke & Co. was never reopened. After the closing of the firm in September, 1873, it soon became evident that it would be impossible to settle its affairs without bankruptcy. Jay Cooke, McCulloch & Co., of London, could not continue without the aid of the parent firm. The First National, of Washington, was also liquidated. As a result Jay Cooke's whole banking organization disappeared.

The partners of Jay Cooke & Co. either retired or entered other firms. Jay Cooke himself never returned to banking. He rebuilt his personal fortune, however, through a venture in silver mining, which he had earlier refused to enter. Thomas, next to Jay Cooke in the Philadelphia house, entered a brokerage firm and eventually became a partner and senior resident in Drexel & Co., of Philadelphia. Fahnestock and Garland of the New York house entered the First National Bank, of New York. Garland gained a reputation as one of the best brokers on the Street; Fahnestock was made head of the bond department of the First National and as such directed a considerable business during the subsequent refunding of the war debt, in which the First National played a leading part. Thus individual partners continued in business, though Jay Cooke & Co. disappeared.

10. Readings

For further details on the business career of Jay Cooke and the work of Jay Cooke & Co. consult Henrietta M. Larson, *Jay Cooke, Private Banker* (Cambridge, 1936).

Chapters on Jay Cooke's personality and character and his interests outside business are found in E. P. Oberholtzer, *Jay Cooke, Financier of the Civil War* (Philadelphia, 1907).

11. Suggested Questions

1. Jay Cooke's system of bond distribution was remarkably successful during the war. Why was it not so effective in selling Northern Pacifics? Has this any general significance for investment banking?
2. Baron Rothschild refused the invitation to join Jay Cooke & Co. in taking over the financing of the Northern Pacific project because it involved too much risk and trouble in management. Was Cooke justified in proceeding contrary to Rothschild's judgment?
3. What errors in policy did Jay Cooke make in 1869–73?
4. Did the completion of the Northern Pacific in 1888 vindicate Jay Cooke's judgment as a banker?

XXI. THE DEVELOPMENT OF THE NEW YORK STOCK EXCHANGE

1. General Statement

The New York Stock Exchange started as a voluntary, unincorporated, private club of members to provide for themselves a trading place and rules governing trade in securities. It attempted to be exclusive, and prizing secrecy it shunned publicity in any form, holding to the ideal that its business was a private matter. Today the Exchange is still a voluntary association of members to provide a market place and rules of trading in securities, but it now stands as an institution weighted with public responsibility. Its operations are regarded as being of deep public concern because they closely affect the value of securities and business conditions that influence the well-being of the public at large.

2. Important Dates in the History of the New York Stock Exchange

1792	Original brokers' agreement.
1817	The New York Stock and Exchange Board organized.
1830	First rail stock, the Mohawk & Hudson, listed.
1863	Name changed to New York Stock Exchange.
1866	Atlantic cable opened.
1867	Stock tickers introduced.
1868	Membership made salable.
1869	Establishment of a governing committee of 28 members. Consolidation of the New York Stock Exchange and the Open Board of Brokers.
1871	Continuous market for stocks established.
1878	Telephones on the Exchange floor.
1879	Forty new memberships authorized to pay for enlargement of the building.
1881	Electric annunciator board installed.
1885	Department of unlisted securities established.
1892	Organization of Stock Clearing House.
1909	"Hughes Investigation" of speculation in securities and commodities.
1912–13	"Money Trust" investigation by the Pujo Committee.
1922	Questionnaire for regular examination of the financial condition of members' firms inaugurated.
1926	Listing committee instructed to give careful thought to the matter of voting control in considering applications.
1930	New high-speed ticker service started.
1932	Membership numbered 1,375.
1933	Federal Securities Act passed.
1934	Securities Exchange Commission established. Active reform movement within the Exchange began to gain way.

3. Beginnings, 1792–1816

"We, the Subscribers, Brokers for the Purchase and Sale of Public Stock, do hereby solemnly promise and pledge ourselves to each other, that we will not buy or sell from this day for any person whatsoever, any kind of Public Stock at a less rate than one-quarter per cent Commission on the Specie value, and that we will give a preference to each other in our Negotiations. In testimony whereof we have set our hands this 17th day of May, at New York, 1792."[1]

The above was the first written agreement among New York stockbrokers. It was the result of a meeting held in March, 1792, at Corré's Hotel by the "merchants and dealers in stocks" at which certain resolutions had been adopted providing for the appointment of a committee on organization and forbidding the members of the group to deal in any sale of stocks at public auction. Previously the auctioneers had endeavored to establish a public stock market by holding daily sales under a joint arrangement.

The following list of quotations in a New York newspaper for May 26, 1792, shows the size of the market at the time:[2]

Stock	Price
6 per cents	22s. 0d.
3 per cents	12s. 8d.
Deferred	13s. 2d.
Indents	12s. 3d.
Final Settlements	18s. 6d.
Half Shares Bank U. S.	50 per cent premium
Shares Bank of North America (Philadelphia)	15 per cent premium

[1] Francis L. Eames, *The New York Stock Exchange* (New York, 1894), p. 14; for list of signers and their occupations see the appendix.

[2] *Ibid.*, p. 15. Twenty shillings equivalent to par.

The above list shows how narrow was the supply of securities in 1792: (1) the "stocks" representing the war debt owed or assumed, from the States, by the federal government and (2) bank stocks. The list was later broadened by the issue of State bonds for internal improvements, and banks and insurance stocks. Few of the securities of business enterprises, however, found their way to the central market. The lack of quick communication, moreover, made security dealings distinctly local, although there were some arbitrage dealings between New York, Boston, and Philadelphia.

For twenty-five years the business of the stockbrokers warranted neither a very close organization nor a definite market place—in good weather they met on the street, in bad weather in the Merchants' Exchange. The increase in trading caused by the borrowing of the government during the War of 1812 and by the rapid growth of banks and insurance companies made necessary, however, a new form of organization among brokers.

4. Formal Organization and the Development of Rules, 1817–43

On February 25, 1817, thirteen individual brokers and the representatives of seven firms held a meeting in the office of Samuel J. Beebe in the old Tontine Coffee House and appointed a committee on organization. This committee reported a set of rules, now known as the Constitution of 1817, which prescribed in detail the methods for transacting the business of dealing in securities. The following articles are quoted from this constitution:

"It shall be the duty of the President to call the Stocks at the hour that may be fixed upon by the Board, from time to time, as the season may require. . . . [The President would stand up on the rostrum and read off each stock in order. Trading in each stock would take place when that stock was 'called.']

"It shall be the duty of the Secretary to keep the minutes of the Board in a book for the purpose, an account of all fines, and to collect the same, and also a register of all actual sales of Stocks made at the Board, the register to be accessible to members of the Board only.

"The election of new members shall be by ballot—he or they must be proposed at least three days preceding the election, and three black balls shall exclude."

The rest of the articles of the constitution deal with the rates of commission, the mechanics of election to the Board, and points of order. A week after the adoption of these articles an amendment was added: [3]

"Passed by unanimous vote, March 15, 1817, that no fictitious sale or contract shall be made at this board. Any member or members making a fictitious sale or contract shall, upon conviction thereof, be expelled from the Board."

The great number of resolutions passed in this formative period shows the difficulties with which the brokers came in contact while trying to establish a permanent organization. The following excerpts from the proceedings of the Board [4] show what their troubles were:

"Saturday, March 15, 1817.

"Resolved, That sales made at this Board are to be settled for on the next day succeeding the day of sale, unless expressed to the contrary."

[3] E. C. Stedman, *The New York Stock Exchange* (New York, 1905), p. 65. The making of such a fictitious contract came to be called a "wash sale." In both a "wash sale" and a "matched order" there is no change of ownership. In the first, two persons engage in a fictitious transaction usually in order to establish an artificial price with no real intention of exchanging money or goods. In a "matched order," an outsider gives one broker an order to sell and another broker an order to buy the same security at the same price and so attempts to manipulate the price of a security. Both brokers could be innocent and still be the unconscious agents of collusion.

[4] *Ibid.*, pp. 65–66.

"Monday, April 14, 1817.

"Resolved, That in all sales of Specie between Brokers, the purchaser shall send for the same, or pay the expense, if any, when the seller delivers it."

"Tuesday, April 29, 1817.

"Resolved, That James Arden is not competent for any Broker to receive an order from."

"November 10, 1817.

"Resolved, That no member of this Board, nor any partner of a member, shall hereafter give the prices of any kind of Stock, Exchange or Specie, to any printer for publication, and that the Secretary of the Board only be authorized to give prices for that purpose."

"November 29, 1817.

"Resolved, That the Secretary be authorized to furnish the prices of Stock but once a week, to one price current only, at his discretion, and that no other quotation be made for publication."

"December 9, 1817.

"Resolved, That all offers made and accepted shall be considered binding, whether called by the President or not, but where there may be more than one claimant the Stock may be put up again at the same or higher rate, or withdrawn, at the option of the person so offering."

The Board evidently had some trouble in keeping their operations secret, for on January 26, 1819, the following resolution was adopted: [5]

"It is mutually understood that the members of this Board do not communicate to persons out-doors what members of this Board are the purchasers or sellers of stocks at this Board, or what members offer to purchase or sell."

The constitution was revised in 1820, but the new regulations did not contain any vital innovations. The Board had always been extremely jealous of its privileges; only one new member had been admitted in 1817, although several outside brokers had made unsuccessful attempts to get in. The revised constitution prescribed an initiation fee of $25 and made still further restrictions upon the rules of admission. Another attempt to raise the standards of the association is seen in article 13 of the revised articles.[6]

"Any member who fails to comply with his contracts, or becomes insolvent, shall be suspended until he has settled with his creditors. On his application for re-admission, a committee of five members shall be appointed to investigate his conduct and the causes of his failure, who shall report the same, and if two-thirds of the members present are for reinstating him, he shall again be entitled to his seat at the Board, excepting when his failure has been caused by speculations on his own account, or for the account of persons whose responsibility is merely nominal; in that case he shall no longer be considered a member of the Board until such engagements are settled."

At this time a set of by-laws was established. These provided that stocks and specie should not be offered in amounts of less than $500. No offer was to be allowed under one-quarter per cent, unless for sums of more than $1,000. When two members claimed acceptance of the same bid or offer, the man making it might withdraw it if he wished. Indecorous conduct on the part of a member made him liable to suspension for not less than a week nor more than a month. A fine of six cents was imposed for nonattendance at the calling of the stocks unless the member was sick or out of town. The fines and fees were to be applied to the payment of the expenses of the Board. If those were not sufficient, the balance was to be equally shared by the members.

Soon after the adoption of the Constitution of 1817 the first regular meeting room was rented from George F. Vaupell at 40 Wall Street for $200 per annum, "he to furnish fire and chairs, when required, and to keep the room in order." [7] Between the years 1819 and 1827 (when

[5] Eames, *op. cit.*, p. 18.

[6] Stedman, *op. cit.*, pp. 67–68.

[7] *Ibid.*, p. 65.

the Merchants' Exchange was built), the Board moved about a great deal from one meeting place to another. Mention is made in the records of the "lower back room in the rear of the Protection Fire Company," a room at Washington Hall, and "Mr. Warren's Room." After 1827 the Board met regularly at the Merchants' Exchange until that building was destroyed by the fire in 1835.[8] From then until the New Merchants' Exchange was built in 1842 the Board moved from one place to another, at one time renting a room once used as a hayloft.

The daily turnover of stocks, even after the regular exchange had been established, was not very large. During 1827 there were some days when the total sales were as low as 14 shares, although 100 shares seem to have been a fair day's trading. During 1830 and 1831 the amount was larger, for "thousand share days" were not unusual.[9]

Besides this buying and selling on the Exchange there was also a certain amount of street selling of varying proportions which could not be controlled by the Board. These sales were at times reported to have been as large as those at the Board, and undoubtedly the prices used were those set by the Board at its morning call. The relation between the Board and the Curb at this time was described in a New York State Assembly document of 1836: [10]

> "One great object of meeting together in the morning as a board, is to ascertain who desires to buy and sell a particular stock, which buying and selling, to a great extent, is done publicly in the street, or at the exchange, after the board adjourns, and after the prices of the morning are made known to those, out of the board, who may desire to buy or sell."

Although the trading list for 1817 was long in comparison with that of 1792, it still contained only bonds of federal and state governments, and banks and insurance company stocks. No industrial or railroad shares were included.[11] Such stocks as would probably fall into the public utility class today were at that time listed as State stocks, being issued by the State governments to finance water companies, highways, and other internal improvements. After the War of 1812 had come a rapid increase in incorporation. By 1818 there were 392 banks in the country,[12] and coupled with this growth in banks was the increase in the number of marine and fire insurance companies.

Speculation then became rampant, especially in such shares as those of the United States Bank. The State of New York tried to curb speculative activity in the security market by passing a law in 1812 aimed primarily at short selling. This act, like its English predecessor passed in 1734, was, however, not very effective.[13] It failed to stop short selling and at the same time it provided a lawful way for the breaking of inconvenient contracts. The act was repealed, and short sales became legalized by an act of the New York Assembly in 1858.[14] If this law of 1812 had not been a dead letter from the start, it is doubtful whether the New York Stock and Exchange Board would have found the increase in busi-

[8] Only a few important records of the Board were saved.

[9] Margaret G. Myers, *The New York Money Market,* vol. i (New York, 1931), p. 18.

[10] Quoted in *ibid.*

[11] Boston, the manufacturing center of the country at that time, had no industrial shares listed on its exchange until 1827 (*ibid.,* p. 15).

[12] Stedman, *op. cit.,* p. 77.

[13] J. E. Dos Passos, *A Treatise on the Law of Stock Brokers and Stock Exchanges* (New York, 1905), pp. 488–489.

[14] This act reëstablishing the doctrine of the common law, provided that "no contract, written or verbal, . . . made for the purchase, sale, transfer, or delivery of any certificate . . . shall be void, or voidable, for any want of consideration, or because of the non-payment of any consideration, or because the vendor at the time of making such contract is not the owner or possessor of the certificate. . . ." (*ibid.,* p. 492)

ness during the panic year of 1819 such as to warrant the revision of its constitution and the adoption of a formal set of by-laws.

Activity upon the Stock Exchange increased after the rise of railroad securities in 1831. While canal stocks were the chief transportation securities during the 'twenties, rails became of great importance during the 'thirties and maintained that position throughout the century. The Mohawk & Hudson was the first railroad listed on the Exchange.[15] By 1831 the value of the steam locomotive as compared to horse power had been demonstrated. Capital poured forth as the speculative propensities of steam railroads were recognized. Part of this capital came from the State legislatures before 1838, but the greater part of it came from individuals. By 1840 there were about 3,000 miles of road in operation; by 1850 about 9,000; and by 1860 about 30,000 miles.[16]

The entrance of transportation securities into the market paved the way for stock manipulations. The first real corner on the Exchange was in 1835 in the stock of the Morris Canal & Banking Co. This corner was probably engineered by John Ward with Jacob Little and Daniel Drew as associates.[17] The stock was quietly bought up at 30 to 40 per cent below par, while the pool went into the street and made enormous time purchases. On settling day the clique unloaded at 150, clearing nearly 300 per cent.

This corner is the first real indication of a major obstacle in the path of the development of the Stock Exchange as a free market. For the rest of the nineteenth century the brokers who were attempting to build up a safe and regularized market for securities had to struggle, not only to curb great stock manipulations but also to maintain their control over the market itself. The abuses to which the market was subject during this period tended to build up an attitude of public hostility to the Exchange from which it has never recovered, despite the fact that business ethics have changed considerably in the meantime.

The dealings of Jacob Little, the first outstanding stock manipulator, are characteristic of the kind of thing which the Board, as an association, tried to regulate. Jacob Little was the pioneer of that class of speculative operators of which Drew, Vanderbilt, and Gould later became conspicuous examples.[18] The use of the convertible bond trick in stock manipulation seems to have originated with him. In 1840 he started a bear campaign against Erie shares, disposing of large blocks of stock on sellers' options running from six to twelve months. An attempt was made to corner him. The price was raised and no stock was available when his contracts matured. However, the crafty manipulator had bought in the London market Erie bonds which were convertible into stock, and he emerged from the crisis unscathed. The result of this coup was the passing of a new rule by the Stock and Exchange Board, which limited the duration of sellers' options to sixty days. This did not, however, prevent future performances of like nature.[19]

In the year of the corner in Morris Canal an audacious corner in Harlem stock was also engineered. When the pool ran the price up to 200, the determined shorts called a meeting of the Board. The brokers elected a committee of four to receive the payment of differences and to act as a committee of arbitration between the parties.

As a result of these operations the

[15] Aug., 1830 (Stedman, *op. cit.*, p. 87).

[16] Myers, *op. cit.*, p. 33.

[17] Stedman, *op. cit.*, p. 102.

[18] It is said that Little made and lost nine fortunes between 1837 and 1857. He was perpetually engaged in speculation, spending his mornings at the cotton exchange and his afternoons at the Stock Exchange (*ibid.*, p. 101).

[19] *Ibid.*, p. 102.

Board appointed a committee to investigate corners in general.

"It was said by a financial writer of that day that 'the system so much indulged in of late of time bargains and cornering will probably be sifted to the bottom. The recent operations in Morris Canal stock, the Harlem Railroad, and the Montauk Railroad have been a series of puzzles to the community, as much so as the roulette table or the faro-bank to the uninitiated in gambling.' "[20]

It is interesting to note the following advertisement of 1835, which reveals a high conception of the function and the ethics of the broker, a conception absolutely contrary to the methods of Jacob Little:[21]

"JOHN THOMPSON, No. 12 Wall St.,

"Pledges himself to his customers and friends that in his stock negotiations he will do nothing on his own account—his time and ability in all cases shall be devoted for the benefit of those who favor him with their orders."

The actions of Little and of that powerful group of speculators of which he was the forerunner damaged the power and prestige of the New York Exchange. In some cases their operations caused a tightening of the rules; in most cases their actions lowered the prestige of the whole group, even of those brokers who were attempting to build up a free, open, and regularized market for securities.

A second effect of the increased activity upon the Exchange caused by the influx of rail securities was the establishment of a rival group of stockbrokers sometime prior to 1836. This was organized by some of the more enterprising, or outside, traders of the curb. This board came to an end in 1848 when most of its members were taken into the old board. The following is taken from a description of the two boards, which was published in 1848:[22]

"The Old Board . . . is very exclusive in its character, and sits with closed doors. As a qualification for admission, a person must have transacted business in Wall Street for one year, and be at peace with all the world, or rather have satisfactorily settled all just obligations, if he has been in any difficulties or embarrassment. The admission fee is $400, and an applicant is excluded if only three black balls are cast into the ballot box. Nothing can entitle an individual to a seat except the votes of the members, and, therefore, there are several applicants refused for one admitted. Members, of course, are not obliged to account for their votes, and, therefore, a person is as likely to be refused from private pique or prejudice as anything else.

"This exclusiveness provoked the formation of another Board of a more democratic character, at which the transactions, prior to 1836, exceeded those of the old association, and the number of its members was also larger. . . . It numbers at present but fifteen or twenty members, and they are mostly small potatoes with small means. It is principally sustained by its gentlemanly and talented President, who was once a large and wealthy operator in the Old Board, and had accumulated some few hundred thousands. He was obliged, however, in common with others, to succumb; but is prevented from reentering on account of his having prudently settled $100,000 on his better half in the height of his prosperity, of which, of course, he refused to deprive her when he surrendered his own resources.

"The Old Board numbers about seventy-five members, who assemble from half-past ten o'clock until noon, and from a quarter of three until three o'clock. Members are called to order by the President, who commences the business of the Board by repeating the names of the different stocks or securities, pausing at each for the members to buy or sell. All transactions are recorded by the Secretary as they occur, and these are generally reported in the leading papers of the day.

"When the brokers are not in session, they,

[20] S. S. Pratt, *The Work of Wall Street* (New York, 1910), p. 12.

[21] Eames, *op. cit.*, p. 30.

[22] *Ibid.*, pp. 34–35.

as well as all other operators and interested persons, assemble promiscuously at the corner of Wall and Hanover Streets . . . and it not infrequently happens that more business is done in the open air than at both the Boards."

A third effect of the rise of railroad securities upon the Exchange was the fact that it helped to provide a more solid foundation for a permanent securities market. The increase of the public debt after 1812 revived the security market; the practical wiping-out of the public debt in 1835 had no material effect since new securities had become definitely established.

It is important to note that in this period the Exchange, though the most important and the most rapidly growing stock exchange in the country, had not yet risen to a dominant position in investment finance. The flotation of new securities was wholly unrelated to the exchange, being done directly by the issuing corporation itself or through local or other agencies, notably commercial and investment banks and bankers working at home and abroad. Leaders among these investment bankers were Brown Brothers & Co., Prime, Ward & King, Nevins, Townsend & Co., the Morris Canal & Banking Co., the Bank of Manhattan Co., and the Phenix Bank. The trade in securities on the market was, moreover, by no means centralized. A large proportion of the securities was traded over the counter, though decreasingly of course as the decades passed. The local exchanges, as in Boston and Philadelphia, were also sufficiently active to take care of much local business.

5. Some Significant New Factors, 1844–61

The upswing in business confidence and activity in the late 'forties and early 'fifties, stimulated by the additions to the national wealth caused by the discovery of gold, inaugurated a new era of speculation and investment. Railroad construction proceeded rapidly and money poured into banks. The banks lent their credit freely to the promotion of new enterprises. The increase in securities caused great activity on the Exchange. Rail stock was watered, fraudulent stock was issued, and forged stock was sold. These developments brought new problems to the stock market in general and to the Exchange in particular.

At this time the growing investment and speculative activity came to be concentrated in New York. Basic to this development were (1) the widening of the investment market through the new telegraph and (2) the general effect of improved transportation on the commercial position of New York.

The rise of New York to commercial leadership brought to that city demand deposits of banks, which were actually bank reserves; and these deposits furnished funds for the development of a strong call-loan market. The early history of call loans in New York is obscure; it is definitely known that collateral demand loans were made in 1837 and that by 1843 call-loan rates were quoted in newspapers and call loans were discussed in *Hunt's Merchants' Magazine.*[23] The term "call loans" came to be commonly used about 1845, and by 1857 such loans were usually included in any account of the market.

Call loans, says a recent study,[24] brought about a new technique for financing the purchase of securities and carrying the burden of marginal sales of stock. Until such loans were established as part of the financial mechanism of New York, most of the security financing had been done on time, and the brokers had not generally assumed responsibility for financing purchases. "As the growth of

[23] Beginning July, 1843, in the "Monthly Commercial Chronicle."

[24] The discussion of the call loan below follows closely Myers, *op. cit.*, chap. vii, in some instances quoting verbatim.

bankers' balances made larger sums available for call loans, the proportion of stocks sold on time declined, and by 1857 daily settlements were more frequent than time settlements on the New York Stock Exchange."

The call loan had several features which made its use attractive to speculators engaged in buying stocks on margin. In ordinary times call loans were available at a lower rate than time loans on a similar security. Of course in times of monetary stringency this was not so, as the call rates rose higher than the time rates; nevertheless, "call loans were nearly always obtainable at a price, while time loans were frequently unobtainable during a panic even though the nominal rate would be low." The question of margin trading provides an interesting problem, for stock speculation on margin has been carried on in America to a greater extent than in any other country. Margin trading is really complementary to the call-loan system, and "it was certainly a factor in the extreme variation of stock prices to which the New York market was subject."

While the call-loan market had a considerable influence upon the investment market, it was also affected by it. Call loans upon collateral security could never have become widespread unless there had existed a security market of sufficient size to offer diversified collateral and ensure the selling of such collateral under normal conditions. Thus the growth of the call-loan market paralleled the growth of the security market, and the use of call loans in the financing of security transactions is linked directly with the development of the New York Stock Exchange.

On the relation of the call loans to banking reserves the effect is not so apparent, but this relationship also exerted an influence upon the Stock Exchange. As the call-loan market developed before the Civil War, it gradually became the central reservoir for the banking reserves of the nation and in time of panic it carried the responsibility for providing the banks with funds. There was no central bank to which the banks could apply for aid, and the New York Clearing House had not yet developed the technique for aiding in an emergency by issuing loan certificates. The New York banks, left to go their own way, invested most of their funds in call loans. If the balances in New York had been merely surplus funds seeking investment which had no relation to bank reserves, the situation would have been different. In reality, however, a large share of the bankers' balances in New York actually consisted of the country bankers' cash reserves. These funds were invested in call loans, which were of a "shiftable" rather than an actually liquid nature. The demand for the return of a deposit by a country bank would necessitate the lowering of the loans and discounts of the New York bank by that sum, thus shifting the burden to another or causing stock prices to decline.

The panic of 1857 advertised the faults of the call-loan system. The panic was precipitated by the failure of the New York branch of the Ohio Life Insurance and Trust Co., which carried heavy balances of western banks which it had loaned out on the call market with rail stocks as collateral. Thus, when falling prices in the stock market lowered the value of this collateral to such an extent that many borrowers could not repay their loans, the country balances which were being demanded could not be sent back. The New York banks were the center of the American banking system, and there was no agency to which they could resort for aid. They had trusted to the call-loan market as a reserve, instead of keeping a supply of specie on hand sufficient to tide them over a crisis, as a central bank would have done.

There had been much criticism before 1857 which recognized the danger to the individual bank, but it had not arrived at what is now considered to be the basic difficulty, namely, the pyramiding of actual bank reserves in New York City which were placed in call loans. After this panic the connection between the actual bank reserves of the country and the call-loan market was definitely recognized.

6. Period of the Great Speculators, 1861–77

The New York Stock Exchange in 1861 is well described in the following: [25]

"Less than a hundred members were accustomed to gather at the sessions of sixty-one. . . . Lord's Court, the Board Room (which was approached through intricate passages), was a crowded scene on busy days. The rostrum, at one end of the chamber, ran nearly the length of the row of four high, arched windows behind it. . . . Tables ornamented with inkstands ran lengthwise through the room, and here sat members scribbling memoranda or following the bids and offers as each security was called. Others crowded into the spaces between the tables, and each man rose from his seat whenever he had occasion to take an active part in the market. The chimney-pot hats of the decade previous still flourished, though a trifle lower in the crown. They contrasted here and there with soft, round specimens of headgear, resembling somewhat the flat, black hats, now favored by a portion of the clergy, and most conveniently designed to skim through the air with buoyancy and speed when tossed away by a facetious neighbor. Practical jokes enlightened the monotony of a dull period of trading, and a serious man would have cause to wonder betimes at the levity of his fellows, being thoroughly disgusted that he could not enjoy a quiet discussion of the money market or the latest news from the front without learning that some light-witted member had pinned an unseemly poster to his respectable coat-tails."

This picture of the Exchange in 1861 is valuable because during the next twenty years many changes were to be made in its organization, in its methods of trading, in the type of its members, and in its relations with the public. A direct repercussion of the panic of 1857 was the influx of young blood and new ideas into American business. Many of the older Stock Exchange members were forced into bankruptcy by the panic, and their places were filled with young men. One young man who forced his way into the Stock Exchange at this time described the situation years afterwards: [26]

"This panic and its immediate results created an entire revolution in the methods of doing business in Wall Street. Prior to this time, the antique element had ruled in things financial, speculative and commercial. This crisis sounded the death knell of old fogyism in the 'street.' A younger race of financiers arose and filled the places of the old conservative leaders.

. . . .

"This struggle for new life in Wall Street was not successfully developed without a serious effort to attain it. The old potentates of the street fought hard to prolong their obstructive power, and their tenacious vitality was hard to smother, reminding one of the nine lives attributed to the feline species. The efforts of the young and enterprising men to gain an entrance to the Stock Exchange were regarded by the older members as an impertinent intrusion on the natural rights of the senior members. It was next to impossible for a young man, without powerful and wealthy patrons, to obtain membership in the New York Stock Exchange at the time of which I speak."

The opportunity for the rising generation to gain a foothold and to become prominent was provided by the Civil War. The two outstanding characteristics of the decade of the 'sixties were the speculation in gold and greenbacks and the struggle of a few strong men for railroad supremacy. Speculation in gold had been brought on by the issuing of irredeemable paper money by the government. The popularity of gold speculation was widespread,

[25] Stedman, *op. cit.*, p. 145.

[26] Henry Clews, *Fifty Years in Wall Street* (New York, 1908), pp. 6–7.

not only because it afforded such rapid-fire action, but also because the uncertain quality of the public money increased the speculative element in all legitimate business. Thus the effect upon all classes, whether merchants or laborers or something else, was pronounced because of the fluctuations in legal tender. In the face of this disturbance, however, the government was buying huge supplies, reducing the number of men available for industry, and paying high prices. Such a general inflation produced temporary stimulation in American business. New enterprises were started, promoters flourished, and stock speculation overflowed the Exchange to such an extent that minor exchanges became active.

Some of those minor exchanges achieved a degree of respectability, but most of them stand as examples of what irresponsible speculative trading can do. Some were short-lived and passing in their importance, while a few helped to influence the old Exchange to make needed reforms. They varied in character from the short-lived speculative bucket shop and evening markets to more lasting exchanges on which legitimate trading was done according to fixed rules. Unhampered by old rules and traditions, the new trading groups introduced new methods of trading and new forms of manipulation which were demoralizing in their effect on stock trading. But some of the minor exchanges had a significant influence on the old Exchange.

The street market for securities, which had existed from earliest times in New York, continued to function at this time. In 1861 the meeting place was in William Street. This market differed from the Curb of today in that it did not confine its activities to securities unlisted on the Exchange. It was in fact, says Stedman, used by members of the Board for the execution through younger brokers of orders which could not be put through at the calls on the Exchange. This street market expanded greatly with the increase in speculation. While stocks were being called on the Stock and Exchange Board, Curb operations were suspended, but for the rest of the time it provided the only continuous market for securities in New York. No records of its transactions were made.[27]

The new exchanges which were established at the time of the Civil War varied in character. There was Goodwin's Room, in which trading followed quotations relayed through a keyhole of the Stock Exchange.[28] Another, known as the Coal Hole, established in 1862 in a gloomy basement, was open to anyone who paid a low annual subscription. Started for the benefit of brokers who were not members of the Exchange, it soon developed into a gold market and moved into more commodious quarters. In "Gilpins' news room" this exchange became the center of a great speculation in gold under somewhat easy rules.

The crystallization of a new speculative movement led to the establishment of another exchange. In 1857 and 1859 unsuccessful mining exchanges had been established, and from 1861 to 1864 mining shares had been traded on the New York Stock and Exchange Board. In the latter year, however, the Mining Board of New York was organized by 41 brokers, with regulations and an initiation fee. The following description is characteristic of the times and of the business conducted on this exchange: [29]

> "Here the magic process of working up the shares of unknown mining companies—the chief assets of which were credit at a job printer's and faith in American prosperity—gratified the eyes and in time appropriated the cash of the beholder.
>
> . . . .

[27] Stedman, *op. cit.*, p. 146.
[28] *Loc. cit.*
[29] *Ibid.*, p. 158.

". . . The age of Coal Oil Johnny had begun.[30] An immense class of illiterate men, suddenly entrusted with a wealth which dazzled them by its newness, were amusing and startling civilization in their efforts to get rid of it. . . ."

In 1866 the brokers dealing in mining and oil stocks united, forming the Petroleum and Mining Board, but the notorious reputation of this exchange soon proved its undoing.

One of the more important of the newer exchanges was the "Open Board of Stockbrokers." This group, the nucleus of which was the more responsible dealers who had frequented the Coal Hole and earlier the Curb, in 1864 formed a definite organization with a constitution and regulations.[31] This organization admitted the public to the board room. It was governed by an executive committee and had an initiation fee of $500. Calls were made on the board at 1 o'clock and 3:15 in the afternoon and later at 10 in the morning. At other hours the Open Board held a continuous market on the street and, beginning late in 1865, in the "Long Room" of the new building of the Stock Exchange. Here brokers of all boards met and operated a continuous market, and the sales at the calls were relatively small.[32]

It is significant to note that during this period the Stock Exchange was only one of the stock exchanges functioning in New York, and its business was only a part—and probably at times a smaller part—of the business done on the "Street." In the brokerage business of New York of 1865, according to the records of the Bureau of Internal Revenue, the three leading firms in the amount of business done were firms apparently connected with the Open Board of Brokers.[33]

[30] Petroleum was first found in large quantities by Edwin L. Drake at Titusville, Pa., in 1859 (*ibid.*, p. 124).

[31] Eames, *op. cit.*, p. 43.

[32] *Ibid.*, pp. 150–151.

[33] Stedman, *op. cit.*, p. 162.

Various classes of traders made up the dealing in the stock market. There were the brokers, the heavy operators, and those smaller occasional investors known as outsiders. A contemporary divided the *habitués* of the exchange into three classes: (1) operators who speculated generally for themselves and sometimes for others; (2) brokers, who bought and sold for outsiders and themselves; and (3) bankers, who were a combination of operator, broker, and moneylender.

The so-called operator was the most conspicuous and the most disturbing individual in the stock market at the time, and he was also the greatest obstacle in the way of free competition on the Stock Exchange. He continued to occupy that position almost till the end of the 1870's.

The outstanding operators of this period were such men as Daniel Drew, Henry Keep, Anthony Morse, Commodore Vanderbilt, James Fisk, Thomas C. Durant, Leonard and Addison G. Jerome, and William H. Marston. Commodore Vanderbilt differed from most of those operators in that his aim was to control in order to build a better system of transportation; the general run of operators were out-and-out gamblers.

The favorite tool of the operator was the pool and his object the corner. The cornering of the market was not so difficult then as it later became for the reason that even the largest corporations had rather small capital. The capital of eight railroads which were the popular subject of speculation ranged from the $6,000,000 of the Rock Island to the $24,000,000 of the New York Central. The other six were the Erie, Harlem, Hudson River, Michigan Southern, Prairie du Chien, and the Fort Wayne.

One notorious operation is described in the following: [34]

"Among the operators who achieved both reputation and bankruptcy in the sixties was

[34] *Ibid.*, pp. 188–189.

William H. Marston, the contriver of the famous Prairie du Chien corner. Marston was formerly the cashier of an Illinois bank. He was attracted to this city by its alluring promises of fortune, and became a commission broker in the Street. His business prospered, and from a broker he developed into a speculator of prominence. In company with Henry Keep, a leading director in the Michigan Southern & Northern Indiana Railroad, he made great profits by bulling the stock of that property. This was in the summer of 1865. In the fall of that year he accumulated a large amount of Michigan & Prairie du Chien Railroad stock, a commodity then known in Street parlance as 'Prairie Dog,' which had been selling at about $60 a share. November saw an exciting corner in these shares.

"The Michigan Southern movement had culminated on October 6th, when a cash sale was made at 84½, a rise of about fifteen points in less than a week. A break in gold compelled a quick unloading by the Keep-Marston clique, and Michigan Southern fell to 76¾ on the following day. But the movement had been profitable. The manipulation of Prairie Dog followed hard on its heels. Marston, it is said, originally planned merely to raise that stock to par, but finding that there was a general disposition on the part of the road's directors to attack it he determined upon a more aggressive campaign for their humiliation. Short sales had hammered Prairie du Chien to $57 a share on October 21st. Marston and his associates kept steadily buying, and by November 4th they had advanced the price to 96. The stock amounted only to about 52,000 shares, and it had been easily oversold. The frightened shorts found it impossible to cover. Some of them obtained private settlements at once, and the newspaper press of the day reported that a single house had paid $125,000 to escape its contracts. On November 6th Prairie Dog sold between 150 and 220 at the first call. Later a sale was made at the astounding price of 275 on the Exchange, the stock touching 212 on the Open Board. The irregularity of the quotations was one of the most startling features of the corner. That very afternoon Prairie du Chien changed hands from 160 to 165; yet the distracted shorts paid 200 and 225 to cover their contracts on the following day. On November 8th the stock fluctuated between 120 and 185, and two days later, the situation having been adjusted, it sold down to 110.

"Marston achieved success in this affair, largely because a great deal of stock was held in the West and was likely to stay there. He took good care, in fact, that it should do so. No thrifty business man or prudent farmer in the region beyond Lake Michigan, who had invested his capital in the shares of Prairie Dog, was suffered to learn of the extraordinary gymnastics then being performed in the East. The reader will doubtless regard it as a striking coincidence that the *Milwaukee Sentinel,* in its New York dispatches of November 6th and 7th, gave the current quotations for Prairie du Chien at 80¼ and 80½, while printing the other stock market prices correctly. The promoter of the corner, not being in control of the road's management, had also to face the danger of a supply of fresh shares brought into existence for his special benefit. The Milwaukee & Prairie du Chien had recently leased the McGregor Western Railroad Company, and was authorized to base an issue of new preferred stock on this transaction. Marston obtained an injunction from Judge Sutherland, restraining the directors from converting this preferred into common stock, with which to make good their short contracts. He had thus provided against the turning of either of his flanks, and he reaped the fruits of victory. One house openly defaulted on its contracts, preferring to fight the matter in the courts. The cornering party, nevertheless, made exceptional profits. A brilliant coup was scored in the unloading of the road, with which they appear to have been saddled. Marston succeeded in selling it to the Milwaukee & St. Paul Railroad, and it is now a part of the Chicago, Milwaukee & St. Paul system."

The most notorious market battles of the 'sixties were those which raged around the Erie Railroad, and there the worst methods of the time were used. Erie was the special football of Daniel Drew. As a director for many years he made much money dealing in its stock. In 1867 a struggle began between Vanderbilt's New York Central and Drew's Erie over freight to Chicago. Vanderbilt decided to buy up Erie and began to do so in 1868. Drew and his two allies, Gould and Fisk, resolved to keep Vanderbilt out. Vanderbilt started in February, 1868, to buy up the $25,000,000 of Erie common and preferred, taking the precaution of securing injunctions from the Supreme Court of New York to restrain Drew from making fresh issues of capital or by other manipulations to upset the value of the road's securities. But through his broker Drew bought heavily an issue of convertible bonds and had them converted into stock. It was a lot for Drew to buy, but he forced Vanderbilt to take the stock. This was followed by the issue of the remainder of the convertible bonds, accomplished by illegal means. In the course of the fight the Erie directors fled to Jersey City with the bonds of the Erie and the $6,000,000 or more of cash paid by Vanderbilt for fresh issues of stock. The battle shifted to Albany, where a corrupt Assembly sanctioned by law the illegal acts of the Erie gang. The Drew-Vanderbilt fight ended in a compromise, but the Erie scandals went on.

In May of 1869 the Open Board of Brokers was merged with the Stock Exchange. The membership of the older exchange was increased at this time from 533 to 1,060. The merger created the largest and most important exchange in the country.[35]

At the same time the whole government of the Stock Exchange was vested in a governing committee of 40 members. This was a great step in the direction of getting action on the part of the Exchange. Previously the only standing committee was the Committee on Securities, established in 1860, which had limited powers to pass on stocks and bonds dealt in on the Exchange.[36] In all matters of legislation the Exchange formed a committee of the whole—it was difficult to get this together because there was no governing committee; every application for readmission and every case for arbitration had to come up before a special committee. With a smaller governing committee it became easier to get action, most important at a time when the exploits of unprincipled stock operators called for regulation.

In January, 1869, a rule was passed by the Exchange requiring that the shares of all active stocks should be registered at the proper agency. This regulation was made necessary by the fact that some companies had secretly been issuing large additional blocks of stock, selling the stock and delivering the certificates before the increase could be made public. All the companies complied at once except the Erie, whose stock was in consequence dropped from the list, but it was not long before the Erie also conformed to the new rule and was readmitted to the Exchange.

New provision was also made at this time for the registration of sales. The old rule had been that a sale was not completed before the stock had been transferred on the books of the company, but during the active speculation of Civil War years this system had been supplanted by delivery by "power and certificate."

During the late 'sixties two inventions were made which were to extend immeasurably the influence of the New York Stock Exchange. They were the Atlantic cable and the stock ticker.

In 1866 the first successful Atlantic cable was placed in operation. Its effect is summarized by Stedman as follows: [37]

> "It immensely quickened commercial intercourse between this country and Great Britain. From the stock broker's standpoint its prime value was in transmitting instantaneous quotations, and orders to buy and sell securities, between the continents. A speedy outgrowth of the new condition was

[35] *Ibid.*, p. 214.
[36] Eames, *op. cit.*, p. 44.
[37] Stedman, *op. cit.*, p. 195.

the arbitrage business, in which stock houses with foreign connections learned to profit by the price differences between the New York and London markets for American shares."

No less revolutionary was the effect of the ticker.[38] Until 1867 stock quotations were noted upon suitable pads by the brokers and clerks on the floor of the Exchange, and these were then carried to the various Wall Street offices and were sent to other cities by telegraph. Though this system was satisfactory for those in New York who could be right at hand during trading, it was far from satisfactory for other brokers or traders, especially those in other cities who had to wait for quotations to be collected and sent by telegraph. The first usable ticker was constructed in 1867 under the Gold and Stock Telegraph Co., which gained permission from the Exchange to go on its floor to gather quotations for this new service. The first instrument, installed in the office of Drew's brokers, created a sensation. Within a few days over one hundred subscribers had been secured for the instruments. A number of other ticker companies were organized. In a few years the tickers were greatly improved and the service was extended to other cities. In 1871 the Gold and Stock Telegraph Co. came into the control of the Western Union Telegraph Co. which gave wide service throughout the country.

The ticker introduced the problem of properly controlling the quotations sent out. As the competition of the several ticker companies became more active, the Exchange came to exert a greater control over the gathering of quotations on the floor, employing its own reporters who turned the quotations over to the ticker companies. The result was that the Stock Exchange was in a position to designate those who should receive such prices and how they should be sent out. Since applications for service had to be approved by an official of the Exchange, bucket-shops could not obtain quotations directly from the instruments. In 1890 a majority interest in the Commercial Telegram Co. was secured by the Stock Exchange. This firm was reorganized as the New York Quotation Co. An arrangement was made with the Gold and Stock Telegraph Co. whereby the New York Quotation Co. would supply quotations to members of the Exchange below Canal Street, and the other company would supply the rest. It was at this time that extensive litigation was carried on in the courts to determine whether or not the Exchange really had the right to say who should and who should not get quotations.

This question of the guardianship of quotations is an old one. As early as 1875 the Stock Exchange began to put restrictive measures on the use of the ticker into its contracts with the telegraph company. In 1878 still more forcible measures were employed, and in 1882 steps were taken by which the Exchange authorities personally inspected the telegraph company's quotation contracts with its patrons. Later this was carried to such an extreme in the determination to protect the public from impositions that even the Exchange members could not install wires from their offices to outsiders until the proper committee of the Stock Exchange had passed upon the application.[39]

A development after the Civil War of fundamental importance was the widening of the source of funds employed in the call-loan market. The principal lenders were the Clearing House banks of New York but these were not the only ones. Savings banks and trust companies, insurance companies, and the large private banks were using the call-loan market as a place for the investment of funds.[40] The activity of the savings banks in the call-loan market was limited in 1875

[38] See *ibid.*, p. 433, for a chapter on the ticker.

[39] W. C. Van Antwerp, *The Stock Exchange from Within* (New York, 1913), p. 149.

[40] Stedman, *op. cit.*, p. 446.

through legislation caused by the disastrous experience of the savings banks during the panic of 1873. Private bankers played an important part, many of them combining the functions of banker, broker, and underwriter.[41] J. P. Morgan & Co. came in to relieve the market in every crisis, and in 1912, witnesses before the Pujo Committee named Kuhn, Loeb & Co., Goldman Sachs, and Speyers, as the three most active lenders on call.[42]

In the actual placing of call loans, brokers played an increasingly important part. This function seemed to gain prominence as the call loan increased in use over the time loan as a means for the financing of security transactions. In 1869 the brokers who specialized in the lending of money and securities were given a separate post at the Exchange, and an element of organization was introduced into what had been up to then a quite unorganized market for loans on Stock Exchange collateral.[43] Since banks and others would naturally tend to conduct their business through these specialists, this definite location increased the importance of this group of brokers. The private bankers were the first to utilize the new facilities, and gradually the commercial banks did likewise.

The war-time period of great speculation in New York suffered a considerable setback in the 1870's. In 1871 the market began to falter, and from then until 1879 the market showed little buoyancy. The toll of this depression was heavy. Of the thousand members of the Exchange 65 failed in 1871, 32 in 1872, 79 in 1873, 34 in 1874, 37 in 1875, 49 in 1876, and decreasing numbers thereafter.[44] Among those failures were important brokerage and banking firms.

In the late 'seventies, also, many of the old operators disappeared. In 1876 Daniel Drew went bankrupt and in 1879 he died. In 1877 Commodore Vanderbilt died.

7. The Growth of the Modern Exchange, 1878–1913

At the end of the decade of the 1870's trading in securities began, after several years of quiet, to pick up again. The amount of business done on the Exchange is shown in Table 1.[45]

[41] Myers, *op. cit.*, pp. 265–266.

[42] 62d Congress, 3d Sess., 1913, *Pujo Committee Hearings,* vol. i, p. 745.

[43] Stedman, *op. cit.*, p. 447.

[44] Eames, *op. cit.*, p. 96.

[45] *Ibid.*, p. 95.

Table 1. SALES AT THE NEW YORK STOCK EXCHANGE, 1878–93

Year	Shares sold	Value of shares sold	Railway bonds sold	U. S. bonds sold	State bonds sold
1878	39,875,593	$2,157,269,581	...	...	...
1879	72,765,762	4,136,633,570	...	...	...
1880	97,919,099	6,819,086,054	...	...	...
1881	114,511,248	8,197,506,403	...	...	...
1882	116,307,271	7,689,453,436	$246,769,410	$18,555,850	$26,571,260
1883	97,049,909	6,260,809,961	284,768,100	17,046,150	6,986,500
1884	96,154,971	5,939,500,000	499,955,200	14,905,150	2,826,900
1885	92,538,947	5,479,859,840	660,659,400	15,261,200	14,678,053
1886	100,802,050	5,885,662,200	587,237,500	12,793,500	20,394,411
1887	84,914,616	4,508,778,899	347,127,330	7,110,400	15,306,800
1888	65,179,106	3,539,519,143	345,914,057	6,573,700	5,188,285
1889	72,014,600	4,059,231,891	398,825,425	3,698,850	5,932,350
1890	71,282,885	3,977,664,193	401,829,220	2,625,500	4,870,400
1891	69,031,689	3,812,247,419	383,715,000	1,460,800	3,475,100
1892	85,875,092	4,874,014,262	485,857,400	1,729,100	4,793,950
1893	80,977,839	4,550,260,916	351,854,450	2,143,250	3,792,800

During the years preceding 1885 there was a turmoil in the security market. Following the breaking-up of the anthracite coal combination, coal shares declined a hundred points during the year. Hostile State legislation in the West rendered many western rail shares practically worthless. The fight of the eastern trunk lines which in 1885 led to a great reduction of rates had placed the trunk line shares in such a position that the public did not want to buy them. The result was that many buyers started to turn to industrial shares as a means of investment. Transactions in industrials increased to such an extent that members of the Stock Exchange felt compelled to buy those shares for customers and to assume the risk of carrying them without the safeguard of a public market. The public demand for industrial stocks during this period when other stocks had become discredited was such that an "Unlisted Department" was established by the Stock Exchange, and stocks which were not in a position to meet the requirements of the Committee on Stock List were admitted to this department. The rapid increase in business caused by the rise of industrial stocks required the addition of more room to the Exchange in 1887.

It was at this time that a new exchange was organized to take advantage of the growing business. The New York Mining Stock Exchange after 1876 provided a market for mining and other stocks; its scope was broadened in 1883; and in 1885 it became the Consolidated Stock and Petroleum Exchange, and railroads were added to its list. Though the Consolidated provided a market for industrials before they were admitted fully on the New York Stock Exchange, it came to be regarded as a rival by the latter exchange, which forbade its members to deal on the newer board.

It was during this period that industrials began to be accepted by banks as stock collateral. The industrials fluctuated more widely than the rails, although it may be doubted whether they were subject to more manipulation. It was many years before the industrials were admitted into the collateral portfolios at all; even as late as 1899 some banks and trust companies would not accept them while others would insist upon a larger margin. By 1911 the industrials had gained enough of a reputation so that they comprised about one-third of the total collateral, the other two-thirds being rails.[46]

The increase in volume of trading on the Exchange caused by the expansion of railroads and later augmented by the incoming of industrial stocks made necessary a more expeditious method of handling the transfer of stocks between buyer and seller. Transfer was then being done through the use of messenger boys, "running at top speed, their hands full of securities." Even more pressing than physical delivery was the need for some kind of credit with which to finance sales.

The obvious solution of these difficulties was some form of clearing-house organization, based on the principles applied to the clearing of bank checks by the New York Clearing House Association and applied to gold accounts by the Gold Exchange Bank. The need for such an organization had been felt as far back as 1857, and repeated attempts had been made to meet the need. After the panic of 1873, agitation for a clearing house became very strong and for the next ten years committees of the Exchange regularly considered the matter but without results. Several systems were tried by the Exchange or by voluntary groups. In 1892, when the banks became fearful of the immense certifications necessary for brokers and threatened to limit them, a committee of the Exchange proposed a plan which was successfully put into action.[47]

[46] Myers, *op. cit.*, p. 281.

[47] Eames, *op. cit.*, p. 93.

Closely associated with the demand for a stock clearing house had been suggestions that term settlements be adopted in New York. Persons who were familiar with the English system under which settlement was made only once in each fortnight considered that such a plan might be successful in New York since it would tend to reduce the amount of credit necessary to carry marginal stock transactions and would cancel short-term transactions. The term plan was actually put into operation, but after less than three months it was abolished. The idea was revived in 1919 "as a means of divorcing call loans from the security market and establishing a new call loan market based on acceptances in the European manner," but no definite step was taken.[48]

Trading on the Exchange showed some important changes in the later part of the century. The outside speculator and investor continued to occupy an important place. But the dominant influence of the individual operator was a thing of the past. Though there were still important individual operators, the preponderant influence was that of the group. Banking houses began to coöperate, and in the floating of an issue the syndicate used the Exchange in a big way to "make a market" for issues they were promoting. Funds moved in large amounts on the Exchange, and operations came to be limited not only to the funds of the individual or even a group of firms but by those wider ramifications which accompanied the growth of large fortunes and the financial integration of the period.

Obstacles to a freely competitive market continued to exist. The corner was not so important, relatively, as it had earlier been. But pools secretly influenced the market in a significant way. And as the elements constituting a pool became more and more powerful, the problem of maintaining a free market became greater. Short selling and margin trading were the two other features of operations on the Exchange which were by many regarded as problems.

If we can believe Henry Clews, who was a Wall Streeter himself, the dominating group on Wall Street in the early years of the century was the Standard Oil group. They "have introduced in their Wall Street operations the same quiet, unostentatious, but resistless measures that they have always employed heretofore in the conduct of their corporate affairs." Beside them "every other man or combination of men that has ever operated in the Street are materially belittled by comparison." They were the greatest operators the world had ever seen, according to Clews, and they controlled Wall Street almost absolutely.[49]

In this period of its history there came considerable reform within the Exchange. In some measure this was in response to outside criticism, but it also represented the victory of reform elements within. One must remember that various interests have always been represented on the Exchange, that is, the big operators, the brokers doing principally a brokerage business (and, as such, representative of the outsiders who bought and sold securities), and the brokers who were also operators. Moreover the various large operators and brokers dealing on their own often were also tied up with rival or competitive interests, individuals or institutions.

One type of reform was instituted by the Exchange in response to the growing difficulty of getting accurate information on the companies whose securities were sold on the Exchange. Obviously, misinformation or the absence of information was the basis of many of the questionable operations. Corporations some fifty years ago looked upon the reports they gave out as a distinct favor to and not a right of the stockholders. Requests for reports were sent to companies that had stock

[48] Myers, *op. cit.*, pp. 305–307.

[49] Clews, *op. cit.*, p. 701.

listed on the Exchange, but the results were not satisfactory. But new listings were accepted on condition that monthly reports be made. At the same time the investment bankers were demanding more information about securities.[50] State railroad commissions and the Interstate Commerce Commission helped to improve railroad reports, and the Hughes investigation of 1909 had some influence.

There was no important legislative control of the Stock Exchange in this period. In 1908 it was proposed that a federal tax on stock sales, such as had been levied during the Civil War, be used as a means of penalizing speculation, but no action was taken.[51] Such a law was enacted by the State of New York in 1905.[52] An investigation was made of the Stock Exchange in 1909 by a commission appointed by Governor Charles Evans Hughes, of New York. Its purpose was to ascertain "what changes, if any, are advisable in the laws of the State bearing upon speculation in securities and commodities." [53] No records of the private hearings were kept, but in its report the committee made some positive recommendations about reforms to be made by the New York Stock Exchange itself.

The recommendations of this committee looked largely to internal reforms to be put into effect by the Exchange itself: the requirement of larger margins; [54] the valuation of securities at average rather than at current prices; the abolition of the unlisted department; the strengthening of listing requirements; and the recommendation that trading be carried on in reasonably small units such as 100 shares. It was also recommended that the board of governors be given the power to decide when a corner existed and to fix a settlement price.[55]

The commission refused to condemn short selling and margin trading, and, since such laws had never been successfully enforced either in the United States or abroad, it would not recommend that legislation be passed designed to stop such practices. Likewise the committee did not recommend the passage of a law against the manipulation of stock prices; its members felt that the manipulation which accompanied the issue of new securities had certain advantages for investors, and that the manipulation which had as its object speculative profit was too difficult to control by means of legislation and could be better handled by the Exchange itself. The committee was, moreover, not prepared to advocate the incorporation of the Exchange, a measure often advanced as a necessary reform.[56]

Many of the recommendations made by the Hughes Committee were put into immediate effect by the Exchange. Among other things the unlisted department was abolished in 1910; [57] the law committee of the Exchange was empowered to examine the dealings of any member whenever it should be deemed to the interest of the Exchange to do so; and members were forbidden to have business dealings with bucket-shops.[58]

The strong position taken by the Pujo Committee of the House of Representatives in 1912–13 in its "money trust" inquiry was quite different from that taken

[50] The *Bond Record* was established in 1893 under the leadership of Harvey Fisk & Sons to publish information of a high quality on investments.

[51] Myers, *op. cit.*, pp. 307–308.

[52] *Ibid.*, p. 308.

[53] *Report of Committee on Speculation in Securities and Commodities* (New York, 1909).

[54] Large enough so that no business would be done on less than 20 per cent (*ibid.*, p. 9).

[55] *Ibid.*, pp. 8 ff.

[56] The Exchange as a voluntary association has greater power over its members than if it were incorporated; also it can subject them to instant discipline which would not be so if legal processes were required (*ibid.*, p. 18).

[57] Most of its 800 issues were admitted to the active list after meeting the requirements (*Commercial & Financial Chronicle*, vol. xc, April 2, 1910, p. 891).

[58] Myers, *op. cit.*, p. 312.

by the Hughes investigation. This inquiry proceeded as if to prove the witnesses guilty and placed the representatives of the Stock Exchange and other New York institutions definitely upon the defensive. The majority report proposed that legislation be passed to bring about the following through the regulation of interstate communication: incorporation of the stock exchanges under State law; full reports of corporations desiring to list their securities upon the Exchange, including reports of commissions paid for floating security issues; prohibition of sales with the purpose of creating an appearance of activity in a stock or manipulating price; judicial review of admission of securities to the trading list or exclusion from it; margins of at least 20 per cent; prohibition of lending customers' securities to other members, and pledging customers' securities for loans with or without the consent of the customer for an amount greater than the unpaid portion; and the opening of brokers' books of account to federal officials.[59]

The bill which embodied these recommendations failed to pass, but during the preliminary hearings it had become apparent that the New York Stock Exchange had already made changes to conform with the suggestions of the Pujo Committee. In 1913 the rule against "wash sales" was strengthened; likewise were the recommendations in regard to the lending of securities and to the adequacy of margins incorporated by the Exchange. Very shortly after this the Exchange appointed a committee of five "to watch the course of prices of securities and examine into the dealings of members whenever it appeared that improper transactions were being carried on." [60]

Several laws were passed by the New York Assembly at the time of these hearings in response to demands for public regulation. The following are some of the things which were made crimes punishable under the penal code of the State: bucketshops, manipulation of stock prices, fictitious sales, false representation of securities, the publication of fictitious transactions, unfair discrimination by exchanges or their members, the pledging of customers' securities without their permission, and the making of transactions by brokers after they had become insolvent. A bill was introduced to compel the Stock Exchange to incorporate, but it was finally defeated.[61]

8. The New York Stock Exchange, 1914–29

The outstanding development in this period was the notable increase in the business which was done on the Exchange, as is shown by Table 2.[62] Behind this increase was an absolute growth in government bonds and in the securities of private corporations and the existence of great reservoirs of savings and credit for use in investments or in speculative operations.

Table 2. TOTAL ANNUAL TRANSACTIONS ON NEW YORK STOCK EXCHANGE, 1914–38

Year	Stocks (Shares)	Bonds (Par Value)
1914	47,431,227	$ 461,649,200
1915	172,496,774	961,698,900
1916	232,633,124	1,148,159,550
1917	184,623,326	1,034,568,500
1918	143,279,573	2,012,365,300
1919	318,272,910	3,676,100,600
1920	227,635,768	3,868,421,700
1921	172,778,535	3,386,159,000
1922	260,890,802	4,145,568,008
1923	236,482,731	2,744,966,900
1924	284,044,082	3,801,963,000
1925	459,717,623	3,427,042,210

59 U. S. Congress, House Committee on Banking and Currency, *Report of the Committee appointed . . . to Investigate the Concentration of Control of Money and Credit,* Feb. 28, 1913, pp. 162–163.

60 Myers, *op. cit.,* p. 312.

61 *Ibid.,* pp. 313–314.

62 *New York Stock Exchange Year Book,* 1938, p. 125.

Table 2. (*continued*)

Year	Stocks (Shares)	Bonds (Par Value)
1926	451,868,353	$3,015,344,915
1927	581,702,342	3,307,239,382
1928	930,893,276	2,835,831,560
1929	1,124,608,910	2,996,398,000
1930	810,632,546	2,730,301,800
1931	576,765,412	2,969,770,600
1932	425,234,294	2,991,244,000
1933	654,816,452	3,355,646,000
1934	323,845,634	3,701,916,000
1935	381,635,752	3,339,458,000
1936	496,046,869	3,576,874,000
1937	409,464,570	2,792,531,000
1938	297,466,722	1,859,865,000

From 1924 to 1929 came the greatest bull market the Exchange has ever known. The Dow-Jones Industrial Average rose from 100 in the early fall of 1924 to a high of 381.17 on September 3, 1929, and rails rose from 100 in September, 1925, to 189.11 on September 3, 1929.

As before, the Exchange in the 1920's opposed laws proposed for the regulation of the Exchange while it took steps looking toward reform. In 1922 the constitution of the Exchange was revised. The authority of the board of governors was increased, the duties and obligations of members were more clearly defined, and additional safeguards were provided to enforce the high standards which the important position of the Exchange required. Offenses were more clearly defined, and the Governing Committee was given more power to enforce penalties, to provide for the settlement of corners, to prevent purchases and sales for the purpose of manipulating prices, and to prevent such business connections of members as might work harm against the interest or the good repute of the Exchange.[63]

This revision of the constitution is characteristic of the attitude of the Exchange in its administrative policies over the last decade. Rules and regulations, especially those dealing with the investing public, were made stronger. Determined efforts were made to place members and members' firms on a high level in character, business integrity, and financial management. Questionnaires distributed regularly to members gave a periodical audit of all members' accounts under the supervision of the Business Conduct Committee and the Accountant of the Exchange.[64] An attempt was made to secure quarterly reports from corporations. Old committees were abolished or consolidated, and new committees were established. The entire decade was marked by the strengthening of the internal organization and by its greater centralization. The association was making a definite attempt to clean house and place itself in such a position that legislative control would not be exercised.

The Exchange also came to take a hand in improving security trading outside its walls. In 1922 it sponsored a Better Business Bureau in New York. This organization was immediately successful and helped a great deal in anti-fraud activities by acting as a fact-finding agency, ferreting out amateurs and professionals in the security swindling business. The Better Business Bureau, which is a national organization with branches in many cities, coöperated so effectively with private business interests, on the one hand, and with State and federal governmental departments, on the other, that fraudulent security activity was definitely checked.

Perhaps the most significant development in the efforts of the Exchange to strengthen itself was its campaign for improving its position in the opinion of the public. It was in 1922 that the Exchange first inaugurated its policy of publicity, which took the form of a consistent and carefully planned campaign of education. Statements, speeches, and articles concerning the Exchange were put out directly to the public by the president. An official emblem for the use of Exchange members in their advertisements was de-

[63] *Report of the President of the New York Stock Exchange,* 1924–25.

[64] *Ibid.,* 1928–29.

vised so that the public could differentiate more easily between members and nonmembers. Likewise certificates for use in members' offices were distributed. In 1933 motion pictures were taken of the floor of the Exchange during the business session, and later another film was made showing all the mechanical operations of the Exchange. These films were shown all over the world. The Committee on Publicity answered thousands of private inquiries for information; a statistical bulletin was regularly issued; and annual reports were rendered.

The emphasis thrown upon the development of public relations by the Exchange since 1920 was helpful in combating fraudulent issues of stock, in weeding out bogus brokers, in acquainting the public with the functions of the Exchange, and in creating a mutually beneficial understanding between world security markets. The most important effect, however, was that the point of view of the Exchange was broadened and the institution became more sensitive to outside opinion.

9. Recent Developments

The crash of October, 1929—when on one day 12,000,000 shares were traded on the Exchange—brought new problems and new programs. The terrific decline in business cut trading on the Exchange very greatly, and the reform movement that came with the depression placed much of the blame for the bad condition of business on the speculation of the 'twenties in general and on the Stock Exchange in particular. The result was reform of the Exchange from both within and without.

This time the federal government stepped in. In 1932–33 the Senate Committee on Banking and Currency conducted extensive hearings on stock exchange practices. The Federal Securities Act of 1933 and the Securities Exchange Act of 1934 marked a revolution in the regulation of exchanges in the United States. The New York Stock Exchange, which had courageously fought to pass and enforce rules to protect the buyer of securities, and the State of New York, which had tried to secure reform through regulation, had been unable to go so far as desired because of the competition of other exchanges. It was thought by many at this time that federal regulation was the only solution.

Behind this legislation was the feeling that there had come radical changes in the ownership and management of securities in the United States, particularly since the World War. This view is expressed in a report of a congressional committee on the securities exchange bill: [65]

"All through these years the machinery of the stock exchanges and of corporate management have only grown bigger without growing different. But this significant growth in size and importance of the exchanges and the business they do with the public has necessitated a real difference in kind in the treatment of that public by the law and by business ethics. Stock exchanges which handle the distribution and trading of a very substantial part of the entire national wealth and which have developed a technique of sucking funds from every corner of the country cannot operate under the same traditions and practices as pre-war stock exchanges which handled substantially only the transactions of professional investors and speculators. And standards of corporate management adequate to inspire investor confidence in the 'caveat stockholder' era of closely held stockholder-managed companies cannot be stably perpetuated in an era where one company boasts over 700,000 stockholders, and 200 corporations control one half the corporate wealth of the country.

. . . .

"When corporations were small, when their managers were intimately acquainted with their owners and when the interests of management and ownership were substantially identical, conditions did not require the regulation of security markers. Even those who

[65] 73d Congress, 2d Sess., 1934, *House Reports*, no. 1383, "Securities Exchange Bill of 1934," pp. 4–5.

in former days managed great corporations were by reason of their personal contacts with their shareholders constantly aware of their responsibilities. But as management became divorced from ownership and came under the control of banking groups, men forgot that they were dealing with the savings of men and the making of profits became an impersonal thing."

The Federal Securities Act, which became effective on May 27, 1933, provided for the application for registration of securities issued in the future with the Federal Trade Commission before the issues could be sold. With the Commission had to be filed a complete financial statement of the issuing company, a list of officers and directors and their salaries, and a complete statement of compensation to be paid to the selling agents. When the application had been approved, the issue could be sold. The statement as to the condition of the issuing company had to be signed by the principal executives, the financial officers, accounting officers, and the directors of the company in question; and they were liable for civil and criminal prosecution if at any time in the future the statements were found to be false.

The Act met much criticism and opposition. Though it was pointed out that it was not so severe as the British Companies Act, the penalties and liabilities involved made business men fearful and were said by many to mean serious obstruction in the flow of capital. Obviously the effect depended on the administration of the Act.

The second important development under the federal government was the Securities Exchange Act of 1934. Among its provisions were the following:

(1) The Securities Exchange Commission was established to administer the Securities Act of 1933 and the Securities Exchange Act of 1934.

(2) Registration of all exchanges (except unimportant ones which the Commission might exempt from the rule) by the Commission under certain rules was made obligatory by the provision that the use of the mails or any instrumentality of interstate commerce was forbidden in connection with the use of any facility of any exchange which was not so registered.

(3) "For the purpose of preventing the excessive use of credit for the purchase or carrying of securities" the Federal Reserve Board should prescribe rules and regulations as to the amount of credit that could be extended on securities, setting the initial amount at 55 per cent of the current market price of the security or 100 per cent of the lowest market price on the last 3 years but not above 75 per cent of current market price. It was further provided that such credit could not be extended directly or indirectly by any member of a national securities exchange or any broker or dealer transacting a securities business through such a member except under certain severe restrictions.

(4) Severe limitations were placed on the borrowing of exchange members or brokers or dealers carrying on business through an exchange member.

(5) Severe restrictions were placed on the manipulation of security prices. Not only short sales and stop-loss orders but other manipulative devices were specifically put under the jurisdiction of the SEC.

(6) With a view to segregating the function of broker and dealer, the Commission was given the power to prescribe rules to regulate or prevent floor trading by exchange members, directly or indirectly for their own account or for discretionary accounts, and to regulate the trading of specialists and odd-lot dealers and brokers who were also dealing on their own account.

(7) Rules were laid down for the registration of securities.

(8) Periodic and other reports were required of the issuer of a security registered on a national exchange.

(9) Restrictions were placed on the use of proxies.

(10) For the purpose of preventing the unfair use—for short sales, for instance—of information obtained by officer, director or large stockholders of a certain security, restrictions were placed on the purchase and sale of such issue by such persons.

On the inside of the New York Stock Exchange reform also took place in the 'thirties. Among the members arose criticism of excessive margin trading, of short selling, and of the participation of specialists in pools in securities for which they were specialists. Rules were adopted to curb such trading by specialists and to minimize short selling. Rules were also made to forbid members to lend customers' securities, to require members to make weekly reports on pool and syndicate operations, on options, and so on. Trained investigators were designated to watch for signs of manipulations, and wash sales were specifically outlawed.

Though President Whitney of the Exchange opposed federal regulation and even worked against some of the reforms within, there has apparently come a strengthening of the element on the Exchange which favors change. In 1934 the Exchange picked ten outsiders to serve as an advisory committee. The Conway Committee appointed by President Gay in 1937 is credited with improving greatly the public relations of the Exchange. There has come at the same time a change in the administration of the association. At about the beginning of 1934 there came to be evident a considerable opposition to President Whitney and the governing board; the opposition, though it saw few of the abuses said by the outside to exist on the Exchange, did not like Whitney's methods of defense, and several large investment houses were said to be dissatisfied with what was considered dominance of the Exchange by "two-dollar brokers" and specialists. In 1935 Charles R. Gay was elected president, and eight new members were elected to the governing board of eleven. Even a greater victory for the reform element came in the election of W. H. Martin, Jr., as head of the Exchange. These changes in leadership have much significance for the Exchange and may help materially to increase public confidence in the institution as a market for securities.

10. Suggested Readings

Edmund C. Stedman, *The New York Stock Exchange* (New York, 1905), vol. i. A useful account of the development of the Exchange and its setting to 1905.

Francis L. Eames, *The New York Stock Exchange* (New York, 1894). This book gives many quotations from early Exchange records.

J. Edward Meeker, *The Work of the Stock Exchange* (New York, 1922). A good account of the workings of the Exchange by its economist.

Margaret G. Myers, *The New York Money Market* (New York, 1931). Though this book contains little that is directly on the Exchange, it is invaluable for anyone who seeks to understand the larger business setting within which the Exchange operated.

Henry Clews, *Fifty Years in Wall Street* (New York, 1908). This is a rambling book of reminiscences from 1857 to 1908 by one who was on the Street.

A number of government reports contain much information on the New York Stock Exchange and its practices. *The Report of the Committee on Speculation in Securities and Commodities,* New York State, 1909, is brief but important. The reports of the Congressional money trust investigation of 1912–13, the hearings on the regulation of the issuance of stocks and bonds by common carriers in 1914, and the hearings on Stock Exchange practices in 1933 all contain important information.

11. Suggested Questions

1. Why was term settlement used more than "cash settlement" before 1857? Why has England kept the term settlement?
2. What were the effects of the introduction of the telegraph?
3. What is the significance of the control of quotations over the ticker by the Exchange?
4. Why was the unlisted department

of the Exchange abolished (upon recommendation of the Hughes Committee)?

5. The Exchange was organized as an aid for carrying on the broker's business. How have its character and functions changed?
6. Do you hold to the view that in recent years outside regulation has been necessary?

XXII. NEW YORK TRANSATLANTIC PACKET SERVICES 1817–1837

1. Introductory Statement

In the early part of the nineteenth century there were three general situations which throw light upon, and constitute a background for, the main theme of this case. One was the growing commercial importance of New York in comparison with Philadelphia and Boston. There were both external and internal factors at work in the decision as to which of the three cities would attain hegemony. Secondly, there was a comparable struggle between a new type of business policy and business leadership on the one hand and an old but well-tried type on the other. The new represented specialization in business function; the old, the combination in one firm of a large number of functions. In the period 1800–30 there was no clear indication as to which would be victorious, perhaps no great consciousness, indeed, of any kind of struggle. Thirdly, there was a developing sense of the importance of time and punctuality. Town merchants had long struggled to force the farmers to pay their debts on time. Banks in the larger centers had striven to compel merchants to meet their obligations punctually. A few business leaders, both in the Old World and in the New, had a vision of the more effective utilization of time in business.

In 1755–56 the British government had established monthly postal packets between Falmouth and New York, resuming this service after the War of 1812; but the vessels employed usually prolonged the voyage by calling at Halifax in the summer and Bermuda in the winter, and they were often referred to as "coffin brigs" because of their tendency to founder at sea. Until the inauguration of the "Old Line" sailings between New York and Liverpool in January, 1818, there had been no commercial service for the dispatch of freight and passengers across the Atlantic Ocean according to a fixed schedule.[1]

To be sure, by the end of the eighteenth century there were many "regular traders," owned by general merchants, plying between America and Europe. In 1783 the French government, in order to encourage trade with the newly formed United States, had secretly subsidized a regular line between Lorient and New York. But regularity in such cases normally meant two complete voyages annually per ship: one ship to Europe in June or July, returning in August or September, and the other leaving in November or December and coming back to America in March or April. Although regular traders were often as large, as comfortable, and as fast as the packets, they were operated primarily to transport goods for their owners, who were general merchants engaged in importing and exporting. Leaving port only when they had a full load of freight and passengers, they frequently called at several ports to complete their cargoes. Most of them were owned by partnerships which rarely possessed more than three ships.[2]

When the first American packet line was founded, the western world had enjoyed

[1] Wesley E. Rich, *The History of the United States Post Office to the Year 1829* (Cambridge, 1924), p. 36; F. B. C. Bradlee, *The Dreadnought* (Salem, Mass., 1920), pp. 10–11.

[2] *Ibid.*, p. 11; Carl C. Cutler, *Greyhounds of the Sea* (New York, 1930), pp. 56–59.

nearly three years of peace following a long period of war. International strife had seriously hampered shipping on the Atlantic, but Great Britain had continued the industrial advance which had begun in the eighteenth century. When circumstances permitted, England exported large quantities of manufactured goods in exchange for the raw materials, especially cotton, obtained from the United States.

2. The Founding of the First Line, 1817–18 [3]

In the New York *Commercial Advertiser* of October 24, 1817, and the two succeeding issues there appeared an advertisement announcing the establishment of a packet line operating between New York and Liverpool. Four ships of about 400 tons each were to be operated, one "to sail from each place on a certain day in every month throughout the year." One was to sail from New York on the 5th and one from Liverpool on the 1st of every month. All the ships were coppered and copper fastened, "known to be remarkably fast sailers," and their accommodations were advertised as "uncommonly extensive and commodious." The owners believed that the experience of the commanders, the regularity of the sailings, and the excellent condition in which they would deliver their cargoes would make the ships "very desirable opportunities for the conveyance of goods."

The founders of this line were Isaac Wright and his son William, Francis and Jeremiah Thompson, and Benjamin Marshall. Isaac Wright was the son of a Long Island blacksmith. Shortly after learning his father's craft he established himself in New York City as a hardware merchant, and by 1817, in partnership with his son, he was importing iron bars, sheeting, canvas, and other goods on a large scale. Francis Thompson, son of a West Riding woolen manufacturer, had come to New York in 1798. Apparently he was an agent selling the cloth which his father and brothers manufactured in England, but he soon became a general merchant, importing iron and other wares as well. He had shared business ventures with Wright, whose daughter he had married. Benjamin Marshall had also come, in 1803, from Yorkshire where he had been in the cotton-textile manufacturing business. He soon joined Francis Thompson in a partnership and attained considerable prominence as an importer of cotton cloth. Jeremiah Thompson, a nephew of Francis Thompson, had come to New York from Yorkshire in 1801. After working for some years in his uncle's firm, he became a general merchant and eventually was regarded as one of the largest exporters of cotton in this country. With the exception of Marshall, all these men were Quakers.

All the men who founded the first line (often referred to as the "Black Ball Line" because of the large black ball which was painted on the fore-topsails of its ships) had, before 1817, become part owners of ships employed in transatlantic and coastal trade; and the Wrights and Francis Thompson had frequently served as shipping agents for vessels belonging to other merchants. The fact that all five were listed in 1816 as owners of the *Pacific* and the *Amity*—possibly to raise funds for this new ship the Wrights and Francis Thompson had sold to Marshall and Jeremiah Thompson part interest in the *Pacific*, which they had owned and operated since 1807—is probably the basis for the oft-repeated but erroneous statement that the first line of Liverpool packets was founded in 1816. The same five men were joint owners of the *Courier*, which was launched in 1817. The three ships were

[3] This case is based primarily upon the doctoral dissertation, The Origins and Early Years of the Trans-Atlantic Packet Lines of New York, 1817–1835, by Conrad P. Wright, on file in Harvard College Library. Only for material from other sources will references be given. As far as possible, all quoted material has been taken directly from the original source to avoid errors in transcription.

used in the regular trade between New York and Liverpool prior to the institution of the packet service which was scheduled to start in January, 1818.[4]

3. Some Problems and Consequences of Operating Transatlantic Packets

The first of the new packet ships to operate, the *Courier,* sailed from Liverpool on January 3, 1818, two days late; the Liverpool agents of the line were apparently never so much concerned about punctual departures as were the owners in America. One day's delay may have resulted from superstition, for January 2 came on a Friday, and sailors generally regarded Friday as an unlucky day for starting a voyage. It must be recognized, too, that northwest winds prevailed at Liverpool, making it difficult to sail from the wharves down the fairly narrow channel to open water. By employing steam towage when necessary, the packet lines eventually overcame difficulty with embarkation at both Liverpool and New York. The first of the packet ships to make the eastward voyage, the *James Monroe,* left New York as scheduled, on January 5, 1818, in the face of a northeast blizzard which made many observers predict postponement of departure.[5]

Even with the addition of a fourth vessel, the owners had to assign to each ship three round trips a year instead of the two which most regular traders made; the result was an exacting schedule for the line. The New York *Commercial Advertiser* of April 2, 1818, published the following news item relating to the packet service:

"REMARKABLE EXPEDITION — The packet ship *Pacific,* Captain Williams, arrived at this port from Liverpool on the evening of the 25th of March and commenced discharging the next day. She has discharged her cargo and reloaded in the short space of *six* days. We understand that she was completely ready for sea this morning at 11 o'clock. She will sail at the appointed time, Sunday, the 5th of April."

When the *James Monroe* set out on her return trip to New York on March 3, 1818, she encountered heavy gales and finally put back to Liverpool with the loss of a topmast and one man. Sailing again on March 26, she reached New York on April 30, just five days before she was supposed to leave on the return voyage. On May 1, 1818, the firm announced that the date of departure of the *James Monroe* and other ships would thenceforth be the 10th of the month rather than the 5th. This allowed 70 days between a ship's date of departure from Liverpool and its scheduled day for leaving New York on the return. Owing to the prevailing head winds and currents, the westward passage usually required almost twice the time taken for the one eastward, the winter voyages being particularly subject to delays on account of weather. It must be remembered also that the packets were driven to the extreme of safety at all times, carrying sail until it meant risking men's lives to reef or furl. In consequence of the severe shocks and strains to which they were subjected, after each crossing the packet ships always needed tightening, refitting, and repairs. On ordinary sailing vessels much of this kind of work was handled en route.[6]

The new sailing date ordinarily made it possible for New York merchants to receive mail which had left England by packet the 1st of one month and to post replies immediately by the packet embarking for Liverpool on the 10th of the following month. The decision to change the date may also have been influenced by the desire to avoid direct competition for mail and passengers with the British Post-Office packets. These were scheduled

[4] Robert G. Albion, *Square-Riggers on Schedule* (Princeton, 1938), pp. 24–25, 112–114.

[5] *Ibid.,* pp. 21–22, 237–238; Cutler, *op. cit.,* pp. 62–63.

[6] *Ibid.,* pp. 58–63; Basil Lubbock, *The Western Ocean Packets* (Glasgow, 1925), pp. 5–7.

to sail on the day after the first Wednesday of the month, so that their departure from New York fell between the 2d and the 8th of the month.

Difficulties were by no means confined to the operation of ships. Mail from Philadelphia, for instance, failed to reach the *Albion* in time for its departure on March 10, 1819, and a man who signed himself "Philadelphia Merchant" charged that the line was deliberately hindering Philadelphia's trade. The New York *Commercial Advertiser* defended the packet line as follows: [7]

". . . the owners of the line of Packets have exerted themselves to give general satisfaction to the public. For the accommodation of Merchants residing at Boston and Philadelphia, they have made arrangements to have bags deposited for letters at those places. In the month of February a notice . . . was published in a Philadelphia paper, stating that during the bad state of the roads, the letters from that city would be forwarded on the 8th of the month. This, however, was not, it seems, attended to at Philadelphia. The Albion sailed on the morning of the 10th at the usual hour, previous to which, a signal had been agreed on, which was to have been displayed, had the mail arrived by half after eleven, and the ship would have waited for the letters. The mail on that day did not arrive until twelve o'clock, consequently the vessel could not be overtaken—We witnessed the anxiety of the owners for the arrival of the mail. . . . The imputing improper motives to the owners is dishonorable to the 'Philadelphia Merchant.' "

A few days later the Philadelphia *Franklin Gazette* closed the dispute with a letter, from which the following is an excerpt: [8]

"When I was called upon, as Post-Master, to know whether I would make up mail for the American Packets, I consented without the slightest hesitation. The proprietors then stated to me the punctuality with which this line started, and that should the roads be bad, or any accident occur to the mail, those letters that would be sent on the 9th might not arrive in time for the packets—for they would start at a certain hour, if the wind was fair. . . . I gave the public notice; and if individuals did not think proper to put their letters in the Post Office on the 8th, they have no one to blame but themselves. I will here remark, that almost all the letters for the packet were deposited in the Post-office on the 9th, as upon a recurrence to the Post Bill, I find the unusual sum of 111 dollars, for paid letters to New York, on that day.

"Richard Bache, P. M."

The Boston mail also missed the *Albion* because of bad roads, but the Boston press made no comment, hostile or otherwise.

The First Line stood alone for four years in providing transatlantic packet service. Seriously depressed business conditions undoubtedly helped to check the emergence of competing packet lines between 1818 and 1822. Foreign trade dwindled to stagnation, and many regular Liverpool traders were compelled to try other routes in search of freight, while those who continued their usual course brought back large amounts of coal and salt as ballast for lack of better cargo. To judge by the small amount of ballast which was carried by the packets at this time, the line must have obtained fairly full loads of more profitable freight.

The chief commodities which the packets carried during 1818 in 12 eastbound passages totaled 2,044 bales of cotton, 10,815 barrels of flour, 1,921 barrels of pot and pearl ashes, 1,558 barrels of apples, and 218 bales of wool. In addition they carried small quantities of grain, fur, bark, lumber, and turpentine. The flour shipments proved to be exceptional, for the British Corn Laws, relaxed in 1818, soon shut down again and closed the British market to New York's chief local product. The return cargoes cannot be determined exactly, but the most important items were textiles, wine, books,

[7] New York *Commercial Advertiser,* March 11 and 16, 1819.

[8] Quoted from the *Commercial Advertiser,* March 24, 1819.

and miscellaneous manufactured goods. Because of their speed and regularity the packets obtained a virtual monopoly of specie shipments, which moved in both directions in large amounts to settle trade balances.[9]

The passengers carried by the packet line in 1818 and 1819 averaged 14 per crossing, and this average dropped less in 1820 than did that of passenger-carrying vessels generally. That the proprietors replaced the old *Pacific* by the fast new *Albion* in 1819, and the *Courier* by the *Nestor* in 1820, is fair evidence that the enterprise was doing reasonably well.

The British Post-Office packets made an early response to the newly formed commercial line by referring to it in their advertisements. One of June 11, 1818, had the appended line: "N. B. Passengers taken for the same price as by Liverpool Packets [40 guineas, including beds, bedding, wines, and stores]." The advertisement of July 1, 1818, indicated that an attempt was being made to speed up and improve the postal packet service. Another, published in February, 1819, openly and rather sneeringly admitted that the decoration of their cabin quarters was not superior "to those of the line," but asserted that the accommodations were "for solid comfort . . . more agreeable."

In general, however, the British postal packets did not offer so much competition as the regular traders, which on the whole sailed more frequently and directly than the postal packets and were often faster ships. Moreover, the "liners" carried goods as well as mail and passengers, while the British postal packets ordinarily transported no freight. But, while some regular traders offered equal speed and comfort, none could match the punctuality of the packets. For example, the *Manhattan*, a fast trader with excellent cabin accommodations, was advertised on October 23, 1819, to sail for Liverpool between November 10 and 15. Ten days later the agents advertised for 250 to 300 bales of cotton to complete its cargo. On November 6, in advertising for 200 more bales, the agents declared that the ship would sail "positively" on November 20. Further appeals for 100 to 150 bales of cotton for cargo were issued on November 15 and 24, and then it was announced that the ship would depart on December 5, weather permitting, whether the ship's cargo was completed or not. This final promise was executed. Such delays and postponements were typical of ordinary sailing vessels at this time.

The *New England Palladium*, of August 28, 1821, reprinted the following statement about packet service from the Quebec *Gazette:*

> "We received our regular file of papers by the American packet ship James Monroe, forwarded from the General Post-Office, at London, which it appears has now determined to send mails to Canada by these ships, which sail regularly from Liverpool, on the 1st of every month, and usually make very short passages. The King's packets do not usually sail from Falmouth till nearly the middle of the month. The new arrangements will therefore give us a regular mail from England about once a fortnight, instead of once a month as formerly, and a much more speedy conveyance for at least one of them."

The year 1822 brought trouble for the first line of Liverpool packets in the form of competition and disaster at sea. In April a severe storm wrecked the *Albion* on a reef off the Irish coast, with a loss of 47 of the 55 persons on board. The owners' share of ship and cargo had been insured for $51,200. In July another ship, on her maiden voyage, struck an iceberg. While the crew and passengers were rescued, the vessel and its entire cargo were lost. Fortunately the owners had ordered two new vessels, which were completed in time to permit the maintenance of the schedule

[9] Albion, *op. cit.*, pp. 36–40 and appendix viii.

by a slight rearrangement of the regular succession of ships.[10]

It may be well here to point out that the five owners of the original line continued after its establishment to engage in other business pursuits. Isaac Wright and his son acted as agents for other vessels, engaged in whaling for at least the years 1819–23, and employed vessels both in coastal trade and in voyages to Europe and China. Francis Thompson acted as shipping agent; he operated ships in the coastal and European trade, often joining Jeremiah Thompson in making triangular voyages between New York, southern ports, and Europe in cotton export ventures; and, in 1819, he started one vessel in regular service between New York and Dublin, apparently inaugurating the practice of bringing back immigrants whose passage had been prepaid by friends and relatives. Both the Wrights served as directors of New York banks, while Jeremiah Thompson participated in private banking and speculated heavily in cotton. Marshall branched out from general trade to the manufacture of cotton textiles in New York State.

4. The Formation of Other Packet Lines

Business conditions in both the United States and Great Britain revived in 1821, and shipping on the Atlantic coast boomed as a result.[11] On January 2, 1822, the New York *Commercial Advertiser* carried an advertisement, which, under the heading "New Line of Liverpool Packets," announced: "The owners of the ships Meteor, Panthea, Manhattan and Hercules, intend one of them to sail from this port on the 25th, and from Liverpool on the 12th of each month." For freight or passage prospective clients were to apply to Byrnes, Trimble & Co., 159 South Street.

Thomas S. Byrnes had been in partnership with Jacob Wood in New York City between 1806 and 1817, the firm engaging chiefly in the business of importing grain, seed, and flour from Delaware, Maryland, and Virginia. Much of their trade had been carried on in association with Silas Wood, a flour and grain dealer of Fredericksburg, Virginia. In 1816 the firm had entered foreign shipping when it purchased a share in the *Hercules* with James and Richard Loines, George Trimble, and another New York merchant as joint owners. The Loines brothers, flour dealers, had entered Liverpool shipping in 1815 by purchasing shares in regular traders. George Trimble, too, had been dealing in grain and flour. With the retirement of Jacob Wood in 1817, the firm of Wood & Byrnes dissolved, and a new one was formed with Byrnes, Silas Wood, and Trimble as partners. Byrnes, Trimble, and the Loines brothers were Quakers. There were also family ties among them, for Byrnes's wife was a niece of Isaac Wright of the "Old Line" and James Loines was a brother-in-law of Wright as well as the father-in-law of Byrnes.

With three good ships among them, these men had attempted to organize their sailings into a regular succession in 1819, and they had even advertised them as packets for a short while. Late in 1820 they began to dispatch their ships about the twenty-fifth of the month, with fair punctuality, and to advertise the fact. In 1821 a fourth ship was acquired. To some extent, then, the Byrnes, Trimble & Co. ships had competed with the First Line of packets for more than a year before the Second Line, often referred to as the Red Star Line, was formally announced. The initial sailing was not auspicious. Although the *Meteor* left the wharf on January 25 as scheduled, ice held it in the East River for three days. After it had been towed through the narrows by steamer on the fourth day, there was further delay; the ship finally got to

[10] *Ibid.*, p. 31.

[11] Willard L. Thorp, *Business Annals* (New York, 1926), pp. 75, 119, 157; Cutler, *op. cit.*, pp. 64–65.

sea on February 1. Subsequent sailings were much more punctual. Three months later the date of departure was advanced to the 24th.[12]

Despite the fact that the owners of the First and Second lines were friends and neighbors connected by religious and marriage ties, a lively competition immediately ensued. Within six weeks (February 14, 1822) the First Line announced that it would add ships and double its service, with vessels departing from both New York and Liverpool on the 1st and 16th of the month. It also reduced its price of passage from 40 to 35 guineas. The new ships were both heavier and faster than existing ones, averaging nearly five hundred tons burden. New York now had three sailings to Liverpool every month, on the 1st, 16th, and 24th. The service on the 1st was usually called the First or Old Line, while that of the 16th was sometimes referred to as the Third Line, since its establishment followed that of the Second. Both the First and Third were also known as the Black Ball Line.

In July, 1822, appeared the Fourth Line (Swallow Tail Line), which closed the remaining gap by scheduling departures from New York on the 8th and from Liverpool on the 24th. Its principal owners were Fish & Grinnell, Thaddeus Phelps & Co., and Abraham Richards, all New York merchants. Preserved Fish had joined Joseph Grinnell in partnership in 1815, after having had experience as a whaler and as a shipping agent in New Bedford. The two men operated as shipping agents and dealers in whale oil, sperm candles, rum, fish, plaster, and other wares. Abraham Richards, a shipping agent and shipowner in New York, was also the New York representative of his brother Silas who, besides being a cotton broker, was shipping agent in Liverpool, serving in that capacity for several ships of the Second Line and for all those belonging to the Fourth. Thaddeus Phelps, a dealer in cotton, rice, and other southern produce, had in 1815 become part owner of a ship trading with Havre. Later he became part owner of ships plying between New York, Savannah, Havre, and Liverpool, and in 1819 he was acting as agent for a regular Liverpool trader.

In addition to these principal owners there were a number of other New York merchants who contributed capital to the Fourth Line but took no part in its management: Verdine Ellsworth, J. S. Crary, Peter Crary, Peter Crary, Jr., John Taylor, James Magee, Gamaliel Smith, James McCall, William Stoddard, and Nash De Cost. Ellsworth was in partnership with Phelps, the Crarys were chiefly interested in importing dry goods and general merchandise, Taylor was a dry goods importer and bank director, Magee concentrated on trade with Ireland, Smith and McCall were cotton merchants who imported cotton from Savannah and exported it to Liverpool, and Stoddard and De Cost were ship captains.

Meanwhile a need had arisen for a packet service between New York and Havre, and in 1818–19 a group of merchants (among them Thaddeus Phelps) had attempted to provide regular service. Unfortunately the trade between France and the United States at that time was seriously hindered by legislative restrictions which each government had made in attempts to favor its own shipping. France had fixed low brokerage fees for French ships using her ports but high ones for American vessels. She had also levied a high duty on cotton which was imported in American bottoms. In 1820 the American government retaliated by levying a prohibitive duty of $18 per ton on goods brought to this country in French ships. Between 1820 and 1822 trade practically ceased as a result, but the commercial treaty which was concluded in 1822 made possible a resumption of normal Franco-American com-

[12] *Loc. cit.*

merce. An opportunity for a packet service was again open, and in 1822 an announcement was published,[13] stating that a line of packets would be established between New York and Havre, "sailing from New York in regular succession every other month in the year, and likewise to leave Havre," commencing on September 10, 1822. "The price of passage is fixed at 140 dollars for which sum passengers will be furnished with beds and bedding, wines and stores of all kinds." The subscribers were Francis Depau, Isaac Bell, and M. R. Burke.

The moving spirit in this enterprise, Francis Depau, was a Frenchman by birth who had become a general merchant in New York after his escape from a Santo Domingo sugar plantation during a native uprising and after having served for a period as commission merchant in Charleston, South Carolina. In partnership with John R. Skiddy, a sea captain, and Gardner Greene Howland, one of New York's greatest merchants of the period, Depau had owned and operated a ship trading with the West Indies, the Gulf Coast, and South America, and also with Havre, Bordeaux, and Charleston. In association with Isaac Bell and Miles R. Burke he had owned and operated a ship trading with Havre, Bordeaux, and Marseilles. Isaac Bell, son of a loyalist family, had returned to New York after the Revolution and had engaged in trade with China and the East Indies. Burke was a sea captain who commanded one of the new line's ships.

In January, 1823, the second line to Havre was announced, offering monthly service, with ships leaving both New York and Havre on the 1st of the month, starting February 1, 1823. The ownership of this line being scattered, even more markedly than in the case of its predecessor, the management was placed in the hands of an agent, John I. Boyd, who owned no share in any of the four vessels used. One of the prime movers was the firm of Le Roy, Bayard & Co., one of New York's leading mercantile houses. This firm had owned and operated many ships trading with Europe, the West Indies, and South America, but had used them almost exclusively for its own cargoes. Another owner was William Whitlock, Jr., who had also participated in the attempt to found a service to Havre in 1818–19. He was a shipping agent and merchant, dealing mainly in cotton. Boyd, formerly employed by Le Roy, Bayard & Co., had subsequently established himself as a shipbroker. He was shortly joined by Dominick Crassous, who with a man named Diaz had previously operated as a shipbroker, apparently the first firm in New York (1819) to specialize in this work; others had combined ship brokerage with importing and other functions. When Crassous retired, Boyd took Edward Hinken into partnership, the firm continuing to act as agents for the line.

Trade between New York and London at this time was considerably less than that with Liverpool or Havre, chiefly because London did not offer a steady market for cotton. London's traffic increased in the 1820's, however, and in May, 1824, a line of packets was announced for the New York–London trade, sailing monthly after July 1. Its agents and part owners were John Griswold and Fish & Grinnell. The latter firm was also part owner of the Fourth Line to Liverpool. The Crarys of the Fourth Line also invested in this one, again taking no part in its management. Griswold had long been an importer, shipowner, and agent. When his partner, Samuel W. Coates, died in 1824, the line was temporarily reduced to two ships, but new associates were soon found, among them being Captain Reuben Brimley.

In 1824 Jeremiah Thompson helped to found a service from New York to Greenock, Scotland. Ships were scheduled to

[13] From the New York *Shipping and Commercial*, July 26, 1822.

embark regularly once a month from Greenock, but sailings from New York were apparently left to circumstance.

5. Some General Consequences of the Packet Lines

The scheduled sailings of the packets soon helped to break down the seamen's established traditions and superstitions, which had previously interfered with prompt departures. They also encouraged a widespread appreciation of punctuality and speed in transportation. After 1821 shipping lines generally began to send off their ships on the dates scheduled and to emphasize speed of passage.[14] The transatlantic packet services also helped to build up New York's shipping and commercial strength, not only because they facilitated her trade with Europe but also because they favored profitable coastwise shipping, particularly with the southern ports. Indeed, the overseas trade depended upon the commerce with southern ports. In 1824 the New York *Evening Post* commented on this as follows: [15]

"We do not think that we can be charged with exaggeration when we state that there is not a city in the world which, in all respects, has advanced with greater rapidity, than the city of New York, within the last ten years. . . . Already our coasting trade is unrivalled; and the amount of duties on imports and tonnage is greater than the whole of Boston, Philadelphia, Baltimore, Norfolk and Savannah put together. . . .

"We have, in New York, . . . a greater number of packet ships than all the ports of the Union collectively. There are sixteen which sail regularly betwixt this port and Liverpool. In the Havre line there are four; in the Savannah, seven; in the New Orleans, four; in the Charleston, ten; besides the brigs, sloops and schooners, which sail on regular days to Boston, Providence, New London, New Haven, and various ports in the South."

[14] Cutler, *op. cit.*, p. 66.
[15] *Evening Post,* Jan. 8, 1824.

While New York packets were prospering, two attempts were made to establish packet service between Boston and Liverpool. The Boston & Liverpool Packet Co., established in 1822 with four ships, had failed by 1827. Another packet line, which started in 1827, lasted only four or five years. Bostonians sensed that New York was capturing important business. In 1825 one of them wrote: [16]

"If it is asked whether New York consumes so many more goods than Massachusetts as to enable her to support so many packets, I answer no; it is owing to her merchants having more enterprize than ours.

"We rest satisfied with supplying . . . western and southern places with the natural products of New England, while the New Yorkers import for them all their European and India goods. . . . New Orleans is increasing every year with the greatest rapidity; and New York is grasping at the whole trade.

"Their packets are excellent, ably commanded, . . . and complete the voyage in nine and sometimes in six weeks. Our packets are three months in performing the same. . . .

"Besides the cotton received for the goods sold to the southern and western states, the New York merchants are constantly receiving large quantities for the express purpose of shipping to Europe. Thus they not only load their regular packets; and others of their own ships; but have lately given full freights to our northern vessels, besides employing a great many to bring the cotton from New Orleans and Mobile. Our Liverpool packets find little or no freight here, and therefore go to Charleston for freight."

Philadelphia, thanks to the enterprise of Thomas Cope, had a packet service to Liverpool after 1821, and Jeremiah Thompson helped to found another line in 1824; but, while Philadelphia shipping expanded, its growth could not compare with

[16] Quoted in Albion, *op. cit.*, p. 75. See Albion's study also (chap. iii) for the only existing account of the coastwise packets, which were so essential to the growth of New York's transatlantic trade.

that which took place in New York.[17] In general American ships at this time were carrying about 90 per cent of the country's ocean trade.

6. Later History of the New York Packet Lines, to 1837

Despite the interference of storms and wrecks—the Old Line lost two more ships in 1824 and the Second Line lost one in 1827—the packets continued to provide regular sailings and became *the ships* of the Atlantic shuttle for both passengers and valuable freight. By 1835 the character of the eastbound cargoes had altered somewhat from that of 1818. The principal commodities carried in 48 voyages to Liverpool totaled 33,384 bales of cotton, 26,121 barrels of naval stores, 5,431 hogsheads of flaxseed, 1,747 barrels of apples, 2,185 barrels of iron ore, and 276 hogsheads of tobacco. Westbound freight continued to consist largely of textiles and other manufactured products, and iron rails were frequently carried to fill up the hold.[18]

Several important changes in ownership had taken place by 1836. Since these changes were chiefly the result of business failures, evidently some of the original owners had been unable to cope with the problems which confronted them as a result of their attempt to handle several different types of business.

Jeremiah Thompson, in addition to carrying on his shipping interests, continued to import cloth and export cotton on a large scale. He lost heavily in 1824–25 when Vincent Nolte of New Orleans, with whom he had joined in cotton speculations, failed as a result of a rapid fall in price. Thompson, too, went to the wall late in 1827. Weakened by this circumstance, Francis Thompson failed in the next year, but despite the loss of their share of ownership he and his nephews continued to serve as agents for the Black Ball Line. Marshall had become deeply interested in cotton manufacturing and finally withdrew from shipping in 1832. Isaac Wright died in the same year, leaving the ownership of the line in the hands of his son, William, and Joseph Walker, a son-in-law of Francis Thompson. In 1834 six of the Old Line ships were sold, Goodhue & Co. becoming the agents. The principal owner of the Black Ball Line was now Jonathan Goodhue, along with Peletiah Perit and Calvin Durand, who were his partners. Goodhue had long been a commission merchant with connections in many ports in Europe, the East Indies, Mexico, and South America. In 1819, Perit had joined him in a firm devoted to "general commission and freight carrying business." Two sea captains, Charles H. Marshall and Nathan Cobb, also became part owners of the line at this time, and Marshall was given the entire management. Subsequently he became the principal owner.[19]

A change in the ownership of the Second Line took place when Byrnes of Byrnes, Trimble & Co. died in 1825. A large share of the business then passed into the hands of S. Hicks & Sons, an important firm of Quaker merchants. Samuel Hicks, after operating successfully as an importer and general merchant, had become part owner of several ships (1817–18) in which the Thompsons were interested, and his firm soon became one of the most active in the shipping business. His firm immediately began to add larger ships to the Second Line so as to compete on more even terms with the Black Ball Line, which had been setting the pace for all in ship construction as well as in service. The Loines brothers gradually withdrew from the line within the next three years.

[17] Cutler, *op. cit.*, pp. 68–72; Lubbock, *op. cit.*, pp. 26–29; Albion, *op. cit.*, pp. 47–48, 74–76.

[18] *Ibid.*, pp. 38–42 and appendix viii. Where there is a discrepancy between the text and the appendix, the latter (according to the author) should be used.

[19] *Ibid.*, pp. 114–118.

A. & S. Richards, who had been among the owners of the Fourth Line, were eliminated in 1825 when their business failed as a result of the same cotton speculations which led to Jeremiah Thompson's bankruptcy. Ellsworth and Phelps sold out their interests in 1826, and between 1827 and 1832 Preserved Fish withdrew. The firm of Fish & Grinnell then became Grinnell, Minturn & Co. Robert Minturn, like the sons of Joseph Grinnell whom he joined in partnership (1830), was a general merchant, but the firm devoted most of its attention to shipping and for fifty years stood among the leading shipowners and operators of this country.

The Havre lines continued in this period without much change. Depau continued to be the principal owner of the First Line; but after William Bayard's death in 1826 the house of Le Roy, Bayard & Co. failed in the hands of his two sons (1827), and William Whitlock, Jr., became the principal owner. Both lines continued to operate profitably for many years.

The London line settled down in 1829, after some changes, to two sailings per month, one on the 1st by Fish, Grinnell & Co., and one on the 15th by John Griswold & Co. In 1832 service was increased to three sailings per month, on the 1st, 10th, and 20th.

Between 1830 and 1833 a new service to Liverpool was developed, the Kermit Line. Perhaps the most notable thing about this new line was that it was essentially a product of the shipping business rather than an outgrowth of a mercantile enterprise. The manager and principal owner was Robert Kermit, who had entered shipping in 1824 when he became associated with Boyd and acquired a share in one of the Havre packet ships. In 1827 he became agent for Stephen Whitney, one of the wealthiest men in New York. Whitney, having made a fortune in groceries, wine, and cotton, withdrew from active trade in 1830 in order to invest in real estate, canals, and railroads. He retained, however, a joint interest with Kermit in two ships which Kermit dispatched in 1832–33 almost as regularly as packets. In the summer of 1833 Kermit added a third vessel, chartered a fourth, and announced regular sailings on the 14th of the month. Such wealthy New Yorkers as Archibald Gracie, Joseph Sands, Rufus King, and Nathaniel Prime invested in the Kermit Line. One of the captains, William C. Thompson, also took a share in it. They sold two ships in 1835 as being unsuitable for packet service, but Kermit continued to operate regularly with the aid of chartered vessels. At the same time his line purchased the Second Line of Liverpool packets from S. Hicks & Sons.[20]

In 1836 the Collins Line to Liverpool was founded. This service, like the Kermit Line, was established by a man who became a specialist in shipping. E. K. Collins had served as supercargo on vessels trading with the West Indies. In 1827 he established a line of packets between New York and Vera Cruz, following shortly with another between New York and New Orleans. His success with these packets led him to establish a monthly service to Liverpool, often referred to as the Dramatic Line because the ships were named after famous actors.[21]

By 1837, then, the transatlantic packet lines of New York were well established and prospering, and their success helped to pave the way for the clipper ship era in American maritime history which was just beginning. Many years of successful operation lay ahead of them, but already in the offing was the steamship, which was to reap the harvest of their emphasis upon speed and punctuality.

In 1838 four different steamships crossed the Atlantic, one of them completing five voyages from Liverpool to New York and

[20] *Ibid.*, pp. 43, 119–121.

[21] *Ibid.*, pp. 123–125; Lubbock, *op. cit.*, pp. 10–11.

back during the year. These ships were not much faster on the eastward run, but they could make the westbound passage in less than half the time required by the sailing packets, and they could offer reasonably regular arrivals as well as punctual departures. In 1839 the British government granted a generous subsidy to the newly formed Cunard Co., which began operations a year later. Fortunately for the New York packets the Cunard Line first chose Boston as its terminus, and for several years no one succeeded in establishing regular steam service between New York and Europe. In 1848, however, the Cunard Co. began regular voyages out of New York and carried off the cabin passenger and fine freight business. The sailing packet lines assumed secondary importance.[22]

7. Readings

Robert G. Albion, *Square-Riggers on Schedule* (Princeton, 1938). The only accurate history of New York's packet services. Readable, rich in detail on all aspects of packet service, and as complete as sources permit.

Robert G. Albion, *Rise of New York Port* (New York, 1939). A carefully prepared study of the growth of New York City as a port, giving attention to both geographical and commercial factors.

N. S. Buck, *The Development of the Organisation of Anglo-American Trade, 1800–1850* (New Haven, 1925). Excellent background on the rise of New York commercially and the channels through which its imports and exports flowed.

8. Suggested Questions

1. What is the significance of the various business interests of the men who founded the packet lines?
2. What difficulties were encountered in establishing regular transatlantic packet service?
3. Why did New York City take the leadership and why succeed?
4. To what extent were the owners of the packet lines specialized in 1822? In 1836?
5. What were the long-time effects of American success with the packet services?
6. What should have been the business policy of a New York–Liverpool packet line in 1838?
7. Do the early efforts to form packet services belong to mercantile or industrial capitalism?

XXIII. CORNELIUS VANDERBILT, 1794–1877

1. General Statement

Cornelius Vanderbilt was the first of the great specialists in American transportation. There is no adequate biography of this striking figure—most judgments of Vanderbilt fail to see him at work against the background of his time—and he is generally pictured as a somewhat vulgar individualist who recognized no law and no right but his own. The material which follows aims to give some insight into his character and his business policy and methods.

[22] Albion, *op. cit.*, pp. 253–266.

2. Important Dates in Vanderbilt's Career

1794	Birth of Cornelius Vanderbilt.
1810	Set up in business as a boatman.
1815	Entered coastwise shipping trade by building small schooner.
1817	Possessed $9,000 in cash, as well as interest in several sailing vessels. Quit the shipping business and annual profits of $3,000 to become a steamboat captain at $1,000 a year.
1829	Set up in steamboat business

1829	for himself with capital of $30,000.
1830–35	Average profit of $30,000 a year.
1836	Cleared $60,000. Worth at this time half a million dollars. Was running a score of vessels.
1849	Entered ocean shipping with a short route through Nicaragua.
1849–53	Cleared $1,000,000 annually in Nicaragua alone.
1853	Sold interest in line. At this time had $11,000,000 invested, making 25 per cent annually.
1854	Again engaged in Nicaragua line, making $10,000,000 in the next nine years.
1861	Worth $20,000,000 and owned nearly 100 vessels.
1862	Began to withdraw from shipping and entered railroads.
1863	Secured control of the Harlem Railroad.
1864	Secured control of the Hudson River Railroad.
1867	Made president of the New York Central Railroad.
1868	Fought Drew, Gould, and Fisk for possession of the Erie. Lost more than $1,000,000.
1869	Consolidated Hudson River and New York Central.
1869–73	Secured control of other roads.
1873	Built the New York Union Depot.
1877	Died, leaving property of over $100,000,000.

3. Summary of Vanderbilt's Business Career [1]

Cornelius Vanderbilt was born in Port Richmond, Staten Island, New York, on May 27, 1794. He came of a long line of farmers, the first of whom had left Holland to settle on Long Island near Brooklyn. Generation after generation of Vanderbilts had toiled hard, practised almost incredible economy, and developed stamina and resistance. Although Cornelius' father was one of the less thrifty members of the family, he is said to have been the first boatman to adhere to a regular schedule in his daily plying between the quarantine ground and New York. In view of his son's future activities it is significant that he had imagination and was interested in speculation, though with unfortunate consequences. His wife possessed the qualities which he lacked—energy, forethought, self-reliance, and thrift—and it seems as if their son inherited the positive characteristics of both. Although Cornelius cared nothing for books (later he regretted his illiteracy), he was strong both mentally and physically and had a retentive memory for those things which interested him. He loved the water and, from the age of twelve, satisfactorily performed responsible tasks connected with the transport of produce on his father's pirogue. Four years later he confided to his mother that he had decided to become a sailor. Finally yielding to her persuasion, he gave up the project on condition that he might buy a boat. His mother reluctantly promised that, if he would plant with grain an eight-acre field, which was so stony that it had never been plowed, she would give him $100 for a boat. Although he was given less than a month—until his sixteenth birthday, he accomplished the task, so it is said, with the help of his friends whose services he enlisted with promises of future rewards in the form of sails in the forthcoming boat.

With his capital of $100 Cornelius purchased a 20-passenger pirogue and announced his readiness to transport freight and passengers to New York City. Cornelius' charge for a single fare was 18 cents. He worked about 16 hours a day. By daylight he carried casual freight and passengers; at night he conveyed parties to the city. At the end of the year he returned to his mother the $100 she had

[1] Summarized from W. A. Croffut, *The Vanderbilts and the Story of Their Fortune* (Chicago, 1886).

given him for his boat and $1,000 besides. At the end of the next year he gave her another $1,000 and had in the meantime bought shares in two or three other boats. At this time strained relations with Great Britain had led to an increased interest in fortification, and Cornelius was kept busy carrying materials to the forts flanking the entrance to the Sound and the Narrows. Sometimes he worked from dawn till after dark without stopping for meals. He was always ready for any difficult or dangerous job, he charged fair prices, and he allowed no one to underbid him. In spite of his rough manners he soon gained a favorable reputation, once (during the War of 1812) being called on to transport a party seeking reinforcements to the Battery. During the war bids were invited for a contract to convey provisions to the posts near New York for three months—the contractor to be exempt from military duty. Many boatmen, anxious to escape service, put in preposterously low bids. Cornelius did not bid until urged to do so by his father, when he put in a bid which he thought to be fair. To his surprise his offer was given preference over the others, which were much lower, the statement being made by those in charge that the work must be done and they knew he would do it.

Throughout his life he followed his custom of doing, in spite of all obstacles, whatever he had set out to do. He could drive himself unmercifully, even when ill. It was perhaps this quality in him which made him ever impatient of weaklings and beggars, with the result that he disliked to be asked for contributions and made it a rule never to put his name to a subscription paper. This does not mean, however, that he did not give aid when he considered the cause a good one. During the time that he was supplying the forts, for instance, he stayed a day and a night with a community of Shakers on one of his cruises up the river. Their refusal to accept compensation for his board and lodging made a lasting impression upon him. Many years later, when he was president of the Harlem Railroad, he astounded his associates by granting the Shakers an important and unusual concession. His later important benefactions —$50,000 to be used in purchasing a church in New York for his wife's old pastor and his gift of $1,000,000 for Vanderbilt University at Nashville—were similarly unsolicited and obviously for worthy causes.

The six forts which Vanderbilt contracted to supply during the war had to be provisioned once a week, and it was a day's job to supply each one. During the day he continued with his Staten Island business, conveying provisions to the forts at night. His large profits made it possible for him to build a small schooner for the coasting trade, which he sent under a captain up and down the Sound or along the coast. The next year he was able to build a very large schooner to ply between New York and Charleston. No work was too small for him; he would even peddle shad or melons up and down the coast or the river. When the war closed, he at once began to study methods of improving ships. He introduced certain novel ideas which were much discussed by shipbuilders in general, and he carried out his ideas in a vessel of his own which he had constructed at this time. He continued in shipbuilding and shipping and in 1817, at the age of 23, he had $9,000 in cash and an interest in various sailing vessels.

By 1810 Fulton and Livingston had four steamboats on the Hudson, as well as one on the Delaware and one on the St. Lawrence. Vanderbilt, along with other shipowners, at first scoffed at these crafts; after careful study and consideration, however, he at last concluded that the future of navigation belonged to the steamboat. He gave up his coasting business, sold his shares in half a dozen vessels, and looked about for an entrance into steamboating.

Fulton and Livingston had a New York monopoly on the new type of navigation, but it was contested by Thomas Gibbons, who had established a combination stage-and-steamer line from New York to Philadelphia. Vanderbilt became captain of the Gibbons steamboat, relinquishing his former $3,000 of annual profits from luffing and tacking for a salary of $1,000. Under his management the line for the first time began to pay, and a year later he supervised the building of a larger steamer. An advertisement in a New York newspaper in the fall of 1826 shows that the steamboat captained by Vanderbilt left the wharf at New York at noon every day except Sunday. The passengers, after their trip to the Jersey shore, 25 miles of land carriage, and a trip by river steamboat, arrived in Philadelphia at 10 o'clock the following morning; the fare was $3.00. Vanderbilt's wife assumed competent charge of the halfway house, where all the travelers had to spend the night. The line at last began to pay $40,000 a year to Gibbons. Vanderbilt's salary was increased to $2,000, and in addition he received profits from the tavern.

Until 1824, when the Livingston monopoly was declared unconstitutional by the Supreme Court of the United States, Vanderbilt was engaged in a constant fight with the New Yorkers. Once they made an unsuccessful attempt to buy him off by offering him a salary of $5,000 a year to take charge of their large boat.

In 1829 Vanderbilt, having $30,000 in cash, decided to reap the advantage of his twelve years' experience and of his knowledge of the construction and operation of steamboats. Over the protests of his wife and Gibbons—who offered to double his salary, sell him half the line at his own price, and let him pay for it out of his profits—he resigned and went to New York City. In 1830 he began to build improved boats, which he ran in opposition to old, established lines. His chief antagonist, thinking that Vanderbilt was backed by Gibbons, withdrew from the fight rather than waste a fortune in cutting rates; his place was taken by Daniel Drew and Dean Richmond. It was Vanderbilt's policy to build better boats than his competitors' and to run them at the lowest paying rates. Whenever he saw a line which was apparently making large profits, he threw himself into competition and drove it from the field by giving better and cheaper service. Between 1830 and 1835 he made $30,000 a year; in 1836 he made $60,000. Though Vanderbilt at one time or another built or bought a hundred vessels, none was ever lost while in his possession. He never insured a vessel, saying, "If corporations can make money out of insurance, I can." In 1836, at the age of 42, he was worth $500,000 and was running a score of vessels.

During the next 15 years he increased his operations greatly. He ran boats to Albany until Robert L. Stevens & Son bought him off. He built greatly improved boats and he established lines to Bridgeport, Norwalk, Derby, New Haven, Hartford, New London, Providence, Newport, and even Boston. He prospered notably from 1840 to 1850.

At the time of the gold rush in 1849 the Pacific Mail Steamship Co. monopolized most of the transportation service, running steamers in connection with both shores at Panama, charging $600 for the round trip and giving poor service. Vanderbilt decided that he could do it for half that price and save 600 miles by crossing at Lake Nicaragua. He built a large steamer and, towing a small sidewheel steamboat, steamed down to Nicaragua. Since his engineers had reported that the San Juan River emptying out of the Lake was not navigable, Vanderbilt took the little steamer up himself. Two steamers were put on the river and a large one on the lake. On the Atlantic side he placed four steamers and on the Pacific side five others. A steamer left New York every fortnight. He made more than $1,000,000 in Nicaragua alone each year; of course he received revenue from other enterprises as well. In 1853 he sold out his Nicaragua route to the Transit Line. At that time he remarked to a friend that he had $11,000,000 invested in such a way that it would bring him 25 per cent annually without risk.

Vanderbilt soon found himself in trouble with the Nicaragua Transit Co., to which he had sold a controlling interest in his short route to California and which now refused to pay him. Because prosecution under these circumstances would be a national affair, Vanderbilt wrote them:

"Gentlemen: You have undertaken to cheat me. I won't sue you, for law is too slow. I will ruin you.

"Yours truly,

"Cornelius Van Derbilt"

Putting another fleet of steamers to work, in two years he had the opposing line in a bankrupt condition. Vanderbilt remained for nine more years in the California shipping business, accumulating thereby at least $10,000,000.

When the Crimean War broke out, the Cunard line of steamers was withdrawn for service between England and the Black Sea. Collins was running a weekly line of good American steamers, but since he gave only half the service required Vanderbilt offered to form a partnership with him and put on two more steamships. Collins, not wishing to be connected with Vanderbilt, refused. Vanderbilt then went to Congress and offered to put on two Atlantic steamers, running once a fortnight, if Congress would pay him the same amount that it paid the English steamers—$16,000 a trip. Collins had been receiving $33,000 a trip and asked Vanderbilt not to lower the price, promising to help him get his proposal accepted if the old price was retained. Vanderbilt declared he was doing this for a patriotic motive and that Collins should retire if he could not meet the price of the Cunard and Vanderbilt lines. Vanderbilt finally agreed as a compromise to carry the mails for $19,750 each round trip, the whole amount to be forfeited if he did not beat the Collins steamers every trip. The Collins influence, however, kept this proposal from being passed by Congress. Yet, when one of Collins' steamers was lost, Vanderbilt offered him the use of another without charge till it could be replaced. Then he built three new Atlantic steamers and organized a new line from New York to Havre. When he had demonstrated the superiority of his line, he offered to carry the foreign mails for nothing. President Pierce vetoed the Collins subsidy and Collins had to quit.

Though Vanderbilt had now secured a firm hold on the Atlantic carrying trade, he did not push it. Believing that railroads were the coming investment, he sold some of his vessels, transferred some to other lines, and gradually withdrew his money from shipping. Thus, when the Civil War broke out, his prosperity did not suffer. At this time he had fewer than a hundred vessels and was worth at least $20,000,000.

In the winter of 1862–63, Vanderbilt became interested in the Harlem Railroad. Charles W. Sanford, its counsel, seeing its stock worth only three cents on the dollar, urged Vanderbilt to become a director. He at first refused but later, on condition that Daniel Drew would also participate, he consented to take a little interest. The Commodore, as he was called, had sold all his ships to Allen & Garrison for $3,000,000 cash and was ready to invest this amount in railroad stock.

The Harlem stock had been going at $3 a share in 1857, $6 in 1859, and $8 or $9 in 1860, and it did not sell at a much higher rate when he began buying heavily. When he had advanced a considerable sum, however, the stock doubled and soon went to 30. The Commodore continued buying, and the rumor went out that he had some new franchise or advantage. Under this stimulus stock went to 50. On April 21, the Common Council of New York passed an ordinance authorizing him to build a street railroad down Broadway to the Battery. Next day Harlem went to 75 and finally to par. Vanderbilt was elected president of the road on May 19.

In June it was observed that the aldermen who had granted this franchise were selling Harlem "short." The Commodore, however, went on buying, getting his friends to buy for him. Soon more shares had been sold than the 110,000 in existence. Then the Council rescinded the ordinance, and the laying of rails was enjoined. The aldermen and their supporters continued selling short. The stock dropped to 72. At that point those who had sold short wanted to deliver, but the stock immediately shot up, for the Commodore held it all. He forced settlement at $179 a share. Vanderbilt and his partners made millions, while the Common Council and their associates were ruined.

Cornelius Vanderbilt made his son, William H., vice-president of the railroad. William had for twenty years been a successful farmer and had left that occupation to become receiver of a bankrupt railroad, the stock of which he had in two years caused to rise from almost nothing to $175 per share. The father and son improved the track of the Harlem, increased the speed of its trains, and soon made it a paying investment. The Vanderbilts' rules for managing a railroad were (1) buy your railroad; (2) stop the stealing that went on under the other man; (3) improve the road in every practicable way within a reasonable expenditure; (4) consolidate it with any other road that can be run with it economically; (5) water its stock; and (6) make it pay a large dividend.

In the fall of 1863 the Commodore began to buy Hudson River Railroad stock, which had been going at 25, and soon obtained control of the road. Wishing to consolidate this line with the Harlem road, he caused a bill authorizing consolidation to be introduced into the legislature; he secured a promise of support from the governor and a majority of the legislature, despite the opposition of the Erie and the Central. Stock went up until at last it stood at 150, the Commodore buying largely. But in February, 1864, some of the legislators, thinking they saw a chance to make some money, began selling "short" and defeated the bill. The Commodore, though informed of these tactics, kept on buying. The stock finally dropped to 90 but there it stayed. Instead of delivering, the gamblers decided to wait until it should go down to 50. Meanwhile the Commodore and some of his friends began to buy stock secretly. When the legislators and their friends tried to buy for delivery, they found themselves in the same difficulty that the New York aldermen once had been in—there was no stock to be had. The Vanderbilt pool had bought 27,000 more shares than the entire stock of the road! The Commodore wanted to put it up to 1,000 but his allies objected on the grounds of the effect it would have on business, and they let it go at 285. Drew compromised for $1,000,000. Many of those concerned were absolutely ruined.

The Commodore made his son vice-president also of the Hudson River Railroad. Young Vanderbilt applied to this road the same methods which had been successful with the Harlem Railroad, with similar results. The Commodore did not at this time endeavor to consolidate his two roads. Instead he put $2,000,000 into the New York Central and soon obtained control of that road, as will be seen later.

In 1867 the Commodore turned his attention to the Erie Railroad, which was largely controlled by Daniel Drew, who used his position as treasurer to exploit the road. Vanderbilt went to work buying large blocks of stock and electing some of the directors. Drew was ousted but by hard pleading finally got back on the board where, assisted by Gould and Fisk, he again became a menace. There arose a rumor of Drew's intention to distribute more stock. Judge Barnard issued an injunction against this, ordering Drew to return to the treasury one-fourth of all the stock already out and also forbidding the conversion of any Erie bonds into stock. Vanderbilt kept on buying and the stock continued rising. Finally the Vanderbilt party had a virtual corner. Drew, Gould, Fisk, and others had been selling short. To ward off ruin, 100,000 shares of new stock were signed in blank and deposited in Drew's office.

On March 10 Drew ordered an employee to transfer the books of stock to another office. On the way he was waylaid by Fisk, and the stock was taken and thrown on the market. Vanderbilt and his supporters kept on buying. One of Vanderbilt's agents, when the banks refused to loan money on the overissue of Erie, succeeded in getting a loan by threatening to throw Central on the market at 50 and ruin them. Vanderbilt kept on at the futile task of buying. As Fisk remarked, "If this printing press don't break down, I'll be —— if I don't give the old hog all he wants of Erie." When things had somewhat settled, Vanderbilt though still solvent was behind six or seven millions, while other buyers were absolutely ruined. Warrants were sworn out for the arrest of the conspirators, who fled to Jersey City, taking with them $7,000,000 in currency, the withdrawal of which created an artificial stringency and caused stocks to fall. Vanderbilt was on the ragged edge of failure, but from some source he secured sufficient funds to carry him through. He sold all the genuine stock he had and carried on a vigorous campaign against the conspirators, procuring attachments against their property as well as warrants for their arrest.

The conspirators were not yet ready to give up. They had made a sum of money worth fighting for, and they succeeded in getting through the legislature an act authorizing the issue of bogus bonds. But at last they surrendered, first Drew, then Gould and Fisk. Vanderbilt was relieved of 50,000 shares at $70, receiving $2,500,000 in cash and $1,250,000 in bonds of the Boston, Hartford & Erie at $80. He was to receive another million, outright, for the privilege of calling on him for his other 50,000 shares at $70 any time within four months. The conspirators were later compelled to pay $9,000,000 to the Erie as restitution for the amount their activities had cost the road. Vanderbilt's little venture in Erie cost him one or two million dollars and he swore never to touch the road again. At its next session the legislature passed an act forbidding consolidation of the Erie and the Central.

Vanderbilt was more successful with his other pools. In the first five years of his railroad venture he had cleared $25,000,000. In two years he advanced to the Central $2,000,000 and with this thoroughly overhauled the road. In 1869 he secured from the legislature the privilege of consolidating the Hudson River and New York Central roads. He bought from the city St. John's Park on Hudson Street for $1,000,000, and on it erected a gigantic freight depot for the Hudson River Railroad. His son, William, was made vice-president of the consolidated system. Then the Commodore hastened to dilute the capital of all his roads, thereby almost doubling his previous wealth. When he was elected president of the Hudson River Railroad its capital was $7,000,000. When he became president of the Central its capital was $28,000,000. Early in 1869 he declared a tremendous dividend of new stock to all stockholders. Eighty per cent was added to the estimated value of Hudson River and 107 per cent to that of the Central. The capital stock of the two roads, in other words, was increased from $35,000,000 to $86,000,000 and later to $90,000,000.

Vanderbilt and his friends profited enormously from these operations. One night he carried away $6,000,000 as part of his share of the profits, and in addition he had $20,000,000 in new stock. In 1869 the stock of the consolidated roads reached 200, though the amount issued had been doubled.

Though advancing in years Vanderbilt continued to extend his railroad empire. Later the father and son took over the Lake Shore and the Michigan Southern, the Lake Shore through the death in 1873 of its president, one of the Commodore's sons-in-law. Very soon Vanderbilt acquired control also of the Canada Southern and the Michigan Central. When almost 80 years old he obtained a charter from the legislature authorizing the erection of a Union Depot at 4th Avenue and 42nd Street, giving him the use of the avenue thence to Harlem for a series of underground or viaduct tracks conducting into the heart of the city the trains of the Central, Hudson River, Harlem, New Haven, and Boston lines. Through this charter the city assumed one-half the cost of the subterranean way, the cost being $6,500,000.

The Vanderbilts now controlled the great northern trunk line to Chicago. They had laid two tracks on the Central for passengers and two for freight. The freight trains could carry enough grain to load 200 vessels a day. The Commodore thus had one continuous road 978 miles in length with side lines greatly increasing the total, which represented an aggregate capital of $150,000,000 of which he owned one-half.

In the ten years from 1863 to 1873 Vanderbilt thus pieced together many independent lines into one continuous system from Chicago to New York. Where passengers going from one of the two terminal cities to the other had formerly had to board seven different trains, after Vanderbilt's consolidations they could go the whole distance in one. Freight, which had formerly been transferred at the many transfer points at great cost, profited especially by the saving from direct service.

At 81 years of age Vanderbilt boasted that he had made $1,000,000 for each year of his life. He died on January 4, 1877, after an illness of almost eight months. His will left nearly $90,000,000 to his son, William H. Bequests to all other persons amounted to $15,000,000; one-half of this went to the four sons of the principal heir, Cornelius (the eldest) getting by far the largest share.

4. Vanderbilt's Methods [2]

"The Commodore acquired possession of his great trunk railroad largely by exercising the brute power of his wealth. He boldly purchased in the open market properties of enormous potential value, which their holders were only too contented to sell. The Vanderbilt fortune is one of the results of two great financial crises—the hard times occasioned by the Civil War and by the panic of 1873. Practically every Vanderbilt railroad with the exception of the New York Central, was in a state of virtual bankruptcy when the Commodore came into possession of it. When he began purchasing the Harlem road, its stock sold for eight cents on the dollar; shares in the Hudson River line, when Vanderbilt began picking them up, went begging at twenty. The panic of 1873 gave the Commodore what is now the most valuable of all the New York Central properties, the Lake Shore & Michigan Southern Railroad. The Commodore's son-in-law, Horace F. Clark, consolidated the roads between Buffalo and Chicago into this great line in 1869; he managed it so badly, however, that when the great crash came in 1873, it had a

[2] From "The Vanderbilt Fortune," *McClure's Magazine*, Nov., 1908, pp. 46–62, by Burton J. Hendrick.

floating debt of $6,000,000 and an overdue payroll of $1,400,000. It had contracted a loan of $2,000,000 from the Union Trust Company in New York, the failure to pay which had forced the trust company into a receivership. When things had reached this pass, Vanderbilt stepped in, wrote his check for $6,000,000 to pay off the Lake Shore debt, and assumed personal responsibility for the Union Trust Company's loan. As his reward, he took the property himself, became its president, and, with Amasa Stone, started in on the work of resuscitation. All his purchasing operations the Commodore made less expensive by his continual manipulations of the stock market. At the time that he was purchasing the Harlem and Hudson River roads, he was constantly speculating in their shares; the several Harlem and Hudson River 'corners' which he engineered furnished the most celebrated Wall Street episodes of the early sixties; in one he made from three to five million dollars' profit—enough to purchase the Harlem River line several times over. That he had other resources, however, Vanderbilt made clear when he started his campaign for the acquisition of the great New York Central line extending from Albany to Buffalo.

"Several powerful millionaires and politicians controlled the New York Central Railroad; it regularly paid dividends, and, for a time, did a large and steadily increasing business. Several members of the old Albany regency—including Dean Richmond, Erastus Corning, and Peter Coggers—actively managed the property. Having purchased a large interest in the stock, Vanderbilt attempted, in 1866, to secure control, and met the first serious setback of his railroad career. In seizing the railroad from these powerful rivals, the Commodore now displayed all his characteristic audacity, resourcefulness, and defiance of public opinion. With the Hudson River Railroad he simply clubbed his way into the Central.

"The Central had two avenues by which it could send its passengers and freight from Albany to New York—the Hudson River steamboats and Vanderbilt's Hudson River Railroad. In the winter time, however, the river was completely frozen over, and the Central was absolutely dependent on Vanderbilt's Hudson River line. The Commodore took advantage of this circumstance to cripple his adversary, decrease its earnings, depreciate its stock, and ultimately to seize the property. In the latter part of January, 1867, the Hudson River road notified the New York Central that it would no longer accept traffic from it. At Albany a new railroad bridge had recently been constructed; over this Hudson River trains passed, and, at Albany, interchanged passengers and freight with the New York Central. Suddenly all Hudson River trains refused to cross this bridge, and established a new stopping place on the east side of the river.

"The very day this order became effective, the thermometer dropped to zero, and one of the most terrible snowstorms of recent years set in. In this snowstorm, western passengers on the New York Central had to walk across the river, dragging their baggage along with them, in order to make connections with the Hudson River trains to New York. When they reached the other side, the Hudson River trains had usually left; this also was part of the general scheme to make the break in connection complete. Meanwhile, western freight began to accumulate at Albany, thousands of cattle, for which no provision could be made, suffered seriously from exposure and hunger. The inevitable then took place: all western freight began to be shipped from Buffalo to New York by way of the Erie Railroad. The Central's earnings immediately decreased; its bankruptcy, under these conditions, could probably not be long postponed. Its stock, which, in the fall of 1866, had sold at $130 a share, declined, as a result of Vanderbilt's onslaught to $95. As it went down, the Commodore purchased thousands of shares, and, in a few months, had $6,000,000 of its $23,000,000 capital in his own name. The more conservative Central stockholders now took up Vanderbilt's cause. They had tired of the old political crowd; Vanderbilt's management of the Harlem and the Hudson River had given him a great reputation as a railroad man. In the fall of 1867, therefore, a majority of the Central's stockholders formally offered Vanderbilt control of the road.

"Thus, in 10 years, Commodore Vanderbilt, at the age of 80, had realized his ambition for a New York–Chicago line. He had introduced, also, a new conception of railroad ownership and control—the one-man idea. Hitherto a congeries of wrangling stockholders had managed these disorganized properties; Vanderbilt became the Caesar of the railroad situation. There have been other great American railroad autocrats—Gould, Huntington, Hill, and Harriman—but no one has held so absolute a position as the Commodore. Railroad ownership is now a complicated affair—a combination of bankers, important financiers with large minority interests, proxy holders, and the like. Hardly any American magnate can point to a great trunk property and say That is mine. This is precisely what Cornelius Vanderbilt could do. No combination of stockholders could oust him from control, for he actually had a majority interest in his own name. When he died, he owned sixty per cent of the stock of the New York Central, a majority interest in the Harlem, the Lake Shore, and the Canada Southern, and many minority holdings in other roads.

"He managed these properties, spent many millions in their reconstruction, and manipulated their securities with absolute independence of all minority stockholders. That the public had any legitimate concern with his railroads would have struck the Commodore as absurd. Once, upon the witness stand, he repeatedly replied, 'None of your business' to a regularly authorized inquisitor who was attempting to get certain first-hand information concerning the Central's affairs. Before he obtained control of the Central, its official reports were fairly complete, afterwards, they did not furnish the most rudimentary information. He had the utmost contempt for the law and its representatives: 'Law!' he once roared, 'what do I care about the law? Hain't I got the power?' Once, observing that a Central director had not voted for a certain proposition which had been under consideration, he asked the reason why. 'Don't you know, Commodore,' his friend replied, 'that each and every one of these transactions is absolutely forbidden by the statutes of the State of New York?' 'My God! John,' said Vanderbilt, 'you don't suppose you can run a railroad in accordance with the statutes of the State of New York, do you?'

"The Central's stockholders submitted to this despotism because they found it a most profitable one. From the *disjecta membra* which he had picked up on the New York Stock Exchange, Vanderbilt developed a smooth, rapidly running, and highly paying trunk line. From New York to his Chicago terminus, he remade the property, physically and financially. He doubled the capacity of the Hudson River division by widening the roadbed and laying a second track. From Albany to Buffalo he laid four tracks,—two exclusively for freight and two for passengers. These four tracks, upon which Vanderbilt spent $40,000,000, were long the wonder of the railroad world.

"All along his line, the Commodore ripped up the old iron rails which had done service for many years and relaid them with steel. It is interesting . . . Vanderbilt had to import these new steel rails from England. He replaced wooden bridges with steel and iron ones, and along the whole length of the line built new passenger and freight stations. He converted the old Harlem station into the terminus for the whole Vanderbilt system. At Forty-second Street Vanderbilt built the Grand Central station, then the country's largest railroad terminal. In Fourth Avenue, he sank the Harlem tracks and constructed the present tunnel—which, 30 years ago, was regarded as a great public improvement. In every department the Commodore introduced new efficiency and economies. When he came into possession of the Central, all its locomotives were covered with dazzling brass work; the Commodore found the polishing of these ornaments an expensive luxury and had them all painted black. He discovered among the employees, according to a contemporary account, 'an army of suckers in the form of ticket and freight agents;' most of these he dismissed and the others he brought firmly into line.

"As a result of all these changes, the earnings and traffic of the road greatly increased. The Central became the favorite passenger route from Chicago to New York; the grain, the cattle, the forest and the farm products of the far West began to move to the seaboard along the Central in enormous quantities. The old bankrupt roads became good dividend payers; their shares, from being the playthings of Wall Street, came to be looked upon as the country's most desirable investments. The Harlem Railroad, which had a large deficit when the Commodore took hold, in 1863, paid eight per cent dividends in 1866. The Hudson River, which had experienced all kinds of reverses before Vanderbilt took charge, paid its eight per cent in 1867. The New York Central also almost immediately went upon an eight per cent basis. The Lake Shore, which was $7,000,000 in debt when the Commodore rescued it from bankruptcy in 1873, had cleared up all its obligations and paid a dividend of three and one-half per cent in 1875. It is not surprising that the Commodore's fame as a railroad man reached everywhere. The New York *Tribune* declared that Vanderbilt had done more to restore confidence in railroad management than any living man. Three times the English stockholders of the Erie road, outraged by the criminal maladministration of their property, begged Vanderbilt to assume its management.

"Vanderbilt did not accomplish all these results without perpetrating gross abuses. There was not much in his management, or that of his descendants, that could be properly described as graft. Inside rings absorbing the profits of the stockholders, or engaging in private operations at their expense—such scandals, during Vanderbilt's management, were practically unknown. That the Commodore constantly speculated in the stock market and that he manipulated the management of his railroads as part of these speculations, is unquestionably true; inasmuch, however, as he never paid less than eight per cent dividends on the Central, his stockholders did not unduly suffer. There is one essential difference between the Gould and the Vanderbilt ideas of railway management. Gould sacrificed his own stockholders to make himself rich; Vanderbilt laid heavy tribute upon the public to make rich the owners of the Central properties. Under the Commodore's control, rebating flourished on a large scale. By granting rebates to the Standard Oil group in the earliest days, Vanderbilt helped to nurture that powerful monopoly which has since gained so strong a hold upon his own railroad system. He practised all those rate discriminations that, in recent years, have been outlawed by federal action. He bribed legislators and corrupted courts.

"With the exception of the Harlem River Road, Vanderbilt remorselessly watered every property he got. He signalized his control of the Hudson River by issuing $7,000,000 worth of new stock, at least one-half of which represented no actual value. A year after taking over the Central, he increased its capitalization by $23,000,000, practically every dollar of which represented inside profits for himself and his friends. Both a legislative and a stock market scandal accompanied this inflation. Vanderbilt went about the matter with characteristic secrecy. Only two members of his board of directors, his son-in-law, Horace F. Clark, and Chester W. Chapin, had any inkling of his intentions. William H. Vanderbilt, his own son, afterwards declared that he had been kept in ignorance, and had even sold, at a great loss, large blocks of Central stock a few days before the operation went through. The Commodore even refused to have the requisite legal documents printed, for fear that the printers might reveal his plans. The three directors, Clark, Chapin, and Vanderbilt formally voted the consolidation, not at the Central's offices, but at Horace F. Clark's house. They met at midnight, and declared a stock dividend of eighty per cent on the outstanding issue of the New York Central Railroad.

"On this occasion Vanderbilt must have voted profits ranging from $8,000,000 to $15,000,000 into his own pockets. His speculative winnings in Central stock at the same time must have been very large. A few days before passing this bonus issue, it was said, he had quietly picked up 130,000 shares of Central stock. The day before the deal became known, Central stock sold at $120 a share; the day after at $160; and Vanderbilt's purchase therefore represented more than $5,000,000 in profits. In November, 1869, Vanderbilt consolidated the two properties into one corporation—the present New York Central & Hudson River Railroad; and on this occasion he again increased their capitalization by nearly $23,000,000's [sic] worth of watered stock. In these years he thus poured nearly $60,000,000 of fictitious value into the Central Railroad—two-thirds its entire stock capitalization.

"The payment of dividends upon these issues sadly taxed the Central's resources. Under this heavy weight, the property Vanderbilt had so brilliantly developed began to show signs of decay. Indeed, these stock inflations explain that parsimonious management which has for many years been associated with the Vanderbilt name. Vanderbilt had to raise annually nearly $7,000,000 for Central stockholders, of which nearly $5,000,000 represented dividends on fictitious issues. To get this money, enormously high freights were levied on local traffic, rolling stock was allowed to depreciate, stations fell into disrepair, and general dilapidation resulted. These stock inflations, however, largely explain the enormous increase of the Commodore's fortune in the last ten years of his life. His stock profits from the three transactions must have aggregated $25,000,000; and upon this he received eight per cent dividends for eight years. These items in themselves therefore account for nearly $40,000,000 of the $104,000,000 of which he died possessed."

5. Vanderbilt on the Witness Stand [3]

The testimony of Vanderbilt given below is revealing of the business man. It was given at Albany, February 5, 1867. The matter in question was the Commodore's action in stopping the Hudson River trains before they reached the terminus opposite Albany.

"Q. Do not the railroads of this state receive franchises and enjoy privileges not possessed and enjoyed by citizens and individuals at large? A. I presume so.

"Q. Why are those franchises granted—for what purpose? A. For the public good.

"Q. The Hudson River R. R. was built first from New York to Greenbush? A. I understood so.

"Q. What was its connection before the Albany bridge was built? A. That I cannot tell you, exactly.

"Q. How were passengers and freight transported across the river before the Albany bridge was built? A. I suppose they were transported by ferry boat.

"Q. Was not that attended with considerable delay and some considerable additional expense? A. I don't think it was attended with any delay or expense by the Hudson River R. R. Co.

"Q. Didn't the people suffer considerable delay and expense by the use of the ferry in place of the bridge? A. I think they lose more by the bridge than they do by the ferry.

"Q. You mean going from and coming to the Delavan House? A. I mean that.

"Q. You are aware that there was a long contest between the citizens of Troy and Albany about its [a bridge across the Hudson] construction? A. Yes, sir.

"Q. That the Legislature finally granted a charter? A. Yes, sir.

"Q. What was the object of the Legislature in granting that charter? A. I don't know. I have not read it.

"Q. That charter gives the bridge company extraordinary powers which otherwise they would not have had? A. Yes, sir.

"Q. Then must not your answer be that the charter was granted for the public good? A. It may be.

"Q. If the Legislature permitted the construction of this bridge to the injury of commerce, was it not to promote the interests of commerce by uniting the Hudson River and Central roads? A. I presume it was, but I don't know anything about that.

"Q. If that was the object of the Legislature, then were the officers of either the Central or Hudson River railroads, so long as there was a legal remedy, justified in breaking the connection, which break might have lasted for months instead of days, and resulted in great loss of time and money? A. That I don't know.

"Q. Take into consideration the whole question—the companies having received these franchises with extraordinary powers to serve the public, and the Bridge company having received the same, were the officers of these great organizations created for the public good, justified in breaking that connection, so long as

[3] New York State, *Assembly Documents,* 1867, no. 19, pp. 205–210. Testimony before the committee on railroads of the Assembly.

there was a legal remedy left to them? A. I answered that a while ago.

"Q. I think I put the question in a little different way? A. I should give about the same answer. If the public suffers in consequence of such a break it is a great misfortune, and I should be exceedingly sorry for it; but at the same time, if the Central railroad says 'you shall run your cars right straight through to Buffalo, and we will not pay anything for them, or anything of that kind,' I say I will not do it. Let me answer your question by asking another, as the Yankee does. Would you think it right for the Legislature to compel me to let them have my cars without compensation because the public good was concerned? Would the Legislature justify such a transaction as that?

"Q. There is a remedy for that also if I am to answer the question, but in the course of this testimony this delay of cars does not appear to have been the cause of this difference. Could not the Hudson River railroad enforce their claim for the $100,000 through the courts of law? A. They might; I will not give an opinion on that point. I stated a while ago that I for one will never go to a court of law when I have the power in my own hands to see myself right. Let the other parties go to law if they want, but by —— I think I know what the law is; I have had enough of it.

"Q. Would you recommend all other citizens to pursue the same course? A. I would recommend them all to pursue the course that I pursue. What is it? To do nothing that is wrong; to pursue a straightforward, direct course, and deal with everybody else as you would like to have them deal with you.

"Q. I would like a straightforward reply to this question. You represent the Hudson River railroad company and Mr. Keep represents the Central railroad company. Jointly the two companies with the Western railroad control the Bridge company. You have admitted that the railroads and the bridge were constructed for the public good. I would like to have you answer the question whether these officers are justified, taking into view the public interest, in breaking the connection between the roads? A. I don't know how I can answer that any better than by saying, if by making the bridge and putting the two roads together, you are going to compel the two to run under an arrangement by which one is sacrificed to the other, I think that is a good ways to go for the public interest.

"Q. If you had no interest in railways, but was a large transporter of property over railways, and a break in the connection of the road should occur, and continue so long that your property would suffer depreciation in value, would you not expect the Legislature to enact a law that would not permit a similar occurrence in the future? A. I am told that such a law is already enacted. I don't care what law the Legislature makes in reference to railroads, provided it is general, and applies to all roads. For if I cannot exist upon the same terms with the rest of them, I will retire and go out of the business. As regards the Hudson River road, we don't ask anything in the way of laws to be enacted, either one way or the other, if they will only treat us as they treat all the roads throughout the state. If they do that I don't see that we have any right to complain.

"Q. The only object I have in putting these questions was with reference to the public interest, for I care very little about the differences between the N. Y. Central and Hudson River railroads? A. I don't suppose you do; but we would not like to have the Legislature turn around and say, 'You shall do just as the New York Central railroad tells you to do.'

"Q. The law is not yet enacted? A. I am not a railroad man. I own a good deal of railroad stock. I invested my money in railroads because I supposed it was going to be a good investment. I intended to let it be there. All I have to say is that if the acts of the Legislature are going to lessen the value of my investments, I shall sell out my interest in railroad stocks, and invest my money in something else.

. . . .

"Q. How much stock have you in the Harlem road? A. I don't know whether it is right for the committee to inquire into how much property I have got.

"Q. It is material to know whether you hold a controlling interest? A. I have a good deal.

"Q. Have you a controlling interest? A. I don't know whether I have a controlling interest. We have a board of directors, and in that board of directors the majority rules.

"Q. How much stock have you in the Harlem railroad company? A. That I cannot tell you.

"Q. Can't you tell how much you have got? A. I don't know that that is a proper question. You might just as well ask me to give you an inventory of my estate. If I am compelled to answer I will answer.

"Q. Do you refuse to answer? A. If I am compelled to answer I will.

"Q. I want to know whether you refuse to answer that question? A. I prefer not to answer it, because I don't think it proper.

"Q. I consider it a very important question —or may be—that depends upon the answer? A. I cannot answer you any other way with all due deference. I don't wish to be disrespectful.

"Mr. Parker: I think you had better make your calculations not to go home tonight until we see what the Legislature says about your refusal.

. . . .

"Q. It does not follow that you have so much invested. Men frequently— A. I cannot tell you how much I have invested in it.

"Q. It does not follow that you have invested all that is in your name; it may not all be paid for? A. I don't buy any stocks that I don't pay for; I don't buy anything unless I have the money to pay for it.

"By Mr. Parker:

"Q. I will repeat the same question with reference to the Hudson River railroad. It has been charged that you control both roads, that you as an individual were assuming to do certain things which were against the interests of the public in this state. This committee meet here as between the companies and the people of the state, and are not here to inquire into the differences between the companies and find out which was originally to blame. A. You are here to inquire. Here is a man who has taken a road when its stock was not worth ten dollars a share, and had not been up for years. He has had a little pride; he said he would bring up that road, and make the stock valuable, and he has got that road in a position—

"Q. I asked you for the purpose of ascertaining if you had a controlling interest in the road, but you refused to answer. I now repeat the same question in reference to the Hudson River road? A. In reference to the Hudson River road—but if I answer that, you will want an answer with reference to the Harlem, and I don't see that you have any right to ask the question.

"Q. You have a right to refuse to answer, but other parties have a right to determine whether you shall or not? A. I cannot tell you that.

. . . .

"Q. Do you know how much you own in the Hudson River railroad? A. I don't know that.

"Q. Do you know whether you own a controlling interest in it or not? A. I don't know; I never found any difficulty with our directors.

"Q. (By Mr. Weed.) Do you own more than half the stock? A. Oh, that is nonsense!

"Q. Do you know how much the capital stock of the Hudson River railroad is? A. I know, or I suppose that there is something like seven millions of stock, and I suppose there is an indebtedness of seven millions more.

"Q. How is it divided? A. In shares of $100 each.

"Q. You refuse to answer as to how many shares you have? A. With all due deference to the committee. I don't think you have any right to compel me to give an inventory of my estate.

"Q. We don't ask that? A. That is about

it, for you may keep on from one thing to another until you have got it."

6. Suggested Readings

On Vanderbilt:

W. A. Croffut, *The Vanderbilts and the Story of Their Fortune* (Chicago, 1886). This book gives the main points of Vanderbilt's career and many anecdotes about him, but it is far from being a satisfactory biography.

General background:

C. F. and H. Adams, *Chapters of Erie* (New York, 1871). A critical portrayal of railroad finance at its worst, which gives details of Vanderbilt's encounter with Erie.

E. P. Oberholtzer, *History of the United States since the Civil War,* vol. ii (New York, 1922), pp. 538–614. This selection deals with notorious railroad scandals in the 'sixties and 'seventies.

Bouck White, *The Book of Daniel Drew* (New York, 1911). A penetrating analysis of one of Vanderbilt's contemporaries and rivals; recommended for comparison.

7. Suggested Questions

1. What were Vanderbilt's chief contributions to railroading?
2. What were the specific elements of strength and weakness in Vanderbilt's business policy as a whole?
3. What was there in public life that made possible the business operations of Drew, Gould, Fisk, and Vanderbilt? Were their practices unethical? Were these men financial or industrial capitalists?
4. Contrast the difficulties of Vanderbilt and the Van Sweringens in railroad consolidation.

XXIV. CINCINNATI SOUTHERN RAILWAY: STRUGGLE BETWEEN TWO RIVAL CITIES FOR METROPOLITAN DOMINANCE, 1860–1929

1. General Statement

The building of the Cincinnati Southern Railway is one of the most extraordinary events recorded in the history of American cities. As a climax to the long rivalry between the business men of Louisville and Cincinnati, the story of the beginnings of the Cincinnati Southern interprets the commercial life of those Ohio River cities. But its greatest significance for business history lies in its portrayal of the forces which were at work: shifting trade routes, the construction of strategic railroads, the creation of new methods of doing business, the rapid rise of the Great Lakes region, and the development of commanding metropolitan cities.

2. Supremacy of Cincinnati, 1820–60

From 1820 until about 1860, Cincinnati was the greatest city west of the Atlantic seaboard. Cincinnati possessed the double advantage of being the chief distributing point of northern manufactures to southern retailers and of being a great market for the purchase of the agricultural products of the West and the South. Its most natural hinterland was Kentucky's rich blue-grass region, and in competition with Louisville it contended very successfully for the trade of that area. In addition, the city was famous as a cloth-manufacturing and pork-packing center.

Cincinnati, located midway between St. Louis and Pittsburgh, gained an early advantage in the trade along the Ohio River. Its "location on the outside of a great bend in the river increased the city's tributary area, making it the focal point of a considerable area of the surrounding country." [1] Settlers often left the Ohio

[1] J. Russell Whitaker, "Cincinnati," *Journal of Geography,* vol. xxi (1922), p. 223.

River at Cincinnati en route to the Northwest.

"Altho the first steamboat passed Cincinnati in 1811, by 1825, 100 were arriving and departing each month. All packet lines on the Ohio made it their terminal. In 1832, 2,231 arrivals were recorded, and 1847 saw the peak with 4,007. Flat boats on the Miamis fed the river traffic to the extent of some 150 boats a year. Construction of the Ohio canals made the river all the more important. The time required for the New Orleans trip dropped from six months to about twenty-four days, with the result that Cincinnati as a river port became vital in the commerce of the West. With the exception of New Orleans, it was the largest city west of the Appalachians.

"The two canals most directly influencing Cincinnati were the Miami-Erie and the Whitewater. The Miami canal, begun in 1824 and completed in 1842, followed Mill Creek to the Big Miami, thence to Lake Erie by the Maumee River valley; the Whitewater Canal ran northwest to the Whitewater branch of the Miami." [2]

Until about 1850 the Miami Canal, which connected Toledo and Cincinnati and gave Cincinnati a water route to Lake Erie, was one of the most important factors in the growth of the city. In 1850 the tolls collected on this canal were over $315,000; 117,655 tons of merchandise were brought to Cincinnati on the canal in that year, while 42,784 tons were cleared in the same time. After 1850 new railroad connections gradually reduced the importance of this traffic link.[3]

An expert in the subject of American internal trade described the commerce of Cincinnati in a report made in 1881. He summarized the description as follows: [4]

"The trade of Cincinnati by river was for many years coextensive with the navigable waters of the Mississippi River and its tributaries. This trade extended from Pittsburgh, Pa., to Fort Benton, in the present Territory of Montana, and from St. Paul, Minn., to the city of New Orleans."

Merchandise came into and went out of Cincinnati chiefly by river. As a distributing center Cincinnati was even able to overlap the area dominated by the merchants of New Orleans, and along with Louisville and St. Louis it practically controlled the best part of the southern trade. The merchants of these three cities understood the wants and peculiarities of southern business and, until the coming of the railroad, had little competition in the distribution of merchandise to the South.

The railroad enabled the jobbers and manufacturers of Boston, New York, Philadelphia, Baltimore, and Chicago to carry on trade with most of the cities and towns in the southern States. Traveling salesmen visited almost every town south of the Ohio, while freight shipments could be made directly to points in that section.

The following population figures illustrate the growth of Cincinnati and competing cities: [5]

Cities	1820	1830	1840	1850	1860	1870	1880
Cincinnati	9,642	24,831	46,338	115,435	161,044	216,239	255,708
Chicago	....	70	4,470	29,963	112,172	298,977	503,304
St. Louis	....	5,862	16,469	77,860	160,773	310,864	350,522
Louisville	4,012	10,341	21,210	43,194	68,033	100,753	123,645

[2] *Ibid.*, p. 225.

[3] Charles Cist, *Cincinnati in 1851* (Cincinnati, 1851), p. 142; C. T. Greve, *Centennial History of Cincinnati and Representative Citizens* (Chicago, 1904), vol. i, pp. 582–583.

[4] Joseph Nimmo, Jr., "Report on the Internal Commerce of the U. S.," 46th Congress, 3d Sess., 1881, *House Ex. Doc.*, no. 7, part 2, p. 76.

[5] *Ibid.*, p. 73.

Cincinnati's closest competitor after 1860 was Louisville. Though originally settled during the American Revolution, Louisville did not grow rapidly until steam navigation had been introduced on the Ohio River. Louisville's situation on the Falls of the Ohio gave it a natural advantage. Steamers on their way down the river from Pittsburgh or Cincinnati were often forced to stop at Louisville because the water was so low. Sometimes they waited five or six months before high water filled the narrow stream below and allowed them to pass. In 1830 a canal was built around the Falls, but such exorbitant tolls were charged for its use that steamers unloaded below the Falls and had their cargoes dragged around it. Louisville continued to exploit this advantage of position until the government increased the size of the canal and took it over in 1874.[6]

3. Louisville Triumphs after 1860

A. Cincinnati business men fail to build or aid railroads.

Realizing that her natural hinterland lay to the south, Cincinnati had early desired a railroad in that direction. In 1835, after several southern cities had joined to agitate for a railway from Cincinnati to Charleston, Cincinnati took part in the movement; and charters for the Cincinnati, Louisville & Charleston Railway were secured from the various States which it was to traverse. In July, 1836, a great railroad convention at Knoxville selected the route from Charleston to Cincinnati, but in the panic of 1837 the enterprise had to be abandoned permanently.

Several other attempts were made in the next twenty-five years to build a railroad into the South. The last important project before 1860 was a proposed extension of the Cincinnati, Lexington & East Tennessee Railroad, then in operation from Nicholasville, Kentucky, to Knoxville, Tennessee. The road agreed to make the connection for a cash bonus of $1,000,000 to be raised by individual subscription, but Cincinnati business men failed to subscribe the necessary sum and the proposition was laid aside.[7]

After the Civil War, Cincinnati merchants continued to refuse to put their money into railroad development schemes, and some new means of financing the road had to be discovered. Other municipalities were able to vote bond issues on their credit and use the proceeds to subscribe to railway companies. Louisville had been able to do this very successfully,[8] but Cincinnati was blocked by a provision in the Ohio Constitution which prohibited cities from lending their credit to railroads. The specific clause, a product of the reaction to the period of wild-cat speculation before 1850, read as follows: [9]

"Sec. 6. The General Assembly shall never authorize any county, city, town, or township, by vote of its citizens or otherwise, to become a stockholder in any joint stock company, corporation, or association whatever; or to raise money for, or loan its credit to, or in aid of, any such company, corporation or association."

B. The Louisville & Nashville Railroad.

Louisville business men desired a southern railway fully as much as the Cincinnatians, for they saw that the city which developed such a connection would be commercially supreme. Accordingly, in 1850 a company was organized in Louisville for the construction of a road to Nashville, Tennessee.

[6] E. C. Semple, "Louisville: A Study in Economic Geography," *Journal of School Geography,* Dec., 1900, pp. 361–370.

[7] J. H. Hollander, *The Cincinnati Southern Railway* (Baltimore, 1894), p. 14.

[8] See *Louisville, Her Commercial, Manufacturing and Social Advantages* (Louisville, 1859), pp. 96–97.

[9] I. F. Patterson, *The Constitutions of Ohio* (Cleveland, 1912), pp. 137–138. This is sec. 6 of art. viii of the second Ohio Constitution, adopted in 1851.

Cotterill, an authoritative writer on the subject, says: [10]

"The Louisville and Nashville had been promoted and was controlled by Louisville men and had been built in the expectation that its profits would mostly be derived from the carrying of southern freight to Louisville."

Out of an original capitalization of three million dollars the city of Louisville subscribed one million, and several counties subscribed three hundred thousand, one hundred thousand, and like sums, to the Louisville & Nashville Railroad. They were richly repaid, for from the beginning the road met with outstanding success. First opened for traffic in November, 1859, it profited greatly during the war years from carrying military supplies—it was the only western railroad connecting the northern and southern railway systems. In addition to paying cash dividends averaging almost 8 per cent between 1863 and 1869, it paid a stock dividend of 10 per cent in 1864 and another of 40 per cent in 1868.[11]

C. Louisville aids other railroads.

By 1859 Louisville had already given $3,225,000 in aid to railroads built or to be built from that city.[12] In order to reach Knoxville the city subscribed $1,000,000 toward the Lebanon branch of the Louisville & Nashville in 1867, while in 1871 Louisville gave $375,000 to the Louisville & Nashville Railroad that it might procure the Nashville & Decatur road before Cincinnati should have acquired it. All parts of Kentucky shared in Louisville's liberality. By 1876 the city had railroad lines to 75 counties and access by water to 33 more, which made it possible to tap the trade of 108 of the 117 counties in the State. For these connections $8,190,000 had been paid.[13]

D. Louisville business men block Cincinnati.

Coulter explains the situation existing before 1869: [14]

"At this time Cincinnati's only practicable route to the South was through Louisville over the Louisville and Nashville Railroad. From Louisville southward she had all the facilities in theory enjoyed by the Falls City. But her route to Louisville was round-about and irregular. She was still using the Ohio River very extensively. She also had railway connections running north of the river; but as long as there was no bridge across the river at Louisville, she enjoyed few advantages in this road. There was also a rail route south of the river by a circuitous route through Lexington and Frankfort. But the lack of a bridge at Cincinnati took much of the practical value of this road away."

In 1869 the Louisville, Cincinnati & Lexington Railroad completed the construction of that division of its route which ran on a direct line from Cincinnati to Louisville, with the idea that, as soon as a right of way was granted to enter the city of Louisville, it would be possible for freight to go directly from Cincinnati to the South via this railroad and the Louisville & Nashville Railroad. This would have given a distinct advantage to the business men of Cincinnati, who were forced to ship a large proportion of their goods by steamer on the Ohio River to Louisville. Goods intended for the southern trade then had to be transferred to the cars of the Louisville & Nashville road after they reached Louisville. The directors of the Louisville, Cincinnati & Lexington expressed themselves as follows in their report for the year 1869: [15]

[10] R. S. Cotterill, "The Louisville and Nashville Railroad, 1861–1865," *American Historical Review,* vol. xxix (1923–24), p. 700.

[11] *A Book about the Louisville & Nashville R. R.* (Louisville, 1923), pp. 3, 11; *Poor's Manual of Railroads,* 1890, p. 373.

[12] *Louisville, Her Commercial Manufacturing and Social Advantages,* pp. 96–97.

[13] E. M. Coulter, *The Cincinnati Southern Railroad* (Chicago, 1922), pp. 8–10.

[14] *Ibid.,* p. 22.

[15] *Third Annual Report of the Louisville, Cincinnati & Lexington Railroad* (1869), pp. 9–10.

"It is very much to be regretted that we are not yet able to announce to you the settlement of the vexed question of a right of way through the city of Louisville to a connection with the Nashville Railroad . . . the Executive Committee passed a resolution offering to change the gauge of the road on the terms proposed by the city authorities [the object of the City Council being to force the Cincinnati line to use a gauge differing from that used by the Louisville & Nashville]. . . . Negotiations to this effect have now been pending for several months, and it seems that the only difficulty remaining in the way arises from the inability of the city councils to agree upon the particular route which should be granted for the connecting line."

The Louisville City Council refused to permit the Louisville & Nashville and the Louisville, Cincinnati & Lexington railroads to connect at Louisville except on condition that a change be made in the gauge of the latter from 5 feet—the uniform southern gauge—to 4 feet 8½ inches, so as to make a break of gauge at Louisville. Otherwise the Council threatened to separate the roads by a distance of a mile and a half.

The Cincinnati newspapers consistently attacked this stand. Reprinted below is an ironic bit from one of the many articles on this subject appearing in their columns at this time.[16]

"A Peanut City.

"Louisville opposes this [railroad connection]. Three hundred of her solid men met in council, discussed and denounced the scheme as a blow at the prosperity of the city, thus admitting that the prosperity of Louisville depends upon a change of freight and passengers at that place. But the managers of the railroad say that if not permitted to make the connection through the city it will be made around it. They argue that they can not compete with seaboard routes for travel and trade between East and South if forced to drive passengers out of the cars at night to buy peanuts at Louisville and to employ drays to haul freight from one depot to another. . . . But the solid men say passengers must stop, and consignees must have freight delayed and taxed whether they 'want to' or not. They will keep open a gap, and thus Louisville will be the Northern terminus of Southern roads, and the Southern terminus of Northern roads, and thus the city will spread and grow."

In 1870 Louisville interests defeated a bill in the Kentucky Legislature for the charter of the Louisville Steam Transfer Co., which with a 5-foot gauge was to join the two railroads. In revenge the Cincinnati road threatened to build around Louisville and not enter the city at all. Finally the Louisville, Cincinnati & Lexington Railroad agreed to enter the city on the changed gauge, and in August, 1871, reduced the gauge from 5 feet to 4 feet 8½ inches throughout its entire length of 174 miles.[17]

E. River traffic hindered.

Louisville also continued to exploit Cincinnati's trade by charging 50 cents per ton on all traffic through the canal at the Falls of the Ohio. Louisville's steamers could employ wharves below the Falls and exempt themselves from this fee, while Cincinnati complained that its boats "paying the lawful 50 cents a ton passage would pay sixteen per cent on total cost of boat; and if six years old, toll equals cost!"[18] Cincinnati newspapers also complained that the "Louisville canal, ditch, or whatever it may be named, is a serious impediment to the river commercial interests of our city . . . by reason of the limited and ill managed water course through which our boats are compelled to pass."[19]

F. The rail rate situation.

Louisville business men had still other methods at their command. Since the

[16] *Cincinnati Daily Gazette*, July 9, 1868.

[17] *Ibid.*, Aug. 3, 1868, p. 2, and Mar. 24, 1870, p. 1; R. H. Collins, *History of Kentucky* (Covington, 1878), vol. i, pp. 214, 216.

[18] Quotation from speech by W. M. Corry in Coulter, *op. cit.*, p. 25.

[19] *Cincinnati Daily Gazette*, Jan. 12, 1867, p. 4.

Louisville & Nashville road was being operated for the benefit of Louisville merchants, they saw to it that "Rail rates between Cincinnati and local points were made by adding the rate between Cincinnati and Louisville to the rate between Louisville and those points. Between Cincinnati and competitive points, the rates were formed by adding an arbitrary charge between Cincinnati and Louisville to the rate from Louisville to such points."[20]

One shipper criticized this practice at a meeting of the Cincinnati Board of Trade, January 4, 1872:[21]

"In the month of November I shipped some goods to New Orleans and paid $1.80 per hundred for shipping it. The party I shipped to complained of freight charges and requested me to send him the bills of lading showing rates. I sent him the bill of lading dated the 8th of November. It stated that the goods occupied more space in a car, there was great difficulty in handling it, and it was in all respects the worst kind of freight. And yet it is shipped from Louisville for 75 cents a hundred, while from Cincinnati it is $1.80."

G. The freight blockade.

An even more critical situation developed with regard to freight movements. The Louisville & Nashville Railroad, having a monopoly of shipments to the South, was at times unable to take care of freight shipments, and embargoes on freight were declared. The Louisville correspondent of the *Cincinnati Gazette* pictured the usual situation in his letter of September 22, 1870:[22]

"There will be no chance for Cincinnati during the fall trade to ship goods to the South. The blockade of freight in the Louisville & Nashville Railroad depots is just as great as it was a year ago and of course there is little chance for Cincinnati freight while Louisville has any use of the rolling stock of that road."

A shipper complained of the holding-up of freight shipments at a meeting of the Cincinnati Board of Trade, January 4, 1872:[23]

"I ship my goods to New Orleans and they lie in Louisville eight days. The Louisville freight is forwarded, and the Cincinnati freight is laid over there, and the sun shines on it."

H. Louisville gains and Cincinnati stagnates.

Louisville advanced rapidly in the years 1860 to 1870. With her powerful railroad monopoly she succeeded in capturing a considerable amount of Cincinnati's trade and in building up her export commerce tremendously.[24] The new situation also favored her manufacturing interests, as is evidenced by Table 1.[25]

[20] Hollander, *op. cit.*, pp. 16–17.

[21] *Cincinnati Daily Gazette,* Jan. 5, 1872, p. 4.

[22] *Ibid.,* Sept. 23, 1870, p. 1.

[23] *Ibid.,* Jan. 5, 1872, p. 4. See also the extract from the *Nashville Banner,* quoted in the supplement to the *Cincinnati Daily Gazette,* Feb. 15, 1870, p. 1.

[24] *Ibid.,* Mar. 13, 1871, p. 1.

[25] *History of the Ohio Falls Cities and Their Counties* (pub. by L. A. Williams & Co., Cleveland, 1882), vol. i, p. 519.

Table 1. MANUFACTURING IN LOUISVILLE

	1860	1870	1881
Number of establishments	436	801	1,191
Number of hands employed	7,396	11,589	21,937
Population of Louisville	68,033	100,753	126,566
Capital invested	$ 5,023,491	$11,129,291	$20,864,449
Amount of wages paid	$ 2,120,179	$ 4,464,040	$ 5,765,387
Value of material	$ 7,896,891	$19,369,556	$22,362,704
Value of products	$14,135,517	$20,364,650	$35,908,338

Meanwhile Cincinnati's business had begun to stagnate. Her long, roundabout, and impractical connections with the South gradually began to cut her off from southern markets. The city's distributive commerce was most drastically affected by the new situation, as is illustrated by figures in Table 2.[26]

Table 2. VALUE OF PRINCIPAL ARTICLES RECEIVED AND SHIPPED AT CINCINNATI 1855–79

Year ending Aug. 31	Received	Shipped
1855	$ 67,501,341	$ 38,777,394
1860	103,347,216	77,037,188
1865	307,552,397	193,790,311
1870	312,978,665	193,517,690
1873	326,023,054	213,320,768
1876	294,214,245	190,186,929
1879	208,153,301	192,338,337

4. Building of the Cincinnati Southern Railway

A. The region in competition.

The problem now before Cincinnati's business men was to find some means by which they might gain a sure grasp upon that region which was naturally their territory. To the northward, lower Ohio and part of southeastern Indiana were still theirs, but the Illinois trade had left them, and most of their Iowa trade was being lost. Chicago and St. Louis, with their great trunk lines and well-located short routes, together with several cities of less importance, had by this time divided the rest of the region north of the Ohio among themselves. The great railway routes had not favored Cincinnati, and little could now be gained from railroad expansion in a northerly direction. South of the Ohio the Kentucky Central Railroad made Cincinnati's trade with central Kentucky fairly secure. But Louisville had encroached upon the export trade of this region because there was no outlet to the southward for the tobacco and horses of central Kentucky except by way of Louisville.

Southern Kentucky still had no road to either city, though both were interested in the territory. Western Kentucky, with the Louisville & Nashville Railroad and its several extensions, was wholly Louisville's. Farther south, Nashville and Decatur probably favored Louisville because of their direct connections with that city, while Chattanooga and Knoxville were not yet under the sway of either rival. Both had such disadvantageous connections with Baltimore, Philadelphia, and other northern cities, however, that a shorter route to either of the Ohio River cities furnished tempting commercial possibilities.[27]

B. The problem.

Decay was threatening Cincinnati. The business men of the city were forced to seek connection with new regions in order to bring about trade expansion. The total situation was reviewed by the editor of one of the Cincinnati daily papers, who at that time was engaged in attacking a park development project: [28]

"One thing is certain, that not only must something be done by Cincinnati for herself, but that the thing done must be something of wider scope and more vital significance than mere local improvements. . . . It is not in the decoration of the city that public expenditure is demanded, but in providing material to make more city. Venice did not perish for lack of palaces. She ceased to command the trade of the Indies. Rome was not saved by her water-works, and London has not grown

[26] Goods which merely passed through the city are not included. The import figures include many raw materials which were later exported in the form of finished products. Nimmo, *op. cit.*, p. 87.

[27] E. A. Ferguson, *Founding of the Cincinnati Southern Railway* (Cincinnati, 1905), p. 62; *The Ferguson Railway Act* (Cincinnati, 1872), pp. 25–26; *Cincinnati Daily Gazette,* Sept. 20, 1867, p. 2, and Nov. 29, 1867, p. 2; Coulter, *op. cit.*, pp. 8, 9, 12, 19.

[28] *Cincinnati Commercial,* Nov. 26, 1868, quoted in *The Ferguson Railway Act,* pp. 20–21.

great because she has parks. The trade that is due Cincinnati has been permitted to drift away from her. . . . The case of our early opulence mis-taught us. It is time that we should emerge from the dimness of our medievial [sic] epoch, and put off the philosophy of indifference that has been cultivated to our cost. We must have parks and avenues and great public edifices, and bigger things generally, to make the city more attractive; but *first* we need to secure for ourselves the imperial dominion that is our rightful heritage, and get the food whereby we are to grow."

C. The Ferguson Act.

Cincinnati business men were fully convinced of the importance of a southern railroad connection by 1867, yet the clause in the Ohio Constitution which prevented aid to private enterprises seemingly made impossible the construction of a road. The City Council appointed a committee to study the situation, but their report was that "they regret that, at present, no direct action can be taken by the Council in furtherance of this great improvement," since the Constitution of Ohio made illegal any action which they might take. They stated that they could only recommend that the city foster and encourage roads already constructed.[29]

The situation appeared hopeless, when a project broached by Edward A. Ferguson in the spring of 1868 presented an avenue of escape. Ferguson, a constitutional lawyer of Cincinnati, urged that the city construct the road. His argument was that the Constitution only prohibited the city from being a stockholder and did not hinder it from constructing the road in its corporate capacity. Being faced with yet another clause in the Ohio Constitution, which prohibited all special legislation, he drafted a bill for cities "of the first class having a population exceeding one hundred and fifty thousand inhabitants." Cincinnati was, of course, the only city in Ohio to come under this classification.[30] The bill was passed by the General Assembly in 1869.[31]

The Ferguson Act provided that, when the City Council of a city of over 150,000 by vote of its members declared it essential to the interests of the city to secure a new railroad with one terminus in that city, a specified court within the city should appoint five trustees to carry out the proposed project. When the project had been ratified by the voters of the city, the trustees could borrow up to $10,000,000 in the name of the city for building the road and should control the disbursement of the funds thus secured in procuring right of way and building the railway.

D. The choice of routes.

The Act passed by the General Assembly of Ohio gave Cincinnati the right to hold an election to decide upon a $10,000,000 bond issue for the construction of the railroad. A southern terminus for the road had to be chosen before a vote was taken on the bond issue. Knoxville, Chattanooga, and Nashville were the cities given primary consideration, and Louisville greatly feared that Nashville would be selected.

Saner policy decided against the Nashville route, for its choice would have forced the Cincinnati Southern into a bitter and unprofitable competition with the Louisville & Nashville. All the interested cities had their representatives in Cincinnati enthusiastically urging the merits of their respective routes, and finally, on June 4, 1869, the City Council of Cincinnati after much deliberation chose the line of way which led to Chattanooga. They were influenced in their decision chiefly by the fact that Chattanooga was the key to the system of southern railways. From this point at least three first-

[29] *Cincinnati Daily Gazette,* Nov. 16, 1867, p. 1.

[30] Hollander, *op. cit.,* pp. 18–20.

[31] *General and Local Laws Passed by the Fifty-Eighth General Assembly of the State of Ohio,* vol. lxvi (1869), pp. 80–81.

class roads radiated, and tracks extended to Knoxville, Savannah, and New Orleans.[32]

E. Cincinnati opinion on the bond issue.

By this time the people were thoroughly aroused. Every important newspaper in Cincinnati favored the bond issue, and scores of editorials were published in its behalf. The general attitude of the press is contained in substance in these remarks by the *Cincinnati Enquirer*, April 14, 1869:[33]

> "But it is useless to argue this question. It is already sufficiently appreciated. Everybody in Cincinnati is for the Southern Railroad. Everybody thinks that it ought to have been built several years since. . . ."

It is noteworthy, however, that everybody in Cincinnati was not for the road. Considerable opposition to the bond issue was evinced by a group of men led by Judge W. M. Dickson, who had been consistently attacking "monopolies, jobbery and public trickery, public dishonesty, office seeking for the mere office. . . ."[34] In this case he "could not conceive of a city engaging in such a project; firstly because the thing to be done was not a governmental affair, and secondly because the movement was stupid and doomed to failure." On this point he said: "If our city owns the road, it is more likely that it will be used against the city than if owned by the individuals. Louisville is our rival in this trade, the pet of Kentucky. How long would it be before she could get discrimination against a road owned by 'a damned abolition city'?" He proposed that the city be given power to vote a gift of $1,000,000 to any corporation that would build the railroad within a certain period.[35]

Other arguments of the opposition were briefly enumerated in the *Cincinnati Daily Gazette:*[36]

> "It proposes to sink ten millions.
>
> "It will tax the personal property the same as the real, although the latter only will be benefited.
>
> "How do we know that the railroad can be built for ten millions? What if we shall expend that without completing the road? Then we shall have no road, and all our money gone.
>
> "Why should Cincinnati alone build the road when other places are to be benefited?
>
> "It is a forced loan. The money will all be squandered by corruption.
>
> "It is a fearful thing to put ten millions into the hands of receivers appointed by the Superior Court."

F. The popular vote on the bond issue.

The opponents of the Cincinnati Southern Railway charged the promoters of the project with submitting it to a popular vote only as a "mere scheme to procure for it the credit of such an indorsement by rushing it through upon a furore of public excitement that could be stirred up in regard to it."[37] Their statements seem to suggest that a small, well-organized group of interested Cincinnati business men was securing the support of Cincinnati's citizens for the passage of this measure, even though most of the citizens of Cincinnati were actually indifferent as to what happened to the project.

It is difficult to procure evidence that either favors or disproves this charge. Certainly the fight for the railroad was skillfully organized. Both the Chamber of Commerce and the Board of Trade favored the road. These two organizations of business men appointed a joint executive committee to manage the campaign.[38]

[32] *Cincinnati Daily Gazette,* 1869, May 1, 7, 8, 21, and 28, and June 2, 3, and 25 (supplement).

[33] Quoted in *The Ferguson Railway Act,* pp. 25–26. Numerous extracts from the other Cincinnati papers are included in this pamphlet.

[34] *History of Cincinnati and Hamilton County* (Cincinnati, 1894), p. 185.

[35] Quoted from the *Cincinnati Commercial* in Coulter, *op. cit.*, p. 33.

[36] May 7, 1869.

[37] *Cincinnati Daily Gazette,* May 15, 1869.

[38] *Ibid.*, June 11, 1869.

In each of the 20 wards of the city a committee, often numbering as many as 100 men, was appointed to get out the vote. On election day, June 26, 1869, the mayor ordered all business houses to close for a portion of the time. To stir up enthusiasm, nine bands of music paraded the streets, the firebells were rung, and the newspapers came out with special supplements devoted to praising the proposed railroad and painting a glowing picture of the prosperity to come for Cincinnati after the railway's completion. No considerable opposition to the Cincinnati Southern was in evidence at the polls. Possibly because no opposition had been expected, or because of a general lack of interest in the railway, only a light vote was recorded. There were 15,435 ballots cast in favor of the road, and 1,500 against.[39]

G. The struggle for a right of way.

The next line of action was to secure from the state legislatures of Kentucky and Tennessee the necessary grants of right of way to Chattanooga. Stubborn opposition on the part of Nashville and Knoxville did not prevent one of the necessary bills from passing both houses of the Tennessee Legislature in January, 1870.[40]

Louisville used every means in its power to defeat the Cincinnati Southern bill, when it came before the Kentucky Legislature, and was ably seconded in this fight by the Louisville & Nashville road. Both Ohio River cities employed thousands of dollars in bribing the Kentucky legislators, but Louisville's tactics were the more successful, and in March, 1870, the bill was defeated after close votes in both houses of the Legislature had been recorded. Only a few weeks later the Legislature granted a right of way to Louisville for an "imaginary railroad" which it had suddenly projected to Chattanooga. Louisville, by proposing the construction of the Louisville & Chattanooga Grand Trunk Railroad a short time before the Legislature met, had cleverly succeeded in forestalling the Cincinnati road. Its bluff had helped to capture the Kentucky Legislature.[41]

These facts aroused central Kentucky against Louisville business men. Protest meetings were held, Louisville jobbers and manufacturers were boycotted, and editorials, similar to the following extract from the *Kentucky Statesman*,[42] appeared in many local papers.

> "This whole portion of Kentucky are deeply feeling the great outrage that the Legislature has done it in order to satisfy the selfish demands of Louisville, and that most infamous of corporations, the Louisville & Nashville Railroad. . . . we have yet to meet the first person along the line of it who does not denounce it as a cold-blooded, powerful thing, that disregards all interests save that of clutching the money of those who are compelled to patronize it. . . . She [Louisville] would force the whole State to pay the duty she would choose to levy."

At the next meeting of the Kentucky Legislature, in January, 1871, not only central Kentucky but also Tennessee and Georgia made every effort in favor of the bill. Seventy-nine members of the Tennessee Legislature signed a memorial for the road, while the governor of Georgia had a delegation at the Kentucky capitol to bring pressure to bear in favor of the bill. All this had little effect. After a closer vote than that taken in the previ-

[39] *Ibid.*, June 25, 26, and 28, 1869; *Circular of Laws and Decisions Relating to the Cincinnati Southern Railway* (Cincinnati, 1873), p. vi.

[40] Coulter, *op. cit.*, p. 40.

[41] *Memorial of Trustees and Speech of Hon. John C. Breckenridge to the General Assembly of Kentucky and Proceedings of the Lexington Railroad Convention* (1871); *Cincinnati Daily Gazette*, Feb. 19, Mar. 10, Mar. 11, Mar. 17, Mar. 24, Oct. 15, all 1870; and Jan. 9, 1871; Coulter, *op. cit.*, p. 47.

[42] Quoted in the *Cincinnati Daily Gazette*, Mar. 10, 1870.

ous year, the bill favoring Cincinnati's project was again defeated.[43]

Louisville's merchants continually exploited latent prejudices against the hated Yankees of Ohio, who, it was declared, had helped to thrust Negro suffrage upon Kentucky. Even campaign songs used in Kentucky against the bill played on anti-northern feeling.

Such tactics, however, eventually proved to be without avail. The greater part of Kentucky wanted the road, and finally on January 27, 1872, succeeded in securing the passage of the Cincinnati Southern bill. Celebrations of the victory were soon staged throughout central Kentucky, while the trustees of the Cincinnati Southern began to draw up plans for construction.[44]

H. Financing and constructing the railway.

Under the direction of the permanent board of five trustees appointed by the Superior Court of Cincinnati the building of the road began in 1873, but the first train was not run to Chattanooga until 1880. The route of the road is indicated on the map opposite p. 29, above. Though the road as completed was only 336 miles long, its construction was made difficult because of an enormous underestimate of the cost of construction, the necessity for securing authorization for three additional construction loans, and the crisis of 1873 which made railroad bonds very unpopular. A total of $18,300,000 of bonds was issued up to 1880, and this enlarged the indebtedness of the city from $5,363,000 in 1871 to $23,953,981 in 1880. The original act required that the bonds be sold at par, which made it necessary for the first ten millions of them to be marketed at an interest rate of 7.3 per cent though some subsequent issues were sold on a more favorable basis. It is likely that the marketing of such considerable amounts of municipal bonds had an unfavorable effect upon the city's credit at the time, because it raised the per capita indebtedness and brought about an increase in the tax levy of as much as 8.76 mills by 1880. If the public had known at the start what the road was going to cost, the city would probably never have built the Cincinnati Southern Railway.[45]

I. Cost of the railway to Cincinnati.

The completed portions of the railway were leased only temporarily between 1877 and 1881, but a permanent lease was drawn up at the latter date with a new group organized as the Cincinnati, New Orleans & Texas Pacific Railway Co. The road was leased to them for 25 years at an annual rental which increased progressively from $800,000 to $1,250,000 during the period. In 1902 the lease was modified and extended to 1966; under this second lease the rental was set at $1,050,000 for the first 20 years, and $1,100,000 for the next 20 years. In November, 1927, the citizens of Cincinnati voted to extend the lease until 2026, in order that the lessee company might have a tenure commensurate with the permanent betterments which they desired to make on the property. The terms of the new lease provided for a payment to the city of $1,250,000 per annum plus 2 per cent of the net profits for the first 19 years; $1,350,000 plus 3 per cent for the next 20 years; $1,450,000 plus 4 per cent for the second 20; $1,600,000 plus 5 per cent for the third; and $1,700,000 plus 6 per cent for the fourth twenty-year period.[46]

The railway has at no time brought revenue to the city treasury. Not until it had been operated about twenty years were the trustees even able in any year to meet the total interest charges with the yearly rental from the leasing cor-

[43] Coulter, *op. cit.*, pp. 51–52.

[44] Collins, *op. cit.*, p. 211; Coulter, *op. cit.*, vol. i, pp. 60–61.

[45] Hollander, *op. cit.*, pp. 74–76.

[46] *Cincinnati Southern Railway Agreements for Operating Road* (1881), pp. 9, 29–30. *The Cincinnati Southern Railway Lease* (1927), p. 6.

poration. Gradually, as this rental increased, the income received began to exceed the charges, but on December 31, 1911, the total expense for this account by the city still exceeded the income received from the railway to that date by $8,258,949. By December 31, 1921, this amount had been reduced to $2,712,439, yet in 1927 a certain amount of accumulated interest charges still remained.[47]

Until the end of 1927 the city had received $53,073,202 in rentals from the lessees.[48] The city had spent $25,200,000 on the road. The entire outstanding interest-bearing bonded debt of the railroad was $21,332,000 in 1927, while the trustees had set up against this a sinking fund which amounted to $4,970,576 on December 31, 1927. The trustees of the railway then valued it at $100,000,000.

J. Cincinnati since 1880.

In 1868 friends of the road had urged its building as a last resort, "a matter of life or death, where our future prosperity or decay is in such scales."[49] The future of Cincinnati, the Queen City of the West, was unmistakably in the balance after 1860.

After 1880 the new road opened up a wide territory in Kentucky, which had never before been developed, and gave Cincinnati's industries cheap sources of coal and lumber.[50] It also brought Cincinnati a greater southern distributing area and made the city the central market for the agricultural products of the eastern and the blue-grass regions of Kentucky.

Cincinnati has progressed absolutely but not relatively since 1880. The first decade after the construction of the railway was one of considerable economic progress; the volume of manufacturing in the city almost doubled in that period. But since that time advance has been painfully slow. Chicago, Cleveland, Detroit, and St. Louis have reached the million class in population and have become great centers, while Cincinnati's commercial area has decreased. Louisville has also fallen far behind in the struggle. Over twenty years ago Cincinnati lost to Cleveland its preëminence in manufacture in Ohio while its chief industries—foundry and machine-shop products, men's clothing, and meat packing—have gradually diminished in importance as the competition of Chicago, St. Louis, Cleveland, Pittsburgh, New York, and other cities has been felt.[51]

5. Suggested Readings

E. M. Coulter, *The Cincinnati Southern Railroad and the Struggle for Southern Commerce, 1865–1872* (Chicago, 1922) This book tells in considerable detail of the position of the two rival cities with respect to southern trade and Cincinnati's struggle for a railroad into the South.

J. H. Hollander, *The Cincinnati Southern Railway,* in Johns Hopkins University Studies (Baltimore, 1894). This book deals only briefly with the need for the road but fully with the legal aspects of the case and the building and operation of the road in its earlier years.

6. Suggested Questions

1. What were the factors responsible for the success of Cincinnati and the relative failure of Louisville before the Civil War?

[47] *The Cincinnati Southern Railway,* published by the trustees, 1912, pp. 7, 8, 11; *ibid.,* 1923, p. 17; *The Cincinnati Southern Railway Lease,* p. 2.

[48] *The Cincinnati Southern Railway,* 1923, pp. 16–17, 26; *The Cincinnati Southern Railway Lease,* p. 2; *Annual Reports of the City Auditor of Cincinnati,* 1923–27.

[49] *Cincinnati Daily Times,* Nov. 28, 1868, quoted in Hollander, *op. cit.,* p. 22.

[50] *Resource Survey of the Commercial Club of Cincinnati,* series 2, no. 1 (June, 1927), pp. 35, 70.

[51] *United States Census,* 1880, *Manufactures* (Washington, 1883), p. xxiv; *Report on Manufacturing Industries in the United States at the Eleventh Census,* 1890 (Washington, 1895), pp. 144–145; *A Biennial Census of Manufactures,* 1925, pp. 1392–1394.

2. Why did Louisville want to keep Cincinnati out of Kentucky?
3. Did Louisville business men and the Louisville & Nashville Railroad gain or lose by endeavoring to block Cincinnati?
4. Should the Cincinnati Southern Railway have been constructed by the municipality?
5. In what railroad group is the Cincinnati Southern at the present time?
6. What light does this case throw upon the relations between business and politics?

XXV. THE DEVELOPMENT OF INTERNAL MARKETS: METROPOLITAN ECONOMY

1. General Statement

The work of the sedentary merchant is the background for the study of the growth of internal markets. Ensconced in Boston, New York, Philadelphia, Baltimore, Charleston, and New Orleans, this type of merchant carried on a variety of mercantile functions in a leisurely fashion, much as his predecessors in Europe had done for centuries. Among these functions were exporting, importing, wholesaling, and acting as commission agent for other merchants.

The common movement toward specialization in Europe, America, and elsewhere would, because of the new and exacting requirements in production and marketing techniques, inevitably pull apart these and the other functions performed by the sedentary merchant. Had there been no opening-up of the American West, this movement would have progressed along the Atlantic Coast as one metropolitan area after another came into existence. With the rapid settlement of the West, however, the change came more speedily.

We should be on the lookout for the many implications of the market changes, such as the mental switch from the Atlantic to the hinterland, from foreign lands to home districts, from ocean to inland routes. Throughout the colonial period England was spoken of as home. This was less common after 1783, and still less after the 1830's, as new routes of transportation and communication promoted western growth.

As the West was peopled and given a social and political pattern, Europe heightened its interest in the development, both for the sake of expanding its sale of goods and gradually as an opening for the investment of its capital. The East did the same and saw both the favorable opportunity for business gains and the unfavorable result arising from the loss of persons who moved to the West.

The West was to create new ideas, or revive old ones, concerning political organization and administration. It was to re-create an emphasis upon economic democracy. We are here interested chiefly, however, in the new pattern of mercantile organization that eventuated. It is important to discover the pattern and the meaning thereof, keeping in mind the change from town to metropolitan economy and the shift from the sedentary merchant to his successors—perhaps these two are counterparts of the same thing. Instead of the sedentary merchant we find at least two prominent combinations of specialists: (a) the importer-commission-agent-retailer group, and (b) the importer-wholesaler-retailer group. Instead of the importer should be put the domestic manufacturer as industry developed in America. These two combinations were to remain till long after the Civil War. Late in the nineteenth century there was a movement to eliminate the middle functionaries, but that belongs to a later story.

2. Significant Dates on Transportation and Communication

1807	Fulton's *Clermont* on the Hudson.
1811	First steamboat, the *New Orleans,* on the Ohio and the Mississippi.
1817	The *Ontario,* the first steamboat on Lake Ontario and the Great Lakes.
1818	First steamboat, *Walk-in-the-Water,* on Lake Erie.
1825	Erie Canal completed.
1829	Welland Canal completed.
1842	Railroad, Boston to Albany. Railroad, Albany to Buffalo.
1845	Cheap postage introduced.
1848	Telegraph, New York to Chicago. Chicago Board of Trade established.
1849–56	Widespread telegraph services in eastern half of United States.
1852	Railroads, New York to Chicago and Philadelphia to Chicago.
1861	Telegraph, New York to San Francisco.
1864	New York a central reserve city.
1867	Stock ticker in New York City.
1869	Railroad, Chicago to San Francisco.
1874	Railroad, Chicago to New Orleans.
1884	Telephone, Boston to New York.
1887	Chicago and St. Louis made central reserve cities.
1892	Telephone, New York to Chicago.
1914	Twelve Federal Reserve cities.
1915	Telephone, New York to San Francisco.

3. Metropolitan Economy in America [1]

"We may think of metropolitan economy as an organization of people having a large city as nucleus, just as town economy had a town as its center. Or we may put it this way, metropolitan economy is the organization of producers and consumers mutually dependent for goods and services, wherein their wants are supplied by a system of exchange concentrated in a large city which is the focus of local trade and the center through which normal economic relations with the outside are established and maintained.

"Just as villages remained when town economy prevailed, so do towns remain when metropolitan economy comes into existence. Towns remain, but in economic subordination to the metropolis. They continue to play a part, but as tributaries to a larger center. Towns exist, but not town economy. This change is marked by many a struggle as independent communities fell beneath the shadow—we can hardly say yoke—of the metropolitan center. Southampton and Bristol became subordinated to London; Rouen to Paris; Salem and Portland to Boston; Albany and Buffalo to New York; Milwaukee and Detroit to Chicago.

"A closer examination of these dependent towns would show different types performing different functions, but all subordinate. And beyond the towns there are more or less scattered communities of producers of foodstuffs and raw materials, such as farmers, miners, fishermen, and lumbermen.

"The large area of many communities, or rather the population, may be called a 'metropolitan market,' and the organization that sustains it 'metropolitan economy.' It is true that in studying this organization we are inclined to emphasize the great metropolitan center; but to forget the large dependent district would be fatal to a correct understanding of the subject. Perhaps, indeed, it is somewhat incorrect to speak of the area as dependent upon the center, for, though that is true, the center is also dependent upon the outlying area with its towns, villages, and scattered homesteads. Interdependence of the parts is really the key to the whole situation.

. . . .

"When we study metropolitan organization in America, not from the standpoint of rivalry but of present-day attainment, we find about eleven metropolitan centers with their

[1] N. S. B. Gras, *An Introduction to Economic History* (New York, 1922), pp. 186–187, 292–299.

respective areas. These are all full-grown; in other words, they have reached the financial phase of their development. These eleven are New York, Chicago, St. Louis, Philadelphia, Boston, Cleveland, the Twin Cities, Kansas City, San Francisco, Baltimore, and Cincinnati. The first nine of these are growing absolutely and relatively, the last two absolutely but not relatively. No one would hesitate to accept the first five and San Francisco. Only a study of the situation would add the others.

"When the Federal Reserve cities were chosen, all the metropolitan centers above mentioned were selected, with the exception of the last two. We are, of course, not specially concerned with the considerations that led to the selection of the twelve Federal Reserve cities, but the failure to choose Baltimore and Cincinnati is interesting.

"Although Baltimore was founded late, as compared with some of its northern rivals, it made rapid progress, doubling its population in one decade. Its early promise has not been maintained, however, for in canal and railroad construction Baltimore lagged behind New York and Philadelphia. Then it made slight effort to extend its hinterland southward. Although its dominance over its rather restricted area westward was very real in general commerce, transportation, and finance, still its outstanding success was as a port of shipment.

"Cincinnati was at first a commercial tributary of New Orleans. Later its trade developed with the eastern cities, notably with Baltimore and Philadelphia. In its manufactures it suffered from rivalry with other centers, in iron wares with Pittsburgh, in meat packing with Chicago, in the clothing industry with New York and Chicago, and in the shoe industry with Boston and Philadelphia. Although Cincinnati has developed a metropolitan organization, that organization is apparently dwindling away. Cincinnati has suffered from three misfortunes. It has no adequate water transportation; it is not favorably located for the iron and steel industry; and it is not on the main line of east and west traffic. When New York triumphed over New Orleans, Cleveland became a rival of Cincinnati. Cleveland is not greatly ahead, but both it and its area are progressing rapidly. Cleveland belongs to the future, Cincinnati to the past, as far as metropolitan economy is concerned, and as indications point at present.

"It would be worth while to determine statistically what a metropolis really is. If satisfactory figures were available, this could be done. The population of the metropolis would be large, as compared with the population of other cities in the district. This comparative advantage, however, would be suggestive, not final. The metropolis would have a relatively large proportion of workers engaged in wholesaling and relatively few in manufacture, when compared with other large cities in the district. And there would be a lack of any marked dependence on a neighboring center for trade and transportation. A city in which such conditions prevailed would at least be in the third phase of its development. If statistics proved that its loans to the surrounding area were large (especially its discounts of commercial paper), then it would be classed as a fully developed (in function) metropolitan center. Or we may put it this way: that city is a full-fledged metropolis when most kinds of products of the district concentrate in it for trade as well as transit; when these products are paid for by wares that radiate from it; and when the necessary financial transactions involved in this exchange are provided by it.

"With these criteria in mind, let us consider Detroit and Pittsburgh. The population of each of these centers, not simply in the narrow municipal limits but in the contiguous territory, is more than one million. But as compared with other centers in the district, Chicago in the first case and Philadelphia in the second, they are not so large. Although both were early trading and military posts, they have developed the manufacture, not the distribution of goods. The prominence of manufacturing in each is due to the phenomenal development of one industry, automobile in Detroit and iron and steel in Pittsburgh. Although the capital, surplus, and deposits of the banks in both cities are large, neither can claim that it performs important banking functions for the surrounding territory. Both of these cities must be classed as industrial tributaries of metropolitan centers, Detroit of Chicago, and Pittsburgh of Philadelphia and New York and (to an increasing extent) of Cleveland, though they are both fairly independent and unwilling tributaries. It may be that Detroit and Pittsburgh will ultimately become metropolitan centers. Older metropolitan cities have entered the metropolitan stage as described in the preceding chapter, but there is no reason why in new countries, or in old ones at a late date, urban centers should not enter through some other avenue, in the case of these industrial tributaries through manufacturing.

"A much more difficult task than discovering the metropolitan centers, is outlining their areas. This sometimes proves difficult even in the case of political states; it is much more so in the case of economic units. Often when political boundaries are decided upon, they are maintained as purely arbitrary marks of sovereignty. Metropolitan boundaries cannot thus be made hard and fast. They keep shifting with conditions, and the land on the confines of two contiguous areas is debatable territory. For one purpose it may belong to one metropolis, for a different purpose to another. The reality of the dependence of the area decreases as you go out from the metropolis: that is the essence of the whole matter.

. . . .

"The easiest areas to determine are around Boston and the Twin Cities, though in both cases there is a strip of debatable territory. The hardest to mark off are the hinterlands of New York and Philadelphia; Cleveland and Cincinnati; Chicago and St. Louis; and Kansas City and San Francisco. The limits of the last two are hard to fix because of the undeveloped condition of parts of the areas; the others because of overlapping. In the case of St. Louis we see a clear example of a metropolis turning from fields once sought after to sections where there is less competition, in this particular instance from a northern to a southern district. In order to make this left-over territory more worth while, the chamber of commerce of St. Louis has been active in a movement for developing town trade and uplifting rural agriculture in certain parts of its tributary area.

"Philadelphia is only two hours from New York. At one time Philadelphia was the unquestioned center of the economic life of Pennsylvania, but New York has so tapped the northeastern part that it is about as much in New York's as in Philadelphia's area. And so with New Jersey. One wonders whether the future is going to witness a revival of Philadelphia, or its submergence into the position of an industrial satellite of New York. For those who wish to draw the line between the areas of the two metropolitan centers, the most profitable suggestion is to follow the systems of transportation, especially where they run somewhat parallel and then veer off towards one metropolis or the other. Go to some of the towns lying midway between two metropolitan centers and ask which is the more dominating. The first and unpremeditated reply favors one metropolis, but a second thought favors the other and so you are left in doubt.

"As one examines the metropolitan districts in the United States, he sees decline and progress, a see-saw of unending struggle, not marked by political elections or military engagements, but by advertising, the circulation of newspapers, the activities of commercial travelers, the struggles of boards of trade, rate wars, and the migration of workers and business men. The observer also notes that where there is approximate equality of function there are inequalities of resources which reflect age, natural wealth of the area, healthfulness of the climate, and character of the people. He sees, too, that some metropolitan organizations, while well rounded in their economic activities, are nevertheless distinguished from their neighbors by their more complete development of agriculture, manufacture, or mining. This is determined in the long run, not by age but by resources. The Boston area has but little agriculture, almost no mining, but a great deal of manufacture. The Philadelphia area has turned from agriculture to mining and manufacture. The Chicago area keeps a fine balance of them all.

"In 1852, it was stated that there were 'no interior markets' in the United States. How marketing conditions have changed since that time, for, while perhaps not yet shaken down into final form, the West is nevertheless well developed, except for the Rocky Mountain section! But the South is different. Shall we say that on the whole it is still in the stage of town economy, and that its one old-time center of metropolitan promise (New Orleans) is relatively declining? New centers will probably arise: Atlanta has already shown powers of growth and commercial and financial organization. During the Civil War the South had railroads and river systems. These met or crossed one another, but there was no economic concentration, except at New Orleans, and that was not comparable with the concentration at New York, Boston, and Philadelphia. The South during the Civil War had an effective military organization but a feeble economic system. With but few towns, and no important metropolis, the South could not mobilize its economic in support of its military forces."

4. Internal Trade, 1843 [2]

"Almost up to the present time, the whole weight of population in the United States has lain along the Atlantic shore, on and near its tide waters, and a great proportion of their wealth was connected with foreign commerce, carried on through their seaports. These being at once the centers of domestic and foreign trade, grew rapidly, and constituted all the large towns of the country. The inference was thence drawn, that as our towns of greatest size were connected with foreign commerce, this constituted the chief, if not the only source of wealth, and that large cities could grow up nowhere but on the shores of the salt sea. Such had been the experience of our people, and the opinion founded on it has been pertinaciously adhered to, notwithstanding the situation of the country in regard to trade and commerce has essentially altered. It seems not, until lately, to have entered the minds even of well-informed statesmen, that the internal trade of this country has become far more extensive, important, and profitable, than its foreign commerce. In what ratio the former exceeds the latter, it is impossible to state with exactness. We may, however, approximate the truth near enough to illustrate our subject.

"The annual production of Massachusetts has been ascertained to be of the value of $100,000,000. If the industry of the whole nation were equally productive, its yearly value would be about $2,300,000,000; but, as we know that capital is not so abundantly united with labor in the other states, it would be an over-estimate to make that state the basis of a calculation for the whole country. $1,500,000,000 is probably near the actual amount of our yearly earnings. Of this, there may be $500,000,000 consumed and used where it is earned, without being exchanged. The balance, being $1,000,000,000, constitutes the subjects of exchange, and the articles that make up the domestic trade and foreign commerce of the United States. The value of those which enter into our foreign commerce is, on an average, about $100,000,000. The average domestic exports of the years 1841 and 1842, is $99,470,900. There will then remain $900,000,000, or nine-tenths, for our internal trade. Supposing, then, some of our towns to be adapted only to foreign commerce, and others as exclusively fitted for domestic trade; the latter, in our country, would have nine times as much business as the former, and should, in consequence, be nine times as large. Although we have no great towns that do not, in some degree, participate in both foreign and domestic trade, yet we have those whose situations particularly adapt them to the one or the other; and we wish it constantly borne in mind, that an adaptation to internal trade, other things being equal, is worth nine times as much to a town as an adaptation in an equal degree to foreign commerce. It may be said, and with truth, that our great seaports have manifest advantages for domestic, as well as for foreign commerce. Since the peace of Europe left every nation free to use its own navigation, the trade of our Atlantic coast has probably been five times greater than that carried on with foreign nations; as the coasting tonnage has exceeded the foreign, and the number of voyages of the former, can scarcely be less than five to one of the latter.

"Now, what is the extent and quality of that coast, compared with the navigable river and lake coasts of the North American valley? From the mouth of the St. Croix to Sandy Hook, the soil, though hard and comparatively barren, is so well cultivated as to furnish no inconsiderable amount of products

[2] J. W. Scott, of Toledo, Ohio, in *Hunt's Merchants' Magazine*, vol. viii (1843), pp. 321–323, 324–325, 327–330.

for internal trade. In extent, including bays, inlets, and both shores of navigable rivers, and excluding the sand beach known as Cape Cod, this coast may be estimated at 900 miles. From Sandy Hook to Norfolk, including both shores of Delaware and Chesapeake bays, and their navigable inlets, and excluding the barren shore to Cape May, the coast may be computed at 900 miles more. And from Norfolk to the Sabine, there is a barren coast of upwards of 2,000 miles, bordered most of the way by a sandy desert extending inland on an average of 80 or 90 miles. Over this desert must be transported most of the produce and merchandise, the transit and exchange of which, constitute the trade of this part of the coast. This barrier of nature must lessen its trade at least one-half. It will be a liberal allowance to say, that 4,000 miles of accessible coast are afforded to our vessels by the Atlantic Ocean and Gulf of Mexico. Of this, only about 2,500 miles, from Passamoquaddy to St. Marys, can be said to have contributed much, until recently, to the building of our Atlantic cities. To the trade of this coast, then, are we to attribute five-sixths of the growth and business, previous to the opening of the Erie canal, of Portland, Salem, Boston, Providence, New York, Albany, Troy, Philadelphia, Baltimore, Washington, Richmond, Norfolk, Charleston, Savannah, and several other towns of less importance. Perhaps, it will be said, that foreign trade is more profitable in proportion to its amount, than domestic. But is this likely? Will not the New York merchant be as apt to make a profitable bargain with a Carolinian, as with an Englishman of Lancashire? Or, is it an advantage to trade, to have the wide obstacle of the Atlantic in its way? Do distance and difficulty, and risk and danger, tend to promote commercial intercourse and profitable trade? If so, the Alleganies are a singular blessing to the commercial men living on their western slope. Some think that it is the foreign commerce that brings all the wealth to the country, and sets in motion most of the domestic trade. At best, however, we can only receive by it imported values, in exchange for values exported, and those values must first be created at home.

. . . .

"Will it be said that, admitting the chief agency in building up great cities to belong to internal industry and trade, it remains to be proved that New York and the other great Atlantic cities will feel less of the beneficial effects of this agency than Cincinnati and her western sisters? It does not appear to us difficult to sustain by facts and reasoning, the superior claims in this respect of our western towns. It should be borne in mind, that the North American valley embraces the climate, soils, and minerals, usually found distributed among many nations. From the northern shores of the upper lakes, and the highest navigable points of the Mississippi and Missouri rivers, to the Gulf of Mexico, nearly all the agricultural articles which contribute to the enjoyment of civilized man, are now, or may be produced in profusion. The north will send to the south, grain, flour, provisions, including the delicate fish of the lakes, and the fruits of a temperate clime, in exchange for the sugar, rice, cotton, tobacco, and the fruits of the warm south. These are but a few of the articles, the produce of the soil, which will be the subjects of commerce in this valley. Of mineral productions, which, at no distant day, will tend to swell the tide of internal commerce, it will suffice to mention coal, iron, salt, lead, lime, and marble. Will Boston, or New York, or Baltimore, or New Orleans, be the point selected for the interchange of these products? Or, shall we choose some convenient central points on river and lake for the theatres of these exchanges? Some persons may be found, perhaps, who will claim this for New Orleans; but the experience of the past, more than the reason of the thing, will not bear them out. Cincinnati has now more white inhabitants than that outport, although her first street was laid out, and her first log-house raised, long after New Orleans had been known as an important place of trade, and had already become a considerable city.

"It is imagined by some, that the destiny of this valley has fixed it down to the almost exclusive pursuit of agriculture, ignorant that, as a general rule in all ages of the world, and in all countries, the mouths go to the food, and not the food to the mouths. Dr. Chalmers says: 'The bulkiness of food forms one of those forces in the economic machine, which tends to equalize the population of every land with the products of its own agriculture. It does not restrain disproportion and excess in all cases; but in every large state it will be found, that wherever an excess obtains, it forms but a very small fraction of the whole population. Each trade must have an agricultural basis to rest upon; for in every process of industry, the first and greatest necessity is, that the workmen shall be fed.' Again: 'Generally speaking, the *excrescent* (the population, over and above that which the country can feed,) bears a very minute proportion to the natural population of a country; and almost nowhere does the commerce of a nation overleap, but by a very little way, the basis of its own agriculture.' The Atlantic states, and particularly those of New England, claim that they are to become the seats of the manufactures with which the west is to be supplied; that mechanics, and artisans, and manufacturers, are not to select for their place of business, the region in which the means of living are most abundant and their manufactured articles in greatest demand, but the section which is most deficient in those means, and to which their food and fuel must, during their lives, be transported hundreds of miles, and the products of their labor be sent back the same long road for a market.

. . . .

"But our interior cities will not depend for their development altogether on internal trade. They will partake, in some degree, with their Atlantic sisters of the foreign commerce also; and if, as some seem to suppose, the profits of commerce increase with the distance at which it is carried on, and the difficulties which nature has thrown in its way, the western towns will have the same advantage over their eastern rivals in foreign commerce, which some claim for the latter over the former in our domestic trade. Cincinnati and her lake rivals, may use the outports of New Orleans and New York, as Paris and Vienna, use those of Havre and Trieste; and it will surely one day come to pass, that steamers from Europe will enter our great lakes, and be seen booming up the Mississippi.

"To add strength and conclusiveness to the above facts and deductions, do our readers ask for examples? They are at hand. The first city of which we have any record is Nineveh, situated on the Tigris, not less than 700 miles from its mouth. Babylon, built not long after, was also situated far in the interior, on the river Euphrates. Most of the great cities of antiquity, some of which were of immense extent, were situated in the interior, and chiefly in the vallies of large rivers, meandering through rich alluvial territories. Such were Thebes, Memphis, Ptolemais. Of the cities now known as leading centres of commerce, a large majority have been built almost exclusively by domestic trade. What country has so many great cities as China, a country, until lately, nearly destitute of foreign commerce?

"To bring the comparison home to our readers, we here put down, side by side, the outports and interior towns of the world having each a population of 50,000 and upwards. It should, however, be kept in mind, that many of the great seaports have been built, and are now sustained, mainly by the trade of the nations respectively in which they are situated. Even London, the greatest mart in the world, is believed to derive much the greatest part of the support of its vast population from its trade with the United Kingdom. [The table of 67 outports, and 142 interior cities, the chief of the world, is omitted.]

"If it be said that the discoveries of the polarity of the magnetic needle, the continent of America, and a water passage to India, around the Cape of Good Hope, have changed the character of foreign commerce, and greatly augmented the advantages of the cities engaged in it, it may be replied, that the introduction of steam in coast and river navigation, and of canals, and railroads, and M'Adam roads, all tending to bring into rapid and cheap communication the distant parts of the most extended continent, is a still more potent cause in favor of internal trade and interior towns. The introduction, as instruments of commerce, of steamboats, canals, rail, and M'Adam roads, being of recent date, they have not had time to produce the great results that must inevitably flow from them. The last 20 years have been devoted mainly to the construction of these labor-saving instruments of commerce; during which time, more has been done to facilitate internal trade, than had been effected for the thousands of years since the creation of man. These machines are but just being brought into use; and he is a bold man who, casting his eye 100 years into the future, shall undertake to tell the present generation what will be their effect on our North American valley, when their energies shall be brought to bear over all its broad surface.

"Let it not be forgotten that, while many other countries have territories bordering the ocean, greatly superior to our Atlantic slope, no one government has an interior at all worthy a comparison with ours. It will be observed that, in speaking of the natural facilities for trade in the North American valley, we have left out of view the 4,000 or 5,000 miles of rich and accessible coasts of our great lakes, and their connecting straits. The trade of these inland seas, and its connection with that of the Mississippi valley, are subjects too important to be treated incidentally, in an article of so general a nature as this. They well merit a separate notice at our hands."

5. Contemporary Statements in City Directories

A. St. Louis, Missouri, 1821–58.

(1) In the St. Louis *Directory and Register* of 1821 we find the crude beginnings of a commercial town. Although old as a trading post and incipient place of commerce, the town had a population of only about sixteen hundred persons in 1810.

In 1821 there were listed many merchants, a storekeeper, a grocer, an auctioneer and commission merchant, an accountant, and a gentleman and a gentlelady. No wholesalers or retailers were designated.

(2) By 1851 St. Louis had attained a population of about seventy-eight thousand.

One firm advertised itself as a "Wholesale and Retail Dealer in Drugs, Medicines, Chemicals, Perfumery, Patent Medicines, Paints, Oils, Dye-Stuffs, Window Glass, Glassware, Brushes, &c. &c."—"direct from eastern Importers and Manufacturers."

"Page & Bacon, Banking House" stated: "Deposits received. Drafts and notes from all points of the Union collected, and Exchange on the East and South for sale at all times." They had a branch in California for the purchase of gold dust, coin, and bullion, and for the sale of exchange on New York.

(3) In the directory for 1854–55, we find wholesalers and retailers put down so as not to be counted twice or oftener, such as dealers in boots and shoes, dry goods, groceries, hardware and cutlery, and hats and caps.

One advertising agent, 9 auctioneers, 48 insurance agents or companies, and 13 engineers and surveyors were listed.

There was a traveling agent for Fairbank's Scales who would "attend to building Railroad, Hay, Cattle, or Coal Scales, and repairing either in the city or country."

(4) In 1857 the directory asserted that the big development in steamboating had occurred since 1834. It called attention to the flourishing condition of the wholesale grocery trade. Also, "Many of these merchants in various classes of business, are the direct importers from Europe of their own stocks."

B. Pittsburgh, 1841 and 1856–57.

(1) From the *Business Directory* of 1841.

In this directory of Pittsburgh there is listed a hotel located in New York City: "The Pearl Street House . . . is situated in the heart of the wholesale district of the city, and is consequently chiefly supported by the patronage of country merchants."

Commission and forwarding merchants number 23. "N.B. Our Commission Houses deal also in groceries and Pittsburgh manufactures."

Wholesale grocers number 53. "The mass of our wholesale grocers, likewise, retail to accommodate regular customers."

Wholesale grocers and liquor merchants number 9. Most of these were also retail.

An example of diversification: one firm

was land agent and commission merchant, received goods on storage, and collected money on notes.

(2) From the *Directory* of 1856–57.

"Importer, Jobber and Retailer of French, English and American Dry Goods. The subscriber invites particular attention to his Large Stock of Silks and Dress Goods of all kinds; Shawls, Talmas, Cloaks, Mantles, Needle Work, Hosiery, Ribbon, Mourning, House Furnishing, and a full assortment of Domestics of every description. As he visits Philadelphia, New York and Boston from six to eight times a year, and has made arrangements with the Leading Houses in each of the above named cities, to furnish us any thing New that may arrive by the European Steamers between times, our customers and the public generally may rely on finding all the Novelties and desirable articles in our line in their season."

"A Wholesale & Retail Fancy & Staple Dry Goods Store." Goods "to be sold for Cash only, at New York wholesale prices."

"The Mercantile Agency . . . B. Douglass & Co. Established New York, June, 1841; Pittsburgh, March, 1852, for the accomodation of the Banking and Mercantile Interest of the United States. Collections made, and Legal business attended to throughout the United States, Canada and Europe."

Commercial Broker and Dealer in Notes, Bonds, Stocks, Real Estate, &c.

C. San Francisco—details from the *Directory* of 1856:

"Commission Merchants, Importers and Wholesale Dealers in Paints, Oils, Varnishes, and Window Glass."

"Importers, Wholesale and Retail Dealers in Stoves, Tin Plate, Wire, Sheet Iron, Copper, Tin Ware, &c."

"Wholesale Dealer in Roasted and Ground Coffee."

A warehouseman provided a fireproof warehouse, advanced money on goods in storage, and acted as "Product Commission Merchant."

One firm, Cartle Brothers, claimed to be "Importers and Jobbers in Groceries, Wines, Liquors, Provisions, and General Merchandise."

There was a branch of a Philadelphia firm —an "Importer and Dealer in every variety of Ladies', Gents', Misses', & Children's Boots and Shoes."

A firm of commission merchants advertised: "Cash Advances made on Flour and Grain and Merchandise Generally."

"House Brokerage, and Real Estate Agency, Attend to Renting Houses, Stores, Leasing Land, etc. Bills collected, Loans negotiated. Goods bought on Commission, etc."

There were at least seven express companies that had offices in San Francisco.

A merchants' exchange had been opened in 1852, and in 1853 it used a telegraph line to report ships sighted nearing the harbor.

D. Types of Business Men in New Orleans, 1858 [3]

Agents—mercantile (1)
—collecting
—general
—house
—insurance
—news
—real estate
—ship
—steamboat
—tobacco
Auctioneers
Boots and shoes—wholesale (11)
—retail (59)
Brokers—cotton (40)
—customhouse (34)
—general
—house
—merchandise
—note, stock, and exchange
—produce (16)
—real estate
—ship
—sugar (10)
—tobacco (7)
Clothing—wholesale (15)
—retail
Commission merchants (456)
Druggists—wholesale (14)
—retail

[3] Taken from *A. Mygatt and Co.'s New Orleans Business Directory,* 1858. For categories especially important to this case figures in parentheses indicate the number of individuals or firms listed.

Dry goods—wholesale importers (38)
—retail
Forwarding merchants (5)
(See also commission merchants)
Grocers—wholesale (72)
—retail
Hardware—wholesale (19)
—retail
Hats and caps—wholesale (6)
—retail
Intelligence (12)
Produce—Havana (6)
—northern (3)
—western (55)
Provision dealers (4)
Tobacco factors (4)
Tobacco leaf dealers (3)
Tobacco manufacturers—wholesale (8)
Variety stores (154)
Vermicella and macaroni (3)
Wines, liquors, etc.—wholesale (70)

6. Internal Markets, with Special Emphasis on Chicago

The following statements are taken from a volume compiled by John S. Wright, editor of a Chicago newspaper. Much of Wright's material is copied from other sources.[4]

A. Chicago *vs.* St. Louis.

"In 1848 I compared the advantages of Chicago with Cincinnati, and from the then wonderful progress of the latter, argued that of the former. The comparison, then considered extravagant, is tame now. Though in 1850 she was nearly four times the size of Chicago, yet her numerical increase is only a little over one-half as much. She is next to be passed, and it will soon be done.

"I then said nothing about St. Louis, it being considered visionary by even most of our own people to suppose we could rival her, and it being perhaps doubtful which would take the lead; and being 300 miles apart, afforded ample room for two great cities. Between the rival centres of the East, New York and Philadelphia, is only ninety miles, Baltimore only ninety miles more.

"Not till within the last six or eight years have I claimed certain superiority for Chicago. The powerful advantages of St. Louis in greater population, immense wealth, established business, and river navigation of thousands of miles of which she is the centre, precluded, in the minds of most, the possibility of our excelling. But impossibility, and even improbability, has been removed. The railroad has meanwhile been opened all over this region, and river navigation on the uncertain, changing waters of the Missouri and Upper Mississippi, has seen its best days. The locomotive, not the steamboat, is to be the carrier of produce, passengers and merchandise, as well west as east of the Mississippi; and in this Chicago has and must have large and increasing preeminence. And besides drawing on her territory west of the Father of waters, we are also fast increasing trade with central Illinois, upon which she has fattened.

"Her river navigation is henceforth far excelled in value by that of the lakes; and for her greater wealth, which is relatively fast diminishing, we have a full equivalent in health and climate, hereafter noticed. In obtaining materials to manufacture, she has no superiority over Chicago, except a trifle on cotton and lead. We can get the best of iron ore from Lake Superior, as cheaply as she can from her Iron Mountain, and in lumber and copper we have the advantage.

"With the influential aids of immense wealth, greater age and established business, particularly by steamboats, all of which have operated relatively far stronger in her favor than they can ever again, she has increased since 1850, on a population of 77,680, only 84,319; while we have increased 79,457, on only 29,963. Notwithstanding her important superiority and *prestige*—the general belief that she was to be the greatest city of the West, she has increased in ten years one hundred and eight per cent., and Chicago two hundred and sixty-five per cent. If within the first decade of railroads, and while they are being constructed, such direct effects as these are visible, what is to be expected of the future?

"I have no desire to disparage St. Louis, and do not. But if one city in the West is certain to outstrip the rest, it is important to know it, and my reasoning seems fair and

[4] John S. Wright, *Chicago: Past, Present, Future* (Chicago, 1868), pp. 75–76, 89–90, 316, 166–167, 152.

conclusive. She will surely grow, perhaps to a great size, and though property is higher there than here, I doubt not in both it will prove a good investment. But however large she becomes, the chances are that Chicago, in only twenty to thirty years, will be twice her size.

"St. Louisians of course deny the possibility of her being excelled. They vainly endeavor to account for the inequality of growth, and the papers spur their wealthy citizens to effort to preserve their business. But the reader, with map in hand exhibiting the railroad system, may judge for himself whether the ultimate and speedy supremacy of Chicago can be questioned."

B. Railroads *vs.* rivers.

"The *Missouri Republican,* December 18th, furnishes thoughts right to the point:

"*Railroads vs. Rivers.*—Nothing is more encouraging to the business men of this city than to observe that an interest is being manifested in regard to the building of railroads, in order to place this city in more direct communication with those portions of the rich 'Valley of the Mississippi,' of which St. Louis is the natural commercial centre.

"In former times, when St. Louis was the principal, if not the only point of business in the far West, it owed its advantages to the great rivers, they being the only highways of trade and means of communication; but the times have changed, and the sooner we realize it the better. What ten years ago was a great advantage, might now be considered a drawback, not that we wish to detract from the value of our natural highways, which will continue to add to our prosperity; but we contend that our city has, in consequence of relying on the rivers as channels of trade, neglected to build railroads, and places less favored by nature, have resorted to the building of railroads, and hence have kept pace with the requirements of the age. This tardiness in constructing railroads and building bridges has given to St. Louis a name of old fogyism.

"It is of the utmost importance that we should build these roads which are being spoken of, and extend others which have been commenced, but we also need railroads running parallel with and in close proximity to the Mississippi river north, to tap the flourishing towns on its banks, in order to be accessible during the entire year. We experience great disadvantages to secure trade in that direction, as parties dislike to change their patronage with the change of the season. The trade of the South being now almost entirely lost in consequence of the impoverished state of that country, the West is but sparsely settled, besides being partly cut off by the railroads passing around us. It will be seen that our territory is quite limited, and if we want to retain our position as a great commercial emporium, we must seek new outlets and regain our old grounds.

"If our capitalists do not want to furnish the necessary means and move in the matter, let our Merchants' Exchange and Board of Trade corporations solicit the Eastern capitalists. All that is necessary is to take hold in good earnest, set forth the advantages, show them that our business men are made of the right material; that the accessions made to them of late years possess as much enterprise as any other community, and the little obstacle will easily be overcome. If this is not done our merchants will seek other points, and the cities which excel us in enterprise will carry off the prize.

"Do not neglect to build the bridge across the Mississippi at this point; nothing is more important at this moment. At the much less important points, Quincy, Keokuk, Burlington, Davenport, Clinton, etc., bridges have been or are being built, with all possible speed, and here we are fighting for it still."

C. Railroads and agriculture.

"Railroads secured to the producer very nearly the prices of the Atlantic markets, which was greatly in advance of any price which could possibly be obtained in western markets. It might be supposed that if the carriage of a bushel of grain from Sandusky to New York was reduced from forty cents a bushel to twenty cents, the gain of twenty cents would inure, in part at least, to the consumer; but experience shows this is not the fact. This gain of twenty cents inures to the producer. In proof of this it will be sufficient to adduce two or three well known facts. The prices of flour and meat at New York (estimating them at the gold standard) have not been reduced in the least, notwithstanding the immense quantities of the products of grain imported into that city. On the other hand the prices at Cincinnati, on the Ohio, have doubled, and in some articles, such as pork, have trebled. The great bulk of the gain caused by the cheapness of transportation has gone to the producer. This depends on a general principle, which must continue to operate for many years. The older a country is, the more civic and the less rural it becomes. That is, the greater will be the demand for food, and the less the production. The competition of the consumer for food is greater than that of the producer for price. Hence it is that Europe, an old country, filled with cities, makes a continual demand on this country for food. Hence it is that New England and New York, continually filling up with manufacturers, artisans, and cities, must be supplied with increased quantities of food from the interior West. And hence, while this is the case, prices cannot fall in the great markets. Hence it is that the cheapening of transportation inures to the benefit of the agricultural producer. New England consumes more than a million barrels of western flour. The transportation is cheapened a dollar per barrel; and thus, in New England alone, in the single item of flour, a million of dollars net profit is put into the pockets of the western farmer by the competition of railroads; for a large portion of this flour is carried over the Massachusetts Western railroad. It is entirely true that the manufacturer of New England shares, on his side, in the gain of cheap transportation; but we are here considering simply the influence of railroads on agriculture.

"In the western markets the gain to the farmer is palpable in the enhanced prices of every article. At Cincinnati, in 1848 and 1849, (which was the beginning of the greatest railroad enterprise) the average price of hogs was $3 per hundred. In 1860 and 1861 it was double that, and has continued to increase. This was a net gain to the farmers of Ohio alone of from three to four millions of dollars. In the entire west it was a profit of more than twenty millions on this single animal. For if there were now no railroads, this product could not be carried to market except on foot, which would take away half the value. No further illustration of this point need be made. Take the market prices of New York and Boston, on the Atlantic, and of St. Louis and Cincinnati, in the West, at an interval of twenty years, and it will be seen that the cheap prices of the West have gradually approximated to the high prices of the East, and this solely in consequence of cheapening the cost of transportation, which inures to the benefit of the farmer.

"By thus giving the farmer the benefit of the best markets and highest prices, railroads have increased the agricultural productions of the interior States beyond anything heretofore known in the world. We have already shown that this increased production, or rather its surplus, could not have been carried to market without the aid of railroads, more than two-thirds of the whole being carried off by that means. Let us now reverse this operation and we find, on the other hand, that railroads have stimulated and increased production. The Northwestern States are those in which the influence of railroads on agriculture is most obvious."

D. Meat packing.

"Not only is Chicago the greatest pork, lumber and grain market, in the world, but it is also the greatest live stock market. This will be established by figures, in the present article. The signs of the times are sadly awry if this child of the prairies and the lakes does not likewise become the greatest manufacturing city in the world, ere its years of adolescence merge into the vigorous, muscular action of middle age.

"Probably no enterprise in the history of Chicago has combined so many corporations and capitalists together into one great company, as the Great Union Stock Yards. Railroad companies, that have heretofore been rivals for the live stock trade of the West, and often at war with each other upon this subject, are now a unit, working together as architects of this great undertaking. Their tracks have been extended to a common centre, and nine of the former competing roads now connect directly with the Great Union Stock Yards. The broad prairie that stretches southward from the city is now traversed and re-traversed by their different branches, all tending toward the great bovine city of the world. Packers and commission dealers, whose extensive establishments have heretofore demanded their entire attention, are now found at this nucleus; prospecting upon the results of the enterprise, laying plans for the future, and prognosticating the prosperity that is to follow the opening of this great cattle mart. Their estimates for the future might be considered chimerical by the Rip Van Winkles of other and less go-ahead cities; but Western men know the extent of the broad prairies of Illinois, and neighboring States, which stretch away like the *pampas* of South America, yielding pasturage for innumerable herds of cattle, found nowhere else in the country.

"Among the first business transactions of the hamlet, now grown into this great city, was buying and selling cattle and swine; large herds of which were easily driven to market here, slaughtered and shipped to other points. The packing business was only another branch of this trade, and beef packed in Chicago was to be found in the marts of Liverpool, long before the growing Western town from whence it came had a 'local habitation and a name' among the cities of the continent."

E. Jobbing trade.

"It is a gratifying fact that our jobbing trade is almost four-fifths the amount of all our produce exports, which are about forty millions of the above list, showing that the trade of the country follows the channels of produce and centers here, instead of going chiefly to New York, as is generally supposed. It should do so, for each of these thousands of merchants, scattered all over the West, can step into a car at night and be here in the morning, and replenish his stock, and be home again the next morning. These frequent supplies of fresh goods are always desirable, and economical of interest. Then, too, the saving in expensive trips to New York is an item; and the Chicago jobber saves something in rent and other expenses over the New Yorker; and shipping in large quantities, can often save a trifle in transportation and insurance. Also, manufacturers in the East are fast learning their interests. For western supplies, it is a useless expense to pay transportation to a sea-board city, and commission there, which could all be saved and more by shipping directly hither. Besides, a Chicago house, that by railways and telegraph is in constant communication with every town, can know the condition of its customers—watch 'lame ducks' and guard against losses—far better than any New York concern, however sharp."

7. Marketing of Agricultural Machinery from Chicago [5]

1839–56 Nearly sixteen thousand reapers, reaper-mowers, and mowers were sold for use in America, though only two sold in 1840.

1851 The first trial of the reaper in England—at the exhibition in London where the reaper won a medal. The later machines were made in England, which was ahead of America in the iron and steel industry.

1856 4,095 reapers sold.

1868 9,975 reapers sold.

1865–70 Advertising and publicity were used but much reliance was put upon agents. Easy credit aided sales. Settlement and railroads were closely followed. The market area was from New York to Texas, and even in California. St. Joseph (Missouri) and Omaha were important centers.

1870 About this time, because of the bad business conditions, the McCormick agents devoted more time to securing and collecting debts than to selling machines.

1872–79 The Grangers gave McCormick trouble.
"Where farmers gained control of the state assemblies they raised the taxes on unsold reapers in the charge of agents, and both by laws and by intimidating the courts they made it more difficult for creditors to distrain upon

[5] W. T. Hutchinson, *Cyrus Hall McCormick*, vol. i, *Seed-Time, 1809–1856* (New York, 1930), and vol. ii, *Harvest, 1856–1884* (New York, 1935).

1872–79 the property of their debtors. . . . In some localities, and particularly in Wisconsin, they [Grangers] urged all farmers not to purchase machinery made outside of their state. In Illinois, Iowa, Missouri, Wisconsin, and Nebraska, they endeavored, with ill success, to manufacture harvesting implements. . . ."

1880 By this time the sun never set upon McCormick machines. There was an interesting competition abroad. American grain and pork, going to Europe in great quantities, impaired the market for reapers in so far as they lowered the price of farm products. European farmers were not so able to buy farm machinery.

The market in Canada was restricted by tariffs and by other regulations, but McCormick reapers were sold there nevertheless.

8. Chicago as a Money Market [6]

". . . While there is a concentration of industry and a convergence of transportation at Chicago, there has not been anything like an equivalent convergence of the financing of this commerce. . . . The capital requirements of agriculture and industry and the marketing of the products give rise to the demand for investment and banking funds. The relative ease with which money and credit flow from place to place through the smooth operations of national and international money market machinery, makes it possible, even though not the most economical and convenient, for money market transactions to take place far removed from the market handling the physical goods.

"The activities of the London money market in financing international trade clearly illustrates this point. Because of the momentum of an early start, New York enjoys much the same position with respect to our national exchange as London does in international exchange. Long-established lines of credit reaching into the East have made the use of the New York draft the traditional method of financing domestic trade.

. . . .

"An extremely important factor in the prestige of the New York money market is the presence of a stock exchange which has no equal in organization and operation. The stock exchange is a fundamental part of the money market machinery. Its money desk furnishes a remarkably elastic demand for loanable funds. The call market attracts funds from all over the world which are seeking investment and surplus funds employed in call loans can be very readily withdrawn in case of need. The great flexibility of this market is indicated by the rapid and sometimes extreme fluctuation of the call money rate.

"Another feature which the New York money market enjoys, by virtue of being in a seaboard town, is that of financing foreign trade. It has been customary for the ocean bill of lading to originate in New York and a prejudice exists on the part of foreign importers against inland bills of lading. Consequently, the financing of foreign trade through New York has developed an acceptance business which is considerably ahead of the feeble beginnings made by Chicago. Yet the Chicago banks with their many foreign correspondents furnish adequate machinery for financing international trade, if the foreign importers and domestic exporters choose these banks as the place for payments.

. . . .

"Chicago has long been identified as an important agricultural credit center. While Chicago is not a seat of one of the twelve Federal land banks, the city has two joint stock land banks, the combined loans of which were, at the close of 1926, approximately one hundred five and one-half millions. The resources of either of these banks were in excess of those of any other of the 53 operating joint stock land banks.

. . . .

"The operations of the commercial paper house are important in the Chicago money

[6] Bureau of Business Research, Illinois University, Bulletin no. 17 (1928), *Chicago as a Money Market,* pp. 9–10, 37–41, 43, 53–57.

market. These firms are for the most part middlemen facilitating the exchange of funds between those possessing funds for short time investment, mainly banks, and those producers in need of credit accommodation in the normal course of their business.

"Chicago possesses a number of nationally-known firms dealing in commercial paper. One representative house with its home office in Chicago has offices in eight important centers from New York to San Francisco, and maintains resident salesmen or representatives in a large number of cities.

"Commercial paper bought by Chicago firms originates in practically every state in the union. This paper is purchased chiefly by Chicago banks, and some of it is resold to correspondent banks.

"The growth of the finance company in recent years has been remarkable. Finance companies as specialized credit firms meet a particular need—that of financing the purchase of consumers' goods. It is interesting to note that the first specialized finance company was organized in Chicago in 1905, and functioned for seven or eight years with practically no competition.

"The automobile industry gave the great impetus to the organization of finance companies; and between 1920 and 1924 the greatest growth took place. In August, 1927, a study was made of these firms and 573 different finance companies reported. Of this number 95 had home offices in Illinois. This was considerably in excess of that of any other state. Approximately 182—almost one-third—were located in the Seventh Federal Reserve District. The reporting finance companies of the country transacted an aggregate business of more than three and one-fourth billions during the year, 1926. Eighty-one per cent of this business represented the purchase of automobile paper.

"It has become customary for the largest finance companies to obtain credit in the open market. This is done by selling their collateral trust notes direct to bankers or commercial paper brokers.

"The growth and development of the Middle West created large demands for financing which were supplied mostly by eastern and foreign capital through the investment houses of Boston, New York, and Philadelphia. These firms soon found it expedient to have local offices in the Middle West and branches were established at Cleveland, Detroit, St. Louis, Chicago, and Minneapolis, but as Chicago began to develop into a great railroad and industrial center, these offices began to gravitate toward Chicago.

"The growth of Chicago and the development of the railroads here brought the need for real estate financing, both rural and urban. Farm mortgage financing reached great proportions until the passage of the Federal Farm Loan Act, when the private firms went out of business because they could not compete with the Federal and Joint Stock Land Banks whose bonds are exempt from taxation.

"The urban real estate business developed with the growth of the city, until now there are a large number of firms engaged wholly or in part in city real estate financing. Specialization in this line has been carried to such an extent that some firms devote their entire resources to such work as the financing of hotels, apartment buildings, office buildings, or bungalows. The larger firms engage in all branches of real estate financing.

"Because of the great wealth of this section of the country, the Middle West has changed from a borrowing community to one capable of financing its own operations, and at the same time of lending to others as evidenced by some recent underwriting of foreign issues. Because of this change eastern investment dealers found it very profitable to distribute their securities in this area, and there arose a network of branches of eastern investment firms throughout the Middle West.

"In recent years, however, the situation has changed somewhat and investment houses with Chicago as the principal investment center have developed rapidly until on June 30, 1927, there were 360 investment houses in Chicago including branches of outside firms. However, this number does not include the commercial banks of Chicago which also do an investment banking business.

"The geographical distribution of investment securities by Chicago firms would in fact cover all the states and the principal cities as well as reach the principal foreign countries. One of Chicago's largest firms with agents and representatives throughout the country has pushed its branch offices into the investment territory of the East and reports at this time two branch offices in the State of Maine from which its salesmen cover the entire state; one main branch office in New Hampshire; one in Albany, and one in Brooklyn, New York; one in Springfield, Massachusetts; two in the State of Connecticut; two in Pennsylvania; one in Baltimore, Maryland; and one in Washington, D. C. This indicates that Chicago firms are able to reach into the old established investment centers of the East and compete on favorable terms. The network of branches and agencies of Chicago investment firms representing all lines of securities—real estate, public utilities, railroads, industrials, and so on—reach every important city in the United States and bring the people of these cities in daily direct touch with the Chicago investment market.

"Only a few years ago large investment issues were almost always underwritten in the East, and Chicago banks and investment firms were asked to participate in the retailing. The recent development of the Chicago investment market has brought with it direct underwriting by Chicago firms. During the year 1913 Chicago firms offered bonds to the amount of $3,450,000 while joining with firms in other cities in the retailing of $470,727,000. In the year 1926, 80 banks and investment houses having their main offices in Chicago offered bonds to the amount of $257,376,000 while joining with firms in other cities in the retailing of $1,186,432,000. One Chicago trust company reports that its bond department during the first six months of 1927 underwrote issues in 43 of the 48 states of the Union. This same company maintains an active market for municipal securities of every city in America with a population of 5,000 or more and handles obligations from every city in this country of 100,000 or more. The underwriting of investment issues by Chicago firms is not confined to this country. One firm in Chicago reports direct underwriting for fourteen foreign countries. This same company maintains retail distribution offices in many of the important foreign countries, including such as those inside the Arctic Circle, Japan, South Africa, India, and Australia.

. . . .

"The payment of the coupons and the bonds retailed by Chicago firms in this area through agents in New York makes it necessary for the corporations issuing the bonds to keep deposits in New York banks to meet these payments, thus increasing the supply of funds in the New York money market. The shipment of these bonds to the East for collection causes inconvenience and loss of interest while the collections are being transferred. Occasionally, an eastern institution is found which insists that western bonds be payable in the East not so much because of the cost of conversion into New York funds, but to avoid the inconvenience and loss of interest entailed by transfers. As more of the bonds retailed by Chicago firms are paid through Chicago, more funds will be made available in the Chicago money market, and economies will result from these savings.

. . . .

"The financing of the fixed capital requirements and the marketing of the commodities of the entire Mississippi Valley center in Chicago by the natural laws of economy. In the early development the needs for capital were supplied from outside markets, just as in the early development of this country, capital was obtained from the older countries. However, with the growth of industry and commerce which has taken place during the last half century in the Middle West this area has become more self-sufficing in capital, and in recent years has contributed largely to the capital needs of less developed areas and to the rehabilitation of the older countries whose capital deteriorated during the World War. Just as the United States sprang from a debtor to a creditor nation because of the large demand for American products as a result of the War, the Middle West with Chicago as its commercial center has developed from a capital-borrowing community dependent upon other money markets to a capital-lending community serving other money markets as well as its own.

. . . .

"The source of funds in the Chicago market would include the cash resources of the Chicago banks, the deposit balances of correspondent banks both domestic and foreign, the cash deposits of traders and investors in the Chicago market, the uncollected deposits due from other banks, the funds of corporations held for the redemption of debt or for the payment of coupons and dividends, and residue balances. This does not pretend to enumerate all the sources but merely to point out some of the origins of the market's money. Of course, there may be imports of gold or an increase in the currency by the issue of Federal reserve notes, or a deposit from another market or central bank, or the purchase of securities in the Chicago market from other centers.

"Many banking changes have been witnessed in the Chicago district during the last quarter of a century. The Federal Reserve Bank providing a bankers' bank for that market has been one of the outstanding developments. The amalgamation of many of the banks into a few large banks has enabled these to take care of the expanding needs of commerce and industry.

. . . .

"Up to the present time, Chicago cannot be said to have a call loan market. The grain, cotton, and produce trades have never developed the use of call loans to the same extent that the securities markets have. The Chicago Stock Exchange does not have a money desk. It may be said, however, in justice to the plan under way that a money desk is contemplated in the near future. The present call money rates in Chicago are largely the rates made by two or three of the principal banks to brokers. These rates are naturally about the same. Chicago money in very large volume is loaned upon call in New York against prime stock exchange collateral. The Chicago stock exchange collateral is not held as favorably as that of New York. In fact, it has been said that Chicago names in New York will command a lower rate than in Chicago. A larger development of trading and market analysis in Chicago would relieve this difficulty.

"The seasonal flow of money to and from Chicago is very pronounced because of the movements of country funds out of Chicago for the planting and harvesting of crops and back into Chicago when the crops are marketed. There is also a seasonal demand of commerce peculiar to the Great Lakes region. This is particularly noticeable in the grain export business. The foreign buying of grain and provisions in Chicago is seasonal as well as the traffic on the Great Lakes. This seasonal movement of funds draws heavily upon the bank deposits and affects the investment and trading in the money market.

"Exact statistics of the amount of funds used in the securities, grain, cotton, and other markets cannot be obtained. In the first place, statistical information on these subjects has never been organized and compiled for the Chicago markets as it has been for the New York Stock Exchange. At any event exact information for any market cannot be obtained because the volume of funds borrowed increases and decreases with the resources of the firms and individuals carrying on the business. It is believed, however, that there is a tendency in Chicago to do more cash business than in the security markets of New York. This may be due to different habits built up in the two centers or it may be due to the lack of organization and the development of credit facilities for trading purposes in Chicago comparable to those of New York.

"It would be a matter of interest to know to what extent Chicago banking and investment houses furnish the credit advances, commercial paper, and long term finance of the automobile industry, the steel mills, the railroads, the merchandising houses, and the mineral production of the district. It is a well-known fact that New York finances figure largely in these industries, but as pointed out above, these New York funds are or may be, in large part, a return to the Middle West of middle western deposits in New York.

"While the extent to which New York enters into Chicago financing cannot be determined, some indication is exhibited by the Chicago branches of New York banking and brokerage firms, insurance companies, manufacturing and selling agencies in the Chicago district. The leading New York investment houses have Chicago offices and distribute in this district a large portion of their New York underwritings. Many of these firms have taken on the characteristics of Chicago firms and prefer to be known as such.

"Many of the major middle western corporations and particularly the railroads maintain their trustee, transfer, and paying agencies in New York. This is probably due in part to the requirement of the New York Stock Exchange for securities listed. At any rate, this concentrates the earnings of these corporations in New York banks and increases the loanable capital of New York. In part, this accounts for the lower money rates in New York at times. The deposits of these funds earned by middle western corporations in Chicago together with the development of Chicago securities markets to serve the middle western people and still use these funds in the same way that they are now being used would bring these increased deposits to Chicago banks. Moreover, the cost of collecting New York drafts by middle western banks and the public is more expensive than would be the cost of collecting these same drafts from Chicago. The requirement of the New York Stock Exchange would not interfere with this readjustment of financial settlements.

"Another point that might be raised here is the failure of these middle western corporations whose securities are owned largely by middle western people to list their stocks and bonds upon the Chicago Exchange. It is said that the listing on the New York Exchange makes it undesirable to have these stocks listed on the Chicago Exchange also, because it would set up arbitrage between the two markets. This argument is very faulty when we consider the securities which are listed on the New York Exchange and also on London and the European exchanges.

"Similar comments might be made concerning the insurance companies who do most of their business in the Middle West and maintain their entire bank deposits in New York and do most of their investment buying on New York security markets. The development of the Chicago security markets serving these investors would be a very great convenience and economy to the investors as well as increase the volume of business and profits for Chicago banks and brokers.

"The relation of agriculture to the Chicago money market cannot be adequately pictured if confined to the middle western states. Since Chicago is the principal national and international market for these products, the crops and live stock of the Middle West, Southwest, Northwest, and in fact of the entire area between the two mountain ranges find that the price base point is the Chicago price. It is probable that the price of these products and their volume affect directly the loans and deposits of Chicago banks and the entire money market through the in- and out-flow of the volume of purchasing power.

"Money flows to and from a market as it does a central bank. The market where money will purchase the most is the market toward which funds will flow. The market in which money purchases the least not only ceases to attract outside buyers but drives its own people to other markets.

. . . .

"The laws of the State of Illinois are for the most part unfavorable to the best economic interests of the State and the community. This may be illustrated particularly by the tax laws, and the corporation, and the banking laws. For example, the State imposes a property tax upon the securities of corporations not organized under the laws of the State. This, in itself, is a factor that tends to drive the securities markets outside of the State. The heavy property taxes which fall upon cash and corporate securities is particularly unfavorable. The corporation laws of the State do not encourage enterprises to maintain their head offices in Chicago because more favorable terms may be obtained from other states. The banking laws are particularly unfavorable as indicated by the prohibition of branch banking, a form of bank organization upon which all money markets have been built."

9. Readings

The materials on this subject are scattered. Their nature is indicated by the excerpts included in the case. Not a little that is valuable for background is found in F. M. Jones, *Middlemen in the Domestic Trade of the United States, 1800-1860* (Urbana, 1937).

A broad study of regions is found in H. W. Odum and H. E. Moore, *American Regionalism: A Cultural-Historical Approach to National Integration* (New York, 1938).

10. Suggested Questions

1. Would you agree that the development of internal markets was as important as the industrial revolution for America?
2. What was happening to market organization in the interior, 1820–60?
3. What has been the importance of metropolitan economy in the history of marketing?
4. What were the signs of growing economic maturity in the West? Explain.
5. What has been the effect of panics and depressions on incipient metropolitan centers?
6. Assume (1) an increase in the north-south trade and (2) a tariff union with Canada. What would be the effect on metropolitan economy?
7. Which metropolitan center has greatest prospects for business during the decade just ahead of us?
8. What is the difference between the influence (1) of old-time sectionalism and (2) of present economic regionalism on the economic and political strength of the nation?

XXVI. JAMES J. HILL AND THE GREAT NORTHERN RAILWAY 1878–1916

1. Introduction

James J. Hill, the great "empire builder" of the Northwest, was one of America's outstanding railroad builders, operators, and financiers. Indeed, he might well be regarded as one of the greatest business men America has ever produced.

When young Hill reached St. Paul in Minnesota Territory in 1856,[1] he found little more than a frontier trading post at the head of navigation on the Mississippi, serving mainly the fur trade of the Red River region. The hinterland gave promise of becoming a farming and lumbering region, but settlers, markets, and capital were necessary for its development. St. Paul then had no railroads—there were only the Mississippi and its branches and the well-worn trails to the Red River. Railroads from Chicago and Milwaukee had reached the Mississippi far below St. Paul, and already plans had been made for roads to St. Paul and from there northward and westward. In 1857 a charter was granted to the Minnesota & Pacific. Its first section, called the St. Paul & Pacific, was built in 1862. This road connected St. Paul and its neighboring sawdust village, St. Anthony, which later became a part of Minneapolis. By the time of the panic of 1873 St. Paul had been connected by rail with Chicago, Milwaukee, and Duluth; Jay Cooke's Northern Pacific had reached the Missouri; the St. Paul & Pacific and its so-called First Division, which were controlled by the Northern Pacific, had reached the Red River and Sauk Rapids, the latter some seventy miles northwest of St. Paul. The panic threw the Minnesota roads into bankruptcy; the settlement of the State, having reached only a little beyond Minneapolis in its movement northwestward, was temporarily halted.

In the meantime Hill had become well established in the business of St. Paul and the Red River region. His varied experience as clerk or agent for packet companies and for the St. Paul & Pacific up to 1866, together with his interest after that time in companies engaged in carrying goods and passengers between St. Paul and Winnipeg, gave him a thorough acquaintance with transportation conditions in the Northwest. His work as St. Paul agent for a group of Canadian rivals of the Hudson's Bay Co., and his association in Red River transportation with Norman Kittson, an old Red River

[1] J. G. Pyle, *The Life of James J. Hill* (Doubleday, Doran & Co., New York, 1917), vol. i, pp. 3–23, gives the early life of Hill.

trader, gave him insight into and contact with the important Red River trade. Through his fuel business at St. Paul, which was his most important business interest, he gained experience, good standing, and some capital. By the time of the bankruptcy of the St. Paul & Pacific, therefore, Hill was a successful business man with a fair amount of capital, good business contacts, and a thorough acquaintance with the Northwest, its geography, economic conditions, and business possibilities.

2. Important Dates in the Life of James J. Hill

1838	Born in Ontario, Canada.
1843–52	Attended school at Rockwood, Ontario.
1856	Arrived at St. Paul.
1856–65	Clerk for transportation companies.
1865	Agent of Northwestern Packet Co.
1866	Agent for St. Paul & Pacific and other railroads; entered general transportation, storage, and commission business, and became agent for "free traders" in Canada.
1867	Formed partnership to carry on fuel business.
1870	Entered transportation on the Red River.
1872	Hill and Kittson formed Red River Transportation Co.
1873	St. Paul & Pacific Railway went bankrupt.
1875	Organized Northwestern Fuel Co.
1878	Hill and three associates agreed with St. Paul & Pacific for the purchase of the road.
1879	Sold fuel business and organized the St. Paul, Minneapolis & Manitoba.
1881–83	Assisted in organizing and building Canadian Pacific.
1882	Became president of St. Paul, Minneapolis & Manitoba.
1889	Organized Great Northern.
1893	Hill roads reached Puget Sound; Northern Pacific bankrupt.
1896	Reorganization of the Northern Pacific followed by purchase of large share of its common stock by Hill and Morgan and their friends.
1901	Burlington purchased by Great Northern and Northern Pacific; Morgan and Hill won fight with Union Pacific for control of Northern Pacific; Northern Securities Co. incorporated.
1904	United States Supreme Court declared Northern Securities Co. illegal.
1908	Hill system gained access to the Gulf through purchase of Colorado & Southern.
1916	Death of Hill.

3. Laying the Foundation of the Hill Roads, 1878–83

In 1873 the St. Paul & Pacific was a bankrupt railroad, poorly built, running through an almost unsettled country to the Red River. Foreclosure extinguished the rights of the stock on which control by the Northern Pacific was based, and the main road became almost wholly the property of bondholders in Holland, while the stock of the First Division reverted to a former owner in England.[2]

A group of men saw that this road—which shared with another bankrupt road, the Northern Pacific, the whole territory northwest of St. Paul—had possibilities (see roads on the map facing p. 29). They were: James J. Hill; Norman Kittson, one-time Hudson's Bay Co. agent and associate with Hill in Red River transportation; Donald Smith of Montreal, formerly chief commissioner of the Hudson's Bay Co. and a friend of Hill; and, somewhat later, George Stephen, president of the Bank of Montreal. Spurred on by the threatened revival of the Northern Pacific,

[2] The material in this section has been taken from Pyle, *op. cit.*, except where other references are stated.

these men in 1878 took steps to gain control of the St. Paul & Pacific.

Failing to get financial aid for immediate purchase, they agreed to buy the road on time. Each of the four associates was to hold a one-fifth interest, and one-fifth was assigned to George Stephen as a means of securing the coöperation of someone who would give financial aid.[3] An agreement was thereupon made with the Dutch bondholders. The associates promised to pay the interest and to take over the outstanding bonds of the St. Paul & Pacific, paying for the various issues at rates from 13.75 per cent to 75 per cent of par in gold or in 7 per cent first-mortgage gold bonds (with a preferred stock bonus of one-fourth of the bonds thus delivered) of the company to be organized, within six months of the pending foreclosure of the various mortgages securing the existing bonds.[4] In addition they agreed to build and complete the extension to St. Vincent on the Canadian boundary (over two hundred miles of road) during 1878 if possible and in not more than two years, giving personal bonds to the extent of $100,000 to bind the promise; they also agreed to pay for a Breckenridge-Barnesville link. The associates deposited $280,000 in gold coin as a guarantee and security for the fulfillment of the whole agreement; in case of failure to fulfill this agreement within the six months after foreclosure sales, this sum and all other sums paid and all bonds acquired were to be forfeited and all rights under the agreements were to cease. J. S. Kennedy & Co., of New York, was made the representative of the Dutch bondholders.

In May, 1879, the agreement with the Dutch having been thus far fulfilled and other difficulties settled, the St. Paul, Minneapolis & Manitoba was organized by the four associates and a representative of J. S. Kennedy & Co. George Stephen was made president; an executive committee, of which Hill was a member, was given full power to act between the meetings of the board of directors. Common stock to the extent of $15,000,000 was issued at once and a mortgage bond issue of $8,000,000 at 7 per cent was authorized, and in September another issue of the same amount at 6 per cent. The first bond issue was used for settling with the Dutch bondholders and such others in this country as had been or could be reached, and all outstanding obligations were gathered in. The indebtedness of the old companies, amounting to $44,000,000, was extinguished. Stocks and bonds were paid over to the original associates "in payment for moneys, stocks, bonds, and other properties furnished by them for the purchase or construction of the various lines." All of the second bond issue that was not held as working capital for the building already under way went to cover outlays of the previous year.

After the organization of the Manitoba, Hill gave his attention chiefly to that road. His fuel and Red River transportation interests were sold. He assisted in the organization and building of the Canadian Pacific from 1880 to 1883, but the rest of his time was given to the Manitoba, first as general manager, then as vice-president, and from 1882 as president.[5]

The policy of the management of the Manitoba from 1879 to 1883 was as follows: to improve the old road, especially by substituting steel for iron rails; to build new lines and extensions and establish relations with other roads so as to reach important points in the region, that is, Duluth, Winnipeg, and Dakota Territory immediately west of the Red River; to acquire feeders for the main lines; to encourage settlement and the improvement of agricultural methods in its ter-

[3] *Ibid.*, vol. ii, appendix 5, gives the whole agreement.

[4] *Ibid.*, appendix 6.

[5] St. Paul, Minneapolis & Manitoba, *Annual Report,* 1883, list of officers.

ritory; to improve terminal facilities; and to manage the road so as to pay for improvements and construction principally out of earnings.

The actual accomplishment is indicated by Table 1, which was compiled from the annual reports of the Manitoba for 1880–83.

Stock dividends of 6.5 per cent and 9.5 per cent were issued in 1882 and 1883, respectively, as a representation of earnings used in construction. In the former year $5,000,000 of stock was issued to stockholders at par; and, in view of what was considered the sound condition of the road and its increased value during those years, the board voted in 1883 to authorize the stockholders to purchase the new consolidated mortgage bonds of the company to the extent of one-half of their holdings at 10 per cent of par.[6] The amount so taken was $10,000,000.

The condition of the road about this time is described in a letter written by Hill early in 1884: [7]

> "During the last two years we have spent a great deal of money for steel rails, ballasting track, transfer yards, terminal facilities, new equipment, new shops, and in fact have put the road in better condition than any railway similarly situated that I know of in the West, and consequently are today enabled to operate our road at a lower rate of expense. We have now more than one thousand miles with a 26-foot maximum grade and only 220 miles with more than a 30-foot maximum grade. The latter we expect to reduce to 26- and 30-foot maximum within the next two years. When this is done no railway in the world of one thousand miles or more will have the same low gradients."

[6] *Ibid.*, p. 17.

[7] Pyle, *op. cit.*, vol. i, p. 389.

4. Extending the Manitoba Westward, 1884–93

By 1883 the Manitoba was a prosperous road in a region fast becoming a great wheat producer. Some of the success of the road in its earlier years resulted from its heavy carrying for the construction of the Canadian Pacific, but the development of the Red River supplied other freight to take the place of the loss experienced when the Canadian road reached Lake Superior.[8]

At this point may be noted a break in Hill's connections which is significant. In May, 1883, he resigned from the board and executive committee of the Canadian Pacific over the question of an extension from the main line of the Canadian Pacific to Lake Superior, which would divert much traffic from the Manitoba.[9] Hill had in 1880 opposed the proposed line on the ground that the Canadian road would better expend its means in building westward than in building an extension which could not be profitable.[10]

Should the Manitoba stop growing or should it move on westward? To the

[8] St. Paul, Minneapolis & Manitoba, *Annual Report,* 1885, p. 14.

[9] H. A. Innis, *A History of the Canadian Pacific Railway* (London, 1923), pp. 113–114.

[10] Pyle, *op. cit.*, vol. i, pp. 314–318.

Table 1. FINANCES OF THE MANITOBA

(Dollars in thousands)

Year ending June 30	Mileage operated	Gross earnings	Operating expenses and taxes	Capital stock	Bonds	To sinking fund from land sales	Dividends %
1880	656	$2,933	$1,387	$15,000	$16,325	$598	...
1881	865	3,701	1,856	15,000	18,108	224	...
1882	1,058	6,630	3,516	15,000	18,646	703	6.5
1883	1,350	9,149	4,595	20,000	20,792	814	9.5

north of the path which the Manitoba might take was the Canadian Pacific, and to the south its old rival, the Northern Pacific. The resignation of Hill from the Canadian road was followed almost at once by the resignation from the board of the Manitoba of its two prominent Canadian members. The situation behind the action of Hill and his associates is not clear. Pyle attributes the action to Hill's realization of the fact that the two roads were "too great and too diverse to acknowledge any sort of common control." A quotation from a letter sent to Hill by the two Canadians is suggestive: [11]

> "We cannot conceive of any reason why the two concerns should not be worked in harmony and to their mutual advantage. As you are aware, it is the intention of the Canadian Pacific Railway Company to push the construction of its line as rapidly as possible to the Pacific Ocean. The traffic accruing to the St. Paul Minneapolis & Manitoba Railway from that source and from the development of the Northwest territories cannot fail to be large, and to much more than compensate your company for any loss arising from the opening of the Thunder Bay and North Superior routes. So far as we know, the entire railway traffic between the Canadian Northwest and the United States may be secured to the St. Paul, Minneapolis & Manitoba Railway for a long period, while the Canadian Pacific Railway will strive to secure as much as possible of the business which naturally seeks its channel through Canadian territory."

The Canadian road was subsidized by the government, both with money and with lands, and the Northern Pacific had a large land grant. The Manitoba could expect no help in going westward, for the day of land grants was past. None of these roads had sufficient through business to support it. What should the Manitoba do? The situation was somewhat similar to that which later troubled the Milwaukee.

[11] *Ibid.*, pp. 324–325.

It is known that as early as 1882 Hill planned sometime to build into Montana. In 1883, however, he wrote to a Montanan as follows: [12]

> "I note all you say in regard to the Milk River Valley and the northern part of Montana, but that country is now served by the Northern Pacific Railway and there is not enough business to warrant this company in undertaking the construction of another line."

And in 1884:

> "I think our policy should be to build only such branches or new lines as we are sure will prove good; and by cutting down our grades, etc., put the whole road in condition to give such low rates that opposition enterprises must be bankrupted."

From 1883 to 1886 the extension of the road slowed up greatly. Only a few miles were completed each year, feeders for older lines or short extensions in Dakota.[13] In contrast with the policy followed by the Northern, Union, and Central Pacific lines, many of the extensions of the Manitoba at this time were made by means of small companies, the Manitoba owning the stock and sometimes a part of the bonds and leasing the roads. The Minneapolis & St. Cloud Railway and other small lines had been built in this way.[14] In the Lake Superior & Southwestern, which provided terminal facilities at Superior, the Manitoba had a controlling stock interest.[15] This road was absorbed by the Eastern Railway of Minnesota, organized in 1887 and also owned by the Manitoba,[16] which provided terminal facilities, including docks and large grain elevators, on Lake Superior. At the same time, extensions were built into Minnesota iron ore territory and into South Dakota by the Willmar &

[12] *Ibid.*, pp. 380, 390.

[13] St. Paul, Minneapolis & Manitoba, *Annual Report*, 1882, p. 12, and 1883, pp. 16–17.

[14] *Ibid.*, 1883, pp. 16–17.

[15] *Ibid.*, 1887, pp. 16–17.

[16] *Ibid.*, 1888, pp. 11–12.

Sioux Falls and the Duluth, Watertown & Pacific Railway, the entire capital stock of both being owned by the Manitoba.[17] The Northern Steamship Co. on the Great Lakes, also a Manitoba concern, was put into operation in 1888; this line was expected to become "a powerful ally in controlling traffic and rates for the country served by our lines," [18] that is, to secure better rates eastward for freight originating on the Manitoba.

While those roads and other lines were being constructed as additions to the Manitoba system in Minnesota and eastern Dakota, the Manitoba itself was moving westward. From June, 1886, to June, 1887, over three hundred miles were put into operation on the Dakota extension to the Montana boundary, and the road was completed to Great Falls, Montana Territory.[19] The *Annual Report* of 1887 indicated what traffic was expected in Montana: [20]

"The region . . . is, in the main, well adapted to stock raising; and large portions of it are also capable of successfully producing all varieties of small grain and vegetables without irrigation. It also abounds in beds of coal, iron and limestone, whence there are excellent grounds for confidently expecting the speedy development of important industries in those minerals.

"At the Great Falls of the Missouri River, where the termini of the Manitoba and Montana Central lines join, nature has provided power ample for the most extensive manufacturing operations."

At Great Falls the Hill road met a local road. The Montana Central had been quietly organized in 1886, ostensibly to build from Great Falls to Helena and Butte. Hill's biographer says of the company: [21]

"It issued $5,000,000 of stock and in May, 1887, the issue of $10,000,000 bonds was authorized. At the same meeting the directors entered into an agreement with Mr. Hill 'to evidence in the main and to supersede a verbal contract between the parties long since made and partly executed,' by which he was to furnish, in addition to past advances, the money necessary to construct and equip the line, and was to receive the stock and bonds of the company in exchange. The Montana Central was, to all intents and purposes, James J. Hill. It was organized to occupy the Montana field until the Manitoba should be ready for the rush westward from Minot [North Dakota], which was to break the world's record for railroad building. When Mr. Hill should be ready for that performance, from which the Indian reservation still barred him, he proposed to fall into friendly hands at the Montana end. . . . He was acting, in the fashion that seemed most prudent, for the railroad; and by August of the same year the Manitoba Company had taken over and assumed the agreement that he had entered into with the Montana Central."

The branch line of the Montana Central according to the Manitoba report of 1888,[22]

"reaches a practically inexhaustible field of excellent coal. . . . The Sand Coulee Coal Company has been organized for the purpose of mining this coal on a large scale and its preparatory operations are already well advanced. Its capital stock is all held by this company. When these mines are sufficiently developed to meet the present demand of the public, they will afford a large traffic for both companies, and effect a large saving in the fuel required for their own engines, depots, etc. . . . The great value to the company of its Montana lines has received prompt demonstration in the traffic already developing along the line of the Montana extension. With the development of industries which the stimulating effect of these new lines is sure to bring about within the next year or two, the company's traffic will rest upon a solid basis, *not to be materially affected by the fate of any one grain crop* [italics added]."

[17] *Ibid.*, p. 13.
[18] *Ibid.*, 1889, pp. 17–18.
[19] *Ibid.*, 1887, p. 10.
[20] *Ibid.*, p. 17.
[21] Pyle, *op. cit.*, pp. 388–389.

[22] St. P., M. & M., *Annual Report,* 1888, pp. 17–18, 20.

In 1888–89 there was a lull in the extension of the Manitoba system. Its builders were uncertain whether to build a new road or join some road already built. Combination with the Union Pacific was considered but was not carried out, possibly because of the heavy floating debt of the road. The Northern Pacific was more seriously considered. In May, 1889, Hill wrote to Stephen: [23]

"The more I think of it the more I am convinced that the thing for us to do is to 'take the bull by the horns' and get control of the Northern Pacific, and by one stroke settle all questions at once. This will cost less money and will bring the best results in the least time. Looking over the ground we find the Northern Pacific is the only interest of any magnitude in the entire territory we want to control. It is pursuing a very aggressive course almost regardless of permanent cost and business judgment, at the same time it is doing both the 'Manitoba' and the Canadian Pacific Railroad great damage and in such a way as to compel both to spend large sums of money to no good end. They are cutting rates in Manitoba to an extent that cannot fail to greatly reduce the revenues of all concerned from that province; and the facts as stated in your letter that their lines in Manitoba will not pay anything for six years (and I think it will be ten) is a permanent reason why they cannot hold to any agreement. A starving man will usually get bread if it is to be had, and a starving railway will not maintain rates. . . ."

[23] Pyle, *op. cit.*, p. 451.

"Lord Mount Stephen" answered: [24]

"I am not clear in my own mind as to our ability to capture the control of the Northern Pacific. That is, I do not see so clearly how it is to be done as I do our ability to build a new line of our own. Of that I have no doubt, and think I can see my way to finance an extension to the Coast on very economical terms so far as the finding of the money is concerned. It may be, when I see you, that the difficulties in the way of capturing the Northern Pacific may disappear. I am very much impressed by what you say as to the advantages of getting to the Coast by a control of the Northern Pacific rather than by building a new line if it can be done. . . . The advantages to the St. Paul, Minneapolis & Manitoba and to the Canadian Pacific Railroad as well, of our getting control of the Northern Pacific are very clear, and I think when you come down we must try to come to some definite conclusion as to the course to be pursued and follow it up vigorously. If we decide that a control of the Northern Pacific is out of reach, then I suppose we ought to go vigorously and promptly to work on a new line."

Comparative figures, in Table 2, on the finances of the two roads for the preceding five years are of interest at this point.[25]

The Manitoba group decided to extend its own line to the Coast, and in prepara-

[24] *Ibid.*, p. 452.

[25] Compiled from the annual reports of the two roads for the years given.

Table 2. FINANCES OF THE MANITOBA AND NORTHERN PACIFIC

(Dollars in millions)

Year ending	Mileage operated		Gross earnings		Operating expenses		Stock		Bonds	
June 30	Manitoba	N.P.	Manitoba	N.P.	Manitoba	N.P.	Manitoba	N.P.	Manitoba	N.P.
1884	1,397	2,547	$8.3	$12.6	$3.7	$6.9	$20	$88.8	$31.4	$66.3
1885	1,497	2,668	7.8	11.2	3.3	6.0	20	87.6	32.4	72.3
1886	1,538	2,801	7.3	11.7	3.7	5.9	20	87.0	32.3	72.9
1887	1,935	3,102	8.0	12.8	4.1	6.9	20	86.8	43.3	76.7
1888	2,648	3,337	9.6	15.8	5.2	9.0	20	86.5	51.2	81.6
1889	3,030	3,465	8.6	19.7	4.8	11.9	20	86.1	61.0	83.4

tion for this move came a change in organization. According to Pyle,[26]

"The original limitation of capital stock to $20,000,000 was a strait jacket for a system that must assimilate the capitalization of the many separate companies under which construction in the West had been carried forward. Mr. Hill desired to build new lines from stock proceeds rather than bond sales, giving him a clear property and a basis for future credit issues if that became desirable or necessary. . . . The needs of the new day demanded an instrument more flexible and of wider reach."

The Great Northern Railway Co. was organized in 1889 on the basis of the liberal charter of the Minneapolis & St. Cloud Co.[27] The old Manitoba was transferred to the new Great Northern on February 1, 1890, with a guarantee of 6 per cent dividends on its stock.[28] The personnel of the boards and the officers of the two roads were almost identical, the only difference being that, while only one member of the board of the Manitoba road was from New York, the Great Northern's board included three New Yorkers.[29] A lot of miscellaneous property of the Manitoba, valued at $21,839,123, was also transferred to the Great Northern. The stockholders of the Manitoba paid to the Great Northern $10,000,000 in cash; the latter assumed and paid a lien of $9,250,000 against the Manitoba and thereupon issued to its stockholders $20,000,000 of Great Northern stock, giving one share for each share held in the Manitoba.[30] The Great Northern leased the Manitoba and the other lines, the stocks and bonds of which it had acquired.

Plans for extension to the Coast followed upon the organization of the Great Northern. The Manitoba, in its lease to the Great Northern, agreed to construct an extension of about eight hundred miles from Fort Assiniboine in Montana to Puget Sound. This extension also was leased to the Great Northern. Payment of the principal and interest of bonds for its construction was guaranteed by the Great Northern.[31]

The Seattle & Montana Railway Co. was chartered in Washington in 1889 to complete the road to Puget Sound.[32] To finance this building £6,000,000 of 4 per cent sterling bonds was issued, payment of the principal and interest again being guaranteed by the Great Northern.[33] Control of two lines already built and cooperation with the Union Pacific in building a third also gave connections with New Westminster (British Columbia) and Portland.[34] These connections were made and the Manitoba was built to the Pacific by 1893.[35]

By June 30, 1893, the road was operating almost four thousand miles. The combined stock of the St. Paul, Minneapolis & Manitoba and the Great Northern—the two roads holding virtually all the stock of the whole system—was $45,000,000; the combined bonds issued totaled $85,310,755.[36] The stock of the Great Northern was increased in 1893 by $5,000,000, the stockholders buying at par when the market value was 140.[37] In that year the Manitoba paid 6 per cent and the Great Northern 5 per cent in dividends, and the surplus of the Great

[26] Pyle, *op. cit.*, pp. 460–461.

[27] Acquired by the Manitoba in 1883 (*Annual Report*, 1883, p. 16).

[28] *Ibid.*, 1890, p. 7; Great Northern, *Annual Report*, 1891, p. 11.

[29] List of Officers in report of 1890.

[30] Brooks Adams, *Railways as Public Agents* (Boston, 1910), pp. 89–90, quoting *Steenerson* v. *Great Northern Ry.*, 69 Minnesota, pp. 400–402.

[31] St. P., M. & M., *Annual Report*, 1890, pp. 7–8.

[32] Pyle, *op. cit.*, pp. 458–459.

[33] G. N., *Annual Report*, 1890, p. 12.

[34] Pyle, *op. cit.*, p. 459.

[35] G. N., *Annual Report*, 1893, p. 15.

[36] *Ibid.*, p. 7; St. P., M. & M., *Annual Report*, 1893, p. 5.

[37] G. N., *Annual Report*, 1893, p. 19; Adams, *op. cit.*, p. 98.

Northern at that time was $1,182,330.[38]

This record may be contrasted with that of the Northern Pacific, which operated a mileage of 5,432 miles, had stock of $85,140,131 and bonds totaling $133,545,500,[39] and went bankrupt in that year.

5. Extension of the Hill System by Consolidation, 1894–1904

After 1893 there was a slowing-down in the extension of the Manitoba and the Great Northern, as in the case of the St. Paul & Pacific in the period of depression following 1873 and of its successor, the Manitoba, in 1883. After 1894 the system was gradually extended year by year from a total mileage of 3,765 in 1894 to 5,622 by 1904.[40]

This increase in mileage, consisting chiefly of feeders and connecting lines,[41] was overshadowed by another development in those years—the consolidation of the Great Northern, Northern Pacific, and Burlington into one great system.

After the bankruptcy of the Northern Pacific, Hill devised a plan for securing that road. An agreement was made with the bondholders to foreclose and reorganize, the Great Northern to take half of the $100,000,000 stock to be issued and guarantee bonds to the same amount. The agreement was held invalid by the United States Supreme Court because it was said to mean monopolistic control in the northern half of Minnesota and farther west where there was no competition with the Union Pacific.[42] In anticipation of this action the road was reorganized; J. P. Morgan & Co. was reorganization manager. The common and preferred stockholders gave up their old shares, receiving in exchange new stock for which they paid $10 and $15, respectively, and gave up to Morgan for five years their power as stockholders.[43] Stephen and Hill of the Great Northern then began to gather in common stock, of which $80,000,000 was outstanding. The preferred stock, of which $75,000,000 had been issued, was to be retired. By February, 1897, they had bought $25,834,000 par value of common stock for $4,133,456, that is, at $16 a share.[44] By 1901 Morgan and Hill had sufficient common to give them control of that stock.

The Union Pacific, a competitor of the Northern Pacific in the Far West, also began to buy up Northern Pacific stock, purchasing $78,000,000 of common and preferred, over half of the preferred and of the total of both common and preferred but not enough to give the Union Pacific majority control of the common stock. This was accomplished by the well-known Union Pacific–Harriman raid on the Northern Pacific in 1901. It appeared that Harriman had gained control, but the control was more apparent than real. There was a clause in the reorganization plan, which was overlooked, to the effect that on any January 1 until 1917 the board could retire the preferred stock, on which Harriman's strength was based. Since the board was a creation of Morgan and his associates, the Union Pacific surrendered.[45]

In the meantime the two Northerns had purchased the Chicago, Burlington &

[38] *Ibid.*, pp. 99, 112; G. N., *Annual Report*, 1893, p. 6; St. P., M. & M., *Annual Report*, 1893, p. 4.

[39] N. P., *Annual Report*, 1893, pp. 40–41, 15.

[40] G. N., *Annual Report*, 1894–1903.

[41] For instance, a circular to stockholders dated April 20, 1899, announcing a new stock issue of $15,000,000, stated that this issue was to be used to buy up the capital stock, debentures, and bonds of the Spokane Falls & Northern, the Nelson & Ft. Sheppard, and the Columbia & Red Mountain in Washington and British Columbia.

[42] *Pearsall* v. *Great Northern Railway*, 161 U. S. 646.

[43] *Oral Argument of the Attorney-General for the United States Supreme Court, Northern Securities Company et al.* v. *the United States*, Oct., 1903, no. 277, pp. 11–12.

[44] *Ibid.*, p. 13.

[45] *Ibid.*, pp. 15–22.

Quincy, a prosperous and well-built road which connected with the Northern Pacific–Great Northern at Billings (Montana) and St. Paul and extended to significant points not touched by the other roads, that is, Omaha, St. Louis, and Chicago.[46] The road was paid for at the rate of $200 a share in joint collateral trust bonds of the Northern Pacific and the Great Northern, secured by the stock of the Burlington.[47] These bonds were supported and retired out of the earnings of the Burlington.

Five different lines had been considered before the purchase of the Burlington, more than two of which were the subject of correspondence. Morgan wanted to buy the Chicago, Milwaukee & St. Paul, a road somewhat similar to the Chicago, Burlington & Quincy in the territory covered and in its financial status, but it was not for sale, at least not on the terms offered.[48] Though Hill preferred the Burlington, for reasons that will be brought out later he was willing to assent to Morgan's wishes. The purchase of the Burlington was possibly hastened, however, by the fact that the Union Pacific was buying its stock. The other roads considered were the Wisconsin Central, Chicago & Northwestern, and the Chicago, Great Western.

On November 12, 1901, the Northern Securities Co., organized by Hill and his associates, was incorporated in New Jersey. Its charter reads: [49]

"The objects for which the corporation is formed are: (1) To acquire by purchase, subscription or otherwise, and to hold as investment, any bonds or other securities or evidences of indebtedness. . . . (2) To purchase, hold, sell, assign, transfer, mortgage, pledge, or otherwise dispose of, any bonds or other securities or evidences of indebtedness created or issued by any other corporation. . . . (3) To purchase, hold, sell, assign, transfer, mortgage, pledge or otherwise dispose of shares of the capital stock of any other corporation . . . and, while owner of such stock, to exercise all the rights, powers and privileges of ownership, including the right to vote thereon. . . ."

The company had an authorized capital of $400,000,000. About 76 per cent of Great Northern and 96 per cent of Northern Pacific stock was purchased by the exchange of Northern Securities stock (the Northern Pacific stock, which had been purchased for $16 a share, was in this exchange valued at $115; the Great Northern stock was valued at $180). The Northern Securities Co. was given the power to choose the directors and officers of the two roads, the earnings were to be pooled, and the dividends were to be issued by the Northern Securities Co.[50]

The reasons for the formation of the Northern Securities Co. are thoroughly brought out in the questioning of its main promoters in the famous Northern Securities case. Admitting the common interest of the roads concerned, why did they not coöperate without a formal organization or through an already established trust? Morgan testified that the purpose of the company was to get an organization with a capital stock so large as to insure the roads against seizure by those who would injure them. It appealed to Hill and Morgan as a means of perpetuating a hold and a policy, which might more easily be broken down in individual or smaller concerns, to insure uninterrupted progress in building and maintaining a great transportation system.[51]

The union of the three great roads in the Northern Securities Co. was a logical

[46] *Ibid.*, pp. 13–15.

[47] Circular sent by Hill to stockholders of the G. N., July 1, 1912; B. H. Meyer, *A History of the Northern Securities Case* (Madison, 1906), p. 231.

[48] *Ibid.*, p. 230.

[49] *Charter of the Northern Securities Company*, p. 1.

[50] Meyer, *op. cit.*, pp. 239–240; *Oral Argument of the Attorney General . . .*, pp. 20–24.

[51] Meyer, *op. cit.*, p. 226.

development of existing economic conditions, particularly as interpreted by Hill.

It is easy to see that the income of a road—both gross and net—within certain wide limits (that is, up to the point of decreasing returns) increases with the increase in traffic. It is another matter, however, to build a road in such places and to manage it so as to make a reasonable approach to maximum efficiency.

Hill built his system with a view to traffic, both actual and potential, both coming and going. He maintained that traffic was fundamentally based on the difference in natural resources in different regions; that Nature and her products governed transportation routes; that railway men must get in line or fall by the way. From east to west the resources tapped by the Great Northern were iron and timber, agricultural lands, grazing lands, mines, timber, and fish.

Thus the industries along the Great Northern were almost exclusively extractive, a condition which made exchange with other regions necessary. The exchange east and west was, furthermore, not sufficiently well balanced to prevent the transportation of "empties"—and Hill considered an "empty" a thief. The necessity of increasing the traffic, balancing the east and west traffic, and connecting with consuming and manufacturing sections was evident. The most obvious need was the last-named, and this was met at first through the establishment of the Northern Steamship Co. on Lake Superior in the late 'eighties [52] and by joint rates with the Northern Pacific, the Burlington, and other roads. Concerning the Burlington, Hill said: [53]

"The territory served by the Burlington produces most of the machinery and implements used on the farms, in the forests, mines and mills of the tier of states reached by the Great Northern and Northern Pacific. It also produces a large part of the iron and steel products exported to Asia via the Pacific Ocean. Chicago, Kansas City, St. Joseph and Omaha are the largest provision centers in the country. At St. Louis it connects with the chief cotton carrying lines of the south and southwest. On the other hand the Burlington territory takes for fattening the live stock raised on the northern and western farms and ranches. It consumes lumber in all shapes on a large scale."

Soon after the Great Northern had reached the West Coast, it was found that the traffic was not sufficiently heavy either way and that eastbound traffic was heavier than westbound. The lumber trade of Washington, said Hill, developed faster than the westbound merchandise trade, even with the trade of Alaska and Honolulu. "The result was that we had more cars of lumber to carry east than we had full cars going west. To make them equal again we had to look for more tonnage from the East." [54] One solution seemed to be the Orient.

The Orient had always lured Hill. He had left his home in Ontario to seek adventure and fortune in the Far East. After his road had reached the Coast, he sent agents to Japan and China to study food and manufacturing problems, and to India to study the possibilities of producing there to meet the Chinese and Japanese demand for food and raw cotton. Hill learned that, if each person in a single province of China should eat one ounce of flour a day, the province would take more than twice the surplus of America. But Hill went even further: he hoped to make his road a link in a new chain of transportation connecting Europe and the Far East.[55]

In 1896 a contract was made with a Japanese steamship company, fixing such rates as would enable the Great Northern to pick up, especially, rails and cotton for

[52] St. P., M. & M., *Annual Report,* 1889, p. 17; G. N., *Annual Report,* 1890, p. 14.

[53] *Ibid.,* 1901, p. 10.

[54] Pyle, *op. cit.,* vol. ii, p. 53.

[55] See chap. viii of his *Highways of Progress* (New York, 1910).

Japan.[56] In 1900 the Great Northern Steamship Co. was organized with a capital of $6,000,000, and contracts were made for building two mammoth ships for the transpacific trade.[57] The trade with the Orient further demanded such connections with the American East as would make possible low joint rates. These efforts gave promise of a reward. From 1893 to 1903 exports of the Puget Sound customs district increased nearly 540 per cent.[58] "Presuming that Japan will come to be a great commercial nation," said Hill, "American trade on the Pacific Ocean should soon rival that on the Atlantic." [59]

To provide for a system which would make possible and certain, in a time of intense competition and consolidation, such rates as would build up the through traffic was the fundamental purpose of the Northern Securities Co. But this meant control, and Hill admitted that it meant the elimination of competition in some places. His defense was that railroad competition, which would always exist between regions (largely because of the impossibility of managing too large systems), would maintain competition between sections and thereby eliminate the evils of monopoly within a section.[60]

It was inevitable at the time that the legality of the Northern Securities Co. should be challenged. After three years of litigation the arrangement was in 1904 held by the United States Supreme Court to be a combination in restraint of trade and, as such, illegal under the Sherman Anti-Trust Act.[61]

On the redistribution of the stock of the Northern Pacific, the Union Pacific interests attempted to secure what they had failed to get in 1901—control of the road. The United States Supreme Court, however, in 1905 upheld the contention of the Northern Securities Co., and redistribution was effected in such a way as to keep control, as before the organization of the company, in the hands of Hill and Morgan.[62]

The immediate result of the action of the courts was explained by Hill: [63]

"What has been the result? What is the difference? To the owners of the properties, merely the inconvenience of holding two certificates of stock [of the Northern Pacific and Great Northern] of different colours instead of one, and of keeping track of two different sets of securities. To the public, no difference at all except that it has missed the advantages which the simpler and more businesslike plan would have secured."

6. Rounding Out the Hill System, 1905–16

By 1905 the essential outline and policies of the Hill system had been established. The result was a reasonably well-built road—as standards were in American railroading at that time—and one that always paid moderate dividends and built up its value through extending or improving the road by means of earnings.

A critical investigator of the history of the finances of the Great Northern about this time made the following statement: [64]

"Mr. Hill has to this point, 1906, succeeded not only in returning to the shareholders $69,000,000 in dividends; in paying $9,-000,000 to the syndicate in 60 per cent interest on $10,000,000 of gilt-edge 6 per cent bonds issued at ten cents on the dollar [referring to issue of bonds for 10 per cent cash in 1883]; returning to them every dollar of share capital they ever paid in and $30,000,000 more through the distribution of ore certificates [from Minnesota iron properties], but every five years on an average he has doubled the value of the property and in addition laid aside for future digestion a handsome nest

[56] Pyle, *op. cit.*, vol. ii, pp. 51–58.
[57] *Ibid.*, p. 59.
[58] Hill, *op. cit.*, p. 166.
[59] Pyle, *op. cit.*, vol. ii, p. 60.
[60] *Ibid.*, p. 343.
[61] 193 U. S. 197.

[62] Meyer, *op. cit.*, pp. 300–304.
[63] Hill, *op. cit.*, p. 131.
[64] F. O. Downes in Adams, *op. cit.*, p. 135.

egg in the form of securities and properties, worth apparently as much as the railway system itself."

Three things stand out in the history of the road from 1905 to 1916: the constant reaching out for traffic, the failure of the plans for the oriental trade, and the consolidation of the Great Northern.

Jim Hill continued to be an expansionist. In a letter to the governor of Minnesota at this time he said: [65]

"The disparity between the growth of traffic and the additions to the railroad mileage and the extension of terminals shown by a new mileage of less than 1½ per cent. a year since 1904, to take care of a traffic increase averaging 11 per cent. a year for ten years past, presents and explains the real problem."

The Hill roads continued to grow rapidly—by 1916 the miles operated totaled over 9,000. Feeders and connections with important points were built or bought. In the western section of the road competition with the Union Pacific and a desire on the part of the Great Northern to draw traffic from a wider area on the Coast brought extensions. In 1905 the Portland & Seattle Railway Co. was organized to build from Spokane to Portland and from Seattle to Portland. At first the stock was directly or indirectly purchased by the Great Northern, and in 1908 by the Great Northern and Northern Pacific jointly. In 1907 water-front rights were purchased at Astoria, and arrangements were made for the carrying of traffic between Astoria and San Francisco. In 1914 the Great Northern Pacific Steamship Co. was organized to carry on this trade. And in 1908 the Burlington acquired control of the Colorado & Southern, which gave the Hill roads access to the Gulf of Mexico.[66]

It is important to note that Hill failed in one great effort. His high expectations for the oriental trade did not materialize. In his *Highways of Progress* he attributes his failure to develop a new route between Europe and the Orient to legislative control of rates. The application of domestic regulation to export rates, and the application of practically the same rule to through rates as to local, made it impossible to establish sufficiently low rail-ocean rates to compete with the ships of other countries, which were operating under lower costs than were American ships.[67] Whether or not trade with the Orient would have developed on Hill's lines, even with the most satisfactory rate conditions, is a pertinent question in this relation.

The third outstanding development in the Hill roads in those years was the consolidation of the Great Northern system. In 1907 all the proprietary companies were purchased and assimilated by the Great Northern.[68] As has been noted, most of the stock and some of the bonds of these roads had been acquired earlier. Payment was made in Great Northern stock. Before retiring from the chairmanship of the board of directors in 1912, Hill planned the consolidation of all the bonds of the Great Northern into $600,000,000 of first and refunding mortgage bonds bearing not over 5 per cent.[69] This consolidation would standardize the securities of the road and provide for later needs.

7. On Hill's Policies and Activities

To the rank and file of the people of the Northwest "Jim Hill" was a great figure. He was regarded as a first-class railroad man and as an authority on social and economic questions, particularly those concerning the Northwest. He was considered a man of character, intelligence, and judgment. But most of all, he was affectionately looked upon as a friend of

65 Pyle, *op. cit.*, vol. ii, pp. 262–263.

66 C., B. & Q., *Annual Report,* 1909, p. 13.

67 Hill, *op. cit.*, pp. 156–184.

68 G. N., *Annual Report,* 1907 and 1908.

69 *Ibid.*, 1911, p. 6; circular of Hill, July 1, 1912.

the common man. It is significant that he was not known as Mr. Hill, or James Hill, or Hill of the Great Northern, but simply as Jim Hill.

Hill commanded respect and admiration in the Northwest for both his accomplishments and his qualities. He had an iron physique and limitless energy; a short, stocky, one might say leonine, figure, dynamic and tense yet under perfect control and capable of long and intense effort. He had a tenacious mind that had both the power of intense concentration and breadth of scope; a remarkable capacity for staying close to reality, of always squaring his plans and ideas with actuality; a way of basing judgments on sound information and careful thought, of thinking things through well in advance of action; and the ability to express himself clearly in simple and terse language. He was also a man of positive character: right or wrong in his principles, he had the power to drive himself but also to forget a battle lost and not to worry over what was ahead.

Jim Hill was especially fortunate in his relations with people. He had an intensely democratic and a genuinely social nature coupled with wide understanding and sympathy: he consulted the workingman on his railroad as if he was a partner; he talked with the farmer as if he himself was a farmer; and he was equally at home with the scholar. He was also notably successful as a public speaker, whether he was addressing a farmers' institute or a university audience. In his relations with people he set rigid standards: he would have nothing to do with sham, dishonesty, or laziness, but he had the deepest respect for honest effort, especially when it was intelligent.

No description of Hill is complete that fails to mention something of his personal interests and his private life. Notwithstanding his impetuosity, he was a temperate man. He was very much of a family man. His interests were varied: his favorite vacations were those spent in wild country; he collected paintings, having, it is said, high standards of judgment; he was a wide reader and could quote at length from literary or other works which had impressed him; he could tell a good story, and he had a lively appreciation of the humorous; and he liked nothing better than a long discussion of a current problem.

An important phase of Hill's work as a railroad man was his emphasis on efficient and long-time planning of production in the area served by his road. He not only encouraged settlement of the Northwest; he urged the drainage of the wet land and other means for more nearly completely utilizing the land resources; he urged diversification of crops in order to maintain the productivity of the land; he spent large sums in improving the quality of cattle in the Northwest; and he was indefatigable in talking at farmers' meetings and, generally, in furthering the improvement of agriculture. Moreover, he was one of the early and effective workers for the conservation of natural resources.[70]

Hill had definite ideas concerning the responsibility of members of boards of directors. His position is made clear in a letter concerning a prominent New Yorker whom Kennedy had suggested for the board: [71]

"I told Mr. Kennedy plainly that unless Mr. —— would agree to spend two weeks at least in every year on the property and would undertake to know its wants I would vote against him; and, further, that I would not again vote for any one as director who did not once a year examine the property and its affairs so that his opinion would be of some value in its counsels. This may seem almost unreasonable, but I know that our greatest weakness has been a want of knowledge on the part of the Board of the property in its relative position to other lines and the reasons

[70] See Hill, *op. cit.;* Pyle, *op. cit.,* vol ii.
[71] Pyle, *op. cit.,* vol. i, p. 429.

that should guide its business policy. I am, as you know, not ambitious, and I assure you that unless the stockholders elect directors who will give the company's affairs time enough to understand them, they must get some one else to take the responsibility besides me."

It was a first principle of Hill to keep out of the stock market. But as this policy became known, speculators began to play with Manitoba stock. Attacks on the stock in the fall of 1887 caused Hill to say: [72]

"While we have both always considered it was not our duty to keep the price of the stock in the market at or near any particular figure, I feel that the stock is worth more money, and that if we can stop the raiders from selling down so low as to make some of the more recent purchasers afraid to hold it, the effort will be worth making."

His policies with regard to capitalization are significant. Contrary to the usual practice of using stock as a bonus, Hill held that railroad construction should be financed out of stock. Moreover,[73]

"every dollar of securities, stock as well as bonds, should have behind it a dollar in cash, material or services rendered. . . . he stated publicly that if the law would compel every corporation to put dollar for dollar of cash or property behind its outstanding paper, and make it pay assessments for that purpose or retire the securities which could not show their title clear, it would need to do little else."

In the earlier years Hill extended his roads to a great extent out of earnings, later issuing stock to cover the expenditures.

This principle of making capital represent real value and earning power was followed in construction as well, as is seen from an order to the chief engineer in charge of construction in 1890: [74]

"We do not care enough for Rocky Mountain scenery to spend a large sum of money in developing it either on the Spokane or elsewhere. What we want is the best possible line, shortest distance, lowest grades, and least curvature that we can build between the points to be covered."

Pyle says that Hill and his associates acted to a great extent as their own financial agents and "paid no big commissions and made no scandalous payments to underwriting syndicates." In so far as this was the case, it was because of the financial strength of Hill and his associates. Mount Stephen and Strathcona were strong in Montreal and London, while Hill was fortified by his excellent reputation and his interest in powerful banks. He was for many years a director of the First National and the Chase National, of New York; he was a director of the First National and the Illinois Trust and Savings Co., of Chicago; and he was interested in a number of banks in the

[72] *Ibid.*, pp. 427–428.
[73] *Ibid.*, pp. 478–479.
[74] *Ibid.*, p. 448.

Table 3. SIGNIFICANT STATISTICS ON THE GREAT NORTHERN FOR SELECTED YEARS

	1916	1929	1936	1937
Miles of road operated	10,469	11,869	11,612	11,596
Gross operating revenues	$ 81,262,478	$125,932,807	$ 89,625,105	$ 94,942,292
Gross operating expenses	$ 43,914,076	$ 82,862,910	$ 56,880,722	$ 61,377,723
Stock outstanding	$249,476,850	$249,004,650	$248,558,750	$249,092,150
Funded debt	$194,863,909	$336,819,515	$345,574,915	$336,628,515
Dividends [a]	7%	5%	—	—

[a] No dividends after 1932.

Twin Cities, as early as 1880 becoming a director of the First National, of St. Paul; and in his later years he bought the stock of both the First National and the Second National, of St. Paul, consolidated the latter with the former, and made of the two banks one powerful institution.[75]

The financial strength of Hill enabled him to help finance the moving of crops on his roads in times of stringency. In 1890 he and his railroad extended credit to grain elevators to the amount of over $2,000,000. In 1891, Hill furnished $800,000 for thus moving the crop.[76]

What were Hill's motives in the aid that he gave to farmers and to others in the Northwest? His biographer takes a definite attitude on that question: [77]

"Probably Mr. Hill . . . would have greeted the statement with astonishment and hilarity if someone had said, at this time when he was fighting for supremacy in the Northwest, that his policy was 'the application of the golden rule to business.' . . . Yet, at this distance, what he did looks very like it. But his action was dictated not by abstract altruism, but by enlightened and far-seeing self-interest."

8. Adjustment to Recent Difficult Conditions

Figures from the reports of the Great Northern for 1916, 1929, 1936, and 1937, as given in Table 3 (p. 417), are very illuminating.[78]

Table 4 shows what was happening to the road's income.[79]

[75] *Ibid.*, pp. 306–310.

[76] *Ibid.*, p. 489.

[77] *Ibid.*, pp. 489–490.

[78] G. N., *Annual Report,* 1916, 1929, 1936, and 1937. Dividends from *Poor's Railroads.*

[79] Years 1917–37 from *Poor's Railroads;* figures for 1938 from the annual report of the Great Northern. The average mileage operated was about the same throughout those years. The figures for total operating revenue include income from other than passenger and freight traffic.

Table 4. FIGURES FROM GREAT NORTHERN'S OPERATING STATEMENTS, 1917–38

(In millions)

Year	Freight revenues	Passenger revenues	Net revenues from operation	Net income
1917	$64.3	$15.8	$29.3	$23.0
1918	76.9	15.7	16.3	13.6
1919	77.4	19.6	19.8	13.4
1920	78.5	17.8	11.9	19.3
1921	74.7	16.5	20.8	28.4
1922	78.1	15.1	23.8	10.8
1923	93.7	15.3	33.3	18.1
1924	86.1	13.7	35.0	17.9
1925	90.1	14.0	39.1	21.4
1926	93.3	13.0	42.1	25.9
1927	94.4	12.7	39.5	23.0
1928	104.0	11.5	43.5	25.2
1929	101.1	11.3	43.1	–25.7[a]
1930	85.8	9.0	32.4	18.0
1931	63.3	6.0	21.8	5.3
1932	46.0	3.9	9.9	–14.0
1933	52.7	3.8	20.4	– 3.3
1934	60.3	4.2	22.1	– 1.1
1935	70.2	4.4	31.1	7.1
1936	77.2	5.0	32.7	9.9
1937	81.6	5.1	33.5	10.1
1938	68.5	4.5	24.7	2.7

[a] Minus sign indicates deficit.

The Great Northern, like the northwest roads in general, complained of hard times in the 1920's. Several reasons were given for this difficulty: (1) the rate of increase in traffic had been slackened by the effect of the retardation of the growth of the Northwest and by Panama Canal competition and a rate structure on railroads making competition with water routes impossible; (2) the low rate level in favor of agricultural products, established by the I. C. C., had not adequately recognized the increase in costs of carrying; and (3) increased taxation had been a heavy burden on the roads.[80]

[80] The material on this question on the pages which follow is largely taken from Wood, Struthers & Co., *Great Northern Railway Company, Northern Pacific Railway Company: A Review of Their Operations in the Period 1916–*

That the rate of growth in population and production in the Northwest had been retarded in those years, as compared with 1900–10, is obvious. Indeed in some States—notably Idaho and Montana—there had been a positive loss. There was no longer brisk business in transporting new settlers and their goods. At the same time, because of the comparatively low prices of agricultural products, there was a relative decrease in the purchasing power of the Northwest.

For several years discussion of transcontinental railway affairs was filled with generalizations about the effect of the competition of the Panama Canal. It is difficult to get concrete statements and figures on this question. The decision of the Interstate Commerce Commission in the Transcontinental Cases of 1922 took the position that competition of the water route for traffic influenced the Pacific Coast to buy its purchases from that part of the East from which low water rates could be secured. In 1922 Moody reported that

> "the diversion of traffic to the canal from all railroads taken together is roughly estimated at 4,000,000 tons annually, and perhaps as much as 2,500,000 tons of this is taken from the Southern Pacific lines."

In 1923 the United States Shipping Board estimated that 2,306,000 short tons of cargo went by way of the Canal from the Atlantic Coast to Oregon and Washington ports. The westbound "empties" became a real and increasing problem for the roads of the Northwest. For the first ten months of the year, reported the Great Northern in 1923, it could have carried half a million more tons of goods westbound without any increase in train miles or crew.[81] The railroads unquestionably lost through diversion to the Canal. That this meant a great loss traffic experts of the Great Northern did not maintain. They said that the actual loss of ton-mileage to the Great Northern was probably less than 5 per cent. But, when a road is working on a narrow margin of profit, a small gain or loss makes a great difference.

One of the issues was railroad rates. The railroads maintained that the long-haul and short-haul obstacle made it impossible for them to meet competition. That is, the raising of rates to Pacific terminals to the level of rates to intermediate points after the World War made the railroad rates to those Pacific terminals too high for competition with water routes.[82] The railroads urged that it was necessary to compete at coast points but that inland rates should be relatively higher.

One of the problems which the Great Northern faced in the 1920's was the possible disruption of the Hill system by action of the Interstate Commerce Commission in carrying out the Transportation Act of 1920. Through an integration of forty years of growth the three large Hill roads had become so dependent on each other and so complementary that, it was alleged, the breaking-up of the system would have been disastrous.[83] Not only would it have been especially undesirable for the Great Northern to have been separated from the Burlington, but the proposed union of the Great Northern and the Milwaukee in 1924 was considered very objectionable by the Hill road.[84]

1923 and a Discussion of Some of Their Most Difficult Problems (New York, 1924).

[81] The whole question is briefly considered in A. K. Henry, *The Panama Canal and the Intercoastal Trade* (Philadelphia, 1929).

[82] See N. P., *Annual Report*, 1922, pp. 13–14.

[83] *Brief and Argument in Support of Consolidation of the Burlington, Great Northern and Northern Pacific, and Subsidiaries, before the Interstate Commerce Commission*, Jan. 5, 1924. Docket no. 12964.

[84] *Brief and Argument in Opposition to Choice of Great Northern rather than Northern Pacific for Separation from Burlington and Association with the St. Paul, before the Interstate Commerce Commission*, Jan. 5, 1924. Docket no. 12964.

In 1927, while the fate of the group had still not been decided by the Interstate Commerce Commission, the Northern Pacific and the Great Northern made an agreement for achieving that unity in organization which had, at least outwardly, been destroyed by the Northern Securities decision. It was agreed to form a new company—the Great Northern Pacific Co.—to acquire as soon as feasible the Spokane, Portland & Seattle, the Great Northern, the Northern Pacific, and bus lines and other interests of these roads. The Burlington, being the property of the two Northerns, would be included in the arrangement.[85] Application was made to the Interstate Commerce Commission to proceed with this consolidation. The petition was not granted. In its plans of December 9, 1929, for the consolidation of railroads the Interstate Commerce Commission proposed the union of the two Northerns and the Spokane, Portland & Seattle, the Oregon, California & Eastern, and some minor lines; the Burlington, however, was to be made an independent system.[86] The question was not settled at the time, and in 1931 it was dropped because of conditions arising from the depression.

From 1930 to the present, like western railroads in particular and American railroads as a whole, the Great Northern has been faced with difficult times. The general depression in business, with its decline in grain, lumber, iron ore, and other shipments, the continued fall in farm prices, the loss of the export farm market, the drought of several seasons, and the competition of motor transport have all worn down the income of the road through decreased carriage and lowered rates. In 1936, even after some recovery, net revenues from operations were less than in 1916, while the stock outstanding was about the same and funded debt very much larger. One important step toward lightening the burden of fixed charges was taken in 1936 in the refinancing of $100,766,000 of general mortgage 7 per cent bonds into general mortgage 4 per cent bonds convertible into stock.[87] The problem of low net income, however, still remained unsolved.

[85] *Poor's Railroads,* 1929, pp. 1495–1496.

[86] *Commerce and Finance,* Dec. 25, 1929, p. 2731.

9. Readings

James J. Hill, *Highways of Progress* (New York, 1910). Pages 101–328 are recommended as giving Hill's ideas on various aspects of railroad building and management.

J. G. Pyle, *The Life of James J. Hill* (Garden City, 1917), 2 vols. This is the authorized life of Hill. While not altogether objective, it is of considerable value because it contains much material from the Hill papers.

B. H. Meyer, *A History of the Northern Securities Case* (Madison, 1906). Though concerned principally with the legal phases of the case, this study also recognizes economic aspects.

Brief and Argument in Support of Consolidation of the Burlington, Great Northern and Northern Pacific, and Subsidiaries, before the Interstate Commerce Commission, Jan. 5, 1924.

10. Suggested Questions

1. The Northern Pacific was built from Duluth to the West Coast principally by means of the one large company; the Great Northern grew through the use of smaller, local companies, partially owned by the chief Hill road and leased. How do you explain Hill's choice of the latter method of organization?
2. Why did not Hill unite with the Northern Pacific ten years earlier than he did and thus save the expense of building to the Coast?
3. Until the 1890's Hill had relied heavily on Montreal and London for finan-

[87] G. N., *Annual Report,* 1930–36.

cial aid, but after that he looked more to New York. Why?

4. Were there any errors in judgment behind the consolidation of the three railroads to form the present Hill system?

5. Was Hill a financial or an industrial capitalist?

XXVII. CHICAGO, MILWAUKEE, ST. PAUL & PACIFIC RAILROAD, 1852–1938 [1]

1. General Statement

The history of the Chicago, Milwaukee, St. Paul & Pacific Railroad [2] typifies clearly the various stages through which many American railroads have passed. In the first stage, short local lines financed by local capital were built in answer to local needs—primarily not for the profits involved in the road's operation, but in order to develop the country. In the second stage came the bankruptcy of these lines, followed by a series of mergers in which capital charges were reduced. In the third, the local lines became regional and developed into excellent systems of transportation. And in the fourth stage, regional lines attempted to become trunk or transcontinental lines.

2. Important Dates in the History of the Railroad

1852	Charter granted to LaCrosse & Milwaukee Co.
1863	Reorganization and formation of the Milwaukee & St. Paul Railway Co.
1864	Company built first grain elevator.
1866	Acquired the Prairie du Chien.
1867	Reached St. Paul by means of the acquisition of Minnesota Central Railroad.
1873	Line completed from Milwaukee to Chicago.
1874	Name changed to Chicago, Milwaukee & St. Paul.
1898–1905	Notable prosperity as regional road.
1905	Board of directors authorized building to Seattle.
1909	Traffic to Coast on new extension.
1913	Milwaukee absorbed company which controlled extension to the Coast.
1915–17	Electrification of 438 miles of line in the West.
1918–20	Government operation.
1920–25	Net earnings failed to cover interest.
1925	$50,000,000 in bonds came due. Receivership and reorganization.
1927	Chicago, Milwaukee, St. Paul & Pacific Railroad Co. chartered.
1928	New company operating.
1935	Receivership.
1935–38	Reorganization proceedings.

3. Beginnings of a Local Railroad [3]

By 1850 the portion of Wisconsin bordering on Lake Michigan with Milwaukee as its commercial center was thickly settled. It was a good agricultural country and had cheap transportation owing to its proximity to the lake. West of the settlements on the lake the population was

[1] The factual material for this case to 1929 was taken chiefly from The Financial History of the Chicago, Milwaukee & St. Paul Railway Company, a thesis prepared at the University of Minnesota by Arthur Borak. Sections of material from this work have been quoted verbatim. Professor Borak has generously read the case and made very helpful suggestions.

[2] Throughout this case the road will be called the Milwaukee, as it has been traditionally in the Middle West, though in financial circles it has come to be known as the St. Paul.

[3] For the beginnings of the Milwaukee, Professor Borak depended chiefly on court records and John W. Cary, *The Organization and History of the Chicago, Milwaukee & St. Paul Railway Company* (Milwaukee, 1892).

sparse. Cheap transportation was needed in the back country. In the 'forties there was talk of canals. One was begun in Milwaukee; before it was well under way, however, the possibilities of a railroad came to be considered. Everyone was willing to back such an enterprise. For the farmer in the back country it meant rising land values; for the townsman, trade; for the community as a whole, the opening of large tracts of good land which had hitherto been useless.

In 1852 a group of Milwaukee business men obtained a charter for constructing a road from Milwaukee to La Crosse. (See the map facing p. 29.) The chief problem was to secure funds for building. There were three possible sources of capital for the enterprise: sale of stock, sale of bonds, and government subsidies.

By difficult, piecemeal financing and contracting the Milwaukee & La Crosse was completed to La Crosse in 1858. In some counties stock was sold to farmers, who paid in notes secured by mortgages on their farms. The farmers assigned their dividends to the payment of interest and principal, the railroads sold the notes in the East, and in the absence of dividends many farmers lost their farms. The city of Milwaukee early lent the road $114,000 in bonds. On the strength of what had been accomplished in the way of grading, the railroad in 1854 sold $950,000 of first-mortgage bonds. A land grant, obtained in part directly in 1856 and in part through a devious and questionable deal with the projected St. Croix & Lake Superior in 1857, became the basis for a substantial "land grant mortgage" loan, which later had a perilous time. In 1858 the road obtained from William Barnes a loan in bonds secured by its property.

Though the road was completed to La Crosse, and other lines were acquired through amalgamation or construction so that the railway became a substantial property, the La Crosse & Milwaukee failed financially. It had trouble with contractors; some of the land grants were not actually turned over to the road by the government; dividends were not forthcoming; and default on interest placed the enterprise in the hands of its creditors.

The result was the wiping-out of the original promoters and owners and the organization in 1863 of the Milwaukee & St. Paul Railway Co. The first step in this change was the securing of control by the bondholders under the Barnes mortgage. Their immediate default on the land-grant bonds actually placed control in the hands of a stronger group. By purchase and merger, exchange of stock for bonds, and much litigation, several small divisions, or roads, which had been more or less a part of the La Crosse were brought together in the Milwaukee & St. Paul. Selah Chamberlain, one of the early contractors on the La Crosse, and several capitalists, outstanding among whom was Russell Sage of New York, were elected directors of the newly organized company.

4. Building a Regional System

The new Milwaukee & St. Paul looked toward the immediate extension of the road to St. Paul. Since entry into that place was blocked by other roads already in the St. Paul territory, the officers of the Milwaukee proceeded to purchase their way. They tried, but failed, in 1863 to buy the Prairie du Chien, with its railhead on the Mississippi, which, together with another road from the opposite bank of the river and a third road (partially built) in Minnesota, would form an almost continuous line to St. Paul. About two years later the Milwaukee secured control of the Prairie du Chien by an exchange of stock with H. C. Stimson, who had bought the Prairie du Chien stock on the New York exchange at prices as high as $250 a share. The Prairie road obtained a 999-year lease of the Iowa road, and in 1866 the Milwaukee purchased the Minnesota Central by exchanging stock, share for share, and assuming the latter road's bonds. As soon as the Milwaukee had gained entrance into St. Paul, it was also able to construct its line up the river from LaCrosse to St. Paul. All these extensions were made possible through separate divisional bond issues. In 1867 the Milwaukee owned and operated 835 miles of road, roughly forming a triangle between Milwaukee, St. Paul, and Mason City, Iowa.

In the next quarter-century the Milwaukee was made into a regional system or network of roads. In 1873 it built into Chicago, and in 1874 its name was changed to the Chicago, Milwaukee & St. Paul. Striking westward the road reached the Iowa-Dakota boundary in 1879, and, continuing westward in the 'eighties, reached Kansas City in 1887. At the same time it secured chiefly by construction or purchase a large system of feeders, many short lines and others which reached into northern Wisconsin and northwestern Minnesota and the Dakotas. By June 30, 1891, the Milwaukee's lines totaled 6,083 miles, located as follows: Illinois, 318; Wisconsin and Michigan, 1,736; Iowa, 1,553; Minnesota, 1,120; North Dakota, 118; South Dakota, 1,096; and Missouri, 140 miles.

These extensions were acquired by various means. The usual rule was that the Company did not build the lines. Local capitalists in each community which desired service had to market the common stock of a new company; the Milwaukee sold the bonds, and usually its approval was required in the letting of construction contracts; the Milwaukee leased the new line when completed; and eventually the larger road absorbed the new at a price based upon its proved value. Other lines were acquired by purchase, many after foreclosure and reorganization.

Items from the report of the road as of June 30, 1891, show what its capital structure was at the end of the period of rapid regional growth: miles of railroad, 6,083; funded debt, $124,105,000; preferred stock, $22,198,900; and common stock, $46,022,440. The funded debt consisted of 35 different issues, mostly divisional, ranging in size from $25,340,000 to $106,500 and in interest rate from 8 per cent to 4 per cent—the newer bonds had the lower rates, maturing at different dates until 1989.[4]

From the organization of the Milwaukee in 1863 throughout this period the preferred stock received its dividend of 7 per cent every year except the years 1888–90, when the rate paid ranged from 3.5 to 6 per cent. During the first few years the earnings were put into improvements and dividends were paid in stock; thereafter cash was paid except for the years 1874 and 1875, when because of improvements the dividends were paid in consolidated bonds. Small amounts were paid in dividends on the common stock at different times but not regularly before 1879; in 1880–84 the dividend on common was 7 per cent; in 1885, 4 per cent; in 1886 and 1887, 5 per cent; in 1888, 2.5; and in 1889–91 no dividend was paid. The road followed a conservative policy in the payment of dividends, leaving a considerable balance for application to the property.

In Table 1 (p. 424), the capital, expense, and earnings of the Milwaukee are compared with figures for the Northern Pacific and the Great Northern.

5. A Strong Middle Western System, 1891–1905

The policy of the Milwaukee, says Professor Borak, was from the beginning of this period to do no more speculative rig-

[4] The source of these and other statistics on the Milwaukee and other roads given in this case are chiefly annual reports, *Poor's Manual of Railroads,* and a report on the road submitted to the president of the road, March 16, 1925, by Coverdale & Colpitts, Consulting Engineers.

ging but straightaway railroading. Speculative interests had been shaken off and expansion had slowed down—from 1891 to 1898 there was an increase of only 70 miles. The chief concern of the road from 1891 to 1898—aside from the problem of earnings in a period of depression—was the physical improvement of its property.

The improvement of the road took various forms. Double tracking was completed between Chicago and Milwaukee and Chicago and the Mississippi. The replacement of iron rails with steel was so rapid that by July 1, 1898, there remained only 517 miles of iron rails. New bridges and stations were built. Large amounts were spent on improving railroad shops. The replacement of equipment was very heavy, and old stock was improved by the addition of power brakes, automatic coupling, electric lights, and others of the newest improvements in railroading. The Milwaukee took over its sleeping car service from the Pullman Co., which meant an investment of $678,965.

In view of the cost of expensive improvements and the increase in total mileage, the capital structure of the road became stronger during this period. The common stock was decreased a trifle; the preferred stock was increased from 22 to 31 million; and the funded debt, from 124 to 130 million. The funded debt was increased by 16 million general 4 per cents and 7 million assumed on the purchase of the Milwaukee & Northern; the debt was decreased by the canceling of 7 million of underlying bonds bearing a high rate and the conversion of 9 million into preferred stock.

Though this period was marked by a severe business depression which brought lower prices for agricultural products, the Milwaukee weathered the depression in good condition. It continued to pay 7 per cent on preferred; over the years 1892–98, it paid a total of 23.5 per cent on common; and, except for a deficit of $403,000 in 1895, it had a considerable balance after the payment of dividends.

With the closing years of the decade came business revival which, coupled with increasing production, travel, and purchasing power along the Milwaukee's lines, brought added earnings to the road. The net revenue from operations shot up from $14,122,000 in 1898 to $20,369,000 in 1905. Though there was some expansion in mileage from 1898 to 1905 the principal change in the road's property was continued improvement of its existing physical equipment.

Financially the road put itself in even a stronger position than before. In 1899–1905 it continued to pay 7 per cent on preferred and paid from 5 to 7.5 per

Table 1. FIGURES FROM REPORTS OF THREE RAILROADS, JUNE 30, 1891

	Milwaukee	Northern Pacific	Great Northern
Stock per mile	$11,214	$20,286	$ 7,016
Bonds per mile	$22,688	$33,187	$18,637
Interest per mile	$1,252	$1,719	$1,427
Gross earnings per mile	$4,817	$5,957	$3,679
Expenses per mile (including taxes)	$3,217	$3,648	$2,115
Ratio of expenses to earnings	66.74%	61.23%	57.53%
Ratio of operating expenses to earnings	63.82%	59.40%	50.22%
Net earnings per mile	$1,600	$2,319	$1,567
Average rate per ton per mile	$0.01	$0.0138	$0.0124
Average rate per passenger per mile	$0.0239	$0.0263	$0.028
Revenue from freight per train mile	$1.5234	$2.024	$2.43
Ratio of freight earnings to total earnings	69.12%	69.70%	74.19%
Ratio of passenger earnings to total earnings	22.82%	25.56%	18.26%

cent on common, besides crediting large amounts to balance. It converted large amounts of underlying bonds into preferred stock and financed itself mostly through common stock rather than bonds. The interest charges decreased $340 a mile during this period.

The financial structure of the Milwaukee was not only absolutely but also comparatively strong, as is shown in Table 2, below.

According to one writer [5] on American railroads, in 1904 the Milwaukee was strong in various ways. It was one system without subordinate lines. The administrative ability of Milwaukee-bred men was recognized in the whole American railroad world. The loyalty of its employees was exceptional. Moreover, the management, which had risen within Milwaukee ranks, was progressive. Its willingness to experiment had made it a leader in adapting improvements which cut costs and improved service. It was said that the Milwaukee had a strong progressive individuality and a hatred of outside dominance.

[5] Frank H. Spearman, *The Strategy of Great Railroads* (New York, 1904).

6. Extension to the Coast, 1905–13

The most important development in Milwaukee affairs from 1905 to 1913 was the building of an extension to the Pacific. The roots of this development lie back in the previous period. Of apparent significance are the growth of the Northwest and the growing conviction of men influential in Milwaukee affairs that the road had to have an outlet to the Coast.

Professor Borak traces the beginnings of the movement for extension. He found a reference to extension in 1901 in a letter of Roswell Miller, chairman of the Milwaukee's board, to A. J. Earling, president. The letter refers to a conversation with E. H. Harriman relative to interchange of business between the Milwaukee and the Union Pacific, in which Miller had claimed that the Milwaukee was treated unfavorably as compared with the Northwestern:

" 'I said to him [Harriman] that there would be just one result of the Union Pacific policy, that we should be compelled to build a line to the coast. He said we could not build a line to the coast as good as his, to which I replied that we could build just as good a road

Table 2. FIGURES FROM REPORTS OF THREE RAILROADS, JUNE 30, 1905

	Milwaukee	Northern Pacific	Great Northern
Stock per mile	$15,555.15	$29,168.23	$21,730.84
Funded debt per mile	$17,676.97	$34,903.43	$17,668.08
Interest per mile	$858.24	$1,307.67	$844.09
Gross earnings per mile	$7,221.19	$9,543.44	$7,605.36
Operating expenses and taxes per mile	$4,674.86	$5,345.26	$4,011.68
Net earnings per mile	$2,546.33	$4,198.18	$3,593.36
Ratio of operating expenses and taxes to earnings	64.74%	56.00%	52.75%
Ratio of operating expenses to earnings	58.96%	52.80%	48.67%
Average rate per ton per mile	$0.0881	$0.0832	$0.0792
Freight earnings per train mile	$ 2.33	$ 3.10	$ 4.20
Average number of miles each ton hauled	175.14	334.40	...
Average tons of freight per loaded car	13.74	16.10	20.00
Average tons of freight per train	264.00	366.52	522.76
Average rate per passenger per mile	$0.0224	$0.0223	$0.02384
Ratio of freight earnings to gross earnings	72.11%	76.67%	75.85%
Ratio of passenger earnings to gross earnings	20.30%	22.34%	18.38%

as he could build. He said why don't you start it tomorrow; I said we were not ready, and it might be five years before we got ready; that we could build a line to the coast and supply terminals for $45,000,000,—⅙ of what his line was capitalized at, which would give us an immense advantage over him.' "

There is some evidence that Hill of the Great Northern was interested in the Milwaukee at this time, the reason being that his road needed a connection with Chicago. There were rumors of a plan to bring the Milwaukee into a Hill-Morgan group. Hill admitted buying Milwaukee stock and even hinted at a traffic arrangement between that road and the Great Northern. In fact the purchase of the Milwaukee by the Hill-Morgan interest was considered, Morgan urging that road as against Hill's stand in favor of the Burlington. Harriman's purchase of Burlington stock may have influenced Morgan's and Hill's decision to purchase control of that road.

In 1902 the Milwaukee came to an agreement with the Union Pacific which allowed the former to run trains over the latter's tracks to the Coast. This might eventually have stopped the Milwaukee from building, since it was a very advantageous arrangement for them. A new factor, however, appeared at this time. Again quoting Borak:

"Negotiations for the acquisition of control of the Burlington by the Northern Pacific and Great Northern were going on. Miller who was alarmed wrote Earling on April 9, 1901 that on that day he had seen Mr. Jacob Schiff of Kuhn, Loeb and Company and had told him 'that if the Northern Pacific and Great Northern tied up with the Burlington we should be compelled to build to the coast.' At that time the St. Paul officials had no clear idea as to what part of the Pacific coast they would build. Various points were mentioned in correspondence being exchanged at the time. Miller still thought $45,000,000 would finance the project and that traffic would be divided with the Northern Pacific and Great Northern from the start. At his request Earling sent an engineer over the Northern Pacific to ascertain the cost of duplicating their line. Before the engineer started on his trip he wrote Miller on April 10, 1901 that he was 'sure that it would not cost as much as $45,-000,000 to build as good as the Northern Pacific to the coast.' On April 25, 1901 Miller wrote to Earling that the board had authorized the expenditure of $10,000 in making a reconnaissance from Evarts, South Dakota, to Butte, Montana, and again stated that 'if the Burlington deal goes through we shall be compelled to build to the coast.'

"In August, 1902 Miller submitted to Mr. William Rockefeller, then very influential in St. Paul affairs, a report on the proposed extension to the Pacific coast at Eureka, California, to reach the vast timber lands of Humboldt County, California. On March 29, 1905 Miller wrote Earling that it looked as though the St. Paul would have to build to the coast. On April 27, 1905 a committee of directors was appointed to take action with reference to the acquisition of right of way. On May 25, 1905 Miller reported to Earling that the Harriman and Hill interests had come to an agreement and that 'it was supposed both interests would use all the influence they could to prevent the St. Paul from building.' However, it seems as though neither Hill nor Harriman feared the threats of the Milwaukee to build to the coast. In May, 1905 Hill wrote the following letter to the president of the Burlington:

" 'If I were at the head of the North Western or the St. Paul I would never be satisfied with a connection over some other line that was a natural competitor from the common point eastward. The North Western and the St. Paul, with over fourteen thousand miles of railway, would if they built to the Puget Sound, be a great acquisition to the business of the Sound and would go far toward putting it on a foundation viewed from the commerce of the world ahead of San Francisco. This would, in my judgment, help our line much more than any possible injury it could do.'

"As late as July, 1905, Mr. W. K. Vanderbilt and William Rockefeller had discussed a line to be built jointly by the North Western and the St. Paul. Rockefeller appeared to favor the idea but Miller did not. On November 4, 1905 Miller advised Earling that in view of a cable from Rockefeller, Earling should go ahead with arrangements for construction. On November 28, 1905 the board formally authorized the building of a line to Seattle and Tacoma. On September 28, 1906 Earling reported:

" 'A careful estimate from the information now available indicates that the completed line from the Missouri River to Butte will cost $20,183,000. The estimated cost of the entire line, Missouri River to Seattle, including equipment is $60,000,000.' "

The Milwaukee men were prompted to build to the Pacific Coast not only by fear of competition but also by the hope of obtaining freight from the territory through which they would pass. They expected to get freight from the Orient to be carried to the East of this country. The Milwaukee men believed that they could construct the western division for a fraction of the cost of the older lines, which would allow them an advantage that would give them the bulk of the through freight. They also expected that the road would receive a great deal of traffic from the development of the western country through which the western extension would pass. Indeed, there was already a real-estate and industrial boom in the Rockies and the Pacific Northwest; it was a country of timber and grass and mines. Transportation would help develop those rich resources and provide freight for the Milwaukee.

Potential competition of the Panama Canal does not seem to have been considered by the executives of the Milwaukee. It should be remembered that for over twenty-five years there had been much talk and some effort in the direction of building a Central American canal. In 1903 the new Republic of Panama had granted to the United States concessions which opened the way for the building of a canal. Only a few weeks before the board of the Milwaukee decided to build to the Coast, the report of engineers investigating the Panama route preliminary to construction by the United States was published. Actual construction began in 1906. It is significant that, in the years of construction of the canal, comments in financial and, especially, railroad journals viewed the project more as an engineering problem than as one having far-reaching significance for American railroads. The Canal was finally opened to navigation in 1914.

The road was built by separate companies incorporated in each of the States through which it was to pass, the companies pledging their stock with the Milwaukee. This method avoided trouble with the various State laws. In 1905 the Pacific Railroad Co. was incorporated in Washington and another company in Montana; in 1906 two more companies were incorporated, in Idaho and South Dakota.

In the fall of 1906 the proposed route of the extension was made public. From Chicago to Seattle the distance was to be 2,305 miles, about 150 miles shorter than by way of the Northern Pacific and 80 miles shorter than by way of the Great Northern, with mountain grades of from 1.66 per cent to 1.88 per cent as against an average of 2.2 per cent on the Northern Pacific.

The stock of the four subsidiary companies was deposited with the St. Paul as security for advances. On December 31, 1908, the Idaho, Montana, and South Dakota organizations were acquired by the Washington organization. The name of the latter was changed from the Chicago, Milwaukee & St. Paul Railway Co. of Washington to the Chicago, Milwaukee & Puget Sound Railway Co. The stock of the latter was increased to $100,000,000 and conveyed to the Milwaukee as security for advances previously made for the construction of the extension. Where the St. Paul was getting these funds will be related shortly. Since the State law in Washington permitted a railroad to be bonded up to twice the amount of its capital stock, this $100,000,000 capital stock would now permit the Puget Sound company to issue $200,000,000 in bonds.

The effect on the financial strength of the Milwaukee of the extension to the Coast is indicated by Tables 3 and 4. The first table gives figures on the capital structure before the extension was built and after the costs of extension had been assumed by the Milwaukee; the second shows in detail the condition of the funded debt at the later date.

Table 3. CAPITAL STRUCTURE OF THE MILWAUKEE, 1905 AND 1913

	June 30, 1905	June 30, 1913
Common stock:		
In the hands of the public and in the insurance fund [a]	$58,183,900	$115,946,000
In the Company's treasury	...	402,200
Total	$58,183,900	$116,348,200
Preferred stock:		
In the hands of the public and in the insurance fund	$49,327,400	$115,931,900
In the treasury	...	343,000
Total	$49,327,400	$116,274,900
Funded debt:		
In the hands of the public and in the insurance fund	$116,264,500	$299,554,455
In the treasury	5,912,000	156,295,512
Total funded debt	$122,176,500	$455,849,967

[a] The Milwaukee did not insure its property with an outside insurance company; it paid the premium into a central fund out of which it paid losses, investing this fund in its own securities.

Table 4. ANALYSIS OF THE FUNDED DEBT, JUNE 30, 1913

Funded debt, June 30, 1905			$122,176,500.00
Increased by:			
Generals issued for improvements to the property	$35,689,000		
Underlying bonds refunded	26,837,000	$ 62,526,000.00	
25-year gold debenture 4's		28,050,000.00	
15-year European gold debenture 4's		48,176,654.66	
Convertible gold debenture 4½'s		48,850,800.00	
Chicago, Milwaukee & Puget Sound Railway 4's assumed		173,525,511.64	361,128,966.30
			$483,305,466.30
Decreased by:			
Underlying bonds refunded		$26,837,000.00	
Convertible underlying bonds exchanged for preferred stock and canceled		619,000.00	27,456,000.00
Funded debt, June 30, 1913			$455,849,466.30

Again quoting Borak:

"Needless to say such financing as that which took place during this period very profoundly affected the financial structure of the company. Each mile of line became heavily burdened with obligations to the owners and to outsiders who advanced money to the company for the purchase of its bonds. The changes in the capitalization per mile during this period were as follows:

	June 30, 1905	June 30, 1909	June 30, 1913
Stock	$15,555.15	$18,207.66	$24,602.43
Bonds	17,676.97	15,865.79	31,782.97
Total	$33,232.12	$34,073.45	$56,385.40
Interest	858.24	802.53	1,213.59

"The middle set of figures is interesting. No securities issued in connection with the extension were included in calculating them. Neither was the mileage of the extension, then under construction, included. These figures show what the financial structure would have been if no extension were being built. The stock per mile exceeded the bonds per mile on the company's old lines, a wonderful financial structure for a railroad. Then, as pointed out previously, large amounts of underlying bonds bearing 5, 6 and 7% interest per annum came due in 1910. With these refunded at 4%, which was actually done, the financial structure on the old lines was improved still more. The financial structure on June 30, 1913 did not look like that of the same railroad the financial history of which is here being related. In fact after the construction and merger of the extension on January 1, 1913 it was not the same railroad."

The most striking part of the affair was the difference between the actual cost and the estimated cost of the extension. As pointed out previously, those in charge of the Company's affairs at first estimated that the cost of the extension would be about $45,000,000, later raising the estimate to $60,000,000. Both estimates (as shown by the financing related above, of which practically all the proceeds went into the extension, its branches, and the equipment for these new lines) were proving to be only a small portion of the total actual investment. The cost only to July, 1909, when through traffic was established, was $99,506,000. Ultimately the cost, with branches, terminals, and equipment, was in excess of $250,000,000.

Various reasons have been given for the great difference between estimated and actual costs. It is claimed that the simultaneous construction of railroads in western Canada, together with expansion by the Union and the Northern Pacific and the Great Northern, increased the cost greatly because it raised contract prices. The engineer in charge of construction west of Butte said that forest fires, floods, and slides added to costs on the one hand, while the decision to build a heavier road than had at first been planned increased the cost on the other hand. Careful investigation has not disclosed losses resulting from dishonest expenditures.[6]

Borak concludes:

"After all is said and done, however, it is clear that the project was started with no adequate comprehension by those controlling the destinies of the St. Paul of its probable cost, particularly in view of the high standard of construction actually attained. The commission found from Pearson's testimony and from the records that little, if any, consideration had been given to the building or acquisition of branch lines and feeders later found necessary to secure traffic."

7. Electrification, 1913–17

According to Borak,

"John D. Ryan became a director of the St. Paul in 1909 upon the request of William Rockefeller, who for many years had a large interest in the Anaconda Mining Company and was a director of that company during the St. Paul's electrification. When Ryan became a director he was president of the copper company, which had extensive interests in

[6] This was brought out before the Interstate Commerce Commission in its investigation in 1925.

Montana, and he was also interested in water power. He and his associates had acquired control of the Great Falls Water Power & Town Site Company from the Hill interests and water power was being developed at Great Falls, Montana, when he became a director. Ryan is reported to have said that he was interested in railroad electrification from two standpoints: (a) as one of the new uses for copper, and (b) in securing an outlet for the great undeveloped water power controlled by him and his associates. As a director of the road he thought that he ought not to be an active party in its power negotiations. He took pains to make his position clear to everyone. He avoided taking parts in the board's discussions concerning electrification and avoided meetings when the question was to come up. In framing the power contracts he was the active negotiator for the power companies and Earling, then president, and Goodnow, his assistant, represented the railroad. Ryan depended on the railroad officials to protect the carrier's interests.

"As early as 1906 electric supply companies had made reports with respect to electrifying the Butte, Anaconda & Pacific Railway, a short line controlled by the Anaconda Copper Company, engaged principally in hauling ore from Butte to Anaconda, a distance of about 25 miles. For many years the St. Paul owned 49% of the stock of this road, but sold it subsequent to the period discussed here. Operation of this road by electricity commenced in May, 1913. The work was done by the General Electric Company under an absolute guaranty of performance. In the meantime that company made various studies and investigations with regard to electrification of the St. Paul."

In January, 1913, it was rumored that the progressive St. Paul system planned to electrify about 450 miles of the Company's lines through the mountains in Montana and Idaho. Actual construction started in April, 1914. The mountain divisions, a distance of 438 miles, were completely electrified by 1916. The electrification of the Coast division brought the total to 648 miles of line.

The Company purchased power instead of providing it itself. In 1912 it made a 99-year contract for one division with the Great Falls Power Co., in which Ryan and his associates owned a half interest. In 1913 a 99-year contract was made for a second division with the Thompson Falls Co., in which Ryan had a half interest. Both these companies were merged in 1913 with the Montana Power Co. Ryan again holding a strong interest. In 1917 a 98-year contract was made for the Coast division with the Intermountain Power Co., a company organized by Ryan and others to purchase power manufac-

Table 5. CAPITAL STRUCTURE OF THE MILWAUKEE, 1913 AND 1917

	June 30, 1913	December 31, 1917
Common stock:		
In the hands of the public and in the insurance fund	$115,946,000	$117,411,300
In the Company's treasury	402,200	...
Total	$116,348,200	$117,411,300
Preferred stock:		
In the hands of the public and in the insurance fund	$115,931,900	$115,931,900
In the Company's treasury	343,000	343,000
Total	$116,274,900	$116,274,900
Funded debt:		
In the hands of the public and in the insurance fund	$299,554,455	$383,044,955
In the Company's treasury	156,295,512	107,259,200
Total funded debt	$455,849,967	$490,304,155

tured by other concerns—the railroad paid a considerably higher rate to the Intermountain than the latter paid for the power.

There has been much question as to the financial results of electrification. The total cost of electrification was $22,990,254. The management of the Company claimed that up to the end of 1924 savings of $12,400,000 had been made through electrification. These figures were, however, based on the cost of steam locomotive power in 1915 for moving 1923 traffic. Investigation by the Interstate Commerce Commission in 1925 disclosed that, with the improved steam equipment of later years, the cost would have been about the same for the two types of power. It appears from the investigations by the Commission,[7] with respect to existing costs under electrification, that more favorable contracts should have been made with power companies.

The effect of electrification on the financial condition of the road is suggested by Table 5 on the preceding page.

8. Governmental Operation, 1918–20

The president of the United States took possession of the road at midnight on December 31, 1917, at a time when the Milwaukee was already in a difficult position. What would have happened if the road had remained under private management is evident. On March 21, 1918, Congress enacted the so-called Federal Control Act. The act provided that the president of the United States should make an agreement with each company whose property was taken over, in respect to compensation, condition of the property on return to owners, and other matters.

An agreement was finally reached by which the Milwaukee received $27,946,771 a year. This was more than a strict average of its previous income in that it included allowance for improvements (extension and electrification in Montana and Idaho), the earning power of which had not yet had an opportunity to make itself felt. Under this agreement the road was operated under the Director General until February 28, 1920. Concerning government operation Professor Borak has the following to say:

"The property was operated at a great loss by the Director General, and when it was returned to its owners they were confronted with inadequate revenues, a high scale of wages, and a troubled labor condition. This situation was relieved somewhat by congressional legislation creating a six months guaranty period which provided that the standard return paid as rental during the period of federal control would be continued for the six months March 1, 1920 to August 31, 1920, inclusive, so as to enable the owners to readjust themselves to the conditions resulting from the war.

"The capitalization per mile at the beginning and end of this period was as follows:

	December 31, 1917	December 31, 1920
Stock	$23,452	$22,725
Funded debt	38,497	40,155
Total	$61,949	$62,880
Interest	1,668	1,713

"The increased burdening of each mile of line with heavier funded debt and interest charges during this period is noticeable. Of course some of this increase was for badly needed equipment. When such is the case the increase in debt per mile of line will more likely have beneficial rather than detrimental effects. The increase of over $40 per mile of line in interest charges is significant. The costs of securing funds in the loan market during the war and post war years had gone up. The company was once more borrowing funds on a 6% basis after many years of borrowing at 3½%, 4%, 4½%, and during the previous period at 5% on one block."

9. The Period Leading up to the Receivership, 1920–24

The years 1920–24 were a trying period for the Milwaukee. Table 6, which

[7] See especially 131 I. C. C.

contains significant figures on income, operating expenses, and other obligations of the road for those years, gives some indication of the source of its difficulties.

Interest charges had been steadily increasing at a faster rate than the net income. From 1921 through 1924 the railroad had failed to cover the charges three out of four years, and the fourth year had just barely covered them.

The western extension had increased gross income but not so much as had been expected. The Panama Canal had made it less expensive to ship through freight by water than by train. The competition of automobiles and trucks was already felt. The country through which the Milwaukee ran had not developed according to plan. The cost of construction had been far in excess of what had been expected. The money had been borrowed during a period of high rates. The period of governmental operation of the railroad had increased operating expenses.

In view of the bad financial condition of the road, it is difficult to explain the further complicating of its problems by the acquisition of two additional short lines at a considerable cost. In July, 1921, the Chicago, Terre Haute & Southeastern Railway Co. was leased for 999 years. This road owned almost 600 miles of track, was weak in earnings and in equipment and general condition, and had poor financial standing. President Byram of the Milwaukee recommended its acquisition especially because it reached into Illinois coal fields. Professor Borak says that a total of $19,584,000 in Terre Haute obligations was assumed by the St. Paul at a time when the Indiana road was not earning fixed charges. According to the I. C. C., by June 30, 1925, these obligations and the cost of necessary betterments of the road amounted to $11,000,000.

In 1921 the Milwaukee acquired control of another road in the same region, the Chicago, Milwaukee & Gary Railway Co. This was a shorter road, but a road in poor condition and with a bad earnings history. Like the Terre Haute, it was said to be valuable to the Milwaukee as an aid in securing freight. The acquisition of this road was also criticized later by the I. C. C. It should be noted, however, that the Commission made no objection in 1921.

In 1923 it became evident to those who knew the actual state of affairs that a

Table 6. FIGURES FROM REPORTS OF THE MILWAUKEE, 1921–24

(Dollars in thousands)

Item	1921	1922	1923	1924
Average miles operated	11,030	11,025	10,990	10,987
Operating revenues	$146,766	$156,951	$169,628	$158,366
Operating expenses	127,957	129,597	134,999	125,550
Net revenue	18,809	27,354	34,629	32,816
Taxes and uncollectibles	9,046	9,662	8,617	9,142
Operating income	9,763	17,693	26,012	23,674
Non-operating income	2,087	2,218	2,373	2,525
Gross income	11,850	19,911	28,384	26,199
Net income available for interest	3,712	12,076	19,793	18,718
Interest on debt	19,960	18,073	19,444	20,448
Net income	–13,248 [a]	–5,997	350	–1,730
Dividend on preferred	...	...	...	...
Dividend on common	...	...	...	...
Total dividends	...	...	...	...
Balance	–13,248	–5,997	350	–1,730

[a] Deficit indicated by minus sign.

receivership for the Milwaukee was inevitable. The condition of the road and of its equipment was not holding up to earlier standards. In 1925, $50,000,000 of bonds would come due and there was no hope of refunding them. In 1923 the National City Bank quietly fed into the market the Milwaukee bonds which it owned.

At that time the road had four large stockholders: William Rockefeller with 150,000 shares; Ogden Armour with 125,000 shares; the George Smith interests in England with $20,000,000 of bonds and stock; and E. S. Harkness with 100,000 shares. The first three liquidated their holdings and were all clear before the crash.

10. The Reorganization, 1925–28 [8]

On March 18, 1925, the Milwaukee passed into the hands of a receiver. Kuhn, Loeb & Co. and the National City Co. had been the road's bankers and had distributed most of its securities; and they promptly undertook the task of reorganization. It is significant to note that the road was still in the control of large interests, all but one (Harkness) of whom had cleared out before the receivership materialized.

The task of the bankers who assumed control was to organize a new company to take over the actual operation of the road, fund all current indebtedness, reduce the fixed charges to a sum which the Company could hope to meet without undue stress, maintain the relative positions of the various classes of bond- and stockholders, and raise the necessary capital.

In June the reorganization managers announced a plan which they believed answered the needs of the situation. This drastic plan met with great opposition on the part of the junior bondholders. A committee headed by George S. Roosevelt of Roosevelt & Sons, New York, presented an alternative plan. The result was that Kuhn, Loeb & Co. modified their plan somewhat in answer to the wishes of this committee. The financial proposals of the three plans are given in Table 7, below.[9]

The first plan of the Kuhn, Loeb & Co. committee was drastic. It provided for the assessment of the stockholders for sufficient money to pay off the current indebtedness; in exchange they were to receive fixed interest bonds and new stock, of the same class as the old which it replaced, upon which assessments were to be paid. The plan also provided for the refunding of some $230,950,796 of fixed interest bonds into adjustment mortgage or income bonds. The road would thus have been put into a strong position. The Roosevelt committee objected to the refunding of the defaulted junior bonds into income bonds exclusively. Stockholders were to be assessed $10 a share, less than half of that called for by the first Kuhn, Loeb plan, but were to be given that amount in income bonds. Of the bonds to be received in exchange, 25 per cent were to be in fixed interest bonds and 75 per cent in income bonds. The modified Kuhn, Loeb plan was the same as the original except that it gave the junior bondholders 20 per cent of their claims in fixed interest-bearing securities and 80 per cent in income bonds. This plan was finally adopted.

During the entire reorganization proceedings the committee had been opposed by Edwin C. Jameson of the Globe & Rutgers Fire Insurance Co. Jameson and his insurance company owned some $14,000,000 of Milwaukee bonds, which had in the main been purchased after the re-

[8] On this topic, the chief sources are the investigations of the Interstate Commerce Commission and the recommendations of Coverdale & Colpitts (Consulting Engineers), referred to above.

[9] This table has been compiled from figures in Borak, *op. cit.*, pp. 516–543 and 708–709 and from sources therein referred to: *Commercial & Financial Chronicle,* vol. cxx, pp. 3062 and 3308, and vol. cxxi, pp. 454, 1903, 2516, and 2269; a pamphlet issued by F. J. Lisman & Co., New York, *C. M. & St. P. Ry. Co., Analysis.*

ceivership. Jameson's main effort was to block the process of reorganization and to force the courts to set a high upset price, that is, the minimum price for which it could be sold, on the property. This he was not able to do.

On November 22, 1926, the property was sold for $140,000,000, subject to the undisturbed mortages, to the company organized under the Kuhn, Loeb & Co. modified plan. The dissenting bondholders were now given an opportunity to deposit their bonds. On January 19, 1927, the court approved of the sale, and the property was transferred to the new company.

The income bonds were not to become cumulative until January 1, 1930. Until then the management of the road was to be in the hands of trustees under a plan by which the stockholders deposited their stock with a board of trustees. When the income bonds became cumulative in 1930, the control of the road was returned to the stockholders.

This entire plan of reorganization was based on the supposition that the Milwaukee's troubles were of a temporary nature and that the only thing needed was time. The reorganization managers believed that, given sufficient time, the traffic of the road would increase until the Milwaukee would be in a strong position financially. Therefore, they devised this plan, which would leave the road until 1930 with very low fixed charges and no cumulative charges. Even though the income bonds became cumulative, the income bondholders could not insist on another receivership until the year 2000, when the bonds would become due.

Table 7. SUMMARY OF RECAPITALIZATION PLANS

	Old capitalization	First Kuhn, Loeb	Roosevelt	Modified Kuhn, Loeb
Undisturbed obligations	$181,370,400	$181,370,400	$181,370,400	$181,370,400
Notes	57,200,000	...	...	...
Bonds to be exchanged	230,950,796	...	...	...
Fixed interest bonds:				
Issued in connection with assessment of preferred stock	...	27,823,656	...	27,823,656
Issued in connection with assessment of common stock	...	32,875,164	...	32,875,164
Issued with new adjustment mortgage bonds in exchange for:				
Old bonds	...	...	57,737,699	46,190,160
Government notes	...	...	50,000,000	...
Adjustment mortgage bonds to be issued for:				
Old bonds	...	230,950,796	173,213,097	184,760,640
Assessment of common and preferred stock	...	...	23,334,320	...
Preferred stock	115,931,900	115,931,900	115,931,900	115,931,900
Common stock	117,411,300	117,411,300	117,411,300	117,411,300
Total capitalization	$702,864,396	$706,363,216	$718,998,716	$706,363,220
Charges:				
Total fixed	$21,836,793	$11,466,845	$12,991,412	$13,776,353
If earned:				
Adjustment mortgage bonds	...	11,547,540	9,827,371	9,238,032
Preferred stock	8,115,233	5,796,596	5,796,595	5,796,595

It is interesting to observe that in 1926 the receivers launched a national advertising campaign for the road, the apparent purpose of which was to encourage settlement, develop traffic, and spread information, generally, concerning the region served by the Company. There is reason to believe that this advertising was intended to impress the investing public in order to facilitate reorganization.

11. After the Reorganization of 1928

Reorganization did not solve the problems of the Milwaukee. Its unfortunate experience in the years that followed is illustrated by Table 8.[10]

The reorganization of 1928 proved not to be sufficiently drastic to meet the difficult 'thirties. In the first two years after reorganization the road earned fixed charges, but in no year since 1930 have those charges been covered. The road's income has suffered from the general depression, from the loss of the export grain market, from several years of extreme drought in its area, and from the increasing competition of motor transport. The road has been kept in good physical condition, but it has borrowed from the federal government. At the end of November, 1938, current liabilities of the Company were $68,767,062, current assets were $26,470,935, while cash on hand totaled $12,933,991.[11] On October 1, 1938, accumulated interest on adjustment bonds, beginning January 1, 1930, amounted to 43½ per cent.

By 1935 the finances of the Company were in a serious way. In June the road was given permission to reorganize; and on July 1 it defaulted on interest on its general mortgage bonds. After consultation with the Reconstruction Finance Corporation and representatives of the bondholders, the directors accepted a plan of reorganization. The Federal Court appointed trustees, including President Scandrett, to manage the road, and the I. C. C. took the reorganization plan under consideration.[12] The proposals made were substantially as follows: [13]

"The $138,000,000 of general mortgage bonds, now bearing interest at from 3½ to 4¾

[10] From *Poor's Railroads* and from the annual reports of the railroad. The items for 1926–29 in the last two categories differ slightly from those for 1930–38, but the effect on the total is very small.

[11] *Standard Corporation Records,* vol. xvii, no. 3778, sec. 7 (Feb. 7, 1939), "Chicago, Milwaukee, St. Paul & Pacific R. R. Co."

[12] *New York Times,* June 28 and 30, and Dec. 31, 1935.

[13] *Ibid.,* June 15, 1935, p. 21.

Table 8. FIGURES FROM INCOME STATEMENTS OF THE MILWAUKEE, 1926–38

Year	Net railway operating income	Gross income	Available for fixed charges	Total fixed charges
1926	$18,394,933	$19,656,082	$19,421,239	$21,820,281
1927	14,072,934	15,407,745	15,241,336	21,561,613
1928	29,027,055	31,771,061	31,598,516	22,336,555
1929	26,274,323	30,361,574	30,205,619	23,151,604
1930	15,954,547	19,174,964	19,049,917	23,917,846
1931	8,334,406	10,419,432	10,336,507	24,149,267
1932	−518,117 [a]	1,001,012	906,187	24,175,865
1933	8,597,320	9,862,270	9,763,726	24,175,867
1934	6,539,054	7,941,063	7,852,135	24,099,756
1935	4,723,983	6,122,334	6,035,714	24,044,462
1936	9,461,358	10,920,938	10,851,331	24,047,440
1937	8,790,661	9,925,302	9,824,734	24,046,005
1938	5,274,539	6,203,350	6,101,866	24,098,136

[a] Deficit indicated by minus sign.

per cent, would have one-third of their interest placed on a contingent basis for a period of years. . . .

"The $106,395,000 of 5 per cent Series A mortgage bonds would become 5 per cent income bonds. The holders of the general mortgage and Series A bonds, which, except for underlying bonds, would be the only ones to survive the reorganization, would control the company as long as interest was in arrears.

"The $182,873,000 of adjustment 5 per cent bonds would be converted into new 5 per cent, voting, $25 par, non-cumulative, preferred stock participating equally in dividends with the common stock after the common dividends reached 5 per cent in any one year.

"Each present $100 par 5 per cent, voting, non-cumulative preferred share would receive one new $25 par preferred share. One new $25 par common share would be exchanged for every three present shares of no-par stock."

No decision has yet (March, 1939) been reached on reorganization. Hearings before the I. C. C. ended on September 20, 1937, without any decision. Commissioner Porter said that, since there was no assurance that either the debtors or the creditors would present a bona fide plan, the Commission would examine the record and see whether it could write a plan or dismiss the case and let the creditors take appropriate legal action. The counsel for the institutional bondholders' committee held that the I. C. C. had no authority to write a plan since there was no plan officially before the commission; the Milwaukee management had withdrawn its support of the 1935 tentative plan and the institutional bondholders would not support it.[14] President Scandrett of the road asked for adjournment for 120 days to enable the debtors and bondholders to revise the 1935 plan to fit 1937 conditions. He maintained that revenues were not up to expectations and expenses were higher than estimated, so that the pending plan was risky, especially since the Brotherhoods were pressing for increased wages. The chairman of the debtors' reorganization committee held that it would be rash and unintelligent to attempt to predicate a plan at that time upon the belief that the necessary additional revenues would be provided, and that any plan predicated upon today's earnings would do great violence to all classes of the road's securities.

On pressure from the management and petition of a group of institutional investors, which held about $80,000,000 of the securities of the road, the I. C. C. ordered a reopening of the hearings to take place in February, 1938. During the following summer a proposal was made by the preferred stockholders of the Milwaukee and the common stockholders of the Chicago & Northwestern, also in bankruptcy, for a merger of the two roads, in the expectation that resulting savings would be considerable.[15] In November M. S. Jameson, examiner for the Commission, proposed the complete wiping-out of $117,000,000 of common stock and the eventual changing of preferred to common. Other adjustments were also proposed which, together with the cancellation of the common stock, would bring the total capitalization down from $857,634,977 to $631,010,668, of which $105,895,179 would be fixed interest debt.[16] Under this plan initial fixed interest charges would amount to $3,864,600. The latest development has been the refusal (January 21, 1939) of the I. C. C. to reopen reorganization proceedings to consider a plan for the consolidation of the Milwaukee and the Northwestern.

12. Suggested Readings

An excellent short article on the road is A. M. Borak, "The Chicago, Milwaukee, and St. Paul Railroad: Recent History of the Last Transcontinental," *Journal of*

[14] *Railway Age,* Sept. 15, 1937, p. 426.

[15] *New York Times,* Feb. 5, March 1, 17, 22, 23, July 16, and Aug. 17, 1938.

[16] *Ibid.,* Nov. 6, 1938; *Standard Corporation Records, loc. cit.*

Economic and Business History, vol. iii (1930–31), pp. 81–117.

On the general history of railroad finance in the United States see Frederick A. Cleveland and Fred Wilbur Powell, *Railroad Finance* (New York, 1923).

On the early history of the Milwaukee only one printed book is worth consideration, John W. Cary, *The Organization and History of the Chicago, Milwaukee & St. Paul Railway Company* (Milwaukee, 1892). The author, a general counsel of the railroad, was primarily concerned with how the road acquired its property. A sensational attack on the policies of the Milwaukee is Max Lowenthal, *The Investor Pays* (New York, 1933).

13. Suggested Questions

1. What different classes of people were concerned with the building of the early lines? What rewards did they expect?
2. What were the actual influences that caused the Milwaukee to build to the Coast? What other courses were open to the railroad?
3. What were the basic causes of the Milwaukee's troubles?
4. Would a federal government planning bureau have advised going through to the Coast?
5. What should the reorganization of 1928 have attempted to accomplish? How could this have been done?
6. What is the present financial condition of the road?
7. Are industrial or financial capitalists responsible for the present condition of the railroad?

XXVIII. DENNISON MANUFACTURING COMPANY, 1844–1938

1. General Statement

The history of the Dennison Manufacturing Co. illustrates many of the typical features of industrial development in the United States. Starting on a small scale as a household enterprise, the concern, through expanding its market at home and abroad and increasing the range of its products, has grown into a highly mechanized factory. Outstanding features of Dennison history have been the stress upon growth from within, the response of the enterprise to the changing phases of the business cycle, the readiness of the management to consider new ideas, whether in the field of merchandising or of personnel policy, and the conscious study of their own history and the candor with which they express their own problems.[1]

2. Dennison Chronology

1844	Andrew Dennison began to manufacture jewelers' boxes.
1855	Sold business to his son Eliphalet.
1858	Started manufacture of merchandise tags.
1863	Partnership formed. Patent for a shipping tag acquired.
1868	Store opened in Chicago.
1875	Foreign selling begun.
1878	Incorporation and adoption of plan for the sale of stock to executives.
1879	Factory purchased at Roxbury.
1881	Began to emphasize products for homecraft work.
1890	Sales to commercial consumers broadened.
1892	Capitalization reached $1,000,000.
1897	Factory at Framingham opened.
1897–1900	Manufacturing centralized at Framingham.
1901	Advertising man employed.
1906	Merchandising committees established.

[1] The material for this case was taken from material in the archives of the Company, from articles in the *Journal of Economic and Business History,* "History of the Dennison Manufacturing Company," by E. P. Hayes, vol. i (1928–29), pp. 467–502, and "History of the Dennison Manufacturing Company—II," by Charlotte Heath, vol. ii (1929–30), pp. 163–202, and from interviews generously given by officials of the Company.

1909	Marketing, management, and all general office work concentrated at Framingham.
1911	Industrial partnership plan adopted.
1912	New stress on foreign market.
1916	Office of employment manager created and consolidation at Framingham completed.
1919	Employees' committee set up.
1920	Business historian appointed.
1922	A box factory established at Marlboro.
1924	Factory established in England.
1930	Factory established in Canada. Selling organization made regional.
1932	Box division reorganized. Company sustained net loss of $481,184.
1934	Year ended with over $1,000,000 in cash but nearly $900,000 owing on debenture stock and cumulative preferred.
1939	Recapitalization plan adopted.

3. Beginnings of the Dennison Enterprise, 1844–74

In 1844 Andrew Dennison of Brunswick, Maine, began to make jewelers' boxes as a home industry. Dennison was a shoemaker by trade, but the making of shoes no longer afforded him a livelihood. He had four children, two daughters at home and two sons. One son, Aaron, was a successful jeweler in Boston. Observing that the delivery of French jewelers' boxes was slow and uncertain, he took some materials and boxes, as samples, to his father and sisters. They began to make boxes, for which Aaron secured orders from jewelers in Boston and New York. It may have been significant for the new enterprise that Aaron Dennison went into watchmaking; he started and carried on in Roxbury an enterprise for the manufacture of watches on the principle of interchangeable parts, which under his leadership laid the foundation for the Waltham Watch Co.

For about five years Andrew Dennison's business remained a home industry. A variety of boxes was made, French and German samples being imitated. A high quality was insisted on by the father. At first he sold his product at cost, including freight, plus 20 per cent. The 20 per cent was later about doubled.

Two major problems arose in those early years: it proved difficult to secure proper materials at reasonable cost, and it was found unsatisfactory to fill small orders for such a large variety of boxes. The other son, Eliphalet Whorf, solved these problems by taking over purchasing and marketing in the fall of 1849. Eliphalet had a record of failure in the jewelry business—his father said he "suffers his outgoes to exceed his income." But Eliphalet was the right man for that particular work at that time. He was an expansionist, willing to take risks in order to build a bigger business, and he was an excellent salesman. The discovery of gold in California ushered in a period of great expansion—a time when credit was easy and market opportunities were great. After 1850 Eliphalet Dennison dominated the business for about thirty years.

Eliphalet was on the alert to find new products; besides boxes, the Dennisons were soon selling tissue paper, cards, fine cotton, and tags. The business grew and an office was opened in New York. The son found it difficult to fill increasing orders; he lost some orders because of the time required to fill them from Brunswick. He, therefore, urged his father to move to Roxbury, near Boston, but the latter would not leave Brunswick. The outcome was that in 1855 Eliphalet bought the business, paying $9,000 for it (apparently mostly on credit).

Little is known of the business from 1855 to 1863. A box factory was established in Boston. In 1858 merchandise tags, other than jewelers', were launched —the eyes were cut by a machine, and the tags were sent to Matilda Dennison to be given out to families in Brunswick for stringing. The business of a New York tag importer was also bought. Tags were destined to become the most important product of the enterprise.

In 1863 came two significant developments in the business. Evidently because he was in financial need, Dennison took three partners into his business. The total original capital was $23,834.38; Dennison's share was valued at $15,540.02, and the three new partners supplied the remainder.

The formation of the partnership and the tag patent, together with favorable conditions resulting from the Civil War, definitely established the Dennisons on a firm basis. For 22 months after the partnership had been formed, profits were the equivalent of 125 per cent of capital per year. From 1863 to 1875 the business expanded rapidly. In 1868, sales totaled $238,000; by 1874 they amounted to $427,000 for the year.

During this period new items continued to be added. These included die-stamped boxes, gummed labels, sealing wax, and colored tissue paper. In 1863 a part of the box manufacturing was returned to Brunswick where it was carried out under the supervision of Matilda Dennison. In those years manufacturing was also carried on in Boston, Newtonville, and Falmouth, and in the Chicago and New York branch stores.

Expansion brought new problems. Other manufacturers offered serious competition not long after the close of the war. They made cheaper grades of tags which appealed to large commercial consumers. The Dennison firm tried to meet competition by buying out competitors—this practice was discontinued when it was found that competitors entered the field to sell out to Dennison's—and by introducing a line of cheaper tags.

The selling of Dennison products reached in this period into the South and West. Several additional branch offices were therefore established: in Philadelphia in 1862, Chicago in 1868, Cincinnati in 1871, and St. Louis in 1873. By 1870 jobbers and printers, receiving a discount of 40 per cent if true wholesalers, were the principal agents for distributing Dennison goods to retailers and consumers. But these dealers did not push satisfactorily the five or six hundred varieties of stationers' goods which Dennison was making, and they would not carry a full line. Dennison's, therefore, began to do some of the selling itself. This attempt at integration aroused the other distributors, and the agreement of Dennison to prepare in Cincinnati "more fully to filter our manufactures through sellers" shows that it was not ready to fight established distributing agencies.

At the beginning of 1875 E. W. Dennison could look back over 25 years of successful business. He found the reasons for that success in part in the policies which his concern had followed:

> "In the first place we have pursued a policy of protecting the seller of the goods, and thus securing their cooperation. This has been very valuable. Next we have as a rule made good goods and especially adapted to the uses to be put to. Next we have been prompt in all business relations. We have systematized many little usefuls of scattered sale but important in the aggregate, but which we could have made but little headway upon without the system that has done more than all other to enable us to attain and hold our position—and now I refer to the system of having our full assortment represented in the principal markets of the union and thus bringing these little usefuls within the reach of the consumers of them. While by this means our expenses have been largely increased I have but to cite the fact that each branch has been more than self-sustaining and we have been enabled by their means to check all formidable competition."

4. Developments under Rapidly Changing Conditions, 1875–97

Competition was clearly becoming a problem for the Dennisons in the early 'seventies. Business conditions following the panic of 1873 aggravated that problem. For the next quarter-century there was a general drop in the price level. Dennison's, depending on a wide variety of consumers, had to adjust itself to declining prices.

The full effects of the panic were felt in 1875 when, for the first time since E. W. Dennison had taken over the business, total sales were less than those of the preceding year. In 1877, however, sales again reached a new high mark. From then on, except in 1884, 1893, and 1896, the trend of dollar volume was upward. The increase for 1878–98 was almost fourfold. The increase over those 20 years was, however, neither rapid nor extreme. Compared with some other lines, the Dennison business experienced a relatively conservative expansion.

It would be reasonable to expect that, even with an increasing volume of dollar sales, it would be difficult to maintain profits under the pressure of a declining price level. Profits did not rise nearly so rapidly nor so far as sales; nevertheless, profits were considerable. The average net profit on sales for 1878–98 was 14.1 per cent.

A. Marketing.

Prior to 1875 Dennison's had set up a sales organization which covered the whole United States and reached into Canada and Cuba. Six sales territories of varying size, centered in six cities, had been established. Each of these had a branch store which served as headquarters for salesmen, a stock depot, and a store principally for wholesale purposes but also reaching out into retailing. The Cincinnati branch store was opened in 1871 and dropped in 1898, and during that time San Francisco was added. Within these territorial divisions the sales organization continued to develop along the same lines as in the earlier period.

As has generally been true of American business which has tended to outgrow a profitable market at home, Dennison's in this period reached out for a larger foreign market. Central and South America were invaded before 1890 with some success. An examination of the possibilities in England in the years 1875–78 led to making a London stationer, from whom Dennison's had bought parchment, its sales agent. A canvass of the English jewelers' trade by young C. S. Dennison in the early 'eighties showed that that market was inaccessible. The London stationer proved to be an unsatisfactory sales agent, and a small wholesale store was set up in London. It was soon learned, however, that the English market wanted cheaper goods. In 1886 the business was again turned over to the earlier agent, who made tags on a Dennison machine and sold them on a royalty basis. One new product was especially designed for the English market —wooden boxes for the parcel post.

Of all the divisions of Dennison's work at this time, none was more sensitive to changing conditions than merchandising. The two dominating individuals in this period were E. W. Dennison and H. K. Dyer, both essentially salesmen. They had a keen feeling for what the market would take, and at what prices.

Concerning price policy in this period we have only scattered items of information. Old lines felt competition most severely. As patents expired and as competitors raised the quality of their products into Dennison's class, the latter's advantage became smaller. Dennison's was clearly forced to meet competition in several important lines by cutting prices or introducing cheaper grades of goods. By 1890 it was necessary to reduce the price of tags 12 per cent; later a cheap tag without the Dennison imprint was introduced. Toward the close of 1895 the competition of domestic crepe paper forced a 50 per cent reduction in Dennison imported crepe—this cut brought a great fall in Dennison's profits. In the gummed label market the Company maintained its place by cutting from 75 cents down to 50 cents a carton.

Further evidence of the drive of competition is the fact that local price concessions were made. The manager of the Chicago store succeeded in getting cheaper lines of tags to meet a highly competitive local situation. Salesmen were even given authority to make their own prices to get orders. It is significant that, on the whole, pricing was in this period controlled by the selling rather than the producing end of the business. Only on less competitive items was the factory management allowed to increase prices to protect itself.

As patents began to expire and as competition became more intense in the late 'eighties and 'nineties, advertising received greater emphasis. For a time Dennison's advertised in city and town directories; it appealed to the home consumer in such periodicals as the *Ladies' Home Journal* and *The Youth's Companion;* it had a booth display at the Chicago World's Fair. For the years 1892 to 1897 expenditures for advertising averaged slightly less than 1 per cent of sales.

It was in the introduction of new items and in meeting new sources of demand that Dennison's did especially effective work in those years.

Despite effective competition in the jewelers' line, the introduction of new styles of boxes and cases and additional findings obviated the necessity for sweeping price reductions in this branch of the business. New items in other lines also helped save the day. Paper napkins proved highly profitable. Imported crepe paper, introduced about 1890, did much to hold up the business in the middle 'nineties—Dennison's began to make crepe in 1897. Glues and paste were also added, as well as additional colors of old items. The only noticeably unsuccessful new product, wooden boxes for the British parcel post, was soon dropped.

In the early 'eighties Dennison's began to build up a market among home consumers. A most significant step was the introduction of materials for homecraft work. In 1881 came colored tissue paper for art work and sealing wax in 20 colors. A pamphlet, *The Art of Sealing a Letter,* was launched. Crepe paper and paper napkins also appealed to the home consumer. The development of products for the home consumer altered the character of Dennison stores. With the establishment of art departments in the 'eighties, and later with the use of demonstrators, the stores began gradually to lose their wholesale character, and by about 1910 they had become essentially the retail centers which they are today.

Dennison's also broadened out among commercial buyers of their products. Until about 1890 sales had been largely to wholesale and retail stationers and jewelers—dealers, as Dennison's called them. At that time the firm undertook to canvass manufacturers, shippers, and the like—those Dennison's called consumers as distinguished from dealers. This development changed the selling organization radically. The number of salesmen was greatly increased. The canvass of consumers was pushed. There came within each selling territory specialization among salesmen as to both area and type of customer.

B. Production.

Production was in this period clearly dominated by selling. This was partly a result of personality within the organization and partly the result of market conditions.

One characteristic of production was the gradual movement toward concentration in one place. By 1885 all stationers' items except sealing wax were made in the Company's plant at Roxbury, purchased in 1879. Because of inadequate labor at Brunswick, box manufacture was transferred to Brooklyn and Roxbury. Some manufacturing was still done in connection with the Chicago and St. Louis stores. In 1896–97, since trucking had become so expensive at Roxbury, a new plant was secured in Framingham where excellent railroad connections were available. About 1905 the Company began to ship large orders from Framingham, and in 1910 to ship practically all business direct from Framingham, except retail stock.

From the apparently low expenditures on machinery [2] it would seem that manufacturing policy as regards machinery was decidedly non-progressive; the machinery investment would seem to have been kept at a minimum throughout this period. In 1883 the investment in machinery was said to have been $111,000—by 1892, only $92,000. This failure to provide for expansion may have been more apparent than real, for there is reason to believe that a great deal of machinery was charged to expense in those days.

On the whole, the management at Roxbury was not progressive. There were individual attempts at improvement. Some office improvement was started in 1881. In 1887 purchasing was put under C. S. Dennison, but it was on a hand-to-mouth, rather than a scientific, basis. The factory was reluctant to try new lower-cost materials—there was no real record of costs—and production costs were pounded down only as forced by the marketing end. It seems that the dictation of policies by the selling end was demoralizing to factory personnel.

C. Organization and control.

The Dennison business was incorporated in 1878. The capital stock of $150,000 was so divided that E. W. Dennison and his son, H. B., held two-thirds, and Metcalf, one of the original partners, one-third. Provision was made for giving stock, out of profits, to principal young executives at the discretion of the directors. Under this provision C. S. Dennison, another son of E. W., and H. K. Dyer were admitted to the firm, together with several men of less importance. It is significant that on the death of E. W. Dennison in 1886 his stock was offered to 13 men, 2 of whom were in the production and 11 in the selling end of the business.

It is clear that the marketing group dominated the firm in this period, both in numbers and in strength of personality. Two men stood above the others in their influence: E. W. Dennison, who gave up the presidency in 1885 and died in 1886; and Dyer, head of the New York office, who became treasurer in 1885 and president in 1892. Both were strong on merchandising and selling. E. W. insisted on a quality product. Dyer was rough in manner, a strong driver of his employees, and very much of an individualist.

A few points from the financial history of the firm reveal something of its financial policy. The capital stock was increased out of profits from the original $150,000 in 1878 to $1,000,000 in 1892. In 1883 and 1890, 100 per cent stock dividends were declared and in 1891, almost 28 per cent. In addition to stock dividends the shareholders received considerable cash or credit dividends. Between 1879 and 1893, inclusive, the lowest dividend paid was 10 per cent (1884) and the highest 35 per cent (1885), while the most common was 20 per cent. Improvements were paid out of profits. A heavy internal debt was acquired in the 'eighties by the fact that shareholders left a part of their dividends with the firm at 6 per cent interest. By 1886 this amounted to $520,000, or more than the capital stock. Apparently under the influence of Dyer, this debt was cleared up by 1893. In its place came a small surplus, known as the Treasurer's Trust Account. For the years 1878–98, on the original capital of the concern was paid a cash dividend of $2,781,000 and a stock dividend of $850,000; and a surplus of $270,000 was created, making a total gain of about $3,900,000 for 20 years. So strong was the firm's financial standing that its stock of $1,000,000 in 1898 was worth from $250 to $300 a share.

It was the firm's policy to pay good wages to its executives. In 1878 the presi-

[2] See Table 3, pp. 459–460.

dent and treasurer received $8,000 and $5,000 annually; and in 1890, $20,000 each; the salaries were again raised in 1895. Lower executives were similarly raised throughout the period.

5. New Developments in Organization and Policy, 1898–1920

Reflecting generally prosperous business conditions, Dennison sales increased rapidly in those years. In 1900 the two-million-dollar mark was passed; in 1910 the five-million-dollar mark; during the World War years there was an abnormal growth which brought sales to the high point of $14,500,000 in 1920. The increase in sales was paralleled by an increase in profits.

The rapid growth of sales put a heavy strain on management. The larger business put a heavier burden on all departments, necessitating considerable reorganization. Production in particular, which had been neglected in the earlier period, presented many problems. It also became necessary to bring about a closer coördination of the various functional divisions of the Company.

Perhaps because production became very important in this period, and doubtless because the strongest leadership lay in the producing end of the business, the coördination of functions came to be centered in Framingham, which was also the center of manufacturing operations.

The years 1898–1920 will be considered under five heads: production, sales organization and methods, merchandising, labor policy, and reorganization.

A. Strengthening production.

The rapid expansion of sales in 1898 to 1920 revealed the weaknesses of factory production, and attention was necessarily turned to that side of the business. One result was the continuation of the policy of centralizing manufacture at Framingham. In 1900 the manufacturing operations in Brooklyn were transferred to the new factory at Framingham. But a certain amount of manufacturing was still being done at some of the branch stores; because of labor shortage at Framingham, box manufacture had to be done at Roxbury; and in 1901, owing to the growing pressure of business, the manufacture of jewelers' boxes was discontinued at Framingham in favor of Philadelphia, New York, and Chicago.

In 1906, however, an investigation of the manufacturing carried on at the branch stores indicated no advantage to the organization as a whole in this arrangement. Indeed, the different accounting methods used, which make comparison difficult, the variations in policy and in quality of product, and the additional overhead costs involved in maintaining several plants were all obvious disadvantages. By 1912 practically all of the work done at these shops had been transferred to Framingham. Labor difficulties, however, continued to make necessary the carrying-on of some manufacturing processes at other points.

It has already been pointed out that the machinery investment of the Dennison plant was very low during the 'nineties. With the opening of the factory in Framingham this figure naturally rose. Shortly after 1900 the growth, especially, of the shipping-tag market made apparent the necessity for new and increased equipment. The box-making equipment was also modernized; and by 1906 there had been an increase in the machinery investment of more than 300 per cent over the 1897 figure. From then until 1915 the increase continued to bear a normal relationship to the growing volume of business. Then rising prices began to curtail additions, and by 1918 the ratio of machinery to total assets was lower than at any time since 1897. As business continued to increase, however, it became necessary to contract for a new building and new equipment, even though it was recognized that prices were abnormally high. The pressure on production during these years also stimulated the substitution of machinery for hand processes.

Even more important than changes in equipment and location were the changes in factory management around 1900. The long stress on the selling end of the business up to the end of the century had resulted in a slump in ability and efficiency at the factory. With the rapid increase in business after 1898 this situation soon became apparent, and in 1901 an outside expert started an investigation of the factory. Largely at his instigation, a number of innovations were introduced. A finished goods department and a raw materials department were created to give a better control over inventory. An improved method was also introduced of adding factory expenses as a fixed contingency charge to the costs of products as charged to the branch stores. While this was largely a matter of bookkeeping, the change did shift a measure of control from the branches to the factory.

It is easy to see that a marked change in emphasis had occurred in the Dennison organization. The expert's investigation in 1901 had revealed to the directors their error in neglecting the factory. Dyer, who had become president in 1892, now gave the factory superintendent greatly increased authority. C. S. Dennison and his nephew H. S. Dennison (son of H. B.) also worked to strengthen the position of the factory. In 1906 H. S. Dennison became works manager. During the early 1900's there were also several changes in the board of directors, the men who came in being more sympathetic to the new régime. In 1906 Dyer resigned, and the control of the organization definitely passed to the manufacturing side.

Between 1910 and 1919 followed other important changes. The process of centralization at Framingham then received increased emphasis, and the stress on management was reflected in the establishment of a research department, a methods department, and a planning department, as well as in increasing functionalization and divisional control.

In 1910 serious attention was turned to the purchasing department, whose policies had up to that time been rather casual. About two years later one of the younger executives was put in charge of the department, and he proceeded to centralize the buying as well as to collect more accurate purchasing information, to spread Dennison purchases in order to avoid too much dependence on a few sources of supply, and to build up goodwill. All this was of vital importance to the factory a few years later, when the World War had broken up many normal trade relations and the securing of supplies in the face of a chaotic raw material market became a very difficult problem.

In 1917 H. S. Dennison became president; and this, with the appointment of two more factory men as directors and in 1920 of the works manager to a similar position, made even more nearly complete the factory's control of the organization. By this time the situation which had prevailed at the beginning of the century was completely reversed: the factory now dominated to as great a degree as the selling organization had at the earlier date. This was all the more true because not only had production activities been concentrated at Framingham but much had been done toward the centralization there of merchandising and marketing functions as well.

B. Selling organization and methods.

The selling organization that had been built up in the early period, when sales were by no means easy, stood the Dennison enterprise in good stead when business began its rapid increase at the turn of the century. The increase made necessary a larger sales force and the opening of many new sales offices. This movement was accentuated by a further stress on the canvass of consumers. By 1906 local or "sample" offices had been established in 22 cities. This development led during 1909–10 to a reorganization of the selling end of the Dennison enterprise. Instead of the former five branch offices, which covered all Dennison sales territory, the country was now broken up into about thirty districts, controlled by four sales managers located at Framingham. The selling staff was almost doubled. The practice had already been established of shipping orders directly from factory to customer rather than through the branch where the order had originated. Many of the branch managers naturally opposed these rather radical changes, but the policies were adopted nevertheless. The branch offices became largely retail stores, while general control of sales was centralized at Framingham. Within the sales districts there was an increasing tendency toward specialization by merchandise lines and by classes of customers. Moreover, in this period Dennison departments began to be established by dealers in their stationery stores.

Meanwhile the increased staff and the emphasis upon consumer sales involved at least a partial abandonment of jobbers and wholesalers, upon whom complete dependence had once been placed. This shift was a part of the general movement toward the elimination of the middleman. It was especially marked in the East; the western offices, with greater distances to cover, were more inclined to continue their dependence on the wholesaler. The geographic difference made itself felt particularly in pricing, which assumed great importance because of the keen competition of the period. This matter will be more fully discussed below.

Reference has already been made to attempts to cultivate the foreign market. In 1912 the Dennison Manufacturing Co., Ltd., was established in London with a store designed to handle both retail and wholesale trade in the British Isles as well as the export business to western Europe. It was found, however, that the former London agent still had the legal right to sell tags under the Dennison name; both he and Dennison's, therefore, continued in the market. In 1912 and the following year, offices were opened by the parent company in Mexico City and Buenos Aires, and a company was incorporated in Berlin. The outbreak of war upset the European market, but new possibilities were cultivated in the West Indies and South America.

An important phase of marketing development in the period from 1898 to 1920 was in the field of advertising. Expenditures for advertising had previously not been large, but partly in order to meet keen competition, especially in the field of crepe, increased appropriations were now made for advertising. In 1901 they amounted to $23,000; by 1906 the figure was $136,000, a sum not to be equaled again during the period. At the same time that increasing amounts began to be expended in this way, a man was hired to give his entire time to advertising, thus coördinating the work which had hitherto been done by store managers. For several years the services of an advertising agency were also employed, but in 1910 the management began to handle its own advertising. In 1908 and 1914, in the face of depressed business conditions, the advertising appropriations were reduced. But during the World War years the rush of business brought home to the administration the desirability of keeping advertising expenditures at a minimum when the volume of business was large, and of increasing that expenditure at times when such a stimulus to business was more necessary.

In 1917 advertising was put on what was called the five-year plan, the arrangements being made for about five years in advance. It was thought that no shorter period furnished an adequate test of success or failure. At about this time, too, the Company again employed an advertising agency to draft the general features of the plan.

C. Developments in merchandising.

In the Dennison organization merchandising has been differentiated from selling as that function which determines the products which are to be sold. This differentiation first became clearly marked in 1906 with the establishment of merchandising committees, a step which had long been under consideration. Six committees were set up, one for each of the six "lines" into which Dennison products were divided: tags, crepe, jewelers' items, adhesives, Christmas items, and consumers' items. Each committee consisted of one or more directors, a chairman who was either store manager or sales manager, several salesmen, and one or two factory men. At first the committees met but once a year, and the chairmen continued to devote most of their attention to sales. But the establishment of these committees constituted one of the most important landmarks in Dennison history, because it did much to harmonize the interests of factory and sales organization and to centralize the control over both. By 1909 the importance of these committees was becoming clear; also in that year two factory men became committee chairmen. By 1911 all the committee chairmen were located at Framingham and were devoting their entire attention to merchandising activities—the planning of new items, fixing price bases, watching production of their items—and making them known to salesmen. These chairmen, of course, also traveled extensively through the sales districts. In 1917 a general merchandise committee was formed, composed of a chairman who had both selling and merchandising experience, the chairmen of the merchandise committees, the purchasing agent, and the works manager. The merchandising committee not only was a clearing house for the different merchandising functions; in reality it coördinated production and selling and provided, theoretically, for keeping the different lines well balanced in relation to the business as a whole.

The increased attention to advertising did much to build up sales, but perhaps equally important were the efforts of the merchandising section in making changes to meet new conditions. At the beginning of the century, shipping tags, boxes, and crepe paper were among the chief items in Dennison sales. The keen competition of the 1890's, as has been noted, had made necessary some price reductions, particularly in the West, and had brought about the introduction of some cheaper lines. This situation carried over into the twentieth century. Some reference has already been made to differences which arose between the eastern and the western sales organizations in this period. The eastern salesmen laid their chief stress on intensive canvass of buyers; the western salesmen, still largely dependent on wholesalers and jobbers, pressed for the introduction of cheaper lines which would appeal to their wholesale trade. This demand was met in crepe paper by giving the western trade a cheaper grade. But difficulties immediately arose in the East, where the cheap paper was not offered. The same question of price arose in regard to shipping tags, another field where competition was very keen. For a time some sales in this field were made at a loss, which was charged to advertising. The price question was not so serious at that time in connection with napkins. The demand for a cheaper grade was met by the purchase of such napkins from another manufacturer. The establishment of the merchandising committees, however, with their tendency to harmonize the needs and demands of the manufacturing and selling sections, helped to solve these price difficulties; and, long before the end of this period, uniform prices had been established for all parts of the country.

Boxes also presented a merchandising problem. Reference has already been made to special difficulties in the production of this item. The increasing volume of sales in the early part of the century made the problem even more serious. Some cheap boxes were bought from other manufacturers, and some boxes were imported, but eventually the merchandisers recognized the importance of the fact that orders for boxes came with a rush every fall, with a slump during the rest of the year. Stress was then placed on securing a more even flow of orders, thus reducing the seasonal fluctuation in labor and production demands.

Several new Dennison products were introduced during this period or assumed greatly increased importance in sales. Crepe paper, production of which had begun before the panic of 1893, rapidly came to the front, especially after the introduction in 1914 of a new and improved quality which sold well not only in the United States but particularly in the foreign market. When the World War brought about a stress on essential products, an attempt was made by the merchandising department to bring the crepe line within this category by introducing a line of paper bandages and surgical pads. Though the War did not last long enough to establish this line permanently, the buying epidemic following the War brought the crepe line fully into its own.

About 1900 a line of Christmas merchandise began to be pushed with considerable success, though it never became so important as crepe. Later, goods for other holidays, especially Hallowe'en, were added to the line. The War put a temporary stop to the development of these goods, but afterwards sales rose rapidly.

As for shipping tags, which had been a major Dennison product since 1863, special stress began to be placed about 1900 on quality, both in material and in printing. This continued to such an extent that the field for cheaper tags was left largely to Dennison competitors, in spite of the price concessions made for a time, especially to the western sales organization. On the other hand, Dennison's retained its major share of the plain tag business, which was with the stationery trade rather than with consumers. In 1917 the profits on shipping tags were 50 per cent greater than for any other single entire line, which seemed to justify the claim that this item then formed "the backbone of the business."

The jewelers' line, with which Andrew Dennison had founded the enterprise, experienced a number of vicissitudes during the period under consideration. Perhaps partly because it was the oldest line there was for a time less stress on innovation than in other fields, thus furnishing competitors an opening. As with other Dennison products, emphasis was placed on quality rather than on price, though cheaper goods were carried to afford an opening with customers who might later be educated to buy the better quality. In 1911 an important step was taken in offering paper boxes to others than jewelers. In 1913 a line was introduced for haberdashers, perfumers, et cetera, and in 1914 a drug-box specialist was employed on the sales staff. It was hoped by these changes to secure a more even flow of orders to the factory. In 1915 there was a heavy loss in jewelry-box sales, and the difficulty of obtaining foreign supplies of cases and trays during the War hindered recovery. In the whole box line the congestion accompanying war conditions resulted in a long-needed standardization of product. The number of box sizes was cut by about half, standard forms were adopted, and interchangeable parts for cases began to be made. The use of machinery was stimulated, even in the making of high-grade boxes, though previously it had always been thought that quality could not be obtained with machine processes.

Among the other Dennison items were wax products and adhesives—passe partout, mucilage, glue, paste, gummed labels and seals, and gummed paper. The greatest difficulty was encountered with gummed paper. The factory, itself a consumer of this item, laid greatest emphasis on sticking quality, while the salesmen wanted paper which could be kept in stock for some time without curling or blocking. This problem dragged throughout the period, not enough pressure being brought on the factory to change its producing methods. After the War, sales of sealing wax increased enormously for several years.

Consumer (business consumers) items in general assumed much greater importance in this period, and a start was made in getting consumers to use Dennison items for advertising purposes. In the years of abnormal business immediately preceding 1920, however, the most important merchandising development was not the introduction of new lines but the cancellation of about fifteen hundred old items, sales of which were no longer important. At the same time attention was being turned to the creation of new items designed to tide over the reaction which was recognized as inevitable.

D. Changing labor policy.

During a time when increased attention was devoted to factory problems of all kinds, labor naturally came in for its share, though the Dennison organization has never had any particularly acute labor problems. The factory investigation of 1901 indicated that labor discipline should be tightened, and efforts were made in this direction. The chronic labor shortage, however, and the strength of the trade unions prevented any very marked change. In 1902, at the request of the employees, there was a reduction in working hours from 58 to 54 per week. In 1911 another reduction, to 51 hours, was voluntarily made by the administration. During these years, too, in accordance both with the general trend in industry and the special stress on management in the Dennison enterprise, personnel policies received considerable attention. A clinic was set up; a lunchroom, restroom, and lending library were established; and recreation facilities, clubs, and a savings fund were introduced. In 1916, in order to centralize employment and personnel management, the office of employment manager was created.

The rapid rise in the cost of living, particularly during the War, caused the wage problem to become acute in the Dennison enterprise as elsewhere throughout the industrial world. The administration, wishing to make only such increase as could be permanently maintained, held back as long as possible. Even so, individual wage increases from 1914 to 1919 averaged 62 per cent. In 1919 a considerable increase was made throughout the plant, and in 1920 a 5 per cent cost-of-living bonus was added, with the understanding that it was temporary, and it was in fact eliminated in 1921.

One of the most important innovations in Dennison labor policy during the period 1898–1920 was the creation in 1919 of the General Works Committee, since called the Employees' Committee. It has already been pointed out that in 1906 H. S. Dennison became works manager; his constant interest in personnel policies played its part as his influence in the Dennison organization mounted. The establishment of the Employees' Committee was the culmination of a prolonged discussion of the best way in which to give the workers a voice in management; it was in itself an outgrowth of a war industries committee of workers. The members of the Employees' Committee, which met once a month, were elected from those below managerial rank in each department. The recommendations of the committee were subject to the approval of the management, the chief function of the committee being to encourage a free interchange of ideas between workers and management.

Within a year the Employees' Committee had demonstrated its usefulness. By 1920 it had made two important contributions to policy. One, a plan for extending profit-sharing to the workers which was accepted by the directors for a five-year trial period, will be more fully described below.

The second contribution of the committee was a plan for minimizing the hardships of irregular employment. This policy had been anticipated in 1916, when management had begun to make provision for an unemployment reserve. Seasonal demand, particularly in the box department, had long created an employment problem for management—layoffs because of seasonal variations often lost to the organization some of its most energetic and skillful workers. The plan which the Employees' Committee helped to formulate provided that a worker who was laid off, though still retained on the Company pay roll, should be paid 80 per cent of his regular wages if he had dependents, 60 per cent if he had none. Before a man was laid off, every effort was to be made to transfer him to another department where employment opportunities existed, any loss in wages to be compensated for up to 90 per cent out of the reserve.

The adoption of these plans, which were designed to give the worker a feeling of security in his job and an interest in the success of the Company, would have been impracticable had not the Dennison organization been operating at that time on a very profitable basis. Sales were on the increase during the whole period and, though selling expenses went up after 1910 owing to changes in the selling organization, net profits were maintained to the end of the period at 10 per cent of sales or more. Even with due attention to the building-up of a reserve, substantial surpluses accumulated. In 1905 the capitalization of the Company was increased to $2,000,000 by the payment of a stock dividend of 100 per cent.

E. Reorganization of the Company and the industrial partnership.

The number of stockholders had increased gradually since incorporation in 1878, but the bulk of the shares was held by sales executives. Since no provision had been made for retaining control within the Company, the retirement or death of original holders gradually left considerable blocks of stock in the hands of outsiders. It became clear that eventually the organization might be controlled by stockholders whose chief interest was in current dividends, a situation directly contrary to the desires of E. W. Dennison when he incorporated the enterprise. In 1906 a certain amount of stock was offered to 15 of the younger executives. But this did not solve the difficulty, and in 1911 C. S. Dennison and his nephew, H. S. Dennison, persuaded the principal stockholders to agree to the organization of a new company. This reincorporation set up the industrial partnership, which was one of the most important innovations in policy during the period under consideration.

As a first step, the existing common stock was all converted into 8 per cent first preferred (later called debenture stock). It was agreed that the earnings in excess of dividend requirements, which had hitherto been distributed from time to time in the form of stock dividends, should henceforth be distributed as industrial partnership stock (later called management stock) to those employees of the Company who had been chiefly responsible for the creation of profits. This group included those who had attained a rank where they undoubtedly could contribute to profits—e. g., principal salesman, foreman, chief clerk, or higher. The industrial partnership stock was to be distributed in proportion to salary, beginning with those who had been with the firm for 7 years and were earning a minimum of $1,200 or for 5 years with a minimum of $1,500. Later variations were designed to stress the managerial factor as a basis for stock distribution, for the plan was considered to be primarily one of management-sharing. It was, of course, found difficult to strike a satisfactory balance between a strictly salary basis and a purely subjective basis for the distribution of stock. The amount of stock distributed in any one year was to depend on the earnings in excess of dividends and reserves during the preceding 12 months. The original stockholders were persuaded to accept this arrangement through the capitalization of the surplus which was already in the treasury as well as $1,000,000 for goodwill, which had hitherto been disregarded on the books.

Since it was part of the policy to share management as well as profits, it was arranged that, when the industrial partnership stock totaled $1,000,000, the voting power of the Company should pass from the first preferred stockholders to the industrial partnership stockholders, who were to continue in control as long as they paid first preferred dividends in full. The industrial partnership stock was made non-transferable, except to and from the Company, in order to ensure the maintenance of control by people actively engaged in the business. In case of death or retirement of a holder, his stock could be exchanged for an equal amount of second preferred stock. Second preferred stock, which was authorized in 1911 to make such exchange possible, bore a return of 7 per cent, was negotiable, and carried no voting power.

The first issue of this new stock was a small amount for cash to 175 employees. The first issue of stock at the end of the first year was for $146,940, one-third the total of the salaries of 198 participants. During the eight years prior to 1920, industrial partnership stock was distributed at an average rate equal to 45 per cent of the managerial salaries. Some of the first preferred stock was bought in during this period. The outstanding capital stock was thus increased from $4,500,000 at the time of incorporation to $5,889,000 at the end of 1919.

Profit-sharing among workers below executive rank had already been reported on unfavorably, the feeling being that such workers had little opportunity to increase profits, and that an annual or semiannual bonus would in any case be ineffective as an incentive. When this question was taken up again in 1919, a different conclusion was reached, and it was agreed to set aside one-third of the surplus profits each year to be distributed in the form of employee industrial partnership stock. The distributions here were based, however, not on earnings but on length of service—it was felt that a worker's influence on profits increased with the length of his employment in the Company. Employee industrial partnership stock did not carry a voting privilege and, being exchangeable for second preferred stock on the death or retirement of a holder, it was not transferable. For 1920 (that is, in 1921), an abnormal year for both sales and profits, $363,000 in stock was distributed to 1,418 newly made employee partners.

The great prosperity of the years 1916–20 was shared by Dennison employees in other ways than through the industrial partnership. On the Company's seventy-fifth anniversary in 1919, more than $66,000 was given to nonpartners in cash; nearly $150,000 for the unemployment reserve; $100,000 for an employee housing fund; and $50,000 for industrial service activities, which amount was later added to the unemployment reserve.

6. Chief Problems, Especially in Marketing, 1920–30

The 1920's were in some respects trying years for Dennison's as for many other business enterprises. From the high point of $14,500,000 in 1920, sales dropped somewhat in 1921 and 1922; this was followed by a recovery, another drop in 1924, and an increase to $16,800,-

000 in 1929. There was a further decrease in sales in 1930. It was impossible during this period to maintain profits at their old level. In no year after 1920 did they reach 10 per cent of sales, a figure which they had steadily exceeded before 1921. Increasing competition, particularly in those lines in which the Company had enjoyed a marked advantage, helped to reduce profit margins.

A. Expansion and decentralization of production.

In 1922, because of the long-standing difficulty in securing skilled labor for this department at Framingham, a box factory was built at Marlboro, Massachusetts. By 1932 all the Dennison boxes were being made there. Tag manufacturing was resumed at Chicago in 1928, the western selling organization still feeling strongly that it required service which was more prompt and better suited to local needs than could be supplied from Framingham.

More important than either of these changes was the opening in 1930 of a new factory at Drummondville, Quebec, to handle the Canadian trade. This factory was built and is being operated by the Dennison Manufacturing Co. of Canada, Ltd. It began by making crepe paper, but other items were soon added, notably shipping tags. The Dennison Manufacturing Co., Ltd., the English subsidiary which was organized in 1912, has had a manufacturing plant in London since 1924. It was the intention, through the development of these two plants, to cultivate more extensively the Dennison market in the British Empire, trading on the "Buy British" movement.

In factory organization the most important changes of the decade 1920–30 were in box-making. It has already been noted that this department lagged behind the enterprise as a whole. Those in charge of the box factory had long maintained that standardized methods and an extensive use of machinery in this field were incompatible with the high quality of the Dennison product. Early in the 1920's, however, new men were placed in the department to introduce more efficient methods, and a survey was made of the whole box division. It was finally decided to treat this as a separate unit in the organization. The box division is now operated quite separately, a policy which is the more feasible, in that most of the box manufacturing is carried on in the Marlboro plant.

In line with the increased emphasis on original investigation in the Dennison organization, a research department established before the War has grown greatly in importance during the decade. More unusual was the creation, at the same time, of the office of business historian.[3] To the historian were entrusted all the historical records of the Dennison enterprise from its inception in 1844. From these records was compiled a history of the Company in manuscript form, which was consulted by the executives or directors of the Company when questions arose as to the policies and practices of the past. For the past few years the policy has been not to write the history in finished form but rather to keep indexed files, from which answers to any questions can readily be secured.

In 1929–30 steps were taken to coordinate the various kinds of research being carried on in the organization through the establishment of a committee on research activities. This committee supervises the work being done in the fields of materials, machinery, merchandising, methods, and markets, and it also prevents duplication of effort and suggests new lines of investigation.

B. A more aggressive marketing organization.

The most important changes which occurred in the Dennison organization in the 1920's were in selling. The foreign

[3] N. S. B. Gras, *Industrial Evolution* (Cambridge, 1930), chap. xiv.

market was further cultivated after the War, not only through the English and Canadian companies but also through the development of exports to South America and the Continent of Europe. Sales in these areas were made partly by men sent out from the head office and partly by local men appointed as agents and salesmen.

Dennison orders have for many years been classified as A, B, or C. "A" orders are those from jewelers and all orders for boxes from any trade. "B" orders include orders from wholesalers, except jewelers, from retailers for resale (as, for example, to stationery stores and the stationery departments of department stores), and from printing establishments and crepe novelty manufacturers. "C" orders are those from consumers and from wholesalers and dealers for consumption, for example, orders for shipping tags and labels used by manufacturers and by the supply departments of department and other stores.

In 1930 the Dennison selling organization was completely altered. As a result of the business depression a good deal of stress was laid by the selling organization on increased service and promptness in the handling of orders. With this object in mind, most of the 30 selling districts (with the exception of 6 in the South and West) were consolidated into 5 sales regions with a regional manager for each. The district and the general sales managers were given up, but from among them were chosen the regional managers. The latter were located in Boston, New York, Philadelphia, Chicago, and Cleveland and were made responsible for all the sales (A, B, and C) in their respective regions. Under the regional managers were specialists in each of the A, B, and C lines; these specialists were responsible for the sales of the region in their particular fields, and they also did some selling. Some of the salesmen in those parts of the country where there was the greatest volume of Dennison sales specialized in A, B, or C orders. Others covering the smaller towns handled two or all three classes. When the sales regions were set up, the service departments—chiefly for correspondence and adjustments—were transferred from Framingham to the regional headquarters.

It was decided that in its stress on direct sales the organization had gone too far in eliminating inducements to the wholesaler to handle the Dennison line. In 1931, therefore, a policy was inaugurated which was new for Dennison's. A service wholesaler plan was established, under which a growing number of the larger wholesalers with whom the Company dealt were granted special inducements to handle a fairly large and representative stock of Dennison merchandise and to push Dennison sales. The service wholesalers, in representative cities throughout the country, secured a 2 per cent cash discount, were allowed freight charges, and received special selling aids for Dennison goods. The policy was to shift the relations with the smaller dealer to the service wholesaler, the salesmen sending their orders to him and goods being dispatched from the service wholesaler rather than directly from Framingham.

C. Merchandising.

In view of the buyer's market which prevailed after 1920, a good deal of attention was paid to merchandising. The prolonged difficulty with the gummed-paper line was solved by curtailing sales for a year or two until a new and more satisfactory product could be turned out. In 1927 Dennison arranged a royalty agreement for the sale of the total output of a manufacturer of metal cases. Similar arrangements have since been made for the sale of several other products. In 1929 Dennison began the packaging and selling of Cellophane.

Because of increasing difficulty in keeping up sales, a number of new items were introduced, including paper handkerchiefs, dusters, and baby pads. Dennison's also began to put on the market some mechanical devices, such as marking machines, which were of importance not so much in themselves as because they would stimulate the use of Dennison products. Considerable stress was placed also on finding new uses for some of the older items, notably for tags. With the increase in shipping by auto truck and in mechanical methods of marking, one of the chief Dennison products was threatened with a serious decline. This was modified, however, by the encouragement of new uses in laundries, shoe-repair shops, garages, and so on; also the use of guarantee and trade-mark tags and of novelty tags for bridge tallies, tag calendars and blotters, and the like. Another merchandising innovation in this important line was a noticeable trend toward standardization and simplification. As might have been expected, the marketing difficulties of the period led to some price concessions and to the introduction of certain cheaper lines, for instance, in crepe paper and napkins. The crepe line during the 1920's obtained precedence over tags as the leading Dennison product.

Merchandising problems, since early in the century, had been handled in the Dennison organization by grouping the products into half a dozen main lines, each of which was a more or less separate unit with its own merchandising committee. About 1930 it was thought that, in view of the similarity of merchandising problems in all lines—in estimating, prices, the development of new products, and so on—a functional division would be more satisfactory than a product division. The merchandise committees were therefore temporarily abandoned,[4] though a general merchandising committee for the whole organization was retained. There were also merchandise line managers, who spent most of their time traveling; and at Framingham a merchandise maintenance staff as well as a merchandise development staff. This set-up was not found completely satisfactory, however, and a new form was devised which combined some of the elements of both the old and the new plan.

D. Labor.

In the field of labor there were no important developments during the decade under consideration. The wage adjustments of the postwar years were made without serious difficulty, and the generally good business during the decade, together with the operation of the unemployment reserve plan, prevented the appearance of any great unemployment problem. A growing stress on measured production tended to increase total earnings. The Works Committee, later called Employees' Committee, continued to demonstrate its importance; it has been a valuable agent in maintaining harmonious relations between management and workers. At the end of 1929 a change in structure was adopted, the general committee giving way to divisional committees, whose chairmen met twice a month as the Council of Nine. The chief motive in this change was the reduction of expense.

An important personnel policy was inaugurated about 1926 in the beginning of educational training. This training was entirely voluntary and not standardized; it was based on an analysis of individual needs and was made the sole responsibility of a trained educator. Wherever possible, small groups were formed around the individual needs disclosed. By 1929 there were as many as 40 different groups; most of the managerial employees were included, and the plan had been extended to the selling group. It was felt that this work was very valuable, especially in view of the Dennison policy of

[4] A few years later the earlier organization was largely restored except that a maintenance and development staff from the newer organization was maintained separately.

promotions from within the organization.

E. A changed capital structure.

In this as in the preceding period, the capital structure of Dennison's went through most significant developments. The first preferred stock of the Company was slowly but steadily being retired, but the second preferred was of course on the increase, as were the two classes of industrial partnership stock. In 1920 the par value of the total outstanding stock was just over $6,500,000; in 1925 it was about $9,225,000; in 1930 it amounted to $10,758,000. In the 1920 distribution (made in 1921) the industrial partners numbered 378 management shareholders and 1,418 employee shareholders; these figures changed to 394 and 2,318, respectively, for 1925, and to 395 and 1,866 for 1929. Meanwhile their stock holdings had increased steadily, from $1,680,000 for management and zero for employees at the end of 1920 to $3,054,000 and $995,000, respectively, at the end of 1929.

The industrial partnership plan, splendid as was its object, brought problems in its administration. There was always the question of how much should be distributed out of earnings. Moreover, if taken in stock by the employee, the money remained in the business just as much as if the profits had merely been added to surplus, and only dividends would be paid out; but, if large amounts of such industrial partnership stock were exchanged for preferred stock bearing a fixed and cumulative rate, a serious situation might well arise. As long as the earnings of the Company were maintained, the additional load would presumably be carried or it could be decreased by retiring some of the stock. Trouble arose, however, from the decline of earnings in the 1920's and from the failure to foresee that decline far enough ahead of time.

In 1927 certain amendments were made for improvements in the capital structure of the Company. The total authorized capital was increased from $11,000,000 to $14,000,000, and the classes of stock were changed in name. The old first preferred was renamed debenture stock; the second preferred, simply preferred; the industrial partnership stock was called management stock; the employee partnership certificates (previously merely scrip) were authorized as employee stock, and provision was made for a new class: $500,000 of class A stock to be issued, at the discretion of the directors, to take the place of the management or employee stock held by employees who left the Company. The dividends of this new class A came before dividends on management and employee stock and prior to the issuance as extra remuneration of new stock of these two classes. No class A stock was issued until 1931.

Under the changed structure of 1927, extra remuneration in the form of management or employee stock was given to two groups: the former to principal employees who had been with the Company at least five years and held responsible positions, and the latter to senior employees selected chiefly on the basis of length of service with the Company.

F. The Investors' Advisory Council.

In view of the fact that Dennison directors gave their whole time to the management of the Company, it was feared that their point of view might become too narrow. An Investors' Advisory Council was, therefore, set up in 1927 to meet this danger. The Council was composed of five men from outside the Company's ranks, chosen for their knowledge of business in general and of investments and investors' interests. The Council met four times a year to look into the affairs of the Company, as would a board of directors, and to advise Dennison management and suggest changes.

7. Adjustment to Depression, 1930–38

The depression brought a great shrinkage in volume of sales and a rapid fall in prices. The effect on earnings was very significant. Earnings after depreciation, which had been $1,275,310 in 1929 and $484,288 in 1930, fell to losses of $316,910 in 1931 and $481,184 in 1932.[5] In 1932 earnings before depreciation were $6,850; though the depreciation figured on plant and equipment in that year was only about half that taken in 1929 and 1930, the total depreciation was increased by a terrific loss on inventory. In 1933 there was a slight recovery, and after that a great improvement in earnings after depreciation, an increase from $461,015 in 1934 to $637,569 in 1936. There was a marked drop again in 1937, and an even greater fall in 1938.

Dividends reflected the drop in earnings. In 1932–38 there were no dividends on the non-cumulative stocks. On debenture and preferred stocks unpaid cumulative dividends totaled $449,901 in 1932, $894,771 in 1934, and $1,063,177 in 1937.[6]

Dennison's at first took the commonly accepted view that the depression would be brief. Accordingly, it continued in 1930 to carry its full labor force, though at a heavy cost, and it also carried out earlier plans for expansion. This amounted to a total expenditure on real estate, plant, and equipment—including the branch in Canada—of $454,369.

With the terrific fall in sales that came in the autumn of 1930, however, Dennison's began to take drastic steps to meet the depression. Some of these could be realized in a relatively short time; others were a matter of longer-time change and policy. One very serious problem persisted and became aggravated throughout the 'thirties: the problem of forecasting the almost unprecedentedly short business cycle. Another serious problem has been social security taxes and State sales and use taxes which the Company has to a large part had to absorb, owing to the price structure and market conditions affecting many of its products.[7]

A. Selling.

In 1930 Dennison's had nine foreign sales offices besides those in Canada and England, but in the depression which followed the foreign market served by those nine offices vanished almost completely. There was no longer a "world" market for Dennison. The work of those foreign offices was, therefore, turned over to foreign agents working on commission.

In the home market Dennison selling became more aggressive than ever. Prices were lowered to meet competition. Small orders were taken from retailers, even at a loss—this was especially true of the box division. To cut the loss on small orders a special department was established to handle them, and much of the small-order business was also turned over to service wholesalers. Orders for new types of special merchandise were sought. Much emphasis was placed on market research, to determine both the actual and the potential market. Selling had to be kept tremendously alive and flexible in order to keep up with rapid changes in methods of reaching the home consumers, for instance such changes as the growth of chain stores. Strangely enough, the chain store has not helped to solve the problem of small orders because orders from chains have come from the individual stores.

The selling organization tended toward decentralization. To facilitate the filling of orders, merchandise was placed in public warehouses at a number of strategic

[5] In addition to these ordinary losses there were heavy charges for unemployment relief and separation allowances and depreciation of foreign balances charged to surplus and reserves.

[6] *Poor's Industrials* and reports of the Company.

[7] From 1935 to 1937 the increase in taxes was $100,000 a year. The 1936 increase was $44,000 for social security and $70,000 income tax owing to recovery of income; the 1937 increase was all in social security. For 1938 the income tax declined and income and social security taxes remained the same.

points, about a score in all. A considerable line was placed in a warehouse at Chicago with the object of filling there all rush orders from the Chicago district. District 6 (western New York) was organized as a training school for salesmen, with seven to ten men under one supervisor. This was an experiment looking toward a reorganization of the sales end of the business. Later, a small squad of trailer salesmen was sent out to show a full line of Dennison products to small dealers.

B. Merchandising.

On the whole, the older and hence more standardized products suffered more from competition than did the others. The tag division was in a difficult way. It suffered a great volume loss and had to make heavy unemployment payments in 1930. Volume loss continued heavy in 1931–32. In 1930 the box division's volume shrank $400,000, or two-thirds of the total shrinkage for all products; by 1933 only about one-fifth of the potential box capacity was used. The crepe business and gummed products stood up relatively well.

The merchandising division, with the close coöperation of selling and production, worked hard to devise means of offsetting volume decrease by devising new merchandise items. A great deal was spent on research for developing new merchandise lines or items. The measures taken varied among the divisions. The Dennison tradition was against dropping old lines, though, of course, actually many individual items were dropped. The effort to add new lines was general. There are those who think, however, that there has been too much preoccupation with paper and stationers' supplies.

The most important single line for offsetting losses incurred in the tag division were the new pinning and marking machines. Observing that string tags were going out of use, Dennison's devised a machine for pinning tags on goods. These machines were assembled in the Dennison plant at Framingham and some of the parts were made there. The tag division met hand-to-mouth buying by speeding up the filling of special orders; such close coördination was made with the selling, estimating, planning, and producing departments that goods ordered could be designed, produced, and shipped in a few hours.

The division having the most unsatisfactory record was the box division. About 1929 it dropped fine jewelers' boxes and all hand-made boxes and turned to the machine manufacture of commercial shipping boxes. In box-making there was great competition, and the loss in volume was tremendous. One explanation may be that Dennison's was making boxes of too high a grade.

The two other large divisions promised to be more successful. The repeal of prohibition brought an unprecedented business in embossed sealed labels, but this demand proved to be only temporary. The crepe division was fairly successful in maintaining volume except for the decline in the sale of crepe paper itself. It went after every business that might help offset volume loss. Special orders were sought on articles which Dennison's had never made. During the year June 1, 1930, to June 1, 1931, the division made 110 changes in merchandise and packages of the different items carried, dropped 212 of the old items, of which 21 were reinstated, and added 241 new items. Among those added were folded napkins, Madeira napkins guest towels for chain stores, gold and silver bronze crepe, and bridge sets. In 1932 a new line of crepe was added, which was offered in a variety of colors. Cellophane proved disappointing as did also a line of gelatine products, two important innovations in the department making waxes, glues, inks, and the like. A new line, developed recently, has some promise though the demand may be limited—that is, window display sets and semi-rigid materials, such as Designcraft, Plan-a-trim, Flexcraft, and Tonecraft. None of the new lines has had the success of older important lines.

C. Production.

Many lines of adjustment are discernible in production, all looking toward the cutting of costs. The tendency toward decentralization of production, already under way before 1929, was carried further. The Canadian plant had been completed in 1930; more and more goods came to be manufactured in Chicago; and the establishment of a plant on the Pacific Coast was considered. More meticulous cost accounting was instituted. Better control was developed of raw-material and finished-goods inventory, with a considerable cutting-down of balances on hand. Machines were speeded up, worked continuously, or improved so as to turn out a larger volume in a given time. New and cheaper processes were introduced, some resulting in producing the same quality of goods at a lower cost and others meeting a demand for a product of lower quality.

There was a considerable cutting of personnel and labor force. The shrinkage of the work of some departments, together with reorganization, brought about consolidation which decreased the supervisory force. Substituting further machinery for men and speeding up machinery made possible a considerable saving in labor cost.

Dennison's liberal labor policy was in part curtailed. Vacations with pay were temporarily abandoned and later reinstated on a basis variable with earnings.[8] Unemployment payments and financial assistance to employees were replaced by participation in the national social security program. The distribution of employee and management stock as an additional compensation automatically declined with the decline of earnings. It is significant, however, that in a time of much labor agitation and uncertainty, Dennison's has had no serious labor problem. It should be noted that the Company has long had a very active Employees' Committee. The problem of heavy labor costs has been and continues to be a serious one. To what extent this is due to location in New England, to the high ideals of the firm, or to

[8] The total expenditures for vacations is as large now relatively as it was in the 'twenties.

Table 1. FROM THE DENNISON BALANCE SHEETS
December 31, 1929–38

	Assets				Liabilities		
Year	Cash in bank and on hand	Accounts and notes receivable	Merchandise, material, and supplies	Total current assets	Money owed to banks for short-time loans	Accounts payable and accrued	Surplus and surplus reserves
1929	$ 595,524	$3,634,970	$4,024,726	$8,364,930	$300,000	$696,457	$1,158,367
1930	399,275	2,975,315	3,876,796	7,357,436	450,000	570,000	1,011,349
1931	595,865	2,335,624	3,072,783	6,108,405	710,000	309,981	302,027
1932	926,927	1,514,412	2,499,071	5,009,545	0 [a]	398,872	670,115
1933	1,062,855	1,587,151	2,390,675	5,166,308	103,000 [b]	335,285	831,497
1934	1,071,263	1,630,729	2,385,476	5,126,462	69,160	478,665	876,592
1935	1,173,635	1,673,818	2,416,596	5,326,435	59,160	578,181	1,053,415
1936	1,116,284	1,902,042	2,636,903	5,708,174	64,100	771,745	1,139,188
1937	645,932	1,779,224	2,870,802	5,295,959	30,000	705,387	1,229,302
1938	641,342	1,874,002	2,500,684	5,016,029	30,000	650,719	975,934

[a] Bank loans were reduced during the depression year 1932 chiefly through the reduction of debts due the Company, by allowing inventories to run low, and by a failure to replace equipment as fast as depreciated.

[b] All those figures for 1933 to 1938, inclusive, represent borrowings for subsidiary companies, odd figures for 1933 to 1936 because loans were in sterling.

the general labor situation it is not easy to make out.

D. Finances.

The finances of the Company were put to a severe test during the depression. Significant financial adjustments are revealed by items from the firm's annual reports as given in Table 1 on the preceding page.

The depression served to bring into clear relief the top-heavy capital structure of the firm. Table 2 shows an attempt to adjust this capital to the lowered level of income.

Earnings showed a creditable improvement in 1936, and all but two dollars of the accumulated dividends on the 8 per cent debenture stock were paid. The existence of $1,063,177 of back dividends and the need of meeting annual dividends of $507,617 created, however, a difficult situation for the Company.

A plan was, therefore, proposed to the stockholders in May, 1937, for strengthening the capital structure. It was not adopted, probably because it did not take into account sufficiently the equity position of the holders of cumulative 7 per cent preferred stock. In 1939 another plan was proposed and was adopted by the stockholders. Under this plan the 8 per cent debenture stock remains unchanged. The 7 per cent preferred and accumulated dividends (totaling about 48 per cent on the stock) will be exchanged for six dollars in cash, one share of new prior preferred stock bearing a dividend rate of 6 per cent of which 3 per cent will be cumulative whether or not earned and 3 per cent cumulative if earned, and four shares of class "A" Common Stock, which is junior to debenture and prior preferred and entitled to 50 cents in dividends when such dividends are declared. Each share of the old class "A" stock and each $10 of interim Optional Receipts will receive 1¼ shares of "A" Common; each share of Employee Stock will receive one of "A" Common; and each share of management stock one share of voting common stock.[9]

The changes made under the present recapitalization plan will not greatly affect the total capitalization. They will improve the position of the Company very greatly, however, in that the obligations arising from dividend cumulations are taken care of and the rate of cumulation in the future is greatly reduced.

E. Administration and management.

[9] Details of the reorganization of 1939 will probably appear in *Poor's Industrials* for 1939.

Table 2. DENNISON STOCK OUTSTANDING, 1929–38

(Not including treasury stock)

Year	Debenture stock, 8% cumulative	Preferred, 7% cumulative	Class A 7%	Interim optional receipts	Management stock	Employee stock
1929	$4,121,400	$2,638,000	....	....	$3,053,920	$ 995,250 [a]
1930	4,114,700	2,754,600	....	....	2,888,220 [a]	1,000,780
1931	4,114,500	2,985,000	$467,690	$ 18,790	1,884,880	672,540
1932	4,064,500	2,943,300	757,790	23,300	1,006,430	304,260
1933	4,025,900	2,786,400	818,740	46,100	944,960	281,980
1934	3,935,700	2,761,500	833,850	41,920	938,770	277,240
1935	3,928,900	2,761,500	829,630	70,520	917,820	269,280
1936	3,928,900	2,761,500	853,070	106,950	864,690	262,540
1937	3,928,900	2,567,600	895,430	104,080	829,730	258,010
1938	3,928,900	2,563,400	915,320	144,840	773,970	253,120

[a] In 1929 there was extra remuneration in the form of additional management and employee stock amounting to $333,859.

President H. S. Dennison and about seven directors combined policy formulation and management in this period. Each is at the head of one division of the company organization. Aside from his general duties as president, H. S. Dennison has financial control. The positions in the management headed by others are as follows: (1) vice-president and director in charge of research and development; (2) treasurer and general manager of marketing; (3) director of merchandise development and retail stores; (4) director in charge of merchandise line management and maintenance; (5) director of manufacturing; (6) director of sales force; (7) director of advertising and sales promotion; and (8) director of office and warehouse. The men now holding those positions are generally regarded as able and effective managers.

Dennison's administrative set-up suggests some important questions. There still remains the problem of getting the broad point of view which the Investors' Advisory Council was supposed to supply. The Council did not prove so effective in aiding management as had been hoped and was not reappointed after 1937. It has been suggested that one other method of avoiding inbreeding of policy and management would be occasionally to bring new and outside blood into the management. There is also the problem of coördinating policy formulation and management. Obviously there is the danger in such an organization as Dennison's that the president and the director-managers will be heavily pressed by their departmental duties to the exclusion of the larger point of view. In the case of the Dennison management, as in other instances of this type of organization, there may be a lack of freshness and incisiveness in general administration. Perhaps one unfortunate aspect of the situation is the dead weight of the debenture holding group of stockholders, in many cases consisting of trustees.

8. Statistics on Dennison's Business, 1878–1938 [10]

Table 3. FIGURES ON ASSETS AND OPERATIONS [a]

(In thousands of dollars)

Year	Sales	Net Profits	Assets	Machinery [b]
1878	$467	$31	$276	$35
1879	556	96	445	34
1880	733	97	578	69
1881	908	146	709	92
1882	1,097	169	799	100
1883	1,172	133	877	111
1884	1,113	102	888	108
1885	1,147	154	937	105
1886	1,260	203	942	81
1887	1,377	206	1,083	105
1888	1,374	207	1,119	108
1889	1,437	210	1,107	100
1890	1,565	265	1,160	101
1891	1,625	224	1,220	94
1892	1,762	288	1,259	92
1893	1,602	256	1,273	106
1894	1,699	259	1,233	97
1895	1,855	306	1,288	111
1896	1,612	205	1,343	100
1897	1,675	198	1,356	157
1898	1,740	182	1,383	157
1899	1,978	230	1,490	174
1900	2,099	188	1,512	183
1901	2,325	296	1,647	282
1902	2,667	394	1,959	298
1903	3,091	465	2,437	460
1904	3,335	509	2,576	560
1905	3,740	556	2,873	641
1906	4,406	607	3,294	641
1907	4,738	613	3,176	715
1908	4,067	561	3,111	671
1909	4,696	651	3,380	465
1910	5,005	604	3,934	500
1911	4,921	491	4,994	582
1912	5,275	495	5,297	600
1913	5,443	587	5,253	671
1914	5,226	552	5,551	749
1915	5,253	534	5,775	798

[a] Figures are consolidated totals after subsidiaries were established.

[b] Capital invested in machinery.

[10] Compiled from table in Heath, *op. cit.*, p. 191, and from records of the Company.

Table 3. (*Continued*)

Year	Sales	Net Profits	Assets	Machinery
1916	6,711	968	6,141	817
1917	7,361	976	6,884	858
1918	8,201	1,028	7,948	593
1919	10,330	1,000	8,792	643
1920	14,478	1,875	10,649	779
1921	12,337	581	9,707	766
1922	13,149	...	10,999	730
1923	15,089	1,331	11,486	921
1924	14,628	801	11,654	1,163
1925	15,695	1,295	12,411	1,223
1926	16,204	1,222	12,192	1,275
1927	16,575	1,175	12,979	1,445
1928	16,375	1,272	13,447	1,483
1929	16,800	1,275	13,621	1,545
1930	14,550	484 [c]	12,790	1,586
1931	12,100	−316 [d]	11,704	1,670
1932	8,950	−481 [d]	10,471	1,606
1933	9,075	59	10,487	1,625
1934	11,100	461	10,470	1,561
1935	11,675	499	10,733	1,565
1936	12,875	638	10,936	1,528
1937	13,775	464	10,739	...
1938	12,525	45	10,413	...

[c] From 1930 to 1934 certain unusual items were charged or credited direct to surplus, that is, depreciation and appreciation of foreign exchange due to abandonment of gold, first by the United Kingdom and then by the United States, unemployment relief and separation allowances, and taxes of other years.

[d] Net loss.

9. Readings

The "History of the Dennison Manufacturing Company," *Journal of Economic and Business History,* vol. i (1928–29), pp. 467–502, by E. P. Hayes, and vol. ii (1929–30), pp. 163–202, by Charlotte Heath, is a short history of Dennison's, carefully and thoughtfully written from the firm records.

N. S. B. Gras, *Industrial Evolution* (Cambridge, 1930), chap. xiv, considers some significant aspects of Dennison's history, especially its labor policy.

10. Suggested Questions

1. What is the nature of the business of this firm?
2. What are the relative advantages and disadvantages of centralization in production and marketing, as exemplified in the Dennison history? Can a permanent balance be reached between the producing and the marketing interest; if so, how?
3. How far, and why, has Dennison history repeated itself, 1873–98 and 1920–present?
4. What do you think of the industrial partnership plan as a management and financial policy (rather than as social engineering)?
5. What do you think of the financial reorganization effected in 1939?
6. In what ways can the office of business history in the Dennison organization be of service to the enterprise?

XXIX. N. W. AYER & SON, ADVERTISING AGENCY, 1869–1939

1. Introduction

The modern advertising agency is one of the most important elements in the marketing structure of today. It emerged and developed during the past century, and the history of N. W. Ayer & Son illustrates every phase of its evolution.

Advertising itself is much older than the agency. In the Middle Ages it consisted of pictorial signboards and the announcements of criers and bellmen. Confined to bare information, advertising then as now served as an aid in bringing the buyer and seller together. With the invention of printing, advertisement by means of handbills, placards, and periodical publications came into use.[1] It was not, however, until the tremendous development of mechanical production and the concurrent expansion of markets in the nineteenth century that advertising at-

[1] Frank Presbrey, *History and Development of Advertising* (New York, 1929), pp. 1–55; *Encyclopaedia Britannica,* 14th ed., vol. i, p. 195.

tained its modern technique and importance.

As the modern phase developed, the newspaper was the chief medium of advertising.[2] The growth of population, improvements in transportation and communication, and the development of more efficient devices for printing and papermaking were among the forces which led to a rapid increase in the number of newspapers published in the United States after 1790. According to one estimate, they increased from 72 in 1790 to 2,800 in 1850 and 5,253 in 1860.[3]

To the advertiser who wished to reach a public beyond his local district the rapid multiplication of media, combined with a high death-rate among individual publications, presented bewildering confusion. A complete lack of reliable information about charges for advertising made matters worse. Publishers as a class were poor business men: they regarded income from advertising as so much extra profit; space was (and is) a highly perishable commodity; and rates varied from paper to paper and from day to day to an extent now almost incredible. Even after some stabilization had taken place, one lot of space which was quoted at $15,000 finally sold for $120, and such wide fluctuations were not unusual. From the publisher's point of view, the potential users of newspaper space presented a widely scattered and relatively inaccessible market which few individual papers could afford to canvass.[4]

The first advertising agent of whom we have definite record, Volney B. Palmer, is said to have started an agency in Philadelphia in 1841.[5] At any rate, on printed notices dated 1844 and 1845 Palmer styled himself "Agent for Country Newspapers," carrying on this business in conjunction with a real-estate, conveyancing, wood and coal office.[6] For some years Palmer's father had been publisher of the Mount Holly, New Jersey, *Mirror,* and there is reason to believe that Palmer began his business career by soliciting advertisements for this paper. The agency grew rapidly; by 1849 Palmer had established branches in Boston, New York, and Baltimore.[7] Meanwhile John Hooper had started an agency in New York. Beginning as a canvasser for the *Tribune,* he was soon accommodating his customers by inserting advertisements in other New York papers, collecting and paying for the advertisements, and receiving a commission from the publishers concerned. The growth of this practice soon led Hooper to set himself up as a general agent.[8] A third agency was opened in Boston in 1849 by S. M. Pettengill, who had previously worked for Palmer.[9]

Palmer solicited orders for advertising, aided in the selection of papers, forwarded the orders and copy to the newspapers, kept a file of publications for reference, and charged his customers the rates which they would have had to pay in dealing directly with the publishers.[10] He demanded a discount (usually referred to as a commission) of 25 per cent of the gross price on all business forwarded by his agency; he tried to obtain the same proportion of

[2] *Loc. cit.;* Joseph P. Bachem, *Das Eindringen der Reklame in die deutschen politischen Tageszeitungen* (Munich, 1929), pp. 26–27.

[3] Daniel J. Kenny, *The American Newspaper Directory and Record of the Press* (New York, 1861), p. 121.

[4] George P. Rowell, *Forty Years an Advertising Agent, 1865–1905* (New York, 1926), pp. 318–320.

[5] Letter dated June 29, 1846, quoted in *V. B. Palmer's Business Men's Almanac,* 1855 (Philadelphia), p. 40.

[6] Palmer advertisements in possession of N. W. Ayer & Son, Inc., Philadelphia. Material in this collection will be referred to henceforth as Ayer Col.

[7] *Ibid.;* also information obtained from two of Palmer's grandchildren in 1922 by a member of the Ayer firm, Ayer Col.

[8] Rowell, *op. cit.,* pp. 140–141.

[9] S. M. Pettengill, "Reminiscences of the Advertising Business," *Printers' Ink,* vol. iii, no. 26 (Dec. 24, 1890), pp. 686–690.

[10] *Palmer's Almanac,* 1850.

any business which was given directly to the publisher by anyone who had once been a customer of his. He attempted to establish himself as sole agent for the publishers with whom he dealt; but he refused to assume the credit risks involved, and he would not pay for advertisements if the advertiser failed to pay him.[11] Other agents apparently modeled their practice on Palmer's, and the 25 per cent commission became the trade custom.

Spirited competition soon forced down rates. However, George P. Rowell, a young man who had canvassed advertising for the *Boston Post,* saw a chance to increase agency revenue. The usual charge for a "square" (about one inch in a column) in country papers was $1.00 for the first and 50 cents for each of several subsequent insertions, but a whole column could be bought for a year for $100 or even less, minus the agent's commission. Thus, if this space could be resold at the low price of $1.00 per square per month, a good profit could be made. In 1865, after ascertaining that publishers would subdivide the space and change the copy monthly, Rowell started his agency. This inaugurated the space-wholesaling era of the agency business.

At the same time Rowell introduced another change: he agreed to pay cash to any publisher who would allow an additional discount of 5 per cent.[12] Before long he had also established the principle that agencies should assume credit risks and pay the publisher for space even when the advertiser had defaulted.[13] Extending Rowell's idea, Carlton & Smith and other agencies began to contract annually with the publications which they represented, paying a lump sum and taking over for the most part the management of the advertising columns. Even before Rowell's time, agents had begun to supplement their income by paying for space, where possible, with type, ink, and other printers' materials on which a second profit could be made.[14]

At this stage of the evolution of the advertising agency the firm of N. W. Ayer & Son was started in Philadelphia.

2. Important Dates in the History of N. W. Ayer & Son

1848	Francis Wayland Ayer born at Lee, Mass.
1868	Began to solicit advertising for the *National Baptist* of Philadelphia, Pa.
1869	Founded agency in partnership with his father, N. W. Ayer, giving the latter's name to the business.
1875	Printing department added to the agency organization.
1876	First contract made charging commission on *net* cost of space.
1877	Ayer agency took over Philadelphia business of Coe, Wetherill & Co., successors to Volney B. Palmer, thereby becoming direct descendant of first advertising agency in the United States.
1878	H. N. McKinney, employee, admitted to partnership.
1879	First formal market survey made for a client.
1880	First edition of *American Newspaper Annual* published.
1880–90	Ayer commission standardized at 15 per cent.
1884	Ayer agency acquired a printers' supply house.
1888	Annual volume exceeded $1,000,000 for first time.
1892	Ayer hired man to work exclusively on advertising copy.
1890–1900	Ayer agency began to stress magazine advertising as well as newspaper advertising.
1898	Outdoor (poster and painted

[11] Rowell, *op. cit.*, pp. 72–73.

[12] *Ibid.*, pp. 63–68.

[13] *Ibid.*, p. 238; James W. Young, *Advertising Agency Compensation* (Chicago, 1933), p. 25.

[14] *V. B. Palmer's New Yorker,* vol. i, no. 1 (Dec., 1851).

sign) advertising begun by Ayer agency.

1903 New York office opened.

1902–06 Firm discontinued advertising of alcoholic liquors and patent medicines.

1905 Boston office opened.

1910 Chicago office opened.

1911 Wilfred W. Fry, employee and son-in-law of F. W. Ayer, admitted to firm. Cleveland office opened.

1918 Death of H. N. McKinney. W. M. Armistead, employee, admitted to firm.

1919 Ayer commission increased to 16⅔ per cent. Annual volume exceeded $10,000,000 for the first time.

1922 Advertising programs over radio inaugurated by N. W. Ayer & Son.

1923 Death of F. W. Ayer. Wilfred W. Fry became head of the agency.

1924 Cleveland office closed. San Francisco office opened.

1926 Annual volume exceeded $25,000,000 for the first time.

1929 The business was changed from a partnership to a corporation. Offices opened in Detroit and London.

1932 Offices opened in Buenos Aires and São Paulo.

1934 N. W. Ayer & Son of Canada established in Montreal.

1936 Death of Wilfred W. Fry. H. A. Batten succeeded him as president.

1937 Canadian division opened a branch in Toronto.

1939 Establishment of the Ayer Foundation for Consumer Analysis.

3. Outline History of N. W. Ayer & Son [15]

In April, 1869, a new agency was started by a mere youth of 21—Francis Wayland Ayer, the son of a New England school teacher, Nathan Wheeler Ayer. For several years Wayland had taught school, hoping to earn enough to permit his going to college; shortly after, he had matriculated at Rochester University. Family circumstances, however, compelled him to find a job. In 1868 he began his business career in Philadelphia by soliciting advertising for the *National Baptist*, a religious weekly newspaper. Before a year had elapsed, he decided to start out for himself. After persuading his father to join him, F. W. Ayer launched his agency with his entire savings of $250 as capital. Actually N. W. Ayer had little to do with the firm; ill during much of the period since the firm's establishment, he died in February, 1873.

The son had all the traditional conservatism, shrewdness, and determination of a Yankee. In addition, he was a devout and active member of the Baptist Church and carried over into his business a strong religious fervor. Although his business experience was very limited, he quickly grasped the essential functions and possibilities of the advertising business. Stern, intensely practical, he reached decisions slowly and cautiously; once a course of action was chosen, however, he worked towards his goal with unfaltering courage and energy.

At first he confined his activities to representing 11 Philadelphia religious weeklies, but by the end of 1871 the firm was forwarding advertisements directly to 325 publications in 27 States and placing business in other papers through other agents. Excerpts from letters written by F. W. Ayer to his father throw light on the early activities:

"Philadelphia,
"July 11th, 1872.

"Now for business! It is dull as you suppose, still we are very much engaged and as

[15] Unless otherwise indicated, all statements about the Ayer firm's history are based upon a study of the agency's private records and upon interviews with officers and employees in connection with the forthcoming volume, Ralph M. Hower, *The History of an Advertising Agency* (Cambridge, 1939).

yet have found no time to close at 5 P.M. as we did all through last summer. The Pat[ent] Med[icine] adv. of Wenzell's is coming back pretty lively. They can't swallow my low figures. Will try & fix them up satisfactorially however. . . . Made good terms with 'Epis [copal] Meth[odist]' & 'Cath[olic] Mirror' of Bato. [Baltimore] for pat. med. adv. also with Wilmington 'Com[mercial] & Tribune' for Evans'. The latter was $100.00 gross. Could not come to terms with the 'Meth. Protestant' but may yet. They want double rates for pat. med. advs. which I am not inclined to pay. . . . I quite improved one arrangement with the 'Epis. Methodist' and they will publish us as their Phila. agents. Was well pleased with the results of my trip. . . . Since returning from Bato. 'The Epis. Register' have accepted the offer which I made them on Monday after writing you. It is $3,600.00 per yr for 3 yrs we to have exclusive control of *all* their advertising. Shall try to close with Rue tomorrow."

"Philadelphia,
"July 22, 1872

"The contract with the Epis. Reg. is not yet closed. They asked for bonds in $1000.—which I declined to furnish. . . . Have closed with Rue provided the arrangement with Epis. Reg. does not fall through. Orders today about $500. $300 from Dauchy small profit if any, $150 for Presb[yterian] through Ambler. This carries business with the Presb. over $3000. for the year. . . . Took a $50. order from Flint last wk. but business was very quiet. Sent an estimate on high cost papers $1000.—against Rowell to Union Pub. Co. Chicago. Hope to get it. But little money in it though."

After his father's death a valued friend called upon Ayer, who later (1916) described the interview as follows:

"He said he had learned to respect me for myself; he was sorry he could not respect me for my business. He looked me right in the eye and said, 'What is an advertising agent? Nothing but a drummer, and he never will be anything else. . . . If you like me to, I think I am in a position to introduce you to a house in this city of recognized standing, with which it would be an honor to you to be associated. . . .'

"He didn't realize that he ran a knife right into me first and then turned it around. I said to him that with his permission I would sleep over that and tell him the next morning what I thought. The next morning I went to him and thanked him for the thought he had expressed, and for his coming to me and telling me that he respected me—for I coveted his respect—but I said, 'The proposition you made to me does not appeal to me. I have put my hand to this plow, and by the help of the Lord, I am going to finish the furrow, and before I have finished it, if we both live, you are coming to me some day and say that you respect me for my business as well as for myself.'"

At the close of 1873 George O. Wallace, the first employee, received a fourth interest in the partnership. Like the partners who have since been admitted, he contributed no outside capital but paid for his interest out of his share of the subsequent earnings of the business.

The business was small at the beginning—the total volume for the first twelve months is reported to have been $15,000 [16]—and was handled by the two partners, who solicited business during the day and toiled early and late at the bookkeeping and clerical work involved. By the end of 1874, however, the firm had changed quarters twice to obtain more room, employed at least ten people, and had reached an annual volume of over $100,000. In the following year a printing department was added for printing the many forms required and turning out proofs of advertisements so that publishers might be shown exactly how the finished copy should appear.

In 1876 the firm inaugurated the now famous Ayer open contract which went far to reform agency-client relations. Competition among agencies had been demoralizing the advertising business. Advertisers had encouraged cutthroat practice by asking agents to submit competitive bids; agents put pressure on publishers; and

[16] Advertisement, *Farm Implement News*, Sept., 1885.

honest service was being forgotten. In 1875 Rowell had announced that henceforth he would refuse to submit bids in competition, since the relation between agent and advertiser should be one of mutual confidence in which the agent would serve his client honestly to the best of his ability and resources, giving the client the lowest gross prices obtainable and taking as remuneration whatever commission the publisher allowed the agent.[17] By this time the commission was as low as 10 per cent for some papers.

Ayer at once saw the point. He also noted one implication which Rowell had overlooked. Ayer's principal partner, who had been an employee in 1875, summed up the situation in a letter dated February 15, 1890:

> "[Rowell's] plan . . . seemed to us to lack one important feature. The advertiser had no means of knowing how much the agent made. In other words he engaged a confidential employee with an indefinite and unknown salary to be fixed by another and known only to the employee.
>
> "We, therefore, adopted the plan, changing it, however, to a definite commission upon the amount of business placed, and this put the matter in such shape that the advertiser was as familiar with the cost and our profit as we ourselves."

Ayer went to one customer whose business had been obtained in 1874 and 1875 by underbidding, got him to admit that the agency was entitled to a fair profit, and finally obtained an agreement whereby the agency was to place all the advertising for one year at the lowest rates obtainable and charge a commission on the net cost of the space. The plan was avowedly an experiment; the first contract was at 12.5 per cent, another was at one-ninth of the net cost, others were at 10 and 15 per cent. Some time after 1878 the agency fixed upon 15 per cent as the proper rate of commission.

[17] Rowell advertisements, 1875, 1878, Ayer Col.

Not all advertising was handled on this basis. Some advertisers could not be trusted to keep secret the prices which would necessarily be revealed to them. Others insisted upon competitive bids; and Ayer, in the hope of eventually landing them as contract customers, sometimes yielded. A number of advertisers, whose volume of business was so small that the cost-plus-commission plan would not provide enough money to cover the agency expense involved, were willing to sign the Ayer contract. Instead of a fixed rate of commission, contracts in such cases provided: "You are to secure the best terms possible . . . and charge to our account at prices which will allow you a satisfactory profit. These charges, however, are not in any case to exceed publishers' rates." Both the competitive bidding and the contract-without-commission plan were later abandoned, but the firm has continued to accept some business from small advertisers on what it calls the fixed-price or order basis. In such cases there is no contract establishing relations over a definite period of time, and the agency charges the advertiser full publishers' rates.

Although for some years the open-contract arrangement was not featured in the firm's advertisements, it rapidly became the basis on which the bulk of the Ayer business was handled. In 1885 the agency announced that nearly three-fourths of its business for 1884 had been on this plan. Since the World War the business handled by the firm on the fixed-price basis has amounted to less than one-tenth of the total volume.

The Ayer contract plan left its mark upon the entire advertising structure. Palmer had been the agent of the publisher. Rowell had started the wholesaling stage, in which the agent (in such transactions really a jobber) bought space in large quantities for as little as possible and retailed it to advertisers for as much as possible. Ayer opened a new era, in which the advertising agent's primary concern was not to sell space for publishers, not to sell space which he himself had acquired, but rather to *buy* space for his customers. The advertising agent thus became the representative and counselor of the advertiser.

Before Ayer's adoption of the open-contract plan advertising agents had been concerned mainly with selling space at a profit. Ayer wanted to get away from price competition; he saw that his opportunity lay in selling service—in serving the advertiser so well that his business would grow, and with it the volume of advertising handled by the agency. Rowell and other agents had groped for this idea, but they had not seen that the agent's judgment as to an advertising plan should be freed from bias. If he owned space in a particular publication, if he received a larger rate of commission from one publication than from another, the fact would influence his judgment as to their suitability for a customer's advertising.

Other agents scoffed, but as the merits of the idea became evident the plan gained ground. Almost immediately the existing agencies split into two groups: some remained as before the representatives of publications, known henceforth as publishers' representatives or special agents; others, like Ayer, went over to the side of the advertiser and became general agents. The special agent solicited advertising for a few publications and represented them with advertisers and general agents. The general agent solicited advertising business in general, helped his clients to make advertising plans, and placed their advertisements with the publishers.[18]

One factor which hastened the movement of the Ayer agency to the side of the advertiser was the admission to partnership of Henry Nelson McKinney on January 1, 1878. McKinney was born in South Africa, the son of an American missionary. Coming to this country at the age of twelve with what education his mother had been able to give him, he spent one term in a public school and one in a business college. At sixteen he arrived in Philadelphia with fifty cents in his pocket, looking for a job. After serving for a short period as bookkeeper for the Presbyterian Board of Publications, he began to sell books and before long was in the book-publishing business, with Ayer placing his advertising. In 1875, when the dishonesty of a partner forced McKinney into bankruptcy, Ayer gave him a place in the agency as bookkeeper. His particular abilities were just what the firm needed. Ayer was an organizer and manager of rare power, Wallace was noted as a cold-blooded and efficient space-buyer, but neither was especially good at obtaining business. McKinney was a poor manager, but he came to be recognized as one of the greatest advertising salesmen in the country. To an extraordinary degree he won confidence and lasting friendships wherever he went; he had a genius for advertising ideas; and he understood how advertising should be combined with selling campaigns. Like Ayer he was an active Baptist and carried over into his daily work a strong religious zeal. Ayer saw his merits and soon shifted him from bookkeeping to canvassing. Unlike Wallace, McKinney realized the significance of the open-contract plan which Ayer had conceived, and he sold it to advertisers with enthusiasm and success. With McKinney in the firm the Ayer agency was equipped to go beyond the mere placing of advertisements.[19]

In 1879 or 1880 McKinney interviewed a manufacturer of threshing machines who usually gave his advertising contract to the lowest bidder. When asked for the list of publications on which bids were to be made, the manufacturer replied that the advertising was to be run wherever threshing machines were used. McKinney ac-

[18] Young, *op. cit.*, pp. 24–28.

[19] Facts about McKinney's life have been obtained from his son; information as to his character and contribution to the business has been obtained from his son, business associates, and Ayer clients.

cepted the challenge implied and hurried back to Philadelphia. The information needed could not be obtained from Washington. Turning to publishers, state officials, and all other possible sources, the agency employees quickly gathered and analyzed data. Considering the circumstances, they made a remarkable survey of grain production in the United States. This was combined with tables showing the publications which reached various markets, together with their rates and estimated circulations. When the manufacturer saw the report, he was amazed and wanted to buy it. McKinney replied that the information was not for sale but was free to Ayer clients. A large order was immediately forthcoming.

This success in gathering information was a factor in the decision, in 1880, to publish the *American Newspaper Annual,* which contained circulation data about publications in the United States and Canada. Until Rowell had broken precedent in 1869 by publishing it in his *American Newspaper Directory,* this information had been the guarded stock-in-trade of the advertising agent. As advertising became a more complicated practice, however, the agent's business depended less upon the secrecy about publication data than upon his ability to buy and use space efficiently for his clients. Indeed, it had become the custom to supply such information as a part of the ordinary soliciting of business among advertisers. Doubtless Ayer was influenced by the fact that advertising space in the directory could be sold to publishers for cash or in exchange for space in their publications. The *Annual,* in fact, was a profitable undertaking until, in 1914, all advertising was eliminated from it and the proceeds came entirely from the sale of copies.

In the 1880's and 1890's the agency found itself assuming another function, that of preparing copy for advertisements. Even Palmer had offered to help his customers to write their advertisements, and McKinney in the Ayer agency had given copy ideas and assistance as a part of his regular work in soliciting business. But agents generally felt that the advertiser must know his own business better than anyone else could know it and that he was therefore better qualified to write his own advertisements. Men like John Wanamaker, who advertised on a large scale, hired their own copywriters; and many others resorted to independent experts in the preparation of advertising copy.[20]

One element forcing this function upon agents was their constant battle for business. Knowledge of rates and circulation and skill in the selection of media, though still important, were being overshadowed by the necessity of offering superior service to discourage advertisers from placing their own advertisements. (Many publishers were willing in this period to accept business directly from advertisers and to allow them the agency discount.) Further, it was only natural that some agencies should try to develop additional services in the effort to get business away from their competitors.

Also important was the growing competition among advertisers themselves for the attention of the public. Originally the problem had been simply to get a message before the consumer; with the rapid increase in the quantity of advertising, however, the problem was to make that message effective. Advertising copy had to become more attractive, more convincing; its preparation called for special ability and experience. Brands, trade names, and packaged goods were increasing in number and importance by 1890; more and better art work was required to present them effectively to the public. Simultaneously the technical advance of the printing industry made possible the introduction of more variety and skill in advertisements. Moreover, after the Ayer agency had succeeded, in 1895, in getting *Harper's Magazine* to insert an advertisement in color, maga-

[20] Presbrey, *op. cit.,* pp. 302–309, 522–526.

zines generally began to print colored illustrations.[21] This innovation, as color-printing processes were improved, gave greater scope for illustrators.

In 1898 the National Biscuit Co. was formed, and McKinney succeeded in getting its advertising contract. The situation called for a national advertising campaign concentrated around a trade mark, a trade name, and a package. McKinney provided the names *Uneeda, Nabisco,* and others which won great vogue at the time; and the Ayer agency, apparently for the first time, gave on a large scale all the modern agency services.[22]

The agency also obtained the advertising contracts of the N. K. Fairbanks Co., the Standard Oil Co. (all divisions, including the Vacuum Oil Co., Atlantic Refining Co., and Corn Products Refining Co.), H. J. Heinz Co., Simmons Hardware Co., and many other manufacturers who were attaining nationwide distribution. As the business of the advertisers increased, their advertising appropriations grew, and the Ayer agency likewise had to expand. In the 1890's the agency had begun to emphasize magazine as well as newspaper advertising, and in 1900 an outdoor advertising department was added to handle the outdoor advertising of the National Biscuit Co. and other clients. The annual volume of business of the agency passed the $2,000,000 mark; the staff increased steadily from 140 employees in 1896 to over 200 in 1903; branch offices were established in Boston, New York, and Chicago; and the organization and management of the agency was rapidly becoming more complex and difficult.

The War's chief effect on the agency was to bring publishing difficulties, through paper shortages and strikes, and to swell agency expenses. On January 1, 1919, the rate of the Ayer commission was increased to 16⅔ per cent. Other agents at this time were allowed commissions ranging from 10 to 15 per cent on the gross price.

Inevitably the management of the agency was put into younger hands. McKinney suffered from constant ill health after 1900. Ayer devoted much of his attention to the affairs of the Merchants National Bank, of Philadelphia (he was director from 1888, president from 1895 to 1910, chairman of the board, 1910, and director of the First National Bank, of Philadelphia, after the merging of the two institutions in 1910); he was active in the local, State, and national organizations of the Baptist Church and the Y. M. C. A. Both Ayer and McKinney gave considerable attention to the Jersey herd and Meridale Farms at Meredith, New York, which they had started as a hobby and which under Ayer's supervision had developed into a sizable breeding and dairy business, not without profit.

Although other partners had been admitted, McKinney and Ayer had remained the great figures of the firm and of the agency business in general. McKinney's ability to evolve constructive advertising and selling ideas has, by general consent, seldom been equaled; and, more than any other person, he was responsible for the growth of the volume of business in the Ayer agency. But it was F. W. Ayer who had built and managed the machine which was required to handle that volume of business successfully. The agencies of Palmer, Pettengill, and Rowell, though profitable, had not survived their founders. At an early stage in his career Ayer had resolved to build an organization rather than an aggregation of advertising men—an organization which would carry on his work and his principles after his hand left the helm. He worked as no one else on his staff worked; when the task of management grew too great for one man, he worked out a practical delegation of

[21] *Art in Advertising,* April, 1895, p. 104.

[22] Interviews with men who were employees of the National Biscuit Co. and the Ayer agency at the time; also correspondence between the two firms in file #6035 of the National Biscuit Co., New York City.

responsibilities; and, as he grew older, he gradually turned over the controls to the men who were to follow him. Thus it was that the passing of the older partners marked no interruption in the activities or policies of N. W. Ayer & Son.

The depression of 1920–21 to some extent checked the postwar boom in advertising, but a rapid rise began again in 1923. By 1926 volume had doubled, and by 1930 it had reached the highest mark ever made in the history of the firm, six times the prewar volume. Meanwhile the Ayer agency, owing to the fact that the American Telephone and Telegraph Co. was a client and had established one of the first radio broadcasting stations, had pioneered in radio advertising, arranging commercial programs as early as the fall of 1922. The use of radio for advertising on a substantial scale dates from 1928.

Since the late 1880's N. W. Ayer & Son had placed advertising from coast to coast and, with the establishment of the San Francisco branch office, the agency made its own business-getting efforts national in scope. In 1928 the firm took steps to meet the ever-pressing problem of adequate quarters for the central offices by erecting a modern thirteen-story building on the historic Washington Square, Philadelphia. In 1929, after the Ayer agency had obtained the advertising business of the Ford Motor Co., branch offices were opened in Detroit and in London, England. After an investigation of the markets and advertising conditions, in 1931 the agency placed representatives in Buenos Aires and São Paulo. In 1934 a Canadian subsidiary was established in Montreal; a branch of this organization was opened in Toronto in 1937. Late in 1938 the firm added an office in Honolulu.

4. Relations with Clients

During the early period the agency's primary task was to convince the prospective customer that advertising would be helpful to his business. The agency gave advice as to the types and circulation of publications likely to give the best results, prepared estimates of the cost of a given campaign, occasionally helped to prepare the copy, had the advertisements set up in type, conducted all the correspondence with the publications, bought and forwarded the necessary plates and electrotypes, kept files of newspapers and checked them to see that the advertisements ordered were inserted at the time and in the manner stipulated, and audited and paid the publishers' bills. After about 1900 the major problem was not so much to persuade the prospective client that he should advertise as to convince him that Ayer service was better for his particular needs than that of other agencies. The following excerpt from a letter of solicitation, written in 1907, sets forth some of the theory behind the open contract:

"To make permanent our connection with an advertiser, insuring him the benefit of an experience which we gather from the care of his business, and also of that gathered from the care of the business of many other advertisers, we devised what is known as our 'Open Contract' plan. . . . It is like the retaining fee of a lawyer; *although there is no fee required.* It insures our standing with an advertiser and gives us the reasonable expectation of serving him right along; this is a marked advantage to both. We know that no short-lived advertising campaign is worth while to an advertiser; while for our part, if at the end of every year we had to begin all over again to get the same business, it would not be worth while to us either. By this plan we become, in reality, the advertising department of our client's business. . . . We can give him honest and impartial advice as to mediums for instance, as one paper pays us as well as another. You doubtless know that this is a very common way of making good on the part of the average agent; by introducing a few papers known as 'sleepers' into the list he transforms loss into profit, as their only value is their value to him. . . . The agreement does not obligate the customer to spend any stipulated amount, it only assures us that what he does in this line shall be done through and with us."

The agency's service rendered to its clients has varied widely, according to individual circumstances and needs. Each situation calls for a determination of the purpose of the advertising and the preparation of a plan which will attain that object. The Ayer agency goes into the general history of each client's business and makes as thorough an analysis as circumstances permit of (1) the product, in relation to consumer demand; (2) the market, with reference to location, possible volume, seasonal and other influences, and competition; and (3) the channels of distribution, including the client's own sales organization and policies.

The agency then determines the aims and scope of the advertising which the client's situation requires, and it selects the advertising media which seem best fitted to carry out the plan, choosing them with regard to their character, the quality, quantity, and location of their circulation, and the cost. Further, every detail connected with the writing, arrangement, and illustration of the advertisement is planned and executed. Lastly, the space must be engaged, the advertisement put in proper form for reproduction and forwarded to publications, insertions checked, and bills audited. It is also customary for the agency to assist in an analysis of the results through studies of sales and calls on dealers and the general public.

The accuracy and completeness of the studies made and the influence of the agency on the client's business cannot be estimated in any tangible way. However, in most cases the agency appears (at least since the War) to have been taken into the confidence of the client and to have worked in close coöperation. There are repeated instances in which the agency has made or obtained remarkably complete and accurate market surveys and has been instrumental in making important changes in the design of products and their packaging, their prices and distribution channels, the client's sales organization, and even in the client's production methods. There have also been instances in which the agency, after a study, has advised against any advertising expenditure on the grounds that the situation was not one in which advertising could be successful. Perhaps an outstanding example of the preliminary work of the agency and its influence upon the client's business is to be found in the history of its relations with the Cannon Towel Co. In this case the agency worked with the client over a period of four years before any consumer advertising was placed; and during the whole of the relationship the Ayer agency aided product design, marketing, merchandising, and sales organization, in addition to preparing and placing advertisements.[23]

After 1930 the work of the agency in market research expanded, and it began to apply various techniques to test the effectiveness of its copy and radio programs. In order to improve and expand its research work the firm established in February, 1939, the Ayer Institute for Consumer Analysis. The Institute was set up as a separate unit so as to make it independent of the agency's production departments in conducting its investigations. The scope of its activities includes consumer habits and attitudes, copy and advertising media, trends in public opinion, and assistance with the scientific testing of commercial products.

In the course of its relations with clients the firm has developed a number of basic policies. As a natural result of the adoption of the open-contract policy, from about 1880 the agency has scrutinized prospective accounts carefully in order to avoid advertising that might give unsatis-

[23] These conclusions find support in those reached in a study of the service rendered by agencies in general to more than a hundred of the leading American advertisers. See Young, *op. cit.*, pp. 45–71.

factory returns to clients. The following excerpt reveals the characteristic attitude of the Ayer agency:

"Philadelphia, Pa.,
"August 5, 1897.

"From our point of view, the first thing to be decided is are both you and we agreed that you have something which it will pay to advertise; next, are we agreed that there is reasonable prospect of our being able to make advertising pay you; further, would a business association be personally pleasant; and finally, is our business reputation and your commercial standing such that we could expect to deal together satisfactorily. In our judgment, this is the way in which the matter should be considered, and if you agree in this view of it, we will be pleased to have one of our representatives call upon you."

The firm has always solicited the accounts of small businesses which seem likely to grow; but, whereas before 1900 it canvassed orders of any size from $10 up, after 1900 it began to ask solicitors to be very careful about seeking accounts which would run less than $1,000 per year in volume. In recent years the firm has seldom accepted an account unless it showed prospects of growing, after a reasonable period of development, to at least $50,000 a year in volume of advertising.

The Ayer agency also selects clients with regard to their character. Lotteries and secret disease remedies have been refused since about 1880, intoxicating liquors since about 1904, and patent medicines of the more objectionable type since about 1905.

By breaking the total agency volume down into the amounts spent in advertising different commodities, some light is thrown upon the changing character of the business handled by the Ayer agency. The following analysis shows the twenty principal commodity groups advertised through N. W. Ayer & Son at each of three different periods:

	Per Cent of Total Identified		
	1877–78 [a]	1900–01	1930
Patent medicines	21.6	8.4	*
Books, tracts, etc.	10.2	1.8	*
Jewelry and silverware	8.6	2.2	1.5
Greeting cards, chromos, etc.	7.7	*	*
Dry goods, clothing, etc.	7.5	7.5	3.3
Seeds, nursery stock, livestock remedies	6.7	4.4	1.5
Machinery, hardware, building materials	5.4	5.2	4.0
Schools and colleges	4.3	5.8	1.5
Tobacco products	4.2	7.2	17.9
Pianos and other musical instruments	3.6	1.0	.9
Household furnishings and supplies	3.5	1.5	2.3
Foods and food drinks	3.2	17.7	15.7
Newspapers and magazines	2.9	6.6	.8
Hotels and restaurants	2.0	*	*
Patents and pensions procured	1.7	*	*
Agents wanted	1.2	*	*
Real estate	1.2	*	*
Drugs and toilet goods	.9	3.2	6.3

(Note: An asterisk simply indicates that the group concerned did not rank among the first twenty in the period. In many cases small amounts were spent in advertising the commodities in question.)

[a] For the years 1877 and 1878 not all expenditures could be identified with particular commodities; the percentages given are based upon the total amount traced, which was 74.4 per cent of the entire volume handled by the agency.

Transportation and communication	.7	1.0	3.6
Farm implements	.5	4.1	2.0
Fuel and lubricants	*	10.1	1.9
Candy and soft drinks	*	4.4	4.3
Correspondence schools	*	3.3	1.2
Carriages	*	2.4	*
Insurance and financial	*	.3	.6
Automobiles, tires, and accessories	*	*	25.4
Chemicals	*	*	4.4
Office equipment and supplies	*	*	1.6

Before 1900 no question was raised about the propriety of the agency's handling the advertising contracts of two or more firms which were in competition with one another. Since about 1900, however, the question of competing accounts has been complicated by the increase in number and size of national advertisers. In general, if there is any chance that a prospective account may be regarded as competing with the business of an Ayer client, the client is consulted about the matter. In some instances, accounts which originally did not compete have, through amalgamations or territorial expansion, become competing accounts.

As clients have gradually determined against sharing the Ayer agency with their competitors, so the agency has since about 1900 opposed sharing the advertising account of a client with another advertising agency. If, however, a given concern has several divisions, each with a separate sales organization, the agency is usually willing to accept the business of one unit even when the advertising of the other units is placed through another agency. Similarly, the Ayer agency has accepted the advertising to be done abroad from firms whose domestic advertising is not handled by the Ayer agency.

Differences of opinion are bound to arise as to the wisdom of agency recommendations. Since results can seldom be predicted with certainty, the agency has frequently yielded when the client has insisted upon a change of plan or idea. However, this is not always true. Occasionally the agency is convinced that yielding to a client's wishes will bring seriously unsatisfactory results to the client or reflect discredit upon the agency. Preferring to risk loss of business rather than to be associated with an advertising failure in such situations the agency has flatly refused to do the client's bidding. Thus the Ayer agency has repeatedly refused to buy testimonials to be used in connection with the advertising of a client's product; also, it has sacrificed business because of its unwillingness to handle sensational "stunt" advertising.

The Ayer agency has consistently refused to reduce its rate of commission both to large advertisers and to advertisers who have wanted to contract for only a part of the Ayer service. In this connection, excerpts from a letter written since 1930 are illuminating. The business at stake was an immediate order for $500,000 and the client was one whose annual volume of advertising is usually in excess of $1,000,000:

"At this point we would like to emphasize the fact that our basis is known and recognized by publishers throughout the world, and it was the basis on which we charged before publishers increased their agents' commission to 15%. . . .

"The confusion seems to lie in the fact that at the present time you may not want any of our creative services and, therefore, we should be in a position to make an allowance for same. As you will see when you understand all the circumstances, we are not in a position to do this. . . .

"Any space broker who offers to split the commission which he is allowed by publishers, must break faith, and in many instances his written word, with the publishers. . . .

"Our charge to all our customers is on the placing basis. In addition to this service, our volume enables us to maintain numerous plus services in creative, merchandising and other phases of the business. Sometimes customers use none of these plus services, others use some, but they are available to all customers. In our agreement with you you will find that we did not obligate you to use advertisements which we prepared, because it reads: 'In the event of our wishing such service, you are to prepare advertising copy, etc.' You will see we obligate ourselves to give you our full service, but we do not obligate you to take it."

No accurate analysis of the reasons for the cancellation of contracts with clients can be made, but a tabulation of the canceled contracts filed since 1895 indicates that the agency has taken the initiative in about as many instances as the client. Of the contracts which seem to have been canceled by the agency the following main reasons for cancellation, in order of frequency, have been given:

The account has been inactive over a long period of time.

The account has become inactive nationally.

The client has gone out of business.

The client's attitude toward the agency recommendations has been unsatisfactory.

The account has come into conflict with that of another client.

The client has not paid his bills.

Of the contracts which seem to have been canceled by the client the main reasons, in order of frequency, have been:

Desire to place business through a local agency.

Dissatisfaction with the service given.

Change in ownership of the client's business.

Financial reasons.

Change in personnel in the client's organization.

Dissatisfaction with Ayer charges.

The average duration of the contracts which were canceled between 1895 and 1933 was three years and seven months. The firm with which the first open contract was made has been a client ever since, and a number of large accounts have remained with the Ayer agency for more than twenty-five years.

5. Relations between the Ayer Agency and Publications

Among the questions arising out of agency-publisher relations, those connected with space rates and agency commissions have always loomed large. As we have seen above, rates during the early years of the Ayer history were not stable. Every publication established official or "card" rates for space, but in practice both space rates and commissions to agents usually differed from those published. The great emphasis upon price led every agent, Ayer included, to seek concessions from publishers. By offering special cash terms or promising to make extra efforts in behalf of a given publication, an agent could frequently buy space at a price well below card rates. Often, when the volume of business forwarded by the agency had reached an agreed figure, an additional rebate was given. One bundle of contracts between the Ayer agency and publishers has survived of which a few are summarized below for purposes of illustration:

Jan. 25, 1886. *Home and Farm.* 25 per cent commission allowed to Ayer in return for $900 of business per month for 12 consecutive months, or $10,800. Other agents not to receive more than 12.5 per cent.

Jan. 26, 1887. Cincinnati *Commercial Gazette.* 35 per cent allowed on all business secured by Ayer west of Buffalo and Pittsburgh and south of Washington.

Aug. 21, 1890. *Farmer's Call.* $1.25 per inch on advertisements running less than 3 months; $1.00 per inch if 3 months or more. Paper not to be quoted on estimates at less than $2.00 net. Ayer to send advertising to this paper whenever client allows Ayer to select publications or instructs Ayer to place advertising in the paper's territory.

Nov. 27, 1891. *St. Nicholas.* 20 per cent commission to Ayer. All other agents 10 per cent except J. Walter Thompson, who has a "slightly better" rate.

Feb. 1, 1892. Boston *Pilot*. If net amount of business during 1892 reaches $1,000, a cash rebate will be made on the basis of 30 per cent commission instead of 25 per cent; if $1,500, 33⅓ per cent; if $2,000, 35 per cent.

Dec. 29, 1892. *Domestic Monthly*. Net rate 21 cents per line on all business to Jan. 1, 1894. Lowest rate to other agents 25.5 cents net except Lord & Thomas who have 5,000 line contract at 22.95 cents.

Jan. 10, 1893. *Home Magazine*. 25 per cent commission; other agents 15 per cent. 5,000 lines for $5,950. All Ayer clients to be charged card rates except those on open-contract basis.

Nov. 17, 1893. *Farm-Poultry Monthly*. Seed advertising to be 10 cents per line net, on condition that paper receives "a liberal share of every seed account placed by Ayer," to season of 1894.

In addition to these general arrangements the Ayer agency constantly made special agreements for particular advertising contracts which it had to place. As a result of the many agreements and constant correspondence with publishers the agency soon acquired a vast fund of inside information and a large number of special rates for advertising. Agreements usually contained a clause providing for strict secrecy about special prices, and in some agreements was a provision that the agency was to charge card rates to its customers. In such contracts, however, an exception was noted to permit the agency to charge its open-contract customers the net cost of space plus its commission rather than the gross card rate.

As the basis of competition shifted from price to service, special space rates lost much of their importance. With a fixed rate of commission based upon the net cost the Ayer agency had less to gain by exacting concessions from publishers. Competition, however, compelled the agency to seek assurance that it was obtaining rates as low as those allowed to other agents. The spread of the Ayer idea, particularly after 1890, was undoubtedly a factor in the stabilization of space rates and agency commissions which took place between 1890 and 1910.[24]

As N. W. Ayer & Son and other general agencies progressed, publishers began to recognize that the advertising agent and the publisher's representative (special agency) were performing different functions. The representative was a special advocate whose job was to canvass existing advertisers and advertising agents on behalf of a given publication. The agent's function was to advance the cause of advertising generally and to develop new advertisers, most of whose expenditures would go to the publications. In addition the agent, unlike the representative, shouldered the burden of credit risks. As this situation became clear, publishers began to protect the general agent by stabilizing rates, allowing no commissions or special concessions to advertisers who placed business directly, and withdrawing recognition from agencies which rebated commissions to their clients or cut the publishers' rates. In a sense, therefore, the advertising agent remained the agent of the publisher, and there was some justification for the stand which Frank Munsey, Cyrus Curtis, and other publishers took (about 1900) when they refused to accept business from any agency which failed to charge card rates to its clients.

On several occasions this particular problem has caused friction between N. W. Ayer & Son and publishers. If a publisher allowed 13 per cent commission, the Ayer agency could buy $1,000 worth of space for $870, for which it would charge its customers $870 plus 15 per cent, or $1,000.50. If, however, the commission allowed was 15 per cent, the Ayer agency bought the space for $850 and charged $850 plus 15 per cent or $977.50; this was less than card rates and gave rise to accusations of price-cutting. Ayer argued that he had fixed his charges on the basis of his own cost of doing business long before this is-

[24] *Ibid.*, pp. 30–35.

sue arose; that he was not consulted by publishers when they fixed their rates of commission; and that they had no right to dictate the terms upon which the Ayer agency was to do business. *McClure's Magazine* refused to see the matter in this light; as a result the two organizations severed all relations between 1902 and 1905. But the agency proved its ability to prosper without placing advertisements in *McClure's,* and in the face of this fact and Ayer's determination the publication eventually yielded.

After rates have been agreed upon, the printing of advertisements calls for a host of details to be attended to by the agency. Plates and mats must fit the publishers' equipment, closing dates must be met, schedules must be followed to the letter, and the published advertisements must be carefully checked. The agency wants a particular position for an advertisement, a client has to change his copy after the closing dead-line, a printer errs in following instructions—an endless variety of problems arises, each calling for technical knowledge, negotiation, tact, and judgment, in order that the agency may reconcile all the interests involved.

Advertising has long been a resource of the swindler and quack; some of it has always been objectionable on moral grounds. Towards the close of the nineteenth century, publishers began to recognize a responsibility to the public and to censor the advertisements which came to them for publication. An attempt was made to eliminate fraudulent offers and misleading claims; many patent medicines came under the ban, and a number of publishers excluded liquor advertising. This was followed by restrictions upon the kind of illustrations used in connection with the advertising. To all this the Ayer agency gave hearty coöperation, but the borderline cases naturally gave rise to difficulty from time to time.

Censorship has also emerged to protect the interests of advertisers themselves. As publishers developed their advertising departments, it became clear that, in the interest of fair play and advertising volume, advertisers had to be restrained from making derogatory statements about competitors' goods and from making claims which could be regarded as unfair competition. Lastly, censorship from the standpoint of the publication was instituted as the race for popular appeal led publishers to give more attention to the typographical appearance of their pages. For example, to prevent a page from having an excessively dark and heavy appearance, publishers frequently make restrictions as to the use of different styles of type, borders, and cuts. Such developments have enormously increased and complicated the work of the agency.

On the other hand, the Ayer agency has itself influenced the contents of publications. It has remonstrated with publishers when advertisements in their columns have reflected upon the products of Ayer clients in a manner which it regarded as unfair or improper; it has taken steps to prevent advertisements of its clients from appearing next to reading or advertising matter which might detract from their effectiveness. More important still, it has influenced the editorial contents of publications. In the early 1900's, when it was handling the advertising of the National Biscuit Co., the Standard Oil Co., and others of the large-scale businesses then coming into prominence, the Ayer agency was faced with "trust-busting" propaganda. Naturally it objected to the hostility which a number of publications, after accepting their advertising, openly displayed towards these enterprises. The agency held that a publisher might take whatever attitude he liked towards big business, but that, if he accepted an advertising contract for one of the companies concerned, he should not destroy the value of that advertising by direct editorial attacks upon the advertiser; to do so was not only inconsistent but was also a plain breach of faith which the agency and its client could not countenance.

This raises the question of what is now called publicity, that is, material in the news columns which refers to products or business enterprises. At the time the Ayer agency was launched, it was the accepted practice for a publisher to insert a "reading notice" calling the reader's attention to an advertisement or product. Offers of advertising contracts frequently stipulated that such notices should appear gratis in connection with the advertising. In other cases the reading notice was simply an advertisement in disguise for which the publisher charged advertising rates. Such material was usually prepared by the advertiser or, when the agency took over the preparation of copy, by agency copywriters. Various influences combined in time to eliminate reading notices from publications unless they were labeled advertisements.

Public interest in commercial and industrial developments today, however, necessitates the publishing of articles relating directly or indirectly to this subject. In the interests of accuracy and self-advancement, business concerns often prepare material for release to the press. Natural forces have led advertising agencies to establish publicity departments. For many years the Ayer agency handled this work in a division of its Copy Department. Rapid growth after the War, however, made it advisable to establish a separate department, with newspaper men rather than advertisement writers in charge. The Ayer agency sends out with every piece of publicity material the statement that it is offered for its news value alone and that its acceptance or rejection will have no bearing on the placement of any advertising which may be entrusted to the agency.

In the course of time the Ayer agency has built up among publishers an unusual reputation for leadership and excellence in every phase of its activities. In recognition of N. W. Ayer & Son's outstanding work in the development of American advertising a group of more than two hundred of the country's leading publishers presented the firm with a silver loving-cup on its fortieth anniversary, and with a gold one on its fiftieth. A New York publisher of long-standing prominence is responsible for the statement that no other agency has ever been accorded a similar tribute.

Relations with other media (especially radio and outdoor advertising interests) reveal problems and policies which resemble those involved in the agency's relations with publishers.

6. Organization and Management of N. W. Ayer & Son, Inc.

In 1912, when the Ayer staff was assembled to go over plans for a complete reorganization, F. W. Ayer said, in part:

> "I knew that I wanted this business to outlive me. . . . No other advertising agency business has demonstrated the fact that this is a business rather than a profession—that it is an organized proposition rather than a profession in that it doesn't need to die with the man who has the skill and strength and determination to build it up."

Some of the steps in the attainment of that goal can be traced. When the business grew too large for the father and son to handle it personally (after 1870), assistants were hired; bookkeeping was apparently made a specialized job with the hiring of the first employee. Within a year or two a separate division, the Registry Department, was set up to keep files of newspapers and to check the insertion of advertisements by Ayer clients as a basis for the payment of bills. In 1875 a Printing Department was added. All other activities of the agency were carried on in the central division known as the Business Department. The men in this department solicited business, prepared lists of papers and estimates, bought space, and executed orders generally. There was no formal direction of solicitors; there was even no very definite delineation of territories.

By 1884 a fundamental step had been taken in creating the Forwarding Department to take over the purchase of space and the forwarding of advertisements to publications. As Ayer expressed it, this was "to separate those who made promises to the advertiser from those who performed the promises made. Although these operations were closely connected, they were distinct in function and like the two leaves of a hinge." By this time had also been created the *Annual* Department, which collected circulation data and published the Ayer newspaper directory; the Merchandise Department, which handled the printers' ink, type, and other supplies sold to publishers; and a Business Advertising Department, which prepared and executed the advertising of the Ayer agency itself. George O. Wallace was in charge of the Forwarding Department; McKinney headed the soliciting efforts; and Ayer, concentrating on the financial side, superintended the business as a whole.

Beginning in January, 1892, copywriters were added to the general or Business Department to put into finished form the ideas of clients; and, in December of the same year, steps were taken to regiment the efforts to get business. In the following year one man was assigned to investigate the credit and character of prospective clients.

From various extant memoranda it is evident that the firm had grown, Topsy-like, without much concerted planning; but it is clear that by 1890 most of the operations had found their way into definite channels. To an increasing extent the agency was composed of specialists, each of whom handled only one or two of the many steps involved in the placing of advertising. Stenographers, typists, rate clerks, order clerks, and messengers had been added; and the number of classifications, as well as the number of employees, was growing rapidly.

After several years of effort to cope with the problems arising out of this growth, Ayer decided in 1899 to reorganize the business as a whole and called in an efficiency expert to assist in the task. The solicitors, relieved of much of the work which they had previously done toward the execution of the business obtained, were put into a separate department devoted exclusively to the canvassing of advertisers. Those engaged in the preparation of advertisements were formed into a Copy Department. The Outdoor Advertising Department was instituted to handle the poster and sign advertising which the agency had just started to place. To coördinate the various routine activities a division bearing the old name Business Department was organized to divide and schedule business among the other departments of the agency and see to its punctual completion. Over all was the Executive Department, which consisted of the four partners and a staff of assistants.

This reorganization established the general lines along which departmentalization has developed down to the present day, but much had to be done before the machine would give the kind of service that was needed. The chief problems were to delegate much of the authority and responsibility, which had formerly been concentrated in the hands of Ayer, and to coordinate all activities and departments properly. In 1905 the creation of three committees solved much of the difficulty: one was to plan and direct all the business-getting efforts and to provide a stronger link between the solicitors and the other departments; the second was to formulate all the plans for the execution of business, including consideration of the distribution of the advertiser's appropriation, style of copy, and the costs and profits involved; the third committee was in charge of the execution of business and was concerned with the efficiency of individual Ayer departments, the adjustment of the working force to the volume of business to be handled, and the control of internal expense.

Meanwhile, the creation of branch offices had complicated matters. Business-getting efforts henceforth were under the immediate direction of branch managers; all the work of preparing estimates and copy, as well as all placing, necessarily remained in Philadelphia. In 1907 Ayer, lamenting that the firm had never undertaken to train or direct its solicitors, announced that steps were being taken to remedy this oversight.

Up to this point the management of the agency had been entirely in the hands of men who had worked up in the business from the bottom. In 1911, however, a man who had been brought in to help with the administration only four years earlier was appointed general manager of the entire business. Under his direction a complete reorganization was again made in 1912. The departments, which had grown unwieldy since 1900, were subdivided into bureaus with chiefs responsible to department heads, who in turn were responsible to the general manager. As before, the division of work among departments and bureaus was along functional lines.

Since 1912 the Ayer organization has grown tremendously both in size and complexity, generally along the lines worked out between 1900 and 1912. Whenever further division of activities offered advantages, a new bureau or department was created; and specialization of work and employees has increased steadily. Likewise, just as the Business Department was organized in 1900 to coördinate the work of the other departments, so bureaus and supervisors have been added to control the movement of business through the individual departments. With the routine activities systematized and placed in the hands of subordinate employees, the executive branch of the agency has concentrated upon the problems of planning, management, and policy. Even here, however, specialization inevitably developed, individual partners concentrating on particular branches or departments of the business, and Wilfred W. Fry (after 1916) overseeing the business as a whole.

To preserve the unity of the organization and the flexibility of its operations, the firm has not drawn sharp lines of authority and function. Moreover, frequent conferences between members of different departments, the practice of making written memoranda of all decisions and instructions, and the general liaison work of the Business Department have combined to avoid the dangers of over-specialization. Some light is thrown upon the success of the specialization and organization by the following facts. In 1901 a staff of 180 employees was required to handle slightly over $2,000,000 worth of business; in 1926 a staff ranging from 574 to 622 employees successfully handled a volume of over $25,000,000. Meanwhile the work of preparing and placing advertisements had increased tremendously and the hours of work had been reduced by at least 10 hours per week.

In 1929 the Ayer firm was incorporated, with Wilfred W. Fry (who, as F. W. Ayer's son-in-law, had inherited the controlling interest) as president. This step was taken to enable members of the Ayer staff to participate in the profits of the business, but it resulted in no important change in the organization of the firm's activities. Upon Fry's death in July, 1936, several of the principal vice-presidents became involved in a fight for control of the agency. This contest terminated in December with the withdrawal of one of the vice-presidents and the election as president of Harry A. Batten, who had begun his employment in the firm in 1911.

7. Readings

Ralph M. Hower, *The History of an Advertising Agency* (Cambridge, 1939). A detailed and fully documented study of the history of N. W. Ayer & Son, Inc.

Frank Presbrey, *The History and Development of Advertising* (New York, 1929). A voluminous compilation with some interpretation by an agent of long experience. Not a scholarly study but a useful source book.

George P. Rowell, *Forty Years an Advertising Agent* (New York, 1905, reprinted in 1926). The reminiscences of one of the pioneer agents. Not well organized but interesting and important.

James W. Young, *Advertising Agency Compensation* (Chicago, 1933). A brief, carefully prepared survey of the origin and development of the "commission system" of agency compensation. Better for the facts presented than the conclusions reached.

8. Suggested Questions

1. Contrast the functions performed by Palmer's agency with those performed by N. W. Ayer & Son, Inc.
2. What evidence is there of the development of a professional attitude in the Ayer agency towards its work?
3. From the point of view of operating expenses, what are the chief problems faced by the advertising agency? What steps should be taken to remedy the situation?
4. What reasons lie behind the tendency of advertisers to use an agency which does not serve a competitor, and behind the agency's insistence upon handling all the advertising for any single business unit?
5. Is the commission plan of compensation sound from the advertiser's point of view? What are the merits of the Ayer policy of one rate of commission to all clients regardless of their size or the service wanted?
6. What should be the attitude of the agency toward the consuming public?

XXX. JOHN WANAMAKER, 1838–1922

1. General Statement

John Wanamaker was of German descent, serious, hardworking, saving, and religious. He imitated contemporaries in some policies and led in others. He was always doing something new. Philadelphia and, later, New York City were never allowed long to forget his presence and activity. Perhaps we may say that he built his business upon aggressive exploitation of service to customers.

Wanamaker kept for use the records of his firm's progress. He was conscious of the importance of business history, probably largely for advertising purposes. In the official publications of the Wanamaker store we learn about sales methods, sources of wares, treatment of employees, public benefactions, and general expansion. The financing of the business (by banks), however, is rarely touched upon. Wanamaker preferred and attained family control (under a joint-stock form of organization) and ownership of the stores and their premises.

When in 1915 the University of Pennsylvania conferred the degree of LL.D. on John Wanamaker, the Provost of that institution spoke of him as "philanthropist, statesman, eminent in the councils of the nation, Christian leader, constructive genius, who on the basis of the Golden Rule, by thought and practice, has revolutionized the business methods of the merchants of the world."

The reader will observe that the sources on which this case is based are not without bias and sometimes are positively inaccurate. They have come mostly from the publicity of John Wanamaker's store or from biographies written to honor his memory. Indeed, the chief biographical material on Wanamaker comes from men who were extremely friendly to him and under the influence of his dynamic personality. Though most of the things that were written about Wanamaker are favorable, many of the things that were said about him are unfavorable. In either instance the statements are strong. This discrepancy only increases the difficulty of the historian who attempts to deal with them. One-sided as is most of the published material on Wanamaker, yet it illustrates the spirit and the methods of one of America's greatest industrial specialists.

2. Dates in the Life of Wanamaker

1838	Born in Philadelphia.
1852	Left school to become an errand boy.
1856	Clerked in retail clothing store at $2.50 a week.
1858	Organized a Sunday school, later famous.
1861	Opened a clothing store with a partner.
1865	Adopted one-price and refund policies.
1869	John Wanamaker & Co. established men's clothing store on Chestnut St., in the fashionable shopping center of Philadelphia.
1876	Opened Grand Depot, a large clothing store. General restaurant installed.
1877	Dry goods, women's wear, and house furnishings added to men's clothing in Grand Depot.
1880	Paris office opened. Bargain room, forerunner of basement store.
1881	Factory for making of Morris chairs (other factories later).
1884	Post office, telegraph, and telephone offices in store.
1888	Berlin office opened.
1889–93	Served as Postmaster General.
1896	Purchased what remained of A. T. Stewart store in New York City.
1900	Early closing: 5:00 in summer, 5:30 in winter.
1907	Almost ruined in attempt to build new stores out of current earnings.
1909	Office opened in Yokohama.
1910	Free delivery of purchases of $5 and over within international postage limits.
1911	London office opened. Cable service introducing Paris fashions.
1913	First free delivery by parcel post.
1914	Saturdays in July and August full holidays.
1918	Closing at 5 o'clock, except a few weeks before Christmas.
1922	Death of Wanamaker.

3. General Background

A. Selling methods.

(1) One price and satisfaction guaranteed.

Most observers agree that selling methods in the 1850's and 1860's left much to be desired. Misrepresentation of quality, short measure, and other sharp practices were frequently encountered, and selling prices almost everywhere depended upon the customer's ability to bargain with the salesman. A change for the better was under way, however, for A. T. Stewart had inaugurated the one-price system in New York at a very early date, and a number of stores in New England (among them R. H. Macy's in Haverhill) regularly advertised that they had only one price for all customers. Moreover, the idea was making headway that the customer should be satisfied with his purchase. Thus a Haverhill store advertised in 1853 "all goods as represented or the money refunded," [1] and in 1855 the clothing store of Smith & Strong, of Oswego, New York, pledged [2] "that we guarantee every article sold to be what it is represented, and that we cheerfully return the money when any dissatisfaction exists." Macy made a similar guarantee as early as 1859; and, a few years later, John Wanamaker began to emphasize one price and satisfaction guaranteed to such an extent that it soon became the standard practice of all self-respecting retailers.[3]

[1] Advertisements in the Haverhill (Mass.) *Gazette*, 1853.

[2] Advertisement, *Oswego Palladium*, April 27, 1855.

[3] R. M. Hower, "Urban Retailing 100 Years Ago," *Bulletin of the Business Historical Society*, Dec., 1938, pp. 94–95.

(2) The rise of the department store.[4]

"In the movement toward adding new lines and functions—toward the modern department store—the New York dry goods firms clearly led the way. But, in Philadelphia in 1877, John Wanamaker began to expand from men's clothing and furnishings into many lines, and F. & R. Lazarus of Columbus, Ohio, also branched out from men's clothing; while the Fair, in Chicago, first began in notions, hardware, and crockery. Again, Eaton's, of Toronto, and Gimbel Brothers, of Milwaukee, evolved into department stores out of the old general store; but most general stores seem to have dropped out of the race or turned into more or less specialized stores.

"Which of these expanded institutions shall we label the first department store? That depends, of course, upon how you define the term. A first requisite is that the store shall be organized into departments for purposes of buying, selling, accounting, and general managerial control. A. T. Stewart usually gets credit for priority in this feature, but no one really knows. It is clear that in the 1840's and 1850's a number of dry goods stores were departmentized, and in the West, in the 1850's, at least two general stores had some sort of departmental arrangement.

"In addition to departmental organization, a retailing concern must have a general line of merchandise to be considered a department store. Hence we must eliminate A. T. Stewart's claim to priority, for his store was still essentially a dry goods store in 1870, when Macy's had clearly gone beyond textile lines. The result seems to be about a tie between Macy's and Lord & Taylor. Macy was first to establish book, china, and silverware departments, but Lord & Taylor was the first to add furniture and shoe departments. Perhaps the important point is that many specialty stores in large cities had grown into department stores by 1880. And John Wanamaker again dramatized the trend and led after 1882 with one innovation after another."

B. Testimony, on the department stores, before the Industrial Commission, 1899–1900.

[4] *Ibid.*, pp. 96–97.

(1) John Wanamaker.[5]

"Q. Will you please name some of those reasons [why department stores can buy at better prices than jobbers]. A. Well, the manufacturer until a very few years ago, took all the risk of creating his production. Necessarily, he had to be in advance of the season from 6 months to 1 year. It required large capital, necessitating the mercantile banker, in the shape of the commission merchant. His principal business was banking—to receive the goods and advance upon them. Generally it was his own paper. That is to say, the manufacturer drew bills on his commission man, who indorsed them. He charged a commission for that, and then the manufacturer . . . had to find the banker to furnish the money, generally a local banker. The commission man sold the goods to the jobber, which necessarily resulted in another building, and the goods were then sold, scattering them over the country, thus necessitating two organizations and two risks, the manufacturer's risk and the commission man's risk. . . . Now that is all gone. The manufacturer does not need the commission man. To be logical, the manufacturer does not need to take the large risk he formerly took, because through the retailer in touch with the consumer he can find out exactly what his mills should make and often has the retailer's order before a thread is in the loom. . . . The manufacturer has less risk, less interest to pay, and less trouble in having his collections made. . . .

"Q. Are not a large number of owners of department stores also owners of factories and control absolutely the product of those factories?—A. I do not believe such a course is general. When I began business I had the idea that the true thing for me to do was to manufacture. I said to myself, if I can get a thing and sell it for just one profit, I can sell a great deal more of it. But I found out in 10 or 15 years that manufacturing is quite another business, and a man had better attend to the business that he knows; and I practically threw away immense plants of sewing machines. . . . I would not have a factory of any kind. I prefer to be in the open market to see what everybody is making. . . .

"Q. . . . You mean that the department

[5] *Report of the Industrial Commission,* 1900, vol. vii, pp. 455–458, 464–467.

stores import their own goods direct from the manufacturers, while the small storekeepers must buy them from the importer?—A. They must buy them from the jobber. The importer of those goods himself sells them to the jobber. That is about all there is for a jobber today.

. . . .

"Q. . . . Has the department store been a great factor in establishing the one-price system in the retail trade?—A. I would say yes to that. The minute that one store adopts a good system the store that competes with it must do the same thing. . . .

"Q. . . . Is not this becoming rather common among department stores [to use leaders, sold at or below cost, as bait]?—A. It is among a great many, but what can you do with it? . . . I want to keep away from the store that tries to catch me with that kind of a fishhook. If they lose on one thing they will put it on something else you do not know of. . . . We would like to go to a place where they have some rule and system, under which we would be sure not to pay too much for a thing, and not to a man that does a catch-all-you-can business. You may want a thing as [sic] he recoups all those losses on; a coat or something of that kind.

. . . .

"Q. . . . Would you give the commission some sort of an idea of the extent of your store in Philadelphia, size of buildings, number of employees, capital involved, and means of distribution by vans and otherwise?—A. The size of the property is 250 feet on Market street by 488 feet to Chestnut. It is a queer old patchwork building. Its floor area covers about 14 acres. The acreage of the warehouse and all that is in use in Philadelphia for the business is just about 20 acres in round figures. The number of employees of the store in Philadelphia last night was 5,660. I suppose there are about 100 more I did not get; I just took it at what they had posted, and they did not have everything entered. The value of the stock in Philadelphia would be about $6,000,000 in the retail. The amount of capital would hardly give you any idea, for the reason that it includes the real estate. I suppose the real estate there would now be worth $10,000,000—from Market to Chestnut, next to the city hall. There is a vast capital besides that that enters into it. First, the goods which are not in the store, but that are on sea and in transit; perhaps not less than a million more going through the works that we are obligated for. Then, also, there are the amounts of the monthly charges. We do not do a credit business, but anything that people will pay us for at the end of the month can go on the books. I should think we have 400 horses in our stables at the present time."

(2) Otto Young, manager of the "Fair" in Chicago.[6]

"Q. What is the economy of many departments under one management?—A. The economy is largely in the quantity of goods that we can purchase, as against the small merchant. We buy our goods for cash. No department store that has to buy goods on credit ever made a success. Department stores do away largely with the middlemen, with the jobbers. They buy nine-tenths of their goods direct from the manufacturer; they do not have to pay two or three profits before the goods get to them. . . .

. . . .

"Q. You would not want [to employ] a girl then who was alone in the world and would have to dress and feed herself out of what she could earn in your store?—A. No; we would not want her.

"Q. Would not want her?—A. No; she had better go into service somewhere where she could earn more money. It is hard work in Chicago to get servants for less than $5 or $6 a week; they are scarce."

(3) Samuel W. Woodward, department store merchant, Washington, D. C.[7]

"Q. What, then, in your opinion, is the reason for the change that has occurred in the last 25 years in the methods of conducting mercantile business?—A. First, the fall in prices; and second, the difficulty of getting any profit at all, have compelled men who had the ability, means, and capacity to extend their lines; and in the third place, so many

[6] *Ibid.*, pp. 696, 701.
[7] *Ibid.*, pp. 734, 736.

men in business after the panic of 1857 had nothing to do in the early sixties but to go to their places of business in the morning and mark up the prices of their goods. When the great change came in the end of the sixties they did not know how to do business on a falling market; that is, as we say, they were not quick sellers enough. When we think that ordinary cotton cloths sold for 60 and 70 cents a yard when the war ended—well, I use cotton cloth as an extreme illustration, but the same was true in every line of what we call textiles—underwear, outside wear, and house furnishings in general. In my experience, on Hanover street, in those days a good many merchants thought they were worth a great deal of money, but it was in stock on the shelf, that was depreciating all the time until prices got down to a level; then it was too late.

"Q. You think that stocks of goods are turned over, that is, converted into cash, more rapidly nowadays than 25 or 30 years ago?—A. Immeasurably.

"Q. That permits the merchant to accept a smaller profit and still do well, does it not?—A. Yes, sir. We could not do business nowadays and carry the stocks that we did 25 or 30 years ago.

"Q. Is there some credit still given in the business of retail merchandising?—A. Yes.

"Q. How long credits, as a rule?—A. Baltimore is the only city that I know of that holds on to the old 6 months' credit system. All good merchants that I know of in the North and East require monthly settlements.

"Q. That is considered practically cash?—A. Practically cash, yes. They get their money before the 10th of the following month. It is practically cash, and I am sure that these accounts are not wanted unless they are paid in that way.

. . . .

"Q. Have the combination stores had the effect to very materially decrease the number of dealers between the manufacturer and the seller of goods?—A. Yes; that is very marked in the jobbing business. As you know, Colonel Clarke, there is almost no jobbing trade in Boston now.

"Mr. Clarke. Only 4 dry goods houses of that class left there, I believe.

"The Witness. Yes; when we started in business, in 1873, Franklin street and Devonshire street and Summer and Chauncey were lined on both sides. You could count them by the dozens. . . ."

4. An Official Wanamaker Appraisal of Wanamaker History, 1861–1911.[8]

"At the close of the first day [in 1861] the cash drawer revealed a total intake of $24.67.

"Of this sum $24 was spent for advertising and 67 cents saved for making change next morning.

"Looking backward to this beginning, the Founder wrote only yesterday:

. . . .

" 'In those days it was the custom to start work at six-thirty in the morning and keep on until seven or half-past at night, except Saturdays, when stores closed from ten to ten-thirty at night.'

" 'There was no selling price for goods—there was an asking price, and the most persistent haggler bought the goods far below the unwary.'

" 'Seldom was cash paid for wages to the workpeople making clothing. The general rule was fortnightly settlements in grocery, coal and other orders, on which the manufacturer had a percentage.'

. . . .

" 'Very boldly we swam out and made for four good landings:

FIRST. Cash payments on the spot to workpeople on completion of the work.

SECOND. Shorter business days.

THIRD. Not two prices,—one price and only one.

FOURTH. Taking back anything sold and returning the money.'

"The first of these pioneering reforms began with the business; the second in 1862; the third and fourth in 1865.

. . . .

[8] *Golden Book of the Wanamaker Stores, Jubilee Year, 1861–1911* (Philadelphia, 1911), vol. i, pp. 27–28, 47, 53–55, 57–58, 61, 68, 77, 85–86, 102–104, 117–118, 120–122, 175–176, 187, 195, 202, 219, 231–232, 249, 275–276. Reprinted with permission of the trustees of the estate of Rodman Wanamaker.

"Few merchants believed the new two-acre store [opened in 1876] could succeed, because

1. *It would not importune anyone to buy.*

2. *The prices of goods were put down at the beginning to the lowest point that they could be sold for and there was no underground way to get them. All were on the ground floor from the first.*

3. *The goods were genuinely trustworthy. Seconds were not sold for anything but seconds, even if the people could not tell the difference.*

4. *A sale could be canceled and money got back easily by return of what failed to please.*

5. *New, fair and most agreeable relations were established between the purchaser and the seller, the poor and the rich, the wise and the unwise—there was no favoritism.*

"This doctrine was rank heresy in trade circles.

"But Wanamaker's was doing business with the public, not with other traders.

. . . .

" 'So you are going to start the Dry Goods business?' [Wanamaker was asked, as reported in a newspaper.]

" 'Yes!'

" 'What is your idea, Mr. Wanamaker, in doing it?'

" 'To do in Ladies' goods just what we have done with Men's goods—first in getting Clothing for the people at reasonable prices; then in reducing the prices of Shoes; then in lowering the cost of Hats. All these are Men's and Children's goods. Now, then, we propose to turn our attention to Women's goods, hoping to bring about beneficial results.'

" 'But this is not in your line?'

" 'Why not, who has a patent on merchandising? We never questioned the right of the Dry Goods stores that began to sell Clothing, nor would we doubt the propriety of dealing in any article that we pleased. If we were just starting in business who would consider it proper to question what business we chose to follow?'

" 'But you have a large business already.'

" 'So we have, and we worked sixteen years for it, and with the large property we now have we can do a great deal more business with no more expense for rent, taxes, gas, and only the addition of needed clerk hire. This is a great advantage for introducing a new department.'

" 'What is the tendency of large establishments?'

" 'Well, the moment the doors of the new Dry Goods Department open the prices will go down throughout the city.'

" 'Why do you suppose that?'

" 'Because the more competition the better it is for a community—the better the people are served.'

" 'What is your plan in conducting the Dry Goods business?'

" 'First. To secure superior men in each department whose undoubted ability will guarantee a good stock.

" 'Second. To sell only good makes of goods.

" 'Third. To stick to One Price.

" 'Fourth. To mark all the stock uniformly low.

" 'Fifth. To exchange all kinds of goods.'

. . . .

" 'What effect will this have on other storekeepers?'

" 'That is not the question; the real question to be considered is whether the people will be served by it or not—it is not the few that are to be thought of, but the many. To answer a polite question, however, unquestionably the new store must have an excellent effect on the city business—two roads to New York serve the city better than one would—by its uniformly moderate prices it will compel low prices everywhere; it will stimulate every one to do their best to serve their patrons; it will attract, by its mammoth stock and its conveniences, crowds of people from the country, who buy all kinds of goods of our neighbors, the Furniture, Glassware and Stove stores, Harness, Grocery and other stores; it will bring money to Philadelphia that otherwise would not come here; it will give employment to hundreds of people, many of whom would otherwise be idle.'

. . . .

" 'I shall always remember that morning [of the opening of the "New Kind of Store," 1877]. I had the privilege of being shown over the new store by the honored proprietor himself,' wrote Dr. James R. Miller. 'I shall never forget his happiness. He told me what he hoped the new store would do for Philadelphia. Goods could be bought a good deal cheaper in Philadelphia that day, he said, than the week before. People would not need any longer to go to New York to do their shopping. Instead of hurting other stores in the city, this new store would do them all good. It would bring new business to Philadelphia from all the surrounding country, and all the stores would get their share of this. It would introduce new ways of trading and doing business, and all the stores would get a fresh impetus.'

. . . .

"On June 3, 1881, in connection with the Wanamaker Store's first advertisement of Morris chairs it was stated that 'They were made in our own factory because the maker whom we had employed threw up his job under threat of a boycott if he worked for Wanamaker.'

. . . .

"The electric lamps lighted the way to expansion in every department, and in the autumn of 1879 the floor space occupied by the business totaled 4¹¹⁄₁₀₀ acres, and there were 40 distinct sections.

"They lighted the way also to one of the most important and widely copied of business innovations—full-page advertisements in newspapers. For in December, 1879, during the great reception given General Grant on his return from girdling the globe, Wanamaker's first made consecutive use of this new generally adopted publicity measure.

"Five months later was introduced the 'Wanamaker style' of advertising. The old-fashioned sort that had under-gone few changes since Franklin's day was replaced with real news, written in plain, straightforward language, and printed in clear, readable type. This in place of prosaic statements repeated from ten to a hundred times, and set in whatever form pleased the printer.

. . . .

"The year 1883 was one of varied growth and expansion. June first the actual value of the stock was $2,500,000—a mint of merchandise. The floor space was now eight acres; the Mail Order Bureau was receiving and answering an average of 1,000 letters daily and Buyers for the store went to Europe by the half-dozen. The ventilating system was so enlarged and perfected that in summer the store temperature was many degrees cooler than the air outside.

. . . .

"Celebrating the Twentieth Anniversary of the move to 'Centre Square,' a signed editorial printed early in 1897 said:

" 'A large slice of our little fortune was lost in establishing this new system of business. Slowly, very slowly, our plans unfolded, and gradually other stores, one after another, began to take our unpatentable forms and principles. We are glad to see what are termed "Wanamaker Innovations" creeping into the general storekeeping of the nation. Instead of hurting the business of the city, as many predicted, the large stores grew larger, and the small stores greatly increased in number, as is apparent to any observer.'

"The closing days of 1897 brought an announcement almost as interesting to the public as to those directly concerned.

" 'Every cent of profit on the excess of the whole month's business over that of December, 1896,' it said, 'shall be set aside for division among our salespeople.

" 'This is not profit-sharing nor an eking out of salaries, for salary lists here are the one thing we are liberal with—it is actually turning a lively business over to the benefit of our helpers for a part of the days.'

. . . .

"It gave to its employes a new standing by recognizing a social duty to them as employes, and requiring from them no concealments in the performance of their duties to customers.

. . . .

"It is a part of the history of the business that some years ago it made a division of profits to the employes, and later adopted a regular system of half-yearly advances of salaries upon their working records and a bonus upon the sales of the month of December.

"It established an Insurance Association, with three classes of sick and death benefits, which has distributed since its formation, June 21st, 1882, almost half a million dollars.

"1st class cost $5.90 a year to each individual.
"2nd " " $2.90 " " " " "
"3rd " " $1.34 " " " " "

3)$10.14
or $3.38 on an average per year.

"It established and maintained at the expense of the founder of the store a pension roll, upon which the aged and disabled receive half pay, and in some cases more than that.

"It established and still maintains the Annie McDowell Circulating Library, containing 4,100 volumes, for the convenience and saving of time of employes.

"It maintains a Saving Fund for employes, with inducements to save.

"The Building Associations instituted and managed by our employes are most successful methods of saving.

"This store organized its schools upon their present practical basis six years ago [1905], not as an advertisement, but as a clear duty to its young men and boys, and they have become a function of the store, in which six thousand and four persons have been students. It is a quite effective and greatly prized work, of which there is no publicity except at graduations, when we are obliged to go outside of the store for a place to hold the Commencements. The Diplomas of Graduation then given are of great value as recommendations to those removing to other cities. It is an inherent part of the store system that there is a social service due from the employer to the employed, full development of which has not been possible in the old buildings, which require the halls and recitation rooms being provided in the new building.

"Education for industry is the wider, broader work of equipment due to employes, who are in more than fifty per cent of cases without definite technical knowledge for best earning power.

"Compare the life of Dry Goods Assistant nowadays with what it was generally before this store opened and you will realize the encouragement to do still better things.

"It seems to me that a tremendous responsibility rests upon employers toward their intelligent, painstaking employes, who spend their lives year in and year out under the same roof. The originality, personality, initiative and inventions of methods and easements of mercantile life are intangible influences; but they exist and are felt, though they may not always be definable in words.

. . . .

"For many years the young men and women and the boys and girls have been taught in the day and night classes of this Commercial Institute which is now a part of the American University of Trade and Applied Commerce.

"Since its founding more than 7,500 students have been enrolled, the younger boys and girls composing the morning school, held during store hours, and the older ones staying two evenings a week, having supper free in the store and afterwards reporting to the class rooms.

"Now this work has broadened into a full-fledged University of practical learning, in which will be taught the science of merchandising; the history, evolution and qualities of all merchandise sold in the Wanamaker Stores, giving at the same time to the whole store family such self-culture, general culture and enlarged outlook as the universities of theory aim to give.

"Text-books and courses are in preparation embracing the principles of hygiene, physiology, ethics, logic, art, music, craftsmanship, and such technical branches as accounting, auditing, investments, finance, banking, commerce and kindred topics.

"These text-books will cover all branches of the curriculum, including seventy or eighty manuals of merchandise—one for each section of the stores.

"To be included also in the University curriculum are certain branches of the trades, such as dressmaking, dress-cutting, shirt-cutting, shirtmaking, millinery, art embroidery, watch and clock repairing, engraving, upholstering, carpet making and laying and other special technical work of a purely trades character.

"University quarters are building as part of the store equipment, with class-rooms, merchandise clinic-rooms, study-rooms, laboratories, gymnasium and rest-rooms.

"It is an effective and greatly prized work, connected with which is no publicity except at commencement time, when parents and friends are invited to the regular graduation exercises.

"Certificates of Graduation from this American University of Trade and Applied Commerce are of great value as recommendations to graduates removing to other cities.

. . . .

" '. . . Having personally created the business, [said Wanamaker in 1909,] the Founder and his son, Rodman, are now its sole owners, which ownership is in shares all held by themselves, in incorporated companies organized only for the future perpetuation of the business. . . .'

. . . .

" 'THE STARTING POINT.

" 'The community of interest;

" 'The humanities—not of theory, but of fact in an individual relation to each individual customer and employe.

" 'Motif—A high and clear ideal with a determination to preserve the balance of fairness between all concerned.

" The ideas underlying the business which has led in the new order of things, and which has grown to such proportions, are specifically

" '(1) AS TO THE PUBLIC.

" '(a) A service exactly opposite to the ancient custom that "the customer must look out for himself."

" '(b) A kind of storekeeping absolutely new in its ensuring protection from statements, printed or spoken, ignorant or wilful, in reference to origins of merchandise, their qualities and actual values.

" '(c) An elimination of so-called privileges to customers, as privileges, when they border on humiliations, because hospitality as well as the return of goods for refunds or reclamations are *rights* that spenders of money are entitled to as rights, and not as favors.

" '(d) Recognizing and practicing the manifest, though unwritten law, that customers are entitled under our system to the maximum of satisfactions at the minimum of cost, for the reason that they pay the usual and ordinary expenses of storekeeping, which are always included in the price of merchandise.

" '(e) Securing to each individual dealing with us to the last analysis exactitude of intelligent service and full value for value received in every transaction.

" '(2) AS TO THE WORKING PEOPLE.

" '(a) An admission as a fundamental principle that workers are entitled to further considerations beyond legal wages, covering their welfare and their education.

" '(b) To see that employes are not overreached or overlooked, and making it possible that there shall be nothing between a man and success, but himself.

" '(c) To provide education to employes as the only means of doing what legislation or combination cannot do, the improvement of their earning capacity, and thereby assisting to remove the antagonisms of labor and capital, adding to the sum of human happiness.

" '(d) That the education provided shall not include the dead languages or other unuseful studies to the detriment of the practical and technical everyday work studies that aid in making a better living.

" '(e) That the education must at the same time go towards the development of character in order to enable a man to better engineer his life to higher living and greater happiness, as well as to earn his daily bread.

" '(f) To keep foremost the observance of the spirit as well as the letter of the laws that govern our business transactions and relations to each other.

" '(g) A fixed plan of retirement of employes on retired pay to give rest and recreation to the old and chances to the younger people for promotion.

" '(h) A Court of Appeal, chosen by the employes, to hear and adjust impartially any complaint the employes desire to lay before such a court of reference.

" 'THE CARDINAL POINTS OF THE BUSINESS.

" '(1) The assembling and distribution of the best products of the world upon the most intelligent and economic basis.

" '(2) The ablest management, most thorough accuracy of service and, because of the fairest treatment of all the workers, from the humblest to the highest, the finest comradeship.

" '(3) The life and soul of the business to be its honor.

" '(4) That the aim and purpose of the

business must always be that as the business rises it must lift every worker with it.'

. . . .

[PUBLIC SERVICES OF WANAMAKER'S]

"IN COMMERCIAL WAYS—By opening sure markets to American and foreign goods. By training their own people in scientific merchandising, and by demonstrating that merchandising is a science.

"IN EDUCATIONAL WAYS—By continual exhibitions, industrial, artistic and instructive; and by organizing the first Store Commercial Institute and the first Store University, the 'American University of Trade and Applied Commerce,' in which store people are given a thorough business training.

"IN INTELLECTUAL WAYS—By revolutionizing book trade methods and prices and by demonstrating practically that publicity is a science.

"IN MUSICAL WAYS—By revolutionizing the piano trade. By inaugurating store concerts. By giving store people vocal and instrumental training.

"IN FURTHERING THE FINE ARTS—By stimulating native talent with competitive exhibitions and by importing the best works of foreign art salons.

"IN LIFTING FASHION TO A RECOGNIZED ART SHOW—The first American stores to plant themselves amid the Paris fashions; to systematically gather and report them by cable; and to give them to America as promptly as Paris herself can get them.

. . . .

"IN WAYS OF PUBLIC ACCOMMODATIONS—By keeping store telephone service in operation night and day.

. . . .

"To bring about the new conditions, however, it was necessary to become a manufacturer of certain classes of goods which could not be bought in the open market.

"And to this day—a sidelight on the tenacity of old customs—the Wanamaker Stores are compelled to make their own laboratory toilet products, their own candy, their own bedding, and to plan, originate and have made to their own specifications many kinds of goods.

. . . .

"Salesmen for years had been giving their customers whatever information they had about the merchandise. The Wanamaker Store now began giving this information publicly to a multiplicity of probable customers.

. . . .

"Wanamaker advertising became news.

"It began to tell the story of the store as the newspapers then were only beginning to tell the story of the world's daily happenings.

"It began to give information about merchandise that was helpful to the customer in making their selections.

"It was not a lever to sell; it was a lever to buy with.

"It had passed beyond the 'announcement' stage of advertising—and had led the way into the 'informative' stage. Into the helpful, friendly stage.

. . . .

" 'Mr. A. A. Butler sails today [December 22, 1879] to open an office in Paris as a permanent facility for buying goods and executing commissions within the scope of our business.'

. . . .

"A Wanamaker Merchandise Bureau was established at Yokohama in 1909, and within the last year has been laid the foundation for the opening of a London office, through which shall be cemented trade connections with another great capital, making the Wanamaker Stores a still more important representative of foreign lands in America.

"The Philadelphia and New York organizations may be called the two legs on which this business stands; the Paris, Yokohama and London Bureaus its hands that reach out to the remotest corners to procure the world's best.

. . . .

"There is probably no other store in the world that has gone into the Paris Salons and purchased the pictures best worth having to decorate its walls. It is largely these paintings and this kind of artistic exhibition, open to all for the coming, that have helped to convert the Wanamaker Stores into vast public museums, quickening the interest of thousands of visitors, and reaching a larger number than many of the museums owned and controlled by the city or the state.

. . . .

". . . A constant stream of letters, cables and information is pouring into headquarters from that side of the sea, and the incessant arrival of Paris merchandise would suggest, as someone has said, 'that there is a Wanamaker tunnel under the ocean.'

"This quick service is specially necessary, with the articles of dress that change in fashion frequently and with great rapidity—as, for example, millinery. So far as known, Wanamaker's is the only store having an exclusive *envoi* of the latest Paris hats once a week; enabling the patrons of its millinery salons to put on the hats that *Tout Paris* is wearing—not a month later, *but on the very same day.*

"The Wanamaker stocks of Paris goods, unique in their design, are seldom duplicated in America. These constant importations have their effect on many of the American-made articles that come into the Wanamaker Stores.

"Back of all this fashion work that the Wanamaker Stores are doing, lies, however, another purpose that rises to the surface once in a while. It is, to guide women to dress better, more simply, and more graciously; to make themselves more attractive by wearing well-bred clothes that express them; to choose these clothes wisely—in a word, to make their own the Frenchwomen's century-old fascination and daintiness of dress. Without doubt, a large share of credit for the general progress made in these directions can be rightly ascribed to the long-continued and never-failing efforts of the Wanamaker Stores to get the right fashions and to present them with an intelligent perception of what the influence of their development will mean."

5. Excerpts from a Recent Biography of John Wanamaker [9]

"The credit for having initiated the one-price system in retail merchandising has often been given to Wanamaker; but he himself wrote on March 2, 1907:

" 'A. T. Stewart first began the one-price rule for dry goods, and our system carried it further than he did.'

"This generous attribution to another of the policy so frequently attributed to him is backed by many authorities. But we find it advertised by other New York stores in 1841 and 1842. It was claimed by Marshall Field in 1867. Both in England and in France one price was made a drawing-card by merchants at least as early as we find it on this side of the Atlantic. The Bon Marché advertised it in 1854, but did not claim to be the first in making the effort to put a stop to haggling and bargaining in the retail trade. The earliest definite claim that we have been able to discover is that of the great Newcastle merchant, Bainbridge, who opened a shop in 1837 with 'a definite fixed price, distinctly marked on all goods, and to this custom he rigidly adhered.'

"In writing about the one-price system at a considerably later date Wanamaker said that it had been ostensibly adopted by several other Philadelphia stores, but that there were ways of getting around it. A varying scale of discounts met almost any condition of customer; and, while in some shops the marked price was paid, a cap, a pair of gloves or suspenders, collars, or sometimes only a handkerchief, was 'thrown in.' There were days when articles were lower than ticketed. It could happen conveniently to be the day on which a customer who insisted on bargaining was in the shop.

"We know, too, that it was a long hard fight to get the buying public to understand that one price had come to stay. This is evi-

[9] Herbert Adams Gibbons, *John Wanamaker* (New York, 1926), vol. i, pp. 85, 91–94, 114, 116, 124–125, 127–128, 148–149, 166–170, 176–178, 214–215, 223–224, 225–226, 233–234, 237–239, 273–275; vol. ii, pp. 16–17, 42. Some footnotes have been omitted. Reprinted with permission of trustees of estate of Rodman Wanamaker.

dent from the frequent announcement of the policy, and insistence on it, by other large establishments in Philadelphia and New York in the early 'seventies. Wanamaker reiterated it in 1871, and again in 1874, as a 'cardinal point' of Wanamaker merchandising policy [since 1865]. . . .

. . . .

"Where Wanamaker led the way in establishing one price as a business principle, later to be universally accepted in retailing, was by announcing in 1865 that the customer could return the article and get his money back. There were no strings to this offer (except, of course, that the article had not been used). We find nowhere that this policy had been advertised before Oak Hall announced it [though then in use in Europe and the United States]. It was really the complement to one price. It gave the buyer faith in the genuineness of the claim that the price he paid was the same to all. Despite the many inconveniences and problems, which we shall mention later, attendant upon return of merchandise, it was a stroke of genius that revolutionized the American mercantile world of the post-Civil War Period.

. . . .

"He concentrated first on buying. The science of buying did not end with knowing goods and where to get them, sensing styles and patterns, and judging quantities. All this was essential, but the price had to be right. The all-wool guaranty could not be maintained unless there was a close margin in buying. The first move was to dispense with local jobbers and go directly to manufacturers and to the great wholesale houses in New York. He had already tried this as an emergency measure at the opening of the war, when he was seeking freshness and variety and credit. Now he decided to eliminate the middleman in order to get his all-wool goods at reasonable prices. Philadelphia jobbers and competitors immediately countered with the threat of boycotting houses that sold to Wanamaker & Brown. Upon the young man of twenty-four was imposed the task of convincing his sources of supplies that they would not lose out by dealing with Wanamaker & Brown. He had a momentary advantage in the purchasing power of cloth that his contract work gave him. But with the ready-made manufacturers the telling argument had to be large orders and cash payment.

. . . .

"Isaac D. Shearer, who lived until the middle of March, 1926, was the cashier of John Wanamaker & Co. He told the biographer recently that John Wanamaker emancipated himself from worries over the machinery of his business and its finances before he was thirty, and that this was one of the principal reasons for Wanamaker's early and sweeping success. The young merchant had an amazing mastery of details and a penetrating eye that took in everything. But he knew what not to get wrought up over and expend his energy in. He used to tell his staff, even when he had only a few executives, that it was their business to attend to the machinery and the money. He refused to occupy himself with matters that others could manage.

. . . .

"As manufacturing in large quantities began to replace articles made by hand, the merchandise gradually became more diversified, and the necessity of carrying large stocks to fit all sizes of customers demanded bigger establishments and greater capital. We have seen how wholesaling and contract work were the underpinning of the Oak Hall retail trade. It was the same with A. T. Stewart & Co. and Field, Leiter & Co. At this period, Marshall Field drew most of his profit from lot sales to country merchants. Stewart loved retailing, and opened in 1863 a retail store ahead of anything else in the United States; but he, too, depended somewhat upon his wholesale trade. There were two tendencies —towards the general store, transplanting to the city the old country store and towards larger specialty shops, depending for their growth upon reaching a wider circle of customers than could be counted upon in the keen competition of city mercantile life.

. . . .

". . . The Chestnut Street store was a triumph in merchandising ability. Among Philadelphians it established, as Oak Hall could never have done, John Wanamaker's reputation for taste and quality of merchandise, and in the merchant's own brain it planted the idea and gave the inspiration for the 'new kind of store.'

. . . .

". . . The Chestnut Street Store [established in 1869], success that it was, did not keep pace with his ambition. And he was eager as a child to carry the gospel of 'one price' and 'money back' to a wider field than he had yet reached. On him was the urge of other worlds to conquer.

"Wanamaker & Brown had for several years been doing business in semi-fit clothing through agents, mostly postmasters. Suits and overcoats were offered unfinished, a local tailor to do the final fitting. Where there was much trade to be had, tailors in small cities were appointed agents. They would take measurements, send them in to Oak Hall, get the partly made garment, and do the finishing. From this to self-measurement and direct order, or order of ready-made clothing on approval, was only a step.

"Wanamaker came close to founding the pioneer mail-order house. He did not follow up this lead energetically, because business by correspondence was too impersonal. He wanted the pleasure of displaying his goods and seeing customers come in and buy them.

"At the end of 1871 Wanamaker & Brown had a surplus in certain cheaper lines, due to widespread unemployment. It was one of the few times in his career that he was heavily overstocked. Studying the situation, he learned that there were good times in the Pittsburgh steel business, where all the mills were working to capacity rolling steel rails. Promptly he shipped the surplus stock to Pittsburgh, and opened a store on Fifth Avenue, advertising the Wanamaker principles. Washington and Richmond stores came next, and then branches in Middle Western cities. It was a great field, and if he had followed it out Wanamaker would have become the originator of the first chain store system in America. The opportunity was within his grasp.

. . . .

"Initiating this policy and maintaining it throughout his life made him at times seem churlish and lacking in the spirit of *camaraderie* in what came to be considered a new classification of retail merchandising. It led him occasionally in his advertising into what competitors believed to be hair-splitting, if not extravagant, claims. It brought down upon his head the condemnation of merchants who stuck to their special lines, and did not win him the friendship of most of those who went along with him into the wider field or who followed and imitated him. On the other hand, the results amply prove that there was nothing quixotic about the conception, and there can be no doubt that it became—and remained until his death—the greatest single factor in establishing the success of the general stores of today.

. . . .

". . . Wanamaker determined to go into general storekeeping . . . gathering distinctive specialty shops under one roof, with a common administrative organization, but with the buying in charge of highly trained specialists . . .

. . . .

"Before the opening, Wanamaker gathered his staff of nearly a thousand around him, and talked to them in his homely fashion. He asked them to look at the design of the store, aisles, and circles, each one larger, until the outer one touched the four great entrances, and eight vertical aisles, leading from the center, and cutting through the five circles. 'It is a wheel,' he said, 'and each of you is a spoke. I am the motive power, and I shall see that the wheel keeps moving. But you must each be in your place at all times, and do your duty, or I can accomplish nothing. . . .'

. . . .

"But Wanamaker realized that if he were going to make his general store what he intended it to be, a group of specialty shops, each with a complete stock, success could be assured only by acquiring the eleven dwellings facing Chestnut Street on the plot from Thirteenth to Juniper Streets, and extending back to Kelly Street. The idea was ambitious and risky. It seems incredible that within a year of the time when he did not know whether he was going to pull through or not Wanamaker should have decided to make so radical an increase in his floor space and his investment. . . .

. . . .

"The completion of the purchase of the block on which the present store stands was celebrated by a 'grand illumination.' On November 11, 1878, it was announced that the store would be open that evening from 7:30 to 10 to show what the Grand Depot had to offer for the Christmas season. Nothing would be sold. . . . An exuberant reporter saw the event thus:

" 'The whole area, as viewed from the galleries and towers, was a sunlit sea of heads. The élite of fashion, the solidity and wealth, the youth and beauty of the city poured through the points of entrance to the Grand Depot in a steady stream of humanity that was at times resistless in its onward rush. . . .'

. . . .

". . . Never before had they [the Centennial visitors] thought of merchandising as a service to customers. And never before had they been in a store that was manifestly a show place, where they could look around without being importuned to buy, and where they could feel as much at ease as if they were strolling down the street. It was a unique experience, too, to find a store in which there was a place to sit down and write letters. Of course they all sent home postcards, furnished free, with a picture of the Grand Depot, one of the features of the Centennial. Along with the guide books and pamphlets purchased or handed out to them at Fairmount Park they put among their souvenirs of the World's Fair the 'Wanamaker Store Book' which explained the new mercantile policies, and described the magnitude of the Wanamaker clothing business.

. . . .

"Wanamaker was delighted when Ogden [a Philadelphian who had since 1852 been in a clothing firm in New York] agreed to join his organization on January 1, 1879. But he came, not to help at the Grand Depot in the new general-store venture, but to give to Oak Hall the time Wanamaker could no longer spare and the high ability and competence as a clothing merchant that Wanamaker knew he had. After four years at Oak Hall Wanamaker invited Ogden to join him at the Grand Depot, putting before him the alluring prospect of association in the great business that had just turned the corner and was now firmly established. He told Ogden that if Oak Hall and the Chestnut Street Store prospered for two years under the management of his brothers and their associates, he would turn the two businesses over to them and invite Ogden to join him in general storekeeping. . . .

"Freed of the responsibility and care of the two clothing establishments [in 1885, by new partnership arrangements], and supported by his old and trusted friend, Ogden, and his eldest son, who had recently graduated at Princeton, Wanamaker now had associates . . . whom he needed in order to cope with an expansion that called for more than he felt that he alone would be able to give. . . .

. . . .

"When the new store buildings were going up in Philadelphia and New York, it is evident from documents in the files that Wanamaker thought for a time of calling his business 'The Wanamaker Composite Stores.' He never used the term 'department store,' and was consistent throughout his career in believing that and asserting that he was not in the department-store business.

"Marshall Field divided his time and talents between the wholesale and retail business, and he always had partners. Virtually all the department stores of Paris, London, New York, Philadelphia, Chicago, Boston, and other cities became stock companies or went to the public for capital with huge bond issues. For nearly half a century John Wanamaker personally directed the enterprise that he had founded and owned, imposing upon himself a life-long sentence of hard labor as a first-hand student of merchandising materials and policies and of the psychology of advertising and the buying public. This is the significance of 'the new kind of store.'

. . . .

"His courage is strikingly revealed . . . when a late warm spell retarded the fall sales, just when he needed money to meet his bills. On October 1, [1873] he told Libbey:

" 'As one warm day after another has slipped away and my receipts have disappointed me and the remittances that I promised myself to make to you had to be withheld I felt I ought to write you to be patient for a few days longer.

" 'The fact is I have paid off nearly all that I owe to others that is overdue and when I get a few goods out of the Customs House that I was foolish enough to have bought abroad I shall have little to do but to pay you. I know I can pay all the money I owe you but I never expect to get out of debt to you what I owe you for kindnesses which I hope soon to talk over with you.

" 'I am glad to fling into some people's faces that you and your house are the exception in dunning me for payments. I mean to have it remain so by pouring money in to you soon.'

"Rumors of a crash not only passed from mouth to mouth during the summer of 1877, but they got into the type of newspaper that used to exist a generation ago but which has long passed into history. The newspapers that lived by scandal and blackmail Wanamaker never advertised in. This was their opportunity. The new enterprise was at first ridiculed, and when financial circles began to speak of Wanamaker's difficulties several Philadelphia papers, which have long since disappeared, so their names have no interest to us, made the most of the critical situation. In one of these, on August 31, 1877, we find:

" 'There's trouble in the big Market Street Wigwam. Protests, extensions, unpaid employes, etc. etc. Not long ago, we predicted that somebody would soon meet the fate of the overambitious frog in the fable, which tried and tried to swell itself up to the size of an ox, and busted itself. Somebody has been trying to swell himself up to the mercantile dimensions of the late A. T. Stewart, and an explosion is imminent. " 'Twas ever thus!" But, there has been something more than foolish ambition and imprudence in this case There has been a greedy, grasping and godless spirit at work in the mind of somebody, prompting him to break down other business and absorb almost every branch of mercantile business in his own establishment. Herein crops out, in a very offensive form, the ambition to imitate A. T. Stewart, who was one of the meanest men and merchants that ever lived. He squelched hundreds of smaller dealers without compunction and ground his employes into the very dust of humiliation and impecuniosity; and his ambitious Philadelphia prototype on a smaller scale, has been trying to play the same heartless game. But, this Philadelphia merchant has had to cope with some very solid business men, and he has found that he has been butting his poor head against some very stubborn stone walls. He's in danger. He is walking on the thin crust of a volcano which threatens to blow him and his wigwam sky-high, scattering hats and haberdashery, shoes and chemisettes, collars and cuffs, trunks and teapots, lawns and lines, boots and broadcloth, furs and flannels, to the four winds.'

"The ill will and active hostility of Philadelphia merchants had been incurred for two reasons: The first was the fear that the general store would prove to be an octopus, stretching out its tentacles in all directions and strangling the small shopkeepers, who could not meet the competitive prices, the advantages and attractions, and the advertising offensive, of large establishments. Retail merchandising had always been carried on by specialty shops. Men with ideas like Wanamaker's were a subversive influence, menacing the existing structure of the business world. The second was that the Wanamaker policy, begun in the 'Opportunity Sale' of April, 1877, and followed by 'Partial Inventory,' 'Mid-summer' and 'Early Fall' sales in the first six months of 'the new kind of store,' of clearing at a sacrifice existing stocks that had not moved quickly, made a radical change in the existing methods of retailing to which specialty shops found difficulty in adjusting themselves. This had already happened in Paris, and it was upsetting the business world in New York and Chicago as well as in Philadelphia.

. . . .

"It is a curious and astonishing revelation to study and record from documents the life of this man. We are unable to find any evidence of the desire or intention to meet a financial crisis by what seems to an ordinary mortal the obvious expedient, a temporary pause, if not actual retrenchment, for the fear of throwing good money after bad. This was not Wanamaker's plan of action. Faced with demands for payments, he ordered a few more buildings on Chestnut Street to be bought, and put his O. K. on blue prints for further construction. Then he would turn his attention to schemes for stimulating sales. He believed that if he could get the right kind of merchandise, display it well, and advertise it effectively, people would buy. The money would come in and the bills would be paid. The results invariably justified this belief.

"Wanamaker's chief anxiety, therefore, was not finding the money to meet the needs of his business which were rapidly increasing. Nor did he seem to fear any heavy falling off in the buying capacity of the people, due to bad times. He put all his thoughts on having goods to offer, that would win and keep the confidence of the buying public in the Grand Depot, to making his store attractive and serviceable, and to presenting through the daily press accurate Wanamaker store news.

. . . .

"To quantity and quality of stocks must be added style. This was Wanamaker's greatest struggle with his early buyers. He had around him some men who were excellent merchants when it came to gauging the quantities and varieties needed to meet the demand, and whose sterling honesty equaled his own. But they had little imagination or taste, and were disinclined to study styles. Wanamaker never felt that his great enterprise would fail for lack of money to carry it on or because of inefficient management. But as long as he lived he did worry over falling behind in the styles of his goods. He had a horror of any department becoming stereotyped, content to jog along handling what manufacturers and importers were offering. This easy road of merchandising it was not in him to follow. Point-blank he refused to follow it.

"Here we have the secret of the hold he got upon the buying public of Philadelphia and the rapid growth of his prestige as a merchant throughout the country. It is interesting to discover from the records that the sales he originated, and which were immediately copied by other merchants, were not inspired by the desire or necessity of increasing the volume of business, but by the determination to keep stocks fresh and up to date. We have proof of this great fact in his notes of the period and in his talks to buyers. For instance:

" 'Let me say that there is no room in the Grand Depot for old stocks. We are increasing our floor space this year, but not for that. If one of your salesmen sees an article around, unsold, until he gets tired of looking at it, how can you expect to find—ever—a satisfied purchaser for it? Mark down goods before they get out of style. That is why we have our sales. We must move the goods while they are still fresh and are still a good buy. Don't think that being able eventually to sell without a loss is good merchandising. I want to repeat that there is only one kind of good merchandising, and that is to sell to people only what they ought to have, not what they will take for a price. The men who will keep this business flourishing are those who are thinking about what is going to be worn and what is going to be used.' [Not a new idea, as there were clearance sales long before this.]

"But mere words and preachments, inspirational talks to buyers, scoldings and ravings, would not have made the Grand Depot a success. Wanamaker created the machinery for enabling his buyers to carry out his ideals, and he stood behind them constantly, discussing their problems sympathetically, finding the remedy when things went wrong, and making it possible for them to apply the remedy.

. . . .

"Wanamaker said that his stores would betray a public trust if they offered for sale any merchandise that was not in good taste. Not long after he had opened his furniture department, he called the head one day and declared that the furniture in the store was a disgrace. 'I wouldn't have it in my house,' he said, 'and I won't have anything in my store that I wouldn't be willing to buy and use myself.' He issued an ultimatum: either John Wanamaker was to carry only the very best of furniture or John Wanamaker would go out of the furniture business. . . . 'Would you have me buy antiques?' asked the head, venturing what he thought was a joke. 'Yes,' said Wanamaker, 'buy antiques. Buy lines of the best furniture you can get your hands on. Through the antiques, people may get interested in good reproductions. . . .'

. . . . .

"And two years later the British Warehouseman of May 15, 1889, said:

" 'Mr. Wanamaker is looked upon by the citizens of Philadelphia as a power in the land. He is the owner of the largest retail establishment in the world, and there are few charitable or commercial movements in the Quaker City with which his name is not associated. He employs fifty heads of departments, who command the vast industrial army, numbering over 4,000 persons, that forms the working force. Whiteley's, of Westbourne Grove, Shoolbred's, the Glasgow Colosseum, Kendal Milnes', or the Paris Bon Marché would be lost in such a gigantic structure as that owned by Mr. Wanamaker.'

"At the time the Grand Depot was turned into a general store many able business men, who had studied carefully or who had themselves had experience in the development of a large retail business, believed that no truly great establishment could be built up without being underpinned by a wholesale business. A. T. Stewart and Co.'s position in New York had been attained by developing simultaneously the wholesale and retail fields in dry-goods; Marshall Field and his associates, Palmer and Leiter, were launching their retail business in Chicago after the great fire on the foundation of supplying dry-goods by wholesale to the merchants of the Middle West. The experience of John Wanamaker had been the same as that of A. T. Stewart and Marshall Field. He had built up the greatest retail clothing store in the country while he was enjoying the advantages of being under the same roof a wholesaler and manufacturer. But the experiment of 'the new kind of store' had been carried through a decade to unrivaled success solely by retailing.

"We have seen how Wanamaker undertook to supply himself with goods only when he could not get what he wanted in the market. But the momentous decade of his merchandising career had been paralleled by the marvelous rise of Marshall Field & Co. in Chicago. Field had partners, of course, where Wanamaker had none, and it was not until the early years of the twentieth century that Marshall Field's retail business equaled that of Wanamaker. On the other hand, the Chicago firm was doing a tremendous volume of business in its wholesale department, and seemed to enjoy certain advantages from wholesaling and retailing together that Wanamaker did not have. The decade had been marked by the rise of other general stores in many American cities, including Philadelphia, and Wanamaker was beginning to have lively competition. These considerations, added to the change in his own position, due to giving up Oak Hall and the Lower Chestnut Street Store and taking in Ogden and Thomas B. Wanamaker as partners, led John Wanamaker to enter the wholesale dry-goods field.

"In the early part of 1887 he purchased the wholesale business of Thomas J. Mustin & Co., and later in the same year that of Riegel, Scott and Co. To house his new wholesaling enterprise he put up a six-story brick building on an opposite corner of Thirteenth and Market Streets. But Wanamaker was never a man to do anything on a small scale. At the end of 1887 he purchased the largest wholesale dry-goods business in Philadelphia from Hood, Bonbright & Co. The newspapers announced:

" 'The sum which Mr. Wanamaker is said to have paid for Hood, Bonbright & Co. is $1,600,000, and he continues that business in the building which had been built for the firm by the Girard Trust, at the southwest corner of Eleventh and Market Streets, paying therefor an annual rental of $67,000.'

"The wholesale dry-goods business of Hood, Bonbright & Co. was third in the United States. Wanamaker entered into the new venture heart and soul. He worked steadily, day and night, on the inventory of the stock. He declared at the time and afterward that he had never had such fun. It was a great adventure, consolidating the business of the three wholesale houses. His leadership had never been more vigorous and successful, and the virtually unlimited scope of his merchandising genius quickly made itself felt in this new field. He was soon doing a wholesale business of $20,000,000 a year.

. . . . .

". . . We have spoken elsewhere of the establishment of his own printing-house in 1876, which issued one million copies of a booklet about Oak Hall and the Grand Depot at the time of the Centennial Exhibition. . . . He tried full pages in weekly and monthly periodicals. This is how the *Farm Journal* originated. It was first published at the Grand Depot in 1876, with the Wanamaker advertising page as its financial underwriting. Wanamaker used full pages in the *Century* and *Scribner's* in the early 1880's. In connection with his book business his advertisements had nation-wide circulation, and were copied everywhere. He conceived the idea of store magazines for 'ladies'—as women were then called. The *Philadelphia Store News*—a complete newspaper—was published first in 1883, devoted to items of interest about the Wanamaker business. *Everybody's Journal,* a little periodical issued as an advertisement for Oak Hall, grew into *Everybody's Magazine,* a pioneer in the ten-cent field. Catalogs . . . , booklets, circulars, and cards, calling attention to sales or specific categories of merchandise, went out through the mails.

. . . .

". . . No matter what he did as a citizen and a churchman the petty-minded and jealous were going to see in every activity the merchant, thinking of his wares. This truth was neatly and forcibly expressed in verses written by a clever New York newspaperman:

" 'My name is John; I run a great big store
And I make money; which is not surprising,
When you reflect that each year I do more
Of advertising.

" 'I advertise in papers great and small
And everybody knows I'm enterprising;
But then, whate'er I do, they, one and all,
Say: "Advertising!"

. . . .

" 'If, as a business man, I take a hand
In a municipal reform uprising,
The others in it are a faithful band;
I'm "advertising."

. . . . .

" 'I've given my employes co-operation,
They will do better work for realizing
A share of profits; but full half the nation
Says: "Advertising!"

. . . .

" 'No doubt 'twill be the same thing when I die.
They'll say I did it for the eulogizing—
Which is not grudged to others dead; but I
"Am advertising!" ' "

6. Recollections on Store Organization and Operation after 1900[10]

A. Mr. Wanamaker managed his own business right up to the December day in 1920 when he turned over his entire common stock interest to his son, Rodman Wanamaker, and went south for his usual winter vacation. He had his key men but he kept close contact with men and women, high and low, in every section of his business, particularly selling sections, so he knew of his personal knowledge what was going on, where he was weak in merchandise and service, where strong. He picked up ideas from everyone, his own people, other stores, here and abroad, but followed no one. Quick to abandon as he was to conceive, he tried out and abandoned many retailing practices long before others had thought of them; he centralized buying with acquisition of the New York store, appointed divisional

[10] Dictated by Rodman Barker in 1938 in answer to specific questions. Mr. Barker is vice-president of the Wanamaker stores and has been with the firm, in the financial end, about forty years.

merchandise managers in the early years of the century, and established unit and desk control of stocks in 1908–09.

Wanamaker did not want everyone poured into the same mold. He wanted to and did develop individuality. He liked to refer to his heads of sections not as buyers but as merchants. Some he found could not work without records, others could not work with records. He encouraged them both. Results counted, and only results.

Since he himself was always in close contact with the handling of the finances, the counting-room became the nerve center of the store; through the counting-room and those in charge of the counting-room everything was routed and cleared. No time was lost in conferences, few reports were made and no circulation given, absolutely none, to the daily, monthly, and yearly statements laid before Wanamaker. There was mutual understanding, things were accomplished quickly, changes in personnel were discouraged and were few. There was a big and growing family, a happy family and not a highly paid family. Wanamaker himself was a past master in keeping peace in the family, in gathering enthusiastic workers about himself without paying them great salaries. His leading men and women for the most part came from the ranks, advanced from the bottom rungs, step by step, gradually.

As the work in the main store grew he shared its administration with those under him; but he watched over it all, not only planning in a broad way but also handling detail when anything went wrong or when anything unusual or difficult to handle came up. He was equally at home in striking an advertising note, in handling a financial problem, or in teaching by example courtesy and patience to employees, as in stepping off a crowded elevator. Ever was Wanamaker's the directing hand of the Philadelphia store.

With the acquisition of the New York store he first sent his long-time partner Ogden to look after it, to watch over it, to guide it; then his son Thomas, and later Rodman to whom he finally gave full swing. He talked of it as Rodman's store and, though he never lost touch with it, the responsibility was definitely placed on Rodman's shoulders—his to pick his aids high and low, his to fix their pay and bonuses.

B. Wanamaker gave his buyers widest latitude. He wanted men and women capable of thinking for themselves, meeting problems as they arose; he wanted managers not buyers, people whose responsibility was to see that service was given as well as merchandise gathered. And this type of men and women were developed from the ranks. So little apparent direction was given that it seemed to be a natural growth. Led by example, influenced by environment, encouraged by advancement, the men and women who were needed were developed—almost unconsciously, seemingly without effort —with years of growing responsibility into the loyal, broad-minded, quick-thinking merchants Wanamaker sought—never perfect, always capable of further improvement, never finished until ready for placement on the retired roll.

C. Wanamaker did not know of accounting controls as we now know them. He did not have them and, of course, did not use them. But he knew at all times the trend of his business and of the many departments making up his business. He knew where there was weakness and where there was strength; where there was growth, where there was not; where profits were being made and where they were not; and above all, by observation more than figure, where there was waste, waste of labor, unoccupied time. The waste was cut off by leveling off sales, so that there were no valleys, no peaks, there were no big days in the week, no small days, no big months in the year, no small ones, save December with Christmas buying and July the vacation month. With months thus evened off and Saturday business no bigger than Monday or Tuesday or Wednesday or Thursday or Friday, there was economy of operation. Pressure was put behind the dull days and dull months, rather than the heavy, so that the dull became less dull and the heavy less top-heavy; and so that things were ironed out until there were no peaks other than December calling for additional help and no dull months other than July which was vacation month, and no week-day heavier than other week-days, save only days of storm. This was the aim, this the accomplishment of the merchant.

Wanamaker and those working under him were not without working controls. Working controls they had, working controls gathered at small cost with no great detail but sufficient for their guidance. Every morning Wanamaker had before him a statement of sales and purchases for the previous day and cumulative for the month, in total and by sections, comparative with previous years. Every morning he had before him a statement of the previous day's receipts, cash sales and collections, cash in bank and accounts and obligations of all kinds due or past due that day. Every day he had before him an estimate of receipts for the balance of the month and the next three months and of commitments for the same months. Current monthly stock reports by sections were always at hand. Then stock reports were kept at cost, not based on present retail method but on a predetermined rate of profit on sales, arbitrary but based on experience. In conjunction with daily sales and purchase reports these stock reports would show at a glance to those experienced, estimated stock for any section any day of the month. If stocks moved up faster than expected or down slower than expected, obviously predetermined profit was not being made. The red light was out and investigation in order. Initial mark-up on bills was at hand, and reductions were at hand. Leak there was, on the surface or hidden. If on the surface, faulty merchandising, to be corrected; if hidden leaks, to be discovered; if carelessness or dishonesty, stopped.

Accounting controls as we now know them were not kept. But figures sufficient to enable the experienced to watch gross margins, costs, and profits were kept. Watched they were and watched so successfully that, in the main, leaks were stopped before dangerous; changes made where necessary with a promptness that kept sections out of the red. Through bad years and good years, while Wanamaker was at the helm, it was rare that any section at the end of any year appeared in the red. Wanamaker at all times had his mind fixed on sales and gross profit, pushing sales ahead and maintaining gross profit, being keenly aware that if sales were pushed ahead expenses in large measure would take care of themselves, at least be easy to control.

D. As the years went by Wanamaker had more and more in mind the retirement of his older people. He never created a fund for this retirement—his mind did not run that way. He looked upon pensions or retired pay as a proper charge against current earnings of the business. He never dreamed of a time when current earnings would not be ample to take care of pension payments. He felt and announced that anyone in his employ, men or women, who had given twenty years or more of loyal service to the business was of right entitled to retired pay when in any way disabled or reaching an age when the lengthening shadows of life gave him the right to spend his remaining years in ease and comfort without being a charge to relatives. This age he finally fixed at 70 years, not when it would be obligatory to go on the retired or, as he stated, the honor roll, but optional with the employee. Minimum retirement pay be fixed at $8.00 a week, maximum $100.00, inside these limits retirement pay to be one-half of current pay. This was long before there was thought of social security acts. Retired pay was never made a contract obligation, was and is given as a pure gratuity and as such grantor is free to give, reduce, or take away as said grantor sees fit.

7. Wanamaker's Treatment of Labor

A. Wanamaker's speech on labor, about 1890.[11]

". . . Mr. Wanamaker, becoming more and more interested in the views of radical reformers, finally consented to meet a body of them in friendly conference.

. . . .

"The address of Professor Frank Parsons ended as follows: 'If men of genius and power devoted themselves to the cause of industrial justice and human development with the same fervor they show in their efforts to accumulate fortunes for themselves, their success in the higher sphere would be as great as it is now in the making of money, and the world would move as it never moved before toward the time when all shall live for each, and each for all, in a universal Brotherhood, a mighty Trust for the production of happiness, a World Cooperation for the benefit of all mankind.'

"Mr. Wanamaker's reply was in substance, as follows: 'Mr. Chairman, Ladies and Gentlemen:

" 'Well, I guess I might as well surrender at the start. Let me tell you first how I came to be here tonight. Some weeks ago my friend Dr. Morgan—I see him now in the audience and he looks like General Howard, —did any one ever tell you, Doctor, that you looked like General Howard?—No, sir. Well, you do very much,—as I was saying Dr. Morgan sent me a paper called the Nationalist containing a criticism that seemed to me pretty severe from my standpoint, and when the Doctor came in we talked about it and I said: "If you'd like to bring the man who wrote that, to see me, I'd like to talk with him," and he did, and I have conversed with him several times, and through his persuasion have come here tonight to talk matters over with you.

" 'I appreciate the kindness and the ability of the address that has been made to me. And if I could believe that the ideas expressed in it were practical, I would give up my partnership and go into the work at once. There is nothing so well worth living for. I have tried in my way,—perhaps not in the right way, but I have tried, and I have become discouraged.

" 'It is a delusion that men do not get what they are worth. Now and then a man is unfortunate, I grant, but as a rule men get what they are worth. Why it's the hardest thing in the world to find a clean, strong, earnest, upright young man,—they're as scarce as hen's teeth. I had a boy working for me once at three dollars a week—I only got two dollars and fifty cents when I began,—and the boy's father who was loom boss in a factory came to me and said he guessed he'd have to take his boy out, he could make more in the factory. "How much?" I asked—"Four dollars a week." "Well, let him alone and he'll be getting five a week here after a while." When the boy was getting eight dollars the father came again, and again I persuaded him to leave the boy with me. When the boy was getting ten dollars a week the father came again and said he was going to take the boy away. "What for?" "He isn't making enough money." "What will you do with him?" "Put him in the factory." "How much will he get?" "Twelve dollars first—fifteen afterward." "Any more?" "Yes, he may get to be loom boss." "What will he make then?" "Seventy-five dollars a month." "Well, then, let the boy alone, he'll be getting a hundred a month here some day." I had the hardest work to get that man to leave his boy, and we are paying that boy now $1,000 a month.

" 'I did not come prepared to make a speech on reform. . . . It seems to me there is nothing for it but education, and such discussions as this. I am working in that way—helping to educate several hundred of young men and women,—some of them are learning stenography, and I ought to have

[11] A brochure on *The Wanamaker Conference; John Wanamaker and the Nationalist,* by F. Parsons (Philadelphia, no date), pp. 2, 5–6.

had one of them here to take down the professor's fine words. I have tried other things. I went one evening, with an earnest worker, into what are called the "slums"—I don't often go, for I like to keep unpleasant things out of my life instead of going to them,—but I went this one evening with my friend, and I talked to some thirty fallen women. I said "Do you like this life?" "No." "Do you expect to stay in it?" "No." "When do you expect to get out of it?" "Don't know exactly when, hope a chance will offer sometime." "Is your mother living?" "Don't ask me that." "You know this gentleman?" pointing to my friend. "Yes." "And trust him?" "Yes." "Well, he will tell you that I am responsible and will do as I say, and I say that if you will leave this life right now, you shall have a good home, and I will do my best to get you employment, and I think I can do it, and you can live an honest life from now on," and how many of those women do you think accepted the offer? Only one and she was sick. I was discouraged.

" 'I have tried profit-sharing also. Years ago Governor Geary appointed me to investigate the Rochdale cooperative undertakings, and I made a report. It is filed away at Harrisburg now, I suppose. I tried profit-sharing in my store; distributed $100,000. But my people had no idea of thrift. One woman took her $150 and bought a piano, another bought a silk dress, and so on,—no idea of saving. I was discouraged. Maybe I didn't try the right way, but it was not a success. I offered to pay them interest if they would save their money and put it into the store—they thought I wanted to increase my capital, and wouldn't do it. I could have borrowed plenty of money for less interest than I offered them. I do not say I have given it up,—a committee of the employes has the matter still under consideration, but they report that at present nothing can be done. There is nothing for it but education.

" 'You must educate the people up to brother-love prices,—if I should charge brother-love prices now I would be in the sheriff's hands in a few weeks. As for men who deal unjustly with their employes, I think you can make a public sentiment that will make it too warm for a man who is robbing labor. No man ever made $150,000,000, or even $50,000,000—he may have captured it in a sort of way, but he never made it. I shall be glad to answer any questions you wish to ask me,—try to answer them, I mean,—for you may ask some I cannot answer.' "

B. Statements made in 1914.

(1) Wanamaker claimed that there were no ill-paid people in his employ, and that the stories of immorality were false. "The young women," he said, "could not do their work as efficiently as they do if they lived the lives they are said to live." [12]

2. "Mrs. Jeannette Smith, a pleasant-faced woman of mature years, went on the stand and declared that she had worked at Wanamaker's for seventeen years. She received $8 a week at the beginning, and when she left the store on December 24, 1913, she was receiving $10 a week. Five minutes before closing time on that day, she says that she was approached by an official of the store and told that her services were no longer required. She said that during the course of her seventeen years' service she had been late at the store twice. She appealed to the employment manager, but could not see him. She then wrote to him and received a reply that he could not 'create' a position for her.

"Preston D. Lynn, manager of John Wanamaker stores, said that he was not opposed to unionism so long as propaganda work was not carried on within the store. An employe, however, who has recently been dismissed, declared that he was told that his services were no longer required because he had been giving information about the store to the union. The store had no objection to his belonging to the union, he was told, but he must not give any information. 'That,' said the witness, 'is like telling me that I can go to church, but must not pray.' " [13]

[12] *New York Times,* June 23, 1914, p. 5.

[13] John A. Fitch, "The Longshoreman's Case and Department Store Conditions," *Survey,* June 20, 1914, pp. 320–321.

8. Wanamaker and the Keystone Bank Failure [14]

John Wanamaker appeared before the Keystone Bank investigating committee and admitted the truth of statements made by previous witnesses that he had been on very friendly terms with Lucas, the dead president of the bank, who stole $998,000 of its funds, and with Marsh, the fugitive president who succeeded Lucas and concealed his predecessor's theft by means of false statements and other deceits; [15] that he enjoyed most unusual favors at the bank during Marsh's presidency; that Marsh once lent him $200,000 of the bank's money on his personal note, without the knowledge of the directors; that although the National Banking Law forbade the granting of discounts beyond $50,000 in amount, Mr. Wanamaker was able to get discounts to the extent of $150,000 based upon his own notes without collateral, and that Mrs. Wanamaker was allowed to overdraw her personal account in the bank to the extent of $1,000, and possibly $5,000. Mr. Wanamaker also admitted that his firm had deposits of nearly $400,000 in the Keystone Bank in November, but these were gradually removed so that when the collapse came there was little or nothing to be lost. He admitted that Marsh told him in August that he could no longer afford to pay 6 per cent on the penny saving fund of the Bethany Church; it was then withdrawn. He confessed that he and President Lucas had entered upon a speculative venture in Reading stock in which the Keystone Bank's money was used with great freedom. They purchased Reading stock on joint account, Lucas supplying certain sums of money as Wanamaker called for them and depositing the same to Wanamaker's personal account in the Keystone Bank, and on this Wanamaker drew checks amounting to $60,000. Upon several occasions when Wanamaker called for money, Lucas gave him Keystone Bank stock, and when Lucas died, Wanamaker held 2,515 shares of this stock which he had used for raising money in various ways. After Lucas' death Wanamaker discovered that no money had been placed to his credit, and that his account at the bank was overdrawn to the extent of about $60,000. He therefore held fast to the 2,515 shares of Keystone stock as security for that loss.

Wanamaker admitted in his cross-examination that when he discovered that Lucas had not put in the $60,000 in money to meet his (Wanamaker's) checks to that amount—checks which the bank had cashed—he held the bank stock as security for the loss; that when he was told the bank stock was fraudulent he refused to believe it and tried to sell it, even after the bank had failed, finally surrendering it to Lucas' estate.

It was shown that Mr. Wanamaker, who had denied holding stock in the Keystone Bank, had actually held 2,625 shares issued to him directly, in addition to the 2,515 shares held by him as collateral. Some of the fraudulent stock had been issued in the name of his secretary and some of the genuine in the name of his office boy. Two bank presidents testified that they had made loans on some of the Keystone stock issued to Wanamaker.

Later it was proved that Wanamaker had tried to secure money from Mrs. Lucas and Marsh for the fraudulent stock, after being told that it was fraudulent, by threatening to inform the comptroller

[14] Notes taken from the *Nation:* "Mr. Wanamaker's Confessions," vol. lii, p. 472, and editorial comment, pp. 452–453, 470, 489; "Wanamaker's Keystone Stock," vol. liii, pp. 1–4, and "Wanamaker's Latest Version," pp. 41, 60–61. It should be remembered that this information is taken from a journal which might be said to present one-sided information, which is often very useful but not always revealing of the whole situation.

[15] *Report of the Comptroller of the Currency,* 1891, p. 64.

of the currency. However, Mr. Wanamaker said that he was not then sure that the stock was false. Other charges were that Wanamaker received $200,000 of city money from the city treasurer through Marsh, the bank president, as a loan.

9. Wanamaker's Fortune at His Death, 1922

The extent of Wanamaker's fortune was apparently never divulged. Some time before his death it was estimated at $25,000,000, but it is believed to have been considerably larger at the time of his death. Of course, gifts to various charities, religious and educational, somewhat restricted the growth of Wanamaker's wealth. It is not unlikely that the net profits of John Wanamaker's business amounted during his lifetime to about $40,000,000. This is necessarily a guess.

Following is a statement of the organization and finances of the two Wanamaker stores about 1923.[16]

A. John Wanamaker, Philadelphia. Incorporated in Pennsylvania, 1909; owns store with subway connection, power house, and outside buildings—offices, factories, garages, stables, etc.

Capital stock, authorized and outstanding, $7,500,000, par $100. All owned by Rodman Wanamaker. Also $1,000,000 preferred stock held in trust with Fidelity Trust Co. for a trust created during the lifetime of John Wanamaker.

Funded debt $10,000,000, first 6 per cent gold bonds due 1932.

Directors, Rodman Wanamaker, Wm. L. Nevin, and J. D. Williams.

B. John Wanamaker, New York. Incorporated in New York, 1907. The store building is owned by the A. T. Stewart Realty Co., the stock of which is owned by John Wanamaker, Philadelphia.

Capital stock, authorized and outstanding, $7,500,000, par $100. All owned by John Wanamaker. No funded debt.

Directors. The same as for the Philadelphia store.

[16] *Poor's and Moody's Manual Consolidated, Industrial Section,* vol. ii (1923), pp. 604–605.

10. Readings

Golden Book of the Wanamaker Stores, Jubilee Year, 1861–1911 (Philadelphia, 1911). An official, uncritical narrative and appraisal.

Herbert Adams Gibbons, *John Wanamaker,* 2 vols. (New York, 1926). A discriminating but friendly biography. Volume i is the more valuable.

J. H. Appel, *The Business Biography of John Wanamaker* (New York, 1930). An illuminating exposition of Wanamaker's character by one who worked closely with him.

11. Suggested Questions

1. What were the chief business methods of John Wanamaker?
2. Have his methods been generally followed? Specify. Wherein has progress been made since?
3. What was there in Wanamaker's policy or methods that pointed to industrial capitalism and what to financial capitalism?
4. Admitting (for the sake of argument) the superiority of labor conditions in the Wanamaker stores over those in other department stores, would you say that the Wanamaker labor situation was still open to criticism? Specify. Do you know the current labor situation?
5. How do you explain Wanamaker's personal capacity for success in retailing? Was it wholly his personal make-up (including his religion) or was there something on the outside that brought him victory?
6. What would happen to a big department store in a régime of communism?

FINANCIAL CAPITALISM

XXXI. TWO METROPOLITAN BANKS: FIRST NATIONAL BANK OF BOSTON AND FIRST NATIONAL BANK OF NEW YORK

Part I

The First National Bank of Boston

1. General Statement

There were two main streams that joined to make the First National Bank of Boston. The first was the old First National which slightly antedated the Civil War, and the second was the Massachusetts Bank which was set up just after the Revolutionary War.

The old First National had an inconspicuous existence from 1859 to 1864, as the Safety Fund Bank. It had been created by local business men who were without distinction—they were honest, careful, and continuous in their efforts. Its chief founders were William H. Hill, a stationer and bookbinder, and Abraham T. Lowe, at various times a doctor, apothecary, member of the State legislature, and, between 1839 and 1859, a director in a number of companies and banks. For the most part the early directors were jobbers and commission merchants. In 1864, however, the directors saw an opportunity: they became the first in Boston to join the new national banking system, which was generally unpopular among bankers. Joining the new system at once helped the institution as a bankers' bank in the New England region. Whether the directors merely seized an opportunity which they only vaguely understood or had a vision of Boston's growing importance as a financial center is not clear. Between 1870 and 1903, one-half the deposits of the First National were normally made up of amounts standing to the credit of other national banks in Boston and outside.

2. Important Dates in the History of the First National Bank of Boston

1859	Formation of the Safety Fund Bank (later the First National).
1864	The Safety Fund became the First National.
1903	Consolidation of First National and Massachusetts National banks.
1904	Consolidation with National Bank of Redemption.
1907	Beginning of general policy of paying interest on accounts.
1908	Safe-deposit boxes available.
1912	Bank's *New England Letter* (weekly) began.
1913	Bank's representative reported on prospects in South America.
1914	Bank opened time-deposit department.
1915	Bank reported largest amount of acceptances in Federal Reserve System. Trust department established.
1917	Branch established in Buenos Aires.
1918	First National Corporation (security affiliate) formed.

1921 International Acceptance Bank established with First National as a shareholder. Bank ended its circulation.

1922 Bank opened office in London.

1923 Consolidation with International National Bank and thereby the acquisition of its first (seven) local branches. Branch opened in Havana.

1925 Office opened in Paris (closed 1936).

1926 Office opened in Berlin (discontinued in 1937).

1927 Notable legal case—*Willett* v. *Herrick* (First National Bank).

1929 The First of Boston Investment Management Corporation established, later discontinued. Purchase of Old Colony Trust Co.

1932 First National took over the deposit assets and liabilities of Atlantic National.

1933 House organ established.

1934 Directors reduced from 84 to 25. First National-Old Colony Corporation (security affiliate) divorced and became The First Boston Corporation.

1937 A personal loan department opened. End of stockholders' double liability.

3. Merger with the Massachusetts Bank, 1903

The Massachusetts Bank had got into great difficulty in the period beginning about 1884. The savings banks of Boston, which were large owners of the stock of the Massachusetts Bank as of other commercial banks in Boston, were anxious to bring about a change so that dividends could be earned. Investment bankers came to the rescue. In 1898 Kidder, Peabody & Co. merged seven small banks under the name of one—the Shawmut. In 1903 Hornblower & Weeks did the same for the Massachusetts and the First National. First, however, they wisely built up the capital, surplus, and deposits of the Massachusetts Bank during the period 1900–03.

The following statement was made about the First National by a well-informed reporter in June, 1903: [1]

> "During the past three years various efforts have been made to get possession of the First. It was regarded as one of the most likely purchases in the city, and it was supposed on the street that it might be possible to buy it, as President Carr was 74 years old and Cashier Draper 69. . . . In the 44 years of its existence the bank has paid dividends averaging 10¼ per cent, and has, in addition, out of its earnings, created a surplus of $1,000,000."

Though to all outward appearances the First National had been very profitable during the 1890's, actually it had maintained a dividend rate of 12 per cent and later 10 per cent a year only by granting as dividends over $200,000 in profits accumulated before 1892. Probably the most important reason for the willingness of Carr and Draper to liquidate their holdings in their bank was, therefore, because they wanted to sell out at a time when their stock would still bring a high market price.[2]

The merger of the two banks was effected very quickly and cleverly. On June 27, 1903, Hornblower & Weeks headed a syndicate which purchased the control of the First National Bank for the Massachusetts National Bank.[3] With the two banks in hand the members of the Massachusetts National Bank syndicate voted, as stockholders in the First National Bank, to purchase the Massachusetts National for $1,040,000 in cash. This same

[1] *Boston Herald,* June 28, 1903, p. 19. John Carr had been president for 22 years and teller for as long before that. C. H. Draper had been cashier for 22 years.

[2] Dividend Book of the First National Bank, vol. ii (1901–05), in Baker Library. See the profit and loss statements, 1892–1903.

[3] Charles G. Washburn, *Life of John W. Weeks* (Boston, 1928), p. 15.

FIRST NATIONAL BANK OF BOSTON MERGERS

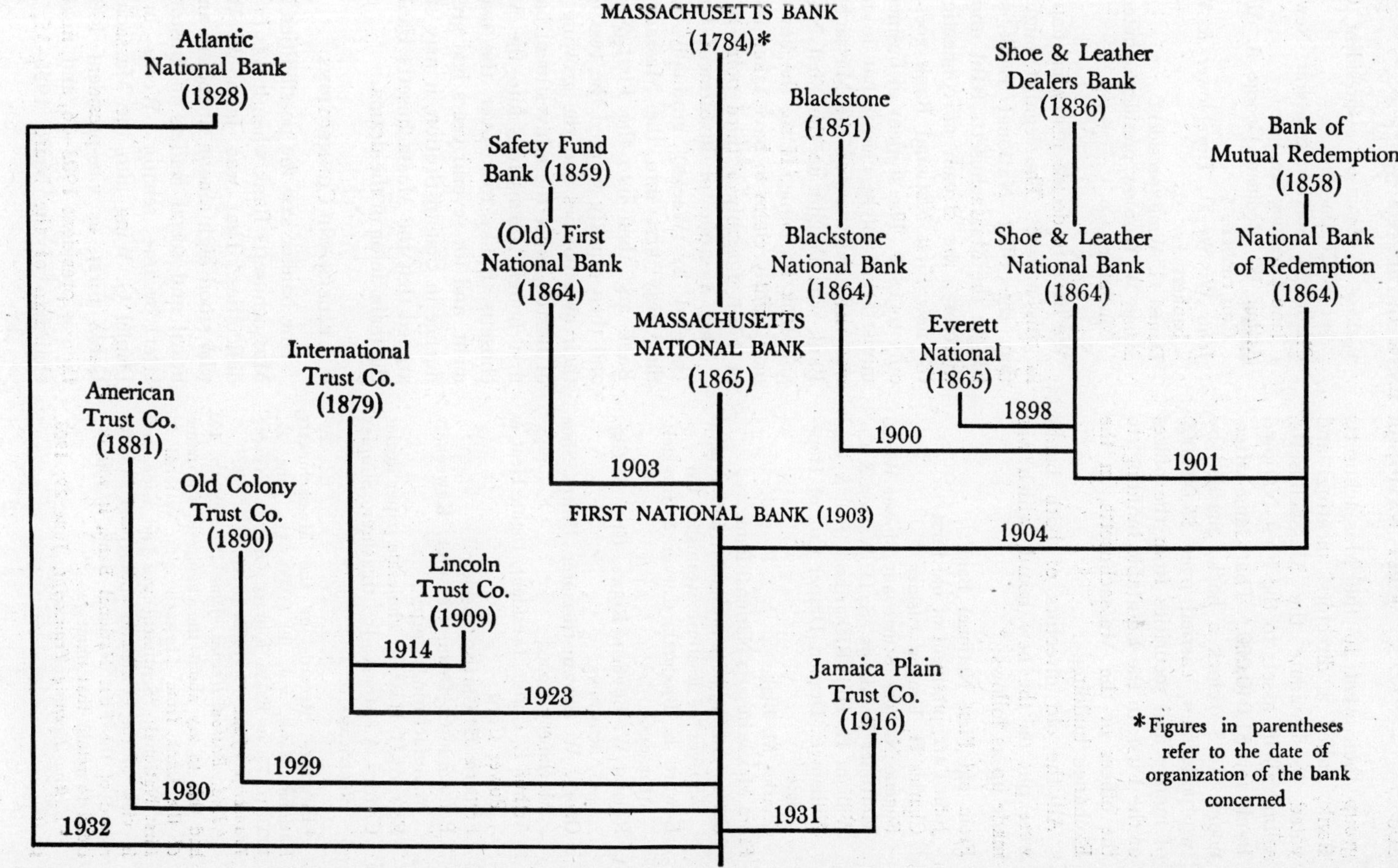

*Figures in parentheses refer to the date of organization of the bank concerned

group then went to the Massachusetts Bank, called a directors' meeting, and voted to liquidate the Massachusetts, selling all its assets to the First National Bank for $1,040,000.[4] That same afternoon, "at 5 o'clock a hack, guarded by two policemen, carried over $5,000,000 of money and securities from the offices of the First, in the Equitable building, to the offices of the Massachusetts, in the Exchange building. . . ."[5]

All the old directors of both banks were put on the new board, which was made up as follows: [6]

From old First National Bank:
- John Carr, president of old First
- Charles H. Draper, cashier
- Eugene N. Foss, Sturtevant Blower Works
- Mortimer B. Mason, S. D. Warren & Co.
- William H. Hill, Richardson, Hill & Co.
- William F. Draper, Draper Co., of Hopedale
- Charles M. Blake

From Massachusetts National Bank:
- Calvin Austin, vice-president, and general manager of Eastern Steamship Co.
- Edward E. Blodgett, Carver & Blodgett, attorneys
- Roland W. Boyden, Ropes, Gray & Gorham, attorneys
- George W. Brown, treasurer, United Shoe Machinery Co.
- Arthur E. Childs, president, Light, Heat & Power Corp.
- Frederic H. Curtiss, cashier
- Benjamin C. Dean, treasurer, Keweenaw Manufacturing Corp.
- Edward H. Haskell, wholesale paper dealer
- Charles A. Morss, Jr., treasurer, Simplex Electrical Co.
- Wallace F. Robinson, ex-president, Chamber of Commerce
- Charles H. Souther, treasurer, New England Dredging Co.
- Arthur W. Stedman, George A. Alden & Co., rubber
- John W. Weeks, Hornblower & Weeks, bankers
- Daniel G. Wing, president
- Sidney W. Winslow, president, United Shoe Machinery Co.

We have to decide just what happened in this merger. The legalist might say that the First National Bank simply bought the Massachusetts Bank and that, therefore, the stream of connections of the new First National Bank goes back only to 1859. The student of business administration might claim that in fact it was the executives of the Massachusetts Bank who bought up the First National and took its name. If so, the new Bank may rightly claim to have taken its start in 1784. Possibly a third point of view is that a group of investment bankers (headed by Weeks) gradually bought their way first into the Massachusetts Bank and then into the First National and then quickly merged the two to suit their own policies and the growing needs of Boston. Since these investment bankers first bought themselves into the Massachusetts Bank, took over the management, and for several years had great influence in that institution, it may still be argued that the Massachusetts Bank was the main actor in the drama.

4. Leaders and Connections

One banker saw the possibilities in the Massachusetts Bank when it was in grave difficulties. That was John W. Weeks, who stood high among financiers and political and social leaders in Boston and later became senator. Weeks brought Daniel G. Wing into the Massachusetts Bank. First, as vice-president 1900–03, then as president 1903–26, and, finally, as chairman of the board 1926–35, Wing

[4] Directors' Records of the Massachusetts National Bank, vol. iii (1900–04), June 27, 1903, p. 73, in Baker Library; *Boston Evening Transcript,* June 29, 1903, p. 16.

[5] *Ibid. Boston Herald,* June 28, 1903, p. 19, had this to say about the change in the name of the Bank from Massachusetts National to First National: "Sentiment was laid aside, and in view of the excellent standing and brilliant record of the First National Bank, it was decided to retain that name. . . ."

[6] *Boston Evening Transcript,* June 29, 1903, p. 16.

was the real force within the Bank. He was the George F. Baker of the First National of Boston and yet followed very different policies. Wing and Baker were notable commercial bankers.

The Shawmut and the First National became the two rival banks in Boston. The question in 1903 was which would win and how. The Shawmut has been strong in the New England region and has belonged to the Kidder Peabody-Kuhn Loeb group, while the First National has reached far beyond New England and has been known as a member of the old Morgan group. Their policies, growth, and institutional strategy in 1929–32 and since 1933 are of significance.

5. Later Mergers, 1904–32

The First National Bank of today has grown largely through consolidation with other banks. Some of the banks taken over had themselves merged with other banks, which in turn had previously merged. It was not a process of "bank eat bank" but adjustment of banking resources and consolidation of functions so as to produce a more up-to-date institution, one better able to care for the needs of changing business. This does not mean, however, that no mistakes were made.

The First National merger of 1903 resulted in an increase in the resources of the Bank to $13,078,050 by September of that same year.[7] But the group in control of the First National had no intention of stopping at this point. Their next step was to absorb the National Bank of Redemption.

The National Bank of Redemption had been formed in 1858 and at first was called the Bank of Mutual Redemption. Originally organized by the country banks for the purpose of combating the Suffolk Bank and effecting the redemption of country money at a lower cost, it met bitter opposition from the start. By April, 1859, however, it already had the accounts of half the banks in New England, and during and after the Civil War it was perhaps better known than any other bank in Boston because of its intimate daily connection with so many country banks.[8]

In 1864, the Bank of Mutual Redemption joined the national banking system and was reorganized as the National Bank of Redemption. Though its work as a bank of redemption ceased when State bank notes were replaced by national bank notes, its business as a bank of deposit for country, State, and national banks, and later trust companies, gained steadily; and until 1900, when the National Shawmut Bank completed its organization, it remained the most important bankers' bank in New England.[9]

It was difficult for the National Bank of Redemption to compete with the Shawmut Bank after 1898 by reason of the latter's enormous size. This was one of the considerations which brought about the combination of the Redemption with the Shoe and Leather National Bank in 1901. The Shoe and Leather National, which had been organized as the Shoe and Leather Dealers Bank in 1836, no longer catered to a single industry, but handled a well-distributed commercial business and also cleared for many out-of-town banks.[10] Having previously merged with

[7] *Report of the Comptroller of the Currency,* 1903, vol. ii, p. 563.

[8] D. P. Bailey, Jr., "History of Banking in Massachusetts," *Bankers' Magazine,* vol. xxxi (1876–77), p. 311; Suffolk Bank Directors' Records, vol. iv (1852–59), Oct. 7, 1858, in Baker Library; *Acts of Incorporation of the Bank of Mutual Redemption* (Lowell, 1860).

[9] Compare figures of balances due State and national banks by Boston national banks between 1866 and 1904. These figures are recorded in each annual *Report of the Comptroller of the Currency,* in the Massachusetts division of his report.

[10] *Boston Directory,* 1865, 1880, 1901; Shoe and Leather Bank Scrap Book, records of officers and directors of the Bank, in Baker Library. See figures in *Report of the Comptroller of the Currency,* 1866–1900.

the Blackstone National and the Everett National banks, its resources were well over $13,000,000 at the time of its combination with the National Bank of Redemption.[11]

On merging with the Shoe and Leather National Bank, John E. Toulmin, the very successful president of that institution, became president of the National Bank of Redemption. The need for a man like Toulmin at the Redemption may have been instrumental in making this merger possible.[12] Toulmin's death in July, 1903, therefore, left the National Bank of Redemption without a strong and capable chief executive despite the fact that James B. Case, the venerable ex-president of the bank, consented to act as president until someone could be chosen to succeed Toulmin.[13]

The plan drawn up for the amalgamation of the National Bank of Redemption and the First National Bank is described in the following circular from the directors of the Redemption to the stockholders of that institution: [14]

"The National Bank of Redemption is to sell to the First National Bank all its assets, good will and business, in consideration of the payment to said National Bank of Redemption of three million two hundred thousand (3,200,000) dollars in cash, and the assumption by the First National Bank of all the liabilities of said National Bank of Redemption.

. . . .

"Upon the death of President Toulmin, Mr. James B. Case assumed the presidency of this Bank, with the distinct understanding that a permanent successor to Mr. Toulmin should be found as soon as possible. Some time ago your Directors requested Mr. Daniel G. Wing, formerly Receiver of the Globe National Bank and now President of the First National Bank, to become President of this Bank. Mr. Wing was unwilling to do this unless the two banks and the various interests represented in each could be harmoniously combined. We believe that this result has been satisfactorily attained. The consolidated Bank will have a capital of $2,000,000, a surplus of $2,000,000, and deposits of about $35,000,000. We believe that the consolidation will result in great benefit to the stockholders and customers of both banks."

As a result of its combination with the Redemption, the First National was now the second largest bank in Boston with total resources of $45,648,700 in 1905, a figure comparing favorably with that of $60,346,702 for the National Shawmut Bank.[15] Sweeping changes in the general banking situation in Boston, brought about in this period of consolidation, are explained by Edwin A. Stone: [16]

"While thirty-two of the Boston National Banks have gone out of existence [between 1895 and 1905] twenty-eight remain, and happily most of them are in a vigorous condition. . . .

"It will be noticed that there has been a net loss in the capital of $25,450,000, a gain in deposits of $53,378,000, and in the surplus of $5,172,000. The latter has not all been earned, as in some cases of reorganization there was a cash contribution to this fund. While the percentage of surplus to capital in 1894 was 36.80, it is now 80.00.

"This improved financial condition is a cause for congratulation. For example, ten years ago twenty of the sixty banks [stocks] were selling below their par value, while at present there is but one bank in this condition.

"The transformation of interests is also

[11] *Ibid.*, 1901, vol. ii, p. 483.

[12] *Boston Evening Transcript*, Oct. 21, 1901, p. 2.

[13] See Scrap Book of the National Bank of Redemption (1901–06), Apr. 25, 1904, in Baker Library.

[14] *Circular to the Stockholders of the National Bank of Redemption*, Apr. 23, 1904, in National Bank of Redemption Scrap Book (1901–06), in Baker Library.

[15] *Report of the Comptroller of the Currency*, 1905, p. 661.

[16] Edwin A. Stone, *Second Chapter in Boston Banking* (Boston, 1906), pp. 7–8.

quite noticeable. In 1894, thirty-two banks had average resources of about four millions while now there are about half this number. Ten of the twenty-eight remaining banks average a little over twenty-two millions each. Two of these, the Shawmut and First National, control about forty per-cent of the total resources.

"The National Shawmut has proved the greatest magnet. 'It has gathered to itself a large portion of the business of twelve banks which had an aggregate capital of $11,500,000 and now carries on its business on a capitalization of $3,500,000. The First National, with a capital of $2,000,000, is the result of the combination of five banks [?], having an aggregate capital of $4,800,000. The Eliot has liquidated two other banks, without increasing its own capital of $1,000,000. The State took in the Hide and Leather with $1,000,000 and its own capital remains unchanged at $2,000,000. The Second National has increased its capital $400,000 to $2,000,000, and so really stands for two banks besides its own, the Suffolk and Washington, whose capital was $2,250,000.' The latest amalgamation has been that of the Webster and Atlas, whose combined capital was formerly $2,500,000 but is now reduced to $1,000,000.

". . . One of the best results has been the saving in the expenses of management and a 'general strengthening and solidification.' This improvement has especially shown itself in the increased net earnings. The average dividend paid in 1898 on a capital of $49,650,000 was 2.3%, while the recent dividend on a capital of $28,400,000 was 6.35%. The total earnings of all the Boston banks for the year 1905 amounted to 9.60% in the aggregate."

The *Boston Commercial* in 1903 refused to sympathize completely with the consolidation movement: [17]

"The big institutions are a distinct advantage to the big corporations and to those who have occasion to use large amounts of money. . . . But woe to the ordinary merchant!

"The man who does a relatively small, though absolutely safe, business cannot get near the management of the big banks. That privilege is reserved for the big customer. No great complaint can be entered on that ground. It is natural enough. The merchant or business man where banking business is not large, according to modern standards, makes a mistake to give that business to an institution so large that his account is lost to sight. The bank may be managed admirably. His money may be absolutely safe; but if the time comes when he desires any favor or accommodation, he will find that it is hard to obtain; that, in fact, he is scarcely considered at all. The loss of his account is not deemed a serious affair by the management, and if he does not like the treatment he receives he can go elsewhere.

"Of course, there are exceptions to this rule, as to all other rules. It is the inevitable tendency of the consolidation of banking institutions, however. However much the managements of such institutions might desire to accommodate small depositors there is a physical limit and if all the energy is used on the bigger customers, there is none left for the smaller.

"In a comparatively small institution, however, conditions are different. As the big depositors, compelled to borrow large amounts of money, cannot do so from the small banks, the latter are free to do business with smaller customers. These latter accounts are fully as safe and profitable as the large accounts. The security offered by a small borrower is likely to be as gilt edged as that offered by a heavy borrower. Often it is of better character.

"It will indeed be an unfortunate day for Boston when all the small banking institutions have been eliminated. We do not believe, however, that it will ever come. A reaction from the consolidation fever will come soon, if, indeed, it has not already begun."

In the interest of brevity we must omit the later consolidations, important as they were. Attention should be called particularly to the merger with the International Trust Co. in 1923 and the Old Colony Trust Co. in 1929. Although such

[17] *Boston Commercial,* Nov. 7, 1903, p. 4.

mergers brought much desired trust business to the First National, still they had some drawbacks. Consolidation, which greatly increased the number of employees till old age and death came to the rescue of the Bank, raised the number on the board of directors to 85—more like a congress for debate than a committee for administrative work.

6. Business and Services

The First National of Boston has grown in two ways, by consolidation and by going out for new business. Some of the new business was new in type, some new only in customers. Additional customers were obtained by offering new services or by interlocking directorates or by business-getting efforts (in recent years through the activities of vice-presidents).

The numerous services of the Bank are performed in the home office, branches at home and abroad, offices abroad, the security affiliate (1918–34), and the Old Colony Trust Co. The services are the usual ones of a big metropolitan bank, integrated to serve a large number of customers. Some of the services (e. g., travel and translation, both unimportant) have not been profitable. Unprofitable branches have been reduced till now (1939) there are only 23 branches in Boston.

7. Statistics on the First National Bank of Boston, 1903–37

Table 1. SELECTED FINANCIAL DATA

1903–38

(Dollars in thousands)

Year	Capital	Surplus and undivided profits	Individual deposits	Dividends %
1903	$ 1,000	$ 1,046	$ 7,355	8
1904	2,000	2,092	18,881	8
1905	2,000	2,129	20,296	8
1906	2,000	2,291	21,060	8
1907	2,000	2,594	22,176	8
1908	2,000	3,088	27,510	11
1909	2,000	3,320	34,667	12
1910	3,000	5,888	34,321	12
1911	3,000	6,383	36,999	12
1912	5,000	10,710	46,102	12
1913	5,000	11,178	49,531	12
1914	5,000	11,672	49,664	12
1915	5,000	11,934	54,096	15
1916	5,000	12,710	73,712	16
1917	7,500	18,577	98,625	19
1918	7,500	20,153	189,991	20
1919	7,500	20,270	157,569	20
1920	15,000	21,665	148,455	17
1921	15,000	23,253	119,862	16
1922	15,000	22,359	146,333	16
1923	15,000	20,960	187,927	16
1924	15,000	19,284	198,038	16
1925	20,000	24,496	220,460	16

Year	Capital	Surplus and undivided profits	Individual deposits	Dividends %
1926	20,000	24,307	247,427	16
1927	20,000	23,720	265,380	16
1928	25,000	31,975	271,333	16
1929	27,500	31,660	284,170	16 [a]
1930	44,500	40,058	454,524	16
1931	44,500	33,029	423,159	16
1932	44,500	29,448	512,627	13
1933	44,500	27,816	468,223	10
1934	44,500	30,068	485,462	10
1935	27,812 [b]	47,879	526,600	16
1936	27,812	49,471	537,406	16
1937	27,812	51,515	519,295	16
1938	27,812	52,371	539,150	16

[a] Four per cent par value, dividend for first quarter; 12 per cent par value, last three-quarters; initial dividend of 80 cents paid on $20 par shares, July 1, 1929, and quarterly thereafter to Jan. 2, 1931, inclusive.

[b] Par value of stock reduced from $20 to $12.50, and $16,687,500 credited to surplus.

Table 2. ANALYSIS OF INCOME

Selected Years

(In per cent)

	1908	1916	1928	1934	1938
Loans and discounts	78.13	76.22	64.75	52.62	49.07
Acceptances	0.00	2.69	2.76	2.92	2.12
Investments	7.40	8.49	14.77	31.16	30.05
Trust division	0.00	.59	2.88	2.04	3.17
Foreign division	2.03	1.80	1.86	1.42	.63
Safe deposit	.33	.60	.65	1.49	1.93
Building income	0.00	1.02	2.98	4.09	4.67
Foreign branches	0.00	0.00	5.33	.31	3.08
Interest banks	8.29	6.75	2.34	.10	0.00
Service charges	0.00	0.00	.58	2.17	3.84
Other income	3.82	1.84	1.10	1.68	1.44

Table 3. MISCELLANEOUS DATA

	December 31, 1937	December 31, 1938
Number of employees (including officers)	3,022	3,040
" " officers	265	260
" " depositors (active)	301,253	305,744
" " stockholders	19,811	20,397

Part II

The First National Bank of the City of New York, 1863–1938

1. Some Important Dates in the History of the First National Bank of New York

1863	The Bank chartered.
1865	New York Clearing House Association admitted Bank to membership.
1877	George F. Baker became president of Bank.
1901	Acquired Bank of the Republic.
1908	First Security Co. set up.
1909	George F. Baker, chairman of the board (until death).
1911	Pension fund established for employees.
1913	George F. Baker testified before the Pujo Committee.
1915	Great increase in "deposits of banks."
1922	Jackson E. Reynolds (formerly professor of law at Stanford and Columbia and later attorney for the Central Railroad of New Jersey) became president.
1924	Gift to Harvard by George F. Baker, Sr.
1931	George F. Baker, Sr., died, leaving fortune of about $73,750,000 (including 14,000 shares of the Bank and 54,833 of American Telephone & Telegraph).
1932	A corporation formed by group of directors of First Security Co. to loan $29,500,000 to the company on its note.
	Lowest reported "deposits of banks" since 1927. New banking house erected on old site.
1933	Dissolution of First Security Co.
1934	No sale of stock to Reconstruction Finance Co.
1935	Leon Fraser, vice-president. Circulation ended.
1936	Leon Fraser succeeded Reynolds as president.
1937	Death of George F. Baker, Jr., whose will established a charitable foundation of 7,500 shares of the Bank's stock.

2. The Bankers' Bank

In 1863, Samuel C. Thompson, Frederick F. Thompson, George F. Baker, and four associates applied for a charter to organize the First National Bank of the City of New York. The capital of this bank was to be $200,000.[18] The president was to be Samuel C. Thompson.

John Thompson, the father of Samuel C. and Frederick F., had been a private banker in New York City but had failed in the panic of 1857.[19] Immediately thereafter he had appeared as the publisher of the *Bank Note Detector,* a periodical listing and describing counterfeit or fraudulent notes in circulation.[20] He was later associated with his sons in conducting their private banking and brokerage establishment, known as Thompson Brothers, at 2 Wall Street.[21] This firm seems to have been the immediate ancestor of the First National Bank; not only did it supply the leading incorporators and the first president for the new institution, but the cashier of the old firm also became the first cashier of the new.[22] The new bank, moreover, was housed in the basement of 2½ Wall Street, while Thompson Brothers continued to occupy the basement of 2 Wall Street.

George Fisher Baker was born in 1840 at Troy, New York. His father worked

[18] *Bankers' Magazine,* vol. xviii (1863–64), p. 155.

[19] *Ibid.,* vol. xii (1857–58), pp. 325–326.

[20] Jay Cooke's Memoirs, Jay Cooke Papers, Baker Library; *Commercial & Financial Chronicle,* Jan. 17, 1925, pp. 275–276.

[21] *Bankers' Magazine,* vol. xviii (1863–64), p. 155; *Commercial & Financial Chronicle, loc. cit.*

[22] *Ibid.; Bankers' Magazine, loc. cit.*

for the *New York Tribune* for a while, but in 1854 became secretary to Myron B. Clark, then governor of New York.[23] The son, that is, George F. Baker (1840–1931), was educated at Seward's school at Florida, New York, but left at the age of sixteen to commence work. In 1856 he obtained a clerkship in the New York State banking department at a salary of $500 a year. He stayed in this department until 1863, when he was approached by the Thompsons about helping in the organization of the First National Bank of New York. (The young clerk's work in the State banking department had made a very favorable impression upon John Thompson.) Baker became the first teller of the First National.[24]

There is a very interesting question as to the source of the $200,000 that was put up as the First's capital. It seems probable that the bulk of it was supplied by the incorporators. Baker is said to have had $3,000 in savings with which he purchased thirty shares,[25] and no doubt the Thompsons had some capital, for they had been brokers at a time when the brokerage business was profitable. It would be interesting to know how much outsiders also invested,[26] and what were the motives that caused men to invest in this new bank. Did outsiders invest because they believed the Bank was going to succeed, or because they wished to receive preferential treatment as far as loans were concerned? Did patriotism enter into the subscriptions for stock, owing to the fact that the Bank would fill a national need?

The Bank commenced operations on July 25, 1863, in the basement at 2½ Wall Street. From the beginning it was highly successful. The organizers must be given credit for seeing the opportunity that existed at that time before other people recognized it, and for moving rapidly enough to take advantage of it. This is all the more important in that there was very much opposition to the establishment of national banks in New York.

It is worth noting at this point an unsuccessful effort to establish a large national bank in New York at the time. With a view to strengthening the prestige of the national banking system, Hugh McCulloch, comptroller of the currency, urged the establishment in New York of a bank with a capital of several million. He invited sixteen of New York's leading financiers to a meeting in October to discuss the project. He insisted that New York, if it wished to maintain its position of financial leadership, must adapt itself to the changed conditions resulting from the establishment of the national system. A bank such as that which he proposed should act as a central bank or depository for the reserves of national banks throughout the country. Moreover, held McCulloch, it would have control over the interest rate, minimize gold shipments between countries, and be very profitable to those who owned it.

A committee of seven members, drawn from New York's leading financiers, was chosen to draw up plans for the organization of such a bank. The committee recommended the establishment of a national bank with a capital of from three to five million, subscription to be open to the public. But nothing seems to have come of the plan. It may be that it died because of the opposition of the large State-chartered banks in New York.[27]

This effort, though unsuccessful, is of interest in relation to the First National in two ways. It illustrates the lack of confidence in and the opposition to the

[23] *Commercial & Financial Chronicle, loc. cit.*

[24] *New York Times,* May 3, 1931; *Commercial & Financial Chronicle, loc. cit.*

[25] *Ibid.; New York Times,* May 3, 1931.

[26] Besides Baker and the Thompsons, George M. Snow of the *New York Tribune* and Charles Blondell were on the first board of directors (*Bankers' Magazine, loc. cit.*).

[27] Another later effort of McCulloch's was successful (see Henrietta M. Larson, *Jay Cooke, Private Banker,* Cambridge, 1936, pp. 140–141).

national system on the part of New York's leading financiers. It is also pertinent to observe that the little First National eventually rose to somewhat the type of leadership anticipated by McCulloch.

From the beginning the First National had a large volume of business. Within six months after organization its capital was increased to $300,000, and, within one year after opening, to $500,000. All was not smooth sailing, however, for the new bank. From the beginning it met with opposition from the older banks in New York City. They refused, as they did with other national banks, to allow it to belong to the Clearing House. In order to get around this difficulty Baker cleared through the Bank of the Republic, until in 1865 the First National was admitted to membership in the Clearing House.

The National Bank Act of 1863 divided banking cities into three classes: country points, reserve cities, and central reserve cities. National banks in country points had to keep cash reserves equal to 15 per cent of their deposit liabilities, 6 per cent in cash in their own vault and 9 per cent on deposit in a reserve or central reserve city.[28] Reserve city banks had to keep cash reserves of 25 per cent of their deposit liabilities, 12½ per cent in cash in their own vaults and the remainder on deposit in a central reserve city bank. Central reserve city banks had to keep reserves of 25 per cent of their deposits

[28] Harold G. Moulton, *The Financial Organization of Society* (Chicago, 1921), p. 482.

Table 1. DEPOSITS IN THE FIRST NATIONAL BANK OF NEW YORK
1867–1938

Date	Banks	Individuals	United States
1863–1866 [a]	....	....	....
1867 Oct. 7	$ 2,388,670	$ 1,996,159	$ 181,046
1868 Oct. 5	3,223,279	3,355,883	293,681
1869 Oct. 9	3,740,040	1,635,680	12,858
1870 Oct. 8	3,997,140	1,066,780	....
1871 Oct. 2	5,135,907	1,208,314	652,041
1872 Oct. 3	4,353,586	874,975	....
1873 Sept. 12	5,333,595	1,572,337	....
1874 Oct. 2	5,488,593	1,748,728	....
1875 Oct. 1	5,696,065	2,286,771	....
1876 Oct. 2	7,914,819	1,562,784	....
1877 Oct. 1	6,348,402	1,752,054	....
1878 Oct. 1	8,855,702	2,128,241	15,703,877
1879 Oct. 2	10,074,558	3,452,364	3,601,550
1880 Oct. 1	13,672,780	3,593,873	....
1881 Oct. 1	14,369,177	5,861,322	....
1882 Oct. 3	12,224,357	6,529,969 [b]	....
1883 Oct. 2	12,912,862	4,762,740	....
1884 Sept. 30	13,182,723	4,361,834	....
1885 Oct. 1	16,424,870	5,202,690	....
1886 Oct. 7	16,777,233	7,463,092	....
1887 Oct. 5	17,070,070	6,203,475	500,000
1888 Oct. 4	19,172,223	7,114,822	77,000

[a] For 1863 through 1866 no records are available.

[b] From 1882 through 1900 we have combined the deposits of individuals and certified checks except for the years 1887 through 1889 when there is no separate item for certified checks.

Date	Banks	Individuals	United States
1889 Sept. 30	$ 17,961,591	$ 5,961,450	$ 47,300
1890 Oct. 2	18,768,079	5,152,629	....
1891 Sept. 25	19,119,133	6,370,097	....
1892 Sept. 30	20,857,642	6,758,887	....
1893 Oct. 3	14,166,236	5,883,849	....
1894 Oct. 2	20,199,110	7,183,426	....
1895 Sept. 28	17,458,911	7,326,637	....
1896 Oct. 6	14,563,938	6,717,691	....
1897 Oct. 5	19,821,134	8,678,044	....
1898 Sept. 20	22,391,358	8,678,938	....
1899 Sept. 7	27,546,843	11,710,986	....
1900 Sept. 5	24,957,695	15,040,201	1,555,000 [c]
1901 Dec. 10	39,558,476	36,609,541	2,678,000
1902 Nov. 25	37,538,760	45,355,265	2,678,000
1903 Nov. 17	35,767,562	28,190,259	2,678,000
1904 Nov. 10	63,041,315	55,911,078	1,610,000
1905 Nov. 9	44,375,506	53,685,114	605,000
1906 Sept. 4	47,481,418	39,741,581	605,000
1907 Dec. 3	40,705,493	41,812,782	12,255,000
1908 Nov. 27	68,500,185	83,991,331	990,400
1909 Nov. 16	47,742,057	53,977,999	1,000
1910 June 30	58,037,035	54,003,080	1,000
1911 Dec. 5	59,008,384	55,148,602	1,000
1912 Nov. 26	52,772,511	57,166,957	1,000
1913 Oct. 21	54,911,842	52,797,711	1,000
1914 Dec. 31	51,845,381	71,494,575	1,000
1915 Dec. 31	96,141,917	108,740,439	1,000
1916 Dec. 27	72,466,148	110,636,577	....
1917 Dec. 31	60,273,280	119,752,678	52,924,931
1918 Dec. 31	57,026,632	153,218,880	4,570,000
1919 Nov. 17	56,413,143	177,268,238	26,624,000
1920 Dec. 29	42,441,383	171,532,758	23,800,000
1921 Dec. 31	60,195,216	161,145,632	8,591,200
1922 Dec. 29	77,034,905	201,489,655	46,628,550
1923 Dec. 31	74,111,213	172,032,986	7,638,500
1924 Dec. 31	90,273,183	217,145,908	3,051,200
1925 Dec. 31	76,101,319	213,318,409	10,479,700
1926 Dec. 31	78,900,974	228,015,289	7,461,800
1927 Dec. 31	140,564,332	201,608,809	7,364,700
1928 Dec. 31	144,458,204	295,099,116	10,803,500
1929 Dec. 31	134,123,408	270,609,865	4,048,000
1930 Dec. 31	144,628,897	274,360,731	4,258,800
1931 Dec. 31	103,459,833	250,943,918	20,753,200
1932 Dec. 31	176,925,591	229,146,731	....
1933 Dec. 30	97,000,625	258,927,849	21,929,976
1934 Dec. 31	117,681,532	295,074,937	29,831,700
1935 Dec. 31	156,203,062	321,617,610	1,530,600
1936 Dec. 31	152,916,479	373,302,037 [d]	....
1937 Dec. 31	121,970,637	317,212,307	16,573,000
1938 Dec. 31	165,263,442	365,278,079 [d]	....

[c] **In addition there was a United States Bond account amounting to $1,000,000.**

[d] Includes United States deposits.

in cash in their own vaults. Central reserve cities were New York and later also Chicago and St. Louis.

The deposits of "country" banks made up a very important part of the total deposits of the Bank. This fact is easily explained when we remember that Baker's bank was the first national bank located in New York City, the first that was designated specifically to hold the reserves of country banks.

Unfortunately we have all too little information about the interest paid on bank balances held by the First National. Toward the end of his life George F. Baker stated that his Bank paid from 2 per cent to 4 per cent on its balances. If, as seems probable, it had done so from the very first, the policy of this bank was in marked contrast to that of many of the older banks of New York City, as for instance the Chemical, which enunciated a definite policy against paying interest on deposits. It was the usual practice, however, among *private* banks to pay for deposits. Table 1 (p. 514) gives the amount of deposits of other banks and of individuals and the United States.[29]

3. Extension of Financial Control, 1877–1908

This period is characterized by the leadership of George F. Baker, who was president of the Bank throughout the years in question. Although we have no adequate information for the period, we seem to find that the dominant feature was the close association of the Bank with the growing big business units. This does not mean that the Bank was ceasing to be a depository for other banks, but that it was developing a new group of customers—depositors and borrowers.

Let us look at Table 1 to observe the course of deposits in the First National Bank, particularly individual deposits. These include personal and corporation accounts. They arise from two general sources: the deposit of actual cash and the credit resulting from a loan, in which the customer gives the bank his note and receives in return an equivalent credit on the books of the bank.

The commercial deposits of the First National are noteworthy, owing to the fact that they are few in number but large in amount. One hundred and fifty-five accounts in 1912 carried balances amounting to $32,426,854, or over 60 per cent of the total commercial deposits;[30] these depositors must have been insurance companies, railroads, industrials, and other very large concerns.

The question arises as to why this group of concerns maintained their accounts with the First National and not with other equally efficient banks. Some light may be thrown on the subject by considering for a moment the Bank's influential officers and directors. In 1912 some of these were George F. Baker, J. Pierpont Morgan, James J. Hill, Henry P. Davison, and Thomas W. Lamont.[31] The following list of corporations, in which the Bank's officers were directors, shows that the Bank was represented on the boards of many of the nation's largest business organizations. Asterisks indicate corporations on whose boards J. P. Morgan & Co. was also represented.

Adams Express Co.*
American Can Co.
American Cotton Oil Co.
American Surety Co.
American Telephone & Telegraph Co.*
Astor Trust Co.*
Audit Company of New York
Bankers' Safe Deposit Co.

[29] Figures for 1867 to 1900 are taken from the *Report of the Comptroller of the Currency* for those years; for 1901 to 1938, from *Statement of the First National Bank of the City of New York.*

[30] *Money Trust Investigation* (Washington, 1913), part ii, p. 1495.

[31] From the records of the Bank.

Baldwin Locomotive Co.*
Bankers' Trust *
Brooklyn Trust Co.
Burlington, Cedar Rapids & Northern Railway Co.
Car Trust Investment Co., Ltd.
Cedar Rapids, Iowa Falls & Northwestern Railway Co.
Central Railway of New Jersey *
Chase National Bank
Chicago, Burlington & Quincy Railroad Co.
Chicago, Rock Island & Pacific Railway Co.
Chicago, Rock Island & Pacific Railroad Co.
Choctaw, Oklahoma & Gulf Railroad Co.
Colorado & Southern Railway Co.
Consolidated Gas Company of New York
Delaware, Lackawanna & Western Coal
Delaware, Lackawanna & Western Railroad Co.
East Jersey Water Co.
Equitable Life Assurance Society
Erie Railroad Co.*
Farmers' Loan & Trust Co.
Fidelity Phenix Fire Insurance Company of New York
First National Bank of New York *
First Security Company of New York *
First National Bank of Groton, N. Y.
Geneva, Corning & Southern Railroad Co.*
Guaranty Trust Company of New York *
Home Life Insurance Company of New York
Jersey City Water Supply Co.
Keokuk & Des Moines Railway Co.
Lake Erie & Western Railroad Co.*
Lake Shore & Michigan Southern Railroad Co.*
Lehigh & Wilkes-Barre Coal Co.*
Lehigh Valley Railroad Co.*
Liberty National Bank of New York *
Michigan Central Railroad Co.*
Mohawk & Malone Railway Co.*
Montclair Water Company of New Jersey
Mutual Life Insurance Company of New York *
Nashawannuck Manufacturing Co.
National Bank of Commerce of New York *
National Biscuit Co.
New England Navigation Co.*
New Jersey General Security Co.
New York & Harlem Railroad Co.*
New York & Long Branch Railroad Co.
New York & Putnam Railroad Co.*
New York Central & Hudson River Railroad Co.*
New York, Chicago & St. Louis Railroad Co.*
New York Edison Co.
New York Mutual Gas Light Co.
New York, New Haven & Hartford Railroad Co.*
New York, Susquehanna & Western Railroad Co.*
Northern Pacific Railway Co.*
Northern Securities Co.
Pennsylvania Coal Co.
Peoria & Bureau Valley Railroad Co.
Phelps, Dodge & Co.
Philadelphia & Reading Railway Co.*
Pullman Co.*
Quincy, Omaha & Kansas City Railway Co.
Reading Co.*
Review of Reviews Co.
Rock Island Co.
Rutland Railroad Co.*
Securities Co.
Southern Railway Co.*
Tide Water Oil Co.
Tobacco Products Corporation
United States Rubber Co.*
United States Steel Corporation *
West Shore Railroad Co.*
Wm. Cramp & Sons, Ship & Engine Building Co.*

Without having access to the Bank's records, of course, we cannot tell which of these companies conducted or conduct their banking business with the First National Bank of New York. Knowing as we do something of the character of the Bank's accounts, we may logically conclude that most if not all the companies on this list conducted part of their banking business with this Bank.

In 1905 George F. Baker testified before the investigating committee of the New York State Legislature that the Mutual Life Insurance Co. carried an average balance with them of over a million dollars, on which 2 per cent interest was allowed.[32] The interesting part of this is the question as to which relationship between the Bank and its customers came first. Did the customer corporation first come to the Bank and, after relationships had been arranged, accept a bank officer on its board of directors? Or did men on the board of directors become interested in the Bank and use their influence to cause the concern to do business with the Bank?

A significant chapter in the history of the Bank would be its relation with the Mutual Life Insurance Company of New York. This company, while one of the largest in existence, was from the first purely mutual in character. The board of trustees was elected by those policyholders having policies of $1,000 or over. As a matter of fact, however, the holders never voted but gave their proxies to the existing trustees who reëlected their successors or occasionally brought in an outsider.[33]

In 1879 George F. Baker became a director in this company.[34] This occurred shortly after Baker had succeeded Thompson as president of the Bank in 1877.[35] It is to be noted that it was after this time that the Bank had its phenomenal growth. Whether that was because Baker was president and because of his connection with a powerful insurance company, or as a result of outside business influences, cannot be learned from available sources of information. What is known is that from this time on, the First National and the Mutual Life had very close relationships: the Mutual owned stock in the First National;[36] the Mutual maintained large balances with the First National;[37] they were in syndicates together.

One very probable reason for the phenomenal growth of the First National lies in favorable early circumstances. The Bank got an early start and received large deposits, thus becoming capable of taking care of the needs of large customers. Because at an early date it was able to meet such needs, the Bank got additional customers; the more that came, the better it was able to serve them. Thus the favorable factors of an early start, strategic location, and early preëminence contributed largely to its growth.

4. Period of the First Security Co., 1908–33.

This period is characterized by the existence and operation of the First Security Co. In 1908 the First National Bank declared a $10,000,000 cash dividend to be used in organizing a security company.[38] The original objects of the company were as follows:

- To acquire real and personal property
- To buy and sell stocks, bonds, and notes
- To buy, hold, and sell bonds or notes secured by mortgages; and to lend money on mortgages

It was forbidden to carry on a banking business or to acquire possession of a common carrier.

The problem was how to organize this security company so that it would be legal, yet owned and controlled by the Bank. The scheme of organization was devised by a man learned in the law. The capital was supplied by a dividend from the Bank to the stockholders. Each stockholder had previously subscribed to his pro rata share of the new stock. The officers of the Bank were to be trustees and

[32] *Testimony taken before the Joint Committee of the Senate and Assembly of the State of New York to Investigate and Examine into the Business and Affairs of Life Insurance Companies* (New York, 1906), vol. i, p. 623.

[33] *Ibid.*, p. 21.

[34] *Annual Report of the Mutual Life Insurance Company,* 1880, p. 2.

[35] Pamphlet published by the Bank in 1903, pp. 1 ff.

[36] *Testimony . . . Life Insurance Companies,* vol. i, pp. 623–626.

[37] *Ibid.*, p. 623.

[38] *Money Trust Investigation,* pp. 1481 ff.

managers of the First Security Co. A notation on the Bank stock stated that it represented share for share an equal amount of Security stock. By this arrangement neither First National nor Security stock could be sold separately.

Thus both companies were identical, but complied with the law. This complicates the history of the First National Bank from 1908 onward, since this company (an integral part of the Bank) did not have to publish any reports (though it was examined by the bank examiners). Much of the interesting part of the Bank's history from 1908 to 1933 is undoubtedly contained within the records of the First Security Co., but these have not been made known to the public.

The First Security Co. has been commonly regarded as the first example of such a concern in the United States. Actually, the First National Bank of New York in 1907 sent a representative to study a subsidiary which the First National Bank of Chicago had set up to hold securities. This was called the First Trust and Savings Bank. Besides holding the securities of the parent bank, it did a trust and savings bank business.

The two balance sheets of the First Security Co. published by the Bank and other significant information follow:

BALANCE SHEET

December 31, 1925

RESOURCES

Cash		$ 2,689.53
Syndicates and Loans		6,927,753.59
Investments		50,504,032.27
		$57,434,475.39

LIABILITIES

Capital	$10,000,000.00	
Undivided Profits	16,012,915.71	$26,012,915.71
Reserved for Taxes		139,293.14
Bills Payable		$31,045,000.00
Other Liabilities		237,266.54
		$57,434,475.39

EARNINGS AND DIVIDENDS [a]

	1924	1925
Earnings for the year	$3,817,559.48	$4,537,450.69
Dividends	2,000,000.00	3,500,000.00
Surplus	$1,817,559.48	$1,037,450.69

[a] A similar statement was made in the Bank's statements at the end of each year, 1927–31, inclusive.

OFFICERS, 1925

Geo. F. Baker, chairman of the board
Jackson E. Reynolds, president
Francis L. Hine, vice-president
Geo. F. Baker, Jr., vice-president
Everett B. Sweezy, vice-president
Samuel A. Welldon, secretary
Henry S. Sturgis, treasurer

DIRECTORS, 1925

Geo. F. Baker	Jackson E. Reynolds
Francis L. Hine	Elbert H. Gary
Geo. F. Baker, Jr.	Lewis Cass Ledyard
Arthur Curtiss James	Francis D. Bartow
Thomas W. Lamont	Myron C. Taylor
J. P. Morgan	Payne Whitney
Louis W. Hill	Everett B. Sweezy
John R. Morron	Walter S. Gifford

BALANCE SHEET

June 30, 1933

ASSETS

Stock of Affiliated Bank Owned	$ 472,750.00
Stock of Other Banks Owned	318,862.79
All Other Investments	37,887,937.65
Amount on Deposit in Affiliated Bank	24,539.92
Total Assets (See Note)	$38,704,090.36

Note: Market value of total assets, June 30, 1933, $27,790,606.

LIABILITIES

Capital	$10,000,000.00
Profit and Loss	3,404,878.87
Bills Payable with Accrued Interest	25,285,652.78
Borrowings from Affiliated Bank	0
Reserved for Taxes	13,558.71
Total Liabilities	$38,704,090.36

The following statement shows the character of business of the above-named affiliate and discloses fully its relations with the above-named bank:

Character of business:—Principally investments in securities for its own account.

Relations with bank:—Stock held by trustees, ratably for stockholders of bank.

STATEMENT OF ASSETS OF COMPANY IN DISSOLUTION

December 30, 1933

Securities listed on the New York Stock Exchange, at last sale	$1,652,161.69
1,895 shares Bank for International Settlements, 25 per cent paid, at cost	228,522.79
Cash in bank	49,148.81

DIVIDENDS OF THE FIRST SECURITY COMPANY[a]

1924	$2,000,000	1928	$8,000,000
1925	3,500,000	1929	8,000,000
1926	2,000,000	1930	8,000,000
1927	3,500,000	1931	3,000,000

[a] From surplus: 1928, $2,414,536; 1929, $1,633,498; 1930, $3,919,143; 1931, $451,877.

The First Security Co. paid throughout its history from May 19, 1908, to January 30, 1934, $67,718,500 in dividends, including the final liquidating dividends. The following quotation from the *Wall Street Journal*, November 3, 1933, is pertinent:

"Dissolution of the First Security Company

"First National Bank of New York has notified its stockholders that directors of the First Security Co., the affiliate of the bank, have resolved that 'it is, in their judgment, advisable that the First Security Co. be placed in dissolution, its debts paid as rapidly as may seem advisable, and its net assets, if any, after liquidation, be distributed.'

"The stock of the First Security Co. ($10,000,000 of $100 par), is held by trustees under an agreement dated February 14, 1908, between trustees and stockholders, under which each certificate of stock of the bank bears endorsement entitling bank stockholders to share ratably in the dividends or profits, and, in case of dissolution, in the distribution of the capital of the First Security Co. Under this agreement the trustees act as absolute owners of the capital stock of the Security Co., except as they receive written directions signed by the holders of two-thirds in interest of the certificates of stock of the bank.

"In his letter to the stockholders, Jackson E. Reynolds, president, states that the Security company as of October 30, owned assets having a value at market quotations on that date of $11,033,652, and that it owed $10,677,448, balance, including interest, on a note, not maturing until January 7, 1937, bearing 'unconditional interest' at 2½%, paid to the last interest date, and 'additional interest' at 3½%, which may, at the option of the company, be postponed in whole or in part to later interest dates or to date of maturity.

"The note contains the usual provisions as to lien on all property of the maker held by the lender, added Mr. Reynolds. It matures at once on insolvency; collateral may be sold on nonpayment when due; it may be assigned with collateral; it may be sold and collateral repledged; but it contains no covenant to maintain collateral at any stated value, nor the right to mature the note on shrinkage in value of collateral. The maker has the right to pay all or part of the principal before maturity, directing withdrawal and sale of collateral for that purpose.

"Note Originally Amounted to $29,500,000

"The note, originally for $29,500,000 is held by a corporation formed in 1932 by a group of directors of the First Security Co.

to advance funds to the company. The only person still remaining interested in the lending corporation is George F. Baker, chairman of the bank, chairman of the Security company, and son of the founder.

" 'Mr. Baker's holdings of First National Bank stock and of beneficial interest in the stock of the First Security Co., through ownership and by control, are such that his directions will probably be necessary in order to obtain the direction of at least two-thirds in interest to terminate the Agreement (of February 14, 1908, between trustees and stockholders),' said Mr. Reynolds. 'Mr. Baker has expressed his intention to give such directions with respect to such holdings,' he added.

"A further commitment of the First Security Co. is to pay the uncalled balance (3,553,125 Swiss francs) of the par value of stock of the Bank for International Settlements owned by the company.

"Accompanying the letter to the stockholders were forms to be signed, directing the trustees under the Agreement to effectuate steps and instructions to the bank to issue new certificates.

'To Issue 'Declarations of Interest'

" 'Upon receipt of signed instructions from the necessary two-thirds, the First Security Co. will be placed in dissolution and the Agreement terminated and notice mailed to you to send in your bank stock certificates for exchange into new certificates without endorsement, which new certificates will then be forwarded to you, together with Declaration of Interest in the dissolution of the First Security Co.,' it concluded.

"Dissolution of the First Security Co. marks the passing of the pioneer in bank affiliates. It was organized by the late George F. Baker, often referred to as the 'dean of Wall Street,' and was designed to undertake operations not provided for under the banking laws. Its dissolution is the result of provisions under the Banking Act of 1933.

'Contributed Generously to Dividends Formerly

"In former years the Security company contributed generously to the dividends paid to the bank's stockholders, paying $80 annually during 1928, 1929 and 1930.

"At the beginning of 1932, the stockholders were informed that while the 'market value of its assets exceeded its indebtedness by more than $38,000,000,' the market value of those assets on January 12, 1932, was 'less than its indebtedness by approximately $6,000,000.' In a subsequent communication—December 13, 1932—the deficit had increased about $5,750,000 'coincident with the market decline in the value of standard securities in the last 12 months,' it was stated.

"In reporting condition of the Security company, as of October 25, last, in compliance with the call of the Comptroller of Currency, it was stated that the company owned $228,522 of stock of other banks and had $78,513 on deposit with its affiliated bank. There were no borrowings from the affiliated bank, it was stated."

It was during the period with which we are dealing, 1908–33, that the First National Bank became identified in public thinking with financial capitalism. To be sure, the foundations of this system were laid in the earlier period but little or no attention was paid to it.

In the Money Trust Investigation of 1912–13 George F. Baker was regarded as one of the central figures in the big financial network. The First National Bank was held to be one of the central institutions in the Money Trust which helped a few men control a large part of the liquid wealth of the country. It was a common view that George F. Baker and J. P. Morgan headed one of the two big financial groups which included the Hill, New Haven, and other railroads, the United States Steel Corp., General Electric, American Telephone & Telegraph, and so on.

One of the chief results of the Money Trust Investigation was the Federal Reserve System, established in 1914, which was designed in part to rob New York banks of their dominance. We can see from the following figures that it had only a slight effect upon the First National Bank.

Following is a record of the Bank's

capital, surplus, earnings, and dividends:[39]

[39] All figures for 1863 through 1866 and the dividend and net profit figures for 1867–1912 are from *Money Trust Investigation,* part ii, pp. 1479–1480; the dividend figures for 1913–19 are from the Bankers Gazette in the *Commercial & Financial Chronicle* for each year, for 1920–25 from a circular issued by Noble and Corwin, April 8, 1927, and for 1926–38 from *Moody's;* the other figures for 1867 through 1900 are from *Report of the Comptroller of the Currency* for those years, and for 1901–38 from *Statement of the First National Bank of the City of New York* for each year.

Table 2. SELECTED FINANCIAL DATA

Date	Capital [a]	Surplus [a]	Undivided profits	Net profits	Dividends [a]
1863	$300	.....	.....	$ 13,016	None
1864	500	.....	.....	266,905	$130
1865	500	$ 100	.....	207,171	100
1866	500	200	.....	187,458	100
1867 Oct. 7	500	300	$ 45,645	57,807	50
1868 Oct. 5	500	400	21,279	146,900	100
1869 Oct. 9	500	400	70,438	173,105	125
1870 Oct. 8	500	250	11,837	64,337	260
1871 Oct. 2	500	250	21,459	98,237	110
1872 Oct. 3	500	350	65,589	281,929	175
1873 Sept. 12	500	500	4,814	242,816	75
1874 Oct. 2	500	500	18,212	62,123	60
1875 Oct. 1	500	300	167,494	277,280	60
1876 Oct. 2	500	300	124,031	146,914	110
1877 Oct. 1	500	500	236,678	753,227	60
1878 Oct. 1	500	1,000	277,444	379,602	295
1879 Oct. 2	500	1,000	804,511	1,345,530	600
1880 Oct. 1	500	2,000	222,347	913,239	200
1881 Oct. 1	500	2,500	414,655	977,969	450
1882 Oct. 3	500	3,000	273,777	510,372	200
1883 Oct. 2	500	3,000	338,403	370,397	200
1884 Sept. 30	500	3,000	777,747	308,444	200
1885 Oct. 1	500	3,000	970,168	739,844	200
1886 Oct. 7	500	4,000	587,250	1,036,773	200
1887 Oct. 5	500	5,000	430,721	732,669	200
1888 Oct. 4	500	5,000	875,794	907,584	300
1889 Sept. 30	500	5,000	1,089,358	573,435	500
1890 Oct. 2	500	5,000	1,701,344	1,049,991	500
1891 Sept. 25	500	5,000	1,799,970	831,177	500
1892 Sept. 30	500	5,000	2,030,461	724,131	500
1893 Oct. 3	500	5,000	2,330,098	544,562	500
1894 Oct. 2	500	5,000	2,274,274	532,577	500
1895 Sept. 28	500	5,000	2,181,089	357,996	500
1896 Oct. 6	500	5,000	2,208,479	402,638	500
1897 Oct. 5	500	5,000	2,069,798	487,551	500
1898 Sept. 20	500	5,000	2,488,208	979,244	500
1899 Sept. 7	500	5,000	2,763,543	1,032,895	500
1900 Sept. 5	500	5,000	4,114,251	2,154,301	500
1901 Dec. 10	10,000	10,000	1,354,376	12,906,357	10,750 [b]
1902 Nov. 25	10,000	10,000	2,666,609	3,415,749	2,000

[a] 000 Omitted.
[b] Includes $9,500,000 dividend applied to increase capital stock.

Date	Capital [a]	Surplus [a]	Undivided profits	Net profits	Dividends [a]
1903 Nov. 17	$10,000	$ 10,000	$ 3,328,885	$ 2,744,170	$ 2,000
1904 Nov. 10	10,000	10,000	4,148,005	3,443,562	2,000
1905 Nov. 9	10,000	10,000	5,882,680	4,669,719	2,625
1906 Sept. 4	10,000	17,883 [c]	....	5,330,207	2,675
1907 Dec. 3	10,000	15,000	4,533,938	3,378,393	3,200
1908 Nov. 27	10,000	15,000	2,072,250	10,677,092	12,900 [d]
1909 Nov. 16	10,000	15,000	4,808,604	4,305,268	4,000
1910 June 30	10,000	15,000	4,855,567	3,627,463	4,000
1911 Dec. 5	10,000	15,000	6,984,399	4,374,886	3,300
1912 Nov. 26	10,000	15,000	6,940,165	2,474,805 [e]	7,000
1913 Oct. 21	10,000	15,000	7,229,299	....	3,000
1914 Dec. 31	10,000	15,000	6,595,063	....	5,000
1915 Dec. 31	10,000	15,000	8,759,023	....	5,000
1916 Dec. 27	10,000	20,000	5,243,436	....	5,000
1917 Dec. 31	10,000	20,000	8,949,252	....	6,000
1918 Dec. 31	10,000	20,000	10,504,000	....	5,000
1919 Nov. 17	10,000	20,000	13,815,022	....	5,000
1920 Dec. 29	10,000	20,000	17,770,339	....	5,000
1921 Dec. 31	10,000	25,000	16,291,984	....	5,000
1922 Dec. 29	10,000	50,000	1,584,266	....	5,000
1923 Dec. 31	10,000	50,000	9,319,036	....	5,000
1924 Dec. 31	10,000	50,000	16,060,059	....	7,500
1925 Dec. 31	10,000	70,000	3,804,041	....	8,000
1926 Dec. 31	10,000	70,000	7,448,682	....	10,000
1927 Dec. 31	10,000	80,000	2,799,068	....	10,000
1928 Dec. 31	10,000	90,000	2,684,391	....	10,000
1929 Dec. 31	10,000	100,000	3,359,751	....	10,000
1930 Dec. 31	10,000	100,000	14,009,524	....	10,000
1931 Dec. 31	10,000	100,000	12,537,242	....	10,000
1932 Dec. 31	10,000	75,000	6,483,357	....	10,000
1933 Dec. 30	10,000	65,000	7,278,379	....	10,000
1934 Dec. 31	10,000	80,000	9,218,068	....	10,000
1935 Dec. 31	10,000	80,000	10,572,171	....	10,000
1936 Dec. 31	10,000	100,000	6,960,885	....	10,000
1937 Dec. 31	10,000	100,000	8,207,633	....	10,000
1938 Dec. 31	10,000	100,000	9,072,832	....	10,000

[c] Includes undivided profits.
[d] Includes $10,000,000 dividend to organize the First Security Co. For 1908–1938 includes dividends of First Security Co.
[e] Net profits for 1913–38 could be roughly estimated from figures available.

5. Experience of the Bank since 1933

Although the First National Bank received some scares in the years of deepening gloom, 1931–33, it escaped many of the heartaches of bankers in the period of the depression. Public indignation was aroused against A. H. Wiggin of the Chase National Bank and C. E. Mitchell of the National City Bank. No charges of financial misconduct were made against an official of the First National. Moreover, the First National felt considerable satisfaction in the fact that it was not a heavy loser from the bonds issued abroad and sold in this country during the period 1923–29. Indeed, it had good reason to congratulate itself on not having lost a dollar from loans to Germany.

The income of the Bank for the year 1936 was broken up and published (for the first time) as follows:

INCOME STATEMENT FOR 1936 [a]

Net earnings from loans and investments	$13,916,683.12	
Other earnings	580,061.76	
Net profits on securities	1,027,999.58	
Miscellaneous credits	107,862.51	$15,632,606.97
Less:		
Operating expenses	$1,536,959.73	
Reserved for taxes and assessments	2,424,000.00	
Miscellaneous debits	282,933.07	4,243,892.80
Net income		$11,388,714.17
Dividends paid		10,000,000.00
Balance to undivided profits		$ 1,388,714.17
Undivided profits, December 31, 1935		10,572,171.20
		$11,960,885.37
Transferred to surplus		5,000,000.00
Undivided profits, December 31, 1936		$ 6,960,885.37

[a] Similar statements have been published annually since this year.

The following statistics for December 31, 1937, are of great interest:

Number of employees	201
Number of officers	15
Number of depositors	1,082
Number of stockholders	5,102

6. Taking Care of Customers

It is said that the chief characteristic of the First National Bank is that the Bank takes care of its customers. Of course, all banks do this. The only question is what the First National does that is exceptional.

The Bank is relatively free of rules in its treatment of borrowers. While the normal course may be to require, say, a deposit of $200,000 and then to extend a credit of $1,000,000 with all loans to be paid for three months each year, the First National has no such rigid formula.

Since the Bank has a very small number of customers, it can assist them in various ways, for instance, occasionally in getting orders. There is nothing peculiar about this except that the strategic position of the Bank and its small number of customers enable it to do a better job than in most cases.

If a customer wanted a loan above the limit permitted to a national bank, then the First National, if it favored the loan, would normally call other banks to inform them of its client's needs and indicate that it was itself lending to the limit. To be sure, this is a common practice in big banks; the only unusual feature in this case is that the institutions which are served are larger than the average.

7. Miscellaneous

It should be noted that the First National Bank has no branches and has merged with only one bank (in 1901), possibly in order to secure more floor space. It does little foreign business. George F. Baker, Sr., sold the First Security Co.'s holdings (majority of the total) in the Chase National partly with the thought that Chase was going into foreign business without having the trained personnel to make such a course safe. He thought that no American bankers had adequate training in the foreign field. He regarded the domestic field as safer and more profitable.

Some students of banking have called the First National an investment trust. How far this condition is temporary remains to be seen.

The First National does not advertise or seek customers. Still it is always ready to consider new business. It will admit a firm or person only for a good reason, because it prefers that relations, once established, shall be enduring and satisfactory both for the customer and for the Bank. It seems to the outsider that the very exclusiveness of the business of the First National is an asset.

Deprived by the law of 1933 of its participation in holding certain equities, through the First Security Co., and prevented by business conditions from making many large loans to its customers, the Bank, like commercial banks generally, may well sympathize with the federal government's policy of taxing undistributed corporate profits. On general grounds, we might argue that, if the big industrialists were forced to borrow at banks, then the federal government might have more control over credit—for better or for worse. The First National is by circumstances put into a position of great interest to the student and challenge to the officers of the Bank.

A good summary of the Bank's career is found in its earnings. From the earnings on a paid-in capital (by April, 1864) of $500,000, plus $8,000,000 capital surplus resulting from the sale of additional shares in 1901,[40] it had, up to December 31, 1937, made payments to stockholders as shown in Table 3.

8. Supplementary Material: Street Loans of the First National Bank of New York, 1929

For many years the First National Bank had employed a portion of its funds, and on occasion very substantial amounts, in street loans to brokers secured by Stock Exchange collateral, which by reason of their safety and liquidity had proved a highly satisfactory medium for the short-term employment of funds. The

[40] In 1901, $4,000,000 par value (40,000 shares) of the capital stock increase ($9,500,000) was sold to George F. Baker, that is, 40,000 shares at $300 a share. Accordingly, we should add to the $500,000 the sum paid by Baker in 1901, that is, the difference between the par value and the price at which the stock was sold, which is $8,000,000.

Table 3. TOTAL PAYMENTS TO STOCKHOLDERS

Total dividends paid by Bank		$193,810,000
Paid by First Security Co.		
Dividends	$65,700,000	
Capital returned to stockholders, January, 1934, on dissolution of First Security Co.	2,018,500	67,718,500
Total		$261,528,500

[This figure becomes more significant when we note Table 4:]

Table 4. STOCKHOLDERS' DIVIDENDS AND EQUITY

1864–1937

Dividends paid	$261,528,500
Present equity: surplus and undivided profits	108,207,632
Total	$369,736,132

Bank had dealt with many borrowers in the street loan market, some of whom were also its depositors, and as a general practice did not call a loan to a broker so long as that loan remained properly secured according to the Bank's requirements. Although some brokers paid off at least part of their demand loans each morning, reborrowing in the afternoon, according to the requirements of their day's business, others continued their demand loans from day to day for long periods, aware of the Bank's practice of not calling properly secured loans, and paid them off only as their borrowing requirements diminished. The rates on such loans were, of course, set daily and were subject to frequent change in periods of activity.

The safety and liquidity of street loans, and the high rates which they carried during the latter part of 1928 and the early months of 1929, had attracted many lenders other than banks and banking houses, including industrial, public utility and other corporations, investment trusts, wealthy individuals, and others.

On October 1, 1929, of the substantial amount of street loans, both time and demand, which the Bank was holding, approximately 30 per cent of the total was for its own account, while 70 per cent had been made for the account of correspondent banks and other customers. As the decline of the stock market, which had begun early in September, gained momentum and the liquidation of securities increased, total street loans held by the Bank for its own account and for customers declined sharply, decreasing 20 per cent in the twenty days between October 1 and October 21. Virtually the entire decrease occurred in the Bank's own loans, which during this period shrank 65 per cent as the debit balances of brokers' customers were reduced and the brokers' loans were paid off. During this period street loans for customers' accounts remained at approximately the same figure.

On October 21, with the demoralization of the market increasing, these lenders began to show an inclination to call in their loans, indicating for the first time concern for the safety of their funds and reluctance to continue to have street loans during a period of great uncertainty and strain.

On October 25 customers, for whose accounts the Bank held loans, instructed the Bank to call loans totaling more than $34,000,000, which the Bank, rather than call the loans and add to the demoralization, took over for its own account, leaving the loans undisturbed as far as borrowers were concerned. In this connection it is important to point out that a broker borrowing from the Bank dealt only with the Bank and was not notified or concerned as to whether his loans were held by the Bank for its own account or for the account of its customers. On the same day, October 25, the Bank placed an additional $20,000,000 in street loans in response to brokers' requests for accommodation, the result of these combined transactions being an increase in the Bank's own street loans on that day of $55,000,000.

Following a reduction of $35,000,000 in its own street loans on October 28, resulting from the payment of loans by brokers, the Bank met heavier demands than ever.

On the day of the panic, October 29, as other banks called loans, it made for its own account over $50,000,000 of street loans, while it took over from customers a total of $26,000,000 of loans which they had ordered called. On that day, at a time of panic and general demoralization, the Bank placed some $76,000,000 of its own funds in the street loan market. Throughout the day it kept the sum of $25,000,000 "on the Board" to meet brokers' requirements, increasing this offering whenever brokers' borrowings brought the figure below $25,000,000. The making of $50,000,000 in new street loans that day involved handling a total of $112,000,000 in loans, $31,000,000 having been paid off and $81,000,000 in new loans having been made.

October 30 saw $35,000,000 of loans ordered called by customers taken over and $12,000,000 additional placed in street loans, an increase of $47,000,000 for that day in the Bank's loans to brokers. Again, the placing of $12,000,000 net in street loans resulted from payment of $63,000,000 by brokers and new loans to them of $75,000,000. The next day, October 31, witnessed a decline of $11,000,000 in the Bank's street loans, resulting from payment of $65,000,000 and new loans of $54,000,000.

By the end of October, although the Bank still had money which it was willing to place in street loans to relieve the situation, the burden suddenly thrown on it was greater than its physical facilities allowed it to handle. A neighboring institution with a larger staff expressed its willingness to make street loans on behalf of the Bank, using its own facilities to place in the market the funds to be supplied by the Bank. It loaned a total of $18,000,000, which was repaid during the next few weeks.

Although the liquidation of securities continued, the next few days saw a return to more normal conditions. Total street loans began to decline rapidly as liquidation resulted in the reduction of customers' debit balances with brokers, and as the stock market began to show greater stability other lenders reëntered the money market. Brokers' loans made by the Bank for its own account during the emergency to supply the demand for money, created by the panic and by the sudden withdrawal of other lenders from the market, shrank almost as rapidly as they had mounted. Total street loans for its own account and for the account of customers decreased by over 50 per cent from November 1 to November 15. The Bank's customers returned to the street loan market and placed small amounts on call, but by November 15 the demand for funds had decreased to such an extent, as evidenced by the decline in the call rate from 10 per cent to 4½ per cent, that brokers were paying off their loans and it was difficult to place new money in street loans.

The changes in the relative position of the Bank and its customers in the ownership of the street loans held by the Bank from October 1, 1929, to November 15, 1929, may be summarized as follows:

	Percentage of Street Loans	
	Bank's	Customers'
October 1, 1929	30	70
October 30, 1929	60	40
November 15, 1929	12½	87½

9. Readings

See N. S. B. Gras, *The Massachusetts-First National Bank of Boston* (Cambridge, 1937), particularly chaps. x and xi.

There is no published history of the First National Bank of New York. The policy of the Bank has always been opposed to publicity.

10. Suggested Questions

1. What policies have been profitable to the First National of Boston?
2. What policies have been profitable to the First National of New York? In what ways (if any) can the First National of New York take care of customers not open to the First National of Boston?
3. What of the future for the two banks (a) under a continued régime of financial capitalism and (b) under a new régime of well-rounded national capitalism?
4. Should the First National of Boston try to grow regionally or nationally?
5. What was the nature of the (First National of Boston) merger of 1903? Should the First National of Boston use "1784" in its advertisements?
6. Under what circumstances might the First National of New York change its policy and merge with other banks?

XXXII. TWO LIFE INSURANCE COMPANIES: THE MUTUAL AND THE EQUITABLE, OF NEW YORK, 1842–1938

1. General Statement

Life insurance, relatively unimportant in the United States a century ago, is now one of the most powerful influences in American business. This striking development has been the outgrowth of a great need and has brought with it many serious problems, which can be best understood in the light of the past experience of the leading companies in the field.

For over half a century the Mutual Life Insurance Co., of New York, was one of the leaders in the development of insurance. Its history encompasses most of the important types of changes which have occurred in the industry, many of which were initiated by the Company itself or by its competitor, the Equitable. Thus a study of the history of either company will contribute to an understanding of the problems of the entire industry.

2. Important Dates

1812–42	Period of proprietary life insurance and trust companies.
1842	Mutual Life of New York chartered.
1843	Mutual began to do business.
1843–47	Revolutionary period in American life insurance.
1847–70	Establishment of general agency system.
1852	H. H. Hyde became general agent of Mutual in Boston.
1859	H. B. Hyde organized the Equitable.
1865	Equitable paid cash dividend. Mutual adopted policy of annual cash dividends.
1868	Mutual increased amount of insurance granted to an individual.
1870–90	Rapid growth of insurance, many failures, public opposition, and competition from assessment companies and fraternals.
1879	Mutual adopted incontestable policy.
1890–1905	Cutthroat competition in insurance. New York State insurance investigation. Control of Equitable placed in hands of trustees.
1906–10	Many laws passed to regulate companies. Housecleaning by companies themselves.
1918	Equitable mutualized.
1919–32	Rapid growth of insurance.
1932–present	Period of testing and of a growing consciousness of problems of costs, public relations, and size.

3. Organization of the Mutual Life Insurance Co.

In 1842 a group of business men in New York City, many of them merchants, secured from the legislature of the State of New York a special act incorporating a company to be known as the Mutual Life Insurance Co. of New York. This Company was mutual in all respects. It had no capital stock. It was not to commence operations until over half a million dollars in insurance had been written. The Company was to be governed by a board of trustees having 36 members, 9 of whom were to go out of office each year. Their successors were to be elected by those having insurance policies in the Company, each member being allowed to cast one vote if he carried insurance of at least one thousand dollars. This board of trustees was to supervise the business of the Company and was to hire the necessary officers to carry on the detailed work.[1]

Every fifth year the Company was to balance its books, and, after deducting from the income all expenses for the period

[1] A leaflet entitled *An Act to Incorporate the Mutual Life Insurance Company of New York*, April 12, 1842.

and setting aside reserves against the outstanding policies, declare the remainder to be profits and prorate it to the policies in accordance with "the original amount of the premium paid." This new amount was to be added to the value of the policy, but it was not to be paid until after the death of the insured.

The Mutual Life Insurance Co. was intended to provide a plan of "insurance at cost." Former companies had been privately owned. Policyholders had had neither a voice in management nor a share in profits. Yet, in order to be safe, insurance companies had to charge rates high enough to provide for all contingencies. Thus every normal year policyholders would pay in a surplus sum which was never returned to them. These alleged disadvantages to the stockholder were overcome by making the Company mutual both as to management and as to earnings.[2]

When the Mutual commenced business in 1843, there was very meager information on mortality in the United States. To supply this lack the Company took the English figures and added something to the probable deaths per thousand each year, thus giving a higher mortality figure than would normally be expected. The Company also weighted the figures against itself by figuring on a very low rate of interest on its assets. It did this by using the English figures at a time when the English interest rate was notably below that existing in this country.[3]

Even though the Company did weight the figures against itself, and therefore charged high rates, it soon began to sell much insurance. Other companies had also been charging high rates, but in the case of the Mutual there was the conclusive argument that high rates merely protected the insured and did not cost the insured anything because all surplus profits were returned to the policyholders.

The Mutual was organized at an extremely fortunate time when public opinion was swinging strongly in favor of insurance. By its form of organization, moreover, many earlier objections were removed. After a difficult first year the Company was able to secure a constantly increasing volume of business.

One problem that confronted this Company, as it has all life insurance companies, was the selection of good risks. While the Company was desirous of selling as much insurance as possible, it was conscious of the undesirability of selling insurance to those who had a strong likelihood of collecting it within a few years. Therefore, the Company early instituted a very careful medical examination of the applicant in order to determine his life expectancy.[4] While that practice conflicted with selling interests, this Company like most others relied heavily upon the recommendations of its medical advisers, with the result that it was unusually fortunate in the type of people insured. The early years of the Company were marked by a very favorable mortality rate.[5] Careful selection of risks and the loading of the mortality figures against itself at the beginning meant that for a long period the actual figures were far more favorable than had been anticipated.

In connection with its study of risks the Company made a geographical survey. At the beginning it had been generally considered that all parts of the country were equally healthful, but a little experience demonstrated that certain regions in the South and Southwest were very unhealthful. The Mutual, in common with many of its predecessors and competitors,

[2] *A Treatise on Life Insurance* (New York, 1844), p. 13. This is a pamphlet published by the Company.

[3] *Ibid.*, p. 14.

[4] Pamphlet, written by "A Lady," *What the Public Ought to Know About Life Insurance* (1858), pp. 39 ff.

[5] *The Twenty-first Annual Report of the Mutual Life Insurance Company of New York* (1864), pp. 26 ff.

by 1855 had learned to be careful of insuring in unhealthful sections of the country and had advanced the rates considerably on new policies in those sections. Before long the Company found even the higher rates not fully remunerative and therefore decided not to continue insuring in the southern and southwestern States.[6]

It was recognized from the very first that the strength of the Mutual would depend largely on the strength of its selling force. That is, to be strong the Company had to have a large volume of insurance in force, a continuous flow of new policies, and a wide geographic distribution of its insureds. The Company succeeded in attaining these objectives by employing an aggressive selling force in all parts of the country where it wished to sell insurance.

The Company's method of selling insurance in the early days was simple. It divided the country into territories and gave each territory to an agent who received a commission on all the insurance he sold in the district. Except for the fact that he had to sell a specified amount of insurance, the general agent was usually extremely independent. He hired salesmen and paid them, and thus the sales organization belonged to him.[7] This situation resulted, in the course of years when rival companies sprang up, in the bolting of discontented general agents, who switched their entire business to some rival company. At first many of these general agents lacked zeal in selling insurance. They believed that, if a man wanted insurance badly enough, he would look them up and buy it and that all the agent needed to do was to advertise the location of his office.

The Company sold a number of different kinds of insurance. At first it sold for the most part one-year, seven-year, and whole-of-life policies. Later came endowment policies and limited-payment life policies.[8] By 1866 the following types of policies were being sold: (1) life policies, issued for the whole of life and entitled to dividends; (2) life policies on the ten-year plan, that is, paid-up in ten years but continuing in force and earning dividends unless surrendered; (3) endowment insurance policies, ten-year or payable at a certain age or at death if earlier, participating in surplus arising from that class of risks, and bearing a surrender value after the first payment (the prevailing practice had been to cancel all policies on which payments had not been kept up); (4) endowment policies for children; and (5) survivorship annuities.[9]

The early success of the Company may in some measure be seen from its early statements. Substantial dividends were declared in 1848, 1853, and 1858; in 1858 the dividend was 40 per cent on premiums paid in the preceding five-year period except premiums on short-term policies which received a 20 per cent dividend.[10] On January 31, 1858, insurance in force was $30,481,302 on 10,390 policies. In the year then ending, claims had been paid to the extent of $1,317,643, commissions amounting to $108,142 had been paid, other costs (advertising, medical examination, salaries, printing, rent, and so on) totaled $283,718, and payments on surrendered policies or reduction of premium totaled $169,031. The net assets of the Company at the time were $4,685,908; the surplus, above reserves to cover all

[6] *The Twenty-third Annual Report of the Mutual Life Insurance Company of New York* (1866), pp. 22 ff.

[7] Amos D. Smith, *A Letter to the Massachusetts and Rhode Island Policyholders of the Mutual Life Insurance Company of New York* (1879), p. 3.

[8] This information was supplied by Mr. J. Owen Stalson, who is preparing for publication a volume on the history of insurance.

[9] *Twenty-third Annual Report,* pp. 56–60.

[10] Circular issued by Lorenzo Burge, agent in Boston, dated Dec., 1853, which contains quotations from the Company's annual report; circular issued by the president of the Company, New York, March 6, 1858, containing the president's quinquennial statement.

liabilities, was $1,142,503. Of assets $148,637 were in cash and $4,321,032 were invested in bonds and mortgages as specified by the charter (that is, in mortgages on unencumbered real estate in New York State and bonds of the United States, New York State, or any incorporated city in New York State).

4. Organization of the Equitable Life Assurance Society of the United States

In 1852 the board of trustees appointed Henry Hazen Hyde general agent of the Mutual for the Boston district. He was commissioned by the president to "visit many cities and towns of the United States for the purpose of extending a knowledge of the strength and high standing of the company, to confer with agents already appointed, to select others, and to inspire all with energy and zeal in their efforts to seek applications for life insurance." [11] This man was a very successful salesman, but he is remembered chiefly because he was the father of Henry Baldwin Hyde.

In the year that his father obtained the position of general agent for the Mutual, Henry Baldwin Hyde commenced work in the office of the Company as a clerk. In the course of time he rose to the responsible position of cashier. In this position he first noticed that the Company restricted to $10,000 the amount of insurance that it would write on any one life. Many applications came into the office for amounts far in excess of that amount. The procedure in such cases was to inform the applicant that the Company would give him $10,000 in insurance but not any more. This may have been a very sensible practice—during the early years a loss above that amount might have crippled the Company severely, but the result was that a large volume of business was turned down each year.

The young cashier proposed to the president of the Mutual that a few men within the Company organize an independent company to insure the business which the Mutual rejected because of its size. There would be no competition between the companies; they would work together, with the new company in a subordinate position. The president not only turned down the proposition, but he also said that no man contemplating the organization of a rival company could retain his position with the Mutual. The result of his proposal was that, though his books were found to be correct, young Hyde found himself discharged from his position as cashier without any recommendation or statement of his honesty.[12]

After some consideration Henry Baldwin Hyde decided to organize an independent insurance company. At that time the State law required that all new insurance companies have a minimum capital of $100,000. Hyde proceeded to hire a suite of offices above those occupied by the Mutual at 98 Broadway. Next he hired a sign painter to paint a sign 30 feet long, "The Equitable Life Assurance Society of the United States." This he hung just above the smaller sign of the Mutual. Then he rented some office furniture and bought a box of cigars. By that time he was ready to commence business. His first step was to hire a force of salesmen to call upon various people who he knew were in the market for insurance. Through this organization over a hundred applications for insurance were obtained.

Hyde secured the capital in an ingenious way. He got a doctor to raise $25,000 on the promise of appointment as physician to the company. A lawyer was promised the position of attorney for the company in return for his investing $25,000. The remaining $50,000 was raised in a similar way. Thus the new company met the legal requirement.[13]

[11] *Henry Baldwin Hyde, a Biographical Sketch* (New York, 1901), p. 14.

[12] *Ibid.*, p. 21.

[13] *Ibid.*, pp. 26 ff.

Not everything was smooth sailing, however, for Henry Baldwin Hyde. Since this new company was his idea and since he had organized it, he believed that he should be its first president. Unfortunately, he and his close friends did not own a majority of the stock and thus did not have legal control. The controlling interest held that an older and better-known man should be chosen president. The directors, accordingly, elected William C. Alexander president and Hyde vice-president. This arrangement did not work out badly, however, for actually Hyde was the manager of the concern.

The first thing that the Society did was to make a strong drive to sell insurance.[14] This was not altogether a new idea; some companies had previously made not a little attempt to sell insurance. But apparently Hyde raised the selling program to a new height of aggressiveness. From the first, results were achieved. One thing that happened was that Henry Hazen Hyde, the father of the manager, switched the bulk of his business to the new company.

The older companies at first regarded the new company as a frivolous interference in the serious business of life. They started by merely ignoring it, but they were soon shocked out of this attitude by the great inroads the Society made upon their business. Some of the companies retaliated by attacking the Equitable. Their statements, which attacked the financial solvency of the concern, the character of its business, and the character of its officers, sometimes slipped over into slander. The Equitable, however, went after its detractors so severely that everyone came to be very careful about his statements concerning that firm.

5. Effect of the Civil War

Anyone looking back on the situation would say that the Equitable had been very unfortunate in starting at the time it did, because it had just time enough to sell a large volume of insurance and be caught by the Civil War, which would raise the mortality rate among its best prospects. As a matter of fact, although the company's officers were disturbed, the war proved not to be so injurious as they had expected. In none of the war years, nor in the years that followed, did the mortality among the Society's insured reach the expected rate for any peacetime year. That was because the Equitable had assumed high mortality rates and had then picked only the most favorable prospects. The real worry during this period came from the competition furnished by the Mutual.[15]

In January, 1865, the Equitable balanced its books and declared a dividend to policyholders, which could either be added to the value of the policies or be taken in cash. Since the country was in need of ready money at the time, this dividend was taken in money, which stripped the concern of all its ready cash. Immediately the Mutual announced that from that time on it was going to balance its books annually and declare an annual cash dividend to its policyholders. Not to be outdone, the Equitable made the same announcement. Immediately a cholera plague broke out in certain sections of the country and seemed to be about to sweep over the entire nation. Under such circumstances it seemed that the Equitable, having no cash with which to meet unforeseen contingencies, was headed for trouble. The actuary, insisting that it had been a mistake to promise to pay dividends annually, wanted an announcement that the Society would return to its former policy of five-year intervals between dividends. Henry Hyde refused to assent to this, unless the other companies did the same. Since they had plenty of cash, they made no motion to do so; and the Equitable went along expecting trouble daily. As a matter of fact it met with none, ow-

[14] *Ibid.*, p. 44.

[15] *Ibid.*, pp. 53 ff.

ing to the fact that the cholera did not spread and deaths were no more numerous than would have been expected under normal conditions.

The war years saw a great increase in the total volume of insurance outstanding in the United States. In Massachusetts alone the increase was from $18,580,402 in 1860 to $180,828,972 in 1865, and $308,467,053 in 1866.[16] In other sections of the country it was equally great. Of this increase the Equitable and Mutual got a large share. They were not without competition, however; during this time over twenty new companies came into existence. After the end of the war the increase was even greater.

This period was marked by the great popularity of life insurance and life insurance companies. Up to this time companies had generally met claims honestly and quickly, and they had proved themselves financially responsible. The result was that the public accepted the idea of insurance. The churches were strongly in favor of it, and it was advocated that no man was so poor that he could not carry some insurance on his life in order to protect his wife and children. Men who were not married and had no dependents should take out insurance in the form of paid-up policies, thus taking advantage of the present low rates to provide for dependents whom they might acquire later. Men of moderate means were urged to take out endowment insurance as a method of forced saving. Rich men were urged that they should insure because many things could sweep away their fortunes, and, since an insurance company could lose every cent of its assets and still be solvent so long as it had its policyholders left, insurance represented an ideal investment. These arguments were devoutly believed by most people, and their belief was helped along by insurance agents who were always on the job to point out that insurance was man's duty to humanity. It was argued that, if each man protected his family through ample insurance, dire poverty would be an unknown thing. These factors caused insurance companies to have a phenomenal growth.

In this period the companies proceeded to build up a large surplus for the protection of the policyholders. As the companies increased the volume of their business over this period, they were able to increase the amount of insurance they would give one man—the original limitation of $10,000 was soon removed. For a long time, however, if one company received a very large policy, it broke it up into smaller amounts and had other companies underwrite parts of it.

The first three or four years after the Civil War were marked by the great strides that occurred in the volume of insurance outstanding, in its popularity, and in the relative honesty and reliability of the concerns. The next period gives a very different picture.

6. Rapid Growth, 1870–1900

Up to 1870 life insurance companies had experienced a phenomenal growth. Although most companies were operating on a sound basis during these years, a number were apparently thriving in spite of their operating under faulty actuarial and underwriting plans. The period 1871–73 was marked by the disappearance of over thirty companies either through actual bankruptcy or through merging with some larger and more stable concern.[17] In most cases of bankrupt concerns, since the insurance outstanding was assumed by some solvent firm, the insured lost very little.

This period also felt the effect of the accumulation of data on mortality figures in the United States. By this time the exact number of deaths per thousand that could be expected in the various parts of

[16] Paul Morton, *The First Fifty Years of the Equitable Life Assurance Society of the United States* (New York, 1909), p. 41.

[17] *Henry Baldwin Hyde*, p. 94.

the country was known. Competition had forced rates for insurance into a narrow range, and experience had convinced the companies that those figures were dependable. The difference in rates came chiefly from the different loading figures which the various companies forced the policies to carry in order to cover the overhead costs. The general tendency then was to make a standard charge for the same type of policy; the practice has been continued from that time onward. Competition has not been in the price-cutting field. Owing to the feeling that a company which cut prices or offered bargain insurance was not likely to be financially secure, those insured have not favored price-cutting as a sales method.

Of utmost importance after 1870 was the development of a highly critical attitude on the part of the public toward insurance. The East had generally been favorable toward insurance, but an insurance investigation conducted by the State of New York in 1877 revealed what were considered unreasonably high salaries, nepotism, and overvaluation of investments to give the appearance of large reserves. The officers of the Mutual Life had their control bolstered by proxies secured by agents from policyholders.[18] During the 'seventies and 'eighties the West was swept by a wave of opposition against large eastern corporations. The insurance companies had to withstand heavy opposition. The result was not only a considerable amount of hostile legislation but also the prejudice of the courts against the so-called "soulless corporation." Thus, in many cases it seems that the insurance companies did not get impartial consideration in suits against them. The result of this hostility was that the insurance companies were faced with a large volume of exaggerated or actually fraudulent claims for compensation. One of the most famous was the Wackerlee case.[19]

This was a case of disappearance in which the beneficiary, Mrs. Wackerlee, the widow of the allegedly deceased man, tried to collect life insurance. The claim was denied by the two insurance companies concerned, the Mutual of New York and the Aetna of Hartford, and the "widow" thereupon brought the matter to trial. The Aetna won a judge's decision in Louisiana, and the Mutual lost in a jury decision in Missouri.

The Mutual, believing that this was important as a test case, decided to appeal to a higher court. In the West public opinion and the press came out strongly for the "widow." Much evidence was introduced which obviously disproved the evidence on which the earlier jury decision in favor of the claimant had been based, and, as final proof, the insured man himself was brought into court. He testified that he had disappeared out of fear of staying with his wife since the policies were made out to her. Though witnesses, including the insured's brother, testified to the identity of the insured, the jury again decided in favor of the "widow," who insisted that the man claiming to be the insured was her husband's brother. The Company again appealed the case to a higher court and then the decision was reversed.

Even though it would often have been much less costly to settle out of court, insurance companies at that time, realizing that the slightest laxity in settling claims would be the signal for a multitude of such dubious demands, seem to have fought every case that appeared to be doubtful. Although this undoubtedly re-

[18] *The Condition of the Life Insurance Companies of the State of New York* (printed from the official stenographer's notes of the investigation by the committee of the State Assembly, New York, 1877).

[19] *The Spectator,* Oct. 26, 1882; letter from the law department of the Mutual to the publishers of the Detroit *Free Press,* dated Oct. 17, 1882, in the collection of source material on the Mutual Life, in Baker Library.

sulted in the defrauding of many honest people who (together with dishonest ones) could not afford to take their insecurely established claims to court, it is not clear that under the circumstances any other line of action could have been followed by the insurance companies.

At this time one important step was taken to protect the interest of the beneficiaries of the insured. During the decade 1870–79 there was considerable trouble about the payment of policies in cases in which the insured died within a short time of the days on which they had taken out the policies. Companies, in many cases charging that the insured had died from suicide, refused to settle. But in 1879 the Equitable announced that any policy that had been in force three years was incontestable, regardless of the cause or source of death, suicide or otherwise. The only preliminary to payment of the policy was definite proof of death. The time period was later cut to one year. Competition soon forced other companies to follow the lead of the Equitable.[20]

The next improvement adopted by the Equitable was immediate payment of claims. Heretofore policies had been paid eventually, customarily "sixty days after due notice and proof of death." The result was that when the money was most needed there was none available. Next came the standard simplified policy. Up to this time, policies had differed one from another even if they were of the same general class. From now on, policies of the same class tended to be alike, and the rights of all parties concerned were made clear. These improvements came to be generally adopted within a short period of time.

One of the forces which was at this time driving the insurance companies to more liberal practices was a new type of insurance company which was rapidly coming to the front, the fraternal or assessment company. The larger companies had by now standardized the cost of insurance so that all charged about the same; but in every case the premium was fairly high, based on an actual knowledge of the costs of insurance. The new type was based on the principle that, if a group of healthy young men got together, they could insure each other at a very low rate by simply assessing the living to pay death claims. The result was that they wrote policies at a very low cost. This new development was especially strong in the West because of hostility there to large eastern corporations. The assessment plan was taken up by many fraternal orders and other groups everywhere, and for a few years it seriously embarrassed the old-line insurance concerns. Not for long, however, for within three decades the advantages originally gained by having a large group of insured of the same age turned to a disadvantage. The percentage of deaths rose rapidly, reaching that of the average population and then passing it, since these organizations were not taking in enough new members to keep the percentage down. The assessment companies were, moreover, burdened with insureds whose health made it impossible to secure insurance in regular companies. Once a high death rate had been reached, the assessment concerns faced what was almost a hopeless situation. Young men, able to get insurance at lower rates from an old-line concern, refused to join the organization. This aggravated the situation, which went from bad to worse until in some cases the fraternal insurance concerns were forced out of existence, others being taken over by regular insurance companies. A small minority raised their rates and put themselves on a firm footing. In order to avoid a repetition of this situation most States have passed legislation forcing insurance companies to build up certain reserves against the amount of insurance in force.

[20] Morton, *op. cit.*, p. 74; George Amrhein, *The Liberalization of the Life Insurance Contract* (Philadelphia, 1933), p. 149.

Though 1870 to 1900 was in the insurance field a period of many failures, much public opposition, and intense competition, the business of insurance grew at a phenomenal rate. The experience of the Equitable is illustrated by Table I, below.[21]

Though the figures given for the Mutual in Table 2 are not exactly comparable, they similarly reveal a remarkable growth.[22]

7. The Insurance Investigation of 1905

All through the period 1870–1905, charges of corruption were made against the insurance companies by outsiders and by each company against the others. Nothing was definitely known except that insurance rates were not being reduced and that dividends to policyholders were constantly shrinking. The companies were, however, meeting payments promptly. Antagonism finally became so strong that in 1905 the State assembly of New York appointed a committee to examine the affairs of life insurance companies.

The committee, headed by William W. Armstrong and advised by Charles Evans Hughes, conducted extensive hearings and published the testimony and a report, which together constitute a truly remarkable collection of information on the administration of life insurance companies. The remainder of this section consists of quotations or abstracts from the reports on the Mutual and the Equitable.

A. On the Mutual Life Insurance Co.[23]

In the investigation of the Mutual Life Insurance Co. the first fact brought to light was that the policyholders actually exercised no control over the Company. The control was vested in the existing

[21] *Report to the Policyholders,* 1894, pp. 22–28; *Growth and Present Condition of the Equitable Life Assurance Society of the United States,* 1901, pp. 10, 24–25.

[22] *Ninety-fifth Annual Report of the Mutual Life Insurance Company of New York,* p. 9.

[23] *Report of the Joint Committee of the Senate and Assembly of the State of New York Appointed to Investigate the Affairs of Life Insurance Companies* (Albany, 1906), vol. x, pp. 9–44 (or vol. vii of the other edition, pp. 9–38).

Table 1. GROWTH OF THE EQUITABLE

1865–1900

Year	Assets	Surplus	Total income	Number of policies	Insurance in force
1865	$ 1,586,524	$ 305,704	$ 971,648	8,097	$ 27,507,739
1870	13,236,025	408,434	7,009,344	36,340	143,970,984
1880	41,108,602	6,957,855	8,735,699	52,272	177,597,703
1890	119,243,744	23,740,447	35,036,683	197,825	720,662,473
1900	304,598,063	66,137,170	58,007,130	..... [a]	1,116,875,047

[a] Not given.

Table 2. GROWTH OF THE MUTUAL

1863–1903

Year	Assets	Contingency fund and funds held for dividends	Total income	Insurance in force
1863	$ 10,611,149	$ 1,479,979	$ 5,158,597	$ 52,615,656
1873	65,346,401	2,754,737	19,457,375	289,505,739
1883	100,912,245	12,514,111	18,500,893	342,946,032
1893	184,935,691	15,148,269	41,953,146	802,867,478
1903	401,821,662	61,994,844	77,333,713	1,445,228,681

officers and directors. This group was in general a closed corporation, and outsiders were taken in only to fill vacancies caused by the death or resignation of members. The men in control had no financial interest in the Company. Because of the practice of obtaining through agents proxies for ten years on new policies, President Richard C. McCurdy and Vice-president Robert A. Grannis held sufficient proxies at all times from out-of-town policyholders to prevent an uprising among any discontented group. McCurdy had at that time been president for twenty years, and during the preceding years he had been first vice-president. Robert A. Grannis had been first vice-president for twenty years and had been second vice-president for a long time before that. Thus these two men had had absolute control of the Company. The power of the president is indicated by the following quotation from the bylaws:

"The president shall also have the general direction and superintendence of the affairs and of the officers of the company and shall establish rules and regulations for the conduct of the business of the company and for the direction of its officers. He may from time to time devolve the performance of his duties upon any one of the vice-presidents under the designation of acting president. He may suspend or remove any agent, manager or general agent at pleasure; and in all cases in which the duties of the subordinate officers, employees and agents of the company are not specially prescribed by its by-laws, or by resolution of the board, they shall obey the orders and instructions of the president."

The trustees apparently exercised no effective check on management. They were supposed to act through six standing committees: finance, agency, insurance, mortuary claims, expenditures, and auditing. These committees, apart from the finance committee, did nothing to justify their existence.

Salaries were not fixed by the board of trustees, and apparently the board had no knowledge of them. They were not fixed by any one of the standing committees. Section 36 of the bylaws relating to the finance committee provides: "It shall also determine all questions of salary and compensation for services when not fixed by the board, the president, or an appropriate committee." As a matter of fact, for some twenty years a subcommittee on salaries, appointed by the finance committee, had determined the salaries of the executive officers. Its proceedings had not been known to the other members of the finance committee, and the matter was so treated that the large increases in salaries were known to only two members of the committee and to the officers themselves. Salaries were very high. At various times in the past ten years the president's salary had been raised to $150,000, one vice-president's to $50,000, another's to $30,000, the treasurer's to $40,000, the general manager's to $30,000, and so on.

Relatives had been conspicuously favored. The president's son, who had entered the office of the general agents of the Company in the New York metropolitan district shortly after graduating from college in 1881, in the years 1889–1904 received from his one-half interest in the agency over half a million dollars. In the years 1886–1905 the same son received from a special account of the same firm —the foreign department—$1,268,390, but of this he paid to another member of the firm one-half of the commissions on business obtained before 1893. From 1893 to 1904 a son-in-law of the president received almost a million from the same firm. The report notes that "these profits were made possible by the allowance to C. H. Raymond & Co. of special and exorbitant rates of commission which were not justifiable from any point of view."

The legal expenses for the Company were tremendous, and no adequate record was kept of them. Large sums of money were paid out to the Company's officers on their signing vouchers labeled "Legal expense." These expenses of the Mutual totaled $364,254 in 1904. What actually became of the money paid out for legal expenses has never been accurately determined. It seems probable that much of it was used to influence legislation.

Andrew C. Fields was in charge of the Company's lobby at Albany. He maintained a house near the capitol where many members of the Assembly were his guests for long periods of time. His salary, the expense of maintaining this house, and many other items were paid by the Company. It appears that the insurance companies kept a close watch on all prospective legislation and spent money freely in an effort to influence it. At the same time the Mutual had the habit of contributing liberally toward campaign funds. This money was also charged to legal expense.

Another heavy expense was for printing, stationery, and "advertising." Though the accounts on payments for supplies and for influencing the press were not clear, and it was therefore impossible to learn who profited, the expenses were enormous. After the disclosures had been made by the investigation, the treasurer estimated that $300,000 could be saved each year on the supply, advertising, and literary departments.

The investments of the Company were extraordinary in view of the relatively low returns that were netted on them. The Armstrong report listed the value of the investments at $440,978,371. Some $34,000,000 of this was real estate on which the average net return was less than 3 per cent. Some $243,000,000 consisted of stocks and bonds on which the return was 4.14 per cent. The stocks owned by the Company were of two general classes. First, there was the stock of New York banks, including the First National, the Bank of America, and the Guaranty Trust; secondly, there was the stock of railroads, such as the New York Central, Pennsylvania, and the Chicago, Milwaukee & St. Paul. The Mutual carried large balances at low interest with banks, balances at the beginning of each quarter in 1904 ranging from $17,509,167 to $22,923,857.

It was the custom of this Company to take part in underwriting syndicates. Insurance companies had a particular advantage in syndicate operations because, with their large reserves, they could purchase those securities which they had underwritten and which had not been sold by the syndicate. The profits on the syndicate participations were used to write down the cost of the real estate which the Company had acquired; they never appeared on the books.

According to the report, officers of the Company profited individually from the investments of the Mutual. "Its officers and members of its Finance Committee have considerable interests in several of the banks and trust companies in which the *Mutual* is interested, and its deposits have been largely used to promote the successes of these companies." They similarly profited from the Mutual's syndicate operations, though, the report adds, "without violating the accepted traditions or departing from the standards of the company's management."

The report says:

"The Business of the *Mutual* has enormously expanded within recent years. In twenty years its outstanding insurance has increased from $368,952,337 to $1,547,611,660, and its annual premium income from $14,768,902 to $62,932,097, and during the same period its surplus has risen from $6,943,764 to $74,357,818 (including surplus to be apportioned in 1905). But this notable expansion has not been of advantage to its policy holders. It has served as an excuse for the increase of expenses and for lavish payments to officers and agents. . . . In 1885, when the premium income was $14,768,902 and the total income $20,214,954, the dividends to policy holders were $3,183,023 and the total payments to policy holders $14,402,050, the expenses being only $3,134,452. In 1904, when the premium was $62,932,097 and the total income

$81,002,984, the dividends to policy holders were $2,674,207, the total payments to policy holders were $34,484,275, and the expenses $16,898,456. It is not simply that the distribution of dividends has been deferred. The plan of deferring dividends for long periods . . . has undoubtedly facilitated large accumulations, providing apparently abundant means for doubtful uses on the one hand, while concealing on the other the burden imposed upon the policy holders by the costly efforts to obtain new business. Annual dividends have been largely reduced, and deferred dividends, when the time for distribution has arrived, have fallen far short of expectation, causing severe criticism on the part of policy holders."

B. On the Equitable.[24]

The investigation of the Equitable Life Assurance Society brought out a similar state of affairs. This company had been organized in 1859. By 1904 its outstanding policies numbered 564,594, representing $1,495,542,842 of insurance. It is a corporation with a capital of $100,000 divided into 1,000 shares. By the charter the holders of the capital stock are entitled to semiannual dividends at a rate not exceeding 3.5 per cent. Before an investigating committee in 1877, President Henry Baldwin Hyde testified that the interest of the stockholders was limited to the semiannual dividends, that there had been no additional advantage given to them in any manner, "past, present or contingent," and that all surplus accumulations were for the benefit of the policyholders. He stated that the market value of a share was a little above $150. Stockholders alone were permitted to vote for directors. President Hyde owned a majority of the stock and dominated the company until his death in 1899. Four years previously, he had placed 502 shares of stock in a trust fund with himself as beneficiary, with the provision that at his death the fund should be held for the benefit of his son, James Hazen Hyde. If the son reached the age of thirty, the fund was to become his actual property. The father made further provision as to the disposal of the shares in case of the son's death.

The investigation of the Equitable also revealed irregular conditions. Salaries were high—the son of Henry B. Hyde was receiving $100,000 a year from the Equitable four years after his graduation from college. Legal expenses were also high; some accounts were obviously kept so as not to be decipherable. The Society swelled its assets for the purpose of its annual statement. Real estate was leased to organizations in which Hyde was interested "for terms of extraordinary duration upon conditions most unfavorable to the society." Moreover, "*pro forma* loans have been made at the end of the year; in order to reduce the cash balances, which it was not deemed advisable to show in the report to the [State Insurance] Department." The Society controlled the Mercantile Trust Co. and owned 48 per cent of the stock of the Equitable Trust Co. and used its relations with the trust companies to aid in carrying irregular accounts. The Society had bought shares in certain concerns at prices far above book values. It carried excessive balances on deposit in certain banks. "The obvious purpose of these deposits," says the report, "was to assist the companies in which the society was interested, whose prosperity was also of concern to individual officers. . . ." A committee, headed by H. C. Frick and appointed by the board of the Equitable to investigate and report upon its management, stated that the Society had stepped out of its position as an investor and had become promoter and manipulator. Officers of the Society participated in syndicate operations, using funds of the Society on which 4 per cent interest was paid. In common with its chief competitors the Equitable showed a large diminution in rates of dividends paid policyholders.

[24] *Ibid.*, pp. 94–149 (or vol. vii of the other edition, pp. 75–118).

"In February, 1905, deeming the control of the stock by James H. Hyde to be prejudicial to the interests of the society, President James W. Alexander with some thirty-five other officers and agents of the society, memorialized the Board of Directors to extend to policy holders the right to vote. The petitioners stated that 'from their practical experience in the conduct of the society's business' they 'have become convinced that its continual welfare and progress and the due administration of the trust funds in its charge render a change necessary, and that it is incompatible with present public opinion, as well as with the interests of the society and its beneficiaries, that the policy holders as the real parties in interest should continue to be without any voice in the administration of these funds, but that the entire power of selecting directors should be vested in and exercised solely by the holder for the time being of a majority of the society's nominal capital stock.' The board then adopted a resolution that in its opinion 'the policy holders should be given the right to vote for directors and that steps be taken for carrying this principle into effect at the earliest possible moment.' A committee was appointed 'to arrange the details for carrying the subject into execution, and in connection therewith the settlement of the allied question of indemnification of stockholders,' and this committee in March, 1905, submitted to the board a report unanimously recommending that the charter should be amended so as to provide that twenty-eight of the fifty-two directors should be elected by the policy holders. The report did not deal with the matter of indemnity. The Board of Directors unanimously adopted the form of amended charter as proposed by the committee, and this was subsequently submitted to the superintendent of insurance for approval."

The Frick report of June 2 severely criticized the management. It became evident that, to restore public confidence, it would be necessary to make a change in control of the stock. The week after the Frick report had been made, the 502 shares inherited by young James Hazen Hyde from his father were sold to Thomas Fortune Ryan for $2,500,000 in cash. Ryan testified that he planned to place the shares, as soon as acquired, in a voting trust composed of Grover Cleveland, Justice Morgan, J. O'Brien, and George Westinghouse. The purchase was opposed by E. H. Harriman for reasons which are not clear. The insurance report, as quoted below, reveals that plans for mutualization were not then carried out.

"The deed of transfer of the 502 shares to the three trustees above named was executed by Mr. Ryan on June 15, 1905. It recited the plan adopted by the directors for the mutualization of the society, the litigation which had prevented its consummation, and that the deed was executed to effect, so far as practicable, the result thus sought to be obtained. Accordingly the trustees were authorized to take, in their discretion, any action necessary or proper to carry the plan of mutualization into effect so as to secure to the policy holders the right to elect directly twenty-eight directors or a like proportion of the entire number of the Board; but no steps have thus far been taken in this direction. The trust deed further provides that the trustees shall so vote the shares that out of every thirteen persons voted for seven shall be policy holders selected in accordance with the wishes of the policy holders to be expressed by written requests addressed to the trustees in November of each year by holders of policies in force for not less than a year, and that the remaining six shall be selected by the trustees in their uncontrolled discretion. The object is stated to be that of the entire fifty-two directors, twenty-eight shall be policy holders 'selected by or on behalf of the policy holders.' The trust deed does not, however, provide explicitly that in voting for directors to represent the policy holders the trustees shall be governed by the voice of a plurality of those indicating their wishes. In a letter dated September 18th, addressed to the Committee by Honorable Grover Cleveland, it is stated that the trustees were at once confronted with the conditions which had resulted in such numerous resignations from the board as to make it essential to reinforce the directorate without delay. They believed it to be their duty to act in the matter in such a way as 'to further the scheme of mutualization, which had become the declared policy of the society,' and therefore determined that the persons to be recommended should be taken entirely from policy holders. On June 16th they issued a notice to the policy holders acquainting them with the provisions of the deed, and requested an expression of preferences with reference to the vacancies. The notice was given wide circulation through the public press, and by mailing copies to numerous policy holders. In response the trustees received representatives from a number of associations of policy holders in different localities, who gave advice concerning the choice of those they represented, but with this and diligent effort in other ways to secure information, they were able to recommend on June 27th only nine persons for election. The next day a further notice was published in the press. The result down to the date of the letter had been that twenty-one members 'of such character and business ability as insures the faithful and intelligent discharge of their duties' had been added to the board, all save two being policy holders. Mr. Cleveland adds: 'There are probably nearly half a million individuals who are policy holders in the Equitable Society and yet it would be giving a high estimate to place the number who have thus far made the least effort, directly or indirectly, to acquaint the trustees with their preferences at 25,000; and their desires when made known have often been so palpably inconsiderate or based upon such misconception that they could not, with safety, be followed. The trustees have derived the best aid from policy holders in cases where their representations have been made through associations of the insured, regularly organized, and thus enabled to sift and reduce to sensible concentration the multiplicity and contrariety and the frequently misdirected want of local sentiment.'

"Mr. Cleveland explained the failure of the trustees to put in operation the plan of mutualization 'made mandatory upon the trustees under the terms of the trust agreement' by reference to the *Lord* suit, in which an appeal was then pending to the Appellate Division of the Supreme Court. In his testimony, Mr. Ryan states distinctly that he will do all in his power to aid the policy holders in acquiring the right to elect a majority of the board if it be held that the Legislature is competent to confer it. In a letter addressed to Mr. Morton, under date of June 26, 1905, Mr. Ryan said that he would not under any circumstances sell the stock except to the society or under some plan for the benefit of the society or its policy holders, but if it were found desirable to retire the stock or to acquire it for the policy holders it would be at Mr. Morton's disposal at cost, with four per cent. interest, less dividends. He testified that he had not considered the retirement upon any other basis. The trust of the 502 shares is to continue for five years from June 15, 1905. In furtherance of Mr. Ryan's declared policy it is provided that it shall continue so long as the trustees shall deem advisable, and Mr. Ryan agrees upon the expiration of any period of five years to execute a deed of continuance. But under section 20 of the General Corporation Law limiting such trust agreements to five years it would seem that such an agreement imposes no legal obligation."

8. Changes Following the Investigation of 1905

There have been several results of this investigation. One is that, fearful of further publicity, the insurance company managers proceeded to a house-cleaning and remedied several of the most obvious abuses. The exact amount of this cannot, of course, be determined, but there seems to have arisen a great desire on their part to avoid adverse criticism. Another result is legislation. Working with authentic actuarial data, the State of New York passed laws regarding the reserves which companies must set up against different types of policies. Another law had reference to the investments which a company might make; one of the worst abuses in this field being the practice of buying real estate and common stock which brought low returns, concerns were forbidden to buy common stocks. Next were listed different types of securities which they could buy. Prominent among these were government and municipal bonds; first mortgages up to 50 per cent of the value of the property were included. In case a company had prohibited investments when the legislation was passed, it was given five years in which to dispose of them.[25] This did away with the two most obvious evils.

The evils arising from control of tremendous reserves were not so easily disposed of. In the case of a company organized on the joint-stock plan, the majority stockholders elected the board of directors who invested the money. Here the difficulty remained that, in the case of a successful company, the reserves so dwarfed the capital that it seemed ridiculous for the stockholders to continue to direct the company. The funds were contributed by the policyholders and the risks were borne by them. However, giving the policyholders a vote for directors did not offer the solution to the problem. That plan had been tried in the case of the mutual companies where it had been found that the policyholders, scattered geographically and not interested in the management of the company, had allowed a small ring of directors and officials to dominate the company to an even greater extent than a few men dominated the joint-stock companies. This situation could be avoided only by making the policyholders take an interest in the company, and this could not be accomplished by legislation. The stockholders in many of the joint-stock companies were willing to have their companies mutualized and be indemnified for their stock.

The mutualization of the Equitable was finally accomplished in 1918. Thomas Fortune Ryan's controlling interest, which as noted was in the hands of trustees, was in 1910 sold to J. Pierpont Morgan for $3,000,000 and in 1915 to T. Coleman du Pont for $4,394,540. The *Commercial & Financial Chronicle*[26] quotes General du Pont's representative as follows:

> "I understand that General du Pont does not intend to sell the capital stock to the policyholders, but that he intends, while retaining the stock, to effect a more thorough mutualization of the company by having all of the fifty-two directors named by the policyholders instead of having only twenty-eight named by them, as at present, and that he intends to make more thorough arrangements to see that all policyholders have a chance to exercise a voice in the management of the company."

Eventually this plan was abandoned, and in 1918 the Equitable was mutualized by the sale of the stock to the policyholders, who paid for it out of the company's surplus. The *Chronicle*[27] describes the arrangement as follows:

> "The plan for the mutualization of the Equitable Life Assurance Society was approved by New York State Superintendent of Insurance Jesse S. Phillips on Feb. 6. The policyholders voted in favor of the plan on Dec. 6, the directors adopted it on July 19, while the stockholders, representing a majority of the stock indorsed the mutualization plans on Aug. 21. Superintendent Phillips in a statement detailing the plan and signifying his approval of it notes that it provides in substance for the purchase from T. Coleman du Pont of 564 shares of the capital of the society at $5,400 per share for 501 shares and $1,500 per share for 63 shares, amounting in the aggregate to $2,799,900. He states that only one criticism can be justly urged against the plan—'the seemingly large price paid for a majority of the shares of the capital stock.' He points out, however, that the price provided in the plan for the purchase of the majority stock is less than the present owner paid in 1915, and considerably less than it sold for in 1910. . . .

[25] *The Investigation of Financial and Monetary Conditions in the United States,* vol. ii (1913), p. 1314.

[26] June 19, 1915, p. 2058; *Annual Report of the Superintendent of Insurance of the State of New York,* 1919, part v, pp. 335–336.

[27] *Commercial & Financial Chronicle,* Feb. 16, 1918, pp. 674–675.

"There has been no serious objection from any reliable interested person urged against the adoption of the plan, except upon the part of certain minority stockholders who sought by legal proceedings in the United States Court to restrain the society from carrying out and submitting the proposed plan. They alleged that the stockholders, and not the policyholders, were entitled to the 'free surplus' [surplus above legal reserve] of the society, and therefore it had not the legal right to pay one stockholder a greater price for his stock than for the stock of the other shareholders, it being their chief contention that all stockholders must be treated upon an equal basis, and the same price should be paid for all the stock. The United States Circuit Court of Appeals, however, held in substance that all the surplus of the company belonged to the policyholders; that there was no obligation upon the stockholders to sell their stock at the price fixed in the plan, and their rights were in no way violated. It having been decided that the stockholders, in the event of a final dissolution of the corporation, had no interest in the surplus, and therefore could not legally complain as to the manner of its disposition, the only question to be now determined is whether the mutualization of the Equitable Life Assurance Society, in accordance with the proposed plan, is in the interest of the insuring public generally, and, if consummated, will it violate the rights of existing policyholders, or affect the security of their obligations?"

An interesting question is: What were the motives which actuated Thomas Fortune Ryan, J. Pierpont Morgan, and T. Coleman du Pont? Certain evidence points to the inference that Ryan wished control of the company in order to control its vast assets, but that public opinion and the active opposition of certain financial leaders forced him to change his plans and sell the control. Perhaps there is no basis for this conclusion. J. P. Morgan may have wished to mutualize the company. If this could have been accomplished, it might have resulted in large profits. Why T. Coleman du Pont bought the control of the company may never be known. One reason, undoubtedly, was that he had recently disposed of his interests in the E. I. du Pont de Nemours Co. and was faced with the problem of reinvesting some $20,000,000—the control of the Equitable came upon the market and he bought it. In some ways it might have proved a very lucrative investment. It may be that du Pont felt that the world would be benefited if he placed the control in strong, disinterested hands. It may be that he bought the company intending to occupy himself with its management, found himself extremely hampered by public opinion and regulation, and in disgust rid himself of the responsibility of the company, although at a loss. Whatever his motive may have been, he bought the control, held it three years, and then mutualized the company at a considerable loss to himself.

9. Recent Developments

Since the War there has been a notable growth in life insurance in the United States. The outstanding insurance of the Mutual increased from $1,445,228,681 in 1903 to $1,598,466,078 in 1913, $2,817,761,195 in 1923, and $3,903,658,890 in 1933. By 1929 there was over one hundred billion in insurance in force in the United States.

This great increase was in part the result of new forms of insurance and new services given by insurance companies. In this the Equitable was especially strong. There was in the 1920's a reawakening of the idea of insuring income, that is, of continuing income after an individual's death in order to care for dependents. There was a significant development of the sale of insurance with provision for using the proceeds to establish a trust account with some trust company; that is, the insured selected the trust company, and the insurance company, on the maturing of the insurance contract, turned the funds over to that trust concern. There was also much insurance for tax purposes, especially to pay inheritance taxes. Great emphasis was placed on business insurance; partners, for instance, carried insurance on each other to enable the survivors to purchase the interest of a deceased partner, and companies insured the lives of important executives.

In its reaching for new business the insurance industry adopted some new methods. Market research, especially the study of "consumer" needs and of sales methods, came to be of some importance—the organization of the Life Insurance Sales Research Bureau in the 1920's represents the beginning of coöperative effort in the industry along this line. The growing popularity of the College of American Life Underwriters as a training school for insurance salesmen shows that the industry saw the need of training for the selling of insurance.

Another interest which came to be of increasing importance at this time was the conservation-of-life program of the insurance companies. In this the Metropolitan was the leader. Prevention of accidents, regular medical examination to discover disease in early stages, proper exercise, healthful diet, and so on, have received much attention in insurance publicity.

The depression of 1929–33 brought special problems to insurance companies. The remarkable continuation of the flow of premiums into insurance bears witness to the strong position which life insurance had come to hold in the United States. And that flow helped to keep the insurance companies liquid in spite of the tremendous total of policy loans and of payments on discontinued policies. The fall in the value of investments of the insurance companies brought serious problems. Foreclosures on real estate mortgages and the collapse of the mortgage machinery that had operated in the past made it necessary for insurance companies to provide for property management. Hotels, apartments, office buildings, and farm properties had to be managed in some way. Temporary means of management were devised, generally through existing

Table 3. PERCENTAGE DISTRIBUTION OF INVESTMENTS OF LIFE INSURANCE COMPANIES SHOWING HIGH POINT OF EACH TYPE
1906–36

Type of investment	Percentage of total 1906	High point of each type of investment: Year	High point of each type of investment: Percentage	Percentage of total 1936 [a]
Farm Mortgages	9.3	1924	18.7	3.7
Other "	19.2	1929	30.0	16.6
Total "	28.5	1927	43:1	20.3
United States Bonds	0.1	1936	15.6 [a]	15.6
State, County, and Municipal Bonds	3.6	1936	5.7	5.7
Canadian Government Bonds	0.8	1932	2.4	2.2
Other Foreign Government Bonds	2.3	1916	2.6	0.0
Total Government Bonds	6.8	1936	23.5	23.5
Railroad Bonds and Stocks	34.8	1906	34.8	13.0
Public Utility Bonds and Stocks	4.7	1936	10.8	10.8
Other Bonds and Stocks	3.7	1936	4.1	4.1
Total " " "	50.0	1936	51.4	51.4
Policy Loans	8.9	1932	17.9	13.4
Real Estate	5.4	1936	8.9	8.9
Collateral Loans	1.8	1906	1.8	0.0
Cash	2.3	1935	3.6	3.6

[a] Figures for 1936 are estimates made by the Association of Life Insurance Presidents on the basis of figures for the first 9 months.

organization and with as little actual centralization as possible. How far this depression machinery may become permanent it is impossible to predict.

Table 3, p. 544, suggests what has been happening to the investments of life insurance companies. It gives the percentage of the total investments of over 90 per cent of the United States legal reserve companies in 1906, at the high point of a given type of investment as compared with the total assets, and as estimated at the end of 1936.[28]

10. Suggested Readings

For interesting but uncritical accounts of the history of the Equitable, the following may be read: *Henry Baldwin Hyde, a Biographical Sketch* (New York, 1901); Paul Morton, *The First Fifty Years of the Equitable Life Assurance Society of the United States* (New York, 1909).

By far the most important single source on American life insurance is the *Report of the Joint Committee of the Senate and Assembly of the State of New York Appointed to Investigate the Affairs of Life Insurance Companies* (Albany, 1905–06). There were two editions of this work, printed about the same time by two different companies. Volume x in one edition and volume vii in the other give a summary of the findings of the committee.

Four articles, edited by S. S. Huebner, in *Annals of the American Academy of Political and Social Science,* vol. lxx (March, 1917), should be read: John B. Lunger, "The Problem of Cash Surrender Values and Cash Loans," pp. 54–61; Miles M. Dawson, "Mutualization of Life Insurance Companies," pp. 62–76; Lee K. Frankel, "Conservation of Life by Life Insurance Companies," pp. 77–91; and Walter S. Nichols, "Fraternal Insurance in the United States," pp. 109–122.

On recent problems and developments see the annual *Proceedings of the Life Office Management Association* and the annual *Proceedings of the Association of Life Insurance Presidents.*

A significant recent work is George Amrhein's *The Liberalization of the Life Insurance Contract* (Philadelphia, 1933).

11. Suggested Questions

1. What factors contributed to the Mutual's success? To the Equitable's?
2. Would the Mutual still have been safe if it had not built up large reserves?
3. Should the Mutual continue to allow the policyholders to elect the directors? Should policyholders be allowed one vote per member or one for every thousand dollars of insurance held?
4. Why did Morgan and du Pont pay such a high price for the control of the Equitable?
5. Should the policyholders of the Equitable have bought out the stockholders?
6. Was it a wise policy to force the Mutual to dispose of its common stocks and buy high-grade securities?

XXXIII. J. PIERPONT MORGAN, 1837–1913

1. General Statement

Born in a period when the non-specialized but broad activities of the sedentary merchant were giving way to a new form of business, J. Pierpont Morgan in his early manhood helped furnish capital to the industrial entrepreneurs of the nineteenth century, and he rose to outstanding leadership at the time when the over-rapid expansion in railroad and industrial fields and the resulting destructive competition had to be curbed. Someone had to bring order out of chaos if the investor and the banker, and indeed private business itself, were to survive. In the fact that Morgan helped to do this lies his claim to recognition in the history of American business. Our interest here is in showing, so far as

[28] These figures are from a comprehensive table on pp. 93–94 of the *Proceedings of the Thirtieth Annual Convention of Life Insurance Presidents* (New York, 1936).

we can, the sort of thing he did, by what means, and with what results.

This is a difficult if not an impossible task. A great deal has been written about J. Pierpont Morgan but little critical research has been done on his business career. Morgan's friends and admirers have been warmed by his outstanding qualities; his opponents and his critics have seen in him mostly the stern and the dictatorial. Marxians have pictured him as the embodiment of that concentration of financial control that they believe leads to the destruction of private business. Politicians and journalists have made him the means, by appeals to prejudice, to win votes and subscriptions. A few impartial and serious students, indeed, have tried to see Morgan as he actually was, but they have met two great obstacles: They have been bewildered by the conflicting nature of the printed material on the subject, and they have been unable to get much other information. Indeed, no satisfactory study of Morgan's business career can be made until more is known than at present of the actual operation of business in his time and, especially, of the work of J. P. Morgan & Co. and of the corporations and firms with which they had close relations.

2. Important Dates

- 1837 John Pierpont Morgan born at Hartford, Conn., April 17.
- 1851 His father entered mercantile partnership in Boston.
- 1852 J. Pierpont in Azores for his health.
- 1854 Father entered banking firm of George Peabody in London.
- 1854–56 J. Pierpont in school in Switzerland.
- 1856–57 Studied at the University of Göttingen.
- 1857 Entered office of Duncan, Sherman & Co., private bankers in New York.
- 1859 Studied cotton business in New Orleans.
- 1860 Established office in New York, as agent of George Peabody & Co. Cousin "Jim" Goodwin a partner.
- 1863 Charles Dabney admitted to firm, which became Dabney, Morgan & Co.
- 1864 J. S. Morgan & Co. succeeded George Peabody & Co. in London.
- 1869 J. Pierpont Morgan led in clash with Gould and Fisk.
- 1870 J. S. Morgan & Co. syndicated French loan during Franco-Prussian War.
- 1871 Drexel, Morgan & Co. established in New York.
- 1873 Drexel, Morgan & Co. participated in unsuccessful distribution of United States loan.
- 1876–79 Participated strongly in selling refunding loans.
- 1879 J. Pierpont Morgan managed sale of New York Central stock in London and became a director of the road.
- 1885 Morgan helped stop war of eastern trunk lines.
- 1887–88 Reorganized several railroads, introducing use of voting trust to protect management.
- 1888 By this time Coster active in Morgan reorganizations.
- 1889–90 Morgan tried to form associations of railroads to curb disastrous competition.
- 1890 J. S. Morgan died.
- 1892 J. Pierpont Morgan entered board of General Electric Co.
- 1893 Beginning of large-scale reorganization of bankrupt railways to take final form in so-called Morgan railroad systems.
- 1894 J. P. Morgan & Co. succeeded Drexel, Morgan & Co. on death of Drexel.
- 1895 Morgan-Belmont Syndicate sold gold bonds to protect the dwindling U. S. gold reserves.
- 1898 Morgan helped finance organization of the Federal Steel Co.

1899	J. P. Morgan & Co. participated in a large Mexican loan offered in Europe.
1901	Organized U. S. Steel. Fight for control of Northern Pacific.
1901–02	J. P. Morgan & Co. subscribed to British government loans in connection with Boer War financing.
1902	Morgan organized International Mercantile Marine and International Harvester. Helped settle anthracite coal strike.
1903	Bankers' Trust Co. organized with a Morgan partner as one of three members of its voting trust.
1907	Morgan took leadership in curbing country-wide currency panic of 1907.
1909–10	Morgan and associates acquired interest in Guaranty Trust Co. and Equitable Life Assurance Society.
1912	Morgan testified in Money Trust Investigation.
1913	Died in Rome, March 31. Heavy fall in securities of New Haven Railroad.

3. Family and Education

John Pierpont Morgan's paternal grandfather was a successful business man. A descendant of Yankee pioneers (farmers, artisans, and traders), he followed various lines of work. For a time he taught school; for several years, including the profitable years of the War of 1812, he was a farmer, but with farming he combined dealing in produce and some investing in real estate; then he became a stage-line and tavern owner; when the steamboat and railway came to revolutionize transportation, he invested in them and bought a large hotel in Hartford; and similarly, as banking and insurance grew to importance, he invested in a number of banks and insurance companies, participating in organizing several banks and the Aetna Fire Insurance Co. As a director he took an important part in the management of the Aetna, at the same time making various investments, dealing in real estate, and continuing his interest in farming.

John Pierpont's father, Junius Spencer Morgan, entered the banking house of Morris Ketchum in New York. He remained with Ketchum for several years and then returned to Hartford as a partner in a dry-goods firm. He was in that business when his son, John Pierpont, was born in 1837.

Julia Morgan, John Pierpont's mother, came from an altogether different background. Her father was a man of striking character and wide reputation. He was a Unitarian clergyman, with the sensitiveness and spirit which made him an ardent participant in the reform movements of his time. Evidence of his interest in education is the fact that he helped found the English High School, of Boston. A fearless and uncompromising man, he stood for the "entire freedom and independence" of the pulpit and refused to resign as head of the Hollis Street Society when he was called upon by a majority vote of the members to give up his position as pastor. At the age of seventy-six, he enlisted as a chaplain in the army at the beginning of the Civil War.

The Morgan family lived in Hartford until 1851. John Pierpont's boyhood was that of the son of a well-to-do and rising business man of good standing in his community. An interesting letter has survived from his school days. The thirteen-year-old pupil asked the teacher why he had been treated "in such an inhumane manner as to send me out of the class for laughing a little too loud which I can assure you I am perfectly unable to control and which no punishment will ever cure me of." The teacher could not say, he wrote, "that I have not tried to behave better in class lately." Threatening to go to another teacher the next term—"going into E II is a long contemplated step," he ended with the hope that "before the term ends we shall be on better terms than at present."[1] Later he protested to the same teacher that he had not been given a mark in arithmetic when he was sure that he had the right answer though it was not the same as in the book—"Father and I studied on that same example for 2 hours last night trying to get the answer in the book which proved unsuccessful and I got $17.42 as I said."[2]

In 1851 Junius S. Morgan entered a mercantile partnership in Boston. The next autumn found John Pierpont at the English High School. The diary of the fourteen-year-old boy is not a little revealing; he had the usual boy's interest in girls but an unusual interest in keeping accounts. He and his cousin Jim in Hartford had a partnership, evidently to make purchases for each other. Pierpont wrote about one purchase: "In regard to Diary I can get a cover made for 50 cents. He had a diary for 1849 which by altering the name of the day of the week will do for 1850. Would you prefer this? If so I can get it for you for 75C and it is a first rate one."

Suffering from illness—probably inflammatory rheumatism—Pierpont was in 1852 sent to Fayal in the Azores, where a friend of the Morgans was United States Consul. He wrote long letters home and offered to get anything that friends or family might want him to buy for them—"if for stockings the size of the foot will be necessary." He left Fayal in the spring much improved in health and joined his parents in England for a tour on the Continent. A year later he was graduated from the English High School in Boston, ranking third in his class.[3]

In 1854 the Morgan family moved to London, where the father had accepted an offer of a partnership in the great banking house of the American, George Peabody. This meant school in Switzerland for Pierpont and a broadening of his experience and his friendships. Though at first somewhat untractable and unadaptable—speaking English when French was supposed to be spoken and not observing the rules about quiet after lights were out, during his second year young Morgan became popular with both teachers and schoolmates. The mathematics teacher and the boys are said to have regarded him as very unusual in mathematics. Though he was ill for several months and was much troubled by eruptions on his face (a weakness which is said to have caused him much distress in his later years and made him shy and reluctant to be photographed), his letters contained enthusiastic descriptions of life at Bellerive and intelligent comments about the state of affairs in Europe. He made several close friends, and on leaving the school he wrote to Jim:[4]

> "On the 4th inst. it became my duty to take leave of my Vevey friends, who for eighteen months through sickness and through health had done all for me that any but a parent could do. Then I had to break intercourses probably forever, and I found that I had remained there much too long to make parting a pleasure. . . . when it comes to leaving friends and true friends at that, whom in all probability we shall never meet again, then it is hard, too hard to part. But Jim you will hardly thank me for writing to you thus sadly, but I feel to tell the truth rather sad, and if you don't want to read it just skip it over. You have been fortunate enough to escape these partings and let me assure you you have been very fortunate to have done so."

Young Morgan next enrolled at the University of Göttingen, where he stayed about two years. Here he met students from many countries, including several American boys who were to become outstanding scholars, and he entered heartily into the conviviality of Göttingen. He

[1] Herbert L. Satterlee, *The Life of J. Pierpont Morgan* (privately printed, New York, 1937), p. 121.

[2] *Ibid.*, p. 122.

[3] *Ibid.*, p. 232.

[4] *Ibid.*, pp. 258–259.

studied German, chemistry, and mathematics, European history, and French drama and literature. He made a mark for himself in mathematics.

While at school in Europe, Pierpont spent his summers at home in London and in travel. In London he often served as a personal conductor for friends of his family from America. It was at this time that he acquired that close acquaintance with the art and culture of Europe that became the basis for the remarkable collection of manuscripts and works of art which he later acquired. Indeed, his familiarity with European ways of life and with the people of England and the Continent was undoubtedly an important factor in his success as a banker.

4. Morgan Enters Banking in New York

The autumn of 1857 found young Morgan, then 20 years of age, in the office of Duncan, Sherman & Co., one of the leading private banking houses of New York. His only experience in business was a summer spent in the office of George Peabody & Co., of London, mostly sorting Peabody's letters. Morgan worked with Duncan, Sherman & Co. as a junior clerk under Charles H. Dabney, an expert accountant. For a time he had no salary.

In 1859 Morgan was sent to Cuba and New Orleans, where he stayed a long time, in order to learn how the cotton business was handled. At New Orleans he spent his leisure time on the levee, and one day he learned of a cargo of coffee from South America consigned to someone in New Orleans who had gone when the cargo arrived. Morgan took samples, got quotations, and bought the coffee, drawing on Duncan, Sherman & Co. He soon received a reprimand from his firm, but by that time he had already made for it a profit of several thousand dollars.

Some time near the end of the year 1860 Morgan set up his own office at 54 Exchange Place.[5] He shared the office and office boy with another young business man who was doing some business for George Peabody & Co. Most of Morgan's work was to collect for the account of George Peabody & Co. and to invest for their English customers, but some business was also done in foreign exchange and some lending for the London house and its clients.

By this time Morgan was well established in New York. He had made many friends, with some of whom he was later to be associated in business. He enjoyed singing parties in his friends' homes, joined a church, and in 1861 married. His wife, whom he had courted for some time and who had contracted a rapid type of tuberculosis, died in only a few months. Some time thereafter we find Morgan with his cousin Jim Goodwin in an association which they called J. P. Morgan & Co., at 53 Exchange Place. The two young men set up housekeeping together, and thus Morgan lived until in 1865, when he married Frances Louisa Tracy, a daughter of Charles Tracy, a prominent member of the New York bar.

Two episodes in Morgan's business during the Civil War are frequently mentioned in writings about him, and are generally used to illustrate his business character and methods. One instance had to do with gold speculation. Morgan as a dealer in foreign exchange was forced to enter the gold market. Where the line should be drawn between legitimate trade and speculation it is impossible to say without knowing the specific circumstances in the individual case. It may be true that Morgan and Ketchum's purchase of gold in the autumn of 1863, when Northern reverses were driving the price upward, was an attempt to profit from cornering the market for the metal. If so, they were participating in a trade in which even high

[5] There is some question whether it was in 1860 or 1861 that Morgan set up his own office—*Who's Who in America* for 1899–1900 gave 1860.

officers of the government in Washington had a hand.[6] The other episode is the Hall carbine affair. The story is too long to recount here, but an extensive search has failed to uncover any contemporary proof that justifies the deductions about Morgan's business character which many writers have drawn from the episode.

The Civil War brought a rapid growth in Morgan's business and the two partners in 1863 admitted Charles Dabney as a third, calling the firm Dabney, Morgan & Co. A recent biographer has described the business of the firm at this time as follows: [7]

> "His firm bought and sold securities, bills of exchange, acceptances drawn against bills of lading and staple products such as grain, dry goods and British iron. They were building up a business in foreign exchange, and of course dealing in gold, the most active of all commodities dealt in during the War. He kept himself well informed about the prices current and the trend of the American markets and above all acted as a source of accurate, confidential, detailed information as to events on this side of the water for his father, who had now succeeded to the business of George Peabody & Company. On October 1 [1864], that firm's name was changed to J. S. Morgan & Company."

5. Growth under J. S. Morgan & Co., 1865–79

In the making of J. Pierpont Morgan's business there were four major factors. One was American investment opportunity; another was foreign capital seeking investment; a third was young Morgan himself; and a fourth was his father and his father's strong position with English investors. We are here particularly concerned with the Morgans, who initially built their American business largely on the flow of capital from Europe to America.

In the late 1860's there were two streams of capital flowing into the United States, one from England and the other from Germany. The European bankers guiding the flow of this capital were the Rothschilds, Baring Brothers, J. S. Morgan & Co., represented by A. Belmont, S. G. Ward, and J. P. Morgan & Co. in New York, and young New York houses with strong European connections, particularly the Seligmans, Jacob H. Schiff who in the 'seventies joined Kuhn, Loeb & Co., and also Morton, Bliss & Co., which had a branch in London.

The strongest of these, especially in the earlier decades following the Civil War, were the Rothschilds, Barings, and J. S. Morgan & Co. J. S. Morgan had the great advantage of being American and having good business connections in America, while at the same time he occupied a high position in London.

Railroads dominated foreign investments in America, just as they dominated its economic activity, after the war. Railroad building on the one hand represented constructive economic effort and on the other gave opportunity for the worst buccaneer practices. J. Pierpont Morgan and his firm bought securities for J. S. Morgan and its clients. One reason for the American firm's later strength was no doubt the fact that it did not participate in the manipulation, corruption, and plunder which were found in railroad finance after the war—the work of industrial capitalists.

J. Pierpont Morgan won his first recognition as a factor in New York banking through a successful contest with the worst railroad manipulators. The issue at stake was the control of the Albany & Susquehanna Railroad, and the contestants were Gould and Fisk and their followers of the Erie and J. H. Ramsey, president of the A. & S. This short road with its eastern ter-

[6] Unfortunately, one can "prove" almost anything by citing New York newspapers on this question. The criticism of the gold speculators was in part induced by Jay Cooke, as agent of the government for the sale of loans, but even Cooke recognized the distinction between legitimate trade and speculation.

[7] Satterlee, *op. cit.*, p. 352.

minus at Albany was in a position to contest the hold of the New York Central on New England trade; its other terminus connected with the Erie at Binghamton, which gave it an outlet westward and into the anthracite region in Pennsylvania.

Ramsey brought Morgan's support to his side, and as a member of the board Morgan became the leader of the Ramsey party.[8] Both force and the courts were used in the fight. In December, 1869, the Supreme Court of the State of New York declared in favor of the Morgan-Ramsey party,[9] and the road was leased to the Delaware & Hudson Co., which has held it ever since. In the words of the *New York Times* (January 24, 1873) "this contest, waged not only by litigation but by force of arms, made Mr. Morgan universally respected as an able financier."

While the Morgans and their clients furnished much capital for financing American railroads after the war, they also took a considerable part in the dealing in government securities. We do not know to what extent they participated in the transfer of the original Civil War loans of the federal government to Europe, but presumably they, like Morton, Belmont, the Seligmans, Speyer, and others, took part in that trade. In 1870 J. S. Morgan made a stroke in French finance which put him head and shoulders above most other bankers dealing in governments. He organized a syndicate of bankers which took a 250,000,000 franc loan of the provisional French government at Tours in 1870, when Paris was under siege and the credit of France was none too good. The success of the loan brought great prestige and a considerable profit to J. S. Morgan & Co.

With the coöperation of its house in London, it was to be expected that J. P. Morgan's firm should want to take a hand in the refunding of the American war bonds which was undertaken in 1871. Jay Cooke, who had had charge of the original sale of most of the Civil War loans, expected to manage the sale of refunding loans as well, and with that objective he established a branch house in London at the beginning of 1871. But other bankers also wanted a share of the business. Cooke's strongest opponent with the administration in Washington was Anthony Drexel of Philadelphia, who was backed by Levi P. Morton of New York. Drexel's firm had carried on domestic and foreign exchange and had taken a strong hand in the sale of railroad securities. It had a solid reputation based on over thirty years of successful banking. Both Morton and Drexel had a strong influence in Washington, which they used in opposing Jay Cooke's plans for refunding.[10]

In view of the Morgans' strong connections abroad and Drexel's at home, it is not difficult to explain the merger of the two firms in Drexel, Morgan & Co. in New York in 1871. There on the southeast corner of Broad and Wall—23 Wall Street, the home of J. P. Morgan & Co. today—the new firm built a seven-story building, which was one of the sights of New York. It may have been in a spirit of envy that Jay Cooke wrote to his partners of the folly of tying up as much money as "Tony" Drexel had done in a bank building. That the Morgan-Drexel combination was strong is seen from the statement of the *Commercial & Financial Chronicle*[11] that "the combination of these two conspicuous banking firms with the branches named must place the new firm among the few leading banking houses of the world."

The story of the bankers' competition for the government refunding loans is told in the case on Jay Cooke & Co., considered

[8] *The People of the State of New York against the Albany & Susquehanna Railroad Company, and Others,* New York Court of Appeals (New York, 1871), vol. i, p. 618.

[9] For the legal proceedings see F. C. Hicks, *High Finance in the Sixties* (New Haven, 1929).

[10] See H. M. Larson, *Jay Cooke, Private Banker* (Cambridge, 1936), pp. 291, 310–311, 319–320, 360.

[11] Vol. xiii (1871), p. 11.

on pages 296–324, above. The combination of Drexel, Morgan & Co. with Morton, Bliss & Co. helped break Jay Cooke's hold on government finance, and the failure of Jay Cooke & Co. in the fall of 1873 left refunding to those other bankers.

The panic of 1873 and the deep depression which followed greatly impaired the value of railroad securities, with the result that the immediate opportunity for the investment banker lay in government loans. During the refunding operations in the period from 1876 to 1879 the most lucrative phase of private banking was distributing new loans to replace the old high-rate securities.

The Morgan firms played an important though not a dominant part in the refunding operations. The bonds were sold from time to time by the government through contracts with syndicates of bankers and capitalists, each of whom subscribed for a stated amount. Different bankers organized the various syndicates. A syndicate for a loan in 1879 was organized by a domestic house, Fisk & Hatch,[12] which had given strong support to Jay Cooke in Civil War finance; and distinctly American bankers or capitalists made considerable subscriptions at times—such as the First National Bank of New York, the Bank of Commerce, Winslow, Lanier & Co., Jay Gould, Cyrus Field, and Russell Sage. But the heaviest subscribers on the whole were foreign banking houses or American bankers with strong foreign connections, that is, August Belmont and the Rothschilds, the Morgans, the Mortons, and the Seligmans.

The refunding operations were important to all these American banking houses, especially perhaps to the Morgans. They helped to strengthen American credit in England. The Morgans were the leading subscribers in the English market as the Rothschilds were on the Continent, and the result was both increased prestige and large profits. It seems fair to say that Drexel, Morgan & Co. came out of refunding operations as the ranking American investment house, first among a large group of strong leaders though not popularly recognized to the extent that Jay Cooke & Co. had been. The dominant figure in the Morgan business was still J. S. Morgan of the London house.

6. J. Pierpont Morgan in Railway Finance, 1879–88

The year 1879 was a turning point in the career of J. Pierpont Morgan. That year closed the government operations which had been the chief investment occupation of the Morgan houses and of other bankers in the 1870's and possibly since the Civil War. It was clear that in the near future the outstanding investment field would be railroads. For taking on new work, no one was in a better position than Morgan—no other banker in New York had the combination of vigor, good standing and support, and experience that he had.

J. Pierpont Morgan's first large operation in railroad finance was in the sale of New York Central stock in 1879. When William H. Vanderbilt decided to sell a large part of his stock in order to counteract the threat of adverse legislation and heavy taxation, he turned to Morgan. Only a powerful banking firm could possibly handle the sale of so large a block of stock without upsetting the market. It was rumored that Vanderbilt was also interested in making through the Morgans a connection with the Wabash, St. Louis & Pacific.[13]

Morgan arranged for the underwriting of 250,000 shares of New York Central by a syndicate composed of J. S. Morgan & Co., August Belmont & Co., Morton,

[12] *Com. & Fin. Chron.*, vol. xxviii (1879), p. 418.

[13] *Railway Gazette,* vol. xi, p. 636 (Nov. 28, 1879) and p. 645 (Dec. 5, 1879). It was suggested in the *Com. & Fin. Chron.* (vol. xxix, p. 530, Nov. 22, 1879) that there was to be an exchange of New York Central for Erie and Wabash stock.

Bliss & Co., and Jay Gould. The shares were purchased at 120 and were sold in London at 130, all without causing any noticeable disturbance on the market. The affair was regarded as a "grand financial operation" [14] and it gave J. Pierpont Morgan and the Morgan houses a strong position of leadership in railroad finance. Morgan became a director of the road in order to protect his clients' interests, and three men influential in Wabash administration were also put on the Central board. This seems to bear out the *Chronicle's* suggestion that heavy capital was anxious to get control of trunk-line stocks in order to secure harmony and prevent the cutthroat competition that meant the end of profits.[15]

The next big operation of the Morgans was in Northern Pacific stock. That road had been laboriously pulling itself out of its failure in 1873. In 1876 earnings for the first time exceeded expenditures, and the road embarked on a policy of cautious expansion. Settlement began to move westward again, and there was prospect of increasing traffic. By 1880 the Northern Pacific was a substantial property in a condition to attract capital, and it turned to New York for funds for building its line from the Missouri to the Pacific Coast. The result can best be shown by quoting from a statement of Drexel, Morgan & Co. which appeared in the *Commercial & Financial Chronicle* on December 4, 1880: [16]

"The largest transaction in railroad bonds ever made in the United States has just been closed by Messrs. Drexel, Morgan & Co., Winslow, Lanier & Co., and August Belmont & Co., they having made a contract with the Northern Pacific Railroad Company for $40,000,000 6 per cent gold bonds having forty years to run. . . .

"The three firms named as contractors have associated with them several of the best-known bankers here and in other cities, as well as in Europe, among whom are the following: Messrs. Drexel & Co., Philadelphia; Messrs. J. S. Morgan & Co., London; Messrs. Drexel, Harjes & Co., Paris. In this city the associates are as follows: National Bank of Commerce, Messrs. J. & W. Seligman & Co., Messrs. Kuhn Loeb & Co., Messrs. Woerishoeffer & Co., Third National Bank, Messrs. L. Von Hoffman & Co., Messrs. J. S. Kennedy & Co., Messrs. Speyer & Co. In Boston associated with them are the following: Messrs. Lee, Higginson & Co., Messrs. Brewster, Basset & Co. In Baltimore: Messrs. Johnston Bros. & Co.

. . . .

"By terms of the agreement with the company, the contractors are to name two directors in the board, and the persons selected for the positions are Messrs. J. C. Bullitt, of Philadelphia, and John W. Ellis, of Winslow, Lanier & Co., of New York."

The prosperity which began in the late 1870's brought a boom in American railroads, but when the boom was ended there was the bill to pay. *Poor's Manual* in 1884 called attention to the "immense increase of fictitious capital" of the railroads in 1880–83. Though they were overcapitalized, the old roads could support themselves as long as they occupied the field alone, but by 1885 there were five trunk lines from New York to Chicago—three tottering on the edge of bankruptcy—and two more were being built. Bitter and destructive war was the result.

On his trip to Europe in the early summer of 1885 Morgan became impressed with the necessity of doing something about trunk-line competition.[17] He was convinced that the points to attack were a road built parallel to the New York Central from New York to Buffalo and another threatening the Pennsylvania from

[14] *Com. & Fin. Chron.*, vol. xxix, p. 554 (Nov. 29, 1879).

[15] *Ibid.*

[16] For further details see J. B. Hedges, *Henry Villard and the Railways of the Northwest* (New Haven, 1930).

[17] The temper of the English investor is reflected in the detailed discussion of the New York Central-Pennsylvania difficulties in the *Economist* in December, 1885.

Pittsburgh eastward. The former had been built by promoters who took heavy profits from promotion and construction and then proceeded to threaten the Central with their bankrupt road; the Pennsylvania road was the work of Vanderbilt, backed by Andrew Carnegie and other iron interests that wanted to break the monopoly of the Pennsylvania eastward from Pittsburgh. A further factor in the situation was the Baltimore & Ohio, which was also fighting the Pennsylvania and, like the Reading, was attempting to obtain access to New York by means of the tracks of the Central of New Jersey.

Morgan saw that the two key men in solving the problem were Vanderbilt and President Roberts of the Pennsylvania, who could stop the threat of parallel lines by purchasing the competitors. Vanderbilt was reluctant, however, to give up the South Pennsylvania and was still smarting under the sting of the heavy price he had paid for the Nickel Plate to remove its competition with his Lake Shore road. Roberts was openly committed to enmity with the South Pennsylvania and hated to make concessions to Vanderbilt and Carnegie. But Morgan could use the argument of necessity. Vanderbilt capitulated first, and, after a long conference on Morgan's yacht, Roberts accepted Morgan's proposals.

Drexel, Morgan & Co. managed the transactions necessary to carry out Morgan's proposals. The New York line was purchased at foreclosure by the West Shore Railway Co., which was organized for that purpose. A Morgan partner became its first president, and several men close to Drexel, Morgan & Co. were on its board. The West Shore was then leased to the New York Central, with a guarantee of principal and interest on $50,000,000 new bonds.[18] It was agreed that the Pennsylvania should buy its enemy at cost, but under the law of the State a direct purchase was impossible. J. Pierpont Morgan, therefore, personally bought a 60 per cent interest in the road from a syndicate consisting chiefly of Vanderbilt and "Rockafellow" interests; he paid for the purchase by means of bonds of another road, which securities were provided and guaranteed by the Pennsylvania.[19]

Morgan's next step was to take the leading hand in reorganizing and refinancing some of the tottering roads. These were the Reading, the Baltimore & Ohio, and the Chesapeake & Ohio.

The reorganization of the Philadelphia & Reading came in 1886–87. That road was suffering from the usual competition and from the terrific capital charges resulting from former President Gowen's policy of expansion. Morgan organized a syndicate which improved the capital position of the Reading, cutting fixed charges and rentals from about $14,000,000 as of 1885 to about $6,500,000. The Morgan syndicate provided $15,000,000 in cash, of which it received 5 per cent as compensation. Morgan is said to have established peace with the Pennsylvania and arranged with other anthracite lines for limiting production and maintaining prices. A voting trust, headed by Morgan, was formed to control the Reading for five years, and it chose a New York banker to be president of the road.[20]

Morgan next undertook to place the Baltimore & Ohio on a sound financial basis and in 1888 organized a group to furnish the money. In the contract with the company this group stipulated that the statements of the B. & O. should be verified, the management of the road should be placed in competent hands acceptable to the syndicate, and agreements should be made with other roads about the New York traffic.[21] In carrying out these

[18] *Com. & Fin. Chron.*, vol. xli, p. 689 (Dec. 12, 1885); *Poor's Manual,* 1886, p. 491.

[19] *Com. & Fin. Chron.*, vol. xli, pp. 445–446 (Oct. 17, 1885).

[20] Jules I. Bogen, *The Anthracite Railroads* (New York, 1927), pp. 63–66.

[21] Stuart Daggett, *Railroad Reorganization* (Boston, 1908), pp. 11–22.

stipulations, Morgan found that the B. & O. and its home community would accept only informal agreements, which virtually meant the continuance of competition. The syndicate did not insist, however, since the road was strengthening its finances under the new president and was trying to improve its operation. But when reform threatened to uncover faults in management under the younger Garrett, the family interests elected their own candidate president and thus blocked Morgan's efforts.[22]

In 1888 Drexel, Morgan & Co. also reorganized the Chesapeake & Ohio. That road was heavily loaded with debt and fixed charges, and it did not have satisfactory connections with the Atlantic Coast or with the Middle West. At Morgan's suggestion a committee, including C. H. Coster who was the Drexel, Morgan expert in this field, was put in charge of reorganization, and voting power for five years was given to J. Pierpont Morgan, John C. Brown, and George Bliss. New securities were issued for buying up the old securities and taking care of floating obligations, for providing working capital and funds for finishing a western extension, and for setting up a reserve. An assessment was levied on the stockholders. Control was gained of the Richmond & Allegheny Railroad, which gave access to Newport News, and the work on the new western division was put under way.[23] Reorganization was followed by the purchase of C. P. Huntington's controlling interest in the road by a syndicate of parties interested in the C. C. C. & St. L. Thus was put together, according to the *Commercial & Financial Chronicle,* a strong system of roads which reached from Chicago to Newport News.[24]

By this time the Morgans were recognized far and wide as conservative forces working for peace and harmony and increased confidence. These early Morgan recapitalizations did not necessarily mean a great scaling-down of the capital or even of the fixed capital charges; they generally simplified the capital structure, however, increased the stock as compared with the bonded obligations, funded the floating obligations, and provided working capital and reserves. Morgan reorganization plans also worked in general for more efficient management and for the establishment of better relations with competitors.

7. Creating the Morgan Railway Systems, 1888–1900

When in 1890 J. S. Morgan died, he left about a million dollars in money to his son and the nominal headship of the Morgan houses—the actual headship the son had already attained in New York. Though he was a man of unassuming demeanor and of few words, brusque and retiring in manner, J. Pierpont Morgan's movements were, in the words of the *New York Sun,* "watched more carefully than those of any other man in the financial world." [25]

At this time, as always, Morgan was supported by brilliant and hard-working associates. After the death of the elder Morgan, the London house was ably headed by Walter Burns, the husband of J. Pierpont Morgan's sister. Outstanding among Morgan's partners in New York was Charles H. Coster. Wall Street bankers still speak of Coster's terrific drive in studying a railroad—its physical properties, its management, and its financial condition—and his skill in drawing up reorganization plans. Equally outstanding on the legal side somewhat later was Francis Lynde Stetson. Morgan himself, however, was always the one to formulate the policy of the firm.

To divide Morgan's career into periods involves a certain amount of artificiality. Morgan's business life was a constant

[22] *Ibid.,* pp. 13–16.

[23] *Com. & Fin. Chron.,* vol. xlvi, p. v (Feb. 11, 1888), and vol. xlvii, p. 199 (Aug. 18, 1888).

[24] *Ibid.,* vol. xlix, pp. 97, 113 (July 27, 1889).

[25] Quoted from the *Sun* of Feb. 29, 1892, by John K. Winkler, *Morgan the Magnificent* (New York, 1930), p. 123.

stream of effort, changing with changing opportunities and needs and at all times geared to the realities of a given situation. One might debate whether he had any but a pragmatic philosophy—whether he looked forward very far or had any systematized scheme in mind, or whether he was the man of decision and action who drove through a difficult situation on the strength of the best information that he could get on existing conditions. The year 1889 may in a general way, however, be said to mark the definite beginning of the effort to secure a broader solution of the problem of the railroads. At first Morgan worked toward order through agreements based on community of interest, but later, beginning in 1893, with the necessity of reorganizing many bankrupt railroads, he followed the policy of securing a strong influence in the administration of the roads, or, as it was called, through Morganization.

The first attack was on the problems of western roads. In 1888 the London Morgan house received deposits of the shares of English stockholders of the Chicago, Milwaukee & St. Paul in order to concentrate in themselves representation on the board, "for the control of the property in the interest of honest and efficient railway management."[26] That was important to the Morgans, whose clients were heavily invested in the Middle West where there was a constant state of warfare.

The situation among western roads in 1888 was well described by Charles Francis Adams, then president of the Union Pacific:[27]

". . . The railroad system of this country, especially of the region west of Chicago, is to-day managed on principles which—unless a change of heart occurs, and that soon—must inevitably lead to financial disaster of the most serious kind. There is among the lines composing that system an utter disregard of those fundamental ideas of truth, fair play and fair dealing, which lie at the foundation not only of the Christian faith, but of civilization itself. . . . Since that [Interstate Commerce] Act went into effect two years ago, there has been what might be called a craze for railroad construction. Great corporations, one after the other, have contracted the madness, and have built hundreds of miles of road, almost paralleling each other. In many cases they have actually paralleled each other across wide tracts of country in which no human being lived. This is true in Wisconsin, in Minnesota, in Nebraska, in Kansas. . . . The Interstate Commerce Act was in operation. It was impossible to pool, and the long haul regulated the short haul. Then followed a depth of railroad morals among freight agents lower than had even previously existed,—and that is saying much. The dishonest methods of rate-cutting, the secret systems of rebates, the indirect and hidden payments made to influence the course of traffic, resorted to or devised during the last two years, I do not hesitate to say are unprecedented in the whole bad record of the past. . . ."

Adams advocated setting up group responsibility through the action of the railroads themselves, but public opinion definitely stood in the way. The next move, he thought, would be the formation of railroad systems of 20,000 miles each, under one common management.

Under J. P. Morgan's leadership, Drexel, Morgan & Co., Brown Brothers, and Kidder, Peabody & Co. in the autumn of 1889 issued a circular invitation for a conference of railroad presidents to form an association for enforcing the Interstate Commerce Act and maintaining rates. The first conference met at Morgan's home in December, 1889. According to one writer on Morgan,[28] the banker talked in no uncertain terms to the railway presidents. Adams of the Union Pacific supported Morgan, but Roberts of the Pennsylvania objected to his "very strong language."

[26] *Com. & Fin. Chron.*, vol. xlvii, p. 401 (Oct. 6, 1888); *Economist*, vol. xlvi, p. 1256 (Oct. 6, 1888).

[27] In a speech given in Boston, Dec. 15, 1888, published in *Addresses on The Interstate Commerce Law*.

[28] Carl Hovey in *The Life Story of J. Pierpont Morgan* (New York, 1912), pp. 139–140.

The *Railway World* took a firm stand against the bankers, while the *Chronicle* as firmly supported them. The concrete results were disappointing. While Morgan had visualized an organization with an executive committee having enforcement power, all that was accomplished at first was a gentlemen's agreement. Necessity made the railway executives more tractable when they again convened late in 1890 but, although Morgan's plan for a representative board with power to establish rates was adopted, little came of the effort because the board had no power of enforcement.

The first effort on the part of the bankers to secure coördination on a large scale had failed. The next step was soon taken, again under the leadership of Morgan, but its methods were far different from the methods of conference and agreement. The objectives were in essence the same.

Morgan's opportunity came with the panic of 1893, which precipitated the failure of many railroads inherently weak from the results of bad management and destructive competition. In 1893 alone, according to one authority,[29] 27,000 miles, with an aggregate capitalization of almost two billion dollars, were taken over by the courts, and in 1894–98 foreclosure sales aggregated 40,503 miles. Among the more important roads failing were the Richmond & West Point Terminal, the Reading, the Erie, the Northern Pacific, the Baltimore & Ohio, the Atchison, and the Union Pacific. Morgan had charge of the reorganization of the first four and was concerned in the reorganization of the B. & O. and the Atchison. He had no competitor in this work—even the Harriman–Rockefeller–National City Bank–Kuhn, Loeb group had not yet risen to a point where they could be classed with the Morgans, though Harriman was soon to rise to first rank in the rehabilitation of the Union Pacific.

The Morgan reorganizations followed a general pattern: (1) the finances of the road were put on a sound basis, with lower fixed charges and a capital stock large in relation to bonded indebtedness; (2) the structure of the roads was greatly simplified by consolidation; (3) by means of voting trusts the Morgans retained control for some time after reorganization, and after the voting trusts had expired Morgan representatives were usually found on the boards—when the managers in one instance objected to turning their roads over to the Morgans, Morgan, himself, is said to have retorted, "Your Roads! Your roads belong to my clients;"[30] and (4) with a nucleus of the roads in which he had a powerful influence, Morgan extended coöperation based on community of interest. Since the reorganizations are treated in detail in E. G. Campbell's *The Reorganization of the American Railroad System, 1893–1900,*[31] they will be considered only briefly here.

The first of Morgan's reorganizations at this time led to the organization of the Southern Railway. Morgan reluctantly went into the Richmond Terminal system to prevent a forced sale that would have destroyed the value of many securities. A reorganization committee headed by Coster drew up a plan for both physical and financial rehabilitation of about 6,000 miles of road (excluding the Central of Georgia). Assessments on stockholders—who received in exchange preferred stock—and the sale of stock and bonds furnished means to replace the old securities, to pay floating obligations and the expenses of reorganization, and to improve the road. The result was an immediate reduction in fixed charges from $9,500,000 to $6,789,000, based on the estimated minimum earning capacity of the system. A relatively large common stock was issued. The addition of the Central of Georgia and the placing of the management under Sam-

29 Daggett, *op. cit.*, p. v.

30 *Wall Street Journal,* April 1, 1913.

31 Published in 1938 by the Columbia University Press.

uel Spencer made the Southern the strongest system in the South. One commentator, whose judgment has weight, stated that the welding of such unpromising railroad material—built to sell rather than to operate—in the most unpromising territory in the country for a railroad was "one of the noteworthy achievements of American railroad history." [32]

Reorganization of the Erie was not so immediately successful. The first plan had to be abandoned because it did not cut deeply enough. Another plan combined under one corporation all the properties involved, reaching from Chicago to New York, and provided for the issue of noncumulative preferred and common stock and bonds at greatly reduced interest. The stock was placed under a Morgan voting trust. The Morgans were to receive cash for all expenses and $500,000, payable in common stock, for organizing a syndicate to take $15,000,000 in bonds and any stock on which assessments were not paid. The *Chronicle* said this plan possessed the special merit characteristic of J. P. Morgan & Co.'s reorganizations "of exceeding frankness in dealing with the different classes of security holders." The London *Economist* (which was constitutionally upset over American railroad securities and management) admitted that, though the reorganization cost meant a perpetual charge of $50,000, the scheme had "the essential qualities of . . . adequacy, justice, and elasticity." [33]

Reorganization of the Reading presented very special problems because of its connections with the anthracite industry. Much-needed funds were provided for improving the road's physical condition and an attempt was made to diversify the traffic,[34] but the fundamental problem was the problem of the anthracite industry and the system of roads which served it. Morgan is said later to have secured, through the purchase of stock, an influence in the Lehigh Valley and the Central of New Jersey. The Delaware & Hudson and the Delaware, Lackawanna & Western were supposed to be under the Vanderbilts, who were in the Morgan sphere of influence. Morgan, as has been observed, was strong in the Erie. By 1901 Morgan had come to be regarded as the most important influence in transportation in the anthracite region.[35]

The next region to be entered by Morgan was the Northwest. He refused an invitation to reorganize the Union Pacific because it involved too much politics; the reorganization was therefore taken over by Harriman (with the backing of Kuhn, Loeb) and he made the road into a remarkably strong system. Morgan took on the reorganization of the Northern Pacific, however, and in doing so won the close coöperation of James J. Hill of the Great Northern. Morgan and Hill first attempted to combine the Great Northern and the Northern Pacific but were blocked by court decisions. The Northern Pacific was, therefore, purchased at foreclosure in 1896 by a reorganization committee, which appointed J. P. Morgan & Co. reorganization managers. The road was rehabilitated in the usual Morgan way.[36]

While participating in these and other less spectacular reorganizations, J. Pierpont Morgan became strongly interested in the New Haven road in New England. He had been elected in 1891 to the road's board, which already had as members such strong representatives of New York inter-

[32] For a detailed discussion of this reorganization, see Campbell, *op. cit.*, pp. 149–159.

[33] *Ibid.*, pp. 160–172.

[34] *Ibid.*, pp. 172–187.

[35] *Ibid.*, pp. 188–189; *Report of the Industrial Commission*, vol. xix, pp. 461–463. Note that the Industrial Commission is cautious in its statements about the details of the Morgans' relations with those roads, though it concludes that the "total [anthracite] output more or less directly controlled by Morgan interests is probably from two-thirds to three-fourths of the entire shipments."

[36] For details on the Northern Pacific see Campbell, *op. cit.*, pp. 196–205.

ests as Chauncey Depew and William Rockefeller. In the 'nineties, the New Haven began to absorb other New England railroads. It acquired the New York, Providence & Boston Railroad, the Housatonic, the Old Colony, and the New York & New England, and it took over other roads on long leases. An alliance with the Boston & Maine practically eliminated competition in New England.

Morgan's reorganization work in the 'nineties had important results. It strengthened many railroads and improved their securities and their services. It gave J. P. Morgan & Co., during the initial years, a considerable control through voting trusts, and it usually established them as bankers to the railroad properties in question. The work, of course, yielded handsome fees to the Morgans. To Morgan himself success meant unquestioned leadership in American finance, a leadership that was backed by strong support among the other New York bankers. Only the Harriman–Rockefeller–Kuhn, Loeb group had sufficient resources and following to undertake completely independent operations of like nature.

It was only in the late 'nineties that the Morgans initiated industrial financing on a public scale. Indeed up to that time industry had been confined to small units, utilizing their local banks, to be sure, for temporary loans but not requiring public financing such as great railroad development required. But the beginning of mass production and the opportunity for constructive and profitable development were already attracting bankers to industry. Morgan's first important industrial connection was General Electric, which he and Charles Coster helped organize in 1892 by combining several concerns.[37] With the revival of business and of the tendency towards consolidations to produce economies in 1897–98, Morgan saw opportunity for stabilizing enterprise in the steel industry which had the reputation of being "a prince or pauper." By far the largest unit in that industry was the all-around development under the dominant direction of Andrew Carnegie, who was a great manufacturer and a superb administrator, and lesser producers began to combine to meet his competition. In 1898 Morgan helped to finance the formation of the Federal Steel Co., an integrated concern with a capital of $200,000,000 in which three large companies were combined. Morgan refused to join the great manipulator, John W. Gates, in organizing his large wire combination.

In United States government finance Morgan carried out one spectacular operation in the 'nineties. When in 1895 the gold reserve in the United States Treasury, as a result largely of the Silver Purchase Act, was nearing extinction—after a long period of monetary uncertainty—and after the government had exhausted every other means of supporting its credit, President Cleveland reluctantly accepted a plan suggested by Morgan. On the basis of an obscure enabling clause in an act passed during the Civil War, Morgan offered to try to organize a syndicate to sell bonds for gold, the bulk of which would be obtained abroad and would be imported to buttress the American government's gold reserve. The task was considered impossible,[38] for it virtually meant an attempt to dam up a natural commercial movement.[39]

The Morgan-Belmont Syndicate took the risk of loss in money and in prestige. But they succeeded in securing enough gold and in stemming the export of gold until recovery in trade solved the difficulty. One close to Morgan recalls that he estimated his profits from the whole trans-

[37] *Com. & Fin. Chron.*, vol. liv (June 25, 1892), p. 1051; *Bond Record*, vol. iv (July, 1896), pp. 594–596.

[38] See, for instance, the *Economist*, for Feb. 23, June 15, July 6, and Aug. 10, 1895.

[39] Alexander D. Noyes, *Forty Years of American Finance* (New York, 1898), p. 240. There is an interesting account of the affair by Cleveland, himself, in the *Saturday Evening Post*, April 7, 1904.

action at about $250,000. But in some quarters the public's notion of the gains he made from what was represented as taking advantage of the dire need of the government was far different, and the episode contributed much towards building up a public opinion unfavorable to Morgan. It is a pertinent question whether the affair was not purposely exaggerated by a prominent New York newspaper as an appeal to popular prejudice in a circulation war which it was waging with another newspaper.

8. The Height of Morgan's Career, 1900–13

In considering Morgan's business career there is always a tendency to deal almost exclusively with spectacular episodes and with the aspects of his firm's work in investment banking which are apparent to the public. J. P. Morgan & Co. as a banking institution is, like other banks, seldom or never seen in the various departments of its business. The result is that much of reality is lost, and that almost nothing is given on the problems and the methods of management and the results to the firm. In such a situation almost any conclusion is likely to be drawn, and there is much room for irresponsible conjecture. This is the almost inevitable result of the policy which the Morgans, like other bankers, have followed of considering their business and that of their clients as entirely private and confidential. One can understand the reason and regret the fact.

In this period, as before, the Morgans had houses in Paris, London, and Philadelphia as well as in New York. From 1902 to 1912 the firm was directly responsible for leading in the marketing of corporate issues totaling almost two billion dollars.[40] Besides its work in reorganizations and in underwriting and wholesaling securities, J. P. Morgan & Co. carried on a large commercial banking business. Some idea of the extent of that business may be gathered from the fact that on November 1, 1912, the New York house had the accounts of over a hundred corporations and had aggregate deposits of $162,491,819.-65.[41] Like other banks (and at the same rate) it paid interest on those deposits and was a considerable lender on the stock exchange, keeping a portion of its quick reserves in call loans. It should also be remembered that the firm and its partners had investment interests in manufacturing, transportation, and banking, though as bankers their first concern had to be to keep their assets in a strongly liquid condition.

As to problems of internal organization and management, one or possibly two individual partners were asked to look after these, but in general all partners were supposed to keep free from too much detail. Obviously, each partner bore a serious load of responsibility and work, besides certain duties as director in various corporations. J. Pierpont Morgan himself after middle life did not follow closely the details of management—when all available information on a question was in hand, he made the final decision, and he left execution to others. It is generally held among those who knew the work of J. Pierpont Morgan's firm that the strain on his partners was terrific and that that strain took a heavy toll.

While the business of the firm grew, the external situation also changed. Early in the century the Harriman–Standard Oil–Kuhn, Loeb group made a strong combination which commanded the respect and not infrequently the coöperation of Morgan himself. Morgan and Harriman each had close associates on whom they could customarily depend for support. One source of Morgan's strength was his personal relations with his clients. From the beginning he applied to his banking house those methods of intimate relationship be-

[40] *Money Trust Investigation, Report,* p. 57.

[41] *Money Trust Investigation, Testimony,* p. 1011, and *Report,* p. 57.

tween banker and client which prevailed generally abroad. "The keynote of that relationship was loyalty," said the *Wall Street Journal.* "Mr. Morgan would go to the extreme in protecting any client or banking house which had been in close and honorable association with him, and he expected from them the same loyal support in times of stress and financial trouble." [42]

The most striking development in the Morgans' influence in this period was their attempt to stabilize the financial situation through gaining the active coöperation of financial institutions. There had long been a strong personal friendship between J. Pierpont Morgan and George F. Baker, and that bond was strengthened when Baker invited Morgan to make a considerable investment in the stock of the First National Bank of which Morgan became a director. He also acquired an interest in the National Bank of Commerce and in the National City Bank of New York.[43]

The closest relations were, however, gradually developed with two trust companies. In 1903 the Bankers' Trust Co. was organized and its control was vested in a voting trust composed of a Morgan partner, a vice-president of the First National Bank who six years afterward became a Morgan partner, and a director in United States Steel, who was also an officer of the Liberty National Bank. The voting trust was renewed in 1908 and 1912. The Morgans also acquired an interest in the stock of the Guaranty Trust Co. and had representatives on the directorate. With the Guaranty were merged early in 1910 three other small New York trust companies. The Guaranty was in 1912, in resources and deposits, the largest trust company in the United States, and both the Bankers' and the Guaranty ranked high among the banks of the country.

In 1909 Morgan also purchased from Thomas F. Ryan a majority of the capital stock of the Equitable Life Assurance Society (George F. Baker and James Stillman sharing in the purchase).[44] All the stock had been placed in the hands of trustees, namely, ex-President Grover Cleveland, George Westinghouse, and Judge Morgan O'Brien.

During this period (1900–13) Morgan continued to advance in transportation. In defense of the Southern against the buccaneer Gates, he purchased for the Atlantic Coast Line Railway the Louisville & Nashville Railroad at a price $10,000,000 above what Gates had paid.[45] He organized the International Mercantile Marine Co., a North Atlantic combination; the results of this unsuccessful venture are shown in a later case.[46] In the Northwest, the Morgan-Hill combination was threatened by Harriman; Morgan and Hill won in a spectacular and destructive contest over Northern Pacific stock on the New York Stock Exchange. Though the Northern Securities Co., which they organized to hold control of the Great Northern, the Northern Pacific, and the Burlington, was declared unconstitutional, the combination was maintained through the joint purchase of Burlington Railroad stock by the two other roads.[47]

Lastly, the New Haven system was extended in New England to include steamship and trolley lines as well as railroads. This was undoubtedly Morgan's greatest mistake. The Morgans felt that the policy originally outlined by Charles Mellen, whom they nominated head of the system, was primarily at fault, and Mellen blamed himself for doing (as he claimed) as he was bidden by Morgan. It may be pertinent to note that the theory behind the New

[42] April 1, 1913.

[43] The directorships held in those banks in 1912 are given in *Money Trust Investigation, Interlocking Directorates,* p. 3, and *Report,* pp. 66–67.

[44] *Ibid.,* pp. 57–60; *Fin. & Com. Chron.,* vol. lxxxix, pp. 1458–1459 (Dec. 4, 1909).

[45] Henry Clews, *Fifty Years in Wall Street* (New York, 1908), pp. 764–765.

[46] See below, pp. 566–596.

[47] See above, pp. 403–421.

Haven system was that New England was, in terms of transportation, a region not of long hauls but of short hauls, and therefore almost completely a terminal proposition. Obviously, high prices were paid for many purchases, but Morgan expected the profits of the combination to carry high fixed charges. It is pertinent to ask whether he should have foreseen the inevitable difficulties in management as well as the changes in transportation which came with the later vogue of the motor car.

More successful were Morgan's industrial combinations. He participated in the formation of several large combinations, such as the American Telephone and Telegraph Co., being dominant in the organization of two or three others. He directed and his firm financed the organization of the United States Steel Corporation. Capitalized at $1,400,000,000, it was by far the largest corporation the world had ever known, and though it contained less than 40 per cent of the industry, it unquestionably became supreme in the steel industry in the United States. The career of this concern is also traced in a later case.[48] One of Morgan's most successful combinations was the International Harvester Co. Both these combinations were holding companies which left the management of operating in the hands of the constituent concerns.

There was much criticism of Morgan's combinations at this time. Capitalization was said to be excessive—Morgan placed a high value on the earning power of the combination and paid for constituent companies accordingly. Morgan profits were said to be high; the many-sided transactions presented many opportunities for fees for services. Only when we get a clearer conception than at present of the profits of the financial capitalist and of the value to the corporation and the investor of his services as a banker will it be possible to judge whether he was worth what he received. The most widespread attack on Morgan grew out of fear on the part of many that he might be gaining a virtual monopoly in corporation finance. Morgan admitted that power could be abused—though it could never be regained if lost.[49]

Two emergencies illustrate the strength of Morgan in this period. He was looked upon as the head of the anthracite industry at the time of the great strike of 1902, but he assented to arbitration only after President Roosevelt had threatened government operation of the mines. And it was Morgan to whom the banking community of New York looked for leadership during the panic of 1907. His thorough investigation of the solvency of the institutions endangered, his unhesitating determination on a program once the facts were in, and his unconditional demands on the terrified bankers who appealed to him to take the situation in hand, illustrate Morgan's capacity for leadership and his methods as a leader.

Though Morgan was strong in his own field of finance, he had a weakness which was reacting against him. He had neglected public relations. Like most business men of his generation he considered business simply as private enterprise, and he did not have the temperament—or perhaps the imagination—to see that in a democracy business must have regard for the voter. That he was feeling his way toward some recognition of the need of informing the public about the work of corporations is seen from the fact that he advocated in 1901 the publication of quarterly statements of earnings and tonnage of United States Steel (which was considered a doubtful innovation at the time!). He felt the force of public opposition when he had to testify in the Money Trust Investigation in December, 1912—it may have been that experience which led him to say shortly before he died that "American business must henceforth be done in glass pockets." Before the full implications of

[48] See below, pp. 596–623.

[49] *Money Trust Investigation, Testimony*, pp. 1050, 1052.

the investigation were seen, however, Morgan was gone. He died in Rome on March 31, 1913.

9. The Money Trust Investigation

The popular fear and criticism of the power of the bankers, which arose early in the century, led to an investigation by the committee on banking and currency, headed by Arsène Pujo, in the House of Representatives in 1912–13. Though there is a difference of opinion as to the validity of some of the conclusions drawn from the findings as published in the reports of the committee, there is no question that the published records of the investigation constitute the most comprehensive source of information on American finance which we have for that time. The student is urged to read some of the testimony, especially that of J. Pierpont Morgan and his partners and associates. Herewith will be reproduced excerpts from the conclusions as to concentration and from a statement on the report made by J. P. Morgan & Co.

A. From the Report on the Investigation.

From an elaborate table showing the affiliations of eighteen leading banks and banking houses, the report draws the following summaries about various groups: [50]

"I. The table shows that J. P. Morgan & Co., the First National Bank, the National City Bank, the Guaranty Trust Co., and the Bankers' Trust Co. together have—

"One hundred and eighteen directorships in 34 banks and trust companies having total resources of $2,679,000,000 and total deposits of $1,983,000,000.

"Thirty directorships in 10 insurance companies having total assets of $2,293,000,000.

"One hundred and five directorships in 32 transportation systems having a total capitalization of $11,784,000,000 and a total mileage (excluding express companies and steamship lines) of 150,200.

"Sixty-three directorships in 24 producing and trading corporations having a total capitalization of $3,339,000,000.

"Twenty-five directorships in 12 public utility corporations having a total capitalization of $2,150,000,000.

"In all, 341 directorships in 112 corporations having aggregate resources or capitalization of $22,245,000,000.

. . . .

"II. That J. P. Morgan & Co., the Guaranty Trust Co., the Bankers' Trust Co., and the First National Bank together have—

"Eighty-nine directorships in such banks and trust companies.

"Twenty-nine directorships in such insurance companies.

"Seventy-eight directorships in such transportation systems.

"Forty-nine directorships in such producing and trading corporations, and

"Sixteen directorships in such public utility corporations.

"In all, 261 directorships.

. . . .

"III. That J. P. Morgan & Co., the Guaranty Trust Co., and the Bankers' Trust Co. together have—

"Seventy-eight directorships in such banks and trust companies.

"Twenty-nine directorships in such insurance companies.

"Sixty-four directorships in such transportation systems.

"Forty-four directorships in such producing and trading corporations, and

"Fourteen directorships in such public utility corporations.

"In all, 229 directorships."

The following excerpts point to the committee's conclusions about concentration: [51]

"Your committee is satisfied from the proofs submitted, even in the absence of data from the banks, that there is an established and well-defined identity and community of interest between a few leaders of finance, created and held together through stock ownership, interlocking directorates, partnership

[50] *Money Trust Investigation, Interlocking Directorates,* pp. 27–28.

[51] *Ibid., Report of the Committee,* pp. 129, 131, 133.

and joint account transactions, and other forms of domination over banks, trust companies, railroads, and public-service and industrial corporations, which has resulted in great and rapidly growing concentration of the control of money and credit in the hands of these few men.

. . . .

"The parties to this combination or understanding or community of interest, by whatever name it may be called, may be conveniently classified, for the purpose of differentiation, into four separate groups.

"First. The first, which for convenience of statement we will call the inner group, consists of J. P. Morgan & Co., the recognized leaders, and George F. Baker and James Stillman in their individual capacities and in their joint administration and control of the First National Bank, the National City Bank, the National Bank of Commerce, the Chase National Bank, the Guaranty Trust Co., and the Bankers Trust Co., with total known resources, in these corporations alone, in excess of $1,300,000,000, and of a number of smaller but important financial institutions. This takes no account of the personal fortunes of these gentlemen.

"Second. Closely allied with this inner or primary group, and indeed related to them practically as partners in many of their larger financial enterprises, are the powerful international banking houses of Lee, Higginson & Co. and Kidder, Peabody & Co., with three affiliated banks in Boston—the National Shawmut Bank, the First National Bank, and the Old Colony Trust Co.—having at least more than half of the total resources of all the Boston banks; also with interests and representation in other important New England financial institutions.

"Third. In New York City the international banking house of Messrs. Kuhn, Loeb & Co., with its large foreign clientele and connections, whilst only qualifiedly allied with the inner group, and only in isolated transactions, yet through its close relations with the National City Bank and the National Bank of Commerce and other financial institutions with which it has recently allied itself has many interests in common, conducting large joint-account transactions with them, especially in recent years, and having what virtually amounts to an understanding not to compete, which is defended as a principle of 'banking ethics.' Together they have with a few exceptions pre-empted the banking business of the important railways of the country.

. . . .

"No railroad system or industrial corporation for which either of the houses named has acted as banker could shift its business from one to another. Where one has made an issue of securities for a corporation the others will not bid for subsequent issues of the same corporation. Their frequent and extensive relations in the joint issue of securities has made such a *modus vivendi* inevitable.

"This inner group and allies thus have no effective competition, either from others or amongst themselves for these large security issues and are accordingly free to exact their own terms in most cases. Your committee has no evidence that this power is being used oppressively and no means of ascertaining the facts so long as their profits are undisclosed."

B. Selections from the Response of J. P. Morgan & Co.[52]

". . . . We ventured to point out to you that such 'concentration' as has taken place in New York and other financial centres has been due, not to the purposes and activities of men, but primarily to the operation of our antiquated banking system which automatically compels interior banks to 'concentrate' in New York City hundreds of millions of reserve funds; and next, to economic laws which in every country create some one city as the great financial centre.

. . . .

". . . . In these tables it is shown that 180 bankers and bank directors serve upon the boards of corporations having resources aggregating twenty-five billion dollars, and it is implied that this vast aggregate of the country's wealth is at the disposal of these 180 men. But such an implication rests solely

[52] *Letter from Messrs. J. P. Morgan & Co., in Response to the Invitation of the Sub-Committee. . . . of the Committee on Banking and Currency in the House of Representatives* (a pamphlet, New York City, February 25, 1913).

upon the untenable theory that these men, living in different parts of the country, in many cases personally unacquainted with each other, and in most cases associated only in occasional transactions, vote always for the same policies and control with united purpose the directorates of the 132 corporations on which they serve. The testimony failed to establish any concerted policy or harmony of action binding these 180 men together, and as a matter of fact no such policy exists. The absurdity of the assumption of such control becomes more apparent when one considers that on the average these directors represent only one quarter of the memberships of their boards. It is preposterous to suppose that every 'interlocking' director has full control in every organization with which he is connected, and that the majority of directors who are not 'interlocking' are mere figure-heads, subject to the will of a small minority of their boards.

"Perhaps the greatest harm in the presentation referred to lay in the further unwarranted inference, to which has been given wide publicity, that the vast sum of $25,000,000,000. was in cash or liquid form, subject to the selfish use or abuse of individuals.

. . . .

"These mergers, however, are a development due simply to the demand for larger banking facilities to care for the growth of the country's business. As our cities double and treble in size and importance, as railroads extend and industrial plants expand, not only is it natural, but it is necessary that our banking institutions should grow in order to care for the increased demands put upon them. Perhaps it is not known as well as it should be that in New York City the largest banks are far inferior in size to banks in the commercial capitals of other and much smaller countries. The largest bank in New York City today has resources amounting to only three fifths of the resources of the largest bank in England, to only one fourth of the resources of the largest bank in France, and to less than one fifth of the resources of the largest bank in Germany. As the Committee is aware, in New York City there are only three banks with resources in excess of $200,000,000., while there are ten such institutions in London, five in Berlin and four in Paris.

. . . .

". . . . Since 1907 co-operation has been more active by reason of the lesson which banks in all large cities then learned that, for self-preservation, they could not—as is possible in other countries—rely upon a strong and elastic banking system, but must gain such protection by concurrent action; and second, that such co-operation is simply a further result of the necessity for handling great transactions. . . . if transactions of such magnitude are to be carried on, the country obviously requires not only the larger individual banks, but demands also that those banks shall co-operate to perform efficiently the country's business.

. . . .

". . . . Many questions were asked as to the wisdom in having representatives of private banking houses sit upon the boards of corporations, whose securities the same bankers frequently offer for sale. This practice which has been in vogue abroad, ever since the creation of limited companies, has arisen not from a desire on the part of the banker to manage the daily affairs of the corporation or to purchase its securities more cheaply than he otherwise could; but rather because of his moral responsibility as sponsor for the corporation's securities, to keep an eye upon its policies and to protect the interests of investors in the securities of that corporation. For a private banker to sit upon such a directorate is in most instances a duty, not a privilege.

. . . .

". . . . On this matter [the absence of competitive bidding] we are pleased to submit certain considerations which, we are confident, are borne out by the facts: First, in general and over a period of time, the sale of such securities is invariably subject to the competition of market conditions. . . . Second, in most of the leading commercial States Public Service Commissions pass with great care upon the prices at which the securities of all transportation and public utility corporations are sold. Third, competitive bidding, in the sense of having railroad and industrial securities offered practically at public auction as in the case of municipal securities, is seldom or never practised.

"The reasons against such practise are

plain. Such corporate issues have neither the security, the steadiness nor the general confidence possessed by municipal bonds, and while in good times it is possible that they might be subscribed for at public auction, in bad times there would be no one to bid for them. . . . Should these latter appeal directly to the proverbially timid investor there can be little question that, in times of stress, support would be totally lacking. We should have the spectacle of numberless corporations failing for lack of strong financial or banking support."

10. Readings

There is no satisfactory biography of J. P. Morgan. The following are interesting and suggestive but quite unsound: Lewis Corey, *The House of Morgan* (New York, 1930); Carl Hovey, *The Life Story of J. Pierpont Morgan* (New York, 1912); John Winkler, *Morgan the Magnificent* (New York, 1930). A biography by Herbert L. Satterlee, which is now in the press, will presumably contain new and important material.

John Moody, *The Masters of Capital* (New Haven, 1919), is a short general history of American finance in the time of Morgan.

The following are recommended on reorganizations and combinations: Stuart Daggett, *Railroad Reorganization* (Boston, 1908); E. G. Campbell, *The Reorganization of the American Railroad System, 1893–1900* (New York, 1938); Jules I. Bogen, *The Anthracite Railroads* (New York, 1927); Eliot Jones, *The Anthracite Coal Combination in the United States* (Cambridge, 1914), and *The Trust Problem in the United States* (New York, 1921).

11. Suggested Questions

1. Morgan, unlike most of the captains of industry and finance after the Civil War, did not rise from poverty. What influence did this have on his career and character?
2. What effect did the international position of Morgan have upon his attitude towards business in the United States?
3. Why did the Morgans acquire an interest in so many financial institutions?
4. If you had been asked to reformulate Morgan policy after the Pujo Investigation, what recommendations would you have made?
5. Was something like the system popularly attributed to Morgan desirable from a public point of view?

XXXIV. THE INTERNATIONAL MERCANTILE MARINE COMPANY, 1901–1937

1. Introduction

J. P. Morgan, convinced of the value of combination and integration in industry and encouraged by the immediate success of the United States Steel Corporation, formed the International Mercantile Marine Co. in 1902. Like the Steel Corporation, it was established to meet and overcome a difficult competitive situation. Unlike the Steel Corporation, the I. M. M. was not a success. It is important to determine why, despite careful thought in its formation, the shipping combine fell far short of success.

Though operating with a deficit during much of its history, the I. M. M. has continued to exist down to the present. Where another company might have been allowed to liquidate on several occasions, or indeed have been forced to do so, the I. M. M. has been kept alive. Certain forces have tended to perpetuate this company in the face of pressure which, according to the classical economists, should have brought its certain downfall.

2. Chronology

1885 First international agreement on transatlantic rates.

1891 New agreement reached by Continental lines, apportioning traffic.

1899	Hamburg-American Line negotiated unsuccessfully for interest in the Atlantic Transport Line.
1901	J. P. Morgan arranged for purchase of the British Leyland Line and its subsidiaries.
1902	International Mercantile Marine Co. started business, December 1.
1903	J. Bruce Ismay succeeded Clement A. Griscom as I. M. M. president.
1912	*Titanic* foundered with heavy loss of life.
1913	Departure from policy of complete company insurance of vessels.
1914	Interest payment on I. M. M. 4½ per cent bonds deferred.
1915	Philip A. S. Franklin appointed receiver of I. M. M.
1916	Receivership ended; Franklin elected president of I. M. M.
1917	Dividend paid on preferred stock.
1918	Sale of British subsidiaries prevented by United States government.
1920	Last dividend paid on preferred stock, leaving 42 per cent accumulations.
1921	United States Shipping Board investigated British Admiralty agreements with I. M. M.
1926	White Star Line sold to a British company.
1929	Readjustment of capital structure.
1931	I. M. M. merged with Roosevelt Steamship Company, Inc. Controlling interest in United States Lines Co. bought by I. M. M. in December.
1934	I. M. M. completed negotiations for control of Munson Steamship Lines.
1936	All ships of I. M. M. under United States flag.
1937	I. M. M. ceased to be operating company. Subsidy agreement with United States.

3. Atlantic Shipping before the Morgan Trust

In order to understand the competitive situation which Morgan designed the I. M. M. to overcome, it is necessary first to review conditions on the Atlantic preceding its formation. Although several attempts were made to secure coöperation among the competing lines of competing nations before 1900, little of a constructive nature was accomplished. The situation was not unlike that in the steel industry in America before the formation of the United States Steel Corporation.

Competition on the transatlantic steamship routes became oppressive about 1880, when Albert Ballin, a German ship operator, and Edward Carr, an English operator, started a new kind of emigration service from Germany and England to New York. The new German line operated cargo boats with accommodations for steerage passengers. These steamers had little in common with the usual passenger steamers which carried both cabin and steerage passengers. The advantage to the emigrants of the new type was that it gave them much more space than was at their disposal in the two- and three-class boats.

The Carr Line soon made itself felt as a serious competitor of the Hamburg-American and North German Lloyd lines, and a strenuous rate-war ensued. In July, 1885, at a conference held in Hamburg, an agreement was concluded by the Hamburg-American, the Lloyd, and the Carr lines, the Dutch, Belgian, and French lines, and a representative of the British lines. All these companies bound themselves to raise their rates from Germany to 100 marks, except that the Carr Line received a recognized differential of 10 marks.

In March, 1886, the Carr Line absorbed another German company, the Union Line of Hamburg, thus strengthening its position relatively to the Hamburg-American Line. The latter company immediately arranged a pool agreement with the Carr Line, appointing Ballin as sole head of its North American passenger department and itself taking over the operation of the Union Line's steamers. After these developments Ballin was able to complete negotiations with the British lines which were satisfactory in that they ended a rate war between the two interests.

A few years' trial showed that these agreements were not sufficiently comprehensive. Something was needed to ensure a fair distribution of the traffic at the new rates. But no agreement along these lines was concluded until January, 1891. Even then the final plan agreed upon was accepted by the Continental lines, excepting the French Line, and not by the British. The pool, known as the North Atlantic Steamship Lines Association, distributed the business among the various members.

The years after 1892 were marked by constant negotiation between the British and Continental interests. Agreements were reached on the division of the steerage and cabin passenger business in 1895 and extended for five years in 1899. Still the organization for coöperation was so loose that constant differences interfered with the smooth operation of agreements.

As early as 1891 we find that Ballin, by that time the outstanding shipping man of his day, tried without success to combine the German and American interests on the Atlantic. At that time he wrote B. N. Baker, of Baltimore, head of the Atlantic Transport Line, offering to sell a considerable interest in the Hamburg-American Line to him, with the idea that the services of the two lines would supplement each other. The Atlantic Transport Line, an American-owned company, was engaged in trade from New York and Baltimore to England, operating its ships under the British flag.

Ballin's suggestion did not lead to any immediate practical result, but it was taken up again eight years later, when Pirrie, a shipbuilder of Belfast, thought it necessary to prevent an alliance between the Atlantic Transport Co. and the British Leyland Line. It then became clear, however, that too great a sacrifice would be required on the part of the Hamburg-American Line to carry through the necessary exchange of shares, and the matter was dropped. The new combination being made between English and American shipping promised to become strong.

4. Ballin and the Organization of the Morgan Trust

These shifts in the organization of transatlantic shipping alarmed the Germans and particularly Ballin, who was determined to put German shipping in the van. Ballin was a superbly able and aggressive ship operator, the strongest in Germany if not in the whole world at the time. Though intensely devoted to the German Empire and its kaiser, like some other German industrialists he saw German business in its wider, international relations. When it was rumored that J. Pierpont Morgan was trying to organize a trust to control the Atlantic, Ballin made a careful study of the situation with an eye to protecting German interests if possible. His alarm was reflected in a report to Prince Henckell-Donnersmarch about Morgan's preparations early in 1901. Parts of the report are given here: [1]

"Quite recently the well-known American banker, Mr. J. Pierpont Morgan, conjointly with some other big American capitalists, has taken an interest in the plan [to restore American shipping to its former prominence]. The following facts have become known so far in connexion with his efforts:

"Morgan has acquired the Leyland Line, of Liverpool. . . . This purchase includes the West India and Pacific Line, which was absorbed into the Leyland Line as recently as a twelvemonth ago. The Mediterranean service formerly carried on by the Leyland Line has

[1] Bernard Huldermann, *Albert Ballin* (W. J. Eggers, translator, London, 1922), pp. 48–50.

not been acquired by Morgan. He has, however, added the Atlantic Transport Company. Morgan's evident intention is to form a big American shipping trust, and I have received absolutely reliable information to the effect that the American Line and the Red Star Line are also going to join the combine. The shares of the two last-named lines are already for the most part in American hands, and both companies are being managed from New York. . . .

". . . . The new American concern would possess a fleet representing 430,000 gross register tons. The corresponding figures for the Hamburg-Amerika Linie and for the Lloyd, including steamers building, are 650,000 and 600,000 tons respectively.

"The proper method of rightly appreciating the importance of the American coalition is to restrict the comparison, as far as the two German companies are concerned, to the amount of tonnage which they employ in their services to and from United States ports. If this is borne in mind, we arrive at the following figures: German lines—390,000 G. R. T.; American concern—about 430,000 G. R. T. These figures show that, as regards the amount of tonnage employed, the Morgan Trust is superior to the two German companies on the North Atlantic route. It can also challenge comparison with the regular British lines—grand total, 438,566 G. R. T.

"In all the steps he has taken, Morgan, no doubt, has been guided by his confidence in his ability to enforce the passing of a Subsidy Act by Congress in favour of his undertaking. So long as he does not succeed in these efforts of his he will, of course, be obliged to operate the lines of which he has secured control under foreign flags. Up to the present only four steamers of the American Line, viz. the *New York, Philadelphia, St. Louis,* and *St. Paul* are flying the United States flag, whereas the remaining vessels of the American Line, and those of the Leyland, the West India and Pacific, the American Transport, the National and the Furness-Boston lines, are sailing under the British, and those of the Red Star Line under the Belgian flag.

"The organization which Mr. Morgan either has created, or is creating, is not in itself a danger to the two German shipping companies; neither can it be said that the Government subsidies—provided they do not exceed an amount that is justified by the conditions actually existing—are in themselves detrimental to the German interests. The real danger, however, threatens from the amalgamation of the American railway interests with those of American shipping.

"It is no secret that Morgan is pursuing his far-reaching plans as the head of a syndicate which comprises a number of the most important and most enterprising business men in the United States, and that the railway interests are particularly well represented in it. Morgan himself, during his stay in London a few months ago, stated to some British shipping men that, according to his estimates, nearly 70 per cent. of the goods which are shipped to Europe from the North Atlantic ports are carried to the latter by the railroads on Through Bills of Lading, and that their further transport is entrusted to foreign shipping companies. He and his friends, Morgan added, did not see any reason why the railroad companies should leave it to foreign-owned companies to carry those American goods across the Atlantic. It would be much more logical to bring about an amalgamation of the American railroad and shipping interests for the purpose of securing the whole profits for American capital.

"This projected combination of the railroad and sea-borne traffic is, as I have pointed out, a great source of danger to the foreign shipping companies, as it will expose them to the possibility of finding their supplies from the United States *hinterland* cut off. This latter traffic is indispensable to the remunerative working of our North American services, and it is quite likely that Morgan's statement that they amount to about 70 per cent. of the total sea-borne traffic is essentially correct."

Ballin was not a man to sit by and let Morgan gain control of the Atlantic without protest; neither was he unaware that to oppose Morgan would be foolhardy. He determined to coöperate in this new venure, while at the same time driving as favorable a bargain for the German companies as was possible. Thus in the early summer of 1901 he went to London to talk over the situation with certain outstanding shipping men. His personal notes contain an interesting reference to that visit: [2]

"When I was in London in July (1901), I had an opportunity of discussing this American business with Mr. Pirrie [a Belfast shipbuilder]. Pirrie had already informed me some time ago that he would like to talk to me on this subject, but he had never indicated until then that Morgan had actually instructed him to discuss matters with me. A second meeting took place at which Ismay (the chairman of the White Star Line) was present in addition to Pirrie and myself, and it was agreed that Pirrie should go to New York and find out from Morgan himself what were his plans regarding the White Star Line and the Hamburg-Amerika Linie.

"Shortly after Pirrie's return from the States I went to London to talk things over with him. He had already sent me a wire to say that he had also asked Mr. Wilding [British ship operator] to take part in our meeting; and this circumstance induced me to call on Mr. Wilding when I passed through Southampton *en route* for London. What he told me filled me with as much concern as surprise. He informed me that the syndicate intended to acquire the White Star Line, but that, owing to my relations with the Kaiser, the acquisition of the Hamburg-Amerika Linie was not contemplated. Morgan, he further told me, was willing to work on the most friendly terms with us, as far as this could be done without endangering the interests of the syndicate; but the fact was that the biggest American railroad companies had already approached the syndicate, and that they had offered terms of co-operation which were practically identical with a combination between themselves and the syndicate.

"In the course of the discussions then proceeding between Pirrie, Wilding, and myself the situation changed to our advantage, and I was successful in seeing my own proposals accepted, the essence of which was that, on the one hand, our independence should be respected, that the nationality of our company should not be interfered with, and that no American members should be added to our Board of Trustees; whilst, on the other hand, a fairly close contact was to be established between the two concerns, and competition between them was to be eliminated."

Terms for an agreement between Hamburg-American and the Morgan trust were discussed in London. They provided that the agreement should run for ten years and that there should be a mutual interchange of shares between the two concerns, the shares thus exchanged to represent a value of 20 million marks (equivalent to 25 per cent of the joint-stock capital of the Hamburg-American Line). Mutual participation was also provided for in the event of further increase in the capital of either company. Ballin was to hold for life the voting rights of the Hamburg shares, and Morgan the rights of the American shares on the same terms. The Hamburg company was to have the option of paying the equivalent of its shares in steamers. Ballin did not believe that, considering German public opinion and the wishes of the Imperial Government, he should recommend an interchange of shares exceeding the amount agreed upon. The Morgan group agreed not to call at any German ports, and the Hamburg company agreed not to run any services to such European ports as were served by the other party. A pool agreement covering the cabin business was also made; the steerage and cargo business was to operate on existing understandings until they expired, after which other arrangements should be made. "For my own part," Ballin said in his notes,[3] "I declared that I could only regard the practical execution of these proposals as possible if they receive the unequivocal assent of the Kaiser and of the Imperial Chancellor."

Ballin undertook to make similar arrangements with the North German Lloyd Co. But negotiations proved to be very difficult, for the director general of that company did not share Ballin's views with respect to the danger to German shipping in the American combination. The Lloyd

[2] *Ibid.*, pp. 50–51.

[3] *Ibid.*, p. 52.

company subsequently altered its opinion, and in later discussions in London the president took part. He still feared, however, that the proposed understanding would endanger the independence of the German lines. He insisted upon the omission of the clauses dealing with financial participation but otherwise agreed to the proposals.

The mutual exchange of shares was thereupon dropped in the final draft of the agreement and was replaced by a provision for mutual participation in the distribution of profits. The Morgan concern guaranteed to the German lines a dividend of 6 per cent, claiming only a share in profits beyond that amount.

Concerning the New York meetings held for the signing of final papers, there is an interesting entry in Ballin's diary: [4]

". . . I took up the position that the combine would only be able to make the utmost possible use of its power if we succeeded in securing control of the Cunard and Holland American lines. I was glad to find that Mr. Morgan shared my view. He authorized me to negotiate on his behalf with Director Van den Toorn, the representative of the Holland American Line, and after a series of meetings a preliminary agreement was reached giving Morgan the option of purchasing 51 per cent. of the shares of the Holland American Line. Morgan undertook to negotiate with the Cunard Line through the intermediary of some British friends. It has been settled that, if the control of the two companies in question is secured to the combine, one half of it should be exercised by the American group, and the other half should be divided between the Lloyd and ourselves. This arrangement will assure the German lines of a far-reaching influence on the future development of affairs."

In 1901 depression in the freight business set in, which seriously affected the prospects of transatlantic shipping companies. The effect was especially severe for the companies in the Morgan group, whose ships were largely cargo boats restricted to the North Atlantic route. Ballin wrote in his notes of this time: [5] "Experience now shows that we were doing the right thing when we entered into the alliance with the Trust. If we had not done this, the latter would doubtless have tried to invade the German market in order to keep its many idle ships going."

Pertinent quotations from the agreement of the Morgan and German interests as finally accepted are herewith given. But first note the comment of the directors and managers of the Hamburg-American Line in submitting the agreement to their stockholders: [6]

"On the one hand it was impossible for us to ignore the danger of this combination. On the other hand, in view of the unsatisfactory state of things created in particular by the mutual jealousy of the English lines, we could not fail to recognize the great value of a comprehensive working combination such as had been an object of vain endeavors for many years past.

"It was out of the question that we should entertain proposals which were calculated to affect, even indirectly, in any form or shape the nationality and the independence of our company. . . . Protracted negotiations led to the conclusion of an agreement between the syndicate on the one side and our company and the North German Lloyd on the other—an agreement which we are convinced entirely corresponds to the objects in view."

Quotations from the agreement follow: [7]

"1. The syndicate undertakes not to acquire shares in the German companies, either directly or indirectly; in like manner the German companies undertake to abstain from the direct or indirect acquisition of shares in the syndicate.

"2. In order, nevertheless, to enable the contracting parties to have a direct interest

[4] *Ibid.*, p. 56.

[5] *Ibid.*, p. 62.

[6] *Annual Report of the Commissioner of Navigation*, U. S. Bureau of Navigation, 1902, p. 395.

[7] *Ibid.*, pp. 395–397.

in the returns of their business, the two German companies have undertaken to pay over annually to the syndicate a portion of their dividends which would correspond to the ownership of at least 20,000,000 marks in shares. This arrangement was made at a time when the capital of each of the two companies in shares amounted to 80,000,000 marks. In the event of an increase in the capital such as has, in fact, since taken place (increased to 100,000,000 marks), the syndicate has the right to raise the amount on which its quota of the dividend is reckoned to 25 per cent of the share capital. Per contra, the syndicate undertakes to pay the two German companies from its own funds an interest of 6 per cent upon the same amount—that is to say, upon at least 20,000,000 marks.

"3. In order to secure the advantageous cooperation of the two parties it has been decided to establish a committee which shall see that the agreement is faithfully carried out . . . [which] shall consist of two representatives of the syndicate and two representatives of the German companies.

"4. The combination is intended to represent a defensive and offensive alliance. . . .

. . . .

"6. The syndicate undertakes not to send any of its vessels to a German port without the consent of the two German companies. On the other hand, the German companies undertake to observe certain restrictions in respect to their traffic with British ports. . . .

. . . .

"9. The North Atlantic saloon passenger traffic of both parties will be regulated by a separate agreement with the object of arranging a pool for this branch of the business. The pool arrangements regarding third-class passengers which have been carried out for more than ten years between the companies concerned will remain in force.

"10. Similar arrangements with reference to freights are not for the present contemplated beyond existing agreements. . . .

. . . .

"13. The agreement is concluded for a period of twenty years. . . ."

5. The Morgan Trust and British Interests

The negotiations with the British interests took an entirely different turn from the arrangements with the German shipowners. The American and German interests provided for the pooling of traffic and the delimitation of spheres of activity as a protection against destructive competition; the American and the British negotiations led to actual combination of ownership.

The first purchase provided for was that of the Leyland Line. The Leyland Line had a fleet of 65 steamers of 321,244 gross tons and two newly acquired subsidiaries, namely, the West India & Pacific Steamship Co. and the Wilson & Furness-Leyland Line. Mr. Ellerman was its head and its heaviest owner. J. P. Morgan & Co. and J. S. Morgan & Co. secured from Ellerman an agreement to sell control of this line through the sale of the majority of its common shares.

Quotations from the speech of the chairman in presenting the proposition to shareholders in May, 1901, are significant as to both this particular purchase and the situation in general.[8]

"That being the position with regard to this matter, you will be surprised to learn, as the circular issued by the company conveyed to you, that . . . the terms and conditions of this contingent sale were not settled by the board, but are the result of negotiations between, on the one hand Mr. Ellerman and on the other Messrs Morgan's representatives and those who are associated with them. The latter included the most experienced and eminent persons well known in the shipping world and actively engaged in the Atlantic trade, and most competent to deal with a matter of this kind in which, moreover, they had a great money stake. . . .

". . . Now, last year the profits of this company amounted to upwards of twenty-five times the sum necessary for the service of the debenture interest. Of course, last year

[8] *Ibid.*, 1901, pp. 315–321.

was an abnormal year, and it is not to be taken—at least I think it ought not to be taken—as a test of the ordinary earning powers of this company. But, taking an ordinary year, the service of the debenture interest is covered anywhere between ten and fifteen times over. Therefore, I think I am justified in saying we may put the debenture holders out of the case.

"As regards the ordinary shareholders, whether this offer of £14 10s. per share is a good offer or a bad one depends upon the view you take of this question—whether you think the great profits of the last year or two are likely to be maintained. I saw it stated somewhere that upon the basis of last year's profits £14 10s. was an inadequate offer for these ordinary shares. (Hear, hear.) Well, I agree—I entirely agree—and if any person could guarantee the continuance of the great profits which were earned last year of course £14 10s. would be an insufficient sum. I will give you my opinion for what it is worth, and I do not ask you to accept it unless you agree with it. Speaking only for myself, I think that that man would be a very rash person who capitalized the value of his shares upon the results of a single year's trading (hear, hear) and that particular year one which, owing to exceptional circumstances, was a record year in a trade invariably subject to many vicissitudes. Still, take one year with another—although I do not for one moment believe that the remarkable figures of last year are likely to be repeated in the near future—and, given the conditions of fair competition, I have no reason to doubt that this company will always earn a fair and probably a good return upon the capital invested in it.

"But we must look at this matter all round, and I am bound to tell you that there are two factors in regard to the shipping trade which, while on the one hand it would be quite possible to exaggerate their importance and take too serious a view of their importance, it would on the other hand be exceedingly foolish to ignore and not give due consideration to. You may accept this offer or you may decline it, as seems best to you in your wisdom, but of one thing be sure—American capital is coming into the Atlantic trade, and is coming into the Atlantic trade to stay. The Atlantic trade is a peculiar trade in this respect, that it is almost entirely an east-bound trade. Your vessels going out to the United States take practically nothing. They do not pay their way, or anything like it. The profit is wholly made upon the return cargo. Now, an east-bound trade means the carriage of produce from the United States to Great Britain and the Continent. Well, the relations of Messrs. Morgan to the great railway systems of the United States are known to everybody, and you can judge for yourselves, without my enlarging upon the matter, whether Messrs. Morgan and their friends coming into the Atlantic trade would or would not come into that trade under very favorable conditions so far as they were concerned and very unfavorable conditions as far as many of their competitors were concerned. That is one factor that you have to take into account—I will not say the probability, but the moral certainty, of further powerful competition in the Atlantic trade. The other factor that you have to reckon with is the large subsidies to American shipping contemplated by the American Government. These subsidies have not yet been voted, but the project has assumed a very tangible form, and there does not seem much reason to doubt that before long it will pass from the region of a project and become law. I will only say this with regard to it: That the near prospect of heavy Government subventions to our competitors must add one further element of precariousness to that trade. It comes to this: The ordinary shareholder has to ask himself this question, 'Is it better that I should sell out my shares to Messrs. Morgan at a very handsome profit or shall I continue in the company as it is and take the risks of increased competition in the Atlantic trade?' Of course there is another view which I can quite imagine some of the ordinary shareholders taking, and I do not in the least wish to combat that view. Some ordinary shareholder may say, 'Yes, I recognize that it is a very good thing that Messrs. Morgan, with their powerful connections, are taking this large interest in our company. The company has been prosperous in the past, and with this influential American backing, which may largely neutralize those dangers of increased competition to which you refer, its prosperity in the future may be still greater, and if it is worth Messrs. Morgan's while to offer me £14 10s. per share for my shares it is well worth my while to keep my shares. . .

"Now, with regard to the position of the preference shareholder. An ordinary shareholder in a shipping company is a speculator, or at any rate a speculative investor. In the case of Leylands, he has been a lucky speculator. On the other hand, a preference shareholder is an investor, and as an investor his interest is in the permanence and security of his fixed preferential charge of 5 per cent. Under the proposals before you it is not intended that his position shall be affected—at least not to his prejudice. If Messrs. Morgan acquire the ordinary stock of the company, they will of course have all the rights which they buy and pay for, and they will therefore be in a position to control the policy of the company. Of that there is no doubt; indeed, they have stipulated that if they desire to do so they shall, upon the completion of their purchase, nominate a majority of the board of directors. That is a perfectly reasonable request; but it means, of course, that on the one hand Mr. Ellerman's management of the company, which has been so successful in the past, will come to an end, and on the other hand, speaking for myself, I do not think it is to be doubted that the control which Messrs. Morgan obtain will be exercised by them in a manner entirely in keeping with the worldwide reputation of that eminent firm. But although they will be the largest shareholders, they are only shareholders. They are buying shares—they are not buying the company. The company continues an English company under all the guarantees and protections of English law and of its memorandum and articles of association. If it should be desired at some future time to liquidate the company with a view to reconstruction or to transferring its assets to some other company, it will have to be liquidated in the English courts and under English law, and the rights both of the debenture holders and the preference shareholders to be paid off at a premium, or to participate in surplus assets, if any, given to them in the case of the debenture holders by their trust deed, and in the case of the preference shareholders by the memorandum of association will be respected. . . .

. . . .

"The outlook for freights for the near future is, in my judgment, an uncertain one. We have had prosperous times, and I feel that the near future may bring, at all events for a time, a reflex of bad times, particularly when the tonnage which is usually employed in the North Atlantic trade, but which is now employed in Government transport work, returns to normal employment, in addition to which a large amount of tonnage is building in America for employment in the Atlantic trade, and ordinary competition may be very difficult to face if it is accentuated by the fact that steamers built and owned abroad are being run alongside of your own in the same trade on a competitive basis, with the bulk of the cargo supplied by the country owning the steamer, and which steamers are heavily subsidized by the foreign country to enable them to compete with you on an unfair basis —in other words, that the competition would not be a fair one. It is idle to suppose that your Government would put any countervailing duty on foreign bottoms; that is opposed to the experience of the past, the Government preferring that the industry should be killed and the trade leave the country rather than assist in any way.

"We are very much injured and restricted in our operations by the obsolete methods and rules of the Board of Trade and acts of Parliament passed years ago to meet the circumstances then existing and not modern conditions of trading, but which have never been repealed, and which are ludicrously inapplicable to the present conditions. . . .

"The labor question, especially in London, is growing to be a very serious one. This and other disadvantages will become gradually accentuated should the American Government subsidize American-owned steamers, as America supplies the bulk of the freight on the round voyage, as, owing to hostile tariffs, there is little trade left between this country and America."

On February 4, 1902, a provisional agreement was made for the purchase by a proposed American corporation, represented by J. P. Morgan & Co., of control of a number of other British and American interests. Portions of the agreement follow: [9]

[9] *Ibid.,* 1902, pp. 381–384.

"FIRST.

"1. The object and purpose of this agreement are the acquisition on or before December 31, 1902, of the maritime properties and business hereinafter described, by a corporation (hereinafter called the 'Corporation'), to be organized under the direction of the Vendors to the satisfaction of the Bankers, under the laws of the State of New York, or such other State as shall be selected by them, for and in consideration of the issue therefor to the Vendors or to their representative of the total capital stock of the Corporation, being $120,000,000, of which $60,000,000 shall be preferred stock, entitled and limited to cumulative dividends (in the same manner as the preferred stock of the United States Steel Corporation), at the rate of six per cent per annum, payable semiannually, and $60,000,000 common stock, limited to dividends of ten per cent per annum, so long as there shall be outstanding any of the debentures hereinafter mentioned, and also $50,000 000 of collateral trust debentures, bearing interest at the rate of four and one-half per cent per annum, payable semiannually, the principal to be payable in twenty years, with the right to the Corporation at any time after five years to redeem the same at 105.

"SECOND.

"The maritime properties and business to be acquired by the Corporation are the following:

"1a. Seven hundred and fifty (750) shares of one thousand pounds (£1,000) each, all fully paid up, of the Oceanic Steam Navigation Company (Limited), of No. 30 James street, in the city of Liverpool (hereinafter called the 'White Star Line'), including the new vessels building for said company, and including all rights in the name of White Star Line and in the flag of such line.

"1b. The business, good will, assets, and property of the firm or partnership of Ismay, Imrie & Co., as carried on by them in the cities of Liverpool, London, or elsewhere, including, so far as the White Star Vendors can sell and dispose thereof, the position of managers of the Oceanic Steam Navigation Company (Limited).

"But excluding therefrom all of the properties and rights mentioned in the special contracts or agreements collateral hereto between the White Star Vendors and the Bankers (identified by their signatures and marked respectively '1a' and '1b'), to which contracts reference is made for a statement of the terms, conditions, consideration, and extent of the transaction agreed upon in respect of such shares, business, good will, assets, and property.

"2a. All the shares of the British and North Atlantic Steam Navigation Company (Limited), (hereinafter called the 'Dominion Line'), including all shares of the Mississippi and Dominion Steamship Company (Limited), including all the new vessels building for said companies, and including all rights in the name of Dominion Line and in the flag of such line.

"2b. The business, assets, and good will of the partnership or firm of Richards, Mills & Co., as managers' agents, forwarding agents, master porters, or otherwise, in connection with the business of the British and North Atlantic Steam Navigation Company (Limited) and the Mississippi and Dominion Steamship Company (Limited), as carried on by them, whether in Great Britain or abroad, but excluding therefrom all of the properties and rights mentioned in the special contracts or agreements collateral hereto between the Dominion Vendors and the Bankers (identified by their signatures and marked respectively '2a' and '2b'), to which contracts reference is made for a statement of the terms, conditions, consideration, and extent of the transaction agreed upon in respect of such shares, business, assets, and good will.

"3. The capital stock, properties, and assets of the International Navigation Company (hereinafter called the 'American Line'), including the new vessels building for said company.

"4. The capital stock, properties, and assets of the Atlantic Transport Company of West Virginia (hereinafter called the 'Atlantic Transport Line'), including the new vessels building for said company.

"5. One hundred and eighteen thousand four hundred and sixty-three ordinary shares and 58,703 preference shares of the capital stock of Frederick Leyland & Co., 1900, Limited (hereinafter called the 'Leyland Line').

. . . .

"FOURTH.

"The relative valuations of the several properties for the purposes hereof are to be as follows:

"1a. The valuation of the shares of the White Star Line shall be a sum equal to ten times the net profits of the company for the year 1900, such profits to be taken as shown by the company's books, subject to the deductions and exceptions, and with the further conditions shown and stated in said agreement '1a' collateral hereto, with respect to the method of the ascertainment of the price and property of the White Star Line involved hereunder, it being expressly understood that all calculations necessary to arrive at the exact sum to be paid or to be accounted for by the White Star Vendors or by the Corporation, respectively, under any of the provisions of this agreement, are, if the parties shall be unable to agree thereon, to be made by Messrs. Price, Waterhouse & Co., of the city of London, chartered accountants, and each party shall accept their calculations and decision thereon as final and binding, and act accordingly, and pay one-half of their charges. [Similarly for Ismay, Imrie & Co., the Dominion Line, and Richards, Mills & Co.]

. . . .

"3–4. The aggregate valuation of the American Line and of the Atlantic Transport Line, including new tonnage, and as to the American Line, subject to $19,686,000 of the five per cent bonds of that line, shall be $34,158,000.

"5. The valuation of the said shares of the Leyland Line shall be $11,736,000, it being understood that there are or will be outstanding £815,000 five per cent preference shares and £500,000 four per cent debentures of the said line, not included hereunder.

"FIFTH.

"The price and the method of payment of the price for the said several properties to be conveyed to the Corporation shall be as follows:

"1a–1b. For the total valuation of the White Star Line, and the business of Ismay, Imrie & Co., determined as aforesaid (exclusive of new tonnage and except as otherwise provided in said collateral agreements), twenty-five per cent thereof in cash, seventy-five per cent thereof in preferred stock at par, and a sum equal to thirty-seven and one-half per cent thereof in common stock at par of the Corporation. [Same for Dominion Line and Richards, Mills & Co.]

. . . .

"3–4. For the total valuation of the American Line and the Atlantic Transport Line (exclusive of new tonnage and also exclusive of proper interest adjustment), $18,314,000 in the preferred stock at par and $9,157,000 in the common stock at par of the Corporation, and also, as and when required, $15,844,000 in cash for new tonnage and indebtedness, and such further cash as may be required for proper adjustment of interest at a rate not exceeding six per cent per annum.

"5. For the said ordinary shares and preference shares of the Leyland Line, $11,736,000 in cash, with a proper addition thereto for interest at a rate not exceeding six per cent per annum.

"SIXTH.

"All of the remainder and residue of the preferred stock and the common stock of the Corporation, and also its said collateral trust bonds for $50,000,000, are to be retained by and are to belong to the Vendors, who, however, are to contribute to the Corporation, as working capital, $786,000 in preferred stock and $6,643,000 in common stock, and are to transfer to the syndicate (if and when formed by the Bankers) for $50,000,000 cash, and in full payment for its services, the said $50,000,000 debentures and $2,500,000 of preferred stock and $25,000,000 common stock of the Corporation.

"SEVENTH.

. . . .

"Second. The Bankers will use their best efforts to form a syndicate (in which the Vendors or any of them may be participants) upon the terms above stated, to purchase from the Vendors the said debentures and the said $25,000,000 of common stock and $2,500,000 of preferred stock of the Corporation for the sum of $50,000,000 in cash. The Bankers, however, shall not incur any pecuniary obligations hereunder except to the extent to which, as syndicate subscribers, they may become personally bound for a share of the obligation of the syndicate when completely formed.

"In case the Bankers shall not have formed such syndicate on or before April 30, 1902, this agreement and all obligations thereunder or collateral thereto shall cease and determine on the 30th day of April, 1902, but if notice under article first of this agreement be not given by the Bankers before that date, this agreement shall continue in full force and effect unless and until notice in writing shall have been given determining the same, by any party hereto, whereupon this agreement forthwith shall cease and determine."

Various subagreements elaborated in great detail the terms of the agreement and how they should be carried out. A letter of J. P. Morgan & Co. brought out one important point, namely, they wished to have it understood "that, in our judgment, it may be an essential condition to the completion of said contract that the majority of the shares of the new Corporation should at the outset be held in America." [10]

It is pertinent to note that a separate agreement was made on the same day with Pirrie's firm, Harland & Wolff, Limited, shipbuilders of Belfast. Portions of the agreement follow: [11]

"1. In consideration of the undertakings given by the Builders in clauses 2 and 3 of this agreement the Purchasers bind and oblige themselves to place or cause to be placed with the builders, on commission, terms as set forth in clause 4 of this agreement, all orders for new steamers or heavy repairs or alterations that require to be done at a shipyard in the United Kingdom of Great Britain and Ireland, including reboilering, reengining, and such like. Nothing herein contained, however, shall prevent the Purchasers from placing orders for new steamers, or heavy repairs, or alterations, reboilering, or reengining at shipyards in the United States.

"2. The Builders shall and do undertake to carry out all such orders to the full capacity of their shipyards and workshops, except as regards the Hamburg-Americanische Packetfahrt Actien Gesellschaft's contract provided for in the following clause:

"3. The Builders shall and do undertake not to build for any other shipowners than the parties hereto, provided orders from the Purchasers suffice to keep the said Builders' works fully and continuously employed, and in any case the Builders are not to accept orders from parties who are competitors of the Purchasers in any trade at the time carried on by them without first obtaining the Purchasers' consent; but this proviso is not to prevent the Builders accepting orders from the Hamburg-Americanische Packetfahrt Actien Gesellschaft.

"4. The commission terms on which the work shall be carried out are to be as follows: The cost to the Purchasers to be—

"(1) The cost as shown by the Builders' books, including wages, materials, direct expenses, and a due proportion of fixed expenses and establishment charges.

"(2) A commission on the whole as the Builders' profit, said commission in the case of new ships and their machinery to be reckoned at five per cent, on new boilers and on engines for other than new ships ten per cent, and on repairs, renewals, alterations, and ship work in connection with reboilering and reengining fifteen per cent."

One large British concern in the North Atlantic shipping business, the Cunard, was left out of the Morgan combination. In Ballin's opinion the inclusion of Cunard would have resulted in a community of interest which would have done away with needless competition and substituted mutual participation in the net profits of each line. Morgan wanted to include the Cunard. The following quotation, from an address of the president of the British Board of Trade, delivered on September 30, 1902, suggests why the British line did not join the combine: [12]

"I desire to avail myself of the opportunity which your kindness affords me to

[10] *Ibid.*, p. 384.
[11] *Ibid.*, p. 394.
[12] *Ibid.*, pp. 399–401.

make a statement with regard to a question connected with one of our most important industries—a question which for several months past has greatly exercised the public mind and has raised grave apprehensions even in the minds of those who are not given to view our industrial position in any spirit of unnecessary and exaggerated alarm. I refer to the formation of what is known as the Atlantic Shipping Combine, or, as I believe it ought properly to be called, the Anglo-American Shipping Combination. Englishmen are naturally jealous of everything that affects the British mercantile position and the interests of the British mercantile marine. It is to our mercantile marine that we owe the erection of that great Empire of which the ocean is the highway, and without which that Empire could hardly continue to exist. It is not from the present year only that the transference of a considerable portion of our shipping in the Atlantic to American financial control dates. It began before this year. Before the formation of the Atlantic shipping combination the fleets of several of our great shipping companies had passed, not indeed away from the British flag—for the vessels of these companies continued to retain their British nationality—but into American ownership. This transfer had already excited considerable attention and caused some uneasiness, but that uneasiness was greatly accentuated after it had become known that two other companies, including the famous White Star Line, with its magnificent fleet, containing some of the finest ocean liners afloat, had gone the same way as the companies to which I have referred. But when these companies had passed under the control of a single corporation domiciled in another country, and when this combination had also been joined by the two great German lines, the Hamburg-American Line and the North-German Lloyd, feeling in this country was still further excited.

"Afterwards it became known that the terms on which the German companies had joined the combination were different from those on which the British companies had joined the combination; for it appeared that while the British companies had been practically absorbed into the American combination, the German companies, on the other hand, preserved their identity, preserved their power of individual development, and had, in fact, entered really as an equal power into the alliance with the American combination, as an alliance which, after a certain period of years might be brought to an end by either party to it. It was not surprising that these arrangements when they became known should have produced a deep impression upon the British public; and it was not unnatural that the British public should look to the Government and should expect the Government to take some action in the matter. (Hear! Hear!) This question, moreover, had a naval aspect as well as a commercial aspect. The White Star Line contained some of the finest cruisers at the disposal of the Admiralty. An agreement, indeed, existed between the White Star Line and the Admiralty, which, for a few years longer, placed its vessels at the disposal of the Admiralty. But we had no guaranty whatever that when that agreement came to an end these vessels, or any others that might be built, would be still at the disposal of the Admiralty, or even that they would continue to fly the British flag.

"What aggravated the position was that the great German lines which had entered into partnership with the combination possessed three vessels, and were building a fourth vessel, of a speed higher than any which was at the disposal of our own Admiralty, to serve as merchant cruisers. Now, let me make for a few minutes a digression. The acquisition by the German companies of these vessels of 23½ knots has often been made as a reproach to the enterprise of our own shipping community, which had no vessel of the same class to set in comparison with them. I think that injustice is done there to our great shipping companies. The plain fact of the matter is that vessels of that high speed can not be run so as to be commercially remunerative, except when aided by a heavy subsidy from the state. The White Star Line or the Cunard Line could undoubtedly have built and run such vessels if they had thought it commercially to their advantage to do so. If they have not done so it was because they did not think it commercially advantageous that such vessels should be constructed and run on such terms as existed. But if it is desirable that we should possess such vessels, that we should have such vessels at the disposal of the Admiralty, that such vessels should be attached to the British navy for possible services in time of war, I think you will see that from the naval point of view also a possible monopoly of the entire Atlantic trade by a foreign corporation was a serious matter, which it was necessary to take seriously into account. That, my lords and gentlemen, was the situation with which the Government has had to deal. It will be for the country to judge whether it has dealt with it successfully.

"But what we have done is this: We opened negotiations both with Lord Inverclyde, the chairman of the Cunard Company, and with Mr. Pierpont Morgan, as representing the Atlantic Shipping Combination; and it is the barest justice to say of both these gentlemen that they have shown the utmost readiness to meet the wishes of the Government. (Hear! Hear!) We have been able to enter into an agreement both with Lord Inverclyde and also with Mr. Pierpont Morgan the general effect of which I shall be in a position to state to you now. (Cheers.) I ought to add that of course the agreement made with Lord Inverclyde will have to be submitted to the shareholders of the Cunard Company; but I do not anticipate that their assent to the agreement is likely to be withheld.

"The Cunard Company have pledged themselves to remain in every respect a British company (much cheering), managed by British directors, with the shares not to be transferred to anybody but British subjects. (Renewed cheers.) Their ships are to be officered by British officers. (Cheers.) They also engage to construct two vessels of 24 to 25 knots (cheers); that is to say, vessels a knot faster than any other in the fleet. These two vessels, as well as the entire Cunard fleet, will remain at the disposal of the Admiralty (cheers), the Admiralty being at liberty to charter or purchase any of them at any time on terms fixed in the agreement. I have already explained that the construction and running of these vessels can not be effected on commercial principles. But in order to reduce the expenditure as far as possible the agreement provides that the capital necessary for the construction of these vessels should be advanced by the Government to the Cunard Company, of course, on proper security and on proper conditions of repayment. (Cheers.) The Cunard Company is also to receive from the Government a subsidy in lieu of the present Admiralty subvention, amounting to £150,000 a year. This sum may, perhaps, appear at first sight a somewhat large one; but I can assure you that the point has been most carefully considered, and that we have come to the conclusion that this sum is not more than a fair remuneration for the services to be rendered. To the principle of paying a subsidy in excess of the remuneration fairly due to the services rendered by any shipping company the Government are perfectly opposed. Such subsidy we regard as merely bounty in disguise, and to the principle of giving bounties we are resolutely opposed.

"Now I come to the agreement made with the Atlantic Shipping Combination. I have already indicated that it is not unnatural that the public should see in the Atlantic shipping combine a design of injuring British shipping and British commerce. I say that such a conclusion, having regard to all the circumstances, was not an unnatural one for the public to form; but, while I say that, I feel bound to utter an expression of my firm conviction that no such design ever entered into the mind of Mr. Pierpont Morgan. He is a great believer in the principle of large trusts. He may be right or he may be wrong—on that I express no opinion whatever; but he is a great believer in the principle of trusts, and he also considers that the conditions of the Atlantic shipping trade were such as to make that principle peculiarly applicable, and owing to the American position he consented to that combination. But I am quite certain that he had no intention whatever of injuring the shipping or the commerce of this country. And the proof is the readiness with which he has met the Government on all these points in which the British interests might seem to be most endangered by the fact that this shipping combination had been called into existence.

"Well, we have made an agreement with Mr. Morgan, and the general effect of that agreement is to secure that the British companies in the combination shall remain British, not merely nominally, but in reality. (Cheers.) These companies shall be kept alive, and the majority of their directors shall always be British subjects. The agreement further provides that every ship now flying the British flag, and half the ships hereafter to be built for the combination, shall continue to be British ships and shall continue to fly the British flag—that they shall be officered by British officers, and manned in reasonable proportion by British crews. In other words, these British companies are to remain to all intents and purposes British companies, while the British Government on its side undertakes that they shall continue to be treated as heretofore on a footing of equality with other British companies in respect of any services, whether postal or military or naval, which His Majesty's Government may require from the British mercantile marine. As regards future construction, the combination has undertaken that at least half the tonnage hereafter built for the combination shall be built for the British companies, and shall continue to fly the British flag and be in all respects British vessels; and a provision has further been added enabling His Majesty's Government in an event, which I trust will not be realized, of the combination's pursuing a policy hostile to the British mercantile marine, or hostile to British trade, to terminate the agreement into which they have entered. (Cheers.) I ought to say that both the agreement with the Cunard Company and the agreement with Mr. Morgan are for a period of twenty years. In the case of the Atlantic shipping combine this period of twenty years is to be prolonged with a notice of five years on either side.

". . . In particular it would be most unreasonable to expect that our cousins on the other side of the Atlantic should not claim a fair and due share of the Atlantic trade. I would only ask you to consider the direction and volume of the trade. The goods America sends to this country are in point of value three to one. We are sending to America, if measured not in value but in bulk, something more than that figure. In these circumstances it is impossible that we should expect that the Americans should be permanently content to remain without a considerable share in the Atlantic trade, nor is it, in my opinion, desirable that they should remain without a considerable share in that trade. . . ."

Pirrie, testifying before the subsidy committee of the House of Commons, pointed to another element in the situation which probably influenced English shipping concerns in joining Morgan's trust: [13]

". . . A dangerous international situation was, I am convinced, rapidly approaching, but by the establishment of this community of interests I feel the future of British shipping—which of course also includes our shipbuilding industry—is assured, or at any rate, that these two great national industries will be in a much more secure position than they were before. What we have in effect been doing is to act on the excellent advice given by the Prince of Wales in his speech on his return from his great tour around the Empire, when he uttered the memorable warning, 'England must wake up.' We have seized the opportunity of making a friendly and profitable arrangement for all our interests, both commercial, national, and even political, as nothing can do so much to promote good relations between the two great Anglo-Saxon communities as the community of business interests."

6. Organization of the I. M. M.

The I. M. M. formally came into existence on October 1, 1902. The basic unit in the combination was the International Navigation Co., a New Jersey corporation chartered in 1893. The International had a long history of successful operation through its predecessor, the old Inman Line. It was popularly known as the American Line, and it had won favor for its fine passenger ships. Though it was an American corporation and had the American-European mail contracts, it had only a few ships under American registry. It had one subsidiary, the Red Star, a Belgian line doing business principally with Antwerp. The head of the I. N. Co. was Clement A. Griscom. An amendment to the charter of this company provided for the establishment of the I. M. M.

The financial arrangements which Morgan made in establishing the I. M. M. had a profound effect on its later history.

[13] *Ibid.*, p. 403.

Bonds were authorized as follows: (1) $20,000,000 of 5 per cent first-mortgage gold bonds inherited from the old International Navigation Co. (secured by a first mortgage on the American and Red Star lines); and (2) $75,000,000 in 4½ per cent mortgage and collateral trust gold bonds of the I. M. M. (secured by its properties not subject to the mortgage of the International Navigation Co. and the deposit, with the New York Security and Trust Co., of stock representing the ownership of subsidiaries)—only $50,000,000 of those bonds were issued. The I. M. M. had an authorized capital of $120,000,000, half common and half preferred, at $100 a share.

As stipulated in the agreements with the English and American concerns given above, Morgan's had the management of the floating of the new securities, which he did through a syndicate. But the sale was accomplished with difficulty. By the end of 1903 the common stock outstanding totaled 499,330 shares, and preferred 523,661 shares, and all the $20,000,000 International Navigation Co. bonds were disposed of. Not until 1906, however, did the syndicate complete the sale of the securities of the I. M. M. The Morgan syndicate furnished the new corporation with $50,000,000 in cash. The initial distribution of the securities of the Company and of the cash received from the syndicate is indicated in Table 1.[14]

[14] *Ibid.*, p. 380.

According to the first annual report of the I. M. M., the balance given in Table 1 was used for the following purposes: $11,000,000 for 25 per cent of the purchase of the White and Dominion lines and their associates, Ismay, Imrie & Co. and Richards, Mills & Co.; $652,429 for expenses, such as counsel fees, transfer entries, and so on; and the balance of the cash "for new tonnage previously contracted for, and other additional properties necessary for the business of the Corporation." While cash was thus used for the payment of 25 per cent of the purchase price of the White and Dominion lines, and their associates, the remainder of the purchase price was paid in stock, that is, preferred to the amount of 75 per cent of the purchase price and common equaling 27.5 per cent of the price.

Thus by purchase the I. M. M. gained control of lines operating principally between Antwerp and British ports on one side of the Atlantic and ports from Montreal to Galveston on the other side. The assets represented by its capital structure consisted of complete ownership in the White Star Line, the Atlantic Transport Line, and the Dominion Line, and part ownership in the Leyland. Ownership in the Leyland Line stock in 1903 was as follows: 118,463 out of a total of 120,000 common shares, and 58,703 out of a total of 141,500 preferred shares. An interest in other lines was held in subsidiary

Table 1. INITIAL DISPOSITION OF SECURITIES AND CASH OF I. M. M.

	Cash	Bonds	Preferred	Common	Total cash and stock distributed
J. P. Morgan & Co.	...	$50,000,000	$ 2,500,000	$25,000,000	$27,500,000
International and Atlantic Transport	$15,844,000	...	18,314,000	9,157,000	43,315,000
Leyland Line	11,736,000	...	...	...	11,736,000
Working capital	...	...	786,000	6,643,000	7,429,000
Balance	22,420,000	...	38,400,000	19,200,000	80,020,000
Total	$50,000,000	$50,000,000	$60,000,000	$60,000,000	$170,000,000

treasuries, that is, in Holland-American by White Star and Atlantic Transport and the National Line, owned also by Atlantic Transport. The Red Star, as noted above, and the American Line were owned by the International Navigation Co. before it became the I. M. M.

The aggregate average earnings of these subsidiary companies, as shown by their books, for the five years immediately preceding 1903 were $6,519,071—this average does not allow any deduction for depreciation of steamship properties. The aggregate capitalization of the individual lines was $29,000,000 as against the capitalization of the I. M. M. of $175,591,000.[15]

To ensure proper management Morgan virtually got control of the I. M. M. into his own hands. A voting trust was provided to hold the great majority of both common and preferred stock, voting trust certificates being issued share for share in lieu of the stock itself. The voting trustees were Pirrie and Ismay, representing British interests, J. P. Morgan and his partner Charles Steele, and P. A. B. Widener, representing Atlantic Transport and other American interests. The rights of these trustees were to last five years, the question of extension resting with the holders of the voting trust certificates—in 1907 and 1912 the voting trust was extended for five years.

It may be significant to list the original board of directors with their other interests, to give an indication of where the final control of the Company actually fell. The list is as follows: [16]

C. E. Dawkins	Partner in J. S. Morgan & Co., London
G. W. Perkins	Partner in J. P. Morgan & Co., New York
C. Steele	Partner in J. P. Morgan & Co., New York
J. H. Hyde	President, Equitable Life and Vice -President, Equitable Trust Co.
J. J. Waterbury	President, Manhattan Trust Co.
B. N. Baker	American ship operator
C. A. Griscom	American ship operator
P. A. B. Widener	American capitalist interested in shipping
E. J. Berwind	American coal and railroad operator
J. B. Ismay	British ship operator
W. J. Pirrie	President, Harland & Wolff, Belfast shipbuilders
C. F. Torrey	British ship operator
H. Wilding	British ship operator

[15] *Wall Street Journal,* Sept. 7, 1915.

[16] *First Annual Report* of the I. M. M.; information concerning other interests obtained from *Who's Who* and *Who's Who in America.*

7. Operation of the I. M. M., 1902–14

I. M. M. almost immediately ran into two serious problems. One of those was internal and the other was external. Some idea of the problem of management is given by Ballin. Shortly after the I. M. M. had begun to operate, the head of the Hamburg-American Line visited America. In his discussions with Morgan he severely criticized the management of the I. M. M. and strongly advocated a change. "Morgan," he writes, "finds it impossible to get the right men to take their places, and he held out to me the most alluring prospects if I myself should feel inclined to go to New York as president of the Trust, even if only for a year or two; but I refused his offer, chiefly on account of my relations with the Kaiser." [17] Though Ballin would not take the place, a change was made. Clement A. Griscom, one of the most important figures in American shipping, was changed from president to chairman of the board, and J. Bruce Ismay, of the White Star, became president and active head of the I. M. M. This change of officers was criticized in America; it seemed that the English shipping men thereby regained control of their

[17] Huldermann, *op. cit.*, p. 63.

own property, which they had sold for American cash, and in addition gained control of the American lines.

The most absorbing problem was that of competition. The I. M. M. followed two lines of effort in strengthening its position: it tried to build up its services and it tried to meet competition in rates.

The I. M. M. attempted to develop new routes and to build a better grade of service. Immediately, however, it ran into dangerous rivalry on the part of the Cunard Line. Subsidized by the British government, Cunard's started a heavy building program. Both the *Lusitania* and *Mauretania* were so notably superior to other ships in the transatlantic service as to draw a tremendous amount of traffic. Even the United States Post Office was forced to alter its subsidy contract with the American Line of the I. M. M. to give those rival ships European mail because rapid delivery was of paramount importance to American business. In 1908 the I. M. M. authorized a new issue of £2,500,000 in 4½ per cent debentures of the White Star in order to provide for payment for new tonnage.

Two unfortunate events marred the prestige of I. M. M. service. At the beginning of its operation, in 1903, the *St. Louis* was allowed to sail from Southampton with leaky boilers rather than to upset the schedule. This alone was enough to cause friction within the Company, but, when she arrived in New York late, there was loss in payment for reinsurance and in prestige.

Most serious was the loss of the *Titanic* in 1912. Struck by an iceberg on her maiden voyage from Southampton to New York this powerful and much-advertised White Star liner foundered, with a heavy loss of life. The utter lack of caution displayed by those in authority made the disaster especially serious for the prestige of I. M. M. Disturbed by the loss of traffic to the new Cunarders, President Ismay had ordered the captain of the *Titanic* to drive her to the limit on her first voyage. Ismay was a passenger on board, and, when the captain received warning by wireless of icefields ahead, he ordered the captain to proceed at full speed. Hours later, an iceberg tore a hole in the side of the boat from bow to stern. The fact that Ismay left the sinking ship in the last life boat, when there were still many passengers on the ship, and the fact that the *Titanic* carried inadequate rescue equipment helped to strengthen criticism of the I. M. M.

After the investigation of the catastrophe, Ismay resigned. He was succeeded by Harold Sanderson, who had been active in White Star management for some time. It is said of him that he "was one of the most popular and universally loved men connected with the shipping industry, which was of the greatest service in tiding the White Star Line over a difficult period." [18]

At no time in the earlier years of this period did the I. M. M.–Hamburg-American–North German Lloyd combination succeed in establishing satisfactory agreements with other lines as to rates on the Atlantic. Cunard was able to challenge them on rates as well as service. After bitter rivalry, the Cunard joined the other North Atlantic lines in 1908 in the association known as the Atlantic Conference, which agreed on the division of the steerage traffic, the most important traffic from Europe to America at the time. I. M. M. and its subsidiaries were allowed 29.46 per cent of the westbound steerage traffic and 34.27 per cent of the eastbound. This agreement stipulated the proportion of the whole traffic which should go to each individual company and provided for a central organization to set rates so as to regulate traffic accordingly. The Conference had "fighting steamers"

[18] F. C. Bowen, *A Century of Atlantic Travel* (Boston, 1930), p. 310.

to compete ruthlessly with anyone who broke the agreement or any outsider who might attempt to compete with them.[19] A congressional investigation of shipping rings in 1914 [20] gives further information on agreements. According to this investigation the passenger traffic was completely controlled by a network of agreements. The first- and second-class passenger traffic was subject only to stipulations as to minimum rates; the steerage business, which was by far the most important in the passenger traffic, was covered by pool arrangements by which the rates of the individual lines were so manipulated, above an agreed minimum, as to control the distribution of the traffic according to agreed percentages.[21] The situation in the freight traffic was on the whole comparable with that in the passenger business.[22] The report of the investigation committee shows that relations with railroads were almost as much a matter of pool agreements of steamship lines as were rates on the ships. It is significant that, according to the report, no railroads entering New York offered concessions to ships.[23]

8. Reorganization

On Friday, September 25, 1914, the following statement was issued to the press:

"As the International Mercantile Marine Company has announced its intention to defer payment of interest due Oct. 1 on its mortgage and collateral trust 4½% gold bonds, dated Oct. 1, 1902, the holders of a large amount of the bonds have requested Otto T. Bannard, Andrew J. Miller, Sidney F. Tyler and Albert H. Wiggin to act as a committee to represent and protect their interest and that of other bondholders who may desire to co-operate with them. Mr. Bannard is chairman of the committee, and the New York Trust Co. has been named as depositary. A deposit agreement is being prepared which will shortly be executed and lodged with the depositary. Bondholders are requested to deposit their bonds with the trust company in negotiable form with the coupons due Oct. 1 and subsequently attached. The depositary will issue transfer certificates of deposits and in due course application to list these will be made to the New York Stock Exchange."

Other protective committees were immediately organized by the various security holders to safeguard their interests in case of a receivership of the Company. The bond-indentures provided for a six months' lapse in time after any deferred interest payment before default could be confirmed legally. Thus April 1, 1915, was awaited anxiously by all concerned. The voting trustees exercised their right to dissolve the voting trust on February 23, 1915. Preferred and common stockholders were then in a position directly to guard against any infringement of their equity during reorganization. Whether there was an equity remaining to the stockholders was very doubtful at that time.

Default became legal on April 1, 1915, when the Company had not met the interest payments due in October on its bonds. Federal Judge Hough then appointed P. A. S. Franklin as receiver for the American property of the I. M. M., with authority to conduct the business. Franklin had been a vice-president of the Company up to that time. The Chancery Court of New Jersey appointed C. G. Parker co-receiver to act in the courts of the State in which the I. M. M. was incorporated.

[19] U. S. House of Representatives, 1911, *Hearings on House Joint Resolution no. 72, providing for an Investigation of the so-called Shipping Trust*, pp. 61–84. *The Report of the Royal Commission on Shipping Rings*, 1909, vol. i, part iii, p. 137, stated that there was no rebate system in the transatlantic trade.

[20] U. S. House of Representatives, 1914, *Report on Steamship Agreements and Affiliations in the American Foreign and Domestic Trade*, vols. i-iv.

[21] *Ibid.*, vol. iv, pp. 21–34.

[22] *Ibid.*, pp. 53–71.

[23] *Ibid.*, pp. 241–271.

The receivership applied only to properties directly owned by the Company, such as the American Line and the Red Star Line. It in no way affected the subsidiary companies, such as the White Star Line, the Dominion Line, and the Atlantic Transport Line, all of which were controlled through stock-ownership.

It looked at first as if a quick reorganization would be effected. Early in April the *Wall Street Journal* said: [24]

"Reorganization of the International Mercantile Marine Co. promises not to be the long drawn-out process of financial reconstruction that such processes usually are. In fact, it is possible that a new mark will be set for a speedy and equitable financial readjustment among large industrial corporations. Mercantile Marine's is the largest receivership in the industrial group that has occurred in many years.

"Steps are already underway looking toward the formation of a definite plan of reorganization. Just what this prospective, though tentative, plan will provide cannot be stated at this time. Any final plan, however, it is said, is certain to provide for a very material scaling-down of the company's capitalization. . . .

"The committee of the 4½% collateral trust bondholders, known as the Bannard committee is in touch, by correspondence, with a committee of bondholders in Amsterdam, formed for the protection of the holders abroad of these 4½% collateral trusts. This Dutch committee represents holdings which amount to about $17,000,000. Dutch interests are reported as holding a considerable portion of the common and preferred stocks of the Mercantile Marine."

Trouble began almost immediately, however, when the committee formed in the interests of the preferred stockholders of the I. M. M. made the following announcement:

"It appears from the records of the Marine company that during March, 1915, it was in a position to pay all interest then in default upon its bonds, and that by order of its board of directors the Chairman of the Reorganization Committee, who is President of the New York Trust Company, the Trustee under the mortgage, was notified of this fact. Such a default cannot be made the basis for declaring the principal of the bonds due, and the Committee is advised that the pending foreclosure suit can be successfully defended; that the present receivership was unnecessary and that it could have been avoided by the board of directors of the Marine Company."

The preliminary report of Ernst & Ernst, accountants for the committee, was quoted to the effect that (1) earnings of the I. M. M., before depreciation and the payment of a new war tax but not including individual earnings of some smaller interests in subsidiaries, for the seven months ending July 31, 1915, were over $18,000,000; (2) default on interest was at no time necessary from a cash point of view; and (3) assets on the books of the Company were greatly undervalued. The statement then went on to say:

"The Committee does not intend to permit this valuable property to pass under the present reorganization plan which presents to the bondholders the entire property, with its present enormous earnings, except the insignificant portion of the equity left to the stock. The examination of the affairs of the Marine company is proceeding and arrangements are being made for the defence of the pending foreclosure suit."

On August 3, 1915, a plan for the reorganization of the I. M. M. was adopted by the committees representing the 5 per cent and the 4½ per cent bondholders. It was proposed to organize a new company which would acquire the ships owned by the I. M. M. and, either directly or indirectly, the stock pledged as security for the 5 per cent and 4½ per cent bonds. The proposed capitalization of the new company and the distribution of the new securities are given in Table 2, below.[25]

[24] Apr. 7, 1915.

[25] Taken from *Plan and Agreement of Reorganization,* dated Aug. 3, 1915, p. 7.

Protests from stockholders immediately became vigorous. At a minority stockholders' meeting held on August 18, many objections were raised, centering for the most part on the argument that receivership need never have been resorted to and should be discontinued at once.

Commenting on this view, a Dow, Jones & Co. *Bulletin,* for August 28, 1915, said:

"Irrespective of the merits of these contentions, the fact remains that early in 1914 the company was undoubtedly in a precarious situation, and current liabilities, loans, etc., exceeded current assets by about $4,000,000. Such liabilities could not be paid in property but must necessarily have been paid in cash. The company's building program was too extensive, requiring additional cash more rapidly than it could be realized out of earnings or assets and loans were held largely in England and could not be readily extended after the outbreak of the war. Earnings for 1914 about met interest requirements. The big improvement did not arrive until 1915. . . ."

The *Wall Street Journal,* on September 28, 1915, made an interesting editorial comment on the position of the I. M. M. in receivership. The question was asked why any reorganization was necessary in view of the successful operation during war years.

"But a very good reason for continuing the receivership until a satisfactory reorganization is effected lies in the company's own record from the time it was launched to the time of the default on bond interest last October. During this period, some eleven years, Mercantile Marine had an average annual deficit of about $290,000, while its depreciation account was eighteen to nineteen million dollars in all, under the standard of best steamship practice. The explanation for this showing is the company's heavy bond and stock capitalization.

"Just how excessive this capitalization was is apparent at a glance. The individual steamship lines which went into and made up the combine launched in 1902 as the International Mercantile Marine, had an aggregate capitalization of about $29,000,000. The new company was capitalized in stocks and bonds at $175,591,000, of which $73,992,545 was bonds, and $51,726,300 6% cumulative preferred stock. This total represented annual charges, including dividends on the cumulative preferred issue, of $6,351,908.

. . . .

"It would seem not only wise, therefore,

Table 2. PROPOSED CAPITALIZATION OF NEW COMPANY AND DISTRIBUTION OF SECURITIES

Outstanding securities of I. M. M., July 1, 1915		Cash assessment		5% Convertible bonds		6% Noncumulative preferred stock [b]		Common stock	
Security	Amount	%	Amount	%	Amount	%	Amount	%	Amount
4½% bonds, principal and accrued interest [a]	$55,552,412		. . .	50	$27,776,206	50	$27,776,206		.....
5% bonds, principal and accrued interest [a]	18,440,133		. . .	50	9,220,067	20	3,688,027	30	$ 5,532,040
Preferred stock	51,726,300	2½	$1,293,157	2½	1,293,157		. . .	20	10,345,260
Common stock	49,872,400	2½	1,246,810	2½	1,246,810		. . .	5	2,493,620
Total	$175,591,245		$2,539,967		$39,536,240		$31,464,233		$18,370,920

[a] Interest accrued, April 1, 1914–July 1, 1915.
[b] To share in dividends equally with common stock after dividends of 6 per cent on common.

but imperative, that the efforts at reorganization commenced some months ago, be continued until a plan which shall be mutually satisfactory to all security holders is devised and which, at the same time, shall make such substantial reductions in capitalization and charges as to insure to the stockholders a reasonable return on their investment in normal trade years. That the company has real earning capacity and an efficient management, cannot be questioned. . . ."

When it became clear that there would be some equity left to stockholders after the claims of bondholders were met, the protective committees for preferred and common stockholders began a battle for their own respective rights.[26] It was not until September, 1916, that a plan of reorganization was finally adopted. Briefly, the plan [27] provided that:

(1) 57 per cent of the outstanding bonds would be refunded through the issuance at once of $40,000,000 new 25-year 6 per cent sinking-fund gold bonds; an additional $10,000,000 being authorized for later issue;

(2) The balance of principal and interest of old bonds was to be paid off in cash (6 per cent gold notes for $10,000,000 being authorized to be used only if needed);

(3) There would be no assessment of stockholders;

(4) The question of payment of back dividends on the preferred stock was to be left to the discretion of a new board of directors; and

(5) The new board of directors would consist of 16 directors to serve a term of 3 years, one-third retiring each year.

Recognition of a past evil was made in drawing up the new bond indentures. A provision was inserted requiring that there should be a depreciation charge on the Company's ships at a minimum rate of 4 per cent per year. The bonds were to mature on October 1, 1941; but a redemption provision allowed for retirement at 110 on any interest date upon four weeks' notice.

The elimination of the two old issues of bonds of the I. M. M. left it with a funded debt of only $40,000,000 compared with $70,000,000 before the readjustment. Although the new issue carried a higher interest rate than the old, fixed charges against earnings were reduced materially.

Directors and officers were elected on October 19, 1916. Franklin's success as a receiver was rewarded by his election to the presidency of the new company. Sanderson became chairman of the remodeled board. The old interests were still represented by Pirrie, Sanderson, and Morgan partners. At least six members can be said to have represented common and preferred stockholders and bondholders. It is significant to note that the voting trust had been dissolved in December, 1914.[28]

With the election of the new board of directors and the new president, the reorganization of the I. M. M. was complete.[29] Since the active members of reorganization committees had been elected to the board, continuity of the good management under the receivership was assured. Furthermore, the abnormal profits of the war period were destined to continue for some time.

In November, 1916, the I. M. M. purchased a controlling interest in the New York Shipbuilding Co., which had a plant at Camden and large water-frontage on the Delaware River. This acquisition gave the Company first-class shipbuilding facilities in the United States.

First fruits of the reorganization were

[26] *New York Times,* Dec. 17, 1915, gives the points on which the two groups differed.

[27] *Plan and Agreement,* dated Aug. 1, 1916.

[28] *Annual Report of the I. M. M.,* 1914; *Who's Who* and *Who's Who in America* were consulted on directors.

[29] For further consideration of reorganization and its results see M. J. Fields, "The International Mercantile Marine Company—an Ill-Conceived Trust," *The Journal of Business,* vol. v (1932), pp. 362–379.

realized with the declaration of regular dividends on the preferred stock during 1917. The year 1916 had been exceptionally profitable, but in 1917 all the ships of the I. M. M.—except the few earlier requisitioned—were requisitioned for use by the United States and Great Britain. Several plans were proposed to liquidate back dividends on the stock. Early in November, 1917, a plan was almost put through providing for full cash liquidation; but reverses of the Allies in Europe added such uncertainty to the future of the Company that the idea was dropped. Another plan suggested market purchases of stock by the management, with a consequent reduction in the liability for back dividends. Still another method considered was to refund the issue at par with a slightly higher interest-bearing security. But the final decision provided for occasional cash dividends on account of back dividends. In this way, accumulations were reduced to 42 per cent by the end of 1920.

9. Americanization of the I. M. M.

Immediately after the War had ended, the I. M. M. began to rebuild its old services. Total loss to the Company from enemy action had been forty-three vessels of 409,967 tons gross register. These ships did not bring financial loss to the Company, since they were all covered by war-risk insurance; [30] but, for the most part, they had to be replaced if the old services were to be operated. Furthermore, a large part of the fleet had been used as transports for troops or as auxiliaries for the Allied navy. These ships all required more or less reconditioning to be fit for regular service.

The Red Star Line under the Belgian flag had been forced to cease operations entirely; and its services, especially to Antwerp, required a completely new organization. A few steamers were engaged in the New York–Antwerp run by the end of 1918.

At this time the I. M. M. began to try to dispose of its foreign holdings. In 1917 it sold most of its shares in Holland-America at a good price. In November, 1918, negotiations with a British syndicate were completed, which arranged for the sale to the syndicate of the British subsidiaries of the I. M. M. While details were being adjusted, the United States government sent word that the sale must not go through. A later communication said that under the circumstances the government was prepared to take over ownership of the vessels upon the terms of the British offer. In April, 1919, however, the United States advised the management of the I. M. M. that the government could not consider further the acquisition of the British tonnage, and the Company was free to proceed with the sale to the syndicate if it still seemed desirable. The board of directors then recommended to the stockholders acceptance of the earlier offer, which had been renewed. The terms of the sale were to be £27,000,000, payable in London. Before the stockholders' meeting, however, two directors organized a committee to oppose the sale. They considered the terms, which netted about $80 a ton for the ships involved, as unreasonable in view of the large earnings of the previous few months. The stockholders voted against the transaction. In December the United States Shipping Board made an offer to the I. M. M. for its British tonnage. The terms offered were about $100 a ton and were acceptable to the Company. President Wilson, however, refused to give his sanction to the offer; and it was withdrawn.

Certain minor changes were made in the holdings of the I. M. M. in the years immediately following the War. These several changes gave the Company prac-

[30] *Annual Report*, 1918, p. 4.

tically 100 per cent ownership and equity in all its subsidiaries.

In 1921 the I. M. M. began to experience a drop in earnings which continued for about five years. One obvious reason was the restriction of immigration by the United States government. Another was, of course, the worldwide decrease in traffic which came in the early 'twenties. Generally high costs tended to keep expenses high. One result of the drop in net earnings was the increase in unpaid cumulative dividends on preferred stock after 1920.

On June 17, 1926, stockholders of the I. M. M. granted authority to sell the entire holding of White Star Line shares owned by the Company to the Royal Mail Steam Navigation Co., Ltd., for £7,000,000. This was the first important step taken by the I. M. M. towards concentrating its shipping under the American flag, a policy determined on by the management about this time. On January 24, 1927, £2,000,000 was paid on account, the balance falling due at three successive dates, the last in 1936.

The Company's directors decided to use the proceeds for the purchase and retirement of bonds under the sinking fund provision as long as the price in the market made that an attractive policy. They left open, however, the possibility of using at a later date some of the proceeds to build or acquire other shipping properties or improve those already owned.

Because of the amount at which the White Star Line properties had been carried on the Company's books, the sale created a profit and loss deficit. A special meeting of stockholders was called for September 29, 1927, to consider a plan for readjustment of the capital structure of the Company and a radical write-down of remaining assets to more nearly representative levels. At the meeting a small minority of stockholders was able to obtain an injunction preventing the carrying-out of the plan proposed by the management. It was not until June, 1929, that the stockholders accepted a substitute plan. The new plan reduced the outstanding shares from 498,718 common and 517,250 preferred shares of $100 par value each to 600,000 shares of no par value shares. Both common and preferred stockholders received an interest in the new stock, the preferred stockholders also receiving $20 per share in lieu of their accumulated dividends. After the removal of the accumulated dividends and the deficit, the Company was in a position to declare a dividend on the new stock. This it did on February 15, 1930, the declaration being $1 per share.

On January 6, 1931, announcement was made that the I. M. M. had been merged with the Roosevelt Steamship Co. Four of the directors of the Roosevelt Co., namely, Kermit Roosevelt, Vincent Astor, Basil Harris, and John M. Franklin, were elected directors of the I. M. M.; and from February 1, 1931, the operations of the two companies were merged. The declared object of this consolidation was for the further development of services under the American flag.

In December, 1931, the I. M. M. concluded negotiations in conjunction with the Roosevelt Steamship Co. for the acquisition of an important interest in the capital stock of the United States Lines Co. This company, formed under the laws of Nevada, had taken over the steamships and other properties previously owned by the United States Lines, Inc., consisting of ships originally operated by the United States Shipping Board, including the *Leviathan,* and also steamers of the American Merchant Line. The terms of the acquisition, like those of the consolidation with the Roosevelt Co., were not made public.

On January 2, 1934, plans were announced for the purchase of control of the Munson Steamship Line by the I. M. M.

and the consolidation of their interests. By this merger the I. M. M. extended into the South American trade for the first time. It is understood that the Munson Line owed the United States Shipping Board large sums which it was unable to pay. The Shipping Board, presumably, forced the Munson Line to sell out to a liquid company, in order that it might receive payment on its debts. The arrangements would provide that the I. M. M. acquire a substantial majority of the common stock of the Munson Line and act as managers of all the Munson properties. It is significant that the Munson Line has very valuable mail contracts with the United States government, which require the use of American ships.[31]

The I. M. M. was, in the meantime, steadily going forward in its policy with regard to its foreign tonnage. Some was sold in 1933. In 1934 most of its interest in the Leyland Line was sold, and a few boats were transferred to American registry. By 1936, having sold the remainder of its Leyland and Red Star holdings, it owned and operated ships under the American flag only.

The depression years of the 'thirties made deep inroads on the I. M. M. Foreign holdings were sold at figures which were much lower than their valuation on the books of the I. M. M. At the end of 1931 the Royal Mail defaulted on a payment of £94,000 due on the White Star purchase. But, most important, the Company operated under heavy loss after 1930.

The year 1937 brought some important changes. A payment of $352,002 was received on the claims against the purchaser of White Star. In that year the I. M. M. ceased entirely to be an operating company. And in that year, while important foreign mail contracts were lost under a new federal law, important subsidy agreements were made with the government of the United States. These provided for subsidies on traffic with Hamburg, London, and Liverpool, and for a construction-differential subsidy on a new large ship which was to put the United States Lines Co., a subsidiary of the I. M. M., in a position to compete with the luxury lines of British and Continental companies. In July, 1937, it was announced that I. M. M. and Pan-American Airways had under consideration a plan for coöperative transatlantic travel arrangements. The *Annual Report* for the year shows a notable drop in losses from operation as compared with 1936.

10. Statistics from I. M. M. Reports, 1903–37

Comparative consolidated balance sheets and income statements are appended here. The balance sheets given are restricted to years of unusual financial adjustment. Thus, 1904 was the first year in which a consolidated balance sheet was published; 1913 was the last year before the war-time receivership; and the 1916 balance sheet was the first to give expression to the changes made. The last year in which the White Star Line appeared on the balance sheet of the Company was 1926. In 1927 the results of the sale of that line appear. Finally, 1929 and 1937 bring the record down to the recent past, including capital adjustments required by the sale of the White Star Line.

Operating statements are included for every three years since the formation of the Company and for unusual years intervening. These supplement the information given by the balance sheets during critical years and are of assistance in any study of minor shifts found in the intermediate years.

[31] The Shipping Act of 1928 provided for heavy subsidies for American ships.

INTERNATIONAL MERCANTILE MARINE COMPANY

Comparative Consolidated Balance Sheets

ASSETS

	1904	1913	1916	1926	1927	1929	1937
Current Assets							
Inventories	$ 792,813	$ 870,864	$ 1,025,991	$ 1,309,375	$ 438,272	$ 212,980	$ 29,365
Accounts Receivable	1,758,121	2,158,929	18,366,551	3,658,458	2,043,560	1,142,530	455,690
Other Receivables	2,361,597	626,466	447,268	3,388,692	1,159,325	2,314,164	106,474 [a]
Marketable Securities	598,742	572,494	17,907,363	18,886,504	14,841,123	4,705,177	489,981
Cash	830,835	2,541,577	5,607,025	7,971,527	5,041,472	2,413,990	562,968
Total Current Assets	$6,342,108	$6,770,330	$43,354,198	$35,214,556	$23,523,752	$10,788,841	$1,644,478
Deferred Charges to Profit and Loss	$1,721,800	$2,676,236	$2,707,537	$4,957,757	$2,174,567	$905,250	$574,635
Capital Assets							
Value of Properties before Depreciation [b]	171,036,213	192,422,310	180,506,008	238,734,322	82,912,312 [c]	34,520,520	26,583,807
Depreciation Reserve	...	22,973,160	37,977,136	70,046,634	35,447,899	7,446,977	10,294,880
Properties Net	$171,036,213	$169,449,150	$142,528,872	$168,687,688	$47,464,412	$27,073,542	$16,288,927
Goodwill, less White Star Goodwill	...	...	...	...	34,230,443	...	...
Investments in Other Companies	12,365,207	12,439,173	11,965,177	...	...	20,130,135	7,036,856 [d]
Exchange Memberships, Government Deposits, and Miscellaneous	595,461	2,878,001	3,732,618	6,662,806	1,667,957	451,955	890,944
Other Capital Assets [e]	...	...	...	537,500	23,017,500	18,697,500	14,733
Total Capital Assets	$183,996,881	$184,766,324	$158,226,667	$175,887,994	$106,380,312	$66,353,132	$24,231,460
Total Assets	$192,060,789	$194,212,890	$204,288,403	$216,060,308	$132,078,630	$78,047,222	$26,450,573

[a] Including $84,523 of receivables not current and cash on deposit in a closed bank.
[b] Cost or below beginning in 1927.
[c] White Star properties sold for $69,050,849.
[d] After a reserve of $750,000.
[e] In 1926, security deposited with mortgage trustee for investment in new tonnage. In 1927 and 1929, cash and receivables held by mortgage trustee and receivables from sale of White Star due on or before the end of 1936. Receivable from sale of White Star not included in 1937 because its value was uncertain.

INTERNATIONAL MERCANTILE MARINE COMPANY (*continued*)

Comparative Consolidated Balance Sheets (*continued*)

LIABILITIES

	1904	1913	1916	1926	1927	1929	1937
Current Liabilities							
Accounts Payable and Accruals	$ 4,834,402	$ 5,911,983	$13,975,046	$ 7,614,043	$4,184,688	$3,287,514	$1,330,318
Loans, Bills Payable, Foreign Bank O.D.'s	10,311,190	4,495,222	2,045,635	1,793,714	480,630	637,455	50,000
Purchase Money Oblig. Payable in a Year	...	...	...	...	...	650,100	650,100
Reserves, for Taxes, Insurance and Other Liabilities [f]	720,156	346,402	2,109,808	7,903,523	6,905,855	259,738	295,850
Total Current Liabilities	$15,865,748	$10,753,607	$18,130,489	$17,311,280	$11,571,173	$4,834,807	$2,326,268
Deferred Credits to Profit and Loss	$1,488,433	$2,483,539	$3,846,706	$9,931,321	$4,356,413	$1,868,018	$691,636
Funds, chiefly Insurance [g]	2,060,518	1,208,646	...	5,942,313	6,462,663	7,384,013	...
Contingent and Miscellaneous Reserves	...	...	5,285,423	13,950,805	7,628,045	3,033,678	400,000
Payable to Wholly Owned Subsidiaries, in Process of Liquidation	...	...	...	...	...	...	4,085,000

[f] In 1904 included reserve for repairs, in 1904–05 reserves for insurance claims and shares of Dominion Line outstanding; in 1926–27 the reserves were for U.S. and foreign taxes; in 1937 they included $100,000 for workmen compensation insurance in New York and a contingent reserve.

[g] For 1904 includes depreciation fund of $115,606.

Comparative Consolidated Balance Sheets (*continued*)

LIABILITIES (*continued*)

	1904	1913	1916	1926	1927	1929	1937
Capital Liabilities							
Preferred Stock [h]	$52,255,971	$51,730,971	$51,725,500	$51,725,000	$51,725,000	...	...
Common Stock [h]	49,932,735	49,931,735	49,872,000	49,871,800	49,871,800	$25,366,580	$26,329,798
Stock of Subsidiaries Outstanding	1,697	1,697	242	25,268	23,813	...	...
Bonds and Debentures							
5% Gold Bonds [i]	20,000,000	17,882,000	...	...	...	...	...
4½% Gold Bonds [i]	50,000,000	52,744,000	...	...	...	...	...
6% Gold Bonds [i]	...	...	39,497,000	35,526,000	24,130,000	19,133,000	11,493,000
Debentures of Subsidiaries Outstanding	1,247,938	5,802,055	10,879,714	4,718,565	...	...	...
Loans on Mortgages	745,496	405,643	365,156	2,051,300	1,720,000	1,620,000	1,160,000
Purchase Money Oblig. for Tonnage Payable over a Period of Years	...	...	...	7,859,589	3,945,589	9,690,600	4,489,800
Total Capital Liabilities	$174,183,837	$178,498,101	$152,339,612	$151,777,522	$131,416,202	$55,810,180	$43,472,598
Surplus	–$1,537,749 [j]	$1,268,997	$24,686,172	$17,147,069	–$29,355,865 [j]	$5,116,527	–$24,524,929 [j]
Total Liabilities	$192,060,789	$194,212,890	$204,288,403	$216,060,308	$132,078,632	$78,047,222	$26,450,573

[h] Less stock held in treasury.
[i] Less held in sinking fund or treasury.
[j] Minus sign indicates deficit. The deficit in 1927 came from the fact that the book value of properties and White Star was written off to the extent of $46,475,460.

INTERNATIONAL MERCANTILE MARINE COMPANY

Comparative Consolidated Income Accounts

1903–1937

	1903	1906	1909	1912	1915 [a]	1916
Gross Voyage Earnings	$29,677,756	$35,931,412	$33,461,485	$42,560,693	$51,056,579	$60,602,010
Miscellaneous Earnings	1,359,664	1,256,397	491,723	1,164,816	4,307,589	9,514,105
Surplus, Insurance Account	1,442,502	791,959	357,461	...	...	...
Gross Expenses,[b] Taxes, Interest on Loans	27,598,779	29,530,915	29,344,329	36,337,714	34,217,231	40,471,441
Interest on Bonds	3,083,346	3,420,099	3,692,121	3,599,883	3,805,910	3,698,023
Depreciation on Steamers	...	5,000,000	91,884	3,655,578	...	... [c]
Surplus Account	1,797,797	28,754	1,182,335	132,334	...	10,134,054
Dividends	...	...	...	...	...	...
Surplus Adjustments	...	...	...	–1,498,855	15,069	43,030 [d]
Balance Sheet Surplus	501,401	278,906	–1,297,355	953,396	14,548,128	24,686,172

[a] Since no operating statement was issued for 1915, the figures given were taken from the report for 1916.
[b] Leyland Line included only 1920–27; all but American lines excluded 1930–37.
[c] In 1916 the sum of $23,134,500 was appropriated to cover depreciation for 1914–16.
[d] Not including insurance fund, which was discontinued in 1915 and restored in 1917.

Comparative Consolidated Income Accounts (*continued*)

	1918	1920	1921	1924	1926	1927
Gross Voyage and Miscellaneous Earnings	$34,668,354	$125,807,453	$98,196,029	$78,054,931	$73,418,927	$35,252,190
Gross Expenses, Taxes, Interest on Loans	18,938,054	110,387,584	85,094,108	72,110,040	68,334,013	31,094,894
Interest on Bonds	2,789,763	2,637,690	2,623,262	2,575,965	2,450,051	1,751,635
Depreciation on Steamers	3,301,511	5,346,376	6,117,981	5,756,208	5,040,416	2,433,136
Surplus Account	9,639,026	7,435,802	4,260,678	−2,387,281	−2,405,553	−27,474
Dividends	5,689,805	5,689,805	3,103,515	...	...	...
Surplus Adjustment	355,919	−1,024,669	446,526	892,404	855,885	−45,955,107 [e]
Balance Sheet Surplus	30,561,058	30,556,973	31,714,136	22,039,440	17,147,069	−29,355,865

	1930	1933	1936	1937
Gross Voyage and Miscellaneous Earnings	$16,081,215	$12,336,536	$10,818,424	$11,174,439
Gross Expenses, Taxes, Interest on Loans	12,661,747	11,839,422	10,368,216	10,764,731
Interest on Bonds	1,095,048	835,420	702,470	689,580
Depreciation on Steamers	1,072,135	1,072,135	830,030	871,092
Surplus Account	1,252,285	−1,411,441	−2,261,974	−1,150,964
Dividends	1,197,936	...	...	...
Surplus Adjustment	444,568	−17,772,180 [f]	−2,092,335	1,148,529
Balance Sheet Surplus	5,170,876	−17,509,418	−23,376,396	−24,524,929

[e] Loss of $46,475,460 on excess of book value of White Star over price received minus $520,353 credit to insurance fund leaves deficit.

[f] Surplus reduced by loss for year, reduction of investments in foreign subsidiaries, and unpaid account on sale of White Star.

11. Suggested Readings

F. C. Bowen, *A Century of Atlantic Travel (1830–1930)* (Boston, 1930).

B. Huldermann, *Albert Ballin* (Translation, London, 1922).

E. N. Hurley, *The New Merchant Marine* (New York, 1920).

E. N. Hurley, *World Shipping Data* (Washington, 1919).

I. M. M. *Annual Reports,* all years.

12. Suggested Questions

1. Was Morgan a realist in founding the I. M. M. Co.?
2. Did Morgan pay an excessive price for the companies which went into the I. M. M. Co.? In view of earlier earnings of those companies, was the I. M. M. Co. overcapitalized? Explain the discrepancy in earnings of the subsidiary companies before and after the merger.
3. Did Morgan effectively control the I. M. M. Co. in 1903?
4. Outline the chief causes leading to receivership of the I. M. M. Co. in 1914. Were the causes corrected in the reorganization?
5. Was the Company justified in defaulting on its bonds in April, 1915?
6. Why has the I. M. M. Co. management changed its policy of development under foreign flags to one of developing its American fleet in the postwar period?

XXXV. ELBERT H. GARY AND THE UNITED STATES STEEL CORPORATION, 1901–1938

1. General Statement

The United States Steel Corporation stands as a striking example of the financial capitalist at work on the problems of industry. Here the principles of vertical and horizontal combination were applied as never before in American industry. At the head of the giant concern was placed, not an industrialist like Carnegie, but a lawyer who was close to the investment banker.

This case is a study in policy, not management. It is concerned almost wholly with the formation of the Corporation and its price and labor policies. The operation of the concern as an integrated producer of iron and steel is not included—management is a problem in itself, which would have to be considered before a well-rounded picture could be drawn of the history of the United States Steel Corporation.

2. Important Dates

1846	Gary born in Wheaton, Illinois, son of a farmer and local magistrate.
1865	Began to study law in uncle's office.
1866	Entered Union College of Law, Chicago.
1868	Graduated. Appointed deputy clerk of the Superior Court.
1871	Became partner in Chicago law firm.
1882–90	County judge.
1892	Helped John W. Gates form Consolidated Steel and Wire Co. of Illinois.
1898	Gary and Morgan formed Federal Steel Co. Gary became president.
1901	Gary and Morgan formed U. S Steel Corporation. Gary became chairman of executive committee.
1905–06	Gary began to get U. S. Steel on a firm footing.
1907	Opened as a boom year and closed with a panic. Purchase of the Tennessee Coal, Iron and Railroad Co.
1907–11	Period of the Gary Dinners.
1911–12	The Stanley Committee of the House of Representatives investigated and condemned the methods of U. S. Steel.
1912–19	Government's dissolution suit against U. S. Steel under Sherman Anti-Trust Act.
1915–19	War-time expansion.

1919–20 The Steel Strike.
1920 Supreme Court decided in favor of the Corporation on the monopoly charge.
1922–24 Gary led in abolishing 12-hour day.
1927 Death of Gary. Myron C. Taylor chairman of finance committee.
1928 Beginning of survey by U. S. Steel of its position in industry and its condition as a producer.
1929 $370,000,000 in bonds redeemed or retired, and over a million shares of common stock sold.
1932 Mr. Taylor chairman of board and chief executive officer.
1933 Beginning of modernizing of plants of U. S. Steel subsidiaries for production of light steels.
1938 Collective bargaining accepted. Mr. Taylor succeeded by Mr. Edward R. Stettinius, Jr.

3. Formation of the United States Steel Corporation

A. The United States Steel Corporation was incorporated in New Jersey, February 25, 1901, for the purpose of acquiring the following subsidiaries:

1. Federal Steel Co. Principal products were coke, pig iron, Bessemer steel ingots, open-hearth steel ingots, steel rails, and other finished steel products. Had large ore properties on the Mesaba Range, Minnesota. Depended on other manufacturers for a market for its semifinished products.

2. Carnegie Steel Co. Chief products were coke, pig iron, Bessemer steel ingots, open-hearth steel ingots, and steel rails. It was the largest owner of coal land in the Connellsville region and, through its control of the Oliver Iron Mining Co., it owned large iron ore deposits in Minnesota. It also controlled the Pittsburgh Steamship Co., which operated a fleet of steamships on the Great Lakes. Was dependent on other manufacturers for a market for semifinished products.

3. Lake Superior Consolidated Iron Mines. Operated iron mines on the Mesaba Range, Minnesota.

4. American Bridge Co. Its subsidiaries made about 90 per cent of the total bridge tonnage of the country.

5. National Tube Co. Controlled the principal tube concerns in the United States, about 90 per cent of total production.

6. American Steel and Wire Co. Produced wire, wire nails, rods, and fencing (including from 75 to 85 per cent of the rod and nail mills).

7. National Steel Co. Produced semifinished products, depending on other manufacturers for a market for them.

8. American Steel Hoop Co. Made steel bands, hoops, bars, as well as Bessemer mill and foundry irons. Had a large output of finished material.

9. American Sheet Steel Co. Main product was sheets. This company was virtually a counterpart of Tin Plate.

10. American Tin Plate Co. Its 265 mills made most of the tin plate produced in the United States.

The stocks and bonds of the various companies were acquired and exchanged for stocks and bonds in the new steel corporation. The capital stock of the new corporation was $1,100,000,000, as compared with $717,550,394, the total capitalization of the 10 companies taken in.

The American Steel and Wire Co., the National Tube Co., the American Bridge Co., the American Tin Plate Co., the American Sheet Steel Co., and the American Steel Hoop Co. were all dependent upon other concerns for a large proportion of their raw materials. However, the American Tin Plate and the American Sheet Steel companies, as well as the American Steel Hoop Co., were all affiliated with the National Steel Co. and therefore were certain of a supply of raw materials and semifinished products. They were known as the "Moore" concerns, all of them having been consolidated by W. H. Moore.[1]

[1] *Report of the Commissioner of Corporations on the Steel Industry,* 1911, pt. i, p. 101.

The Federal Steel, National Tube, and American Bridge companies made up what was called the Morgan group, while the American Steel and Wire Co. was in a somewhat independent position. The Carnegie concern, specializing in semifinished products and rails, was the largest of them all, yet it had no special connections with any finishing mills, as did the National and Federal Steel companies.[2] One outstanding steel man expressed the following judgment about the situation: [3]

"There was no question that if the Carnegie Company, with its unlimited means and efficient organization, went into the manufacture of wire, tubes, sheets, or tin plate it would be more than able to hold its own against the respective large consolidations which produced those products, and which in their efforts to monopolize the business had been constrained to include in their respective organizations many plants of inferior character."

B. Gary's testimony before the Stanley Committee in 1911 on the formation of U. S. Steel.[4]

"MR. YOUNG. Now, you will remember when we adjourned last night you were just starting to make a statement of the competition which existed between the different units of the United States Steel Corporation before they were consolidated into that company. . . .

"MR. GARY. The Carnegie Steel Co., the subsidiary companies of the Federal Steel Co., the American Steel Hoop Co., and the National Steel Co. were to some extent in competition. The four companies were not competitive with one another on all the lines of the production of the respective companies. . . .

"The American Wire & Steel Co., the National Tube Co., the American Tin Plate Co., the American Sheet Steel Co., the American Bridge Co., and the Lake Superior Consolidated Iron Mines were not in competition with one another or with the other companies. When we commenced business—

"MR. YOUNG (interposing). Before you go on with that, will you state what were the articles manufactured by these companies in the first group; what competing company did compete?

"MR. GARY. I stated that the other day about as fully as I can. I would say that the principal competition was between the Illinois Steel Co. and the Carnegie Co. in the sense of making the same articles or some of the same articles; they were substantially in competition. I do not wish to minimize that. That is true in the manufacture of rails particularly. So far as products are concerned, they were in substantial competition, and I would say that those were the principal articles.

"However, as you know, the freight rates from Pittsburgh to Chicago are quite large and I believe at that time were in the neighborhood of $3 per ton. The market of the Illinois Steel Co. was in the great and growing West largely. That is, they supplied largely the western railroads who had terminals in Chicago, and of course they did, to some extent, furnish rails to railroads which came from the East and had their terminals in Chicago, but the Carnegie Steel Co. in turn had a natural market which surrounded its plant—that is, the railroads having terminals in Pittsburgh—and when you consider the respective territory or fields of the two, there was not so much competition as it would appear, although it is the fact that the Carnegie Co. did in time come into the western field and into territories which were not controlled to the extent at that time at least of selling rails, I believe, as low as $16 a ton, at a time when the Illinois Steel Co. was considering going into the hands of a receiver and came very near it. It did not pay any dividends, so far as I know, and I believe it did not pay any dividends at all, up to 1899.

"MR. BARTLETT. Right there. When was the Federal Steel Co. formed?

"MR. GARY. In 1898.

"I believe, perhaps, if unrestricted and unchecked destructive competition had gone on the Illinois Steel Co. would undoubtedly have been driven out of business and, perhaps, I might say more. I do not say it with a view of casting any reflection upon anyone's management, but it is not at all certain that if

[2] *Ibid.*, p. 105.

[3] *Ibid.*, p. 104.

[4] *Hearings before the Committee on Investigation of United States Steel Corporation,* House of Representatives, vol. i, 1911, pp. 219–221, 205–210.

the old management or the management which was in force at one time had continued, the Carnegie Co. would not have driven entirely out of business every steel company in the United States. Perhaps you are sufficiently familiar with the facts to determine whether that is a justified statement, but certainly that is the opinion of a great many different people, notwithstanding conditions had improved after the Federal Steel Co. was formed and everyone was getting on a better basis and we had reached the point where we saw it was possible to organize a company which would be self-contained and which would, as I have said, secure a very large proportion of the export business.

. . . .

"MR. YOUNG. While these two companies, the Illinois Steel Co. and the Carnegie Steel Co., each had its field, is it not, nevertheless, true that if the Carnegie Steel Co. had reduced considerably its price for rails, for instance, that it would have necessitated a corresponding reduction on the part of the Illinois Steel Co. in its field?

"MR. GARY. Of course, that is true. If any manufacturer of any importance reduces the price of its commodity, others are compelled to reduce their prices. There is no doubt about that. . . . Mr. Schwab [then president of the Carnegie Co.], some time in 1900, spoke to me about the Federal Steel securing the Carnegie properties, and said he believed that Mr. Carnegie would sell those properties, and I promised to speak to Mr. Morgan about it. I knew it would require some very able financing, so I promised to speak to Mr. Morgan about it. I did speak to Mr. Morgan about it, but did not receive at that time any encouragement whatever. In fact, I do not think he paid enough attention to familiarize himself with the properties. He had been a member of the board of directors of the Federal Steel, but had never taken any active interest with reference to the management, as he never has with reference to the United States Steel Corporation, I might say. I did not report to Mr. Schwab I had talked with Mr. Morgan about it. He spoke to me again about it once or twice, but nothing whatever was done as a result. But along about that time Mr. Simmons, who was, I think, president of the clearing house and president of one of the leading trust companies or banks— . . . at the request of Mr. Frick, gave a dinner in New York, and invited Mr. Schwab, Mr. Morgan, and various other people to the dinner. Mr. Schwab made a little statement at that dinner concerning the steel business that made quite an impression on Mr. Morgan.

"MR. YOUNG. Do you remember what the nature of that statement was—what it related to?

"MR. GARY. It was concerning the great ability of the Carnegie Co. and concerning its cost of production, concerning its export business, which at that time, though small from the present standpoint, was considerable; and of course I have no doubt what Mr. Schwab had in mind was the idea of showing that it would be a great thing if the Federal Steel should see its way clear to acquiring the Carnegie Steel Co.

"MR. YOUNG. Did he say anything about the conditions of competition in the steel business at that time?

"MR. GARY. I was not there, and I do not know that he did. I am not sure about that. I doubt it. But the next thing I heard about it, one Sunday morning early, Mr. Robert Bacon came to my home.

"MR. YOUNG. What was that?

"MR. GARY. Mr. Robert Bacon, who was then a partner in the firm of J. P. Morgan & Co.—then a member of the firm—came to my home early Sunday morning, and said that the night before Mr. Schwab had surprised Mr. Morgan by bringing him a letter from Mr. Carnegie stating that he, Mr. Carnegie, would sell his properties and take his pay in bonds secured on the properties, as I remember. . . .

. . . .

"MR. YOUNG. Did he fix any price on them?

"MR. GARY. Yes; the price was fixed; the price afterwards paid in bonds. Mr. Bacon said Mr. Morgan requested him to come and see me early in the morning and present the whole question to me and get my opinion as to whether or not it was a practical business proposition. . . . I went into that subject very carefully with Mr. Bacon on that day. . . .

. . . .

"MR. GARY. . . . And it was then agreed between us that I should meet Mr. Morgan at his bank at 11 o'clock on Monday. I did meet him there, and he and I spent some time going over this matter, and I explained to him in detail the business reasons for entertaining this proposition, at least, and finally said to him, 'It seems to me, if you think of this being practicable, we should start from the Federal Steel Co., and therefore the first thing to do is to call in the Federal Steel people who are in the management—practically in control—of this corporation.'

. . . .

"After a good deal of discussion and consideration, while there was some opposition—a considerable opposition in the first place, particularly on the part of Mr. Porter—these gentlemen assented; and that is where we started.

"MR. YOUNG. At that time was anything contemplated except the joinder of the Federal Steel Co. and the Carnegie Co.? Had it grown any larger?

"MR. GARY. It had grown in the conversation, yes; no doubt about it. Various other companies were mentioned, particularly the Wire Co., the Tube Co., and the Bridge Co., and later the National Steel Co., because I believe it is true that Mr. Carnegie insisted that the National Steel should be acquired. I never knew until I read Mr. Gates's testimony that that was the result of Mr. Moore going to Mr. Carnegie and suggesting that. That may be true. I have no knowledge on the subject, but I do remember, during the negotiations, during the conversations, that the National Steel was spoken of.

"MR. YOUNG. Was Mr. Moore largely interested in the National Steel at that time?

"MR. GARY. Yes; he was the dominant factor there. There was a group of men consisting of Mr. Moore, Mr. Reid, and Mr. Leeds, who were dominant in that company, and three other companies, the Tin Plate Co., the American Sheet Steel Co., and the American Hoop Co., whatever its technical name may have been; and, since you have asked that question, later came the consideration of the Rockefeller ores, with what was attached. The first proposition was as to whether or not we could organize a complete corporation which should be self-contained, which should be in a position to operate at the lowest cost of production, and which would have sufficient finishing mills and sufficient capital to be able to compete with other manufacturers throughout the world.

"It was on that basis we started this organization; it was on that basis we completed it.

. . . .

"MR. YOUNG. Was the value largely increased by the elimination of competition between some of these component factors?

"MR. GARY. I do not think it was so much that. I think the valuation depended upon the fact that it had a proposition the nearest perfection in its line that had ever been formed, with sufficient capital and sufficient opportunities for improvement in the business, to extend its lines of business, and to manufacture at reasonable cost, more than anything else.

. . . .

"MR. YOUNG. You are sure you heard no conversation by Mr. Morgan in regard to that railroad proposition?

"MR. GARY. I do not remember to have heard anything about it, but I do not say that he did not speak about it. Of course others might correct me. I had heard, I know, that Mr. Carnegie talked of building a railroad from Pittsburgh to New York because he got into some altercation with the Pennsylvania Railroad Co. in regard to freights from Pittsburgh to New York."

C. Gates's testimony before the Stanley Committee in 1911 on the formation of the U. S. Steel Corp.[5]

"THE CHAIRMAN. I am speaking now about that period that elapsed between the demoralization of prices in 1896 and the formation of the United States Steel Corporation. There was an interregnum there in which these various concerns that afterwards became component parts of the corporation were themselves organized?

"MR. GATES. Yes.

"THE CHAIRMAN. They were organized by the absorption of hundreds of hitherto competing concerns. Were they not, Mr. Gates?

[5] *Ibid.*, pp. 39–44.

"MR. GATES. No. . . .

"THE CHAIRMAN. The more of these concerns you were able to get the better you were able to secure the prices you desired, were you not?

"MR. GATES. The control of the market necessitated getting a majority of the producers.

"THE CHAIRMAN. Exactly, I understand. Now, this was the situation, I believe, for a while: These various concerns practically had control of the markets to which they sold; that is, for a while the Federal Co. had control of the market to which it sold its product?

"MR. GATES. No—

"THE CHAIRMAN. And the Tube Co. had control of the market to which it sold its product?

"MR. GATES. The Tube Co. had control, and the Wire Co., but the Carnegie and the Federal were fighting it.

"THE CHAIRMAN. They were fighting. Now, it was to prevent that competition or that fight from getting general all along the line that this organization was created and perfected?

"MR. GATES. That is a pretty hard question to answer. You are asking me what was in Mr. Morgan's mind.

. . . .

"THE CHAIRMAN. I am now trying to get at what was the trouble. Was it not competition and threatened competition between these companies?

"MR. GATES. It was the threat of Carnegie to build a railroad from Ashtabula to his works at Pittsburgh and to build a tube plant in competition with the National Tube Works, which Morgan had just finished.

"THE CHAIRMAN. Was not he also threatening to go into the entire iron and steel business—that is, to compete with the Bridge Co. and with the Steel Hoop Co. and the Sheet & Plate Co.? Was he not threatening to do all those things?

. . . .

"THE CHAIRMAN. Mr. Carnegie was also threatening to go into the tin-plate business, was he not, at that time?

"MR. GATES. I guess he was threatening the whole line.

"THE CHAIRMAN. He was threatening the whole line?

"MR. GATES. He was trying to sell out, and he bought, you see, at a good price. (Laughter)

"THE CHAIRMAN. And the result of this threat along the whole line enabled him to sell this property that he had given an option on at $150,000,000 for about $500,000,000?

"MR. GATES. That is inference on your part. The facts are that he gave an option for $100,000,000 or $160,000,000 and got $320,000,000 a little later.

. . . .

"MR. BEALL. At the time this consolidation was made, what was the general line of manufacture that the Carnegie Co. was engaged in?

"MR. GATES. Outside of tin plate, light sheets, hoops, wire, and tubes, they made a very full product.

. . . .

"MR. BEALL. What was the general character of the manufacture of the National Tube Co.?

"MR. GATES. The National Tube Co. was an acquisition of the principal tube mills of the United States into one concern, where they could get a very handsome profit out of the manufacture of tubes, and that had been done by Mr. Morgan.

"MR. BEALL. There had been a combination of those tube mills by which competition had been very largely destroyed, resulting in an increased price for their product, had there not?

"MR. GATES. I would say 85 or 90 per cent of the total tube tonnage of the United States was in the National Tube Co. at that time.

. . . .

"MR. BEALL. Was it [The American Bridge Co.] any wise connected with the Carnegie Co.?

"MR. GATES. The Carnegie Co. owned the Bridge Co.

. . . .

"MR. BEALL. At the time of this consolidation the American Steel & Wire Co. controlled what per cent of this business?

"MR. GATES. Eighty-five per cent.

. . . .

"MR. BEALL. Some time ago you said there was a fear that Mr. Carnegie would demoralize the railroad business and the tube works just as he had done the steel business, as I understood it.

"MR. GATES. That was Mr. Morgan's statement.

. . . .

"MR. BEALL. In what way had he demoralized the steel business prior to this consolidation?

"MR. GATES. Well, in those days we used to have a few agreements . . . ; the boys would make them, and Andy would pick them over.

. . . .

"MR. BEALL. The real cause of complaint against Mr. Carnegie was that he would not abide by the agreement, but would insist on cutting the price?

"MR. GATES. He was like a bull in a china shop. He would get a thing into his head once in a while and go and do absurd things, that I really think he did not think much about.

. . . .

"MR. BEALL. The fear was that if he carried out his plan there might be a competing line of railroad, as well as—

"MR. GATES. I cannot state it any plainer than Mr. Morgan stated it to Mr. Schwab and me—that if Mr. Carnegie should build this tube works at Ashtabula and a railroad from Ashtabula to his works in the Pittsburgh district it would demoralize the whole situation. That was Mr. Morgan's statement and not mine."

D. Carnegie and Carnegie Steel, 1900.

(1) Plans of the Carnegie Steel Co.:

(a) As stated in contemporary periodicals.

"A very interesting item of news is the announcement that the Carnegie Steel Company are about to enter into the manufacture of Rods on a large scale, and that they may also decide to manufacture Hoops, Bands and Cotton Ties."[6]

"Carnegie Co.—Proposed Railway to Tidewater.—The company, it is asserted, has determined to build a railway of its own from Pittsburgh to tidewater in order to secure the transportation of its product to the seaboard at the lowest possible cost. The route for the line has not been chosen, but it is said may extend either easterly through Pennsylvania or southeasterly to Norfolk, Va."[7]

(b) As considered by Board of Directors of Carnegie Steel Co.[8]

"MR. PEACOCK. I can report that we succeeded in selling the National Transit Company, during the past week, plates enough to keep them supplied until we can arrange for the tubes complete about 50,000 tons. The price is 1.15¢. per pound for the narrow, and 1.20¢. for the wider plates.

"Moreover, the National Tube Company are likely to want to purchase any moment, they having suspended orders for machinery for their new open hearth plant, hoping we will not go into the tube business, as it is rumored we are likely to do.

"MR. SCHWAB. When I was in New York last week, J. Pierpont Morgan sent word he would like to see me. I did not comply for several reasons. I thought it was about railroad matters, but I did meet Mr. Steele, who is his chief assistant, and was informed it was in reference to tubes; that the Morgan people had financed and put through this new tube combination, and were much alarmed about our going into tubes.

"I think when Mr. Carnegie comes out here next week and we have definitely decided as to site [for the new tube plant], we should make a definite announcement of our intentions."

(2) Carnegie on steel competition in 1900.[9]

[6] *Iron Age*, July 26, 1900 (vol. lxvi), p. 22.

[7] *Commercial & Financial Chronicle*, vol. lxxi (Sept. 22, 1900), pp. 603–604.

[8] *United States* v. *United States Steel Corporation and Others*, Government Exhibits, vol. vi, 1914, p. 1901.

[9] *Hearings on U. S. Steel*, vol. iv, 1912, p. 2507.

"THE CHAIRMAN. I see that Mr. Herbert Knox Smith, in his report on the steel industry, makes this statement. . . .

"'. . . . The "secondary" companies began to reach back, acquiring ore reserves and crude steel plants. For example, in 1900, the Steel & Wire Co., whose supply of materials had previously been purchased mainly from the Carnegie or the Federal Co., planned to make its own steel; likewise the National Tube Co. The "primary" concerns, finding these, their chief customers, turning into rivals, retaliated by reaching forward to the manufacture of finished products. . . .'

. . . .

"MR. CARNEGIE. I think that is remarkably well described. I think that gives you the situation."

(3) Sales reports to the board of directors of the Carnegie Steel Co., March 25, 1901.[10]

"Mr. H. P. Bope, as Assistant General Sales Agent, submitted the following reports:

"'We submit herewith a statement in gross tons, of the total sales of Standard Rails—first quality—reported to the New York Committee by the different members of the Rail Association since September 21st, 1900:

Carnegie	430,307
Illinois	467,185
Cambria	163,799
Colorado	108,390
Pennsylvania	189,014
Lackawanna	206,597
National	166,302
TOTAL	1,731,594'"

4. Purchase of the Tennessee Coal, Iron and Railroad Co.

The Tennessee Coal, Iron and Railroad Co. was purchased on November 4, 1907, by the United States Steel Corporation. Previously it had been well known as an independent. It held the largest body of ore in the Birmingham district and was the most important concern operating in the South.

[10] *U. S.* v. *U. S. Steel Corporation and Others*, p. 1919.

A. Report on mineral lands of T. C. I. and R., December 31, 1906.[11]

"The knowledge that your Executive Committee has acquired as to the tonnage and character of the iron ore, coal and limestone owned in *Fee Simple* by your Company, satisfies them that, *in wealth of raw materials* required for the manufacture of iron and steel, your Company *ranks as second to only one in the World,* and is far in advance of any other iron or steel producer in cost of assembling its raw materials for manufacture.

"The Mineral Reserves of coal and iron contained in your lands, as computed by competent authorities, are estimated to be 700,000,000 tons of iron ore and 2,000,000,000 tons of coal. Approximately one-half of your coal supply is of a *superior coking quality,* and your iron ore is largely of a *self-fluxing character,* analyzing approximately 38 per cent metallic iron. . . ."

B. Directors' statement to stockholders of U. S. Steel, 1907.[12]

"In November, 1907, the Corporation acquired a majority of the common stock of the Tennessee Coal, Iron and Railroad Company. . . . The purchase was made during the financial panic of October, 1907. The parties owning or controlling a majority of the Tennessee Company's stock offered the same to the Corporation on terms which were satisfactory both as to price and manner of payment. The purchase of the property promises benefit to the Corporation and also aided promptly and materially in relieving the financial stress at the time existing. The Tennessee property is very valuable. Its mineral resources are large. The location of the iron ore and coal deposits in the immediate proximity of the manufacturing plants enables the production of iron at reasonable cost. It is believed the lines of business of the Tennessee Company can be materially extended. During the last two years about $6,250,000 were expended in rehabilitating, modernizing, and enlarging the furnaces and steel plant. Additional expenditures of considerable magnitude in 1908 are con-

[11] *Forty-seventh Annual Report of Tennessee Coal, Iron and Railroad Co.,* 1906, p. 32.

[12] United States Steel Corporation, *Annual Report,* 1907, pp. 29–30.

templated to complete the plans for improvements which were under way when the Corporation acquired the property. It is believed that when these improvements and extensions shall have been completed and the operating management perfected the business of the company will be profitable."

C. Gary's testimony on the T. C. I. and R. purchase.[13]

"MR. GARY. In one way or another the stock of the Tennessee Coal & Iron Co. had been offered to the United States Steel Corporation, I will not say authoritatively or by the owners exactly, but by people who assumed to be acting between, or acting for the Tennessee people. Our people had been opposed to the purchase of the property at any price or on any basis, and had distinctly said so. Finally, I think sometime in the early part of 1907 . . . Mr. Morgan sent for me and said that Mr. George Kessler . . . had approached him, Mr. Morgan, with the statement that the stock of the Tennessee Coal & Iron Co. could be purchased at about 130, and asked me my opinion. I told Mr. Morgan I did not think it was worth half of that; I did not think we could afford to take it at any such price. . . . Mr. Frick expressed about the same opinion. The matter was then dropped. I believe that Mr. Morgan told me afterwards he found out that Mr. Kessler represented only himself, and did not represent the other people, as Mr. Morgan had supposed.

"Along about the 23d day of October, 1907, Mr. Morgan requested me to come over to the bank, and said Mr. Schley was very much in need of money, or securities which he could use at the bank. . . . the business finally resulted in my accommodating Mr. Schley by loaning him $1,200,000 par value of our second bonds, and taking . . . from him as security for the fulfillment of his agreement, $2,000,000, par value, of the stock of the Tennessee Coal & Iron Co.

"The agreement provided, as I remember, that if the $1,200,000 par value of bonds were not returned by April 23, 1908, the ownership of the $2,000,000 par value of the stock of the Tennessee Coal & Iron Co. should be and remain in the United States Steel Corporation. . . . That, you see, would be taking the Tennessee Coal & Iron Co. stock as security on the basis of 60.

. . . .

"MR. LITTLETON. Is it or is it not a fact that Moore & Schley held the stock of the Tennessee Coal & Iron Co. for and on behalf of a syndicate of gentlemen?

"MR. GARY. A majority of the stock.

"MR. LITTLETON. A majority of it; on behalf of a syndicate of gentlemen comprising O. H. Payne, who had 10,300 shares; L. C. Hanna, who had 10,300 shares; J. P. Duke, who had 10,300 shares; E. J. Berwin, who had 10,300 shares; J. W. Gates, who had 10,300 shares; A. N. Brady, who had the same amount; G. A. Kessler, who had the same amount; Oakleigh Thorne, who had the same amount; E. W. Oglebay, who had 5,150 shares, H. S. Black, who had 5,150 shares; F. D. Stout, who had 5,150 shares; J. W. Simpson, who had 5,150 shares; G. W. French, who had 2,500 shares; S. G. Cooper, who had 1,500 shares; and J. A. Topping, who had 1,000 shares?

"MR. GARY. I think that is correct, except I do not think Kessler was in the original syndicate. I think he bought outside, and Schley finally took his stock with the rest and made some advances on it.

"MR. LITTLETON. With that qualification, then, the situation at that juncture was that Moore & Schley held, for and on behalf of these gentlemen who comprised the syndicate, 118,300 shares of the Tennessee Coal & Iron Co.; that is your understanding?

. . . .

"MR. GARY. I understood from Mr. Ledyard that Moore & Schley had loaned to their customers who had bought this stock and put it in, sums of money, and then they, Moore & Schley, in turn had pledged this stock with these banks as collateral security, in a great many different banks, aggregating, in all, about $6,000,000. . . .

"Mr. Morgan said to me, 'I do not know whether the United States Steel Corporation can afford to buy this stock or not; I will express no opinion on that subject. But I will

[13] *Hearings on U. S. Steel,* vol. i, pp. 126–130, 134–135.

say that, in my opinion, if it does not buy the stock, or unless it or someone else furnishes relief at this particular time, there is not any man on earth can say what the result will be in the financial circles of this country. . . . if you can see your way clear to buy this stock, there is no doubt it will help the situation. . . .' I said to Mr. Morgan, 'In the first place, I would not think of considering the purchase of this stock without going to Washington first and taking the matter up with the President or the Department of Justice, or both. . . . Here is a financial crisis, and from your standpoint the object of buying this stock would be to allay this storm, to assist in overcoming this panic, and if the Department of Justice or the President should find out we had purchased, or were about to purchase it, and should enjoin us from purchasing on the ground that it would add to our holdings and thereby raise the question of creating or adding to a monopoly. . . .'

. . . .

"MR. GARDNER. Here is what I want to get at. You said you and Mr. Frick decided that the stock was worth from 60 to 65, in your opinion.

"MR. GARY. Not more than that.

. . . .

"MR. GARDNER. But on account of Mr. Morgan's representation to you that if Moore & Schley failed it would be followed by a financial panic whose size could not be measured, you finally gave them 100 for that which you thought, only as a business venture taken by itself, to be worth only $65. . . ."

D. President Roosevelt and the T. C. I. and R. purchase.

(1) Letter sent by Roosevelt to the attorney general at the request of Gary.[14]

"The White House,
"Washington, November 4, 1907.

"My dear Mr. Attorney General:

"Judge E. H. Gary and Mr. H. H. Frick, on behalf of the steel corporation, have just called on me. They state that there is a certain business firm (the name of which I have not been told, but which is of real importance in New York business circles) which will undoubtedly fail this week if help is not given. Among its assets are a majority of the securities of the Tennessee Coal Co. Application has been urgently made to the steel corporation to purchase this stock as the only means of avoiding a failure. Judge Gary and Mr. Frick inform me that as a mere business transaction they do not care to purchase the stock, and under ordinary circumstances they would not consider purchasing the stock because but little benefit will come to the steel corporation from the purchase; that they are aware that the purchase will be used as a handle for attack upon them on the ground that they are striving to secure a monopoly of the business and prevent competition—not that this would represent what could be honestly said, but what might be recklessly and untruthfully said. They further inform me that as a matter of fact the policy of the company has been to decline to acquire more than 60 per cent of the steel properties, and that this purpose has been persevered in for several years past, with the object of preventing these accusations, and, as a matter of fact, their proportion of steel properties has slightly decreased, so that it is below this 60 per cent, and the acquisition of the property in question will not raise it above 60 per cent. But they feel that it is immensely to their interest, as to the interest of every responsible business man, to try to prevent a panic and general industrial smash up at this time, and that they are willing to go into this transaction, which they would not otherwise go into, because it seems the opinion of those best fitted to express judgment in New York that it will be an important factor in preventing a break that might be ruinous; and that this has been urged upon them by the combination of the most responsible bankers in New York who are now thus engaged in endeavoring to save the situation. But they asserted they did not wish to do this if I stated it ought not to be done. I answered that while of course I could not advise them to take the action proposed, I felt it no public duty of mine to interpose any objection.

"Sincerely, yours,
"THEODORE ROOSEVELT

"Hon. Charles J. Bonaparte,
"Attorney General."

[14] *Ibid.*, pp. 140–141.

(2) Roosevelt's testimony on the T. C. I. and R. purchase, 1914.[15]

"A. (Continuing). My knowledge was simply this, that it was a matter of general opinion among experts that the Tennessee Coal & Iron people had a property which was almost worthless in their hands, . . . and entirely worthless to any financial institution that had the securities the minute that any panic came.

. . . .

"Q. But did you know that the men who were then in control were spending about eight million dollars in developing this property?

"A. I knew nothing about what they were spending.

"Q. Did you know that prior to this interview, somewhat prior thereto, but within a year, the United States Steel Corporation had certain experts investigate this property and had received reports upon it?

"A. I knew nothing of it; but from my knowledge of the Steel Corporation I should have taken it for granted that they were not buying a pig in a poke.

"Q. Did you know, Col. Roosevelt, that shortly prior to this time the Tennessee Coal, Iron & Railroad Company had placed an order for 157,000 tons of steel open-hearth rails with the Harriman lines?

"A. I knew nothing of such details at all. I have given you, Judge, all that I can remember."

E. Ledyard's testimony before the Stanley Committee.[16]

"MR. LITTLETON. Now will you tell the committee at what time, if you recall, your attention was first attracted to the fact that the firm of Moore & Schley had in their loans a goodly amount of Tennessee Coal & Iron Co. stock?

"MR. LEDYARD [counsel for Oliver Payne]. I should say it must have been within the last week of October, 1907, Col. Payne said to me that the firm of Moore & Schley were very largely indebted to him, and that he was very much concerned over their condition. . . . Col. Payne said that Moore & Schley had a great lot of Tennessee Coal & Iron stock in their loans. . . . He also told me that his understanding of the reason was that the stock was regarded as a pooled or a pegged stock, with only nominal quotations without any real transactions occurring in it, and was a stock of a character that a bank could not realize upon in a time of panic, and he said he did not see any way for Moore & Schley to be saved, except through the acquisition of that stock by the United States Steel Corporation. He said that that would be an extension of the United States Steel Corporation's business, and they might be a purchaser for that stock.

. . . .

"MR. LEDYARD. Col. Payne had lent to them securities to help them along, and he subsequently lent more securities, the securities which he lent being of a class upon which loans could readily be made, and he taking as collateral for those securities uncurrent securities of Moore & Schley, upon which no loans could be made in those times. For instance, Col. Payne would lend them Northern Pacific and Great Northern and standard railroad stock, and they would secure that by giving him uncurrent and unactive securities that did not command a ready market and could not be used to any extent in connection with normal loans in Wall Street.

"MR. LITTLETON. The extent of those securities was what?

"MR. LEDYARD. . . . I think those securities on the one side and other of this account came to $7,000,000 or $8,000,000 on a side.

. . . .

"MR. LEDYARD. I went at once the next morning to Mr. Morgan, as they asked me to do; they asked me to lay their condition before him and I did so.

. . . .

"MR. LITTLETON. Did you tell him that it had been suggested to you, in the first instance, by Col. Payne?

"MR. LEDYARD. I did. He knew my relations with Col. Payne, and how close they had been, and I told Mr. Morgan that Col.

[15] *United States of America* v. *United States Steel Corporation and Others, Testimony,* vol. viii, 1914, pp. 2921–2923.

[16] *Hearings on U. S. Steel,* vol. ii, pp. 933–937.

Payne suggested it to me some days ago, and Mr. Schley the night before had sent for me and given me the situation, and asked me to lay it before Mr. Morgan. . . .

"There were a good many conferences that took place between Mr. Morgan, Judge Gary, and Mr. Frick and other representatives of the Steel Co. through that Saturday and Sunday, and one or two conferences at which I was present with Mr. Frick and Judge Gary. Judge Gary was the reluctant one. He expressed very great reluctance to buy this stock. . . . Judge Gary said, 'It is not worth it, and it is not worth 60 or 65 per share at the outside.' I said, 'Judge Gary, I do not know what it is worth. I know nothing about the stock and its value. I think very likely, however, you will get it, if you wait, if you want it, at $25 a share. I should not be surprised if, by the time it reaches $25 a share, the Steel Co. is not in the market to buy anything; I do not believe it will be.'

. . . .

"There was a suggestion made by Judge Gary to me that they lend Mr. Schley, or Moore & Schley, $5,000,000, I think the amount was. I spoke to Mr. Schley about that. Mr. Schley said it would be perfectly useless; that it would not pull them out, and would not do them, and would not be effective."

F. Schley's testimony before the Stanley Committee.[17]

"MR. LITTLETON. Mr. Schley, what bank, amongst the banks with which you had loans, if any banks, called the loans which were based in part upon Tennessee Coal & Iron or requested the elimination of Tennessee Coal & Iron from the collateral?

"MR. SCHLEY. I can not name any specific bank. It was done frequently by all of them. That would come to my cashier.

"MR. LITTLETON. What is your information as to when the first request was made by any bank that Tennessee Coal & Iron be taken out of the loan and something else be put in its place, if such a request was made.

. . . .

"MR. SCHLEY. I do not remember any specific occurrence of the kind. I know, generally, that it was a collateral not acceptable to the banks.

. . . .

"MR. LITTLETON. Now, coming down to the time of the panic, at the time when the panic set in and everybody was suffering the distress of it, what was it that happened to the Tennessee Coal & Iron stock, if anything did happen, which sort of outlawed it as compared with any other industrial stock?

"MR. SCHLEY. It was in a very bad way as to market price, and there is no bank that will loan on a stock that has not a market.

. . . .

"MR. LITTLETON. That had been true from 1905 and 1906, had it not?

"MR. SCHLEY. Well, some bankers would not at that time.

"MR. LITTLETON. The point I am getting at is whether at the beginning of the panic a general drive was made at Tennessee Coal & Iron?

"MR. SCHLEY. I never knew of that. I never saw anything of that kind."

5. Price Policy under Gary

Up to the time of the formation of the United States Steel Corporation the steel industry had experienced a succession of disastrous price wars. Steel prices reeled dizzily up and down until Gary took control. From that time on they gradually settled into a condition of reasonable stability. Gary endeavored to keep steel prices high and steady. To refrain from any act which might be regarded as a violation of the law, he attempted to stabilize prices by holding a series of meetings known as the Gary Dinners and by organizing the American Iron and Steel Institute.

A. The Gary Dinners.

(1) Gary's statements about the first Gary Dinner.[18]

"MR. GARY. The Chairman inquired yesterday whether or not representatives of the press were admitted to the dinners, and I

[17] *Ibid.*, pp. 1063–1065.

[18] *Ibid.*, vol. i, pp. 75–77.

answered in the negative, except as to the editors of three of the trade journals. The real reason for not making it an open meeting is found in the fact that there is always more or less risk of a misstatement of exactly what occurred, unless the representatives are thoroughly familiar with the subject matter.

. . . .

"Now, at the time of the panic in New York there was, of course, great demoralization temporarily in business, and the fear existed that that would be spread and might be prolonged. . . . We had no lawful right . . . to make any agreement . . . to maintain prices. . . . On the other hand, considering this same question of sustaining, so far as practicable, the equilibrium of trade, we believed we had no moral or legal right to become involved in a bitter and destructive competition, such as used to follow any kind of depression in business among the iron and steel manufacturers, for the reason that if we should go into a competition of that kind it meant a war of the survival of the fittest; it meant that a large percentage, as in old times, of the people engaged in the manufacture of steel would be forced into bankruptcy. . . .

"Now, the question was how to get between the two extremes of securing a monopoly by driving out competition, however good-naturedly, in a bitter, destructive competition or without making any agreement, express or implied, tacit or otherwise, which should result in the maintenance of prices, and so, gentlemen, I invited a large percentage of the steel interests of the country to meet me at dinner. . . . I said that it seemed to me the only way we could lawfully prevent such demoralization and maintain a reasonable steadiness in business . . . was for the steel people to come together occasionally and to tell one to the others exactly what his business was. . . . In other words, to state it simply, if three men, gentlemen on this committee, were practicing law in a certain town and each one knew that the customary fee for services in court was $50 a day and a gentleman from another part of the country should locate in that town and make a totally different price, very much lower, he would immediately get up some sort of competition amongst these professional men. If those three men . . . were in daily conference and each one knew that the others did not propose to change the fees, probably this outsider would not make very much headway in creating a demoralization."

(2) Committees appointed after the Dinner on November 20, 1907.[19]

"It is hereby stipulated and agreed between counsel for petitioner and for the defendants represented by Messrs. Lindabury, Depue & Faulks that, shortly after the dinner given by Judge Gary on November 20, 1907, to the leading representatives of the iron and steel industries, there was a general committee appointed.

. . . .

"That shortly thereafter, and prior to December 26, 1907, the general committee appointed the following subcommittees" (summarized as follows): ore and pig iron; rails and billets; structural material; plates; steel bars; pipe and tubular goods; sheets and tin plate; wire products."

(3) Crawford, president of McKeesport Tin Plate Co., on subcommittee meetings.[20]

"A. I would not like to attempt to say just how many meetings there were, but we held meetings frequently, perhaps sometimes every month, sometimes two months apart, or more.

. . . .

"A. As I remember it, at the first meeting held after the Gary dinners were started Mr. Campbell explained to us that he had been appointed on a committee with others representing the tin plate and sheet manufacturers, and that it was the duty of this committee to have a meeting of the sheet and tin manufacturers from time to time. . . .

. . . .

"A. . . . there was no attempt at the allotting of business; there was no attempt at controlling production. If I would get up and say for our company 'We will name $3.50 a

[19] *United States of America* v. *United States Steel Corporation, Testimony*, vol. ix, 1914, pp. 3745–3747.

[20] *Ibid.*, vol. v, 1914, pp. 1774–1777.

box on tin plate until we feel that there is some reason to change that,' there was no penalty in case I would walk out of a meeting and name $3.00, or any other price.

"Q. Would or not a price be suggested?

"A. A price would always be suggested.

"Q. State whether or not, before they left, there was any difference as to what each one said he was going to charge, or whether it would be the same.

"A. It was always unanimously agreed, or the statement was unanimous on the part of all, that they would quote a certain price."

(4) Proportion of the industry represented at the Dinners.[21]

"MR. GARY. At some of the dinners there have been as high as 90 per cent in tonnage capacity represented."

(5) Remarks by Gary at a typical Dinner, January 11, 1911.[22]

"At the present time the question of maintaining or changing the prices of the commodities in which we deal is uppermost in our minds, because we read and hear about this question every day and almost every hour. I have been pained, I admit, from time to time, to read in the newspapers that the United States Steel Corporation carried a big stick, and was in the habit of inviting the Independents, so-called, to come together for the purpose of lecturing them, or, worse than that, of threatening them in case they proposed to reduce prices. I call upon you as witnesses to refute these insinuations. . . . If any of you desire to lower prices at any time, and will make the fact known to me, you will find that I am a follower and not a stubborn opposer.

. . . .

"Now, my opinion is that it would be a mistake to reduce prices at this time; that it would do more harm than good; that instead of getting more business we would get less business; that the average purchaser, perhaps without exception, is not so much in favor of the reduction of prices, as he is in favor of making it absolutely certain his prices are the same prices that another has to pay for the same commodity. And the only reason in the mind of the proposed purchaser now, able and ready, willing and anxious to buy—the only reason for hesitation—is that he gets the impression in one way or another through the newspapers, and I fear frequently from our own subordinates, that there is a possibility in the future of a reduction in prices, and he is therefore waiting for that time to come."

(6) Answers to Gary at the Dinner of January 11, 1911.[23]

"JOHN A. TOPPING [Chairman, Republic I. & S. Co.]. I am more convinced than ever that any efforts at this time to reduce prices with a view to stimulating consumption will be met in about the manner that Mr. Felton has illustrated. The price line will go down much faster than the production line will go up.

. . . .

"C. S. PRICE [Pres., Cambria Steel Co.]. I will only speak of the business situation and endorse the fact that I consider it very inopportune at this time to make any change in prices.

. . . .

"I. M. SCOTT [Pres., La Belle Iron Works]. Speaking for our Company, we are in favor of maintaining the situation. Logically I do not consider that there is anything else to do. (Applause.)

. . . .

"A. F. Huston [Pres., Lukens I. & S. Co.]. I believe the buying movement will come just as well if we stand up to-day as if we were to make a radical cut in the price. (Applause.)

. . . .

"F. W. WOOD [Pres., Maryland Steel Co.]. I can only express my sympathy with what has been said so much better than I can say it, concerning the advantages of co-operation, and particularly what has been said concerning Mr. Farrell. We have only a sin-

21 *Hearings on U. S. Steel,* vol. i, p. 99.

22 *Addresses and Statements by Elbert H. Gary,* vol. i, H., pp. 10–11.

23 *Ibid.,* pp. 23, 26, 36, 38, 39, 22, 25. Many other iron and steel manufacturers also made speeches of the same tenor.

gle product, steel rails, and there is no indication whatever that any change in price would affect the demand. . . .

. . . .

"E. C. FELTON [Pres., Pennsylvania Steel Co.]. If there is anybody who thinks the present business situation will be improved, stimulated, by cutting prices, he ought to consider just one branch of our business. . . . Let him look at the pig iron situation . . . prices have been met by everybody as they saw fit, and things have gone . . . down, down, down.

. . . .

"E. A. S. CLARKE [Pres., Lackawanna Steel Co.]. While I think it is well to coach salesmen, we must put into them the very same spirit I think we all have here that we are in honor bound not to change our prices without letting the other man know it, because then the salesman knows that he has an answer to give to that proposition."

B. The American Iron and Steel Institute.[24]

"Chartered in 1908, as an outgrowth of the Gary dinners, the institute held its first general meeting in New York on Oct. 14, 1910. In 1911 no general meetings were held, but in 1912 and subsequently two general meetings have been held each year, with the single exception of the year 1918, when the October meeting was omitted because of war activities.

"Judge Gary has been the one president of the institute and his addresses at the semiannual meetings have been the outstanding features. Technical papers of a high order have been read, but always the rallying point was the morning session, and always the meeting place was crowded with men from all departments of the industry, from every part of the country, intent on knowing what their leader would say as to the immediate developments in the industry, and what might be looked for in the months ahead.

. . . .

"It may fairly be said that Judge Gary's presidential addresses brought many to the New York meetings who but for them would not have made the journey. The president covered a wide range of economic, industrial and civic questions—the relations of the Government to business, the relations of steel companies to labor, the competitive relations of producers of steel, and the problem of legal cooperation to prevent demoralization in the steel market and to protect the interests of stockholders, consumers, workers, and the public. The president's appearance and his taking up of the gavel were uniformly a signal for warm applause."

C. Gary on policy of U. S. Steel as to competitors.[25]

"Large corporations are confronted with two extreme opposite points of view. Public sentiment as well as the laws are opposed to combinations in restraint of trade which I suppose would include positive agreements between large interests to maintain prices, restrict output, divide territory, etc., etc., in accordance with the practice of other countries. On the other hand, public sentiment is bitterly opposed to such competition as will result in the destruction of the business of competitors whose opportunities or resources are weak in comparison, because in the end it is certain to secure an absolute monopoly and in the meantime bring great harm to the employees and others.

"We have endeavored to maintain a position between the two extremes. We are perfectly satisfied to limit the amount of our business to our proportion of capacity and to do everything possible we can to promote the interests of our competitors; and by frequent meetings and the interchange of opinions we have thus far been able to accomplish this result without making any agreements of any kind."

D. Testimony of an "independent" producer on the power of U. S. Steel.[26]

[24] "Steel Industry's Great Leader Passes," *Iron Age*, vol. cxx (Aug. 18, 1927), pp. 415–416.

[25] Letter of Gary to Attorney-General Bonaparte, Feb., 1908, quoted in Ida M. Tarbell, *Life of Elbert H. Gary* (New York, 1925), p. 212.

[26] E. R. Crawford, president of McKeesport Tin Plate Co., before Ways and Means Committee of House of Representatives, Jan. 10–11, 1913, as reported in *Iron Trade Review*, vol. lii (Jan. 16, 1913), p. 216.

"He said that if the tariff was cut so that foreign competitors of the Steel Corporation were let in he feared that Corporation would retaliate by adjusting things so as to crush foreign competition, and that the independents here would go down with the foreigners.

" 'The United States Steel Corporation,' he added, 'simply suffers us to do business. It is strong enough to put us out of business in less than a week if it cared to.'

. . . .

" 'Do you think,' the representative [James] asked, 'that the Steel Corporation ought to be subsidized to the extent that you ask in order to enable the independents to do business?'

" 'I don't regard it as a subsidy,' returned Mr. Crawford."

E. Steel prices after the War.

(1) Gary's views, in letter to comptroller of currency: [27]

"Soon after the armistice, which was signed Nov. 11, 1918, I asked the leading steel manufacturers of the country to meet for the purpose of discussing the question of reducing selling prices for recommendation at a meeting which had been called by the War Industries Board for Dec. 9. After a long and interesting discussion it was finally voted to refer the subject matter to a subcommittee with full power. That committee met and decided to make a reduction of between $5 and $6 per ton, and these prices were adhered to until March 21, 1919. At that time the steel manufacturers, through their representatives, met the Industrial Board, appointed by Secretary of Commerce Redfield by the approval of the President, and after a conference of two or three days agreed to make further reductions of about $6 per ton. These prices have been strictly adhered to by the Corporation from that time until the present, notwithstanding wages in February, 1920 were increased about 10%, and also freight rates have been increased about 35% or more.

"During a large portion of this time many of the steel products have been sold at about or below actual mill cost. Taken as a whole, however, the Steel Corporation has been able to make some profit, and I am glad to say has been permitted to maintain its wage rates. . . ."

(2) The comptroller's reply: [28]

"Your position seems to be that because the Government fixed *maximum* prices you were compelled to charge them, regardless of how gross and excessive your profits might be. There was no such compulsion. You were free to forego profit entirely or to reduce it to a really 'reasonable' rate. You could have done this without crushing weaker competitors. There was then plenty of market for all. The Government fixed the maximum prices high because there was need for more material than the United States Steel Corporation could supply and consequent necessity for encouraging smaller producers. *It did not require anybody to exact the maximum rates.* Your legal right to exact those rates was unquestionable. The ethical right is another matter and for your corporation to judge."

F. Gary on place of U. S. Steel in the industry, 1926.[29]

"We are not seeking to unduly extend our activities or to increase our fair percentage of the trade. Quite the contrary. But we are endeavoring to modernize and strengthen our existing plants; to maintain our proper position in the iron and steel industry. During the past twelve years, since January 1, 1914, our steel ingot and casting capacity has increased by 19.7%, while that of our competitors has increased 68%. As a result we now have about 40% of the productive capacity of the country compared with 47.9% at close of 1913, equal to a loss of 7.9% of the entire capacity of the country. This is not right nor fair to our stockholders. In order to properly take care of our natural and legitimate customers, and to protect our stockholders generally, we must expend large sums from year to year."

[27] Letter to John Skelton Williams, Feb. 28, 1921, published in the *Com. & Fin. Chron.*, vol. cxii (Mar. 5, 1921), p. 899.

[28] *Ibid.*, April 2, 1921, p. 1351.

[29] At annual stockholders' meeting, reported in *Com. & Fin. Chron.*, vol. cxxii (April 24, 1926), p. 2291.

G. Statistics on steel production and prices.

Table 1. STEEL PRICES IN THE UNITED STATES, 1890–1928 [30]

(Average wholesale price per gross ton)

Year	Pig iron foundry No. 2 Northern	Bessemer steel Billets	Rails
1890	$17.16	$30.47	$31.78
1891	15.40	25.33	29.92
1892	13.77	23.63	30.00
1893	12.44	20.44	28.13
1894	10.85	16.58	24.00
1895	11.68	18.48	24.33
1896	11.77	18.83	28.00
1897	10.10	15.08	18.75
1898	10.03	15.31	17.63
1899	17.35	31.12	28.13
1900	18.51	25.06	32.29
1901	14.72	24.13	27.33
1902	21.24	30.60	28.00
1903	19.14	27.91	28.00
1904	13.63	22.18	28.00
1905	16.41	24.03	28.00
1906	19.27	27.45	28.00
1907	23.87	29.25	28.00
1908	16.25	26.31	28.00
1909	16.41	24.62	28.00
1910	15.98	25.38	28.00
1911	14.52	21.46	28.00
1912	15.09	22.38	28.00
1913	16.01	25.79	28.00
1914	13.90	20.08	28.00
1915	14.87	22.44	28.00
1916	21.07	43.95	31.33
1917	41.39	69.86	38.00
1918	34.46	47.27	54.00
1919	30.31	40.54	47.26
1920	44.90	56.26	51.83
1921	25.10	34.39	44.04
1922	27.03	33.99	40.69
1923	28.16	41.65	43.00
1924	22.51	38.00	43.00
1925	21.65	35.45	43.00
1926	20.62	35.00	43.00
1927	19.75	33.27	43.00
1928	18.88	32.67	...

[30] *Wholesale Prices,* Bureau of Labor Statistics, July, 1927, pp. 138–147, Jan., 1929, pp. 174–175; *Survey of Current Business,* Feb., 1929, pp. 35–36, are sources for Table 1.

Table 2. PERCENTAGE OF TOTAL OUTPUT PRODUCED BY U. S. STEEL 1901–27 [31]

	1901	1911	1913	1919	1927
Iron ore	45.1	45.8	46.37	42.05	41.35
Blast-furnace products	43.2	45.4	45.47	43.97	37.70
Steel ingots and castings	65.7	53.9	53.21	49.61	41.14
Steel rails	59.8	56.1	55.51	61.96	53.26
Heavy structural shapes	62.2	47.0	54.03	43.77	38.80
Plates and sheets	64.6	45.7	49.13	44.30	36.49
Wire rods	77.6	64.7	58.44	55.42	47.42
Total finished products	50.1	45.7	47.81	44.60	37.70
Wire nails	65.8	51.4	44.55	51.86	41.99
Tin and terne plates	73.0	60.7	58.64	48.44	40.46

H. Supreme Court on U. S. Steel, 1920.[32]

"Suit against the Steel Corporation and certain other companies which it directs and controls by reason of the ownership of their stock, it and they being separately and collectively charged as violators of the Sherman Anti-Trust Act. . . .

"It is prayed that it and they be dissolved because engaged in illegal restraint of trade and the exercise of monopoly.

. . . .

". . . We have seen that the judges of the District Court unanimously concurred in the view that the corporation did not achieve monopoly, and such is our deduction, and it is against monopoly that the statute is directed; not against our expectation of it, but against its realization, and it is certain that it was not realized. The opposing condi-

[31] Table in Arundel Cotter, *United States Steel, A Corporation with a Soul* (New York, 1921), p. 308, arranged from exhibits in the dissolution suit and reports of the American Iron and Steel Institute; *Annual Statistical Report of the American Iron and Steel Institute, 1927* (New York. 1928), p. 73, are sources for Table 2.

[32] *U. S.* v. *United States Steel Corporation,* 251 U. S. 417. Decision written by Mr. Justice McKenna.

tions were underestimated. The power attained was much greater than that possessed by any one competitor—it was not greater than that possessed by all of them. Monopoly, therefore, was not achieved, and competitors had to be persuaded by pools, associations, trade meetings, and through the social form of dinners, all of them, it may be, violations of the law, but transient in their purpose and effect. They were scattered through the years from 1901 (the year of the formation of the corporation) until 1911, but, after instances of success and failure, were abandoned nine months before this suit was brought. There is no evidence that abandonment was in prophecy of or dread of suit; and the illegal practices have not been resumed, nor is there any evidence of an intention to resume them, and certainly no 'dangerous probability' of their resumption. . . . It is our conclusion, therefore, as it was that of the judges below, that the practices were abandoned from a conviction of their futility, from the operation of forces that were not understood, or were underestimated, and the case is not peculiar. . . .

"What, then, can now be urged against the corporation? Can comparisons in other regards be made with its competitors and by such comparisons guilty or innocent existence be assigned it? It is greater in size and productive power than any of its competitors, equal or nearly equal to them all, but its power over prices was not and is not commensurate with its power to produce.

"It is true that there is some testimony tending to show that the corporation had such power, but there was also testimony and a course of action tending strongly to the contrary. The conflict was by the judges of the District Court unanimously resolved against the existence of that power, and in so doing they gave effect to the greater weight of the evidence. It is certain that no such power was exerted. On the contrary, the only attempt at a fixation of prices was as already said, through an appeal to and confederation with competitors, and the record shows besides that when competition occurred it was not in pretense, and the corporation declined in productive powers—the competitors growing either against or in consequence of the competition. If against the competition we have an instance of movement against what the government insists was an irresistible force; if in consequence of competition, we have an illustration of the adage that 'competition is the life of trade' and is not easily repressed. The power of monopoly in the corporation under either illustration is an untenable accusation."

6. Labor Policy under Gary

A. Attitude toward organized labor, 1901–19.

The United States Steel Corporation under Gary's leadership maintained a remarkably consistent attitude toward organized labor. Immediately after the corporation had been organized, it refused to allow the Amalgamated Association of Iron and Steel Workers to extend the union to all the mills of the American Sheet Steel Co. and defeated the union in the strike that followed. In 1904 the Amalgamated struck against the Carnegie Co. and was so badly beaten that it was forced out of the Carnegie plants. By 1909 the American Sheet and Tin Plate Co. felt strong enough to order the Amalgamated out of its mills. After the unsuccessful strike of 1909–10, the Amalgamated was put out of the United States Steel Corporation's plants.

The World War found labor in a particularly strategic position, for the steel industry was increasing production and was in no position to risk discontinuance of work as an outcome of labor difficulties. Desiring to make use of their temporary advantage, the convention of the American Federation of Labor, in June, 1918, resolved to organize the steel industry. In August the 24 unions that had decided to organize steel came together in a meeting called by Samuel Gompers, and in September their work got under way. At the annual convention of the Federation in June, 1919, it was reported that 100,000 men had joined the unions organizing the steel industry. Samuel Gompers wrote Judge Gary asking him to meet a group of union men for a conference, but Gary never answered this letter. A strike vote of the workers authorized a strike in case the corporation continued to hold to its "no-conference" policy. It was reported that 98 per cent of the union men had voted in favor of a strike.

B. Steel strike, 1919.

(1) Basis of U. S. Steel wages.[33]

". . . it follows the usual procedure of not basing wages upon the needs of workers but upon the market rate. The market rate is paid for labor as for any material commodity. The size of the Corporation enables it to play an important part in determining the market rate. . . . Judge Gary told the present writer that he regards it as utterly impracticable to base wages upon family budgets. He said that wages respond to the law of supply and demand.

"The second reason is that, from the viewpoint of the management, it is more important to pay regular dividends, and to build up a huge reserve than it is to pay workers in excess of the market rate, even though this rate is insufficient for the maintenance of a decent or comfortable standard of life."

(2) Anti-union attitude of U. S. Steel.

Page quotes the conclusions in the report of the Commission of Inquiry of the Interchurch World Movement of 1920:[34]

"Maintaining the non-unionism alternative entailed, for the employers, (1) discharging workmen for unionism, (2) blacklists, (3) espionage and the hiring of 'labor detective agencies' operatives, (4) strike breakers, principally negroes.

"Maintaining the non-unionism alternative entailed, for communities, (1) the abrogation of the right of assembly, the suppression of free speech, and the violation of personal rights (principally in Pennsylvania); (2) the use of state police, state troops and (in Indiana) of the U. S. Army; (3) such activities on the part of constituted authorities and of the press and the pulpit as to make the workers believe that these forces oppose labor. . . ."

(3) Labor Committee asks Gary for a conference, August 26, 1919.[35]

"Dear Sir:

. . . .

"This work has been carried on to a point where we feel justified in stating to you that we represent the sentiment of the vast majority of the employees in this industry, and, acting in behalf of them, we solicit of you that a hearing be given to the undersigned committee, who have been selected by the duly accredited representatives of the employees, to place before you matters that are of vital concern to them, and concerning hours of labor, wages, working conditions and the right of collective bargaining.

"The committee called at your office at 3 p.m., Tuesday, August 26, and requested a conference. We were advised by your messenger that you wished to be excused from a personal interview at this time and requested us to have our business in writing . . ."

(4) Demands of the organizers of U. S. Steel workers.

The 12 demands to be considered by the organizers of the workers, in their proposed conference with Judge Gary, were as follows:[36]

"1. Right of collective bargaining.
2. Reinstatement of all men discharged for union activities, with pay for time lost.
3. The eight-hour day.
4. One day's rest in seven.
5. Abolition of 24-hour shifts.
6. Increase in wages sufficient to guarantee American standards of living.

[33] Kirby Page, *The United States Steel Corporation* (New York, 1922), p. 21.

[34] These are from the *Report on the Steel Strike of 1919* (Harcourt, Brace & Co., 1920), p. 197. According to the report, these conditions were the policy of Gary and the U. S. Steel Corporation. The Commission held the Corporation responsible for fixing labor conditions in the steel industry. Communities which acted against the strikers were usually those steel towns belonging to or controlled by the Corporation.

[35] 61st Congress, 1st Sess. (1919), *Investigation of Strike in Steel Industries, Hearings,* pp. 16–17.

[36] *Ibid.,* p. 469.

7. Standard scale of wages for all crafts and classification of workers.
8. Double rates of pay for all overtime work and for work on Sundays and holidays.
9. Check-off system of collecting union dues and assessments.
10. Principle of seniority to apply in maintaining, reducing, and increasing working forces.
11. Abolition of company unions.
12. Abolition of physical examination of applicants for employment."

(5) Gary's reply to the committee, August 27, 1919.[37]

"Gentlemen: Receipt of your communication of August 26 instant is acknowledged.

"We do not think you are authorized to represent the sentiment of a majority of the employees of the United States Steel Corporation and its subsidiaries. We express no opinion concerning any other members of the iron and steel industry.

"As heretofore publicly stated and repeated, our corporation and subsidiaries, although they do not combat labor unions as such, declined to discuss business with them. The corporation and subsidiaries are opposed to the 'closed shop.' They stand for the 'open shop.' . . . In view of the well-known attitude as above expressed, the officers of the corporation respectfully decline to discuss with you, as representatives of a labor union, any matters relating to employes. In doing so no personal discourtesy is intended."

(6) Extracts from committee's reply to Gary, August 27, 1919.[38]

"You question the authority of our committee to represent the majority of your employees. The only way by which we can prove our authority is to put the strike vote into effect and we sincerely hope you will not force a strike to prove this point.

. . . .

"We read with great care your statement as to the interest the corporation takes in the lives and welfare of the employees and their families, and if that were true even in a minor degree, we would not be pressing consideration through a conference of the terrible conditions that exist. . . . You may not be aware that the standard of life of the average steel workers is below the pauper line, which means that charitable institutions furnish to the pauper a better home, more food, clothing, light, and heat than many steel workers can bring into their lives upon the compensation received for putting forth their very best efforts in the steel industry. Surely this is a matter which will be discussed in conference.

. . . .

"You also made reference to the attitude of your corporation in not opposing or preventing your employees from joining labor organizations. It is a matter of common knowledge that the tactics employed by your corporation and subsidiaries have for year[s] most effectually prevented any attempt at organization by your employees. . . .

"Some few days are still at the disposal of our committee before the time limit will have expired when there will be no discretion left to the committee, but to enforce the decree of your employees whom we have the honor to represent."

(7) Gary declines to arbitrate.[39]

"Judge Elbert H. Gary was informed in writing last night at the Hotel Ritz-Carlton, where he was a guest at a dinner, that John Fitzpatrick, leader of the steel strikers, had informed the Senate investigating committee that twenty-four unions were willing to submit all issues of the strike to arbitration, the arbitrators to be selected by President Wilson, and that Fitzpatrick had said this would end the walkout. Asked what his attitude would be toward Fitzpatrick's proposal, Judge Gary wrote the following comment:

"'The Board of Directors of the United States Steel Corporation are the representatives of nearly 150,000 stockholders . . . and are selected to represent and protect their interests. . . . Moreover, I believe our corporation is under great obligation to the general public concerning the issues involved in the pending strike.

"'In these circumstances I would not at

[37] *Ibid.*, p. 17.
[38] *Ibid.*, pp. 17–18.
[39] *New York Times*, Sept. 26, 1919, p. 1.

present answer the question propounded to me. However, I will say for myself that questions of moral principle cannot be arbitrated nor compromised, and, in my opinion, such questions are included in the present unfortunate struggle. I also think we cannot negotiate or confer with Mr. Fitzpatrick and his associates as union leaders concerning our employes whom these gentlemen have volunteered to represent.' "

(8) Gary's view on the "fundamental question." [40]

"It will be observed that the strike is not the result of any claim by any workman for higher wages or better treatment, nor for any reason except the desire and effort on the part of union labor leaders to unionize the iron and steel industry. . . .

"Judging by experience, we believe it is for the best interest of employer and employee and the general public to have a business conducted on the basis of what we term the 'open shop,' thus permitting any man to engage in any line of employment, or any employer to secure the services of any workman on terms agreed upon between the two, whether the workman is or is not connected with a labor union. . . ."

(9) Strikes in the fall of 1919.[41]

"The strike data that follow were obtained from the Department of Labor and from other sources at Washington. These show that there are 121 strikes now under way in the country, indicated on reports received in the seven days preceding September 18. . . .

"Fifty-three strikes are threatened. At the head stands the menace of the strike of the country's steel workers, due for a walkout tomorrow. Beyond the largest cloud is that of the miners, which looms for Nov. 1 unless peace is made.

. . . .

"On the brighter side is the fact that many of the strikes are apparently of short duration. Nineteen are reported to have been settled in the seven days preceding Sept. 17. In most cases the strikers gained an advantage. . . ."

(10) Steel men on strike, 1919.[42]

On September 29, according to one authority, there were 365,600 men out on strike, and 109,300 were out on December 10. These figures may be somewhat exaggerated in each instance, but they serve to represent the situation. There had been approximately 500,000 men employed in the steel plants before the strike.

C. Twelve-hour day.

(1) Twelve-hour day, 1885–1922.

It is certain that by 1890 several operations in steel manufacture had been developed entirely on the basis of the twelve-hour day and a seven-day week. Blast furnaces, Bessemer converters, open-hearth furnaces, and blooming mills require continuous operation in order to produce on the most profitable basis, and at one time almost 100 per cent of the workers in these branches of the industry were employed twelve hours per day. Between 1885 and 1894 the unions had actually resisted the introduction of the three-shift system in some of the plants, but after 1900 the worker's chief complaint was against the long hours of work. Between 1910 and 1914 the United States Steel Corporation took the lead in reducing the seven-day week, and the independents followed; yet during the war years very little progress was made along this line, and the number of twelve-hour men increased. The eight-hour day was an important issue in the strike of 1919, but after its failure the Corporation was able to go along in its old way, and in 1920 there were approximately 85,000 [43] of the Corporation's men on the twelve-hour shift.

[40] "Speech before American Iron and Steel Institute, October 24, 1919," printed in *Review of Reviews* (Nov., 1919), p. 488.

[41] *New York Times,* Sept. 21, 1919, pt. iv, p. 1.

[42] Figures from William Z. Foster, *The Great Steel Strike and Its Lessons* (New York, 1920), p. 191.

[43] Charles A. Gulick, *Labor Policy of the United States Steel Corporation* (New York, 1924), p. 40.

(2) Investigating committee on the twelve-hour day.[44]

A committee of the steel industry, headed by Judge Gary and organized at the instance of President Harding to investigate the twelve-hour day, brought in the following report after a year's study. The report was read at the annual meeting of the American Iron and Steel Institute by Judge Gary on May 25, 1923:

. . . .

"Whatever will be said against the twelve-hour day in the steel industry, investigation has convinced this committee that the same has not of itself been an injury to the employees, physically, mentally, or morally.

. . . .

". . . The workmen, as a rule, prefer the longer hours because it permits larger compensation per day.

. . . .

"Our investigation shows that if the twelve-hour day in the iron and steel industry should be abandoned at present, it would increase the cost of production on the average about 15%; . . . If labor were sufficiently plentiful to permit the change it would be necessary to add to the selling prices certainly as much as the increase in cost.

"But it would [not] be possible, under existing conditions, to obtain a sufficient number of men to operate the plants on a three-shift basis up to a capacity which would supply the present necessities of the purchasing public. There are not now, under a two-shift practice at the furnaces, enough men to meet the demand for iron and steel.

. . . .

"Therefore, under the present conditions, in view of the best interests of both employes and employers, and of the general public, the members of the committee cannot at this time report in favor of the total abolition of the twelve-hour day."

[44] American Iron and Steel Institute, *Year Book,* 1923, pp. 12–14.

(3) Popular reaction to the report.

From the time that the investigating committee made its report, the United States Steel Corporation was attacked in hundreds of news articles, editorials, and speeches. The height of the outburst of public opinion came in July, 1923. The following are examples of criticism in the press:[45]

"Two impressive manifestations of the popular reaction to the Gary report in favor of the twelve-hour day are now available. The document given out by the representatives of 50,000,000 Catholics, Jews and Protestants expressed the humanitarian sentiments which one would expect to find in the average American church of any and all faiths. If it be objected that it is founded on lack of expert and intimate knowledge of the steel industry, there lies to hand the report on continuous industries presented some time ago by the Federated American Engineering Societies, which was financed by the Cabot fund of Boston. This is an expert report. Mortimer E. Cooley, the president of the societies and dean of the engineering schools of the University of Michigan in an interview within a few days reiterates the opinions on the long day in steel which are contained in the formal report of the societies' committee. That committee spent two years on its task, and, says Dean Cooley, 'found indisputably that the twelve-hour shift is not economically necessary and that continuous industry can be run with a profit with the shorter working day.' . . ."

New York Herald[46]—"Mr. Gary's statement refusing to abolish the twelve-hour day in the steel mills is quite what was expected. Why should the steel trust give up the twelve-hour day? There's money in it, the mills are running full, with orders six months ahead; the churches have quit agitating; Congress is not in session; President Harding, who asked that the evil be abolished, is going to

[45] *Boston Herald,* June 8, 1923, p. 24. The first report referred to above is *The Twelve-hour Day in the Steel Industry,* published by the Federal Council of Churches of Christ in America (June, 1923).

[46] This and the quotations that follow are from the *Literary Digest,* June 9, 1923, p. 9.

Alaska, and steel-mill labor remains disorganized, deflated and leaderless."
Buffalo Express—"The religious leaders have not worded their condemnation too strongly."
Washington Evening Star—"The twelve-hour day . . . is out of harmony with existing industrial conditions. It is an anachronism."
Chicago Journal—"The twelve-hour day and the long turn at change of shift are relics of barbarism. Other industries can get along without such overwork. . . ."
Chicago Evening Post—"The conscience of America . . . will not rest satisfied or remain silent until this great industry has ended what it admitted, in better moments, to be an evil. And may that day come speedily." [47]
Philadelphia Public Ledger—"It is time for the Lords of Steel to harken and give ear."

(4) Gary says U. S. Steel will abolish twelve-hour day.

Interview of July 6, 1923: [48] "I can't say exactly when the United States Steel Corporation or any other company will get rid of the twelve-hour day entirely, but I can positively state that they will begin to act in that direction very soon and be very diligent in their efforts."

(5) Gary calls a conference on the twelve-hour day.[49]

Judge Gary brought together the presidents of the subsidiaries of the U. S. Steel Corporation on July 26, 1923. In explaining the meeting he said:

"The purpose of the conference . . . is to consider ways and means of putting into effect the elimination, at the earliest possible moment, of the twelve-hour day, which involves facts and figures more or less complicated."

(6) The Carnegie Steel Co. prepares for the change.

The first unit of the United States Steel Corporation to announce the cutting of hours under Gary's plan was the Carnegie Steel Co. The statement to the press was as follows: [50]

"The twelve-hour day in the plants of the Carnegie Steel Company will be eliminated August 16. . . . Thousands of additional workers will be required under the new schedule.

"Laborers who have been working ten hours or more and who will go on the eight-hour turn will receive 50 cents an hour instead of 40 cents. If the mills are unable to obtain sufficient labor for the extra turn which will be necessary operations may have to be curtailed until such time as the shortage can be made up. . . .

"It is understood that the other subsidiaries of the United States Steel Corporation will also eliminate the twelve-hour turn at an early date. Plans of like nature are being worked out both by the Youngstown Sheet and Tube and the Republic Iron and Steel Companies."

(7) General report of U. S. Steel for 1923.

"The improvement in the demand for iron and steel products which developed in the early fall of 1922, after nearly two years of depression in the industry, continued in very satisfactory volume until June, 1923, following which there was for several months a decided diminution in the amount of new business offered. In the closing months of the year, however, there was a noticeable improvement in tonnage entered and this has continued to the date of writing this report. At the close of 1923, the tonnage of unfilled orders for various classes of rolled steel products was 4,445,339 compared with 6,745,703 tons at close of the preceding year. . . .

"Entering the year 1923 with a large tonnage of unfilled orders on the books which was increased by liberal buying during the first five months . . . total tonnage output of materials produced for sale . . . has been exceeded in only two previous years, 1916 and 1917. As a result of these larger operations, together with improved selling prices, the earnings for the year show a substantial

[47] *Ibid.*, June 30, 1923, pp. 33–34.
[48] *New York Times*, July 7, 1923, p. 1.
[49] *Ibid.*, July 26, 1923, p. 1.
[50] *Ibid.*, Aug. 8, 1923, p. 21.

increase over those of the preceding two years."

7. Earnings of U. S. Steel under Gary [51]

Table 3. EARNINGS OF U. S. STEEL
1901–27

1901	$ 84,779,298	1915	$130,396,011
1902	133,308,763	1916	333,574,178
1903	109,171,152	1917	295,292,180
1904	73,176,522	1918	199,350,680
1905	119,787,658	1919	143,589,063
1906	156,624,273	1920	176,686,898
1907	160,964,673	1921	92,726,058
1908	91,847,710	1922	101,529,310
1909	131,491,414	1923	179,646,674
1910	141,054,754	1924	153,114,812
1911	104,305,466	1925	165,538,465
1912	108,174,673	1926	199,058,869
1913	137,181,345	1927	164,324,376
1914	71,663,615		

8. Recent Developments

A. Earnings.

Table 4. EARNINGS OF U. S. STEEL
1928–38

1928	$193,304,927
1929	258,722,453
1930	152,116,864
1931	41,048,595
1932	−18,028,417 [a]
1933	12,840,580
1934	30,180,757
1935	55,590,482
1936	107,415,395
1937	155,819,019
1938	44,010,357

[a] Loss.

B. Production policy.

(1) Relative volume produced.[52]

Table 5. RATE OF OPERATION OF U. S. STEEL AND INDEPENDENTS
1927–38

Year	Percentage of capacity: U. S. Steel	Independents
1927	78.5	69.2
1928	83.2	77.5
1929	89.3	83.7
1930	67.1	57.6
1931	39.7	36.6
1932	19.5	20.0
1933	29.3	35.4
1934	32.2	41.1
1935	41.6	53.0
1936	61.1	71.8
1937	71.2	75.2
1938 [a]	29.6	32.5

[a] For 33 weeks.

(2) Taylor's summary of recent changes in production.[53]

"While the financial structure was being simplified and the burden of fixed charges lightened, the fundamental investigation as to whether the Corporation was unduly losing its position in the industry and what could be done about it was put under way. This survey was begun and carried forward until 1935 entirely by the engineers within the Corporation . . . and in 1935 we retained the firm of Messrs. Ford, Bacon & Davis to go through all of our properties, methods, personnel and markets and, in collaboration with our engineers and executives, to formulate definite recommendations.

. . . .

". . . The problem before us was to appraise the various markets for steel, the extent of our participation in those markets as contrasted with what should be our reasonable participation, and, where we were falling off, to discover why. In all the markets for the heavier main rolled products, the Corporation stood well, but in the markets for the lighter flat rolled products, the Corporation did not stand so well. This, it appeared, was largely due to a lack of the proper equipment to produce the kind of finished steel

[51] *Poor's Industrials*. Net earnings after deducting expenses for ordinary repairs and maintenance, employees' bonus funds, and also interest on bonds and fixed charges of subsidiary companies, but before depreciation, depletion, or obsolescence.

[52] *New York Times*, Aug. 21, 1938.

[53] Myron C. Taylor, *Ten Years of Steel* (an extension of a speech delivered to the stockholders of U. S. Steel on Apr. 4, 1938), pp. 10–20.

as and when the new generation of customers wanted it. The property survey disclosed that a large number of the plants needed a considerable amount of money spent on them and that many were so located with respect to markets or raw materials, or both, that no amount of money could make them over into economical units. . . .

"It was determined, after a great deal of study, that the Corporation could achieve its highest efficiency by grouping its main producing units in the Pittsburgh district, the Chicago district and the Birmingham district. . . .

. . . .

"During our ten-year period, the changes in the science of steel making came into our problem in a decisive way. The demand for open hearth steel made many plants obsolete that were built around the Bessemer process. . . . A second and greater change was the demand for a character of finished steel that could be made only on continuous mills with highly refined processes. Such mills represent large capital outlays and, while they are very economical if running full, they are very costly if running only on part time. Thus the concentration of production became a factor of such importance as sometimes to outweigh freight rates.

. . . .

"During the ten years, there were thus abandoned, dismantled or sold plants with an annual finished product capacity of 1,700,000 tons and an ingot capacity of 2,225,000 gross tons. . . .

. . . .

"Much of the overlapping of activities was overcome by combining the Carnegie Steel Company and the Illinois Steel Company and later merging with them the American Sheet & Tin Plate Company.

. . . .

". . . the Corporation from January 1st, 1928 to December 31st, 1937, spent for additions, betterments and modernization the sum of $562,569,358 [$457,330,172 on manufacturing properties]. . . .

"These expenditures do not represent the carrying out of a program of expansion. The program has been primarily one of rehabilitation in order to meet trade demands . . . in the ten years, the Corporation has abandoned nearly five million tons of finished rolled capacity, while the new facilities already built or under way will have a capacity of about six million tons. . . .

"Considerable expenditures have been made for the making and rolling of alloy and stainless steel, for the substitution of seamless pipe for lap weld pipe and for the substitution of welding mechanism for riveting in the fabrication of steel, but the greatest expenditures have been made to provide modern facilities for the production of flat rolled products. It is here that the revolution in steel products has taken place.

. . . .

"Including the mills now under construction, the Corporation has installed 4-high mill [for making newer products] capacity of 4,321,200 gross tons of hot rolled flat products. The largest development has been the new Irvin plant on the Monongahela River above Pittsburgh in the heart of the Corporation's producing area. . . . The second largest installation is at Fairfield, Alabama, on the Tennessee Coal & Iron property which will make cold reduced tin plate for the Southern and Far Western markets. . . .

". . . But the making of steel is most certainly not a financial job and neither is it one that can be managed at long range. Therefore, as early as 1932, we planned to separate the actual making and selling of steel from the overall and financial administration and in that year we incorporated the United States Steel Corporation of Delaware. Events postponed the carrying out of that plan, but as of January 1st, 1938, it was put into execution and the coordination of all the iron and steel making activities of the subsidiaries of the Corporation has been concentrated in the new corporation with headquarters at Pittsburgh. Thus henceforth steel making and selling will be carried on in a steel making atmosphere—that is, on the ground—while the financial and general policies will remain with the Corporation."

C. Labor policy.

(1) Agreement on collective bargaining, 1937.[54]

"The Company recognizes the right of its employees to bargain collectively through representatives freely chosen by them without dictation, coercion or intimidation in any form or from any source. It will negotiate with the representatives of any group of its employees so chosen and with any organization as the representative of its members, subject to the recognition of the principle that the right to work is not dependent on membership or non-membership in any organization and subject to the right of every employee freely to bargain in such manner and through such representatives, if any, as he chooses."

(2) From *Annual Report to Stockholders,* 1938.

"Important questions having to do with wages, hours and conditions of employment were satisfactorily adjusted through discussion with employes, or their designated representatives. Expiring agreements with labor organizations were renewed, and new agreements were entered into in conformity with the collective bargaining policy of the subsidiary companies of the Corporation."

D. Price policy.

(1) From *Annual Report to Stockholders,* 1938.

"On June 24, 1938, certain of the subsidiary companies announced lower prices on many of their products, these reductions varying in amount depending partly upon the product and partly upon the point of manufacture. The new prices were approximately on the same level as the prices in effect prior to 1928, and were made to meet a competitive condition and with the hope that such reductions would stimulate a demand for steel products. Concurrently, the new mill prices for these products eliminated the price differentials between Pittsburgh, Chicago and Birmingham."

(2) From the *Wall Street Journal,* June 25, 1938.

"Leading subsidiaries of U. S. Steel Corp. yesterday announced a reduction in steel prices to a point at or below the 1928 levels. The price cut, which has been expected for some days, nevertheless had some unexpected, not to say surprising, features.

"One such feature was the extent of the cut. In sheet and strip, two important automotive products, the reductions range from $4.50 a ton in Pittsburgh to $6.40 in Chicago and $7.50 in Birmingham.

"Another feature was the practical elimination of differentials between Pittsburgh, Chicago and Birmingham as basing points. This went almost to the extent of eliminating the basing point system, which has long been attacked in political circles and generally defended by the steel industry.

"Independents Perturbed

"Both features were perturbing to the independent competitors of the big steel company in the Pittsburgh district. Naturally, they will be forced to meet the cuts inaugurated by the Big Steel subsidiary in that district. In addition, they have lost a differential of almost $2 a ton for steel sold to Chicago area customers.

. . . .

"The independents were taken by surprise by the move, and their first question was whether U. S. Steel, in an attempt to stimulate business, had embarked on a price policy without regard to the rest of the industry."

E. New leadership in U. S. Steel, 1937.[55]

"Never before in the history of the organization have the executive personnel changes of the U. S. Steel Corp. been as many and as important as those announced Tuesday. . . .

"Edward R. Stettinius, Jr., who becomes chairman of the board of directors on April 5, next, was 37 on October 22, last. Benjamin F. Fairless, who assumes the presidency of the corporation on January 1, will be 48 on May 3, next, and Enders M. Voorhees, who

[54] First publicly announced by Myron C. Taylor in his address to stockholders, Apr. 4, 1938. Printed in *Ten Years of Steel,* p. 34.

[55] *Wall Street Journal,* Oct. 28, 1937, pp. 1, 7.

becomes chairman of the finance committee next April is 45.

"The rise of Mr. Stettinius is by far the most spectacular. He is the son of the late Edward R. Stettinius, a former partner of J. P. Morgan & Co. He joined General Motors upon completing his work at the University of Virginia in 1924 and was vice president of the General Motors Co. until he came with U. S. Steel Corp. in 1934.

"Mr. Stettinius is recognized for his liberal views, particularly on labor, and is expected to continue the labor policies of Myron C. Taylor, who will continue his offices in U. S. Steel Corp.'s building here after his retirement as chairman of the board next April. It is generally believed that Mr. Stettinius will have the advice and guidance of Mr. Taylor whenever he desires it.

"Mr. Fairless, known to everyone in and out of the steel industry as 'Ben,' is perhaps the most popular individual in the steel industry today. He was born at Massillon, Ohio [the son of a coal miner].

"His business career dates back to June, 1913, when he became civil engineer for the Wheeling & Lake Erie Railroad. In August of that year he took a similar position with the Central Steel Co. of Massillon, and advanced rapidly through that organization and others, during mergers, etc., finally being made president and general manager of United Alloy Steel Co. beginning in April, 1928.

"In April, 1930, when United Alloy was merged into the new Republic Steel Corp., 'Ben' became executive vice president of the latter. It was his remarkable record during five difficult depression years as a master sales executive and a successful operating head that won for him recognition throughout the industry and resulted in his becoming president of Carnegie-Illinois Steel Corp., two years ago. . . ."

9. Suggested Readings and Sources

For its information on the steel industry in the 1890's, as well as its picture of the industry's leading figure, the first five chapters of volume ii of Burton J. Hendrick's *The Life of Andrew Carnegie* (Garden City, 1932) are strongly recommended.

George Harvey's *Henry Clay Frick* (New York, 1928) is the story of another steel man. It contains an interesting chapter on the United States Steel Corporation.

There is no satisfactory life of Gary, but Ida M. Tarbell's *The Life of Elbert H. Gary* (New York, 1925) is useful even though uncritical. A valuable source on Gary is *Addresses and Statements of Elbert H. Gary, 1904–1927,* 8 vols. An intimate and friendly picture is given in Arundel Cotter's *The Gary I Knew* (Boston, 1928).

An interesting defense of Theodore Roosevelt's action on T. C. I. and R. is found in his article, "Steel Corporation and the Panic of 1907," *Outlook,* vol. xcviii (Aug. 19, 1911), pp. 865–868.

A critical study of the first six years of the company is Abraham Berglund's *The United States Steel Corporation* (Columbia University Studies, 1907).

On recent problems and policies of the steel industry see pages 1071–1157 of *Economics of the Iron and Steel Industry,* vol. ii (New York, 1937), by C. R. Daugherty, M. G. de Chazeau, and S. S. Stratton.

On the labor policy of U. S. Steel the following may be used: for a fair presentation of policy, Charles A. Gulick, *Labor Policy of the United States Steel Corporation* (Columbia University Studies, 1924); on the twelve-hour shift, Charles R. Walker, *Steel, the Diary of a Furnace Worker* (Boston, 1922); for an account of the steel strike, unfavorable, by one of the strike leaders, William Z. Foster, *The Great Steel Strike and Its Lessons* (New York, 1920).

Records of various government agencies are mines of information on U. S. Steel. *The Report of the Industrial Commission,* 1901, contains information on the companies which became a part of U. S. Steel. The hearings and the report of the Stanley Committee on the United States Steel Corporation, 1911, are concerned with both the formation and the subsequent history of the company. The largest collection on the company is the records of the case, *United States of America* v. *United States Steel Corporation and Oth-*

ers, in the District Court of the United States for New Jersey beginning in 1914 and the Supreme Court of the United States beginning in 1916.

10. Suggested Questions

1. Why was the United States Steel Corporation formed?
2. What part did the Corporation play in the integration of the steel industry? Consider the previous progress of Carnegie.
3. What caused Gary and Morgan to buy the Tennessee Coal, Iron and Railroad Co. for the United States Steel Corporation?
4. Would the United States Steel Corporation have a lower or a higher standing in the industry today if it had not adopted the Gary price policy?
5. Why did Gary refuse to accept the workers' demands in 1919 and yield to them in 1923?
6. In view of previous developments and present tendencies, what would you say with reference to the future of the United States Steel Corporation?

XXXVI. ARMOUR & COMPANY, 1867–1938

1. General Statement

The last quarter of the nineteenth century brought the development in the United States of two great food industries on an unprecedented scale. The one was flour milling and the other meat packing. Both were essentially the result of two great forces, the opening-up of endless agricultural and ranching areas in the West and the growth of a great urban market in the United States and in Europe. Both industries were based on new techniques of production; both experienced a period of rapid growth around large business organizations; and both ran into the difficulties of maturity and old age.

Among the leaders in the development of the packing industry has been Armour & Co., which was created by Philip Danforth Armour. Not an innovator so much as a great organizer and a great buyer and seller, Armour was one of the leading industrialists of his generation. With expansion as his leading star, and terrific energy and keen judgment urging him on, he drove on through a promising but difficult business to profit and power.

J. Ogden Armour succeeded his father as head of the Armour interests in 1901, and he led the concern until in 1923. His leadership ended in disaster for the Armours. Here a nice problem presents itself. Did J. Ogden fail because of mistakes in policy and management or because of conditions affecting the industry? Causation perhaps never works singly in business.

2. Important Dates in Armour History

1832 Philip D. Armour born at Stockbridge, New York.

1852 Tramped to California.

1859 Partner in produce business in Milwaukee.

1862 H. O. Armour & Co., grain and provision commission merchants, established in Chicago.

1863 Philip D. Armour in Plankinton & Armour, pork packers, Milwaukee.

1865 Plankinton, Armour & Co., established in New York in commission business, headed by H. O. Armour. Joseph F. Armour in charge in Chicago. Union Stock Yards built.

1867 Chicago house began to pack hogs under name of Armour & Co.

1868 Cattle first slaughtered by Armour's. First practical refrigerator car invented.

1869 Plankinton & Armour, Kansas

City, headed by Simeon B. Armour, began killing cattle for pickling and export.

1874 First large chillroom built at Armour's Chicago plant.

1875 Philip D. Armour moved to Chicago, taking Michael Cudahy from Milwaukee plant to head production.

1879 Armour Brothers' Banking Co. was organized in Kansas City under management of A. Watson Armour. Armour & Co. began canning meat for export.

1884 Philip D. Armour retired from Milwaukee house. First Armour branch house opened in New York to sell canned meats. Philip D. Armour and John C. Black established Continental National Bank, Chicago. Armour's purchased Wahl Glue Works.

1885 Second Armour branch house opened at Albany, with facilities for smoking meats.

1887 Armour-Cudahy Packing Co. organized at South Omaha.

1890 Armour retired from Omaha firm. Armour's had forty branch houses.

1891 United States inspection inaugurated.

1893 Armour Institute of Technology opened.

1894 Fertilizer business started by Armour's.

1896 Armour Soap Works began operations.

1897 Omaha plant opened. Glycerine plant started.

1900 Armour & Co. incorporated in Illinois with capital of $20,000,000.

1901 Philip D. Armour died, also Kirkland B. and Herman O. Armour. Purchase of Sioux City plant marks beginning of great expansion under J. Ogden Armour.

1902 Armour's joined in organization of National Packing Co.

1907 Grape juice and soda fountain supplies first made by Armour's.

1912 Packers acquitted of charge of violating Sherman Anti-Trust Act. Dissolution of National Packing Co., Armour's taking several of firms in the holding company.

1915 Plant opened at La Plata, Argentina.

1916 Four hundred per cent stock dividend increased stock of Armour & Co. to $100,000,000.

1920 Voluntary consent decree entered in United States court whereby packers agreed to give up interests in stockyards and lines other than meat products. Armour Leather Co. organized with $20,500,000 common and preferred stock. Plant at Hamilton, Ontario, closed.

1921 Terrific loss on inventories.

1922 Armour & Co. of Delaware organized.

1923 Reorganization. Commercial bankers gained heavy representation on board. J. Ogden Armour retired from presidency and was succeeded by F. Edson White. Physical assets of Morris & Co. purchased.

1928 General Stockyards Corporation of Delaware formed to take over Armour stockyard interests.

1931 T. G. Lee became president of Armour & Co. Tremendous shrinkage in prices caused heavy loss.

1933 Recapitalization plan proposed to stockholders.

1934 Banker representatives on board of directors gave place to F. H. Prince and two of his associates. Backed by Mr. Prince, R. H. Cabell, 43 years with Armour's, became president.

3. Background of the Industry to 1875 [1]

In the history of the meat-packing industry the period prior to the Civil War in America is characterized as the slaughterhouse period. Killing was done locally, with pork or other meat the only important commercial product. Processing was very primitive. Fresh meat cut from warm carcasses was left on shelves to cool or in pickle for curing. Trim and taints were ignored. Lard was rendered in open kettles and sold unrefined. Hours of work were from dawn to dusk.

The first of the specialists in this work (of whom we know) was William Pynchon, who devoted his activities to slaughtering for local farmers in Springfield, Massachusetts, about 1650. At that time some of the products of the slaughterhouses found their way as dried or smoked meat in barrels or bulk into the export and plantation trade.

As settlement moved westward in the late eighteenth century, Cincinnati became the center of livestock trading and slaughtering activities, becoming known as "Porkopolis." Even then great numbers of animals were raised and fattened in the Ohio Valley and driven to the East to be killed. From the building of the first real packing plant in Cincinnati in 1818 until the Civil War that town remained the center of the packing industry. New forces were at work, however, which were soon to make Chicago the center of activities.

Until means to ship fresh meat from the Middle West to the East had been developed, the local slaughterers in the East were destined to perform most of the killing operations. They were still predominant when Philip Armour appeared on the scene. First of the packers to stress the need for refrigeration, he took advantage of the invention as soon as it was a reality. Finding opposition to his plans, he devised means to overcome it. That the industry would have developed without him is a certainty, but that he played an active part in speeding its development cannot be doubted.

[1] See Rudolf A. Clemen, *The American Livestock and Meat Industry* (New York, 1923), pp. 21–145.

4. Philip D. Armour Builds a Packing Business

A. The growth of the business.[2]

In 1859 Philip D. Armour entered business in Milwaukee. He was then 26 years of age, and he had a money capital of about $6,000 and a fund of experience, both gained from five years in California. On his return from California young Armour had become impressed with the possibilities of Milwaukee, where his brother Herman had entered the grain and provision business.

After a brief and unsuccessful venture in soap making and a trip to St. Paul—where he dealt in hides and met Jim Hill—Philip D. Armour in March, 1859, joined Frederick B. Miles in a partnership to carry on a "produce and commission business" in Milwaukee. Their object was to sell produce to westbound immigrants; each contributed $500 to the business; and both pledged themselves not to draw more than $100 a month.[3]

In 1862 Armour made a trip to Cincinnati, which he had visited some years before. He married Malvina Bell Ogden, the daughter of a successful merchant and real estate dealer. At the same time he observed the great prosperity which the Civil War had brought to the pork packers of Cincinnati. Shortly thereafter he persuaded his brothers Herman and Joseph to set up in the grain business in Chicago, and he himself joined the big-

[2] Much of the information on Armour in this section is from the *Armour Magazine,* April, 1927.

[3] Harper Leech and John Charles Carroll, *Armour and His Times* (New York, 1938), pp. 25–27.

gest packer in Milwaukee—one of the largest in the country—in a partnership for slaughtering and packing hogs.

The Armour-Plankinton business proved very prosperous. The Civil War took great quantities of hams and barrel pork at rising prices. In 1865 Herman Armour was sent to New York City to open a branch under the name of Armour, Plankinton Co., commission merchants. From its beginning the branch was successful, and it served as a valuable contact with the greatest consuming market and financial center of the country.

Though he was very successful during the war, Armour's great *coup* came at the end of the war. Foreseeing victory for the North and a slump in pork prices after peace, he in 1864 contracted for heavy future deliveries of pork. The contracts were filled after the great drop in prices following peace had come, and Plankinton and Armour are said to have made well over a million.

How far Armour's success continued to be a matter of shrewd timing it is impossible to say. This is true, that it was not necessary for him to take such risks on the market. The development on the Chicago Board of Trade during the war of trading in pork for future delivery took off the packer the risk of price change and of finding a market. Before this development, says R. A. Clemen,[4] "pork packing was considered the worst and most risky operation possible because the packer himself had to carry his products until a cash demand came for them, unless the packers were able to break prices of hogs to a safe figure." How far Armour continued later to speculate in pork, it is impossible to say. His heavy speculation in grain suggests that he probably also traded in pork, but at least such speculation was not a necessary part of the packing business after hedging became possible.

By the time of the opening of the Union Stockyards on Christmas Day, 1865, Chicago took its place as the leading packing center of the country. To take advantage of this shift, Armour & Co. was established in Chicago in 1867 to pack hogs. The grain business still continued as a side issue under the name H. O. Armour & Co. The next year saw the Armours beginning to slaughter cattle in Chicago, and two years later sheep were slaughtered. Philip Armour at this time bought the Griffin House with a capacity for killing 30,000 hogs a year. In 1870 Armour & Co. took over all the Chicago interests of the Armours.

"About 1870," says Clemen,[5] "was the beginning of the second era in the history of meat packing. One might say that not until then was it struck by the forces of the industrial revolution." About this time a number of forces combined to drive the industry forward. In the East was a rapid increase in population beyond the point where the local meat supply was adequate. In the Southwest and West beef production had become a specialized industry, particularly in the great cattle country from Texas northward, and the producers were looking for a market.

By 1870 three principal routes to eastern markets had developed. The first was to New Orleans by steamer, up the Mississippi River to Cairo, Illinois, and thence to Chicago and eastward by railroad; the second was by trail to the Red River of the South, thence by river to Cairo, and on by railroad; the third route was by cattle trail to the railheads, the first reaching Abilene, Kansas, in 1867.

The railroad proved, however, to be an unsatisfactory long-distance carrier of livestock to the eastern market. In the 1870's there was much dissatisfaction with rail rates among shippers. Moreover, transportation was slow and facilities for handling livestock were so bad that the

[4] Clemen, *op. cit.*, p. 379.

[5] *Ibid.*, p. 173.

loss was large. In the report for 1870 the Massachusetts Railroad Commissioners stated that shrinkage between Chicago and Boston was between 10 and 15 per cent, and that under the most favorable circumstances the animals left the train unfit to kill, while under the least favorable circumstances a regular percentage of animals died.[6]

The obvious answer was to ship dressed meat, and Armour saw the trend of the times early. Indeed, in 1868 he had started to slaughter cattle in Chicago and, two years later, sheep. Since Kansas City was so advantageously situated, he persuaded his brother Simeon B. Armour to take charge of a branch there in 1869 under the name of Plankinton & Armour. The next year saw the erection of a new plant with a daily capacity of 1,000 cattle for pickling and export purposes.

The Armour business grew fast in the 1870's. In 1875, since Joseph F. Armour's health was failing, Philip D. moved to Chicago, taking Michael Cudahy with him to supervise operations. This move recognized Chicago as the center of Armour operations, as it had indeed become for packing operations for the whole country. In 1879, in the absence of adequate banking facilities in Kansas City, the Armour Brothers' Banking Co. was established there under Andrew W. Armour.

By 1875 the Armours, who had been primarily pork packers, were going heavily into beef. The basis for this change was the invention of new methods of refrigeration, which were to revolutionize the industry. The first practical application of refrigeration to meat storage and transportation in the United States had come immediately after the Civil War. After the railway consolidation between Chicago and the Atlantic Coast had been completed in 1869, making possible single car operations for the whole trip under one agreement, dressed beef was sent to Boston in one of the new Davis refrigerator cars (patented in 1868). Its arrival marked the turning point of the fresh meat industry from one of local significance to national and even international importance.

It was several years, however, before the refrigerator cars were improved sufficiently to be satisfactory. It was Gustavus Swift who finally hit upon the true principle in building refrigerator cars, and he was the leader in developing the dressed meat traffic.[7]

Gustavus F. Swift, born in Sandwich, Massachusetts, in 1839, had built up a wholesale slaughtering business in several communities in eastern Massachusetts. As the local supply of cattle became inadequate he moved his buying westward —to Albany, to Buffalo, and finally to Chicago in 1875. Though he entered Chicago as a cattle buyer in the stockyards, within two years, seeing the possibilities of shipping dressed beef, he started slaughtering in that city.

Swift at once ran into the opposition of railroads in the Trunk Line Association. The railroads feared that the new traffic meant lower income from freight and loss on investment in livestock cars and in stockyards in eastern markets (both the Pennsylvania and the New York Central had heavy investments in yards). Swift, therefore, designed and had refrigerator cars built for his own use and ran them via the Grand Trunk, of Canada, which was not in the Trunk Line Association.

Armour's, as has been seen, entered the dressed beef business in the West before Swift did, but it was in 1876 that the Kansas City branch began the killing of beef to be distributed fresh in refrigerator cars to markets other than local.

A number of difficulties impeded the development of the fresh meat business for about ten years. The railroads con-

[6] *Ibid*, pp. 195–203.

[7] *Ibid.*, p. 221.

tinued for some time to discriminate in rates and other ways. Industries which had grown up in connection with feeding and caring for livestock in transit opposed the new development. Local butchers, who were alarmed by the lower prices possible under the new scheme, fought with propaganda, boycott, and even legislation. In 1886 the National Butchers' Protective Association took up the fight against dressed beef. Consumers, moreover, preferred the fresh meat from the local slaughterhouse, feeling that the other was not wholesome. But gradually the opposition waned, and by 1894, according to R. A. Clemen, came the complete triumph of dressed beef.[8]

Armour attacked at several points the problems confronting the new business. First, he made sure that his product was as good as possible at that time. Then he looked to costs. The refrigerator cars saved a large transportation cost. Since still greater economy was needed, he turned to the problem of waste. A large part of the animals he slaughtered was being thrown away, and part of the waste was expensive to dispose of under sanitation laws. He, therefore, encouraged the fostering of by-product industries to use these discarded materials. In 1879, the Company began the canning of meats for foreign trade. Since certain meats which are unsuitable for sale fresh are adapted to canning, Armour by this move salvaged some animal parts which had previously been waste. Similarly, oleomargarine, put on the market first in 1880 by Armour, used certain parts which had formerly been discarded. In 1882 Armour began to use blood, bones, and meat scrap for the first time on an important scale. This use still further utilized previously discarded materials.

Armour recognized that the most difficult problem was that of selling. While Swift had the advantage of established contacts with butchers in the Boston area, Armour had the advantage of a wide system for the distribution of pork products and a high reputation for quality. In the early 'eighties Armour's disposed of most of its meats through wholesalers, the wholesalers dealing with local butchers and other retailers. The wholesalers lacked aggressiveness, however, and the Armours had no way of directly influencing the consumers.

The solution was found in establishing more branch offices—two had been established early to sell pork. In 1884 a second branch was established in New York, to sell canned meat; in 1885 another was established in Albany, with facilities for smoking meat; five years later, forty branches were listed, some with minor packing facilities, but all with the major purpose of selling directly to retailers. The branch houses were controlled from headquarters at Chicago, a branch-house accounting department being established in the Chicago office in 1889.

The large packers, recognizing that selling should be handled as a common problem, began in about the middle 'eighties to combine in order to eliminate price competition. A committee of the United States Senate reported in 1890 that they had found agreement on prices and the division of territory and business between Armour & Co., Swift & Co., Nelson Morris & Co., and Hammond & Co. The Sherman Act of 1890 did not break up this practice—at least, it is known that from 1893 to 1902 the big packers conducted an almost continuous pool to divide the territory and business among the members.[9]

Several changes in the partner relationships of Armour's occurred from 1878 to 1884. In 1878 John Plankinton retired from the Chicago house. Joseph F. Armour

[8] *Ibid.*, p. 251.

[9] United States Federal Trade Commission, *Report on the Meat-Packing Industry,* 1920, summary and part i, pp. 46–47.

died in 1881. Herman O. Armour withdrew from the central partnership in 1882, taking over complete control of the New York plant. John Plankinton retired from the Kansas City house in that same year, and it became the Armour Packing Co. Philip's son, J. Ogden Armour, left his studies at Yale to help relieve his father. In 1884, Ogden was admitted to partnership in all his father's companies. In the same year Philip D. retired from active management of the Milwaukee house, which became John Plankinton & Co.

It may be noted that, although he had retired from the management of the New York and Milwaukee houses, Philip Armour was still in control of the Chicago, Kansas City, and Omaha houses, which were more strategically located than the other two. He also held the control of the distributing organization, which was fast spreading. He was assured of good banking connections through the Armour Brothers' Banking Co., of Kansas City, and through the Continental National Bank, which he had established with John C. Black, of Chicago, in 1884. Taking the place of Joseph F. Armour, the first of the brothers to die, was J. Ogden Armour, the first of the next generation to step into the business.

Expansion continued after these readjustments of the business partnerships. In 1884 Armour purchased the Wahl Glue Works, which had been established as an industry subsidiary to packing. In 1885 Armour's began the sale of beef extract and pepsin in London. Michael Cudahy, formerly superintendent of the Chicago plant, in 1887 went to East Omaha, where he established the Armour-Cudahy Packing Co. Cudahy wanted his own company, and the profits from the Omaha partnership with Armour proved sufficient in three years to enable him to buy Armour's share. The name of the East Omaha company then became the Cudahy Packing Co.—this concern was destined later to become one of the really great packing firms.

Changes were less marked during the last decade of Philip D. Armour's life, being chiefly along the line of diversification of products. Mincemeat became an item in the Armour line in 1890. Dry sausage was added the next year. The Armour Soap Works began operations next to the Glue Works in 1894. In 1897 Armour's pork and beans were first marketed. A separate glycerine plant was built in the same year. At that time also a new plant was built in Omaha to compete directly with Cudahy. A very successful new department was the fertilizer department, which was established to utilize waste. It had been urged upon Armour by one of the foremen in the Chicago plant, who organized the department and made it an important part of the Armour business.

Philip D. Armour, Jr., was admitted to partnership with his father and brother in 1889. The father took a half-share in the partnerships with his sons, dividing the other half equally between them. Presumably, at his death they were to divide his share, thus creating an equal partnership for the two brothers. As it happened, Philip, Jr., died one year before his father and J. Ogden received his father's share intact. Another personnel factor of passing interest at this time was the admission of F. Edson White into the business in 1894. He was assigned the job of organizing the new sheep department, which he did so well that he was later advanced to the presidency of the Company.

The packing business was strengthened in 1891 by the inauguration of government inspection of slaughtering. The big packers backed this move from the first because it established the quality of their meats in contrast with the uninspected meats of small local slaughterers. Indirectly it increased the costs of the small competitors, who were forced to improve their standards.

In 1891 the general offices of the Company, which had been located on LaSalle

Street, were moved out to the Union Stockyards, where more intimate touch could be kept with the activities of the business. The fact that an advertising department was inaugurated in 1896, during the "buyers' market" which then prevailed, shows that Armour's was adopting new techniques in marketing.

Armour extended into a new field in 1900, when the Armour Car Lines took over the management of the Earl Fruit Co. This marked the assumption of a new function, the distribution of food products other than meat with a view to more nearly complete utilization of the cars and marketing organization of the packers. The condition which made this possible was Armour's ownership of refrigerator cars which were suitable for the transportation of any perishable products.

In 1900 Armour & Co. was incorporated under the laws of Illinois. Various legal complications had led to the separation of the Armour interests into several groups. These groups are outlined below as they existed in 1905 (substantially the same as in 1900): [10]

(1) Packing interests owned by Armour's.

Armour & Co., of Illinois, incorporated in 1900 at $20,000,000.

This company does business only in Illinois and Nebraska and owns the Armour packing houses at Chicago, East St. Louis, and South Omaha, as well as the following which are not incorporated: Armour Fertilizer Works, Armour Soap Works, Armour Glue Works, Armour Curled Hair and Felt Works, and Armour Printing Works.

Other packing interests, owned by or through corporations which are owned by stockholders of Armour & Co. (the three largest in the same proportion as Armour stock):

Armour Packing Co., a New Jersey corporation dating from 1893 with a capital of $7,500,000, which operates the Kansas City packing house. This was at first controlled by the branch of the family residing in Kansas City, but before Philip D.'s death a complete community of interest was established between this house and Armour & Co., of Illinois.

Armour & Co., of New Jersey, a corporation with stock of $100,000. This concern operates practically for the sale of the products of Armour & Co., of Illinois, and owns Armour packing houses at Sioux City and Fort Worth. Its accounts are carried on the books of Armour & Co., of Illinois.

Armour Car Lines, a New Jersey corporation with a capital stock of $100,000. This concern owns the refrigerator and other cars of Armour's; also the Continental Fruit Express, an Illinois corporation with a capital of $1,000,000, whose cars are used for the transportation of fruit.

Armour Packing Co., Ltd., a Louisiana corporation with a capital stock of $5,000, engaged in marketing Armour products.

Armour & Co., a copartnership organized by Armour stockholders for handling the business in Pennsylvania.

Stockyard companies in which Armour's owns stocks: Union Stock Yards Co. of Omaha; Sioux City Stockyards; National Stock Yards, East St. Louis; Fort Worth Stock Yards Co.; and Kansas City Stock Yards Co.

(2) Allied concerns.

Chicago Junction Railways and Union Stock Yards Co. Armour & Co. in 1891 made a contract with this company to maintain its packing-house at this stockyard for fifteen years.

United States Leather Co. A consolidation of many tanneries with $125,000,000 in stock outstanding. Armour's has a substantial voice in its affairs.

(3) Grain interests of Armour's.

Armour Grain Co., a New Jersey corporation capitalized at $1,000,000, controlled by Armour interests.

Armour Elevator Co., an Illinois corporation capitalized at $100,000.

[10] U. S. Bureau of Corporations, *Report of the Commissioner on the Beef Industry,* 1905, pp. 33–35, 291–293.

B. Financial result of operations, 1869–1900.[11]

Table 1. FINANCIAL HISTORY OF ARMOUR & CO. 1869–1900

Year	Reported net profit	Net worth	Profit as per cent of net worth
1869	$ 120,000	$ 160,000	75.0
1870	49,000	200,000	24.5
1871	18,000	240,000	7.5
1872	69,000	240,000	28.8
1873	199,000	258,000	77.1
1874	126,000	408,000	30.9
1875	300,000	500,000	60.0
1876	500,000	750,000	66.7
1877	450,000	1,200,000	37.5
1878	524,000	1,500,000	34.9
1879	705,000	2,000,000	35.3
1880 [a]	2,000,000	2,500,000	64.0
1881	1,850,000	4,250,000	43.5
1882	1,705,000	5,500,000	31.0
1883	510,000	6,500,000	7.8
1884	1,618,000	6,750,000	24.0
1885	1,100,000	7,500,000	14.7
1886	1,050,000	8,000,000	13.1
1887	1,000,000	8,250,000	12.1
1888	1,700,000	9,000,000	18.9
1889	1,550,000	10,000,000	15.5
1890	1,550,000	10,500,000	14.8
1891	1,100,000	11,000,000	10.0
1892	1,886,000	11,250,000	16.8
1893	2,000,000	12,000,000	16.7
1894	729,000	13,000,000	5.6
1895	1,400,000	13,250,000	10.6
1896	2,070,000	14,000,000	14.8
1897–1900 [b]	8,105,000	16,000,000	...

[a] 15 months.
[b] 1897 to incorporation, April, 1900; individual years not available.

The story told by the above table is simple. Profits were generally high during the developmental years to 1885. They fluctuated violently during those years, a condition which was then common in new industries. Although in this period the price trend was downward, the industry was able to make profits because of the new services it had to offer. (Note the effect of collapse in 1893.) In view of the fact that no additional capital was contributed to Armour's business from its inception in 1868 to its incorporation in 1900, the growth of net worth is significant.

The balance sheet of Armour & Co. at about the time of incorporation was as follows:[12]

Assets		
Cash	$ 834,642.22	
Receivables	10,416,770.43	
Inventories	21,564,763.91	
		$32,816,176.56
Investments:		
Stock, Bonds, Member-ships	$ 679,637.32	
Investments —London	450,746.33	
Properties	12,201,561.72	
Deferred Charges	88,967.79	13,420,913.16
		$46,237,089.72
Liabilities		
Notes Payable	$10,025,000.00	
Accounts Payable	2,773,108.31	$12,798,108.31
Capital Stock		20,000,000.00
Surplus		13,438,981.41
		$46,237,089.72

C. Philip D. Armour, the man, and his ideas.

In his early years Armour showed a high capacity for seizing business opportunity. Restless at home on the farm in Stockbridge, New York, at the age of nineteen he organized a party of four to tramp to California to join the gold rush. The trip took six months. One of his companions died, and the others turned home;

[11] *Report on the Meat-Packing Industry,* 1920, part v, p. 21.

[12] Leech and Carroll, *op. cit.,* p. 342.

but Philip Armour went on. Not taken by the gambling spirit of the gold rush, he organized the business of digging ditches for prospectors on a straight-pay basis, hiring others to do the digging while he directed it and drummed up new business. In five years he had saved over $8,000, and he set out for home to buy a good farm and marry. On the way he observed carefully business conditions and opportunities, and after a short visit home (where, it is said, he found the girl married to another) he doubled back to Milwaukee which he considered a place of great promise.

Armour had striking perseverance and vitality. It took both these qualities to force him on to California when his companions turned back. Until late in his active life he is said to have begun work at six o'clock in the morning, greeting those who came to the office after seven with a "Good afternoon!" During the first few years of his business life four o'clock was the order of the day. In later years he took occasional vacations, but these vacations were taken either in branch territories which he wished to examine or in livestock areas. He never returned from a vacation without some recommendation for the business which had come from careful observation. His life was that of a specialist, concentrated at one point and unbalanced.

With all his one-sided interest, Philip Armour was a very human individual. Kind and thoughtful, he held a strong friendship for his associates. In return he won the respect and affection of his friends. He expected and received the utmost loyalty from those who worked closely with him, which was no doubt an element in his success. He placed members of his family in important positions, in some cases with most fortunate results but in others incurring criticism because of unfitness for the jobs given.

Armour was a born leader of men. His attraction for men rose largely from his power, physical as well as mental. Though a man of six feet and great breadth, yet he moved easily. His face was once described as "the face of one so much the master of himself he can afford to be gentle." The description continues: "Voice kindly in its tone and low; and while his eyes twinkle and all around them are the lines of good humour, there is in them all the shrewdness, all the searching quality that you can imagine a man of his record to possess."

Philip Armour was generous with his employees, paying top prices for the services of good men. His theory was: "No general can fight his battles alone. He must depend on his lieutenants, and his success depends upon his ability to select the right man for the right place." Asked where he got his best men, he said, "I raise them." But in doing so he also raised some first-grade competitors. Most notable of these was Michael Cudahy, whose packing firm has since become one of the four largest. It is certain, however, that Armour opposed collective bargaining and the organization of labor, and he seems to have believed that the "good employer" was the solution of the labor problem.

It is no wonder that a man of this sort got things done effectively. When he gave an order, he was sure of its being completed swiftly by able lieutenants. A story is told of how his enemies once tried to ruin him. He had made heavy future commitments in wheat for May delivery. His enemies bought enough wheat to fill all the elevators in Chicago and left it there. Since he must deliver the wheat in elevators, they expected to put him in a position where he would have to buy them out at ruinous prices. But exactly twenty-eight days before delivery was due, he discovered the plot. He gave orders. In twenty-seven days the largest elevator to be built up to that time was completed. He not only had filled the contract, but he had entered another profitable business. His elevator was better situated and more modern than any of the others.

Armour showed the same resourcefulness in eluding the Leiter corner in the late 1890's.

As a manufacturer Armour constantly sought economy and efficiency by preventing waste. He stressed simple modifications of by-products to make them attractive for sale, guaranteeing their excellence and selling at the lowest possible prices. He is quoted as saying, "Anybody can cut prices, but it takes brains to make a better article."

In financial matters he stuck to one principle: to have at all times more cash on hand than the most unlikely contingency could possibly necessitate. To maintain this rule he was often in debt to the banks when ordinary business did not demand the funds. It is probable that this policy prevented the Company from getting into financial trouble during the depression of 1893. Indeed, at that time he was able to buy a half-million dollars in gold in Europe and offer it as support for the big financial houses of Chicago to stem the tide when the city and the Columbian Exposition alike were threatened.

One time, when Philip Armour was off inspecting some St. Paul Railroad lines, it is said, he heard a rumor that his company was in financial trouble. His first action, after catching the first train to Chicago, was to look up the source. It appeared that a bank president had demanded thirty-day payment of a ninety-day note for $100,000. The cashier, in Armour's absence, had refused. The next day Philip went to the president, gave him a calling-down loud enough to be heard by all present in the bank, and ended by throwing $100,000 in currency in his face.

Most revealing of the man and his ideas are the letters Armour wrote to his nephews and sons as they gradually took over the work of running the Armour interests. Quotations from those letters clearly state some of the policies of the "Old Man" and show in what ways he was trying to guide the next generation to good business methods.

(1) To a nephew, Kirk Armour, October 26, 1900: [13]

"I think if you don't look out, you will have a big stock of these goods next year, and I think it is just as well to be a little foxy on your prices. I don't think you boys realize what a big stock of canned goods mean . . . you fellows are not close enough to the trade, and the first thing you know, you will turn a complete somersault, and spill all your profits yourselves."

(2) To the same nephew, May 3, 1897: [14]

". . . The bull always pays a carrying charge, and sometimes a little more, and a future always brings more money; and on general principles as a merchant, it is a good thing to do. In fact, I got my position in life by being a good seller. . . .

"But I notice I am not near so good a merchant as I used to be when I was a good seller, as we are always buying the stuff, and you ought to bear this in mind, too; in fact if you will look over your account for the last three years, or four or five, you will find that all the money you have lost has been by holding goods; you have never lost any by being a seller. And I should like to see you more of a seller and a better seller than you have been. You have such an awful big hitchup, and do such a small business, that it is difficult for you to make any money. Your hitchup is about as expensive as ours, and you don't do one fourth or one third as much business [in Kansas City] as we do [in Chicago], and even we are not doing enough for our hitchup."

(3) To his sons, J. Ogden and Philip D., Jr., December 19, 1899: [15]

"While I am about it, I will say to you how fully you can realize with this pinch of money, how necessary it is for Armour and Co., and the Armour Packing Co., to have more money in their business. I don't want any one to draw out personal money, but

[13] *Ibid.*, p. 98.
[14] *Ibid.*, p. 99.
[15] *Ibid.*, pp. 121–122.

keep it in the business as more money is needed badly.

"It would be a good deal better for some of the partners if their money had been kept in the concern, instead of being taken out and put into what may perhaps turn out to be visionary investments induced by a high rate of dividend. This Biscuit [New York Biscuit stock] may turn out all right, but the firm has got too much of it. . . .

"I think both of you boys have a great deal to learn about investments and you should be careful not to learn it too expensively. You should feel your way along and consult others, as I feel you were not born with the idea of what is really sound and what is not sound, as you cannot always go on an isolated or flippant earning power. . . .

"I have a feeling that we don't know anything about Biscuit and I feel I am correct in my feeling . . . it needs to be well managed in order to get out of it all there is in it, and I feel I don't know anything about the management. . . . I think most of these industrials are full of wind and water, and this will have to be gotten out of them before they are on any safe basis. . . . In fact, I am not a bull on anything that is sold on Wall Street."

(4) To his son, J. Ogden, 1899: [16]

"You of course want to be good and kind to your men. You don't want to be stuck on any of them, but simply just with them. You certainly must permeate the concern from one end to the other that you are not dependent on any one, two or three men to keep the business afloat, but that you can float it yourself, even if you are left without any of them. I say this much as I feel there is a feeling around the concern that the young element isn't as resourceful or as strong in its determination as the 'old man' has been; but you can cultivate this greatly and improve on it a great deal by having it on your mind."

(5) To his sons, 1899: [17]

"You cannot be too careful of yourself in husbanding your money. Don't try to get rich too fast and never feel rich. I have had a little feeling that both of you boys felt your oats a little too much since the closing of the books. But you will have a year before you that will test you a little and show whether there is any ability in you. . . ."

5. Under J. Ogden Armour, 1901–23

A. Expansion of production.[18]

With the incorporation of Armour & Co., a new phase in the history of the Company began, a period of expansion under J. Ogden Armour. Among the early additions to the Armour productive equipment after J. Ogden took charge were three plants: the first by purchase, at Sioux City, in 1901; and the second a newly constructed plant at Fort Worth, Texas, in 1903, and another new plant at East St. Louis. A more far-reaching step was about to be taken. During 1902 there were persistent reports in the press that all the big packers were about to consolidate into a single corporation. Since Schwarzschild & Sulzberger, a large New York packing firm, refused to be a party to it, the plan was never carried out. Instead, in March, 1903, a $15,000,000 corporation, the National Packing Co., was organized under New Jersey laws. This company acquired the capital stock in various properties which had previously been purchased by Armour, Swift, and Morris interests.

The organization of the National Packing Co. established a strong community of interest among the three great packers who contributed to its formation. Armour and Swift had equal representation on its board of directors, each contributing four members; and Morris interests were represented by three directors. At the same time, the combination reduced the number of strong national packers. Only two other companies of importance in the interstate meat trade remained outside the combination: Schwarzschild & Sulzberger

[16] *Ibid.*, p. 222.
[17] *Ibid.*, p. 340.

[18] Most of the facts in this section are from the *Armour Magazine*, April, 1927.

Co. (now Wilson & Co.), of New York, and the Cudahy Packing Co.

From the organization of the National Packing Co. to the entrance of the United States into the World War in 1917, several changes occurred in the physical equipment of Armour & Co. In 1908 the general offices were set up in a new building in the downtown district of Chicago, reversing the move made in 1891, when the offices were moved to the stockyards district. In 1910 William E. Pierce, superintendent of the Chicago plant, was sent to La Plata, Argentina, there to undertake the construction of the greatest meatpacking plant in South America. He completed the task in five years, opening the plant in time to take advantage of the boom war market. In 1912 the National Packing Co. was dissolved, Armour, Swift, and Morris dividing its assets according to their respective interests in the company. As its share Armour & Co. took over large plants in New York, Kansas City, and St. Joseph (Missouri), and other smaller properties. In 1913 Armour purchased a plant at Jersey City; and in 1916 a plant at Indianapolis. The Company extended its activities to the West Coast in 1917 with the purchase of a majority of the stock of the E. H. Stanton Co., meat packers in Spokane, Washington.

During the War, Armour's capacity was taxed to the limit to provide food for the soldiers in Europe. Facilities were improved to this end in 1917, when the largest meat cooler in the world was completed in the Chicago packing plant.

After the close of the War, Armour's acquired plants in Tifton, Georgia, and in South St. Paul. Following these increases in slaughtering capacity, the Armour Leather Co. was organized, to acquire all Armour's leather business, with a capital stock of $10,500,000 common and $10,000,000 of 7 per cent preferred. Also, in 1920 new South American plants were opened at São Paulo, Brazil, and Santa Cruz, Patagonia. The capacity of the meat cooler in the Chicago plant was matched at this time with a freezer having a capacity of some fifty million pounds of product.

In the meantime a plant had been opened at Hamilton, Ontario, which had to be closed in 1920 for lack of satisfactory operation. The number of animals raised in Canada for slaughter was insufficient to support a large plant, and Armour's organization required large plants for overhead coverage. The failure of management better to gauge the conditions in Canada at this time is notable.

While adding new plants, Armour was also continually adding new equipment. On the other hand, it is said that he neglected maintenance seriously. This apparent inconsistency in policy contains much food for thought.

B. By-products under J. Ogden Armour.

By the time J. Ogden Armour assumed control of Armour & Co. the firm had absorbed most of the numerous small independent establishments the function of which in earlier days had been to handle by-products collected from the packing plants. Chemical laboratories had also been installed—after the example of Nelson Morris. The main divisions of by-products had already begun to be recognized as distinct branches of the business. Classified broadly, the by-products which Armour processed in 1900 fell into three major groups: hides, oleo products, and offal (minor products having little or no value). The value of hides was generally greater than the combined value of all other by-products derived from a beef animal. Oleo products were distinctly the next division in importance. From these the main finished products derived in 1900 were oleomargarine, butterine, and compound lard. Salable offal fell into the following chief groups: tongues, sold either fresh or in cans; minor food products, like livers, brains, sweetbreads, ox-tails, hearts, and so on; and a third group which required further processing before they could be sold, such as intestines, blood, heads, feet, and tripe.

The major growth in the manufacture of by-products by Armour & Co., as indeed in the whole industry, has taken place within the last thirty years. Some of these by-products were developed to utilize waste materials in the manufacture of useful goods, like toilet soaps introduced by Armour in 1902. An important recent development has been the study of glandular derivatives. Other products handled were a function of the distribution system, for example, grape juice and soda fountain supplies, both of which were added to the Armour line in 1907. It would be instructive to study the steps of integration of Armour & Co. which this growth has entailed and to examine the forces which led to each addition.

C. Marketing.

The method of selling changed but little under J. Ogden Armour. He accepted the branch house system of distribution as he found it and extended it more in size than in new developments. When he took control of the Company, there were two hundred branch houses; when the bankers assumed control, there were over five hundred. The introduction of the automobile changed somewhat the problems of territory coverage. A trucking control department was established to meet these problems.

After the War, Armour's productive capacity proved too great for its market. In 1923 Armour's bought the physical assets and goodwill of Morris & Co. It was hoped in this way to establish sufficient market for the combined productive capacity of both companies after duplications had been eliminated. This will be discussed in greater detail in the section dealing with the reorganization of the Company.

D. Public relations of Armour & Co.

It has been seen that by 1885 Armour & Co. had passed out of the period of phenomenal growth accompanying the building of a new industry. At that time there were started informal pools among the big packers to improve market conditions and probably to manipulate price. Agreements of one sort or another continued until 1902, when the packers discontinued them in deference to public opinion. In 1903, however, as has been noted above, the National Packing Co., a holding company owning meat-packing stocks, was formed by Armour, Swift, and Morris. Since all three of these packers had an active part in the management of the new company, it was possible for them to continue their informal agreements under the guise of managing the jointly owned company. Following this move the public became even more disturbed than it had been before.

Expressing the feeling of the country in 1904, Congress ordered an investigation of the beef packing industry. The resulting *Report of the Commissioner of Corporations* was an honest attempt to determine to what extent the big packers controlled prices. The report indicated that the conditions of the markets for livestock and meats in the United States were such that very little control could be exercised by the packers. The report did not, however, consider the early pools as conducive to fair market operations. In 1905 the government succeeded in obtaining an injunction against the packers forbidding any device the purpose or effect of which was to restrain commerce. The Supreme Court unanimously held that there had been illegal combination.

The packers continued to operate the National Packing Co. after this injunction; and the government brought suit against them in July, 1905, claiming that the defendants were still carrying on business in opposition to the injunction. The packers denied the charge but because they had been forced to give evidence against themselves to the commissioner of corporations, they requested immunity from suit. The request was granted by the Supreme Court in 1906 in a decision that met with considerable popular disfavor, being commonly known as the "Immunity Bath." The National Packing Co. continued in business as before.

In 1910 the government brought civil suit against the National Packing Co. under the Sherman Anti-Trust Act. At the same time, criminal suit was brought against Armour, Swift, and others concerned, under the same act. The civil suit was later withdrawn to give the other suits greater chance of success. The defendants won the suits, a Chicago jury ruling that there was no criminal action in the conduct of their businesses.

It had become evident to the legal profession by 1912 that the Sherman Anti-Trust Act did not perform the function for which it was intended. Examples like the foregoing court decisions indicated that certain practices which were not acceptable to the public were still legal. The movement which was to end in the Clayton Act pressed forward in Congress. The packers, probably afraid, dissolved the National Packing Co.

The World War came soon after the Clayton Act had gone into effect, and in the rush for efficiency of production the public forgot its concern over monopoly. When the United States entered the War, the government licensed the plants of the big packers, limiting profits to 9 per cent on capital investment. There was no reason to push prosecution against the packers under the licensing arrangement; indeed, public opinion did not justify such prosecution.

After the War prices rose to new heights as did profits. The public had to pay more and more for food products, and the cost of living was becoming oppressive. Superficially it seemed that the packers were bound to extend their operations into virtual monopoly of large sections of the food supply. Already, for example, Armour & Co. dealt in fruits, vegetables, fish, milk, butter, eggs, and all varieties of canned goods. The public turned against the packers once more to protect their markets from complete monopoly control. The Federal Trade Commission was ordered to make a study of the situation to disclose the extent to which control had already progressed. Its report, completed in 1919, condemned the packers at every point and added to the public distrust. The *Report of the Federal Trade Commission* was distinctly unfair in its treatment of the matter, even going so far as to claim illegality of action in matters which the 1904 *Report of the Commissioner of Corporations* had cleared of stigma. But there was enough of truth in it so that the packers preferred not to face trial in court, especially under a heated public opinion. In 1920, therefore, a consent decree was confirmed in the District of Columbia Supreme Court, which provided that (1) the packers should sell their interests in stockyards, terminal railroads, market newspapers, and public cold storage warehouses; (2) they should cease handling food lines unrelated to meat, such as canned fruit and vegetables, canned fish, grape juice, and condiments; and (3) they should refrain from operating retail stores. In return it was agreed by the government that the packers had not been guilty of any illegal action.

Not satisfied with the consent decree as an expression of public disapproval, the next Congress passed an act known as the Packers and Stockyards Act, which prohibited unfair practices of any description. Further, it provided that the secretary of Agriculture should have power to investigate the packers at any time and, if he felt it desirable, to enjoin them from doing anything not specifically prohibited by the consent decree or the Packers and Stockyards Act.

In 1922 Armour established a department of public relations. This was the last action taken by J. Ogden Armour before he gave up the control of his Company.

E. Financial result of operations, 1900–23.[19]

Table 2. FINANCIAL HISTORY OF ARMOUR & CO.
1900–23

(Dollars in millions)

Year	Reported net profit [a]	Net worth [b]	Profit as per cent of net worth
1900 [c]	$ 725	$ 33,439	...
1901	5,736	34,164	16.8
1902	2,500	38,900	6.4
1903	2,250	41,400	5.4
1904	1,850	43,650	4.2
1905	2,800	45,500	6.2
1906	3,000	48,300	6.2
1907	3,100	51,300	6.0
1908	7,800	54,400	14.3
1909	7,500	62,200	12.1
1910	6,500	69,700	9.3
1911	2,510	74,200	3.4
1912	5,702	76,710	7.4
1913	6,028	100,195	6.0
1914	7,510	104,223	7.2
1915	11,000	109,733	10.0
1916	20,100	118,733	16.9
1917	26,929	136,833	19.7
1918	19,747	156,127	12.6
1919	... [a]	173,092 [b]	...
1919	14,099	208,870	6.68
1920	5,320	231,382	2.30
1921	−31,710 [d]	214,158	−14.81 [d]
1922	−7,629 [d]	259,704	−2.94 [d]
1923	15,691	278,587	5.68

[a] 1900–19, before depreciation and interest charges; 1919–23, after these charges.
[b] 1900–19, basis undetermined; 1919–23, all capital stock and surplus.
[c] Six months.
[d] Loss.

F. Financial trouble, 1918–23.

Table 3, compiled from financial statements of the Company, indicates the increasing financial trouble through which Armour & Co. went from 1918 to 1923.[20]

[19] *Report on the Meat-Packing Industry,* 1920, part v, p. 21; and financial statements of the Company.
[20] *Ibid.*

Table 3. WORKING CAPITAL AND FUNDED DEBT OF ARMOUR & CO.
1910–23

(Dollars in millions)

Year	Current assets	Current liabilities	Ratio of of C. A. to C. L.	Funded debt
1910	$ 62.77	$ 10.79	5.82	$30.00
1911	67.41	14.83	4.55	30.00
1912	79.73	25.46	3.13	30.00
1913	88.85	30.80	2.88	30.00
1914	105.10	45.94	2.29	30.00
1915	119.58	52.02	2.30	30.00
1916	137.74	41.02	3.35	50.00
1917	210.37	101.50	2.07	50.00
1918	280.39	115.58	2.34	106.27
1919	342.99	164.15	2.09	81.60
1920	358.79	169.35	2.12	117.64
1921	302.63	145.28	2.08	115.56
1922	187.01	77.11	2.42	100.00 [a]
1923	220.52	84.04	2.62	145.65

[a] Also about $70,000,000 preferred stock sold.

With the exception of preferred stock issued in 1922, there was only one issue of stock, that being $100,000,000 par value of common stock. To the outsider examining the reports of the Company, there were indications of trouble long before 1923. In 1916 working capital was improved by an issue of $20,000,000 4½ per cent mortgage bonds. (At the same time a stock dividend raised stock from $20,000,000 to $100,000,000.) In 1918 a $60,000,000 issue of 6 per cent serial debentures more than doubled the outstanding debt. These bonds were convertible at the holders' option into 7 per cent cumulative preferred stock, authorized for that purpose; and it was proposed to retire them in six yearly lots of $10,000,000 commencing in 1919. Both these series of bonds were issued to retire commercial paper outstanding.

When the debentures were issued, the Company explained that "It has long been the desire of the owners of the Company that the public should be given an opportunity to share in its responsibilities and profits; hence the conversion privilege offered in the debentures." By the end of 1919 the preferred stock standing on the books amounted to $28,390,600. The Company chose to call for redemption only bonds which had been converted in this way, thus avoiding any cash payment to satisfy the serial feature of the issue.

In July, 1920, the Company announced a change in capital structure, again reiterating its desire to give the public more opportunity to share in its management and profits. Gold notes amounting to $60,000,000 were sold to increase working capital. The notes, sold to yield 7.75 per cent, were made convertible into common stock; and it was provided that the ratio of quick assets to current liabilities should at all times be maintained as high as 150 per cent.

Deflation continued through 1921 and, to a lesser degree, through 1922. Aggregate losses from operations in those two years exceeded $39,000,000. With a very heavy burden of fixed charges to meet, this condition could not continue for long. J. Ogden Armour, who a few years previously could have raised sufficient cash from his own estate to save the day, was caught in a position where most of his assets could be sold only at great sacrifice. He lost millions in selling 50,000 shares of Milwaukee Railway stock and all his holdings in Chicago banks. Finally the Company's bankers stepped in to save the investment of their clients and keep the business going.

In 1922 Armour & Co. of Delaware was organized as a principal subsidiary of Armour & Co. It had an authorized common and preferred stock of $161,000,000. This subsidiary was formed to take over unencumbered property of Armour's to use as collateral. On this collateral the corporation raised $110,000,000 by the sale of securities.

The *New York Times* of February 15, 1923, contained an article on the rumored reorganization of Armour & Co. It was said that Armour was to relinquish control, temporarily at least, to three bankers by the creation of a voting trust to hold 51 per cent (out of Armour's 80) of the common stock.

Armour & Co. issued a public statement, following reports of this sort throughout the country, which is quoted here:

> "The active management will be lodged as at present. The bankers mentioned are to be added to the Board of Directors, and to this Board other prominent men of wide experience in business affairs are also to be added. This is in line with making Armour & Company a public rather than a private corporation, and the financing now completed is in line with this accomplishment."

During the period following the War, Armour & Co. had been expanded to handle the business anticipated from a disorganized Europe. When the business proved to fall far short of what was expected, some means of maintaining the activities of the Company at a point approaching capacity had to be devised. Before the bankers took over the business, therefore, they completed a plan whereby Armour & Co. should buy the physical assets of Morris & Co., one of its chief competitors. The Armour & Co. organization was to handle the business of Morris & Co., thus saving a considerable overhead. Wherever duplications arose, they would be eliminated—some promptly, others as the physical equipment became worn out and could be economically scrapped.

Morris & Co. was bought on very favorable terms, the transaction being tied in with the reorganization of Armour & Co. The *New York Times* reported the purchase as follows:

> "With reference to the plan to make Armour & Company a public corporation, it is understood that part of the common stock will eventually be offered to the public. The first block of stock to be disposed of by Mr. Armour, it is said, will be in connection

with the acquisition of Morris & Co. This deal calls for payment of $10,000,000 in cash, $10,000,000 worth of preferred stock, and $10,000,000 worth of common. It is said in banking circles that Mr. Armour would sell enough of his own common stock to Armour & Company to make up the cash, the preferred stock would come from the treasury of the Company and the common from Mr. Armour's holdings. The value of this stock would be adjudged by James B. Forgan, Chairman of the First National Bank of Chicago, and Albert H. Wiggin, president of the Chase National Bank of New York. Later, it is understood, Mr. Armour will transfer his interest in Morris & Company to Armour & Company which may then issue securities against the assets represented by Morris & Company and repay him."

G. J. Ogden Armour and his other business interests.

The *New York Times* of August 17, 1927, characterized J. Ogden Armour thus:

"He took after his mother rather than his father, both in appearance and in ways. In contrast to his father's impulsiveness, J. Ogden was deliberate even to a point of coldness. He was cautious, modest, conciliatory, well-poised and generous. He liked leisure, though he was devoted to his business. . . . He had comparatively few diversions, grand opera being one of them. He cared nothing for social life and rarely accepted invitations to fashionable functions."

Twenty years after J. Ogden had assumed control of Armour & Co. the firm passed into the hands of a group of bankers who took the responsibility of rehabilitating the distressed firm. In 1923 Armour ceased to be the active head of his Company; and his personal estate, once one of the largest in the country, passed into virtual bankruptcy. What were the factors behind this failure? The contrast between his failure in the meat packing business and his father's success is noteworthy.

While Philip D. Armour devoted his life to the single purpose of developing his Company, J. Ogden spread his attention over a broad field of interests. The Company was not always foremost in his mind; indeed, it is suspected that he used it as a convenient means to power rather than as an interest in itself. Previous to financial reverses in 1921 he was a director in a score of railroads, banks, and financial institutions, and he took an active part in grain trading. In reviewing his life the *Chicago Tribune* of August 17, 1927, said in part: "These activities, combined with the great financial influence that his banking connections and his dealings in the grain and stock markets brought him, once led financial experts to believe that he was the logical successor to Edward H. Harriman as the ruler of the super-empire of money." At the height of his power, various estimates of his holdings ran from $100,000,000 to over $200,000,000.

He invested $10,000,000 in an irrigation project in the Sutter River Basin in California. He spent an even larger amount developing a show farm on the North Shore in Chicago, with the purpose of demonstrating just how cattle raising should be done. Considerable sums went toward the cutting of a freight tunnel in Chicago. Kansas City utilities caught his fancy for a while, and much capital went into their development.

It is said that from 1906, when he became interested in the grain market, to the time his power disappeared, he was the largest operator in the Chicago wheat pit. During those years he took part in all the important "squeezes" that occurred. Like some of the executives of the late New Era, he was fed on the phenomenal rise in fortune that accompanied all he did. He grew bold and careless, and loving speculation he continued to spend the major part of his time in speculative pursuits.

J. Ogden Armour apparently believed that his great wealth eliminated the danger involved in his speculative enterprises.

His friends described him as thinking that he was performing a real social advance in the Sutter Basin project. There is little doubt that he felt Melody Farm was an example for mankind to follow.

In J. Ogden Armour's favor let it be said that he was greatly liked by his employees and associates. He had a fondness for old employees and was loath to see one leave. It is related that on one occasion a department head complained of a subordinate whom he had discharged as incompetent, whereupon Armour replied, "He has been here fifteen years. If it has taken you fifteen years to find out that he is incompetent, take him back and keep him as long as he lives."

With all the criticism of J. Ogden Armour, it must not be forgotten that he built a great company from a comparatively small one. When he assumed control, annual sales were $182,000,000; when he turned over the rule to his successors, annual sales were near $1,000,000,000. From a net worth of $33,000,000 in 1900, he built the Company to a point where its net worth was over $250,000,000.

In 1923 his grain company handled more grain than any other concern in the world; his leather business was the second largest of its kind; he conducted one of the foremost fertilizer businesses in America; and he controlled more refrigerator cars than any railroad system in the country. Furthermore, he was the largest individual employer of workers of his time.

Under the severe pressure of postwar deflation Armour's wealth was threatened. Trouble arose on all sides at once. The liquid assets of Armour & Co. were sapped by terrific losses when great inventories at home and abroad had to be sold under production costs. Armour was forced to use his equity in Armour & Co. in an attempt to save his other enterprises and became indebted to the Company for about $50,000,000. At his death he still owed the Company several million dollars. After the smash the chief properties which he had left were the California project, a large block of stock in the Universal Oil Production Co., and his country estate—all then apparently of little worth.[21]

6. Banking Control

After the reorganization a financial committee was established to take charge of the management of Armour & Co. The new committee consisted of five men: J. Ogden Armour, as chairman of the board; Philip L. Reed, as treasurer of the Company; Samuel H. McRoberts, a former treasurer of the Company and then president of the Metropolitan Trust Co., of New York; Arthur Reynolds, president of the Continental and Commercial National Bank, of Chicago, always closely associated with Armour & Co.; and Albert H. Wiggin, president of the Chase National Bank, of New York, of which J. Ogden Armour had long been a director. McRoberts, because of his familiarity with the operating problems of the business, assumed the chairmanship of the committee, which essentially made him the head of the Company.

A few points will be noted about the management of the Company during the years in which the bankers were in control. F. Edson White, who was the president of the Company after the reorganization, had risen from the ranks. He was a practical meat packer and, as such, took charge of the processing operations. T. G. Lee was put in charge of branch houses and merchandising problems, with which several years of service in the branches and central office had made him thoroughly familiar. The financial committee, acting through J. Ogden Armour and Philip L. Reed, guided the management in matters of general policy and finance.

[21] It is interesting to note here that the Universal Oil stock eventually proved very valuable. Mrs. J. Ogden Armour lived in comfort on the income which it yielded; and on her death in 1932 she willed $15,000,000 to Armour & Co. to pay off her husband's debt with interest.

That finance took precedence over other phases of the business cannot be doubted. Table 4, compiled from statements of the Company, shows the extent to which the financial structure of Armour & Co. was strengthened in 1923–32, that is, under the new management.

Table 4. WORKING CAPITAL AND FUNDED DEBT, 1923–32

(Dollars in millions)

Year	Current assets	Current liabilities	Ratio of C. A. to C. L.	Funded debt
1923	$220.52	$84.04	2.62	$145.65
1924	205.80	61.72	3.33	145.04
1925	207.32	55.96	3.70	142.86
1926	209.98	53.89	3.88	138.85
1927	203.20	53.23	3.82	138.00
1928	197.53	32.76	6.03	135.85
1929	203.75	39.06	5.21	133.64
1930	175.95	24.50	7.18	123.51
1931	138.62	13.72	10.10	118.43
1932	118.20	11.43	10.32	96.25

In 1928 the banking element lost its specific interest in Armour & Co., although retaining three positions on the board of directors. The drop in current liabilities in the annual statements from 1923 to 1928 represents mostly short-term notes held by the bankers themselves. Until these notes had been paid, the bankers were able practically to dictate any policy of management they desired. After the payment their influence was limited to their proportional representation on the board.

In the four years from 1919 to 1922, inclusive, average losses amounted to slightly less than 2 per cent on net worth, including a profit in the first two years. From 1923 to 1928, average profits were about 4 per cent on net worth. (Net worth in the latter case was about $75,000,000 more than in the former case.) Even the year 1927, which was one of recession for the packing industry, showed a small profit.

7. After Banking Control

J. Ogden Armour died in August, 1927. Thus passed any influence which he may have exerted after the reorganization. The banking element on the board of directors remained after 1928, but active management passed to the officers of the Company. F. Edson White assumed charge of operations. T. G. Lee kept his position in charge of merchandising while acting also as vice-president in charge of beef.

Times were trying when the board of directors had to begin the search for a new president, after the death of F. Edson White in 1931. An aggressive man of some merchandising ability was needed to carry on the job, and T. G. Lee was the logical choice. A man of middle age, he had shown ability and aggression in his control over merchandising functions of the business. His experience, mostly developed within Armour & Co., included work in the production plants at Chicago and Kansas City, besides some time spent in managing a branch house.

The year 1931 was one of the worst years in the history of meat packing, with tremendous shrinkage in prices, both of the animals bought to be slaughtered and of the finished meats and by-products. Armour showed an operating loss for that year as compared with a profit before dividends shown by Swift & Co., its chief rival.

At the end of 1932 Armour showed a slightly improved statement when compared to that of Swift & Co. Armour earned something toward its fixed charges, while Swift operated at a loss. Sales in the two companies had dropped approximately the same percentage, while in each instance the physical volume of business handled was practically stationary after 1930.

Two things stand out in the Armour statements for 1931 and 1932 which are noteworthy. Current ratio advanced to over ten to one, with current liabilities in both years less than at any time since 1910. The funded debt, which had become large after 1918, dropped to about $96,000,000 at the end of 1932. It was the purchase, at a discount, of bonds for retirement that created the profit for Armour in 1932. The drop in prices during the three years ending at that time freed a large amount of capital previously tied up in inventories, these being reduced accordingly by December 31, 1932, to 47 per cent of their 1930 value on the books.

Branches, which in 1927 numbered five hundred, were reduced to about four hundred; and the smaller number did a more efficient business. Furthermore, the large branches were cut down severely, being moved into smaller quarters with greatly reduced forces wherever leases had run out. Production costs were in the same way cut to a minimum.

One difficulty survived, however, from the reorganization. The heavy fixed charges imposed on earnings by the two large issues of preferred stock made it practically impossible for common stockholders to receive a return on their investment. Furthermore, because of the lack of earnings, dividends were allowed to lapse on the parent company's preferred stock in 1931. In June, 1933, the directors of Armour & Co. notified stockholders that a plan of recapitalization was being designed. This had to be done to write down inflated book values, to bring assets up to capitalization, to make the payments of dividends possible under Illinois law, and to dispose of accumulated dividends. Under the plan proposed, preferred stock was to be eliminated, the equity to be represented by only one class of stock.

The plan met such strong opposition that it was dropped in September, 1933. Later it developed that the chief opposition had come from Frederick H. Prince, a Boston capitalist with heavy holdings in stockyards securities. Already a holder of Armour preferred stock, he had been buying common stock in the open market throughout the summer. Early in 1934 Mr. Prince secured three places on the board of directors for himself and two associates. A partner in Kuhn, Loeb & Co. also became a member of the board. To make room for the new members, McRoberts, Reynolds, and Wiggin resigned their positions on the board which they had held since the reorganization in 1923. After this rearrangement it was announced that Mr. Prince had come to an agreement with the management which would result in submitting to stockholders a modified plan of recapitalization.

The new plan of recapitalization was adopted in July, 1934. This plan was more favorable to the preferred and less favorable to common stock than the earlier plan. Under this plan each share of the old 7 per cent cumulative preferred stock (plus cumulated dividends) was exchanged for one no-par share of $6 cumulative convertible prior-preferred stock and two shares (par $5) of new common stock. Class "A" common was to be exchanged for a share of new common and class "B" for one-half share of new common. Preferred and common bore equal voting rights, one vote to a share.

In the fall of 1934 R. H. Cabell was elected president of Armour & Co., T. G. Lee having died a few weeks before the annual meeting. Mr. Cabell had been with Armour's 43 years, recently as head of Armour interests in London. He was regarded as a Prince man.

For several years Armour's experienced a considerable improvement. Sales and earnings went up greatly until in 1937, after which there was a heavy drop which lasted till after the middle of 1938; this drop was accompanied with a heavy fall in the value of inventory. From 1932 to the end of the year 1938 (Armour's year ending in October), the ratio of earnings to fixed charges, including preferred dividends of subsidiary, was as follows:

1932, 0.22; 1933, 1.46; 1934, 1.76; 1935, 1.62; 1936, 1.79; 1937, 1.74; 1938, 0.32. At the end of October, 1938, funded debt was $77,557,000.

Armour's situation at present is complicated by conditions and developments which are of significance to the whole industry. Though there was a short recovery in 1936–37, depression has prevailed throughout most of the 1930's. More significant in the long run may be changes coming in the industry in the direction of decentralization. In the past eight years the old setup in the meat industry has been going to pieces. Freight rates, changes in areas of production of the livestock, changes in the consuming market, chain store competition, developments which have made a small plant more efficient, and the truck and the radio have all been factors in the change. Even the famous consent decree, which still holds in spite of many efforts to have it removed, is one factor which stands in the way of cheaper distribution on the part of the large packers.

8. Suggested Readings and Sources

On the meat packing industry two books by Rudolf A. Clemen are very good: *The American Livestock and Meat Industry* (New York, 1923), and *By-Products in the Packing Industry* (Chicago, 1927).

The history of the western cattle industry is set forth in an interesting and scholarly way in E. E. Dale, *The Range Cattle Industry* (Norman, Oklahoma, 1930).

Two reports of government investigations give much information on individual packing firms and on the whole industry: *The Report of the Commissioner of Corporations on the Beef Industry,* 1905; *Report of the Federal Trade Commission on the Meat-Packing Industry,* 1919, parts i–vi. For comparison with Armour, the following study of Gustavus Swift is recommended: Louis F. Swift, *The Yankee of the Yards* (Chicago, 1927).

A recent book on Philip D. Armour is recommended as interesting and especially valuable in that it quotes from Armour's letters: Harper Leech and John Charles Carroll, *Armour and His Times* (New York, 1938).

On the history of the firm since the World War the chief sources are the *Armour Magazine,* the *National Provisioner,* the *New York Times,* the *Chicago Tribune,* and business manuals and information services.

9. Suggested Questions

1. Outline the development of production problems and distribution problems in Armour & Co.
2. What do you think of the attitude of the packers toward public opinion (a) in 1905 and (b) in 1920?
3. Did Philip Armour make a mistake when he let Cudahy go?
4. Contrast and compare as personalities Philip Armour and J. Ogden Armour.
5. Has the maintenance of individual control of Armour for so long been to the benefit or to the detriment of (a) the public and (b) the Company?
6. Why have the packers been so anxious to handle unrelated food products?
7. Did the temporary control of Armour & Co. by commercial bankers really establish a régime of financial capitalism?

XXXVII. THE FLOUR-MILLING INDUSTRY IN THE UNITED STATES (AN OUTLINE)

1. General Statement

The history of American flour milling is in many respects like the history of industry in general. From its beginning, but especially since about 1870, the industry has gone through most significant changes in market, in technique of production, and in business organization. The experience of flour milling like that of many American industries has been complicated by the rapid westward extension of agricultural production. One of its problems, however, has been somewhat peculiar to itself: The wheat crop is relatively uncertain as to amount and quality from year to year and it tends to deteriorate in an older area over a period of years.

The entire history of flour milling illustrates special developments which stamp it as unusual. Few American industries have changed centers of production so widely or rapidly. Perhaps no other business has experienced such frequent shifting of equipment, capital, and labor. Hardly any other has reached out so continuously and broadly for improved supplies of raw material.

2. Important Dates in the History of American Milling

1626 Construction in New York City of first flour mill in the thirteen colonies.

1750 Philadelphia leading flour center. Boston importing foodstuffs.

1791 Oliver Evans received patents for improvements in flour-milling methods.

1825 Baltimore leading flour-milling center. Erie Canal opened New York's hinterland.

1848 Chicago Board of Trade established.

1858 Richmond at height of its flour output.

1860 St. Louis and Rochester leading flour-manufacturing centers.

1871 "New Process" introduced in Minneapolis.

1874 C. A. Pillsbury & Co. organized.

1879 John Stevens invented a corrugated roll for making flour.

1880 Minneapolis produced over two million barrels of flour.

1885 Invention of dust-collecting machinery.

1889 Organization of Pillsbury-Washburn Flour Mills Co., Ltd. Eighty-seven per cent of Minneapolis milling in four corporations.

1899 Attempt to organize a monopoly of the milling of flour from hard spring wheat through the formation of United States Flour Milling Co.

1902 Millers' National Federation established.

1903 Washburn-Crosby Co. established a mill at Buffalo.

1904 Introduction of the Alsop process of artificial bleaching.

1917 War-time control of flour milling.

1920 Interstate Commerce Commission rate changes practically destroyed milling-in-transit privileges for Minneapolis mills.

1923 Incorporation of Pillsbury Flour Mills, Inc.

1928 Incorporation of General Mills, Inc.

1929 Standard Milling Co. consolidated with Gold Dust Corporation.

1930 Grain Stabilization Corporation formed under the Agricultural Marketing Act. Millers' National Federation voted to enter a trade practices conference with the Federal Trade Commission.

1932 Supreme Court of the United States annulled the order of the I. C. C. whereby grain rates in the western districts were reduced.

1933 New low level of domestic per capita consumption reached.

3. Flour Milling in the Colonial Period

The first mills, and the rise and spread of merchant milling; milling methods; marketing the flour.

4. Beginnings of Large-scale Milling

Oliver Evans' inventions; growth of market and wheat production; Baltimore as a milling, production, and marketing center, and its conflict with country mills; the Gallego and Haxall Mills at Richmond; milling in northern New York, especially at Rochester; St. Louis as a milling center.

5. Spring Wheat Flour and the Leadership of Minneapolis

Early milling in Minneapolis; the "new process" makes possible milling superior flour from spring wheat; growth of milling at Minneapolis, 1870–90, procuring wheat, production, and marketing.

6. Combinations in Minneapolis Milling

Loss of Minneapolis' advantages makes its mills combine; Pillsbury-Washburn Flour Mills Co.; Northwestern Consolidated; United States Flour Milling Co.

7. Expansion and Decentralization

Factors influencing milling since 1900, changes in wheat area, transportation, and large-scale commercial baking; growth of Kansas City as a milling center; the rise of Buffalo milling to leadership.

8. Recent Developments in Organization

Problems of millers, competition in flour marketing, and changes in flour consumption; the local mill or group; intraregional combinations; national combinations, especially Pillsbury Flour Mills, General Mills, and the flour milling subsidiaries of the Gold Dust Corporation.

9. Sources of Information on Flour Milling

J. Russell Smith, *Industrial and Commercial Geography* (New York, 1922); C. B. Kuhlmann, *The Development of the Flour-Milling Industry in the United States* (Boston, 1929); Henrietta M. Larson, *The Wheat Market and the Farmer in Minnesota, 1858–1900* (New York, 1926); *Moody's* and *Poor's Industrials;* Annual reports of Pillsbury Flour Mills, Inc., General Mills, Inc., and other companies (see especially *The First Five Years of General Mills, Inc.*, a pamphlet issued by General Mills in 1933); *United States Census,* on location and size of milling units from time to time; *Report of the Industrial Commission,* 1901, vol. xiii; Federal Trade Commission, *Bakery Combines and Profits,* 1927, and *Competition and Profits in Bread and Flour,* 1928; Food Research Institute, Wheat Studies, vol. ii, no. 8, *The Decline in Per Capita Consumption of Flour in the United States* (Stanford University, 1926), and vol. ix, no. 3, *The World Wheat Situation, 1931–32* (Stanford University, 1932).

10. Suggested Questions

1. Why have there persistently existed side by side relatively large-scale and small-scale milling units?
2. Why did Chicago not develop flour milling as it did meat packing?
3. Around 1900, combination in flour milling was local or within regions; by 1930 there were several national, or inter-regional, combinations. Explain the change.
4. Does flour milling promise to be a good field for investment in the future? Would you prefer to invest in Pillsbury or General Mills?
5. If you had been seeking employment in the management of milling in 1790, 1880, and 1935, to what region would you have gone? What size or type of organization would you have favored?
6. Do you think that flour milling is likely to be socialized early in a regime of national capitalism?

XXXVIII. HUGO STINNES, GERMAN INDUSTRIALIST

1. General Statement

The combination movement began in the German iron and steel industry in the 1870's, but until 1914 it took the form mainly of cartels designed to limit production and maintain prices. The cartels were in the nature of pools, the members retaining their legal autonomy. From the outbreak of the World War the cartels were doomed. The danger of overproduction immediately disappeared, prices soared, and the appearance of a producer's market removed the necessity of defensive agreements among entrepreneurs. Thus it was that most of the cartels which had been built up since the 'seventies were during the War either broken by their members or allowed to lapse.

From the outbreak of the World War until the end of the inflation period in 1923, stress was laid rather on vertical combinations, including all the steps in production. Such combinations were designed to guarantee supplies of raw materials and markets for the products at each stage. Integrated or, as they were called in Germany, "mixed" plants had become general in the German iron and steel industry before 1914. In the following decade, however, a number of giant combinations were established, some of which went beyond the basic industry and established connections with the electrical industry, the locomotive and automobile industries, navigation and shipping, and other fields. While the central authority in these combinations was much stronger than the usual cartel, in many cases the member firms still retained their legal independence. The practice of purchase by large enterprises of controlling blocks of stock in numerous smaller concerns, often through holding companies, became common.

Among the greatest of these concerns was that of Hugo Stinnes. His family had been prominent in the Ruhr for two generations, active chiefly in coal mining and in shipping on the Rhine. Stinnes started as a young man with his own independent company, but he based his Konzern [1] on the coal mines which constituted a family holding separate from the other enterprises of the members. During the War and postwar period, he extended his Konzern to include a wide variety of enterprises, including lignite mines, overseas trade, hotels, and the newspaper and publishing industries. Stinnes' Konzern, like others, was not permanent; the return of normal currency conditions brought difficulties which, after the death of Stinnes in 1924, ended in the almost complete dissolution of the combination.

2. Chronology

1808	Mathias Stinnes established a coal and shipping business at Mülheim on the Ruhr.
1817	The Stinnes brothers established a navigation line from Cologne to Rotterdam in Holland.
1820	Mathias Stinnes had 66 coal ships on the Rhine and the Ruhr.
1870	Hugo Stinnes, grandson of Mathias, was born.
1893	Hugo established a coal-trading firm with a capital of about $12,500.
1898	The Rhenish-Westphalian Electric Co. was established.

[1] The literal English equivalent of this word is "concern," but we have used the foreign form because in Germany the word has acquired a specialized meaning; that is, it refers to a group tied together legally to some extent, but principally bound by a community of interest and centered in the influence of one person. *Konzern* has in no sense the connotation of a closely knit, centrally controlled organization such as the trust or combine, as these terms are understood in the United States.

1903 Hugo Stinnes helped establish the Coal Bureau.

1905 The Hugo Stinnes Coal Shipping Co. established.

1907 Stinnes became president of the German-Luxemburg Mining and Smelting Co.

1911 Community of interest established between German-Luxemburg and the Smelting Co. of Ramelange Saint-Ingbert, Luxemburg.

1914 Stinnes chiefly responsible for the Department of Raw Materials, a central war authority in Germany.

1916 Under Hugo Stinnes' leadership, three joint-stock companies were formed to exploit Belgian industry, transportation, and agriculture. Principal shareholders were the industrialists, Krupp, Thyssen, Haniel, and Stinnes.

1916–18 Stinnes extended his ocean shipping interests.

1917 Stinnes purchased large landed estates to secure wood for his coal mines. These holdings later furnished basis for advances in paper industry. Established Hugo Stinnes Company for Navigation and Overseas Trade.

1918 Stinnes lost all his interests in Luxemburg and Lorraine, and most of his shipping on the Rhine.

1920 Through the Siemens-Rhein-Elbe-Schuckert-Union, community of interest established between German-Luxemburg, the Gelsenkirchen Mining Co., the Bochum Mining and Cast Steel Co., and the Siemens-Schuckert combine.

1920–23 Stinnes entered into the manufacture of chemicals, explosives, and paper, and into printing and publishing; he expanded his ocean shipping and foreign trade and developed interests in South America, Dutch West Indies, China, and particularly southeastern Europe.

1921 The Austrian Alpine Mining Co. acquired.

1922 Interest acquired in the bank called the Berlin Trading Co. (Handelsgesellschaft).

1923 Interests acquired in the Upper Silesian iron and steel industry.

1924 Death of Hugo Stinnes. His Konzern passed into the control of his sons, Hugo and Edmund.

1925 The Konzern became insolvent.

1925–26 The Konzern liquidated.

3. Stinnes as Described by a Contemporary [2]

"Hugo Stinnes has reached the age of fifty. He has the appearance of a worker and can go about in the clothes of a foreman or a miner without attracting attention. He is like a piece of coal wandering about among his own coal mines. His thick head is set upon a stocky trunk. His black hair is cut close. the face is pale and expansive, the beard is black as coal, the nose is curved and the eyes are heavily underlined. A German paper recently called him the 'Assyrian King.' His external appearance is devoid of pose, he seems heavy and solid. He walks with a slight stoop and shuffles along like a sailor. Clothes, habits and bearing denote a man of simple tastes. 'His pale face, his rather tired eyes and his modest clothes make him look more like a labor secretary than a German Rockefeller'—to quote a French reporter who saw him in Spa."

4. The Social and Economic Principles upon Which Hugo Stinnes Operated [3]

Only reality interested Stinnes. Since he recognized its force and its complexity,

[2] Hermann Brinckmeyer, *Hugo Stinnes* (Alfred Kuttner, translator, Viking Press, Inc., New York, 1921), pp. 1–2.

[3] Adapted from Gaston Raphaël, *Le Roi de la Ruhr* (Paris, 1924), pp. 12, 14–20, 45–48, 57–58, and 66–67.

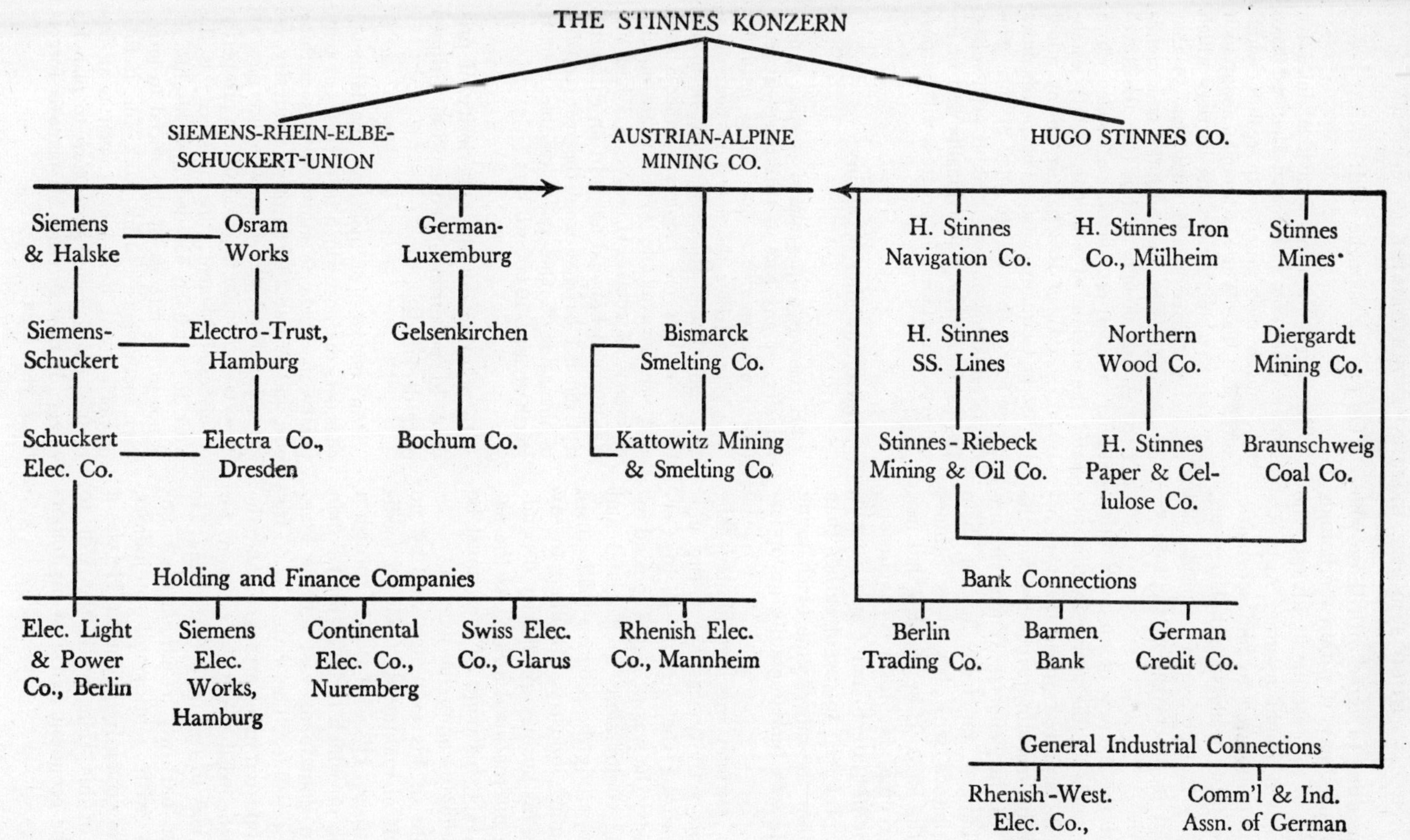

A diagrammatic representation of the most important member groups with some indication of their legal interrelationships, about 1924. Adapted from *Konzerne der Metallindustrie*, p. 72.

he was unwilling to agree with those who wished to encompass it within the bounds of a theory, or to prescribe in advance the forms which it might assume. Any systematization appeared to him schematic, and hence false, useless, and dangerous. He not only had no system himself, but he detested in others the attempt to establish one.

Without the agency of an even fairly coherent synthesis, his active intelligence seized on facts and arranged them, in order to derive certain principles for the guidance of his efforts. When circumstances changed, far from forcing them into compliance with his ideas Stinnes modified the ideas. If he decided that new facts discredited his former conclusions, he did not hesitate to make new conclusions. He preferred to recant rather than fail to follow the movements of changing reality. He was fundamentally an opportunist.

Stinnes' horizon was not limited—the field of his activity was the entire universe. Realizing the weaknesses of German industry, he was prepared to send investigating commissions to England and America to study the progress made there in the mining industry. He liked to say that, since his business prosperity depended on the international as well as the national market, his point of view must be correspondingly comprehensive.

The aim of his existence was by no means that of making shift with a mediocre enterprise. His idea was to furnish a foundation on which to build for German industry a domain as vast and as long-lived as possible. The date 2000 frequently appeared in his arrangements (the Siemens-Rhein-Elbe-Schuckert-Union, for instance, was to run until that date). He was never narrowly reactionary or encumbered with sentimental prejudices, nor was he driven by chimeras. He was a creature of his time, with the will to fashion the economic world of his tomorrow.

On one occasion he said:

"In human life, only individual initiative counts. The War has shown that we have not enough men gifted with real individuality. . . . The War has brought about such reverses that for a time the barriers which restrict initiative should disappear, so that adaptation can be made to the new conditions. As was done in France after the Revolution, all barriers should be broken down and the régime of economic liberty established. . . . What is appalling, to my mind, is that in Germany outstanding personalities are so scarce that we are ruled by men who no longer know how to think as economists. If this decadence of individuality and of intelligence continues, no progress will be possible."

And on another occasion:

"If there is a question of starting a new industry, or any sort of enterprise—at least this is my experience, one begins naturally by asking whether the necessary conditions, geographical and otherwise, have been fulfilled. But then one inquires whether a suitable man is available. Workers are equally necessary, of course. However, if I had 10,000 workers, I should not start an enterprise if I did not have at hand the man capable of managing it. One really capable man is worth at least 10,000 workers."

In pointing out the superiority of private to government enterprise, Stinnes once declared:

"An official [of political appointment] considers the post which he occupies as temporary; he ought to move on to something else, and he wants to. In private industry, on the other hand, the man who occupies an important position is proud of the prosperity of his establishment; this prosperity is the work to which he has dedicated his life. It is not to the interest of the official to introduce innovations into his work, for, if they do not succeed, he is looked upon as an imbecile who does not know how to plan his career; if they succeed, his name is forgotten a year later."

Stinnes was a strong believer in concentration of industrial enterprises and in unified control of those combinations. He once said:

"It is necessary to subordinate the various enterprises [in a group] to a general director who looks at the industrial situation from a broad point of view, and who sees as many aspects as possible."

Stinnes declared that to this supreme direction it was desirable to give a large measure of authority, in order to secure a management which would not hesitate to be ruthless and tireless in its striving for efficiency. The *raison d'être* of groupings should not be, in his estimation, the usual one of permitting economies within the administration. On the contrary, the administrative costs of a vast organization might well be higher than those of several smaller independent ones. But this more expensive administration was also better. It allowed for the improvement of industrial processes, for the better division of labor, and for the intensification of production. "It is foolish," said he, "to want to save small businesses; they know neither how to live nor how to die. To speak frankly, it is necessary that they perish."

In another connection:

"Concentration is the true mold of modern industry. But this concentration is inconceivable unless the large groups are given a free hand. It is necessary to accord an absolute sovereignty to the direction of the large, well-organized groups and to impose no restrictions; otherwise it would be impossible for them to work for the greatest possible good of our whole economic life."

Stinnes was perhaps the greatest German exponent of vertical concentration. He carried it further and developed it more extensively than did any other industrialist. And yet it would be wrong to attribute to him a rigid partiality for vertical concentration. He understood both horizontal and vertical concentration and made use of both. He said:

"Vertical organization is the product of its time and horizontal organization is the product of its time. When you have a scarcity of money or materials, you employ vertical combination in order to achieve the desired result with the least possible expenditure of money and materials. When you have an abundance—and that day will return to Germany, horizontal combination will again have the preference. I collaborated actively in the horizontal organizations which we had before the War, at the time when we were comparatively rich in money and materials; and I hope, if I live long enough, to be able to change my weapon again, if that is in the interests of our national economic life."

Stinnes had a clearly worked-out plan of economic organization, which was in fact the culmination of the business organization which he sponsored. He discussed this plan at length and supported it actively during the period of political and social reorganization following the German Revolution. A thoroughgoing socialization of industry had at that time many advocates in Germany; and it was Stinnes' claim that, by resorting to his plan, large industrial combinations could be quite simply converted to a socialized form. With regard to this plan, he once said:

"I have two guiding principles. One of them is coöperation between enterprises. I do not agree with the creators of the great American trusts that each branch of industry ought to be separate from the others and prosper independently, its sole aim being to secure the largest possible profit. Rather, they should be consolidated. I begin, for instance, with coal, the basis of all industry. I go from that on the one hand to the metal industry, then to finishing industries, thence to ships, navigation, and commerce. On the other hand, I pass from coal to lignite, then to wood, paper, and to newspapers. Thus I have arranged my enterprises into a hierarchy, so as to achieve the maximum sales at the minimum costs. . . . My second guiding principle is coöperation with communities and with workers. My enterprises in the Rhine region function by this sort of coöperation. I myself have passed months among the workers, as a common laborer, in order to understand them; and now I am able to interest them in their work by constantly improving their condition."

In connection with projects of socialization, Stinnes conceived and gave voice to a plan for economic organization which had the double merit of consummating his plan of vertical concentration and of leaving him absolute master of it. He urged the regional organization of the nation on the basis of economic relationships, and the setting-up of economic provinces delimited according to the consumption of such products as gas or electricity or according to industrial resources or production areas. The direction of the producing units, which would be very large, was to be left to technical experts; the regions would be called upon to assist in financing production, and there would be a complete division between ownership and industrial direction. Production would, under this plan, retain the stimulus of private initiative; the Stinnes principle of large-scale enterprise would be completely realized; and all the steps in production would be subordinated to a director who could afford to maintain a broadly social point of view.

5. Stinnes' Business Interests, 1893–1918 [4]

The basis of Hugo Stinnes' strength was laid in the coal industry on the Rhine and the Ruhr. In 1893 Stinnes founded a coal-trading firm with a capital of about $12,500. He early began to participate actively in the creation and development of the powerful horizontal cartels of the Rhine region. He was only 23 years old in 1893 and had scarcely left the family firm when the great industrialist, Emil Kirdorf, founded the Coal Syndicate. And yet he became one of the leaders in this association in the production and sale of coal which controlled almost the whole of the Ruhr coal production, disposed of the product of each firm, so far as it was not absorbed by the firm's own cokery or metal-working plants, and arranged the division of the tonnage between the participating firms. On December 12, 1903, the Coal Syndicate created in coöperation with several powerful firms that other association, called the Coal Bureau for the sake of brevity. The Bureau was a subsidiary of the Coal Syndicate; it had the double purpose of the resale of the coal within a specified area and its transportation on the Rhine. It became a unit in the Steel Association, the steel cartel established in 1904 which was dissolved after the War and was replaced by the Iron Combine.

While his uncles and brothers in the firm of Mathias Stinnes had been content to increase their coal production steadily Hugo branched out into other fields. He early began to purchase stock in the German-Luxemburg Co., established in 1901, which was in coal mining in the Ruhr region and in the iron industry in the Rhineland and in Luxemburg. After serving for a time as a director, Stinnes in 1907 became president of this company, and he was thereafter the controlling influence in its operation. By 1914 the German-Luxemburg Co. had become one of the most important integrated concerns in Germany, with subsidiary plants producing a variety of iron and steel products and with some shipping interests.

[4] The facts in the remainder of this case are chiefly from the following: Raphaël, *op. cit.;* Paul Ufermann, *Der deutsche Stahltrust* (Berlin, 1927); Paul Ufermann and Carl Hüglin, *Stinnes und seine Konzerne* (Berlin, 1924); K. Albach, *Tragödie des Hauses Stinnes* (Essen, 1925); *Konzerne, Interessengemeinschaften, und ähnliche Zusammenschlüsse im deutschen Reich, Ende 1926* (Berlin, 1927); *Konzerne der Metallindustrie* (Stuttgart, 1924); and Nassen, "Auflösung des Stinnes-Konzerns," in *Wirtschaftsdienst,* vol. x (1925), pp. 1193–1196.

In Stinnes' control of the German-Luxemburg Co. he developed the principles which were later of such importance in the building-up of the Stinnes Konzern. He made full use of the possibilities of the joint-stock principle, buying a controlling interest in many of the plants but leaving them their autonomy and avoiding the tying-up of too much capital.

Even before he took control of the German-Luxemburg Co. Stinnes had established connections with another enterprise, the building-up of which was one of his first successes. This was the Rhenish-Westphalian Electric Co., which he and Thyssen, another important industrialist, helped to establish in 1898. At Stinnes' invitation, municipalities and public utilities, which were the chief consumers of the electrical power supplied by the company, furnished the major part of the capital. Direction, however, was left in the hands of Stinnes. This company bought up lignite mines, thus securing a cheap basis for power production. The area to which it supplied electricity widened until it reached from Düsseldorf and Cologne to the Dutch frontier, the Hanover region, and the valley of the Ahr.

At the same time Stinnes' fingers were reaching out to other branches of industry—coal mining, coal-selling agencies, and river and overseas transportation. By the outbreak of the War, Stinnes was one of the powers on the Ruhr. His deeds and words carried weight, his stockholdings were numerous and varied, and he appeared on the board of directors or as president of several enterprises in addition to his own companies. Furthermore, his personality was such that where he had an interest, even a minority interest, his influence was felt. His methods did not always meet with the approval of his associates, but his hand was a sure one and he usually achieved his purposes. It is said that the banks disapproved of his methods in the German-Luxemburg Co.; the Deutsche Bank, which had been interested, withdrew from the enterprise. It is well known that he did not long work in harmony with Thyssen.

The War destroyed many of Stinnes' arrangements, but it proved a great stimulus to industry and particularly to coal, iron, and steel, those industries in which Stinnes was most interested. The War furnished him increased opportunities to plan things in a big way and to shape the situation to his own advantage. Stinnes was one of the chief leaders in the establishment of the Department of Raw Materials, which helped to mobilize German resources during the War. He took a prominent part in planning the war management of Belgian industry and was largely instrumental in the formation of the three companies established for this purpose—the Industrial Association, the Transport Association, and the Agricultural Association.

Meanwhile, the enterprises in which he was interested were expanding in size and increasing in number. In common with other iron and steel entrepreneurs Stinnes made great war profits which subsequently facilitated further expansion. He developed his shipping and foreign trade interests, claiming that he expected to become one of the outstanding entrepreneurs in this field. His chief enterprise in this line was the Hugo Stinnes Company for Navigation and Overseas Trade, established in 1917. His hotel interests date from this period, and he invested in several landed estates which were to supply wood for his mines. It was these lumber holdings which later led him into the cellulose and paper industries.

With the unsuccessful outcome of the War the Stinnes interests lost at one blow the German-Luxemburg holdings in Lorraine and Luxemburg, so that the basis of operations for that company was seriously disrupted. At the same time much of the Rhine shipping, in which Hugo Stinnes was one of the most outstanding figures, had to be turned over to the Allies. There was, however, compensation in both cases; one writer estimates that Stinnes' share alone was between two hundred and three hundred million marks.[5] Moreover, the French group which took over the Luxemburg properties guaranteed a supply of iron for a period of years.

6. Growth of the Stinnes Konzern

For a man of Stinnes' temperament the situation in which the German iron and steel industry found itself at the end of the War was a golden opportunity. Everything was in a state of flux, reorganization on a large scale was essential, and the capital with which to carry it out was at hand. Vertical combination was already the prevailing tendency; and the unhealthy inflation which prevailed at once facilitated and encouraged expansion. "Be anything so long as you are not conservative;" "do anything with your capital except hold it in reserve"—such were the current business mottoes.

The Stinnes Konzern, which attracted such widespread attention, was built up during these years. Until 1920 Hugo Stinnes was consolidating his position steadily; from that time forward, he burst into a fever of expansion. It is difficult to measure his progress quantitatively because of the steady depreciation of the mark, because the nature of the interests acquired by Hugo Stinnes varied widely, and because they were attached, some to the German-Luxemburg Co., some to Hugo Stinnes Co., and some to other enterprises in the Stinnes sphere of influence.

The German-Luxemburg Co. furnished the basis on which one large division of the Konzern was built. As a substitute for its properties lost as a result of the War, this company acquired new German holdings in iron and steel and in the finishing process. More important, in 1920 a community of interest was established with the Gelsenkirchen Mining Co., one of the leading integrated firms in the Ruhr district. The holding company set up was called the Rhein-Elbe-Union (after the most important mine of the Gelsenkirchen Co. and the chief integrated plant of the German-Luxemburg Co.); it was to run until 2000 A. D., and it had a capital of only 300,000 marks. Profits were to be pooled and divided upon an agreed basis.

Later in the year, after a struggle in the stock market, this consolidation acquired a large block of stock in the Bochum Mining and Cast Steel Co., another very large integrated firm in the Ruhr which dated from 1854. Stinnes became president of the Bochum Co. An agreement was made by which the various enterprises were to specialize in production to their mutual advantage. Another step taken at about this time was the acquisition of Böhler Brothers Co., a Berlin firm with iron and steel interests in Austria and Czechoslovakia as well as in Germany. These were among the first foreign interests of the Stinnes Konzern. A most important step, also taken in 1920, was the absorption into the Rhein-Elbe-Union of the Siemens-Schuckert interests, which next to the General Electric Co. formed the most important of the German electrical enterprises. The name of the company holding these important groups was changed to the Siemens-Rhein-Elbe-Schuckert-Union. It began with the modest capital of 517,000 marks, and an agreement was made as to division of profits between the firms, which enabled them to retain their legal autonomy.

The vertical combination had thus, by a swift series of steps, consolidated its position in both directions—back to the raw materials and forward to the finished products and even to the consumer. All the companies concerned were important in themselves, and their consolidation resulted in one of the largest combinations in Germany, producing 16 per cent of the coal, almost as much of the iron and

[5] Raphaël, *op. cit.*, p. 108.

steel, and sharing control of the electrical industry with the General Electric Co.[6] The public was properly astounded and a bit awe-struck at the position which Stinnes had assumed. He was no longer merely a Rhineland industrialist; he had become a figure of national, not to say international, importance.

The center of the second large division of the Konzern was the holding company, Hugo Stinnes Co. Its greatest acquisitions at this time were in the fields of lignite and chemistry and explosives. From cellulose Stinnes went into paper and printing and publishing. He acquired several newspapers, of which the most important was the *Deutsche Allgemeine Zeitung*. At this a cry of protest went up from the public, which had already become suspicious of this spider-web of enterprises being spun across the whole country and even beyond the national boundaries. It looked as though Stinnes was assuring himself of the kind of publicity he wanted, but he disclaimed all ulterior motives and said he was interested merely in completing his production chain—cellulose, paper, and newspapers.

The list of interests acquired by the Konzern in Germany continued to receive additions. Brass and copper works, automobile factories, oil interests, all phases of the iron and steel industry, the film industry, and many branches of trade and shipping, foreign and domestic, fell in some measure within the Stinnes sphere. The iron and steel industry and its allied interests were controlled largely through the Siemens-Rhein-Elbe-Schuckert-Union, while the trading interests were centered chiefly in the Hugo Stinnes Company for Navigation and Overseas Trade.

This latter company was also a holding company with a broad range of interests. Its chief function was, of course, navigation and the export business; it set up many trading offices at home and abroad; it assumed control of many of the oil interests; and one of its special functions was dealing in foreign exchange. In his various lines of business Stinnes naturally dealt on a large scale in bills of exchange, and this company acted as a reservoir for the sums which came in as a result of the export business, the carrying trade, and commission business, and were paid out again for imports of raw materials.

A logical step following the acquisition of so many industrial and trading interests was taken by Stinnes in 1922 with the purchase of a large block of stock in the Berlin Trading Co., a Berlin bank. This was a sound banking concern of considerable prestige, which itself had holdings in numerous industrial enterprises, including Krupp and the General Electric Co. Stinnes denied that his penetration into this new field had any special significance; he implied that he had simply made a profitable investment of some of the surplus funds of his Konzern. It is easy, however, to see behind that motive a thought that, when the time came for a return to normal conditions, intimate and strong financial connections would be of inestimable value.

The initial step into finance was followed by the acquisition of an interest in the Barmen Bank. This was the greatest of the German provincial banks: it had 133 branches and agencies, chiefly in Rhineland and Westphalia; it was an outstanding issuing and financing bank for the iron implement and textile industries; and it had a friendly connection with the

[6] It was often said that it was only a matter of time before the General Electric Co. would fall into the hands of Stinnes. Stinnes had good reason to, and in fact did, try to extend his influence to this enterprise. There were many points where the two concerns touched. There was no community of interest between them, but there were mutual interests in independent enterprises, and there were holding companies and other groupings where the two came in contact. Among these were the Berlin Trading Co., the common interests in Osram, the Electro-Trust, the Telephone Co., and the Linker-Hoffmann-Lauchhammer group.

greatest Saxon institution (the German Credit Institution in Leipzig) and with the greatest Bavarian bank (the Bavarian Mortgage and Exchange Bank in Munich). Holdings in this sphere were further increased by the acquisition of an interest in the North Star Insurance Co.

The Stinnes influence was thus extended to the most important of the provincial institutions. In addition to centralizing the Stinnes interests in the Ruhr region, Hamburg, Berlin, and the Central German lignite region, the new acquisitions in the field of finance acted as an additional centralizing factor, weakening the independent business interests of the various districts in Germany and tending actually to exclude them.

At first this entrance of the mammoth Konzern into the banking field appeared as a sign of strength, but perhaps it really looked forward to a later time when the difficulties of financing would be increased by a return to normal currency conditions. In any case the growth of the Konzern illustrated the increase in the importance of industrial capital at the expense of banking capital. The contrasts pointed out by the anti-Semites and the National Socialists between the "creative" and the "appropriative" capital ceased to hold. Stinnes himself, primarily a coal magnate, synthesized the two kinds of capital, not only from an organizing point of view but also in his personal affairs in his relations with men whose activities were almost purely speculative.

Long before this, the Stinnes Konzern had reached far beyond the national boundaries in its acquisition of new interests. Foreign trade had already led Stinnes into South America, the West Indies, and China. Several of the enterprises of the Konzern, notably the Siemens-Schuckert Works, had important foreign holdings at the time they were brought in. The iron and steel interests soon expanded into Switzerland, Austria, Czechoslovakia, and Rumania, as well as into Poland, culminating in the acquisition of the Austrian-Alpine Mining Co. Oil was even more international, and the Konzern not only penetrated into Russia and Rumania (Hugo Stinnes–Riebeck Mining and Oil Works), but established connections in North and South America and, according to some rumors, in Africa and Mexico.

By 1924 the Stinnes Konzern had at least an interest in the following foreign undertakings: 24 coal mines and fields, 21 iron mines, 7 oil fields and refineries, 16 earth, stone, and ceramic works, 29 smelteries, 20 metal and machinery works and wagon and locomotive factories, 3 telegraph companies, 4 shipyards, 80 electrical plants, 8 paper and chemical plants and sugar works, 4 shoe factories, 47 electrical and gas works, 10 railways, 9 shipping companies, 14 newspaper and printing companies, 9 forests, sawmills, and agricultural holdings, 3 cotton and coconut plantations, 10 banks and holding companies, and 254 selling agencies, trading companies, branches, and the like. Of a total of 572 foreign holdings, according to one authority, 254 were in the neighboring countries to the east of Germany.[7]

Thus, it is seen, the Stinnes interests fell into two main groups centering in the two covering or holding companies, the Siemens-Rhein-Elbe-Schuckert-Union and the Hugo Stinnes Co. Both were interested in the Austrian-Alpine Mining Co. but were otherwise relatively independent of each other. The first of these groups covered two smaller groups. One, the Siemens-Schuckert electrical interests, contained 3 important production companies and 1 large holding company which had interests in 6 other holding companies whose "most important interests" numbered 72 companies. The other, the Rhein-Elbe or coal and iron group, as has al-

[7] Ufermann and Hüglin, *op. cit.*, p. 79.

ready been seen, was made up of 3 large concerns. The Hugo Stinnes Co., according to *Konzerne der Metallindustrie,* in 1924 included 60 enterprises, some of which, of course, reached out to others.

7. Nature of the Konzern

The Stinnes combination was not closely knit like a trust. It was built up in a variety of ways: by complete fusion, as was the case with a number of coal mines bought up by the German-Luxemburg Co.; by the purchase of a majority or even a minority stock interest through agreement or through purchase on the open market, as in the purchase by German-Luxemburg of the Bochum Mining and Cast Steel Co.; by the interlocking of directorates (Stinnes was on the board of numerous companies); and by the agreement between enterprises to carry on operations under one general director, usually under a covering or holding company as in the Siemens-Rhein-Elbe-Schuckert-Union, with a definite arrangement as to the division of profits.

It is clear that the capital involved in these combinations was small in comparison with the total capitalization. It was Stinnes' policy to acquire only minority interests when that would serve his purpose. Many of the interests were acquired on short-time credits, reliance being placed on future profits to wipe out the indebtedness. Though Stinnes was the unifying element in the Stinnes Konzern, the capital he held was relatively small. It has been estimated that about 15 per cent was his share in the majority of the companies.

It was to be expected, therefore, that the units in the Stinnes Konzern should retain a large measure of autonomy. In principle, it is said, Stinnes allowed even to the most modest of the firms concerned the greatest measure of independence compatible with the good functioning of the whole Konzern. What he built up was a confederation in which the members, of varying size, guarded their autonomy. As time went on, this measure of autonomy tended to increase. As an outgrowth of his faith in individual initiative it was the policy of Stinnes to choose first-class subordinates and put on them a large amount of responsibility in their own field.

As the complexity of his organization increased, however, Stinnes tried to bind together—especially within Hugo Stinnes Co.—those enterprises with like interests (creating a sort of horizontal combination within the vertical) and to subdivide the whole Konzern into sections, including (1) shipping and trade, (2) press, printing, and publishing, (3) iron and steel, (4) eastern European interests, and so on. Each of these was to be directed by a subordinate, one of whom, in charge of the trade and navigation group, was his son, Hugo, Jr., at Hamburg. This grouping was designed to minimize duplication in plant and production, to reduce production costs, and to weed out inefficient firms. In effecting this reorganization it was inevitable that stockholders in many of the subsidiary companies should become antagonistic.

The most closely knit part of the Konzern was the Siemens-Rhein-Elbe-Schuckert-Union. Its administration was in the hands of the general council and the managing directors. The managing directors were the members of the managing committees of the companies in the Union; they had to do with the carrying-out of the community of interest and the solution of a number of specified problems common to all. The general council was composed of the members of the boards of directors and the managing committees of the contracting companies; the council had final decision in all matters in which the Union was concerned. The general council was headed by three chairmen of equal importance. Stinnes was one of the three chairmen, by virtue of his position as chairman of the managing committee of German-Luxemburg. But his temperament, as well as the important interests he contracted outside the combination, gave him more influence than his official position necessarily implied. Indeed, it was his personality rather than his capital and position which made him such a power.

It is important to recognize that the principle underlying the Stinnes Konzern was not monopoly but integration. The object of the Konzern was to make as many profits as possible in the handling of one product from the raw material to the consumer. Thus on the production side it covered all stages of production and included the production of necessary auxiliary materials and by-industries or by-products. Both the Hugo Stinnes Co. and the Siemens-Rhein-Elbe-Schuckert-Union reached from the primary raw material to the last stage of the finished product and both controlled large users of their product. The principal difference between the two large groups lay in the fact that, while the Union was centered in the Rhenish-Westphalian smelting industry, the Hugo Stinnes group developed more strongly on the side of marketing or trade. Indeed, the latter even controlled transportation and various enterprises contributing to marketing, such as newspapers and commercial banking. In investment finance it began to build up support through acquiring interests in banks.

While Stinnes visioned a closely knit Konzern in which every part played an essential rôle, reality did not conform to that ideal. It is hard to avoid the conviction that here was no Konzern, in the sense of a group held together by some community of interest, but an incoherent collection of enterprises linked together only by the one stockholder they had in common. Albert Ballin, head of the Hamburg-American Line until 1918, said of Stinnes: "He cannot see a business opportunity without seizing it; even if it belongs to someone else, he proceeds to possess himself of it."

8. The Breakdown of the Stinnes Konzern

Even before the death of Hugo Stinnes in April, 1924, difficulties had begun to appear in his Konzern. Whether, if he had lived, he could have solved them satisfactorily will never be known. A serious period of readjustment would undoubtedly have come with stabilization of the currency and the deflation of 1925–26. It would have been necessary, also, to meet the hostility to the Stinnes Konzern that had risen on the part of other industrialists and banks, workers, and consumers—indeed, the public in general. There is evidence that Stinnes was already beginning to prepare for readjustment before his death.

Stinnes' two sons (Edmund, 30 years of age, and Hugo, 28) had for some time been active in the management of the Konzern with their father and were thus not lacking in experience and background for the solution of their problems. Whether they approached their father in ability is a question answered differently by different authorities. One thing is certain: there were wide differences in their temperament and interests, Edmund being primarily a technician and Hugo a business man.

In June, 1925, it became evident that the Stinnes Konzern had ceased to be solvent and could not return to solvency by its own strength. It would have been difficult in itself to carry on the uncorrelated and in many cases unprofitable undertakings; this was made impossible by the taking-over of several new acquisitions by the sons, after their father's death, thus increasing interest charges and destroying liquidity. The organization was no longer able to carry on the burden of continuous expansion. The dividing of the Konzern between the two elder sons of Hugo Stinnes, which was the first solution attempted, proved not to be a final one. In the group taken over by Edmund Stinnes the automobile plants could no longer avoid bankruptcy, and the share in the North Star Insurance Co. had to be sold in Holland. Very soon it became evident that even the remainder of the Stinnes Konzern could no longer be preserved as a unit. With the help of a banking consortium a complete breakdown was avoided, and a gradual liquidation in more or less independent sections was planned.

Even the heart of the Konzern in the mining industry was broken up. The old family holdings (coal mines and the coal trade) were retained, but the Siemens-Rhein-Elbe-Schuckert-Union was broken up. The shares of German-Luxemburg, upon which the influence of the Stinnes family in the group had rested, were sold in England. The stock in the Siemens firm reverted to the Siemens family. Thus a breakdown in the whole community of interest was arranged. The Baroper Rolling Mill, which was controlled by Stinnes through the ownership of preferred stock, went into the possession of a Berlin metal trading firm which already had a share in the company.

In close connection with the mining interests in the Ruhr region had always stood the Rhenish-Westphalian Electric Co., the building of which had been one of the first accomplishments of Hugo Stinnes. The Stinnes share in the stock of this enterprise went over to the Prussian Fiskus, which at the same time acquired the holdings in Pomerania and the port frontage in Hamburg. The Braunschweig lignite holdings of German-Luxemburg and Gelsenkirchen, which had been designed to increase the influence of the Konzern in the electrical industry, were for the most part taken over by the Rhenish-Westphalian Electric Co. and the national electrical plants.

The lignite holdings and the oil wells of the Hugo Stinnes Oil Well and Refining Co., through which the Stinnes Konzern had secured a leading position in the mineral oil industry, were acquired by the Aniline Combine. The interests in the paper industry were turned over in the winter of 1925–26 to the English Inveresk group. The holdings in bank stocks—the Berlin Trading Co. and the Barmen Bank—went to friends of the respective administrations. As for the Hamburg interests of the House of Stinnes, the export business was taken over by the firm of Arnold Otto Meyer, the shipping interests by the Austral and Kosmos lines.

To the Stinnes family in addition to the old family possessions there remained of important enterprises only the hotel holdings, which could not at once be realized upon.

After the breakdown of the House of Stinnes, the foreign holdings were also divided. The foreign enterprises in the electrical industry were taken over by the Siemens Konzern. Some of the foreign branches remained in the hands of the Stinnes heirs. Others, connected with the Stinnes navigation interests, together with the shipping companies were transferred in 1926 to the Hamburg-American Line. There still remained the mining enterprises which were in the Rhein-Elbe-Union. The greater part of these were handed over to the Steel Combine, notably the Austrian connections, of which the Austrian-Alpine Mining Co. was the head.

9. Readings

M. F. Bruck, *Social and Economic History of Germany from William II to Hitler, 1888–1938* (Cardiff, 1938). This work is recommended for general background.

Paul Neubaur, *Mathias Stinnes und sein Haus* (Mülheim a. d. Ruhr, 1908). This book was published as a centennial volume for the firm of Mathias Stinnes. It furnishes a background for the work of Hugo Stinnes, showing the rise of the family.

Hermann Brinckmeyer, *Hugo Stinnes*

(Alfred Kuttner, translator, New York, 1921). A popular study of Stinnes, written at an early date in the development of the Stinnes Konzern. It furnishes a good starting point for the study of the Konzern.

Gaston Raphaël, *Le Roi de la Ruhr* (Paris, 1924). A very good favorable study of Stinnes, his work, and his principles. It should be noted that it was written shortly before the breakdown of the Stinnes Konzern and did not, therefore, have the advantage of the perspective of the later years.

Paul Ufermann and Carl Hüglin, *Stinnes und seine Konzerne* (Berlin, 1924). This work gives the background and the history of Stinnes' career and a mass of detail on the individual units of the Konzern.

Konzerne der Metallindustrie (published by the Vorstand des Deutschen Metallarbeiter-Verbandes, Stuttgart, 1924). A study of the combination movement in the metal industry, the point of view being that of the laborers. The attitude toward Stinnes is hostile.

Paul Ufermann, *Der deutsche Stahltrust* (Berlin, 1927). An historical study of the combination movement in the steel industry, leading up to the formation of the German Steel Trust. A description of the Stinnes Konzern is given, the general attitude being adversely critical.

Konzerne, Interessengemeinschaften, und ähnliche Zusammenschlüsse im deutschen Reich, Ende 1926 (Statistisches Reichsamt, Berlin, 1927). A study of the combination movement, mainly statistical, prepared by the National Statistical Bureau and finished after the breakdown of the Stinnes Konzern.

10. Suggested Questions

1. What were the chief public and general developments that entered into the life and business of Stinnes?
2. What are the relative advantages and weaknesses of horizontal and vertical combinations, as brought out by the Stinnes Konzern?
3. Would it have been possible to finance the Stinnes Konzern had it not been for the abnormal currency conditions in Germany, 1920–23?
4. What was Stinnes' policy with regard to the banks?
5. Had Stinnes lived for ten years longer, could he have held his Konzern together?
6. Which American firm or firms might come near to repeating the experiences of the Stinnes Konzern under similar external conditions?

SECULAR TRENDS IN BUSINESS HISTORY

INTRODUCTION TO THE CASES ON BUSINESS TRENDS

The cases on business trends which follow are experimental and should be used as such by the reader. They are designed to set forth an hypothesis, to present samples of the types of material or evidence now available on the subject, and to point to tentative conclusions and further work on the subject.

These cases are concerned with the major cyclical pulsations or secular swings in business which lie between the short and ever-recurring business cycle and the long-time changes, such as the Commercial Revolution and the Industrial Revolution or the rise and decline of the various types of capitalism, which have been observed in the preceding cases.

The secular trend has recently received increased consideration from economists. While many students had previously touched upon the idea and Marxians had developed it considerably, it is only in the past twenty years that the secular trend has been the object of careful statistical investigation.[1] In 1926 the Russian economist, N. D. Kondratieff, published in a German periodical his conclusions from several years of investigation of many time series.[2] He concluded that the western world has experienced two and one-half long waves since the late years of the eighteenth century, the first wave from 50 to 60 years in duration, the second from 40 to 50 years, and the third wave beginning in the 1890's. In the United States a number of scholars connected with the National Bureau of Economic Research have been doing work on secular trends which has significance to American business history both in a theoretical and in an historical way. First should be mentioned Simon S. Kuznets' statistical investigations which are set forth in his book, *Secular Movements in Production and Prices* (Boston, 1930). Invaluable as a study of changes in various industries and products, though for a relatively short space of time, is Arthur F. Burns' *Production Trends in the United States since 1870* (New York, 1934). A useful qualitative approach to the problem is presented in Willard L. Thorp, *Business Annals* (New York, 1926). For a general discussion of secular trends and what has been accomplished in investigating them the reader is referred to Wesley C. Mitchell, *Business Cycles* (New York, 1927 and 1930). Professor Mitchell concludes that it is "no wonder that a field which requires the fusion of statistical technique with historical learning and theoretical finesse has not yet been explored." Yet, he holds, "the time may be near when the problem of secular trends will have as definite a standing in economic research, attract as many investigators, and

[1] See W. C. Mitchell, *Business Cycles* (New York, 1927), footnotes, pp. 213–214.

[2] N. D. Kondratieff in "Die langen Wellen der Konjunktur," *Archive für Socialwissenschaft und Socialpolitik,* vol. lvi (Dec., 1926), pp. 573–609, and S. S. Kuznets, *Secular Movements in Production and Prices* (Boston, 1930). A translation of Kondratieff's article was published, somewhat abbreviated, in *The Review of Economic Statistics,* vol. xvii (1935), pp. 105–115.

yield as interesting results as the problem of the business cycle."[3]

The hypothesis on which these cases are based is that there have been secular trends in business profits and in the ease or difficulty of business management, which correspond roughly to secular trends in prices. The hypothesis had its origin in general observations and in the study of the experience of many firms.

The implication of this hypothesis is not that the price trend stands in a simple causal relationship to trends in business. Business management, profits, and prices are clearly the resultants of many common factors, changing and varying in their combination from time to time. Indeed, business administration itself is no doubt one of the factors that have been influential in driving prices downward through helping to make more goods and services available at lower costs. Among the many factors, more or less exterior to business, which influence price may be new markets, new inventions, new sources of power, new raw materials, political change, and war. The last, it should be noted, has a significance in business history which can scarcely be over-rated, and it should be weighed heavily in the study of business change. In some respects, prices may well be considered as the secondary or derived factor which is a resultant of other factors and as such a *barometer* rather than a causal factor. Yet, of all the *factors* exterior to his own organization which influence a business man's operations and his success or failure, none is generally so directly significant as price, for success or failure is in large measure a question of adjustment to a price situation. Perhaps all we can safely say at present as to causal relationship, however, is that the price trend may act as a catalyst which precipitates a change in the form and policy of business.

The price trend has been taken as the basis for period divisions in the history of American business. The divisions used are those which appear in outstanding statistical studies of American prices.[4] Omitting the first half of the secular swing which began in the late 1780's, the first case begins with the high point of that long cycle and ends with its low point in 1843; the second case is concerned with the upward movement beginning in 1843 which culminates in the high point in 1866 of the second long swing; the third begins at that point and follows the downward trend to the low point in 1897; the fourth case is concerned with the upward secular movement, ending in 1920, of the major cycle in the downward swing of which business is at present. The general price movement which is the basis for these divisions is shown in the chart below.[5]

One of the objects of these cases is to test whether the pattern of business profits and management in a general way tends to conform to the pattern of price change. We may tentatively characterize a downward secular trend in business somewhat as follows: there is an increasing difficulty, fluctuating with the cycle, on the part of normal industries to earn profits; marginal and submarginal firms go to the wall; collections are difficult; the strains on management force it to become more efficient; employment declines; crises or panics introduce depressions that are deep furrows in the field of business and not simply dramatic financial flurries as they are likely to be in an upward trend. In such a downward swing there is no reason to think of a decline of progress in production, either quantitative or

[3] *Op. cit.*, pp. 232–233.

[4] Anne Bezanson, Robert D. Gray, and Miriam Hussey, *Wholesale Prices in Philadelphia, 1784–1861* (Philadelphia, 1936); Arthur H. Cole, *Wholesale Commodity Prices in the United States, 1700–1861* and its *Statistical Supplement* (Cambridge, 1929); George F. Warren and Frank A. Pearson, *Prices* (New York, 1933).

[5] Constructed from the annual average index in George F. Warren and Frank A. Pearson, *Gold and Prices* (New York, 1935), pp. 11–14 and for 1935–38 from the index of the Bureau of Labor Statistics.

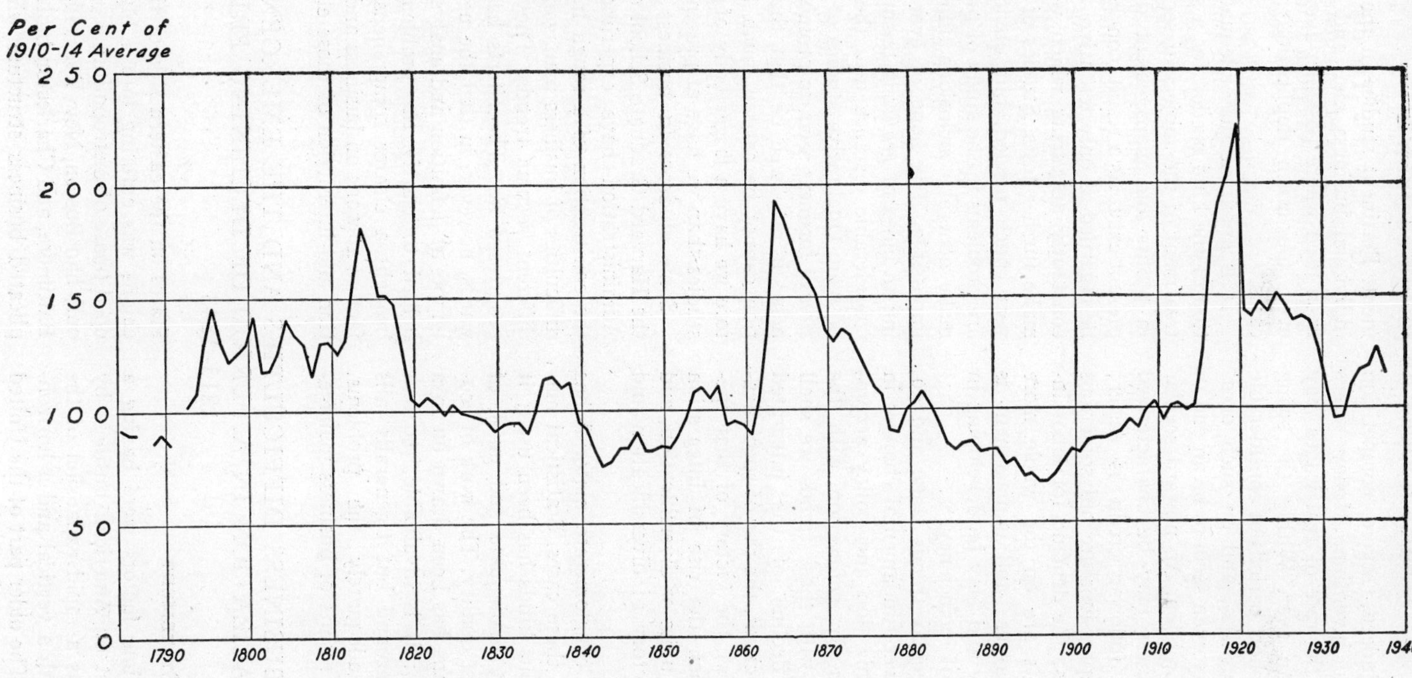

MOVEMENT OF WHOLESALE PRICES IN THE UNITED STATES, 1786–1938

qualitative; indeed, severe competition may stimulate invention. Money wages may fall but the rate of real wages may be higher than ever. Within the swing itself may be short periods of considerable promise in business, and on such occasions there may even seem to be an end to the larger depression. An upward secular trend in business may be characterized somewhat as follows: credit is easier; panics and depressions are not so serious in their effects; the demand for labor increases; profits are on the whole more certain and larger; and management is relatively easy and may be developing in the direction of inefficiency.

As these secular trends come and go, we may discover fundamental changes in business organization and policy accompanying them. In connection with the cases dealing with these trends we shall observe the decline of the integrated sedentary merchant, the rise of specialization in business, the victory of that specialization, then the rise of integration of specialized units or diversification, and finally the victory of diversification and integration.

A mass of conglomerate material has been put into these cases. Statistical material of various kinds has been used; it is of necessity inadequate and much of it is not of first quality. The work of economic historians has been drawn on in a great measure; it is invaluable, particularly for background, but it generally fails to consider adequately the problems, methods, and results of business management. Pertinent studies in the history of individual business men and firms have been used where possible, avoiding, however, too much duplication with other cases.

It is apparent that adequate information of the kind needed for a satisfactory treatment of the subject of secular trends in profits and management does not at present exist. As a result, conclusions must be regarded as only tentative. Studies are constantly appearing which will help us make further tests. Studies of profits are very much needed, but obviously there are problems in the study of profits which make general conclusions difficult if not impossible. The hope of ever constructing an index of *profits* in business for any considerable distance into the past may be vain. Qualitative studies of the *operation* of business seem to promise the most help; it may well be that the investigation cannot be carried much further before we have a larger body of qualitative studies than we have at present.

Some students in business history at the Harvard Graduate School of Business Administration have experimented with the construction of a rough index of the difficulties of business management in the different secular trends. They have not progressed far. The efforts had their rewards, however, in that the necessary attempts at definition and analysis not only helped to clarify the problem but also brought a clearer comprehension of the factors at work on business and of the action and interaction of those elements.

XXXIX. BUSINESS DIFFICULTIES AND THE EMERGENCE OF SPECIALIZATION IN A PERIOD OF DECLINING PRICES 1815–1843

1. General Statement

Two long-time factors were having a powerful effect on American business by 1815. One was a rapid expansion of the market, in both a vertical and a horizontal direction. The older part of the United States on the eastern side of the Appalachians was entering into a highly developed phase of metropolitan economy. Not only had Boston, New York, Philadelphia, Baltimore, and Charleston built up a complicated business structure which served as the market center for large areas, but some of those cities had even built up a considerable machinery for financing trade in their areas. The rapid extension of settlement westward after the war hastened the growth of business in the old centers and brought new markets in the hinterland.

Another significant long-time development was the revolution in transportation and manufacture which had scarcely begun in the United States before 1815 and which was to bring a greater division of labor industrially, commercially, and regionally. The impact of the Industrial Revolution on the developing metropolitan economy was to bring radical changes in the business structure. In other words, specialization was to take the place of the diversified business, and mercantile capitalism was to give way to industrial.

Such long-time developments in business progress in both good and bad times. The behavior of business in the period 1815–43 seems to support the observation, however, that a declining price level, if not too severe, speeds up the rate of change. Never in the history of American business has there been a more rapid growth of new ventures in new fields than in this period, when the drive of prices was downward.

2. General View of the Period

1815	Postwar crisis in March. Auction system came into extensive use in New York for sale of foreign goods.
1815–19	Rapid expansion of foreign trade. Depression in manufactures.
1815–21	Financial chaos, deflation of prices.
1816	Slightly protective tariff passed.
1817	Rapid westward movement began. Second Bank of the United States opened. New York Stock and Exchange Board organized. First big issue of State securities. First dividend, Boston Manufacturing Co. First steamboat on the Great Lakes. First steamboat, New Orleans to Ohio.
1818–20	Banking in bad condition.
1819	Financial panic.
1821–43	Slight downward trend of prices.
1822–25	Prosperity.
1823	Champlain Canal completed.
1824	Mania for chartering banks began.
1824–25	Cotton speculation, corner, collapse.
1825	Panic and bankruptcy of merchants. Erie Canal completed.
1825–29	Revival and prosperity.
1827	Movement of capital from foreign trade to domestic investments notable.
1828	Beginning of rapid development of New England textile manufacturing.
1829	Heavy influx of foreign capital began.
1829–33	Relatively low cotton prices.
1830	First division of Baltimore and Ohio completed.
1830–36	Unfavorable trade balance increased.
1830–43	Prices of domestic products higher than imported goods.
1831	First successful use of locomotive.
1831–34	Heavy import of foreign capital. Many corporations formed.
1833	Incorporation of Chicago.
1833–34	Contraction by second Bank of United States.
1834	Panic. First corner, New York Stock Exchange. Canals connected Philadelphia and Ohio.
1834–37	Rapid rise of prices, boom in trade, land, and securities.
1835	First financial article in New York paper.
1836	United States Bank rechartered by Pennsylvania.
1837	Panic and widespread failure.
1837–39	Pegging cotton prices to stop

	deflation. Activity in internal improvements.
1837–43	Foreign trade declining with slight tendency toward a favorable balance.
1839	Revival, resumption of specie payments, collapse of cotton, panic. *Hunt's Merchants' Magazine* established, first general business periodical in United States.
1839–43	Depression and many failures. Banks almost disappeared in West.
1840–42	Inflow of foreign capital ceased.
1842	Railroad completed, Boston to Albany and Albany to Buffalo.
1843	Bottom of downward price trend.

3. Review of Business Conditions in the Preceding Period

Before considering the years 1815–43 it is well to review briefly business conditions in the preceding period.[1] The year 1789 marked the end of the period of deflation in business and prices which followed the Revolutionary War. From 1789 (or 1788) to December, 1814, both business and prices went through a number of cycles, culminating in the inflationary movement of the war of 1812–14.

The recovery movement which got under way in 1789 lasted until in 1792. The spirit of speculation, which had been stimulated by profits from the rise in government securities and had turned to bank stocks and lands, collapsed in the spring of that year. Bank stocks, government securities, and land dropped in value. Banks tightened their loans and many enterprises and individuals met financial ruin.

Then followed a revival in prices and business which lasted until about 1797. It was based on an increasingly profitable foreign trade though the many difficulties in international relations brought temporary setbacks. In 1797–98 came declining prosperity with the insecurity of commerce and the threat of war with France. In 1799 prices were uncertain. In 1800–02 trade went through the cycle of revival, prosperity, and collapse. For America, the Peace of Amiens (which released European shipping to trade) brought idle ships, diminution of exports, unemployment, and business failures.

Renewal of war in Europe in 1803 was followed by business revival in America, and by 1805–06 this country was again in the flood tide of prosperity. But the British Orders in Council, the Napoleonic Decrees, and Jefferson's Embargo brought stagnation in business by 1808. With the removal of the Embargo and improvement in our export market came a mild revival in 1809–12, but the uncertain relations with England injured trade.

War with England from June, 1812, to the end of 1814 brought higher commodity prices. Foreign goods rose faster than domestic, and the high price of the former gave a strong impetus to domestic manufacturing. The rise in prices was in part the result of the great inflation in the currency which came from the establishment of a large number of weak banks after the disappearance of the first Bank of the United States in 1811.

At the end of the War of 1812, American business was in a dangerously inflated condition. There were many new banks resting on a weak base, and currency was in a chaotic condition. Agriculture had been stimulated by war demands, and manufacturing by the dearth of foreign-made products. While the merchant marine had suffered greatly in the war, it had built up a heavy trade, owing in part to the long wars in Europe. The general price level had risen to more than twice what it had been in 1789.

[1] On conditions in this period see Thorp, *Business Annals,* pp. 113–117, and W. B. Smith and A. H. Cole, *Fluctuations in American Business, 1790–1860* (Cambridge, 1935), pp. 8–33.

4. The Price Trend

From 1815 to 1843 there was a downward trend in the wholesale commodity price level in the United States. From the end of 1814 to about 1821 there was a rapid, though interrupted, downward thrust of the price level, essentially a postwar deflation; thereafter, the decline was slower, according to one investigation of prices during the period, averaging 0.5 per cent a year from 1820 to 1843.[2] As usual the downward movement was cyclical in character, the higher points appearing in 1818, 1825, 1837, and 1839, and unusually low points in 1823, 1830, and 1843. It is important to note not only that there were cycles but also that successive cycles on the whole ended at a progressively lower price level.

All commodity prices did not move in the same direction at any given period of time or at the same rate. The situation is illustrated by studies of important groups of commodities. Figures in Warren and Pearson's *Prices*[3] show significant differences in the behavior of groups of commodities. Farm products and foods lagged noticeably behind textiles and metals and metal products, especially in the two major declines beginning in 1814 and in 1837. Throughout the 1820's, also, the first two groups decreased less than the last two. Smith and Cole similarly found that the drop in agricultural products lagged in the two major declines; indeed, there was no serious break from 1837 to 1839 in farm products. They found a cyclical swing in the agricultural index from 1825 to 1830 but not in the industrial.[4] It is significant that in 1843 cotton reached an all-time low.

A recent study of prices reveals some interesting facts about price movements in Philadelphia, which have a general significance. Agricultural prices were on the whole much less stable than industrial. While industrial products dropped radically from 1814 to 1817, agricultural products continued upward until sometime in 1817. In 1821 they fell below industrial products, soon recovered their higher position and remained higher than industrials, going very much higher at times, until early in 1843.[5]

Another significant comparison is made of Philadelphia prices. In 1814 the average price of 49 imported commodities, which had throughout the Embargo and war years risen far above that of 69 domestic products, began a radical decline, at the beginning of 1816 falling below the domestic price. Throughout the 1820's the differences between the two groups were not marked, though changes in domestic commodity prices tended to lag behind the imported, but from 1831 until the end of 1843 the domestic commodities experienced a strong rise to 1837 and a decline thereafter which did not appear in the prices of imported commodities.[6]

It would be very useful to have sufficient regional studies of prices to consider the relation of business conditions to prices by regions. Prices in New England, Philadelphia, and the South have been compiled carefully for various periods before 1861. For the West, however, where poor transportation facilities kept prices relatively low, we have little price information in a useful form.

The study of Charleston wholesale prices from 1818 to 1842 illustrates regional conditions in price movements.[7] The South Carolina export staples, cotton and rice, changed more violently in

[2] Smith and Cole, *op. cit.*, p. 60.

[3] George F. Warren and Frank A. Pearson, *Prices* (New York, 1933), p. 25.

[4] *Ibid.*, pp. 63 and 66.

[5] Anne Bezanson, Robert D. Gray, and Miriam Hussey, *Wholesale Prices in Philadelphia, 1784–1861* (Philadelphia, 1936), chart opposite p. 4.

[6] *Ibid.*

[7] G. R. Taylor, "Wholesale Commodity Prices at Charleston, South Carolina, 1796–1861," *Journal of Economic and Business History*, vol. iv (1931–32), pp. 859 and 861.

Charleston than the prices of imports or of domestic commodities other than export staples; the export staples rose to unusual heights after 1814 and also in 1825, 1833, 1835, and 1836, while those same export staples fell below the other groups in 1823, and from 1826 to 1833 were almost always lower than the others. Prices of imports in Charleston generally held above other prices until in the early 'thirties.

About changes in wages, interest, and security prices, all of which are important in the whole price picture, even less is known than about changes in commodity prices. Both wages and interest were significant from the point of view of costs. About wages in this period almost nothing is known. Smith and Cole have studied interest rates and stock prices. They concluded that the former fluctuated more violently than either stock or commodity prices, and that the peak and bottom of the movement of interest rates were generally reached later than the corresponding points in the movement of stock and commodity prices.[8]

5. Changes in Business Management

A. The decline of the sedentary merchant.

The largest single field of American business in 1815 was foreign trade. In the years 1786 to 1815 that trade, encouraged by the wars in Europe (1793–1815) which weakened competition and created a great demand for neutral carriers, had grown to a position of dominance in American business. The American foreign merchant commanded much capital, employed many ships and men, and had business contacts the world over. The special province of the American merchant was the Northwest Coast fur trade with the Orient, but his ships sought every port in the world where there was brisk trade, often roaming about from port to port for years without returning home.

From 1815 to 1819 there was a rapid expansion of American foreign trade. The ship tonnage of American registry increased greatly for a time; the Canton trade in particular and foreign trade in general experienced a few years of rapid growth. For a time American merchants had an advantage. Not only did they have strong business contacts built up during the Napoleonic Wars, and furs, cotton, food, and forest products with which to supply the foreign market, but they had also a growing market at home.

Although foreign trade was growing in amount, its prosperity did not increase with its size. The continuous fall in both import and export prices after the war meant that the merchant would be in danger of losing heavily because of the long time taken in carrying goods from market to market.

Certain fundamental factors were behind the change in mercantile prices and profits. The postwar deflation in Europe and America drove prices downward. The textile revolution in England and America was already undermining the western market for oriental cottons and linens. Very significant was the fact that foreign trade had to meet greater competition after the coming of peace. Indeed, so rapid was the increase in trade that the western tea markets had become glutted and hence thoroughly demoralized by 1826. Another factor must also have been important—that the international trade had reached a static point of maturity in which the profit margin tended to decrease, at least until some revolutionary change, such as in power, appeared. Essentially this was a buyer's rather than a seller's market. For the American merchants two other elements entered into the situation. Their oriental trade, especially, had been closely tied up with the trade in sandalwood from the Hawaiian Islands and the fur trade. The

[8] Smith and Cole, *op. cit.*, p. 83.

sandalwood trade was already in a decline owing to the exhaustion of the forests when a heavy tax in 1826 practically made the trade prohibitive.[9] The period of pioneer exploitation in the fur trade was also over. The demand for beaver in Europe was weakening, and competition was keeping profits down to a minimum for the fur companies, while the exhaustion of their production along the coasts was driving them to seek furs farther inland.[10]

This does not mean that profits were not made in the foreign trade in the 'twenties but rather that the making of profits became increasingly difficult. New techniques had to be used. Those merchants were most successful who had not only skill in management but also a considerable capital and a large continuous trade. John Jacob Astor could bargain well; because of his strong capital position and because of the great volume of his business, he could demand the best terms. The time was passing, however, when a young man without capital could begin as a supercargo and work to the top. The powerful concern was the one most likely to succeed.

By the late 'twenties even the most successful American merchants saw that they were in a declining business. They had for some time been withdrawing capital for investment at home, but now they, themselves, began to withdraw from foreign trade. If they had sons, their sons often chose other work. The year 1826 marks the end of John Jacob Astor's active participation in foreign trade. John P. Cushing came home from China in 1827 and gradually withdrew his capital from trade, which he felt was no longer profitable. The same was done by Bryant & Sturgis and Perkins & Co. There was a slight revival of the trade in the good days of the early 'thirties, but only temporarily.

The decline of American foreign trade created some serious problems. What should those merchants do? Cushing could retire to his estate and find satisfaction in beautiful flowers and trees; T. H. Perkins was too old for active work. But what was there for the younger men still in their prime? Moreover, where could mercantile capital find safe and profitable investment? And what of all the young men of the seaboard who had earlier looked to the sea?

Closely linked to foreign trade was the American fur trade. Like the former, the latter had before the war promised satisfactory returns to an adventurous man who was a good trader though he had little capital. Peace brought competition on the ocean which only the strongest could survive, but peace and consequent developments drove some of the strongest operators—the British—out of the American fur empire. It might seem that this should have been favorable to the small man in the fur business, but such was not the case. Large American companies had grown up, and they dominated every large fur region. The strongest was John Jacob Astor's American Fur Co. Though this company had suffered greatly during the war, after the war it was driven by Astor's power—a combination of political influence, superior management, capital, and an extensive and varied trade—till it virtually became the dictator in the American fur business by 1827.

Astor remained in the fur trade until 1834. He retired then because he was getting old. But he seems to have believed that the fur market was getting difficult; he feared that the making of hats from silk instead of beaver would soon break the demand for any but the very finest beaver.[11] Beaver had been the backbone of the fur trade.

[9] K. W. Porter, *John Jacob Astor, Business Man* (Cambridge, 1931), vol. ii, pp. 666–667.

[10] H. M. Chittenden, *The American Fur Trade of the Far West* (New York, 1902), vol. i, pp. 364, 375–395.

[11] *Ibid.*, p. 364.

In the years 1834 to 1843 the American Fur Co. encountered serious difficulties. Rival concerns, with their base not in foreign trade but in the depths of the fur country, threatened its leadership. It clung to its unprofitable Rocky Mountain business in order to maintain its prestige with the Indians. Though the company succeeded in maintaining its leadership against powerful rivals, an authority on the history of the trade said of the American Fur Co. in 1843 that "it required no prophet to see that the sun of its prosperity, so far as the fur trade was concerned, was on the decline." [12] That was as true of the fur trade in general, for the days of great profits had passed away.

In foreign trade, especially, and in the fur trade we have interesting illustrations of business behavior in a period when declining prices pressed on the profit margin. The old business tended to become more keenly competitive, and its management looked for methods with which to meet competitive menaces, the keener and the more powerful in size and resources surviving on the strength of greater efficiency, bargaining power, or reserves. For the rank and file of business, prosperity or even survival could be found only in other fields, where special conditions promised to offset somewhat the downward drive of prices. Those special conditions might be cheaper production through the lowered cost of labor, raw materials, capital, or management, or a shift to something like a seller's market by providing new goods or service, the demand for which exceeded the supply.

B. The rise of the specialist.

The decline in mercantile profits was one factor which turned American business management and capital rapidly into new lines of business; it made greater the comparative advantage of investments at home. The result was the shifting of the focus of activity from the foreign to the domestic, the shifting of capital from mercantile to industrial uses (in the broad sense), and the change of business management from diversification to specialization.

This movement toward specialization took two forms. First, specialization in function—as contrasted with the diversification of the merchant capitalist—in some fields favored the small man. The small manufacturer could find a market through agent-distributors; the agent-distributor did not need a large capital since he might be merely a middleman; the exchange dealer could work on commission until he had built up a capital through earnings. Second, the corporate form of enterprise made for the organization of specialization on a larger scale. The availability of foreign and domestic mercantile capital and the credit of banks made possible the massing of larger amounts of capital in one enterprise with a minimum of risk. The small individual enterprise and the large corporate undertaking grew simultaneously, side by side.

Domestic business took many forms in this period: manufacturing, transportation, insurance, banking, trade, storage, speculation, and investment in stocks, bonds, produce, or real estate. Four of those fields are considered below.

(1) Manufacturing.

Developments in manufacture may be indicated by changes in two industries.

The boot and shoe industry in New England [13] was able to expand in spite of the dreary drizzle of falling prices. It did this by producing in larger volume by means of cheaper processes for new markets. Until about 1810 the shoemaker had been an independent artisan serving mostly a local, custom trade. But the merchants found that the West Indies, South America, the South, and the West —which had few if any shoemakers—

[12] *Ibid.*, p. 374.

[13] See Blanche Evans Hazard, *The Organization of the Boot and Shoe Industry in Massachusetts before 1875* (Cambridge, 1921), pp. 42–96.

would buy cheap boots or brogans for heavy work. As the fall in prices caught the small independent shoemaker serving the custom trade, the new markets gave the first opportunity for meeting the fall of prices.

The leadership in the change was taken by men who could combine some capital with skilled management, chiefly merchants and master shoemakers. The essence of their system was cheap volume production for a low-priced market. The cutting was done in a central place, and different processes or parts were given to different workers. Unskilled women and children worked on the "uppers," which were later given out with cut soles to more skilled workers, who "lasted" the soles and sewed on the uppers.

During the depression following 1837, management in the boot and shoe industry became wholly specialized. The entrepreneurs gave their whole time to the business. They began to seek the high-grade trade, which the custom shoemakers had retained, by producing high-quality shoes in standard sizes. This necessitated greater control over production. The work formerly put out was done in workshops, where a group of unskilled or less skilled men worked under skilled shoemakers. Thus cheap labor was used to make a high quality of shoes.

The textile manufacturers similarly met the situation with lowered production costs. Power-spinning had been introduced in the United States in 1790, but the other processes had been left to the old methods of production. In 1813 was established the Boston Manufacturing Co.; this company introduced the machine factory which carried on all processes of manufacture.[14]

[14] Material on this section has been drawn chiefly from an unpublished study of the Boston Manufacturing Co. by Ralph W. Ells, from Caroline F. Ware, *The Early New England Cotton Manufacture* (Boston, 1931), and J. G. Martin, *History of the Boston Stock and Money Markets* (Boston, 1898).

The experience of the Boston Manufacturing Co. illustrates the problems and methods of the new textile manufacture. The Waltham mill established by this concern adopted the use of power machinery for both spinning and weaving and carried on all processes in one mill. With such a setup, labor without skill or physical strength could be used. The result was that women and children were hired. Because of the heavy fixed investments, capital became a prime consideration under this form. Since capital was expensive, machines had to be used regularly and efficiently, labor had to be disciplined, adequate raw materials had to be on hand, and an inventory was needed to supply the market. It also became necessary to have a regular market. As the work grew, management became more and more important. In the work of the Boston Manufacturing Co., three specialists came to stand at the head: P. T. Jackson, the treasurer and financial manager; Paul Moody, the engineer and production man who had charge of the mill; and the Wards, of Boston, who took over the marketing function.

Although the textile mills were improving in efficiency, tapping cheap labor supplies, using raw material falling in price, and serving an expanding market, the dividends of even the more efficient mills fell with the decline of prices. From 1837 to 1843 the stronger textile mills cut their dividends greatly, frequently passing them altogether.[15] At the same time there was a great mortality among smaller mills. The small, old-form mill was strong only in that it might escape some of the worst effects of competition by producing finer goods. In all matters that depended on an abundance of capital and the economies of mass production and marketing, the large mechanized mill had the advantage.

Table 1 (p. 672), gives the dividends of

[15] Martin, *op. cit.*, p. 128.

New England textile firms which survived through the period.[16]

The textile mills gave rise to an important machine industry, especially in New England. The manufacture of textile machines or tools had been made a separate industry in 1810, when David Wilkinson opened his shop in Pawtucket, Rhode Island. Out of the machine shop of the Waltham Cotton Mill developed what in 1825 became a separate shop for manufacturing machines at Lowell, Massachusetts. Many shops also developed which made various kinds of mill equipment. Worcester, for instance, had nine concerns making pickers, cards, jacks, and

[16] *Ibid.* Companies through "L" given in Table 1.

Table 1. DIVIDENDS OF NEW ENGLAND TEXTILE MANUFACTURING COMPANIES, 1817–43

In per cent of par value of stock except where given in dollars

(Year of establishment indicated)

Year	Amoskeag 1831 (?)	Appleton 1828	Bartlett 1838	Boott Cotton Mills 1836	Boston (Waltham) 1813	Chicopee 1824	Cocheco 1822	Dwight 1842	Great Falls 1825 (?)	Hamilton Cotton 1825	Jackson Co. 1831	Lawrence 1833, '34	Lowell 1828
1817					17								
1818					12½								
1819					12½								
1820					15								
1821					20								
1822					27½		...						
1823					25		...						
1824					25	...	...						
1825					15 [a]	...	...		...	...			
1826					8	...	...		...	...			
1827					9	4	...		...	...			
1828		...			12	8	...		...	7			...
1829		3			7	0	...		...	8			...
1830		11			7	6	...		...	6			...
1831	...	24			$110 [b]	10	...		...	18½	...		5
1832	...	14			$100	14	...		...	24½	...		14
1833	...	16			$100	8	...		...	10	$100 [c]	...	9
1834	6	11			$ 70	8	...		...	11	$70	4	13
1835	15	13			$ 80	10	...		8	14	$154	10	12
1836	8	7		...	$ 70	10	...		5	13	$104	10	15
1837	4	0		...	$ 30	5	...		5	0	$ 80	5	5
1838	3	25 [a]	...	4	$ 30	5	...		0	9	$ 50	4	3
1839	9	5	...	10	$ 60	5	$42 [c]		0	23 [a]	$100	10	25 [a]
1840	0	5	13	4	$ 30	0	0		0	5	0	3	0
1841	6	6	14	10	$ 60	3	$42		4½	8	$200 [a]	7	11
1842	4	0	0	3	0	0	0	3	5	0	$ 50	2	4
1843	7	6	12	5	$ 30	0	0	11	6	6	$ 30	7	3

[a] Paid in stock.

[b] Par of this stock was $500 at first but was raised to $750 about 1835.

[c] Par was $1,000.

so on, by 1830. A very important establishment for making textile machines, the Whitin Shops of Northbridge, Massachusetts, was established in 1831. The work was not limited to New England alone; there were, for instance, the Jenks Works at Philadelphia, as well as early works at Paterson (New Jersey) and Newcastle (Delaware).[17]

(2) Transportation.

The prospects for American transportation development in those decades may be indicated by examples of charges for carriage. In 1821 it cost about as much to carry one ton thirty miles inland as to carry it from Europe to the United States. In 1818 the charge for freight between Philadelphia and Pittsburgh was $8 per hundredweight. In 1820 the charge for a ton from New Orleans to Pittsburgh was from $67 to $112; the time consumed from New Orleans to Pittsburgh was four months, while the return trip could be made in one month.[18]

The first enterprises to profit by these high charges used the steamboat. Fulton and Livingston of New York first established themselves on the Hudson River on the strength of a charter from New York State, and later on the Mississippi and Ohio rivers by virtue of a charter from Louisiana. They were able to maintain practical monopolies on those riverways until 1824, when their monopoly was broken by a decision of the United States Supreme Court to the effect that the regulation of commerce on interstate waterways was a province of the federal government.

Another element was holding back transportation on the inland waterways. The steamboats were subject to many disasters; before 1826, 41 per cent of all the steamboats constructed on the Ohio were destroyed by fire or by the bad condition of the River.[19] This was an engineering problem for which it was difficult to find any solution.

One of the early successful specialists who at this time came to the fore in domestic water carriage was Cornelius Vanderbilt. In 1815 he started in coastwise sailing vessels; but in 1817, deciding that the future was with steam, he hired out to Gibbons, who ran a combination stage and steamboat line from New York to Baltimore. In 1829, with $30,000 in savings, Vanderbilt established his own line. He is said to have averaged a profit of $30,000 a year in 1830–35; in 1836 he cleared $60,000. He never insured and never lost a boat, it is said (his boats were unusually well built). He plowed his profits back into his business, building more boats and establishing regular service for many eastern ports.

One transportation need could not be solved by individual effort or often even by private capital, that is, to connect regions with no common waterways and furnish better means for the hinterland to reach the waterways. That problem was, therefore, largely left to public effort. The canal was the way most commonly favored until the 1840's. Many States undertook to build canals. New York State built the Erie and Champlain canals which connected the Lake Champlain country and the Great Lakes region in 1825. In 1834 the Pennsylvania canal system, built in part by funds from a State lottery, connected the Great Lakes and Pittsburgh with Philadelphia and reached into the anthracite fields. Similarly, the States of Ohio, Indiana, and Illinois undertook to build great canal systems.

In the meantime the railroad came into being in the United States. Railroads were too big undertakings to appeal to individual enterprise, and at first there

[17] V. S. Clark, *History of Manufactures in the United States, 1607–1860* (Washington, 1929), pp. 519–520.

[18] B. H. Meyer, *History of Transportation in the United States before 1860* (Washington, 1917), pp. 88–90.

[19] *Ibid.*, p. 108.

was no certainty that they would be profitable. They therefore were built by corporations. The first incentive to support railroads came from cities or towns which wanted increased business. The Baltimore & Ohio was started by Maryland and Baltimore as a public enterprise to enable them to compete with their northern neighbors. Similar efforts were made by other cities or States, which lent their credit to the new ventures.

The earliest railroads in the United States (as in England) were experimental. The Baltimore & Ohio experimented with every form of track construction and gauge, wasting millions of dollars. Locomotives were unsatisfactory—for instance, they would not run in rain. Vested "interests" opposed them, such as turnpikes, bridge companies, and stage lines, as well as inns, which claimed they were injured by the new roads—even farmers objected because railroads destroyed some of their hay market.

As the railroads proved their worth, however, private capital began to be interested. The commercial interests of Baltimore invested heavily in the Baltimore road, notably Brown Brothers, who had so much to do with its early management. The Boston & Lowell, Boston & Worcester, and others radiating from Boston were similarly heavily backed by Boston commercial and textile capital.

In spite of panics, depressions, and falling prices, many of these earliest railroads were apparently financially successful from the outset. All but one of the roads built from Boston paid moderate dividends from 1835, when the first was opened, until 1843.[20] The railroad and canal investments of J. P. Cushing, who invested heavily in New England railroads in this period, yielded (income to capital) 15.1 per cent in 1836, 1.3 in 1837, 4.5 in 1838, with progressive increases to 1842, and a slight drop in 1843.[21] The most ambitious project at the time, the Baltimore & Ohio, had considerable difficulty, perhaps because in spite of business conditions it was rapidly pushing westward.[22]

From these developments in transportation came another new industry, the manufacture of engines. In 1816 a shop for the manufacture of marine engines was established in New York City. Beginning in 1828 large engine builders were established in several places near seaports. These built stationary as well as marine engines. The construction of steam engines became the special task of western works. By 1830 there were foundries at Pittsburgh, Wheeling, and other places on the Ohio which were devoted chiefly to the manufacture of steam engines. In that year 100 engines were built at Pittsburgh and 150 at Cincinnati. In 1832 was established the Baldwin Works, and in 1834 the Norris Works for building locomotives in Pennsylvania. In the latter year the Locks and Canals Co. of Lowell began to build locomotives, and in 1837 the Rogers Works at Paterson took up this manufacture.[23]

(3) Banking and the brokerage business.

The growth of banking in this period was phenomenal. The local discount bank, serving mainly foreign trade, had developed earlier. But in the years covered by this period banking grew rapidly and developed greatly in function. Chartered

[20] Martin, *op. cit.,* p. 147. Since these roads were small and managed by their owners, who were chiefly conservative Boston merchants, they probably paid dividends from earnings only, though without provision for depreciation or obsolescence.

[21] H. M. Larson, "A China Trader Turns Investor," *Harvard Business Review,* vol. xii (April, 1934), p. 357.

[22] E. Hungerford, *The Story of the Baltimore & Ohio Railroad, 1827–1927* (New York, 1928), pp. 48–215.

[23] J. L. Bishop, *A History of American Manufactures,* vol. ii (Philadelphia, 1864), pp. 818–821, gives dates of establishment of foundries; Clark, *op. cit.,* pp. 506–508.

banks, alone, from 1815 to 1840 increased in number from 208 to 722 and in capital from $82,200,000 to $358,400,000.[24]

In the eastern cities much of the banking development was sound. One of the striking facts about banking is the large amount of mercantile capital which went into that field. Boston, New York, Philadelphia, and Baltimore banks were often headed by members of mercantile families. John Jacob Astor, Bryant & Sturgis, and J. P. Cushing illustrate the transfer of capital from trade to banking. Banks to serve industrial needs, particularly, also grew up, such as the shoe and leather banks and mechanics' and manufacturers'. How profitable the banking business was may be seen from Table 2.[25]

[24] 26th Cong., 2d Sess., *House Reports,* no. 111, "Condition of the State Banks," p. 1456.

[25] Martin, *op. cit.,* pp. 97–98.

Table 2. DIVIDENDS OF BOSTON BANKS
1814–43
In per cent of par value of stock
(Year of establishment indicated)

Year	Atlantic 1828	Atlas 1834	Boston 1803	City 1822	Columbian 1822	Eagle 1822	Freeman's 1836	Globe 1824	Granite 1833	Hamilton 1832	Market 1832	Massachusetts 1784
1814			4									6
1815			4									3
1816			6									6
1817			8									6
1818			8									6
1819			7									6
1820			6.33									4.85
1821			4.40									6
1822			5.33	...	...	...						6.20
1823			5.33	5.75	7	6.50						6
1824			5.06	7.60	5.50	6.25		...				6
1825			5.33	7.25	5.50	6		5				6
1826			4	5.25	6	6		5				6
1827			4	5	6	6		6				3.70
1828	2		4.66	6.50	5.50	6		5.50				4.50
1829	5.50		2.66	6	6	6		5.50				4.50
1830	4		3	4.50	4.50	6		5.50				4.50
1831	3		6	6	5	6		6				4.50
1832	6		6	6	6	6		6		2.50	...	4.90
1833	6		6.50	6	6	6		6	...	6	6.25	5.50
1834	6	...	7	6	6	5		6	4.50	6	6	5
1835	6	7	7	6.50	6	6		6	3	6	6	5
1836	6	6	7	6.50	6	7	...	7	6	6	6	2.50
1837	6	0	6.50	6.50	6	6	6	6.50	6	6	6	6
1838	3	0	6.50	6	6	6	6	6	3.50	6	3	4.50
1839	6	0	7	6	6	6	6	6	6	6	4.75	5.50
1840	2	2	7	6	6	6.50	6	6	5	6	0	5
1841	6	5	7	0	6	6.50	7	6	6	6	3.50	6
1842	6	4.50	7	2	6	0	7	6	4.50	6	6	5.60
1843	5	4	7	3.50	5	5	7	6	5	5	6	4.80

These banks were soundly based on a commercial or industrial clientele which had capital and entrepreneurial experience and which had a legitimate need for banking. These banks were on the whole quite conservative, and accordingly they did not attempt to meet some of the demands for banking services of the time.

Other banks, accordingly, sprang up to manufacture credit through currency issue. In Pennsylvania there was a wild inflation of banking in the smaller towns. Some of the western and southern States established banking as a State monopoly, generally to further internal improvements. The Planters' Bank of Louisiana was aided by the Barings directly, while several State banks sold to European investors great amounts of State bonds to finance internal improvements. Those banks were not successful as banks and collapsed in the early 'forties.

The second Bank of the United States illustrates some of the problems and policies of banking in the period concerned. Badly managed in its first years, a time of general deflation and trouble, it recovered in the 1820's under Nicholas Biddle. The bank had a salutary effect on currency by refusing to accept poor bank notes; it set up a splendid system of domestic exchange; and it tried to follow a fairly conservative policy in its discounting. In doing this, however, Biddle came into sharp conflict with the needs of the new West, which tended to absorb the capital of the bank in loans which had to be renewed. The bank was virtually killed by its political enemies, principally from the debtor West. It was rechartered by Pennsylvania and continued under Biddle. Two things, in particular, worked against its success: (1) it had inherited large blocks of securities from the bank under the federal charter, which fell rapidly in value in the depression following the panic of 1837; and (2) the depression destroyed much of its business. Biddle tried to save the bank by supporting the credit of the country in Europe through the pegging of cotton prices, cotton being the commodity used to settle our foreign balances. This effort failed; in 1839 Biddle resigned; and in 1841 the bank permanently closed its doors. It is not impossible that, if Biddle had worked in an upward movement of prices, his bank would have been successful.

One of the remarkable aspects of banking in this period is the rise to importance of the private banker and broker. Some private banking developed out of the mercantile business, as for instance Brown Brothers and Girard's Bank. Such banks were especially fitted to carry on foreign banking. More closely associated with American domestic development were the brokers and private bankers known as the stock and exchange brokers. They rose to prominence soon after the War of 1812, the product of the chaotic condition of the currency, the widening and growth of trade which increased the business of transferring funds, and the ambitions of capital-less young men to get on in business. These men usually started on a small scale, and, if successful, established branch partnerships in many business centers.

Throughout the whole country the exchange brokers performed a number of functions. They did most of the work of transferring funds, except during the height of the Bank of the United States. In the fluid state of business at the time, this was a risky business which local chartered banks could not do so well as the private concerns with branch partnerships but little capital at stake. They also did a considerable loan business in this period, partly on their own account but chiefly on commission. It was common for individuals or firms seeking loans to go to the broker, who secured the loan from a bank or an individual. By 1843, however, this business had developed so far that private brokers or bankers were borrowing money from banks to loan out at their own risk.

Private brokers or bankers also found much to do in issuing and trading in securities. Industrial concerns, banks, and insurance companies usually sold their stock directly without much use of middlemen. The seller or buyer of stock already on the market, however, looked to the broker. Canals, especially, and some railroads, which were essentially speculative, had to satisfy their need for large funds through middlemen. During the period between the issue of New York State "stock" in 1817 (to finance the building of the Erie Canal) and the widespread repudiation of State loans for internal improvements, the middlemen came to be of great importance in the investment market. They both served the domestic market and brought over much capital from Europe. In the 1830's some of the private bankers who dealt in stocks developed into real investment bankers. Prime, Ward & King and S. & M. Allen & Co. were firms which had, respectively, a strong foreign and a domestic business. They both traded on commission and invested heavily for themselves, at times virtually underwriting loans.

The stock and exchange brokers and bankers were far from safe enterprises. They often did business on little capital. They had an unstable and a risky business. They were easily carried away by boom movements, and deflation characteristically found them too heavily invested in securities and extended on loans to meet their obligations.

There seems normally to have been a high mortality among such enterprises. The panic of 1837 broke many of them, even large ones, and the succeeding years were difficult. Under the uncertain condition of banking, currency, and business in general after 1837, the exchange business was very risky but the possible profits were high. The widespread failure of banks threw much of the inland business into the hands of private concerns, and the harvest was rich for those among them which had good connections in distant places, the best of information on the value of the paper handled, and good standing with banks.

At the end of the period, 1815–43, commercial banking in the large eastern cities, though crippled by the panic of 1837 and the consequent depression, was essentially sound. Country banks in Pennsylvania had suffered severely, and in several States in the newer South and West chartered banks had disappeared almost altogether, leaving the field to private banking. Investment banking had shrunk to small proportions under the downward drive of security prices and widespread repudiation.

(4) Middlemen in the commodities trade.

Between the manufacturer or importing merchant and the consumer the distance of time and space grew greater in this period, and as a result new agencies arose. There were important changes in both retailing and wholesaling.

There was one important new development in retailing. Specialization increased greatly in the larger markets. In New York the retail stores of the importing merchants and wholesalers changed widely in the direction of specialty shops. The beginning of the departmentalized store came later, though A. T. Stewart's —at one time the most famous store in the United States—was established in New York in this period. In the larger inland markets, however, wholesaling and retailing were still combined, and in the small towns and villages the general store predominated. In the Indian country the chain trading posts of the fur companies were the principal trading unit.

The opening of the inland and the growth of large-scale production of manufactured goods created new needs and opportunities in the wholesale field. Increased competition and the downward drive of prices made merchants and manufacturers sell aggressively. This led to great changes in marketing agencies and methods [26] and the building-up of a large domestic marketing system.

The first serious break in the old system of wholesale distribution came with the employment on a large scale of the auction system of selling at the end of the War of 1812. British merchants, loaded with goods, shipped them to American ports, particularly to New York. The simplest and quickest way was to sell at auction. As competition grew in the textile industry, manufacturers also found the auction a convenient way to dispose of surplus goods. The auction system became very important in the distribution of goods in the 1820's—between 1822 and 1830 as much as 70 per cent of the dry goods sold in New York is said to have been sold in this way.

The auction system cut seriously into the business of importers and jobbers and the old marketing system in general, and as a result an anti-auction movement arose. In the general improvement in business in 1830–37 this opposition decreased, and as time passed other marketing agencies arose which were in general more suitable to the needs of the time and, therefore, displaced the auction system in large part.

Neither the auction nor the great merchants in the eastern ports were fitted to take care of the rapidly growing inland market, especially at a time when the downward price trend forced a narrowing of the profit margin. For the same reason and because they were short of capital, the new wholesale marketing agencies were reluctant to assume ownership.

Generally speaking, the agent-distributor was tending to become more important than the owner-distributor. That is, the manufacturer, the importing and wholesaling merchant, and the jobber who owned the goods which he sold were being displaced by the man who did not generally own a stock of goods but performed the functions of a distributor on commission. This was especially true in the West. The owner was by no means entirely displaced in marketing in this period. The New England boot and shoe manufacturers are known to have sold directly to retail distributors, even financing them. In the wholesale trade, the merchant-owner continued to hold a strong place; apparently he was strongest in those lines which had not developed highly specialized wholesaling, such as cotton textiles, and as a jobber in the secondary wholesaling centers, such as the inland wholesale markets.

It is impossible to say how far the commission merchant displaced the others, for the reason that our present knowledge of those marketing agencies is still incomplete. It is certain, however, that it was very common for one concern to do wholesaling both as owner and as agent. In fact, that was apparently the prevailing situation in most places and most lines of trade. That is, the wholesale owner-distributor and the commission agent or broker were frequently merged. In some lines of trade specialized agent-distributors developed, as will be seen later.

The functions of the commission merchants or factors varied. They frequently provided storage; they looked after shipping and insurance in transit; they might extend credit to buyers and guarantee sales; they very frequently gave banking services, such as collecting, remitting payments, and endorsing, accepting, or collecting on bills of exchange; some of them extended credit to manufacturers or planters, even giving advice on what to produce.

These commission merchants or factors varied not only as to their agency or

[26] Material for this section has been drawn considerably from F. M. Jones, *Middlemen in the Domestic Trade of the United States, 1800–1860* (Urbana, 1937).

owner position in the trade but also as to the variety of goods handled. Generally they handled related groups, such as hardware, drugs, dry goods, leather goods, certain groups of groceries, and so on. The forwarding and commission men in the produce trade usually handled all kinds of produce, but in some lines a high degree of specialization arose. Two outstanding instances of agent-distributors handling a narrow product were the cotton factor and the textile selling agent. The latter even came to specialize in handling the product of one firm, as for instance the Wards, who sold the products of the Boston Manufacturing Co.

A less important agent in the distribution of goods was the broker. His services were not so numerous as those performed by the commission merchant or factor. Generally he brought the buyer and seller together and was most important in the produce market—that is, aside from the stock and exchange broker considered earlier in this case.

The traveling agent or commercial traveler was a somewhat slow and late development in this period. He was employed occasionally in the earlier years but apparently not to any considerable extent before 1839. His earlier use seems to have been by small manufacturers to maintain themselves in an increasingly competitive market. For instance, S. W. Collins tells, in his "Reminiscences," of how in 1832 his firm attempted to meet competition: "The hardware trade in the cities manifesting a strong disposition to push other axes against ours we sent out several travelling agents this year to show samples of our work and circulate our hand bills to the Southern and Western States." [27] So little is still known about the traveling agent that it is impossible to speak of him with any degree of certainty.

One extremely important change in marketing occurred in the 1820's and 1830's in the development of several wholesale markets in the interior. Pittsburgh, Cincinnati, and St. Louis were the trans-Allegheny and noncoastal towns which then rose to importance in wholesaling. They imported directly from abroad and assembled goods from New Orleans, Philadelphia, New York, Boston, and from domestic manufacturers. Those western markets remained for a long time financially dependent on coastal cities, but they took over much of the latter's function as distributors. The small wholesale or retail merchants of the interior, who had earlier gone to New York or Philadelphia to buy goods, went instead to those inland centers to make their purchases.

One of the significant features of this marketing setup was the extent to which it functioned on credit. In the West, wrote a Missouri merchant in 1833,[28] "a universal credit system is pursued." The western merchant owed the merchant in Cincinnati or Pittsburgh, who owed the manufacturers' distributor in the East or the importing merchant, who had probably drawn on his credit with some English banker. If the flow in either direction should decrease materially, there would obviously be trouble.

6. The General Condition of Business, 1815–43

In the preceding sections two changes were observed during 1815–43: the shift of capital and management from foreign trade to internal development; and the rapid spread of specialization in transportation, manufacture, banking, and trade. Judging by mercantile records, some of this change was in response to a falling price level. Did it help to balance

[27] A typed copy of Collins' "Reminiscences" is in Baker Library, Harvard University.

[28] James Aull to Siter, Price & Co., Philadelphia, quoted in Lewis E. Atherton, "James and Robert Aull—A Frontier Missouri Mercantile Firm," *Missouri Hist. Review*, vol. xxx (Oct., 1935), p. 26.

the bad effects of the price fall? This subject will be examined with respect to fluctuations in conditions within the period, as expressed in the business cycle, and profit and loss throughout the period.

A. The business cycle and the general trend of business.

In the successive business cycles of 1815–43 (see Table 3) there were longer periods of hard times than of good times.[29]

Table 3. LENGTH OF THE VARIOUS PHASES OF THE BUSINESS CYCLE 1815–44

Prosperity	Recession	Depression	Revival
1815	1815	1815–21	1821–22
	1822		1823
1824–25	1825–26		1826
1827–28	1828	1829	1829
1830–33	1833	1834	1834–35
1835–36	1837	1837–38	1838–39
	1839	1839–43	1843

This situation was not peculiar to the United States, however, for England and Europe in general suffered from postwar deflation. England also had recession or depression in 1826, 1829, and 1839–43.

The above representation of the business cycle would have to be refined greatly to give a true picture of conditions in a particular region or field of business. The years 1815 to 1818 were especially difficult for American manufactures, many establishments being driven out of business by cheap wares from England.[30] In 1818 a crisis developed out of a shift in the demand for American staples. Cotton, flour, and rice prices collapsed in a short time. This meant lessened incomes for farmers and losses for merchants. In 1819 came the first great American banking crisis, and it brought widespread bankruptcy, unemployment, and depression. An Englishman's diagnosis of the causes of this depression was that America had during her period of neutrality increased beyond precedent in wealth, commerce, arts, and population, and she had to go through a distressing period of adjustment until she had "returned to that which is her natural condition." [31]

In the early 1820's, when the price decline slowed up, there was a general revival, with a set-back in 1822. In 1824 new banks were chartered with a large aggregate capital. The year 1825 brought very active speculation in wool and cotton which collapsed in the fall, breaking many merchants and seriously depressing business. From 1828 to about 1833 the cotton South was depressed, though in 1830 the general price level turned upward. At about the same time began a strong movement for investing in banks, textile mills, canals, lands, and even railroads. This may have come in considerable measure from declining profits in foreign trade, which turned both British and American mercantile capital into American domestic investments. The coming of British capital is especially significant; while previously the American deficit from purchases abroad had been carried by the earnings of our merchant marine, in the 'thirties it was settled by the import of capital for investment.

The second Bank of the United States under Biddle acted as a curb on one aspect of the inflationary movement, the demand for credit in the newer West and South. This action was apparently the material basis for Jackson's opposition, which led Biddle in 1833–34 to reduce the discounts of his bank. The effect on the country was severe: money became tight, wages and prices fell, unemployment increased, and bankruptcies were numerous.

The year 1836, and through the early part of 1837, was a time of great invest-

[29] Willard L. Thorp, *Business Annals* (National Bureau of Economic Research, New York, 1926), p. 94.

[30] Smith and Cole, *op. cit.*, p. 20.

[31] *Ibid.*, p. 21.

ment and speculative activity. Prices were good, trade was very active, and business was generally flourishing. There was an unusually strong importation of foreign investment capital and of mercantile credit secured by American concerns in England. This was reasonably safe as long as the upward price movement continued, which supported speculation in spirit if not altogether in body.

Early in 1837, however, prices experienced a decline which soon became precipitous. Jackson's specie circular, requiring that only specie should be accepted in payment for public land, struck a blow at inflated bank currency and applied the spark to a situation that was ready to explode. The fall of cotton prices endangered our foreign credit, which was weakened at the same time by stringency in England. This was highly dangerous, since American expansion had been built on a highly pyramided credit structure which had its base in England. A major panic came in the spring of 1837, breaking six hundred banks and countless mercantile and marketing firms and manufacturers.

One dramatic attempt was made to stem the tide of liquidation. Biddle's Bank of the United States, of Pennsylvania, aided by a few large New York bankers, attempted to support American credit abroad. They secured large loans with which to meet matured obligations and to finance cotton planters and factors, so as to enable them to hold their cotton till the price rose, and to carry on internal improvements.

If the price decline had been short, as in preceding cycles since the postwar deflation this might have worked. But Biddle's scheme could not hold out against the break in cotton prices which came with the collapse of the textile industry in England in 1839. The situation was further complicated by a rapid fall in western produce which also began in the same year.

The price break of 1839 caused a collapse of the whole debt structure. The result was panic, suspension by banks, widespread failures, the cessation of the import of foreign capital, and a depression which lasted until 1843.

B. Profit and loss, 1815–43.

There is no question that this was a period of a great deal of difficulty in business. The exact effect on profits, however, it is impossible to estimate.

It would be helpful to have an index showing the trend of failures in the period, but there is no statistical record of failures. Newspapers and other contemporary sources point to the conclusion that the proportion of failures was very high, particularly in the depression phases of the cycles. Banks, small manufacturing concerns, and middlemen in exchange, securities, or commodities apparently had a very high mortality. But this may have been because the prevailing optimism of a rapidly expanding society led to ventures by individuals far beyond what their capital or experience would justify.

Concerning business profits there is the same lack of conclusive information. Enterprises in the newer West were avoided by conservative eastern investors, which bears out the general impression that western business was uncertain. Dividend records of incorporated banks, insurance companies, and manufacturing concerns in New England, however, reveal moderate profits, generally decreasing toward the end of the period. These concerns were largely in the hands of a class of business men with long experience and considerable capital. There was also a considerable measure of success in and around other eastern commercial cities, some of the success owing no doubt to appreciation in the value of property brought by the increase in the business of important cities.

It is clear that there were many great fortunes in the United States at the end of the period. The largest were those, however, which had their beginning in the foreign trade of the preceding period. Merchants such as Astor, Girard, Perkins, Cushing, Sturgis, and the Browns had gradually shifted their mercantile capital into real estate, textiles, banks, insurance companies, railroads, and canals, as well as good State "stocks," and conservative mortgages. As investors they had fair success but apparently not the great success (except, for instance, Astor in New York real estate) which they had gained in foreign trade.

Some entrepreneurs who arose in this period not only survived but even built up a fund of experience and capital. Though failures were more spectacular than successes, there were new banks, bankers, brokers, manufacturers, and merchants who were in a safe though not a flourishing condition when the low point was reached in 1843. There is considerable basis, however, for the tentative conclusion that even a moderate success over the whole period was less common than failure.

7. Suggested Readings

W. L. Thorp, *Business Annals* (New York, 1926), pp. 117–123. This work gives a year-by-year description of business conditions.

Anne Bezanson, R. D. Gray, and Miriam Hussey, *Wholesale Prices in Philadelphia, 1784–1861* (Philadelphia, 1936). Chaps. vii and ix are especially recommended.

W. B. Smith and A. H. Cole, *Fluctuations in American Business, 1790–1860* (Cambridge, 1935). Pages 37–84 are concerned with the years 1820–45.

Caroline F. Ware, *The Early New England Cotton Manufacture* (Boston, 1931), chaps. iv and vii. This work gives considerable on the administration of an important industry that developed in this period.

Blanche Evans Hazard, *The Organization of the Boot and Shoe Industry in Massachusetts before 1875* (Cambridge, 1921), chaps. iii and iv. This work shows the impact of new developments on an old industry which experienced at that time no significant changes in mechanical techniques of production.

8. Suggested Questions

1. What is your conception of a secular trend in business?
2. Why does specialization in business make such a great advance in this period as compared with the earlier and still surviving unspecialized business units (such as sedentary merchants)?
3. How do you reconcile economic progress with business difficulties during the period 1815–43?
4. What qualities in the business man would you expect to make for survival in such a period as that of 1815–43?
5. Compare business conditions in 1837–43 with those in 1929–35.
6. Compare the secondary postwar panics of 1819 and 1929. What year in the period 1815–43 corresponds to the present year in the downward trend after 1920?
7. If you had been a Boston merchant withdrawing from the China trade in 1830 with a capital of $100,000, but not ready to retire from business, what new work would you have entered into?

XL. BUSINESS PROSPERITY AND THE VICTORY OF SPECIALIZED BUSINESS IN A PERIOD OF RISING PRICES 1843–1866

1. General Statement

The dominant development in American business between 1843 and 1866 was the growth of specialization. This was the form of activity most commonly chosen by business men in their effort to obtain profits in that time of rapid increase in production for a growing market. The sedentary merchant became the specialized banker; the general blacksmith became a manufacturer of reapers. Only in newer or smaller communities did the general merchant and the blacksmith still conduct business in the old nonspecialized way.

How can we explain this rapid advance of specialization? Probably there was in the movement something of imitation, for there is fad and fashion in business as in other lines of social activity. It is a nice question how far the growth of specialization was owing to the growth of the metropolitan market and how far to the spread of the Industrial Revolution. A challenging problem is to discover the relationship between the general upward trend of prices and the growth of specialization in business. In attempting to see this problem one must remember that specialized effort had been the resort of many business men in the previous period of falling prices.

2. General View of the Period

1843	Price trend turned upward.
1843–48	Business uncertain, with tendency to improve.
1844	Cyrus McCormick turned to the West for a market.
1846–48	War with Mexico.
1847	Panic in England felt in United States.
1848	Gold discovered in California. California boom began late in year. Chicago Board of Trade organized.
1849–53	Prosperity.
1849–57	Land speculation and rapid railroad building. Considerable rise in prices.
1850	Singer produced first practical sewing machine.
1852	Railroad, New York to Chicago.
1853	New York Clearing House established.
1854	Financial panic and depression. Railroad reached the Mississippi. First trade association organized.
1855	Dealing in wheat futures started in Chicago.
1855–56	Revival and prosperity.
1857–58	Panic and depression.
1857–61	Prices declined.
1859	Comstock (silver) Lode discovered. Petroleum discovered in Pennsylvania. Shoe and Leather Exchange established in Boston.
1859–60	Revival, prosperity, and recession.
1860–66	Severe fall in tonnage of American vessels clearing for foreign ports.
1861	Business depressed until autumn. Civil War began. Federal borrowing for war began. Banks and government suspended specie payments. Telegraph extended to San Francisco. Jay Cooke & Co. established.
1862	Issue of greenbacks began.
1862–65	War activity and inflation drove business and prices to unprecedented heights, with occasional sharp recessions.
1863	National Banking System established. Speculation in gold began.
1864	Peak in currency prices. New York Mining and Petroleum Board established.
1865	Civil war ended. First Bessemer steel produced in America. McKay machine used in shoe manufacture. Mild boom at end of war followed by recession. Economic and business chaos in South.
1866	Peak in prices in gold.

3. A Rising Price Level

A. The trend of prices.

The most significant price phenomenon from 1843 to 1866 was the general upward movement of prices.[1] This meant a reversal of the downward tendency of 28

[1] This is seen in three indices for the period in the following: G. F. Warren and F. A. Pearson, *Prices* (New York, 1933); Anne Bezanson, R. D. Gray, and Miriam Hussey, *Wholesale Prices in Philadelphia, 1784–1861* (Philadelphia, 1936); and W. B. Smith and A. H. Cole, *Fluctuations in American Business, 1790–1860* (Cambridge, 1935). The last two end in 1861 and 1862, respectively.

years which had reached its nadir in 1843. The movement was very irregular, showing great variation in the rapidity and direction of change from time to time and great differences in the behavior of different commodities or groups of commodities.

First, as to the movement of the general price level. For an indication of the situation until 1861, the course of Philadelphia commodity prices may be examined. The major part of the rise before 1861 occurred between 1849 and 1857. "As is characteristic of periods of rising prices, the length of the advances culminating in peaks in 1845, 1847, 1851, 1855, 1857, and 1859 were usually longer than the periods of recession ending in 1846, 1849, 1852, 1856, 1858, and 1861." [2] The most extreme movement, however, occurred after the war began: by 1864 prices in currency were about double prices in gold in 1861, and by 1866 prices in gold had risen more than one-third since 1861.[3]

Second, as to the movement of individual commodities or groups. An illustration of an important commodity which diverged greatly from the general level is cotton, which in 1843 reached an all-time low and in the 'fifties was quite consistently low. This situation may have had a considerable regional importance.[4] A recent study of Philadelphia prices makes the following significant statements about the relative price movements of groups of commodities. Revival began with imported foods and wines in 1843, followed by farm derivatives, industrial raw and semifinished materials, fish and fur in 1844, and farm crops, finished industrial products, and lumber products and naval stores in 1845. The marked rise in the general index in 1847 came from the unusual rise of farm crops and farm derivatives. The recession in 1848–49 affected all groups. Farm derivatives and lumber products and naval stores were the only groups which in every one of the early 'fifties contributed to the rise of the general index. In 1853–54 all groups rose except furs. In 1854 three groups rose 15 per cent while the other five rose less than 10 per cent. In 1856 occurred serious recessions in farm crops, farm derivatives, and lumber and naval stores. In that same year industrial commodities began to decline and did not rise again until in 1861. In 1857 all groups declined, but at varying rates: imported foods fell 23.7 per cent; fish, farm crops, and farm derivatives, 13 to 16 per cent; furs and the industrial groups, 7 to 9 per cent; and wines and lumber products and naval stores, 2.5 to 3 per cent. In 1859 all groups except imported foods and finished industrial commodities rose, that is, industrial raw and semifinished goods, farm crops, farm derivatives, and so on. In 1860 farm derivatives, industrial raw and semifinished articles, and fish fell 1 per cent or less; finished industrial goods, lumber and naval stores, and furs dropped 2 to 5 per cent, while farm crops fell 8.4 per cent.[5] According to Warren and Pearson's tables,[6] the peak of the currency prices of farm products and foods, of metal and metal products, and of house furnishings was reached in 1864; in 1865 came the peak in textiles, fuel and lighting, and chemicals and drugs; while spirits reached their peak only in 1866.

The study of railroad-stock prices for 1843–62 by Smith and Cole shows the trend of an important type of securities. From February, 1843, to May, 1844, there was in general a very great rise—the greatest until greenback inflation in the Civil War. Though there were minor recessions and a marked advance in 1847, there was no decisive movement until in

[2] Bezanson, Gray, and Hussey, *op. cit.*, p. 230.
[3] Warren and Pearson, *op. cit.*, pp. 26–27, 76.
[4] *Ibid.*, p. 32.
[5] Bezanson, Gray, and Hussey, *op. cit.*, pp. 249–252.
[6] *Op. cit.*, p. 26.

1849. From then until the end of 1852 there was a steep ascent, followed by a rapid descent which late in 1857 reached a low not far above the low of 1843. After 1857 there were sharp rises and drops until inflation in the war sent prices up rapidly.[7]

Smith and Cole found a significant regional difference in railroad-stock prices. New England roads, which had not fallen greatly before 1843, rose slightly from 1843 to 1854 when they began to fall, reaching a low in 1857 below that of 1843; a steady recovery came in 1858–62. The Central Atlantic roads, in contrast, started very low in 1843; after an erratic course reached a high point in 1854; fell to a low in 1858, which was considerably above the low of 1843; rose rapidly until late 1860, when there was a setback from which recovery became strong in 1862. Western roads followed the Central Atlantic roads to a low point in 1858; recovered sharply at once, but fell even lower at the beginning of 1860; then followed a sharp ascent, and a steep descent which turned upward in 1861.[8]

Apparently, wages rose at a rate favorable to industry. There are no reliable statistical studies of wages for this period, though students of wage history regard wages as rising more slowly than living costs or prices. David A. Wells, an astute contemporary observer, made the significant observation that wages did not rise so rapidly as prices in the 1860's.[9] This, if true, may have been the result of the almost complete absence of labor organization[10] at a time when there was a heavy immigration of adult labor.

Money rates apparently on the whole ruled fairly high during this period. Smith and Cole found high rates common in New York, especially from 1846 to 1857. In this matter, however, there were great variations as between time, place, and type of loan. One investigator found great ease in the money market late in 1843, money loaning at 3.75 per cent, while in 1848 the average was nearly 15.5 per cent.[11] In the West rates were generally much higher than in the East. Call loan rates were very low as compared with others. It is significant to note that, in spite of heavy gold production, increase in bank credit, and imports of foreign capital, money was high.

Whether or not a firm profited by price changes depended, of course, on how closely its situation and policy allowed it to take advantage of price rise as compared with the increase in costs involved. In times of rising prices, long-time costs decrease relatively, wages usually rise less quickly than prices, and real estate, capital, equipment, and inventory rise in value relatively to the original cost (minus, of course, depreciation and obsolescence). On the other hand, a manufacturer might well find that there was a considerable increase in costs between the time of accepting an order at a given price and filling it. And money rates might well be raising costs.

B. Factors affecting price movements.

No attempt will be made here to explain the rise of commodity prices, but it should be noted that there were certain important conditions or developments which had an influence on some commodities or on the general price movement. On the side of demand there were three events of unusual importance. Crop failures in Europe in 1846 and 1847 account for the substantial rise in the price of farm crops and farm derivatives until the abundant crops of 1848 were harvested. The Crimean War increased the demand for many goods in 1853–55—the rise in prices which

[7] Smith and Cole, *op. cit.*, pp. 108–109, 184.

[8] *Ibid.*, pp. 112–113.

[9] David A. Wells, "The Recent Financial, Industrial, and Commercial Experiences of the United States," *Cobden Club Essays*, 1871–72, p. 482.

[10] See Selig Perlman, *A History of Trade Unionism in the United States* (New York, 1922), chaps. i–ii.

[11] Smith and Cole, *op. cit.*, pp. 125–127.

began in 1853 coincided with the movement of fleets to the Dardanelles just before the outbreak of war between Russia and Turkey,[12] while the formal declaration of war by England and France against Russia in 1854 not only brought an increase in demand for industrial, forest, and agricultural products but also removed Russian wheat from the world market. The third important influence on the demand side was the American Civil War. This gave a spur to business in the North such as had never before been experienced in the United States, and it pushed production to the limit of capacity.

Intimately related to the rise in prices were changes in gold, currency, and credit. Specifically on the monetary side two events were significant. One was the discovery of gold in California and Australia. The effect of the new gold on prices is, of course, controversial.[13] Contemporary business comment makes much of the inflationary effect of even the anticipation of the inflow of gold. A conservative position is that taken by Bezanson, Gray and Hussey: [14] "Undoubtedly this discovery aided in the beginning of an underlying upward trend in the prices of imported commodities and in the acceleration of the upward trend in the prices of domestic commodities." Gold production in the United States continued high throughout the period. It brought an unprecedented amount of gold into the money stock of the United States. Most of this went abroad to settle unfavorable balances, but enough remained at home to add greatly to our monetary stock. (See Table 1.) Another important monetary event was the issue of almost half a billion dollars of legal tender notes, or greenbacks, during the Civil War, which brought suspension of gold payments. The greenbacks were a very significant factor in the rise of war prices far above earlier domestic prices and even above contemporary world prices.[15]

Throughout the period, bank notes constituted an important part of the money in circulation in the United States. Table 1 shows that this increased rapidly but not so rapidly as gold.[16]

Table 1. MONETARY CIRCULATION IN THE UNITED STATES 1843–66

Year	Estimated specie in the United States [a]	Estimated bank notes outstanding [a]	Total monetary circulation [a, b]	Circulation per capita
1843	$ 90	$ 59	$ 147	$ 7.87
1844	100	75	167	8.68
1845	96	90	177	8.95
1846	97	106	193	9.43
1847	120	106	224	10.59
1848	112	129	232	10.66
1849	120	115	233	10.34
1850	154	131	279	12.02
1851	186	155	330	13.76
1852	204	172	361	14.63
1853	236	188	402	15.80
1854	241	205	426	16.10
1855	250	187	418	15.34
1856	250	195	426	15.16
1857	260	215	457	15.81
1858	260	155	409	13.78
1859	250	193	439	14.35
1860	214 [c]	207	442	13.85
1861	270	202	488	15.11
1862	283	184	629	18.52
1863	260	239	1,001	27.78
1864	203	210	1,063	29.60
1865	189	289	1,180	31.18
1866	167	301	1,068	26.49

[a] In millions.

[b] Circulation is total of two preceding columns minus a small amount of specie in the Treasury.

[c] Beginning in 1860 this column was labeled gold coin and bullion in the source.

[12] Bezanson, Gray, and Hussey, *op. cit.*, p. 243.

[13] See, for instance, R. S. Tucker, "The Myth of 1849," in C. O. Hardy, *Is there Enough Gold?* (Washington, 1936), pp. 177–199.

[14] *Op. cit.*, p. 238.

[15] According to a comparison by Warren and Pearson, *op. cit.*, pp. 75–76.

[16] *Annual Report of the Comptroller of the Currency*, 1919, vol. ii, pp. 34–36; *Annual Report of the Secretary of the Treasury*, 1928, p. 552.

These figures show nothing about two other important factors, deposit currency and credit. There is no way of measuring the former though checks came to be used quite extensively in the period. Concerning credit more is known.

Available figures on the expansion of bank credit, while by no means complete, may be said to show that there was an almost continuous increase, as Table 2 shows.[17]

Table 2. LOANS, DISCOUNTS, AND SECURITIES OF ALL BANKS REPORTING TO THE FEDERAL GOVERNMENT, 1843–66

Year	Amount [a]	Per capita
1843	$283	$14.89
1844	288	14.69
1845	309	15.30
1846	334	16.01
1847	330	15.42
1848	371	16.82
1849	356	15.75
1850	385	16.52
1851	436	18.09
1852	453	18.19
1853	431	16.77
1854	601	22.59
1855	629	22.96
1856	683	24.22
1857	743	25.62
1858	643	21.51
1859	721	23.49
1860	762	24.19
1861	774	23.94
1862	746	22.67
1863	840	25.00
1864	705	20.55
1865	930	26.50
1866	1,165	32.54

[a] In millions.

Government credit also came to have an important bearing on the general credit situation. While a national debt is not wealth, it may be the basis for credit expansion. Significant developments came in those years. In 1850 the federal debt was $63,000,000; in 1857, $10,000,000. The Civil War sky-rocketed it to a high of $2,675,000,000 in 1865.[18] These loans became the basis of the issue of currency by national banks and were given the highest rating as security for loans.

Considerable encouragement to American enterprise also came at times in the form of credit from abroad. The secretary of the Treasury estimated that $222,000,000 of foreign capital was invested in the United States in 1853. By 1860 the estimate was $400,000,000. Half of this was returned during the war. In the 'fifties, therefore, foreign credit was important, but relatively to the amount of business done it was of small significance during the Civil War.

4. Business Activity and Administration

In this period American business men drove rapidly in the direction of greater specialization. With the market broadening and industrial technique improving, they took the new path of specialization in their search for profits.

The focus of their interest was domestic. It is true that American economy was closely tied to European in this period. We still had a great carrying trade on the ocean and we still depended on London to furnish us credit; but the most important contribution of American effort to foreign needs was raw materials. Vastly important was the fact that the United States was in itself a large, and rapidly expanding, producing and consuming area. And, at the close of the period, the Civil War provided an unexpected and large opportunity for American business.

For business the problem was one of organization and management. A great and growing market was there; resources were abundant; and the labor supply was increasing rapidly, with great additions of adult labor through immigration; capital

[17] *Report of the Comptroller of the Currency*, 1931, pp. 1023–1024.

[18] National Monetary Commission, *Statistics of the United States, 1867–1909*, vol. xxi, p. 255.

was optimistic. How were these various factors organized by business men for profit under the spur of a rising price level?

A. The business of transportation.

This period was a time of dramatic advance in transportation. The American clipper ship, designed for speed in the California and Australian gold trade, marked the last great effort of the American merchant marine before it went into a decline in the 'sixties. On inland canals and waters all kinds of craft, from the palatial steamboats of powerful packet lines to the smaller tramp steamer, carried a heavy and remunerative trade. New Orleans, St. Louis, Chicago, Buffalo, and New York were among the markets which owed much to water transportation. But the steamboat on the canal and the river had distinct limitations: there were large hinterland areas which the waterways could not reach; the waterway was uncertain at best; and it did not follow the east and west trade lines which were rapidly growing in strength. The railroad was obviously the answer to this need.

The railroad had its beginning in the earlier period, essentially an experiment with a new medium under adverse business conditions. Then, as later in less promising undertakings, the promotion of railroads depended largely on local public support under the leadership of enterprising business men organized to extend the market area of a city by means of improved transportation.

In 1843–66, however, the railroad, by then proved sound in principle, came definitely to be recognized as a *profitable* field of enterprise. It became the great new industry of the 1850's, absorbing much promotion and speculative effort. By the middle 'forties and thereafter, the railroad was appealing to capitalists for investment both at home and abroad. For instance, in 1848 Baring Brothers took $1,000,000 of Maryland bonds issued to aid the Baltimore & Ohio, which put the Barings definitely behind the road because of their interest in its success; and in 1851 a group of Boston capitalists took over the projected Illinois Central and its land grant.[19] The smaller or less promising enterprises, such as the Philadelphia & Erie, had to finance themselves largely with State or municipal aid.

The growing importance of the railroad is indicated by the fact that railroad stocks shared with land the distinction of being the chief medium of speculation in this period. This speculative activity was not constant in amount. It broke out strongly in 1847. It increased with the discovery of gold in California and remained active for several years; it lessened sometime before 1857; and it rose to great fervor under war inflation. There was an important regional difference in railroad speculation. Smith and Cole show that the securities of New England roads were the most stable and the least subject to speculation, that the securities of the Middle Atlantic roads were in an intermediate position, while the western roads were subject to the greatest speculation.[20] But, though speculative interests in railroads fluctuated with prices and business conditions and differed as between regions, the idea remained constant that the railroad had a good future.

The increasing interest in the railroad is shown by Table 3, which gives the growth of mileage.[21]

Table 3. RAILROAD MILEAGE IN THE UNITED STATES, 1844–66

Year	Miles in operation	Annual increase
1844	4,377	192
1845	4,633	256
1846	4,930	297

[19] B. H. Meyer, *History of Transportation in the United States before 1860* (Washington 1917), pp. 408–409, 532–534.

[20] *Op. cit.*, pp. 112–114.

[21] *Poor's Manual of Railroads of the United States*, 1874–75, p. xxvii.

Year	Miles in operation	Annual increase
1847	5,598	668
1848	5,996	398
1849	7,365	1,369
1850	9,021	1,656
1851	10,982	1,961
1852	12,908	1,926
1853	15,360	2,452
1854	16,720	1,360
1855	18,374	1,654
1856	22,016	3,643
1857	24,503	2,486
1858	26,968	2,465
1859	28,789	1,821
1860	30,635	1,846
1861	31,286	651
1862	32,120	864
1863	33,170	1,050
1864	33,908	738
1865	35,085	1,177
1866	36,827	1,742

As the railroad became more attractive to capital, important changes in organization and administration occurred. First, the roads grew in length. In 1851 New York City's Erie reached to Lake Erie; in 1853 the Pennsylvania reached Pittsburgh, and the Baltimore & Ohio reached the Ohio River. In the 1850's the Illinois Central was built from northern to southern Illinois. Before 1866 several lines had been projected to extend to the Coast. In the same period railroad consolidation made great headway. Though the railroad reached westward to Chicago in 1852 and to the Mississippi in 1854, it was in the 1860's that consolidation of shorter lines formed trunk lines reaching into the Middle West.

Second, this growth in size necessitated changes in administrative setup and policy. Administration began to be further removed from ownership; it had to become specialized. This is the period when railroad administrators came to be important figures in business, for example, men like Vanderbilt of the New York Central, Thomson of the Pennsylvania, and Garrett of the Baltimore & Ohio. The last two, especially, were railroad builders and operators whose object it was to build roads and manage them well.

The administration of the railroad, even so early, brought serious problems. In the middle 'forties William Sturgis of Boston—a China merchant who had become a railroad director—urged upon the president of a certain road not to go too heavily into debt, not to buy property for which there was no direct need, and to seek the goodwill of the public by charging moderate rates rather than paying exorbitant dividends. In the 'fifties the fraudulent issue of stocks for the New Haven advertised the possibility of dishonesty in corporate management. The evils of the next period were thus foreshadowed.

B. Rapid communication by telegraph.

The demonstration in 1844 of the practicability of the telegraph introduced another new form of business. One of the great problems of business men in the preceding period, when communication and transportation were slow, was the long time between the beginning and the completion of an enterprise, as for instance the purchase of goods in Canton and their sale in London. This spread between the beginning and the end of a production or distribution process put on the business man the heavy risk of a long period of price change. The telegraph promised to lessen risk by making possible almost instantaneous transmission of information. Obviously, here was a service for which business men would pay well.

Since little capital was needed for building a telegraph line, the telegraph system grew rapidly. Two types of policy were followed with respect to the telegraph: one looked toward profits from operation; the other, from promotion. Unscrupulous persons wishing to make money from construction would organize a company, secure the names of prominent men as directors (perhaps by the gift of a few shares), and sell shares, probably by a door-to-door canvass. Lines might not even be built. If they were, contracts might be let at a rate many times the actual cost, to be paid in stock. Whatever the contractors could secure for their stock above the cost was profit.[22]

The ease with which lines could be financed and built made the actual or potential competition great. It therefore was necessary either to have monopoly control of patents or improvements or to be financially so strong and offer such excellent service at satisfactory rates that possible competitors would be discouraged. Such service could be realized fully only by a national system.

In the 1850's and 1860's there was open warfare between various telegraph companies.[23] Out of this struggle Western Union emerged with almost a national monopoly. Organized to form a small line in 1851—by building, but mainly by outright purchase and consolidation or acquisition of a controlling interest—by 1869 Western Union was to acquire 66,263 miles of line, within 6,773 miles of the total mileage of the telegraph system of the United States.[24]

C. Exploiting natural resources.

The basis of business activity in the United States in this period was the exploitation of natural resources. Those resources provided the raw material for our national industry; they provided most of the tonnage for our carriers; and they settled our foreign balances. It was to be expected, therefore, that business would reach out more and more for raw materials.

One manifestation of the interest of business men in natural resources was the increased trading in public lands. Soldiers' land warrants (rights to public lands issued to war veterans), which were thrown on the market in large amounts after the War with Mexico, were dealt in extensively by eastern bankers. Individuals and groups of business men on joint account bought warrants and sent representatives out into the new West to select the lands. They also bought railroad lands, notably in the 'fifties those of the Illinois Central. They sold the lands, usually to settlers, through western land agents. Capital did not move in large amounts in this business. But, since it was the usual thing for eastern business men to take a flyer in western lands, the total thus invested was large.

The land business was handled chiefly through more or less specialized real-estate firms in the West. Detroit, Chicago, and Dubuque and Fort Dodge, Iowa, were representative of western cities which had an active trade in public lands. Since these firms had to collect payment and frequently extend credit to buyers, they often became private bankers, thus putting to work eastern funds entrusted to them.

Like other business, the land business was cyclical in character. The curve of total public land sales (chiefly in the West) began to rise in 1842; rose until 1847; fell until 1849; rose and fell sharply in the next two years; rose very high until 1854; fell sharply from 1855 to 1859, and then slowly until checked by the war.[25] The movement of land sales did not clearly follow commodity prices but rather anticipated them.

There was also much reaching out for other resources, largely through individual initiative. Placer gold mining in California was largely carried on by a relatively capital-less individual, though—like agriculture—gold mining gave rise to much business activity and contributed greatly to the settlement of our foreign balances. Individual enterprise was also seeking out copper deposits in Michigan and Wis-

[22] See the *Annual Report of the Western Union Telegraph Company,* 1869, pp. 34–37.

[23] The telegraph became the object of much criticism and congressional investigation around 1870.

[24] *Annual Report of the Western Union Company,* 1869, pp. 6–8, 33.

[25] Smith and Cole, *op. cit.*, p. 57.

consin, iron in Minnesota, and silver in the western mountains. Lumbering was then moving westward in the Great Lakes States, where there were virgin forests and expanding markets; it was carried on by countless partnerships or individual enterprises in which capital and management were relatively important.

The extractive industries during this period became, however, to some extent the object of large corporate enterprise. In 1851 the Delaware, Lackawanna & Western began mining coal for sale. In 1864 the Lehigh Valley Railroad also began to mine coal. During the Civil War, iron, coal, petroleum, and silver became the object of corporate enterprise and of a great deal of speculation. Petroleum and silver investments were regarded as very risky, but they created many fortunes in New York.

The growing importance of petroleum and minerals is shown by Table 4.[26]

D. Growing demands stimulate manufacturing.

Nowhere was the drive toward profits by means of specialized industry more marked than in manufacture. This was clearly not a result of any great technological change. It grew out of the day-to-day attempts to meet new needs and new opportunities in an expanding economy. These attempts led to improvements of various kinds: a great advance in the use of interchangeable mechanism and in the application of automatic machinery to produce standard parts; more efficient power; and improvements in the management of both production and marketing. The drive behind them was clearly the profit motive encouraged by a rapidly growing economy and rising prices.

There was on the whole no radical change in the form of the business unit that carried on the increased production. The corporation was growing in prominence, especially in mining and some forms of manufacturing, particularly during the war. But more commonly the individual or partnership form still prevailed. This meant that ownership was still close to management. Indeed, even when manufacturing did adopt the corporation form, as in textiles and iron manufacture, ownership was fairly close to management. Much of the iron and machine industry, shoe manufacture, clothing manufacture, food processing, and lumbering were still in the partnership form.

The result was that growth was more in numbers than in size. Though the situation is still largely unexplored, it appears that very commonly expansion of production began with the small concern—individual or partner—and that the unit progressed largely out of profits, especially during the war. This growth is shown by Table 5 (p. 692) on manufactures for 1850, 1860, and 1870.[27] Note that the number of establishments increased at about the same rate as the number of workers, and that the capital—allowing for the difference in prices—did not increase greatly per establishment on the average. This

[26] Compiled from United States Geological Survey, *Mineral Resources of the United States,* 1900, pp. 107–108, 141–142, 543; and 1911, part i, p. 126, and part ii, p. 27.

[27] *Census,* 1900, vol. viii, *Manufactures,* pt. ii, pp. 982–983.

Table 4. PRODUCTION OF MINERALS AND PETROLEUM, 1845–70

Year	Gold	Silver	Copper (Long tons)	Iron ore (Long tons)	Coal: Bituminous (Short tons)	Coal: Anthracite (Short tons)	Petroleum (Barrels)
1845	...	$50,000	100	...	1,829,872	2,480,032	...
1850	$50,000,000	50,000	650	...	2,880,017	4,138,164	...
1860	46,000,000	150,000	7,200	2,873,460	6,494,200	8,115,842	500,000
1870	50,000,000	16,000,000	12,600	3,831,891	17,371,305	15,664,275	5,260,745

was a time of high interest rates. Note the marked effect on the price index.[28]

Though most manufactures were relatively small, one development shows that there appeared a recognition of the need for unity and policy within an industry. That was the rise of manufacturers' associations. The first of which we have any record was the American Brass Association organized in 1853 which was designed to meet ruinous competition. By 1856 the organization had become a pool "in which prices and discounts were fixed and production was apportioned and allotted. Penalties for violation were agreed upon." [29] In 1854 the Hampton County Cotton Spinners' Association was organized to meet problems growing out of competition. In 1855 the American Iron Association was organized, the forerunner of the Steel Institute, and in 1864 the National Association of Wool Manufacturers. The first association to be organized on a national scale was the United States Brewers' Association, which dates from 1862.[30] Did these developments have any general meaning as to the condition of those industries at the time? Perhaps they were merely depression phenomena. If so, why did they strike particular industries?

Business was unusually aggressive at this time in entering new lines and building up old lines. Table 6 [31] (on p. 693) shows that in the 1850's several lines came to be manufactured commercially on a sufficiently large scale to be included in the Census. The relative growth of various lines is also significant. The production of cotton goods, for instance, had evidently reached a point of stability, while hosiery manufacture was experiencing the rapid growth of an industry recently brought into the factory. The growth in agricultural implements and pig iron calls attention to the heavy advance of producers' goods.

These figures give the results, but they do not show the process by which the results were obtained. Business history needs to know more of the efforts and activities of the business men who brought this growth, that is, the process by which they pushed the development of manufactures.

A few salient characteristics of several industries may be noted. They point to new problems and new methods.

In the food industries, more and larger concerns were established to supply the demands of a growing domestic urban market and to take advantage of war needs. No great advances were made in processing in this period, except in canning during the war. Interest centered more in the securing of adequate raw materials at good prices; shifting the danger

[28] United States Bureau of Labor Statistics, *Index Numbers of Wholesale Prices in the United States and Foreign Countries,* 1921, p. 158.

[29] J. H. Foth, *Trade Associations* (New York, 1930), p. 8.

[30] E. H. Naylor, *Trade Associations* (New York, 1921), p. 23.

[31] *Census,* 1870, *Industry and Wealth,* pp 588 ff. The price index is from U. S. Bureau of Labor Statistics, *op. cit.*

Table 5. GROWTH OF MANUFACTURING IN THE UNITED STATES
1850, 1860, 1870

	1850	1860	1870
Number of establishments	123,025	140,433	252,148
Capital employed	$533,245,351	$1,009,855,715	$2,118,208,769
Average number of wage earners	957,059	1,311,246	2,053,996
Wages	$236,755,464	$378,878,966	$775,584,343
Cost of material used	$555,123,822	$1,031,605,092	$2,488,427,242
Value of product	$1,019,106,616	$1,885,861,676	$4,232,325,442
Total population	23,130,329	31,303,834	38,456,839
Price index	89.2	100.0	144.4

of loss from price fluctuations during the manufacturing process; securing good transportation rates and adequate credit; and marketing in a national as contrasted with a local market. Hence the processors moved westward with agriculture; they sent buyers out into rural districts; flour millers probably began to hedge on the wheat exchanges; processors generally stayed close to railroad administration and banking to get good transportation and money rates; and they worked hard to strengthen their contacts with big consumers' markets such as Boston, New York, and Philadelphia. These things could not be done effectively by small concerns. But both small and large had one advantage in this period: the greater part of the time they were favored by the upward movement of the market value of their inventory—it would be interesting to know how important to manufacturing profits in this period was inventory appreciation.

In the boot and shoe industry we have clearer evidence of improvements in methods of manufacture. In the 1850's the manufacturers, to save time and to hold markets by prompt delivery of large orders of standardized shoes, brought all the processes into the factory. More capital and a larger stock accordingly were required. In 1860 steam power was introduced to speed up the work. During the Civil War large orders of shoes for Union armies and the scarcity of labor encouraged the adoption of the McKay machine (for sewing uppers on soles).[32] Thus, what was virtually a long-time seller's market brought the machine factory into shoe manufacture.

The building-up of McCormick's manufacturing of reapers is an excellent illustration of the creation of a new industry.[33]

[32] Blanche Evans Hazard, *The Organization of the Boot and Shoe Industry in Massachusetts before 1875* (Cambridge, 1921), pp. 123–124.

[33] This material on McCormick has been taken from W. T. Hutchinson's *Cyrus Hall McCormick,* vols. i and ii (New York, 1930, 1935).

Table 6. INCREASE IN MANUFACTURE OF CERTAIN PRODUCTS
1850, 1860, 1870

(000 Omitted except in Price Index)

	1850	1860	1870
Population	23,130	31,303	38,456
Price Index	89	100	144
Pig iron	$12,748	$ 20,870	$ 69,640
Steel	.....	6,607	12,210
Agricultural implements	6,842	17,487	52,066
Machinery	.....	51,887	138,519
Sewing machines	.....	4,255	14,097
Cotton goods	65,501	115,681	177,489
Silk	.....	6,607	12,210
Woolen goods	43,207	61,894	155,405
Boots and shoes	53,967	91,891	181,644
Hosiery	1,028	7,280	18,411
Men's ready-made clothing	48,311	80,438 [a]	147,650
Women's " " "	.....	.....	12,900
Sugar and molasses	9,898	42,241	108,941
India rubber goods	.....	5,768	14,566
Fire arms	.....	2,342	5,582
Musical instruments	2,580	6,548	13,968

[a] Includes $7,219,000 of shirts, collars, and furnishings, given separately by Census.

From 1839 to 1844 Cyrus McCormick had been experimenting with a mechanical grain reaper in his father's blacksmith shop in Virginia, a shop using the family slaves and an occasional hired man. A number of reapers had been built and tried out in that region but had met severe competition from another machine. In the meantime the McCormicks had fallen deeply into debt.

From 1844 to 1848 Cyrus McCormick reached out for a wider market for his reaper. There was obviously a growing need of labor-saving farm machinery, but it was a need which many others besides McCormick were trying to meet. McCormick's problem, therefore, was to obtain orders in a competitive market. He devoted some of his time to improving the reaper, but he had trouble getting patents on his own improvements. He carried on a heavy advertising campaign in farm papers, and he held demonstrations of his machine in many places, particularly at fairs. Much of his time he spent in traveling about and directing traveling agents in the grain States from New York to Illinois. They interviewed dealers and farmers, taking orders for the next season.

To fill the orders was a problem. The McCormicks were in debt and had only their Virginia blacksmith shop. This shop was entirely inadequate and the transportation charge to a distant buyer was prohibitive. Cyrus McCormick, therefore, contracted with several manufacturers, at Richmond, Rochester, Cincinnati, Chicago, and other places, to manufacture on order on a commission basis. Some were allowed to seek orders for themselves and manufacture reapers, paying McCormick only for the use of his patent rights (say, $20 per machine, or $1,000 for supplying four counties).

This method of manufacture and sale was moderately profitable but it was not satisfactory. It was impossible to secure uniformity of quality under this system of manufacture, and there was the serious difficulty that manufacturers frequently failed to make the number of machines promised—a poor machine or an unfilled order gave a strong advantage to McCormick's competitors. Moreover, McCormick was left with many machines undelivered because they were built too late in the season. These difficulties brought McCormick to the decision that he himself had to have direct control of manufacturing operations.

To manufacture the reaper, McCormick entered into partnership with one of his contracting manufacturers, who was located in Chicago. This manufacturer had experience, some capital, and wide contacts with farmers; and he was located in the heart of the new wheat country.

The year 1851 saw McCormick strongly established in manufacture. In that year he bought out his partners and set up in manufacture alone. In 1848 he had made $30,000 from his partnership besides patent fees from other manufacturers; in 1849 his profits and fees had been about $65,000; and, in 1850, he had sold 1,550 machines, which probably netted a good profit. In 1851 manufacturing rights sold to other manufacturers expired, and McCormick's reaper won a great victory at the World's Fair in London.

In the next ten years McCormick expanded his business greatly. In spite of patent battles, keen competition, occasional poor crops, and depression toward the end of the decade, he forged ahead, not as an inventor but as a business man. He established the supremacy of his machine on the harvest field, increased his sales force, enlarged his factory, and secured good transportation rates. By 1860 he was a millionaire.

During the war McCormick's success continued though great difficulties arose. The southern market was lost and with it the hope of making collections in the South. In the North the problem was no longer to sell reapers but to sell only to those farmers who would pay for them. Drought and poor crops hurt the market in 1863. Farmers paid old bills in depreciated currency. Costs of materials and of transportation rose rapidly. Strikes interfered with manufacture. Substitutes had to be hired for experienced selling agents who were drafted. Yet so strong was competition that the pre-war price of the reaper held until 1864 when it was raised 15 per cent. Still McCormick made profits.

In the face of depreciating currency the McCormicks hedged against losses. They invested their profits as well as loans (their credit was high) in farm lands, Chicago real estate, and even gold. By 1867 Cyrus McCormick's real estate in Chicago, alone, was worth almost twice what he had paid for it, and he was receiving an annual income in rents of $95,000.

E. The middleman in the commodities trade.

The development of the specialized middleman continued at an accelerated rate in this period. There was the same pushing westward and a continued change in organization, technique, and policy. Altogether, there was a notable increase in the number of middlemen in proportion to the population.

The changes in the marketing of agricultural staples were almost revolutionary. Increased production—in the decade of the 'fifties cotton production about doubled, wheat rose around 75 per cent, and corn about 33.5 per cent [34]—and the widening distance between the agricultural producer, the processor or manufacturer, and the consumer gave opportunity for the appearance of new methods and agencies. In the farmers' wheat market there were probably no great changes, the local general store, commission and forwarding agent, or wheat buyer being the chief agency according to the amount of wheat handled. The local producer, commission agent, or trader sold or consigned the wheat to a buyer (a dealer, flour miller, or exporter) or a commission agent in a so-called primary market. As the telegraph reached into the country markets and credit developed for financing the trade, the local wheat buyer grew, as compared with the commission agent who consigned the grain to a primary market such as Chicago.

In the primary markets came the greatest changes. Specialized wheat middlemen appeared, though they were not clearly differentiated as to function; the commission dealer, trader, and storer were often one man. Out of this situation rose great opportunities for profit; for instance, since public and private storage were combined a storage man might store in the same bin his own wheat and that owned by another, with the object of raising the grade of his own. Trading in the primary markets came to be centralized in organized exchanges. In 1848 was organized the Chicago Board of Trade and about the same time the St. Louis Board.[35] In 1858 grading of wheat in Chicago came to be based on weight, an important step toward standardized grading.[36] Futures trading came at about the same time; it was practised in Chicago as early as 1855, while it became active just before 1865.[37] This made possible the shift of risk of price change to the specialized dealers by means of hedging.

The marketing of cotton went through similar developments though more slowly. The cotton exchanges did not rise until after the war. In the 'fifties the northern spinner bought through a broker or directly from a cotton factor in a southern port. But the cotton factor, who financed the cotton trade and therefore occupied

[34] "Agriculture," *Eighth Census of the U.S.*, 1860.

[35] B. H. Hibbard, *Marketing Agricultural Products* (New York, 1921), pp. 118–119.

[36] *First Annual Statement of the Trade and Commerce of Chicago*, 1859, pp. 10–12.

[37] Hibbard, *op. cit.*, p. 122.

a strategic position, was ruined by the war.

Producers' goods were sold through an altogether different system. Domestic bridge iron and rails as well as rolling stock for railroads were apparently sold in large part directly by the manufacturer to the railroad—indeed, it was not unusual for the two companies to have one or more owners and officers in common. Machines and tools for factories, of domestic production, were also apparently sold in this way. Farm machinery on the contrary was sold in various ways, from the full-time traveling agent to the local general store. Some domestic and probably almost all of the imported iron for railroad or industrial uses went through brokers or commission dealers. It was not unusual for bankers who were financing a certain road to purchase iron on commission for their road, apparently helping to finance the purchase or to make payment in the form of bonds.

Consumers' goods were distributed through a more complicated system, differing considerably as between kinds of goods. The domestic producer sold to the wholesaler directly (as in shoes and flour or clothing), through an agent representing one or more mills (as in textiles), or through commission merchants (as in shoes, textiles, iron, or flour). The wholesale importer or jobber was a merchant who sold to other wholesalers and also retailers. The wholesalers—who specialized in large groups of products, such as boots and shoes, groceries, dry goods, clothing, hardware, drugs, and so on—then sold to the retailer or other middlemen.

In consumers' goods, as in agricultural staples, wholesale trading became centralized near the source of production. The shoe trade was at first centered in Boston. Up to about 1850 the domestic textile trade was centered in Boston and Philadelphia, and the trade in imported cloth in New York. After that, however, there was a movement toward New York on the part of Boston and Philadelphia houses.[38] This grew out of the fact that New York had stronger and wider contacts with both foreign and domestic buyers.

In retailing two developments stand out. In the larger cities the specialized shop increased, faster apparently than the growth of business. By 1850 specialization was regarded as normal. But before the Civil War broke, a reaction had begun to set in and a counter movement combined in one firm lines of merchandise and marketing functions. Leaders in starting this change were A. T. Stewart, whose store in New York had some of the characteristics of the department store in this period, R. H. Macy, Marshall Field, Jordan Marsh, and John Wanamaker. Though integration gained a foothold, specialization was still the general order in retailing.

What is the explanation of the intricate marketing organization that grew up at this time? Was it a matter of growth in the size of the market, of inadequately developed marketing technique, or insufficient capital? Was this extensive specialization in marketing a phase in the development of a system to replace the sedentary merchant? Or did rising prices increase the chance of profits for middlemen?

F. Banks and banking.

Expanding production and trade in the United States increased the opportunities for banks and bankers. Those opportunities were of a very wide character, ranging from the developed business communities in the East to the new but rapidly growing West. Working on such a varied and fluid base, banking took different forms and employed different techniques from time to time and place to place. One characteristic of it all was the tendency toward specialization.

[38] M. T. Copeland, *The Cotton Manufacturing Industry of the United States* (Cambridge, 1917), pp. 200–201.

There were two general types of banking organization, the corporate and the private, and within each there was wide variation of form and function. The chartered banks in the eastern cities on the whole built a strong and profitable deposit and discount business in this period. Banks like the Bank of Commerce and the Bank of North America became powerful institutions in New York. Such banks very largely financed trade in their cities. They apparently on the whole followed conservative policies as to reserves, note issue, and discounts. At the other extreme of the chartered banks were the western banks. In the preceding period State-owned and operated banks had become discredited everywhere except in Missouri, and in some States the result was an antipathy to banking which expressed itself in the legal prohibition of corporate banking. The chartered banks which later developed in the West tended to issue currency on a small capital base. In other words there was much weak or definitely fraudulent banking. On the whole, corporate banking failed to meet all the banking needs of the time. The chartered bank was restricted both in the area in which it operated and in its function.

The most aggressive factor in banking at this time was the private bank. There were practically no legal restrictions on the private bank, except occasionally as to note issue. It could be established with little capital, particularly since it was so flexible in form as to be able to do a great variety of work. It could combine banking with mercantile or real-estate business; it could do a commission loan business, serving as a go-between for the borrower and the individual or bank that had money to lend; it could do exchange business on commission; it could establish branches anywhere; and, in its freedom from legal regulations or the control of stockholders, it could change rapidly its place of location or kind of business. The private bank, in other words, was peculiarly fitted to adapt itself to a dynamic business situation.

Because of the ease with which it could be entered and because of its adaptability, private banking grew very rapidly in the 'forties and 'fifties, both in commercial and investment banking, its growth tending to be in the direction of specialization. Its advantage in foreign business is clear. Its organization also fitted it well for the domestic commercial business since its branches enabled it to set up a system of banks reaching out from eastern business centers. Apparently this was the reason why domestic exchange was then in the hands of private banking firms like E. W. Clark & Co., Drexel & Co., and Corcoran & Riggs. Some good private bankers were also able, through the use of bills of exchange, circulating drafts, and certificates of deposit, to supply the equivalent of a circulating bank currency in parts of the West where there was no legally recognized bank currency. George Smith of Chicago was the most successful western banker in devising a sound, though illegal, bank currency.

The national banking system practically destroyed the basis of the private bank's position in domestic exchange. By setting up uniform national standards for individual banks chartered by the federal government, it provided a sound and uniform currency and a nation-wide system of banks through which domestic exchange could be carried on.

A significant aspect of banking in this period was the tendency of funds to move toward New York. This was in keeping with the movement of trade, and it was encouraged by the fact that New York banks began to pay interest on deposits. It was in the later 'forties that New York came forward as the leading center of bank reserves for the country, and by the 'fifties its supremacy was recognized everywhere. It was then the outstanding money market of the country.

A very important development in this

period was the investment business. Earlier, long-time loans and investments had been made chiefly outside banking, except in so far as the business had been handled by the private mercantile or exchange bankers. Even in this later period, investments and long-time loans were to a great extent handled through individuals. The individual who had a surplus frequently invested directly or through a friend in a local individual or corporate enterprise or even in a distant one.

The private bankers came more and more into this work as time passed. They handled much of the western land business, but their chief contribution was in the trade in securities. A large proportion of the new securities for banks, insurance companies, or manufacturing concerns was distributed without the aid of banks. The private bankers had early taken over the handling of trade in securities on the market, but in this period they also entered heavily into the issue of new securities.

Two developments in the investment field gave opportunities to the private bankers: the need of large funds for railroad promotion; and the requirements of the federal government in the Mexican and Civil wars. The bankers sold the securities on commission, only to a small extent taking responsibility for floating new issues. They were, on the whole, just passive middlemen feeling their way into a new and profitable business.

Under the pressure of government demand and the leadership of Jay Cooke, one important development came in the selling of securities during the war. Subscriptions of individual bankers and capitalists were soon found inadequate, and it became necessary to search out the savings in even the humble homes of every corner of the country. Through the combination of a remarkable sales organization and skillful and persistent use of advertising, Jay Cooke was able to sell hundreds of millions of bonds in a few months. There was no underwriting—it was all done on commission. It took careful managements to pay advertising, traveling agents, local agents, regional agents, and Jay Cooke, himself, from three-eighths of one per cent.

When the war was over, an effective system existed for floating new issues. Jay Cooke & Co. and a number of their leading agents, particularly in New York, had become specialists in selling on commission, the bankers helping to finance purchases. Contacts had been established with bankers and banks which led to the door of the smallest savings in the country. And strong contacts had been built with European capitalists through the establishment in New York during the war of the banking houses of J. P. Morgan, the Seligmans, Jacob Schiff, and L. P. Morton, who all had their base in English or German finance.

G. The growth of speculation.

One of the strongest expressions of the optimistic spirit of 1843–66 is the interest that was taken in speculation. Two forces were behind speculation at this time. One was monetary, coming from the increased gold production in California and currency inflation during the war. The other was the belief that the new enterprises and expansion would bring greater national wealth and greater profits —"In the New England States," said *Hunt's Merchants' Magazine* in 1849, "the rapid increase of railroads has been productive, since their regular operation, of a rise in the value of property in Boston alone, to an amount greater than the whole cost of all the railroads in New England."

One development which favored speculation on a large scale was the large accumulation of idle funds in New York. These were loaned out through the call-loan market on collateral security and were used in the securities market. It is interesting that, when interest rates were high in other places, funds were readily available in New York. In the early 'fifties in New York, says a contemporary, "The banks aided speculation with a free hand. Brokers with only $1,500 on deposit would draw checks for $100,000 or even $300,000 which were promptly certified by paying tellers. . . . Clerks who could not raise even a hundred dollars freely speculated, and brokers took their orders without question, so absolutely plentiful were loans." [39]

There was a setback in the market in 1854 and again in 1857. But the Civil War years and those immediately following saw tremendous activity in the New York call-loan market. It had again become easy to get credit on which to speculate in securities.

It is not the intention to imply that the availability of loans in New York was independent of expansion and speculation. The call-loan market was no doubt in large measure a response to the profitableness of loaning surplus funds to the investment market—in other words the result of speculation on the anticipation of profits from investments. Though it was not a primary cause, it is quite probable that its existence did encourage the speculative market.

The speculation centered in New York at this time was concerned principally with stocks and gold. In the 'fifties railroad securities were the object of speculative interest, and in the early 'sixties railroads and also petroleum and mining shares. Suspension of specie payments by the banks and the federal government also brought trading in gold, and gold exchanges were set up. Some of the trade in gold arose from the actual needs of industry and commerce, but the trade came to be dominated by speculators. Gold speculation came chiefly from professionals in New York, though politicians, reporters, and others from different parts of the country point to speculation on something like a national scale.

In this period the professional operator rose to a place of importance on Wall Street. In the 1850's Jacob Little and Daniel Drew were important, but most of the work of Drew and of Vanderbilt, Gould, Fisk, Tobin, Keep, and numerous other professional operators was done subsequently to 1860. With them came intense corners and battles—the decade of the 'sixties has fair claim to being the most striking and possibly the most important decade until the 1920's in the history of speculation in New York.

5. The Condition of Business

The question at this point is whether business was in fact relatively prosperous in this period of a rising price trend and rapid change in institutions and techniques. This question may be approached through a consideration of the general condition of business, profits, and other evidence.

A. Fluctuations in business conditions. It is obvious that business was not always good in this period. The condition of business conformed with the general cyclical fluctuations of prices. As appears to be usual in a period of rising prices, however, the periods of prosperity were long as compared to the periods of depression.

Table 7. BUSINESS FLUCTUATIONS IN THE UNITED STATES, 1843–66 [40]

Revival	Prosperity	Recession	Depression
1843–44	1844–45	1845–46	1846
1847	1847	1847	1848
1848	1849–53	1853–54	1854–55
1855	1856–57	1857	1857–58
1859	1860	1860	1861
1861	1862–65 [a]	1865	1866

[a] In the North more than the South.

It is significant that there was a decided likeness in the movement of the business cycle in the United States and

[39] James K. Medbery, *Men and Mysteries of Wall Street* (Boston, 1870), pp. 306–307.

[40] W. L. Thorp, *Business Annals* (National Bureau of Economic Research, New York, 1926), pp. 76–77.

in certain countries of Western Europe which have been studied in this connection.[41] England, France, and the United States all shared in the panic of 1847; in 1857–58 panic came to those countries and to Austria and Germany. Though the different phases of the cycle were not felt with equal intensity or at exactly the same time in all those countries, on the whole there was a remarkable sympathy in the sweep of the cycle.[42]

Fluctuations in the United States were in general as follows: from 1843 to 1848 business was very uncertain. The revival which began in 1843 was only partial in 1844; agriculture was depressed from either poor crops or low prices. Similarly in 1845 the degree of prosperity varied from time to time and from industry to industry. The war with Mexico and the settlement of the Oregon boundary dispute with England in 1846 gave some impetus to dull business, and conditions were greatly improved in 1847. The panic in England in the fall of that year depressed a none-too-buoyant business. In 1848 business was in general mildly depressed.

In 1849 began that strong expansive movement which, with a short interruption, continued to be effective throughout 1849–66. There seems to be a connection between the revival of business in 1849 and the discovery of gold in California. News of the discovery was confirmed by the president of the United States on December 5, 1848; on December 11 the Philadelphia mint announced that its first assay of California gold dust proved it to be 98⅜ per cent pure.[43] In January, 1849, *Hunt's Merchants' Magazine* noted that "already the prospect of great abundance of gold has promoted a desire to speculate." [44] In March the same journal commented that: [45]

> "The operation of the California gold fever has been to impart a strong spirit of speculation, and to induce enterprise in all commercial countries of a character more bold than any that has marked commercial operations of the past few years. . . . England is now rapidly recovering from that revulsion [of 1847]. American produce is again selling freely at higher prices, and every element of prosperity is in action. The result is, that in all directions the desire to extend bank credits is manifest. In Illinois, Michigan, and Ohio, paper schemes are being projected. In Pennsylvania, a change in government favors the renewal of those money charters that expire in a short time; and in New York the multiplication of banks under the new law is very rapid. All these are symptoms of growing speculation; but as yet the ground is firm, the national wealth great, and the floating capital of the country never greater than now."

Though the gold discovery had aroused a spirit of enterprise, little gold had actually come into circulation. By June it was estimated that gold worth $3,000,000 had left San Francisco, and in September it was said that $1,237,000 had actually been converted into coin.[46]

From 1849 to 1857 American investment activity was concerned with industrial expansion, railroad building, and western development. Up to about 1852 California was the center of interest in the West, and in 1853–57 the Upper Mis-

[41] *Ibid.*, pp. 88, 94.

[42] The international character of the business cycle, historically, has not been given very much attention by students of this period. An interesting study published recently by a German scholar (Hans Rosenberg, *Die Weltwirtschaftskrisis von 1857–1859*, Stuttgart-Berlin, 1934) on the panics of 1857–59 illustrates one approach to the subject. D. Morier Evans, *The History of the Commercial Crisis, 1857–58* (London, 1859), deals with the crisis in England and America.

[43] *Hunt's Merchants' Magazine*, vol. xx (1849), pp. 56–57, 91.

[44] *Ibid.*, p. 79.

[45] *Ibid.*, p. 310.

[46] *Ibid.*, p. 638 and vol. xxi (1849), p. 318.

sissippi Valley. There was a rush of farmers, miners, merchants, and capital into those regions. At the same time, particularly from 1853 on, railroad construction was making rapid strides all over the country, especially out from the leading business centers. Merchants, manufacturers, and professional men now invested in lands and railroads, often on credit. There was in those years a large foreign trade; California's gold, more than the import of capital, accounts for the fact that we could maintain an otherwise unfavorable balance of trade.[47]

The years 1849–57 were broken by a minor panic and a severe but brief depression. Recession in railroad stock prices and business activity took place early in 1854. A stock exchange panic in July, 1854, was followed by financial stringency the country over. There were many private bank failures. Those interested in the California business were hard hit. Business soon, however, recovered from this shock. Capital continued to pour into the Upper Mississippi Valley; there was very active land speculation in that region from 1855 to the fall of 1857.

The panic of 1857 put a sudden stop to speculation and expansion. Since that event was so important and was so revealing of conditions, we shall stop to note the immediate situation out of which it arose and something of its progress.

Dunbar's study of the crisis of 1857 is the best work on the subject.[48] His analysis of the situation out of which the difficulty arose is illuminating. The general business condition at the beginning of the year 1857 was as follows: Foreign trade, while expanding rapidly, was not overdone.[49]

"Internal trade had been pushed forward with a great expansion and lengthening of credits; the railroad system in its rapid growth had absorbed much circulating capital and had also contributed a large share toward the increase of the vast system of credit on which our domestic affairs rested. And finally, this mass of credit was managed by the aid of a great number of banks established upon unlike and often insecure systems, acting upon no common principle, and with no important guaranty for the faithful and prudent discharge of their functions."

The first half of 1857 was characterized by uncertainty in the tone and activity of business. Speculation slowed down; the prices of railroad securities fell; money was not so easy throughout the country; the consumer seems to have been holding back somewhat, and the mercantile interests found greater difficulty in disposing of their goods; shipment of gold continued; and the banks of New York were heavily loaded with country-bank deposits and loans on call.

At the beginning of August there were disquieting symptoms. The export of specie was increasing, and since Europe had good crops there was little hope that the export would be lessened. It was becoming increasingly difficult to make collections in the West. A drain on New York deposits came from country banks, and during the second week in August the New York banks began to contract. The uneasiness and drain on the money market reacted unfavorably on the stock market. There was a decline of railroad securities, thirteen leading railroad stocks falling 11 per cent on the New York Stock Exchange in two weeks.

The spark which set off the explosion was the failure of the Ohio Life Insurance and Trust Co. on August 24. The closing of this bank, says Dunbar, "was the signal for uncontrollable panic, the disastrous course of which was inevitable

[47] *Foreign Commerce and Navigation of the United States,* 1900, vol. i, pp. 38–39, gives figures for the whole period.

[48] C. F. Dunbar, *Economic Essays* (New York, 1904), pp. 266–293.

[49] *Ibid.,* pp. 273–274.

in the absence of any real unity of counsel among the banks. . . ."[50] This was followed first by bank failures in New York and Boston, and thereafter by failures among country banks in the middle and western States and among mercantile firms of good standing throughout the country; at the same time came a slackening of production in manufacturing, which was embarrassed by the failure of commission houses and agents. A California boat sank with $2,000,000 in gold which had been expected to relieve the monetary stringency. The hoarding that was going on was one of the factors which contributed to the suspension of gold payments by banks, which began in Philadelphia and spread to most of the banks of the country. This further broke confidence, and many more failures followed. On October 9 the notes of the Reading Railroad were protested; the suspension of payment by the Erie followed; the Illinois Central made an assignment to its creditors; and the Michigan Central asked for more time to pay its floating debt. The havoc brought by the panic was serious everywhere except in parts of the South.

In the next three years the country was busy with bankruptcies and reorganizations and a general cleaning-up of obligations. There was some speculation, especially in copper, and there was a too rapid extension of banking in parts of the West. On the whole, however, it was a time of fairly careful finance and management. The foreign trade situation was at first much improved, though 1860 saw heavy imports. Industrial and commercial sections recovered more rapidly than agricultural. The West suffered from a lessened demand from Europe but in 1860 was favored by excellent crops.

On the whole the country was well on the way to recovery when the political situation late in 1860 became serious. Secession and the outbreak of the Civil War brought panic and depression.

The war soon had a strong effect on business in the North. War purchases and currency inflation brought about a veritable price revolution. Foreign trade fell, exports falling more than imports, apparently because prices rose rapidly in the United States as compared with Europe. The clothing, food, and iron industries received a tremendous impetus from war demands. New manufacturing and marketing firms and many chartered and private banks were established. Speculation in gold, stocks, and commodities reached unheard-of proportions. Never had the North enjoyed such prosperity.[51] In the South the story was not the same; there the progress of the war brought poverty and economic chaos.

In the North there was a slight boom on the ending of the war, but this was soon followed by recession and a minor depression. As happened after the recent war (1914–18), the depression which came shortly after the war closed did not mature into a serious upset of business; it proved not to be the main postwar upset of business.

B. Profit and loss, 1843–66.

Though this period had the usual ups and downs in business, on the whole it seems to have been a time of very considerable prosperity. We know from contemporary accounts that it was an era of great optimism, and one gains the general impression that much of the industrial and mercantile expansion grew out of profits. As to specific profits, however, this period reveals very little factual evidence.

[50] *Ibid.*, p. 279.

[51] A useful survey of economic experience in the North at the time is E. D. Fite, *Social and Industrial Conditions in the North during the Civil War* (New York, 1910).

Information is, therefore, not available on which to base any general statements as to income from capital and business effort in those years. A mass of miscellaneous data is at hand which has some meaning for specific industries or enterprises.

Joseph G. Martin's *History of the Boston Stock and Money Markets* (Boston, 1898) contains an extensive collection of dividends for several types of corporate enterprise in New England. Dividends are by no means an accurate index at any given time to the prosperity of a concern, for they depend too much on financial and accounting policies to give positive insight into the actual condition of earnings. Consideration of depreciation and of inventory valuation varied very greatly, and it became common in the later part of the period for railroads and mining concerns to inflate their capital and pay dividends out of loans. Yet, over a long period of years dividends do have some meaning.

Table 8 gives the dividends for the first nine in an alphabetical list of New England textile concerns which operated throughout the whole period.[52] Here is an industry which had become very competitive and which did not experience during this period any very significant technological improvement.

[52] J. G. Martin, *History of the Boston Stock and Money Markets* (Boston, 1898), pp. 129–133.

Table 8. DIVIDENDS OF NEW ENGLAND TEXTILE MANUFACTURING COMPANIES, 1843–66

(Percentage of par value of stock)

Year	Appleton	Bartlet Mills	Chicopee	Columbian	Dwight	Great Falls	Hamilton Cotton	James Steam Mills	Lawrence
1843	6	12	0	..	11	6	6	..	7
1844	11	11	7	..	18	17½	13	..	15
1845	12	9½	12	..	20	20	14	..	14
1846	12	8	6	25	16	22½	10	12	15
1847	3	4	6	12	9	10	6	6	10
1848	5	3	0	3	6	8	5	0	3
1849	6	6	3	10	8	6	6	6	6
1850	6	6½	5	10	7	6	6	0	7
1851	0	2	0	3	2	6	3	0	2
1852	6	6½	0	6	6	6	8	6	7
1853	8	8½	4	12	4	9	10	8	9
1854	8	8	0	11	5	11	9	7	8
1855	8	6	0	6	3	8	8	3	7
1856	8	6½	0	6	3	8	8	6	8
1857	8	3	0	3	5	7	7	0	4
1858	9	3	0	0	0	0	7	5	0
1859	10	8	0	4	3	3	8	11	8
1860	10	11	8⅓	6	7	9	9	18	9
1861	10	6	4	6	6	8	6	13	8
1862	10	16	12	7	8	9	10	20	8
1863	10	8	12	7	9	15	8	30	15
1864	10	6	16	7	6	10	6	35	6
1865	25	25	26	5	3	5	5	30	2
1866	20	15	45	10	6	8	5	20	3

Table 9. DIVIDENDS OF BOSTON BANKS
1843–66
(Percentage of par value of stock)

Year	Atlantic	Atlas	Boston	City	Columbian	Freeman's	Globe	Hamilton
1843	5	4	7	3½	5	7	6	5
1844	5	3	7	5	4½	7	6	4½
1845	6	6	7	6	5½	7	6	6
1846	6	6	7	6	6	8	6½	7
1847	6½	6½	7	6	6	8	7	7
1848	7	6½	8	7	7	8½	7½	7
1849	8	7	8	7	7½	9	8	7
1850	8	7	8	7	7	9	8	7
1851	8	6½	8	7	7	9	8	8
1852	8	7	8	7	6½	9	8	8
1853	8	7	8	7	6½	9	8	8
1854	8	7½	8	7	7	10	8	8
1855	7	8	8	7	7	10	8	8
1856	6	8	7	7	7	10	8	8
1857	6	7½	7	7	7	10	8	8
1858	6½	8	7	7	7	8	8	8
1859	7	8	7	6½	7	8	8	8½
1860	7	8	7	7	7	9	8	9
1861	3	7	6	6½	6½	7	8	8½
1862	5	6	0	6	6	6	8	8
1863	5	6½	6	7	6	6½	8	9½
1864	7	8	7	8	7	8	8	14 [a]
1865	9	15 [a]	8	8	18 [b]	29 [a]	32 [a]	7 [a]
1866	10	10	10	8	10	10	10	12

[a] When these banks turned national, most of them declared an extra dividend.
[b] 3 per cent of this was in gold worth 150.

Table 9 gives dividends for eight Boston banks which operated throughout the period.[53] The reader is reminded that the Boston business area was, of all sections of the country, the most conservative in its business at this time. Boston bank dividends for 1843–66 were high in this period relatively to preceding and succeeding periods.

Table 10 on the next page gives the profits of a Philadelphia firm.[54]

One of the notable characteristics of the period is the fact that large fortunes were built up. Speculative fortunes were made in a day in gold, copper mines, or other stocks.[55] But more conservative business also yielded great gains. Jay Cooke, who had made a small competence in the 'fifties, started in banking for himself with little capital in 1861. His share of profits from his banks for succeeding years was as follows: $36,000 in 1862; $300,000 in 1864; $270,000 in 1865; $76,000 in 1866.[56] In 1848 Andrew Carnegie, aged 12, arrived in America with his family (who had borrowed money for the passage); in 1863, when only 27, according to his biography, he had an income

[53] *Ibid.,* pp. 99–101.

[54] Generously supplied by Miss Elva Tooker, who compiled the figures from the account books in Baker Library of Nathan Trotter & Co.

[55] See E. C. Stedman, *The New York Stock Exchange* (New York, 1905), and Medbery, *op. cit.*, for the period.

[56] *In the Matter of Jay Cooke . . . Bankrupts* (Philadelphia, 1875), "Statement of Bankrupts as to causes of Insolvency of Firm," p. 21.

Table 10. PROFITS OF A PHILADELPHIA METAL FIRM
1843–66

Year	Gross profit on merchandise	Interest, discounts, commissions,[a] etc.	Expenses,[b] contingent fund,[c] etc.	Total profits
1843	$23,537	$ 6,905	$ 3,155	$27,287
1844	25,777	1,851	3,226	24,402
1845	32,817	11,620	6,438	37,999
1846	31,820	11,772	3,899	39,693
1847	42,061	14,371	4,432	42,000
1848	34,398	19,076	12,388	41,087
1849	45,707	21,219	6,926	60,000
1850	38,671	17,369	10,042	46,000
1851	32,459	13,447	9,907	36,000
1852	54,789	18,107	12,896	60,000
1853	71,718	26,943	8,662	90,000
1854	50,871	25,160	19,032	57,000
1855	36,263	22,883	14,147	45,000
1856	49,376	20,497	15,873	54,000
1857	28,639	33,756	41,396	21,000
1858	32,178	26,206	13,385	45,000
1859	31,971	33,402	14,373	51,000
1860	36,882	32,934	18,816	51,000
1861	44,641	34,186	18,828	60,000
1862	85,618	30,542	17,161	99,000
1863	47,313	34,548	12,826	69,000
1864	62,921	45,695	15,616	93,000
1865	37,020	48,785	16,805	69,000
1866	58,099	48,096	12,196	93,000

[a] These merchants did a considerable business on commission.

[b] The figure for the cost of merchandise in the ledger includes expenses which do not appear here.

[c] The firm early began to take a round sum for total profits and put the remainder into a contingent fund.

for the year of $47,860.[57] Many illustrations could be given of large incomes.[58]

At the end of the Civil War the United States was in a prosperous condition. Never had this country had so great a productive system, so large a liquid capital, or so strong a credit in Europe as by 1866. The setback to business experienced at the end of the war had been short-lived. There were many who believed that the great prosperity which America had attained was going to continue in the future.

[57] Burton J. Hendrick, *The Life of Andrew Carnegie* (New York, 1932), vol. i, p. 120.

[58] *The Annual Report of the Commissioner of Internal Revenue,* 1873, pp. 164–165, gives income tax figures for 1863–73. Since three different rates were used in those years, the figures are not useful for our purposes.

6. Suggested Readings

W. L. Thorp, *Business Annals* (New York, 1926). See the graphs of cyclical changes in business in different countries and annual summaries of business conditions.

Anne Bezanson, R. D. Gray, and Miriam Hussey, *Wholesale Prices in Philadelphia, 1784–1861* (Philadelphia, 1936). Pages 230–260 are on prices from 1843 to 1862.

W. B. Smith and A. H. Cole, *Fluctuations in American Business, 1790–1860* (Cambridge, 1935). Pages 85–138 are on general conditions, commodity and security prices, public land sales, banking and finance, etc.

C. F. Dunbar, *Economic Essays* (New York, 1904), "The Crisis of 1857," pp. 266–293. This is the best discussion we have of the crisis of 1857.

7. Suggested Questions

1. Is there sufficient evidence to justify calling this a period of business prosperity? If so, what is meant by business prosperity?
2. What were the factors at work bringing about the expansionist optimism of this period?
3. Why did specialization in business gain such a victory in this period?
4. How would you characterize the business cycles within this period? What were the forces behind these cyclical changes?
5. Should the period be closed at 1866 or 1873? Also, consider these two dates with reference to Europe.
6. Do you agree that this was the Golden Age of the common man?
7. How can you explain the relatively slight price rise up to the Civil War? Consider technological progress.

XLI. BUSINESS DIFFICULTIES, WITH A TENDENCY TO COMBINE AND INTEGRATE, IN A PERIOD OF DECLINING PRICES, 1866–1897

1. General Statement

No period in American business history is more challenging to the student of the history of business than the years 1866–97. True, it is difficult to see exactly what was happening in that mad economic effort to build a greater system of production, but even to gain some comprehension of the problem is in itself worth while.

While the years 1843–66 in general had the appearance of good times for business, this later period bears the marks of much struggle and difficulty. Were these real or only apparent? If they were real, can we go so far as to say that there was a fairly consistent and continuous downward trend of business over a considerable period? If there was such a downward trend, how might it be explained? Was it merely the aftermath of the Civil War? Perhaps business was difficult in the period 1866–97 because there was a decline in the rate of increase in world gold production. Or there may have been a dislocation in the equilibrium of demand and supply in goods and services. It may be that relatively too much capital was invested in producers' goods. We should also think in this connection of the fact that the rapid fall in agricultural prices throughout the world may have been of some significance. And the management problems in a rapidly changing economy should not be forgotten.

This period brings up a consideration to which it is worth while giving attention. Relatively to the growth of population, the physical volume of production increased at an accelerating rate. This suggests that 1866–97 was a good time for business. Yet here an essential distinction must be drawn: an increase in productivity need not point to greater income for capital and for the entrepreneurial factor, and it may even be a symptom of ill health in business. It is possible at one and the same time for the social income to be great and the business income to be, on the whole, relatively small. This has been called profitless prosperity.

The concern in all these studies is primarily with the administration of business. In 1866–97 business drove toward persistent change in the mechanical technique of production, in organization, and in management in general. Power-driven machinery, the corporate form of organization, combination into larger units, and the integration of related processes came to characterize American business at this time. The device known as reorganization and the rise to importance of the banker in industry and transportation also became significant. Were these essentially readjustments to a tightening-up of business owing to the downward trend of prices, or adjustments necessary in a business system becoming increasingly complex?

2. General View of the Period

1864	Bessemer steel first produced in America.
1866	First successful Atlantic cable.
1866–67	Depression.
1866–79	Rapid decline in prices.
1867	Beginning of postwar protective tariff movement.
1868–69	Revival and prosperity.
1869	Black Friday gold panic. New York Central reached Chicago. First transcontinental railroad completed.
1869–75	Agricultural discontent attacked railroads.
1870	Depression. New York Cotton Exchange established.
1871	"New process" for milling flour adopted. First modern un-

	derwriting syndicate used in sale of United States loan.
1871–72	Mixed prosperity.
1873	Major postwar panic. Jay Cooke & Co. failed.
1873–78	Unbroken depression.
1874	Inflation bill vetoed.
1877	Severe coal strikes.
1878–82	Revival and prosperity.
1878–97	Bimetalism threatened gold standard.
1879	Resumption of specie payments. First important bankers' syndicate in American railroad finance.
1880–89	Unprecedented railroad construction.
1881	American Federation of Labor established.
1882	Standard Oil Trust established. Taylor began "scientific" management.
1882–85	Recession and depression.
1883–97	Almost continuous price decline.
1884	Severe coal strikes.
1885–87	Revival and prosperity.
1886	Severe railroad strikes.
1887	Interstate Commerce Act passed.
1888	Slight recession.
1889	Carnegie Steel Co. organized.
1889–90	Prosperity.
1890	Sherman Anti-Trust Act passed. National City Bank established.
1890–91	Recession and depression.
1891–92	Revival and prosperity.
1893–95	Panic and depression. United States gold reserve almost depleted.
1894	Pullman and Carnegie strikes.
1895	Depression and revival.
1895	Bryan and "free silver" frightened business.
1895–97	Recession and depression.

3. Declining Prices, 1866–97

A. Behavior of prices.

In 1864 wholesale commodity prices in currency began to fall, and in 1866 prices in gold. From then until 1897 there was a strong general downward movement of prices; excepting a slight recovery in 1880–83 and a few other years, the movement downward was constant. The general index in Warren and Pearson's index numbers of wholesale prices shows a fall from 174 in 1866 to 68 in 1897.[1] The prices of different groups of commodities did not fall at the same rate, however. Farm products fell from 140 in 1866 to 60 in 1897; foods from 173 to 71; hides and leather products from 166 to 71; textiles from 245 to 76; fuel and lighting from 160 to 64; metals and metal products from 278 to 76; chemicals and drugs from 283 to 87; and building materials from 128 to 68. The most severe fall came in metals and metal products, chemicals and drugs, and textile products.

The behavior of a few individual commodities shows a relatively rapid fall. One index gives the fall in cotton textiles from 294.7 in 1866 to 66.0 in 1897, and raw upland middling cotton in New York from 234.4 to 55.9.[2] Another index gives the drop in wheat as from 108.4 in 1866 to a low of 48.9 in 1894.[3] In the same period pig iron fell from $33.26 to $12.10 in gold per ton, and Bessemer steel rails from $120.18 in 1867 to $18.75 in gold per ton in 1897.[4]

B. Explanations of price change.

Various explanations have been made of the downward change in prices. The drop from 1866 to 1879, when the gold standard was restored, was to a decreasing extent owing to the fact that currency was working back to its gold value. It may be that changes in the supply of money had some effect: a decline in world gold production began in the 'sixties, and not till 1892 did world production reach that of 1866.[5] In other words, the rate of

[1] G. F. Warren and F. A. Pearson, *Prices* (New York, 1933), p. 26.

[2] S. S. Kuznets, *Secular Movements in Production and Prices* (Boston, 1930), pp. 346–347, 392–393.

[3] *Ibid.*, pp. 334–335.

[4] *Ibid.*, pp. 364–365, 368–369.

[5] Warren and Pearson, *op. cit.*, p. 97.

increase of gold slowed down during the period. At the same time silver was demonetized in many western countries, which lessened the specie basis for money and increased the burden on gold. In the United States, however, silver was purchased under the Bland-Allison Act of 1878 by the United States Treasury to use as money. Another consideration in the United States was the fact that bank currency was curiously inflexible—it was regulated wholly by the market value of United States bonds and had no direct relation to business needs. The per capita monetary supply in circulation in the United States increased only from $18.28 in 1867 to $22.87 in 1897.[6]

Other things must also be considered as factors in price change. Technological improvements in production, for instance, made possible cheaper production in many fields, and competition tended to drive prices down accordingly. This view is supported by the fact that the price drop seems to have been heaviest in those fields where production was being cheapened most rapidly, as for instance in wheat production, textiles, and iron. Improvements in transportation had a similar effect.

4. Methods and Problems of Business Administration

At the end of the Civil War American business found itself in a highly inflated condition. The question confronting many business men was whether they should retrench or seek new work. Instead of retrenchment, however, came a movement toward expansion immediately following the war, which, except during a few depression years, continued at an accelerating rate.

The amount of expansion in the United States was very great. One index shows that from 1866 to 1897 population about doubled, total production of commodities increased fourfold, agricultural production tripled, mineral production increased almost eight times, and manufactures almost five.[7] From 1870 to 1890 the output of Minneapolis flour mills rose from 193,000 barrels to 7,400,000, while production for the whole country increased almost fourfold. In the twenty years following the early 'seventies, textile mills more than doubled their consumption of cotton, and from 1879 to 1899 the production of shoes also doubled—the relatively slow rate of increase in those lines may be significant. It is in iron and steel that we come upon a veritable epoch of growth. Pig iron increased from an annual output of a little over 2,000,000 tons in the middle 'seventies to between 7,000,000 and 9,000,000 in the 'nineties, while steel rose from an insignificant amount to 7,000,000 tons in 1897.

This tremendous increase in production, far greater than the increase in population, points to a very active business. It was the business man who organized and directed the factors which produced those results. How was this done? Why was it done so rapidly? What problems arose in the process? And how were they met?

These questions all turn on business administration. The object at this point is to examine business administration at work in this period, but there is no satisfactory way of handling the subject from a general point of view. It is impossible to proceed from cause to effect, to touch all aspects of business and all lines, or to follow developments chronologically throughout the period. Only a few essential features of business organization and operation will therefore be touched upon. Something of the pattern of activity and change during the period may be seen therefrom.

Business in this period, as generally in the United States throughout most of the nineteenth century, rushed madly into

[6] National Monetary Commission, *Statistics for the United States, 1867–1909,* p. 158.

[7] W. M. Persons, *Forecasting Business Cycles* (New York, 1931), pp. 170–171.

newly opened regions to exploit virgin resources. One may well ask whether those resources did not absorb much of the shock of the business difficulty arising out of the price decline of the period. There were new raw materials to be found in the copper and iron areas of the Lake Superior region, the forests of the Upper Mississippi, the wheat fields of the prairie and plains States, and the precious mineral resources of the mountain States. The markets provided by the settlement of those newly opened regions were a tremendous field for the middleman; while the railroad found new work as carrier for the developing trade.

It is notable that growth in manufactures came chiefly in two fields. One was the production of such consumers' goods as were close to raw materials, like flour, meats, textiles, and lumber. The other was the production of producers' goods. Service industries were developed very slowly as were also those consumers' goods which were not clearly necessities. The advance in the facilities which made for easier living was not comparable to the advance in productive equipment. In other words the processing and refining of raw materials and the manufacture of producers' goods—for railroads, factories, and farms—and their distribution were the dominant interests of American business in this period.

At this time the movement toward specialization in business reached its height. By specialization is here meant not the fine specialization of the handicraft worker or the specialization in economic functions—which followed the decline of the sedentary merchant—in which finance, transportation, manufacture, and marketing were separated from each other. It was rather a greater specialization within the separate functions. One firm made steel rails, another bridge iron, and still another made parts or even a part of the engine. One banker became predominantly an investment banker, another came to specialize in farm mortgages, and still another in commercial paper. One wholesaler dealt chiefly in woodenware; another in iron and tinware.

The movement toward large units which was observed in the earlier period continued at this time. Manufacturing units grew in large measure out of profits, while railroads were constructed mostly by means of funds from bond issues. The device of consolidation brought about the union of many small firms. Bankers and middlemen took on increasing business. The result was manufacturing firms employing thousands, railroad systems consisting of trunk lines reaching halfway across the continent and fed by countless branches, and middlemen of national importance.

What was behind this drive toward size? It was no doubt partly unconscious imitation, but generally it was the belief that in many fields the optimum size was large. The larger size was made possible by experience in administration and by the fact that capital was available in larger amounts. The device of the corporation, the aggressiveness of the investment banker working with a new technique, and large savings (especially in England and America in the late 'sixties and early 'seventies) gave a tremendous impetus to the movement.

Fundamental to the growth in production by large specialized units was a great technological development. Hobson states that in the fifteen to twenty years preceding 1886 replacement of hand labor by machinery represented a gain in productive power in various industries ranging from 50 per cent to 300 per cent.[8] This was the time when the skilled craftsman was definitely displaced in many important industries by unskilled machine operators. How rapidly machine technique was improved at this time may be illustrated by the fact that in the history of the United

[8] J. A. Hobson, *Evolution of Modern Capitalism* (New York, 1902), p. 172.

States patent office before 1860 some 36,000 patents were issued while in the remainder of the century 640,000 were granted.

The continued improvement of the steam engine, since it made possible the use of steam instead of water power as a prime mover, was probably the most important development of the period. The changes in the steam engine which were significant had to do with the amount of power it could produce, relatively to its weight and fuel consumption, and the controllability of its speed. By the middle 'seventies, improvements in the steam engine brought the great railroad mogul engine and spelled the doom of the sailing vessel. And the first practical steam turbine in 1882 paved the way for the central power plant of the 'nineties.

Other important inventions can only be mentioned. In 1867 came the micrometer caliper and the beginning of that astounding accuracy which is the real secret of automatic production. The Goodyear welting machine, developed in 1862–75, and the trimming and lasting machines, of 1877–83, were the final steps in mechanizing shoe manufacture. Innovations in textile machines were countless; they made the machinery more nearly automatic and increased its speed. The revolution in flour milling began in 1871, when the first successful purifier made possible the manufacture of a high-grade flour from spring wheat, and was completed with the adoption of the chilled iron rolls in 1879. The twine binder was the last great step in mechanizing grain harvesting. Refrigeration in the 'seventies marked the beginning of the fresh meat and fruit industries. No less revolutionary than these developments were improvements in mining, such as the use of dynamite, the power rock drill, and coal-cutting machines. Man power was also largely displaced by machine power in lumbering. Most dramatic in a sense were the improvements in iron and steel. Most significant was the development in steel manufacture which began in about 1865 with the adoption of the Bessemer process. Hydraulic hammers, presses, and improved rolling machinery came in the late 'seventies and early 'eighties. Steel rails formed the backbone of the business, but barbed wire of the 'seventies and structural steel of the 'eighties were also important. Significant to the American industry was the fact that it could produce more cheaply than the English iron masters—in the late 'nineties Carnegie stated that he could make steel rails at the same cost that the English could turn out pig iron.

As this great mechanized and specialized industry developed, serious problems arose. They cannot be said to have occurred at any particular time or because of any given general condition. The most important single factor in bringing them on may have been the downward drive of prices. But the time and nature of their appearance depended, of course, in large measure on the particular condition of a given industry or firm.

For the whole system the biggest problem in this period was perhaps that arising out of the lack of coördination among different branches of economic life or within those branches. Emphasis on capital goods, railroads, factories, and machines set up a great productive system which seems to have produced beyond the ability of the market to consume. Railroads were built in undeveloped regions where there was little traffic, and farm machinery was sold to farmers who could not pay. The rapid expansion of agriculture shows how optimism outstripped the market. One may well ask whether there was not too blind a faith in the appreciation of future values. It may be questioned whether some of that faith did not come from the existence at the end of the Civil War of great savings in the United States in the form of federal securities, which England came eagerly to buy, and from the work of promoters who hoped to make money out of the sale of securities and the construction of enterprises rather than from their operation. The rapid growth of railroads promised a great market for steel and agricultural machines and offered an outlet for agricultural products. Unfortunately there was a limit to the loads available for the railroad to carry, to the iron they could consume, and to the wheat that might be eaten. There was in all this a notable failure to develop, comparably, consumers' lines. Improvements in lighting, plumbing, housing, ready-made clothing, and prepared foods made only slight headway. There seem to be good grounds for believing that the hard times which followed 1893 were an expression of the over-expansion of facilities for producing non-consumable goods.

It may be questioned whether this emphasis on producers' goods was owing to a lack of insight on the part of industrial leaders into the possibilities of the market. It may be that adequate purchasing power did not exist for developing consumers' goods and services; surely, it was not a time of great purchasing power on the part of the farmer or the laborer. One thing is clear, however, that in some fields—notably in railroads—expansion outran the immediate prospects of profitable operation.

Another characteristic of this period which was a cause of much difficulty was the growing weight of capital. Is one secret of the hardships of this period to be found in the dislocations which came when capital was called upon to make rapid adjustments to new conditions? Let us examine the consequences which followed in the train of the increased mechanization of production. In 1845 an English economist (McCulloch) estimated that fixed capital in well-appointed cotton mills, then the most progressive of all manufactures, amounted to about two years' wages per operative. In 1890 Professor Marshall assigned capital in plant a value of about five years' wages for every worker. Turning to tables of capital invested per dollar of value added in manufacture, we arrive at comparable results, though naturally these differ widely in different lines. Average capitalization per establishment increased eight times between 1850 and 1880; value of product, seven times; average number of wage earners employed, three times.

The capital of the small factory owner, who had been the rule during the 'fifties and 'sixties, tended to be rapidly absorbed by machinery. Moreover, increasingly as the new technique differed more widely from the old, it required the scrapping of forms of wealth which had previously had value. Within the business itself it caused a shift in the ratio of fixed to liquid assets.

The shift to machinery once accomplished and machine production established, the repercussions on capital were unfortunately not at an end. A greater proportion of fixed investment means a relatively greater burden of fixed charges: depreciation, maintenance, repairs, power, indirect labor. The danger of heavy loss through enforced idleness becomes greater. What is worse, the temptation to run at a loss in order to meet the most pressing of overhead charges, and thereby still further undermine the price structure, is increased. This is bad enough where the standard that would bring in new capital in an industry remains higher than that which would cause existing capital to contract operations. But where not only is the return from the products of manufacture diminishing but also improved equipment is constantly available at lower cost, the position of the older plant is precarious indeed. This was particularly serious in the decades following the Civil War when prices declined so very rapidly.

Particularly was the above true where the original financing resulted in a rigid capital framework. That is well exemplified in the railroads of the period, the bonded indebtedness of which constituted so large a proportion of total capitalization

—indeed often practically constituted the whole. The railroads showed remarkable ingenuity in finding new bases for bond issues in this period. The weight of the heavy bonded indebtedness was increased by the fact that interest rates were falling throughout the period.

There is reason to believe, moreover, that the weight of the capital liabilities of many railroads was made unduly heavy by fraudulent or inefficient management. The Northern Pacific and Union Pacific were two long roads which clearly paid more for construction than was justifiable. Indeed, it was not unusual for promoters of a road to be primarily interested in the profits that could be made from construction. In the same way, high commissions to bankers for selling bonds—no doubt often necessary if weak bonds should find a market—inflated bonded indebtedness without giving tangible return.

Another problem grew out of specialization and was aggravated by size. That is, a specialized firm with a heavy fixed capitalization was in an especially vulnerable position. The specialized unit, whether it was a bank, a railroad, a factory, or a wholesaling concern, had no control either backwards or forwards in the production process of which it was a part. Yet, especially when it had a heavy fixed capital, its very life depended on a regular flow of business. This was particularly true of railroads and industrial and mining concerns and also of banks which paid interest on heavy deposits.

Closely related to growth in size was the increase in problems of internal management. There was the intricate problem of coördination of various parts of a firm's activity, the matter of supervision of those various parts, and the whole matter of personnel management. The growth in size increased the distance between management and labor and rendered impossible the personal relation which had earlier existed, and the use of automatic machinery made it unnecessary to have so much skilled labor as before. Indeed, business could even profitably employ low-grade labor brought in on contract, such as the coolie of the Orient. The result was that labor came to be looked upon more and more as a commodity. This brought a feeling of insecurity, which made for great unrest among laborers, and it encouraged the feeling of labor class consciousness.

In what ways did business administration try to meet its difficulties? In general, one or more of several courses were followed: costs were cut; control was moved backward or forward to related processes; and a larger volume of production was sought, either by deliberately stimulating demand or by competing for a larger share of the existing demand. These failing, outside interests intervened to coördinate and improve management or to cut fixed capitalization by reorganization.

The problem of costs was attacked on several lines. The cutting of costs by more efficient use of labor and capital was the motive behind mechanical improvements, and also to some extent behind the growth in size considered above. It was the machine that made the greatest saving in costs. This method of saving was felt in every line of mining and industry, in transportation, and in the market distribution process in general. How far costs were reduced by using larger producing units it is impossible to say. Undoubtedly too much was expected of large size, but there is no doubt that in many lines the optimum size was larger than that previously used. For instance, in the production of iron and steel the large furnace was more efficient, and it was best to operate several as one unit. Tremendous saving in mechanical handling, the efficient use of waste gas, heat, and by-products, all favor size. In flour milling, although it was conceded before 1880 that small mills had the advantage, thereafter economies in construction, operation, and superintendence were so marked that the large mill of 1890 had five times the capacity of the large mill of

1870. The meat-packing industry is one of the finest illustrations of the efficient use of by-products in the larger plant. There were two dangers in large size: the danger of developing beyond the efficient size and the possibility that in trying to achieve the technical optimum the limitations of the market would be overlooked.

The larger unit forced at the same time consideration of how to run the concern most efficiently. As early as 1851 McCormick had been experimenting with "little railways" on which raw materials approached machines "apparently on schedule," and with "transfer mechanisms to handle material from one conveyor system to another," thus producing "an ordered progression of operations" in the words of one enthusiastic commentator. But it was to be a generation before this engaged the attention of the specialized technical expert. Scientific job analysis—to determine mechanical speed and efficiency, standardization of tools, routing of work, and so on—was undertaken by Frederick W. Taylor in 1882. In the following years, as the rising tide of unskilled labor and the growing size of the producing unit threatened to swamp management, scientific management came to be a regular means for securing greater efficiency in operation.

In the field of labor, management was not too successful in its struggle to reduce costs. In its efforts to cut wage costs by lowering wages, by lay-offs in slack times, or by long hours, business ran into great resistance. At first labor resorted to political means; in the 1870's it backed the Greenback party. The great railroad strike of 1877 introduced physical force as another method of defense on the part of labor. Thereafter the wage earner's resistance became economic. In periods of hard times, when employers attempted to reduce wages, the reply was organization and strikes. In 1885 there were 645 strikes in 2,284 establishments, with 158,584 strikers and a total of 242,705 workers thrown out of work. In 1886 strikes numbering 1,432 in 10,053 establishments threw over half a million out of work. Year after year the story was the same.[9] "Labor organizations," says a student of the labor movement, "assumed the nature of a real class movement. The idea of the solidarity of labor ceased to be merely verbal and took on life! General strikes, sympathetic strikes, nation-wide boycotts and nation-wide political movements became the order of the day. . . . The failure of strikes brought into use the other weapon of labor—the boycott."[10]

On the whole, in this period of falling prices the greatest disturbances came on the downward side of the cycle. Labor was on the defensive; that is, it was opposing the wage reductions which declining prices often forced on employers. A strange paradox appears here. While labor almost always lost in its struggles with the employer, the real wages of labor apparently did not decline greatly. Although the great collection of wage data for the period—the *Aldrich Report* on which most of the studies of wages in those years are based—is far from reliable, it appears safe to conclude that for labor as a whole daily money wages, over the period, did not fall so rapidly as the decline in the cost of living.[11] We know practically nothing about unemployment during this time, however, or the extent to which changing living conditions among the workers made for a greater reliance on wages, which would be significant in determining real wages.

One result of the struggle between the employer and the employee is fairly clear.

[9] U. S. Commissioner of Labor, *Strikes and Lockouts,* 1906, p. 15.

[10] Selig Perlman, *A History of Trade Unionism in the United States* (New York, 1922), pp. 84–85.

[11] It is significant that Paul Douglas began his study of *Real Wages in the United States, 1890–1926* (New York, 1930) in 1890 and apparently did not use the Aldrich data. For another study see U. S. Bureau of Labor Statistics, *History of Wages in the United States from Colonial Times to 1928,* Bulletin no. 499, pt. 2.

The laboring class was weak in organization and methods—resorting often to undisciplined force—and the employing group was at times ruthless in its methods. Employers used the injunction, the lockout, and government militia to fight labor. There were "good" employers, but their attitude was frequently paternalistic. Not uncommon were the Carnegies or Fricks, self-made men, who resented any show of power on the part of the workers and hated labor organization like the plague. For labor and capital it was a time of open warfare. Never has America had more destructive labor disturbances. The great coal and railroad strikes of 1877, 1885, and 1886, and the Pullman strike of 1894 were milestones in the history of our labor disturbances. The bitterness then engendered in labor by the policy of employers has persisted in certain fields of labor to this day. John L. Lewis is the product of one of the two fields—coal mining and steel—in which the employers were notably ruthless in their treatment of labor in the 'seventies, 'eighties, and 'nineties.

One of the characteristic ways in which specialized business tried to strengthen itself in this period was by means of vertical combination, that is, expansion backward and forward in the production process. Sometimes this was to assure regular supplies and business, sometimes to cut costs, and sometimes, it seems, for no good reason at all. Vertical combination occurred in almost all fields of business. Bankers entered into the insurance business and into the promotion and direction of business in order to get work and more work. The manufacturers—in order to be certain of an outlet—took to pushing marketing by advertising (adopting brands and trade names) and by setting up their own wholesaling agencies, even establishing foreign marketing agencies. Manufacturers reached back to raw materials in various ways: the lumber companies bought forest lands—this was not a new development at the time but an enlargement of an old one; iron concerns bought the sources of their raw materials; and flour millers of Minneapolis established lines of elevators for buying wheat on good terms from the farmers and excluding the competition of Chicago and Duluth buyers. Railroads similarly tried to strengthen their traffic: for instance, Pennsylvania coal roads bought coal lands and northwestern railroads established wheat storage and purchase agencies to assure themselves of freight.

Throughout all this effort ran the drive to get more work to do, to produce larger volume. Up to the point where diminishing returns set in this was profitable, and, even after that point had been reached, it was not unwise if something could be done toward carrying a heavy fixed overhead. But pushing forward toward the consumer was not enough. The ultimate test was price. The struggle became essentially a price struggle and it reached into all fields of business. Only those concerns which produced unique goods or services escaped its worst effects.

The struggle is seen dramatically and clearly in transportation. The facts about railroad rate competition are too well known to require repetition. The results were important. The large shippers—the Minneapolis flour millers, the Carnegie iron interests, or the Rockefeller oil concerns—could bargain with the railroads to their own advantage, to the disadvantage of other shippers, and at great cost to the roads concerned. Between competitive points all shippers had an advantage as compared with noncompetitive traffic. One result of this system of favoritism was severe restrictive legislation in the 1870's in the Middle West.

Since business soon saw that the final effect of price competition would be failure, its next step was to seek salvation in union. Rate pools and traffic associations appeared among railroads. Although early efforts at coöperative action in industry were viewed by industrialists themselves with suspicion (except efforts to secure higher tariffs or in general to influence legislation) as attempts to expose trade secrets and undermine private ownership, the pool, the trust, and the merger came successively as expressions of the exhaustion of business. Turning from a hopeless race to reduce costs as fast as prices fell and maintain profits by ever-increasing volume, the captains of industry welcomed restriction of production and control of price as the way out.

The results of such attempts varied. Pools and gentlemen's agreements in general proved quite ineffective. More successful was the trust, which held actual control, or the merger, which meant complete amalgamation. The trust movement received its first impetus from the Standard Oil Trust of Rockefeller, which after years of effort toward coöperation, was finally realized in 1882; and by the late 1880's it was widely copied. Its power was great though the Sherman Anti-Trust Act of 1890 tried to break it. Actual combinations or mergers proved legally more sound. Both succeeded in a considerable measure in controlling production and price, thus, so far as they succeeded, attacking the evils of large-scale specialization. They extended into almost all fields of business; they were found in banking (notably the National City Bank), in manufacture, and in railroads.[12]

The trust and combination proved only a partial solution. They aggravated the problems of those who were left on the outside. And, even when successful, they had to carry heavy fixed charges and they could not do much to counteract the downward movement of prices.

In the 'eighties and 'nineties one business figure came to the front in the administration of railroads and industrial concerns—the investment banker. He had three interests at stake: his own funds, those of his depositors, and the goodwill of his customers. The failure of Jay Cooke in 1873 advertised the banker's necessity of protecting himself from the bad results of poor or fraudulent management in enterprises which he financed. When the banker after the panic of 1873 was asked to finance a project, he began to ask for a strong position in the administration of the firm to be financed. Indeed, railroads and manufacturing concerns were often glad to turn their problems over to the banker. Thus gradually the banker came to assume the rôle of administrator and conservator, though in his work he was not always wise and he was often swayed by a desire for immediate profits. In this work Morgan was the outstanding figure.

No device of organization or management could, however, turn the direction of the price movement. The efficient and the powerful were better able to meet the downward movement—indeed, the efficient operators were in large measure a cause of falling prices. Those who produced something for which the demand was strong, relatively to supply, escaped somewhat the general downward trend of prices. But those who were in a weak competitive position, who had too heavy a fixed burden of capitalization, or who were inefficient, found conditions extremely difficult. Outright failure or reorganization, which cut the burden of fixed charges, was the fate of many such enterprises.

5. The General Condition of Business, 1866–97

This period has been regarded very generally both in England and in the United States as a time of great difficulty in business. If the alleged basis for such a view is that the fall in prices was increasing the difficulties of business, then it must be remembered that the fall in costs was also very significant. The question of whether or not this was a time of difficulty in business can be approached in three ways:

[12] See table of industrial combinations effected between 1887 and 1900 in Eliot Jones, *The Trust Problem in the United States* (New York, 1921), p. 39.

first, the difficulties which business administration had in this period; second, the general condition of business; and, third, the situation as to profits. The first has already been considered; the other two follow.

A. The business cycle and the general condition of business.

The business cycle is a phenomenon of good times as well as bad. There is some variation, however, as to the relative length of the different phases of the cycle. Table 1 gives the distribution of the various phases of the cycle for this period.[13]

Table 1. LENGTH OF THE PHASES OF THE BUSINESS CYCLE
1866–97

Depression	Revival	Prosperity	Recession
1866–67	1868	1869	1870
1870	1871	1871–73	1873
1874–78	1878–79	1879–82	1882–83
1884–85	1885–86	1887	1888
		1889–90	1890
1891	1891	1892	1893
1893–95	1895		1896
1896–97			

To a considerable extent cyclical movements coincided in the United States and the large countries of Western Europe, particularly after 1871. Both experienced deep depressions in the middle 'seventies, 'eighties, and 'nineties. Indeed, it seems that there were in the larger and more advanced countries of the western world relatively long periods of bad times as compared with good times. Conditions in the United States were a part of the larger situation of the industrialized world.

From merely superficial observation it would appear that business was good in the years 1866–73, the years between the minor and major postwar panics. Physical production continued to increase. New railroads were built rapidly; indeed, a tremendous mania for railroad building doubled our mileage between 1865 and 1873.[14] Speculation flourished, and there was more conspicuous spending for consumption than the country had ever known.

In spite of this appearance of good times, there was much in the years 1866–73 that was precarious for business. It has already been noted that in 1866–67 and 1870 business was on the whole in a depressed state. The business literature of the time shows that business men were—especially until the inauguration of President Grant—continually harassed by uncertainty as to what Congress would do about government finance and monetary matters. The money market was set in turmoil by the merest rumor from Washington. This was advantageous to the clever speculator. But recurring corners in currency, gold, and stocks made times difficult for business in general. The gold panic of 1869 brought many failures and a considerable recession.

Business continued to function but it had lost its buoyancy. Business men were conscious of falling prices and values as compared with war standards. Profits were not so easily secured. Here, again, it is necessary to note that the situation was not uniform for all regions and types of business. The price experience of various groups of commodities differed over the years immediately following the war. The agricultural regions appear, on the whole, to have felt the severe change in the market earlier than the industrial or commercial interests—indeed, it was probably a better time for industry than for agriculture. The decidedly protective tariff established during and after the war helped industry to some extent. It must be remembered, also, that the prices of agricultural staples were strongly influenced by foreign prices, while industry was more

[13] Willard L. Thorp, *Business Annals* (National Bureau of Economic Research, New York, 1926), pp. 77–80.

[14] *Poor's Manual of Railroads*, 1874–75, p. xxvii.

dependent on the protected home market.

There is no doubt, moreover, that railroad building and the various industries and activities contributing thereto were sustained largely by European credit. This situation was not unlike the relationship of Europe to the United States after the recent war.

During the Civil War the credit of the United States had not been good in Europe. David A. Wells, special commissioner of internal revenue, said that our securities held abroad had been returned to the United States so that "the country in 1863 may be said to have exhibited a clean national ledger in respect to foreign indebtedness." [15] Two things changed the situation after the war: the United States proved her intention and ability to pay her war debts; and the breakdown of the European boom which was climaxed by the Overend-Gurney panic in England in 1866 made Europe look elsewhere for a place to invest her savings. Our war debt was rapidly transferred to Europe, and a considerable amount of railroad bonds was sold in England and Germany. With the aid of Jay Cooke & Co., Wells made an investigation into the extent to which our securities were held in Europe toward the end of 1869. The conclusion was that almost a billion and a half dollars of American securities, two-thirds in federal securities, were held in Europe. After 1869 Europe invested in the United States more cautiously, but a large portion of the federal loan of 1871 was taken abroad and there was a considerable sale of railroad bonds in England and Germany in the early 'seventies.

It is clear from a close study of the work of one of the largest banking houses participating in the sale of federal bonds abroad that a large part of the funds realized therefrom was reinvested in American railroad bonds, which bore higher interest rates than the government securities. The actual amount of money that went into railroads is not known. According to *Poor's Manual* the total capital account of the roads in the United States rose from $1,850,000 in 1869 to $3,784,543,034 in 1873.[16] A large portion of the investment went into new railroads in undeveloped regions, which could not pay fixed charges from earnings.

Even with all this activity it is clear that there were weaknesses in the business situation. David A. Wells in 1869 called attention to particular elements in business which he considered quite undesirable: (1) an adverse foreign balance of payments, amounting to about $210,000,000 a year; and (2) decreased productiveness relatively to the size of the business system (owing to overdevelopment of distributive as compared with producing elements), a decrease in the productiveness of labor, and the lessened productivity of capital.[17]

There were certain disturbing elements in the early 'seventies which were serious to business. The fall in prices continued; the decline was especially severe in the West, a fact which not only helped bring on the Granger movement that legislated harshly against railroads but which also cut down the income of western railroads and other business concerns. The deficit in foreign trade continued to mount—in 1872 the excess of imports over exports of merchandise, specie, and gold was $116,283,646, even though $66,133,845 in gold had been exported.[18] Railroad bonds could be sold only at an increasing cost, and the European market was becoming especially wary.

Early in 1873 there appeared a strong feeling of uncertainty among business men and apprehension that a crisis was com-

[15] *Report of the Special Commissioner of Internal Revenue,* 1869, p. xxvi.

[16] *Poor's Manual of Railroads,* 1869–70, p. xxviii, and 1874–75, p. lv.

[17] For a discussion of these, see *Report of the Special Commissioner of Internal Revenue,* 1869, pp. xxix ff.

[18] *Foreign Commerce and Navigation of the United States,* 1901, vol. i, p. 49.

ing.[19] In April and May the money market became tight; the sale of railroad loans practically stopped in Europe. There were several heavy mercantile failures "showing recklessness in credits and overtrading on limited capitals." [20] Word of decreased railroad earnings heightened the prevailing fear, and there were rumors that certain railroad banking houses were in difficulty. A number of those houses had extended credit to railroads far beyond the point of safety.

The summer was dull and relatively uneventful. In August shipments of currency to the interior began, and at the same time came a contraction of loans in the East. The contraction was especially severe in those banks that held the largest country-bank deposits, which were also most heavily loaned out on call. On September 13 the reserves of the New York banks were below legal requirements, particularly the reserves of the banks which were the largest holders of country deposits.[21]

There were some failures in the summer, but in September big houses began to go.[22] First the New York Warehouse and Security Co., which was heavily involved in the Missouri, Kansas & Texas. Next Kenyon, Cox & Co., which had endorsed paper of the Canada Southern to the extent of $1,500,000. On September 18 came the most spectacular failure, that of Jay Cooke & Co., which fell under the weight of its loans to the Northern Pacific and investments in other western railroads. Jay Cooke & Co. and other railroad houses failed because they were unable to raise loans on their railroad collateral to meet demands. On the failure of Jay Cooke & Co. the stock market and the call-loan market became so demoralized that there was practically no chance to get aid. Other railroad bankers, stockbrokers, and a few large banks (one of which had advanced $1,750,000 to the Michigan Southern) failed within a few days after the Cookes.

On September 20 the Stock Exchange was closed. Four days later the New York Clearing House banks practically suspended cash payments. This was followed by widespread suspension of cash payments by inland banks—some had already suffered from the failure of banks in New York.

The first opinion on the panic expressed by the leading financial paper of the country was that this was merely a financial flurry growing out of the fact that certain railroads had over-reached themselves.[23] This proved not to be true, for a long and severe depression followed. The question arises whether the depressing elements were of a later development or whether down beneath the surface there had existed in the business system fundamental weaknesses. Indeed, business in 1866–73 may well be looked upon as resting on the inflation of the war years, and the panic of 1873 as the major postwar panic.

From late 1873 until late 1878 business in the United States—as indeed in Europe also—was in deep depression. "Business since 1873," said the *Commercial & Financial Chronicle* of January 18, 1879, "has been like a retreating army on a terrible march." Prices of commodities, land, and securities fell greatly. There were widespread failures; railroads suffered severely, especially those in the West, a region which was hit very badly. There was stagnation in trade and industry, and unemployment was severe. There were severe labor strikes and railroad rate wars. Chaos reigned in the anthracite in-

[19] The most useful treatment of the panic of 1873 is O. M. W. Sprague's "History of Crises under the National Banking System," in *The National Banking System,* a publication of the National Monetary Commission (Washington, 1911).

[20] *Bankers' Magazine,* June, 1873, p. 997.

[21] Sprague, *op. cit.,* p. 34.

[22] *Commercial & Financial Chronicle* beginning Sept. 13, 1873, records the progress of the difficulties with emphasis on conditions in New York.

[23] *Ibid.,* Sept. 20, 1873, p. 374.

dustry, where combinations had broken down. And there was agitation for currency inflation in the West. Foreign trade decreased greatly, imports falling off more than exports, and gold and silver exports being heavy in most of those years.

Late in 1878 business began to loosen up, and from 1879 to 1882 there was revival and prosperity.[24] Prices rose, there was a strong upturn in foreign trade, and industry and trade showed considerable activity. Railroad construction reached a new high in 1882, and in the same year immigration rose to an unprecedented peak. At times there was unusually active speculation. These years appear to have been good as far as profits were concerned.

But in 1883 business men began to lament over the narrowing margin of returns. This became more or less chronic. "Trade large, competition keen, profits small, and prices showing a weakening tendency," was the burden of the refrain in the business press. In May, 1884, came a severe financial panic. Until 1885 there was a considerable drop in prices and a heavy liquidation of firms. There was depression in industry and trade, followed by severe unemployment, strikes, and a falling-off in railroad construction. Unrest was general.

Business began to revive in 1885, and by 1887 it was on the whole flourishing. In the latter year came a boom in western lands, tremendous railroad construction, and widespread activity. In 1888 business became somewhat spotty. In the next year, however, there was great activity which lasted into 1890. In the last half of 1890 came severe recession, with declining commodity and stock prices, tight money, and many failures among bankers and brokers in November. Conditions improved late in 1891; and 1892 saw great business activity, active foreign trade (especially imports), and declining commodity and railroad stock prices but advancing industrial securities. There was strong agitation for cheaper money and much labor disturbance.

The year 1893 began with recession. The fear that gold payments would break down under the weight of silver, with resulting inflation, made the federal government act to protect the gold reserve and maintain gold payments. In May came a violent panic: prices collapsed; foreign trade and business activity in general declined greatly; failures were widespread; railroad receivership piled up to a terrific total. In the West came the ugly twins of poor crops and low prices.

This was the beginning of four years of almost continuous deep depression: prices pressed downward; failures and reorganizations were heavy; foreign trade fell off; business in general stagnated; unemployment was severe; strikes were common. And the farmer was leaning toward radical measures for stimulating recovery.

B. Profit and loss, 1866–97.

Throughout most of the years 1866–97 business men in general were dissatisfied with profits. Indeed, contemporary comment contains a considerable amount of lament over low profits. Of course the contemporary is notoriously incapable of estimating the amount of good or evil, but his judgment concerning the existence of good or evil is worthy of every attention.

Unfortunately there exists little trustworthy information on profits of the kind that would be most useful to this study. Manufacturing profits too often depend on fortuitous circumstance, such as the buying of the raw material during a break in the market. Dividends, for a variety of reasons, do not always represent earning. The scraps of information which do exist have meaning only of a general kind.

If the most important part of business is profits, then we are at this point confronted with the crux of the whole matter. It is to be regretted that there are so few data concerning business earnings for this period. Probably bank earnings, as re-

[24] For more details on business conditions in this period see Thorp, *op. cit.*, pp. 133–134, 137.

flected in dividends over a long period, are indicative of conditions in business as a whole. Bank earnings and dividends, as given in Table 2, exhibit a remarkable steadiness throughout the decade of the 'eighties; but it is noteworthy that they do not regain the ground lost in the 'seventies and that a decided drop comes in the 'nineties.

Table 2. NET EARNINGS AND DIVIDENDS OF NATIONAL BANKS 1870–97

Year ended March 31	Dividends to capital	Dividends to capital and surplus	Net earnings to capital and surplus
	%	%	%
1870	10.5	8.8	11.8
1871	.1	8.3	10.4
1872	10.0	8.2	10.2
1873	10.3	8.4	10.7
1874	9.9	7.9	10.3
1875	10.1	7.9	9.5
1876	9.8	7.8	8.1
1877	8.9	7.0	6.3
1878	8.6	6.8	5.3
1879	7.6	6.1	4.8
1880	7.8	6.2	6.7
1881	8.2	6.4	8.4
1882	8.6	6.7	9.5
1883	8.6	6.7	8.6
1884	8.2	6.4	8.6
1885	7.8	6.1	6.9
1886	7.9	6.1	7.3
1887	7.9	6.1	8.5
1888	7.9	6.1	8.8
1889	7.9	6.0	8.7
1890	8.1	6.1	8.6
1891	7.9	5.9	8.9
1892	7.5	5.6	7.8
1893	7.5	5.5	7.4
1894	6.8	5.0	5.6
1895	6.9	5.0	5.0
1896	6.9	5.0	5.4
1897	6.7	4.8	5.4

The biggest corporate employer of capital in the United States in this period was the railroad. The dividend record of railroads is not a clear indication of success because financial and accounting policies varied greatly; weak roads frequently paid dividends out of loans and, in case of reorganization, were freed from part of their burden of debt. There was, however, generally a downward trend in railroad dividends during the period. This is seen even in the experience of the most successful roads. The dividends of the New York, New Haven & Hartford fell from 10 per cent in 1867 to 8 per cent in 1897; the New York Central's from 6 per cent in 1866 to 4 per cent in 1897; and the Chicago, Burlington & Quincy's from 10 per cent in 1866 to 4 per cent in 1897.[25] A compilation of railroad dividends which begins with 1882 reveals a steady attrition of earnings. The average dividend rate on all roads fell from 2.93 per cent in 1882 to 1.49 per cent in 1897, while the average rate on those actually paying dividends fell from 6.10 per cent in 1882 to 5.17 per cent in 1897.[26] The larger eastern roads and a few middle western ones on the whole showed the best results. In all sections there were unprofitable roads, as Table 3 indicates,[27] but the northeastern section of the United States consistently showed better results than did the Far West and the South.

Table 3. PERCENTAGE OF RAILROAD STOCK NOT PAYING DIVIDENDS 1882 and 1897

	1882	1897
New England Group	30.26	19.96
Middle Group	40.44	61.40
North Central Group	50.39	52.94
South Atlantic Group	69.04	91.73
South Central Group	77.56	90.24
Southwestern Group	67.26	95.17
Northwestern Group	53.15	76.93
Pacific Group	44.89	93.47
United States	51.89	71.13

[25] Joseph G. Martin, *History of the Boston Stock and Money Markets* (Boston, 1898), pp. 149–157.

[26] *Poor's Manual of Railroads*, 1900, p. lxv.

[27] *Ibid.*, pp. lxii–lxv.

Table 4 indicates even a more significant trend in yields of railroad bonds over the period.[28] A very scholarly and detailed study of the yield of railroad bonds, by Dr. F. R. Macaulay, shows the same general movement.[29]

On manufacturing we have less information than on railroads. Table 5 (p. 722) gives the dividends of the first twelve in an alphabetical list of New England textile companies which operated throughout the whole period.[30]

Some industries more recently organized on a large scale gave excellent returns throughout most of the period. An illustration is flour milling. Minneapolis millers showed increased profits after important technical improvements had enabled them to make good flour from spring wheat. In 1871, the first year of the "purifier," profits are said to have been 50 cents a barrel; in 1872, $1.00; in 1873, $2.00; in 1874, $4.00 to $4.50. It must be remembered that the increase in output was very great at the same time. These excessive increments did not persist during the later part of the 'seventies, but the introduction of the roller process gave fresh impetus to the rise, and profits are said again to have reached $3.00 a barrel. Competition soon thereafter became very severe, and in the later 'eighties the passing of dividends was general.[31]

Several individual companies for which we have profit figures bear witness to the fact that high profits were possible even in this period. The profits of Carnegie's company, for example, were considerable. In the years 1881–88 the lowest annual profit was 20 per cent and the highest 69 per cent. In 1890 the net profit was $5,500,000; during the next five years it fell off to $3,000,000 and $4,000,000. From 1875 to 1900 this company rolled up a total of $133,000,000.[32] Armour & Co., for which we have figures for 1869–96, except the one year 1880, in those years never made less than 5.6 per cent on net worth and even made as high as 77.1 per cent.[33] Another case of success is that of the Dennison Manufacturing Co. From 1879 to 1893, inclusive, improvements were made out of profits, and stock dividends raised the capital stock from $150,000 to $1,000,000; and yet during this period the lowest cash dividend was 10 per cent and the highest 35 per cent.[34]

[28] Standard Statistics Co., Inc., *Standard Statistical Bulletin, Base Book,* Jan., 1932, p. 134.

[29] F. R. Macaulay, *Some Theoretical Problems Suggested by the Movements of Interest Rates, Bond Yields and Stock Prices in the United States since 1856* (New York, 1938).

[30] Martin, *op. cit.*, pp. 131, 133, 136.

[31] C. B. Kuhlmann, *The Development of the Flour-Milling Industry in the United States* (New York, 1929), p. 119.

[32] Burton J. Hendrick, *The Life of Andrew Carnegie,* 2 vols. (Garden City, New York, 1932).

[33] *Report of Federal Trade Commission on the Meat-Packing Industry* (1920), part v, p. 21,

[34] See case on the Dennison Manufacturing Co., p. 442.

Table 4. PERCENTAGE YIELD OF HIGH-GRADE AMERICAN RAILROAD BONDS, 1866–97

Year	Average	Year	Average	Year	Average	Year	Average
1866	6.389	1874	5.901	1882	4.198	1890	3.668
1867	6.327	1875	5.458	1883	4.218	1891	3.834
1868	6.259	1876	5.169	1884	4.166	1892	3.713
1869	6.523	1877	5.183	1885	3.967	1893	3.820
1870	6.408	1878	5.103	1886	3.695	1894	3.604
1871	6.334	1879	4.763	1887	3.760	1895	3.474
1872	6.185	1880	4.468	1888	3.686	1896	3.518
1873	6.214	1881	4.141	1889	3.543	1897	3.322

In contrast with the foregoing moderate or high profits is the large number of failures in business. The bankrupt we have always with us; he is the incapable or the unfortunate. When prices are good and trade brisk, his chance of failure is less than when business presses downward and depression sets in. In good times he may be carried along by others if he gets into distress, but in depression he must stand alone. Statistics on failures do not tell the whole story. Liabilities involved in failures are of much greater importance from an economic point of view than are the crude numbers or percentages of firms failing. Liabilities, more-

Table 5. DIVIDENDS OF NEW ENGLAND TEXTILE MANUFACTURING COMPANIES, 1866–97

(Percentage of capital)

Year	Amoskeag	Androscoggin	Appleton	Atlantic Cotton Mills	Bates	Boott Cotton Mills	Boston	Boston Duck	Chicopee
1866	22	45	20	14	35	16	10	14	45
1867	20	25	10	3	5	10	16	8	28
1868	16	10	20	7	5	15	15	8	35
1869	17	11	12	7	0	12	16	8	40
1870	10	8	9	3	6	11	10	3	18
1871	13 [a]	5	14	8	4	20	11	10	70
1872	18	10	12	8	10	20	12	11	50
1873	14	10	9	8	8	16	8	10	30
1874	14	10	3	0	8	12½	6	10	10
1875	9	9	0	3	0	8	6	8	5
1876	9	6	0	0	3	8	6	6	7
1877	8	6	0	3	6	9	6	7	7
1878	10	3	0	6	3	7	6	7	7
1879	10	3	0	6	8	10	6	8	8
1880	10	8	3	8	9	10	7	9	10
1881	11	10	6	10	12	10	6	10	12
1882	10 [b]	10	6	10	13	12	6	10	12
1883	13	10	6	10	12	12	6	10	11
1884	10	10	3	6	10	3	6	8	7
1885	10	7	0	0	6	5	6	6	0
1886	10	6	0	0	6	5	6	9	0
1887	10 [a]	7	0	3	7	7	7	10	6
1888	10	8	0	6	8	8	8	10	6
1889	10	10	0	6	9	8	5	10	6
1890	10	10	4	6	9	8	8	10	6
1891	10	10	4	5	9	8	7	10	6
1892	10	10	4	5	9	8	6	10 [a]	6
1893	7½	10	2	6	9	6½	4½	10	6
1894	4 [c]	8	0	3	6	3	2	8	5
1895	7	6	0	2	6	6	4	8	2
1896	7	6	0	4	6	4	0	8	3
1897	5	5	0	2	6	0	0	8	2

[a] Extra dividends this year.

[b] 5 extra, March.

[c] Changed dividend periods from Feb. and Aug. to June and Dec. in 1871, and back to Feb. 1 and Aug. 1 in 1895.

over, are expressed in dollars, which fact conceals their importance to a certain extent.[35]

Table 6, which obviously does not provide an adequate basis for comparison, nevertheless gives some interesting figures on business failures in the United States.[36] It shows the same ups and downs as in other series of business statistics, but on the whole the average ran high for the years 1873–97. The panic year 1873 did not have relatively so great an increase in the number failing as in the average liability. The number failing increased greatly in the next five years, but the average liability was much smaller. This suggests that there may be a sequence in the timing of failures which has some relationship to size.

Bankruptcy statistics must be used with care. Not all failures in business end in bankruptcy, for some result in sale of the business, in reorganization, or in merger with other units. In any interpretation of bankruptcy statistics, moreover, we must give most attention not to the absolute figures but to the ratio to population or, even better, to the total business situation.

In the United States, bank failures have been something of a barometer of business conditions. Unfortunately, statistics on State and private banks, which constituted a large proportion of banking in those years, are not available. National bank failures followed the business cycle. Table 7 (p. 724) is significant only as it illustrates a trend.[37] A large number of banks went into voluntary liquidation or were consolidated with other banks; many of them were probably in a weak condition.

[35] Carl Snyder, *Business Cycles and Business Measurements* (New York, 1927), pp. 182–183.

[36] Roger W. Babson, *Business Barometers,* 1925, pp. 251–253, and 1931, p. 103. This table was compiled from figures of R. G. Dun & Co.

[37] For an explanation as to how this table was compiled see National Monetary Commission, vol. xxi, *Statistics for the United States, 1867–1909,* pp. 40–41.

Table 6. FAILURE STATISTICS FOR THE UNITED STATES 1866–97

Year	No. of failures	Liabilities in millions	Percentage of failures to total no. of firms	Year	No. of failures	Liabilities in millions	Percentage of failures to total no. of firms
1866	1,505	$53.8	.94	1882	6,738	$101.5	.83
1867	2,780	96.7	1.33	1883	9,184	172.9	1.06
1868	2,608	63.7	.94	1884	10,968	226.3	1.21
1869	2,799	75.0	.79	1885	10,637	124.2	1.16
1870	3,546	88.2	.83	1886	9,834	114.6	1.01
1871	2,915	85.2	.61	1887	9,634	167.6	...
1872	4,069	121.1	.77	1888	10,679	123.8	...
1873	5,183	228.5	.93	1889	10,882	148.8	...
1874	5,830	155.2	.97	1890	10,907	189.9	...
1875	7,740	201.0	1.21	1891	12,273	189.9	...
1876	9,092	191.1	1.33	1892	10,344	114.0	...
1877	8,872	190.7	1.36	1893	15,242	346.8	1.28
1878	10,478	234.4	1.55	1894	13,885	172.9	1.25
1879	6,658	98.1	...	1895	13,197	173.2	1.09
1880	4,735	65.8	...	1896	15,088	226.1	1.31
1881	5,582	81.2	.71	1897	13,351	154.3	...

Table 7. NATIONAL BANK FAILURES
1866–97

Year	Total number in operation	Number of failures
1866	1,644	2
1867	1,642	7
1868	1,643	3
1869	1,617	2
1870	1,615	...
1871	1,767	...
1872	1,919	6
1873	1,976	11
1874	2,004	3
1875	2,088	5
1876	2,089	9
1877	2,080	10
1878	2,053	14
1879	2,048	8
1880	2,090	3
1881	2,132	...
1882	2,269	3
1883	2,501	2
1884	2,664	11
1885	2,714	4
1886	2,852	8
1887	3,049	8
1888	3,140	8
1889	3,290	2
1890	3,540	9
1891	3,677	25
1892	3,773	17
1893	3,781	65
1894	3,755	21
1895	3,712	36
1896	3,676	27
1897	3,610	38

For no business group are such complete statistics on business difficulties available as for railroads. Railroad receiverships in those years tell a story of almost chronic hard times. Receiverships were most frequently the result of failure to pay interest on mortgage bonds. This might be the result of a number of circumstances—too heavy indebtedness, too low earnings, or both. See Table 8.[38]

Table 8. RAILROAD RECEIVERSHIP
1870–97

Year	Receiverships established: Number	Receiverships established: Percentage of total mileage	Number in receivership January 1	Percentage of total mileage in receivership January 1
1870	3	1.00	...	...
1871	4	1.07	...	...
1872	4	0.81	6	1.56
1873	10	1.93	9	2.17
1874	33	6.10	17	3.31
1875	43	9.91	45	8.87
1876	25	6.14	75	16.56
1877	33	3.91	85	18.19
1878	27	2.90	94	16.42
1879	12	1.27	95	15.51
1880	13	1.01	73	11.67
1881	5	0.11	54	7.31
1882	13	0.79	29	3.66
1883	12	1.68	27	3.35
1884	40	6.96	23	2.82
1885	44	5.86	54	7.47
1886	12	1.17	76	12.41
1887	10	0.74	68	8.54
1888	22	2.05	51	5.76
1889	24	2.35	52	5.28
1890	20	1.48	50	5.16
1891	29	1.18	54	5.61
1892	40	2.46	60	4.13
1893	132	15.51	77	4.84
1894	50	2.31	191	19.41
1895	32	1.78	182	18.60
1896	39	2.03	171	17.10
1897	21	0.83	146	9.68

[38] H. H. Swain, *Economic Aspects of Railroad Receiverships* (New York, 1898), pp. 68, 70–71.

6. Suggested Readings

W. L. Thorp, *Business Annals* (New York, 1926), pp. 131–138. This work provides a year-to-year description of business conditions.

Simon S. Kuznets, *Secular Movements in Production and Prices* (Boston, 1930), chap. i. Very suggestive on retardation of industrial growth in the United States.

Alfred E. Cowles, 3rd, and Associates, *Common-Stock Indexes, 1871–1937* (Bloomington, Indiana, 1938).

A. F. Burns, *Production Trends in the United States since 1870* (New York, 1934). Though this is primarily a theoretical treatment of the subject of retardation of industrial growth, it has great value to the historian.

L. H. Haney, *Business Organization and Combination* (New York, 1920).

D. A. Wells, *Recent Economic Changes* (New York, 1890), is good on conditions shortly after the Civil War.

E. C. Kirkland, *A History of American Economic Life* (New York, 1939). For general economic background this book is good.

B. J. Hendrick, *The Life of Andrew Carnegie*, 2 vols. (New York, 1932). This work is suggested since it illustrates something of the business opportunities and methods of the time. It gives a striking picture of a leading industrial capitalist.

7. Suggested Questions

1. If you assume that there is a secular trend of business, when was the beginning of the trend with which we are dealing (1866, 1873, or at some other time) and when was the end? Give reasons for reply.
2. What factors do you think responsible for the trend of business between 1866 and 1897?
3. If you had been entering business in 1896, which industry would you have preferred to be associated with, if living in each of these cities: Minneapolis, Chicago, New York, Boston?
4. How could you reconcile general progress in production with a downward trend in business in this period? Compare 1815–43.
5. If you had been asked to advise John Wanamaker in 1874, what general long-range policies would you have recommended to him? To the management of Armour & Co.?

XLII. BUSINESS PROSPERITY AND THE RECOMBINATION OF BUSINESS FUNCTIONS IN A PERIOD OF RISING PRICES 1897–1920

1. General Statement

In this period a hundred-year cycle was completed in the organization of American business. Early in the nineteenth century the diversified functions of the sedentary merchant had begun to break down into specialized units; specialization had become the rule in 1843–66; in 1866–97 business men had come to see the grave dangers from competition in a system made up of specialized units with heavy investments in capital. In 1897–1920, therefore, business leaders sought to overcome those dangers. They sought security in control, both horizontal and vertical. In doing this they again combined the various functions in one organization, thus returning to the system of the sedentary merchant, but the new system differed from the old in that it was a combination of *specialized* units.

The growth of combination during the period 1897–1920 was assisted, if not made possible, by the upward trend of prices. The exact relationship between the two cannot be indicated. Certainly this is true: where there is a change in the price structure and a chance for business to adjust itself, business usually does the thing that is most pressing. In the earlier period the old system of specialization seems to have ceased making satisfactory profits. Under the downward drive of prices something could be done in the way of adjustment, particularly along technical and mechanical lines, but two things were clearly necessary before there could be a genuine reorganization of business to meet the mounting problems of specialization. It was a long and difficult process to learn how to manage a large and complicated business organization and to build up a management personnel; before that had been done, large combinations were not practicable. Beyond that was the fact that capital was not available for reorganization on satisfactory terms before there were prospects of profits. The upward turn of prices and the promised and realized profits which came with improving prices made capital eager to enter into the reorganization of business along new lines. This fact had an important bearing on the whole combination movement.

2. General View of the Period

1897	Price trend turned upward. Republicans returned to control of federal government. High protective tariff. Great increase in world production of gold. Excellent crop in United States.
1897–98	Revival.
1897–1903	Formation of many great combinations.
1898	United States acquired possessions in Caribbean and Pacific.
1898–1903	Unusual prosperity.
1899	Boom in immigration began.
1900	Gold Standard Act.
1901	Roosevelt became president. United States Steel Corporation formed.
1902	Federal intervention in anthracite coal strike.
1903	Laws for federal regulation of corporations. Recession.
1904	Northern Securities decision dissolved railroad holding company. Depression and revival.
1905–06	Prosperity.
1906	Further regulation of corporations.
1907	Panic.
1907–08	Depression.
1909	Revival. Higher tariff.
1910	Recession. Prewar peak of commodity price index.
1911	Mild depression. Standard Oil and American Tobacco trusts dissolved.
1912–13	Revival and prosperity.
1913	Wilson elected to curb big business. Recession.
1914	Depression. Federal Reserve System established. Clayton Anti-Trust Act passed. Federal Trade Commission established. Panama Canal opened.
1915	United States Steel Corporation upheld by Supreme Court.
1915–18	War prosperity.
1917	United States entered War. Extensive government regulation of business for war began.
1918	Postwar recession.
1919–20	Revival and prosperity.
1920	All-time peak in commodity prices in United States. Transportation Act recognized weakness of competition.

3. Upward Price Trend, 1897–1920

A. The behavior of prices.

In 1897 began a rise in the price level which, with some short interruptions and with rapid acceleration during the World War, continued until it reached a climax in 1920. The general price index rose at an average annual rate of 2.35 per cent from 1896 to 1913 and very rapidly thereafter until some time after the War was over. Warren and Pearson's general index of commodity prices rose from 68 in 1897 to 102 in 1913 and 226 in 1920.[1] Concerning the significance of the price change

[1] G. F. Warren and F. A. Pearson, *Prices* (New York, 1933), pp. 26–27.

at this time, F. C. Mills makes the following statement: [2]

"The rising tendency in the level of prices during the two decades prior to the war, a tendency shared by every commodity group in the United States, provided one of the most fundamental of the conditions under which business men of that era worked. It affected manufacturing methods and buying and selling habits, and was reflected in numerous business practices. . . ."

The long-time trend of the general price level does not tell the whole story of price change. The great variability in prices of individual commodities from time to time was a significant feature of the change. Commodity prices changed relatively abruptly from month to month and from year to year. This instability tended to decline just before the War, but it became relatively high again during and right after the conflict.[3] "These changes," says Mills, "introduced a considerable degree of uncertainty into business operations, and enhanced the speculative features of business operations." [4] On the whole, manufactured goods were more stable than raw materials.[5]

There was also great variability in the rate of change of different commodities. One investigation gives the average annual percentage rate of price change for 1896–1913 for groups of commodities as follows: [6] all commodities, 2.3; farm products, 3.4; foods, 2.3; building materials, 2.4; metal and metal products, 0.8; fuel and lighting, 2.1; cloth and clothing, 1.8; house furnishings, 1.4; chemicals and drugs, 0.5.

Another study gives the percentage change for other groups of commodities.[7] From 1896 to 1913 raw materials rose at an average rate of 3.02 per cent each year (forest products, 4.13 per cent; minerals, 2.05 per cent; farm products, 3.73 per cent; animal products, 3.05 per cent); producers' goods increased at the rate of a little below 1 per cent; while consumers' goods increased at the rate of 2.32 per cent. The difference in the rate of change in producers' and consumers' goods may have been the result of a change in costs, one probable source of difference being that the decline of distribution costs (which weigh more heavily on consumers' goods) may not have been comparable to the decline of other costs.

On the significance of this type of price variation, F. C. Mills has the following to say: [8]

"In the high variability of individual prices prior to the war, and in all that that implies, we have, I think, one of the most significant conditions which gave to prewar economic life its characteristic tone, and in the downward trend of this variability we have one of the most important of the tendencies which marked the economic development of this period. The conditions of high price variability and marked disturbance in price relations offer opportunities to business men for those conjunctural profits which result from faulty economic adjustments and temporary dislocations. A rising price level, coupled with variable individual prices, represents a happy hunting ground, indeed, for the speculative elements in the business world."

In looking at individual business units and industries one can see how those who were fortunate and farsighted in the conduct of their business could make profits out of price variability. In a static condition there would, presumably, be no such profits. Business usually stands, moreover,

[2] Conference on Unemployment (1921), Committee on Recent Economic Changes, *Recent Economic Changes* (New York, 1929), vol. ii, p. 609.

[3] *Ibid.*, p. 612.

[4] *Ibid.*, p. 613; also see F. C. Mills, *Economic Tendencies* (New York, 1932), pp. 54–55.

[5] *Ibid.*, p. 63.

[6] *Recent Economic Changes,* vol. ii, p. 623.

[7] F. C. Mills, "Post-War Prices and Pre-War Trends," *Proceedings of the American Statistical Association,* 1928, pp. 54–57.

[8] *Recent Economic Changes,* vol. ii, pp. 613–614.

to profit from a rise in prices. The cost of fixed capital and wages tends to lag behind wholesale prices. Inventories appreciate in value. A constant adjustment is going on, it is true, but it is an adjustment which is advantageous to capital and management on the whole.

B. Monetary changes, 1897–1920.

In this period we note the coincidence of rising prices and an unusually high world gold production, a striking contrast to the falling prices and the relatively low gold output of the previous period. Table 1 indicates the changes in gold production and illustrates Warren's and Pearson's theory regarding the relationship of gold output and prices.[9]

The relationship of gold production and prices is, of course, an extremely controversial matter. On the one side is the gold school of theorists who maintain that the amount of monetary gold stocks (relative to the amount of money work to be done) is the fundamental factor; on the other side are those who hold that it is the velocity of monetary circulation, including the various uses of credit, which is the more significant.

The increased gold production of the late 1890's, however, affected both the amount of monetary gold and the velocity of circulation. The first is obvious; the second requires explanation. Ever since the Civil War a strong fight had been raging in the United States over monetary inflation which had come to involve the question of maintaining the gold standard. This was in reality a part of a world movement toward a bimetallic standard. The movement introduced uncertainty about money, which no doubt had something to do with the deflation of the early 1890's.

[9] George F. Warren and Frank A. Pearson, *Gold and Prices* (New York, 1935), p. 133.

Table 1. WORLD GOLD PRODUCTION, MONETARY STOCKS OF GOLD AND PRICES IN THE UNITED STATES, 1845–1929 [a]

Five-year periods	Average annual world's production of gold, 000 fine ounces	Estimated world's stock of monetary gold at end of the year, 000,000 fine ounces	Ratio of gold production to monetary stocks (in per cent)	Per cent change in index numbers of wholesale prices (1880–1914 = 100)
1880–1914	12,293	231	5.3	...
1845–49	1,780	49	3.6	0
1850–54	5,570	63	8.8	+ 9
1855–59	6,502	89	7.3	+12
1860–64	5,885	107	5.5	Civil
1865–69	6,309	122	5.2	War
1870–74	5,640	136	4.1	− 1
1875–79	5,285	146	3.6	−17
1880–84	4,921	154	3.2	+ 5
1885–89	5,361	162	3.3	−17
1890–94	7,109	178	4.0	− 7
1895–99	11,907	209	5.7	− 9
1900–04	14,391	249	5.8	+20
1905–09	20,246	304	6.7	+10
1910–14	22,116	362	6.1	+ 7
1915–19	20,285	433	4.7	World War
1920–24	16,876	481	3.5	+ 1
1925–29	19,401	525	3.7	−10

[a] Based on averages for periods.

The Bryan free silver campaign of 1896 helped further to drive capital into hiding and to frighten the entrepreneur into inactivity. The increase in gold production which began to be apparent in 1897 destroyed the basis for the bimetallists, the free silver movement, and currency depreciation in general. The Gold Standard Act of 1900 recognized in law that the cheap-money bogey, which had been harassing American business ever since 1862, had been destroyed. Altogether, these developments resulted in confidence which helped to bring inactive funds back into activity.

A further change came with the Federal Reserve System. Under the new system the relatively inelastic bank currency of the preceding fifty years was increased by the new Federal Reserve notes based on the discounting of commercial paper. Though the discount rate affected the supply of commercial paper, the flexibility of note issue was much greater than when the national bank notes alone supplied bank currency.

4. Business Administration

A. The rise of new industries.

A significant indication of the activity of business in any period is its production of goods and services. For the earlier periods we had no definite measure of either, though services were probably of small importance compared with goods. No very helpful measurements of the growth of service industries are available for any period, but one may conclude from general observation that there has been in recent decades a progressive increase in those industries which have had to do with the production of services rather than goods. The railroad, telegraph, telephone, and the gas and electric industries (fundamentally, of course, manufacturing industries) have grown with great rapidity since the later decades of the nineteenth century. It is on commodity production, however, that we have the most conclusive and most useful information.

One study of the production of goods, *Production Trends in the United States since 1870,*[10] by A. F. Burns, points to some very important developments in American business in 1897–1920. It reveals fluctuations in the total physical production from time to time, but a slight increase in the annual rate of production over the period. Dr. Burns found a close relationship between the two rhythms of the secular trend and the cycle. "Each time the national economy has experienced an exceptionally rapid secular advance, the production trends of different industries have diverged so widely as to suggest a partial loss of balance, and progress has been checked by a business depression of great severity." [11] Does this suggest that depressions are more frequent in an upward secular trend of production?

Dr. Burns emphasizes the variations in the behavior of different industries. He shows that there were great differences in the relative amplitude of the swing of different types of products away from the general pattern of business fluctuations. Farm products, the precious metals, and petroleum were more or less erratic. Producers' goods experienced larger fluctuations than consumers' goods. Those branches of production which were subject to close business control conformed more closely to the movements of general business than did those industries which were highly competitive.[12]

It is obvious that the rates of long-time change of different groups of industries vary. Persons' index of the annual physical production [13] shows for the years 1897–1920 that the production of manufactured goods increased less rapidly than the production of minerals, but both increased

[10] Published in 1934 by the National Bureau of Economic Research.

[11] *Ibid.*, pp. xviii–xix.

[12] *Ibid.*, pp. xix–xx.

[13] Warren M. Persons, *Forecasting Business Cycles* (New York, 1931), pp. 170–171.

faster than crop production. The last of these conformed more closely to changes in population.

Greatest of all are the variations among individual industries. Burns believes that there is some reason to think that the life of industries was becoming shorter. "A growing share of production is assuming the form of luxuries, superfluities and style goods; the demand for such products has no such stability as the demand for staples. Hence an increase in the birth-rate of new products means an increase in the death-rate among old products and a decline in the average life-span of individual industries."[14]

For the period 1897–1920 the birth of new industries was more striking than the death of old ones. The electrical and automotive industries, with all the related industries, such as rubber, metals, and so on, showed a tremendous growth. The airplane industry was in its beginning. These changes had far-reaching effects on other industries. A few, such as the manufacture of buggies and bicycles, almost disappeared.

The changes in production suggest some general observations. The years 1897–1920 were a highly dynamic period. There was a tremendous competition between the new and the old in industry. There was apparently great opportunity for the business man who scrapped the old and entered the new industry in time to take advantage of the rapid upward swing which new industries generally experience in their earlier years. We should like to know the generating forces behind this dynamic situation. It will be remembered that in the earlier period of falling prices there was a similar expansion in production. Was this not, however, expansion in basic industries which were already established? Is it probable that a more favorable price situation encouraged new ventures of a type which might not have been risked in the earlier situation?

[14] Burns, *op. cit.*, p. xviii.

B. Business turns to combination.

The directing element in this dynamic situation in production was the business administrator. It was he who drove toward the search for new materials, new mechanical and scientific techniques, and new markets or demands; and it was the business leader who shaped the organization of business with a view toward profits and greater profits. How did business organize itself in 1897–1920? What forms did its efforts take, and why? What larger forces did business bend to its needs?

Three developments in the organization of business in this period are of fundamental significance. First, the corporation —which in America reached back into the eighteenth century in banking and insurance, to the beginning of railroad history, and to 1813 in textile manufacture—began about 1890 to be adopted much more widely than before by all types of business; within the present period it became the rule in large American business concerns. Second, the movement toward horizontal combination, that is, the combination of units performing like processes or functions, increased greatly the size of units performing a specialized function. And, third, the movement toward vertical combination, which characterized this period, brought the union of successive or related processes or functions.

The combination movement, both horizontal and vertical, was well under way by 1897. From 1898 to 1903 there was a real mania for combination. It came in every field where large-scale business was possible. Among the industrial combinations organized from 1897 to 1903 were the American Tin Plate Co., American Car and Foundry, International Paper, Otis Elevator, Standard Oil of New Jersey, United Shoe Machinery, Standard Sanitary Manufacturing Co., American Radiator, United States Steel, American Can, International Harvester, Corn Products Co., and International Nickel. Similarly, great combinations were organized to control gas, electric lighting, and street railways of large sections of the country. The railroads were also combined into great systems, a movement which had started in the earlier period. Among these the Hill-Morgan, the Harriman, and, later, the New Haven group were conspicuous.

The movement quieted down after 1903. Various reasons for this are given, such as the Northern Securities decision, government hostility in general, and the stock-market panic of 1903. The fact that most of the available industries had by then been organized and that there was a depression following 1903 would be sufficient to explain the slackening of the movement.

In 1907 the movement revived. From 1907 until the War the organization of holding companies flourished, but in the meantime government opposition had become very strong. In 1911 several "monopolies" were dissolved by the Supreme Court. Beginning in 1914, however, the government, as will be seen later, differentiated more clearly than before between "good" and "bad" monopolies and aimed to restrain and correct rather than to destroy.

Various explanations have been made of the combination movement. Capital, which had long lain dormant out of fear, was eager to buy the issues of the new concerns. Investment bankers, who had suffered from a dearth of work for many years, pushed the movement for what they could earn from the organization and reorganization involved. Mere megalomania, the fashion for size, was undoubtedly a factor; how important, it is impossible to say. There was also a widespread belief that there were economies in size and in integration. And certainly an important element in the movement, probably the most important, was the need of controlling competitive excesses, which were especially hard on business firms with a heavy investment in fixed assets.

The most powerful form of control—more powerful even than a monopolistic organization within an industry—was that which the investment bankers came to hold over business in this period. The active participation of the banker in industry and transportation was seen in its beginning in the earlier period. Its golden age was, however, the period 1897–1920. Again, the motives were probably varied: to secure more efficient management, to bring about a better coördination in a business system suffering from chaotic competition, and to assure bankers of a hold on potential business.

Banker control assumed various forms. The Pujo Committee of 1912–13 reported that such control was accomplished through the consolidation of banks and trust companies into sympathetic groups which secured influence "in the management of insurance companies, railroads, producing and trading corporations, and public utility corporations, by means of stockholdings, voting trusts, fiscal agency contracts, or representation upon their boards of directors, or through supplying the money requirements of railway, industrial, and public utilities corporations and thereby being enabled to participate in the determination of their financial policies." [15]

This aggressive and powerful business system drove ahead on several fronts. It pushed its control backward into the sources of the materials with which it worked. It drove toward cheaper processes in production. It extended its control in marketing and sought new markets. And at all stages it tended to expand horizontally.

The movement toward obtaining control of raw materials by manufacturing concerns had begun in the earlier period but reached its highest point in 1897–1920. Manufacturing concerns did not attempt to control agriculture; tradition and

[15] *Report of the Committee Appointed . . . to investigate the Concentration of Control of Money and Credit* (62nd Congress, 3rd Sess., 1913, *House Report*, no. 1593), p. 56.

problems of finance and management made such control impractical if not impossible, while the existence of a high degree of competition in the agricultural market made it unnecessary. Control of raw materials was sought chiefly in the extractive industries, that is, in lumbering, mining, and oil production. This was the time when the Weyerhaeusers, U. S. Steel, Standard Oil, U. S. Rubber, Guggenheim copper, and other similar interests reached out for control of resources both at home and abroad. The objects of this reaching back to raw materials were several, but apparently the main one was to obtain an assured supply in the face of possible monopoly or to take advantage of the chance to buy at a good price undeveloped resources in the control of weak governments or financially weak individuals.

In the long process of production, advance was made along several lines. The characteristic development was the application of research to the improvement and cheapening of production. Technical improvements in the earlier period had come largely through the work of men who had risen in the business or of engineers trained in the young technical schools. Research by such men continued in this period, as is illustrated by the work of Edison and Ford, but the tendency was toward specialization in research by men trained especially in the theoretical aspects of a science. Business hired the scientist and the engineer trained in universities and technical schools and put them to work in its own laboratories on its own problems, sometimes even going far out into pure science. Thus, business put to work the phenomenal advances then recently made in chemistry, physics, and engineering.

These commercial scientists discovered new products; they also made improvements which formed the basis of important industries and cut the costs of old. The electrical industry, automobile and airplane construction, the making of rubber, stronger steels, and metal alloys, the beginnings of wireless communication and the radio, and the making of new synthetic materials (such as rayon and composition wood) are striking results of science in business. The remarkable utilization of by-products also came through research.

In the management of production great advances were made. This was the period of the flowering of scientific management. "Taylorism" became both a fad and a necessity. Efficient routing and conveying of work in process, improvements in machinery used, mechanization of the work, specialization of the individual worker's task in order to get the greatest efficiency, speeding up the rate of work, and departmentalizing under specialized managers were all a part of the drive toward cheaper and more closely controlled production.

The same type of development came in office management. Office machinery, efficient filing systems, the employment of specialized workers such as accountants, and departmentalization under specialized managers developed to handle the enormous volume of routine work in large concerns.

The growth of the expert on the outside hired to do a given task on the fee basis was another development in this same direction. Here comes to the front that important type known as the business auxiliary. Although the corporation lawyer had appeared long before this time, it was in 1897–1920 that he attained his full stature. The university professor came to be called upon more and more for advice in given situations. But the newest developments were the public accountant, the commercial geologist, the commercial laboratory technician, the consulting engineer, and the public relations counsel, who specialized as consultants on individual problems in their fields in return for a fee.

In no part of its work did business drive forward harder in this period than in marketing. The specialized business concern and the firm with a heavy fixed investment had to be sure of outlets for their goods. The need of reaching the optimum size in production and the pressure of increasing competition in a sense made marketing the most strategic process in business. As a result, marketing became a highly specialized part of a manufacturing concern's work. It became highly organized and looked toward new methods.

Producers were remarkably successful in this period in extending the market for their goods—indeed, herein may lie the key to the great development of business in the period. They advanced both at home and abroad. In the home market some important developments may be noted. Domestic manufacturers came to be protected by a high tariff wall, largely of their own making. The Republican tariffs of 1897 and 1909 did much to eliminate foreign competition in manufactured goods, while the lower Democratic tariff of 1913 was made ineffective by the fact that the War turned the flow of goods toward Europe. No other highly developed industrial country had so large and varied a free trade area of its own. At the same time the needs and the purchasing power of the home market grew greatly. From 1900 to 1920 the population of the United States increased from 75 million to 105 million. More important to business was the fact that a growing portion of the population came to be engaged in specialized work and had to purchase much or most of its necessities. Most important, perhaps, was the rise in the purchasing power of large groups.[16] The price index of farm products prepared by the Bureau of Labor Statistics shows an increase from 58 in 1897 to 218 in 1920.[17] At the same time the index of money wages of those in the manufacturing, transportation, and coal-mining industries (after allowing for unemployment) rose from 92 to 351; this meant not only an increase in dollar earnings but also a definite increase in real income.[18] And one must not forget that the great number of well-to-do and extremely wealthy people in the United States gave an unprecedented market for luxury goods and services.

The increase in specialization on the part of producers, improved transportation, and the rising purchasing power of all large groups resulted in a market situation such as had never been known on so large a scale. It brought a revolution in production as well as in marketing.

In production there was a striking increase, both absolute and relative, in consumers' goods and services. Prepared and packaged foods, factory-made clothing for women, pianos, phonographs, house furnishings, improved plumbing and heating, household conveniences, particularly electric lights and appliances, and automobiles are a few of the lines of which there was greatly increased sale. The consumption of gas and electricity and the growth in urban and interurban transportation facilities and in travel for leisure as well as work similarly show the same increase in purchasing power. The increase in house building made that field one of the largest consumers of materials and labor.

At the same time American producers were also finding a wider market abroad. They were able to take advantage of changes in world production and demand. The development of new regions made for increased production of agricultural goods for the old-world markets, but it also provided a new market for manufactured articles and machines. The old world continued to take American food products. Capital goods—farm machinery, railroad rails, rolling stock, and engines, mining machinery, and textile machines—found

[16] See W. I. King's work on *The Wealth and Income of the People of the United States* (New York, 1915, 1922, 1930).

[17] United States Bureau of Labor Statistics, *Index Numbers of Wholesale Prices in the United States and Foreign Countries,* Bulletin no. 284, 1921, p. 131.

[18] According to Paul H. Douglas, *Real Wages in the United States, 1890–1926* (New York, 1930), p. 468.

ready sale in the newly developed regions. The War of course brought an unprecedented increase in demand for consumers' necessities, some producers' goods, and war materials.

The trend may be illustrated by figures on exports from the United States for the two five-year periods, 1896–1900 and 1916–20. The proportion of nonagricultural exports rose from an average of 33.8 per cent to 57.9 per cent of the total; finished manufactures rose from 21.3 per cent to 39.6 per cent; semi-manufactures from 9.6 per cent to 15.4 per cent; manufactured foodstuffs fell from 24.0 per cent to 17.7 per cent; and crude materials from 26.1 per cent to 18.2 per cent.[19] The growing importance of manufactured goods reflects the changing pattern of American production. Indeed, without the development of foreign sales of manufactured goods, it would hardly have been possible to expand American industry as it was expanded.

A remarkable shift came in the location of those sales. The proportion sent to Canada almost doubled; South America took almost twice as much at the end as at the beginning of the period; Europe's share fell from 76.7 per cent to 63.2 per cent; Asia's more than doubled; Oceania's and Africa's dropped slightly.[20] For the War years the picture was different, but the very heavy exports to England and France are somewhat obscured by the use of five-year averages.

To sell goods in so extensive a market, oftentimes highly competitive, required new marketing techniques. These developed particularly along the lines of advertising and selling.

It was in this period that advertising as we know it today developed. One distinctive feature was advertising on a national scale under standard brands or trade names. Large concerns began to engage specialists in advertising and employed specialized advertising agencies.

For selling, large companies built up a great system of branches and agencies far beyond what they had earlier had. Flour millers and meat packers came to have sales offices in large domestic wholesale and export markets and also abroad. Machine manufacturers and oil companies similarly had selling agencies in large domestic and foreign markets. With this extension abroad went branches of New York banks, especially among our neighbors to the south, and even branch factories. The new American business man abroad was no longer only a general exporter and importer like the earlier foreign merchant; he was, instead, a representative of Washburn–Crosby Mills, Singer Sewing Machine Co., National City Bank, or Standard Oil.

It must not be concluded that large and powerful combinations carried on all American business in the period. There were still countless small manufacturers, bankers, and middlemen. Some did a local business and some specialized on a small product for a wide market. A firm specializing within one particular function depended on many other firms to serve it in various ways. But the dominant and possibly the most dynamic element in business in 1897–1920 was the powerful combination.

Some questions may be asked at this point about the great combination. Did concentration of control under a few banking firms accomplish anything material toward remedying the evils of poorly coordinated specialization? Did it curb the worst evils of cutthroat competition and thus give to business that measure of security necessary for gaining both profits and the stability which made possible long-time planning? Were the great mergers or the combinations through holding companies successful as administrative de-

[19] United States Bureau of Foreign and Domestic Commerce, "Foreign Trade of the United States," *Trade Information Bulletin*, no. 749, 1930, pp. 16 and 18.

[20] *Ibid.*, pp. 18, 31–32.

vices; that is, were they efficient from the point of view of costs in relation to product? One investigation of the experience of 35 large consolidations found that the earnings of the individual concerns preceding consolidation "were between a fifth and a sixth greater than the average for the ten years following consolidation."[21] Another consideration of importance to business in general is the extent to which the great combinations tended to control, stifle, or stimulate smaller producers working in their fields. And, lastly, what justification was there for the charge that combinations were injurious to the interests of the consumer?

It is impossible at this stage to form any final judgment about the efficiency of the large combination and the value of banker control of business. There were no doubt great weaknesses in administration and there was danger in the misuse of power, but there was also something to be gained from the control of certain competitive menaces. The movement was not, however, allowed to develop completely. Partly because of the consumer's and the small business man's fear of monopoly and partly because of the flagrant misuse of power by the big business man, political movements arose which tended to curb business and which aimed to foster regulated competition.

C. Public regulation.

This development had its roots in the preceding period. In 1866–90 the farmer, laborer, and an occasional business man had combined to check the "evils" of corporations and monopolies. State laws were passed to maintain competition on the part of railways and to regulate other corporations. The counterpart of those laws appeared on the national stage in the Interstate Commerce Act of 1887 and the Sherman Anti-Trust Act of 1890. This legislation, however, did not prove so effective as had been hoped.

[21] A. S. Dewing, *The Financial Policy of Corporations* (New York, 1926), pp. 885-898.

With the return of prosperity at the end of the century came a recrudescence of criticism of business. This was reinforced by recruits from the more conservative elements. Theodore Roosevelt, who succeeded to the office of president in 1901, became its political leader. Its intellectual and emotional leadership came from academic observers, such as Van Hise of the University of Wisconsin, who called attention to the tremendous waste of natural resources at the hands of business; social workers, like Jacob Riis, who made known conditions in the slums; and the new journalism, the muckrakers, who exposed the evils of business.

The muckrakers spoke to the reading public in the main through the new popular magazines, which reached the large middle class. In 1903 *McClure's Magazine* began to publish Ida Tarbell's *History of the Standard Oil,* a critical investigation into the past practices of Rockefeller's concern. Frank Norris wrote the *Octopus,* a story built around speculation; Upton Sinclair's *Jungle* exposed the evils of the meat-packing industry; Churchill's *Coniston* concerned itself with railroads and big business in the political arena.

Thus were advertised the evils of business. The criticism was made effective by what business itself was doing. The formation of huge combinations called attention to its growing power. The uncompromising attitude of the employers in the great anthracite and steel strikes gave further evidence of its strength. At the same time the slums and poverty seemed to get worse.

The result of this agitation was a strong movement to curb big business, which wove a whole network of restrictions around business. This took two directions: one, to broaden the control of the government by the voter; the other, to use government for regulating business.

The first of these took various forms in different States: the direct primary, the initiative and referendum of laws, the recall of judges, popular election of judges, and, finally, the direct election of senators in 1913. The theory underlying these changes was that they would remove judges and legislators from the control of business and make them more responsive to the will of the mass of voters. Some of these devices were undoubtedly helpful in breaking corporations' hold on the government, but on the whole the expectations of the originators have not been realized.

The movement, however, brought a considerable activity on the part of the government, which activity was undoubtedly in part a result of the new governing devices. Some States were especially active. The outstanding one was undoubtedly Wisconsin. Authorities differ as to the ultimate effect on business of the laws in Wisconsin; one thing is certain, however—the dominance of railroad and lumber interests in the State was broken. This instance illustrates how business men may follow a decidedly anti-social policy and thereby arouse antagonism which strongly reacts against them.

The federal government entered upon its new economic policy under the leadership of Theodore Roosevelt. In the great anthracite coal strike of 1902, President Roosevelt forced both sides of the controversy to accept investigation by a commission. This was quite different from the federal government's earlier use of injunction and troops to maintain law and order in labor disturbances.

In 1903 Congress proceeded to bring about more effective regulation of industrial corporations and railroads. The Expedition Act speeded up prosecutions under the Sherman Anti-Trust law. The Elkins Anti-Rebate Act struck at the railroads' practice of giving rebates, which aided monopoly through discrimination. The Department of Commerce and Labor was organized to look after the interests of the "people." In 1904 the Northern Securities decision broke up the holding company combining the Great Northern, Northern Pacific, and Burlington railroads in the Northwest. This decision meant the enforcement of the Sherman Anti-Trust law.

In 1906 came further legislation. The Hepburn Act, which greatly extended government control over railroads, provided for uniform accounting methods and abolished free passes. The Pure Foods Act made the government the protector of the consumer as against the manufacturer of adulterated and harmful food. President Roosevelt also led the movement for the conservation of natural resources, with the view especially to preventing illegal exploitation by business interests.

The effects of the Roosevelt attack on business were manifold. The government by no means accomplished what was expected of it—it became evident that, where business men could not directly break a law, they could go around it. The attack had two effects, however, about which there is no question. On the one hand, it heightened criticism of business and raised hopes of more effective action in the future. On the other, it put restrictions on business and showed business that it would be supervised in the future. The effect on business is suggested by the *Commercial & Financial Chronicle* (January 1, 1910): "During Mr. Roosevelt's term, the business world never knew what to look for next, and was in constant fear of a new blow while yet it was staggering from the effects of a long antecedent series of blows." The *Chronicle* noticed, however, a brightening and revival of conditions and a restoration of confidence in business. The reason, it said, referring to President Roosevelt whose term had ended, was that the "removal of that source of irritation operated to promote recuperation and convalescence."

The measures of importance to business taken by Taft's administration were considerable. A very high tariff was adopted. The first corporation tax originated in 1909. The income tax amendment, initiated at the same time, was finally adopted in 1913. The Mann-Elkins Act enlarged the powers of the Interstate Commerce Commission and provided for a new federal court for hearing appeals from the decisions of the Commission.

During Taft's administration a number of trust cases, started under Roosevelt, came to an end. The Standard Oil Co. of New Jersey, a holding company for 37 subsidiaries, was held a monopoly in restraint of trade under the Sherman Act and was ordered to be dissolved. The Tobacco Trust and the Powder Trust were similarly dissolved. This gave a tremendous blow to the trusts, but it by no means destroyed them. They found other means of getting together. Political prosecutors of trusts came to see that there was something besides a formal organization which held combinations together. They became aware of finance capitalism, banker control, and interlocking directorates.

From 1911 on through Taft's administration, business journals complained of the complete lack of enterprise, which they attributed to the fact that confidence in the government was gone. Wilson brought no relief. He had a record for corporation reform as governor of New Jersey, and his New Freedom, advocating equal opportunity for the small man, was anything but reassuring to the larger business men of the country.

No administration had ever made such attacks on business as were made under Wilson. The Underwood-Simmons Act brought a drastic downward revision of the tariff in the face of a powerful lobby. The new administration did not work, however, for the dissolution of combinations through court action. Legislation looked toward the elimination of bad combinations and unfair practices. Unfair practices were defined; interlocking directorates were forbidden; and the Trade Commission was created to serve industry as the Interstate Commerce Commission was serving transportation. Thus came into being the forerunner of the N. R. A.—the codes and the machinery for enforcement.

Most significant perhaps of all the business legislation passed at this time was the Federal Reserve Act. The system which it established had a double origin and a double purpose. The Republicans had planned it as a centralized bank designed to eliminate some of the evils existing in American banking and currency, particularly to give such flexibility to the system as would help prevent the recurrence of panics like that of 1907. The Democrats changed it to a decentralized system with the purpose of breaking the concentration in finance revealed by the Pujo report.

Before the Wilson legislation could be tested adequately to show what effects it might have, the War changed business conditions greatly. After the United States had joined the Allies all efforts were bent toward winning the War, and enforcement of regulatory laws gave way to encouragement of business. After the War a different spirit toward business was manifest. The Transportation Act of 1920 legalized pools and regional groupings in transportation. With the victory of the Republicans in 1920 conservative business again returned to power. We could never entirely go back, however. A tradition and a machinery for regulation had been established. Business knew that regulation had come to stay.

5. A Time of Relative Prosperity

It is generally believed that the period covered by the years 1897–1920 was a time of prosperity and widespread well-being. On the whole that belief seems to have substantial foundation in fact. How far that meant profits for business, good earnings for capital and entrepreneur, it is difficult to say. The evidence which follows points out the direction of change though it does not give an exact measure.

A cursory perusal of the *Commercial & Financial Chronicle* reveals that a decided spirit of optimism prevailed throughout much of the period. Except for the year 1903, the good feeling was almost unbroken until late in 1907. Indeed, at no time since the Civil War had the setting for business seemed so fortuitous as around 1900. The election of McKinley had given assurance that the federal government would be friendly to business and would support the gold standard and a sound currency. Prices began a long upward swing. The Spanish-American War strengthened the United States in Caribbean and far eastern markets. Capital was coming out of hiding and was flowing into the United States because of a favorable trade situation. And, very significant, costs had been greatly deflated in the preceding years of hard times. Everything was set for good times. From 1907 until the War period (1914–18) the spirit was somewhat changed. There was marked criticism of government policy as a disturbing factor of fundamental importance, but that was undoubtedly not the whole story. The difficulty was, however, a national one because the depression was more serious in the United States than elsewhere. The War prevented the working-out of the situation under normal conditions.

Studies of the business cycle reveal that there were in those years the usual ups and downs in business. The frequency and duration of cycles are indicated by Table 2.[22]

There are some very interesting things to be noted in this relation. One is that business cycles, according to Professor Mitchell and others, were shorter at this time than in the preceding period.[23] But more significant as an indication of the general tone of 1897–1920 is the relative length of the different phases of the cycle. Dr. Thorp concludes that in the United States there was 0.9 year of prosperity to 1.0 year of depression from 1865 to 1896, while in the succeeding period to 1920 there were 3.1 years of prosperity to 1.0 of depression.[24]

It is interesting to compare the situation in the United States with that of other highly developed or rapidly developing industrial countries. The United States seems to have had a larger ratio of prosperity to depression than England, France, and Germany, and a slightly smaller ratio than Canada. We escaped a wide depression in the early years of the century but our depression of 1911 was almost unique.[25]

Those studies of the business cycle seem to indicate that in the period 1897–1920 there was a somewhat unusual amount of good times. But what was the experience

[22] J. M. Clark, *Strategic Factors in Business Cycles* (National Bureau of Economic Research, New York, 1934), p. 11.

[23] See Willard L. Thorp, *Business Annals* (New York, 1926), p. 50, and W. C. Mitchell, *Business Cycles* (New York, 1927), p. 415. Dr. Mills thinks that there may be such a thing as a trend toward a decrease in the length of the business cycle while a country is undergoing rapid development, and an increase in its length as the rate of economic change slows up (*ibid.*, p. 413).

[24] *Ibid.*, p. 411.

[25] This conclusion is based on charts in Thorp, *op. cit.* Its validity, of course, depends on the basis for those charts.

Table 2. STANDARD REFERENCE DATES FOR BUSINESS CYCLES IN THE UNITED STATES, 1897–1920

Expansion					Contraction				
Revival			High		Recession			Low	
July	1897	to	June	1899	July	1899	to	December	1900
January	1901	to	September	1902	October	1902	to	August	1904
September	1904	to	May	1907	June	1907	to	June	1908
July	1908	to	January	1910	February	1910	to	January	1912
February	1912	to	January	1913	February	1913	to	December	1914
January	1915	to	August	1918	September	1918	to	April	1919
May	1919	to	January	1920	February	1920	to	September	1921

with respect to different industries or units? To secure satisfactory information on this question is almost impossible. To get data on the income of individual units or partnerships for all but the later years is out of the question. Reports of individual corporations should throw some light on the subject, but irregularities in accounting methods make almost fruitless the difficult task of collecting the information. Series of figures on earnings, dividends, bankruptcies, and receiverships have, however, some significance in this relation.

The United States Bureau of Internal Revenue has collected figures on corporate earnings beginning with 1909. Table 3 gives the percentage of corporations showing net income rather than loss for the years 1909–20.[26]

Table 3. CORPORATIONS IN THE UNITED STATES WITH NET INCOMES, 1909–20

Year	Percentage of total
1909	20 [a]
1910	20 [a]
1911	19 [a]
1912	20 [a]
1913	60
1914	58
1915	52
1916	61
1917	66
1918	64
1919	65
1920	59

[a] Returns showing net income in excess of $5,000 exemption from taxation.

The only groups of corporations for which separate income figures are available are railroads and banks. Table 4 shows that there was an increase in the number of railroads paying dividends on common stock, though at all times in the period a large proportion paid no dividends.[27] Earlier years are included for comparison; unfortunately the series ended with 1917. After 1917 there was a considerable drop in income of railroad investments; the Interstate Commerce Commission has reported returns of 3.51 per cent, 2.46 per cent, and 0.09 per cent for the three years 1918–20 on Class I railroads, which included approximately 90 per cent of the mileage of the country.[28] For comparison with bond yields, Dr. Macaulay's study is recommended.[29]

Table 4.
DIVIDENDS ON RAILROAD STOCK
1888–1917
(In per cent)

Year [a]	Stock yielding dividends	Average rate on dividend-yielding stock	Ratio of dividends to all stocks
1888	38.56	5.38	2.08
1889	38.33	5.04	1.93
1890	36.24	5.45	1.97
1891	40.36	5.07	2.05
1892	39.40	5.35	2.11
1893	38.76	5.58	2.16
1894	36.57	5.40	1.97
1895	29.94	5.74	1.72
1896	29.83	5.62	1.68
1897	29.90	5.43	1.62
1898	33.74	5.29	1.78
1899	40.61	4.96	2.01
1900	45.66	5.23	2.39
1901	51.27	5.26	2.70
1902	55.40	5.55	3.08
1903	56.06	5.70	3.20
1904	57.47	6.09	3.50
1905	62.84	5.78	3.63
1906	66.54	6.03	4.01

[a] Year ended June 30 to 1916; later, Dec. 31.

26 United States Treasury, Bureau of Internal Revenue, *Statistics of Income for 1931* (Washington, 1933), p. 46.

27 United States Interstate Commerce Commission, *Thirty-First Annual Report on the Statistics of Railways in the United States for the Year ended December 31, 1917* (Washington, 1919), p. 26.

28 Bureau of Railway Economics, *Statistics of Railways of Class I*, 1911–20, sheet i.

29 F. R. Macaulay, *Some Theoretical Problems Suggested by the Movements of Interest Rates, Bond Yields and Stock Prices in the United States since 1856* (New York, 1938).

(In per cent)

Year	Stock yielding dividends	Average rate on dividend-yielding stock	Ratio of dividends to all stocks
1907	67.27	6.23	4.19
1908 [b]	65.69	8.07	5.30
1909	64.01	6.53	4.18
1910	66.71	7.50	5.00
1911	67.65	8.03	5.42
1912	64.73	7.17	4.64
1913	66.14	6.37	4.22
1914	64.39	7.97	5.13
1915	60.45	6.29	3.80
1916	60.38	6.48	3.91
1916	62.02	6.75	4.19
1917	62.32	6.81	4.24

[b] Beginning with 1908, does not include returns for switching and terminal companies.

A study of the yield of high-grade American railroad bonds gives some idea of the trend of change in such securities though it does not cover railroad bonds as a whole. From 1885 to 1912, inclusive, those bonds yielded between 3.13 per cent and 3.96 per cent, the low figure in 1899 and the high in 1885; beginning with 1914 there was a fairly regular rise to 5.16 per cent in 1920.[30] These railroad figures are all averages.

No study has been made of percentage earnings of industrial corporations in this period. The yearly dollar totals of dividend payments collected from the *Journal of Commerce* for 1902 to 1920 show a fall in 1904, a rise to 1907, fall in 1908, followed by a continuous rise to 1918, and then a fall again in 1919.[31] But until a great deal of work has been done on this subject nothing definite can possibly be said about it.

The reports of the Comptroller of the Currency of the United States give useful information on national banks. Table 5 gives the earnings of national banks for the whole United States.[32]

Table 5. DIVIDENDS AND NET EARNINGS OF NATIONAL BANKS, 1896–1920

(In per cent)

Year [a]	Dividends to capital	Dividends to capital and surplus	Net earnings to capital and surplus
1896	6.9	5.0	5.4
1897	6.7	4.8	5.4
1898	6.9	5.0	5.2
1899	7.4	5.4	5.8
1900	7.9	5.6	8.2
1901	8.1	5.7	10.0
1902	9.8	6.8	10.5
1903	8.7	5.9	10.1
1904	9.9	6.6	10.4
1905	9.2	9.1	9.0
1906	10.4	6.8	9.5
1907	17.2 [b]	10.8	16.4
1908	10.89	6.75	9.10
1909	10.12	6.18	8.72
1910	10.89	6.65	9.67
1911	11.38	6.83	9.35
1912	11.66	6.93	8.59
1913	11.40	6.75	9.06
1914	11.37	6.80	8.39
1915	10.63	6.33	7.08
1916	10.76	6.38	8.76
1917	11.61	6.79	10.52
1918	11.82	6.78	11.09
1919	12.15	6.83	12.11
1920	12.10	6.70	12.78

[a] Until 1906, year ended March 1; thereafter July 1, until 1920 when it ended June 30.

[b] The figures for 1907 cover from March 1, 1906, to July 1, 1907.

The above figures are averages and do not therefore reveal individual or regional variations, which were very marked. Table 6 gives variations from place to place.[33]

Another test of prosperity may be found in statistics of bankruptcies and receiverships. It is true, of course, that the corre-

[30] Compiled by Dr. F. R. Macaulay, National Bureau of Economic Research and published in *Standard Statistical Bulletin, Base Book,* Jan., 1932, p. 134.

[31] Information secured from the National Bureau of Economic Research.

[32] *Report of the Comptroller of the Currency,* 1919, vol. ii, p. 260; 1920, p. 257.

[33] Compiled from the *Annual Reports of the Comptroller of the Currency.*

Table 6. PERCENTAGE OF DIVIDENDS TO CAPITAL OF NATIONAL BANKS, 1900, 1905, 1910, and 1915

Groups of States	1900 [a]	1905 [a]	1910 [b]	1915 [c]
New England	5.97	6.48	8.55	8.63
Middle Atlantic	8.60	10.09	11.03	11.84
Southern	8.86	10.03	10.98	9.57
Central	8.14	9.42	10.21	10.04
Western	8.06	10.94	15.61	13.25
Pacific	9.09	10.31	13.51	10.33
Important cities				
Boston	5.39	6.19	13.64	9.24
New York	9.82	10.36	12.42	13.66
Philadelphia	7.94	8.76	10.61	11.82
New Orleans	10.60	9.85	13.36	11.10
Chicago	8.89	9.98	9.63	11.21
Minneapolis	5.25	7.48	30.49	11.30
Omaha	2.65	6.05	8.48	8.82
San Francisco	7.84	7.46	8.38	13.62

[a] Year ended Sept. 1. [b] Year ended July 1. [c] Year ended June 30.

Table 7. BANKRUPTCIES IN THE UNITED STATES, 1899–1920

Year [a]	No. of merchants	No. of manufacturers	Total no. of cases	Total liabilities	Percentage of total firms in business failing
1899	5,894	506	19,780	$379,156,517	...
1900	5,286	463	20,712	292,158,153	.92
1901	3,315	304	14,473	173,952,347	.90
1902	3,127	322	14,162	198,146,547	.93
1903	3,974	459	12,734	127,614,944	.94
1904	4,264	408	12,335	116,127,227	.92
1905	4,571	502	12,703	151,908,807	.85
1906	2,868	609	10,316	102,765,231	.77
1907	4,517	953	12,220	126,030,103	.82
1908	4,203	617	11,879	120,638,006	1.08
1909	4,576	662	11,862	120,891,340	.80
1910	5,295	927	14,829	225,194,507	.80
1911	4,993	790	14,186	165,014,725	.81
1912	5,354	841	15,615	170,153,496	.98
1913	6,612	853	17,703	227,083,214	.99
1914	6,339	894	18,794	244,721,826	1.10
1915	7,510	1,216	21,294	245,055,005	1.32
1916	9,140	1,229	24,014	313,646,570	.99
1917	8,716	1,206	25,358	323,557,440	.80
1918	7,090	966	23,530	277,580,913	.58
1919	5,626	843	19,351	241,720,008	.38
1920	3,887	673	15,622	201,626,264	.49

[a] Year ended June 30 for all columns except the last.

lation between bankruptcies and receiverships on the one hand and prosperity on the other is by no means perfect. Bankruptcies (see Table 7,[34] p. 741), seem to have been more closely correlated with cyclical changes than with any secular trend. The very large number of bankruptcies in 1899 and 1900 was no doubt in a measure the result of the new federal bankruptcy law of 1898 of which many debtors immediately took advantage.

[34] The figures for the first four columns are from the *Annalist,* vol. xxxv (1930), pp. 691–692, and 742; and the last column from Roger W. Babson, *Business Barometers,* 1931, pp. 103–104.

The course of railroad receiverships, as given in Table 8,[35] is also significant. It shows a rapid adjustment after the hard times of the middle 'nineties with occasional hard years, which became more or less chronic beginning in 1912. We have other evidence which suggests growing difficulties for business around 1912. Were certain changes under way then which did not have a chance to mature because of the War?

[35] United States Interstate Commerce Commission, *Thirty-First Annual Report of the Statistics of Railways in the United States for the Year ended December 31, 1917* (Washington, 1919), p. 16.

Table 8. COMPARATIVE STATEMENT REGARDING RAILROAD RECEIVERSHIPS, 1894–1917

Year [a]	Miles of road operated by receivers at close of year	Net change during the year	Number of roads under receivers at close of year
1894	40,818.81	. . .	192
1895	37,855.80	2,963.01 [b]	169
1896	30,475.39	7,380.41 [b]	151
1897	18,861.68	11,613.71 [b]	128
1898	12,744.95	6,116.73 [b]	94
1899	9,853.13	2,891.82 [b]	71
1900	4,177.91	5,675.22 [b]	52
1901	2,497.14	1,680.77 [b]	45
1902	1,475.32	1,021.82 [b]	27
1903	1,185.45	289.87 [b]	27
1904	1,323.28	137.83	28
1905	795.82	527.46 [b]	26
1906	3,971.43	3,175.61	34
1907	3,926.31	45.12 [b]	29
1908	9,529.03	5,602.72	52
1909	10,529.80	1,000.77	44
1910	5,257.03	5,272.77 [b]	39
1911	4,592.89	664.14 [b]	39
1912	9,785.83	5,192.94	44
1913	16,286.18	6,500.35	49
1914	18,608.21	2,322.03	68
1915	30,223.05	11,614.84	85
1916	37,353.45	7,130.40	94
1916	34,803.59	2,549.86 [bc]	80
1917	17,375.51	17,428.08 [b]	82

[a] Year ended June 30 until 1916, after which it ended Dec. 31.
[b] Decreases.
[c] Represents last six months of the year.

The number of bank suspensions (see Table 9 [36]) seems high for a time that was considered relatively prosperous. They reveal one or both of two things: (1) weaknesses in the banking organization; (2) an unstable business situation.

For most of the tables in this case we do not have comparable figures for the earlier periods or any other definite basis for comparison. There is some significance, however, in the fact that the relatively bad years were few. There seems to have been a trend toward less profitable times immediately before the War. Was this the beginning of a secular downward trend? Or was it merely another low point in the business cycle? Though bankruptcies and railroad receiverships were high, bank earnings, railroad dividends, and corporate earnings, in general, point to relatively good times during the War and for a short time after the War was over.

[36] *Annual Report of the Comptroller of the Currency*, 1931, pp. 1040–1041.

Table 9. BANK SUSPENSIONS, 1894–1920
(Dollars in thousands)

Year ended June 30	Number: All Banks	Number: National	Number: State	Number: Private	Capital: All Banks	Capital: National	Capital: State	Capital: Private	Deposits: All Banks
1894	122	51	71	..	$10,332	$7,220	$3,112	...	$ 16,086
1895	150	35	115	..	8,291	4,385	3,906	...	14,775
1896	98	20	78	..	6,141	2,740	3,401	...	11,060
1897	170	48	75	47	12,360	7,902	3,427 [a]	$1,031 [a]	48,262
1898	63	10	20	33	2,988	1,350	914	724	10,599
1899	33	7	11	15	1,382	550	503	329	11,440
1900	38	6	16	16	2,532	1,450	731	351	17,299
1901	67	11	15	41	3,345	1,760	685	900	19,865
1902	46	3	23	20	1,740	250	1,051	439	10,671
1903	31	5	9	17	1,584	800	411	373	7,394
1904	125	23	52	50	7,463	3,990	2,376	1,097	37,268
1905	74	17	22	35	2,808	1,035	1,005	768	14,933
1906	51	14	24	13	2,912	1,530	1,097	285	14,672
1907	38	4	14	20	1,654	575	640	439	24,095
1908	153	21	79	53	10,598	5,825	3,610	1,163	226,453
1909	75	15	27	33	3,887	1,929	1,234	724	29,877
1910	32	4	16	12	1,269	275	731	263	19,332
1911	59	3	34	22	2,412	375	1,554	483	21,003
1912	62	7	34	21	3,115	1,100	1,554	461	16,571
1913	44	4	25	15	2,121	650	1,142	329	10,495
1914	115	19	69	27	8,680	4,935	3,153	592	40,927
1915	124	14	71	39	5,775	1,675	3,244	856	37,522
1916	56	15	29	12	2,523	935	1,325	263	18,189
1917	41	6	20	15	2,423	1,180	914	329	15,423
1918	28	3	15	10	1,030	125	685	220	10,962
1919	44	2	41	1	2,120	225	1,873	22	11,057
1920	47	3	35	9	1,926	130	1,599	197	20,725

[a] Capital of State and private banks estimated from 1897 to 1920.

6. General Readings

See the books recommended in the preceding case. The following additional works are recommended:

F. C. Mills, *Economic Tendencies in the United States* (New York, 1932).

Conference on Unemployment (1921), Committee on Recent Economic Changes, *Recent Economic Changes* (New York, 1929).

J. M. Clark, *Strategic Factors in Business Cycles* (New York, 1934). While this is a study of business cycles in general, it contains much material on recent American experience.

A. F. Burns, *Production Trends in the United States since 1870* (New York, 1934). Is invaluable for the study of changes in various industries and products.

F. R. Macaulay, *Some Theoretical Problems Suggested by the Movements of Interest Rates, Bond Yields and Stock Prices in the United States since 1856* (New York, 1938). Contains significant tables.

7. Suggested Questions

1. Were the years 1897–1920 a time of economic advance? Was it a time of good business?
2. Does the evidence presented indicate a clear relation between the trend of prices and of business profits?
3. What factors, other than the price change, may have had an effect on profits over a considerable part of the period?
4. Do you observe any similarities or dissimilarities in the situations leading to panics or depressions in the two periods 1866–97 and 1897–1920?
5. Is there any reason to believe that American business was running into trouble just before the War (1914–18), and that it was "saved" by the War?
6. Do you accept it as true that since 1920 we have been in a downward secular trend of business?

NATIONAL CAPITALISM

XLIII. RECENT ECONOMIC SYSTEMS

1. General Statement

Our ideas, which are commonly miscellaneous and oddly assorted, prove on analysis to be capable of orderly treatment. They belong to larger syntheses of ideas, theories, or systems of thought. It is helpful to go back to these systems of thought—in this case economic systems—so as to discover the larger implications of otherwise fragmentary concepts.

So far as is known the economic thoughts of the ancient peoples were not much developed into organized theories. The Greeks had ideas about house management and wrote about the subject. The Romans were eager students of agriculture and, learning much from the Carthaginians, set down on parchment their rich store of practical husbandry.

It was the Middle Ages which, abhorring or at least fearing commerce, developed ideas and ideals about how trade and general business should be carried on. A business man had better be careful in gaining wealth that he lose not his soul. He must charge only a just price and he must charge nothing for a loan of money, except in certain instances such as those involving great risk.

The national state has brought in the great dominating ideas of modern times. Between the discovery of America and the death of Shakespeare they were developed, at least in outline. In a general way the main emphasis was to make the national state strong economically, commonly by restrictions and regulation and even monopolies. This was the doctrine of mercantilism—strength through merchandising. Those dissenting adhered to economic liberalism, but they got nowhere until centuries later, when England had become a master of mechanical technique. But these two systems embody much of the uncertainty and conflict in modern economic life.

2. Important Dates

1879	Germany returned to protection.
1881–92	France returned to protection.
1895–1915	F. W. Taylor expounded scientific management of capital and labor in production—efficiency and materialism emphasized.
1897–1929	Era of prosperity and extreme individualism.
1913	Wilson's "New Freedom" from big business domination.
1917	Communist revolution in Russia.
1922	Beginning of Fascism.
1928–29	New Era of business—many excesses.
1932	Depth of the depression.
1933	National socialism gains power in Germany, under Hitler. The New Deal begins in America.
1935	Modified "new deals" in France and Belgium.

3. Survey of Recent Economic Systems

In a case presented above appears a diagram[1] of economic systems of policy and thought. To be sure, names appear where whole books should be; but we can

[1] See p. 99.

individually follow up the various topics dealt with, in case we are not already familiar with them.

We may again note that men are compelled by circumstances to work out policies, largely grounded in economic conditions and necessities, in order to govern. Theorists reflect on the economic aspects and give rise to economic theory which is logically arranged and appears for the time at least to be all-embracing and cogent. Persons far on the outside—in the pulpit, in the teacher's study, on the soap box, or in the journalist's office—deny these theories or oppose the policies of governments. They establish church doctrines, utopian schemes, theories of reconstruction, opportunistic radicalism, and so on. Such doctrines are valuable, even if disturbing to those responsible for the orderly procedures of business and government. Such doctrines as they champion never succeed and never fail: some part of them gets into the main stream of policy and thought.

We do not need to contemplate for long the growth of policy, theory, and protest doctrines, before we learn that there is an essential background of factual development that contains the key to all three. This factual background is business history. In this history we find the now familiar stages of petty, mercantile, industrial, financial, and national capitalism.[2]

Mercantile capitalism was reflected in mercantilism or the politico-economic policy of the nation and empire. Industrial capitalism was largely responsible for the new economic policy of liberalism and for the classical economic theory of Adam Smith, David Ricardo, and others. Classical economics became more and more a system of logic with fine distinctions and special terminology. The business man liked it on the whole without understanding much of it. Later, when the system of neo-classical economics arose with its further ramifications, broader sympathies, and new techniques, the business man had in effect to fold up his tent and withdraw from the field of economic theory. To amplify these thoughts:[3]

"There were two mistakes in classical economics on the side of policy and much that was left undeveloped on the side of theory. The assumption or conclusion had been that free trade was good alike for England and the other countries. Certainly England which had advanced farther in trade, manufacture, and banking than other countries wanted only an unrestricted opportunity to trade with the rest of the world. Free trade was fair weather for the English trading vessel. In reality, no other nation was in a place to profit from free trade. That peoples varied vastly in their preparation for the new system became apparent in the period 1840–80. Friedrich List was one of the first to see this. There arose in Germany the historical school of economics, under first Roscher and then Schmoller, that urged the relativity of policies and ideas. The historical school insisted that the classical economists had considered but one time and one place: in short that they had founded classical economics upon the temporary condition of England in the period about 1760–1840. The protagonists of the historical school were not business men but professors of economics.

"First, the classical economists made the mistake of forgetting the less advanced nations. Secondly, they followed their predecessors in forgetting the non-profit-taking classes, especially the workers, at a time when the concentration of workmen in factories was calling attention to evil conditions. In allowing the business men of the eighteenth and nineteenth centuries to operate without restraint, classical economists gave moral sanction to an exploitation of the working class that shocked the sensibilities of intelligent citizens. To put material wealth above human welfare was a perversion of society that could not last. Accordingly, to redress the balance, a new system, social economics, came into existence, first as a policy and then

[2] See the Introduction to this casebook and also *Business and Capitalism* (New York, 1939) by N. S. B. Gras.

[3] N. S. B. Gras, "The Business Man and Economic Systems," *Journal of Economic and Business History,* vol. iii (1930–31), pp. 178–184.

as a body of doctrines. Although Robert Owen, the benevolent manufacturer of Manchester and New Lanark, espoused the cause of the workers, and Charles Booth, a Liverpool ship-owner, collected volumes on the subject of labor conditions in London, it was generally left to non-business men to urge the new point of view and formulate the new social-ethical code. In the doing of this, teachers and preachers, labor leaders and socialists have predominated. Social economics has lacked the cogency of classical economics. As its point of view gains victory after victory, it is likely to disappear as a system or emphasis.

"In other matters the classical economists had erred, notably on the theoretical side. A reformulation of theories concerning wages, interest, rent, and value was needed. To meet this need the school of neo-classical economics came into existence, with Jevons and Marshall in England, Menger and Böhm-Bawerk in Austria, and Clark and Taussig in America, among its leading protagonists. This school has emphasized the psychological background of economic situations, particularly in the explanation of prices. It has endeavored to use mathematics for both the determination and demonstration of economic truths. It has accepted a large measure of the relativity of the historical school and a large measure of the human emphasis of the social-economic school. It has recognized the process of change in business, notably the business cycle.

"But above all, this neo-classical school, which is the leading theoretical school today, has been the work of professional economists. It has so elaborated economic theories that the business man not only cannot assist in the process but can find no patience with the effort. A system of economics which is founded upon mathematics, logic, psychology, history, and a social point of view can have no spontaneous attraction for the business leader. Certainly the business man has lost his place completely in the field of creative effort in theorizing. This situation is paralleled in medicine, in which the physician learns from the laboratory worker, and in engineering, in which the engineer learns from the physicist and the chemist.

"In the divorce between business and economics, the man of affairs has not been content to live in a vacuum. He has a policy and he has ideas as to the nature of economic forces and relationships. That some of these are crude is clear enough. That some of them are based on common sense and are worthy of attention, on the part of the economist, has been clearly recognized in recent years. It would be of great service if we could have these ideas formulated. In the face of the elaborate economic theorizing of the professional economist, the business man has naturally not had the courage, to say nothing of the leisure, to erect his ideas into a cogent system. But there is a body of unassimilated doctrine of considerable bulk and of great importance which we may call neo-mercantilism. This is a mingling of unformulated economic thought and economic policy.

"It is difficult to arrive at a clear idea of what the neo-mercantilism of our day really is. We note only a few points and these on the side of policy. There is a group of business men, largely manufacturers, small tradesmen, and local bankers who want to bring back restraint and regulation in business. The reaction from free trade came in France and Germany in the 1870's, when in accordance with the teachings of the historical economists and in answer to an inquiry into actual facts, business men perceived that free trade put them at a disadvantage in competition with a people so advanced as the English. *Manchesterthum* soon appeared to be a Greek present for unsuspecting Trojans. Then set in almost an epidemic of tariff making which comprehended almost the whole Continent of Europe. In America the policy of protection had never been overthrown because of the obvious immaturity of American industry. But there can be no doubt that the swing to protection in Europe made an ever higher tariff wall in America more excusable.

"Manufacturers, small tradesmen, local bankers, and others seek regulation and restraint not only through national tariffs but through local municipal legislation and regional action. Of course this is more than a return to the mercantilism of the early modern period: it is, in part, a return to the urban economic régime of the Middle Ages. There is, however, at least this one difference that, while the advantage of the merchants of one town may be considered, for example in the campaigns for community buying as against chain stores and mail-order houses, there is commonly a broader basis in the demand for regional alignment and planning. The town of the Middle Ages, the state of the early modern period, the world of the nineteenth century, each seemed the proper emphasis of its time. In the twentieth century there is not a little to indicate that there is a regional mercantilism that is growing up, if not to supplant other points of view at least to urge its own. The efforts of the New England Council, the plans of the American Northwest, and the hopes of the Maritime Provinces of Canada all point in the same direction. Regionalism has been the object of the united consideration of natural and social scientists in a conference in the city of Washington in 1930. During the Great War and since, regionalism has received official sanction in France.

"The modern trade association, taking its start in England in the late eighteenth century and in America largely in the late nineteenth, has served the purpose of promoting the general interests of the trade in question. At times it has been an agency in combating the claims and aggression of workmen. But in recent years there is more than a suggestion of its use in upholding the small and weaker business man in the face of competition with the big corporation. Accordingly, it may be that this trade association will become the spiritual successor to the medieval gild which was the basic institution in the urban economic régime. The neo-mercantilism of today may find in the trade association the support which urban mercantilism received in the gild during the Middle Ages.

"But the neo-mercantilists have won no easy victory. In fact, there are business men who adhere to the old classical economic policy of unrestricted trade without, of course, ignoring the relativity of ideas and the social point of view. Prominent among these are the international bankers and the leaders of those big corporations which have the strength to stand alone. The view of this group was set forth in the bankers' manifesto of 1926, in which the merits of economic freedom were urged and the dangers pointed out in the adoption of any other system.

"The great bankers and the leaders of the bigger corporations turn to no associations for support or assistance. Leadership is vital to their positions. They want only to be left alone to plan and pioneer. There are no marginal firms in their midst, needing the support of open-price associations. They belong to the nineteenth and twentieth centuries, not to the early Middle Ages.

"It is this group of men who are developing a policy that at least in practice is quite new. They are finding it practical to establish a fixed or pegged price or wage. It was demonstrated during the Great War that economic conditions could be manipulated—at least for the time being. It remains to be seen whether we can start out from the side of low prices and high wages and arrive at the goal of great profits. If so, here is a new form of benefit such as the earlier classical leaders had not dreamed of. It is true that such a policy may be regarded as artificial, but the initiative and control come from the men of business and not through the agency of government.

"Today we find in our midst five groups of persons or schools of thought and policy. These are the neo-mercantilists, the classical adherents, the neo-classical economists, the social economists (the Russian communists being the extremists of the group), and the farmers holding to an agricultural and agrarian policy which is at bottom now physiocratic and now neo-mercantilistic. Out of the welter of interests and claims may come a victory, but it is difficult to discern precisely what it is to be. It is very likely that there will be at least two broad opposing groups, no matter how many subdivisions each may contain. On the one hand, there will be business men who will see large profits in restraint and monopoly. On the other hand, there will be men who will find it to their interest to espouse the cause of freedom in some form or other, like the interlopers of the late medieval and early modern periods who sought to trade outside of the monopolistic commercial companies. Between these two it is not likely to be so much a question of absolute victory as a seesaw of effort. So long as there are the alternatives of regulation and free trade, or indeed a combination of the two, there is a chance to adjust public policy in accordance with the changing needs of business.

"In the meantime there is a small but notable effort in England and America to create a business economics. Business and economics were apart, until mercantilism united them. They separated again after mercantilism had developed into a one-sided classical school. Now, in business economics we may see them reunited. The effort arises in schools of business where the glaring differences between neo-mercantilism, surviving classical economics, and the neo-classical school are most disconcerting. To the teacher the neo-classical school has most of the correct theories, whilst business has the facts, if one may be permitted to make such a contrast. Business economics most certainly may hope to apply many of the sharp distinctions of neo-classical theory to the problems of business. It must concern itself with the ups and downs of business, both the secular trend and the cycle. It will probably assume that private business, if and when enlightened, will be carried on in the best interest of society and most effectively and economically when least controlled from the outside. What it will do with international, national, regional, and local conflicts, it is difficult to surmise; but there is reason to believe that a combination of a regional and an international point of view may gradually win as against the prevailing nationalism. Perhaps we may also expect from business economics an approach to both economic theory and business policy that is at once realistic and dynamic.

"One of the outstanding practices in a school of business today is to study business by means of individual concrete instances. It may be true that this eats heavily into the time of student and instructor, but it has the supreme advantage of keeping both learner and teacher in the world of facts. Perhaps schools of business should regard the study of cases as the preparation not simply for actual business but also for a larger synthesis of economic ideas. If such schools do not turn to the broader aspects of their subject, they will lose their opportunity for leadership. A new philosophy of business and of the relation of business to life is required to meet the needs of our rapidly changing material world."

4. Economic Liberalism in the United States

The United States of America was born in the midst of mercantilism—British mercantilism. The people learned to hate the restrictions of the British Navigation Laws and never fully appreciated the privileges extended to them in shipping. When independence had been won, it was necessary to establish a régime of mercantilism, but since it was American mercantilism it was more palatable. Alexander Hamilton was the chief formulator and very accurately judged that it was most effective to turn national enthusiasm in the direction of manufactures. The tariff became the chief weapon in furthering industry. From 1789 to 1816 the tariff was chiefly for revenue, from 1816 to 1833 protection of home industries was the dominant note, from 1833 to 1846 protection was fairly balanced by free trade sentiment, and from 1846 to 1861 free trade predominated.

In the controversy over free trade versus protection the most distinctive parts were taken by members of Congress and officers of the federal government, for example, Clay, McDuffie, Webster, and Walker. Business leaders as such were not prominent in the contest. There were a few exceptions, however, such as Henry Lee and Abbott Lawrence, both of Massachusetts. Both Matthew Carey and his son Henry, who were at once business men and economists, favored protection. On the other hand Condy Raguet, merchant, lawyer, and writer, of Philadelphia, was an outstanding supporter of free trade doctrine. It would be useful for us at this time to go back and read Raguet's statement of the advantages of free trade.[4]

The intervention of the Civil War and the consequent need for higher taxes led to the high tariff of 1861 and of subsequent years. America gradually slipped over from the call for the protection of infant industries to the demand for the protection of the standard of living of the American workman.

With no strong and enduring economic

[4] See Condy Raguet, *The Principles of Free Trade* (Philadelphia, 1835), pp. 2–4.

liberalism we have had no effective political and intellectual liberalism. With some intolerance surviving from Puritan days and with the narrowness of the petty business man and self-confident farmer, we have missed the liberalism that means broad sympathies with other classes and peoples. This means that there is a lack of strong liberal feeling in the margin between conservatism and radicalism, a lack of a convenient middle ground of political compromise and intellectual refuge of understanding and toleration.

In the universities, to be sure, we have had followers of Adam Smith, David Ricardo, John Stuart Mill, and Alfred Marshall. Their voices have been raised at times with effect, but they have made no very wide conquests in America as they did in England and France in the nineteenth century.

There is no thought of denying to America the existence of individualism, but just the existence of the broad economic doctrines that have embodied it and made it into a system. Of course our law, both constitutional and statutory, has accepted the individual as the source and object of freedom, with necessary restrictions. This has been in part a substitute for economic liberalism which indeed it has to some extent embodied. Perhaps you will say that, so long as we have the rugged individualism of most farmers and business men, we need not worry about the economic liberalism to which they would adhere but of which for various reasons they have not become a part.

5. General Economic Developments, 1865–1913

After the Civil War there developed a spirit of business adventure, individual conquest, and ruthless conduct that knew no precedent and has had few successors. It included reckless speculation, unprincipled manipulation, and shameless perversion of public institutions. In 1873 came not only the panic that halted the development but the national expansion of the Granger movement that ushered in both a protest and a suggestion of a remedy in the form of public regulation. The Interstate Commerce Act of 1887 registered the will of the people to regulate the abuses in railroad transportation.

Business units kept getting bigger and more aggressive. Mere growth was supplemented by merger, especially in the period 1898–1903. Small units were crushed to the ground by big corporations like the Standard Oil companies. The fact that there was some measure of greater stability and efficiency brought little consolation to many people. Into the midst of this situation came a demand for justice for the little fellow who wanted not much more than a living and independence in business. President Woodrow Wilson embodied the inner cry of the small man in his New Freedom of 1913.

6. Woodrow Wilson's New Freedom [5]

"We have seen tariff legislation wander very far afield in our day—very far indeed from the field in which our prosperity might have had a normal growth and stimulation. No one who looks the facts squarely in the face or knows anything that lies beneath the surface of action can fail to perceive the principles upon which recent tariff legislation has been based. We long ago passed beyond the modest notion of 'protecting' the industries of the country and moved boldly forward to the idea that they were entitled to the direct patronage of the Government. For a long time—a time so long that the men now active in public policy hardly remember the conditions that preceded it—we have sought in our tariff schedules to give each group of manufacturers or producers what they themselves thought that they needed in order to maintain a practically exclusive market as against the rest of the world. Consciously or unconsciously, we have built up a set of privileges and exemptions from competition behind which it was easy by any, even the crudest, forms of combina-

[5] G. M. Harper, editor, *President Wilson's Addresses* (New York, 1918), pp. 10–11, 188–194.

tion to organize monopoly; until at last nothing is normal, nothing is obliged to stand the tests of efficiency and economy, in our world of big business, but everything thrives by concerted arrangement. Only new principles of action will save us from a final hard crystallization of monopoly and a complete loss of the influences that quicken enterprise and keep independent energy alive.

"It is plain what those principles must be. We must abolish everything that bears even the semblance of privilege or of any kind of artificial advantage, and put our business men and producers under the stimulation of a constant necessity to be efficient, economical, and enterprising, masters of competitive supremacy, better workers and merchants than any in the world. Aside from the duties laid upon articles which we do not, and probably cannot, produce, therefore, and the duties laid upon luxuries and merely for the sake of the revenues they yield, the object of the tariff duties henceforth laid must be effective competition, the whetting of American wits by contest with the wits of the rest of the world.

. . . .

"The Republican Party was put out of power because of failure, practical failure and moral failure; because it had served special interests and not the country at large; because, under the leadership of its preferred and established guides, of those who still make its choices, it had lost touch with the thoughts and the needs of the nation and was living in a past age and under a fixed illusion, the illusion of greatness. It had framed tariff laws based upon a fear of foreign trade, a fundamental doubt as to American skill, enterprise, and capacity, and a very tender regard for the profitable privileges of those who had gained control of domestic markets and domestic credits; and yet had enacted anti-trust laws which hampered the very things they meant to foster, which were stiff and inelastic, and in part unintelligible. It had permitted the country throughout the long period of its control to stagger from one financial crisis to another under the operation of a national banking law of its own framing which made stringency and panic certain and the control of the larger business operations of the country by the bankers of a few reserve centers inevitable; had made as if it meant to reform the law but had faint-heartedly failed in the attempt, because it could not bring itself to do the one thing necessary to make the reform genuine and effectual, namely, break up the control of small groups of bankers. It had been oblivious, or indifferent, to the fact that the farmers, upon whom the country depends for its food and in the last analysis for its prosperity, were without standing in the matter of commercial credit, without the protection of standards in their market transactions, and without systematic knowledge of the markets themselves; that the laborers of the country, the great army of men who man the industries it was professing to father and promote, carried their labor as a mere commodity to market, were subject to restraint by novel and drastic process in the courts, were without assurance of compensation for industrial accidents, without federal assistance in accommodating labor disputes, and without national aid or advice in finding the places and the industries in which their labor was most needed. The country had no national system of road construction and development. Little intelligent attention was paid to the army, and not enough to the navy. The other republics of America distrusted us, because they found that we thought first of the profits of American investors and only as an afterthought of impartial justice and helpful friendship. Its policy was provincial in all things; its purposes were out of harmony with the temper and purpose of the people and the timely development of the nation's interests.

"So things stood when the Democratic Party came into power. How do they stand now? Alike in the domestic field and in the wide field of the commerce of the world, American business and life and industry have been set free to move as they never moved before.

"The tariff has been revised, not on the principle of repelling foreign trade, but upon the principle of encouraging it, upon something like a footing of equality with our own in respect of the terms of competition, and a Tariff Board has been created whose function it will be to keep the relations of American with foreign business and industry under constant observation, for the guidance alike of our business men and of our Congress. American energies are now directed towards the markets of the world.

"The laws against trusts have been clarified by definition, with a view to making it plain that they were not directed against big business but only against unfair business and the pretense of competition where there was none; and a Trade Commission has been created with powers of guidance and accommodation which have relieved business men of unfounded fears and set them upon the road of hopeful and confident enterprise.

"By the Federal Reserve Act the supply of currency at the disposal of active business has been rendered elastic, taking its volume, not from a fixed body of investment securities, but from the liquid assets of daily trade; and these assets are assessed and accepted, not by distant groups of bankers in control of unavailable reserves, but by bankers at the many centers of local exchange who are in touch with local conditions everywhere.

"Effective measures have been taken for the recreation of an American merchant marine and the revival of the American carrying trade indispensable to our emancipation from the control which foreigners have so long exercised over the opportunities, the routes, and the methods of our commerce with other countries.

"The Interstate Commerce Commission is about to be reorganized to enable it to perform its great and important functions more promptly and more efficiently. We have created, extended and improved the service of the parcels post.

"So much we have done for business. What other party has understood the task so well or executed it so intelligently and energetically? What other party has attempted it at all? The Republican leaders, apparently, know of no means of assisting business but 'protection.' How to stimulate it and put it upon a new footing of energy and enterprise they have not suggested.

"For the farmers of the country we have virtually created commercial credit, by means of the Federal Reserve Act and the Rural Credits Act. They now have the standing of other business men in the money market. We have successfully regulated speculation in 'futures' and established standards in the marketing of grains. By an intelligent Warehouse Act we have assisted to make the standard crops available as never before both for systematic marketing and as a security for loans from the banks. We have greatly added to the work of neighborhood demonstration on the farm itself of improved methods of cultivation, and, through the intelligent extension of the functions of the Department of Agriculture, have made it possible for the farmer to learn systematically where his best markets are and how to get at them.

"The workingmen of America have been given a veritable emancipation, by the legal recognition of a man's labor as part of his life, and not a mere marketable commodity; by exempting labor organizations from processes of the courts which treated their members like fractional parts of mobs and not like accessible and responsible individuals; by releasing our seamen from involuntary servitude; by making adequate provision for compensation for industrial accidents; by providing suitable machinery for mediation and conciliation in industrial disputes; and by putting the Federal Department of Labor at the disposal of the workingman when in search of work.

"We have effected the emancipation of the children of the country by releasing them from hurtful labor. We have instituted a system of national aid in the building of highroads such as the country has been feeling after for a century. . . .

. . . .

"There is one circumstance connected with this program which ought to be very plainly stated. It was resisted at every step by the interests which the Republican Party had catered to and fostered at the expense of the country, and these same interests are now earnestly praying for a reaction which will save their privileges,—for the restoration of their sworn friends to power before it is too late to recover what they have lost. They fought with particular desperation and infinite resourcefulness the reform of the banking and currency system, knowing that to be the citadel of their control; and most anxiously are they hoping and planning for the amendment of the Federal Reserve Act by the concentration of control in a single bank which the old familiar group of bankers can keep under their eye and direction. But while the 'big men' who used to write the tariffs and command the assistance of the Treasury have been hostile,—all but a few with vision,—the average business man knows that he has been delivered, and that the fear that was once every day in his heart, that the men who controlled credit and directed enterprise from the committee rooms of Congress would crush him, is there no more, and will not return,—unless the party that consulted only the 'big men' should return to power,—the party of masterly inactivity and cunning resourcefulness in standing pat to resist change.

"The Republican Party is just the party that *cannot* meet the new conditions of a new age. It does not know the way and it does not wish new conditions. It tried to break away from the old leaders and could not. They still select its candidates and dictate its policy, still resist change, still hanker after the old conditions, still know no methods of encouraging business but the old methods. When it changes its leaders and its purposes and brings its ideas up to date it will have the right to ask the American people to give it power again; but not until then. A new age, an age of revolutionary change, needs new purposes and new ideas."

7. World War and Aftermath, 1914–1929

The World War directed the energies of men into the narrow channel of producing war services and war materials. It led men to save their income and economize on their expenditures. Moreover, all efforts were accompanied by deep emotion and the unsettling of nervous systems never very well held in poise.

The end of the War saw adjustments of great import. While Europe struggled to get back on its feet, America rushed forward to secure a new leadership in trade and finance, a leadership for which it was prepared neither by experience nor by knowledge. From 1923 to 1929 it loaned vast sums to foreign peoples and thereby sustained its export trade: it loaned money to otherwise bankrupt peoples that they might buy American goods.

The focus of the great prosperity of the postwar period came in 1928–29 and was most clearly marked in New York City. It is not too much to say that American business men had gone mad. They thought that prosperity would not end and that the rate of acceleration would not even decrease. Ill-conceived enterprises became the order of the day. Old conservative houses lost all perspective. National political leaders and economic theorists proclaimed a new day. Europe might languish, but America had discovered the secret of perpetual prosperity. Herbert Hoover, first secretary of Commerce and then president, rode the crest of the new wave. His words are worth considering.

8. Hoover's New Day, 1928 [6]

"The Government and Business

"I do not favor any general extension of the Federal Government into the operation of business in competition with its citizens. It is not the system of Lincoln or Roosevelt. It is not the American system. It not only undermines initiative but it undermines state and local self-government. It is the destruction of states' rights. Democracy, however, must be master in its own house. It can assure the conservation of our governmentally controlled natural resources in the interest of the people. It has demonstrated that by the power of regulation it can prevent abuse; it can and must control natural monopolies in full public interest. It can do so without abdicating the very principles upon which our nation has been founded and through which we have reached a standard of living and comfort unparalleled in the world. Violations of public interest by individuals or corporations should be followed by the condemnation and punishment they deserve, but this should not induce us to abandon progressive principles and substitute in their place deadly and destructive doctrines. There are local

[6] *The New Day, Campaign Speeches of Herbert Hoover, 1928* (Stanford University, 1928), pp. 106–107, 31–32, 155–159, and 126–128; Herbert Hoover's recent speeches are collected in *Addresses upon the American Road* (New York, 1938).

instances where the government must enter the business field as a by-product of some great major purpose, such as improvement in navigation, flood control, scientific research, or national defense; but they do not vitiate the general policy to which we should adhere.

. . . .

"With the growth and increasing complexity of our economic life the relations of government and business are multiplying daily. They are yearly more dependent upon each other. Where it is helpful and necessary, this relation should be encouraged. Beyond this it should not go. It is the duty of government to avoid regulation as long as equal opportunity to all citizens is not invaded and public rights violated. Government should not engage in business in competition with its citizens. Such actions extinguish the enterprise and initiative which has been the glory of America and which has been the root of its pre-eminence among the nations of the earth. On the other hand, it is the duty of business to conduct itself so that government regulation or government competition is unnecessary.

"Business is practical, but it is founded upon faith—faith among our people in the integrity of business men, and faith that it will receive fair play from the government. It is the duty of government to maintain that faith. Our whole business system would break down in a day if there was not a high sense of moral responsibility in our business world. The whole practice and ethics of business has made great strides of improvement in the last quarter of a century, largely due to the effort of business and the professions themselves. One of the most helpful signs of recent years is the stronger growth of associations of workers, farmers, business men, and professional men with a desire to cure their own abuses and a purpose to serve public interest. Many problems can be solved through co-operation between government and these self-governing associations to improve methods and practices. When business cures its own abuses it is true self-government, which comprises more than political institutions.

. . . .

"Proposals Now Menacing This System

"There has been revived in this campaign [1928 presidential campaign], however, a series of proposals which, if adopted, would be a long step toward the abandonment of our American system and a surrender to the destructive operation of governmental conduct of commercial business. Because the country is faced with difficulty and doubt over certain national problems—that is, prohibition, farm relief, and electrical power—our opponents propose that we must thrust government a long way into the businesses which give rise to these problems. In effect, they abandon the tenets of their own party and turn to state socialism as a solution for the difficulties presented by all three. It is proposed that we shall change from prohibition to the state purchase and sale of liquor. If their agricultural relief program means anything, it means that the government shall directly or indirectly buy and sell and fix prices of agricultural products. And we are to go into the hydro-electric power business. In other words, we are confronted with a huge program of government in business.

"There is, therefore, submitted to the American people a question of fundamental principle. That is: shall we depart from the principles of our American political and economic system, upon which we have advanced beyond all the rest of the world, in order to adopt methods based on principles destructive of its very foundations? And I wish to emphasize the seriousness of these proposals. I wish to make my position clear; for this goes to the very roots of American life and progress.

"Centralization Fatal to Self-Government

"I should like to state to you the effect that this projection of government in business would have upon our system of self-government and our economic system. That effect would reach to the daily life of every man and woman. It would impair the very basis of liberty and freedom not only for those left outside the fold of expanded bureaucracy but for those embraced within it.

"Let us first see the effect upon self-government. When the Federal Government undertakes to go into commercial business it must at once set up the organization and administration of that business, and it immediately finds itself in a labyrinth, every alley of which leads to the destruction of self-government.

"Commercial business requires a concentration of responsibility. Self-government requires decentralization and many checks and balances to safeguard liberty. Our Government to succeed in business would need become in effect a despotism. There at once begins the destruction of self-government.

"Unwisdom of Government in Business

"The first problem of the government about to adventure in commercial business is to determine a method of administration. It must secure leadership and direction. Shall this leadership be chosen by political agencies or shall we make it elective? The hard practical fact is that leadership in business must come through the sheer rise in ability and character. That rise can only take place in the free atmosphere of competition. Competition is closed by bureaucracy. Political agencies are feeble channels through which to select able leaders to conduct commercial business.

"Government, in order to avoid the possible incompetence, corruption, and tyranny of too great authority in individuals entrusted with commercial business, inevitably turns to boards and commissions. To make sure that there are checks and balances, each member of such boards and commissions must have equal authority. Each has his separate responsibility to the public, and at once we have the conflict of ideas and the lack of decision which would ruin any commercial business. It has contributed greatly to the demoralization of our shipping business. Moreover, these commissions must be representative of different sections and different political parties, so that at once we have an entire blight upon coördinated action within their ranks which destroys any possibility of effective administration.

"Moreover, our legislative bodies cannot in fact delegate their full authority to commissions or to individuals for the conduct of matters vital to the American people; for if we would preserve government by the people we must preserve the authority of our legislators in the activities of our government.

"Thus every time the Federal Government goes into a commercial business, five hundred and thirty-one Senators and Congressmen become the actual board of directors of that business. Every time a state government goes into business one or two hundred state senators and legislators become the actual directors of that business. Even if they were supermen and if there were no politics in the United States, no body of such numbers could competently direct commercial activities; for that requires initiative, instant decision, and action. It took Congress six years of constant discussion to even decide what the method of administration of Muscle Shoals should be.

"When the Federal Government undertakes to go into business, the state governments are at once deprived of control and taxation of that business; when a state government undertakes to go into business, it at once deprives the municipalities of taxation and control of that business. Municipalities, being local and close to the people, can, at times, succeed in business where federal and state governments must fail. We have trouble enough with log-rolling in legislative bodies today. It originates naturally from desires of citizens to advance their particular section or to secure some necessary service. It would be multiplied a thousandfold were the federal and state governments in these businesses.

"The effect upon our economic progress would be even worse. Business progressiveness is dependent on competition. New methods and new ideas are the outgrowth of the spirit of adventure, of individual initiative, and of individual enterprise. Without adventure there is no progress. No government administration can rightly take chances with taxpayers' money.

. . . .

"The Tariff Issue

"One of the most important economic issues of this campaign is the protective tariff. The Republican Party has for seventy years supported a tariff designed to give adequate protection to American labor, American industry, and the American farm against foreign competition.

"Our opponents, after seventy years of continuous opposition to this Republican doctrine, now seek to convince the American people that they have nothing to fear from tariff revision at their hands. The Democratic platform states that they will revise the duties to a basis of 'effective competition.' They did this once before. When the Underwood tariff bill was introduced to Congress in 1913 the Democratic Ways and Means Committee of the House presented it to the country as a 'competitive tariff.' That measure was surely not a protective tariff. It greatly reduced the tariffs on American manufactures and it removed almost the whole protection of the agricultural industry. The competition which it provided was competition with foreign wages and standards of living. The Democratic tariff was subjected to test for only a few months prior to the outbreak of the war. Those few months showed the beginnings of disaster in both industry and agriculture. The production of goods abroad competing with our goods ceased during the war and tariff rates became relatively unimportant. It was not until peace was restored that its ill effects were completely disclosed to the American people. It would seem fair to assume from the declarations of the authors of the measure at the time the Underwood Bill was passed that it was the ideal of an 'effective competitive' tariff. Be this as it may, competition, to be effective, must mean that foreign goods will have opportunity of successfully invading our home markets. The effect of the formula there set forth means a reduction of the tariff and a depression in American wages and American farm prices to meet foreign competition. It means a flood of foreign goods, of foreign farm produce, with the consequent reduction of wages and income of not only workers and farmers but the whole of those who labor, whether in the field, at the bench, or at the desk.

"The Republican Party stands for protection, and on coming into power in 1922 it enacted again a protective tariff to both agriculture and industry."

9. Fascism, 1922–39

In Italy the end of the War brought troubles that were at once economic and political. The national debt was heavy, there were few colonies, merchant shipping was slight, and internal economy was disintegrating. Trade unions were striking on the least provocation. Striking trainmen deserted trains in the country. Radical socialism was sweeping through the ranks of Italian workmen. The intellectuals were increasingly atheistic. The business men were without hope. The moral fiber of the nation was gradually disintegrating.

A few years of this (1918–22) were enough. One of the first to see this was Mussolini. The son of a blacksmith with only a secondary school education, steeped in radical socialism, and himself the leader of socialists, he turned to lead the middle class in the direction of law, order, and strength.

The Fascists were a group of Italians who sought to bring back into the Italian fold some outlying provinces and towns, notably Fiume. This group Mussolini brought over into the larger field of effort —the regeneration of Italy. He saw that he must add to the middle class Fascists other groups, notably the conservative workmen and cultivators of the soil, if he was to have a party able to make any headway.

Marching on Rome with his black shirts in 1922, he seized power from the hands of politicians who were debaters rather than statesmen. While they were talking, Italy was falling to pieces. Henceforth government was to be a matter of force. Mussolini made the Fascists strong and they gave new life to Italy. National vigor was now to take the place of the growing international proletarian solidarity. Political considerations were to stand above class and economic interests. The spirit of Italy was to go forth. Men were to rear large families and all Italians were to be brothers in arms to win for Italy a position of honor and dominance.

In 1926 a constitution was promulgated for Italy. It was to establish the corporate state, or, as we should say, the state of associations. There were to be six associations of employers and six of employees—for industry, agriculture, merchandising, water and air transportation, land transportation, and banking. The thirteenth association was to be made up of intellectual or professional people. These associations were to be formed only when required. They were put into effective operation only in 1939.

Apparently Mussolini was to be the president and another Fascist the vice-president of each association. A great national assembly was to be formed of the representatives of these associations, and presumably was to take the place of the lower house of parliament. This was accomplished only in 1939. Already the National Council of Fascists was in operation to function as the other house of parliament.

There were to be no strikes or lockouts in Italy: these were not in the interest of the state. The Pope was officially won over to support the new régime. Economic improvements—great public works—were undertaken, such as the draining of swamps and the development of the African colonies.

Workmen have felt that Fascism has meant the dominance of employers. They have had no real freedom of action. Intellectual liberals have felt the heavy hand of terrorism. Racketeering and banditry have been suppressed. Honesty in business has been enforced. The glory of Rome has been revived and the ambitions of a warring empire made to live again. The League of Nations could not dominate Italy. France has had to look to her supremacy on the Mediterranean. Germany has lost her blue ribbon on the high seas.

Already it appears that there are two phases in the brief history of Fascism that have been unfolded up to date. The first is 1922–35, which may be characterized as a period of formulation and substantial growth and consolidation of Fascism in Italy. The second period is since 1935, which appears to warrant the designation "costly aggression." Ethiopia was conquered in 1935–36. Troops were sent to help Franco in Spain in 1936–39. The Jews were severely dealt with in 1938. Albania was seized in 1939. A military alliance with Germany was signed in 1939, one which seems to commit Italy to a policy of warfare. As the years go by, Italy seems to be rolling up a heavy debt which must be met some day, and it seems to be getting nearer to a crisis which will not be solved by postponement.

10. National Socialists (Nazis) in Germany

A. Recent history of Germany.

1914–18	War.
1919–21	Heavy reparation exacted from Germany.
1921–23	Inflation which reduced the mark to nothing—necessitated by the drainage of capital.
1924–29	Borrowing abroad to make up for reparations helped to bring considerable prosperity. Borrowed money became permanent capital or wealth, sometimes unproductive.
1929–32	Reparations continued but their continuance became difficult because foreign borrowing ceased and depression arrived.
1933–	National Socialism gained power.

B. Bases of Nazi power.

The middle class supported the Nazis in the expectation of economic betterment. This was the backbone of the whole party.

The industrialists (such as Thyssen and the Lahusen brothers) and gentry supported them in the expectation of honor and freedom abroad. This involved the danger of war and lessened the likelihood of the repayment of debts.

C. Program.[7]

"The programme of the German Workers' Party is limited as to period. The leaders have no intention, once the aims announced in it have been achieved, of setting up fresh ones, merely in order to increase the discontent of the masses artificially, and so ensure the continued existence of the party.

"1. We demand the union of all Germans to form a Great Germany on the basis of the right of self-determination enjoyed by nations.

"2. We demand equality of rights for the German People in its dealings with other nations, and abolition of the Peace Treaties of Versailles and St. Germain.

"3. We demand land and territory (colonies) for the nourishment of our people and for settling our superfluous population.

"4. None but members of the nation may be citizens of the State. None but those of German blood, whatever their creed, may be members of the nation. No Jew, therefore, may be a member of the nation.

"5. Anyone who is not a citizen of the State may live in Germany only as a guest and must be regarded as being subject to foreign laws.

"6. The right of voting on the State's government and legislation is to be enjoyed by the citizen of the State alone. We demand, therefore, that all official appointments, of whatever kind, whether in the Reich, in the country, or in the smaller localities, shall be granted to citizens of the State alone.

"We oppose the corrupting custom of Parliament of filling posts merely with a view to party considerations, and without reference to character or capability.

"7. We demand that the State shall make it its first duty to promote the industry and livelihood of citizens of the State. If it is not possible to nourish the entire population of the State, foreign nationals (non-citizens of the State) must be excluded from the Reich.

"8. All non-German immigration must be prevented. We demand that all non-Germans, who entered Germany subsequent to August 2, 1913, shall be required forthwith to depart from the Reich.

"9. All citizens of the State shall be equal as regards rights and duties.

"10. It must be the first duty of each citizen of the State to work with his mind or with his body. The activities of the individual may not clash with the interests of the whole, but must proceed within the frame of the community and be for the general good.

"We demand therefore:

"11. Abolition of incomes unearned by work.

"12. In view of the enormous sacrifice of life and property demanded of a nation by every war, personal enrichment due to a war must be regarded as a crime against the nation. We demand, therefore, ruthless confiscation of all war gains.

"13. We demand nationalisation of all businesses which have been up to the present formed into companies (Trusts).

"14. We demand that the profits from wholesale trade shall be shared out.

"15. We demand extensive development of provision for old age.

"16. We demand creation and maintenance of a healthy middle class, immediate communalisation of wholesale business premises, and their lease at a cheap rate to small traders, and that extreme consideration shall be shown to all small purveyors to the State, district authorities, and smaller localities.

"17. We demand land reform suitable to our national requirements, passing of a law for confiscation without compensation of land for communal purposes; abolition of interest on land loans, and prevention of all speculation in land.

"18. We demand ruthless prosecution of those whose activities are injurious to the common interest. Sordid criminals against the nation, usurers, profiteers, etc., must be punished with death, whatever their creed or race.

"19. We demand that the Roman Law, which serves the materialistic world order, shall be replaced by a legal system for all Germany.

"20. With the aim of opening to every capable and industrious German the possibility of higher education and of thus obtaining advancement, the State must consider a

[7] See Paul Einzig's *Germany's Default, the Economics of Hitlerism* (Macmillan, London, 1934), pp. 125–128.

thorough reconstruction of our national system of education. The curriculum of all educational establishments must be brought into line with the requirements of practical life. Comprehension of the State idea (State sociology) must be the school objective, beginning with the first dawn of intelligence in the pupil. We demand development of the gifted children of poor parents, whatever their class or occupation, at the expense of the State.

"21. The State must see to raising the standard of health in the nation by protecting mothers and infants, prohibiting child labour, increasing bodily efficiency by obligatory gymnastics and sports laid down by law, and by extensive support of clubs engaged in the bodily development of the young.

"22. We demand abolition of a paid army and formation of a national army.

"23. We demand legal warfare against conscious political lying and its dissemination in the Press. In order to facilitate creation of a German national Press we demand:

"(a) That all editors of newspapers and their assistants, employing the German language, must be members of the nation.

"(b) That special permission from the State shall be necessary before non-German newspapers may appear. These are not necessarily printed in the German language.

"(c) That non-Germans shall be prohibited by law from participation financially in or influencing German newspapers, and that the penalty for contravention of the law shall be suppression of any such newspaper, and immediate deportation of the non-German concerned in it.

"It must be forbidden to publish papers which do not conduce to the national welfare. We demand legal prosecution of all tendencies in art and literature of a kind likely to disintegrate our life as a nation, and the suppression of institutions which militate against the requirements above-mentioned.

"24. We demand liberty for all religious denominations in the State, so far as they are not a danger to it and do not militate against the moral feelings of the German race.

"The party, as such, stands for positive Christianity, but does not bind itself in the matter of creed to any particular confession. It combats the Jewish-materialist spirit within us and without us, and is convinced that our nation can only achieve permanent health from within on the principle: The Common Interest before Self.

"25. That all the foregoing may be realised, we demand the creation of a strong central power of the State; unquestioned authority of the politically centralised Parliament over the entire Reich and its organisation; and formation of Chambers for classes and occupations for the purpose of carrying out the general laws promulgated by the Reich in the various States of the confederation.

"The leaders of the party swear to go straight forward—if necessary to sacrifice their lives—in securing fulfilment of the foregoing points."

D. Events in the Nazi régime.

1. Propaganda against big stores—because big and because commonly Jewish.

2. Persecution of the Jews.

3. Standstill Agreements (beginning in 1931 and continued by the Nazis) as to the payment of short-term liabilities, chiefly of German banks due to foreign banks.

4. Public works carried out in large part by the retention of money due to foreign bondholders.

5. Increase of employment.

6. Abandonment of the League of Nations.

7. Recovery of the Saar.

8. Seizure of the Sudetenland and Czechoslovakia.

E. Hitler labor policy, 1934.[8]

"Hitler's coming to power and Germany's all-time record of unemployment coincided when more than 6,000,000 people registered as unemployed on January 31, 1933. Soon after its installation, the new administration issued a message pledging itself to eliminate all unemployment within four years. This announcement came as a great surprise to those acquainted with the unemployment problem, because it had become evident that present-time unemployment is not merely caused by temporary business depression but is also a symptom of a deeply rooted malad-

[8] See Friedrich Baerwald, "How Germany Reduced Unemployment," *American Economic Review,* vol. xxiv (1934), pp. 617–630.

justment between the structure of the population and the tendencies of economic development. . . ."

Employment was provided directly by means of public works—

". . . flood regulation, underground works organized by public authorities, the opening and the improvement of territories for the use of farmers, and the construction of new automobile highways."

"Special funds and facilities have been made available for the reconditioning of public and private buildings and the remodelling of large apartments into smaller ones."

Agriculture had come to employ many more hands by January, 1934. In order to prevent some of these laborers from going off to the towns as soon as conditions there should be improved, a law was passed in May, 1934, to prevent the laborers from moving to the cities and to prevent city people from hiring rural laborers.

With the object of bringing agricultural prices nearer to industrial prices, taxes were lowered on farms and minimum prices were established for agricultural products.

The number of domestic servants was increased by making it easier to employ them. Employers were given tax exemptions for hiring additional servants; and household servants were exempt from making contributions to the unemployment insurance fund.

The furniture industry was aided by encouraging matrimony. A woman might be given a loan of 1,000 marks when she married, to be paid back in five years. But deduction of 200 marks a year was made for each child she bore. The loan could be used only to buy furniture.

To help employment in the tobacco industry the use of machines was restricted. Socialists and Jews were dismissed from jobs, many of the latter leaving Germany.

"A voluntary labor service" has been established for various groups of laborers. For six months prior to entering the university, students are forced to join this service. The idea is to inculcate the ideal that employing men is a patriotic national service.

11. The New Deal in America, 1933–35

America had considered itself almost immune to the troubles that ate into the vitals of European lands. The stock-market crash of 1929, however, disclosed a weakness that continued to grow until the very foundations of the nation were being questioned by timid souls. The New Era or the New Day was giving way to a day of atonement.

Down and down went prices of goods and securities, and down went the fortunes and hopes of individuals and families. At last the turn came on July 8, 1932. The price of hogs began to rise slightly. The cotton and shoe industries showed life. Men could hardly believe their eyes. Then came the election of 1932 and new fears. To conservative business men the last prop had gone when the Democrats and Roosevelt were elected: here were the muddle-headed money people on the threshold of power—the friends of debtors.

When President Roosevelt came into power, the banks of the country had just been closed: fear stalked in the land. One and all turned to the new president as a deliverer. Never did the circumstances of events so favor an official. Almost anything that he could do would bring about improvement. The new president saw the point only too clearly; he was the emancipator of the nation of slaves.

Instead of a reformer, the president became a Messiah. He was going to substitute human rights for property rights. He would drive the money-changers from the temple. He gathered about himself a number of radicals from universities and law offices. There flowed the fourfold policy of reform, retribution, relief, and recovery. This was the New Deal. Whether the New Deal is a program or an attitude of mind is not clear. Some think that when President Roosevelt declared that no one would suffer from the depression—that is, through any fault of his—we entered a new era in our history. This means that henceforth the national state is responsible for the individual rather than the individual for the national state.

Let us learn of the new deal from the President's own words.[9]

"By almost general acceptance the people have adopted the habit of calling it the New Deal; and it has been well suggested that the phrase expresses a satisfactory combination of the Square Deal and the New Freedom. The appropriateness of this suggestion is indicated by the fact that some of the achievements of the past year will be the fulfilment of the progressive ideas expounded by Theodore Roosevelt of a partnership between business and government and also of the determination of Woodrow Wilson that business should be subjected, through the power of government, to drastic legal limitations against abuses. Thus we have recognized that in some respects government sits down at a table of partnership with business; but in others, it exerts the superior authority of police power to enforce fairness and justice as they should exist among the various elements in economic life. This combination of remedies is made necessary by the fact of revolutionary changes in the conditions of modern life.

. . . .

"Yes, the money changers have fled from their high seats in the temple of our civilization. We may now restore that temple to the ancient truths. The measure of the restoration lies in the extent to which we apply social values more noble than mere monetary profit.

"Happiness lies not in the mere possession of money; it lies in the joy of achievement, in the thrill of creative effort. The joy and the moral stimulation of work no longer must be forgotten in the mad chase of evanescent profits. These dark days, my friends, will be worth all they cost us if they teach us that our true destiny is not to be ministered unto but to minister to ourselves and to our fellow men.

"Recognition of that falsity of material wealth as the standard of success goes hand in hand with the abandonment of the false belief that public office and high political position are to be valued only by the standards of pride of place and personal profit; and there must be an end to a conduct in banking and in business which too often has given to a sacred trust the likeness of callous and selfish wrongdoing. Small wonder that confidence languishes, for it thrives only on honesty, on honor, on the sacredness of obligations, on faithful protection, on unselfish performance: without them it can not live.

. . . .

"It is wholly wrong to call the measures that we have taken government control of farming, control of industry, and control of transportation. It is rather a partnership between Government and farming and industry and transportation, not partnership in profits, for the profits would still go to the citizens, but rather a partnership in planning and partnership to see that the plans are carried out.

"Let me illustrate with an example. Take the cotton goods industry. It is probably true that ninety per cent of the cotton manufacturers would agree to eliminate starvation wages, would agree to stop long hours of employment, would agree to stop child labor, would agree to prevent an over-production that would result in unsalable surpluses. But, what good is such an agreement if the other ten per cent of cotton manufacturers pay starvation wages, require long hours, employ children in their mills and turn out burdensome surpluses? The unfair ten per cent could produce goods so cheaply that the fair ninety per cent would be compelled to meet the unfair conditions. Here is where government comes in. Government ought to have the right and will have the right, after surveying and planning for an industry to prevent, with the assistance of the overwhelming majority of that industry, unfair practice and to enforce this agreement by the authority of government. The so-called anti-trust laws were intended to prevent the creation of monopolies and to forbid unrea-

[9] Taken from Franklin D. Roosevelt, *On Our Way* (New York, 1934), pp. x–xi, 257, 76–78, 85–86, 194–196.

sonable profits to those monopolies. That purpose of the anti-trust laws must be continued, but these laws were never intended to encourage the kind of unfair competition that results in long hours, starvation wages and over-production.

"The same principle applies to farm products and to transportation and every other field of organized private industry.

"We are working toward a definite goal, which is to prevent the return of conditions which came very close to destroying what we call modern civilization. The actual accomplishment of our purpose cannot be attained in a day. Our policies are wholly within purposes for which our American Constitutional Government was established 150 years ago.

. . . .

"The first method sought to apply to industry a concept new in our history. The transfer of national supremacy from the agricultural population to the owners of industry and finance which took place at the turn of the century, together with the creation of great concentrations of business management, had led a generation ago to what we called the attack on the trusts.

"After the World War, a wholly unplanned pyramiding of production and of speculation had left the country in such condition that methods of recovery used in previous periods of depression were useless.

"It is not stretching the point to state categorically that there was not a major industry in the United States in the spring of 1933 that was not suffering either from overproduction, or destructive competition, or unfair practices, or complete lack of planning. Industry itself blamed the anti-trust laws. Industry was wrong. The anti-trust laws were aimed at the prevention of monopolies which through restraint of trade would prevent honest competition and gouge the public.

"I suppose it is human nature for business men, like other men, to be selfish when business is good and they are making handsome profits. I suppose it is also human for business men, like other men, in times of dire distress when everything is going wrong to be very ready to agree to some new plan which they hope will make things right.

"In any event, the overwhelming majority of the business men in May, 1933, were entirely willing to go along with a great cooperative movement directed by the Government and working towards the elimination of the costly practices of the past.

. . . .

"If I were asked to state the great objective which church and state are both demanding for the sake of every man and woman and child in this country, I would say that that great objective is 'a more abundant life.'

"The early Christians challenged the pagan ethics of Greece and of Rome; we are wholly ready to challenge the pagan ethics that are represented in many phases of our boasted modern civilization. We have called on enlightened business judgment, on understanding labor and on intelligent agriculture to provide a more equitable balance of the abundant life between all elements of the community.

"We recognize the right of the individual to seek and to obtain his own fair wage, his own fair profit, in his own fair way—just so long as in the doing of it he shall not push down nor hold down his own neighbor. And at the same time, we are at one in calling for collective effort on broad lines of social planning—a collective effort which is wholly in accord with the social teachings of Christianity.

. . . .

"This younger generation is not satisfied with the exposure of those in high places who seek to line their own nests with other people's money, to cheat their government of its just dues or to break the spirit of the law while observing its legalistic letter. This new generation seeks action—action by collective government and by individual education—toward the ending of practices such as these."

12. National Capitalism

It will be apparent that in considering Fascism, Naziism, and the New Deal, we are confronted with forms of national capitalism. We are so near to this new system that we have difficulty in developing a perspective. Some day, when we can see it longer drawn out, we may decide that, generally speaking, the system has three phases: democratic, autocratic, and Napoleonic. True, Italy and Germany started with the autocratic and seem to proceed to the third, Napoleonic. The United States and France (and soon possibly Great Britain) will proceed from the democratic to the autocratic if present indications mean anything for the future. The common goal promises to be Napoleonic.

Beyond national capitalism lies an extreme system, such as communism in Russia and possibly an excessively radical régime as in the United States.

Far as Roosevelt was willing to go, there were others who would go further. There were intellectual radicals, socialists, communists, inflationists, share-the-wealth people, Townsend pension advocates, and the National Union of Social Justice.

In 1934 this National Union was formed by Father Coughlin, the radio priest of the air. It reflected the need that many felt of going further than Roosevelt was willing to go. Increasingly was this feeling strengthened as men saw Roosevelt turn back from the excessive demands of reconstructionists and hungry debtors.

The sixteen points of the Union are approximately as follows:

1. The liberty of conscience and education.
2. The right of all to work and receive a wage.
3. The nationalization of such public necessities as banks, power, and natural resources.
4. The right of the individual to own property.
5. Public control over private ownership.
6. End of the Federal Reserve in favor of a central bank.
7. Transferring the issuing of currency from the banks to Congress.
8. A central bank should determine the value of the dollar.
9. The farmer should be guaranteed a fair profit.
10. The workman has a right to organize as he will and should be encouraged by the government to organize.
11. Bonds not issued for production purposes should be recalled.
12. Abolition of tax exemption of federal bonds.
13. Wealth should be taxed according to its ability to pay.
14. Lower taxes for the poor.
15. Wealth should be conscripted in time of war.
16. Personal right must be put above property rights.

It is approximately true to say that this is the Catholic economics of the Middle Ages, with some additions and amplifications. It is essentially a charitable policy for aiding debtors—the lower middle class. It is designed to tear down big business and to put the small business man in its place.

Many of the ideas of Father Coughlin are immature or based on ignorance and prejudice. Oratory takes the place of knowledge, and, as it flows, judgment flies out the window. And yet there is a substratum of truth in it all—men are in want and demand aid. They will not pay the price of their own incompetence and misfortune. It is true that in good times manufacturers and bankers have had the upper hand. The towns have flourished, while since 1920 the countryside has languished. But since 1929 all have suffered together.

Despise the logic of Father Coughlin, if you will, but recognize the facts of a situation.

13. Realism in Economic Thinking: a Larger Synthesis

The business man often protests against the artificiality of economic theory based on static conceptions and oversimplifications. At the same time, he is guilty of a similar offense: he is striving for a monistic system based on free competition, fundamentally much like the inner core of economic liberalism. Big business men, Jews, and international bankers hold to a price economics and a profit system. International freedom of trade is as important as individual freedom. In depression the unfortunate nation and person has only bankruptcy to fall back upon. There is no god but wealth, no worship but profits, and no faith apart from trust in managerial competence in the material world of affairs.

In truth, this system of economic individualism has never been accepted by a very large group of persons in America, partly because of historic traditions and partly because of class experiences and interests. The Catholic Church leaders have never accepted it; laborers have not; farmers have not; small business men have not; the bond-holding class has not; and the consumers have not. It may be that at any particular time these groups participate in the general cash nexus of the extreme laissez-faire group, to either their own profit or loss, but they have never understood nor sympathized with the system of even approximately complete freedom of economic activity.

There is a widespread acceptance of certain types of production and at the same time a suspicion or rejection of other types. Most or all people accept commodity production and the production of a form and a place utility. The situation is very different when we come to time and possession utilities. As we know, also, there is a widespread view that we have now come to a period in our development when the supplying of capital can be done by the national state.

It is not a very useful reply for anyone to say that the attitudes of various non-business classes are false, idealistic, fuzzy, or radical. Economic realism is what the business man needs above all things else. Realistic thinking recognizes the economic ideas of all groups, not tested by the concepts of laissez-faire economists or of big business, but as the representations of human interests and class advantages. It may be true that big business has been or is still on top, but, if it were overthrown and an agrarian state established, then something like physiocracy would prevail. In socialistic Russia the labor-consumer point of view prevails.

Such considerations as these lead us to inquire what we are to make of such a heterogeneous situation in the fields of education and government. Few would deny that a state which does not make the main lines of education, business, and government converge has little chance of surviving long.

It is not a mere matter of expediency to conclude that we must compromise. In an age of great social challenge and change we must accept heterogeneity, class interest, and group divergence. Doing this will lead us to a balanced state in which extremes will be avoided and upsets obviated. Our business civilization may give way to another type.

14. Readings

Encyclopaedia of the Social Sciences, vol. v (1931), "Social Economics," pp. 377–381, and "Socio-Ethical Schools," pp. 381–385.

W. G. Welk, *Fascist Economic Policy* (Cambridge, 1938).

Adolf Hitler, *Mein Kampf* (first German ed., 1924; English, 1933 and 1938).

Franklin D. Roosevelt, *On Our Way* (New York, 1934).

Howard S. Piquet, *Outline of the New Deal Legislation of 1933–34* (2nd edition, New York, 1934).

Charles E. Coughlin, *Eight Lectures on Labor, Capital and Justice* (Royal Oak, Michigan, April, 1934).

N. S. B. Gras, *Business and Capitalism* (New York, 1939).

15. Suggested Questions

1. Some scholars think that political policy is just a camouflage for economic policy. Do you agree?
2. What economic situation in the world makes prolonged peace difficult? Can you go so far as to say that, under existing circumstances, war is a concomitant of business?

3. Contrast the general economic problems of the United States on the one hand with those of Germany and Italy on the other. Is national capitalism the solution?
4. What brands of liberalism are there? Which have existed in America?
5. Do you agree that Fascism is likely to be more enduring than is Naziism?
6. Do you think it reasonable to expect three phases in national capitalism: (a) democratic, (b) autocratic, and (c) Napoleonic?
7. What is economic realism? Can it be reconciled with "the immutable laws of economics?"

(3)

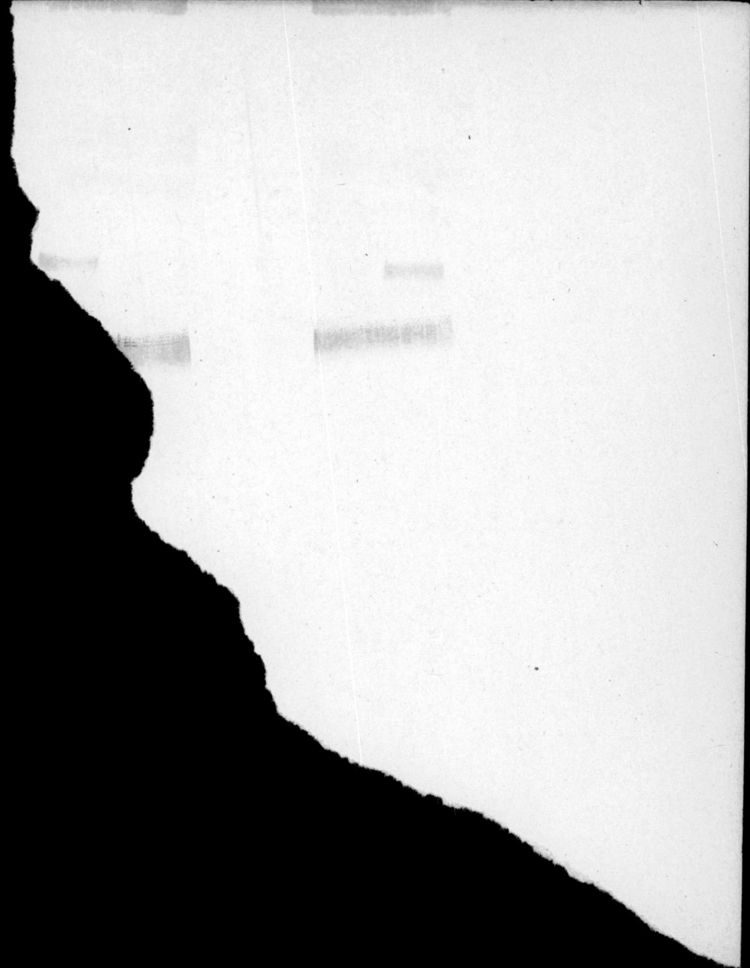